Dictionary of **African Biography**

Dictionary of
African Biography

EMMANUEL K. AKYEAMPONG
and HENRY LOUIS GATES, JR.

Editors in Chief

VOLUME 1 : ABACH—BRAND

OXFORD
UNIVERSITY PRESS

OXFORD
UNIVERSITY PRESS

Oxford University Press, Inc., publishes works that further
Oxford University's objective of excellence
in research, scholarship, and education.

Oxford   New York
Auckland   Cape Town   Dar es Salaam   Hong Kong   Karachi
Kuala Lumpur   Madrid   Melbourne   Mexico City   Nairobi
New Delhi   Shanghai   Taipei   Toronto

With offices in
Argentina   Austria   Brazil   Chile   Czech Republic   France   Greece
Guatemala   Hungary   Italy   Japan   Poland   Portugal   Singapore
South Korea   Switzerland   Thailand   Turkey   Ukraine   Vietnam

Published by Oxford University Press, Inc.
198 Madison Avenue, New York, NY 10016
www.oup.com

Oxford is a registered trademark of Oxford University Press

Library of Congress Cataloging-in-Publication Data

Dictionary of African biography / Emmanuel K. Akyeampong and Henry Louis Gates, Jr. Editors in Chief.
p. cm.
Includes bibliographical references and index.
ISBN 978-0-19-538207-5 (v.1–6 : alk. paper) 1. Africa—Biography—Dictionaries.
I. Akyeampong, Emmanuel Kwaku. II. Gates, Henry Louis
CT1920.D52   2012
920.06—dc22   2011014871

1 3 5 7 9 8 6 4 2

Printed in the United States of America
on acid-free paper

Contents

Dictionary of African Biography

List of Entries

Preface

It is particularly satisfying to see this immense effort to compile a multivolume *Dictionary of African Biography* (*DAB*) with over 2,100 entries, covering the lives of individuals who lived or live in every historical period over the whole of the African continent, come to fruition under the auspices of the Oxford University Press. The *DAB* joins a select number of national biographies also published by Oxford University Press, including the *Oxford Dictionary of National Biography*, the *American National Biography*, and the *African American National Biography*. There were also several hundred biographies in *Africana: The Encyclopedia of the African and African American Experience* published by Oxford University Press under the editorship of Kwame Anthony Appiah and Henry Louis Gates, Jr., in 2005. The *DAB* builds on two important initiatives spearheaded by W. E. B. Du Bois. The first consisted of his three attempts to edit an international, Pan-African "Encyclopedia Africana," which he conceived in 1909, attempted again in the 1930s under the title "The Encyclopedia of the Negro," and evolved once again into a continental-focused "The Encyclopedia Africana" in its final iteration, of which Du Bois served as editor in chief in Ghana between 1961 and his death in 1963. Following his death, Du Bois's Ghanaian compatriots decided to embark on the completion of his encyclopedia indirectly by producing a projected twenty-volume *Africana Dictionary of National Biography*. Edited by L. H. Ofosu-Appiah, only three volumes of this proposed work were ultimately published between 1975 and 1995, covering about 650 individuals from eight countries. The coverage of the *Africana Dictionary of National Biography* was understandably limited, with very few living subjects included. Since that time, other biographical dictionaries have been regional or national in scope, and those that have aimed at continental coverage—especially in a single volume—have generally been quite cursory in their coverage, because of limits of space and resources. At the level of national biographies, the *Encyclopaedia Aethiopica* has set a high standard. The first four volumes containing four thousand subject entries, including biographies, were published in Hamburg by the Institute of African and Ethiopian Studies between 2003 and 2010.

The *DAB*'s ambition is to achieve—through this first edition and then through an ever-expanding online edition in the Oxford African American Studies Center—the most comprehensive continental coverage (including Africa north of the Sahara) available to date, a degree and depth of coverage that will dramatically increase our understanding of the lives and achievements of individual Africans who lived across the full range of continental Africa from ancient times to the present. The publication of such a reference work, we perceived, could have a transformative impact on teaching and research in African studies, narrating the full history of the African continent through the collective lives of the women and men who made that history. The original design proposed to encompass the full scope of history from people such as the first humans, who were born in Africa, the pharaohs and other exemplars of the ancient world, through a surprising range of individual Africans who thrived in Africa, the Middle East, and Europe during classical antiquity, the Middle Ages, the Age of Discovery and the Renaissance, the Enlightenment and the era of colonization, all the way to the independence movements of the 1950s and 1960s. We proposed to end with representatives of the 1 billion Africans living in the twenty-first century. The final result met all of those goals and provided a remarkable tapestry of more than two thousand Africans who shaped their times by the life choices they made.

The print edition of the Dictionary includes 2,126 entries in six volumes dealing with individuals drawn from all walks of life including philosophers, politicians, kings, queens, traders, entertainers, scholars, religious figures, activists, and everyday people whose lives have contributed richly and variously to African history. In entries ranging from two hundred to three thousand words, each contributor was challenged to produce highly readable essays of substance and reliability that would make the *DAB* the starting point for researchers interested in Africa's historical actors, living and deceased. Unavoidably, personalities known to be historically significant, but on whom there is very little reliable information for even the creation of a sound one hundred–word entry, were unfortunately dropped. Each entry is followed by a guide to further reading, and the entries are extensively cross-referenced to promote an integrated reading of historical actors whose lives overlapped.

With an eye to a comprehensive coverage of African personalities, the published *DAB*, which will be available online, will be complemented by an online edition that aims to add an additional ten thousand entries over the next several years. We have been deeply gratified and impressed by the collaboration of scholars from all over the world to produce these biographies. The acknowledgments section below briefly mentions the area editors who identified entries and contributing authors, and they are also listed facing the title page. The online edition will allow us to expand this biographical database—the largest yet published—even further, on a scale that Du Bois could scarcely imagine when he first conceived his "Encyclopedia Africana" in 1909.

Scope and Organization

Key decisions were made about geographical and temporal scope that framed the parameters of the *DAB*. First, we decided to include the entire continent of Africa. Second, we decided to let the availability of historical evidence determine the temporal framework or how far back we could go in historical time, provided that a detailed entry of at least five hundred words could be written on each historical figure. In deciding which subjects should be included, we resolved that:

1. Each subject should have had a significant impact on the historical development of Africa as a whole or, more often, on local communities, regions, and nations within Africa.
2. Living subjects should have had a significant impact on contemporary society, culture, and politics of Africa.

Although the vast majority of entries were on subjects who were born and remained in Africa, we have also included representative entries on subjects born outside of Africa, but whose lives had an enormous impact on the development of the continent and its peoples: foreign monarchs such as Sebastian of Portugal, Victoria of Britain, and Leopold II of Belgium; explorers such as Vasco da Gama; missionaries such as Mary Slessor; returned descendants of African slaves such as Matilda Newport in Liberia, Edward Wilmot Blyden in Liberia and Sierra Leone, and W. E. B. Du Bois in Ghana; and colonial officials like André Latrille in French Africa and Sir George Goldie in Nigeria. Likewise, we included representative examples of African-born subjects who were forcibly removed from Africa or voluntarily relocated to other continents and made significant historical contributions to the histories of other continents: Juan Garrido, Mohammah Gardo Baquaqua, Phillis Wheatley, Ottobah Cugoana, Olaudah Equiano, and others. This third criterion acknowledges the growing interest in diaspora and transnational histories to which the editors in chief and several of the area editors have made contributions. (See, for example, Henry Louis Gates, Jr., and Kwame Anthony Appiah, *Africana: The Encyclopedia of the African and African-American Experience* [Oxford University Press, 2005], and Emmanuel Akyeampong, "Africans in the Diaspora; the Diaspora and Africa," Commissioned Article for Centenary Issue, *African Affairs*, 99 [April 2000], 183–215.)

We are especially pleased with the quality and number of entries on women, which form 20 percent of all the entries. By contrast, the *Oxford Dictionary of National Biography* includes only 10 percent of its entries on women and the *American National Biography* 15 percent. Thirty percent of the entries in the *African American National Biography* are on women.

With 436 entries on women, this makes the *DAB* the largest biographical dictionary of African women ever published and for this we are grateful to Kathleen Sheldon, one of our area editors, who guided the selection of female subjects for the Dictionary. Moreover, 15 percent of the entries on women are of subjects born before 1800, indicating significant coverage of what is usually defined as "early" Africa.

For the distribution of entries over time and space, about 10 percent of subjects are from before 600 AD, and 25 percent of all subjects were born before 1800 (of which 9 percent are women). We had hoped for a larger percentage of pre-1800 entries and encouraged the area editors to solicit more entries on early Africa, but were limited in terms of subjects that could attract substantial essays and contributing authors. Many area editors highlighted the decline in scholarly interest in precolonial Africa, a trend noted in Joseph C. Miller, "History and Africa/Africa and History," *American Historical Review*, 104 (1999): 1–32.

Approximately one-quarter of the entries deal with living people. Still, there was a clear post–World War II focus by all the editors, whose remit was the period between 1800 and 2000, and we saw in this, perhaps, the desire to highlight African achievement in the postcolonial era, plus the rapid expansion of populations in post-1945 Africa. The twentieth-century focus, however, increased the number of entries on living women (33 percent of the total of living subjects), a result we consider quite satisfying.

Using twenty-first-century borders and grouping subject categories in ways that overlapped with the research expertise of our area editors, we divided Africa into seven regions: **North and East Africa**: Djibouti, Egypt, Eritrea, Ethiopia, Somalia, and Sudan; **Greater Maghreb**: Algeria, Libya, Mauritania; Morocco, Tunisia, and Western Sahara; **East Africa**: Kenya, Madagascar, Mauritius, Seychelles, Uganda, and Tanzania; **Southern Africa**: Botswana, Lesotho, Malawi, Mozambique, Namibia, South Africa, Swaziland, Zambia, and Zimbabwe; **French-speaking West Africa**: Benin, Burkina Faso, Ivory Coast, Guinea, Mali, Niger, Senegal, and Togo; **English-speaking West Africa:** The Gambia, Ghana, Liberia, Nigeria, and Sierra Leone; and **Central Africa and Portuguese-speaking Africa:** Angola, Burundi, Cameroon, the Central African Republic, Chad, the Republic of the Congo, Democratic Republic of the Congo, Equatorial Guinea, Gabon, Rwanda, and São Tomé and Príncipe. In terms of a breakdown of entries by region, we have balanced the more extensive historical record of Northern Africa with the greater modern population of sub-Saharan Africa. Thus, West Africa represents 25 percent of all entries, North and East Africa 25 percent, Southern Africa 16 percent, Central Africa 14 percent, Greater Maghreb 11 percent, and East Africa 10 percent. In terms of the percentage of entries for the period after 1800, West Africa constitutes 26 percent (Anglophone West Africa 14 percent and Francophone West Africa 12 percent), North and East Africa 20 percent, Southern Africa 19 percent, Central Africa and Lusophone West Africa 17 percent, East Africa 12 percent, and the Greater Maghreb 6 percent.

Acknowledgments

A large project like this accumulates many debts. We acknowledge the invaluable role of Casper Grathwohl, our brilliant reference publisher at Oxford, whose support for this project was unflagging. Executive Editors Steven Niven, at Harvard, and Stephen Wagley, at Oxford University Press, managed the organization and logistics of the *DAB* with admirable finesse and grace. They also worked closely with the editors in chief and the area editors to ensure the timely completion of the project. At OUP, Robert Repino, Holly Seabury, and Jenny Keegan played vital roles at various stages, in planning, in maintaining contact with the area editors and hundreds of contributors, and in receiving and processing articles, thereby keeping the project on track and up to a high standard of quality. Mark O'Malley guided the project through copyediting, page makeup, and proofreading. The *DAB* undoubtedly benefited from the earlier and continuing collaboration between Oxford University Press and the W. E. B. Du Bois Institute on *Encyclopedia Africana* and the *African American National Biography*.

Although the area editors are listed facing the title page of the Dictionary, we want to end this preface by acknowledging their indispensable role in making this project successful.

These area editors helped finalize our table of contents, suggested authors for specific entries, and approved the historical accuracy of all entries in their field. Our area editors were Stanley Burstein, Chouki El Hamel, Allen Fromherz, Israel Gershoni, Lidwien Kapteijns, Ray Kea, Christopher J. Lee, Paul Lovejoy, Ghislaine Lydon, Jonathan Miran, Evan Mwangi, Jeremy Rich, Kathleen Sheldon, Jay Spaulding, and Thomas Spear. In the final review process Steven Niven, Stephen Wagley, and Jenny Keegan were aided by the careful editorial skills of Sara Byala of the University of Pennsylvania, Gregory Byala of Temple University, and Jeremy Rich of Middle Tennessee State University. It must be noted that in addition to his editorial responsibilities Professor Rich authored a remarkable 287 high-quality biographical entries for the *DAB*. We give special thanks to Professor Steven Pinker of Harvard for sharing his knowledge on human evolution and genetic diversity in Africa.

EMMANUEL K. AKYEAMPONG
HENRY LOUIS GATES, JR.

African Lives: An Introduction

I

Africa is the most continuous site of the evolution of the human species on our planet. The human lineage is 6 million years old. The first member of the genus *Homo* appeared about 2.6 million years ago; anatomically modern *Homo sapiens* emerged between 100,000 and 200,000 years ago, and behaviorally modern humans emerged between 50,000 and 80,000 years ago. And during these millions of years of human prehistory, the main events unfolded on the African continent. The nameless subjects who created this common ancestry and history of the human community are our anonymous common ancestors, and we owe our existence to them.

Despite their remarkably important significance to our shared heritage as human beings, we cannot memorialize these people as individuals, although we can, through DNA analysis, reconstruct our Mitochondrial Eve and Y-chromosomal Adam, our most recent common matrilineal and patrilineal ancestors, who lived some 200,000 and 60,000 to 90,000 years ago, respectively. And thus, the oldest subject chronologically in the *Dictionary of African Biography* is the metaphorical mother of the human race, who appears as **African Eve** (all names in boldface in this introduction refer to an entry in the Dictionary).

We think that by sampling some of the more fascinating figures who thrived between 3100 BC and the twenty-first century, we might give readers an idea of the astonishing richness and variety of the lives of the women and men included in the six volumes of the *Dictionary of African Biography.* "Africa," for us, is a vast continent that is the home of the most genetic diversity in the entire human community, not a signifier for the color of a people. Indeed, the "Africans" whose biographies are found in these pages are black, white, and several shades of color in between. Fortunately, early African history is rich in detail about some of the more colorful men and women who, as we say, made a name for themselves between 3100 BC and 641 AD, the first historical era that we cover in the Dictionary.

A man named **Narmer** is generally thought to be the earliest pharaoh, the first king of a united Egypt, who ruled between the Predynastic Age and the First Dynasty. Narmer's kingdom is assigned Dynasty 0, and although we don't know much about him, his is the oldest entry in our dictionary of a human being we know by name.

The earliest nonruler in this volume is the well-known architect and administrator **Imhotep,** who lived during the earlier part of Egypt's Third Dynasty (c. 2686–2613 BC). Imhotep was a high-ranking courtier who held many important positions. But he is best known, without a doubt, as the architect of Egypt's first stone building, the Sakkara Step Pyramid, built for King Djoser (Netjerikhet). Upon his death, Imhotep became one of the few nonroyal Egyptians to be deified.

We remember an adventurous man named **Kharkhuf,** a provincial nobleman in Upper Egypt who lived between 2315 BC and 2190 BC, for his writings about his explorations through sub-Saharan Africa. Kharkhuf led several expeditions to Kush (or Nubia), south of the second cataract of the Nile. He documented the early ethnic topography of what today is northern Sudan. Kharkhuf, who apparently had a healthy sense of himself, identified himself as "him who brings royal luxury products from all the foreign lands" and lists such items as incense, ebony, oil, wheat, panther skins, ivory tusks, throw sticks, and cattle.

Much of late has been speculated about the color of the ancient Egyptians, and indeed arguments about their "blackness" have become something of a passionate spectator sport. But there is no doubt that the Twenty-fifth Dynasty—also known as the Nubian or Ethiopian or Black Dynasty (760 BC to 656 BC)—was ruled by black pharaohs from the Kingdom of Kush. Two of the most colorful of these were **Piankhy** and **Taharqa.** Piankhy, sometimes known as Piye, ruled between 752 BC and 721 BC. His conquest of Egypt established the period of the Kushite supremacy in the Nile River valley. Piankhy is depicted as quite chivalrous, instructing his army not to attack at night or to attack unexpectedly, but to fight the enemy only "when he says [he is ready]." He always offers a town he is about to besiege a proposal to surrender. He is firm, but he is merciful as well, seeking to avoid death when possible. He is also impressively pious; after the fall of Memphis, he sent his guards to the temples to prevent pillage. Taharqa is mentioned in the Hebrew Bible as Tirhakah in two places: 2 *Kings* 19:9 and *Isaiah* 37:9. During the reign of King Hezekiah of Judah, Taharqa prevented Sennacherib from destroying Jerusalem and dispersing its inhabitants, an intervention pivotal to the history of Israel. He reigned between 690 BC and 664 BC. His father was Piankhy, the king of Napata, who first conquered his northern neighbors in Egypt.

We tend to think of **Henry the Navigator** when we think of early explorers down the West African coast. But **Hanno the Navigator** got there first, some two thousand years before Henry's intrepid sailors did. Hanno was a Carthaginian explorer who traveled down the coast of Africa, perhaps as far as Cameroon, around 500 BC. His journey marked a high point in the Phoenician-Punic exploration of Africa. The written account of Hanno's journey was rediscovered in the Renaissance and inspired European explorers between the sixteenth and the nineteenth centuries. One of the scholars who wrote about Hanno was **Juba II,** the king of Mauretania.

Juba II was a great scholar, whose earliest works of scholarship focused on Roman history, the history of the theater, and linguistics. In 25 BC, the Emperor **Augustus** placed Juba on the throne of Mauretania (essentially modern Algeria and Morocco), which he ruled with his wife, **Cleopatra Selene,** the last surviving child of **Cleopatra VII** and **Mark Antony.** He wrote a lengthy treatise, entitled *Libyka,* about the history, geography, and ethnography of northwest Africa, including the Canary Islands. He also wrote about the source of the Nile and the now-extinct North African elephant. His final treatise, *On Arabia,* included the first detailed discussion of the Arabian peninsula and summarized the most accurate knowledge of the routes to India. In fact, when taken together, *Libyka* and *On Arabia* provided the first seamless discussion of the southern portion of the known world, from the Atlantic coast of Africa to India.

Just as the various queens named Cleopatra did, other women played signal roles in the early history of Africa. **Elissa** or Dido, a mythical figure, was the legendary founder of Carthage in the late ninth century BC. **Nehanda** is known as the founding mother of the southern African kingdom of Mutapa, which flourished from the fifteenth to the eighteenth century AD. And perhaps the best known, along with Cleopatra, was **Makedda,** better known in the West as the Queen of Sheba, who Ethiopians believe hailed from that country in the tenth century BC, and whose son Menelik, putatively fathered by King Solomon, founded the Ethiopian monarchy that Ethiopian tradition says culminated with Ras Tafari, who became the emperor **Haile Selassie I.**

Just as fascinating as Makedda and Cleopatra was **Ameniras,** another great female historical figure, who flourished in the first century BC and was the Meroitic queen of the ancient empire of Kush. By then the southern city of Meroe had become the capital of Kush, after the Egyptians had pushed the Kushites from Piankhy's northern heartland at Napata. Because of Ameniras's brave and effective defense of Kushite sovereignty against the Romans, the Meroitic title for queen mother—*kdke*, translated as "Candace"—became popular during the Roman era. It is mentioned in the *Book of Acts*, in fact. The Greek geographer **Strabo** writes of the "one-eyed" Candace, queen of Kush, who resisted Roman attempts to subjugate and annex Kush. After the Kushite and Roman armies fought to a stalemate, Ameniras's ambassadors established peace with Augustus. Augustus subsequently abandoned the idea of making Kush a vassal state and therefore relinquished the tribute he had initially imposed and retreated from northern Nubia. Ameniras's historical significance is that she protected the territorial integrity and independence of the Kushite state and inaugurated a period of economic prosperity that encouraged the flourishing of trade, commerce, and intercultural exchange between Kush and the Mediterranean world. This era is often called the Golden Age of Meroe, and it lasted until the middle of the fourth century AD.

Africa and Africans played key roles in the early history of the Christian church. **Tertullian** (Quintus Septimus Florens Tertullianus), who lived between 160 and 240, was the earliest Christian apologist and theologian to write in Latin. His *Apologeticum* is a bitingly sarcastic and yet unassailably logical indictment against the imperial policy of arresting and trying Christians. His *Adversus Praxean*, a response to a heretic, articulates the theology of the Trinity for the first time. Tertullian's theology tended toward the enthusiastic, hardline brand of African Christianity most famously characterized by martyrs such as **Perpetua and Felicity.** He was a major influence on both **Cyprian of Carthage** and **Augustine of Hippo.**

Perpetua was that rarest of beings, an educated woman in third-century North Africa. Along with her slave, Felicity, she was imprisoned and sentenced to death by the Romans for her faith in about 200. While imprisoned and awaiting her execution, she kept a diary of her experiences and her dreams. She gave the diary to a friend, who added a description of the women's fate in the arena: they were mauled by a wild cow, while others in the group of martyrs were attacked by other beasts. When the cow did not succeed in killing Perpetua, a gladiator was summoned to complete her execution. He struck her with his sword, but accidentally hit her shoulder. Perpetua guided his hand to cut her throat. Her diary was preserved and venerated by early Christians, ensuring her influence within the early church.

The first female scholar of whom we have reasonably detailed and firm knowledge on the African continent was **Hypatia** of Alexandria. As glorious as was her public career, Hypatia's tragic death is the stuff of legend, revealing the complexity of Christian belief and behavior in the early centuries of the church's history. Hypatia lived between about 355 and 415, and she was an astronomer, mathematician, and a philosopher. She was quite active as a public figure and took a leading role in the civic affairs of Alexandria, delivering public lectures on philosophy. Hers was a Neoplatonist philosophy heavily influenced by mathematics. She taught students the intricacies of technical mathematics and astronomy. While her career alone was sufficient to accord her a pioneering role in African history, the lurid nature of her death would have done so as well. She died in 415, murdered by a crowd of Christian zealots who declared her a heretic, seized her, stripped her, and proceeded to dismember her and then burned her mangled corpse. Christians were not the only martyrs in the early centuries after Christ.

Black Africans also played key roles in the early history of the Muslim religion. **Bilal ibn Rabah,** who lived from the late sixth century to 641, is universally known in the Muslim world as the first muezzin (*mu'addin*) in the history of Islam. Originally a slave born in Mecca, he had an "Ethiopian" (or more precisely, a black Sub-Saharan) ancestry, which explains his nickname "al-Habashi," which means "the Abyssinian," the name by which Ethiopia was known. Bilal came to know Islam at its first inception and was one of the earliest converts to the new faith. In 630, when Mecca was eventually reconquered by Islamic forces, Bilal had the honor of calling the Muslim faithful to prayer, launching the *adhan* from the roof of the holy Kaaba.

II

The *DAB* entries covering the period from the early Middle Ages through the Enlightenment in the eighteenth century, roughly from 600 to 1800, highlight the impact of both Islam and Europe on the African continent and the African continent upon Europe and Islam. This is a history of contact and conquest, war, the rise and fall of empires, great intellectual and scientific achievements, and the expansion of trade, travel, and cultural interaction between Africa and the broader world.

Whereas the history of cultural and political contact between Europeans and Africans, especially in the modern era, has been widely discussed by scholars, the role of Africans in Muslim religion and culture (and the role of Islam in Africa, north and south of the Sahara), especially in its earliest years of creation and propagation, is much less well known. The biographies of individuals who played an historical role in the birth, growth, and spread of Islam are quite riveting. Let us start in the year 690. Resistance to the Damascus-based Umayyad Caliphate in northern Africa was first led by **Kusaila ibn Lamzam,** a king of the Berber Empire (parts of Morocco, Algeria, and Tunisia). Kusaila, known as Aksel (meaning Tiger) by his own people, was likely a Christian member of the semisedentary Awraba people, who converted to Islam around 670. While remaining a Muslim, he later allied with the Byzantines and confronted the Umayyads at the Battle of Mems (c. 686–690), where he led a force against Arabic troops commanded by Zuhair ibn Qais al-Balawi. Greatly outnumbered, Kusaila was killed.

The semilegendary queen of the Aures Mountain Berbers in what is now Algeria continued resistance. Since the main sources describing the Arab conquest of the Berbers were written by the conquerors, she is most often known as **Kahina**, meaning "Sorceress." Nonetheless, the Arab chronicles portray her as a noble adversary against the spread of Islam and Arabic power. Kahina most likely represented an actual woman—or perhaps a group of different female queens or leaders. She first appears in the sources in 695 as the head of a group of nomadic Berbers who waged a guerrilla war against Hasan ibn al-Nu'man, the Arab governor of North Africa. Her constant harassment slowed his attempt to consolidate control over the region. She is most often depicted with long flowing hair and with a supernatural power to foresee the future, including an ability to outwit enemy forces by predicting their movements. Kahina also came to embody a pastoral Berber ideal that contrasted with Arab plunder. One chronicle has her proclaiming that "The Arabs search for towns, for gold and for silver, but we only seek pasturage." Hasan finally encircled the Berbers, but legend has it that he offered Kahina a chance to escape. She refused, declaring, "Kings do not flee," and led her forces into the face of the enemy, with sword drawn and her long hair flowing, before finally surrendering. Hasan decapitated her near a place called Kahina's Well.

Musa ibn Nusayr, Umayyad governor of North Africa in the early eighth century, stabilized Muslim control over the region and incorporated the majority Berber population into the army and administration. He also expanded Muslim rule from Tunisia to the Atlantic coast in Morocco. Musa's generals brought many Berbers under Islamic rule, leaving local chiefs in authority over their tribes once they agreed to embrace Islam.

One convert was **Tariq ibn Ziyad**, a Berber slave belonging to Musa, who rose to become his deputy governor. With an army of twelve thousand soldiers, most of them Berbers, Tariq launched the Muslim conquest of Spain in 711. They landed first at the Rock of Gibraltar, which ever after would bear Tariq's name (Arabic: *Jabal Tariq,* corrupted by Europeans as "Gibraltar"). Soon thereafter, Tariq and his forces occupied Algeciras and Torre de Cartagena. Upon hearing of Tariq's success, Musa took his own army of eighteen thousand across the Straits of Gibraltar in 712 and conquered portions of the Iberian peninsula not yet taken by Tariq.

The Idrisid dynasty extended Islamic rule in North Africa in the eight and ninth centuries, notably in Morocco, where **Idris II** built the city of Fez. In the centuries that followed, northern and western Africa became a hotbed of trade, scientific discovery, and literary innovation. Among the most notable of many outstanding historical figures in this period were **Constantinus Africanus** (Constantine the African), an eleventh-century trader and scientist, who lived in Tunis and brought Arabic medical and scientific knowledge from North Africa to the European Mediterranean. Among his most popular works in Europe were his writings on sex and gynecology, which contained remedies for many sexual and reproductive ailments.

Constantinus Africanus's near contemporary was the Sunni scholar, **Abu Bakr Muhammad al-Turtushi,** who is noted for *Siraj al-muluk,* a major treatise on the ideal form of Islamic government, completed in 1122. Turtushi was also a gifted poet of erotic verse and included among his students **Muhammad Ibn Tumart,** who founded the Almohad dynasty, which ruled North Africa and Islamic Iberia until the early thirteenth century. The most well known polymath of the Almohad era was **Ibn Rushd** (Averroes), who famously stated that there was no inherent inconsistency between Greek rational thought and Islam. Less well known was his close friend in Marrakech, **Ibn Tufayl**, author of *Hayy ibn Yaqzan*, a philosophical tale about a man raised on a desert island that later influenced similar works by Daniel Defoe, John Locke, and Baruch Spinoza.

Biographical dictionaries such as the *DAB* are indebted to predecessor texts created by scholars such as the prolific thirteenth-century Egyptian writer **Ibn al-Qifti**, whose surviving texts include biographical dictionaries of several hundred scientists and scholars, *Ta'rikh al-Hukama* and *Inbah al-Ruwat*. Our understanding of early Mali and other western African kingdoms in the thirteenth and fourteenth centuries likewise owes an immense debt to the great North African explorers and writers **Ibn Battuta** and **Ibn Khaldun**. Khaldun served in the royal courts of Tunis and Fez before moving to Algeria to write the *Kittab al-ibar*, an extensive history of North Africa, on which many *DAB* entries rely as a source. He was also the author of the *Muqqaddimah*, one of the earliest philosophical examinations of the philosophy of history. Drawing on oral tradition, he provided the first written accounts of the exploits of the great king **Sunjata Keita**, the founder of the Mali empire, and his successors, including **Mansa Musa**, whose 1324 pilgrimage to Mecca, via Cairo, was noted both for the fact that a black African monarch did it and for the emperor's wealth in gold. (Mansa Musa also told an encyclopedist in Cairo that he was a surrogate for the real emperor, Mansa Muhammad, who had embarked with twelve hundred canoes to find the land beyond the sea, on the other side of the Atlantic Ocean.) Ibn Khaldun also wrote of a later Mali emperor, **Mansa Sulayman**, as did Ibn Battuta, a native Berber raised in an elite Muslim family in Tangier.

Ibn Battuta provides a vivid firsthand account of Mansa Sulayman's court in 1352–1353. He documents the power and wealth of the Mali kingdom, based on trade in gold and salt. Mansa Sulayman commanded the largest army in the Western Sudan and his court matched the finest in Europe for pageantry and sartorial elegance. Ibn Battuta's account depicts Sulayman as a capable and effective ruler who adjudicated disputes with fairness, but he also noted an attempted coup d'état against the ruler, incredibly, by his own queen, **Qasa**. Ibn Battuta also visited the kingdom of Songhay and traveled the full extent of the Muslim world, from West Africa to Asia Minor and Central Asia, India, Sri Lanka, China, and Southeast Asia. The seventy-five thousand miles of his journey exceeded by fivefold the distance traveled by his more famous European contemporary, Marco Polo.

The brilliance of Ibn Khaldun and Ibn Battuta was matched—and perhaps exceeded—in the sixteenth century by the Moroccan diplomat, writer, and traveler al-Hasan ibn Muhammad al-Wazzan. Al-Wazzan, known to his European contemporaries as **Leo Africanus**, traveled throughout West Africa on behalf of the sultan of Fez, visiting Timbuktu, Gao, and Bornu in 1513, when the Songhay Empire was at its peak. Five years later he was captured by Spanish corsairs off the coast of Tunisia, who sold him as a slave to Pope Leo X, who convinced Leo Africanus to convert to Christianity. He thereby gained his freedom, learned Latin, and taught many of the leading figures of the Renaissance about Arabic, Islamic religion and culture, and African history and civilization. Leo Africanus's *Description of Africa* was a bestseller throughout Europe and was the main source of sixteenth- and seventeenth-century European knowledge about the continent. Some scholars speculate that Shakespeare may have based the character of Othello on Leo Africanus.

Leo, Ibn Battuta, and Ibn Khaldun all wrote about the glories of the West African Mali and Songhay empires. The rulers of those empires in turn recognized and encouraged religious and intellectual scholarship. As **Sonni Ali Ber**, the fifteenth-century founder of the Songhay, stated, "Without Islamic scholars the world would cease to be good." Among the Islamic scholars whose work continued to enlighten the world in the centuries that followed, special mention must be given to the learned **Mahmoud Kati** of Timbuktu, who penned the *Ta'rikh al-fattash* (*The Chronicle of the Seeker: Serving as an Account of the Towns, Armies, and Leading Figures [of the Takrur]*), a lively portrait of the rise and fall of the Songhay dynasty of the Askiyas. The chronicle is viewed by many scholars as Africa's most important historical document of the late medieval era. In it Kati reveals the wealth, diversity, and complexity of one very important

West Africa society in the fifteenth and sixteenth centuries. Another Timbuktu scholar, **Ahmad Baba al-Massufi al-Tinbukti,** author of a biographical dictionary of the best-known Sahelian scholars of Maliki law, was the most famous West African scholar of the late medieval period.

Ber's successor, the powerful **Muhammed Ture,** who consolidated and expanded the Songhay kingdom, died in 1538. The following year, 1539, witnessed the deaths of two other Africans whose lives show the surprising degree of engagement between Africans and the wider world in the sixteenth and seventeenth centuries. Contrary to most assumptions, the traffic between the African continent and Europe went two ways; Africans were as curious about Europeans as Europe was curious about Africa. One such African traveler was **Tsega Ze'ab,** a sixteenth-century cleric who represented Ethiopia as its ambassador at the court of Portuguese king João III. He also traveled to India.

The earlier explorations of **Henry the Navigator** and **Vasco da Gama** had spurred Portuguese interest in trade with Africa. Through Tsega Ze'ab, the Christian Ethiopian emperor **Lebna Dengel** (Dawit II) began a dialogue with Pope Clement VII. Such ties would help restore Christian rule after the invasion of Ethiopia by the Islamic forces of **Ahmad ibn Ibrahim al-Ghazi** in the 1530s. At the time of Lebna Dengel's death in 1540, it seemed that the Ethiopian empire was doomed, but Lebna's son **Gelawdewos** enlisted Portuguese support and defeated Ahmad's armies at the Battle of Wayna Daga in 1543. While grateful to his allies in Portugal and the Vatican, Galawdewos nonetheless made clear in his 1555 Confession of Faith that he had no intention of abandoning the doctrines of the Ethiopian Orthodox Church for Roman Catholicism.

Tsega Ze'ab's contemporary, **Esteban de Dorantes,** exemplifies the beginning of five centuries of engagement between Africa and the Western hemisphere. A Moroccan-born slave, Esteban is the earliest known person of African descent to have set foot on what is now the United States of America. He arrived in Florida on Good Friday, 1528, died in Mexico eleven years later, and is remembered in Zuni spiritual traditions to the present day.

III

The *DAB* entries from the fifteenth, sixteenth, seventeenth, and eighteenth centuries show the growing importance of the Atlantic slave trade, as well as the first flowering of Christianity south of the Sahara. In southern and eastern Africa, powerful oral traditions tell us something of semimythical rulers in the fifteenth century, such as **Kimera,** an early king of Buganda, and **Nyanhehwe,** who consolidated the Mutapa empire in present-day Zimbabwe and Mozambique. The oral tradition highlighting well-established kingdoms and states in the region is confirmed by the Portuguese engagement with the sophisticated Kongo Kingdom in the late fifteenth century. The Kongo king Nzinga Nkuwu, later called **João I,** initially welcomed trade with the Portuguese, who provided troops and firearms, and certainly benefited from Portuguese assistance to defeat his rivals. Along with many Kongo nobles, however, João came to resent efforts to end polygamy and other traditional practices.

After João's death, his son **Afonso I** enlisted Portuguese support to defeat his non-Christian rivals and consolidate his rule over the kingdom. The price for that support was Afonso's complicity in the Atlantic slave trade, including supplying Kongo slaves for Portuguese sugar plantations on the previously uninhabited island of São Tomé, off the West African coast. The powerful and charismatic Queen **Nzinga a Mbandi,** for example, was an effective negotiator on behalf of the Mbundu people, who still live in present-day Angola. When the Portuguese exiled her, she abandoned Catholicism, enlisted fugitive slaves, and allied with Dutch forces in a long resistance campaign. Nzinga ultimately accepted a diplomatic agreement with the Portuguese, returned to Catholicism in 1656, and embraced the international slave trade.

Slavery is as old as civilization itself. Africa—from whence human civilization evolved—cannot possibly be an exception. Slavery on the African continent preceded the presence of Europeans, of course, by millennia; in the modern era, African elites from West Africa to Central Africa collaborated with Europeans in the transatlantic slave trade. Despite centuries of contact between sub-Saharan Africans and Europeans, since classical Greco-Roman antiquity and continuing through the Middle Ages (as amply documented in *The Image of the Black in Western Art*), Europe's knowledge of Africa grew within the context of trade from the early modern era—the "age of discovery" and the Renaissance—especially because of the trans-atlantic slave trade. As a result, the slave trade and European trading relations with African rulers and merchants loom large in European writings from the seventeenth century, shaping whole historiographies such as that of Dahomey in the eighteenth and nineteenth centuries (see Robin Law, "Dahomey and the Slave Trade: Reflections on the Historiography of the Rise of Dahomey," *Journal of African History* 27 [1986]: 237–267).

The occasional African source reflects similar preoccupations among the African elite, as can be seen in the diary of Antera Duke (see below). These European sources thus document close collaboration with Africa's political and mercantile elites, although they tell us very little about what ordinary Africans thought of this trade. We know, though, that the kingdom of Benin in its early contact with the Portuguese prohibited the sale of Benin nationals, thus reducing Portuguese enthusiasm for trade in Benin. Also, the peoples of coastal Ivory Coast and the Kru of Liberia remained aloof from the export slave trade throughout its history. Yet, like the Kongo and Angola monarchs, other African kingdoms, such as Asante and Dahomey, also found it in their economic interests to participate actively as partners in the international slave trade. The Dutch, French, Spanish, Portuguese, and British built their empires in the New World on the backs of African slave labor, with the complicity of African rulers.

To take just one example, the military might and wealth of the eighteenth-century West African kingdom of Dahomey was fueled by the slave trade. **Tegbesu,** one of Dahomey's most powerful rulers, symbolized his rule with a blunderbuss musket as a sign of the importance of the slave trade in providing him with modern weaponry. He controlled the official prices for slaves and forced French and Portuguese merchants to accept the slave trade on his terms. By 1750 his authority was such that he sent ambassadors to Bahia, the Brazilian destination of millions of slaves.

His successor, **Kpengla,** vied with rival monarchs in Oyo to make Dahomey the center of the slave trade and was deeply concerned by the growth of abolitionist sentiment in Britain in the 1780s as a threat to Dahomey's military and economic power. Similar views were expressed by **Antera Duke Ephraim,** Kpengla's contemporary in the port of Calabar (in present-day Nigeria). The Calabar slave trade was mainly with British merchants, and Antera Duke Ephraim learned enough English during his contacts with them to keep a diary. That record provides a rare—and candid—glimpse of the slave trade as experienced and perceived by one of its principal African promoters. Antera Duke Ephraim and other leading African traders who formed the elite Ekpe (Leopard) Society enjoyed harmonious, even convivial, relations with their British counterparts.

If African elites could play a role as autonomous agents in their home countries in the slave trade, some also experienced a remarkable degree of autonomy in European societies, as free people from Africa, as former slaves liberated in Europe, and even a few as academics. The existence of Africans in European courts goes back at least to the early sixteenth century. One person, identified as Christophle le More and described as an African prince, had his portrait painted by Jan Mostaert, sometime between 1520 and 1530; le More was listed at the Flemish Court. **Jacobus Elisa Johannes Capitein,** born in 1717, was one of the first persons of African descent to earn a doctorate at any European university. Capitein was enslaved at about age eight and later sold to an agent of the Dutch West Indies Company. Brought to the Netherlands (where he became free), he was baptized a Christian and educated at the prestigious Latin School in The Hague, where he learned Latin, Greek, and Hebrew. In 1737 he gave a public lecture, later published as "On the Calling of the Heathen." He then studied theology at the University of Leiden and published his doctoral treatise defending the institution of slavery as compatible with Christianity. He returned to his home in the Gold Coast and founded a boy's school. In the mid-eighteenth century Africans were also becoming prominent in English elite circles, as evidenced by the portraits of Job Ben Solomon (Ayuba Suleiman Diallo) and William Sessarakoo in *The Gentlemen's Magazine* in 1750.

In both West and Central East Africa many of the Africans involved in the eighteenth- and nineteenth-century slave trade were women. In many respects this is not surprising because most slaves in Africa were also women, as is made clear in the seminal study by Claire Robertson and Martin Klein, *Women and Slavery in Africa* (Madison: University of Wisconsin Press, 1983). Women slaves were valued for production and reproduction, relieving free women of burdens in these two spheres. Moreover, throughout Africa women were deeply involved in merchant trading, more generally, and the slave trade was in many ways an extension of broader merchant networks.

Among those slave traders included in the *DAB* are **Elizabeth Frazer Skelton** of Guinea; **Fenda Lawrence** of Gambia; and **Bibiana Vaz** and **Aurelia Correia** of Guinea-Bissau. Fenda Lawrence is just one example of how fluid the generally rigid institution of slavery could be for those Africans instrumental in the trade. It will surprise many of our readers to learn that Lawrence actually sailed to British North America in the 1770s. Georgia's colonial government issued her a certificate stating that she was "a free black woman and trader in the Gambia River on the Coast of Africa" and had voluntarily "come to be and remain for some time in this province" with permission to "pass and repass unmolested with the said province of her lawful and necessary occasion." Other members of the African elites from Kongo and Angola traveled freely to Brazil to negotiate terms of the sale of their slaves with the Portuguese; some people from a variety of African kingdoms even served as crew members on the slave ships, freely traveling back and forth between Africa and the New World.

Still another female slave trader was **Ana Joaquina dos Santos e Silva**, born to a Portuguese father and an African mother, who was a leading merchant, moneylender, entrepreneur, and slave trader in Angola. She had extensive links to the Brazilian slave trade and was perhaps the wealthiest of all merchants in Portugal's Angola colony in the early nineteenth century. Although Brazil abolished the slave trade in 1850 (it would not abolish slavery itself until 1888), Ana Joaquina continued to prosper, having diversified her business links beyond the slave trade. The more we learn about the institution of slavery the more peculiar, indeed, it becomes, as entries such as these in the *DAB* make clear.

Africans are as complex as any other peoples, with motives as mixed, as selfish, and as selfless as those of any other human beings. If some African elites avidly participated in the slave trade, many Africans did not and fought it most valiantly, if in vain. The Dictionary contains many examples of Africans who resisted the slave trade and the institution of slavery from the beginning: the slaves themselves. These include people such as the following: **Bayano**, who established a maroon colony in Spanish Panama in the mid-sixteenth century; **Amador**, leader of a major slave revolt in 1595, which almost succeeded in defeating the Portuguese colonial authorities in São Tomé; **Kofi**, who led Akan slaves in resistance to the Dutch authorities in eighteenth-century Guyana; and **Makandal**, who was burned alive in 1758 under a sign reading, "Seducer, Profaner, Poisoner," after leading a revolt on the French West Indian colony of Saint-Domingue (Haiti).

While the primary focus of the *DAB* is on Africans in Africa, as we have seen, we also have included a sampling of entries about Africans who made a historical contribution of some sort both in Europe and in the Western Hemisphere. A small group of Africans, who described themselves in their writings as such, invented the Anglo-African literary tradition, writing in Boston and London after 1770. This group of pioneers includes the inventors of the slave narrative genre **James Albert Ukawsaw Gronniosaw, Olaudah Equiano**, and the celebrated poet **Phillis Wheatley,** the first person of African descent to publish a book of poetry in English ("El negro" **Juan Latino** was the first African to publish a book of poetry, in Latin, in 1573). Less famous is the West African–born slave **Belinda**, the author of the first known slave testimony by an African woman in the United States; she was owned by Isaac Royall, Jr., whose estate helped found the Harvard Law School. When Royall, a loyalist, returned to England, Belinda successfully petitioned the Massachusetts state legislature for reparations from Royall's estate for her unpaid labor.

Among several free Africans who rose to prominence in Europe in the eighteenth and nineteenth centuries was **Kwasi Boakye,** the son of Kwaku Dua *Asantehene* (king of Asante), who lived in Europe from 1834 to 1867. Kwasi Boakye was brought with another young Asante prince to the Netherlands and was educated at a boarding school in Delft. He was baptized into the Reformed Church in 1843 and studied civil engineering at the Royal Academy in Delft. Although he experienced racism in both Holland and Indonesia, where he worked as a mining engineer, the Dutch government awarded him a pension and land in Jakarta, where he died in 1904.

The *DAB* also includes entries on the descendants of Africans such as **Lott Cary, John Brown Russwurm**, and **Edward Wilmot Blyden**, who returned to the land of their forefathers and foremothers, and **Martin Delany**, who died before he could do so. Job ben Solomon, Alexander Crummell, Henry Highland Garnet and other notable returnees to Africa will appear in the online *DAB*. One of the earliest Liberian settlers was **Matilda Newport**, born free in Philadelphia in 1795. Very little is known about her life in the new nation. She came to be celebrated as a pioneer of Liberian independence, however, because of an account—possibly fictitious—by Alexander Crummell, which praised her role in the settlers' victory over the Dei natives of Liberia. Several of Sierra Leone's founders are included, notably the Baptist preacher **David George** and the Methodist minister **Boston King.**

Another was **Thomas Peters**, born in West Africa, purchased by French slave traders, and brought to Louisiana to work in the sugar fields. Peters tried to escape from his masters on several occasions and was sold to William Campbell, a North Carolina planter, some time in the 1770s. In early 1776 when Patriot forces abandoned Wilmington, Peters joined the Loyalist army of Black Pioneers, who responded to Lord Dunmore's call for slaves to rally to the loyalist cause—and abandon their rebel masters. After fighting for five years and reaching the rank of sergeant, Peters then joined the 2,775 African Americans the British Navy evacuated from New York City to Nova Scotia in 1783. Racism by white settlers, a hostile climate, and a lack of economic opportunities led Peters to London in 1790 where he successfully petitioned the British government to allow Loyalist blacks to settle the new colony of Sierra Leone. Peters was one of the key leaders of the exodus of over one thousand black Nova Scotians who left Halifax for Freetown in 1791. He died less than four months after his arrival.

The development of Africa within an emerging Atlantic system of trade and cultural exchange should not distract us from historical changes driven by forces from within Africa itself in the same era. Among the most important were the leading Sufi religious thinkers and political leaders who inspired the formation of the Fulani theocratic and jihadi states of West Africa in the eighteenth and nineteenth centuries. These began with Fouta Djallon in present-day Guinea in the 1720s; Futa Toro, established along the Senegal River in 1776; and Macina in Mali by the nineteenth century. The most powerful of the Fulani theocracies, however, was the Sokoto Caliphate founded by **Uthman Dan Fodio**, a Fulani cleric, who in 1808 conquered and united the Hausa states located in present-day Northern Nigeria. He was succeeded by his son **Muhammad Bello**, who influenced ʿ**Umar Tal,** a Senegalese apostle of the Tijaniyya Sufi religious brotherhood who lived at Bello's court in the 1830s. ʿUmar Tal married Bello's daughter, and their son succeeded Tal as ruler of the Mali-based Toucouleur Empire in the late nineteenth century.

In terms of indigenous cultural developments, the Dictionary also recognizes the flourishing in East Africa of Swahili verse in Ajami script from the eighteenth century onward. These authors include **Mwanakupona Binti Msham**, a female poet who was born in 1820 on Pate Island in the Indian Ocean off Kenya's north coast and who is best known for her "Utendi wa Mwanakupona" (The Epic of Mwanakupona). Another was **Hemedi Abdallah bin Said el-Buhriy**, who was born in 1850 on Pemba Island (now part of Tanzania) to a long line of Islamic scholars and poets. His best-known poem is "Utenzi wa Vita vya Wadachi Kutamalaki Mrima," about the 1888–1889 war waged by coastal peoples against German occupiers in which Hemedi was a spy. It praises the leadership of **Bushiri bin Salim**, while depicting the Germans as drunken infidels, lacking civilization. Both poets drew on the recognized progenitor of the Swahili oral tradition, **Fumo Liyongo**, who probably lived in the twelfth and thirteenth centuries. In 1913 **Muhammad Kijumwa**, published the most authoritative source on *Liyongo Utendi wa Fumo Liyongo* (The Epic of Liyongo).

IV

In the nineteenth century, Europeans began to exert a much greater influence on the African continent than they had even during the history of the slave trade. The *DAB* thus includes King **Leopold II** of Belgium and Queen **Victoria** of the United Kingdom, whose imperial designs profoundly shaped the changing map of Africa. African leaders from this period include **Muhammad Ahmad ibn ʿAbdallah**, the Sudanese religious figure known to the British as the Mahdi; **Sayyid bin Sultan**, the Omani ruler based in Zanzibar and its East African mainland dependencies; the Nyamwezi leaders **Mirambo** and **Msiri**; and the Swahili merchant and slave trader **Tippu Tip** in East and Central Africa. In southern Africa, the powerful Zulu kingdom established by **Shaka Zulu** by the early 1800s was continued by his nephew **Cetshwayo ka Mpande**. At the beginning of the 1879 Anglo-Zulu War, Cetshwayo inflicted a number of defeats on the British Army, but was ultimately defeated and his kingdom dismembered by the superior weaponry of the British. Notable also is **Rabih al-Zabayr Fadl Allah** in Sudan, whose military campaigns were the last major African threat to French rule in Central Africa; he was defeated and killed in 1900.

We have included some explorers and adventurers, including the French **Pierre Savorgnan de Brazza** in French Central Africa and **Louis Archinard** in French West Africa; and the Britons **Cecil John Rhodes**, General **Charles George Gordon**, **David Livingstone**, perhaps the most famous missionary in the history of colonialism, and the equally famous journalist who tracked Livingstone down, **Henry Morton Stanley**.

In West Africa, the advantages and limits of trade with the Europeans are exemplified by the case of the merchant and king **Jaja of Opobo.** Jaja was born in the Niger delta and kidnapped and sold into slavery as a child to a Bonny palm oil trader, who recognized the boy's intelligence and business acumen. Within a few years, remarkably, the former Igbo slave became a Bonny chief and, through his dominance of the delta's hinterland and good relations with European merchants, became one of the wealthiest traders in the region. In 1870 he established a settlement in Opobo and declared himself king.

The British recognized Jaja's kingdom—and cultivated good relations with him. In 1873–1874 during the Third Ashanti War on the Gold Coast, King Jaja supplied the British with some of his fighting men from Opobo. In recognition of that effort and strong relations with the British Empire, Queen Victoria awarded Jaja a ceremonial silver sword in 1875. Those good relations changed when Jaja became too powerful and threatened Britain's efforts to control the oil trade and oil prices. As a result of the 1884 Treaty of Berlin initiating the "Scramble for Africa," Britain declared the Niger delta a "Protectorate of the Crown." When Jaja protested, colonial officials first promised to negotiate, but then reneged, kidnapped him, brought him to Accra, found him guilty of obstructing trade, and exiled him to the West Indies. He was later allowed to return to Opobo, but died on route.

Somewhat more successful in negotiating for their people were **Khama III, Sebele I,** and **Bathoen I**, three chiefs of the Bechuanaland Protectorate. In 1895 they traveled to Britain to meet Queen Victoria and succeeded in preventing their territories from being absorbed into what became the country of Rhodesia. Following their audience with Victoria, Sebele of the Bakwena said, "Her Majesty is charming. She has a kind face and a sweet voice. But I had no idea that she was so short and stout."

Between the "Scramble for Africa" and World War I, Europeans began to color the map of Africa in shades reflecting their dominance of these "possessions." The borders often split apart traditional groupings and even families. On many maps the British gave "their" countries a pinkish-red hue, colored the French territories of North and West Africa beige, and marked German possessions in Tanganyika, Rwanda-Urundi, South West Africa, Cameroon, and Togoland in light green. While Portugal's colonies on both coasts were aquamarine, the Central African expanse of the Belgian Congo—Joseph Conrad's "Heart of Darkness"—was shaded a bright blue. Italy's growing imperial ambitions were reflected by the bright purples of Libya and parts of the Horn, while Spain's tiny enclave on the Guinea coast, like its possessions in the Sahara, was crimson. In terms of territory the French Empire was largest and the British Empire the most populous. Only in Abyssinia and Liberia did a pale yellow reflect the independence of African nation states from colonial control. The former was one of the most ancient of nations; the latter was first settled in 1821 and established as a republic in 1847, a date that preceded the unified Italian and German states. At the beginning of the twenty-first century that map had been transformed to reflect fifty-three sovereign African independent states. The sovereignty of a fifty-fourth territory, Western Sahara, was in dispute, claimed by both the Kingdom of Morocco and the Sahrawi Arab Democratic Republic. In July 2011 these independent states were joined by the Republic of South Sudan. Some have proposed that Africa's newest state should be named the Republic of Kush after the ancient kingdom of that name located in Egypt and Sudan.

The process of decolonization and the rise of independent African nation-states is told through the lives of many writers, intellectuals, cultural, religious, and political leaders in these pages. A good starting point is 1900, the year of the first Pan-African Conference, which was held in London. It was convened by the Trinidadian barrister **Henry Sylvester Williams** and was attended by thirty delegates, mostly from the West Indies, Britain, and the United States, including **W. E. B. Du Bois,** a recent PhD from Harvard. Du Bois served as chairman, Committee on Address, and it was in that capacity, in a communiqué from this conference, that he first, famously, stated that the "problem of the Twentieth Century is the problem of the color line." The conference also called on Queen Victoria to place African and West Indian colonies on an equal standing with white-majority British colonies like Canada and Australia. That call echoed the views of some earlier West African thinkers like **Edward Wilmot Blyden, James Beale Africanus Horton**, Bishops **James Holy Johnson** and **Samuel Ajayi Crowther**, and **J. E. Casely-Hayford,** who sought greater promotion and recognition of African talents and greater autonomy for Africans within the British imperial structure.

By the World War I era and the 1920s a more radical nationalist edge began to emerge, notably among lawyers like **John Mensah Sarbah** of the Gold Coast Aborigines' Rights Protection Society and the crusading Nigerian journalist and political leader **Herbert Macaulay**. Two of the most intriguing figures of the early twentieth century are the South African **Solomon Tshekisho Plaatje** and **James Emman Kwegyir Aggrey** of the Gold Coast. Plaatje began his career as a crusading journalist exposing racism, injustice, and the exploitation of black South African workers. In 1912 he was the first secretary-general of the South African Native National Congress, the forerunner of the African National Congress, and later was the first translator of Shakespeare into the African language of Setswana.

Aggrey was born to a prominent Gold Coast family, but unlike many of his contemporaries he sought an education in the United States, first at Livingstone College, a historically black college in Salisbury, North Carolina, and then at Columbia University. In the 1920s he visited and lectured in eighteen African countries for the Phelps-Stokes Fund as part of a project to highlight the educational needs on the continent. Aggrey was a compelling and graceful speaker, and thousands of Africans came to hear him speak on that tour. Above all, Aggrey advanced the idea of Africa as a cultural whole. He encouraged the promotion of a distinct pan-African consciousness at the expense of tribal and territorial identities. Among those he met and directly influenced were **Benjamin Nnamdi Azikiwe** (first president of Nigeria), **William Tubman** (the long serving president of Liberia), **Sylvanus Epiphanio Olympio** (first president of Togo), **Hastings Kamuzu Banda** (first president of Malawi), and **Kwame Nkrumah** (first president of Ghana).

Many of these political leaders would attend the next four subsequent Pan-African Congresses held in 1919, 1921, 1923, and 1927, which attracted more African participants than the first, including many from Francophone Africa. (The fifth, and perhaps most memorable, would be held in 1945.) Most notable was **Blaise Diagne,** born on Gorée Island in Senegal, which had been a leading center of the transatlantic slave trade. Diagne was a powerful opponent of racial discrimination within the French empire, but he was less sympathetic to

Pan-Africanist solutions that viewed Africa as a distinct entity with common goals and needs. His focus was rather on achieving equality for Africans within a Francophone context. The development of the concept of Négritude by **Léopold Sédar Senghor** and **Aimé Césaire** in the 1930s thus marked a radical departure from Diagne among Francophone nationalists in Africa and brought them closer to the Anglophone nationalists influenced by James Aggrey. And while they clashed and differed in many ways from Du Bois, who first visited Africa (Liberia) in 1937, Senghor and Césaire in the 1930s and 1940s brought into black and African nationalist thought an increasing identification with Marxist ideas, at the same time that Du Bois was moving in that direction.

The 1945 Pan-African Congress, organized by the Trinidadian **George Padmore** brought the major intellectuals and activists of twentieth-century Pan-Africanism together in one place: Manchester, England, the heartland of the British industrial revolution and the city of Friedrich Engels. It was there that Du Bois met Nkrumah, a meeting that would have lasting consequences for both men, eventually leading Nkrumah to invite Du Bois to settle in Ghana, which he did in 1961. The Manchester congress set the agenda for the decolonization of African nations, which gathered pace quickly in the decade that followed. Decolonization was assisted by the postwar exhaustion of the European imperial powers and by allies of African self-rule within the British and French socialist and labor movements. Increasingly African nationalists would seek to take advantage of divisions between the United States and the Soviet Union in the cold war.

Most Africans remained under colonial rule until World War II, although an independent South Africa was established with white minority rule in 1910, and Egypt ended British and French control over all but the Suez Canal in 1922. While Ethiopia reasserted its historical independence in 1941 after a five-year period of Italian occupation, the first country to establish independence after World War II was another Italian territory, Libya, under King **Idris** in 1951. Sudan followed in 1956, with **Isma'il al-Azhari** coming to power and ending joint British and Egyptian control. In that year **Gamal Abd al-Nasser** came to power in Egypt, bringing with him a new strain of anticolonial thought and action in North Africa–modernist pan-Arab nationalism. The French Empire decolonized rapidly, resulting in two independent states in 1956: a Moroccan kingdom under **Mohammed V** and a Tunisian republic led by **Habib Bourguiba**. In 1957 Ghana under Kwame Nkrumah became the first British colony to declare independence. A republic in Guinea was established in 1958 led by **Ahmed Sékou Touré.** It was, however, the year 1960 that signaled the new order of independent African states. On the first day of that year independence was declared in Cameroon, led by **Ahmadou Ahidjo.** Sixteen nations followed over the next eleven months: Togo (Sylvanus Olympio); Senegal (Léopold Sédar Senghor); Mali (**Modibo Keïta)**; Madgasacar (Philibert Tsiranana); Republic of the Congo (Leopoldville; later Zaire, now Democratic Republic of the Congo) (**Joseph Kasa-Vubu**); Somalia (Aden Abdullah Osman Daar); Benin (**Coutoucou Hubert Maga**); Niger (**Diori Hamani**) Upper Volta (later Burkina Faso) (Maurice Yaméogo); Ivory Coast (**Félix Houphouët-Boigny**) Chad (**François Tombalbaye**), the Central African Republic (**David Dacko**), Congo (Brazzaville) (**Fulbert Youlou**); Gabon (**Léon M'ba**); Nigeria (Nnamdi Azikiwe); and Mauritania (**Moktar Ould Daddah**).

Sierra Leone (**Milton Augustus Strieby Margai**) and Tanganyika (**Julius Nyerere**) declared independence in 1961, with the latter country becoming Tanzania after union with Zanzibar in 1964. Ugandan independence in 1962 was led by King **Muteesa II**, who took the name Frederick Edward Mutesa; that same year Algeria finally achieved independence from France, after a long and brutal civil war. In 1963 **Ahmed Ben Bella** became president of the new Algerian republic, while **Jomo Kenyatta** became the first prime minister of independent Kenya. These were followed by Malawi (Hastings Banda, 1964), Zambia (**Kenneth Kaunda**, 1964), Gambia (Sir **Dawda Kairaba Jawara**, 1965), Botswana (Sir **Seretse Khama**, 1966); Lesotho (King Moshoeshoe II, 1966); and Swaziland (King **Sobhuza II**, 1968). Equatorial Guinea achieved independence from Spain in 1968, becoming a republic under **Macías Nguema**.

Perhaps the most intriguing story of the independence era comes from Congo (Leopoldville), where Joseph Kasa-Vubu was the first president. He was however, eclipsed by his fellow independence leader **Patrice Emery Lumumba**, who was only thirty-four years old when elected as the first prime minister of an independent Congo in 1960. Lumumba developed close links with the like-minded Nkrumah at All-African Peoples' Conferences held in Accra in 1958 and Tunis in 1960. Both were socialists determined to forge unity among the emerging African states. Lumumba's fate may have been sealed by his dramatic Independence Day speech, which condemned the atrocities of Belgian colonialism and reminded the watching King Baudouin that Congo had only achieved its independence through bloodshed and struggle. An internal struggle between Lumumba and Congo's more moderate first president Joseph Kasa-Vubu came to a head in 1961 with Lumumba's assassination, perhaps by Belgian agents and perhaps with the complicity of the CIA, as a result of Lumumba's growing support by the Soviet Union. At any rate, the unstable Congo republic that followed, and its overthrow by Joseph-Désiré Mobutu (**Mobutu Sese Seko**), foreshadowed similar military takeovers or the establishment of one-party states in several other new African nations.

Lumumba, however, remained an inspirational figure, notably for the anticolonial leaders in Portuguese Africa, such as **Amílcar Lopes Cabral** and the African Party for the Independence of Guinea and Cape Verde, **Samora Moïses Machel** in Mozambique, and **Agostinho Neto** in Angola. Portugal, the first European country to colonize Africa, was the last to decolonize, with Guinea Bissau becoming independent in 1974, followed a year later by Mozambique, Cape Verde, São Tomé and Príncipe, and Angola. Lumumba—as well as Du Bois, Nkrumah, Malcolm X, and other pan-African nationalists—was also an influence on **Steve Biko**, the key figure in the Black Consciousness movement in South Africa in the 1970s and 1980s. The election of **Nelson Rolihlahla Mandela** as president of the first truly democratic state in South Africa in 1994 perhaps serves as a fitting—and hopeful—endpoint of a century of anticolonial struggles on the continent.

V

We in the West often tend to think of Africa primarily in terms of slavery and colonialism, but Africa has a long tradition of excellence in the arts and sciences, including, for example, a number of Nobel laureates in a variety of disciplines, beginning in 1952. The *DAB* contains biographies of nineteen Nobel laureates, sixteen of whom were born on the African continent. **Doris Lessing** (Literature, 2007) was born in Persia, before moving to colonial Rhodesia as a child. Two others were born in Europe, but, like Lessing, have a strong connection to the African continent: the French citizen and humanitarian **Albert Schweitzer** (Peace, 1952), who died in Gabon, at his famous hospital; and **Jean-Marie Gustave Le Clézio** (Literature, 2008), a joint citizen of France and Mauritius, who spent his childhood in Nigeria. The French-Algerian **Albert Camus** won the prize for Literature in 1957.

It is worthy of note that in addition to Schweitzer, nine of Africa's Nobel prizes have been for peace. Four winners of the Peace Prize have been South Africans, including **Albert John Mvumbi Luthuli** (1961); **Desmond Mpilo Tutu** (1984); Nelson Mandela (1993) and **Frederik William De Klerk** (1993); three have been Egyptians: **Muhammad Anwar al-Sadat** (1978); **Yasser Arafat**, the Palestinian leader, who was born and educated in Cairo (1994); and **Mohamed ElBaradei** (2005); one, **Kofi Atta Annan** (2001), was from Ghana and one, **Wangari Muta Maathai** (2004), the only African woman to win the prize, was from Kenya. In 1986 Nigerian **Wole Soyinka** was the first African to win the Nobel Prize in Literature. Subsequent winners are the Egyptian **Naguib Mahfouz** (1988) and the South Africans **Nadine Gordimer** (1991) and **J. M. Coetzee** (2003).

Perhaps less well known are the two Africans who have won a Nobel Prize in the field of science. In 1951 the South African **Max Theiler** received the Nobel Prize in Physiology or Medicine. Theiler developed the first effective yellow-fever vaccine, which eliminated yellow fever as a threat to public health in West Africa in the late 1940s. **Ahmed Zewail,** an Egyptian-born American citizen educated at the Universities of Alexandria and Pennsylvania, won the 1999 Nobel Prize in Chemistry for his work in founding the field of femtochemistry. Using rapid laser technique, Zewail showed how atoms in a molecule move during a chemical reaction, thereby transforming scientists' understanding of intramolecular behavior. Zewail, the Linus Pauling Professor of Chemistry and professor of physics at the California Institute of Technology, is also President Barack Obama's special envoy for science to the Middle East and Africa. In February 2011 Zewail returned to Egypt to assist the transition to democracy in his native land.

There are, of course, many other realms of renown recognized in the *DAB*. We include great track athletes, including the Ethiopian distance runners **Abebe Bikila, Haile Gebrselassie, Kenenisa Bekele** and **Derartu Tulu; Kip Keino** of Kenya; **Maria Lurdes Mutola** of Mozambique, the greatest female 800-meter runner in history; and **Hicham El Guerrouj**, the Moroccan 1,500-meter champion known as the "King of the Mile." Two other Olympic golds were won in Atlanta in 1996, by the Nigerian-born basketball star **Hakeem Olajuwon**, who competed for the United States, and **Augustine Azuka** "Jay Jay" **Okocha** of the Nigerian Super Eagles soccer team. Other soccer greats included are the Mozambican-born **Eusébio**, the most prolific striker of his era; Cameroon's **Roger Milla**, the oldest player to play and score in a World Cup; and **George Manneh Weah**, the first African selected as World Footballer of the Year. In 2005 Weah was defeated in a run-off for the presidency of Liberia by **Ellen Johnson Sirleaf,** who became the first elected female head of state of an African nation.

The *DAB* also includes entries on a wide range of artists, musicians, and writers. Playwrights range from the ancient Roman playwright **Terence** and the thirteenth-century "Arab Aristophanes," **Shams al din Muhammad Ibn Daniyal**, to contemporary playwrights like Kirundi-language writer **Marie-Louise Sibazuri** of Burundi and Tanzania's **Penina Muhando**, the first female playwright of the Swahili language. Well over one hundred poets are included, reaching across the borders of nations and centuries: **Muyaka bin Haji al-Ghassaniy**, an influential nineteenth-century Kenyan poet in the *mashairi* tradition, influenced the later work of Tanzanian writers like **Shaaban Robert** and **Saadani Abdu Kandoro**. The Senegambian-born poet Phillis Wheatley famously wrote in praise of the American Revolution, while the modern-day Gambian **Lenrie Peters** explores in his poems the corrupting influences of colonialism on African societies. **Abu al-Qasim al-Shabbi's** "The Will of Life" became a rallying cry in the 2010–2011 uprisings in his native Tunisia as well as in Egypt. The Greek-Egyptian writer **Constantine Cavafy** won acclaim for his poems dealing with themes of classical history and homosexual eroticism, and **Kabelo Sello Duiker's** novels controversially explored sexual experimentation and exploitation in apartheid-era Cape Town.

Our musical entries range from traditional singers like Egypt's **Umm Kulthum**, recognized as the greatest singer in Arab music history, **Cheb Khaled,** the undisputed king of Algerian Rai music, and **Reuben Tholakele Caluza**, whose combinations of ragtime rhythms and traditional Zulu lyrics brought modernist African musical traditions to the attention of international audiences. We also include the radical Nigerian musician and activist **Fela Anikulapo Kuti** (who happens to be Wole Soyinka's first cousin) and the Somalian rapper **K'Naan Warsame**, whose lyrics are inspired by his childhood in the war-torn streets of Mogadishu.

Entries on African film explore the lives of numerous path-breaking artists. **Tsitsi Dangaremgba**'s 1996 film *Everyone's Child* was the first feature film directed by a black Zimbabwean woman. **Omar Sharif** and **Djimon Hounsou** were among the first African-born actors nominated for Academy Awards. The Senegalese filmmaker **Djibril Diop Mambéty** has been widely acclaimed for the innovative style and narrative structure of his films, which include a documentary about the making of Burkinabe director **Idrissa Ouédraogo**'s *Yaaba* (1989).

The artists included have produced pieces in a wide array of artistic media and traditions. The bronze sculpture "Anyanwu" (*sunshine* in Igbo), created by the modernist artist **Benedict Chukwukadibia Enwonwu,** stands as an enduring symbol of Nigerian independence. Self-taught visual artist and actress **Younouss Seye** of Senegal incorporates pan-African symbolism into her mixed-media paintings through her regular use of cowrie shells. The Nigerian woodcarvers **George Bandele Areogun** and **Lamidi Olonade Fakeye** helped to create the artistic genres of Yoruba-Christian and Yoruba-Neotraditional art, and **Sokari Douglas Camp**'s steel sculptures draw upon the Kalabari traditions of the healing powers of art.

VI

Some readers may be surprised that we have no entry on the most famous and powerful person of African descent on the planet, Barack Obama Jr., the president of the United States of America since 2009. Yet since President Obama was born in the United States and spent no significant period of his life in Africa, he is instead properly included in our companion title, *African American National Biography*.

The *DAB* does, however, include essays on the president's father, **Barack Obama Sr.**, and his grandfather, **Hussein Onyango Obama**, both born in Kenya. Hussein Obama was an herbalist, cook, and farmer, whose life was typical of many Africans growing up in East Africa under British rule. He learned to read and write from Christian missionaries and may have converted to Catholicism before later becoming a Muslim while living in Zanzibar. He worked at various times for the British Army as a cook and laborer, but after World War II, like many Africans he began to note the irony that he had helped defeat fascism while remaining a colonial subject. Details are sparse but he may have supplied information to leaders of the Kenya African Union. In 1949 he was jailed for two years for anticolonial activities and emerged from jail more embittered toward the British than he had been before. Like most ethnic Luos, he had no involvement in the later Kikuyu-based Mau Mau resistance movement against British rule in Kenya.

Hussein Obama's focus in the 1950s was to farm, raise his children, and advance the educational future of his bright eldest son, Barack Obama Sr. That goal was achieved by an airlift of eighty-one Kenyan students to study in America. That 1959 airlift was sponsored by African American civil rights leaders such as Harry Belafonte and organized in Kenya by **Tom Mboya,** a young socialist who a year earlier had served as conference chair of the All-African Peoples' Conference convened by Kwame Nkrumah in Accra. Barack Obama Sr. was one of the Kenyan students in that airlift. Shortly after arriving in Hawaii in 1959, he met and married a young American woman named Ann Dunham. Barack Obama Jr. was born to the couple in Honolulu two years later in 1961. After Barack Obama Sr. and his wife divorced, he returned to Kenya in the mid-1960s, with an economics degree from the University of Hawaii and a master's degree from Harvard. He worked as an economist in the Kenyan Ministry of Economic Planning and Development, then headed by Mboya, and was later a senior economist in the Ministry of Finance. Though talented and ambitious, his career never reached the heights many had predicted. His political fortunes waned with the assassination of his fellow Luo Mboya, in 1969, and stalled in the 1970s after he openly criticized Jomo Kenyatta. Among the other Kenyan scholars assisted by Mboya's airlift was Wangari Muta Matthai, who would later become a leading environmentalist, and in 2004 became the first African female winner of the Nobel Peace Prize.

VII

Perhaps the most gratifying aspect of editing this Dictionary is that, even at its first stage of completion with two thousand entries, it constitutes the largest database of biographies of individuals who, in such a wide range of ways, helped to make the history of the African continent, from the ancient Egyptians to the present. And we expect it to grow to include ten thousand entries on line. Why is this so especially important in the context of African history? For so very long, Africa was depicted in the West as a continent frozen in a static present, a continent immune to progress and change, a continent housing a people without a past. The German philosopher Georg Wilhelm Friedrich Hegel's attitude, expressed in 1790, is typical: "At this point we leave Africa, not to mention it again. For it is no historical part of the World; it has no movement or development to exhibit. Historical movements in it—that is in its northern part—belong to the Asiastic or European World. . . . What we properly understand by Africa is the Unhistorical, Undeveloped Spirit, still involved in the conditions of mere nature, and which had to be presented here only as on the threshold of the World's History." Writing about half a century after Hegel, the American lexicographer Noah Webster affirmed Hegel's opinion: "of the wooly haired Africans, who constitute the principal part of the inhabitants of Africa, there is no history, & there can be none. That race has remained in barbarism from the first ages of the world." And lest we think that such attitudes about Africa and its Africans are remnants of an era framed by the slave trade and colonialism, the English historian Hugh Trevor-Roper, quite infamously, wrote as recently as 1965 that "Perhaps, in the future, there will be some African history to teach. But at present there is none, or very little: there is only the history of the Europeans in Africa."

And what do these three assertions, and others like them, share in common? On what premises are they based? We might put it like this: if Africa has no major tradition of writing before the onset of European "discovery" and colonialism, then it can have no history; with no history, it can have no formal, reliably repeatable memory. And with no memory, Africans can have no subjectivity, in the Cartesian sense of that term, connoting the self-reflection inherent in any meta-narrative. As Trevor-Roper put it, "History, I believe, is essentially a form of movement, and purposive movement too. It is not a mere phantasmagoria of changing shapes and costumes, of battles and conquests, dynasties and usurpations, social forms and social disintegration . . . we may neglect our own history and amuse ourselves with the unrewarding gyrations of barbarous tribes in picturesque but irrelevant corners of the globe: tribes whose chief function in history, in my opinion, is to show to the present an image of the past from which, by history, it has escaped."

The other thing that Hegel, Webster, and Trevor-Roper share in common is an almost total ignorance of the African subjects (and their historical contexts) who actually shaped the course of events that unfolded on the African continent in drama and detail as complex as human history unfolded in Europe, the Middle East, or Asia. Africans made their own history and told stories about that history, just like everyone else. The problem is that we, in the West, are only just bothering to learn about it. Even the scholarly recuperation of African cultural forms such as music and art, in the twentieth century, unwittingly, perhaps, fostered the illusion that traditional African creativity was "collective" and "functional" and somehow, therefore, inescapably anonymous, faceless, nameless: works created by objects, not subjects, in the Cartesian sense of that term.

Africans, in other words, were not only human beings purportedly without a past; they were human beings ostensibly without a discrete presence, the presence of individual thought, action, and achievement—all because these accomplishments have not been adequately recorded, passed down, and anthologized in encyclopedias and dictionaries such as this one. It is to preserve, archive, and disseminate these rich and compelling stories of the thousands of Africans whose hopes and dreams, ideals and foibles, achievements and failures, are collected in these pages, and the thousands more to be added to our database, that is one of the principal purposes of this *Dictionary of African Biography*. We tell the history of Africa in these pages by retelling the individual histories of the complex human beings who made that history. This collective history of individual African lives stands as an implicit critique of the aspersions such as those Hegel, Webster, and Trevor-Roper cast upon both African history and the historically significant Africans who made that history.

EMMANUEL K. AKYEAMPONG

HENRY LOUIS GATES, JR.

Executive Editors' Note

Editorial work on the *Dictionary of African Biography* began in summer 2008. The first invitations to contributors were sent in October 2008 and the last manuscript arrived in March 2011, just over thirty months later. In the meantime, the son of a Kenyan was elected president of the United States and several long-serving African heads of state left office. The print version of the Dictionary was intended to include biographies of two thousand of the most important people who made the history of Africa. As the project was being developed and as articles were reviewed, contributors and editors suggested other names, with the result that there are 2,126 entries in the Dictionary, comprising over 2.1 million words. We hope that no major figure has been left out; many more biographies will be included in an expanded online version of the Dictionary.

The entries are arranged in alphabetical order letter by letter, not word by word, up to the first comma. Readers will therefore find the sequence, "Baba, Sidiyya," "Baba ʿAruj," "Babalola, Joseph Ayodele," "Babangida, Ibrahim Badamosi," and "Baba of Karo."

Because the Dictionary is intended primarily for an English-speaking audience, the headwords are forms of names most familiar to that audience from the media, recognizing that the forms may not always be the most accurate. We have, for example, chosen to use "Nasser, Gamal Abd al-" rather than "ʿAbd al-Nasir, Jamal." The variants of Gadafy/Gaddafi/Gadhafi/Kaddafi/Kadhafi/Qaddafi/Qaddafi/Qadhafi will be well known; we have chosen to use "Qaddafi." The common form of Ethiopian and Eritrean names is the given name and the father's name; there are no surnames, although Western media outlets often treat the father's name as a surname. For example, the marathon runner Haile Gebrselassie is usually referred to as "Gebrselassie." The editors of the Dictionary have decided, in most cases, to follow the Ethiopian custom; the runner is therefore found under "H" and the headword is "Haile Gebrselassie."

The Dictionary includes blind entries directing readers from familiar variants of an entry term to the entry term itself. For example, the blind entry for "Abiodun, Christiana" tells the reader to look under "Emanuel, Christiana Abiodun."

To guide readers from one biography to related biographies, a selective bibliography appears at the end of almost every biography. These references are not exhaustive, but they are intended to direct the reader to the main sources of further information on the subject of the entry and his or her historical context. The bibliographies will enable the reader seeking to pursue a topic in greater detail to the most useful works in English and the most important scholarly works in any language. For entries on writers, we have included those authors's most important works within the body of the text. The Dictionary also includes 224 illustrations.

The contributors have sought to write in clear language with a minimum of technical vocabulary. We have respected the individual voices of the contributors as far as possible and appropriate. The biographies give important terms and titles in their original languages, with English translations when needed. With regard to technical matters of style—such as capitalization and italics—we have followed *The Chicago Manual of Style*, sixteenth edition; for spelling, we have followed *Merriam-Webster's Collegiate Dictionary*, eleventh edition; for proper names, *Merriam-Webster's Biographical Dictionary* and *Merriam-Webster's Geographical Dictionary*, third edition. As might be expected from a dictionary that spans the entire continent and covers several millennia of African history, there are many exceptions.

African names and terms take many forms depending on the languages of the people who bear them, how those languages were understood by non-Africans (usually colonialists and imperialists who spoke Arabic or European languages), and the many ways in which non-Africans decided to render those languages, and their sounds, in their own alphabets.

For names and terms in Arabic, Ethiopian languages, Hausa, Yoruba, and other languages, we have generally avoided a scientific or technical transliteration that employs diacritics and accents, underdots and macrons, punctuation, and special letters that may be distracting and incomprehensible to the nonspecialist. We have chosen to use simplified transliteration systems that are consistent, accurate, and accessible to the English-speaking general reader.

For Arabic names and terms, we show ayns and hamzas, but not underdots, macrons, or other special characters. The particle al- is rendered as it is spelled (al-), not as it is pronounced (ad-, an-, ar-, as-, at-, and other forms before sun letters); it may appear as el or El in some names (for example, Muhammad ElBaradei). We have not imposed a single spelling on commonly encountered names, recognizing that there are variants and regional variations in the spelling of the same name, especially if the name is in a language other than Arabic: just as in English some people are named Stephen and some Steven, so in African languages people may be named Muhammad, Mohamed, or Mehmet.

In Ethiopia and Eritrea, there are three main groups of languages: Arabic, other Semitic (Geez, Amharic, Tigrinya, and Tigre) and Cushitic (Oromo, Afar, and Somali). Because of this complexity and because of the fact that there is no one accepted method of transliteration for the Semitic and Cushitic languages, we have followed a simplified system used in the most authoritative and widely read books published in English on the history of Ethiopia as well as most academic journals in the English-speaking world. Readers will therefore come across usages such as "Haile Selasse" rather than "Haylä Séllase" and "Menen" rather than "Mänän."

The final volume contains listings of subjects by dates of birth or periods of activity, by places of birth or major involvement, and by occupations and realms of renown; a list of current heads of state; the directory of contributors; and a comprehensive index that lists all the topics covered in the Dictionary, including those that are not headwords themselves.

In the listing by dates of death or periods of activity, periods are broadly delineated as before 640 CE (the Arab conquest of Egypt), 640–1800, 1801–1900, 1901–2000, and 2001 to the present. In the biographies, there are many instances of c. (for circa) and fl. (for flourished).

In the listing by places of birth or major involvement, designation of regions follows the divisions set by scholars working on the various regions, for example, the Greater Maghreb or French-speaking West Africa. For assignment of subjects to countries, we have recognized modern borders, with some adjustments for premodern states and jurisdictions. Thus, the early Christian theologian Tertullian is listed under Ancient Roman Africa/Tunisia rather than Tunisia and Augustine of Hippo and his mother, Monnica, under Ancient Roman Numidia/Algeria rather than Algeria. The lists of regions and countries accommodate some interlopers who came from outside Africa, but who had an impact on its history, figures such as Asurbanipal (listed under Ancient Assyria), who never set foot on African soil, but whose seventh-century BCE empire included Egypt; or the cartographer and explorer Keith Johnston (Scotland), who died within six weeks of arriving on the continent, but whose research and surveys proved invaluable to our understanding of African geography. The two countries named Congo are distinguished as Congo (Brazzaville) for the Republic of the Congo (formerly French Middle Congo, part of French Equatorial Africa) and Congo (Kinshasa)—and in a few instances Congo (Leopoldville)—for the Democratic Republic of the Congo (formerly Congo Free State, Belgian Congo, and Zaire).

Occupations and realms of renown presented special challenges to the editors and required the greatest care in interpretation and wording. Subjects were assigned to classifications by the editors, not by the contributors, based on what we found in the biographies. Perfect consistency was difficult, if not impossible, to achieve. Some of our headings may seem bland. Many include the word figure, which avoids having to distinguish leaders from followers. The wording is usually American, so that we use "Labor Union Figure" rather than "Trade Union Figure."

We have tried to describe, not judge, recognizing that what may be offensive to some is descriptive to others and vice versa. We do not have a category "Dictator" or "Mass Murderer." Other occupations that may raise eyebrows or hackles are "Chief," "Imperialist," "Pirate," and "Rebel." We intend no political critique in listing subjects under "Imperialist"; we mean only leaders of extra-African empires in the modern period and only when so described in the text of their biographies; agents of colonial empires are listed under "Colonial Administrator/ Governor/Agent." Instead of "Pirate" we considered the heading "Maritime Figure," which would include sailors, admirals, and other seafarers. But we decided that it was too vague and nondescriptive, and it seemed ludicrous, as we began drafting this note in late February 2011, to say that four Americans were killed by "Somali maritime figures." We settled on "Corsair/ Pirate."

The two most difficult categories were religion and rulership. For religion, we listed subjects under "job description" and added extensions for different religions and denominations, for example, "Saint, Early Christian," "Saint, Ethiopian," "Saint, Islamic," and "Saint, Roman Catholic." Subjects are listed by occupation—for example, "Bishop/Archbishop, Roman Catholic"—and also all together under "Roman Catholic Figure."

With regard to rulers, one contributor's *big man* is another's *traditional ruler*. Most contributors avoided the terms *chief* and *chieftain*. "Monarch" designates the ruler of a major territory, country, or empire; "Ruler" designates the ruler of a smaller jurisdiction. There are separate headings for "Ancient Egyptian Ruler/Pharaoh," "Ethiopian Emperor/Empress/ Monarch," and the like.

We avoid listing occupations under higher-level taxonomies, such as economics, politics, religion, or society; readers should not have to guess where an occupation might be found. It is easy to find "Bishop" under religion, but is "Feminist" under politics or society or something else?

We have tried to be accurate. While some might list Sarah Baartman under "Actress" or "Entertainer" we put her in her own singular occupation, "Hottentot Venus," the term by which she was known during her lifetime and by which most people will look her up; no one will expect to find her under "Human Exhibit." Other categories with only one representative include the entry on the "Earliest Human" (African Eve), our common matrilineal ancestor, who lived 200,000 years ago in Africa, and the youngest "Windmill Inventor" (William Kamkwamba, born in Malawi in 1987).

The biographies in the Dictionary were up to date as of August 2011, when some 504 subjects, or 24 percent of the total, were still alive. Although reference works properly survey the state of knowledge about a topic and should avoid journalistic currency, contributors and editors struggled in early 2011 to keep up with current events, for example, Laurent Gbagbo's and Alassane Ouattara's contesting the results of the presidential election in the Ivory Coast, the overthrow of Zine el-Abidine Ben Ali in Tunisia, the resignation of Egyptian president Muhammad Husni Sa'id Mubarak, and the defiant clinging to power of Mu'ammar al-Qaddafi in Libya. On 9 July 2011, between the completion of the Dictionary and its publication, the southern provinces of Sudan became the world's newest independent country, the Republic of South Sudan.

We wish to acknowledge the many people involved in the making of *Dictionary of African Biography*: the editors in chief, Emmanuel K. Akyeampong and Henry Louis Gates Jr.; the members of the editorial board; the contributors; the staffs at the W. E. B. Du Bois Institute and at Oxford University Press; and numerous freelance editors and proofreaders. Four editors— Allan Fromherz, Jonathan Miran, Jeremy Rich, and Kathleen Sheldon—deserve our special thanks for their advice and direction and their willingness to take on extra duties and help us deal with unexpected crises.

STEVEN J. NIVEN
STEPHEN WAGLEY
APRIL 2011

Common Abbreviations Used in This Work

AH   *anno Hegirae*, in the year of the Hajj
b.   born
BCE   before the common era (= BC, before Christ)
c.   *circa*, about, approximately
CE   common era (= AD, *anno Domini*)
cf.   *confer*, compare
d.   died
diss.   dissertation
ed.   editor (pl., eds), edition
f.   and following (pl., ff.)
fl.   *floruit*, flourished
l.   line (pl., ll.)
n.   note
n.d.   no date
no.   number
n.p.   no place
n.s.   new series
p.   page (pl., pp.)
pt.   part
rev.   revised
ser.   series
supp.   supplement
vol.   volume (pl., vols.)

Dictionary of **African Biography**

Abacha, Sani (1943–1998), Nigerian military officer and military head of state, was born on 20 September 1943 to the Abacha family in the northern state of Kano, Nigeria. Abacha attended the City Senior Primary School in Kano before proceeding to the Provincial Secondary School in Kano (renamed Government College) in 1957 for his secondary education. Abacha completed his secondary education in 1962 and decided to pursue a military career. Abacha enrolled at the Nigerian Military Training College in Kaduna in 1962. In 1963 he attended the Mons Defense Officers' Cadet Training College in Aldershot, United Kingdom, and was commissioned as a second lieutenant in the Nigerian army in the same year.

Abacha was promoted to lieutenant in 1966 after attending the School of Infantry in Warminister, United Kingdom. He became a captain in 1967 and was promoted to major in 1969, lieutenant-colonel in 1972, colonel in 1975, and brigadier in 1980. Similarly, Abacha attended the Command and Staff College in Jaji in 1976 and the National Institute for Policy and Strategic Studies in Kuru, Jos, Nigeria, and the Senior International Defense Course in Monterey, California, in 1981 and 1982, respectively. Also between 1966 and 1980 Abacha served as platoon and battalion commander, commander, second infantry division, and the commanding officer, second infantry brigade.

While Abacha remained very active in his military service, he was an unknown figure in the Nigerian political and public space until 31 December 1983 when he announced the military coup that overthrew the democratic government of President Shehu Shagari. The television and radio broadcast introduced Abacha to Nigerians, and he never left the public space until his death in 1998.

When General Muhammadu Buhari became the head of state after the December 1983 coup, Abacha was appointed the general officer commanding, second mechanized division of the Nigerian army. Abacha also announced the August 1985 coup and became the chief of army staff to General Ibrahim Badamosi Babangida, who became the head of state. With his new position, Abacha became a member of the Armed Forces Ruling Council (AFRC). In 1987 Abacha was promoted to lieutenant-general by Babangida, for whom he helped to plan and execute the 1985 coup that ousted the Buhari regime. Abacha became the chairman of the joint chiefs of staff in 1989 and was appointed minister of defense by Babangida in 1990.

Babangida handed over power to the Ernest Shonekan–led interim national government in August 1993 following the annulment of the 12 June 1993 presidential election allegedly won by Moshood Abiola, and Abacha became the secretary of defense in the new cabinet. On 17 November 1993 Abacha forced Shonekan to resign and became the head of state because he was the most senior military officer at the time. Abacha's five-year rule was marred by gross violations of human rights, stifling of dissident voices, and massive corruption. For instance, Abacha ordered the immediate arrest and trial of Abiola for treason after the latter presented himself as president-elect on 11 June 1994.

Although Abacha supported the democratic efforts in Liberia and Sierra Leone and insisted that he was committed to returning democratic governance back to Nigeria, his actions proved otherwise. Abacha banned all forms of association except for strictly religious ones and clamped down on human rights advocates and campaigners. The National Democratic Coalition (NADECO) that asked Abacha to release Abiola and declare him president was one example of such groups proscribed by the Abacha-led government. Members of NADECO were harassed, imprisoned, tortured, and killed while some lucky ones went into hiding or into exile. The Nigerian writer and Nobel laureate Wole Soyinka was one of those critics who had to flee the country to escape the brutalities of Abacha. While the likes of Soyinka might be considered lucky to escape Abacha's tyranny, others such as Kudirat Abiola, wife of the then detained winner of the 1993 elections, was killed by gunmen suspected to be members of Abacha's killer squad.

Apart from those murdered by Abacha's government, other activists and politicians were arrested and imprisoned by him. Interestingly, military officers were not spared because Abacha did not hesitate to arrest officers whom he considered disloyal to his government. These officers were linked to phantom coup plots, and some of these officers included Olusegun Obasanjo, who remained in prison until Abacha's death and later became Nigeria's civilian president; Shehu Musa Yar' Adua, who was allegedly poisoned and died in prison; and Oladipo Diya, who was Abacha's chief of army staff. Obasanjo, Diya, and other political detainees were released by General Abdulsalam Abubakar, who succeeded Abacha as head of state.

Other victims of Abacha's tyranny included the renowned environmentalist and martyr Ken Saro-Wiwa and other members of the Movement for the Survival of the Ogoni People (MOSOP) who were sentenced to death on spurious charges and hurriedly executed by Abacha's government. In reality Ken Saro-Wiwa and his group condemned the indiscriminate practices of Shell and other oil companies in the Niger delta and criticized the government for tolerating the environmental degradation of the oil companies. Saro-Wiwa's execution attracted international condemnation and sanctions for Nigeria, including suspension from the Commonwealth for three years.

These sanctions notwithstanding, Abacha retained his resolute hold on power and surrounded himself with about three thousand loyal soldiers, including Major Hamza Mustapha who served as his chief security officer and was alleged to be the mastermind of the regime's tyranny. Abacha made very few public appearances, although he did receive the late Pope John Paul II in March 1998.

Abacha died on 8 June 1998 of what military authorities claimed to be a heart attack. Unofficial sources contended that Abacha died from poison administered by some Indian prostitutes whose company he kept that night. The unconfirmed sources noted that the poisoning was arranged by Abacha's political opponents and was meant to end his tyranny. Abacha was buried on the same day in his Kano home according to Islamic burial rites. At the time he died Abacha had already been adopted as the sole candidate of the five political parties that he allowed for the election scheduled for August 1998. According to Abacha Nigeria was to return to democratic rule on 1 October 1998.

After his death, the Olusegun Obasanjo government accused Abacha of corruption and looting the treasury. Obasanjo sought and got the approval of Swiss authorities to freeze the accounts of Abacha's family and their associates. Abacha was accused of looting about $4 billion, but his family denied these charges. The Obasanjo government arrested his eldest surviving son, Mohammed, but he was released after the family agreed to pay back about $1 billion to the government. In 2004 Transparency International named Abacha as the fourth most corrupt leader in recent history while his name continues to attract negative reactions from Nigerians. Abacha was survived by his wife, Maryam Sani Abacha, who bore him six sons and three daughters. His eldest son, Ibrahim Abacha, died in a plane crash in 1996.

[*See also* Abiola, Moshood Kashimawo Olawale; Babangida, Ibrahim Badamosi; Obasanjo, Olusegun; Saro-Wiwa, Ken; *and* Soyinka, Wole.]

BIBLIOGRAPHY

Adebanwi, Wale, and Ebenezer Obadare, eds. *Encountering the Nigerian State*. New York: Palgrave Macmillan, 2010.

Falola, T. *The History of Nigeria*. Westport, Conn.: Greenwood Press, 1999.

Fawole, W. Alade. *Paranoia, Hostility, and Defiance : General Sani Abacha and the "New" Nigeria Foreign Policy*. Ile-Ife, Nigeria: Obafemi Awolowo University Press, 1999.

Soyinka, Wole. *You Must Set Forth at Dawn: A Memoir*. New York: Random House, 2007. A memoir that demonstrates Abacha's tyranny against human and civil rights activists.

"Times Topics." *New York Times*. http://topics.nytimes.com/topics/reference/timestopics/people/a/sani_abacha/index.html. An online resource that provides news articles on Sani Abacha.

CAJETAN N. IHEKA

Abani, Chris (1966–), Nigerian novelist, poet, dramatist, educator, and political activist, was born Christopher Uchechukwu Andrew Abani, on 27 December 1966, in Afikpo, Nigeria. Abani's life has been dramatically shaped but not defined by the political violence associated with the Nigerian state. Born in the Igbo heartland of southeast Nigeria to an Igbo father and British mother, Abani was six months old when the Biafran War began. His mother fled to Britain with him and his siblings, an experience that he would later narrate in poetic form in *Daphne's Lot* (2003). Returning to Nigeria after the war, Abani demonstrated precocious literary talent, publishing his first short story at age ten and finishing his first novel, *Masters of the Board* (1984), at sixteen. The novel, a political thriller, imagines a Nazi plot to return to power by using unwitting Third World governments as its pawns.

Abani was arrested in 1985 because Nigeria's military government claimed that *Masters of the Board* had provided the blueprint for a failed coup. After being imprisoned and tortured, on his release Abani became a vocal political critic, writing and producing plays for an antidictatorship guerrilla theater group. He also produced a novel, *Sirocco* (1987), that was seized by the state on publication. His literary activity resulted in two more periods of imprisonment (including at the notorious Kiri Kiri maximum-security prison, nicknamed "Kalakuta Republic"). After his release, repeated attempts on his life forced him into exile in Britain in 1991.

In London Abani continued his political activism and was closely associated with the black British artistic scene. He also earned an MA in gender and cultural studies from the University of London. Around 1996 he began composing poems about his experience in prison, which were collected in *Kalakuta Republic* (2000). The work, written in an unassuming yet penetrating style, memorializes his experiences and those of his prison mates without succumbing to anger or vengeance. In 1999, after a neighbor was murdered (Abani believed himself to be the intended victim), Abani fled into exile a second time, settling in Los Angeles.

In Los Angeles Abani continued to write poetry, releasing *Daphne's Lot* and *Dog Woman* (2004) in

quick succession. The former weaves together his family's experience during the Biafran War with vignettes of ordinary citizens caught in the violence. The latter "represents a reaction to and a reinterpretation of works by artists from a great range of historical periods and genres, including Portuguese painter Paula Rego and French poet Charles Baudelaire as well as Rainer Maria Rilke and Bartolomé de Las Casas" (Okpala, 2009, p. 8). Both collections of poetry feature powerful women as focalizing figures.

Abani returned to fiction with *GraceLand* (2004), which won several literary awards including the PEN/Hemingway Book Prize. The story traces the survival and redemption of Elvis Oke, a teenage Elvis impersonator in postcolonial Lagos, as he negotiates between poverty, domestic abuse, and political predation. *Becoming Abigail* (2006), Abani's first novella, is a meditation on suffering and survival. It tells the story of Abigail, a young girl who is kidnapped to Britain from Nigeria and forced into prostitution by her cousin.

The lyrical, elliptical style Abani adopted for *Becoming Abigail* gave the novella an experimental quality that was mirrored in the poetry of *Hands Washing Water* (2006). These poems, frequently addressed to close friends and fellow writers, include the American Civil War sequence "Buffalo Women," which imagines the correspondence between two separated lovers. In 2006 Abani earned a PhD in literature and creative writing from the University of California, Riverside, where he has subsequently served as a professor of writing and literature.

Abani's recent fiction continues to examine the limits of experience, narrative, and imagination. For Black, the emotionally lost hero of *The Virgin of Flames* (2007), his body and the city of Los Angeles become canvases on which he continuously reinvents his racial and gender identities. In *Song for Night* (2007) Abani returns to Africa as his subject. Although his teenage protagonist, "My Luck," a mine-sweeper in the Biafran War, has been violently silenced by his military trainers, in telling his story Abani insists that fiction can provide a compassionate alternative voice. His collection of poetry, *Sanctificum* (2010), develops a highly personal mix of allusions to Catholicism, literature, music, and his personal history to explore such topics as the power of ritual and belief; memory and forgetting; and violence, love, and survival.

By the early twenty-first century Abani was increasingly considered a leading voice in African letters. His capacious imagination incorporates both political thriller and postmodern experimental verse; the megacities of Los Angeles and Lagos; a voiceless child soldier; and his own parents' love life. By confronting readers with stories of ambivalence, complicity, and bewilderment alongside shocking depictions of violence, Abani's work demands a place for itself in humanistic struggles against tyranny, exploitation, and meaninglessness. As he has stated in an interview, "Artists were essentially shamans or priests or seers in the old days and I think art is still the primary focus of looking for ways to deal with the questions of being human" (Archibeque, 2005).

Abani has received several additional literary awards, including the PEN USA Freedom-to-Write Award (2001), a Lannan Literary Fellowship (2003), and a Guggenheim Award (2009).

BIBLIOGRAPHY
Archibeque, Carlye. "An Interview with Chris Abani." *Poetix: Poetry for Southern California*, 2005. http://www.poetix.net/abani.htm.
Datcher, Michael. "West Coast Kinsfolk." *Black Issues Book Review* 7, no. 3 (2005):34–35.
Okpala, Jude Chudi. "Chris Abani." In *Dictionary of Literary Biography*, edited by R. Victoria Arana. Vol. 347: *Twenty-First-Century "Black" British Writers*, pp. 3–12. Farmington Hills, Mich.: Gale Cengage, 2009.

ARIEL BOOKMAN

Abar (fl. seventh century BCE), queen of Kush, was the mother of Taharqa (ruled c. 690–664 BCE), the most remarkable king of the period of the Kushite domination in Egypt (the Twenty-Fifth, "Ethiopian," Dynasty). Her name is also interpreted in specialist literature as Abala, Abale, Abalo, Abiru, and Ibart.

The information about Abar is extremely scanty. The main sources are several stelae of her son Taharqa found during excavations at Gemeten (near the modern village of Kawa, south of the Third Cataract of the Nile), one of the major sanctuaries of Kush. The relief at the top of one of the stelae represents Abar, in two symmetrical scenes, playing sistrum behind Taharqa as he presents bread and wine to the god Amun. Similar representations of her were found in a wall relief in the so-called Temple B 300 at Jebel Barkal (the main temple complex of ancient Sudan, situated between the Third and Fourth Cataracts) and in the Amun Temple at Sanam (not far from Barkal, on the opposite bank of the Nile).

From the textual material about Abar it appears that she was a niece (sister's daughter) of Alara, the earliest, semi-legendary ruler of the Kushite kingdom, who is known by name and was probably the founder of the royal dynasty. From the circumstantial evidence it has been assumed that Abar was a daughter of Kashta, the first historically attested Kushite king, and a sister-wife of the king Piankhy, the conqueror of Egypt and the first of the "Ethiopian" dynasty pharaohs.

The biographical references to Abar in Taharqa's stelae are concentrated on two episodes. The records on his two stelae of regnal year six (one from Gemeten in Kush and the other, its duplicate, from Tanis in Lower Egypt) mention the visit of the "King's mother" to Egypt after an extraordinary flood and several natural phenomena ("four goodly wonders within one year") took place. It is stated that Abar came to see Taharqa after a long separation (as he had departed from her at the age of twenty) and rejoiced exceedingly when she saw her son crowned and invested with all the attributes of royal power. The text compares Abar with the goddess Isis who "saw her son Horus on the throne of (his) father Osiris after he had been a youth in the nest of Chemmis" and flatteringly remarks that "Isis, when she found Horus, was like the King's mother (now that) she has been reunited to her son."

The record seems to be alluding to a mythological reunion of the Egyptian principal goddess Isis with her son Horus, son of Osiris, after a long period of separation, but paradoxically no extant accounts of the Osirian cycle of myths, Egyptian or others (as Plutarch's *On Isis and Osiris*), seem to mention such an episode. On the other hand, similar references to the reunion of the queen mother, identified with Isis, and her son soon after his enthronement may be seen in some other Kushite kings' official records (e.g., stela of Anlamani and an inscription of Irikeamannote, both from Gemeten). This suggests that a certain ritual action is being implied in all such cases, which was to take place in the course of the Kushite king's induction procedure, even if it was to happen, as in Taharqa's case, six years after his coronation. No Egyptian parallels of this have been attested, so it might be an innovation of the Kushite domination in Egypt or an Eyptianizing transformation of some traditional Kushite custom(s).

It seems most likely that the king's "reunion" with his mother was meant to somehow confirm his genealogical right to the throne. In the case of Taharqa and Abar this is particularly obvious.

In his two Gematen stelae, of regnal years six and ten, respectively, it is claimed that his rise to power had been predetermined by an old petition of his maternal great-uncle (mother's mother's brother) Alara, the founder of the dynasty. As alleged in Taharqa's text, his ancestor at one time, perhaps celebrating his victory over some rival(s), had "committed" several of his sisters to the god Amun of Gematen, praying him to grant that their descendents "attain prosperity (and) the appearing as king, as you have done for me," and, according to one of the versions, particularly favoring one of these sisters, the future "mother's mother" of Taharqa. Thus it is clear that the relationship, through Abar, with her glorious ancestor Alara was a most important argument of Taharqa's legitimation.

It seems probable that the standing of Taharqa as the overlord of the Egypto-Kushite kingdom had somehow weakened by his sixth regnal year (it is assumed that his first years were difficult, perhaps lean, years as a result of natural disasters), the more so since, judging from some indirect considerations, his rights to the throne were not indisputable. The appearance of the queen mother at this period must have remedied the situation and allowed Taharqa to rule for another twenty years.

Brief though they are, the references to Abar show how influential a queen mother could be in the Kushite society, where—as it seems, much stricter than in Egypt—there was a taboo on putting on the names of the kings' earthly fathers (due to the religious dogma of the kings' divine sonship), each of the ruling kings being declared to be a (re)-incarnation of the god Horus, risen on the throne of his father, Osiris.

The Kushite sources may yield some other pieces of evidence in this regard. A hint may be found, for instance, in the closing lines of the Triumphal stela of King Piankhy (eighth century BCE), the earliest considerable written monument of Kush, where the "cow (that) bore the bull" is praised. More explicit is the evidence of the Election stela of king Aspelta (sixth century BCE), where his matrilineal female relatives for seven generations are retrospectively enumerated in support of his rights to the throne, while it is known that Aspelta's mother was also mother of his predecessor, King Anlamani. Much more fragmentary is the textual evidence of the queen mothers' role during the following centuries of the history of Kush, partly to be complemented by the iconographical material.

The result of the evolution of this institution may probably be seen in the numerous allusions to the Kushite ruling queens (who may have been widows or regents) in the late period. Some similar references have survived in the accounts of foreign visitors (a Greek inscription in Dakka and a Latin one in Musawwarat es Sufra) and, though sometimes in a somewhat exaggerated presentation, in the works of some Greco-Roman writers (Strabo, Pliny, Nero, Plutarch, Cassius Dio, Eusebius, and others).

The precedent of Abar is particularly important as the earliest of the more or less distinct relevant pieces of evidence regarding the development of queenship as a political institution of Kush.

[See also Alara; Aspelta; Piankhy; and Taharqa.]

BIBLIOGRAPHY

Eide, T., T. Hägg, R. H. Pierce, and L. Török, eds. *Fontes Historiae Nubiorum*, Vol. I: *From the Eighth to the Mid-Fifth Century BC*. Bergen, Norway: Bergen University Press, Klassisk Institute, 1994.

Lohwasser, A. "Queenship in Kush: Status, Role and Ideology of Royal Women." *Journal of the American Research Center in Egypt* 38 (2001): 61–76.

Török, L. *The Birth of an African Kingdom: Kush and Her Myth of the State in the First Millennium BC*. Lille, France: Université Charles-de-Gaulle, 1995.

Troy, L. *Patterns of Queenship in Ancient Egyptian Myth and History*. Uppsala, Sweden: Almquist and Wiksell Intl., 1986.

A. K. VINOGRADOV

Abba Bagibo I (1802–1861), king of one of the five Oromo states of the Gibe region in southwestern Ethiopia during the first half of the nineteenth century. He was the richest prince, whose reign marked the golden age of the Gibe states. He was born in 1802 in Sappa, the first capital of the kingdom of Limmu Ennarya, where he received a rudimentary form of Islamic education. As a young man, the tall, handsome, well-built, and eloquent Abba Bagibo is said to have possessed a considerable share of his father Abba Mogol's vigor. He spent many years in learning the art of war in his father's army. It was during those years of training that Abba Bagibo demonstrated his exceptional qualities of leadership, organizational ability, management of information, and wise use of resources.

In 1825 Abba Bagibo overthrew his father, seized power, and adopted a commercial policy that made his new capital, Saqqa, the commercial capital of the region, where traders from different nationalities met and traded with each other. By 1840 Abba Bagibo's policy of expansion through warfare and diplomacy almost brought him close to realizing his deepest ambition of uniting the Gibe region and the surrounding Oromo groups in the regions of Wallaga, Illubabor, and western Shewa. However, by 1841 Abba Bagibo had abandoned his aggressive policy and profitably exchanged it for the image of a patient and exceptionally peace-loving king, strong-willed, passionately devoted to the maintenance of peace and order in the region, earning him the reputation of "the new Solomon of the [Oromo]"(Massaia, 1978, p. 371). For the next twenty years Abba Bagibo dominated the Gibe region through a sophisticated policy of political marriage, gift-giving, and changing outdated and unproductive policies.

Abba Bagibo married twelve queens from the ruling classes of the Gibe region and the surrounding states. Of his sons, more than twenty married women from either the ruling houses of the surrounding countries or the wealthy men of their country. His numerous daughters were given in marriage to wealthy men of the surrounding countries. Thus, Abba Bagibo held together his own country and sought to hold together the surrounding countries through political marriages.

Abba Bagibo was not only the wealthiest king in the region but also knew how to use that wealth to impress his nobility as well as foreign visitors, including Europeans. He distributed precious commodities as gifts to the nobility of the Gibe region and the Christian princes in northern Ethiopia. Through his generosity he won many friends and neutralized enemies. As part of his strategy of impressing people, he used the artists and builders of the Gibe region to build fifteen elegant, relatively splendid, well-designed, and artistically well-executed royal residences during his reign. Royal residences were the busiest industrial centers in his kingdom. The most famous royal residence was that of Garuqqe, whose entrance gate was decorated with a design of Chinese fashion that had produced a strong impact on his subjects. According to the Italian missionary Cardinal Guglielmo Massaia, "the fruits of the royal residence, the walls built with such magnificence and skills could not find a match in the whole of Ethiopia."(Massaia, 1885–1895, p. 159). Abba Bagibo was one of the rare Oromo kings who understood the importance of changing outdated and counterproductive policies. For instance, in 1847 he took two immediate measures—one political and the other economic—with which he revitalized his administration, created prosperity at home, and maintained relative peace abroad up to 1861. First, he injected fresh vitality into his administration by replacing old officials with young and vigorous ones. He dismissed corrupt provincial governors and replaced them with more honest ones. Second, Abba Bagibo abolished the prohibition on trading with Kaffa and removed many restrictions on trade and traders. He even lifted the monopoly on some important commodities.

Finally, though Muslim himself, Abba Bagibo was the most liberal of all the Oromo kings, the protectors of Christians in the region. It was he who helped Massaia, the first Catholic bishop of Oromoland, to establish centers of missionary activities in the Gibe region and the kingdom of Kaffa. He was an exceptionally able leader and consummate politician, during whose reign Limmu Ennarya was the economic center and political powerhouse of the Gibe region. He died in 1861. "His death was a great misfortune not only for the Catholic mission but also for the kingdom of Ennarya, for all the [Oromo states]. . . . Even for European science" (Massaia, 1885–1895, p. 283). He symbolized the hope for unity in the Gibe region, which died with him.

BIBLIOGRAPHY

Abir, Mordechai, *Ethiopia: The Era of the Princes, The Challenge of Islam and the Re-Unification of the Christian Empire, 1769–1855*. London: Longmans, 1968.

Cecchi, A. *Da Zeila alle Frontiere del Caffa*, vol. 2. Rome: Ermanno Loescher, 1886.

Hassen, Mohammed. *The Oromo of Ethiopia A History 1570–1860*. Cambridge, UK: Cambridge University Press, 1990.

Massaia, G. *I miei trentacinque anni di mission nell'Alta Etiopia*, vol. 6. Milan: Coop. Tipografica Manuzio, 1885–1895.

Massaia, G. *Lettere e scritti minori 1836–66*. A Cura di Antonio Rosso, vol. 2. Rome: Istituto Storico dei Cappuccini, 1978.

MOHAMMED HASSEN ALI

Abba Jifar II (1861–1932), Oromo king of the Gibe region, in southwestern Ethiopia, was crowned in 1878. A year after his accession to power, Abba Jifar invaded the neighboring Oromo state of Gera with around twenty thousand men. This attack on a flimsy pretext was a show of force for the neighboring Oromo leaders, demonstrating his determination to dominate the political landscape of the Gibe region through threat or use of military power, diplomacy, and marriage alliances. He was not destined to dominate the Gibe region as the king of Shewa soon occupied it. Though Abba Jifar could mobilize tens of thousands of men for war, his army suffered from major weaknesses and lack of modern firearms and training.

In fact, Abba Jifar came to power at a time of dramatic change in modern Ethiopian history, when the clouds of conquest and destruction were hanging thick and low over the future of all the Oromo in Ethiopia. In 1878 two rival Abyssinian princes, Emperor Yohannes IV of Tigray (r. 1872–1889) and King Menilek of Shewa (r. 1865–1889), met at Boru Meda in Wallo and issued an ominous edict: all Muslims had to convert to Christianity within two years. Emperor Yohannes, who was determined to obtain unity in northern Ethiopia under the guise of religion, banned Islam in 1879. This ban, which lasted for a decade, was characterized by tremendous loss of life and wanton destruction of property. All over Wallo, Muslim schools were closed and mosques were turned into churches, leading to the exodus of a large number of people from Wallo.

Abba Jifar could not offer military aid to his fellow Muslim Oromo in Wallo, but he did aid Muslim refugees from Wallo by settling them in his kingdom, to its benefit. Some of those who settled in Jimma were scholars and jurists, who increased the number of Muslim teachers in that land. Abba Jifar also encouraged various Muslim religious orders to settle in the countryside, where they were supported by land grants from the king and gifts from wealthy Muslims. Those orders became centers of Islamic learning and religious culture. Although the famous market of Hirmata (about eight miles south of the capital) was the commercial emporium of the southwestern part of what is today Ethiopia, Jiren became the center of Islamic learning. Both attracted talented individuals from all over Oromo territory.

Learned Muslim refugees from Wallo contributed to the growth of Islamic education in Jimma. By the 1880s Jimma boasted of having sixty madrasas (schools of higher education) and hundreds of qur'anic schools as most mosques had one qur'anic school where children were taught reading and writing. It was because of the growth of higher education that Jimma became the famous center of Islamic learning for all Oromo. Oromo scholars in Jimma pioneered the practice of producing poetry and religious literature in their native language. In short, Abba Jifar's pragmatic policy of helping refugees from Wallo left behind a legacy of growth in Islamic education and the beginning of written Oromo literature in the Gibe region.

A second problem that faced the Oromo states was the rivalry that developed between the Amhara kings of Gojjam and Shewa over control of the Gibe region. Of the two, King Menilek of Shewa had well-armed, European-trained soldiers and the political ambition to conquer all Oromo from Wallaga in the west to Hararghe in the east, from Wallo in the north to Borana in the south. Menilek's conquest of the Gibe region was accomplished by Ras Gobana Dacchi, himself of Oromo origin. Gobana arrived in the Gibe region in 1881 and offered Oromo leaders the choice of peaceful submission to him or destruction. At that dark hour Abba Jifar turned to his mother, Genne Gummiti, who urged her son not to fight an unwinnable war. Accepting the counsel of his mother, Abba Jifar submitted to Gobana peacefully, thereby averting the destruction of his kingdom. Menilek granted Abba Jifar internal autonomy in exchange for an annual payment of 300,000 Maria Theresa thalers in cash and goods including animals, ivory, and coffee. This tax, which placed a heavy burden on Abba Jifar's people, was to be delivered to Menilek in person each year.

When Gobana Dacchi was removed from the administration of the Gibe region in 1886, Abba Jifar did not join other Oromo kings who rebelled in support of Gobana and, indeed, may have counseled them not to rebel. The kings of Gera, Gomma, Guma, and Limmu-Ennarya would spend their last days in the dungeons of Abba Jifar. In addition to his high annual tax Abba Jifar was required to participate in Menilek's wars, among them wars against Kullo in 1888, Walyeta (Walamo) in 1894, and Kefa in 1897. Because Abba Jifar was so careful not to anger or raise the suspicion of Menilek, he maintained the internal autonomy of his kingdom. As a result, no Amhara officials were appointed in his country, churches were not established, and armed settlers were not settled, thus saving his people from the confiscation of land, economic exploitation, political subjugation, and cultural devastation to which many of their neighbors were subjected.

While participating in Menilek's wars against his neighbors, Abba Jifar also continued with his own expansion. He attacked and captured land from the small kingdoms of Janjero and Garo, enslaving some prisoners of war while settling others in his land. He freed the prisoners from Janjero and recruited them into his army. He even appointed one man, a former member of the royal family of Janjero, as a governor of the district and stationed him on the Janjero border, where in 1888 they made war on "their own ex-countrymen and kinsmen" (Lewis, 2001). As Menilek used Gobana Dacchi to conquer extensive Oromo territory, Abba Jifar used a member of the royal family of Janjero for the same purpose.

Abba Jifar was the fifth king of Jimma, the longest-lasting Oromo state in southwestern Ethiopia. He was the best-loved king of Jimma, for his character and his relation with his people, and the richest and most popular Oromo leader, whose fame, prestige, and wealth were widely known within and beyond Ethiopia long after his time. When Abba Jifar became seriously ill, his grandson, Abba Jobir, succeeded to the throne in 1930. Emperor Haile Selassie immediately increased the tax burden on Jimma, which the new king was unable to pay. Using that as a pretext the emperor effectively ended Jimma's internal autonomy. When Abba Jifar died in 1932 Haile Selassie abolished the kingdom and reduced Jimma to a mere district in the province of Kefa.

[See also Gobana Dacchi; Haile Selassie I; Menilek II; and Yohannes IV.]

BIBLIOGRAPHY

Cerulli, E. Etiopia Occidentale, 2 vols. Rome: Sindicato Italiano Arti Grafiche, 1933.

Cerulli, E. Folk Literature of the Galla of Southern Abyssinia. Harvard African Studies, vol. 3. Cambridge, Mass.: Harvard University Press, 1922.

Hassen, Mohammed. "Islam as an Ideology of Resistance among the Oromo in Ethiopia." In "Islam in Africa," special issue, American Journal of Islamic Social Sciences 26, no. 3 (Summer 2009): 85–109.

Hassen, Mohammed. The Oromo of Ethiopia: A History, 1570–1860. Cambridge, UK: Cambridge University Press, 1990.

Lewis, Herbert S. Jimma Abba Jifar, An Oromo Monarchy: Ethiopia 1830–1932. Lawrenceville, N.J.: Red Sea Press, 2001.

MOHAMMED HASSEN ALI

Abba Jobir (1900–1988), last king of the kingdom of Jimma in Ethiopia, scholar, was born in Jiren, the political capital and commercial center of southwestern Ethiopia. As a young man Abba Jobir received the best Muslim education under several prominent Muslim scholars who settled in Jimma

during the reign of his famous grandfather Abba Jifar II (r. 1878–1932).

His grandfather was the most famous, wealthiest, and most popular Oromo king throughout Ethiopia during the second half of the nineteenth century. He was a very foresighted politician who had an excellent grasp of the importance of firearms in warfare. He sent agents to the expanding kingdom of Shewa and realized that King Menilek had superiority in weapons; therefore, he peacefully submitted to Menilek. Although four other Oromo kings who resisted Menilek were destroyed, Abba Jifar II signed a peace treaty with the Christian king of Shewa in 1882. In exchange for local autonomy Abba Jifar II was required to pay annually 300,000 Maria Theresa thalers in cash or in kind, which was the single largest tribute paid by any regional leader in Ethiopia. When Abba Jifar II became seriously ill in 1928, it was his grandson Abba Jobir who took over the reins of power. In 1930 the people of Jimma celebrated the crowning of Abba Jobir as their new king. However, Emperor Haile Selassie curtailed the local autonomy of Jimma. As if that were not enough, in 1932, when Abba Jifar II died, the emperor abolished the kingdom of Jimma, the once famous state was reduced to an awrajja (district) of the Kefa governorate, and for the first time Christian Amhara governors and settlers became the new masters in Jimma, confiscating extensive Oromo lands. Abba Jobir himself was removed from power and detained in Shewa until 1935.

Abba Jobir, who hated the Amhara administration, secretly corresponded with the Italians even before they occupied Ethiopia (1936–1941). The Italians freed Abba Jobir and returned him to power in Jimma. In fact, the Italians used his name and fame for their pro-Oromo and anti-Amhara policy. They appointed Abba Jobir as the head of the "Oromo-Sidama governorate," one of the six autonomous regions into which the Italian East African empire was divided. As one of the six most powerful local leaders in the Italian East African empire, Abba Jobir visited Italy, where he was treated with respect as a distinguished guest of honor. He also toured Egypt and the Middle East in support of the Italian pro-Oromo and pro-Muslim policies. However, when Emperor Haile Selassie was restored to power by the British in 1941, he removed Abba Jobir from power. Abba Jobir was detained from 1944 to 1946.

After he was released from detention Abba Jobir abandoned his political ambitions and devoted his quiet life to wide-ranging studies of Oromo and

Ethiopian history, geography, Islamic law and theology, and Muslim history. He wrote *Notes on Oromo History and Islam in Ethiopia*, in which he strongly attacked the gross distortion of Oromo history in the Ethiopian historiography and set out to correcting it. He also wrote a long manuscript, which contains an extensive history of the kingdom of Jimma and other Oromo Gibe states. His manuscript also deals with Oromo political, social, cultural, and religious institutions. Neither of his works was published, for fear of persecution. In 1976 Abba Jobir went on pilgrimage to Mecca, where his grandfather had built apartment buildings (as well as in Medina) where Oromo Muslims could stay while on pilgrimage. In 1982 he was still unwilling to allow the publication of his works because he feared for the safety of his son Abba Biyya Abba Jobir, who was in detention in Addis Ababa from 1979 to 1990. Abba Jobir lived in exile until his death in 1988 and was buried in Mecca.

[*See also* Abba Jifar II; Haile Selassie I; *and* Menilek II.]

BIBLIOGRAPHY

This article is based on interviews by the author with Abba Jobir (10–13 June 1982 in Mecca) and with Abba Biyya Abba Jobir, his son (1991, Washington, D.C.); on an unpublished manuscript by Abba Jobir in the possession of the author; on Abba Jobir's unpublished *Notes on the History of Oromo and Islam in Ethiopia*; and on personal correspondence with Elias Kedir (13 July 2009). I am indebted to Elias Kedir for providing useful information about Abba Jifar II as well as his grandfather, Abba Jobir.

Greenfield, Richard. *Ethiopia: A New Political History.* London: Pall Mall Press, 1965.

Sbacchi, Alberto. *Ethiopia under Mussolini, Fascism and Colonial Experience.* London: Zed Books, 1985.

Sbacchi, Alberto. *Legacy of Bitterness: Ethiopia and Fascist Italy, 1935–1941.* Lawrenceville, N.J.: Red Sea Press, 1997.

MOHAMMED HASSEN ALI

Abbas, Ferhat (1899–1985), Algerian politician and public intellectual, was born on 24 October 1899 in the village of Chahna, located six miles south of the Algerian town of Taher. His parents belonged to a peasant family, and his father, Said Ahmed ben Abbas, was a local chief and cattle trader. Abbas had eleven siblings. His father was the state-appointed leader of Chahna from 1889 to 1928.

As a boy Abbas attended primary schools at Jijel and then entered secondary school at the lycée at Skikda in 1909. After Abbas passed his baccalaureate examinations, he entered the French army medical service for three years. Afterward, Abbas enrolled in the pharmacy school of the University of Algiers. In 1931 he set up his own pharmacy in Sétif after having graduated from university. Abbas strongly supported the ideal of equal rights for Arab and Berber Muslims and European Christians in Algeria under French rule. Abbas and his fellow assimilationist colleague Mohammad Saleh Bendjelloul led the Fédération des Élus Indigènes (FEI; Federation of Elected Natives), a group of Algerian intellectuals who called for moderate reforms and continued French rule.

Abbas faced a serious challenge in the 1930s from Messali Hadj and his Étoile Nord-Africaine movement, who promoted independence from French rule rather than equal rights for all under the French republic. By contrast, Abbas served as a municipal councilor for Sétif in 1935 and then held the same position for the larger city of Constantine in 1936. He had great hope that the Popular Front Socialist and Communist political coalition's victory in the national French elections of 1936 would bring about dramatic reforms in Algeria despite the determination of most European settlers to maintain their economic and political privileges over most Algerians. The Popular Front government proposed to grant between twenty thousand and thirty thousand Algerians full French citizenship under the Blum-Viollette Bill, but settler opposition eventually blocked its passage in the French parliament.

This failure deeply disillusioned Abbas but he declared in a famous essay in *Entente*, a newspaper that he created in 1935, that no Algerian nation had ever existed and that the future of all people living in Algeria would always be tied to France. Naturally, this assertion made many Algerian nationalists associated with Hadj and his Parti Populaire Algérien (PPA) reject Abbas entirely. Meanwhile, moderates in the FEI broke up into several groups between 1936 and 1938. Abbas formed his own moderate party, the Union Populaire Algérienne (UPA), on 28 July 1938. When war with Germany commenced in 1939, Abbas volunteered to serve in the French army. However, France's defeat in 1940 followed by the establishment of the Vichy regime in southern France and Algeria under Philippe Pétain disgusted Abbas. The Vichy administration refused to countenance any reforms.

The Allied occupation of Algeria in 1942 and the new Free French government under Charles de Gaulle offered a new but fleeting sense of hope to Abbas. He helped to produce a famous 1943 set of demands for more political rights for all Algerians in February 1943, the Manifeste du Peuple Algérien. Abbas then put together the Association des Amis du Manifeste et de la Liberté (AML) movement that brought together some PPA supporters and reformist Muslim scholars with moderate assimilationists. Abbas ceded leadership to Hadj. Although de Gaulle provided full citizenship to some Western-educated Algerians in 1944, the massacre of Algerians protesting against the deportation of Hadj and continued settler domination in May 1945 in Sétif and Guelma displayed the French government's determination to reject nationalist parties. Abbas himself was placed under house arrest following the massacre. Once he was released from prison Abbas formed the Union Démocratique du Manifeste Algérien (UDMA) in 1946, which called for an autonomous Algerian state within the French Union.

The creation of the French Fourth Republic in 1946 led to a long struggle among settlers, French officials, and different nationalist parties to determine political rights. Abbas boycotted the 1946 elections on the grounds the French government still had done too little to promote real democratic reforms, but he served on the Algerian Assembly from 1947 to 1955. By the early 1950s Abbas's effort to reconcile Algerian aspirations for equality with Europeans was viewed as a failure by more radical nationalists, while French settlers remained intransigent in their resistance to moderate reforms. Once the Front de Libération Nationale (FLN) launched an armed struggle for full independence in November 1954, Abbas tried in vain to find a peaceful way to resolve disagreements between the FLN and the French government. Abbas, horrified by the violence employed by both the French military and the FLN, eventually decided that he had to commit to the FLN. The rebel movement chose to make Abbas the leader of its provisional government in exile in Tunis on 19 September 1958, even though many FLN military and political leaders still viewed Abbas as too moderate. Abbas proved to be a very skillful diplomat as he presented the FLN's case to various foreign governments in North Africa and elsewhere. Abbas was removed from his leadership position in August 1961 by more radical figures in the FLN.

The Evian Accords, which settled the French government's acceptance of Algerian independence in the spring of 1962, did not lead to the democracy envisioned by Abbas. He was the head of the new Algerian parliament from 1962 to August 1963 but resigned on the grounds that the FLN's new constitution had largely ignored parliamentary recommendations and that FLN leader Ahmed Ben Bella was too authoritarian. Abbas was dismissed from the FLN and arrested in 1964. When Houari Boumedienne overthrew Ben Bella's government in 1965, Abbas chose to stay out of politics. In 1976 Abbas openly criticized Boumedienne's dictatorship and was arrested as a result. After Boumedienne died in 1978 Abbas was liberated again but concentrated on writing books and essays regarding the failures of the postcolonial Algerian state. He died in Algiers on 23 December 1985. Abbas was one of the most important figures in Algerian politics in the twentieth century, even though his hopes were dashed so often in the colonial and independence periods.

[*See also* Ben Bella, Ahmed; *and* Boumedienne, Houari.]

BIBLIOGRAPHY

Abbas, Ferhat. *L'indépendance confisquée*. Paris: Flammarion, 1984.

Kaddache, Mahfoud. *Histoire du nationalism algérien 1919–1951*. Paris: Paris-Méditerranée, 2003.

Stora, Benjamin. *Les sources du nationalisme algérien*. Paris: L'Harmattan, 1989.

Stora, Benjamin, and Zakya Daoud. *Ferhat Abbas une utopia algérienne*. Paris: Denoël, 1995.

JEREMY RICH

ʿAbbas Hilmi II (1874–1944), the third and last khedive of Egypt, ruled the country from 1892 to 1914. ʿAbbas was the seventh ruler in Mehmet ʿAli's dynasty, which was established in the early nineteenth century. ʿAbbas came to the throne at the very young age of eighteen in January 1892 after his father, Khedive Tawfiq (r. 1879–1892), died unexpectedly. Born in Cairo ʿAbbas was educated by tutors at the Thudicum in Geneva and later in the Theresianum Military Academy in Vienna.

Unlike his father, a weak ruler who was considered a puppet of the British colonial rule, the young ʿAbbas strove to restore the original khedival status as sovereign ruler, patterned after the model established by his grandfather Ismaʿil (r. 1863–1879), and to assert Egypt's unique status as a semiautonomous province within the Ottoman Empire. ʿAbbas's aspirations clashed with British rule, particularly with

'Abbas Hilmi II. Engraving after a photograph by Van Bosch, Paris. (Private Collection/Photo © Tarker/The Bridgeman Art Library)

the authority of the powerful agent and consul-general Evelyn Baring, Lord Cromer (r. 1883–1907). 'Abbas challenged Cromer by attempting to appoint his own prime minister, Husayn Fakhri, rather than accept the consul-general's choice, Mustafa Fahmi, and in his public criticism of Sir Horatio Herbert Kitchener, head of the Egyptian armed forces, for neglecting to maintain high professional standards. 'Abbas's provocative efforts proved unsuccessful—he was forced to accept Riyad Pasha as a compromise prime minister and to apologize to Kitchener. However, these incidents generated tremendous support among anti-imperialist Egyptians, who saw 'Abbas as a charismatic, independent leader prepared to confront colonial rule. More specifically, these actions drew the attention of the emerging Egyptian Nationalists, headed by Mustafa Kamil (1874–1908). 'Abbas had supported early nationalist activities by Kamil and the seminal nationalist movement, and he secretly formed the Society for the Revival of the Nation, which eventually became the basis for Kamil's Nationalist Party. He also financially supported Shaykh 'Ali Yusuf's anticolonialist publication *al-Mu'ayyad* and Kamil's French and English editions of *al-Liwa'*. The Ottoman orientations of the khedive and the Nationalists also played a role in their early collaboration. The association between an ambitious khedive and a young nationalist leader laid the foundations for the emergence of the Egyptian nationalist movement with a defined national agenda to struggle for the country's liberation and independence.

However, this self-serving relationship did not last long. The French-British Entente Cordiale (1904) dashed national expectations for French support and marked the beginnings of an independent national struggle against British rule, led by Kamil who preferred allegiance to the Ottoman Empire. 'Abbas distanced himself from the Nationalist Party in an effort to improve his relations with the British rule, particularly in the new context of Cromer's retirement and the subsequent appointment of Sir Eldon Gorst (1907). Gorst was much more receptive to the khedive's ambitions and granted 'Abbas greater authority and freedom of action. With the support of Gorst, 'Abbas contributed to pioneering Egyptian cultural and educational projects that culminated in his assistance in the establishment of the nucleus of the Egyptian University in 1908. Another important step in this new policy was the appointment of the pro-British Copt leader Butrus Ghali to prime minister (1908–1910). Ghali's government, backed both by the khedive and the British, reinstated the 1881 Press Law (1909), which imposed constraints on the freedom of the press, particularly the nationalist press. Ghali's assassination by a militant nationalist (1910) heightened the tension between 'Abbas and the Nationalists.

However, the year 1911 augured additional change: Gorst died and Sir Herbert Kitchener was appointed consul-general (1911–1914). Kitchener worked to reassert full British colonial authority and 'Abbas quickly became his rival. British fear of nationalist militant activity led to increasing British pressure on the Nationalists and to a growing suspicion that the khedive supported their anti-British activities. Their pro-Ottomanism, on the eve of World War I, brought tensions to a peak in the summer of 1914. Kitchener took advantage of 'Abbas's extended vacation in Istanbul (the result of an assassination attempt that led to an injury and the need to recuperate) and through the British Embassy in Istanbul notified 'Abbas that he would not be allowed to reenter Egypt.

In December 1914 the British authorities, already in the war, announced their decision to depose 'Abbas. In his place they appointed his uncle Husayn

Kamil with the title of sultan. They simultaneously declared Egypt a British protectorate, which de facto severed Egypt from the Ottoman Empire. The former khedive attempted to establish relations with the Ottoman government as a means of convincing them to liberate Egypt from British rule and to reinstall him as the country's leader. But his relations with the Ottoman leaders were problematic and permeated with mutual suspicions. Old rivalries and mistrust prevented him from finding ways to collaborate with the exiled Nationalists led by Muhammad Farid. Thus, the former khedive found himself wandering through Austria, Switzerland, and Germany during the war. He declared support for Germany in the hope that they would reinstall him to his previous position, to no avail.

After the war, unable to return to Egypt, 'Abbas repeatedly attempted to assert control over his assets in Egypt but was denied by Egyptian and British authorities. In May 1931 'Abbas officially renounced his claim to the Egyptian throne in favor of King Fu'ad. In the beginning of the 1930s he was involved in peace initiatives between Zionist and Arab leaders in an effort to solve the Arab-Jewish conflict in Palestine. He strove to use this political involvement to return to the local political arena but his efforts again failed. 'Abbas wandered around European capitals with little purpose other than minor business enterprises and real estate investments. During World War II he supported the Axis Powers in yet another desperate attempt to return to the local political arena. Again he failed. 'Abbas Hilmi II died in Geneva in 1944, leaving substantial memoirs and diaries that recorded his life from his own unique angle.

[*See also* Farid, Muhammad; Fu'ad I, Ahmad; Isma'il; Kamil, Mustafa; *and* Kitchener, Horatio.]

BIBLIOGRAPHY

Abbas Hilmi II. *The Last Khedive of Egypt: Memoirs of Abbas Hilmi II*, edited and translated by Amira Sonbol. Reading, UK: Ithaca Press, 1998.

Baring, Evelyn (Earl of Cromer). *Abbas II*. London: Macmillan, 1915.

Baring, Evelyn (Earl of Cromer). *Modern Egypt*. 2 vols. London: Macmillan, 1908.

Goldschmidt, Arthur, Jr. "The Egyptian Nationalist Party: 1892–1919." In *Political and Social Change in Modern Egypt*, edited by P. M. Holt, pp. 308–333. London: Oxford University Press, 1968.

Mayer, Thomas. "Dreamers and Opportunists: 'Abbas Hilmi's Peace Initiative in Palestine, 1930–1931."
In *Egypt and Palestine, A Millennium of Association (868–1948)*, edited by Amnon Cohen and Gabriel Baer. Jerusalem: Ben Zvi Institute; New York: St. Martin's Press, 1984.

Owen, Roger. *Lord Cromer: Victorian Imperialist, Edwardian Proconsul*. Oxford: Oxford University Press, 2004.

ISRAEL GERSHONI

Abbe Gubegna (1933–1980), Ethiopian intellectual, novelist, playwright, and poet, was born on 1 July 1933 in Gojjam Province, Ethiopia. He was one of the prominent literary figures in modern Ethiopian literature, the author of some twenty-three books between 1956 and 1977; two are in English and the rest in Amharic, his native language. The works comprise eight novels, five plays, three poetry collections, and another five on various subjects, including translation of biographies and works on land tenure.

His mother, Yirgedu Belay, died young, leaving him to be raised by his father, Gubegna Ambaye. It was her expressed wish that Abbe should go to school, which Ambaye fulfilled by sending him to a church school, as was usual. He attended different schools in Gojjam and Begemeder for twelve years and attained a high level of excellence in the traditional curriculum, which included Geez poetry, hymnody, and liturgical dance, all rooted in the tradition of the Ethiopian Orthodox Church. He then joined the so-called modern school in a neighboring town and completed high school.

He moved to Addis Ababa to begin a career in journalism with the Ministry of Information in 1958–1959. In 1960, a few months before an ill-fated coup, his first play, *YeRom Awwedadek* (The Fall of Rome), which was prophetic about where the country was heading unless curative steps were taken against the ills of Ethiopian society, appeared. But more telling was his novel *Alewwelledem* (I Won't Be Born), published in 1962–1963, a vivid description of the abject poverty of a society into which a baby refused to be born. It was seized and burned by the police on the order of the emperor, but the suppression of the novel made Abbe's reputation. He was called to the imperial palace and given an audience by Emperor Haile Selassie I, who expressed appreciation of Abbe's concern for the nation with a tone suggesting that a man of his stature should try his hand in administration, about which Abbe remained ambivalent. The following year, he wrote *Melke'am: seyfe nebelbal* (Melke'am: Sword of Flame), a novel of social criticism that advocated a democratic transformation against a backdrop of autocracy, which the Ethiopian state was. It became a best seller with twenty-five thousand copies sold in just a few months.

With this book Abbe became a prominent public individual and decided to run for parliament. While making his first public address, he was apprehended for allegedly causing public unrest and for having contact with foreigners. He was considered dangerous to the state and forced into exile, first to Gore and then to Mocha, two of the most inaccessible towns in the country at that time. There, he stayed for four years, living on a meager allowance of only 50 birr a month (about 25 USD at the time).

After he returned to Addis Ababa in 1969, Abbe published his longest novel, *And lennatu* (A Mother's Only Son), a historical description of the rise and tragic fall of Emperor Tewodros, a visionary and unifier in nineteenth-century Ethiopia. Abbe wrote it with a view to making an exposé of the conservative attitude of the imperial leadership of Haile Selassie toward reform. The book was a success in terms of publicity, with several reprints made of it. After that, Abbe started earning his living by writing.

Until the change of government in 1974 Abbe had been in a head-on confrontation with the state and the Orthodox Church, which he condemned for its complacency. After the change he turned his attention to the leftists, whom he exposed as power mongers in his play *Poletika enna poletikegnoch* (Politics and Politicians), just as he was against the military junta that took power and its manifestly socialist doctrinaire. He openly told some of the members of the junta that they had no legitimacy to lead the country. His vision was a constitutional monarchy with an elected parliament exercising power, which was also the theme of his novel *Melke'am: seyfe nebelbal*.

Prolific as he was, Abbe was not acclaimed for his literary craft. In fact, he accused some of his contemporaries, such as Solomon Deressa and Dagnachew Worku, for being too formalist, a charge that Asfaw Damte attributes to Abbe's minimal exposure to literary theory.

Abbe was living in Bahr Dar among relatives when he went to Addis to publish a book that was a critique of socialism, the state ideology. On 1 February 1972 he was found lying in the street and died in hospital the following day, at the age of forty-seven. His death has remained a mystery, but associates and relatives believe it was a political killing.

Abbe will be remembered by generations of Ethiopians as a literary giant who dealt with issues that cut across the sociopolitical spectrum of the Ethiopian state and beyond, as his 1962 book on the death of Patrice Lumumba suggests. Already his works have attracted many young talents who have read him at length and produced graduate theses at Addis Ababa University. Furthermore, Abbe would remain an exemplar of a literary idol of great valor.

[*See also* Haile Selassie I; *and* Tewodros II.]

BIBLIOGRAPHY

Azeze, Fekade. "Abbe Gubäñña." In *Encyclopaedia Aethiopica*, vol. 1, edited by Siegberg Uhlig, pp. 30–31. Wiesbaden: Harrasowitz, 2003. Includes a list of Abbe Gubegna's writings.

Kane, Thomas L. *Ethiopian Literature in Amharic.* Wiesbaden: Harrassowitz, 1975.

Molvaer, Reidulf. *Black Lions: The Creative Lives of Modern Ethiopia's Literary Giants and Pioneers.* Lawrenceville, N.J.: Red Sea Press, 1997.

BAYE YIMAM

'Abd al-'Aziz, Muhammad (c. 1947–), secretary-general of the Popular Front for the Liberation of Saguia El Hamra and Rio de Oro (Polisario Front) and president of the Sahrawi Arab Democratic Republic, was born on 17 August 1947 near Smara (he is also reported to have been born in Marrakech around 1948). His name is also spelled Mohamed Abdelaziz. He is a member of the Foqra faction within the tribal confederation of Rguibat.

In 1958 the French and Spanish colonial forces launched a military campaign against the southern liberation movement. His family was forced to resettle in Tan-Tan. In the early 1960s he did his primary and secondary schooling in Smara and Bou Izakarn. By the late 1960s he had moved to Casablanca and then Rabat, where he continued his university undergraduate education at Mohamed V University. In 1970 he became a member of the Rabat-based Embryonic Movement for the Liberation of the Sahara. During his stay in Rabat he met El Ouali Mustapha Sayid and Omar El Hadrami, two key founders of the movement. In the early 1970s the Saharan Liberation Movement relocated to the Spanish-controlled Western Sahara and began an armed rebellion against the Spanish forces. On 10 May 1973 the Polisario Front was founded and 'Abd al-'Aziz became one of its key military leaders.

When Spain withdrew its troops from the Spanish Sahara before the death of General Francisco Franco in 1975, the Algerian-backed Polisario Front launched a guerrilla war on Morocco and Mauritania after they annexed Saguia El Hamra and Rio De Oro, respectively. In June 1976 El Ouali Mustapha Sayid, one of the founders of the Polisario Front and its leader, died in a raid on Nouakchott. Mahfoud Laroussi replaced him as the temporary new secretary-general of the Polisario Front until the third general congress of the Sahrawi people was held on 26–30 August 1976. Since then, 'Abd al-'Aziz has been confirmed as the secretary-general of the Polisario Front. In 1979 Mauritania renounced its claims to a share of territories after being unable to fend off the numerous incursions of the Polisario Front. King Hassan II annexed the area under Mauritanian authority after its government recognized the rights of the Sahrawi to the territory and relinquished its claims over its share. A Polisario Front guerrilla war against Morocco would continue under 'Abd al-'Aziz's leadership until the late 1980s. During the fifth general congress of the Sahrawi people in October 1982, 'Abd al-'Aziz became president of the Sahrawi Arab Democratic Republic.

Based in the Algerian city of Tindouf, 'Abd al-'Aziz has been influenced heavily by secular Arab and socialist nationalist ideologies. Accordingly, under his military leadership the Polisario Front adopted a guerrilla war in its fight over the Saharan territories. However, when Morocco completed its 1,550-miles of walls in the mid-1980s, the Polisario Front's ability to strike Moroccan military targets was limited. This forced Muhammad 'Abd al-'Aziz to change his political and military strategy toward Morocco. With the support of the Algerian government, 'Abd al-'Aziz used diplomacy to seek worldwide support for his cause.

He stressed the Sahrawi right of self-determination as the driving point in his diplomatic missions. Despite the fact that many African, Latin American, and European countries have backed 'Abd al-'Aziz, he had little support from key powers in Europe (especially France) or the United States. In 1982, and with the full backing of Algeria, the Organization of African Unity granted the Polisario Front a seat as a member, leading Morocco to leave the organization. During the twenty-first summit of the Organization of African Unity in 1985, 'Abd al-'Aziz was elected vice president. In 2002, and after the first summit of the African Union, he was elected vice president. Since the foundation of the Polisario Front, he has always enjoyed full support from Algeria despite his lower status in the early period of the organization. He has faced tremendous opposition from other forces within the Polisario Front for different reasons. One of his key critics in the Polisario Front is the Khatt al-Shahid (Line of the Martyr) faction, which supports armed resistance against the Moroccan government. This group has also accused him of internal corruption and nepotism.

As the president of the Sahrawi Arab Democratic Republic and the secretary-general of the Polisario, 'Abd al-'Aziz has played key roles in negotiations and political discussion with Morocco, the United Nations, and other countries regarding the Western Saharan conflict. On 14 September 1976 he requested a new United Nations resolution on the question of self-determination. In 1991 he reached a cease-fire agreement with the Moroccan government with the understanding that the United Nations would organize a referendum on the independence of Western Sahara. This plan has yet to take place because of disputes over voters' eligibility. In the meantime, 'Abd al-'Aziz and his close associates continue to fight a public-relations war with the Moroccan government over the rights and status of Sahrawi refugees in Tindouf. In the last decades, Morocco has offered royal amnesty and monetary support to Sahrawis and managed to lure high- and low-level figures from the Polisario Front. In addition, the government has even relied on 'Abd al-'Aziz's father, Muhammad al-Bashir al-Rguibi, who is a member of the Royal Advisory Council for Saharan Affairs, to put pressure on 'Abd al-'Aziz to renounce his support for the independence of Western Sahara. With the full support of the Algerian government, 'Abd al-'Aziz has maintained his internal and external political grip on the Polisario Front despite many forces of opposition.

[See also Hassan II.]

BIBLIOGRAPHY

Damis, John. *Conflict in North East Africa: The Western Sahara Dispute.* Stanford, Calif.: Hoover Institution Press, 1983.

Pazzanita, Anthony. *Historical Dictionary of Western Sahara.* Lanham, Md.: Scarecrow Press, 2006.

Zunis, Stephen, and Jacob Mundy. *Western Sahara: War, Nationalism and Conflict Irresolution.* Syracuse, N.Y.: Syracuse University Press, 2010.

AOMAR BOUM

'Abd al-Hamid ben Badis (1889–1940), Algerian nationalist, was born in Constantine in East Algeria on 5 December 1889 to a scholarly and religious household. His family claimed to have descended from the founder of Algiers, Bologhine Ben Ziri, and held the position of notables who valued learning both Eastern and Western.

Ben Badis's brother studied law in French establishments, while he pursued a career in religious studies at the Mosque-University of Zeituna in Tunisia. Prior to that, he studied in Constantine under the patronage of his tutor Hamdane Lounissi, a follower of the Zawiya al-Tijania religious order.

While in Tunisia he came under the influence of the Islamic Salafi movement, which called for the purification of Islam from the effects of charlatanism and obscurantist practices through teaching Muslim communities about the *salaf* (early Muslim leaders) and their pure Islamic ways. This often involved attacks on the shaykhs of religious orders as well as official imams employed by the French administration.

Among the Islamic scholars who left an indelible mark on the personality of ben Badis and his standpoint on Islam were Shaykh Mohammed Al-Taher Ben Achour who introduced him to the magnificence of the Arabic language; Shaykh Mohammed Al-Nakhli whose teachings convinced him of the urgent need to purge Muslim communities of deviant religious practices that made them easy prey to colonialism; and Shaykh Al-Bachir who brought him a wide awareness about the state of the Muslim nation which, from the Atlantic to the Gulf, was lingering under colonial rule and ignorance.

His academic circle expanded even wider during his pilgrimage to Mecca as he spent three months in Medina lecturing to circles of Muslims from all over the world about Islamic reform and the ills suffered by Muslim societies across the globe.

His stay in Medina was also an opportunity for him to meet other Muslim reformists of the likes of his compatriot Shaykh Bachir Al Ibrahimi, with whom he spent long hours planning a reformist movement for Algeria as the only way to fight colonialism. These ideas were also discussed with Sayed Husain Ahmad Madani, a scholar from India who, from his religious base as Shaykh al-Islam, fought for the independence of India and opposed the two-nation theory and the migration of Muslim Indians to Pakistan.

Among the ideas ben Badis took from Sayed Husain was the founding of the Jam'iyat Ulama' al-Muslimin al-Jaza'iriyin (Union of the Algerian Muslim Ulama) as a prototype of Jam'iyat Ulama' al-Hind, of which Sayed Husain was president until his death in 1957.

In Medina ben Badis also came into contact with the Wahhabi movement, which influenced many of his reformist views. From Medina he traveled to Syria and Cairo, staying for some time at the al-Azhar, where he met with many distinguished Islamic scholars.

His journey in the Middle East came to an end in 1913 when he decided to return to Constantine and start his mission as an Islamic reformist on a wide scale. Believing in the benefits of education as a means to eradicate obscurantism, he started his mission as a teacher in the Sidi Qammouch mosque, where he taught male and female children during the day and adults in the evening. Islamic sciences, history, language, and literature were among the subjects he taught. His efforts were lauded by the Algerian people who attended his classes in huge numbers, which led him and his followers to open many more schools.

By the 1950s 124 schools had been created where 274 teachers taught around 40,000 pupils. Most of the teachers taught on a voluntary basis, and the schools were financed by local donations. Some of the graduates of these schools were sent to al-Qarawiyin in Fez (Morocco), al-Zeituna in al-Qayrawan (Tunisia), and al-Azhar in Cairo, all of which are religious centers of learning.

Although many believe that ben Badis established the Jam'iyat Ulama' al-Muslimin al-Jaza'iriyin single-handedly, one has to set the record right by stating that the terrain was prepared by the emergence of many Algerian religious scholars from across the country who were of the generation of ben Badis and that the visit of Muhammad 'Abdu to Algeria in 1905 did indeed play a major role in introducing the reformist idea to the country's scholars, among whom we may cite Shaykh Medjaoui, Shaykh Ben Smaïa, and Shaykh Benali Fekhkhar, who like ben Badis condemned the backward practices of many religious charlatans who were tools in the hands of colonial France.

What ben Badis achieved, however, is grouping the Algerian Ulama, some of whom were his disciples, under the aegis of a union, namely, the Jam'iyat Ulama' al-Muslimin al-Jaza'iriyin, in 1931, whose ideology is very much anchored in the teachings of Muhammed 'Abdu and Rashid Reda and in some areas those of the Wahhabi movement. At the head of this association were prominent figures who played major roles in Algeria's modern history, namely, al-Tayeb al-Oqbi, Larbi Tebessi, Moubarak al-Mili, and Bachir al-Ibrahimi.

This Muslim organization of religious scholars and leaders played a very important role in the building of the Algerian national identity during the colonial period and formed a base for some of the Islamist movements that emerged in postcolonial Algeria. The ideas of this association were voiced regularly in its monthly magazine *Al-Chihab* and the many publications of ben Badis, which include the following titles: *Mabadi' al-Usul* (1980), *Al-'aqa'id al-Islamiya min al-ayat al-Qur'aniya wa al-Ahadith al-Nabawiya* (1985), and *Majalis al-Tadhkir* (1991).

On 16 April 1940 ben Badis died prematurely in Constantine, leaving behind him many disciples and companions who continued his unfinished oeuvre. His memory is celebrated as the National Day of Knowledge in independent Algeria on 16 April of every year.

Shaykh ben Badis is an emblematic figure of the Islamic Reform Movement in Algeria, often remembered for his famous verse "Arabic is my language, Algeria my country and Islam my religion." This verse became a slogan of resistance in the face of French colonialism, which dangerously interfered with the identity of Algerian people through a relentless acculturation campaign.

[*See also* Buluggin ibn Ziri.]

BIBLIOGRAPHY

Merad, Ali. *Ibn Badis: Commentateur du Koran*. Paris: Geuthner, 1971.

Merad, Ali. *Le Réformisme Musulman en Algérie de 1925 à 1940*. Algiers: SNED, 1967.

Quandt, William B. *Revolution and Political Leadership: Algeria, 1954–1968*. Cambridge, Mass.: MIT Press, 1969.

Ruedy, John. *Modern Algeria. The Origins and Development of a Nation*. Bloomington: Indiana University Press, 1992.

ZAHIA SMAIL SALHI

'Abd al-Karim (fl. late sixteenth–mid-seventeenth century), political leader and legendary founder of the Chadian kingdom of Wadai, was born in the late sixteenth century. Since the early nineteenth century, a number of competing narratives have emerged about his origins. Several Wadai notables told the North African traveler Muhammad al-Tunsi during his stay in the kingdom in 1810 and 1811 that Saleh 'Abd al-Karim came to their land from Mecca via Egypt. Thus he was an Arab whose family may have fled the Ottoman occupation of the Hejaz in 1517. In the mid-nineteenth century the German travelers Heinrich Barth and Gustav Nachtigal both recorded stories about

'Abd al-Karim's origins, which stated that the founder of Wadai was a member of a Sudanese Arab clan or a member of a Guimir community located on the modern Chadian-Sudanese frontier. However, a number of elderly Wadai men interviewed by historians in the 1960s and 1970s claimed that he was a Maba-speaking man born in the village of Djamé, located in the Wadai region. Still another Arabic written account contended he was a member of an Arab tribe who fled to Morocco and then entered Wadai from the west after spending time in the kingdom of Bornu, located by Lake Chad. Such divergent explanations show how difficult it is to find verifiable information about him.

A complicated and often contradictory set of stories about 'Abd al-Karim's career revolve around his role in spreading Islam into the Wadai region. In one story, a Meccan scholar carried a tablet to Wadai that Arabian leaders had asked him to bury. 'Abd al-Karim traded a copper drum for the tablet and used it to support his legitimacy as a Muslim leader. A number of accounts suggest the king of the Toundjour resisted 'Abd al-Karim's calls to convert to Islam. In Wadai and its northeastern neighbor Darfur, the Toundjour are recalled as a non-Muslim dynasty. 'Abd al-Karim was said to have slipped away with the Toundjour king's daughter, the king swearing revenge against the foreign interloper. Then he followed the model of the Prophet Muhammad by withdrawing from the Toundjour. 'Abd al-Karim drew together many Maba and Arab tribes and drove the Toundjour from power. A colorful tale that ties together political and religious divisions described a conversation between 'Abd al-Karim and Daoud, king of the Toundjour. After Daoud allowed 'Abd al-Karim to marry his daughter, the ruler asked the cleric to pray for him. However, 'Abd al-Karim prayed to God for himself instead of his father-in-law, and the king died. Other versions argue that the Toundjour people welcomed 'Abd al-Karim's teachings. Despite all these disagreements, there is general agreement that 'Abd al-Karim built a series of mosques in Wadai in the early or middle decades of the seventeenth century.

Sometimes 'Abd al-Karim is simply presented as a Muslim preacher, perhaps one who had studied at Islamic schools in Arabia. One narrative associates 'Abd al-Karim with al-Jarmiyu, a reformist Muslim scholar executed by the king of Bornu in 1591. A more plausible account links 'Abd al-Karim to the Muslim scholarly center of Bidderi, located to the west of Wadai in the Muslim kingdom of Baguirmi.

These versions highlight his piety and observe that a number of Muslim scholars entered Wadai with him, including Muhammad Dinar, Shaykh Mahamat Abou Gar, Mahamat Ibnou Dirim, and Dédé. Yet other histories state he led a small army into battle against non-Muslim enemies. One legend described how 'Abd al-Karim's Arab allies tied branches to their camels' tails to raise so much dust that the Toundjour troops fled, believing that a much bigger army lay in wait for them.

Some historians have argued that 'Abd al-Karim's rise to power fit with a series of changes that swept through the Sahel and the southern borders of the Sahara after the Moroccan invasion of the Songhai kingdom in the West African interior. The chaos brought by this event may have led to political and religious divisions all the way to Bornu, Baguirmi, and Wadai. 'Abd al-Karim also seems to be linked to a group of nomadic people who took power in Wadai, as evidenced by references to camels or the legend that he established his capital of Wara in a mountainous region after searching for some stray calves. The ruins of Wara are still visible today. They include the foundations of large houses, mosques, and an extensive cemetery. It became a trade center. Later rulers of Wadai continued to live in Wara until the mid-nineteenth century, when the kingdom's capital was moved to Abéché.

'Abd al-Karim fused various models of political rule common among Sudanese Muslim states with local political practices, although oral traditions claim that he destroyed sites associated with spiritual practices opposed to Islam. Like many other kingdoms from Sennar to Bornu, 'Abd al-Karim was believed to be a sacred monarch. He appears to have continued royal rituals to show spiritual authority, such as lighting the first fire of the year that his subjects had to use to rekindle their own fires. 'Abd al-Karim was associated with royal drums, which became part of the insignia of later kings. Yet he did not act as a completely independent sovereign. It is very likely that he paid tribute to the Kayra sultans who controlled Darfur.

To add to the confusion based on the varied histories of 'Abd al-Karim, it is unclear how long he ruled over Wadai. Some contend he ruled as long as sixty-six years. It is more likely that he reigned for about twenty years or so in the middle of the seventeenth century. What is clear is that many later generations viewed the corpus of narratives about 'Abd al-Karim as a means of creating a common sense of solidarity as members of the Wadai kingdom.

BIBLIOGRAPHY

Fage, J. D., Richard Gray, and Roland Oliver. *The Cambridge History of Africa*, vol. 4. Cambridge, UK: Cambridge University Press, 1975.

Hoenig, Karen Haire. "Identity Imaged in History and Story: Re/constructing the Life of Abd-al-Karim, Founder/Renewer of Islam in Wadai, Chad." *African Identities* 5, no. 3 (2007): 313–330.

Insoll, Timothy. *The Archaeology of Islam in Sub-Saharan Africa*. Cambridge, UK: Cambridge University Press, 2003.

Tubiana, Marie-José, Issa Hassan Khayar, and Paule Deville. *Abd el-Karim: propagateur de l'islam et fondateur du royaume du Ouddaï*. Paris: Editions du Centre National de la Recherche Scientifique, 1978.

JEREMY RICH

'Abdalla, Abdilatif (1946–), Kenyan poet, is East Africa's most renowned contemporary Kiswahili poet, even though he has published only one collection of poetry and one epic poem. He is a political activist and scholar and teaches Swahili at Leipzig University in Germany.

Abdilatif 'Abdalla was born in 1946 in Mombasa, Kenya. He was raised by his grandfather Ahmad Basheikh bin Hussein, who was a poet and teacher. 'Abdalla attended primary school in Faza and Takaungu and did secondary studies through the British Tutorial College. He worked briefly as an assistant accountant for the Mombasa City Council. In the late 1960s Abdalla wrote and distributed a political pamphlet, *Kenya Twendapi?* (Kenya, Where Are We Headed?), in support of the opposition party the Kenya People's Union (KPU). During the government crackdown on KPU activities, 'Abdalla was arrested on 20 December 1968 and detained for three years. He was held first in Kamiti prison in Nairobi and later at Shimo la Tewa prison outside of Mombasa. While held in Shimo la Tewa prison, 'Abdalla wrote the poems that were later published in the collection *Sauti ya Dhiki*. Although the poems in *Sauti ya Dhiki* do not make direct reference to the Kenyatta government, many of them may be read as being harshly critical of that regime. In one of the most well-known poems in the collection, two brothers, Ali and Badi, whose voices sound like those of then president Jomo Kenyatta and opposition leader Oginga Odinga, debate the use of a coconut tree, symbolizing Kenya, and its products. The poem begins as follows:

> Alii: Ndugu ulo mnazini, wanitafuta balaa You
> up there, you're looking for trouble!

Nakwambiya shuka tini, katakata wakataa I
     keep asking you to come down, but you take
     no notice.
Wafanya ni masikani, mustarehe ʿmekaa You seem
     to have made a comfortable home up there
Utashuka au la? Will you or won't you come
     down?

Badi: Ndugu tini ya mnazi, nilo juu nakujibu
     You down there, you listen to me
Haya ni ya upuuzi, unambiyayo swahibu What
     you're telling me is a whole load of nonsense.
Kushuka tini siwezi, pasi kujuwa sababu I've no
     intention of coming down without good
     reason
Hiyo ni yangu jawabu That's my reply (Author's
     trans. in Mnazi).

This poem, like most of the others in the collection, is written in the Mombasa dialect of Swahili;
and ʿAbdalla, in this poem as in others, uses conventional rhyme and meter patterns, although he
uses a variant here in the fourth line of each verse
by shortening it to an eight-syllable half line.

ʿAbdalla's other well-known work is *Utenzi wa
Maisha ya Adamu na Hawaa*, an epic poem on the
life of Adam and Eve that he wrote when he was
sixteen. This poem is written in the classic Swahili
narrative style, and large sections of it are written as
a dialogue between Adamu and Hawaa. Although
the story is a classical religious one, the dramatic
element is that of a poet who also explains in the
poem why he has written the epic in Swahili:

Natunga kwa Kiswahili I compose in Swahili
Kila neno kwa dalili Each word intentionally
     [chosen]
Mpate kutaamali So that you comprehend
Vyema na kuwaeleya. Well and understand
     them [Adam and Eve].

When the collection *Sauti ya Dhiki* was awarded
the Kenyatta Prize in Literature, ʿAbdalla went into
exile in Tanzania in 1972. While living in Tanzania
he worked as a senior researcher on the *Kamusi ya
Kiswahili Sanifu*, produced by the University of Dar
es Salaam's Institute for Swahili Research, and
edited the journal *Mulika*. He also edited a number
of works, including his brother Ahmad Nassir's
anthology of poetry *Taa ya Umalenga* (1978). In
addition, he published poetry in a number of
Tanzanian journals during this period.

ʿAbdalla subsequently moved to London, where
he worked for the Swahili service of BBC radio and
later became editor in chief of the news magazine
Africa Events. In 1988 ʿAbdalla published his only
poem in English, "Peace, Love, and Unity for
Whom?" The title of the poem uses the slogan of
the Daniel arap Moi government of Kenya, "peace,
love, and unity." The poem was written in response
to an effort by the Moi government to bribe ʿAbdalla
to stop his work with Ngugi wa Thiong'o in the
United Movement for Democracy in Kenya. The
poem is a rejection of the offer and a sharp critique
of the Moi government.

[*See also* Kenyatta, Jomo; Ngugi wa Thiong'o; *and*
Odinga, Jaramogi Oginga.]

BIBLIOGRAPHY

Works by Abdilatif Abdalla

Utenzi wa Maisha ya Adamu na Hawaa. Edited by
     Abdilahi Nassir. Nairobi: Oxford University Press,
     1971.
Sauti ya Dhiki. Nairobi: Oxford University Press, 1973.
"Mnazi: The Struggle for the Coconut Tree." *Index on
     Censorship* 12, no. 4 (1983): 32–33.
"Peace, Love, and Unity for Whom?" In *UMOJA's
     Struggle for Democracy in Kenya: Special Report
     on the 1988 General Elections in Kenya*. London:
     United Movement for Democracy in Kenya,
     1988.

Works about Abdilatif Abdalla

Nyaigotti-Chacha, Chacha. *Ushairi wa Abdilatif
     Abdalla: Sauti ya Utetezi*. Dar es Salaam: Dar es
     Salaam University Press, 1992.
Walibora Waliaula, Ken. "Prison, Poetry, and
     Polyphony in Abdilatif's *Sauti ya Dhiki*." *Research in
     African Literatures* 40, no. 3 (2009): 129–148.
                                        ANN BIERSTEKER

Abdallah al-Ghalib (1517–1574), second sultan of
the Saʿdian dynasty, reigned between 1557 and 1574.
He was also known Abdallah al-Ghalib Billah. In
1549 Muhammad al-Shaykh occupied Fez, but the
Wattasids sought the Ottomans' help and regained
control of Fez in 1554. Muhammad al-Shaykh was
able to control Fez and named his son Abdallah
al-Ghalib as its governor. Under the authority of
al-Ghalib, Fez regained the political stability and
economic prosperity that it had lost under the
Wattasids. However, it also remained a center of
opposition to the emerging Saʿdian dynasty that
had already controlled southern Morocco and captured Marrakech from the Wattasids. In 1557 Turkish
officers assassinated Muhammad al-Shaykh, and

Abdallah al-Ghalib became the new Sa'dian sultan after intense family infighting over the legitimate successor.

Abdallah al-Ghalib faced major internal and external challenges. He moved from Fez to Marrakech in 1558 and made it his new capital. The Ottoman Turks were challenged in Morocco by the religious and political authority of the Sa'dians, who threatened their authority over the whole Maghreb. The dominance of the Qadiriyya order and other religious scholars in Fez led by 'Abdul al-Wahid al-Wansharisi, the son of Ahmad al-Wansharisi, posed a primary obstacle for the Sa'dians. Before his assassination, Muhammad al-Shaykh waged a political and religious war against the Sufis of Fez and confiscated the property donated to them by Wattasid rulers. Abdallah al-Ghalib continued his father's campaign against the Sufi orders, which saw him as a weak sultan against the Portuguese and Spanish presence on the Moroccan coasts. In Marrakech Abdallah al-Ghalib assassinated Abou Abdallah al-Andalusi, a jurist who influenced many followers to rise against his rule. Despite these clashes with religious brotherhoods and scholars, al-Ghalib tried to strengthen his political and religious relationships with the leaders of the Sufi Jazzuliyya brotherhood. He projected himself as a pious Muslim caliph despite rumors that he entertained singers, held parties where drinking was permitted, and wore silk and gold. In addition to his support of the Jazzuli preachers, al-Ghalib tried to negotiate truces with other Sufi orders that sought refuge in the Atlas Mountains.

Abdallah al-Ghalib was criticized by religious brotherhoods, mainly because of his external relationships with the Iberian powers (Spain and Portugal), France, and Great Britain. From the time he came to power and in order to limit the influence of the Ottoman Turks in Morocco, al-Ghalib followed one of the most balanced external policies toward European powers by a Sa'dian sultan. Unlike his father, al-Ghalib saw that the only way to save the young Sa'dian dynasty from crumbling was to build diplomatic relationships with his Mediterranean enemies through truces. Unlike the Wattasids, who built their power around the Sufis' support, al-Ghalib limited the role of Sufi brotherhoods in waging jihad against the European powers despite their critique of his strategy.

In addition to these challenges, family members had challenged al-Ghalib's succession from the beginning. Some of al-Ghalib's brothers fled to Algeria after they refused to accept his son Muhammad al-Mutawakkil as his heir. Al-Mamoun settled in Tlemcen (Algeria) until al-Ghalib's agents assassinated him. 'Abd al-Malik and Abu al-Abbas Ahmad (al-Mansour) moved to Istanbul. 'Abd al-Malik pleaded with Sultan Murad to support his political claim as the legitimate sultan of Morocco. Before al-Ghalib settled in Marrakech, 'Ali ibn Abi Bakr Aznag, the governor of Marrakech, massacred his uncle Ahmad al-Aaraj and his uncle's children for fear that the population would pay allegiance to his uncle before his arrival in Marrakech. Al-Ghalib became known for getting rid of any member of his palace or family who would threaten or challenge his authority. He was also able to defeat many independence movements from the young Sa'dian dynasty. These included the internal revolutions of 'Uthman in Sous (February 1558), 'Umar in Debdou (April 1558), and 'Abd al-Mouman in Marrakech (December 1558). After successfully limiting the power of the religious opposition and the threat of his family members, Abdallah al-Ghalib focused on the external threats to his rule. In the beginning he built a strong alliance with Spain and limited his diplomatic relationships with the Ottomans after he succeeded in eliminating their internal challenges by 1560. At the same time he signed economic deals with France by giving it access to Ksar al-Saghir. In return, he was promised military support and training of his troops. These strategic external relationships not only saved his reign but also led to the survival of the Sa'dians amid all the external Spanish, Portuguese, and Ottoman interests in Morocco.

Abdallah al-Ghalib also played a major role in the development of the city of Marrakech. In 1570 he restored the Ali ibn Youssef madrasa that had been previously built on the site of the Marinid madrasa of Abd al-Hassan. The school included a dormitory and was the largest in Marrakech. Al-Ghalib also built the dome on Muhammad al-Shaykh's tomb and restored many buildings built during the Almohad reign in the Casbah including the palace, the mosque, and its minaret. He built the mosque of al-Mawasin al-A'dam and the hospital of al-Tal'a. Finally, al-Ghalib established the Jewish quarter of Marrakech (*mallah*) close to the palace and provided protection for the Jewish population of Marrakech. The *mallah* had its own gardens, synagogues, schools, a cemetery, and shops. Al-Ghalib's rule proved to be one of the most important phases in the history of the Sa'dian dynasty. His internal and external policies ensured the future survival of the whole dynasty despite all the challenges of its neighbors.

[*See also* 'Abd al-Malik I; *and* Muhammad al-Shaykh.]

BIBLIOGRAPHY

Deverdun, Gaston. *Marrakesh des Origines à 1912.* Rabat, Morocco: Éditions Techniques Nord-Africaines, 1959.

Gottreich, Emily. *The Mellah of Marrakesh: Jewish and Muslim Space in Morocco's Red City.* Bloomington: Indiana University Press, 2007.

Terasse, Henri. *Histoire du Maroc des origins à l'établissement du Protectorat français.* Casablanca, Morocco: Éditions Atlantides, 1972.

AOMAR BOUM

Abdallahi Muhammad al-Ta'aishi (1846–1899), the Khalifa Abdallahi of the Sudan, was born at Turda in Darfur, the son of Muhammad Adam, a holy man of the Ta'aisha Baqqara whose grandfather had migrated from farther west. Living among the Rizayqat as a soothsayer, Abdallahi was taken prisoner in 1873 by the forces of al-Zubayr Rahma Mansur, the Ja'ali Arab merchant prince, who was on the verge of conquering Darfur. Later, in a famous episode, Abdallahi professed belief that al-Zubayr might be the Mahdi, the deliverer prophesied in certain Islamic traditions. At some point after his release Abdallahi, with his father and brothers, set out on the pilgrimage to Mecca, but he settled in southern Kordofan.

From the time of their earliest acquaintance, at al-Masallamiyya, Abdallahi appears to have been convinced that Muhammad Ahmad ibn 'Abdallah was the Mahdi. What role he played in the Mahdi's manifestation in 1881, and in some critical events immediately thereafter, is uncertain, as is the date of the Mahdi's appointment of Abdallahi as one of four *khalifa*s. As such, the Mahdi reckoned him the successor of Abu Bakr, the first *khalifa* ("caliph") of Islam. Abdallahi commanded the Black Flag division of the Mahdist forces, which was composed mainly of Baqqara tribesmen, and he alone was entitled commander of the armies of the Mahdiyya. Responding to others' jealousy, the Mahdi in 1883 proclaimed Abdallahi's unique status, which was further enhanced on several occasions before the fall of Khartoum in 1885.

The period following the Mahdi's untimely death in June 1885 witnessed a contest between Abdallahi and another *khalifa*, Muhammad Sharif, a relative of the Mahdi whose followers included the Mahdi's family (styled "Ashraf") and sedentary Arabs of the Nile valley generally, the *awlad al-balad*. The eschatological basis of the Mahdi's appeal had precluded plans for succession, and his death might have destroyed the unity of his nascent state. As against dynastic claims, Abdallahi had the advantages of military superiority and the Mahdi's own apparent wishes; subsequently, Abdallahi's personal role in Mahdist theology was enhanced through prophetic revelations and propaganda. A theme of Abdallahi's reign, however, would be the irreconcilable opposition of the Ashraf. In 1891 this assumed the character of open rebellion, which the *khalifa* put down with skill; Muhammad Sharif was imprisoned, and the Ashraf were suppressed.

The policies Abdallahi pursued to maintain control included the enforced residence at Omdurman of leading Ashraf, of other Arab notables, and eventually of whole ethnic groups, especially of Baqqara westerners, to limit their scope for rebellion. Abdallahi himself rarely strayed from the environs of Omdurman. Provincial governors and others were replaced with loyalists, notably including the *khalifa*'s kin. Abdallahi's pursuit of a campaign to conquer Egypt has been ascribed, controversially, to a desire to rid himself of its commander, the great emir 'Abd al-Rahman al-Nujumi, whose defeat and death at Tushki (Toski) in 1889 effectively ended the Mahdist threat to Egypt. Abdallahi's arms were more successful elsewhere: at al-Qallabat (Gallabat) in March 1889 the Sudanese decisively defeated the Abyssinians; in western Sudan the Mahdists managed, with great difficulty, to suppress rebellions by Fur princes and Baqqara tribesmen.

After the battles of 1889 and in the wake of a devastating famine, Abdallahi initiated political changes. These involved a tacit end to the jihad beyond Sudan, conciliation of opponents at home, and, after ruthless exploitation of the agricultural Gezira to feed the motley population of Omdurman, a new economic policy. Steps to relieve the conditions of the *awlad al-balad* included removing oppressive governors, appointing locals to positions of authority, encouraging agriculture, and rescinding the prohibition of trade with Egypt, both along the border and through Suakin.

Through these and other means, the *khalifa* consolidated his rule. Although Mahdism remained the official ideology, the regime evolved into a Muslim monarchy. State apparatus inaugurated by the Mahdi was extended and regularized, reformed and adjusted as required. Abdallahi's immediate family, notably his brother Ya'qub and eldest son

Uthman Shaykh al-Din, were ensconced in powerful positions, and dynastic succession was assumed. Conditions were far from those depicted in contemporary European accounts—and the enormous literature thereafter based on them: many Sudanese who had fled the Mahdiyya to Egypt willingly returned.

The mortal threat to Abdallahi and the Mahdist state was external as the encircling European powers relished the great prize of the upper Nile. In the 1890s Italy annexed Eritrea, and the Belgians entered western Equatoria and the western Bahr al-Ghazal, en route to the Nile. In 1895 the French government authorized the Marchand mission. International agreements carved up the region. British propagandists agitated constantly to "avenge Gordon" and thwart the French. In 1896 the British government finally authorized an advance from Egypt to Dongola to distract the Mahdists from threatening Italian Eritrea. Anglo-Egyptian forces moved thereafter inexorably up the Nile toward Omdurman.

Abdallahi's room for maneuver was limited. The decision to hold back for a final battle near Omdurman was determined by the need to provision his huge army. The invasion force had obvious modern advantages, but the outcome of a single great battle was far from inevitable. In the end, however, the tactics of Abdallahi's commanders on the field of Karari on 2 September 1898, and the invaders' advanced weaponry, determined the outcome. The Mahdist army was routed, Omdurman was occupied, and Abdallahi fled into Kordofan with a still considerable force.

The *khalifa* managed to hold out for another year. On 24 November 1899 he was brought to battle by an Anglo-Egyptian force at Umm Diwaykarat in southern Kordofan. When the day was lost the *khalifa*, with his leading emirs, heroically sat down on their sheepskins and were killed in the melee.

The historical record of the Khalifa Abdallahi has been written largely by enemies. Grotesque caricatures, based on contemporary British propaganda, continue to be retailed in popular works, fiction, and film. These depict him as a monster whose overthrow relieved the Sudanese of tyranny and ushered in an era of colonial progress. There is no biography in English.

[*See also* Gordon, Charles George; Muhammad Ahmad ibn 'Abdallah; *and* Zubayr Rahma Mansur, al-.]

BIBLIOGRAPHY

Holt, P. M. *The Mahdist State in the Sudan, 1881–1898*. 2d ed. Oxford: Clarendon Press, 1970. Outstanding account in English of the Mahdiyya, providing a critical account of Abdallahi's rule.

Sanderson, G. N. *England, Europe, and the Upper Nile, 1882–1889*. Edinburgh: Edinburgh University Press, 1965. Details the complicated diplomacy leading to the destruction of the Mahdist state.

Shuqayr, Na'um. *Ta'rikh al-Sudan wa'l-qadim wa'l-hadith wa jughrafiyatuh*. Cairo: 1903. The most important published primary source.

Zulfo, Ismat Hasan. *Karari, the Sudanese Account of the Battle of Omdurman*. Translated by Peter Clark. London: Shoe String Press, 1980. Provides a useful military history of the *khalifa*'s reign.

M. W. DALY

'Abdallah Jamma' (1482–1562), patriarch of the 'Abdallab group and cofounder of the first Muslim state in Sudan, the Blue Sultanate, in the sixteenth century, was born 'Abdallah bin Mohammed al-Baqir.

Shaykh 'Abdallah Jamma''s father, Mohammed al-Baqir, was a member of the elite Meccan Qawasma tribe, whose members claim to have descended from Hussein, the grandson of the Prophet Muhammad. Mohammed al-Baqir is reported to have migrated from Mecca to Sawakin on the Red Sea, where he married Hosna, daughter of Abdallah al-Qareen of the Rufa'a tribe and where their son 'Abdallah was born. When the young 'Abdallah turned seven, his father took him back to Mecca, where he studied the Qur'an and other religious sciences until the age of twenty-three, when Shaykh 'Abdallah returned to Sawakin in Sudan.

In Sawakin, he married the daughter of the sharif of Sawakin, Shaykh Abu-Dhanana, and began his efforts to unite the dispersed Arab tribes. His noble heritage is likely to have provided him with decisive moral authority over the tribes as he adjudicated their disputes and settled old feuds. Having united the Arab tribes and earned the name "Jamma'" or "unifier," he entered into an alliance with Amara Dongos, the leader of Fonj. The united Arab and Fonj forces were able to defeat the then ruling Christian tribes in the famous battle of Soba in 1505, thereby establishing the first Arab-Muslim rule in Sudan. Although some historians have indicated that the formal alliance between the Fonj and Shaykh 'Abdallah's followers, the 'Abdallab, may have occurred after the establishment of the Blue Sultanate, they still concede that prior Arab alliances are likely to have existed under the leadership of Shaykh 'Abdallah Jamma'.

Although overall political control of the newly established Blue Sultanate was nominally in the hands of the Fonj, the sheikhdom of 'Abdallab in Gharri retained not only spiritual leadership but also political rule over the northern portion of the sultanate on behalf of the Fonj, who exercised direct rule over the southern part. In one incident, Shaykh 'Abdallah is reported to have corresponded with the Ottoman sultan Saleem when he intended to invade Sudan and convinced him that the people of Sudan were fellow Muslims and thus the invasion could not be justified on religious grounds.

With the establishment of Islam as the new state religion, a religious renaissance was under way in Sudan. Shaykh 'Abdallah Jamma' set out to further spread Islam in Sudan, and he selected a number of learned scholars and sent them to Sudan's various regions to teach the tenets of the religion to the new converts. He also invited a number of prominent scholars from outside Sudan, including Morocco and Iraq, and lavished them with gifts to entice them to remain in Sudan. Noteworthy among those scholars was Shaykh Taj al-Deen al-Bahari, who spread the Sufi teachings of Shaykh Abdul-Qadir al-Jilani among the 'Abdallab and their followers. Shaykh 'Abdallah Jamma' is also reported to have sponsored some Sudanese to travel to study Islam at al-Azhar in Egypt and elsewhere and return home to share their learning with their countrymen.

After his death Shaykh 'Abdallah Jamma' was succeeded by nineteen sons, including King Ajeeb al-Manjilik, who led the first Sudanese pilgrimage to Mecca, having commissioned the building of a road from Gharri to Mosawa' on the Red Sea. The descendants of Shaykh 'Abdallah Jamma' continued to rule the shaykhdom for three centuries until the Turkish invasion of Sudan in 1821.

BIBLIOGRAPHY

Mohyieddeen, Mohammed Salih. *The Abdallab Sheikhdom and Its Impact on Sudan's Political Life.* English translation of *Mashiakhat al-Abdallab wa Atharaha fi Hayat al-Sudan al-Siyasiyya,* 1972.

Mohyieddeen, Salah. *Ajeeb al-Manjilik,* 1975.

Shibaikah, Makki. *Sudan Through the Centuries.* English translation of *Al-Sudan Abr al-Quroon,* 1964.

AHMED T. EL-GEILI

'Abd al-Malik I (1541–1578), Moroccan ruler, was one of the sons of Muhammad al-Shaykh of the Sa'di or Saadian dynasty, which ruled a region roughly coterminous with modern Morocco from 1525 until c. 1610. He was born Abu Marwan Abd al-Malik to a woman called Sahaba al-Rahmaniyya who accompanied her son on his later travels through the Mediterranean. The Sa'di dynasty came to power at an important historical juncture. During the fifteenth and early sixteenth centuries, Portugal had constructed numerous trading enclaves (*feitorias*) along Morocco's Atlantic seaboard and imposed its control on much of the Gharb plain. In the last decades of the fifteenth century, Spain had finally conquered Muslim Granada and established a series of footholds on the Mediterranean coast of Africa. At the same time both countries had established vast overseas empires. At the other end of the Mediterranean, the Ottomans acted as a Muslim counterbalance, conquering the Levant (1516) and Egypt (1517) and then dispatching corsairs to secure the coasts of North Africa against the Spanish Habsburg advance.

The Ottoman Habsburg contest for Mediterranean hegemony and Portugal's aspirations to conquer Morocco deeply marked the life of 'Abd al-Malik. The Sa'di lineage had used the prestige generated by their family's claim of descent from the Prophet to secure the support of numerous Arabic-speaking tribes in the Dar'a valley in southern Morocco for a jihad against the Portuguese. Using new gunpowder technology acquired from Dutch and English black marketeers, Muhammad al-Shaykh managed to oust the Portuguese from Santa Cruz (Agadir) in 1541, the year of 'Abd al-Malik's birth. The Ottomans, who had established a foothold in Algiers by this time, perceived in their Moroccan coreligionist a useful thorn in the side of Portugal and Habsburg Spain but also a possible threat. They therefore dispatched a corps of Janissaries, who were instructed to pretend that they had deserted, to enter his service as spies, according to al-Ifrani. The Sa'di army also included migrants from the Iberian Peninsula, Muslims forced to leave by the punitive policies of the Spanish crown, which included forced conversion to Catholicism. 'Abd al-Malik therefore grew up in an international environment in which indigenous Moroccan, Ottoman, and Iberian aspects mingled.

In 1557 the Ottoman sultan instructed the Janissaries to assassinate Muhammad al-Shaykh, whose establishment of a united Moroccan sultanate suggested the emergence of an assertive sovereign state on the frontier between Spain and Ottoman Algiers rather than a supine client regime. Muhammad al-Shaykh was succeeded by his eldest son, Abdallah al-Ghalib, at which point the sixteen-year-old 'Abd al-Malik and his younger brother Ahmad fled the sultanate with their mothers fearing a purge. They were joined by another brother, 'Abd al-Mu'min, shortly afterward. 'Abd al-Malik spent some time in Tlemcen just within Ottoman territory but then moved on to the safer confines of Ottoman Algiers.

During this period, which lasted for about a decade, 'Abd al-Malik became a cosmopolitan product of the Mediterranean world of his day. The greatest influence on 'Abd al-Malik was naturally that of the Ottomans. He not only learned Turkish and adopted Ottoman dress, but also joined the Janissary corps and became a skilled military man in the Ottoman mode. He also married the daughter of an Ottoman, Hajj Murad, and became a trusted member of the Ottoman establishment. The Ottoman sultan Murad III granted him an army commission in Egypt in 1568, and he participated in the battle of Lepanto in 1571. He was captured at Lepanto and held prisoner in Oran by the Spanish for a year, during which time he mastered Spanish. He also learned other European languages and adopted manners of attire and behavior that enabled him to mix easily with Christian Europeans.

After his release he returned to Ottoman service and served as a commander under Sinan Pasha during the successful siege of Tunis in 1574, a victory that vindicated the Ottomans' previous defeat at Lepanto. Although the chronology of this period is slightly confused, 'Abd al-Malik and his mother, who was in Istanbul, petitioned Murad III for military assistance to seize the Sa'di throne from his nephew Muhammad al-Mutawakkil, who succeeded his father, Abdallah, in 1574. The Ottoman sultan remained reluctant until after the victory at Tunis had confirmed Ottoman supremacy throughout North Africa except Morocco. 'Abd al-Malik, now a proven Ottoman commander, offered the attractive proposition of making Morocco an Ottoman vassal with minimal effort on the part of Istanbul. The Ottoman sultan gave his blessing to the project, and 'Abd al-Malik returned to Algiers to collect a substantial Janissary force, assisted by his younger brother Ahmad.

He marched against his nephew Muhammad al-Mutawakkil and defeated him at the battle of Rukn, largely because many of Muhammad's Spanish Muslim troops defected on the battlefield. Fez fell

shortly afterward and then Marrakech. After his victory 'Abd al-Malik took the regnal title al-Mu'tasim Bi'llah. He sent the majority of his Ottoman troops back to Algiers at this point in favor of relying on indigenous and Spanish Muslim fighters, suggesting that he had a looser concept of "vassalage" than the Ottoman sultan may have supposed. The deposed Muhammad al-Mutawakkil sought refuge at the Portuguese court of Dom Sebastian, a young king with his sights set on what turned out to be a quixotic ambition to conquer Morocco.

The internecine struggle between Muhammad al-Mutawakkil, disparagingly known as "The Portuguese," and 'Abd al-Malik thus became a proxy war between Portugal and the Ottomans for control of Morocco. 'Abd al-Malik, however, benefited from being able to depict the war as a jihad against the infidel and to denounce his nephew as an apostate for seeking Christian help. The struggle came to a head at the battle of the Three Kings in 1578, also known as the battle of Alcazar or Wad al-Makhazin. 'Abd al-Malik fell sick before the battle commenced and delegated the active command to his younger brother Ahmad, who had accompanied him to Istanbul and become his right-hand man in the struggle to capture Morocco. As the battle turned against him, however, he masterfully rallied his troops to cut into the Portuguese ranks. He dropped dead shortly afterward, but his army held together and routed the Portuguese. Muhammad al-Mutawakkil drowned trying to flee across the river; Dom Sebastian and numerous Portuguese nobles were also drowned, killed, or captured. 'Abd al-Malik's brother Ahmad, his nominated heir, was recognized as the next Sa'di sultan on the battlefield. It was thus Ahmad who benefited from his brother's endeavors and lived to become the most famous of the Sa'di sultans, relegating 'Abd al-Malik, his brother and mentor, to the sidelines of history.

[*See also* Abdallah al-Ghalib; Mansur, Moulay Ahmad al-; *and* Muhammad al-Shaykh.]

BIBLIOGRAPHY

Cook, Weston F. *The Hundred Years War for Morocco: Gunpowder and the Military Revolution in the Early Modern Muslim World*. Boulder, Colo.: Westview Press, 1994.

Cornell, Vincent. "Socio-economic Dimensions of Reconquista and Jihad in Morocco: Portuguese Dukkala and the Sadid Sus." *International Journal of Middle Eastern Studies* 22, no. 4 (1990): 379–418.

García-Arenal, Mercedes. *Ahmad al-Mansur: The Beginnings of Modern Morocco*. Oxford: Oneworld, 2009.

Hess, Andrew. *Forgotten Frontier: A History of the Sixteenth Century Ibero-African Frontier*. Chicago: University of Chicago Press, 1978.

Ifrani, Muhammad al-Saghir al-. *Nozhet-elhadi; histoire de la dynastie saadienne au Maroc (1511–1670)*, edited and translated by O. Houdas. 2 vols. Paris: Leroux, 1888–1889.

AMIRA K. BENNISON

'Abd al-Mu'min (d. 1163), builder of the Almohad Empire and great Moroccan military leader and able administrator, led the Almohad movement for *tawhid*, absolute monotheistic unity, after the death of the Mahdi Ibn Tumart, the Almohad founder, in c. 1130. His full name was 'Abd al-Mu'min ibn 'Ali ibn 'Alwi bin Ya'la al-Kumi Abu Muhammad.

After defeating the Almoravid Empire at Marrakech, he established the administrative and military foundations of the Almohad state while securing a caliphal succession for his descendants, the Mu'minid dynasty. In a matter of decades 'Abd al-Mu'min and his followers transformed the Almohads from a vigorous but vulnerable ideological movement in the small Atlas Mountain town of Tinmal to one of the largest and most successful Islamic empires in North African and Andalusian history.

Effectively an outsider, 'Abd al-Mu'min's ancestry was different from the noble Masmuda ethnic groups that made up the core of the Almohad army and hierarchy. He was born into the Arabicized Berber group of the Kumya of the Zanata confederation in the province of modern Oran. Although he was not a member of the original Almohad groups of the Moroccan Atlas who so vigorously followed the Mahdi Ibn Tumart, he was well suited for leadership and could use his status as an outsider to mediate intergroup jealousies. Only later, in the writings of the *Kitab al Ansab*, a book found, like many Almohad sources, in a collection of manuscripts at the Escorial in Spain, did 'Abd al Mu'min claim an illustrious Arab and Berber ancestry that tied him to pre-Islamic prophets as much as the Berber Queen Kahina.

Ibn Tumart singled out the young man in a mosque full of others and told 'Abd al-Mu'min that he need go no further in search of the light of knowledge; everything he needed to know was in front of him. Al-Baydhaq, the chronicler, biographer, and fervent Almohad panegyrist, witnessed this encounter between Mahdi and the future caliph around the year 1117. He seemed to have embellished the story as a way of legitimizing the succession of 'Abd al-Mu'min and to lend a sense of fate and inevitability to the rise of so humble a young man. In al-Baydhaq's version of events, the Mahdi and 'Abd al-Mu'min were talking in the middle of the night when al-Baydhaq brought an unidentified red book, most likely the Qur'an or possibly a *jafr*, a book of divination; the Mahdi then declared, "The cause on which the life of the faith depends, will only succeed with 'Abd al-Mu'min ibn 'Ali, lamp of the Almohads; your conversion will be the conversion of the world from sin." It was from this declaration that 'Abd al-Mu'min would later legitimize his title as caliph. Whereas the Almoravid sultans remained nominally loyal to the Abbasid caliphs in Baghdad, the Almohads under 'Abd al-Mu'min had ambitions to conquer and restore the entire Islamic world to its former glory under the inspired teachings of the Mahdi.

In many ways the personalities and abilities of Ibn Tumart, the idealistic spiritual Mahdi, and 'Abd al-Mu'min, the practical, shrewd, but still loyal administrator and warrior, were perfectly compatible. Their combined efforts, along with the support of a select core of followers, the Council of Ten, including that model of loyalty and tribal legitimacy Abu Hafs 'Umar al-Hintati, forged a powerful tribal army confident enough to attack the capital of the powerful Almoravid sultan at Marrakech. Fought on the open plains, the Almohad mountain warriors were mowed down by the experienced Almoravid cavalry. But the battle of al-Buhaira in 1130 was only a short-term disaster for the Almohads. Although sorely defeated, they learned an important tactic that would be followed almost unfailingly by 'Abd al-Mu'min as he conquered the entire Maghreb: always keep the high ground, and consolidate mountain territory before invading the lower plains.

It was the death of Mahdi Ibn Tumart in 1130, shortly after the disaster at al-Buhaira, that may have saved the Almohads from further idealistic but tactically disastrous front-end assaults on the Almoravids. Such was the vulnerability of the movement in 1130 that the news of Ibn Tumart's death was not made available outside a tight circle led by 'Abd al-Mu'min until 1133. His body was kept preserved in his house as proclamations, allegedly from the mouth of the Mahdi but in fact from the administrative mind of 'Abd al-Mu'min, were issued to the various ethnic groups and the

Almohad hierarchy of shaykhs and scholars. It was only after these three years that 'Abd al-Mu'min received the allegiance of all of his followers, using the Mahdi's spiritual charisma even though the Mahdi himself was no longer alive.

Ruler of the Almohads from his day of proclamation in 1133 until his death in 1163, the beginning of 'Abd al-Mu'min's career was marked by rapid military success along the entire range of the Atlas Mountains and the Rif. He thus secured the entire mountainous backbone of the Maghreb, before even attempting to venture out onto the open plains. Often using guerilla tactics, he first attacked the Almoravid fortresses built along the High Atlas, quickly conquering the Sus region. Then he turned his attention north to the Middle Atlas, where he conquered the strategically important Tafilalt oases in 1140–1141. Then he moved still farther north, easily gaining the allegiance of mountain peoples before finally returning to his own birthplace at Tagra.

Having secured the mountains and gained a vast army of fierce mountain warriors, 'Abd al-Mu'min finally felt ready to confront the Almoravids directly. The Almoravid leadership was also seriously weakened at this point after the death of the able sultan 'Ali ibn Yusuf who was succeeded by his son Tashfin ibn Ali and the skilled Christian general Reverter (al-Ruburtayr), who led the Almoravid Christian contingent. Many of the founding Almoravid peoples were in open revolt. Tashfin was defeated at Tlemcen. Fleeing to Oran, the Almoravid sultan died after falling from his horse and off a cliff in 1145. Although they put up some local resistance to the mountain groups, the great cities of Fez, Meknès, and Salé were quickly conquered by 1146.

Finally, seventeen years after the infamous battle of al-Buhaira, 'Abd al-Mu'min turned confidently toward the Almoravid capital of Marrakech in 1147. Marrakech finally fell after a bloody siege and heroic resistance that included the women of the city. Almoravid rule was then extinguished when 'Abd al-Mu'min killed the young prince Ishaq ibn 'Ali ibn Yusuf. Although he chose the old Almoravid palace in Marrakech as his new home and Marrakech as the new capital of the empire, some accounts record that the caliph refused to reenter the city until all the religious buildings and mosques of the Almoravids had been destroyed and their qibla, or direction of prayer, had properly reoriented according to Almohad standards. With the construction of the great Kutubiyya Mosque, whose magnificent and austere minaret still defines much of Maghrebi architecture, 'Abd al-Mu'min aimed to cleanse Marrakech of the Almoravid past and refound the city as a symbol of Almohad Islam, a manifestation of the austere Almohad doctrine in stone. 'Abd al-Mu'min's architectural standards would set the tone for much of Almohad architecture, including the Giralda of Seville and the Hassan Tower of Rabat, impressive symbols of Almohad ambitions.

Having soundly defeated the Almoravid state at Marrakech, 'Abd al-Mu'min soon turned his attention northeast to Ifriqiya, or modern Tunis, where Normans led by Roger II and Arab Bedouin had all but destroyed any semblance of central power. 'Abd al-Mu'min declared jihad, or holy war, against the Christian Normans, who had established fortress bases on formerly Muslim North African soil. On his way to Ifriqiya he secured Algiers, Bougie, and Setif, subduing the descendants of restive Arab nomads in the area. Distracted by engagements in the Iberian Peninsula, Ifriqiya itself was not conquered until some eight years later when 'Abd al-Mu'min defeated Roger II at Mahdiyya in 1160 and went on to gain control of the entire coastline to Tripoli.

Almohad campaigns began early in 1145, even before the conquest of Marrakech. The former admiral of the Almoravids, Ibn Maymun, soon joined the Almohads, allowing them to build a navy and assault the coastline of southern Spain, taking Cadiz early in the campaign. Jerez, Niebla, Silves, Beja, Badajoz, and, most importantly, Seville, the future northern capital of the Almohads, as well as Granada all surrendered in 1154. Almería was recaptured from the Christians in 1157. Indeed, it was the growing Christian ambition to conquer all of Al-Andalus that convinced 'Abd al-Mu'min to become personally involved in the campaign. In 1162 'Abd al-Mu'min built up a huge army at the newly established city of Rabat, where he may have had ambitions to conquer not only Andalusia but also much of the Christian world. These ambitions were cut short, however, by his death in May 1163. He was buried next to the simple grave of the Mahdi Ibn Tumart in Tinmal, the great spiritual leader who had inspired him to join the Almohad movement more than forty years before.

[*See also* Ibn Tumart, Muhammad; *and* Kahina.]

BIBLIOGRAPHY
Brett, Michael. "The Lamp of the Almohads:
    Illumination as a Political Idea in Twelfth-Century

Morocco." In *Ibn Khaldun and the Medieval Maghreb*. Rugby, UK: Variorum, 1999.

Fromherz, Allen. *The Almohads: The Rise of an Islamic Empire*. London: IB Tauris, 2010.

Le Tourneau, Roger. *The Almohad Movement in North Africa*. Princeton, N.J.: Princeton University Press, 1969.

ALLEN J. FROMHERZ

'Abd al-Nasir, Jamal. *See* Nasser, Gamal Abd al-.

'Abd al-Rahman, 'A'ishah (Bint al-Shati' or Daughter of the Riverbank; 1913–1998), Egyptian Islamic scholar and prominent writer of Arabic literature, was born on 18 November 1913 into a conservative religious household in Dumyat (Damietta) in the Egyptian Delta. She was a descendent, on her mother's side, of a shaykh of the Al-Azhar, the prestigious mosque and university in Cairo, and her father taught at Dumyat Religious Institute. Well acquainted with her family history, 'Abd al-Rahman sought to continue this proud tradition. She began learning basic reading and writing skills before the age of five in a *kuttab* in her father's village. This early instruction prepared her to read the Qur'an. 'Abd al-Rahman's later education became more difficult, however, as her father did not believe that girls should be educated outside the home because secular education did not provide proper instruction for them. As a result, 'Abd al-Rahman's mother would continually intervene to help her daughter attend both primary and secondary school when her father traveled. When 'Abd al-Rahman's father returned from his journeys, he would insist that she leave school and be educated at home. 'Abd al-Rahman, though, believed that her father's actions did not deprive her of an education but that her home schooling provided additional instruction to the knowledge that she received in school.

For her secondary education, 'Abd al-Rahman made repeated appeals to the Ministry of Education to allow her to attend a teacher-training school for women in Tanta. Her efforts proved successful, but when her father found out that she was going out to school, he again forced her to be educated at home. 'Abd al-Rahman agreed to her father's demands but planned to borrow the teachers' books to complete secondary school. Finally, with her mother's aid, she graduated from a teacher-training school for women in Mansourah. While still at school, she began writing poems, which she sent to the magazine *al-Nahdah al-Nisa'iyah* (The Women's Renaissance) for publication. *Al-Nahdah al-Nisa'iyah* began as a strictly women's journal, but by the 1930s the magazine was covering more issues about Islam. 'Abd al-Rahman met with the owner of the magazine, Labibah Ahmad, who had aided many Egyptian women in their attempts at becoming established in the field of journalism. Ahmad rewarded 'Abd al-Rahman with the directorship of the magazine in 1933.

Well on her way to becoming an important contributor to not only *al-Nahdah al-Nisa'iyah* but also some of the most prestigious periodicals in Egypt, 'Abd al-Rahman produced articles as well as pieces of literature. She wrote for *al-Misriyah*, the Arabic equivalent of Huda Sha'rawi's feminist journal *L'Egyptienne* (The Egyptian Woman); *al-Balagh* (The Report); and *Kawkab al-Sharq* (Star of the East). Because of 'Abd al-Rahman's concerns about her family's acceptance of seeing her real name in print, she began writing under the pseudonym Bint al-Shati'. In her articles for *al-Ahram* (The Pyramids), Egypt's leading newspaper, she wrote about the Egyptian countryside and the unfair treatment of the peasantry. Her articles became the basis for two books, *The Egyptian Countryside*, published in 1936, and *Qadiyyat al-Fallah* (The Problem of the Peasant), published in 1938. Few writers, let alone women writers, took up the issue of the suffering of the peasantry and the devastating impact of the Depression on the Egyptian countryside. In fact, many Egyptian writers during this period tended to view the peasant as a romantic, timeless icon of the pharaonic period and not part of the very real contemporary problems facing Egypt. Since 'Abd al-Rahman grew up in the countryside and continued to return there while in university, she had firsthand knowledge of the situation.

After years of struggle, in 1934 'Abd al-Rahman attended Cairo University and majored in Arabic literature and Islamic studies. Islamic studies would become her focus for the rest of her life. She also studied foreign languages, including English, French, and Italian. Having to provide for her material support, 'Abd al-Rahman taught at a girls' school in Giza close to the university. She took classes with the eminent Islamic scholar Amin al-Khuli; he later became her mentor. They married in 1947 and had three children. He died in 1966. While attending university 'Abd al-Rahman noticed that many of the books in the curriculum for Islamic studies and classical Arabic were written by foreigners who were not Arabs or Muslims, providing her with added incentive to make major contributions to both discourses.

She received her BA in 1939, working as an assistant lecturer for the university in the same year. In 1941 she was awarded an MA. The Ministry of Education appointed her inspector for the teaching of Arabic literature the following year. Her first novel, *Secret of the Beach and Master of the Estate: The Story of a Sinful Woman*, appeared in 1942. In 1950 'Abd al-Rahman received her PhD and became assistant professor of Arabic literature from 1950 to 1957 at Ain Shams University in the Misr al-Gadida (Heliopolis) area of Cairo. She became chair of her department in 1962. She later served in various capacities as a visiting professor at some of the most renowned universities in the Arab world, including Al-Qarawiyin University in Morocco, Beirut University, and Emirates University.

Aside from her literary contributions, which include her semiautobiographical compilation of short stories entitled *Sirr al-Shati'* (The Secret of the Riverbank), in which she details vividly life in the countryside, 'Abd al-Rahman is probably best known as an Islamic scholar. Undoubtedly, her most famous work on Islamic history includes a series of volumes on the women in the Prophet Muhammad's life, which she completed in the 1960s. She also wrote commentaries on Islamic scripture and jurisprudence as well as literary criticism. 'Abd al-Rahman held numerous government positions for Egyptian culture, including membership on the Supreme Council of Islamic Affairs and the Supreme Council of Culture. She also won awards for her contributions to Islamic studies and Arabic literature in Egypt and in the Arab world. Clearly, 'Abd al-Rahman remains one of the foremost female Islamic scholars in the world to date and one of the greatest literary figures in Egyptian history. She died on 1 December 1998 in Cairo.

BIBLIOGRAPHY

'Abd al-Rahman, 'A'ishah. *'Ala Jisr: Usturat al-Zaman* (On the Bridge: A Myth of Time). Cairo: Dar al-Hilal, 1967. In her autobiography, the author relates the important events of her life from birth through her years at university.

Badran, Margot. *Feminists, Islam, and Nation: Gender and the Making of Modern Egypt.* Princeton, N.J.: Princeton University Press, 1995. One of the best sources for information on the lives of prominent Egyptian women in the twentieth century.

Baron, Beth. *Egypt as a Woman: Nationalism, Gender and Politics.* Berkeley: University of California Press, 2005.

Elsadda, Hoda, and Emad Abu-Ghazi. *Significant Moments in the History of Egyptian Women.* Cairo: National Council for Women, 2001. This book recounts the important contributions of Egyptian women to the history of their nation from the eighteenth to the twentieth century.

Zeidan, Joseph T. *Arab Women Novelists: The Formative Years and Beyond.* Albany, N.Y.: SUNY Press, 1995. An excellent source for information on important Arab women novelists, including 'A'ishah 'Abd al-Rahman.

CATHLYN MARISCOTTI

'Abd al-Rahman al-Mahdi (1885–1959), leader of the Mahdist movement in Sudan, was the posthumous son of Muhammad Ahmad ibn 'Abdallah, the Mahdi, and of Maqbula bint Nurayn Muhammad al-Fadl, a princess of the Fur royal house. He spent much of his childhood at Omdurman, where he and his relatives were subordinated to the Khalifa Abdallahi. During the Anglo-Egyptian pacification of the country after the battle of Omdurman (1898), he was wounded in an affray that left two of his brothers dead.

Until World War I the family of the Mahdi suffered from the colonial regime's policy of suppressing the Mahdist cult and guarding against religious heterodoxy in general. Alarmed, however, at the possible effects in Sudan of the Ottoman sultan's alliance with the Central Powers in 1914, the Anglo-Egyptian regime conciliated the major Sufi leaders and 'Abd al-Rahman, the generally accepted successor to leadership of the Mahdist movement. Proving himself both loyal to the government and even more charismatic than they had expected, Sayyid 'Abd al-Rahman soon rivaled Ali al-Mirghani, the hereditary leader of the quietist and anti-Mahdist Khatmiyya Sufis, for preeminence.

By the early 1920s the British rued their wartime rehabilitation of the Mahdi's son. He had already accrued considerable wealth from agricultural projects, notably at Aba Island, the cradle of Mahdism in the White Nile. In 1921 a serious rising in Darfur was blamed on his growing influence there, and attempts were made to check his activities. Yet he was thought instrumental in keeping the protonationalist uprising of 1924 from spreading to his supposedly fanatical followers. His role was evolving, in both theory and practice, to encompass what would be called "neo-Mahdism," a movement relying on his religious prestige for mass support but with moderate, modern political aims.

Those crystallized in 'Abd al-Rahman's patronage of the Sudanese independence movement. This was divided into two camps: unionists allied with Egypt and ostensibly favoring the unity of the Nile valley, with whom the Khatmiyya became associated, and those favoring "the Sudan for the Sudanese" while tolerating a British role to prevent union with Egypt. This dichotomy dominated politics until independence, in ways that both hastened change and retarded development. All aspects of political activity were affected: local government, the press, students' unions. Constitutional reform and electoral politics reflected the fluctuating fortunes of religious sects rather than secular ideologies. Proindependence elements as disparate as educated moderates, conservative tribal leaders, religious radicals, and communists chose pragmatic alliance or sullen opposition but were unable on their own to win a mass following. Meanwhile, the advantages accruing to support for independence were vitiated by 'Abd al-Rahman's presumed monarchical intentions, regal lifestyle, and a political apparatus built on patronage rather than expertise.

In parliamentary elections in 1953, therefore, the unionists under Isma'il al-Azhari won a stunning victory over 'Abd al-Rahman's party, the Umma (which was nominally led by his son al-Siddiq), and formed the first Sudanese government. 'Abd al-Rahman's continuing power was amply demonstrated, however, when the ceremonial opening of parliament in March 1954 was marred by tens of thousands of rioting Mahdist tribesmen; the answer to union with Egypt appeared to be civil war. But the support of the Khatmiyya for union had always been a strategy for foiling a Mahdist monarchy. Now in power, Isma'il al-Azhari led the unionists to independence in 1956.

'Abd al-Rahman's role in and above Sudanese politics continued thereafter. In July 1956 his differences with Sayyid Ali were patched up to the detriment of secularists, and Isma'il al-Azhari's was replaced by the Umma politician and former general Abdallah Khalil as prime minister. He in turn apparently colluded in the military coup of November 1958 that ended Sudan's brief democratic experiment.

Sayyid 'Abd al-Rahman al-Mahdi died in March 1959. Knighted by the British and a pasha of Egypt, he was arguably the single most important Sudanese of the colonial era. He oversaw—and indeed epitomized—in Sudan a process of routinization

characteristic of Islamic messianism in Africa. Yet he signally failed either to reestablish Mahdism as synonymous with the Sudanese independence of his father's day or to manage its evolution into a vehicle of modern nationalism. The ambiguous character of the movement continued after his death to bedevil his family—and his country. His son al-Hadi was killed in opposition to the military dictatorship of Ja'far al-Nimeiry in 1970, and his grandson al-Sadiq al-Mahdi, who was sometime prime minister in the 1960s and 1980s, was overthrown in the coup of the National Islamic Front in 1989.

[See also Abdallahi Muhammad al-Ta'aishi; Azhari, Isma'il al-; Mirghani, Ali al-; Muhammad Ahmad ibn 'Abdallah; and Nimeiry, Ja'far al-.]

BIBLIOGRAPHY

Daly, M. W. *Empire on the Nile: The Anglo-Egyptian Sudan, 1898–1934.* Cambridge, UK: Cambridge University Press, 1986.

Daly, M. W. *Imperial Sudan: The Anglo-Egyptian Condominium, 1934–1956.* Cambridge, UK: Cambridge University Press, 1991. Together with the above they cover the political history of the colonial period.

Hasan, Ahmed Ibrahim. "Imperialism and Neo-Mahdism in the Sudan: A Study of British Policy towards Neo-Mahdism, 1924–1927." *International Journal of African Historical Studies* 13 (1980): 214–239. This and other works by the same author deal with the emergence of neo-Mahdism.

Warburg, Gabriel. *Islam, Sectarianism and Politics in Sudan since the Mahdiyya* (London: C. Hurst, 2003). This and other works by the same author deal with sectarian politics during the colonial period.

M. W. DALY

'Abd al-Rahman ibn Ahmad Bukr (c. 1725–1801), sultan of the Sudanese kingdom of Darfur from 1785 to 1801, was born to Sultan Ahmad Bukr and an unknown woman. The youngest of four sons of Ahmad Bukr who ruled Darfur, many thought him a weak choice. He became a very successful monarch, after overcoming internal opposition. During his reign Darfur's system of sultanic estates (*hakuras*) flourished, and the sultanate became Egypt's main supplier of trans-Saharan goods, including ivory, ostrich feathers, and slaves.

After a series of wars and intrigues involving internal factions, the rival Musabba'at dynasty in

Kordofan, and Wadai, sultan Muhammad Tayrab ibn Ahmad Bukr made peace with Wadai to the west and successfully invaded Kordofan. This war took the Fur armies far from home (reputedly to the Nile), and the sultan was forced to turn back in 1786. By the time the army reached Bara, the sultan was dying, and the succession struggle began. After many plot twists, this became a classic uncle-nephew confrontation between 'Abd al-Rahman and Ishaq ibn Muhammad Tayrab, his father's chosen successor. The forces gathered in Bara favored 'Abd al-Rahman precisely because he was not a powerful military leader but rather a childless man of about sixty, with few allies, a Beigo slave woman (Umm Busa) as his only concubine, and a reputation as a *faqih*, or holy man. A well-placed royal eunuch, Muhammad Kurra, ultimately ensured 'Abd al-Rahman's selection.

A three-year civil war (c. 1786–1789) ensued between 'Abd al-Rahman and his nephew, backed by one royal faction and strong support from the Zaghawa. The new sultan confirmed old sultanic land grants (*hakura*s), made new ones to reward his allies in the civil war, and gained support from regional governors and immigrant groups including *fuqara* (Muslim holy men), the Bagirmi general Ahmad Jurab al-Fil and his followers, and nomadic Arab groups. The net effect was to create a new multiethnic ruling coalition, with common interests as *hakura* holders, slaveholders, and courtiers with access to the sultan.

In Kordofan the Musabba'at leader Hashim had returned and ousted the Fur governor. In 1791–1792 a new invasion defeated Hashim, and Muhammad Kurra, one of the victorious generals, became governor of Kordofan. By 1799 the sultan grew wary of Muhammad Kurra's power and had him forcibly removed and brought to Al-Fashir. Muhammad Kurra cleared himself of suspicion and returned to his post.

During 'Abd al-Rahman's reign, Darfur's role in supplying Egypt with slaves greatly increased owing to the conquest of Kordofan. In 1796 the traveler William G. Browne accompanied a caravan that included five thousand slaves from Darfur to Egypt. When the French invaded Egypt in 1798, they reported that "Each year, two caravans come from Dar Fur, each made up of four to five thousand camels . . . the number of slaves brought to Egypt in an average year is five to six thousand, of whom three-quarters are young girls or women. The slaves are from six or seven to thirty or forty years old. They are sold in the various cities where the caravan stops but nearly exclusively in Cairo." After the sultan sent a congratulatory letter to Napoleon, the commander of French forces in Egypt, he replied on 30 June 1799: "I request that you send me two thousand strong and vigorous black male slaves over the age of sixteen by the next caravan: I will buy them all."

Later the French purchased some slaves from the Darfur caravan to replace soldiers lost to the plague. Because his designated successor Muhammad al-Fadl ibn Abd al Rahman was about fourteen years old, the sultan entrusted Muhammad Kurra with overseeing the transfer of power. Sultan 'Abd al-Rahman died in 1801.

BIBLIOGRAPHY

Browne, William G. *Travels in Africa, Egypt, and Syria, from the Year 1792 to 1798.* 2d ed. London: T. Cadell and W. Davies, 1806. Browne traveled to Darfur and met sultan 'Abd al-Rahman.

La Rue, George Michael. "The Export Trade of Dar Fur, ca. 1785–1875." In *Figuring African Trade*, edited by G. Liesegang, H. Pasch, and A. Jones. Kolner Beitrage zur Afrikanistik, vol. 11, pp. 636–668. Berlin: Dietrich Reimer, 1986. Provides many details on the sultanate's trans-Saharan trade.

Tunisi, Muhammad ibn Umar, al- (El-Tounsy, Le Chaykh Mohammed Ebn Omar). *Voyage au Darfour.* Translated by Dr. Perron. Paris: Benjamin Duprat, 1845. Al-Tunisi traveled to and lived in Darfur during the reign of 'Abd al-Rahman's successor; provides many details that are otherwise unavailable.

GEORGE MICHAEL LA RUE

'Abd al-Raziq, Ali (1888–1966), Egyptian jurist, government official, and author of one of the most important and controversial books of the twentieth century on Islam and politics, *Islam and the Foundations of Governance*. This short book, published in 1925, caused a storm of protest, and 'Abd al-Raziq was arraigned before a jury of Egyptian religious leaders (including the grandfather of the late-twentieth-century al-Qaeda leader Ayman al-Zawahiri) and officially stripped of his status as a religious scholar ('*alim*).

Abd al-Raziq was born in the Upper Egyptian province of Minya to a well-known and relatively well-off family. He studied at Al-Azhar University. Although he was too young to have known the prominent Egyptian 'alim Muhammad Abduh (d. 1905), his work appears to have been influenced by Abduh's break with prevailing orthodoxy.

Abduh was the highest jurisconsult (mufti) in Egypt at the time of his death. In 1915 'Abd al-Raziq became a judge in the Islamic (*shar'i*) court system, which still provided much of the administration of justice to the Muslim population of Egypt. Egypt still had a dual court system, with both Islamic courts and the so-called mixed courts, that provided judgments in cases in which foreign residents or foreign interests had a role. 'Abd al-Raziq was a founding member of the Eastern Bond society, which was formed in 1922, and editor of its journal in the later 1920s. Other members of his family played an important role in Egyptian politics, primarily in the Liberal Constitutionalist Party. The Liberal Constitutionalists are usually seen as political opponents of the more populist Wafd Party that emerged from the wave of revolutionary protest against British rule in the spring of 1919.

The massive revolt of 1919 led the British, who had occupied Egypt in 1882 and turned it into a protectorate in 1914, to think that they could no longer directly control the country. After several years of study and discussion, the British government decided to return nominal sovereignty to Egypt with a powerful royal authority and an elected but relatively weak national assembly.

In June 1925, not long after the Turkish Republic abolished the caliphate, 'Abd al-Raziq published *Al-Islam wa usul al-hukm* (Islam and the Foundations of Governance). The distinguished Egyptian historian Yunan Labib Rizq called it the most renowned book ever published in Egypt, although it is more read about than read. In it, 'Abd al-Raziq, still formally a *shar'i* court judge in El Mansura, argued that the caliphate was not a requirement of Islamic religion and that Muhammad was, in fact, primarily a spiritual, rather than a temporal, leader. 'Abd al-Raziq noted that neither the Qur'an nor accounts of Muhammad's statements or actions (the hadith literature) utilize the word "caliph" or describe a caliphal form of government. He therefore concluded that Muslims were free to adopt any form of government they wished and that Islam was compatible with any and all forms of government.

The book created an immediate sensation for two distinct but somewhat related reasons. First, in the immediate aftermath of the abolition of the Ottoman caliphate the book argued that Islam was a purely spiritual faith and not a religion with a legal structure that encompasses worldly life. This was at odds with the understanding of Islam widespread among the population and certainly among scholars in religious institutions at the time. Second, in the context of Egyptian politics at the time, it struck a blow at the pretensions of the monarchy domestically and internationally. Although the book recognized that Islam was compatible with monarchy, it made a strong case that the legitimacy of the state in Muslim societies arose from popular sovereignty and consent. 'Abd al-Raziq did not countenance that the religious authorities could clothe the state in legitimacy apart from wider social groups. King Fu'ad's power, however, depended primarily on his constitutional control of the bureaucracy and the armed forces and his relationship with the religious authorities. Fu'ad had no intention of ceding power, for example, to the popular nationalist party, the Wafd, which frequently commanded a majority in the parliament. The book also struck a blow at Fu'ad's brief flirtation with the idea of re-creating the caliphate in Cairo and thus at his hope to transform his kingdom into a center for international Islamic politics.

The trial and expulsion of 'Abd al-Raziq from official status as a member of the *ulama* entailed, under the existing law regulating the Azhar, that he be removed from the *shar'i* judiciary. The governing parliamentary cabinet was therefore forced to address the issue that roiled the political world for several months and led to the collapse of the governing coalition in which the Liberal Constitutionalists, the party to which 'Abd al-Raziq and many explicitly secularizing reformers were linked, had participated.

'Abd al-Raziq was the first author from within Islamic tradition and discourse to pose the possibility that there was no specifically Islamic form of governance or, as he put it, that there was no such thing as an Islamic state. Although time has vindicated 'Abd al-Raziq's argument about the many ways in which government can be organized and still be called Islamic, his book and its argument remain powerfully troubling to contemporary activists of Islamic politics. The Moroccan and Saudi monarchs both claim to have instituted Islamic states in the form of kingdoms. The Islamic Republic of Iran was formally established through a referendum on 1 April 1979 and has a very different structure of government from the Islamic Republic of Pakistan. In Iran the religious establishment has a formal role in the government, whereas in Pakistan it does not. Significant Muslim communities also now live in secular states where the majority of the population is not Muslim. These diverse realities would have seemed beyond the realm of possibility to 'Abd al-Raziq's critics.

'Abd al-Raziq's slim book was the first of several important assaults on accepted doctrines of the time. In 1926 Taha Hussein (Husayn) published his famous study of pre-Islamic verse, *Fi al-shi'r al-jahili* (On Pre-Islamic Poetry), which also became the subject of intense criticism. The same political forces that had attacked 'Abd al-Raziq arrayed themselves against Hussein, who was a professor of literature, and the still newly founded Egyptian University. Hussein retained his position at the Egyptian University and later (1950–1952) served as minister of education, as well as playing a prominent role as a leading liberal intellectual.

In his important study of Muhammad Husayn Haykal, a leader of the Liberal Constitutionalist Party, Charles D. Smith proposes that 'Abd al-Raziq had a real but diffuse influence on the thinking of other Egyptian liberals including Haykal, Husayn, his brother Mustafa 'Abd al-Raziq, and Mahmud Shaltut, who served as rector of Al-Azhar from 1958 until his death in 1963. Shaltut had, in the 1920s and 1930s, participated with Ali 'Abd al-Raziq in vigorous criticism of Azhari *ulama* including al-Zawahiri.

In 1947 'Abd al-Raziq published his second book on *ijma'* (consensus) and its role in Islamic law. *Ijma'* is generally taken to be one of the sources of Sunni law, but there is some question about how broad the agreement on consensus must be or can be. This book was largely uncontroversial, although it may have broken some new ground by citing contemporary scholars from the university along with classical Islamic sources.

'Abd al-Raziq himself was rehabilitated as a political figure when he served as minister of religious endowments in the 1948–1949 government of Ibrahim 'Abd al-Hadi, a position his brother Mustafa had already held in several previous governments beginning in 1938. 'Abd al-Raziq was also made a pasha, one of the highest ranking social designations bestowed by the government on citizens at the time. 'Abd al-Raziq ceased to be a prominent public figure after the 1952 Free Officers Movement toppled the monarchy.

Although still a controversial and consequently not widely quoted work, *Al-Islam wa usul al-hukm* proved to be both prescient and influential. It was an important contribution to Islamic modernism as conceived by figures such as Muhammad Abduh and Jamal al-Din al-Afghani. Some contemporary intellectuals, such as Muhammad Salim al-Awwa, the prominent Egyptian attorney, now argue that democracy is embedded in Islamic thought. Others, however, such as the Egyptian writer Khaled Muhammad Khalid (in 1950) and the Moroccan philosopher Muhammad Abid al-Jabiri (in the 1980s and 1990s), have followed the structure of his argument. Although neither has referred directly to 'Abd al-Raziq, both have asserted that the Qur'an and the hadith literature do not provide necessary guidance to contemporary Muslims about the structure of the state, thereby leaving them free to adapt what institutions they see best.

[*See also* 'Abduh, Muhammad; Afghani, Jamal al-Din Muhammad al-; Fu'ad I, Ahmad; *and* Hussein, Taha.]

BIBLIOGRAPHY

Gershoni, Israel, and James P. Jankowski. *Egypt, Islam and the Arabs: The Search for Egyptian Nationhood, 1900–1930.* New York: Oxford University Press, 1986.

Rizq, Yunan Labib. *Ta'rikh al-wizarat al-misriyyah.* Cairo: Al-Ahram Center for Political and Strategic Studies, 1975.

Smith, Charles D. *Islam and the Search for Social Order in Modern Egypt: A Biography of Muhammad Husayn Haykal.* Albany: State University of New York Press, 1983.

ELLIS GOLDBERG

'Abd al-Wahhab, Muhammad (c. 1910–1991), Egyptian composer, musician, and film star, was born in the early 1900s, either in Cairo or in the village of Abu Kibir, Sharqiya Province. There is confusion regarding both the date and the place of his birth. Two official identification cards in his possession listed his birth in 1910 but in the two different locations named above. 'Abd al-Wahhab's contemporaries have suggested that he was born sometime between 1896 and 1907; their suggestions are supported by reported incidents of his early musical life and encounters with important historical figures of the 1910s. His early years were spent in the Bab al-Sha'rani quarter of Cairo, where his father, Muhammad Abu 'Isa 'Abd al-Wahhab, was shaykh (religious scholar and caretaker) of the neighborhood mosque. 'Abd al-Wahhab was one of five children born to his father and Fatima Higazi, his mother. Early on, 'Abd al-Wahhab was enrolled by his father in a *kuttab*, a religious school, where he developed his vocal skills through *tajwid*, the art of recitation of the Qur'an. Although he was praised for his recitation, he demonstrated greater interest in singing popular songs of the day and, against his family's wishes, began singing in Cairo's clubs and theaters at a young age.

Around 1919 he began his performance career in earnest, joining the musical theater troupes of impresarios 'Abd al-Rahman Rushdi and then 'Ali al-Kassar. In 1921 he was heard by Sayyid Darwish, then a singer and composer for the musical theater, who offered him a brief role in the operetta *Sharazad*. Although the performance itself was not a success, 'Abd al-Wahhab found inspiration for his own musical innovation in Darwish's modernist compositional style. In 1922 he left the musical theater and enrolled in formal music education at the Oriental Music Club, an organization that in 1929 became the Arab Music Institute.

In 1925 'Abd al-Wahhab developed a relationship with poet Ahmad Shawqi, who exerted a formative influence on the young performer. Shawqi, known as the "prince of poets," was closely connected with Egypt's aristocracy and introduced 'Abd al-Wahhab to influential writers, artists, and political leaders. Shawqi supplemented 'Abd al-Wahhab's religious education with real-world experiences. He taught 'Abd al-Wahhab French and invited him to accompany him to France and Lebanon, where the young musician absorbed international music and culture. Until his death in 1932, Shawqi acted as a patron and a mentor, encouraging 'Abd al-Wahhab in his composition and providing elegant texts for several of his early songs, including "Ya Jarat al-Wadi" ("Oh Neighbor of the Valley," 1928) and "Ahun 'Alayk" ("Did I Become of Little Importance to You?," 1928). Even in these early works, 'Abd al-Wahhab departed from conventions of Arab music by minimizing spontaneous ornamentation and improvisation, both features of *tarab*, the traditional style that had been popular through the early twentieth century, and by adding instruments, such as the accordion, to his accompanying ensemble.

By the 1930s 'Abd al-Wahhab was already recognized as a leading singer and composer; he now entered into the burgeoning world of Egyptian musical film. 'Abd al-Wahhab starred in seven films between 1933 and 1946 and composed all the songs for these films, as well as songs for other artists in other films. The songs he wrote for film exhibit a keen awareness of the demands of this medium. They tended to be shorter and often more colloquial in their language, although he did set to music a handful of *qasa'id* (sing. *qasida*, a poetic form in classical Arabic) that were used in his films. Musically, the film songs demonstrate a progressive incorporation of European elements. 'Abd al-Wahhab expanded the *takht*, the traditional Arab music ensemble that includes one musician playing each of the characteristically Arab instruments ('*ud*, *qanun*, *nay*, violin, *riqq*), and added cello, bass, accordion, and numerous violins. He used other Western instruments more sparingly to achieve a particular sound or mood: piano, oboe, flute, piccolo, tympani, castanets, and sometimes an entire brass section. With a constant desire to effect musical progress, 'Abd al-Wahhab utilized techniques of orchestration and choral arrangements derived from European classical music and not infrequently borrowed and adapted musical quotations of well-known works from the Western orchestral tradition.

'Abd al-Wahhab's reputation grew, facilitating collaboration with the best poets, musicians, and producers of the day. Through his films, a number of female singers/actors were introduced to the Egyptian public, including Layla Murad, who went on to have an extremely successful career as a film star. After the death of Ahmad Shawqi, 'Abd al-Wahhab worked for a period of time with Ahmad Rami, a renowned poet who is generally more closely associated with 'Abd al-Wahhab's female rival, Umm Kulthum. While he was working on his fourth film, *Yum Sa'id* (Happy Day), he was introduced to poet Husayn al-Sayyid, with whom he collaborated extensively in subsequent years. Al-Sayyid allowed 'Abd al-Wahhab a larger collaborative role in the process of writing a song text. He also set to music poems by the Lebanese poet Bisharah al-Khuri, whom 'Abd al-Wahhab credits with introducing him to a new and "modern" style of poetic expression.

In the 1940s 'Abd al-Wahhab started to write songs that were longer and more complex, composed with radio performance in mind rather than film or 78-rpm recordings, which had necessitated shorter songs. These "grand songs," as they were termed by the composer, had texts in either classical or colloquial Arabic and invoked themes of grandeur, for example, of nature, such as "al-Nahr al-Khalid" ("The Eternal River," referring to the Nile), and of ancient Egypt, such as "Karnak" and "Cleopatra." These songs revived the *takht* as the primary instrumentation, and although multiple violins and some other orchestral instruments were featured, these "grand songs" of the 1940s did not include many of the European instruments featured in his film songs, such as the accordion and castanets. The oud, 'Abd al-Wahhab's primary instrument and a favorite instrument to accompany solo singers, was featured more prominently as 'Abd al-Wahhab chose to accompany himself in sections of these pieces. These songs also featured long instrumental introductions, partly intended by the composer to help develop an audience for instrumental music. The enjoyment of purely instrumental music was something 'Abd al-Wahhab admired in European classical music and felt was necessary for Arab music's progress.

Throughout the 1950s and 1960s, instrumental music continued to take a larger role in 'Abd al-Wahhab's composition, as well as further exploration of elements of European orchestration. He worked with several arrangers skilled in orchestration during this period. Although he had firmly established his reputation as Egypt's premiere musical innovator and modernist, he now faced increasing competition from younger composers, including Baligh Hamdi and Muhammad al-Mugi, and singers, such as his own protégé 'Abd al-Halim Hafiz. Following the revolution of 1952, encouraged by new national institutions governing Egyptian media, 'Abd al-Wahhab (like most of his contemporaries) composed a number of nationalistic songs.

By the 1960s 'Abd al-Wahhab had retired from singing in public, turning his attention entirely to composition. In 1964 'Abd al-Wahhab finally collaborated with his most prominent rival, the female singer Umm Kulthum. The collaboration was reportedly motivated by a request from Jamal 'Abd al-Nasir, who wished to see these two superstars of Egyptian music share the stage during his presidency. "Inta 'Umri" ("You Are My Life"), composed by 'Abd al-Wahhab and sung by Umm Kulthum, premiered 6 February 1964. In typical 'Abd al-Wahhab fashion, the song featured a lengthy instrumental introduction with solos played on qanun and electric guitar. The song lasted more than two hours, a long song even by the standards of the day, and was received as a great success by the audience in the theater as well as audiences throughout the Arab world who had tuned in to the live radio broadcast. The resulting recording became the best-selling Egyptian recording ever. These two artists, remembered as the leading lights of a golden age in Egyptian music, collaborated on nine other songs between 1964 and 1973, including "Laylat Hubb" ("Night of Love") and "Wi-Daarit il-Ayyam" ("The Days Have Passed").

'Abd al-Wahhab continued to compose in the 1970s and 1980s, although his later compositions have not achieved the same prominence as his earlier works. His last composition, "Min Ghayr Leh" ("Without Asking Why"), was released in 1989 and sold over 2 million copies. 'Abd al-Wahhab died on 3 May 1991, of heart failure.

He married twice, first to Zubaydah al-Hakim, whose wealth provided him with the resources to hire the best musicians, technicians, and producers for his films. He had five children with al-Hakim. Following a divorce, his second marriage was to a Jordanian, Nahla al-Qudsi.

Muhammad 'Abd al-Wahhab is popularly known as a modernist, an innovator, and perhaps the most significant male figure in twentieth-century Egyptian music. He left an extensive catalog of over 250 songs and some 50 instrumental pieces, many of which remain widely performed by top musicians (such as Shaheen, 1990). His legacy of musical innovation and integration of international elements continues to inspire composers and musicians throughout the Arab world and the Arab diaspora.

[*See also* Shawqi, Ahmed.]

BIBLIOGRAPHY

Armbrust, Walter. *Mass Culture and Modernism in Egypt.* Cambridge, UK: Cambridge University Press, 1996.

Azzam, Nabil. "Muhammad 'Abd al-Wahhab in Modern Egyptian Music." PhD diss., University of California, Los Angeles, 1990.

Danielson, Virginia, Scott Marcus, and Dwight Reynolds, eds. *The Garland Encyclopedia of World Music.* Vol. 6: *The Middle East.* New York: Routledge, 2002.

Sahhab, Fiktur. *Al-Sab'a al-kibar fi'l-musiqa 'l-'arabiyya al-mu'asira.* Beirut: Dar al-'Ilm li-'l-Malayin, 1987.

Shaheen, Simon. *The Music of Mohamed Abdel Wahab.* Axiom Records 422-846 754-2, 1990, compact disc.

ANNE ELISE THOMAS

'**Abdel-Kader** (1808–1883), Algerian emir and anti-colonialist leader, was born on 6 September 1808 near Mascara in the west of Algeria. His full name was 'Abd al-Qadir bin Muhieddine; he is known in the Arab east as 'Abdel-Kader al-Jaza'iri and in Algeria as al-Amir 'Abd El-Kader.

His father, Muhieddine al-Hassani, was a Sufi shaykh who followed the Qadiriyya religious order and claimed to be a Hasani (*sharif*) descendent of the Prophet with family ties with the Idrisi dynasty of Morocco. As a young boy, 'Abdel-Kader trained in horsemanship, and from this he developed his love for horses, about which he wrote some beautiful poetry. He was also trained in religious sciences; he memorized the Qur'an and read in theology

'**Abdel-Kader.** Lithograph by August Bry, nineteenth
century. (Private Collection/The Bridgeman Art Library)

and philology. He was also known as a poet who
recited classical poetry and wrote his own poetry,
mostly centering on war and chivalry.

In 1825 'Abdel-Kader set out with his father on a
long pilgrimage to Mecca. En route they stopped at
many centers of Islamic learning such as Zitouna in
Tunisia and visited shrines of venerated Sufis such
as those of Ibn 'Arabi and 'Abd al-Qadir al-Jilani,
the patron saint of Algiers who was buried in
Baghdad. There both father and son were given an
ijaza (license) to instruct by the imam of the Qadiri
Sufi order. On their return route to Algeria, 'Abdel-
Kader and his father visited Al-Azhar in Cairo and
studied there for a few months. 'Abdel-Kader was
deeply impressed by Muhammad 'Ali Pasha's
reforms in Egypt. The long pilgrimage ended in
1832, and the return of father and son was celebrated
with much glamour as 'Abdel-Kader was elected
emir al-Mu'minin (commander of the faithful) by
his fellow tribesmen. Many other surrounding
groups in the western region paid him allegiance
and rallied under his leadership. By this time
French troops had occupied parts of northern
Algeria and started to advance toward the interior.
As the elected leader, 'Abdel-Kader took it upon

himself to organize a resistance movement to fight
the French occupation troops and declared jihad
against them.

Between 1832 and 1842 'Abdel-Kader's troops
scored many victories as well as some defeats, leading the enemy, under the command of the fierce
Marshal Thomas Bugeaud, to sign the Treaty of
Tafna in 1837. Bugeaud was sent to Algeria in 1836
to consolidate the French armies and bring an end
to 'Abdel-Kader's successes with the use of the
harsh techniques he was known for, killing indis-
criminately and looting the various groups of their
livelihood by setting fire to their crops and killing
their animals. By able negotiation 'Abdel-Kader
convinced Bugeaud to sign the Treaty of Tafna in
1837, which delimited the territories of the two parties. This, in fact, further increased 'Abdel-Kader's
territory and political strength, making him master
of the whole interior of Oran and the Titteri, with
the French having to be content with a few ports.
This truce was used by 'Abdel-Kader to found a
modern state by allying and uniting the various
ethnic groups and cultivating a consciousness of an
independent Algeria. He consolidated his military
ranks and established a well-trained army of some
two thousand troops, to which he allied a good
number of trained volunteers. To do so, he established a juridical equality system between the tribes
and a regularized taxation system.

This truce, however, lasted for only two years as
French troops marched through Algerian-liberated
territory in 1839, which broke the Treaty of Tafna
and made 'Abdel-Kader renew his resistance and
call for jihad in October of the same year, attacking
French strongholds. In the following year the French
launched a wide action to occupy all Algerian territory and caused 'Abdel-Kader's army to shrink,
especially after the loss of Oran in 1841 and of
Tlemcen in 1842. This resulted in the shattering of
his army and livelihood. At this stage he fled to
Morocco, where he sought protection from its
sultan, Mawlay 'Abd ar-Rahman ibn Hisham
(r. 1822–1859), remaining there until 1846, when he
returned to settle in southern Algeria. However, the
French continued to attack him and his people,
leading him to leave for Morocco once more; but
this time he failed to obtain the sultan's protection,
leaving him with no other option but surrender to
the French in 1847 on the condition that he and his
family be allowed to settle in Syria. Instead, they
were imprisoned in France for five years, after which
they were released to settle in Bursa (Turkey) and
then moved to Damascus, where he died in 1883.

As a man, 'Abdel-Kader was known for his chivalry and his military and political leadership. He enjoyed a physically impressive figure and a very charismatic character. On the other hand, he is remembered as a devout Muslim and Sufi shaykh whose *baraka* (divine blessing) attracted many followers. On the diplomatic level, the emir was known as a world-famous advocate for religious tolerance and cultural openness. This is due not only to the way he treated his French prisoners, whom he fed better than his own and released when food supplies were scarce, but also to the heroic role he played while in exile in Syria, saving the lives of some twelve thousand Syrian Maronite Catholics during religious riots in 1860. He acted as a peacemaker between Muslims, Druze, and Christians and often repeated that Christians and Muslims were not destined to fight the Crusades over and over again. For this role he won the praise of many world leaders, including President Abraham Lincoln, Queen Victoria, and many French priests and bishops. In the climate of today's religious intolerance, Prince Hassan bin Talal of Jordan praised the emir for his true sense of jihad as an inner struggle to remain true to one's religion.

He died on 26 May 1883 in Damascus, where he was buried in the same mausoleum as Ibn 'Arabi. His remains were moved to Algeria on 5 July 1966 on the fourth anniversary of independence.

[*See also* Muhammad 'Ali.]

BIBLIOGRAPHY

"'Abdel-Kader." In *Encyclopaedia Britannica*. 11th ed. Cambridge, UK: Cambridge University Press, 1911.

Abun-Nasr, Jamil. *A History of the Maghrib in the Islamic Period*. Cambridge, UK: Cambridge University Press, 1987.

Kiser, John W. *Commander of the Faithful: The Life and Times of Emir Abd el-Kader: A Story of True Jihad*. Rhinebeck, N.Y.: Monkfish, 2008.

Werner, Louis. "Prince of Brotherhood." *Saudi Aramco World*, July–August 2010: 2–9.

ZAHIA SMAIL SALHI

Abderrahman El Majdoub (1506–1568), Moroccan troubadour poet and Sufi figure, was born in 1506 in the village of Tit near the city of Azemmour. He is also known as al-Shaykh Abu Zayd Abderrahman al-Majdoub Ibn Ayyad Ibn Yaacub Ibn Salama Ibn Khashan al-Sanhaji al-Dukkali and as al-Majdoub; his contemporaries nicknamed him El Majdoub. He moved with his father to Meknès in 1508. His father was a renowned Sufi trained by al-Shaykh Ibrahim Afham al-Zarhuni, a disciple of al-Shaykh Ahmad Zarruq. Zarruq was a North African Sufi who lived through the fifteenth-century Marinid religious turmoil. He called for new interpretations of Islam based on juridical sainthood that stressed religious form. Accordingly, Zarruq asked Sufi authorities of Fez to avoid opportunistic notions of jihad that scapegoat some Muslims in order to increase the accusers' political status. Abderrahman El Majdoub was influenced indirectly by some of Zarruq's ideas regarding the nature and role of Sufi authorities in the context of political turmoil and economic decline.

During Zarruq's period, a Sufi community called the "mad holy people of Fez" had a large influence on society and attracted a large number of common people in the context of the political decline of the Marinid dynasty. These Sufis were known as *majdoubs*. As holy madmen, it was believed that the capacity of reasoning of the *majdoubs* is disjointed by their attraction to God. In this state of madness, their routine personality was disrupted, although they were thought to have the capacity to perform miracles in public. *Majdoubs* were not crazy; they were simply in a state of possession that allowed them to point to the truth. Zarruq was critical of these holy madmen, yet, as a shaykh, he managed to attract some of them as his religious disciples. Al-Shaykh Ibrahim Afham al-Zarhuni, a former *majdoub*, was one of his famous disciples. As the Iberians began to invade the Moroccan coasts and the Wattasids failed to curb their military conquest, the *majdoubs* of Fez and Meknès aligned themselves with the emerging Sa'dian dynasty and the Jazzuliya brotherhood. Ali Sanhaji, Abu Rawayin, and Sayyida Amina were some of the *majdoubs* who led this revolt against the Wattasids, opening the doors for the Sa'dian control of Fez in 1549. It is in this period that Abderrahman El Majdoub would emerge as a famous Sufi intellectual in Meknès. El Majdoub had a strong religious relationship with Amina, who saw him as her spiritual brother. El Majdoub established a new Sufi community that combined Sufi ideas from Zarruq and the holy madmen. However, his movement was more influenced by Jazzuli notions of Sufi authority than Zarruq's legal reformism. That is, El Majdoub applied the juridical interpretation stressed by Zarruq but rejected his disdain of Sufi sainthood. This social movement would be known as the Tariqa Zarruqiyya al-Majdoubiyya. As a Sufi El Majdoub never lived the life of the holy madmen; instead, he married and had children.

Abderrahman El Majdoub was educated in Meknès before he moved to Fez. There is little information about his intellectual life in Fez. However, while in Fez he attended religious circles organized by Ali Sanhaji, himself a disciple of Zarruq. In Meknès Abu Rawayin, al-Shaykh Ahmad al-Shabih, al-Shaykh Said Ibn Abi Bakr al-Mishnaza'i, al-Shaykh Abd al-Haq al-Zaliji, and al-Shaykh Sayyidi Umar al-Khatab al-Zarhun Abderrahman were some of his teachers. By looking at the intellectual genealogy of his teachers, it is clear that El Majdoub was influenced largely by Zarruq's social and intellectual movement through Ali Sanhaji and the Jazzuli brotherhood through Umar al-Khatab al-Zarhuni. In this context and given the religious connections between the al-Zarruqiya and al-Jazzuliyya movements, El Majdoub was a Shadhili.

El Majdoub's poetry was about political, moral, and social issues. His *Diwan Sidi Abderrahman El Majdoub* (Collected Poems) provides his mystical views on love, death, emotions, women, science, education, religion, age, etc. El Majdoub is known throughout North Africa and Morocco in particular for his poetry, which was so popular that it became part of the daily proverbs of Moroccan society. He was not only a mystic but a social reformer who lived the life of a troubadour whose main concern was to raise social awareness about the issues that faced his society.

Muhammad 'Abduh. (Private Collection/The Bridgeman Art Library)

BIBLIOGRAPHY

De Premare, A. L. *Sidi 'Abd Er-Rahman El Mejdoub: Mysticisme populaire, société et pouvoir au Maroc au 16è siècle.* Paris: Éditions du CNRS, 1985.

Kugle, Scott. *Rebel between Spirit and Law: Ahmad Zarruq, Sainthood, and Authority in Islam.* Bloomington: Indiana University Press, 2006.

AOMAR BOUM

'Abduh, Muhammad (1849–1905), Egyptian Muslim theologian, modernist, and reformer, was born in the Gharbiya Province of Lower Egypt, the son of 'Abduh ibn Hasan Khayr Allah, a peasant farmer, and his wife, who was descended from the Bani 'Adl clan. He grew up in the village of Mahallat Nasr and received a traditional education, learning the Qur'an by heart. In 1862 he was sent to the madrasa (Islamic college) in Tanta. There, he perfected his Qur'an recitation and started to learn Arabic grammar, by the then normal method of memorizing texts and commentaries without explanation from his teachers.

Reacting against this, according to his own account, he ran away from the college and returned to his village, intending to become a peasant rather than a scholar. In this condition he married in 1865, at the age of sixteen. But after various vicissitudes he resorted to his great-uncle, Shaykh Darwish Khadr, who carefully taught and explained to him both qur'anic and Sufi (mystical) texts and inculcated in him the importance of high ethical and intellectual standards.

In 1866, thus reinvigorated, he entered the famous traditional mosque-university of Al-Azhar in Cairo. There he embraced especially the study and practice of mysticism and asceticism, withdrawing as much as possible from human contact. In the early 1870s he came under the influence of Sayyid Jamal al-Din al-Afghani (1839–1897), an influential Iranian scholar and revolutionary, at that time resident in Cairo, who not only drew 'Abduh out of his ascetic reclusiveness but also widened his theological and philosophical education along rational and even modernistic lines. At the same time he interested him in politics, which mainly took the form of a pan-Islamic concern to unite the Muslim *umma* (worldwide community) in the face of European imperialism.

This enthusiasm led 'Abduh to take up journalism, writing patriotic, educational, and reformist articles for the newspaper *Al-Ahram*. He graduated from Al-Azhar in 1877, despite having aroused the antagonism of the authorities there by his rationalist attitudes, which he imparted also to his fellow students. He then took up teaching, not only in Al-Azhar but also in two secular colleges recently established by the government of Khedive Isma'il. After the latter was deposed in 1879, 'Abduh was dismissed from these posts and exiled to his native village, only to be appointed in the following year as editor of the official newspaper *Al-Waqa'i' al-Misriya*. In this role he continued to advocate for educational and social reform and to oppose the increasing European interference in Egypt, throwing his weight behind the nationalist movement led by Ahmad 'Urabi (1840–1911). He maintained this support, despite his reservations about the involvement of the military, until the British invasion and suppression of the movement in September 1882. He was then tried and sent into exile.

After a year in Beirut, he joined al-Afghani in Paris and published with him in 1884 the short-lived but influential periodical *Al-'Urwa al-Wuthqa* (The Firmest Bond), advocating pan-Islamic resistance to European imperialism. During this period he traveled as an agitator to Tunisia, recently occupied by France, and sought to make contact with the Mahdi (Muhammad Ahmad ibn 'Abdallah) in Sudan, in the hope of securing his help in the liberation of Egypt. Eventually, though, he returned to Beirut and resumed teaching and writing on reform.

In 1888 he was pardoned by the khedive and returned to Egypt. Having abandoned his former militancy but still a proponent of religious and civil reform, he occupied a series of influential and responsible posts: as *qadi* (judge), permanent member of the Legislative Council, founder-member of the Muslim Benevolent Society, and, most importantly, grand mufti (supreme legal interpreter) of Egypt from 1899 until his death in Alexandria (from kidney cancer) in 1905.

As well as his influential journalistic writings and articles and his commentaries on qur'anic verses and classical Islamic authors, 'Abduh wrote and published at least two full-length theological treatises: *Risalat al-waridat* (Treatise on Mystical Inspirations, Cairo, 1874) and *Risalat al-Tawhid* (Treatise on the Unity of God, Cairo, 1897, and

many later editions and translations). Some of his articles were also collected into thematic volumes, notably those defending Islam against Western critics. Other works remained in manuscript form and have only recently been discovered.

But his influence derived at least as much from the impression that he made on those who heard him speak, either in addresses and lectures or in conversation, and then transmitted his ideas and teachings. In fact, a significant body of such disciples developed his ideas and methods in the first half of the twentieth century, notably the Syrian (resident in Egypt) Muhammad Rashid Rida (1865–1935), whose newspaper, *Al-Manar*, did much to propagate 'Abduh's reformist principles; Qasim Amin (1863–1908), advocate of women's emancipation; Sa'd Zaghlul (1859–1927), nationalist politician and leader of the 1919 Egyptian revolution; and 'Ali 'Abd al-Raziq (1888–1966), a jurist who advocated separation of religion and state.

'Abduh's thought was broad enough to give rise to quite different, and ultimately conflicting, tendencies. On the one hand, he was a staunch defender of his homeland and of the Muslim world in general, against both political and spiritual encroachment by Christian Europe; and he sought to free Islam from the debilitating accretion of corrupt and obscurantist practices, which rendered it vulnerable. This tendency was developed, particularly by Rashid Rida, into a movement known as the Salafiya, which aimed to revitalize Islam by reclaiming the purity of its original doctrines and sources of authority and strict adherence to them. Some see in this the origins of modern Islamic "fundamentalism." On the other hand, 'Abduh was also a rationalist who welcomed modern philosophy and science, even from Europe, and sought to build a reformed and modern Muslim society compatible with them. This tendency has inspired many who have subsequently attempted, not always successfully, to modernize the political and intellectual life of Egypt and other Muslim countries in a changing world. The conflict between these two tendencies has remained unresolved.

[*See also* Amin, Qasim Muhammad; Isma'il; Muhammad Ahmad ibn 'Abdallah; Rashid Rida, Muhammad; 'Urabi, Ahmad Muhammad; *and* Zaghlul, Sa'd.]

BIBLIOGRAPHY

Adams, Charles C. *Islam and Modernism in Egypt: A Study of the Modern Reform Movement Inaugurated by Muhammad 'Abduh.* London: Oxford University Press, 1933. Reprint, London: Routledge, 2000.

Haj, Samira. *Reconfiguring Islamic Tradition: Reform, Rationality, and Modernity.* Stanford, Calif.: Stanford University Press, 2009. Includes a "close reading" of the works of 'Abduh.

Kedourie, Elie. *Afghani and 'Abduh: An Essay on Religious Unbelief and Political Activism in Modern Islam.* London: Frank Cass, 1966. Reprint, London: Routledge, 2008. Argues, not entirely convincingly, that 'Abduh held esoteric beliefs incompatible with orthodox Islam.

Kerr, Malcolm H. *Islamic Reform: The Political and Legal Theories of Muhammad 'Abduh and Rashid Rida.* Berkeley: University of California Press, 1966.

GEOFFREY ROPER

Abdul-Hayy, Muhammad (1944–1989), Sudanese poet, critic, and academician, was born in Ad Damer on 1 January 1944, after which he moved across Sudan with his family. His father was Abdul-Hayy Mahmoud, an architect who studied country planning in Britain. His mother, Aziza Ismaeel Fawzy, was a daughter of an architect as well. Abdul-Hayy married Dr. Aisha Moussa and had four children. He graduated from Khartoum University and obtained his PhD in comparative literature from Oxford University. He published many important volumes of poetry and produced many books and critical essays in both Arabic and English. In the 1970s he held some cultural and academic posts. For his last nine years, a series of ailments caused his health to decline and his linguistic memory to die until he was completely paralyzed. After a long struggle with illness, he died on 23 August 1989 in Sopa University Hospital.

Abdul-Hayy was among those who called for a national literature that highlighted the cultural, geographical, and historical specificity of Sudan. Some scholars have dealt with his literature as belonging to the school of "forest and desert." This school of poetry highlights the combination of the Arab cultural component (symbolized by the desert) and the African cultural component (symbolized by the jungle).

Abdul-Hayy's awareness of Sudan's cultural specificity was a motive for him to write about the kingdom of Sennar. This kingdom was founded in 1504 after some Arab and African tribes were united. It ruled large parts of Sudan until its fall in 1821. This kingdom was always presented in his poetry as a symbol of the perfect coexistence between races and cultures incarnated in the Arab and African cultures. His poem "The Return to Sennar" received huge acclaim when it was first published in 1963 and provided him with widespread popularity around the Arab world even though he was still an adolescent. Despite the fact that Abdul-Hayy himself denied that his poetry belonged to the "forest and desert" school, the issue of Sudanese identity dominated his poetry. His poetic works include *Moa'alakat al isharat* (The Signals, 1977); *Al-samandal yughanni* (The Newt Sings, 1977); *Hadiqat al-ward al-akhirah* (The Last Rose Garden, 1984); and *Allah fizaman al'unf* (God in the Time of Violence, 1993). His *The Return to Sennar* (1973) received the most popularity and attained great interest from critics.

Abdul-Hayy not only produced volumes of poetry but also wrote a play, *Ru't al-malik* (The King's Vision, 1973), and translated selections of African poetry into English and published them under the title *Tribal Masks.* His writings on comparative literature in general and on the relationship between Arabic literature and Western literature in particular were of extreme significance in the field of Arabic studies.

Abdul-Hayy was not only a distinguished poet but also a distinguished scholar. As soon as he completed his studies in the Department of English, University of Khartoum, in 1967, he traveled on a scholarship to England in 1968. Two years later, he obtained his MA degree from Leeds University. His thesis revolved around the works of the British poet Edwin Muir (1887–1959); it was published by the University of Khartoum under the title *The Angel and the Girl: Necessity and Liberty in Edwin Muir's Works.* In 1973 he obtained his PhD from Oxford University in comparative literature; his dissertation was published in London in 1982 under the title *Tradition and English and American Influence in Arabic Romantic Poetry: A Study in Comparative Literature.*

Having obtained his PhD, Abdul-Hayy returned to Sudan and taught English and comparative literature in the Department of English, University of Khartoum, serving as head of the department from 1978 to 1980. Before that, he established the journal of the faculty of arts and was its editor in chief. Throughout his academic life, Abdul-Hayy wrote a number of scholarly works in Arabic and English, including *Conflict and Identity: The Cultural Poetics of Contemporary Sudanese Poetry* (Khartoum, 1967), *The Greek Myth in Contemporary Arabic Poetry (1900–1950): A Study in Comparative Literature* (in Arabic) (Cairo, 1977), *English Poets in Arabic: The Arab Romantics' Knowledge of English*

Poetry (1900–1950): A Study in Comparative Literature with a bibliography of Arabic translations of English and American poetry, 1830–1970 (Khartoum, 1980), and *Vision and Words: A Reading in al-Tijani Yousuf Basheer's Poetry* (Khartoum, 1985).

Abdul-Hayy did not indulge in political activity. When he attempted to join the National al-Ummah Party, he was rejected; subsequently, he joined the National Unionist Party instead. He was a member of the Sudanese Socialist Union for a short time when he accepted the post of director of the Department of Culture in the Ministry of Culture and Information from 1976 to 1977. During this short period he established the Child Culture Centre and tried to strengthen cultural ties with the Arab world by inviting Arab writers to Sudanese cultural festivals.

Since his death Abdul-Hayy's presence on both the academic and the literary levels in Sudan has not waned. His academic works are being translated into Arabic and what has been released is getting republished, and his poetry is receiving increasing levels of critical attention.

BIBLIOGRAPHY

Abdul-Hayy, Mohammed. *al-Amal al-shi'riyah al-kamilah*. Cairo: Markaz al-Dirasat al-Sudaniyah, 1999.

Jayyusi, Salma Khadra, al-. *Trends and Movements in Modern Arabic Poetry*. Leiden, Netherlands: Brill, 1977.

EMAD ABDUL-LATIF

Abdulla, Muhammed Said (1918–1991), Swahili novelist, was born in Makunduchi village in Zanzibar (now part of Tanzania) in 1918. Even though he was a Muslim, he was educated in a missionary school. After completing his secondary education in 1938, he worked for the Civil Health Department and edited the *Swahili Bulletin* in the Department of Agriculture on his island. His complete biography remains obscure. He lost all his family in January 1964 during the bloody revolution that overthrew the sultan of Zanzibar and his mainly Arab government but took a heavy toll of victims among the population as well.

Abdulla's first novelette, *Mzimu wa watu wa kale* (Graveyard of the Ancestors, 1960), aroused lively interest among the critics for its innovations: the abandonment of the folktale tradition, omnipresent in Swahili fiction of those days, and the concern for literary style. It won first prize in the East

African Literary Competition of 1957–1958, and this fact was a great encouragement for Abdulla's literary career.

The novelette is the first of a series of detective stories linked through the character of Bwana Msa ("Msa" being an acronym of the author's name), an amateur detective, and his friend Najum, who have been labeled by the critics the African Sherlock Holmes and his Watson. The grim mystery of a corpse found in a graveyard with his head chopped off is resolved with incredible ease by Bwana Msa, and such is also the case in his subsequent stories. In *Kisima cha Giningi* (The Giningi Well, 1969) the richest woman of a village is murdered by her greedy uncle. *Duniani kuna watu* (There Are People in the World, 1973) is a story of unintentional incest between a tender heiress and her father's driver; only after their secret wedding do they discover that they are sister and brother. In *Siri ya sifuri* (The Secret of Zero, 1974) the fiancé of another rich heiress is killed by his rival. *Mwana wa Yungi hulewa* (Even the Devil's Child Is Brought Up, 1976) is the story of two illegitimate children of an Arab princess and a rich Goan, entrusted to a wicked servant who steals the children's money and, on top of that, engages a killer to murder them. Finally, in the last novel, *Kosa la Bwana Msa* (Bwana Msa's Fault, 1984), the famous detective commits a mistake when investigating a case of bigamy. The protagonist marries a rich woman and, secretly, another one, younger and prettier. The first wife discovers the deceit and sends two killers after the husband, but it is she who eventually dies. Rather than a thriller, it is a sentimental story with some suspense.

A great shortcoming of Abdulla's novelettes is their unconvincing, overcomplicated plots. All the stories are situated in prerevolutionary Zanzibar among extremely rich people, for the most part wealthy Arab landowners. Their present is intertwined with the past; in fact, crime or any other mystery on which the plot is built derives from the complex relationship that brings together the various characters in the story. Vengeance and greed are the most powerful motives for the criminal actions.

For some critics Bwana Msa is a black European with a job or hobby that does not exist in Africa. Other characters, however, especially village people, are without doubt truly Zanzibarian and so is the setting of all the stories. Abdulla's philosophical attitude appears distinctly in his later works. While solving an entangled problem, Bwana Msa finds the opportunity to discuss all kinds of topics—linguistic, social, historical, and others—but these excursions are never boring.

Abdulla's ability to write on even banal themes in an interesting and witty manner makes him particularly successful in feuilleton and essay. He also produced a novelette, *Mke mmoja waume watatu* (One Wife, Three Husbands, 1975), which is different from the others as it has no mystery or standard characters. In this story the author states that every woman needs three men to be satisfied, illustrating his absurd thesis on the problematic marriage of his hero. Finally, there is the brilliant short story, "Mke wangu ("My Wife"), published in the volume *Kinywa jumba la maneno* (The Mouth Is the Palace of the Words, 1977) by various authors. In it a rich and spoiled young man from the town wants to marry a simple village girl in order to form her character as he likes, only to discover that the girl, who is sharp-witted and has a strong personality, is not at all disconcerted by urban "civilization" and does not consent to being manipulated.

Much has been written on Muhammed Said Abdulla, especially about his first novelette, *Mzimu wa watu wa kale*. Most critics have discussed the character of Bwana Msa, his resemblance to European detectives like Auguste Dupin and Sherlock Holmes, and the credibility of his sharp deductions. Only a few of them have pointed out Abdulla's realism and stylistic ability. His main innovations are abandonment of the folktale tradition and the use of a Western literary style. His first novelette, *Mzimu wa watu wa kale*, already contains the best of his style: a faithful description of the milieu, an accurate reproduction of the speech and gestures of the characters, a subtle sense of humor, colorful but polished language.

Thus, Abdulla is the first Swahili novelist who succeeded in blending local traditions with Western literary form and creating the modern Swahili novel.

BIBLIOGRAPHY

Bertoncini Zúbková, Elena. "Two Contemporary Swahili Writers: Muhammad Said Abdulla and Euphrase Kezilahabi." In *The East African Experience: Essays on English and Swahili Literature*, edited by Ulla Schild, pp. 85–90. Berlin: Dietrich Reimer, 1980.

Bertoncini Zúbková, Elena, Mikhail D. Gromov, Said A. M. Khamis, and Kyallo Wadi Wamitila. *Outline of Swahili Literature: Prose Fiction and Drama.*

2d ed., extensively revised and enlarged. Leiden, Netherlands: Brill, 2009.

Garnier, Xavier. *Le roman swahili.* Paris: Karthala, 2006. In the chapter dedicated to investigations and enigmas, Abdulla's novels are analyzed in depth.

Lindfors, Berth. "The Element of Mystery in the Novels of Mohamed Saidi Abdalla." *Kiswahili* 50, no. 2 (1983): 48–57.

Lindfors, Berth. "Sherlock Holmes in Africa. Part I: Kenya. Part II: Zanzibar." *Baker Street Journal* 15, no. 2 (1965): 67–74.

ELENA BERTONCINI ZÚBKOVÁ

Abdurahman, Abdullah (1872–1940), South African medical doctor and politician, the most significant political leader of the South African Coloured community during the first half of the twentieth century, was born in Wellington near Cape Town on 12 December 1872. He was the eldest son of nine children born to Abdul Rachman, a greengrocer, and his wife Kadija Dollie. Descended from grandparents who were manumitted slaves, his graduation as a medical doctor from the University of Glasgow in 1893 was a signal achievement. After two years of postgraduate study in London, he returned to Cape Town in 1895.

Abdurahman entered public life in 1904 when he became the first black person to be elected to the Cape Town City Council. Except for 1913–1915 he represented Wards 6 and 7 (District 6) for the rest of his life. Abdurahman exerted substantial influence on local government because of the exceptional support he enjoyed among Coloured voters and through his energetic chairing of several council committees. As chair between 1923 and 1937 of the most important of these, the Streets and Drainage Committee, he wielded considerable clout. In 1914 Abdurahman became the first Coloured person to be elected to the Cape Provincial Council. He held the Castle Division seat until he died.

It was, however, as president of the African Political Organization (APO), the first substantive Coloured political body, founded in 1902, that Abdurahman made his most important political contribution. Elected to the post in 1905, he dominated its leadership for the thirty-five years he served as president. Under his direction, the APO grew from an insignificant, faction-ridden body into an organization of several thousand members with a national network of branches by 1910, making it the country's largest black political organization of the day. From 1909 it also published the bilingual *APO* newspaper, in its words, "to champion our just cause for political equality with whites." Abdurahman contributed extensively to the paper. For the next three decades the APO remained the most important Coloured communal organization, dominating black protest politics. Through the APO Abdurahman waged a futile struggle to stem the erosion of Coloured civil rights and coordinated wide-ranging efforts for the socioeconomic uplift-ment of the Coloured people, especially in the fields of education and public health.

It was particularly in education that Abdurahman left an enduring legacy. He was instrumental in the establishment in 1911 of the Trafalgar High School, the first to offer secondary education to Coloured students. He also played a catalytic role in the founding of the Teachers' League of South Africa in 1913. It was, in addition, largely through his initia-tive that several other educational institutions, such as the Rahmaniyeh Institute in 1913, the Schotsche Kloof Primary School in 1931, and Livingstone High School in 1934, among several others, were created.

Although he of necessity focused on the advance-ment of Coloured interests, Abdurahman recog-nized the need to foster interracial cooperation. His most notable contributions in this regard were to participate in the 1909 South African Native and Coloured People's Delegation to Britain, to protest the racially discriminatory clauses in the draft South Africa Act, and to jointly convene four Non-European Conferences with D. D. T. Jabavu between 1927 and 1934, to mobilize opposition to prime minister J. B. M. Hertzog's segregationist policies. Such was Abdurahman's reputation that, although he was not Indian, the South African Indian Congress in 1925 asked him to lead their delegation to request that the Indian government intervene in anti-Asian legislation about to be tabled by the Union government. Abdurahman was the only black member of the Wilcox Commission appointed in 1934 to enquire into the socioeconomic condi-tion of the Coloured people. He and a minority of liberal commissioners consistently opposed the segregationist ethos of its recommendations, espe-cially protoapartheid ones of the sort that sexual intercourse between Coloureds and whites be out-lawed, that residential segregation of Coloured people be implemented, and that a separate univer-sity for Coloureds be established.

The mercurial Abdurahman was a gifted orator and a charismatic leader. In the earlier part of his career it was in particular his fiery rhetoric that animated supporters. Much of his attraction as a leader lay in the confidence with which he negoti-ated the intimidating environment of the domi-nant society and the fearlessness and flair with which he attacked the injustices inflicted upon Coloured people. Adurahman's sway within his constituency, which consisted largely of the Coloured petite bourgeoisie and the "respectable" stratum within the black working classes, lay not only in the eloquence with which he articulated their political desires and the vigor with which he strove to achieve them but also in the degree to which his personal bearing and achievements embodied their highest social aspirations. Part of Abdurahman's charisma lay in his unaffected, amicable manner and the ease with which he related to all sectors of his community, especially those less privileged. His indefatigable campaign-ing to improve their socioeconomic conditions and personal acts of generosity such as paying the school fees of destitute but deserving students, not charging indigent patients, and taking time out of a busy schedule to secure a youngster an appren-ticeship won him a reputation as a champion of the poor.

The political legacy of Abdurahman has been a matter of controversy. Liberals have tended to regard him as the most accomplished leader to have represented Coloured interests, while those within the radical movement have generally despised him as collaborationist. There can, however, be no denying that for three and a half decades before his death in Cape Town on 20 February 1940 Abdurahman was by far the most influential and popular political leader within the Coloured community. His political acumen also won him widespread respect within the white political estab-lishment as well as grudging acknowledgment from many diehard opponents.

Because he represented a marginal social group during an era of tightening segregation, Abdurahman's achievement lies less in tangible political gains than in the degree to which he was able to unite his constituency in a stand against racism and autocracy over nearly four decades. In 1999 president Nelson Mandela honored Abdurahman by posthumously awarding him the Order for Meritorious Service, class I (gold).

[*See also* Hertzog, James Barry Munnik; Jabavu, Davidson Don Tengo; *and* Mandela, Nelson Rolihlahla.]

BIBLIOGRAPHY

Adhikari, Mohamed. *Not White Enough, Not Black Enough: Racial Identity in South Africa's Coloured Community.* Athens: Ohio University Press, 2005.

Lewis, Gavin. *Between the Wire and the Wall: A History of South African "Coloured" Politics.* Cape Town: David Philip, 1987.

Shifrin, Thelma. "Abdullah Abdurahman." In *Dictionary of South African Biography*, vol. 1. Cape Town: Tafelberg, 1968.

van der Ross, Richard. *"Say It Out Loud": The APO Presidential Addresses and Other Major Political Speeches, 1906–1940, of Dr. Abdullah Abdurahman.* Bellville, South Africa: University of the Western Cape Institute for Historical Research, 1990.

MOHAMED ADHIKARI

Abebe Bikila (1932–1973), Ethiopian athlete, was born on 7 August 1932 in Jato, a village located some eighty miles from Addis Ababa, outside the town of Mendida in Shewa Province. His father died before he was born, and young Abebe was adopted by Bikila Demisse, a shepherd. Having completed his studies at age twelve at the local traditional school, he followed in his adopted father's footsteps. At the age of twenty, he decided to venture out of peasantry and made his way on foot to the capital, to join the Imperial Bodyguard. In 1954 he married Yewibdar Welde-Giyorgis, with whom he fathered four children. He distinguished himself as a talented player of *gena*, a traditional Ethiopian hockey game, but remained an anonymous soldier until the age of twenty-four. At that time, while guarding the departure of the Ethiopian delegation to the 1956 Olympic Games in Melbourne, he decided to begin competing as a runner. His exceptional abilities caught the eye of the Swedish coach of the Ethiopian team, Major Onni Niskanen, and Abebe Bikila, now an army captain, won Ethiopia's national championship in the marathon and made it to the next Olympic Games in Rome. It was there, on a September evening in 1960, that he began to make history.

The marathon race began and ended near the Colosseum and the Arch of Constantine, and Italian youngsters dressed as Roman soldiers stood along the road, adding to the atmosphere. The unknown Abebe Bikila defeated all favorites and won in a record time of 2:15:16.2, finishing 26 seconds ahead of his main rival. Not only was he the first black African to win an Olympic gold medal, but he captured all eyes, running in a majestic style and barefoot. Just prior to the race he took off his shoes because they were new and uncomfortable, and his appearance in Rome was engraved in the memory of all who witnessed the race: the barefoot son of a shepherd winning for Ethiopia. At the time this victory in Rome was conceived by many as a noble Ethiopian response to Mussolini's brutalizing of Ethiopia in 1936–1941. Abebe Bikila himself emphasized this when he answered the question of why he ran barefoot: "I wanted the world to know that my country, Ethiopia, has always won with determination and heroism." However, from a later perspective, it seems that Abebe Bikila's victory in Rome instead contributed to the ensuing process of Ethiopian-Italian reconciliation. The Abebe Bikila Bridge, built in 2010 in the town of Ladispoli, near Rome, attests to this legacy.

Between 1961 and 1963 Abebe Bikila, now a celebrity, won all the marathon races he entered except for the Boston Marathon of 1963. Forty days before the 1964 Olympic Games in Tokyo, during a training run near Addis Ababa, he collapsed, was diagnosed with acute appendicitis, and was operated upon. He was not expected to compete. However, he did enter the marathon and won against all odds, setting a new world record of 2:12:11.2 and becoming the first athlete ever to win two Olympic marathons. At the 1968 Mexico City Olympic Games, Abebe Bikila, who had injured his knee, had to withdraw after 17 kilometers, enabling his compatriot Mamo Wolde to win the gold medal.

In 1969 Abebe Bikila was seriously injured when he lost control of his Volkswagen Beetle, a present from Emperor Haile Selassie, and landed in a ditch. He underwent surgery in England but remained a paraplegic. In 1970 he competed in archery at the International Paraplegic Games; and he bowed out of the international scene at the 1972 Munich Olympic Games as a guest of honor, admired by all. On 23 October 1973 Abebe Bikila died in Addis Ababa at the age of forty-one from a complication related to the accident of four years earlier.

In the history of international athletics, Abebe Bikila remains one of the greatest long-distance runners. The International Athletic Committee listed him among the top ten athletes of the millennium. In the wider context of African history, he contributed to the continent's regained respectability in sport and beyond. His performances in international arenas inspired new generations of African athletes, who grew to dominate middle- and long-distance running and break all world records. Abebe Bikila ushered in the appearance of dozens of young Ethiopian athletes, men and women, who would follow him in advancing the image of Ethiopia as being identified with abilities and achievement. Ethiopia entered the twentieth century as a victorious nation, the only one in Africa capable of maintaining independence in the face of European imperialism. This sense of pride was greatly eroded by the Italian conquest of the 1930s and was restored in part also by the great victories of Abebe Bikila and his Ethiopian successors, men and women, notably Miruts Yifter, Haile Gebrselassie, Kananisa Bekele, Mesaret Difar, Tirunash Dibaba, and many others. Abebe Bikila died during the last months of the old imperial regime of Haile Selassie, but his fame has outlived all political changes. As the son of a peasant who made it to fame, he has remained a popular figure in Ethiopia: the central stadium in Addis Ababa is named after him, and his bronze statue stands in the capital's Saint Joseph Cemetery. The international sport community commemorated his legacy by establishing the annual Abebe Bikila Award, presented in New York since 1978 to an individual who has made an outstanding contribution to distance running and helped to promote the spirit of noble sportsmanship.

Abebe Bikila was one of the most famous athletes in history, the man who put Africa on the map of modern international sport and, in the eyes of many, a symbol of Ethiopia as a land of respectability and high achievement.

[*See also* Haile Gebrselassie; *and* Haile Selassie I.]

BIBLIOGRAPHY

Gebeyehu, Berhanu. "Abebe Bikila." In *Encyclopaedia Aethiopica*, edited by Siegbert Uhlig, vol. 1, pp. 22–23. Wiesbaden: Harrassowitz, 2003– .

Judah, Tim. *Bikila: Ethiopia's Barefoot Olympian*. London: Reportage Press, 2008.

Martin, David E., and Roger W. H. Gynn. *The Olympic Marathon: The History and Drama of Sport's Most Challenging Event*. Champaign, Ill.: Human Kinetics, 2000.

Rambali, Paul. *Barefoot Runner: The Life of Marathon Runner Abebe Bikila*. 2d ed. London: Serpent's Tail, 2007.

HAGGAI ERLICH

Abiodun, Christiana. [*See* Emanuel, Christiana Abiodun.

Abiola, Moshood Kashimawo Olawale (1937– 1998), Nigerian entrepreneur, philanthropist, politician, and publisher, was born on 24 August 1937 in the southwestern town of Egba, Abeokuta, in the present-day Ogun State, to Alhaji Salawu Adelekan Akanni Abiola and Zeliat Wuraola Ayinke Abiola (née Kassim). Although Abiola was the twenty-third child of his parents, he was their first surviving child as his older siblings had died at infancy or were stillborn. Because of several deaths that had plagued the family, Abiola was named "Kashimawo," meaning "Let us wait and see." It was not until his fifteenth birthday that his parents gave him a regular name, Moshood, having been convinced that the young Abiola had come to stay.

Although he was born and raised in a poor family, the young Abiola exhibited some entrepreneurial tendencies when he started gathering and selling firewood at the tender age of nine. With the proceeds from his business, he was able to support his family. At the age of fifteen, Abiola founded a band that played music at ceremonies in exchange for food. Later the band became so famous that it started charging fees for performances. With the

Moshood Kasimawo Olawale Abiola, 1993. (AP Images/ Dave Caulkin)

proceeds from his musical engagement, Abiola was able to support his family and his education.

The young Abiola not only was gifted in entrepreneurship but also had some academic talents. He attended Nawar-ud-Deen School and Africa Central School, both in Abeokuta, for his primary education between 1944 and 1950. For his secondary education, Abiola enrolled at Baptist Boys High School, Abeokuta, from 1951 to 1956. At the Baptist School Abiola served as editor of the school magazine, *The Trumpeter*, while Olusegun Obasanjo, who later became Nigeria's military and civilian president, served as the deputy editor.

On completing his secondary education in 1956, Abiola started his professional career as a clerk with Barclays Bank in Ibadan, the capital city of present-day Oyo state. From Barclays Abiola moved to the Western Region Finance Corporation, where he worked as an executive accounts officer. In 1961 Abiola proceeded to the Department of Management and Accountancy of Glasgow University, Scotland, where he graduated in 1963 with a first-class degree in political economy, commercial law, and management accountancy. From 1963 to 1965 Abiola was at the Institute of Chartered Accountants of Scotland, where he also graduated with distinction.

On his return to Nigeria Abiola served as a senior accountant at the University of Lagos Teaching Hospital, from where he moved to Pfizer. Abiola later joined International Telephone and Telegraph Corporation (ITT), where he rose to become the vice president for Africa and the Middle East. While serving as vice president, Abiola was also the chair of the Nigerian subsidiary of ITT. During this time Abiola invested his resources in West Africa, particularly in Nigeria. Specifically, he set up Concord Press, Concord Airlines, and Summit Oil International Limited, which was the largest indigenous oil exploration firm in Nigeria at the time.

Besides his successful career and expansive business empire, Abiola was a philanthropist. In fact, his rise to prominence has been attributed largely to his philanthropic engagement. Abiola constructed several schools for the education of the young. He also built mosques and churches (even though he was a Muslim), donated libraries, and sponsored water projects in various Nigerian states and communities, among other projects. In addition to his local acts of social responsibility, Abiola was involved in some international philanthropic projects. For example, he was a Pan-Africanist who contributed to the black struggles in the United States and in South Africa, where he donated funds toward the dismantling of the apartheid regime. He also expended his energies and funds in the campaign to gain reparations for slavery and colonialism in Africa and the diaspora.

In recognition of his business and philanthropic activities, Abiola was honored with about two hundred chieftaincy titles from several Nigerian communities, including the Bashorun of Ibadanland (1987), the Aare Onakakanfo of Yorubaland (1987), and the Jagungbola of Lagos (1989). Abiola was also named the international businessman of the year in December 1988, after being bestowed with the key to the city of Washington, D.C., earlier in 1987. Similarly, Abiola occupied such honorary positions as president of the Nigerian Stock Exchange; patron, Kwame Nkrumah Foundation; chair, G15 Business Council; trustee, Martin Luther King Foundation; and Pillar of Sports in Africa. He was also chancellor of Ladoke Akintola University of Technology, Ogbomoso.

Although Abiola's philanthropic engagement helped his rise to prominence, his political activities also attracted local and international acclaim. Abiola's political trajectory can be traced to his joining the National Council of Nigeria and the Cameroons at the age of nineteen. He later rose to become the chair of the ruling National Party of Nigeria in the early 1980s. However, the military truncated Abiola's political career when it staged the coup that ended civilian rule in December 1983. Nevertheless, Abiola remained a close associate of the military regimes, especially during the reign of General Ibrahim Babangida. Given his popularity with the Nigerian masses and the goodwill that he enjoyed from the military government at the time, Abiola ran in the 1993 presidential elections that would have ushered in the third republic in Nigeria. Running on the platform of the Social Democratic Party, Abiola defeated Bashir Tofa, the candidate of the National Republican Convention, in an election that has been described as the freest and fairest election in Nigerian history. Abiola's victory in that election was so significant because he got a majority of votes across ethnic and religious divides. In fact, he won the election in Tofa's own region of Kano State.

When the Babangida-led federal military government annulled the 12 June 1993 elections, citing what seemed to many as frivolous excuses, Abiola refused to accept the annulment and instead galvanized the support of Nigerians and the international community to restore his mandate. As a result of such pressure at home and abroad, Babangida handed over power to an interim national government headed by Ernest Shonekan in August 1993. In November 2003 General Sani Abacha overthrew Shonekan and established another military government. Returning from a foreign trip in 1994, Abiola declared himself president on 11 June in Epetedo, Lagos. In reaction, the Abacha-led government arrested and charged him with treason. While in custody, several human rights and political activists, including Kudirat, one of Abiola's wives, mounted pressure on Abacha to release Abiola. However, Abacha agreed to release the president-elect only if he renounced his mandate. Abiola refused and several activists were either killed or imprisoned by the Abacha-led government for their activism. Kudirat, for instance, was allegedly killed by agents of the military government in Lagos.

Abiola remained in custody until the death of Abacha in June 1998. His successor, General Abdulsalami Abubakar, was planning to release him when Abiola died of a heart attack on 7 July 1998. Abiola was meeting with a US government delegation when he developed difficulty breathing. He was rushed to the hospital, where he died afterward. Although Abiola's supporters claimed that he was poisoned, independent autopsy reports indicated that he died of heart-related diseases. Despite criticisms of his close association with the military regimes in Nigeria and alleged corruption, as mentioned in Fela Anikulapo Kuti's song "ITT," Abiola enjoyed the support of Nigerians and the international community. He had several wives and was alleged to have fathered more than a hundred children. In his will, Abiola instructed that his children had to pass a DNA test to ascertain their paternity before benefitting from the wealth he left behind. Some of his alleged children failed the test.

[*See also* Abacha, Sani; Babangida, Ibrahim Badamosi; *and* Kuti, Fela Anikulapo.]

BIBLIOGRAPHY

"Hope Rises—MKO Abiola: Nigeria." http://www. hope-rises.com. An online resource that portrays the life of M. K. O. Abiola and his contributions to Nigeria and the world.

CAJETAN N. IHEKA

Abo, Wassis Hortense Léonie (1945–), Congolese activist and prominent member of the Kwilu rebellion in the Democratic Republic of the Congo, was born in Malungu on the banks of the Kwilu River in the Belgian Congo on 15 August 1945. In 1963 she joined the armed uprising led by Pierre Mulele, the leader of the rebellion and the former minister of education in Patrice Lumumba's cabinet.

Her mother, Labon, died in childbirth, so Abo, whose name means "mourning" in Kimbundu, was raised by her adoptive parents, Awaka and Mabiungu. Despite the violent protestations of her grandmother Aney, Abo started attending primary school in the village of Lukamba in 1952. She transferred to a boarding school at the Totshi mission at the age of nine. There she was baptized and renamed Léonie Hortense. In 1957 Abo and thirteen other young girls made up the first class of assistant midwives and pediatric nurses at Foreami, a foundation promoting health care for the Congolese created by Belgium's Queen Elisabeth. She received her diploma shortly before her fourteenth birthday.

Léonie Abo's arranged marriage to Gaspar Mumputu (September 1959) was marked by domestic violence. During her early married life in Kikwit, she learned about the political activities of the Parti Solidaire Africain (of which Pierre Mulele was the secretary-general), national independence, and the death of Lumumba; but it took the maquis experience to politicize her. On the brink of leaving her husband (June 1962), she fell in love with Rémy Makoloni. After her husband took them to court, Abo spent a month in prison. Thwarting her dreams of domestic bliss, her brothers tricked her in August 1963 into accompanying them into the maquis (armed resistance based in the forest), where her medical skills were in demand.

The first violent incidents of the rebellion in the Kwilu occurred in January 1964 when Mulelist insurgents attacked government outposts, mission stations, and company installations. By April the army had already gained the upper hand, but administrative reoccupation took several months. Rebel forces in various regions established control over a large part of the country for a period of nearly two years. This control ended in December 1965, shortly after Mobutu Sese Seko's coup in November of that year. Mulele and his partisans finally left the maquis in 1967.

An estimated 90,000 to 100,000 people participated in the Kwilu rebellion, an estimated 20 to 35 percent of whom were women. Many women, like Abo, were taken to the maquis against their will. Nevertheless, qualitative distinctions are frequently made between the 1960s rebellions in other parts of the Congo and that in the Kwilu. In the Kwilu women were part of assault teams, commanded troops, gave political lessons, and executed individuals considered traitors. Furthermore, a woman served as a judge on a tribunal, whereas elsewhere women were relegated to the subaltern tasks of informing, surveillance, and preparing meals.

Within a month of her arrival in the maquis Mulele took Abo as his wife. In this role she was both revered (people believed that she shared the magical powers they attributed to him) and targeted. Her primary function was to provide medical care and run the pharmacy. She also worked with Mulele in the explosives department. Although she was physically robust, underwent rigorous training, and was considered as a candidate for commanding troops, she was too soft-spoken to fulfill this role.

In addition to advancing both a Maoist-inspired, rural-based revolution and a second "liberation," the maquis advocated equality among women and men, husbands and wives. Women's roles in the public realm evolved despite local resistance (among women and men, partisans and villagers). But the extraordinary circumstances that had opened up new spaces for women in the public sphere did not produce new roles in the so-called private sphere of marriage or in sexual relations. Traditional customs were respected, and bride price was paid for marriages contracted in the maquis to keep the peace with the villagers, on whom the rebels depended for food and information. Having embraced the revolution after her initial misgivings, Abo was distressed when Mulele took a second wife (Monique Ilo in December 1964) and announced his intention to take a third (Bernadette Kimbadi in January 1967).

Nevertheless, as the situation in the forest deteriorated and the number of rebels continued to dwindle, Abo alone remained with Mulele until his death. Once everyone else had left, purportedly in order to regroup, the two of them made the five-hundred-mile journey to Brazzaville in a canoe. Unable to connect with Lumumbists, Mulele, supposedly amnestied by Mobutu, was taken to Kinshasa, where he was tortured and killed in October 1968. Abo spent several months in prison. Shortly after her release in January 1969, she learned that she was about to be rearrested and fled to Brazzaville, where she hoped to join other revolutionaries. Remaining in exile until shortly before Mobutu was ousted, she worked as a nurse and gave birth to two daughters, Eulalie in 1971 and Ghislaine in 1974.

Upon her return to the Congo in 1996 she lived and worked in Kinshasa. She helped establish local women's organizations for undernourished children and, along with a handful of sympathizers, managed a farm in the Maluku area about sixty miles outside of Kinshasa, growing produce destined for the popular quarters of the city. She cofounded la Fraternité des Patriotes Congolais (FRAPAC), an organization bringing together the combatants of the Kwilu/Kwango maquis, and was an active member as well as honorary president of the nonprofit organization l'Union des Femmes Congolaises pour le Développement (UFCD). Under Laurent Kabila she worked on rural reconstruction in Abdoulaye Yerodia's cabinet. In the 2006 elections she was a candidate for the Union des Patriotes et des Nationalistes Congolais (UPNAC) in the Kikwit region.

In the maquis Abo had noted the discrepancies between the words and actions of the leaders concerning gender equity. After the death of Mulele, empowered by the new roles espoused in the maquis, she eschewed traditional family responsibilities. In two short texts Abo, while she staunchly defends Mulele's contested legacy, emphasizes her role as his companion in struggle, thereby validating her own contribution to decolonization and shedding the dependence associated with the role of wife. Nevertheless, for Abo the fight for women's rights cannot be separated from the broader struggle against capitalism and imperialism. An avid spokesperson for Mulele, she also managed to say, "Women are standing tall, they have shouldered more than their share of the burden in this revolution" (Martens, 1994, p. 219).

[*See also* Kabila, Laurent-Désiré; Lumumba, Patrice Emery; Mobutu Sese Seko; *and* Mulele, Pierre.]

BIBLIOGRAPHY

Abo, Léonie. "3 Octobre 1991: vingt-troisième anniversaire de la mort de Pierre Mulele." *Lire les femmes écrivains et littératures africaine.* http://www.arts.uwa.edu.au/AFLIT/IneditAbo.html.

Abo, Léonie. "Un témoignage risqué." *Lire les femmes écrivains et littératures africaine.* http://aflit.arts.uwa.edu.au/IneditAbo2.html.

Bouwer, Karen. "Léonie Abo: The Political Lessons of the Maquis." In *Gender and Decolonization in the Congo: The Legacy of Patrice Lumumba*, pp. 101–130. New York: Palgrave Macmillan, 2010.

Coquery-Vidrovitch, Catherine. "Abo: Revolutionary Woman or Tool of the Revolution?" In *African Women: A Modern History*. Translated by Beth Gillian Raps, pp. 186–188. Boulder, Colo.: Westview Press, 1997.

Coquery-Vidrovitch, Catherine, Alain Forest, and Herbert F. Weiss, eds. *Rébellions-révolution au Zaire, 1963–1965*. 2 vols. Paris: L'Harmattan, 1987.

Martens, Ludo. *Abo: Une femme du Congo*. Brussels: EPO; Paris: L'Harmattan, 1994. Martens's strong ideological bent makes his publications suspect to some scholars. He nevertheless remains the most important source on women's participation in the rebellion, complementing with detail the brief allusions to women's roles by the preeminent scholar of the rebellions, Benoît Verhaegen. Martens's copiously documented book *Pierre Mulele ou la seconde vie de Patrice Lumumba* (Brussels: EPO, 1985) focuses significantly on women in the maquis and includes records from Herbert Weiss's personal archives as well as interviews with partisans and extracts of Abo's maquis journal.

KAREN BOUWER

Aboubaker Ibrahim Chehem (c. 1810–1885), pasha of Zeila (1857–?), an Afar Hassoba, was born at Ambado on the north coast of the Gulf of Tadjoura (present-day Djibouti). During the first half of the nineteenth century, the most lucrative trade in the area was traffic in slaves, although political disorders in the Abyssinian highlands later led to a vigorous trade in arms. Aboubaker also provided guides and supplies for various European expeditions from the coast up into Abyssinia.

Aboubaker and his eleven sons became wealthy, but their trading activities brought them into direct and frequently bitter competition with Ali Chermarke Saleh, the pasha of Zeyla. Chermarke, a Somali Issa (born c. 1775), held a contract with the Turks to collect taxes on goods passing through the ancient port of Zeyla. Britain was the first European power to establish a naval facility in the region, at Aden in 1842, and Ali Chermarke maintained their trust and confidence.

Although Aboubaker's role in the development of what became the French colony of Obock and dependencies, later French Somaliland, was secondary to his broader lifetime business achievements in the Horn of Africa, he is accorded special mention in French colonial history. In a letter to the French government posted in 1859, he laid out the advantages that would accrue to France in establishing a counterweight to the British position in Aden. He was later instrumental in unveiling information about the murder of Henri Lambert, the French consul in Aden. After signing a treaty with France for the purchase of territory around Obock in 1862, during years of French indecision about actually establishing a colony on the Gulf of Tadjoura, he protected the French claims from being overtaken by other imperial powers.

Lambert's death was engineered by Ali Chermarke Saleh, who had been contracted by the Ottoman Empire to collect taxes on all goods transiting Zeyla to and from the Ogaden and the Abyssinian highlands. He therefore opposed the emergence of French interest in the Red Sea and the Gulf of Aden as a development that would harm his political and commercial influence. It is in this context that he allegedly, on 29 June 1859, plotted the death of the French consul, then traveling by boat between Moussa and Maskali, two small islands facing Cap Jiboutil, site of the present-day city of Djibouti.

The death of the French consul under suspicious circumstances required a reaction from Paris. Before sending a punitive expedition into the area, permission was easily obtained from the Turkish Porte in Istanbul. Admiral Fleuriot de Langle was sent to the region to make a formal investigation. The French admiral already had in his possession various letters from Aboubaker laying out the facts of Ali Chermarke's duplicity. In his first meetings with Turkish officials in Hodeida, Fleuriot de Langle produced the Royal Turkish *firman* authorizing his mission and demanded the arrest of Chermarke. Despite trickery by both Chermarke and local British agents, Chermarke was arrested, but he died before he could be taken to France.

Aboubaker became pasha, and he gave loyal service to the Egyptian authorities who occupied the former Turkish holdings in the Horn of Africa between 1875 and 1885. He lived to see his dreams in the Gulf of Tadjoura fulfilled when, in 1884, after the British had closed Aden's coaling facilities to French warships, Léonce Lagarde, a young colonial administrator, opened a coaling station at Obock and unified French possessions on both sides of the gulf. This led, in 1888, to the opening of a new administrative capital at Djibouti, then a succession of coral reefs and mangrove swamps but with a good natural harbor. Bourhan, the seventh son of Aboubaker, was selected as the first chief of the new village of Djibouti.

[*See also* Bourhan, Ali Aref.]

BIBLIOGRAPHY

Fontrier, Marc. *Abou-Bakr Ibrahim, Pacha de Zeyla–Marchand d'Esclaves: Commerce et Diplomatie dans le Golfe de Tadjoura 1840–1885*. Paris: L'Harmattan-Bibliothèque Peiresc, 2003.

Joint Daguenet, Roger. *Aux Origines de l'Implantation Française en Mer Rouge: Vie et mort d'Henri Lambert Consul de France à Aden–1859*. Paris: L'Harmattan-Collection racines du présent, 1992.

WALTER CLARKE

Aboulela, Leila (1964–), Sudanese writer, was born in Cairo, Egypt, to an Egyptian mother (Sudan's first ever female demographer) and a Sudanese father. She was brought up and educated in Khartoum, at the Khartoum American School, and graduated in 1985 from the University of Khartoum with a degree in economics, before moving to London in her mid-twenties to study for her master's degree in statistics at the London School of Economics. In 1990 she moved to Aberdeen, Scotland, with her husband and three children, and she started writing in 1992 while working as a part-time research assistant and lecturer. She explains that the Gulf War, and the anti-Islam/anti-Arab sentiments that it triggered, provided the initial impetus for her writing. Aboulela has lived in Cairo, Khartoum, Jakarta, Dubai, London, Abu Dhabi, Doha and Aberdeen, where she wrote most of her fiction.

Aboulela is a devout Muslim, and her fictional work engages with the role of faith in the life of her multifaceted characters. She states that both her grandmother, who studied medicine in the 1940s, and her mother, who was a university professor, imparted faith in Islam as a "personal and private thing" and that her idea of religion "wasn't about a woman not working or having to dress in a certain way" (Sethi, 2005, p. 1). It was in Britain, where she felt alienated, that she started to wear the hijab because she wanted to show her faith more visibly.

Aboulela's first novel, *The Translator* (1999), is about a young Sudanese widow, Sammar, who works in Aberdeen as a translator for the Scottish Middle Eastern scholar Rae, for whom she translates Arabic manuscripts into English. The novel is set both in Khartoum and in Aberdeen and explores the possibility of a love relationship between the two main characters in spite of their many potentially divisive differences. Central to the plot is Rae's conversion to Islam, without which their marriage would be impossible. Particularly noteworthy are the passages in the novel where the memory of a childhood and early adulthood in Sudan before departure structures the protagonist's perceptions of her present life in a different place. The novel was long-listed for the Orange Prize in 2000 and the IMPAC Dublin Literary Award in 2001 and short-listed for the Saltire Scottish Book Prize in 2000. In 2002 the text was serialized and broadcast on BBC Radio 4. This drama serialization was short-listed in 2003 for the Race and Media Award. The novel has been translated into Spanish, German, Dutch, and Arabic and was voted a "notable book of the year" by the *New York Times* in 2006.

Aboulela's short story "The Museum" won the inaugural Caine Prize for African Writing in 2000. This story could be regarded as Aboulela's most political piece; the narrative engages with colonial discourses on Africa, as epitomized in the museum displays, and the way such representations still have currency in the present-day reality of the main characters. The story also appears in her collection of stories *Coloured Lights*, which was published in 2001; and it was broadcast on BBC Radio 4. Aboulela wrote several radio plays that were broadcast, including The Mystic Life (2003) and the historical drama The Lion of Chechnya (2005).

Aboulela's second novel, *Minaret*, published by Bloomsbury in 2005, was long-listed for the Orange and IMPAC prizes. It tells the story of Najwa and her twin Omar, who, after a sheltered and elitist childhood in Sudan, struggle to make sense of their lives as exiles in London. Omar, unable to adjust to his much reduced lifestyle, ends up in jail after being arrested for dealing in drugs. Najwa, on the other hand, finds friendship in a group of women who meet at the local mosque, while she works as a cleaner and childminder. She falls in love with her employer's younger brother, and the family, once they discover this love affair, direct their energy at driving the couple apart.

The most recent novel *Lyrics Alley* (2010) is set in Sudan, Egypt, and Britain of the 1950s and portrays the trials of the extended Abuzeid family against the backdrop of Egypt's crumbling monarchy and the end of British rule in Sudan. The text traces the intricate connections between personal desire, suffering, and art as the main character Nur struggles to find meaning after a diving accident leaves him paralyzed. He becomes a famous popular poet, while having to completely rearrange his life and that of his family. The novel's finely drawn and detailed descriptions of the characters' inner conflicts are superbly balanced against the backdrop of historical events.

Aboulela's novels, as well as most of the stories in her collection, investigate, in nuanced and often lyrical ways, questions of home and belonging as she portrays the conflicts of migration and the difficulty of creating a "home" in the new place of residence. Her fiction explores the complex cultural encounters and the possibilities of living in a secular society while being rooted in Islam. Her characters are not static but learn about themselves and others, misunderstand their new environment, and form relationships across cultural divides. Fadia Faqir argues that Aboulela's "halaal fiction," while propagating "an Islamic world view," is also a good example of "transcultural and transnational literature" (Faqir, 2004, p. 169). Aboulela's fiction mainly focuses on the marginalization of North African Muslim women in Britain and locates the causes in the interstices of Western and Islamic patriarchy, as well as in the misunderstandings of cultural differences. She asserts the transnational character of Islam but points out that the memory of local, African, and specifically Khartoumian experience is crucial for her characters' understanding of themselves in their new environments.

BIBLIOGRAPHY

Cooper, Brenda. *A New Generation of African Writers: Migration, Material Culture and Language.* Woodbridge, UK: James Currey, 2008.

Faqir, Fadia. "Lost in Translation. *Index on Censorship* 33, no. 2 (April 2004): 166–170.

Nash, Geoffrey. "Re-siting Religion and Creating a Feminised Space in the Fiction of Ahdaf Soueif and Leila Aboulela." *Wasafiri* 35 (Spring 2002): 28–31.

Sethi, Anita. "Keep the Faith." *The Observer*, June 5, 2005. http://books.guardian.co.uk/departments/generalfiction/story/0,6000,1499352,00.html.

TINA STEINER

Abraham Afewerki (1966–2006), Eritrean Tigrinya singer and performer, songwriter, instrument player, and music composer, was born in the city of Asmara. During the Eritrean war of liberation (1961–1991), Abraham Afewerki and his family, like hundreds of thousands of other Eritreans, sought refuge in Sudan.

Abraham Afewerki became attracted by music and musical instruments at an early age. As a young child, he started playing *famfam* (harmonica) and singing at school events. As a young boy with great artistic potential, he joined the Qeyyahti Embaba

(Red Flowers) of the Eritrean People's Liberation Front (EPLF) at the age of twelve. The Red Flowers was a cultural troupe composed of young artists who performed cultural and revolutionary music and theater within Eritrea (in areas controlled by the EPLF) and Sudan. A branch of the troupe of which Abraham Afewerki was a member was active in Khartoum. By writing and composing his own lyrics and melodies, he started performing songs related to the situation in Eritrea in 1979.

After staying in Sudan for some time, Abraham Afewerki traveled to Italy, where he struggled to realize his dream of becoming a good musician. Until the 1990s he managed to become one of the most admired Eritrean musicians of his generation. Apart from singing, he also learned to play the *kerar* (a five- or six-string lyre) and guitar. Moreover, he wrote lyrics, composed melodies, and developed a singing style. He made some albums in the 1990s on which he included many songs comprising themes related to Eritrean nationalism, love and romance, social issues, and entertainment. Between the years 1991 and 2006 he continued to play, perform, and sing and demonstrated his capacity to become one of the greatest Eritrean musicians of his time. After living in Italy for many years, Abraham Afewerki moved to the United States, where he also studied management and information systems and acquired a BS degree with honors.

He released his first music cassette, entitled *Wegahta* (The Dawn), in Tigrinya genre, in 1991. As its release coincided with Eritrea's independence, some of its lyrics were related to success and happiness. In one of the songs, "Wegahta," Abraham Afewerki sang that the darkness had gone and the dawn had come for Eritrea's people. In 1994 he released his second cassette, *Tesfaya Sinqey* (Hope Is My Source of Food). This release comprised songs that appealed to the Eritrean public, and most of its lyrics dealt with love, hope, and hard work. In 1997 Abraham Afewerki released *Meley* (Beautiful), a CD that contained some of his songs from 1979 and the early 1980s. In 1998 he released *Mestir Fiqri* (The Secret of Love), a CD whose content resembled that of his earlier releases.

During the border conflict between Eritrea and Ethiopia (1998–2000), Abraham Afewerki played a considerable role in performing nationalistic music. One of his famous songs during the time, entitled "Abzelena Alina" ("Wherever We Are"), illuminated the unity and heroism of Eritreans. Abraham Afewerki's performance of this song was greatly admired all over Eritrea. It was played almost everywhere during the war. In 2000 Abraham Afewerki released yet another CD, *Hadera* (Allegiance).

The most important of Abraham Afewerki's albums was *Semay* (The Sky), which was released in 2006 and, again, carried a strong emotional appeal to the Eritrean public. For most Eritreans many of the lyrics on this album reflected their actual concerns and their country's contemporary situation. Among the songs contained on this album was "Semay Iyu Deretey" ("The Sky Is My Limit"), which entered into popular memory among Eritreans and is one of the most played songs in the country. Other songs include "Sedray" ("My Family"), "Kihilewelki iyye" ("I Will Live for You"), "Fikri kem tsehay iyyu" ("Love Is Like the Sun"), and "Maryam asmereyti" ("St. Mary of Asmara"). Abraham Afewerki's musical artistry is also loved in the countries that neighbor Eritrea, particularly Ethiopia and Sudan.

Abraham Afewerki drowned off the Red Sea coast Dahlak Islands, near the port city of Massawa, on 7 October 2006. It was thought that he went to Eritrea to produce his last album in the form of a movie musical. Just before he died, he performed in several places in Eritrea, most remarkably in Sawa military camp. His sudden death shocked most Eritreans at home and abroad.

Apart from his great artistic talents, Abraham Afewerki is also remembered by Eritreans as a humble, honest, and sociable artist. Above all, his interpretations of Tigrinya lyrics and melody have enshrined him in popular memory, and he remains one of the most renowned artists in Eritrea.

BIBLIOGRAPHY

Delina Solutions. "Interview with Abraham Afewerki." http://www.delinasolutions.net/abraham_afewerki_interview.htm.

Mengisteab, Hezbawi. "The Star Has Fallen: A Short Biography of the Renowned Singer, Abraham Afewerki." *Meftih*, October 3, 2006, 3–4a, b, c.

MUSSIE TESFAGIORGIS

Abrahams, Peter Henry (1919–), South African-born poet, journalist, essayist, and novelist, was born on 19 March 1919, in Vrededorp, a slum in Johannesburg, though he later became an adopted citizen of Britain. His father was James Henry Abrahams Deras (or De Ras), an Ethiopian itinerant who settled in Johannesburg as a mine laborer. His mother, Angelina DuPlessis, was a Coloured woman whose first husband was a Cape Malay resident, with whom she had two children. His parents met and married in Vrededorp. Abrahams grew up as a Coloured, "a by-product of the early contact between black and white" (Abrahams, 1981, p. 10), which made him aware of the social and political consequences of racial formation in South Africa. His father died when he was still young. Upon his father's death, his family was thrown into poverty. Abrahams later wrote that his mother "went to work in the homes of white folk, usually living in and looking after their children" (Abrahams, 2000, p. 2). It was after his father's death that he briefly moved to Elsburg, in Johannesburg, where he lived with his aunt. He later returned to Vrededorp, which, along with Fordsburg, was the dominant milieu of his childhood. His work and intellectual odyssey are testaments of his struggle to "rid ourselves of the vast mythological superstructure of blood and race and color which has been part of 'the black man's burden' in the twentieth century" (Abrahams, 2000, p. 62).

Abrahams took menial jobs at an early age. He was illiterate until he began to go to school on the insistence of an older white woman with whom he worked at a smithy, at the age of ten. It was reading, in particular literature, that forged "a new consciousness" (Abrahams, 1981, p. 161) within him. It was a fortuitous encounter with a man who referred him to Peter Dabula of the Bantu Men's Social Center that landed him a job working in the office of the Pathfinders, the black section of the racially segregated Boy Scout movement. It was here that he became acquainted with the national African newspaper *The Bantu World* and the writings and works of African Americans such as Paul Robeson (1898–1976), W. E. B. Du Bois (1868–1963), Alain Locke (1885–1954), Countee Cullen (1903–1946), and Claude McKay (1890–1948), an experience through which he forged his "color nationalism through the writings of men and women who lived a world away from me" (Abrahams, 1981, p. 197).

Work at the Pathfinders office of the Boy Scout movement soon expired and at the beckon of Peter Dabula, Abrahams wrote to P. S. Woodfield, then the principal of Diocesan Training College, Grace Dieu at Pietersburg, where he began his studies in 1936. He began to write and publish poetry in *The Bantu World*. He then enrolled at Saint Peter's Secondary with the intention of matriculating there. Es'kia Mphahlele (1919–2008), the noted writer and fellow Saint Peter's attendee, remembered Abrahams in his autobiography *Down Second Avenue* (1990) as "vividly talking about Marcus Garvey, taking it for granted that we must know about him.... Abrahams wrote verse in his exercise books and gave them to us to read.... I remember now how morose the verse was: straining to justify and glorify the dark complexion with the I'm-black-and-proud-of-it theme." The intellectual milieu of Saint Peter's exposed Abrahams to Marxism, a political philosophy he felt had "offered a reasonable explanation of the world in which I lived"; but he questioned whether it had "any room for the compassionate humanity that pervaded the life and teaching of Christ" (Abrahams, 1981, p. 251).

Abrahams left Saint Peter's in 1938. By then his writing was gaining some public recognition. Early in 1938 Oliver Walker published a feature article, "Coloured Boy Poet," an appraisal of Abrahams, in the *Daily Express*. Abrahams matriculated from Saint Peter's and subsequently left for Cape Town, where he taught briefly. He became involved in protests against the Hertzog Bills that had effectively done away with the franchise for Africans and Coloureds. Here Abrahams was an active participant in intellectual discussions of the racial politics of the time. It appears that at this time he had already decided that he wanted to leave South Africa for England in pursuit of a career as a writer. Having failed to secure a passport, he left Cape Town for Durban, where he edited a magazine. However, he could not raise enough money for his passage. He finally left South Africa in 1939, working as a stoker's trimmer on a ship.

It took more than a year at sea before Abrahams arrived in wartime London in October 1940. There he met the Trinidadian-born Pan-Africanist and Marxist intellectual and activist George Padmore (1903–1959) and began a friendship with him. He published two volumes of poetry, *Here, Friend* (1940), followed by *A Black Man Speaks of Freedom* (1941). Abrahams had by now settled into a routine of writing that alternated with his tenure as a dispatch clerk at Central Books, a socialist bookstore. He later worked as a subeditor of *The Daily Worker*. The collections of poetry were followed in 1942 by the publication of *Dark Testament*, a collection of short stories. In this year he married Dorothy Pennington, who was also involved in left-wing politics and a friend of Padmore. It was under the direction of Padmore that Abrahams was involved in the planning of the Fifth Pan-African Congress held in

Manchester, England, in 1944, which was opened by Du Bois. It was during this time, however, that Abrahams had begun to feel disillusioned by the recalcitrant specter of "color consciousness" among those who controlled the movement of the left-wing radicals. This led to his break with both Marxism and the British Communist Party, although he was not a card-carrying member of the organization.

After World War II ended, Abrahams and Dorothy went on a fortnight's holiday in the south of France. On this excursion he began working on the manuscripts of novels that would become *Mine Boy* and *The Path of Thunder*. Whereas *Mine Boy* explored the exigencies of racial capitalism in South Africa and the incipient struggle of a migrant laborer to find the means of resisting the exploitative regime of labor while developing a positively nonracial ethic, *The Path of Thunder* follows the interracial love of a young couple whose relationship is tantamount to a transgression of the norms that have been prescribed by the racial state of South Africa. A period of financial difficulty ensued when he returned to London and lost his job because he was not a registered member of the British Communist Party. A referral to the Worker's Educational Association made by Padmore enabled him to generate some income through lectures about South Africa. When *Mine Boy* was published in 1946, the pressures of making a living eased. *The Path of Thunder* was published about two years later. In the mid-1940s his marriage to Dorothy took a turn for the worse. In 1946 he met Daphne Elizabeth Miller, who was then a student at an art school in the south of London. The couple moved to Paris on 1 June 1948 and later married. They had three children.

In Paris Abrahams was acquainted with the African American writer Richard Wright (1908–1960), the South African artist Gerard Sekoto (1913–1993), and the larger community of writers and intellectuals in the city. *Wild Conquest*, a historical novel that explored the origins of racial tension in South Africa, was published in 1950. He again left Paris with his family for Britain in the middle of 1950. The family settled in Debden, Essex. In 1952 Abrahams traveled to East and South Africa on a trip sponsored by the BBC Third Programme, the Paris edition of the *New York Herald Tribune*, and *The Observer*. *Return to Goli* (1953) came out of those experiences. Closely related to Abrahams's experiences in Africa was his novel *A Wreath for Udomo* (1956), which sought to capture some of the ironies and difficulties of political nationalism in Africa.

Abrahams's first autobiography, *Tell Freedom* (1954), which it appears he had been working on since the end of World War II, not only chronicles his personal life but also examines the horrors of apartheid.

In the middle of 1955 he was commissioned by the Corona Library to write a book on Jamaica. Before leaving for the Caribbean, Abrahams briefly went to the United States, where he spent some time with Langston Hughes in New York before traveling to the South by train. He then visited the University of Atlanta in Georgia before returning to Harlem to end his trip. He returned to England briefly and made his departure to the Caribbean from there early in September 1955.

Abrahams's journey to the Caribbean entailed a "visit to all the main islands of the English-speaking Caribbean and what was then British Guiana" (Abrahams, 2000, p. 167). *Jamaica: An Island Mosaic* was published in the Corona Library series in 1957. It seems that Abrahams decided to settle his family in Jamaica once he returned from his trip to the Caribbean. Once he had submitted his manuscript for the book, he and his family left Debden for Coyaba. He began working as the editor of the "independent nationalist paper" (Abrahams, 2000, p. 184) *Public Opinion* in 1956. The newspaper soon folded, and in 1958 he began to "broadcast a daily five-minute news commentary on Radio Jamaica" (Abrahams, 2000, p. 208), work that he was involved in until 1999, when he was eighty years old.

The period of Abrahams's life in Jamaica has been described as marking the "third phase" of his literary and intellectual life. He published *A Night of Their Own* (1965), which explored the perils of race in apartheid South Africa. With *This Island Now* (1966), a novel set in the Caribbean, Abrahams widened his scope, anticipating the problems to be faced by newly independent nations. His most recent novel is *The View from Coyaba* (1985), which follows four generations of a Jamaican family and the struggle for independence. Living in Coyaba in 2000, Abrahams published his second memoir, *The Black Experience in the 20th Century: An Autobiography and Meditation.*

[*See also* Du Bois, W. E. B.; *and* Padmore, George.]

BIBLIOGRAPHY

Works by Peter Henry Abrahams
Tell Freedom. London: Faber and Faber, 1981.
The Black Experience in the 20th Century: An Autobiography and Meditation. Bloomington: Indiana University Press, 2000.

Works about Peter Henry Abrahams
Ensor, Robert. *The Novels of Peter Abrahams and the Rise of Nationalism in Africa.* Essen, Germany: Die Blaue Eule, 1992.
Killam, J. D., and Ruth Rowe. "Peter Abrahams." In *The Companion to African Literatures.* Oxford: James Currey, 2000.
Masilela, Nongela. "Peter Abrahams in the Modern African World." *Current Writing* 16, no. 2 (2004): 31–45.
Ogungbesan, Kolawole. *The Writing of Peter Abrahams.* New York: Africana Publishing Company, 1979.
Wade, Michael. *Peter Abrahams.* London: Evans Brothers, 1972.

KHWEZI MKHIZE

Abranches, Henrique (1932–2004), Angolan anthropologist, writer, and political activist, was born Mário de Carvalho Moutinho in Lisbon on 29 September 1932. Portuguese by birth and Angolan by nationality, Henrique Abranches also used the pseudonyms "Mwene Kalungo" and "Mwene Kalungo-Lungo." In 1947 he and his family left Portugal to settle in Luanda, where he attended the Liceu Salvador Correia, a pioneering institution of secondary education in Angola whose students included several names that were later important in Angolan literature. After five years in Luanda, Abranches moved to the city of Sá de Bandeira (now Lubango) in the Huíla Plateau in southern Angola, where he became interested in the customs and traditions of the people of the region. He returned briefly to Portugal, where he finished secondary school and attended the Society of Fine Arts. He returned to Lubango on his own and began working for the Bank of Angola. In 1952 he was transferred to Namibe in the southeast region of Angola.

Two years later he entered the Portuguese colonial army, an experience that determined Abranches's awareness of the injustice of Portugal's colonial domination of Angola. Returning to Lubango, he began his political activities with the African workers of the region, organizing meetings and assemblies and attempting to establish cooperatives in order to improve working conditions. During that time he also began collaborating with newspapers and reviews such as *Cultura*, from the Cultural Society of Angola, an association founded in 1942. Later he also worked with *Mensagem*, publishing ethnographic and literary texts that revealed his knowledge and observations of the region and its inhabitants. He was also politically active in Namibe, where he tried to organize a clandestine labor union for the fisheries workers. That brought about his contact with members of the Movimento Popular de Libertação de Angola (MPLA; People's Movement for the Liberation of Angola), which he joined when it was founded in 1956.

The attack on the prisons in Luanda on 4 February 1961, organized by various Angolan nationalist groups with the goal of liberating political prisoners, marked the beginning of the armed struggle against colonialism in Angola and was a significant event in Abranches's life. Following the attack, he was detained by the Polícia de Intervenção e Defesa do Estado (PIDE), the Portuguese secret police, and taken to the São Paulo jail, where he wrote the first draft of his novel *A Konkhava de Feti*. He also produced his first literary publication in the volume *Diálogo*, which was published in 1963 by the Casa dos Estudeantes do Império, an institution created in Lisbon in 1944 to support students from the colonies that quickly transformed into a center of activity for the anticolonial movements of Portuguese Africa.

In 1962 Abranches was deported from Angola and sent to Lisbon, where he lived clandestinely before fleeing to Paris. In Paris he contacted the president of the MPLA, Agostinho Neto, and with other militants left for Algeria, where they settled in Algiers and founded the Center of Angolan Studies in 1964. The principal objectives of the center were to make a documentary collection about Angola, collecting diverse materials and producing monographs and studies about various areas of knowledge. They also developed propaganda for the MPLA, which included such activists and intellectuals as Pepetela, Fernando Costa Andrade, and Adolfo Maria, among others. In 1969 the Center of Angolan Studies moved to Brazzaville, in the Democratic Republic of Congo, where it continued to be active until 1972. Among the works produced by the center, a notable book was the *História de Angola*, written in 1965 and then published in Portugal much later. The center activists also created a comic strip, *Contra a escravidão* (Against Slavery). Abranches, known by the name André Bufo, is considered the father of Angolan comics.

His participation in the liberation struggle and his notable work in various areas of Angolan studies led Abranches to take Angolan citizenship and, after independence in 1975, to accept responsibility in the military, politics, science, and cultural sectors. He served as captain in the People's Liberation Army of Angola, and he was director of the National Museum of Anthropology in Luanda, part of the Angolan Museums Service and the National Anthropological Laboratory, which he created.

He produced a range of articles and studies, published in international reviews, about the history, myths, and traditions of the diverse Angolan culture; and he formulated projects to integrate the differences and to combat tribalism, seeking to develop an Angolan national culture and identity. The study *Reflexões sobre cultura nacional*, published in Lisbon and Luanda in 1980, became a reference work in Angolan studies, an exemplary work of Abranches's thinking and of his intellectual and political development. It clearly presents the historical and anthropological research in the construction of an Angolan nation that met the ideology and vision of the MPLA.

In literary production Abranches wrote poems, stories, and novels, especially historic and ethnographic novels alongside such authors as Pepetela. In his novels *A Konkhava de Feti* (1981), *O Clã de Novembrino* (published in three volumes in 1989), *Kissoko de Guerra* (published in two volumes in 1989), *Misericórdia para o Reino do Congo* (1996), and others, fiction is mixed with history and ethnography; he re-created the myths and traditions of the people of southern Angola, such as the *kuvale* and the *kwanyama*, and gave life to events linked to precolonial history, the liberation war against the Portuguese army, and the war against the South African army, which invaded the country in 1975. If his poems in *Cântico Barroco* (1987) express the grief and disenchantment surrounding the civil war that broke out in Angola in 1975 between the MPLA and União Nacional para a Independência Total de Angola (UNITA; National Union for the Total Independence of Angola), founded in 1966 and led by Jonas Savimbi, the historic novels reaffirmed the heroism of the Angolan people and their faith in national unity.

A "man of seven talents," as he was described during a tribute organized by Irene Marques Guerra (Luanda, 2003), Abranches was a member of the Union of Angolan Writers, formed in 1975, and participated in the founding of the National Union of Visual Artists in 1977. He passed away in South Africa following a heart attack.

[*See also* Pepetela; *and* Savimbi, Jonas Malheiro.]

BIBLIOGRAPHY

Afolaby, Niyi. *The Golden Cage: Regeneration in Lusophone African Literature and Culture.* Trenton, N.J.: African World Press, 2001.

Helgesson, Stefan. *Transnationalism in Southern African Literature: Modernists, Realists and the Inequality of Print Culture.* New York: Routledge, 2009.

Laban, Michel. *Angola: encontro com escritores.* 2 vols. Oporto, Portugal: Fundação Eng. António de Almeida, 1991. A book of interviews with writers.

Leite, Ana Mafalda. "Angola." In *The Postcolonial Literature of Lusophone Africa*, edited by Patrick Chabal. London: C. Hurst, 1996.

Padilha, Laura Cavalcante. *Entre Voz e Letra: o Lugar da Ancestralidade na ficção angolana do século XX.* 2d rev. ed. Rio de Janeiro: Pallas, 2007. About the oral tradition in contemporary Angolan fiction.

Padilha, Laura Cavalcante, and Margarida Calafate Ribeiro, eds. *Lendo Angola.* Oporto, Portugal: Edições Afrontamento, 2008.

JESSICA FALCONI
Translated from the Portuguese by Kathleen Sheldon

Abreha Tesemma (1901–1967), Eritrean intellectual, businessman, and politician, was born in the village of Ma'ereba, southeast of Asmara. Abreha Tesemma is the son of one of the famous Eritrean chiefs and statesmen, Raesi Tesemma Asmerom Untura. As a young man, Abreha Tesemma attended both local church and Western school, which enabled him to become one of the most accomplished Eritrean scholars and politicians of his time, as well as a renowned agriculturalist and artist. He mastered a number of languages including Italian, Geez, and Amharic; his paintings fused Eritrean and Western themes and styles. For the greatest part of his life, he was engaged in agricultural activities, business, politics, and painting.

Abreha Tesemma's father, Raesi Tesemma Asmerom, served as principal chief of at least two districts in the province of Akkele Guzay—Hadegti and Egella-Hames. Based on oral sources, Raesi Tesemma was highly respected for his strategies of local conflict resolution in areas of Eritrea that fell within his administrative domain. During the post-Italian period he played a significant role as a politician, participating in proindependence organizations such as Mahber Feqri Hager (Association for Love of Country), which he helped to found in 1941, and parties like the Liberal Progressive Party and Independence Block that advocated for Eritrea's independence.

Between 1918 and 1929 Abreha Tesemma served as a secretary and representative of his father. He also served as an administrator of the Hadegti District and governor of other districts at different times. After the Italian occupation of Ethiopia, Abreha Tesemma was appointed by the Italians as counselor of the Italian governor of the Amhara domain (1940–1941). Abreha Tesemma returned to Eritrea after its occupation by the British in 1941. There he served as a district chief, assistant to the British Military Administration's political secretary, and political counselor in the city of Asmara until 1952, when the British Military Administration promoted him to the position of secretary of internal affairs. Despite his tasks as secretary and counselor, Abreha Tesemma was highly engaged in business: he founded a bus company called SATAYE (Sociéta Anonima Transporti Automobilistici di Eritrea), for which he later served as chair. SATAYE would continue to function as the largest bus company in Eritrea throughout the post-British and Ethiopian occupation period, providing the chief means of land transport between Asmara and Addis Ababa for most of the 1970s and 1980s. Abreha Tesemma also became increasingly involved in agriculture, implementing new farming and forestry practices in his home village, and in social justice issues. Starting in the late 1940s he served as the president of the Arbitral Court, which dealt with activities of local conflict resolution, and he was an active member and chair of the Eritrean Children Welfare Society.

Like his father, Abreha Tesemma was a highly engaged Eritrean politician. He demonstrated his deeply nationalist political orientations in a number of activities. For instance, he played a significant role in the foundation of one of the major Eritrean movements, called Ertra n'Ertrawyan (Eritrea for Eritreans); aided in establishing the Liberal Progressive Party; and became an active member of the Eritrean Independence Block. At one point in 1944 Abreha Tesemma expressed his opinion of the intended establishment of "Tigray-Tigrigni" (the incorporation of Tigray with Eritrea), which would eventually lead to the political independence of the Tigrinya-speaking domain. In an article in an Eritrean weekly newspaper, Abreha Tesemma demonstrated that Eritrea's future should hold political autonomy and that Ethiopia would not be able to provide credible political administration for the territory. Unity with Ethiopia, he argued, would create turmoil and not peace for the population of the Tigray territory. Later he was an active participant in the unsuccessful convention of political parties and politicians commonly known as the Convention of Bet Giorgis in 1946. Unhappy with the political relations of most of the existing political parties in

Eritrea, Abreha Tesemma founded the Liberal Progressive Party in 1947.

By 1950 Abreha Tesemma and other political figures agreed to form a coalition of several parties that eventually came to be known as the Independence Party. After the establishment of the Eritrea-Ethiopia federation in 1952, he was elected to the Constituent Assembly, in which he served until his rival Tedla Bairu alleged that Abreha Tesemma was involved in a number of illegal activities, mainly assassination plots. As a result of this rivalry, Abreha Tesemma was imprisoned in October 1953 without any legally established reason or evidence. Although he repeatedly demonstrated that he was innocent and that Tedla Bairu's accusations were unfounded, his appeal received no just adjudication. To Abreha Tesemma, this illegal imprisonment demonstrated that the federal arrangement between Eritrea and Ethiopia was not functioning and could not function in the future. During the Ethiopian occupation period (after 1962), he remained politically inactive, simply because he was extremely unpopular with the Ethiopian authorities in Eritrea. His demonstrative stand for Eritrea's independence revealed that he would not be a politician to be used for Ethiopia's political interests in Eritrea. However, he continued to engage in business and community activities, as well as agricultural practices until his death in 1967.

Abreha Tesemma is still remembered for his abilities as a great administrator, outstanding thinker, lucid speaker, and highly dependable counselor, as well as for his commitment to freedom and social improvement in Eritrea.

[See also Tedla Bairu.]

BIBLIOGRAPHY

Gebre-Medhin, Jordan. *Peasants and Nationalism in Eritrea: A Critique of Ethiopian Studies*, pp. 83, 93–94, 161–163. Trenton, N.J.: Red Sea Press, 1989.

Killion, Tom. *Historical Dictionary of Eritrea*. London: Scarecrow Press, 1998.

Negash, Tekeste. *Eritrea and Ethiopia: The Federal Experience*. Uppsala, Sweden: Nordiska Afrikainstitutet, 1997.

Saulsberry, Nicole Denise. "The Life and Times of Woldeab Woldemariam (1905–1995)." Ph.D. diss., Stanford University, 2001.

Tafla, Bairu. "Abräha Täsämma." In *Encyclopaedia Aethiopica*, edited by Siegbert Uhlig, vol. 1, p. 43. Wiesbaden, Germany: Harrassowitz Verlag, 2003.

Tesfay, Alemseged. *Let Us Stay United: Eritrea 1941–1950. English translation of Aynefelale: ertra 1941–1950.* Asmara: Hidri Publishers, 2001.

MUSSIE TESFAGIORGIS

Abu al-Hasan 'Ali ibn Uthman (1297–1351), tenth sultan of the Moroccan Marinid dynasty, came to power in the aftermath of the long and largely peaceful reign of his father, Abu Sa'id Uthman (r. 1310–1331). The greatest builder of the Marinids, Abu al-Hasan constructed mosques in Fez and Tlemcen, as well as madrasas in numerous Moroccan cities and a hospital in Fez. The accomplishments of his reign are chronicled in a history written by his secretary, Ibn Marzuq, making Abu al-Hasan the best known of the Marinid sultans.

With Marinid power firmly established in Morocco, Abu al-Hasan sought to expand the dynasty's influence, first in southern Spain and then throughout the Maghreb. His attempt to reconstitute the former Almohad Empire, though seemingly successful at first, proved to be disastrous in the long run. Abu al-Hasan's reign ended with his eastern possessions in rebellion and his son Abu 'Inan usurping his power in Tlemcen and Morocco. Unable to restore himself to the throne, Abu al-Hasan ended his life as a refugee among the Hintata Berbers in the High Atlas Mountains of southern Morocco.

Abu al-Hasan's initial foreign adventures took place in the Iberian Peninsula. In 1333 the Marinid army took Gibraltar, from which it attempted to force the Castilians out of the fortress of Tarifa. This town had served as the Marinid advance post in Spain during the reigns of their earliest sultans; however, the Castilians had captured it in 1292. Abu al-Hasan's attempt to recover Tarifa was a dismal failure. In fact, the majority of the sultan's initiatives in Spain were unsuccessful, culminating in his devastating defeat to the Castilians at the Salado River in 1340. Following this disaster, Abu al-Hasan turned his attention to expanding Marinid domains in North Africa.

His efforts on that front initially appeared to be much more successful. Launching his army against the neighboring Zayyanid state in 1335, Abu al-Hasan captured most of the Zayyanid holdings in the central Maghreb during a little more than two years of fighting. His Algerian campaign culminated in the successful conquest of the Zayyanid capital of Tlemcen in 1337. This was a tremendous accomplishment, one his predecessors had sought many times but had been unable to achieve in almost a hundred years of Marinid rule. Tlemcen quickly became Abu al-Hasan's new eastern capital. But the sultan's ambitions had still not been satisfied.

Abu al-Hasan next turned his attention to the Hafsid dynasty in Ifriqiya (modern Tunisia). The Hafsids had long claimed to be the true heirs of the Almohads, maintaining their allegiance to the teachings of the Almohad founder, Ibn Tumart. The Marinids had long coveted Hafsid religious legitimacy, to the point that early Marinid sultans sought to obtain this legitimacy by professing allegiance to the Hafsid sultans in Tunis. Abu al-Hasan attempted to achieve the same thing through marriage alliances with the Hafsids. He first married the sister of the Hafsid ruler, Abu Bakr, but she was killed in the military disaster on the Salado River. In 1346 Abu al-Hasan sought another marriage alliance with the Hafsids, this time agreeing to marry Abu Bakr's daughter. However, Abu Bakr died in October 1346 while his daughter was en route to join Abu al-Hasan in Tlemcen. A succession crisis followed, in which Abu Bakr's son killed the designated heir, Abu al-Abbas.

At the same time Abu al-Hasan was meeting with Abu Bakr's former chamberlain, Muhammad 'Abdullah ibn Tafrajin, who convinced the Marinid sultan that the time was ripe for him to lay claim to the Hafsid domains. Riding eastward with his army Abu al-Hasan received the submission of one Tunisian town after another. In late 1347 he arrived in Tunis, which submitted to his authority, after which he rode to the south to secure the ancient cities of Qayrawan and Mahdiyya. Everything seemed to be falling into place for the Marinid sultan to finally reunite the Maghreb under his authority.

However, as it turned out, Abu al-Hasan had dangerously overextended himself and there was more opposition to his rule than had appeared at first. Soon the Arabian tribes in the Tunisian countryside rebelled against the Marinids, even as the Hafsid elite, who had first recognized Abu al-Hasan's authority, abandoned him in the cities. Before long most of Tunisia and eastern Algeria were in open rebellion.

Circumstances went from bad to worse for Abu al-Hasan. Back in Tlemcen, his son Abu 'Inan heard about the rebellion in Tunisia. Assuming that his father had been killed and wanting to get a jump on competitors for the sultanate, Abu 'Inan declared himself to be sultan over Marinid domains in summer 1348. Raising an army Abu 'Inan defeated his nephew Mansur, the governor of Fez, in a battle outside Taza, after which the remaining cities of Morocco offered their submission to him. When this news reached Abu al-Hasan in Tunis, he left the eastern Maghreb by sea at the end of 1349, bound for Morocco, where he hoped to reclaim his authority. But it was too late. His army was defeated outside Tlemcen by the Zayyanids, who had reclaimed the city following Abu 'Inan's departure. Shortly thereafter Abu al-Hasan was turned away from Marrakech by an army led by Abu 'Inan. Taking refuge in the High Atlas among the Hintata Berbers, Abu al-Hasan ended his life in disgrace in May 1351.

Although earlier Marinid sultans had overestimated their ability to establish a broader empire, none miscalculated quite so disastrously as Abu al-Hasan. During long absences from Morocco on his frequent campaigns, the sultan lost the support of his own society. The siren song of renewing the old Almohad Empire led to his ultimate downfall. Unable to see the infeasibility of such a project, the sultan succumbed to his natural aggressive and ambitious impulses. Although he seemed to obtain his objective, it proved to be an ephemeral empire, which held together for less than a year. In the end Abu al-Hasan lost even those domains where his rule was more substantial. In pursuit of a great empire, he lost everything.

[*See also* Abu 'Inan Faris; *and* Ibn Tumart, Muhammad.]

BIBLIOGRAPHY

Ibn al-Ahmar, Abu al-Walid. *Rawdat al Nisrîn*. French translation *Histoire des Benî Marîn, rois de Fâs intitulée Rawdat al Nisrîn (Le Jardin des Églantines)*. Edited and annotated translation by Ghaoutsi Bouali and Georges Marçais. Paris: Ernest Leroux, 1917.

Ibn Khaldun, 'Abd al-Rahman. *Kitab al-'Ibar*. French translation *Histoire des Berbères et des dynasties musulmanes de l'Afrique septentrionale*, new ed., 4 vols. Translation by Baron de Slane. Paris: Casanova, 1968–1969.

Ibn Marzuq, Muhammad ibn Ahmad. *Al Musnad*. Spanish translation *El Musnad: hechos memorables de Abu l-Hasan, sultán de los benimerines*. Edited and translated by María J. Viguera. Madrid: Instituto Hispano-Arabe de Cultura, 1977.

Shatzmiller, Maya. *The Berbers and the Islamic State: The Marinid Experience in Pre-Protectorate Morocco*. Princeton, N.J.: Markus Weiner, 2000.

STEPHEN CORY

Abu al-Qasim (c. 798–c. 871), Egyptian author and historian, was born in Cairo. A famed historian and writer of the *Futuh Misr*, or the *Conquest of Egypt*, the oldest preserved work on the subject, Abu al-Qasim 'Abd al Rahman bin 'Abd Allah Ibn 'Abd al-Hakam is also known for his description of the Muslim conquest of North Africa and Iberia. Abu al-Qasim was a member of a prominent Egyptian family of legal scholars. His father, 'Abd Allah, wrote a refutation of al-Shafi'i, the famed founder of the Shafi'i school of Islamic law, and was brought to Baghdad to swear to the createdness of the Qur'an. He refused and was sent back to Egypt by the caliph al-Ma'mun. Indeed, despite their wealth and initial prominence, the 'Abd al-Hakam family was often persecuted for standing up for their principles, especially for the preservation of traditional Maliki law, an early version of Islamic law. In 851 they were fined around 1.5 million dinars on trumped-up charges by officials unhappy with their independent stance on legal matters.

Although he wrote as a legal scholar, not strictly as a historian, his narrative style was lively and full of colorful anecdotes. His history of the conquest of Spain is especially famous for its accounts of cannibalism on the island of Umm Hakim and of secret doors and golden tables. Writing as much through analogy and anecdote as through straight chronology, he weaved legends into his narrative that seemed to confirm the inevitability of Islamic conquest, an inevitability willed by God. The story of the door of many padlocks is often cited.

> There was a house in Andalus, the door of which was secured with padlocks, and on which every new king of the country placed a padlock of his own, until the accession to power of the king against whom the Muslims marched. They therefore begged him [the Christian King] to put a padlock on it. . . . But he refused saying, I will place nothing on it, until I shall have known what is in . . . but behold inside were portraits of the Arabs, a letter in which it was written, "when this door shall be opened, these people will invade this country."

Abu al-Qasim also wrote important information about the early topography of Fustat, the city that would become the core of Cairo, and issues related to the early finances of Islamic Egypt. He was especially vehement in his defense of Coptic Christians, whom he said should be protected at all times as members of the People of the Book, who were to be respected under Islam. He died around 871 and was buried near his father's tomb in Fustat.

[*See also* Ma'mun.]

BIBLIOGRAPHY

Al-Kindi. *The Governors and Judges of Egypt*. Edited by R. Guest. Leiden, Netherlands: Brill; London: Luzac, 1912.

Brockopp, Jonathan. *Early Maliki Law: Ibn 'Abd al Hakam and His Major Compendium of Jurisprudence*. Leiden, Netherlands: Brill, 2000.

Ibn 'Abd al-Hakam. *The History of the Conquest of Spain*. Translated by John H. Jones. New York: Burt Franklin, 1969.

Kennedy, Hugh. *Muslim Spain and Portugal: A Political History of Al-Andalus*. London: Longman, 1997.

ALLEN FROMHERZ

Abu Bakr al-Maliki (d. 1081 or 1097), Tunisian historian, was born in the city of al-Qayrawan to a father trained as a scholar of Islamic law and hadith. His full name was Abu Bakr 'Abd Allah bin Muhammad al-Maliki. Al-Maliki's father was a historian in his own right, and he is known to have authored a hagiography of the renowned Tunisian jurist Abu al-Hasan al-Qabisi (d. 1012). Al-Maliki received his early education in al-Qayrawan under several influential figures, including Abu Bakr ibn 'Abd al-Rahman (d. 1040 or 1043) and Muhammad bin 'Abbas al-Ansari (d. 1036). He also appears to have spent a brief period in Sicily studying with several scholars there.

Upon his return to al-Qayrawan, al-Maliki embarked on a career teaching the various branches of the Islamic sciences. Among his pupils was the important jurist Abu 'Abd Allah al-Mazari (d. 1141), who cites al-Maliki affectionately in one of his extant legal opinions. Al-Maliki elected to remain in al-Qayrawan following the destruction of that city by Bedouin tribesmen in 1057, choosing not to join the exodus of the city's scholarly community to the coastal city of Mahdia. He is best known as a historian, and his biographical account of the Maliki scholars of al-Qayrawan remains an important source for our understanding of the growth and dissemination of the Maliki school of Islamic jurisprudence in the region of Ifriqiya. The work, entitled *Riyad al-nufus* (The Meadow of Souls), contains biographical notices of some 275 scholars and men of religion active in the region of Ifriqiya from the time of the early Islamic conquests until the eve of the ruinous Bedouin invasions of the mid-eleventh century. Many of the biographical sketches al-Maliki included in the *Riyad* are remarkably detailed, and they have allowed modern observers to reconstruct the social and intellectual history of Islamic North Africa in its formative period, particularly that of al-Qayrawan and its environs, to a notable degree.

The title al-Maliki chose for the work is significant, and it conveys well the unmistakable tone of nostalgia that suffuses the various entries. Al-Maliki witnessed a number of dramatic reversals to Islam in the western Mediterranean during his lifetime, gravest of which were the aforementioned sack of al-Qayrawan and the Norman conquest of Muslim Sicily; it is likely that his motivation in composing the *Riyad* issued from a desire to preserve from oblivion the intellectual and religious heritage of a region that appeared increasingly under threat, both internally and externally, in the final decades of the eleventh century.

Al-Maliki's *Riyad* served as an important source for later Muslim historians, and it appears that al-Qadi 'Iyad al-Sabti (d. 1149) drew heavily from it as he composed his biographical account of Muslim scholars. Another figure of note who relied on al-Maliki's work is the Andalusian jurist Abu Bakr al-Turtushi, who made use of the work while writing his treatise on heretical innovations in Islam.

[*See also* Abu Bakr ibn 'Abd al-Rahman al-Khalwani; Mazari, Abu 'Abd Allah Muhammad al-; *and* Turtushi, Abu Bakr Muhammad al-.]

BIBLIOGRAPHY

Abu Bakr al-Maliki. *Kitab riyad al-nufus fi tabaqat 'ulama' al-Qayrawan wa Ifriqiya*, edited by Bashir al-Bakkush. Beirut: Dar al-Gharb al-Islami, 1994.

Rosenthal, Franz. *A History of Muslim Historiography*. Leiden: Brill, 1968.

RUSSELL HOPLEY

Abu Bakr ibn 'Abd al-Rahman al-Khalwani

(d. 1040 or 1043), Islamic jurist, born to an Arab family with origins in the region of Jazira Sharik (present-day Cap Bon, Tunisia). A close companion and later rival of the North African jurist Abu 'Imran al-Fasi (d. 1039), Abu Bakr ibn 'Abd al-Rahman was fortunate to receive his early education in al-Qayrawan under two eminent scholars of Islamic law, Ibn Abi Zayd al-Qayrawani (d. 996) and Abu al-Hasan al-Qabisi (d. 1012). Abu Bakr was considered to be among the most talented of al-Qabisi's many pupils, and it was under his tutelage that Abu Bakr learned

to compose Islamic legal opinions, otherwise known as fatwas. He subsequently embarked on the journey eastward in 987, both to undertake the pilgrimage to Mecca and to further his education with established scholars in the cultural capitals of the Islamic east. Abu Bakr is reported to have spent time in Egypt during his sojourn in the east, and it was in the rarefied intellectual milieu of Cairo that he came into contact with two figures of note, Abu Bakr Muhammad al-Na'ali (d. 990) and Abu al-Qasim 'Abd al-Rahman al-Ghafiqi al-Jawhari (d. 995).

Following the completion of his studies in the east, Abu Bakr returned to al-Qayrawan and took to teaching the various branches of Islamic jurisprudence. The list of pupils he trained over the next four decades is extensive and includes Abu Bakr al-Maliki (d. c. 1080), a figure who would subsequently compose an important biographical history of the jurists of al-Qayrawan. It would appear that Abu Bakr ibn 'Abd al-Rahman, along with Abu 'Imran al-Fasi, largely oversaw the legal training of an entire generation of North African jurists in the first half of the eleventh century. Their influence was not limited to the dissemination of Islamic law in North Africa, however. Students traveled to al-Qayrawan from as far afield as Andalusia, Sicily, and the *bilad al-Sudan* to attend lectures given by Abu Bakr and Abu 'Imran in the various fields of Islamic law. Moreover, Abu Bakr was frequently consulted by Andalusian jurists as they sought to formulate rulings on a host of issues. Among these jurists of Muslim Spain, one finds mention of Ibn Sahl, an important mufti from Granada, and Abu 'Abd Allah al-Baji, a jurist from Seville. It is with these two figures and their frequent consultation with Abu Bakr on legal matters of considerable import that one can discern the influence that North African Malikism brought to bear on the development of Islamic legal practice in Andalusia. Such reliance also points to the formation of a common legal culture in these highly disparate regions of the Islamic west, largely under the guidance of several prominent jurists from al-Qayrawan, Abu Bakr foremost among them.

Abu Bakr played a significant role in the consolidation of a distinctly North African school of Maliki jurisprudence centered in the metropolis of al-Qayrawan. The foundations for such a school had been set in place during the previous generation by the aforementioned Ibn Abi Zayd al-Qayrawani and Abu al-Hasan al-Qabisi and, before them, by Sahnun al-Tanukhi (d. 855). That Sahnun studied in Egypt with Ibn al-Qasim

(d. 807), a pupil of Malik ibn Anas, the eponymous founder of the Maliki school of Islamic jurisprudence, establishes a firm chain of transmission between the legal practice of Medina during the time of the Prophet and its articulation in Ifriqiya during the era of Abu Bakr ibn 'Abd al-Rahman some four centuries later. The destruction of al-Qayrawan at the hands of Bedouin tribesmen of the Banu Hilal in the decade following Abu Bakr's death would not bring an end to this development. Rather, the flight of several jurists from al-Qayrawan to the coastal city of Mahdia in the latter half of the eleventh century effectively preserved the Ifriqiyan branch of Malikism; indeed, under the aegis of a number of distinguished legal scholars, al-Imam al-Mazari (d. 1141) most notably, Malikism in Ifriqiya was effectively restored to its earlier prominence, albeit in the coastal setting of Mahdia.

The Maliki school of Islamic jurisprudence in North Africa was thus confronted with a number of distinct challenges in the period following the death of Abu Bakr ibn 'Abd al-Rahman, the gravest of these being the aforementioned sack of al-Qayrawan in the mid-eleventh century. The second such challenge came with the growth in the early twelfth century of the messianic doctrine of the Mahdi Ibn Tumart, founder of the Almohad state; the tension between Almohad messianism and orthodox Malikism would culminate at the end of the twelfth century with the public burning of Sahnun's *Mudawwana*, an important compendium of Maliki jurisprudence, during the reign of the Almohad caliph Abu Yusuf (r. 1184–1199).

Abu Bakr appears to have had a somewhat strained relationship with the political authorities of his day, most notably with the Zirid sovereign al-Mu'izz ibn Badis (d. 1062). Indeed, several remarks made by Abu Bakr cast al-Mu'izz in a decidedly unflattering light. He publicly criticized the Zirid ruler for allowing Fatimid coinage to circulate freely in Ifriqiya following the departure of this latter dynasty for Egypt in 972. The use of the Fatimid regnal insignia and implements at the Zirid court in al-Qayrawan likewise drew the opprobrium of Abu Bakr. Accounts of this nature occur with some frequency in the biographies of Abu Bakr, and they appear designed to emphasize the role he played in overseeing the eradication of Shi'ism from North Africa during the early eleventh century. The frequent criticism he directed at the Zirids for their close association with the Fatimids very possibly prompted al-Mu'izz ibn Badis to make a decisive break with the rulers of Egypt, a move that marked the triumph of orthodox Sunni Islam in Ifriqiya.

As is well known, however, the Fatimid response to this rupture was disastrous for the Zirids and the city of al-Qayrawan, both of which suffered considerably at the hands of the Bedouin tribesmen unleashed on Ifriqiya by the Fatimids.

Abu Bakr ibn 'Abd al-Rahman died in 1040 or 1043 and was buried alongside his father at the cemetery of Bab Tunis in al-Qayrawan. A large mosque bearing his name was subsequently erected in the Granadan quarter of that city.

[*See also* Abu Bakr al-Maliki; Fasi, Abu 'Imran al-; Ibn Abi Zayd al-Qayrawani; Qabisi, 'Ali ibn Muhammad al-; Sahnun, Abu Said al-Tanukhi; *and* Tamim ibn al-Mu'izz ibn Badis.]

BIBLIOGRAPHY

Bekir, Ahmed. *Histoire de l'École malikite en Orient jusqu'à la fin du moyen age*. Tunis: Imprimérie de l'U.G.T.T., 1962.

Idris, Hady Roger. "Deux maîtres de l'école juridique kairouanaise sous les Zîrîdes (XIe siècle): Abû Bakr b. 'Abd al-Rahman et Abu 'Imran al-Fasi." *Annales de l'Institut d'Etudes Orientales* 13 (1955): 30–60.

Talbi, Mohamed. *L'Émirat aghlabide, 184–296/800–909, histoire politique*. Paris: Librarie d'Amérique et d'Orient, 1966.

RUSSELL HOPLEY

Abu Bakr ibn 'Umar (d. 1087), chief of the West African Lamtuna, one of the Sanhaja Berber peoples, and leader of the Almoravid movement that eventually conquered Morocco, western Algeria, and Islamic Spain in the north and Mauritania and portions of Mali in the south. Although he became leader of the Almoravids following the death of the movement's founder, 'Abdallah ibn Yasin, in 1059, his notoriety was surpassed by that of his cousin, Yusuf ibn Tashfin. Yusuf would lead the Almoravids to multiple conquests in the north, while Abu Bakr remained with his Sanhaja warriors in the south, where he continued to lead jihad against the infidels of sub-Saharan West Africa. His accomplishments included defeating the kingdom of Ghana, but he was never able to establish full Almoravid control in the region. Abu Bakr ibn 'Umar was killed in battle in 1087, after which Almoravid authority in the south rapidly disintegrated.

The Almoravid movement arose among the Sanhaja of the northern Sahara after one of their chiefs (Yahya ibn Ibrahim of the Juddala group) made the pilgrimage to Mecca in 1035–1036. While on pilgrimage, Ibn Ibrahim became aware of the vast differences between orthodox Islam, which he encountered in the holy lands, and the folk Islam practiced by his own people in the desert. For this reason, the Juddala chief sought a teacher who would come back with him and instruct the Sanhaja in proper Islamic practices. He eventually met Ibn Yasin, who had been referred to him by a holy man in the Sus valley and was himself a member of the Jazula group of the southern Sahara. Ibn Yasin agreed to accompany Ibn Ibrahim back to the desert, where he undertook to train the Sanhaja in orthodox Islam, beginning in 1039 or 1040.

Ibn Yasin's mission had its successes and failures. Upon his arrival among the Sanhaja, the holy man established an outpost (ribat) for training tribal warriors in their Islamic duties and establishing an army to spread God's rule through jihad. Thus, his followers became known as "the people of the ribat" (al-murabitun, or Almoravids). Many of the Juddala initially responded to his message, and they formed a tribal army that began to conquer their neighbors in the name of Islam. However, others chafed at the harsh methods used by Ibn Yasin to instill orthodox Islam. Upon the death of Ibn Ibrahim, the Juddala rebelled against Ibn Yasin, and he had to run for his life. Nevertheless, Ibn Yasin soon obtained a second chance to establish his movement when he was invited to take up residence among the Lamtuna by their chief, Yahya ibn 'Umar, and his brother, Abu Bakr ibn 'Umar.

Ibn Yasin experienced great success through his new alliance with the Lamtuna. In 1042 they began their conquest of the main Sanhaja groups, including the Juddala and the Massufa. Ibn Yasin determined to take control of the Saharan caravan trade, which motivated his conquests of Sijilmasa (the northern terminus of the trans-Saharan trade route) and Awdaghust (the southern terminus). Following this accomplishment, the Almoravids began to target southern Morocco, particularly the Sus valley. In every place they conquered, the Almoravids implemented their own harsh interpretation of Maliki Islamic law.

However, trouble arose again when the Juddala rebelled for a second time, following the Almoravid conquest of Awdaghust. In the ensuing battle (1056), Yahya ibn 'Umar was killed, leaving leadership of the Lamtuna to his brother Abu Bakr. Yet the Almoravid conquests continued. Under Abu Bakr's leadership, the Almoravids conquered the heterodox tribes of southern Morocco (Dar'a and Sus valleys) between 1057 and 1059. In 1059 Ibn Yasin was killed while fighting the Barghawata, a group

that seems to have combined Christian and Muslim teachings to form its own religious sect. The death of Ibn Yasin left Abu Bakr ibn 'Umar as the undisputed leader of the Almoravid movement.

However, Abu Bakr's leadership would not remain unchallenged for long. Concerned about disturbances among the Sanhaja in their homeland, Abu Bakr returned to the Sahara to restore order. He left his cousin Yusuf ibn Tashfin in charge of continuing the Almoravid advance in the north. The sources disagree as to whether Abu Bakr's departure took place in 1061 or in 1071. At any rate, it seems to have taken him a couple of years to reestablish his authority in the central Sanhaja domains. However, upon his return to Morocco, Abu Bakr discovered that his cousin had usurped his authority, apparently upon the instigation of Ibn Tashfin's wife, Zaynab, who was herself a former wife of Abu Bakr.

Faced with another crisis, Abu Bakr decided to take the path of peace rather than risk splitting the Almoravid movement again. He delegated authority in the north to Ibn Tashfin, telling his cousin that he preferred to live in the desert in the central Sanhaja lands. Thus, the two parted company on a cordial basis, after which Ibn Tashfin launched a series of conquests that would lead to the establishment of the city of Marrakech as the northern Almoravid capital and would eventually extend Almoravid domains all the way into southern Spain. All these accomplishments were undertaken while Ibn Tashfin was technically the deputy of Abu Bakr ibn 'Umar, the senior chief of the Lamtuna and the one who had been personally appointed by Ibn Yasin.

Meanwhile, Abu Bakr continued his conquests in the south, making his capital in the desert town of Azukki. He appears to have won a number of battles against sub-Saharan tribes, with his greatest victory taking place when he defeated Ghana, site of a formerly great West African empire. Yet, Abu Bakr's southern conquests would not long survive his own death in 1087, which was ironically the year of Ibn Tashfin's triumph in Spain. Although the northern Almoravid Empire would prosper for several more generations, its holdings in the south were quickly lost as divisions among the Lamtuna contributed to the breakup of the southern empire.

[See also Yusuf ibn Tashfin, Abu Ya'qub.]

BIBLIOGRAPHY

Farias, P. F. Moraes. "The Almoravids: Some Questions Concerning the Character of the Movement during Its Periods of Closest Contact with the Western Sudan."

Bulletin de l'Institut Français d'Afrique Noire 24, ser. B, nos. 3–4 (1967): 794–878.

Hopkins, J. F. P., trans. "Al-Bakri," "Ibn al-Athir," "Ibn Khallikan," "Ibn Idhari," "Ibn Abi Zar," "Al-Hulal al-Mawshiyya," and "Ibn Khaldun." In *Corpus of Early Arabic Sources for West African History*, edited by Nehemia Levtzion and J. F. P. Hopkins, pp. 62–87, 157–166, 216–232, 234–248, 309–342. Princeton, N.J.: Markus Wiener, 2000.

Levtzion, Nehemia. "Abd Allah b. Yasin and the Almoravids." In *The Cultivators of Islam*, edited by John Ralph Willis. Studies in West African Islamic History, vol. 1, pp. 78–112. London: Frank Cass, 1979.

Miranda, A. H. "La salida de los Almorávides del Desierto y el reinado de Yusuf b. Tashfin." *Hespéris* 3–4 (1959): 155–182.

STEPHEN CORY

Abu 'Inan Faris (1329–1358), eleventh sultan of the Moroccan Marinid dynasty, claimed the sultanate by rebelling against his father, Abu al-Hasan 'Ali, in 1348 while the latter was fighting a rebellion in Tunisia. Reassembling his forces in Algiers, Abu al-Hasan faced off against a larger army led by Abu 'Inan in 1349. Following a crushing defeat, Abu al-Hasan retreated to the desert town of Sijilmasa, where he was welcomed by the tribal leader Ouenzemmar. But his ally soon abandoned him when Abu 'Inan's troops descended upon Sijilmasa, so Abu al-Hasan fled to Marrakech. There, he recruited supporters from among Masmouda Berbers and local Arabs. In May 1350 the army of Abu al-Hasan battled the forces of Abu 'Inan near the Umm al-Rabia River, where Abu 'Inan was again victorious. After being rescued by one of his soldiers, Abu al-Hasan was provided refuge among the Hintata peoples of the High Atlas Mountains. Pursued by Abu 'Inan, the aged sultan abdicated his position and was allowed to stay with the Hintata, where he died on 24 May 1351.

Abu 'Inan was now the unchallenged ruler of Morocco. His first task was to recover the lands of the eastern Maghreb that his father had lost. To start out, Abu 'Inan launched a siege of Tlemcen in 1352. Within a few months, the Marinid army had routed and scattered the Zayyanid troops, capturing their sultan. Shortly afterward Abu 'Inan triumphantly entered the city. But, like his father, the new sultan would not be satisfied with Tlemcen alone. In rapid succession his armies conquered the other towns of the central Maghreb, including Chelif, Medea, and Bougie. Once he appointed governors for these cities, Abu 'Inan returned to Tlemcen to celebrate the end of the fast of Ramadan.

But these conquests would not be as easy as they first seemed. Shortly after leaving Bougie, the Marinid sultan would face a revolt led by Sanhaja Berbers. Although he quickly regained the city, Abu 'Inan had to arrest more than two hundred suspects from among the populace, along with a number of Berber chiefs, to restore order. Further trouble arose through the instigation of Abu 'Inan's brother Abu al-Fadl, who was plotting rebellion among the Masmouda in southern Morocco. But the sultan was able to convince his brother's protectors to surrender the fugitive in 1354, after which he had Abu al-Fadl strangled in prison. In 1355 Abu 'Inan faced a rebellion by his brother Eicha, who had been granted authority over Marinid possessions in southern Spain during the reign of Abu al-Hasan. But when Eicha's closest adviser backed the sultan and Abu 'Inan's fleet arrived in Gibraltar, the rebel prince was arrested along with his son. Both were consigned to prison for several months, only to be brutally executed following the Feast of the Sacrifice.

Despite these troubles, Abu 'Inan remained intent upon uniting the Maghreb under Marinid authority. In 1356 the city of Constantine submitted to the Marinid sultan following the arrival of a large army with siege engines outside its walls. However, the Marinid governor, Abu al-'Abbas, soon led the city in rebellion, issuing a declaration of independence from Abu 'Inan. During the following year, Abu 'Inan and his army left Fez with great pomp, intending to recapture the cities of the central Maghreb and carry out the long-awaited conquest of Ifriqiya (Tunisia). Ibn Khaldun describes these troops as a "powerful army that marched with flags deployed and whose feet shook the earth [so that] the inhabitants, filled with fear, abandoned their sultan and threw themselves down before the Marinid sovereign, offering their submission" (Ibn Khaldun, 1968–1969, pp. 4, 313). The rebel Abu al-'Abbas was arrested and sent off in chains to a prison in Ceuta.

Abu 'Inan's plan to conquer Tunis involved the use of his fleet, from which he intended to besiege the city by sea. In late summer of 1357 the forces of the Marinid sultan took the city and proclaimed the sovereignty of Abu 'Inan. But the Marinids soon faced a rebellion led by Arab tribes, who did not want to pay tribute to Abu 'Inan. With the aid of a local chief, the Marinid army put down the tribal resistance, extending its authority into the desert.

Although the sultan's expedition seemed to have achieved success, it became necessary for the army to return to Fez because of a shortage of supplies, which had been exhausted during the long campaign. In addition, Abu 'Inan had been informed of a planned coup in Morocco, the goal of which was to replace him with another pretender. Thus, the sultan and his army returned home in November 1357, after which he imprisoned his vizier, Faris Ibn Maimun, whom he suspected of complicity with the rebels. A few days later he had the vizier executed, and he also rounded up and punished a number of Marinid chiefs who were involved in the plot. But this rapid retreat came at a price. The Marinid garrisons in Tunisia were soon besieged by rebels and the Marinid troops were finally forced to retreat back to Morocco.

Abu 'Inan resolved to launch another expedition the following year. In spring 1358 he prepared and dispatched his army under the command of Sulayman ibn Dawud, governor of the Marinid possessions in Spain. In addition, he assigned the governor of Zab, along with his troops, to join Ibn Dawud in putting down the rebellion in Tunisia. However, the armies would be drawn back to Morocco by the sudden illness and death of the sultan on 5 December 1358. As Abu 'Inan lay ill, a power struggle within the court ultimately led to the defeat of the heir apparent, Abu Zayyan, in favor of the five-year-old prince al-Sa'id. This prince's protector, the vizier al-Fududi, then had Abu 'Inan strangled in his bed. Like his father, Abu 'Inan had spent the majority of his reign seeking to establish Marinid dominion throughout the Maghreb, and, like his father, his plans were ultimately doomed to failure.

[*See also* Ibn Khaldun.]

BIBLIOGRAPHY

Basset, H., and E. Lévi-Provençal. "Chella, une nécropole mérinide." *Hespéris* 2 (1922): 1–92, 255–316.

Ibn al-Ahmar, Abu al-Walid. *Rawdat al Nisrîn.* French translation *Histoire des Benî Marîn, rois de Fâs intitulée Rawdat al Nisrîn (Le Jardin des Églantines).* Edited and annotated translation by Ghaoutsi Bouali and Georges Marçais. Paris: Ernest Leroux, 1917.

Ibn Khaldun, 'Abd al-Rahman. *Kitab al-'Ibar.* French translation *Histoire des Berbères et des dynasties musulmanes de l'Afrique septentrionale,* new ed., 4 vols. Translation by Baron de Slane. Paris: Casanova, 1968–1969.

Shatzmiller, Maya. *The Berbers and the Islamic State: The Marinid Experience in Pre-Protectorate Morocco.* Princeton, N.J.: Markus Weiner, 2000.

STEPHEN CORY

Abu Kamil Shuja (850–930), Egyptian Muslim mathematician, also known as al-Hasib al-Misri, the Egyptian Calculator (or Reckoner). His full name was Abu Kamil Shuja' ibn Aslam ibn Muhammad ibn Shuja. Very few biographical details are known concerning Abu Kamil, but his productive peak appears to have been at the end of the ninth century. The year of his birth and the year of his death are known with a decent degree of certainty as he is known to have died before al-Imrani (who died in 955) but to have lived well beyond al-Khwarizmi (who died in 850). A direct successor in the development of algebra to al-Khwarizmi, his texts on algebraic theory helped to form the groundwork for later mathematicians, including al-Karaji. Fibonacci would later adopt his mathematical techniques.

Abu Kamil worked to perfect many of al-Khwarizmi's algebraic methods, including work with the multiplication and division of algebraic objects and the addition and subtraction of exponential and radical objects. Abu Kamil was also the first known author to have treated irrational numbers as algebraic objects. He was also the first to accept that irrational numbers—such as cube roots, square roots, and fourth roots—could be solutions to quadratic equations. He also was the first to treat irrational numbers as possible coefficients in an equation. His works contain the earliest known example of the techniques used to solve three nonlinear simultaneous equations with three unknown variables.

Abu Kamil is known primarily for his works in algebraic and numerical theories, of which three of the surviving texts are known to have formed important foundations in the development of algebraic systems: *Algebra, On Measurement and Geometry,* and *Book of Rare Things in the Art of Calculation.* Other texts have survived as well, including works on linear equations, combinatorics, and other algebraic fundamentals.

The first of these texts, *Algebra* (or *Book on Algebra*), focuses on the application of algebraic methods to geometrical problems. Its techniques appear to draw heavily from methods developed by previous Greek and Babylonian mathematicians, combined with al-Khwarizmi's methods. This text makes the important leap of developing the ability to work with exponential powers of an unknown variable higher than that of the square. Although no notation is developed, the text clearly deals with exponential powers of a variable of cubes or higher, up to the power of eight. The work survives in a single, but nearly pristine, manuscript. However, it has been commented upon several times and influenced a great deal of early Spanish mathematical texts, particularly Johannes Hispalensis's *Liber mahemeleth*, which is an extension of the first two sections of the text.

The second of these texts, *On Measurement and Geometry* (also given as *Book on Surveying and Geometry*), is not a text designed for mathematicians but instead is intended for land surveyors. It presents a number of rules for solving various geometrical problems that a surveyor may encounter. A number of these rules are quite complicated, but each is illustrated with a numerical example of the rule, worked through.

The third of these texts, the *Book of Rare Things in the Art of Calculation*, is concerned with solutions to indeterminate equations. This text represents the first known case of indeterminate equations of the types found in Diophantus's works being solved by an Arabic mathematician. This is particularly interesting as, assuming the dates given for the time of Abu Kamil's work are correct, he wrote before Diophantus's *Arithmetica* had been studied in depth in this part of the Arabic world. This likely means that the solutions Abu Kamil develops within this text were independently created and not sourced from Diophantus's works. Moreover, Abu Kamil includes a number of methods for dealing with such intermediate equations that are not found in any of the known books of the *Arithmetica*. His work in this text appears to have inspired research into real numbers, solutions to polynomials, and the finding of roots by al-Karaji and Ibn Yahya al-Maghribi al-Samaw'al.

A number of smaller works, each dealing with a particular type or application of algebraic methodology, also survive. The *Book of the Birds* deals with a set of example problems focused around the purchase of different types of birds and the various combinations of purchases made based on given amounts spent or quantity purchased. Another such work, *Estate Sharing Using Unknowns* (also *Estate Sharing Using Algebra*), focuses on using algebraic methods to solve issues of inheritance, based on the requirements of Muslim law and the opinions of select jurists. It is also believed that there existed a number of other works that did

not survive, including one text on the rule of false position.

BIBLIOGRAPHY

Levey, Martin. "Abu Kamil Shuja' Ibn Aslam Ibn Muhammad Ibn Shuja." In *Dictionary of Scientific Biography*, edited by Charles Coulston Gillispie, pp. 30–32. New York: Charles Scribner's Sons, 1970.

Levey, Martin. *The Algebra of Abu Kamil*. Madison: University of Wisconsin Press, 1966. Edition of the Hebrew translation of part A.

Sesiano, Jacques. "Abu Kamil Shuja." In *Encyclopaedia of the History of Science, Technology, and Medicine in Non-Western Cultures*, edited by Helaine Selin. Dordrecht, Netherlands: Kluwer Academic, 1997.

Sesiano, Jacques. "Islamic Mathematics." In *Mathematics across Cultures: The History of Non-Western Mathematics*, edited by Helaine Selin. Dordrecht, Netherlands: Kluwer Academic, 2000.

NESS CREIGHTON

Abu Madyan (1115–1198), Sufi leader who has been referred to as "the Junayd of the West," played an important role in the early development of Sufism within North Africa. One of his disciples, 'Abd al-Salam ibn Mashish, was later the spiritual master for Abu al-Hasan al-Shadili, founder of one of the most influential North African Sufi movements.

Abu Madyan was born in the town of Cantillana, near Seville in Muslim Spain. He lost his parents early in life and was raised by his older brothers, who regularly mistreated him. The Moroccan biographer al-Tadili (d. 1229/30) included biographical comments from Abu Madyan's writings, such as the shaykh's explanation of how he finally escaped from the control of his brothers. Abu Madyan relates that he fled from his home only to be captured by a brother who intended to kill him because of his many escape attempts. His brother attacked him with a sword, and Abu Madyan could defend himself with only a piece of wood. However, when the brother hit the piece of wood, his sword shattered into small bits. Visibly shaken by this, Abu Madyan's first recorded miracle, the brother allowed him to leave.

Finally free, Abu Madyan wandered for several months around southern Spain, in search of knowledge. This thirst for knowledge eventually sent him across the Strait of Gibraltar. After working for a time with fishermen in Sabta (modern Ceuta),

Abu Madyan made his way to Marrakech, where he served for a while in a mercenary army defending the Almoravid capital. He finally left for Fez, after being told that it was the best place in the country to learn about religion. In that city, he studied under some of the most prestigious local shaykhs, including the Berber holy man 'Ali ibn Hirzihim (better known as Sidi Harazim), at whose *zawiya* he stayed for several years. There he met a number of important shaykhs from both Andalusia and the Maghreb (North Africa). He also developed a strong ascetic ethic and would frequently retreat into the ruins of an old mosque near Fez in order to meditate in seclusion. Under the influence of Ibn Hirzihim and Abu al-Hasan ibn Ghalib, Abu Madyan established himself as an "orthodox," or *shar'i*, mystic (i.e., one who placed an emphasis upon keeping his practices in line with the teachings of sharia law). His example would later be critical in the establishment of Sufi orders that maintained this emphasis, as opposed to more radical orders that deviated extensively from sharia-mandated behavior. This is why Abu Madyan has been referred to as "the Junayd of the West," since al-Junayd ibn Muhammad (d. 910) played a similar role in the eastern Islamic world.

While still based in Fez Abu Madyan traveled to visit shaykhs in other parts of Morocco. One of these was Abu Ya'za Yalannur ibn Maymun al-Dukkali (d. 1177), who had a *zawiya* in the Middle Atlas Mountains where Abu Madyan stayed for a short time. Though Abu Ya'za was illiterate and spoke only Berber languages, Abu Madyan seems to have been impressed with his spiritual power (*baraka*) and insight. Some accounts indicate that Abu Madyan also made the pilgrimage to Mecca, where he studied under the famous shaykh 'Abd al-Qadir al-Jilani. Professor Vincent Cornell doubts that this meeting ever took place but thinks it more likely that Abu Madyan could have met Ahmad al-Rifa'i (founder of the Rifaiyya Sufi order) while in the east. Among earlier eastern shaykhs who influenced Abu Madyan was al-Ghazali, whose works he studied intensively while in Fez and whose combination of sharia knowledge and mystical experience Abu Madyan seems to have imitated.

Having completed his formal training, Abu Madyan departed from Fez and settled in Bijaya, a fairly large city in western Algeria. Unfortunately, historical sources tell us little about the several decades he spent in this city. Cornell speculates that Abu Madyan may have been attracted to Bijaya because of its regional importance as a center of trade or because there was a sizeable Andalusi community there. Whatever the reasons for its appeal, Abu Madyan established his *zawiya* in Bijaya, attracting students from all over the Islamic world, especially from the Maghreb. To these students, Abu Madyan became known as a shaykh who emphasized teaching, often tailoring his instruction specifically to their needs. An important part of his teaching was his "sessions of admonition," at which inquirers could discuss different doctrinal issues or obtain advice on personal, legal, or political matters.

Cornell argues that Abu Madyan, like Junayd in the east, became a synthesizer of different Sufi traditions and that he formulated a coherent mystical doctrine, the first time this had been done in the Muslim west. He became known as the Spiritual Axis (*qutb*) of his time, and his program of Sufi knowledge and practices would have a profound influence upon shaykhs who came after him. Abu Madyan's branch of Sufism drew from the dominant North African Maliki school of Islamic law, highlighted orthopraxy and piety, and was less metaphysical than the eastern Sufi orders. Abu Madyan especially emphasized ascetic practices, such as extensive fasting, reliance upon God alone, quiescence, and poverty. However, social responsibility was also a key aspect of Abu Madyan's teachings, and he took a stand against abuses carried out by both the Almoravid and the Almohad governments. His message created a following among western Muslims eager to explore new ways of achieving religious certainty during troubled times.

It was within this context of political upheaval that Abu Madyan eventually got into trouble. Fearing that his orthodox influence would steer people away from their own reformist doctrine, the Almohad government called Abu Madyan to appear in Marrakech in 1198, to defend his teachings. However, en route to this meeting, Abu Madyan died outside the city of Tlemcen in western Algeria. Ironically, his shrine is now located in that city, where he had little direct involvement during his lifetime, rather than his beloved Bijaya, where his influence was so dramatically felt.

[*See also* Ibn al-Mashish al-Alami, Moulay Abdasalam; *and* Ibn al-Zayyat al-Tadili.]

BIBLIOGRAPHY

Abun Nasr, Jamil M. *Muslim Communities of Grace: The Sufi Brotherhoods in Islamic*

Religious Life. New York: Columbia University Press, 2007.

Barges, Abbé J. J. L. *Vie de célèbre marabout Cidi Abou-Médien*. Paris: Ernest Leroux, 1884.

Bel, Alfred. "Sidî Bou Medyan et son maître Ed-Daqqaq à Fès." In *Mélanges René Basset*, pp. 31–68. Paris: Editions Ernest Leroux, 1923.

Cornell, Vincent J., ed. and trans. *The Way of Abu Madyan: Doctrinal and Poetic Works of Abu Madyan Shu'ayb ibn al-Husayn al-Ansari (c. 509/1115–6–594/1198)*. Cambridge, UK: Islamic Texts Society, 1996.

STEPHEN CORY

Abu Mahasin Taghribirdi (c. 1409–1470), Egyptian historian, was born in Cairo possibly around the year 1409, three years after the death of his distinguished predecessor Ibn Khaldun. He was the son of a Mamluk. The Mamluk system relied on the recruitment of fresh slave soldiers and usually excluded the sons of Mamluks. Although his father became chief of the Egyptian armies under Sultan al-Faraj and governor of Damascus, Abu Mahasin Taghribirdi did not have the same opportunity to rise to the same levels in government as his father. Although he was welcomed into the Mamluk court and even provided with a fief to maintain his income, he concentrated as much on his writing and study as on the maintenance or expansion of his political powers. He took an active part in the campaigns of Sultan Barsbay, who patronized the work of the historian al-'Ayni. It was customary at the time for histories to be recited orally at court, and it appears that Abu Mahasin was enthralled by the work of al-'Ayni and wished to attempt his own historical writing.

His first major book was a biographical dictionary, an account of the lives of important sultans, scholars, and Mamluks from 1248 to 1451. These biographical dictionaries, called *tabaqat*, were a well-established form that had been popular in Arabic historiography since the first attempts to understand the character of the companions of the Prophet Muhammad. As with *Plutarch's Lives*, these incredibly rich and varied biographical accounts were seen as a means of learning from the experience and leadership of past lives. His next work was a history of Egypt from 641 to the 1450s. He did not claim sole authorship of this work but said it was a collective effort involving himself and his friends.

When the historian al-Maqrizi died, Abu Mahasin Taghribirdi became the most respected historian and chronicler in Mamluk Egypt. He compiled the stories and lives of his contemporaries and wrote about social and economic conditions as well as political concerns. Although he never approached the interpretive mastery of his predecessor Ibn Khaldun or even of his immediate successor al-Maqrizi, his work remains a vital source for understanding the history of fifteenth-century Egypt and Africa.

Like most historians of the period, Taghribirdi also dabbled in other genres, writing a long mystical work of poetry and compiling several literary anthologies. After a fairly long life of writing and study, he finally gathered all his manuscripts in one place—a mosque he had built for himself in Cairo. He died and was buried there, surrounded by his precious papers and writings, in June 1470.

[*See also* Barsbay; Ibn Khaldun; *and* Maqrizi, al-.]

BIBLIOGRAPHY

Abu Mahasin Taghribirdi. *Egypt and Syria under the Circassian Sultans*. Translated by William Popper. New York: AMS Press, 1995.

Philipp, Thomas, and Ulrich Haarmann, eds. *The Mamluks in Egyptian Politics and Society*. Cambridge, UK: Cambridge University Press, 2007.

Raymond, André. *Cairo*. Cambridge, Mass.: Harvard University Press, 2001.

ALLEN FROMHERZ

Abu Muhammad 'Abd al-Haqq I *See* Marinid Dynasty.

Abu Muhammad 'Abd al-Haqq II (1419–1465), thirtieth and final sultan of the Moroccan Marinid dynasty, became titular head of the state at the age of one, after his father, Abu Sa'id Uthman III, was murdered. This development allowed 'Abd al-Haqq's regent, Abu Zakariyya Yahya al-Wattasi, to rule the state in his name. Upon Abu Zakariyya's death in 1448, his nephew, 'Ali ibn Yusuf, took power, once again in the name of 'Abd al-Haqq, whom the Wattasids kept excluded from real authority. Ten years later, in 1458, 'Ali ibn Yusuf al Wattasi died, and Abu Zakariyya's son, Yahya, took over the all-powerful position as 'Abd al-Haqq's regent.

It was at this point that 'Abd al-Haqq rebelled against Wattasid dominance in order to exercise his authority independently. After executing every member of the Wattasid family living in Fez, 'Abd al-Haqq proceeded to punish Fezzi *ulama*, who had countenanced the Wattasid co-optation of power.

His most drastic measure was to remove the tax exemption that the *shurafa'* (descendants of the Prophet Muhammad) as well as the Sufi shaykhs had traditionally enjoyed under Marinid rule. Isolated from most of the local religious establishment and uncertain whom to trust, the sultan appointed several Jews to positions of authority within his administration, including Harun al-Batas as vizier of the state.

'Abd al-Haqq's new tax policies were driven by more than simply the desire for revenge against the *ulama*. His state was in dire need of resources, especially because his actual area of control was limited to the immediate region surrounding Fez. His Wattasid opponent, Muhammad al-Shaykh, was in control of the coastal town of Asila and much of northern Morocco. At the same time, the Portuguese were establishing a string of fortresses along the Moroccan Atlantic coast, while the Castilians eliminated the last Marinid outpost in Spain, taking Gibraltar in 1462. In order to fund an army to fight against these myriad enemies, 'Abd al-Haqq increased taxes within the area under his control. In fact, some historians assert that his appointment of Jews to high office was connected with his desire to ally himself with wealthy Jewish merchant families within North Africa.

However, by alienating the Fezzi religious establishment, 'Abd al-Haqq had exacerbated conditions that would result in his downfall. During the previous several decades, the *shurafa'* had been gaining influence throughout the country, especially within the city of Fez. Many Moroccans viewed them as a holy lineage that was endowed with abundant *baraka* (spiritual power and blessing), even looking to the *shurafa'* to lead them against the encroaching Christian forces of Castile and Portugal. This fact is illustrated by the increasing prominence of Sufi orders led by holy men claiming descent from the family of the Prophet. The most influential of these holy men was Shaykh Muhammad al-Jazuli, founder of the Jazuliyya Sufi order. Although he grew up in the Sus valley, al-Jazuli had spent several years in Fez and had a number of supporters within the city. After an extended trip to the Islamic east, al-Jazuli established his order in the southern city of Safi, from which he called for Islamic revival under sharifian leadership. His sudden death in 1465 led to charges that the shaykh had been poisoned.

The Wattasids had recognized the increasing influence of the *shurafa'* for several decades and had attempted to control this impulse by co-opting the movement. To curry the favor of the *ulama*, the Wattasids had even financed the construction of a shrine over the grave of Idris II, the sharifian founder of Fez. In fact, Abu Zakariyya had made a point of associating himself with the discovery of Idris's tomb in old Fez, in conjunction with the *mizwar al-shurafa'* (leader of the sharifian families of Fez), in 1437. Through allying with the *shurafa'* the Wattasids had hoped to solidify their position as heads of state, despite their dubious credentials. Thus, 'Abd al-Haqq's deposition and execution of the Wattasids in Fez had created tension between himself and the religious establishment even before he removed their tax exemption.

Historical details regarding the ultimate showdown between 'Abd al-Haqq and the Fezzi religious establishment remain somewhat hazy as different accounts record alternate versions of the events of 1465. Most reports state that an altercation broke out within the city during that year as the result of a Jewish tax collector's assault on a *sharifa* who had refused to pay taxes. Popular outrage was fanned into flame by local preachers who called for the city to rise up against the regime of 'Abd al-Haqq. The tax collector was killed, and there were violent attacks against inhabitants of the Jewish quarter carried out by enraged Muslims. The sultan and the vizier Harun al-Batas were away from Fez at the time, engaging in military action against the Wattasids. Upon their return to the city, most of the army revolted against 'Abd al-Haqq. Stating that they no longer wanted to submit to a Jew, the dissident soldiers killed Harun and took the bound sultan into Fez, where he would be executed in the city streets a few hours later. Some accounts indicate that the sultan had his throat slit, as is done to sheep during the ritual sacrifice of Eid al-Adha.

With the death of 'Abd al-Haqq came the end of the Marinid dynasty. Leadership within Fez passed to the *mizwar al-shurafa'*, Muhammad ibn Imran al-Juti, and Fez was run as an independent sharifian city-state for several years. In 1472 the Wattasid Muhammad al-Shaykh managed to subdue the city and to briefly reassert Wattasid control throughout the country. But the Wattasids soon lost functional supremacy in the south, first to the Berber Hintata confederacy, which seems to have ruled sporadically in Marrakech since the mid-fifteenth century, and later to the sharifian Sa'di family that arose from the Sus valley in the 1520s. By 1554 the Wattasids themselves had fallen from power in Fez, and the Sa'dis established sharifian rule over

Morocco, a tradition that has remained in place within the country to the present day.

[*See also* Idris II; *and* Jazuli, Muhammad al-.]

BIBLIOGRAPHY

Beck, Herman L. *L'Image d'Idris II, ses descendants de Fas et la politique sharifienne des sultans Marinides (656–869/1258–1465).* Leiden, Netherlands: E. J. Brill, 1989.

Cour, Auguste. *La dynastie marocaine des Beni Wattas (1420–1544).* Paris: P. Geuthner, 1920.

Garcia Arenal, Mercedes. "The Revolution of Fas in 869/1465 and the Death of Sultan 'Abd al-Haqq al-Marini." *Bulletin of the School of Oriental and African Studies* 41, no. 1 (1978): 43–66.

Nasiri, Ahmad ibn Khalid, al-. Kitab al-istiqsa'. Translated by I. Hamet. *Archives Marocaines* 33 (1934): 468–476.

STEPHEN CORY

Abu Salih the Armenian (fl. fourteenth century), Egyptian Christian author, was a patron of Copto-Arabic historical literature, long presumed to be the author of *Churches and Monasteries of Egypt and Some Neighboring Countries*, a twelfth-century topographical survey of Christian sites and traditions in and around Egypt. The original author of the majority of that work was, in fact, Abu al-Makarim Sa'dallah Ibn Jirjis Ibn Mas'ud, an elder of the Coptic Orthodox Church of Alexandria. Despite confusion regarding its authorship, *Churches and Monasteries* has proven to be a crucial text for the study of Coptic tradition, Christian-Muslim relations, and the twelfth-century Egyptian state and society in general and was in turn an important source to later medieval chroniclers and topographers.

Although little is actually known about the specifics of the life of Abu Salih, his patronage of this important piece of medieval Egyptian historical literature suggests that he was of a well-to-do socioeconomic class, and his nomenclature suggests that he belonged to the influential Armenian community that had relocated to Egypt during the so-called Armenian period of the Fatimid dynasty beginning in the late eleventh century. His name became associated with *Churches and Monasteries* by its inclusion on the earliest extant manuscript when Orientalist scholars, who often took a keen interest in indigenous Christian communities of the Islamic world, labored in the late nineteenth century to collect, translate, and edit this important work. B. T. A. Evetts identified Abu Salih—whose name was evident at the front of the manuscript—as the author, and the text has carried that name beginning with Evetts's edited translation of the first volume of *Church and Monasteries* in 1895. Johannes Den Heijer has since clarified that it was Abu al-Makarim who, in fact, composed substantial portions of the twelfth-century parts of the text. However, it appears to have been a prominent source in its own day: later authors contributed to the version of the text that came down to Abu Salih in the fourteenth century, and their identities have since disappeared from evidence in the manuscripts.

Authorship aside, the text of *Churches and Monasteries* contains an astounding and widely varying amount of information regarding the world of the Copts of Egypt in the twelfth century. The clear focus throughout the text is to provide a survey of the sacred Christian sites of Egypt and its environs (primarily churches and monasteries, as the title suggests), including physical descriptions as well as discussions of the historical traditions about them and their resident communities. In terms of the former, the text describes the structures and conditions of sites both prominent and obscure throughout Lower and Upper Egypt, often including sites that had been destroyed by nature, neglect, or violence in or before the author's own time but the historical memory of which local communities had maintained. This has provided a fascinating time capsule for historians as many of the sites that were prominent in the author's day remain as such for comparison: the Mu'allaqa ("Hanging") Church of Old Cairo and the Monastery of Saint Anthony by the Red Sea, for example.

One of the most striking features of the historical traditions preserved by *Churches and Monasteries* is the nature of interaction between the variety of Christian communities present in that era, as well as between them and their surrounding predominately Muslim society and authorities. Its depictions of the former are often antagonistic: the volume included in Evetts's 1895 translation, for example, includes an account of the strange case of Marqus Ibn al-Qanbar, a contemporary priest whose flirtation with Byzantine doctrine and liturgical practice drew the ire of Coptic Orthodox authorities and eventually encompassed not just his local congregation in Damietta but also the prominent Monastery of Saint Anthony. The author of *Churches and Monasteries* relates this account as part of its survey of that monastery, in fact, and takes care to note that this crisis of doctrine and interconfessional rivalry remained unresolved until Coptic officials appealed to a sympathetic Islamic judge for arbitration. Throughout the text the author is careful to identify the Christian sect that held ownership of each church and monastery, drawing a sharp dividing line between the Chalcedonian (Melkite/Greek Orthodox) and anti-Chalcedonian (Coptic and Armenian, primarily) factions that had characterized the Christian community in Egypt since the fifth century.

As this example suggests, the text of *Churches and Monasteries* also draws attention to the complex and constantly shifting relations between the Copts and their Muslim neighbors and rulers. It includes a surprising number of accounts of Muslim authority figures who were amenable to their Christian subjects, even downright sympathetic at times: in addition to the story of the Islamic judge who mediates an inter-Christian dispute, for example, the author retells al-Shabushti's account of Khumarawayh ibn Ahmad ibn Tulun, governor of Egypt in the late ninth century, who often visited the Qusayr Monastery outside Old Cairo in order to gaze at a particularly beautiful icon of the Virgin Mary as he enjoyed a cup of the abbey's wine.

However, *Churches and Monasteries* does not shy away from recording the animosity that also regularly appeared between the dominant community and local non-Muslims. Most evident are the exceptional moments of oppression that appeared at times of dynastic transition or regional instability, such as the destruction of sites during the infamous persecution of Christians by al-Hakim in the early eleventh century, the pillaging of churches and monasteries by Turkish and Kurdish soldiers during the chaotic collapse of Fatimid authority in the mid-twelfth century, and the enforcement of sumptuary laws against non-Muslims by Saladin in the 1170s during the establishment of his rule and struggle against the Crusaders (measures that he eventually repealed). These examples, consistent in tone and content throughout the multiple volumes of *Churches and Monasteries*, are illustrative of the nature of Christian-Muslim relations in Egypt throughout the Islamic Middle Period: although they often coexisted in a state of normalcy and even cooperation, the status of Christians and other non-Muslims waxed and waned as a result of the same dynamics of flux and instability that periodically impacted all of the Egyptian state and society.

[*See also* Saladin.]

BIBLIOGRAPHY

Atiya, Aziz S. "Some Egyptian Monasteries According to the Unpublished MS. of Al-Shabushti's 'Kitab al-Diyarat.'" *Bulletin de la Société d'Archéologie Copte* 5 (1939): 1–28; and Abu al-Hasan 'Ali al-Shabushti. *Kitab al-diyarat*. Edited and annotated by Kurkis 'Awwad. Baghdad: Matba't al-ma'arif, 1951. Al-Shabushti was a tenth-century Muslim author whose fascination with Christian monasteries pours through every account of this expansive work, and the author of *Churches and Monasteries* regularly refers to this work in his own topography. The former, useful only for Arabic readers, includes the full text of his survey of monasteries from Iraq to Egypt; the latter includes a critical edition of portions of the Arabic text along with an accurate English translation but only those sections devoted to Egyptian monasteries.

Den Heijer, Johannes. "The Composition of *The Churches and Monasteries of Egypt*: Some Preliminary Remarks." In *Acts of the Fifth International Congress of Coptic Studies, Washington, 12–15 August 1992*. Vol. 2: *Papers from the Sections*, part 1, edited by David W. Johnson. Rome: Centro Italiano Microfiches, 1993. This is the most comprehensive and informative work to date on the complicated and confusing authorship of *Churches and Monasteries*.

Sa'dallah Ibn Jirjis Ibn Mas'ud Abu al-Makarim (published under the name Abu Salih the Armenian), *The Churches and Monasteries of Egypt and Some Neighboring Countries*, reprint ed. Edited and translated by B. T. A. Evetts. Piscataway, N.J.: Gorgias Press, 2001. This is currently the most accessible version of the text in question, in terms of both language and availability, although it includes only the first volume of the original text. Evetts includes both a readable (if archaic) English translation and the edited Arabic transcription of an original manuscript. The remaining portions of the text may be found in Arabic, without translation, under the following: Sa'dallah Jirjis Abu al-Makarim. *Tarikh al-kana'is wa-l-adyara*. 4 vols. Edited by Fr. Samuel al-Suryani. Cairo: Dayr al-Suryan, 1984.

KURT WERTHMULLER

Abu Yahya ibn 'Abd al-Haqq (c. 1207–1258), fourth sultan of the Moroccan Marinid dynasty, took over leadership in the aftermath of a significant military defeat in 1244 when his predecessor Muhammad ibn 'Abd al-Haqq was killed. Ibn Khaldun states that Abu Yahya divided Morocco between the Marinid clans, assigning each a specific portion of land in perpetuity, even before he conquered the country. With this motivation, the leading families of the Marinid alliance increased the number of troops that they contributed to the army, thus augmenting their forces for the struggle against the Almohads, the de jure rulers over Morocco.

The Almohads had allied with the Banu Asker, a dissident Marinid clan, along with Yaghmurasan, chief of the Banu ʿAbd al-Wad, rulers of Tlemcen. But at a critical moment, these forces switched sides and joined the Marinid army against the Almohads, who were then defeated in battle. The Banu Asker then submitted to Abu Yahya, while Yaghmurasan returned to Tlemcen with his troops. Despite these victories, the Marinids still had a legitimacy problem that would hinder them in establishing their authority over the whole of Morocco. After all, the Almohads had ruled the region for almost 150 years in the name of their religious doctrine, but the Marinids had no leadership credentials other than their tribal forces. For this reason, Abu Yahya established an alliance with the Hafsids, masters of Ifriqiya (present-day Tunisia), to rule Morocco in their name. The Hafsids claimed to represent the true authority of Ibn Tumart, founder of the Almohads, whose teachings they believed had been betrayed by the later Almohad caliphs. This alliance would provide a semblance of legitimacy for the Marinids.

By the late 1240s the Almohads were in desperate straits, having lost most of their territory to former allies. Thus, they gathered all their troops for a showdown with the Marinids in 1247–1248. With their caliph al-Said at its head, the Almohad force marched to the Beht River. Upon seeing this large army, Abu Yahya called for reinforcements from allied Marinid clans. Meanwhile, the Almohads advanced upon Meknès, where the inhabitants quickly submitted. Following this triumph, the Almohads headed toward Taza, while Abu Yahya and his troops faded back into the Banu Iznacen Mountains. He then sent emissaries to the Almohad camp to offer Marinid submission in exchange for a pardon for past hostilities. The ambassador even promised al-Said that Marinid troops would join his forces to take on Yaghmurasan and the Banu ʿAbd al-Wad.

The Almohad caliph, however, suspected a trap. Abu Yahya offered to send five hundred warriors to join the Almohads, but al-Said instead left Taza, intending to do battle himself with the army of the

Banu ʿAbd al-Wad. However, he was killed in the mountains of Temzezdekt, after which the Almohad forces retreated toward Marrakech under the leadership of al-Said's son, ʿAbd Allah. Abu Yahya had received news of al-Said's death, and Marinid warriors ambushed the Almohad army near Guerif, routing them completely. Some of the Almohad troops switched sides and joined the Marinids.

Following the Almohad defeat, Abu Yahya hastened to establish his authority throughout Morocco. One of his first stops was in Fez. By September 1248, two months after the death of al-Said, the Marinids had established their authority in the citadel of Fez. Within four months, the Marinid army had besieged and conquered Taza, after which Abu Yahya received envoys bearing promises of submission from all the important cities of northern Morocco. In Fez Abu Yahya proclaimed the supremacy of the Hafsid sultanate, mediated through their allies, the Marinids. He promised a just and stable administration under the leadership of the sharif Abu al-Abbas, whom he appointed governor over the city, while the sultan himself left to conquer further territory.

In Marrakech the sharif Abu Hafs Umar al-Mortada took control in the name of the Almohads. Upon leaving Fez with his army to meet this new threat, Abu Yahya appointed his client al-Saud ibn Khirbash to guard the city. However, after the departure of the Marinid troops in January 1250, a group of conspirators assassinated al-Saud and plundered his possessions. They then sent emissaries to declare their submission to al-Mortada. Abu Yahya was quickly informed of this rebellion, and he returned to Fez to lay siege to the city. When the inhabitants' pleas for help went unheeded by al-Mortada, they appealed next to Yaghmurasan, who sent an army of ʿAbd al-Wad warriors to alleviate the siege of Fez. But the army of Abu Yahya met them in battle on the plains outside Oujda, and there they defeated the army of Yaghmurasan. Abu Yahya then returned to his siege, eventually forcing the Fezzis to declare their submission to Marinid authority. The victorious emir entered Fez for the second time in 1250. When the Fezzis were slow in paying the agreed-upon reparations, Abu Yahya had the qadi Abu ʿAbd al-Rahman executed, along with several of his supporters, and their severed heads placed upon the walls of the city.

Following the reconquest of Fez, Abu Yahya sent his troops to take the coastal cities of Salé and Rabat in 1251–1252. In 1255 al-Mortada assembled a large army to force a climactic showdown with the Marinids. The two sides met in the mountains of Behloula, near Fez. The victory went to the Marinid army, which despoiled the Almohad camp, al-Mortada escaping with his life and little else. In 1257 the army of Abu Yahya defeated Yaghmurasan at Abu Salit, thus securing Marinid control over the regions of Sijilmasa and Draʾa, key locations in the Saharan caravan trade.

After appointing a governor over Sijilmasa, Abu Yahya returned to Fez, where he began to plan for his next campaign. However, there would be no further campaigns for the great Marinid conqueror, who died in Fez in July 1258. He was replaced by his brother Yaqub ibn ʿAbd al-Haqq. Still, Abu Yahya had done much to solidify Marinid control over Morocco. His successor would build upon his work, finally eliminating the Almohad Empire.

[*See also* Abu Muhammad ʿAbd al-Haqq I; Abu Yusuf Yaʿqub ibn ʿAbd al-Haqq; Ibn Khaldun; *and* Yaghmurasan.]

BIBLIOGRAPHY

Ibn Abi Zar, Abu al-Hasan. *Kitab al-anis al-mutrib bi-rawd al-Qirtas.* French translation *Roudh El-Kartas: Histoire des souverains du Maghreb (Espagne et Maroc) et annals de la ville de Fès.* Translated by A. Beaumier. Paris: LʼImprimerie Impériale, 1860.

Ibn al-Ahmar, Abu al-Walid. *Rawdat al Nisrîn.* French translation *Histoire des Benî Marîn, rois de Fâs intitulée Rawdat al Nisrîn (Le Jardin des Églantines).* Edited and annotated translation by Ghaoutsi Bouali and Georges Marçais. Paris: Ernest Leroux, 1917.

Ibn Khaldun, ʿAbd al-Rahman. *Kitab al-ʿIbar.* French translation *Histoire des Berbères et des dynasties musulmanes de lʼAfrique septentrionale,* new ed., 4 vols. Translation by Baron de Slane. Paris: Casanova, 1968–1969.

Shatzmiller, Maya. *The Berbers and the Islamic State: The Marinid Experience in Pre-Protectorate Morocco.* Princeton, N.J.: Markus Weiner, 2000.

STEPHEN CORY

ʿAbu Yaʿqub Yusuf (d. 1184), second Moroccan caliph of the Almohad (Muʾminid) dynasty (r. 1163–1184), was a great patron of philosophy and architecture, a defensive leader, and statesman. The beginning of his reign was rocked by conflict over succession. His father, ʿAbd al-Muʾmin, had designated Muhammad, the older brother of a different mother as his successor. Muhammad was in power

from a few weeks to a few months. The sources differ on the exact length of his reign.

However, it was clear from the beginning that Muhmmad did not have the ambition or the ability to lead the vast administrative and military apparatus his father had created. ʿAbu Yaʿqub Yusuf had the support of a powerful woman, his mother. It seems this formidable woman and her other son, the powerful vizier Abu Hafs ʿUmar, conspired to elevate ʿAbu Yaʿqub Yusuf as caliph. ʿUmar claimed that the caliph ʿAbd al-Muʾmin had declared to him on his deathbed that Yaʿqub Yusuf, not Muhammad, should be the heir apparent. Yaʿqub Yusuf was quickly summoned from Seville, where he was governor, and proclaimed caliph by the Almohad tribal hierarchy in Rabat. Soon, however, other members of ʿAbd al-Muʾminʼs large family began to protest. Another brother, ʿAli, then governor of Fez, as well as the governors of Bijaya and Córdoba, also brothers, refused to recognize the new caliph. Only after five years of Shakespearean conspiracy, intrigue, and mysterious deaths could Yaʿqub Yusuf gain enough authority to be declared *amir al-muʾminin* (prince of believers) rather than the less prestigious *amir al-muslimin* (prince of the Muslims).

Family intrigue was not the only concern of ʿAbu Yaʿqub Yusuf. When internal threats were not rocking his personal power, external threats and revolt were threatening the internal unity of the Almohad Empire. Soon many of the more freedom-loving groups in the northern Rif area near Ceuta began to rebel, including the powerful Ghumara confederation. He also faced a local rebellion in Gafsa, in what is now Tunisia, and a serious threat from Ibn Mardanish who had ambitions to conquer Almohad territory in Andalusia. It was only after the defeat of Ibn Mardanish and the suppression of the Ghumara and Gafsa revolts that he was declared caliph in 563/1168. The Almohads were then threatened by the rapid rise of Giraldo sem Pavor of Portugal who captured several strategic towns and laid siege to Badajoz. The Christian King Ferdinand II of León (r. 1157–1188), an Almohad ally, saved the important city for the Almohads.

In 1171 ʿAbu Yaʿqub assembled a great army in Marrakech in order to finally quell the disruptions and disorders of al-Andalus. Some ten thousand Almohads and ten thousand Arab tribesmen were part of the army. The caliph reviewed the troops at a grand and sumptuous feast in the Buhaira gardens outside the city gates. The Arabs, having been introduced from elsewhere, were constantly quarreling with the local Almohads. Ominously, there was less than total obedience paid to the caliph himself. There was some good news. The two sons of Ibn Mardanish of al-Andalus, once a great threat to the Almohad hold in Andalusia, soon declared their loyalty to Ya'qub after their father's death and defeat. In an extraordinary turn of loyalties, the caliph later married the daughter of Ibn Mardanish in 1175 and incorporated the Mardanish clan into the tribal hierarchy. In 1172 the two sons of Ibn Mardanish suggested the siege of Huete, a major Christian threat to the Almohads. The city was only lightly defended and should have been an easy victory. According to one source, the Almohads were on the verge of victory but the caliph, surrounded in his tent by scholars and immersed in questions of religious dogma and theology, refused to appear before the troops. His dispirited commanders soon lost the momentum and fell back into a long siege and eventual defeat. Ya'qub's army was routed.

The growing ferocity and unity of the Christian armies, inspired by the crusading spirit and increasingly determined to defeat the Almohads for religious purposes, rather than simply political or military intrigue, was a constant threat to Ya'qub Yusuf and the Almohads. The Christian pilgrimage to the shrine of Saint James at Santiago de Compostela was becoming more than simply an Iberian exercise, but an event that made all of Europe aware of the so-called Western Crusade against the Almohads. Unlike the Christians, who were increasingly inspired and united by the pope's crusader call, the Almohads were beginning to lose their original, expansive ideology of jihad that had supported the rise of 'Abd al Mu'min. Unlike his father, an aggressive conqueror of lands for the cause of the Mahdi, Ya'qub Yusuf was much more interested in defending existing Almohad territory from attack. There was some justification for this defensive posture. A great plague had spread throughout the empire. The caliph was himself infected even as the Christians led by Alfonso VIII (r. 1158–1214) were laying siege to the important town of Cuenca forcing this strategic fortress to surrender in 1177. Sancho of Portugal (r. 1158–1211) invaded the valley of the Algarve to the mouth of the Guadalquivir, forcing the evacuation of Muslims once again.

By 1184 the situation in Iberia was becoming increasingly serious. Ferdinand, once an Almohad ally, had sealed the peace of Fresno-Lavandera and renounced his connections with the Muslims. Castile and León were now united in their efforts against the Almohads. Even so, Ya'qub was determined to quell the Portuguese invasions and prepared a grand army of warriors to eliminate the constant harassment of the northwest border. In late June 1184 he assembled his army near the Portuguese fort of Santarem, a strong and almost impregnable fortress. The large but ineffective Almohad army was quickly bogged down near the river and was finally routed at the approach of Ferdinand II. The Christian King, who had once been a trusted ally, would now lead his own army against Ya'qub Yusuf. Mortally wounded, the caliph died near Evora on the way back to Seville on 29 July 1184.

Although the rule of Caliph Ya'qub Yusuf was often beset by military disaster, especially in Andalusia, his reign was far from a failure. He fostered a unique and brilliant combination of Almohad, Berber, Arab, and Andalusian culture, philosophy, and architecture. 'Abu Ya'qub was born a Berber but his life in Andalusia and the great cities of North Africa exposed him to a diversity of Arab and Andalusian cultural influences. In 579/1183 he began the building of an entire imperial quarter in Marrakech, al-Saliha. Using a combination of Andalusian and Berber architects, this palace would be an emblem of Almohad magnificence and power. It would also symbolize, like Marrakech itself, the establishment of the Berbers and the Berber ethnic groups as a people capable of uniting, building, and maintaining a civilization, separate and independent in ideology and scope from the Eastern Islamic world. Whereas the Almoravids borrowed the Maliki doctrine and proclaimed allegiance to the Abbasid caliph, the Almohads and the caliph Ya'qub maintained exclusive Almohad claims. The doctrine of the Mahdi and Almohad unitarianism *tawhid* remained a strong, cohesive force. The Almohad hierarchy of the ethnic groups maintained their positions, leading the army into battle even as the bureaucracy of trained scholars and administrators were prepared to rule, conscript soldiers, and collect taxes at the empires most distant outposts. Except for those individual rebellions mentioned above, the tax revenue collected by the Almohads from client groups was continuous and steady, allowing the caliph to spend generously on cultural and architectural projects even as he was engaged in military defense in Iberia and elsewhere.

This possibly legendary story of the caliph discussing religion and theology, even as a vital battle raged at Huete, sheds important light on the nature and priorities of 'Abu Ya'qub. The caliph was constantly surrounded by the most eminent scholars and thinkers from all parts of his realm. Poets, doctors, philosophers, qadis, and historians all made up his closest entourage. The purpose and direction of these discussions was not, however, pointless sophistry. Where his father was a conqueror, Ya'qub was a consolidator of empire and of the ideas that would define the Almohad movement as a whole. His discussions on religious works were as much a struggle, a jihad, to fit the Almohad movement into a legitimate and lasting religious theology as the battles raging outside the gates of Andalusian towns.

The maturing of the Almohad Empire under 'Abu Ya'qub led to a new and exciting intellectual era, inspiring experimental approaches to reason and faith, approaches that would come to fruition with the works of Ibn Rushd (Averroes). Ibn Rushd's teacher, Ibn Tufayl, was Ya'qub's personal doctor and one of his most trusted advisors. Ibn Tufayl wrote an Arabic and Berber novel about the life of a man created with no family, no human relations, only his life and his realization of God's existence. The decendants of Ibn Zuhr (d. 1162), the great physician who died in Seville a year before Ya'qub's reign, and Ibn Rushd were similarly patronized and encouraged by the caliph, producing some of their greatest works. Treatment of Jews did worsen. Many were forced to move or were executed. This was not a perfect reign of interreligious understanding. Nevertheless, far from destroying the culture of Andalusia through invasion and oppression, the Almohads provided the unified conditions for a new flowering of Andalusian, Berber, and Arab thought. Seville and Marrakech were endowed with vast public works projects, bringing water inside, allowing magnificent gardens and palaces to sprout into existence. The fine arts of textile weaving, ceramics, and book illustration were increasingly refined. Finally, trade with Europe and sub-Saharan Africa made the Almohad Empire a stepping-stone between two continents.

By not engaging in continuous, offensive, and potentially reckless military campaigns of expansion, Ya'qub preserved and internally strengthened the empire his father had conquered. He accomplished this consolidation challenged not only by divisions within his own family, but by divisions between the old Berber groups who had founded the empire and the new Arab warriors that were brought into the vast military-bureaucratic, moving tent city that was the peripatetic caliphate.

Despite his many defeats in the fields of war, his greatest victory was in the fields of thought, culture, architecture, those things associated with the civilization: not simply an effective army but an effective internal state. He paved the way for the further flowering of Almohad civilization under his successor al-Mansur.

[See also 'Abd al-Mu'min; and Ibn Rushd.]

BIBLIOGRAPHY

Fromherz, Allen. *The Almohads: The Rise of an Islamic Empire.* London: I.B. Tauris, 2010.

Kennedy, Hugh. *Muslim Spain and Portugal: A Political History of Al-Andalus.* London: Longman 1996.

Le Tourneau, Roger. *The Almohad Movement in North Africa in the Twelfth and Thirteenth Centuries.* Princeton, N.J.: Princeton University Press, 1969.

ALLEN J. FROMHERZ

'Abu Ya'qub Yusuf (d. 1307), sixth sultan of the Moroccan Marinid dynasty, seized power in 1286 after his father, Abu Yusuf Ya'qub, had consolidated Marinid authority throughout Morocco. With this seemingly secure base, 'Abu Ya'qub spent most of his reign engaging in external battles. The Moroccan sultan was involved in the numerous struggles of southern Spain for several years, seeking to strengthen the Marinid position in that key area. In the final twelve years of his reign, 'Abu Ya'qub sought to expand Marinid rule throughout the Maghreb by bringing down the neighboring Zayyanid dynasty, which had often been a thorn in the side of earlier Marinid sultans. Although he initially made some progress on these two fronts, in neither case was 'Abu Ya'qub fully able to achieve his aims.

Like his father before him, 'Abu Ya'qub spent his first two years as sultan putting down revolts within Morocco. His main opponents were family members who disputed his right to succession, including a cousin, a brother, and even one of his sons, Abu Amr. 'Abu Ya'qub forcefully suppressed these rebellions, executing the insurgents, with the exception of his son, who he pardoned. Further revolts were launched by groups of Ma'qil Arabs in the southern part of the country. The sultan's army marched throughout the region for several months, repressing the unrest. In some cases, rebels fled to Tlemcen to take refuge among the Zayyanids, who refused to turn them over to 'Abu Ya'qub in the name of hospitality. Such incidents further aggravated hostilities between the Marinid and Zayyanid regimes.

The sultan's interest in Spain seems to have originated at the beginning of his reign, when he traveled to Algeciras to succeed his father, who had died in that town. The new sultan devoted a couple of months to establishing alliances in Spain, including a personal meeting with the Nasrid sultan, Ibn al-Ahmar. 'Abu Ya'qub's opportunities in the Iberian Peninsula increased as a result of conflict between the two Christian kingdoms of Castile and Aragon. With the Christians fighting one another, the Marinid sultan was able to maintain neutrality between them, while seeking to expand his influence along the southern coast. As he reinforced his outposts in Tarifa, Algeciras, and Ronda, 'Abu Ya'qub kept a watchful eye on the struggles between the Iberian states.

However, matters took a turn for the worse for the Marinids after Castile and Aragon agreed to a peace treaty in 1291. Now able to focus its full attention on its Muslim rivals, the army of Castile captured Tarifa from the Marinids in 1292, while the Granadans remained on the sidelines. Despite sharing the same Islamic faith, the Nasrids of Granada were not any more interested in strengthening the hand of their coreligionists than they were in seeing Castile or Aragon become too powerful. In fact, despite their early friendship, Ibn al-Ahmar began to suspect ulterior motives on the part of 'Abu Ya'qub, believing that the Marinid wished to establish his own Iberian kingdom. Lacking cooperation from Granada and having lost his main fortress in Spain, 'Abu Ya'qub decided to withdraw from the peninsula in 1294, leaving his remaining Iberian possessions in the hands of the Nasrids.

His withdrawal from Spain did not deter 'Abu Ya'qub from foreign adventures however. He next turned his attention to the Zayyanids of the western Algerian city of Tlemcen. This dynasty had long served as an adversary to the Marinids, particularly under the leadership of its founder, Yaghmurasan. In fact, Ibn Khaldun maintains that hostility between the Banu Marin and the Banu 'Abd al-Wad (from which the Zayyanids arose) dated back long before either of these Zanata Berber tribes had established individual dynasties. This conflict was continued by 'Abu Ya'qub and his Zayyanid adversary, Uthman ibn Yaghmurasan. 'Abu Ya'qub first laid siege to Tlemcen in early 1290, after Uthman refused to relinquish the Marinid rebel, Muhammad ibn Wattu. However, the Marinid sultan ended the siege in early 1291, after the king of Castile broke his treaty with the Marinids, attacking their outposts in the peninsula.

In 1295, after the failure of his Iberian sorties, 'Abu Ya'qub recommenced hostilities with the Zayyanids. He launched numerous offensives against his neighbors to the east, successfully capturing most Zayyanid holdings to the west of Tlemcen. In 1299, the Marinid army began an extended siege of the Zayyanid capital itself. Determined to finally conquer the city that had long held out against the Marinids, 'Abu Ya'qub constructed a wall around Tlemcen, with a deep moat to keep anybody from entering or leaving the city. He established ties with a number of Algerian tribes, who agreed to recognize Marinid supremacy over that of the Zayyanids. 'Abu Ya'qub even won the support of the Hafsids in Ifriqiya (modern-day Tunisia). And yet, Tlemcen still refused to fall. The death of the Zayyanid sultan, Uthman, in 1304 apparently had no effect as his successor, Muhammad, continued to resist Marinid attempts at conquest. The siege finally came to an end after eight years, when 'Abu Ya'qub was assassinated by one of his eunuchs in May 1307. Once again, the Marinids had failed to take Tlemcen.

The long siege of Tlemcen came at a high price for the Marinids. While 'Abu Ya'qub's army bided its time outside the city walls, tribal rebellions and would-be sultans arose within Morocco. Sometimes these troubles were encouraged by rivals in Spain. Although he successfully put down these rebellions, 'Abu Ya'qub's obsession with foreign wars weakened the internal stability that he had inherited from his father. In fact, his immediate successors would need to withdraw from further expansion in order to restore Marinid authority throughout Morocco. By the early fourteenth century, the competing powers within North Africa and Spain were too evenly matched to allow for the reestablishment of a Maghreb state on the level of the Almohad Empire, although the Marinids would periodically attempt to achieve this goal. As later Marinid sultans would eventually realize, the goal of establishing a greater Marinid Empire would prove unattainable.

[See also Ibn Khaldun.]

BIBLIOGRAPHY

Ibn Abi Zar', Abu al-Hasan. *Kitab al-anis al-mutrib bi-rawd al-Qirtas*. French translation *Roudh El-Kartas: Histoire des souverains du Maghreb (Espagne et Maroc) et annals de la ville de Fès*. Translated by A. Beaumier. Paris: L'Imprimerie Impériale, 1860.

Ibn al-Ahmar, Abu al-Walid. *Rawdat al Nisrîn.* French translation *Histoire des Benî Marîn, rois de Fâs intitulée Rawdat al Nisrîn (Le Jardin des Églantines).* Edited and annotated translation by Ghaoutsi Bouali and Georges Marçais. Paris: Ernest Leroux, 1917.

Ibn Khaldun, 'Abd al-Rahman. *Kitab al-'Ibar.* French translation *Histoire des Berbères et des dynasties musulmanes de l'Afrique septentrionale,* nouv. ed., 4 vols. Translation by Baron de Slane. Paris: Casanova, 1968–1969.

Shatzmiller, Maya. *The Berbers and the Islamic State: The Marinid Experience in Pre-Protectorate Morocco.* Princeton, N.J.: Markus Wiener, 2000.

STEPHEN CORY

Abu Yusuf (d. 1769), Mamluk bey of Upper Egypt and head of the Hawwara (a Berber people), was the emir and the de facto ruler of Upper Egypt during the mid-eighteenth century who was part of the opposition to 'Ali Bey's rule of Egypt. Abu Yusuf and the tribe belonged to Nisf Haram, which would become closely associated with the Qasimmi Mamluks. His full name was Humam ibn Yusuf ibn Ahmad al-Hawwari, also sometimes given as Humam Abu Yusuf.

Like previous Hawwara leaders, the power base of Abu Yusuf was in Farshut, in the province of Qena. From here, their influence extended westward, encompassing large sections of the Sa'id. Initially, Hawwara claims under Abu Yusuf came into conflict with both the Bardisi and the Akhmim claims. Humam was successful in eventually eliminating both of these rivals.

Abu Yusuf oversaw a brief period of comparative prosperity and tranquility in the history of Upper Egypt during the mid-eighteenth century after he established power. He consolidated power sometime around 1740, after a decisive defeat of the Bardisi emir. Other defeats would eventually lead to the extinction of the Akhmim dynasty as well, extending the territory of the Hawwara and eliminating his only rivals of any note in the region. He, rather than the various transient Ottoman or Mamluk governors, was the primary centralization of power in the region, owing to the distractions of the governors by the intrigues within the Mamluk power base in Cairo. However remote from Cairo he was, he did play several crucial roles in the Mamluk power struggles during the eighteenth century.

This entanglement came in the form of support offered to the exiled Qasimi faction members, and it played a key role in later political events in Cairo, in which he became inextricably involved. Qasimi Mamluks fleeing Lower Egypt after their political power had collapsed following their defeat in 1730 found sanctuary with Abu Yusuf and entered his service. There, the Qasimi faction began to integrate with the Hawwara and other local peoples. This refuge and alliance allowed the Qasimi faction to rebuild power during their exile.

He was drawn in to a quarrel between 'Ali Bey and Salih Bey, and this quarrel would prove to be his eventual undoing in the long term. He was particularly close to Salih Bey, the last Qasimi political head who had been exiled by 'Ali Bey in 1765 and who had been his friend and ally before exile. When Salih sought exile with him in Farshut, Abu Yusuf agreed and allowed him and his followers to settle there. When 'Ali himself sought asylum in Upper Egypt two years later, Abu Yusuf forced the two to reconcile their differences, which forged an alliance that enabled the two beys to retake Cairo.

This alliance was short-lived as Salih was assassinated by 'Ali in 1768. And again, when the followers of Salih sought help to capture Asyut to hold out against the governor appointed by 'Ali for Upper Egypt, Abu Yusuf assisted. However, 'Ali Bey's forces defeated the Hawwara and the rebels who had once been Salih's supporters. Abu Yusuf, defeated and shamed, fled Farshut to Esna, where he died in December of 1769. After his exile and death, the Hawwara chiefs either surrendered to Muhammad Bey Abu'l-Dhahab or fled into exile themselves.

Accounts of Abu Yusuf's rule differ in terms of their treatment of both his personal character and the characteristics of his reign. Al-Jabarti's account holds him to be a fair, hospitable, and loyal ruler—a paragon of Arab *shaykhly* virtue as a ruler. On the other hand, Burckhardt records that he was a ruler who oppressed the Copts, extorted merchants, and generally was disliked by those he ruled. Both accounts may be true and merely different interpretations of his actions. Accounts in both cases mention his wealth, power, and prestige, as well as his religious devotion. He is recorded to have extended hospitality to several influential *ulama*, as well as to have supported *ulama* in Cairo.

After Abu Yusuf's exile and eventual death on 7 December 1769, the political power of the Hawwara was at an end. While his son, Darwish, succeeded him, the heir never enjoyed the political influence of his father and proved to be a relatively weak ruler. However, the tribe retained some of its social and economic importance until the time of Muhammad 'Ali Pasha. And, come the rule of Ibrahim Pasha, the Hawwara would find their sources of wealth and influence confiscated or diverted. They were, eventually, absorbed into the rest of society in the region.

[See also 'Ali Bey the Great.]

BIBLIOGRAPHY

Burckhardt, Johann Ludwig, ed. *Travels in Nubia.* London: J. Murray, 1819, pp. 531–533.

Jabarti, Abd al-Rahman al-. *'Aja'ib al-athar.* Cairo: Bulaq, 1873.

Khanam, R., ed. "Hawwara: Tribe of Algeria, Egypt, Morocco, Sicily, Spain, Sudan, Tunisia, and Yemen." In *Encyclopaedic Ethnography of Middle-East and Central Asia.* New Delhi: Global Vision Publishing House, 2005.

NESS CREIGHTON

Abu Yusuf Ya'qub ibn 'Abd al-Haqq (d. 1286), fifth sultan of the Moroccan Marinid dynasty, took over from his brother, Abu Yahya, in October 1258. Abu Yahya brought the Marinids to the brink of controlling all of Morocco and eliminating the Almohad caliphate, which had ruled over much of North Africa for the previous 150 years. During the twenty-eight years of his reign, Abu Yusuf Ya'qub finished the job begun by his predecessor and established Marinid predominance throughout Morocco. However, he was unable to reestablish Moroccan authority either in the central and eastern Maghreb or over Islamic Spain, as the Almohads had done. Like his brother, Abu Yusuf accepted the nominal sovereignty of the Hafsids of Tunis in order to establish religious legitimacy for ruling Morocco. The Hafsids claimed to be the true successors of the Almohads and to have remained faithful to the original doctrines of Almohad founder Ibn Tumart. Since the Hafsids were far away, this allegiance did not restrict the Marinids from serving as the independent rulers of Morocco.

Upon accession to the throne, Abu Yusuf encountered opposition from a number of sources. In addition to his ongoing battles with the Almohads, he faced hostility from the Zayyanid ruler of Tlemcen, Yaghmurasan. Afraid that a strong Marinid state would threaten his hold on the central Maghreb, Yaghmurasan often allied with the Almohads so that the Marinids faced a two-front war with the Almohads, who did not respect the sovereignty of the Hafsids in the south, and the Zayyanids in the north. In addition, Abu Yusuf worried about the Castilian threat from southern Spain. On multiple occasions he felt compelled to send troops into the Iberian Peninsula to prop up the Muslim buffer state of Granada. Abu Yusuf's main goal seems to have been to retain a balance of power in Spain so that at times he even came to the assistance of Castile in putting down local rebellions. He also made an alliance with the Christian kingdom of Aragon to help him bring the local emir of Ceuta, Abu al-Qasim al-'Azfi, under control.

But the biggest threats to Abu Yusuf's rule were the internal challenges that he faced. Arising from a confederation of northern Berber tribes loosely related to one another, the Marinid state was never lacking in multiple claimants to the throne. In 1259, Abu Yusuf encountered a rebellion led by his nephew, Ya'qub ibn Abdulla. Ya'qub had managed to capture the coastal towns of Rabat and Salé as well as to obtain military support from Castile, which hoped to gain entrée into Morocco by backing the pretender. It took 3 years for Abu Yusuf to put down this rebellion. His efforts were often hindered by the fact that he was frequently drawn away from combating the rebels by Zayyanid incursions in the east. Nevertheless, by 1262, Abu Yusuf had made peace with his rebellious relatives, sending them off to the holy war in Spain, where they could cause trouble for the Castilians rather than himself. With problems in the north temporarily under control, Abu Yusuf turned his attention back to the Almohads. He finally captured Marrakech in 1269, effectively uniting Morocco under Marinid rule. By 1275, the remaining Almohads had been rounded up and executed—except for a few who retreated to remote mountain hideaways.

The second internal threat came from the Marinid capital of Fez. The Fezzis saw their city as the religious center of the country, and they viewed the Marinids as unsophisticated upstarts who lacked true legitimacy to rule. After dealing with numerous revolts and problems with the Fezzi elite, Abu Yusuf decided to build his own capital on the outskirts of Fez. In 1276, he began construction on Fez al-Jadid (New Fez) right next to the old city (Fez al-Bali). This new city would serve as the administrative capital of the country, where the sultan's palace would be located and the army barracks were built. Eventually, the Marinid sultans would also move the Jewish population into Fez al-Jadid, into a neighborhood that became known as "the Mellah." This was because the Jews served many useful functions for the Marinid state and, behind the fortifications of New Fez, they could be better protected from the religious prejudices of the larger populace. At the same time, the existence of the Marinid capital directly next to Fez al-Bali provided the sultans with the opportunity to keep an eye on religious dissidence and to work on establishing ties among the city's influential religious scholars.

By the early 1270s, Abu Yusuf felt his rule to be more secure, and he was in a better position to attempt an expansion of Marinid power beyond the borders of Morocco. In 1272, he took on the Zayyanid threat, defeating Yaghmurasan at Isly and destroying his fortress at Oujda. Although he also laid siege to Tlemcen, Abu Yusuf was unable to conquer the city. In 1274, the Marinids captured the southern desert city of Sijilmasa, wresting it from the authority of the Zayyanids. This victory allowed Abu Yusuf to gain more direct control over the prosperous caravan trade from West Africa, which passed through the desert outpost. It also provided additional security for the southern parts of the country. After agreeing to a truce with Yaghmurasan, Abu Yusuf began to pursue active involvement in Spain. From 1275 to 1286, the Marinid sultan led four expeditions across the Strait of Gibraltar, frequently involving himself in internal struggles among the Castilians and Granadans in an effort to stabilize his northern frontier.

By the time of his death on 20 March 1286, Abu Yusuf Ya'qub had successfully consolidated Marinid authority throughout Morocco. He had eliminated the Almohads, defeated the Zayyanids, gained an interest in the caravan trade at Sijilmasa, and constructed a new capital that stabilized the Marinid administration, even as it helped to keep Fezzi religious opposition under control. Although Marinid rule lacked the scope and religious legitimacy of the earlier Almohads, the Marinids had at least established their supremacy in Morocco and demonstrated themselves to be a dynasty that neighboring states would need to take seriously. It was a feat in which the old sultan could legitimately take pride.

[See also Abu Yahya ibn 'Abd al-Haqq; and Yaghmurasan.]

BIBLIOGRAPHY

Ibn Abi Zar', Abu al-Hasan. *Kitab al-anis al-mutrib bi-rawd al-Qirtas*. French translation *Roudh El-Kartas: Histoire des souverains du Maghreb (Espagne et Maroc) et annals de la ville de Fès*. Translated by A. Beaumier. Paris: L'Imprimerie Impériale, 1860.

Ibn al-Ahmar, Abu al-Walid. *Rawdat al Nisrîn*. French translation *Histoire des Benî Marîn, rois de Fâs intitulée Rawdat al Nisrîn (Le Jardin des Églantines)*. Edited and annotated translation by Ghaoutsi Bouali and Georges Marçais. Paris: Ernest Leroux, 1917.

Ibn Khaldun, 'Abd al-Rahman. *Kitab al-'Ibar*. French translation *Histoire des Berbères et des dynasties musulmanes de l'Afrique septentrionale*, nouv. ed., 4 vols. Translation by Baron de Slane. Paris: Casanova, 1968–1969.

Shatzmiller, Maya. *The Berbers and the Islamic State: The Marinid Experience in Pre-Protectorate Morocco*. Princeton: Markus Weiner, 2000.

STEPHEN CORY

Abu Zayd, Nasr Hamid (1943–2010), Egyptian thinker and academic, was born in Quhafa in Tanta. His father was a grocer and his mother a housewife. He had two sisters and two brothers. He married Ibtihal Younes, a professor of French literature at Cairo University. Though his family could not afford to give him a university education, he obtained an industrial secondary diploma in 1960 that enabled him to work as a radio technician between 1961 and 1972.

Abu Zayd joined the Department of Arabic, Faculty of Arts, Cairo University. Upon his graduation in 1972, he was appointed as a teaching assistant in Islamic studies. He obtained his MA degree in 1976 and his PhD. in 1982. During the preparation of his Ph.D., he attained a Ford Foundation Grant to study at the American University in Cairo between 1976 and 1977. Then, between 1978 and 1980, he obtained a grant from the Middle East Center at the University of Pennsylvania. He also worked as a visiting professor at the University of Osaka from 1985 to 1989.

After a controversial court sentence demanding the divorce of Abu Zayd from his wife, on the basis of Abu Zayd's being an apostate, he had to leave Egypt. In October 1995, he settled in the Netherlands to work as a visiting professor at the University of Leiden. In 2002, he was appointed as professor to the Averroes (Ibn Rushd) Chair at the University of Utrecht. He died in Cairo on 5 July 2010 after contracting a virus during a visit to Indonesia.

Abu Zayd devoted the majority of his academic work to the study of both the traditional and the contemporary Islamic discourses. In a brief statement summarizing the purpose of his academic project, Abu Zayd says that it is "the production of scientific awareness of religion and rational interpretations of the texts wherein history and human interests are seen as essential factors" (Abu Zayd, 1994, p. 48).

To achieve this aim, Abu Zayd tackled many fundamental issues related to the major trends in the interpretation of the Qur'an in Islamic tradition. He dedicated his M.A. thesis to dealing with the problem of metaphor in the Qur'an; it was published under the title *Rationalism in Exegesis: A Study of the Problem of Metaphor in the Writing of the Mutazilites* (*Al-Ittijah al-'Aqli fi al-Tafsir: Dirasah fi Qadiyat al-Majaz fi al-Qur'an 'inda al-Mu'tazilah*, 1982).

His doctoral thesis tackled the basis of the Sufis' hermeneutics of the Qur'an in the writings of Ibn Arabi. It was published under the title *The Philosophy of Hermeneutics: A Study of Ibn al-'Arabi's Hermeneutics of the Qur'an* (*Falsafat al-Ta'wil: Dirasah fi Ta'wil al-Qur'an 'inda Muhyi al-Din ibn al-'Arabi*, 1983). Moreover, in his book *The Foundation of Moderate Ideology in Islamic Thought by al-Shafi'i* (*al-Imam al-Shafi'i wa-Ta'sis al-Idiyulujiyah al-Wasatiyah*, 1993), Abu Zayd explored al-Shafi'i's concepts of the Qur'an and Sunnah, which had a great influence on many traditional interpretations of the Qur'an.

Before leaving Egypt, Abu Zayd wrote *The Concept of the Text*, which produced much controversy. In this book, Abu Zayd argues that the qur'anic text is a product of the interaction between the revelation and the social, political, and economic conditions that surrounded its descent, understanding, and interpretation. To understand the impact of cultural factors in the production of the meaning of the qur'anic text, he employs linguistic and philosophical approaches and methodologies such as semiotics, discourse analysis, and hermeneutics. These approaches allow him to present new perspectives on some of the central concepts in qur'anic studies, such as the revelation, the burner and the abrogated, Mecca or Medina verses, and the reasons behind the descent of the Qur'an.

Abu Zayd pursued his project in Islamic discourse critique by working in two directions. First, he developed methodologies for analyzing texts and talk; his coedited book *The Systems of Signs* (*Ilm al-'Alamat*, 1986) is considered one of his most prominent contributions to this field. Second, he studied critically contemporary Islamic discourses such as salafism, fundamentalism, political Islamic groups, and what Abu Zayd termed the "Islamic left." *Critique of Islamic Discourse* (*Naqd al-Khitab al-Dini*) is considered one of his most important books in this field.

Abu Zayd spent the period from 1995 until his death in 2010 outside Egypt except for short visits. During this period, he achieved a high international profile in the field of qur'anic studies. He wrote many of his works in English, and his major writings have been translated into different languages such as Dutch, English, French, German, Turkish, Persian, Indonesian, and Spanish.

During this period, Abu Zayd paid great attention to two major issues, the first being human rights, especially the rights of women. His book *Circles of Fear* (*Dawa'ir al-Khawf*) analyzes the religious discourse that could be employed to legitimize sorts of domination and discrimination against women in some Islamic societies. The second issue is the development of a humanistic hermeneutics approach to the Qur'an that gives a key role to the human historical and cultural context that accompanies the descent of the Qur'an in comprehending and reproducing its meaning. He attempted to put his approach into practice through the establishment of an institute of qur'anic studies in Indonesia; he was working intensively toward its establishment in the months immediately preceding his death.

Abu Zayd received many awards, including the Prize of Democracy, awarded by the Association of Muslim Democrat, Copenhagen, Denmark (2006); the Ibn Rushd Prize for Freedom of Thought, Berlin (2005); and the Jordanian Writers Association Award for Democracy and Freedom, Jordan (1998).

BIBLIOGRAPHY

Abu Zayd, Nasr. *Dawa'ir al-Khawf: Qira'ah fi Khitab al-Mar'ah.* (Circles of Fear: Analysis of the Discourse about Women). Beirut and Casablanca: al-Markaz al-Thakafi al-Arabi, 1999.

Abu Zayd, Nasr. *Mafhum al-Nass: Dirasah fi 'Ulum al-Qur'an.* (The Concept of the Text: A Study of the Qur'anic Sciences). Cairo: General Egyptian Book Organization, 1993.

Abu Zayd, Nasr. *Naqd al-Khitab al-Dini* (Critique of Islamic Discourse), 2d ed. Cairo: Sina, 1994.

Abu Zayd, Nasr. *Reformation of Islamic Thought: A Critical Historical Analysis.* Amsterdam: Amsterdam University Press, 2006.

Abu Zayd, Nasr. *Rethinking the Qur'an: Towards a Humanistic Hermeneutics.* Utrecht: Humanistics University Press, 2004.

Abu Zayd, Nasr, and Esther R. Nelson. *Voice of an Exile: Reflections on Islam.* New York: Praeger, 2004.

Abu, Zayd, Nasr, and Siza Kasim. (eds.). *'Ilm al-'Alamat.* (The Systems of Signs). Cairo: Ilias, 1986.

EMAD ABDUL-LATIF

Acheampong, Ignatius Kutu (1931–1979), army officer and military head of state of Ghana, was born in Trabuom in the present-day Ashanti Region of southern Ghana and then part of Britain's Gold Coast colony. He was the son of James Kwadwo Kutu Acheampong and Akua Manu. Raised as a Roman Catholic, he attended Trabuom Elementary School and St. Peter's Catholic School in Kumasi, before receiving his secondary education at the Central College of Commerce at Swedru in the Central Region of Ghana. Having obtained his West Africa Secondary School General Certificate of Education at the ordinary level (popularly known as GCE O level) and a diploma in commerce, he worked in various places and positions. From 1945 to 1951, he was a stenographer/secretary at the Timber Sawmill in Kumasi, a teacher at Kumasi Commercial College, and the vice principal at Agona-Swedru College of Commerce.

Acheampong subsequently enlisted as a private soldier in the British colonial army in 1951 and was sent for further training at Aldershot, England, one of the top military training centers of the British army. Having served with a British army contingent in Germany, Acheampong returned home and in 1959 was commissioned as an officer in the Ghana army with the rank of second lieutenant. He rose quickly through the ranks and received advance training, including a personnel administration course at the United States Army Staff College, in Fort Leavenworth, Kansas. He subsequently became the commanding officer of the 5th and 6th battalions of Ghana's army. In the early 1960s, he served with the Ghanaian contingent in the United Nations Peacekeeping Force in Congo. At the rank of lieutenant colonel he served in the administration of the first military regime of Ghana, the National Liberation Council, as the chair of the Brong-Ahafo Regional Committee. Between 1971 and 1972, he served as the commander of the First Infantry Brigade. Prior to his coup, he was appointed as the commander of the Southern Brigade of the Ghana Army, from where he plotted and executed his coup d'état against the democratically elected government of Dr. Kofi Abrefa Busia on 13 January 1972.

Although the election of Busia heralded a return to civilian rule, his government faced many challenges in the early 1970s, particularly in the economic sphere. Busia's austerity measures, notably his decision to devalue the Ghana currency—the cedi—by 48.6 percent, provoked widespread discontent and served as the primary motivation for the military coup. Acheampong struck while Busia was in London receiving medical care. The coup was bloodless, and Colonel Acheampong moved quickly to seize and consolidate power. He constituted the National Redemption Council (NRC) government, of which he was the chair and, as such, the head of state of Ghana. He suspended the 1969 constitution, banned party politics, and detained some people perceived to be threats to the NRC. The NRC was later reorganized as the Supreme Military Council (SMC), again under the chair of Acheampong.

Associating himself with the nationalist and anti-imperialist ideology and rhetoric of Ghana's first president, Kwame Nkrumah, Acheampong implemented certain populist economic policies that reversed Busia's fiscal conservatism. Historian Kevin Shillington notes that the new regime canceled the 5 percent development levy, revalued the cedi, and, using the popular cry of "*Yentua, yentua*" ("We won't pay, we won't pay"), repudiated many of the country's debts. Acheampong popularized the ideal of self-reliance and launched Operation Feed Yourself, an agricultural project aimed at promoting self-sufficiency in food production in Ghana. As part of this project, the regime implemented the Tono and Vea irrigation projects in the drought-prone Upper Region (now Upper East Region) and the Dawenya irrigation project on the Accra plains. As Roger Gocking observed in his *The History of Ghana*, Operation Feed Yourself was the most successful program of the NRC because Ghana was able to produce enough food that it could feed its population and even export rice in 1973. In addition, the NRC managed to lift the country from a trade deficit of $56 million in 1971 to a trade surplus of $204 million in 1973.

However, the initial successes of Operation Feed Yourself and Acheampong's economic policies were short-lived. Subsequently, mismanagement, corruption, and unfavorable international economic factors (like the global oil crisis of 1973) combined to plunge the Ghanaian economy into perhaps the worst crisis that it has ever faced since independence. Inflation reached 116.4 percent in 1977—because Acheampong's only solution to the mounting budget deficits was to print more money. In the face of this crisis the Acheampong government had few solutions, save for launching an essay competition seeking suggestions on improving the economy. Acheampong even declared a week of prayer for the economy in 1977, an act of disorientation, if not delusion, in the face of the economic crisis. At the same time Acheampong and his colleagues in the NRC/SMC continued to loot the state coffers for their personal enrichment and that of their cronies. The high-level corruption and nepotism that marked Ghanaian politics during the 1970s military regime resulted in a new word—*kalabule*—being coined to capture the situation.

In order to maintain power indefinitely, Acheampong devised a system of nonparty government known as the Union Government (UNIGOV) by which the army, the police, and civilians ostensibly governed the country together—with himself at the head of this coalition. His declared—and to many Ghanaians, plausible—reason for proposing the UNIGOV was that party politics "brought in divisions, tribalism, victimization and various forms of social evil." Using the nationalist appeals of Nkrumah and borrowing the rhetoric of American president Abraham Lincoln, Acheampong declared his commitment to "a government of the people for the people" to which "everybody must belong" (Gocking, 2005, p. 175). However, his UNIGOV proposal sparked protests by students and other professional bodies, like the Ghana Bar Association, which strongly opposed it as a thinly veiled front for a one-party military dictatorship headed by Acheampong. In 1977, the National Union of Students organized demonstrations at the three universities in Ghana at the time (University of Ghana, University of Cape Coast, and University of Science and Technology) against the UNIGOV and called for Acheampong to resign. He refused and, determined to implement his UNIGOV proposal, used the police to crack down on the student demonstrations, resulting in the death of one student at the University of Ghana and the closure of the universities.

By 1978 the regime had become increasingly unpopular. Acheampong secured a referendum victory for his UNIGOV plan but was believed to have manipulated the referendum results. Matters came to a head on 5 July 1978, when members of his own SMC government and trusted commanders of his army units, led by General Fred Akuffo, his army chief of staff, and General Neville A. Odartey-Wellington, commander of the Ghana Army, ousted Acheampong from power in a bloodless coup. In June 1979, Akuffo's SMC II was also overthrown by J. J. Rawlings; and in the midst of the public anger against corruption in the upper echelons of the military, former military rulers, including Acheampong and Akuffo, were executed by a firing squad.

Acheampong's tenure as head of state is popularly associated with political corruption and economic mismanagement in Ghana. Moreover, political scientists like Dennis Austin have argued that the coup d'état against Busia was unjustifiable since Busia, unlike Nkrumah, was a democrat who had done nothing to block competitive and periodic elections. Nonetheless, the regime enjoyed some successes, notably its agriculture policies. Irrigation projects established under Acheampong in the 1970s continued to serve as a source of food security for people who lived near them in the decades that followed. He also won respect in many quarters for giving Kwame Nkrumah a state funeral befitting the nation's founding head of state.

[*See also* Akuffo, Fred; Busia, Kofi Abrefa; Nkrumah, Kwame; *and* Rawlings, Jerry John.]

BIBLIOGRAPHY

Austin, Dennis. "The Ghana Armed Forces and Ghanaian Society." *Third World Quarterly* 7, no. 1 (January 1985): 90–101.

Gocking, Roger. *The History of Ghana.* Westport, Conn.: Greenwood Press, 2005.

Oquaye, Mike. *Politics in Ghana 1982–92: Rawlings, Revolution and Populist Democracy.* Accra, Ghana: Tornado Publications, 2004.

Shillington, Kevin. *Ghana and the Rawlings Factor.* New York: St. Martin's Press, 1992.

JASPER AYELAZUNO

Achebe, Chinua (1930–), Nigerian novelist, was born Albert Chinualumogu Achebe on 15 November 1930 at Saint Simon's Church, Nneobi, near Ogidi, in British colonial Nigeria. His father, Isaiah Okafo Achebe, was a teacher and evangelist and his mother, Janet Anaenechi Iloeghunam, was from the Awka area of eastern Nigeria. Until the age of five, Achebe was brought up at a church school, where his father taught. When his father went into semiretirement in 1935 in Ogidi, Achebe became a child of two worlds, the modern world and the world of indigenous tradition. He began primary school at Saint Philip's Central School at Akpakaogwe, Ogidi, moving on to Nekede Central School near Owerri in 1942. Achebe developed into a studious young man, passing entrance examinations for two prestigious secondary schools.

It was at Government College Umuahia, which had a good library and extremely able and dedicated teachers, that Achebe cultivated his love of literature. The school's insistence on correct grammatical expression and use of English outside the classroom afforded Achebe the opportunity to

Chinua Achebe, 2002. (AP Images/Craig Ruttle)

master the language exceedingly well. In 1948, he left Government College with great distinction, winning a scholarship to study medicine at the newly founded University College Ibadan, which was then affiliated with the University of London. After the first year, he switched from medicine to English, history, and geography, later replacing geography with religious studies.

Even more critical to Achebe's formation as a writer was the English syllabus at Ibadan, which offered a full historical coverage of English literature. It was particularly the inclusion of novels such as Joseph Conrad's *Heart of Darkness* and Joyce Cary's *Mister Johnson* that provoked Achebe into

becoming a writer. While at the university Achebe began to write essays, poems, and short stories that he published in two campus journals, *The Bug* and *The University Herald*, the latter of which he was the editor. He received a second-class B.A. degree, which must have disappointed him and clearly came as a surprise to his teachers. Even so, a University of London B.A. was a passport to greater things.

After graduating, he returned home, eventually becoming a teacher at the Merchants of Light School, a private school in Oba that was a far cry from the well-resourced government school he had attended. Achebe put together a rudimentary library and taught English and history, picking up teaching skills that would stand him in good stead as a university don in Nigeria and the United States. He left this post in 1954 to join the Nigerian Broadcasting Service (NBS) in Lagos, where he established himself as a reliable and innovative editor and producer and developed an appreciation of the difference between the spoken and written word, especially regarding English. In 1957, he became department head.

Around this time Achebe began to write seriously, beginning work on what would become the novel *Things Fall Apart* in 1955 and completing a full draft by the time he attended a course at the BBC Staff Training College in 1956. One of his tutors there encouraged him to submit it for publication, and on his return to Nigeria, Achebe revised and submitted it to publishers in London. In the view of Achebe scholar Simon Gikandi, the novel's publication in 1958 inaugurated modern African writing in English. The novel presents a complex picture of the precolonial African past, and its depiction of the meeting of Igbo and Europeans rebuts colonial stereotypes of the continent.

In 1958, Achebe was promoted to NBS controller of the Eastern Region in Enugu, in recognition of his innovative programming. Around this time, he met his wife, Christie Chinwe Okoli, from Umuokpu, Awka, who was then working at Broadcasting House, whom he married on 10 September 1961 in Ibadan. Soon after his marriage, Achebe became director of external broadcasting, making him one of the most influential people in postcolonial Nigeria, especially in adapting broadcast media to the needs of the nation, which became independent in October 1960 and a republic in 1963. With access to the new political elite, Achebe was one of the first to sense that all was not well with the new state, and his writing began to reflect this. Originally conceived as part of a trilogy, the novel *No Longer at Ease* (1960) depicts Obi Okonkwo, grandson of Okonkwo, the protagonist in *Things Fall Apart*, as culturally deracinated and lacking any morals. In Achebe's third novel, *Arrow of God* (1964), Ezeulu, a chief priest, accommodates Christianity and Western influence with a view to employing it strategically, should it be efficacious, to bolster his own position; but his wager proves a miscalculation. *A Man of the People* (1966), published after his 1962 elevation to editor of the Heinemann African Writers Series, would be considered prophetic of the crisis that engulfed Nigeria from 1966 to 1970.

Hardly had *A Man of the People* been published than Nigeria had its first coup, in January 1966, led by junior officers predominantly of Igbo origin. There was suspicion in some government quarters that Achebe's novel might have been informed by his being privy to the plans for the coup, something he has denied and dismissed as improbable. The coup was generally seen in the Northern Region as a usurpation by one particular ethnic group, the Igbo; and as a result, unspeakable violence was targeted on them in the north, spreading to other parts of the country, including Lagos. In July a countercoup by northern officers, presided over by General Yakubu Gowon, established a new government. Most of the Igbo and other groups from the east, such as the Ijaw and Effik, fled to the Eastern Region, where in 1967, under the leadership of Colonel Chukwuemeka Ojukwu, the Republic of Biafra was proclaimed. Achebe, a reluctant separatist, remained in Lagos; but with his commitment to the ideal of a united Nigeria shattered, he went east and committed himself wholly to the defense and consolidation of the new republic as a roving ambassador, a senior member of the Ministry of Information, and chair of the National Guidance Committee that drafted *The Ahiara Declaration: The Principles of the Biafran Revolution* (1969).

Achebe was unable to do much writing during the war, but he did publish a collection of poetry, *Beware Soul Brother* (1971), and another of short stories, *Girls at War* (1972). Both collections drew upon the difficulties of day-to-day life in Biafra. With the poet Christopher Okigbo, he set up a publishing house that planned to publish *How the Leopard Got His Claws*; but Okigbo died at the battlefront and the publishing house was bombed, so it was published in 1972 by Nwamfe Publishers. The story shows Achebe's ability to use oral tradition as a political and a moral weapon. It was not easy for him at this time to continue as editor of the Heinemann Series, and he relinquished the position in 1972. In addition, he founded the Centre for African Studies at the University of Nigeria, Nsukka, during the war. After the end of the war, on 12 January 1970, he returned to the university, establishing *Okike*, a journal of creative writing and criticism, and contributing to the rebuilding of the university.

In September 1972, Achebe left for the United States to take up an appointment at the University of Massachusetts, Amherst, and a visiting professorship at the University of Connecticut before returning in 1976 to a chair in English at the University of Nigeria, which he occupied until his retirement in 1981. In 1975 he published a collection of critical essays, *Morning Yet on Creation Day*, which included his most influential essay, "The Novelist as Teacher." Achebe was also consolidating his position as a literary critic. In most of his lectures in Nigeria during this period, he offered an alternative vision of the country, in which he saw education as central to the task of transformation. He continued to travel abroad, giving numerous lectures and receiving countless honors. In 1979, he accepted one of the highest honors in the country, the Nigerian National Merit Award, and appointment as officer of the Order of the Federal Republic of Nigeria. Although some expressed surprise as to why Achebe would accept a military government award, he contended that he needed to encourage the recognition of merit in Nigeria and especially the contribution of the arts. During this time, he organized the tenth-anniversary celebration of *Okike* and resuscitated the Association of Nigerian Authors, of which he had been president before the civil war. In many ways, this was Achebe's firm return to the ideal of one Nigeria, though he continued to worry about the underlying instability of the country.

After retiring from the university, he entered politics, in 1983 joining the People's Redemption Party, led by Aminu Kano, who Achebe believed offered the possibility of radical change, and becoming party chair. However, just before the national elections that year, Kano died; and with his successors resurrecting the old xenophobic politics, Achebe resigned from the party but continued to analyze and comment on public affairs. By this time he had published his important treatise *The Trouble with Nigeria* (1983), in which he argued that the trouble with Nigeria was a failure of leadership.

In 1983, the civilian government of Shehu Shagari was overthrown by General Muhammadu Buhari, who, after promising to rectify things, settled into business as usual, leading to his own overthrow by General Ibrahim Babangida in 1985. Achebe was one of the first people to recognize that the new leader was also sly and autocratic. In 1986, he and Wole Soyinka pleaded with Babangida for clemency for Major General Mamman Vatsa and other alleged coup plotters, but they were executed. In the 1980s, Achebe refused Babangida's offer to chair a public body responsible for radio and telecommunications. On the literary front, the two-day Heinemann conference of African and Caribbean Writers at the Institute of Contemporary Arts, London, which brought together Ngugi wa Thiong'o and Nuruddin Farah, among others, put Achebe

center stage when he argued that, though indigenous languages in Africa were important, writing in English was a legitimate exercise and one that helped in nation building.

However, it was the publication of Achebe's long-awaited fifth novel, *Anthills of the Savannah*, in 1987 that crowned that decade for the writer. The novel revisited the ground covered by *A Man of the People* but did so with greater perceptiveness of the subtle personality shifts that lead to dictatorship. The following year Achebe published a collection of essays, *Hopes and Impediments*, covering his thinking between 1965 and 1987, particularly in the essay on Joseph Conrad's *Heart of Darkness*. Despite criticism of the essay by some, Achebe had made his point and his views now became part of the canonical critical opinion on *Heart of Darkness*.

A number of celebrations were held in honor of Achebe's sixtieth birthday in 1990, most poignantly at the University of Nigeria, where he had spent much of his time as a teacher. Despite a car accident that year which left him paralyzed, he took up the Charles Stephenson Professorship of Literature at Bard College, New York, where in the early 2000s he continues to teach. Confined to a wheelchair, he adopted the philosophy that "one learns as one suffers and one is richer" (Ezenwa-Ohaeto, 1997, p. 254). His travels and public lectures continued apace, notably his 1993 Ashby Lecture at Clare College, which reflected on his early formation as a writer and intellectual. Among the honors bestowed on him in the 1990s were the 1998 MacMillan-Stewart Lectureship at Harvard University and the Presidential Fellow Lectureship at the World Bank.

Although he spent most of the 1990s outside Nigeria, he remained engaged in the political process. When General Sani Abacha seized power in 1993, Achebe campaigned for the reinstatement of civilian rule. On a visit to Nigeria in 1999 he met the new civilian leader, President Olusegun Obasanjo, a retired army general. Achebe praised the return to democracy, albeit with reservations. His caution was proved correct by the continuation of corruption and evidence of electoral fraud in Obasanjo's reelection in 2003. In 2004, Achebe rejected the second highest honor in Nigeria, commander of the Federal Republic of Nigeria, which Obasanjo had granted him.

Achebe's seventieth birthday in 2000 was celebrated by an international gathering of writers, critics, and friends at Bard. Nelson Mandela saluted him as "a fellow freedom fighter in whose company the prison walls fell down" (Jaggi, 2000). The Nobel

Prize laureates Wole Soyinka and Nadine Gordimer also congratulated him. The same year, his reflections on life away from Nigeria were published in *Home and Exile*. In 2007, he was awarded the Man Booker International Prize, correcting what many perceived as a great injustice to African literature, that the founding father of African literature had not won some of the key international prizes. In 2008, the fiftieth anniversary of the publication of *Things Fall Apart* was celebrated at Birkbeck College and the Institute of English Studies in London and at Princeton and Bard College in the United States. The following January, Achebe returned to Nigeria for the first time in 10 years to give the 2009 Ahajioku Lecture as part of an International Festival of Igbo culture. That year he also published a collection of essays, *The Education of A British-Protected Child*, and joined Brown University in Providence, Rhode Island, as the David and Marianna Fisher University Professor and professor of African studies.

In six decades as one of Africa's leading thinkers and writers, Achebe's main concern has been with the wider implications of the continent's place in history and the world. In years to come, the Chinua Achebe Centre for African Literatures and Languages and the Chinua Achebe Fellowship in Global African Studies at Bard College will provide an educational and financial resource for African writers and scholars to continue in that tradition.

[*See also* Abacha, Sani; Babangida, Ibrahim Badamosi; Farah, Nuruddin; Gowon, Yakubu Jack; Gordimer, Nadine; Kano, Muhammad Aminu; Mandela, Nelson Rolihlahla; Ngugi wa Thiong'o; Obasanjo, Olusegun; Ojukwu, Chukwuemeka Odumegwu; Okigbo, Christopher Ifekandu; *and* Soyinka, Wole.]

BIBLIOGRAPHY

Ezenwa-Ohaeto. *Chinua Achebe: A Biography*. Oxford: James Currey, 1997.

Gikandi, Simon. *Reading Chinua Achebe*. Oxford: James Currey, 1991.

Jaggi, Maya. "Storyteller of the Savannah." *Guardian*, January 18, 2000.

Lindfors, Bernth. *Conversations with Chinua Achebe*. Jackson: University Press of Mississippi, 1997.

Pilkington, Ed. "A Long Way from Home." *Guardian*, July 10, 2007.

Sallah, Tijan, and Ngozi Okonjo-Iweala. *Chinua Achebe: Teacher of Light*. Trenton, N.J.: Africa World Press, 2003.

Sengupta, Somini. "A Storyteller." *New York Times*, January 10, 2000.

MPALIVE-HANGSON MSISKA

Achmat, Adurrazack (1962–), antiapartheid, gay rights, AIDS, and human rights activist, was born in Johannesburg in South Africa. Adurrazack ("Zackie") Achmat was of Cape Malay heritage. His father, Suleiman Achmat, was a member of the South African Communist Party and his mother, Mymoena, was a trade union shop steward. Achmat's entry into politics began at the age of 14 with his participation in the 1976 student uprising. He was detained in 1977 for burning down his high school in Salt River to demonstrate his support for the uprising. Achmat obtained a bachelor of arts honors degree in English literature from the University of the Western Cape in 1992.

He spent much of the period between 1976 and 1980 in detention for his opposition to the apartheid system. It was also in this period that Achmat read the then-banned works of Karl Marx and Leon Trotsky and the progressive academic journal *Work in Progress*. In conjunction with other student activists, he also provided critical support to the strike-related boycotts of Fattis and Monis and Wilson Rowntree's products (Carson, 2008).

Achmat was recruited into the African National Congress while being detained in 1980. In the 1980s and early 1990s Achmat was a member of the Trotskyite Marxist Workers' Tendency. In 1984 he cofounded the Bellville Community Health Project with Jack Lewis.

Achmat was diagnosed as being HIV-positive in 1990. Following his diagnosis, Achmat focused on gay rights activism. In 1992 he cofounded the Association of Bisexuals, Lesbians and Gays (ABIGALE) with his sister Midi Achmat in Cape Town. ABIGALE worked effectively with its gay rights allies to advocate for the inclusion of the sexual orientation nondiscrimination clause in the interim constitution of 1993. In 1994 he cofounded the National Coalition for Gay and Lesbian Equality. This organization succeeded in advocacy for the clause's retention in the final constitution of 1996 and obtained extensive law reform through equality litigation for lesbian, gay, bisexual, and transgendered persons (Croucher, 2002; Thoreson, 2008). Achmat also promoted gay rights through his work as a filmmaker. He cofounded Idol Pictures with Jack Lewis in 1993 and the Out in Africa Film Festival in 1994.

In late 1994 Achmat began to work at the AIDS Law Project, which had been formed by a human rights lawyer, Edwin Cameron. Achmat cofounded the Treatment Action Campaign (TAC) in December 1998, calling for its formation at the funeral of activist colleague Simon Tseko Nkoli. He was most widely known and fêted both in his own country and internationally for his role as chairperson of TAC (1998–2008).

Achmat played a critical role as its media spokesperson. At a time when AIDS activists such as Gugu Dlamini were murdered for revealing their diagnosis, he placed a strong emphasis on openness about living with the disease and designed TAC's iconic "HIV POSITIVE" T-shirts. TAC's strategies were newly radical in the history of AIDS activism. The movement effectively drew on antiapartheid imagery to claim moral and political legitimacy (Robins, 2004). And it did so in a credible manner, largely because most of its more experienced activists such as Achmat had a history of antiapartheid organizing. The movement also effectively used film to advance its cause. Lewis produced and directed a film *(Patient Abuse, 2001)* and a television series *(Siyayinqoba Beat It!,* 1998–) dealing with TAC (Hodes, 2010). Achmat also starred in a biographical documentary by Brian Tilley *(It's My Life,* 2001).

From 1998 to 2001 the overwhelming focus of the movement's activism was its opposition to litigation by the main multinational pharmaceutical industry body—the Pharmaceutical Manufacturers' Association—against Nelson Mandela's government. This litigation was aimed at blocking legislation to enable wider access to affordable, essential generic medicines. In 2000 Achmat led a successful global campaign for the Pharmaceutical Manufacturers' Association to drop its suit, with tactics including civil disobedience. He also made an extraordinary pledge (2000–2003) to refuse to take combination antiretroviral therapy until the pharmaceutical industry and government enabled universal access to it in South Africa.

In 2001 TAC embarked on constitutional litigation to force the South African government to provide nevirapine for the prevention of mother-to-child transmission of HIV infection at all public-sector antenatal facilities. This was necessary because President Thabo Mbeki and his health minister, Manto Tshabalala Msimang, adhered to AIDS dissidence (Mbali, 2003; Nattrass, 2007). In 2002 the Constitutional Court upheld a Pretoria High Court judgment which ordered comprehensive public-sector provision of the drug on the basis of the right to access to health care (Heywood, 2003).

Achmat remained a key movement strategist and spokesperson throughout this campaign. Achmat also led TAC's second civil disobedience campaign (2003), when activists were arrested en masse to highlight their demand that the government adopt a national HIV treatment plan. In 2003 the government announced a plan for public-sector provision of the drugs.

Achmat received numerous awards for his TAC activism. Most notably, he was named one of *Time* magazine's Heroes of 2003 and the Quaker American Friends Service Committee nominated both him and TAC for the Nobel Peace Prize (2003). He also obtained an honorary masters degree (University of Cape Town, 2002), an honorary doctor of law degree (University of Natal, 2003), and an honorary doctorate (University of the Western Cape, 2005). Both Achmat and TAC decried the suboptimal antiretroviral rollout, which was substantially driven by the minister's continued AIDS dissidence. And greater political will to optimally provide treatment was only in evidence in the administrations that followed Mbeki's ousting as president. In 2008 TAC assumed new leadership, but Achmat remained a member of the movement.

He married his long-time partner Dalli Weyers in Cape Town in 2008.

Achmat went on to cofound the Social Justice Coalition (2008) and Equal Education (2008). In addition, he served as the director of the Centre for Law & Social Justice in Cape Town (2009–).

[*See also* Cameron, Edwin; Mandela, Nelson Rolihlahla; *and* Mbeki, Thabo Mvuyelwa.]

BIBLIOGRAPHY

Carson, Tracy. "Black Trade Unions and Consumer Boycotts in the Cape Province, South Africa 1978–1982." PhD diss., Oxford University, 2008.

Croucher, Sheila. "South Africa's Democratization and the Politics of Gay Liberation." *Journal of Southern African Studies* 28, no. 2 (2002): 315–330.

Heywood, Mark. "Current Development: Preventing Mother-to-Child Transmission in South Africa: Backgrounds, Strategies and Outcomes in the Treatment Action Campaign Case against the Minister of Health." *South African Journal on Human Rights* 19 (2003): 278–303.

Hodes, Rebecca. "Televising Treatment: The Political Struggle for Antiretrovirals on South

African Television." *Social History of Medicine,* accessed 20 May 2010; doi: 10.1093/shm/hkp105. http://shm.oxfordjournals.org/cgi/reprint/hkp105?ij key=xFxv674nnShVOi6&keytype=ref.

Mbali, Mandisa. "HIV/AIDS Policy-Making in South Africa." In *State of the Nation: South Africa 2003–2004,* edited by John Daniel, Adam Habib, and Roger Southall, pp. 312–329. Cape Town, South Africa: HSRC Press, 2003.

Nattrass, Nicoli. *Mortal Combat: AIDS Denialism and the Struggle for Antiretrovirals in South Africa.* Scotsburg, South Africa: University of KwaZulu-Natal Press, 2007.

Robins, Steven. "Long Live Zackie, Long Live: AIDS Activism, Science and Citizenship after Apartheid." *Journal of Southern African Studies* 30, no. 3 (2004): 651–672.

Thoreson, Ryan Richard. "Somewhere over the Rainbow Nation: Gay, Lesbian and Bisexual Activism in South Africa." *Journal of Southern African Studies* 34, no. 4 (2008): 679–697.

MANDISA MBALI

Acholonu, Catherine Obianuju (1951–), Nigerian writer, also known as Catherine Obianuju Acholonu-Olumba, was born on 26 October 1951 in Orlu of Igbo parentage. The daughter of Chief Lazarus Emejuru Olumba and Josephine Olumba of Umuokwara Village in the town of Orlu in Imo State, southeastern Nigeria, she obtained her early education at local primary and secondary schools in Orlu. At age seventeen, in an arranged marriage, she became the wife of Douglas Acholonu, a surgeon then living in Germany, by whom she had four children: Ifunanya, Nneka, Chidozie, and Kelechi. In 1974 she registered as a student of English and American language and literature and Germanic linguistics at the University of Dusseldorf and earned a master's degree in her chosen field in 1977.

Upon returning to Nigeria in 1980, she accepted a teaching appointment at Alvan Ikoku College of Education in Owerri. While teaching, Acholonu was also writing her PhD dissertation. In 1982 she defended her doctoral thesis and scored two *magna cum laude* and one *cum laude*, becoming the first African woman to earn both a master's and a doctoral degree at the University of Dusseldorf.

In addition to teaching, Acholonu began writing poetry and critical essays which she presented at conferences throughout Nigeria and outside Nigeria. In 1982 she founded AFA Publications and *AFA: A Journal of Creative Writing*, which she edited. It published book reviews, critical essays, interviews, and poetry by scholars and students of African literature. In 2006 she became the first person to publish eight books in one day in Lagos, Nigeria. As a specialist in women's studies and an activist, Acholonu was the only Nigerian and one of two Africans assigned by the United Nations Division for Women and Sustainable Development to participate in the Expert Group Meeting held in Santo Domingo in 1986, with the goal of mainstreaming gender into the plans of action of the three UN Conferences of Rio de Janeiro, Brazil; Cairo, Egypt; and Beijing, China.

In the 1980s Acholonu conducted two years of field research that led to the discovery of the native Igbo roots of the African ex-slave and abolitionist Olaudah Equiano (also known as Gustava Vassa), the author of the first autobiography by an African and African American published in English, *The Interesting Narrative of the Life of Olaudah Equiano or Gustavus Vassa, The African, Written by Himself* (London, 1789). Acholonu's success in finding Equiano's African roots and family in Imo State, Nigeria, earned her a Fulbright Scholarship, as well as a sponsored lecture tour of American and British universities. She was also writer-in-residence at the Westchester Consortium for International Studies (1990–1991) and a visiting professor at Manhattanville College, Marymount College, Iona College, and the College of New Rochelle in New York State. At Manhattanville College, Acholonu initiated conversations with the administration and faculty that led to the development of an African American studies program. She was asked to head the unit she helped to create, but family pressures in Nigeria did not allow her to continue her stay in United States. In 1991 she gave the annual Hitachi Lecture at the college, entitled "The African Feminist Challenge in Life and Literature." The issues raised in this paper were later developed into her theory of African gender called Motherism.

After the publication of *The Igbo Roots of Olaudah Equiano,* Acholonu pioneered a series of groundbreaking research works in African literature and scholarship. Her book *Motherism: The Afrocentric Alternative to Feminism* (1995) has been described as the first fully articulated and sustainable theory of African gender studies. Her theory of Motherism is said to be the basis of the maternal theory being introduced in Canada and other Western countries. Another work, *They Lived Before Adam: Prehistoric Origins of the Igbo* (2009), won her the Flora Nwapa Award for Literary Excellence and the Phillis

Wheatley Award for Work that Transcends Culture, Boundary, and Perception in 2009 at the Schomburg Center for Research in Black Culture, in New York.

They Lived Before Adam is the sequel to another equally seminal publication, *The Gram Code of African Adam: Stone Books and Cave Libraries, Reconstructing 450,000 Years of Africa's Lost Civilizations* (2005). Both works make use of a new method of transcription that Acholonu and her team used to transcribe the prehistoric stone inscriptions of ancient forest dwellers in southeastern Nigeria. As a result of her work, these stone monoliths have been listed by the World Monument Fund as "writings of ancient Nigerians before 2000 B.C." Her work on these stone inscriptions has opened up a new frontier of research into African linguistics, establishing that prehistoric Africans had an indigenous system of writing. Acholonu has made a persuasive case that these prehistoric stone inscriptions are a form of written communication and that ancient Africans made undeniable contributions to world civilizations that include the first writings known to man.

Acholonu was the first Nigerian woman to have a research center named after her, The Catherine Acholonu Research Center, based in Abuja and Owerri, Nigeria, a state-of-the-art resource in African cultural research and information technology, with a publishing arm called CARC Publications, an extension of Acholonu's AFA Publications. She was appointed African Renaissance Ambassador by the African Renaissance Conference in Benin. She was until 2002 the special adviser on arts and culture to the president of the Federal Republic of Nigeria. In 2003 she was Nigeria's sole representative to the global Forum of Arts and Culture for the Implementation of the UN Convention to Combat Desertification (UNFAC).

In recognition of her groundbreaking contributions to African scholarship, Acholonu was honored with the title of professor of African history and philosophy by the Nigerian campus of Pilgrim's University and Theological Seminary in Aba, Nigeria. Her most recent publication, *The Lost Testament of the Ancestors of Adam, Unearthing Heliopolis/Igbo Ukwu, The Celestial City of the Gods of Egypt and India* (2010), is a sequel to *They Lived Before Adam*.

[*See also* Equiano, Olaudah; *and* Nwapa, Flora.]

BIBLIOGRAPHY

Berrian, Brenda F. *Bibliography of African Women Writers and Journalists: Ancient Egypt–1984.* Washington, DC: Three Continents Press, 1985.

Ezenwa-Ohaeto. *Contemporary Nigerian Poetry and the Poetics of Orality.* Bayreuth, Germany: E. Breitinger, 1998.

Miller, Jane Eldridge, editor. *Who's Who in Contemporary Women's Writing.* New York: Routledge, 2001.

MARIE UMEH

Acogny, Germaine (1944–), Senegalese dancer and choreographer, was born in Benin, the daughter of a Senegalese colonial civil servant and the granddaughter of a Yoruba priestess. When she was ten years old, her family moved to Dakar, Senegal. From an early age, Acogny showed exceptional talent for and love of dancing. After pursuing a degree in physical education, she went to France in the early 1960s, where she studied ballet and modern dance. Upon returning to Senegal, she began teaching dance classes in the courtyard of her home and in the lycée, where she was hired to be in charge of physical education. In these classes she began to develop a codification of what she calls "African dance." Establishing an inventory of positions and steps as well as a spatial stability to each position's appearance, she developed a dance technique based on an aesthetic of groundedness, a sense of dynamism moving up through the feet and then inhabiting the entire body, which she describes as specifically African.

Acogny was brought to the attention of President Léopold Sédar Senghor of Senegal after she choreographed his poem "Femme Noire, Femme Nu." Senghor had recently argued for the importance of music and the visual arts in defining African identity, and she impressed upon him the need to include dance within this theory of Négritude. As a result, he sent her to Brussels to work with the Belgian-Senegalese choreographer Maurice Béjart, who was director of the prestigious Ballet du Vingtième Siècle. In part because of her interest in codifying a lexicon of steps, Acogny was chosen by Senghor and Béjart to assist in the creation of Mudra Afrique, one in a network of schools that Béjart hoped to establish to promote contemporary dance in relation to distinctive dance traditions worldwide. Initially, Béjart specified the curriculum: daily classes in ballet, Martha Graham's modern dance technique, Acogny's African technique, dance composition, and drumming. But then he selected a Belgian director, who, in turn, chose the dance instructors, all of whom were of African ancestry and who came from Haiti to teach the Graham technique and from the United States to teach ballet. Both men claimed to know African dance better than Acogny, and they attempted to take over her portion of her curriculum. Acogny defiantly opposed this, confronting Béjart and refusing to continue with the project unless she was acknowledged as the sole director and authority of the school. Béjart consented, and Acogny, asserting her own leadership and reputation, allowed the foreign teachers to continue to teach their specialties. Thus, Acogny invited a colonial project into dialogue with her own dance practices but never allowed it to dominate and ultimately replaced Béjart's colonial structure with her own leadership.

As head of Mudra Afrique, Acogny invited European students to participate alongside students from Africa. She learned to accept that their sincere efforts simply looked different and began to integrate their variations into her teaching. Thus, rather than force conformity to a canonical repertoire, she developed an ever-changing, constantly renewing practice. Even as the National Ballet of Senegal (Ballet National du Sénégal) achieved increasing prominence, touring the world with its showcase of traditional tribal dances, Acogny defied the Western concept of an opposition between tradition and innovation upon which the National Ballet was based. Instead, she constructed an ongoing inquiry into African dance, treating its tradition as perpetually self-renewing, and began to forge a pan-African aesthetic, a hybrid product of the encounter between European contemporary dance and African forms that extended beyond region or nation to invite participation from choreographers all over the continent.

Acogny published her *Danse Africaine/Afrikanischer Tanz/African Dance* in 1980, a pathbreaking work that demonstrated Senegalese dance as consisting of a clearly specified vocabulary with identifiable criteria of competence of execution. In this it defied traditional Western assumptions about the African dancing body, which had been encoded as natural, impulsive, lascivious, or chaotic. Contrary to these racist assumptions, *African Dance* proposed a clear and progressive curriculum of study. In 1985, Acogny and her husband, Helmut Vogt, established Studio-École-Ballet-Théâtre du Troisième Monde in Toulouse, France. There, she continued to promote African dance and to cultivate awareness of an Africanist aesthetic with great success.

In 1995 Acogny returned to Senegal to solicit support for the establishment of a new dance school, and in 1998 she celebrated the opening of the École des Sables, in the village of Toabab Julau located some 40 miles south of Dakar. As in Mudra Afrique, Acogny strove to create a strong sense of community between local inhabitants and the international students who attended the school. By inviting villagers to performances and integrating their labor and resources into the school's economy, Acogny keeps the village from turning into a museum, while affirming the lengthy history of its *habitus*. Acogny has further ensured that rejuvenation by canonizing a vocabulary, one she continues to teach into the twenty-first century, that also acknowledges the flexible interplay among all bodies that learn it. École des Sables boasts an exquisite, open-air dance studio with a sand floor and a view of the ocean and surrounding baobab trees. Students practicing technique experience the uneven terrain, the slight changes in pitch and texture of the ground, with each step they take. Thus, her approach affirms one's ability to respond to the earth in idiosyncratic or improvised ways, rather than simply executing steps derived from universal principles of movement.

Beginning in 1998, Acogny embarked on a series of major collaborative projects with her company Jant-Bi and foreign choreographers who worked with her on the creation of new evening-length dances. Three major projects, with the German modern dance choreographer Susanne Linke, the Japanese butoh artist Kota Yamasaki, and the African American choreographer Jawole Willa Jo Zolar, have toured internationally to great acclaim. Acogny has also been instrumental in developing pan-African contemporary dance techniques, establishing an annual competition in choreography for new works modeled on the French Bagnolet tradition and promoting the work of younger choreographers from across Africa. Acogny was awarded the Chevalier of the Order of Merit and Officer of Arts and Letters of the French Republic and Knight of the National Order of the Lion of Senegal.

Acogny's leadership in developing African dance and her visionary collaborations with international artists have created a crucial model for how to participate in concert dance on the global stage. She is seen as a leading force by dance artists around the world who desire to pursue both the preservation of traditional aesthetics and the creation of new local and global dance works.

[*See also* Senghor, Léopold Sédar.]

BIBLIOGRAPHY

Acogny, Germaine. *Danse Africanine/Afrikanischer Tanz/African Dance*. Unterhaching, Germany: Weingarten, 1980.

Castaldi, Francesca. *Choreographies of African Identities: Négritude, Dance, and the National Ballet of Senegal*. Urbana: University of Illinois Press, 2006.

Thompson, Robert Farris. *African Art in Motion: Icon and Act in the Collection of Katherine Coryton White*. National Gallery of Art, Washington, DC; Frederick S. Wight Art Gallery, University of California, Los Angeles. Los Angeles and Berkeley: University of California Press, 1974. Exhibition catalog.

Welsh-Asante, Kariamu. *African Dance: An Artistic, Historical, and Philosophical Inquiry*. Trenton, N.J.: African World Press, 1996.

SUSAN LEIGH FOSTER

Adandozan (d. 1818), king of Dahomey, was born sometime in the middle of the eighteenth century. His father was Agonglo, king of Dahomey from 1789 to 1797. Adandozan was the eldest son of Agonglo. Oral narratives collected later in the nineteenth century presented him as incompetent and mentally deranged, but it should be kept in mind that rival royal family members eventually ousted Adandozan from power and would have had a vested interest in deriding his achievements. Adandozan ascended to the throne of Dahomey in 1797, in a time marked by difficulties for the kingdom. The royal slave-trading monopoly ran aground on international difficulties, particularly the decision of the French government to abandon the slave trade from 1794 to 1802 and the British and US governments' decision to abandon the slave trade in 1807 and 1808, respectively. The British government began to send warships to stop other countries from purchasing slaves from Dahomey. These issues placed strains on Adandozan's ability to maintain the patronage necessary to please his large royal household and Dahoman aristocrats.

Most written and oral narratives about the king were negative. Adandozan launched a series of bloody wars against the Yoruba kingdom of Oyo and refused to pay tribute. The king commanded all Catholic priests to leave Dahomey on the ground that the Fon god Legba was the true deity of his lands. He annoyed Afro-Portuguese slave-trading families by expelling and taking prisoner Portuguese slave traders in his domains as well as from neighboring city-states such as Porto-Novo and Badagry. Adandozan confiscated hundreds of slaves from African slave traders in the port city of Ouidah, a vassal of Dahomey. According to oral tradition, Adandozan even sold off his own half-brother Gakpe's mother, Agontime, into slavery. Gakpe barely escaped being sold off himself, according to the same reports, but managed to fool the king by pretending to be insane.

Slave trader Nicolas d'Oliveira introduced the legendary Brazilian slave trader Francisco Felix de Souza to Adandozan, who allowed de Souza a special grant to buy slaves in Ouidah. However, Adandozan did not supply the numbers of slaves he had agreed to sell to de Souza annually after several years. de Souza grew so annoyed with the situation that he went to the Dahoman capital of Abomey to settle the affair. Once de Souza threatened to leave Ouidah entirely, Adandozan is said to have replied, "When a bird lays eggs in a nest and leaves, he leaves the eggs behind." This meant all of de Souza's merchandise and slaves would henceforth belong to Adandozan. The king then imprisoned de Souza for eight months. De Souza managed to contact dissident members of the royal family like Gakpe, who arranged the escape of the Brazilian. Some twentieth-century historians have argued that Adandozan was demonstrating his sovereignty over his territory and sought to reduce his kingdom's dependence on slave exports, but this thesis was still far from universally accepted. Gakpe led a revolt against Adandozan and seized the throne in 1818. He died in prison, while Gakpe held power under the name of Glele for the next four decades.

[*See also* Agonglo; *and* Glele.]

BIBLIOGRAPHY

Bay, Edna. *Wives of the Leopard: Gender, Politics, and Culture in the Kingdom of Dahomey*. Charlottesville: University of Virginia Press, 1998.

Law, Robin. *Ouidah: The Social History of a West African Slaving Port, 1727–1892*. Athens: Ohio University Press, 2004.

Monroe, J. Cameron. "Continuity, Revolution or Evolution on the Salve Coast of West Africa? Royal Architecture and Political Order in Precolonial Dahomey." *Journal of African History* 48 (2007): 349–373.

JEREMY RICH

Adda, Gladys (1921–), Tunisian labor activist, women's rights activist, and journalist, was born in the town of Gabes in southern Tunisia. Adda rose to prominence owing to her mother's emphasis upon female education, although her parents were of modest means. One branch of Adda's family, who are North African Jews, was originally from Batna in Algeria; her maternal grandfather had left French Algeria to seek his fortune in Tunisia, where he managed a small hotel in the south. For her parents' generation, it was somewhat unusual for women to attend school; to achieve the "certificate of study," as Adda's mother did, was a noteworthy achievement. Gladys Adda's life trajectory illustrated a number of important regional and global social and political currents: nationalism and anticolonialism, organized labor and workers' movements, socialism and communism, women's emancipation, and fascism and anti-Semitism against the backdrop of World War II.

In primary school, Adda attended classes with Muslim, Jewish, and European girls; but once admitted to secondary school, she studied with both boys and girls. In this period, no native Tunisians taught in secondary education; thus, all teachers were French or European. The experiences of undisguised racism on the part of the European teaching staff awakened Adda to the harsh realities of colonial schooling. As was true for many girls during this era, she was forced by her family to give up her studies at the age of fifteen and marry in 1936 a man from the Jewish community in Gabes who was much older than she, by twelve years. Two years later, attacks against Jews in the south were fomented by Italian Fascists resident in Tunisia, and several Jews were killed. In order to prevent more deaths, the Muslims of Gabes protected the Jewish neighborhood where Adda, her husband, and his large extended family lived.

After more than seven years of marriage, Adda decided to divorce her husband and move to Tunis to work with her friend, Bice Slama, another Tunisian Jewish woman, who was politically committed to a number of causes in the capital city. This was a particularly dark period for Tunisians, above all Jews, since the country was occupied by German and Italian military forces from 1942 until 1943, when the Allies liberated it. During the occupation, Adda covertly distributed anticolonial and anti-Nazi tracts, which marked the first stage of her political activism. In 1944, she joined a Tunisian branch of the Communist Party since she found that it was the only organization simultaneously fighting against fascism and for the rights of the oppressed, notably the workers. In Tunis, Adda and Slama distributed communist newspapers to male laborers in factories to cultivate a collective awareness of worker exploitation, a rather remarkable activity at the time for women. Nevertheless, this form of activism brought another realization for Adda—the need to militate for women's rights.

In 1944, Adda became one of the cofounders of the Union of Women of Tunisia (UFT) led by Nabiha Ben Miled, a Tunisian Muslim. In the same period, she met her second husband, Georges, a fellow communist activist, with whom she had twins during a financially difficult time, attenuated by assistance of friends in the women's movement. From the double perspective of mother and militant, Adda realized the urgency of educating women, many of whom were illiterate. The UFT also took on the cause of Tunisian soldiers fighting in Europe as well as the wartime crises of shortages of basic supplies and foodstuffs. After World War II, the UFT tackled the pressing problems of Tunisian independence from France and democratic rights for the people, many of whom were refused access to colonial schools. Another area of activism was native women's health, which had been deliberately neglected by the colonial regime, so Adda and her colleagues organized free women's clinics well as adult female literacy schools.

In this period of intense resistance to colonialism, Adda's husband was imprisoned by French authorities for his active involvement in the nationalist movement then struggling to force France to give Tunisia independence. The issue of nationalists condemned to prison or to death for "subversive" activities by colonial officials was also taken up by the UFT, which petitioned the French parliament in Paris, demanding the implementation of civil and human rights for political prisoners. In the colonial prisons, the nationalists organized courses in the French language for the incarcerated Tunisians condemned to death since they wanted to "learn the language of the oppressor to better fight against them." Adda managed to slip a French dictionary to her husband in prison for this purpose. Once Tunisian independence was granted in 1956, the UFT turned its attention to neighboring Algeria, where a colonial bloody guerilla war raged that endured until 1962 with terrible consequences for Algerian women, children, and civilians. Adda and the women of the UFT organized medical and financial support services for Algerian combatants, many of whom traveled clandestinely to Tunisia for assistance. Significantly, at the same time, the UFT drew into its network anti-imperial French women living in Tunis to help with the Algerian war effort in a period when France's colonial army still occupied Tunisia.

With Tunisian independence, Adda's life took a curious twist for someone who had earlier been committed to communism but later broke with the party altogether. She accepted a post with the newly created Tunisian National Bank, where she worked until retirement in 1981. After 1956, Tunisia lost its financial and banking managers, so Adda regarded it as important for social justice and equality that the country enjoy a solid banking sector; she continued to work for women's rights both in North Africa and globally. Because they regarded Tunisia as their native land, neither Adda nor her husband, also Jewish, left the country in the 1950s, when many Tunisian Jews relocated mainly to France or to Israel after Tunisia's independence from France in 1956. Retirement did not end Adda's activism since she taught university courses in business management and participated in the Tunisian branch of the Ligue des Droits de l'Homme, an international human rights organization. When interviewed in the early 1990s about her personal vision of life, Adda summed it up with these revealing words: "I remain an optimist."

BIBLIOGRAPHY

Kazdaghli, Habib, ed. *Mémoire de femmes: Tunisiennes dans la vie publique, 1920–1960.* Tunis: Éditions Média Com, 1993.

Larguèche, Dalenda, ed. *Femmes en villes.* Tunis: Centre de Publications Universitaires, 2006.

Perkins, Kenneth J. *A History of Modern Tunisia.* Cambridge: Cambridge University Press, 2004.

JULIA A. CLANCY-SMITH

Adé, King Sunny (1946–), Nigerian pioneer of *juju* and world music star, was born Sunday Adeniyi Adé in the southwestern Nigerian city of Ondo on 22 September 1946. His father was a Methodist pastor and the organist for his church, while his mother engaged in various trading enterprises. Through his maternal grandfather, who lived in the town of Akoure, near Ondo, Ade was of royal lineage. By the time he reached his adolescent years, Adé had moved with his family to the town of Oshobo. Although he completed primary school, Adé ended up dropping out of secondary school before completing his studies. His lack of financial resources cut short his formal education. He already had developed eclectic tastes in music through his childhood and adolescent experiences. Traditional Yoruba music featuring drums fascinated the young boy, as did the occasional use of drums at church. Adé remembered in a 2005 interview that when he was a child he would chase after vans that drove through his neighborhood playing music. His parents had enough money to purchase a phonograph, so Adé listened to Brazilian and other foreign musical groups. American rhythm and blues, country, and blues music also appealed to him. Since his family had no interest in paying for Adé to take

music lessons, he joined a band run by the Boys Brigade, a youth group similar to the Boy Scouts.

His family did not look kindly on Adé's ambitions to commence a career in music, however, so in 1962 he tricked them into permitting him to move to the large Nigerian city of Lagos. Adé lied to his parents and told them he had won a scholarship to attend the University of Lagos, when in reality he just wanted to pursue his dream of a musical career. Adé joined the musical group of singer Moses Olaiya and his Rhythm Dandies in 1963. When the band told him he was too young, Adé told them he was almost 20 rather than barely 17 years of age. This group closely imitated the popular West African highlife style that dominated mid-twentieth-century Nigerian and Ghanaian music. Olaiya eventually chose to enter the theater and became a star in his own right as an actor. Adé then brought together many former members of the Rhythm Dandies and formed his own group in 1966, the Green Spots. Adé then followed his passion for the *juju* musical style derived from traditional Yoruba music and followed the pioneering sound of musician Isaiah Kehinde Dairo and his band, I. K. Dairo and His Blue Spots. His first group was a ten-man band, and it originally signed with Tunde Amuwo before making Jide Smith its manager, who rented out instruments to new groups like the Green Spots.

Adé's adaptation of pedal steel, his birdlike dance moves, and the incredibly talented percussion and guitar playing skills of his group made him a star in Nigeria. His band cut many albums with the Nigeria-Africa Song label owned by wealthy businessman Bolarinwa Abioro between 1967 and 1972. Adé's lyrical subjects ranged widely, from celebrating victories by the Nigerian federal government against Biafran rebels in 1968 to incorporating Yoruba proverbs and Christian messages into various individual songs. Local soccer clubs also became the subject of praise songs. Eventually, he brought in accordions, bass guitars, and other instruments rarely heard in West African music, thanks to Abioro's patronage. Adé earned enough to buy out Smith in 1969, which was a good thing given that Smith collected up to two-thirds of whatever audience members donated to Adé and other band members. In twentieth-century Nigeria, artists made their money at live concerts, where fans would walk to the stage and put money on performers in a practice known as "spraying." Adé first put his new Western instruments to work on a 1970 single entitled "Alújónù Onígítà," Adé's nickname in Yoruba, which translates into English as "Wizard of the Guitar." The B-side featured raunchy lyrics put to an arrangement of a popular hymn that also included traditional drumming styles. Such a blending of the sacred and the profane and of Western and Yoruba styles was typical for Adé and his band.

As with so many Nigerian musical groups, troubles emerged between Adé's band and their financial patron. Abioro and Adé split in 1972 over royalties and financial arrangements. They engaged in a long court battle as a result, and even thirty years later Adé claimed he could not rerelease his Green Spots records because of this long dispute. Adé renamed his band the African Beats in the same year, in part to avoid legal problems with a company that sold cigarettes under the Green Spot trademark. He set up his own record label, Sunny Aldade Records, in 1974. By the late 1970s, Adé was becoming an international star. His beloved 1976 album *Synchro System Movement* drew influences from Fela Kuti's Afro-Beat style and American soul music. Like Kuti, Adé abandoned the typical Western model of two- to five-minute songs in favor of performances that could last over half an hour. This practice reflected traditional Yoruba music far better than the single-song model brought in from Europe and North America. Wealthy fans who were profiting from the oil boom in the 1970s paid Adé handsomely. By 1979, his group had expanded to roughly twenty members and featured expensive synthesizers, tenor guitars, and many dancers. European and North American audiences began to listen to Adé as well. Reggae music record label owner Chris Blackwell decided to sign the African Beats in 1982. The band recorded an album in Togo designed to draw in Western audiences and had some success outside of Africa.

Adé toured the United States for the first time as a result of this venture. However, Island Records dropped Adé in 1984 as it was clear he had reached only a small but devoted audience. He continued to tour Europe and the United States on occasion from the mid-1980s to the end of the first decade of the twenty-first century. Eventually, the African Beats broke up, but Adé formed new bands, like Golden Mercury and The Way Forward. In the early twenty-first century, he became head of the Nigerian musicians' union and spent much of his time fighting the rampant piracy of music in his country. He was the most popular *juju* artist of his lifetime.

[*See also* Dairo, Isaiah Kehinde; *and* Kuti, Fela Anikulapo.]

BIBLIOGRAPHY

Adé, King Sunny, interview with Afropop Worldwide, May 1, 2005, accessed 27 April 2010, http://www.afropop.org/multi/interview/ID/79/King+Sunny+Ade%2C+2005-part+1.

Ajayi, Tunji. *King Sunny Ade The Legend! Cultural Communication via a Genre of African Music.* Parker, CO: Outskirts, 2009.

Ajirire, Tosin, and Wale Alabi. *King Sunny Ade: An Intimate Biography.* Lagos: Showbiz Publications, 1989.

Waterman, Christopher Alan. *Juju: A Social History and Ethnography of an African Popular Music.* Chicago: University of Chicago Press, 1990.

JEREMY RICH

Ade Ajayi, Jacob Festus (1929–), pioneering historian of Africa, was born on 26 May 1929 in Ikole-Ekiti, southwestern Nigeria. He had his early education at Saint Paul's School, Ikole-Ekiti and Ekiti Central School, where he later taught as a pupil teacher. He proceeded to Igbobi College, Lagos, and later to University College, Ibadan (now the University of Ibadan), as a foundation student in 1948. In 1951 Ade Ajayi obtained his BA Honors degree in general history, Latin, and English. In 1952 he took another BA Honors degree in history at Leicester University, in England, which he completed in 1955 with first class honors. In 1958 Ade Ajayi completed his doctorate degree at the University of London, where he was one of the first African doctoral students of the eminent historian of Africa Roland Oliver. He then returned to Nigeria to join the history department at the University of Ibadan as a lecturer grade two. By 1963 and barely thirty-six years old he had become a full professor of history.

Ajayi's contribution to African history and historiography is diverse. Most importantly he has argued against the undue weight given colonialism in African history, arguing that colonialism was just an "episode" against the larger history of Africa. He also argues that African institutions survived the colonial episode and remain central in defining African societies. He has sought to demonstrate this in his scholarship, especially on precolonial Yoruba societies, where he has been a major influence in the understanding of a chaotic nineteenth-century Yorubaland characterized by incessant warfare, but also by sociopolitical innovation.

Together with Kenneth O. Dike, he was central in shaping the Ibadan school of history, notable for distinguished studies of precolonial Nigerian societies that stressed African agency and institutional innovation, and drawing on oral and written sources. Ade Ajayi's immediate concern at Ibadan was the need to chart a new course for historical scholarship in Africa. Together, they transformed the history curriculum in Nigeria from its Eurocentric perspective to emphasize its African contents and, specifically, to make historical studies relevant to Africa and its environment. He, along with others, laid the building blocks for the noted Ibadan school of history and African history, as a distinct branch of historical scholarship. In addition, Ade Ajayi emphasized change and continuity as fundamental to understanding events, epochs, and personages in African history. He orchestrated a critical view of historical events as weathering episodes, which, notwithstanding apparent changes, still live behind the core of African culture.

As an African historian, Ade Ajayi's extensive use of oral and written sources fostered the rise of African historiography as well as raising awareness on oral sources as veritable and credible sources in historical writing. Arising from his marriage of oral and written courses, he redefined the study of British colonization of Nigeria; emphasized the place of religion, Christianity and Islam, in Nigeria's nationalism; and, with gradation, expressed a much more critical stance on pan-Africanism as the foundation of African nationalism. In a prodigious scholarly career, his most significant works have included his doctoral thesis, published as *Christian Missions in Nigeria, 1841–1891: The Making of a New Elite* (1964), *Yoruba Warfare in the Nineteenth Century* (1964), and *A Thousand Years of West African History* (1965). In 1992 he published *Patriot to the Core*, a short biography of one of his heroes, Samuel Ajayi Crowther, the linguist and Nigeria's first African Anglican bishop. The historian Toyin Falola collected twenty-nine of Ade Ajayi's most important essays in a festschrift, *Tradition and Change in Africa: The Essays of J. F. Ade Ajayi* (2000). In a review of the latter collection, the historian J. D. Y. Peel honored Ade Ajayi as "the Moses of Nigerian Historiography." He was an important figure with other like-minded historians such as Albert Adu Boahen on the International Committee for the UNESCO General History of Africa, which came up with the eight-volume *General History of Africa* to counter the *Cambridge History of Africa*, which in the opinion of African historians foregrounded the activities of Europeans in Africa. He was also the editor of *UNESCO's General History of Africa,* volume six (1989).

Ade Ajayi also held many important administrative positions in Nigeria's academic sphere.

Between 1959 and 1962 he was assistant warden and warden, Sultan Bello Hall, and later served as master of Nnamdi Azikwe Hall from 1966 to 1972. Between 1964 and 1966 he was dean of arts at the University of Ibadan, and later, between 1966 and 1969, he was head, department of history. He was promoted deputy vice chancellor between 1966 and 1968. In 1972 he was appointed vice chancellor of the University of Lagos, a position he relinquished following a controversial anti-fee students' demonstration termed "Ali-Must-Go," which led to the death of a student, Akintunde Ojo, by the Nigerian police in 1978. Following his controversial removal from the University of Lagos by General Olusegun Obasanjo's military administration, Ade Ajayi returned to the University of Ibadan, where he continued his efforts in historical scholarship.

A scholar with a global audience, Ade Ajayi has served as a visiting professor of African history at the University of California, Los Angeles; El Colegio de Mexico; Amherst College; University of Bergen, Norway; and the Ohio State University, in Columbus, Ohio. He has also lectured at several American universities, including Columbia, Cornell, Harvard, Howard, Northwestern, Princeton, Stanford, and the University of Wisconsin. He was also a guest lecturer at the first university inaugural lecture at Makerere University, Uganda, in 1971. He has also served as a member of council of Cape Coast University, Ghana; the National University of Lesotho; and the University of Science and Technology, Kumasi, Ghana. He was a member of the board of the International Association of Universities. Between 1980 and 1990 he was a member of the executive board and later vice president of the Association of African Universities. Ade Ajayi was also a member, and later chairman, of the Governing Council of the United Nations University between 1974 and 1980.

For his numerous contributions to global educational development and lifetime service, Ade Ajayi was awarded the Nigerian National Merit Award by the Federal Government of Nigeria and the Distinguished Africanist Award by the African Studies Association in 1993. His other awards include Honorary Doctor of Letters, Birmingham University; Honorary Doctor of Letters, Ondo State University (now University of Ado-Ekiti); Honorary Fellow, School of Oriental and African Studies (SOAS), London; Foundation Fellow, Historical Society of Nigeria and Fellow, Ghana Historical Society; former chairman, Committee of Vice-Chancellors of Nigerian Universities; 25th Anniversary Gold Medal Winner, University of Lagos; Honorary Vice

President for Life, Royal African Society, London; *Bobapitan* of Ado-Ekiti; *Onikoyi* of Ile-Ife; and Emeritus Professor of History, University of Ibadan.

As of 2010 Ade Ajayi had published more than a hundred works, more than half of which he wrote and published while technically in retirement. In his eighth decade, Ajayi continued to teach a course in the historiography of Africa at the University of Ibadan.

[*See also* Crowther, Samuel Ajayi; Dike, Kenneth; Falola Toyin; *and* Obasanjo, Olusegun.]

BIBLIOGRAPHY

Ade Ajayi, J. F. "On the Politics of Being Mortal." *Transition* 59 (1993): 32–44.

Ade Ajayi, J. F. *Tradition and Change in Africa: The Essays of J. F. Ade Ajayi*, edited by Toyin Falola. Trenton, N.J.: Africa World Press, 2000.

Hess, Robert A. "J. F. Ade Ajayi and the New Historiography in West Africa." *African Studies Review* 14, no. 2 (September 1971): 273–285.

Peel, J. D. Y. "The Moses of Nigerian Historiography." *The Journal of African History* 43, no. 3 (2002): 532–533.

ADEYEMI BUKOLA OYENIYI

Adherbal ('drb'l, Atarbas; first century BCE), ruler of a portion of Numidia (118–112 BCE), was the son of King Micipsa of Numidia. When his father died in 118 BCE he was named joint heir with his brother Hiempsal I and cousin Jugurtha (who had served under Roman command in Spain), with the latter, who was older, as primary heir. The Romans, already involved in the affairs of Numidia (the territory south and west of Carthage), saw this arrangement as the potential disaster that it was and at first adopted a hands-off policy. Animosity between the three heirs, which may have predated Micipsa's death, erupted almost immediately. Hiempsal was soon eliminated by Jugurtha, and Adherbal promptly fled to Rome. He and Jugurtha entered into a competition as to who could spread money more lavishly around the city, and both were invited to address the Senate. Adherbal emphasized his character and his cousin's deficiencies, Jugurtha his service to Rome in Spain. The Senate sent a commission to Numidia, led by L. Opimius (consul of 121 BCE), who, upon his arrival in Africa, was entertained lavishly by Jugurtha. The commission divided the kingdom between the two heirs but in a way favoring Jugurtha.

Matters were quiet for a few years, and Rome believed that any problems with Numidia were over. Jugurtha evidently was biding his time and attacked his brother in 112 BCE. Adherbal established himself in Cirta, the Numidian capital (modern Constantine in Algeria), and enlisted the aid of a substantial resident Roman mercantile population, whose existence is a hint as to why Rome was so deeply involved in Numidian affairs. Adherbal was promptly besieged by Jugurtha, and when another Roman commission arrived, they were hosted by Jugurtha but not allowed to consult with Adherbal. A third commission had little effect. What happened next is uncertain, but when the Romans in Cirta urged surrender, Adherbal did so, only to be tortured and killed by his cousin. Allegedly many others, including members of the Roman community, were also killed; and news of this "massacre," probably exaggerated, quickly reached Rome. This resulted in a full-scale war between Rome and Jugurtha, now surviving king of the entire territory. This war, which lasted nearly a decade, substantially shifted the balance of power between Rome and the North African territories and precipitated the instability that was to plague Rome for the next century.

Although Adherbal remains shadowy, he is an important figure in the developing relations between expanding Rome and the North African world. Roman involvement in the Numidian kingdom, perhaps in large part to protect its mercantile population in the region, eventually led to total Roman control of the area. Almost all that is known about Adherbal comes from Sallust's biographical essay on Jugurtha, written perhaps 75 years after the events. Sallust has presented a detailed study of Rome's relations with allied kingdoms on its frontier and why Rome became more deeply involved in the destinies of these states.

[*See also* Jugurtha.]

BIBLIOGRAPHY

Roller, Duane W. *The World of Juba II and Kleopatra Selene: Royal Scholarship on Rome's African Frontier*. London: Routledge, 2003. The most recent study of the Numidian kingdom of the period, including all the evidence for Adherbal.

Sallust (Gaius Sallustius Crispus). *Catiline's Conspiracy, The Jugurthine War, Histories*. Translated by William W. Batstone. Oxford World's Classics. Oxford: Oxford University Press, 2010.

DUANE W. ROLLER

Adichie, Chimamanda Ngozi (1977–), Nigerian creative writer and essayist, was born on 15 September 1977 in Enugu, Nigeria, the fifth of six children, to James Nwoye and Grace Ifeoma Adichie. The Igbo family's ancestral hometown was Abba in Anambra State, but Adichie grew up in Nsukka, where her parents worked. Her father was professor of statistics at the University of Nigeria and later became the institution's deputy vice-chancellor, while her mother, a graduate in sociology, was its first female registrar.

Adichie began writing stories as a child. Her first pieces were heavily influenced by the British children's literature of which she was an avid reader; her early prose was, more specifically, modeled on the books of English author Enid Blyton. When Adichie was about ten years old, she discovered African novels such as *Things Fall Apart* (1958) by Nigerian Chinua Achebe and *The African Child* (originally published in French as *L'enfant noir* in 1953) by Guinean Camara Laye. In later essays and interviews, she described the reading of these books as a turning point in her development as a writer, for they led her to understand that her own literary creations need not be cast in European molds but could mirror her own African experiences.

Adichie completed her primary and secondary education at the University of Nigeria School, winning several awards for her academic excellence. She then studied pharmacy and medicine at the university for a year and a half but rapidly realized that she did not want to enter the medical profession. In 1997 she published a collection of poems entitled *Decisions* and left Nigeria for the United States to study communication at Drexel University in Philadelphia on a scholarship. The following year she published a play, *For Love of Biafra*, which deals with the Nigerian civil war. This work marked the author's first imaginative exploration of the Biafran conflict, which had divided the country between 1967 and 1970 and had claimed both of her grandfathers.

After two years at Drexel, Adichie moved to Connecticut to live with her sister Ijeoma, who had recently established a medical practice in Coventry. The writer transferred to Eastern Connecticut State University and graduated summa cum laude in 2001 with a major in communication and a minor in political science. When she was a senior at Eastern, she started writing *Purple Hibiscus*, a narrative that was to become her first published novel in 2003. The story, set in Nigeria in the late twentieth century, focuses on a fifteen-year-old Igbo girl,

Kambili, and follows the evolution of the heroine's attitude toward her father—a highly respected businessman who, as an extremist Catholic, rules his family with a rod of iron.

Shortly before the publication of her debut novel, Adichie began to gain recognition on the international literary scene as several of her short stories won, or were nominated for, prestigious awards. In 2002, she was declared joint winner of the BBC Short Story Competition for "That Harmattan Morning" and made the short list of the Caine Prize for African Writing with her piece "You in America." She further won the 2002–2003 David T. Wong International Short Story Prize for "Half of a Yellow Sun" and the 2003 O. Henry Prize for "The American Embassy."

Adichie's reputation was further enhanced by the critical success of *Purple Hibiscus*. Among other distinctions, the novel won the 2004 Hurston/Wright Legacy Award for Best Debut Fiction and the 2005 Commonwealth Writers' Prize for Best First Book; in 2004 it was shortlisted for the Orange Prize for Fiction and long-listed for the Booker Prize. Significantly, the narrative was also praised by Adichie's illustrious compatriot Chinua Achebe, whose own *Arrow of God* (1964) she had by then consistently cited as her favorite novel.

Meanwhile, Adichie continued to combine her literary and academic work. In 2004 she obtained a master's degree in creative writing from Johns Hopkins University; in 2005–2006 she was granted a Hodder Fellowship from the University of Princeton, where she taught a class in introductory fiction. In the fall of 2006 she enrolled in a master's program in African history at Yale University. At the same time, she pursued her writing career, publishing numerous stories in international journals such as *Granta* and the *New Yorker* and several essays in prestigious newspapers, including the *Guardian* and the *Washington Post*. Although her short fiction has dealt with themes ranging from the Biafran war to contemporary Nigeria and Igbo immigrants in the United States, her essays often express her complicated attachment to her country of origin, fiercely denouncing its corrupt political system and the hypocrisy of its religious leaders.

The late summer of 2006 saw the publication of Adichie's second novel, *Half of a Yellow Sun*, which once again testified to the author's concern with the complexities of the Biafran war. Indeed, the book centers on several Nigerian protagonists and an English character before and during the conflict and masterfully associates a vigorous condemnation of the brutalities of war with a sensitive portrayal of individual destinies. The novel, blurbed by Achebe, gained instant critical praise and received major accolades. Most notably, it won the Orange Broadband Prize for Fiction in 2007 and was short-listed for the Commonwealth Writers' Prize for Best Book (Africa region) the same year. *Half of a Yellow Sun* was also a commercial success, especially in the United Kingdom, and sealed the writer's status as one of the leading figures of early twenty-first-century African literature.

While studying in the United States and touring the world to promote her work, Adichie regularly returned to Nigeria, actively supporting emerging local literary talent by organizing workshops for aspiring writers in Lagos. In May 2008 she graduated from Yale and moved to Columbia, Maryland. In September of the same year, she received a fellowship from the MacArthur Foundation, a $500,000 so-called genius grant awarded to promising researchers and artists.

Adichie's first collection of short stories, *The Thing around Your Neck*, was published in April 2009. The book features revised versions of eleven previously published pieces and a new thought-provoking story that interweaves themes such as religion, homosexuality, and illegal immigration to the United States.

[*See also* Achebe, Chinua; *and* Laye, Camara.]

BIBLIOGRAPHY

Works by Adichie

Purple Hibiscus. London: Harper Perennial, 2005. A paperback edition that contains a profile of Adichie, some biographical information, and an essay by the writer.

Half of a Yellow Sun. New York: Knopf, 2006.

The Thing around Your Neck. London: Fourth Estate, 2009.

Works about Adichie

Cooper, Brenda. *New Generation of African Writers: Migration, Material Culture and Language.* Oxford: James Currey, 2008. A study of diasporic African writing that features two chapters on Adichie's work, respectively devoted to *Purple Hibiscus* and *Half of a Yellow Sun.*

Tunca, Daria. *The Chimamanda Ngozi Adichie Website.* http://www.L3.ulg.ac.be/adichie. An academic page including a biography of Adichie, an introduction to her writing and a full bibliography of works by and about the author.

DARIA TUNCA

Adoula, Cyrille (1921–1978), Congolese politician, was born on 13 September 1921 in Kinshasa, then part of the Belgian Congo and subsequently the capital city of the Democratic Republic of Congo. His father was a dockworker from the Bangala ethnic community from the northwestern Équateur Province. Adoula attended a Catholic missionary primary school and then graduated from the Saint Joseph Institute in Kinshasa. He then worked from 1941 to 1952 as a clerk in a series of different commercial firms. The Central Bank of Congo hired Adoula to a senior position in 1952, which marked the first time any African had held an important post with this firm. He joined the Conseil pour le Travail et la Prévoyance in 1948, a group of well-educated Congolese calling for limited social services from the government.

In 1954, Adoula joined the Belgian socialist party. He then joined the Fédération Générale de Travailleurs Belge (FGTB), a major coalition of Belgian trade unions. On becoming one of the head Congolese delegates in the FGTB, he left his position in the bank. Adoula immersed himself in political activity. He attended the 1957 International Labor Conference in Geneva and the following year was a signatory on a famous August 1958 manifesto of liberal Catholic intellectuals calling for equal political and legal rights for Congolese and Belgians. Adoula was one of the founding members of the Mouvement National Congolais (MNC) political party with Joseph Ileo and Patrice Lumumba. The MNC aspired to attain independence and create a democracy that would unite the country rather than promote regional autonomy or even the breakup of the Congo, as advocated by other organizations such as Joseph Kasa-Vubu's Alliance des Bakongo (ABAKO) party or Moïse Tshombe's Conakat party. While Lumumba became more strident in his nationalist and anticolonial rhetoric, Adoula remained fairly moderate, even if he pushed for the creation of a separate Congolese trade union outside of the FGTB in 1959. He visited Israel and West Germany in his position as a trade union leader and was even made a member of the International Congress of Federated Trade Unions, but he resigned because of his political duties. Adoula worked with Albert Kalonji, a politician from Kasai Province, to try to oust Lumumba from his post in 1959. This plan failed, although it did succeed in splitting the MNC into two separate factions. Adoula considered Lumumba to be too willing to entertain the idea of aid from communist countries. He and Kalonji formed the MNC-K party, which then allied with Kasa-Vubu and ABAKO. After briefly serving as an elected senator for the city of Mbandaka, Kasa-Vubu and Ileo selected Adoula to become the minister of the interior in February 1960.

The advent of independence in June 1960, followed by Lumumba's demand for Belgian troops to leave the country and Tshombe's declaration that Katanga was now an independent country, helped to create a very chaotic situation in Congo in 1960. Adoula strongly endorsed the United Nations intervention to force Katanga to stay as part of the Congo, even as he distanced himself further from Lumumba. With both Kasa-Vubu and Lumumba declaring themselves head of the national government in September 1960, the United States Central Intelligence Agency officer Larry Devlin became increasingly impressed with Adoula as a liberal anticommunist alternative to the radical Lumumba and the embarrassment of the Katanga secession. Although some far-right politicians in the United States preferred Tshombe to the uncharismatic Adoula, the latter did not alienate many African and Asian nations in the same way as Tshombe. After Devlin and Belgian intelligence allowed military officer and future dictator Mobutu Sese Seko to arrest Lumumba and to force Kasa-Vubu to create a new government, Adoula was well-placed to guide a fragile coalition known as the "Binza group." Adoula condemned the Katanga secession and did nothing to act against Lumumba's abduction to Katanga, where Lumumba was executed in January 1961. The Central Intelligence Agency, the United Nations, and the governments and secret services of other Western countries launched a campaign involving bribery to ensure that Adoula became the new prime minister in early 1961. Adoula managed to bring some radicals such as Christophe Gbenye into his cabinet, but leftists like Antoine Gizenga eventually denounced Adoula as a pawn of Western imperialism and formed a dissident government based in the eastern Congolese city of Kisangani.

Although he managed to bring Gizenga into his government and lead the diplomatic struggle to keep United Nations troops in Congo until they finally defeated Tshombe's Katanga scheme once and for all, Adoula had no firm base to resist the growing armed rebel movements led by Pierre Mulele, Gbenye, and others who claimed Lumumba's mantle. As his government lost control over much of eastern and northern Congo by 1964, Kasa-Vubu forced Adoula to resign in favor of former Katanagan leader Moïse Tshombe. His effectiveness turned out to be valuable once Mobutu definitively seized power from Kasa-Vubu in a November 1965 coup. Adoula proved very accommodating to the new regime and worked as an ambassador to the United States and Belgium. He briefly was Mobutu's foreign minister in 1969 and 1970 and then retired. Adoula passed away from an illness in Lausanne, Switzerland, on 24 May 1978.

[See also Gbenye, Christophe; Gizenga, Antoine; Kasa-Vubu, Joseph; Lumumba, Patrice Emery; Mulele, Pierre; Mobutu Sese Seko; and Tshombe, Moïse Kapenda.]

BIBLIOGRAPHY

Devlin, Larry. *Chief of Station, Congo: A Memoir of 1960–1967*. New York: Public Affairs, 2007.

Verhaegen, Benoît, ed. *Rébellions au Congo*, 2 vols. Brussels: CRISP, 1966 and 1969.

Young, Crawford. *Politics in the Congo*. Princeton, N.J.: Princeton University Press, 1965.

JEREMY RICH

Adrian of Canterbury (c. 635–710), Christian saint, North African–born abbot active in England, was a well-known scholar and the abbot of St. Augustine's Abbey in Canterbury, England. Another form of his name is "Hadrian."

According to the medieval English writer the Venerable Bede, Adrian was a Berber native from a Greek-speaking family in North Africa, likely in Libya Cyrenaica, who had fled the Arab invasions into the region when he was about ten years of age, evacuating to Naples, which was then controlled by the Byzantine Empire. At an unknown age, though still quite young, Adrian joined one of the Benedictine monasteries in the area and would eventually become abbot of a monastery near Naples called Monasterium Hiridanum (also given as Niridanum, and both may be errors for Nisidanum, the Niridian monastery on the Isle of Nisida in the Bay of Naples). Bede describes Adrian as being "by nation an African, well versed in holy writ, experienced in monastical and ecclesiastical discipline, and excellently skilled both in the Greek and Latin tongues."

He is known from other sources to have met and eventually become an ambassador for the eastern emperor Constans II in the year 663 during his campaigns in the region. It is likely Constans who introduced Adrian to, or was responsible for, Adrian's meeting Pope Vitalian when the emperor visited Rome in that year. Adrian was apparently much liked by Vitalian and was quickly considered to be a close adviser to him. In 667, Pope Vitalian offered Adrian the position of archbishop of Canterbury, apparently twice, which Adrian declined, citing his own unworthiness. Other sources, including Bede, indicate that Adrian suffered some sort of infirmity that he saw as preventing him from taking on the workload of a bishop or other higher office than that of abbot.

In his place after the second invitation, which occurred after another individual selected had unexpectedly died, Adrian suggested Theodore of Tarsus, who was a friend of Adrian's and had previously lived first in Tarsus both under the Byzantine Empire and under the Persian Empire and then in Constantinople. Theodore was, by this point, in Rome at the time of the second invitation and had been living with a community of other eastern monks near the city. Pope Vitalian relented and accepted Adrian's recommendation, with the condition that Adrian accompany Theodore to England. After Theodore was ordained on Sunday 26 March 668, the two left Rome on 27 May of the same year.

They traveled by sea to Marseilles, then overland to Arles. In Arles they delivered a set of letters to Archbishop John from the Pope but were detained there until passports could be obtained from the mayor of the palace, Ebrion, who ruled that section of Gaul for the king, Clotaire III. Yet even when the documents had been secured, the two were forced to remain in northern France over the winter, each in different locations. Theodore was invited to stay with the bishop of Paris, and when spring arrived, he was sent for by King Ecgbert of Kent, who had sent his prefect Redfrid to escort him, and reached England in May of 669, only a year after having left Rome.

Adrian, however, was not so lucky. He had wintered first with Emme, the bishop of Sens, and then with Faro, the bishop of Meaux. When spring came, he too was ready to depart but was detained on the order of the mayor of the palace, Eboïn. Ebroïn or King Theuderic III of the Franks suspected Adrian of being on some errand either for the kings of Britain or for an ambassador from the eastern emperor and in either case of being out to cause strife for King Theuderic's country. Eventually, the king changed his mind, and Adrian was allowed to leave for England.

From this point forward in Adrian's life, there is some uncertainty as to the order of events, owing to discrepancies in an early part of this account.

In one version, as soon as Adrian arrived in Canterbury, he was made the abbot of St. Peter's—today known as St. Augustine's Abbey—as it is given that this was in accordance with the papal instructions given to Theodore upon his departure. In another version, Adrian was not made abbot until after Benedict Biscop resigned. Biscop was, in this account, supposed to have traveled with Theodore and Adrian from Rome, and it was he whom the pope instructed be made the abbot of the monastery of St. Peter at Canterbury. If this is the case, Biscop is said to have held the position of abbot for two years, before he resigned.

In either case, it is during the tenure of Adrian as abbot of the monastery of St. Peter that he and Theodore, as the archbishop, established the well-known school in Canterbury. It is reported in at least one version of Bede's account of Theodore's time as archbishop of Canterbury that he and Adrian traveled England together in search of scholars and students for their school. The school taught not only theology, scripture, Latin, and Greek but also Roman law, rhetoric, writing, medicine, music, physical science, and mathematics. Adrian himself is said to have taught poetry, astronomy, math, scripture, and virtue. St. Aldhelm, traditionally said to be the first English scholar, is also said to have been one of his students.

The school at Canterbury is said to have surpassed even the best of the schools in the rest of Western Europe. Bede even speaks of a few remaining students of the school when he writes in the eighth century, whom he praises as reading and speaking Greek and Latin as easily as they did the languages to which they were born.

Adrian of Canterbury died on 9 January 710 and is buried in the church at the monastery of St. Peter at Canterbury—now St. Augustine's at Canterbury. Theodore, who died well before his friend, in 690, is buried in the same church, which is the traditional burial place of the archbishop of Canterbury.

His tomb has been the recorded site for a number of miracles, and a report in 1091 states that his body was found incorrupt in its tomb when it was opened during reconstruction of the monastery.

BIBLIOGRAPHY

Bede. "Lives of the Abbots of Wearmouth and Jarrow." In *Ecclesiastical History of the English Nation*, edited by J. A. Giles. London: J. M. Dent, 1910.

Bede. *Bede's Ecclesiastical History of the English People.* Edited by Bertram Colgrave and R. A. B. Mynors.

Oxford Medieval Texts. Oxford: Clarendon Press, 1969.

Bede. *Bede's Ecclesiastical History of the English People: A Historical Commentary*. Edited by J. M. Wallace-Hadrill. Oxford Medieval Texts. Oxford: Clarendon Press; New York: Oxford University Press, 1988.

Bede. *Historia Ecclesiastica Gentis Anglorum (The Ecclesiastical History of the English Nation)*, edited by Paul Halsall, book 4, ebook edition. London: J. M. Dent 1997, accessed June 1, 2010, http://www.fordham.edu/halsall/basis/bede-book4.html.

Benedictine Monks of St. Augustine's Abbey. *The Book of Saints: A Dictionary of Servants of God Canonized by the Catholic Church*. London: A & C Black, 1989.

Delaney, John J. *Dictionary of Saints*. Garden City, N.Y.: Doubleday, 1980.

Serralda, Vincent, and André Huard. *Le Berbère— Lumière de l'occident*. Paris: Nouvelles Editions Latines, 1984.

NESS CREIGHTON

Afewerk Tekle (1932–), Ethiopian artist, was born in Ankober in Shewa Province, Ethiopia. As a young student Afewerk excelled in mathematics and draftsmanship. Recognizing these talents, the government of Emperor Haile Selassie provided a scholarship in 1947 for Afewerk to study mining engineering in England. Showing great promise as a visual artist, Afewerk soon received the emperor's permission to transfer to London's Central School of Arts and Crafts. Subsequently, he attended the Slade School of Fine Art, University College London. While studying there, he made several trips to the European continent to see and experience works of art firsthand.

Afewerk's first solo exhibition of paintings in Addis Ababa, held at Municipality Hall in 1954, was not universally well received. In particular, an abstract interpretation of the Crucifixion inspired by European modernism, now in the National Museum of Ethiopia, was the subject of debate and controversy in a city with a centuries-old tradition of sacred imagery. However, the emperor expressed approval of the artist's work and purchased two of the canvases. Soon thereafter Afewerk returned to Europe, where he traveled on the continent for two years and pursued further studies in London. Afewerk was profoundly influenced by his studies in Europe and throughout his career has moved fluidly between figural and abstract imagery based on his interpretations of Western artistic styles. His love for his Ethiopian heritage is expressed more directly in the subject matter than the style of his paintings and sculptures. In his choice of themes the artist has been sufficiently flexible to benefit from the patronage of three successive regimes, the imperial government of Haile Selassie (overthrown in 1974), the Derg regime of Mengistu Haile Mariam (1974–1991), and the government of Prime Minister Meles Zenawi (1995–present).

Afewerk has won numerous national and international awards including the Prix de Rome in 1955. He was the first recipient of the Haile Selassie Prize Trust Award in 1964 "for his outstanding drawings, paintings, landscapes, and portraits which eloquently express his particular world environment, and for his contribution in being among the first to introduce contemporary techniques to Ethiopian subject matter and content" (Pankhurst, p. 43). His *Self-Portrait* was the first work of art by an artist from the African continent to be acquired for the permanent collection of the Uffizi Gallery in Florence, in 1981. His paintings are well represented in the National Museum of Ethiopia, and in 2004 his painting *Homage to Russian Ballet* from 1968 entered the collection of the National Museum of African Art, Smithsonian Institution, as a gift of Joseph and Patricia Brumit. This painting is related in style to Afewerk's stained glass window designs, in which he introduced the use of a bold network of curved and straight black lines that overlay an abstract linear pattern over a traditional figural composition.

Afewerk's first major commission from the Ethiopian government was for murals and mosaics at St. George's Cathedral in Addis Ababa, including his interpretations of Solomon and the Queen of Sheba and the Last Judgment, a project that occupied him for three and a half years in the late 1950s. During the same period, he completed a series of stained glass windows of Ethiopian warrior heroes for the military academy in Harar. Also for Harar he executed a bronze equestrian monument to Ras Mekonnen Welde Mikael, father of Emperor Haile Selassie, in the stylistic tradition of European Renaissance equestrian ruler portraits. In 1959 Afewerk received the commission to design a stained glass window for the Africa Hall of the United Nations Economic Commission for Africa in Addis Ababa. The resulting composition, *The Struggle and Aspiration of the African People*, incorporates pan-African themes in a strong statement about the negative impact of colonialism. The monumental window, measuring 150 square meters, is among his best-known works. Its three sections represent Africa's troubled history, present struggles, and hopes for the future. From the time of this project on, Afewerk received national and international recognition for his prodigious output of easel and mural paintings, stained glass windows, and designs for stamps, national ceremonial dress, and other ephemera in the service of the Ethiopian government. His oeuvre includes portraits, landscapes, genre scenes, and sacred subjects. In the 1960s and the following decades the artist was invited to exhibit his work and to lecture widely in the United States, the Soviet Union, and numerous countries of Europe and Africa.

A retrospective exhibition of Afewerk's work in 1961 in Addis Ababa included a painting of an elegant Ethiopian woman in aristocratic attire titled *Maskal Flower*, which was subsequently exhibited in the Soviet Union, the United States, and Senegal. The artist was criticized by some of his countrymen for choosing a wealthy aristocratic woman to represent Ethiopia, where so many struggle in poverty. He responded that this painting, together with another of around the same date titled *Mother Ethiopia*, represents his hope for the future of Ethiopia. "It may never be achieved, but they are examples of my vision for the eventual Ethiopian—beautiful, well-fed, full of life and serene" (Fosu, p. 25).

Afewerk designed his imposing house, studio, and gallery in 1959 and completed construction over the course of fifteen years. Known as Villa Alpha, the structure is modeled on historic Ethiopian stone architecture in ancient Aksum and medieval Gondar in the north and the old walled city of Harar in the east. It is open to visitors by appointment and functions as a museum of his works and career. The artist has spoken of his desire to leave the house and the numerous works of art in it as a gift to the nation (Afewerk, conversation with the author: November 1, 2002). Although Afewerk was not on the faculty of the Fine Arts School in Addis Ababa (now the School of Fine Art and Design of Addis Ababa University) and did not teach or take apprentices, his national and international recognition, awards, prominent commissions, and financial success have made him a role model for many Ethiopian artists.

[*See also* Haile Selassie I; Mekonnen Welde Mikael; Meles Zenawi; *and* Mengistu Haile Mariam.]

BIBLIOGRAPHY

Fosu, Kojo. *20th Century Art of Africa*, pp. 21–28. Zaria, Nigeria: Gaskiya Corporation, 1986.

Hassan, Salah M., and Achamyeleh Debela. "Addis Connections: The Making of the Modern Ethiopian Art Movement." In *Seven Stories about Modern Art in Africa*, edited by Clémentine Deliss, pp. 129–130. Paris: Flammarion, 1995.

Pankhurst, Richard. *Afewerk Tekle*. Addis Ababa: Artistic Printers of Ethiopia, 1987.

REBECCA MARTIN NAGY

Afewerq Gebre Iyesus (1868–1947), Ethiopian painter, diplomat, customs director, entrepreneur, linguist, university professor, and novelist, was born in Zage, Gojjam province of Ethiopia, on 10 July 1868. His father, Gebre Iyesus Denke, was a priest serving a local church, and his mother, Fenta Tehun Adego Ayechew, was presumably a housewife. In Zage, then a center of learning, Afewerq learned the painting, poetry, church music, and liturgical dancing of the Ethiopian Orthodox Christian tradition.

Afewerq was related to Empress Taytu Betul, wife of Emperor Menilek (1844–1913), on account of which he was brought to the palace to continue what he had started in Zage. He was later sent to Italy to further his studies at the Accademia Albertina di Belle Arti in Turin. Upon his return from Italy, he began to produce mural paintings by order of the palace and decorated the churches at Entotto, then the capital city. However, he soon lost favor of the empress who believed that he was too Europeanized. With the help of Alfred Ilg, a Swiss adviser to the emperor, Afewerq left for Switzerland. Shortly before the Italo-Ethiopian war in 1896, Afewerq left for Eritrea. He returned to Italy after the war and joined the College Internazionale in Turin. In 1902 he took up a teaching position at the Istituto Orientale in Naples, where he taught Amharic and also wrote a pedagogical grammar of the language. In 1904 he married Eugenia Rossini, an Italian, with whom he had a daughter and three sons.

The same year, Afewerq moved to Eritrea again, started an import-export business, became adviser to the Banka Cooperative Populare Eritrea, and went into commercial farming with others. Politically, he opposed the Ethiopian state, which he believed to be inefficient, corrupt, conservative, and badly in need of change. He expressed these opinions in his book *Guide du Voyageur en Abyssinie*. He supported Lij Iyasu's accession to the throne after Menilek, whose biography he also wrote during the same period in Italy. Unfortunately, Lij Iyasu did not stay long in power; he was deposed and replaced by Zewditu, the emperor's daughter, with Teferi, (later Haile Selassie I) as regent and heir designate. The new leadership invited Afewerq to join the government and serve the country; he accepted the offer and went on a trade mission to the United States in 1918. In 1922 he was appointed director of customs at Dire Dawa with the accompanying title of *Negadras*. After three years as *Negadras*, he was appointed president of the special court that dealt with cases involving Ethiopians and foreigners. He presided over this court for five years, until he retired due to poor health.

In 1931 Afewerq was made *chargé d'affaires* of Ethiopia to Italy, a position he held until he was recalled when Italy invaded Ethiopia in 1935. He openly supported the invasion, became the editor of a newspaper called *yeKesar Mengest Melektegna* (Messenger of the Government of Caesar [King of Italy]), and wrote extensively against the patriotic resistance movement. He was given the title *Afe Kesar* ("spokesman of Caesar") and served as supreme head of the natives judiciary. He believed that the invasion would bring an end to the age-old feudal system and transform the country into a modern state. When Italy lost the war and left the country in 1941, Afewerq faced trial for treason. Eventually, his death-sentence was commuted to life imprisonment. He was exiled to Jimma, where he lost his sight and died in prison in 1947 at the age of seventy-nine.

His book *Lebb welled tarik* (A Story Born by the Heart), published in Rome in 1908, heralded the beginning of modern Amharic literature. It deals with the theme of conflict between Paganism and Christianity and the victory of the latter over the former. Afewerq also wrote various manuals and texts on linguistic matters relating to Amharic.

Afewerq is considered a traitor by the state and a nationalist by those close to him. He envisioned a modern Ethiopian state like that of Italy, where he lived for forty years and with which he was enchanted.

[*See also* Menilek II; *and* Taytu Betul.]

BIBLIOGRAPHY

Gerard, Albert. "Amharic Creative Literature: The Early Phase." *Journal of Ethiopian Studies* 6, no. 2 (1968): 39–59.

Pankhurst, Richard. "The Foundations of Ethiopian Education." *Ethiopian Observer* 13 (1962): 241–290)

Rouaud, Alain. *Afa-Warq, 1868–1947: un intellectual éthiopien témoin de son temps*. Paris: Presses du CNRS, 1991.

Yonas Admasu . "Afewerq Gebre Iyesus." In *Encyclopaedia Aethiopica*, vol. 1., pp. 122–124. Wiesbaden, Germany: Harrassowitz Verlag, 2002.

BAYE YIMAM

Afghani, Jamal al-Din Muhammad al- (1839–1897), philosopher, pioneer of Islamic reformist thought, pan-Islamic nationalist as well as a staunch opponent of British penetration in the East, also known as al-Asadaabadi and al-Husayni, Afghani, was born in October/November 1839 in the Iranian village of Asadaabad. However, he endeavored to hide his origins so as to conceal his Shiite identity. It was with this in mind that he assumed the surname al-Afghani (of Afghan origin).

His father, Sayyid Safdar, is said to have been a modest farmer, but a learned Muslim. From the age of five to ten, Afghani was apparently educated at home, focusing on Arabic and the Qur'an. Thereafter, he was sent to school in Qazvin and later Tehran, where he received the standard Shiite education.

After several years of study in the holy city of Najaf, Afghani moved to India in approximately 1855, where he first encountered British colonialism. By the time he reached Afghanistan in 1866, he was already considered a sworn enemy of British rule in Islamic lands and a proponent of waging a struggle against imperialism. While in Afghanistan, the charismatic thinker presented himself as a Rumi (i.e., from Turkey) and even assumed the name Istanbuli. Moreover, he formed ties with Prince Muhammad A'zam Khan (the emir of Afghanistan from 1866 to 1868) and tried to convince the monarch to adopt an anti-British stance. Toward the end of 1868, A'zam was defeated on the battlefield and fled to Iran. His successor, Shir 'Ali Khan, had al-Afghani expelled from the country.

Afghani arrived in Istanbul in the fall of 1869 and was appointed to the reform-minded Council on Education. As such, he was chosen to give one of the speeches at the dedication ceremony of the Darulfunun (the local university). In his speech Afghani implored Muslims to awaken from their deep slumber of prolonged neglect and emulate the "civilized nations" of the West. In early 1871 he was banished from Istanbul at the request of the Seyhulislam (the Ottoman Empire's supreme religious authority) for publicly defining prophecy as an inspired craft rather than an acquired one.

In the spring of 1871, Afghani came to Cairo at the invitation of an Egyptian politician, Riyad Pasha, who had promised him a monthly stipend. During his stay, Afghani regularly taught in his house and attracted a circle of young intellectuals, among them Muhammad 'Abduh, who went on to become one of the most prominent Islamic reformists; the Christian-Syrian novelist Adib Ishaq; the journalist and novelist 'Abdallah al-Nadim; and Sa'd Zaghlul, who eventually led Egypt's struggle for independence against Britain following World War I.

The 1870s was a decade of westernization in Egypt. The Egyptian ruler, the Khedive Isma'il, presided over development and modernization projects that mired the country in heavy debt, which ultimately prompted the British to occupy Egypt in September 1882. Correspondingly, foreign powers (especially Britain) became increasingly involved in the country's affairs, and the local European community steadily expanded. In 1878 Afghani began giving fiery public speeches in which he excoriated the British and clamored for the preservation of Egyptian independence. As a result, Khedive Taufiq, who had succeeded the exiled Isma'il to the throne, banished Afghani from the country in August 1879.

From Egypt, Afghani headed back to India, where he wrote his important work *The Refutation of the Materialists*. Three years later Afghani set sail for Europe. Following a short stay in London, he moved on to Paris and started publishing articles with an anti-British and pan-Islamic bent. In early 1884 he was joined in France by his friend Muhammad 'Abduh after the latter was also deported from Egypt (by the British). 'Abduh and Afghani established a newspaper, *Al-'Urwa Al-Wuthqa* (The Firmest Bond). However, the enterprise folded after less than a year, and the two exiles parted ways.

With the assistance of Wilfrid Blunt, an anti-imperialist poet, Afghani entered informal negotiations with the British over their presence in Egypt and the Sudan. Afghani resided in Blunt's home in England for part of 1885, but the talks proved to be fruitless. From early 1886 until the spring of 1887, Afghani lived in Iran and even met Nasir al-Din Shah, to whom he reportedly offered himself "as a sword to be used against the shah's foreign enemies." On account of his belligerent anti-British positions, Afghani was ordered to leave Iran and subsequently moved to Russia.

Afghani spent the next two years in Russia where he sought to convince government officials to launch a war against Britain. Against the backdrop of the tense relations between Russia and Iran, the shah invited him back to Tehran at the end of 1889. Afghani indeed returned and surrounded himself with a group of disciples. In talks with his followers, the peripatetic intellectual contended that the time

had come for an aggressive policy against British infiltration throughout the area. After circulating a leaflet that lambasted the Iranian government for granting a tobacco concession to the British, Afghani was asked to leave the country yet again. Upon arriving in London, via Iraq, he waged a heated campaign to oust the shah, whom he labelled a tyrant.

In the summer of 1892 Afghani arrived in Istanbul at the request of Sultan Abdulhamid, who intended to keep a close eye on the outspoken thinker so as to prevent him from compromising the empire's important relations with Britain. The sultan was amicable toward Afghani at first, but his attitude soured over the course of 1895 when senior clergy accused Afghani of being a heretic and a fraud. In the meantime, the reigning Egyptian Khedive, 'Abbas Hilmi, came to Istanbul and met with Afghani in secret. They apparently discussed the reestablishment of the caliphate, an idea that was perceived as a threat by the sultan. Soon after the court's officials foiled Afghani's plans to leave the Golden Horn in December on a British visa. The following May, the shah was murdered by one of Afghani's disciples, who had come to Istanbul prior to the assassination in order to consult with his mentor. The Iranians demanded that the intellectual be extradited to Teheran, but the sultan rejected their wishes.

A lecture given at the Sorbonne by the French Historian Ernest Renan appeared in *Journal de Dèbats* in March 1883. In his lecture Renan opined that Islam and the Arabs are inherently hostile to philosophy and science. What is more, this is the reason that these fields were developed in the Islamic world by non-Arabs. Two months later Afghani responded to Renan's argument in the same newspaper. Afghani argued that, at its inception, no nation can march to the light of pure wisdom. At the dawn of civilization, mankind was unable to explain many commonplace occurrences. Therefore society needed guides, namely prophets, to make sense of nature and promulgate commandments in the name of a supreme being. No religion is rational or tolerant, Afghani continued. In this respect, the lone difference between Islam and Christianity is tied to age. He expressed his hope that Islam would extricate itself, just as Christianity had, from the shackles of religion and noted that Islam had already enjoyed a scientific and cultural blossoming during the Middle Ages, when Europe was shrouded in ignorance.

Afghani's longest and most renowned work is the above-mentioned *Al-Radd 'Ala al-Dahriyyin*

(Refutation of the Materialists), in which he assailed the views of Sayyid Ahmad Khan, a reform-minded Islamic intellectual. Materialism, in Afghani's estimation, embodies the modern Western approach of attempting to explain the world in an entirely rational manner, without taking into account the possibility of a supreme force. Afghani claimed that the materialists are ruining human felicity and the natural order, whereas Islam reinforces them. More specifically, human progress and happiness are dependent on people's wherewithal to purify the consciousness of "the pollution of superstitions and false images," and only Islam is fit for this task. He also averred that every nation is best advised to have two specific groups of intellectuals, each of which is responsible for educating the people in the sciences and in ethics, respectively. However, only Islam commands the faithful to maintain both groups.

There are those who ask, Afghani wrote, if Islam is so beneficent, why is it in such a sorry state? His answer to this question is rather simple: "When they were [truly] Muslims, they were what they were and the world bears witness to their excellence." In other words, his generation of Muslims had veered off the judicious path of their predecessors. Afghani thus concluded that it is incumbent upon Muslims to take their fate by the hand, as stated in the following qur'anic verse: "Verily, God does not change the state of a people until they change themselves inwardly." Over the years, this verse has indeed become a favorite aphorism of modernists who beseech Muslims to take palpable steps to improve their lot.

Afghani's philosophy is pan-Islamic. It proceeds on the axis between the aspiration to modernize and rationalize Islam and, conversely, the rejection of the Occident as a model for imitation. In his view, rational interpretation and judicious implementation of the Qur'an by means of *ijtihad* (a religious concept meaning discretion), rather than the imprudent imitation of the European "materialists," are the keys to helping Muslims adapt themselves to the modern world. Whoever rejects this route to progress, according to Afghani, must bear responsibility for the stagnation (*jummud*) and mimicry (*taqlid*) that have taken hold of Islam. Afghani made no distinction between religion and politics, for Islam, in his opinion, is a system that encompasses all areas of life. The reforms that he pressed for are designed to empower Islam so as to enable his co-religionists to stand up to the West and prevent it from encroaching upon their lands. Similarly, he called upon Muslims to unite and preserve the heritage of their forefathers.

Afghani died at his home in Istanbul on 9 March 1897. Although rumors were spread that he had been poisoned, the cause of death was cancer of the pharynx.

[*See also* 'Abduh, Muhammad; *and* Isma'il.]

BIBLIOGRAPHY

Works by Jamal Al-Din Muhammad Al-Afghani

Al-Aathar al-Kamila (Afghani's Collected Works), edited by Sayyid Hadi Khasru Shahi. Vols. 1–2. Cairo: Maktabat al-Shuruq al-Dawliyya, 2002.

Works about Jamal Al-Din Muhammad Al-Afghani

'Amara, Muhammad. *Jamal al-Din al-Afghani, Muwaqiz al-Sharq wa-Faylusuf al-Islam* (al-Afghani, the Man Who Woke Up the East and the Philosopher of Islam). Cairo: Dar al-Mustaqbal al-'Arabi, 1984.

Asadaabadi, Mirza Lutfullah Khan al-. *Jamal al-Din al-Asadaabadi al-Ma'aruf bi-al-Afghani—Al-ta'arif bihi wa bi-Aatharihi* (Introducing al-Afghani and His Works), translated into Arabic by 'Abd al-Na'im Muhammad Husayni. Beirut: Dar al-Kitab al-Lubnani, 1973.

Hourani, Albert. *Arabic Thought in the Liberal Age, 1798–1939*. Cambridge, UK, and New York: Cambridge University Press, 2001.

Keddie, Nikki R. *An Islamic Response to Imperialism: Political and Religious Writings of Sayyid Jamal ad-Din "al-Afghani."* Berkeley: University of California Press, 1983.

Keddie, Nikki R. *Sayyid Jamal ad-Din "al-Afghani," A Political Biography*. Berkeley: University of California Press, 1972.

Kedourie, Elie. *Afghani and 'Abduh: An Essay on Religious Unbelief and Political Activism in Modern Islam*. New edition. London: Routledge, 2008.

EFRAIM BARAK

Afigbo, Adiele Eberechukwu (1937–2009), Nigerian scholar, professor of African history at the University of Nigeria, Nsukka, was born on 22 November 1937 in Ihube, Okigwe, in present-day Imo State, southeastern Nigeria. He had his early education at Methodist Central School, Ihube, Okigwe, between 1944 and 1950 and won the Okigwe Native Administration scholarship, which enabled him to attend St. Augustine's Grammar School, Nkwerre Orlu, in Imo State between 1951 and 1956. With a scholarship from the government of Eastern Nigeria, he proceeded to the University

College, Ibadan (now University of Ibadan, Ibadan), to study history. Afigbo graduated at the top of his class and therefore won the University of Ibadan postgraduate scholarships, which enabled him to study and complete his doctorate degree, also a first among his colleagues, among whom were Obaro Ikime and Philip Igbafe. Afigbo, thus, became the first person to receive a doctoral degree in history from a Nigerian university.

Afigbo's meteoric rise could be attributed to enterprise and luck. As a pupil at the Methodist Central School, Ihube, Afigbo was tutored by Mr. Oji Iheukumere, the head teacher and a disciplinarian. At St. Augustine's Grammar School, Mazi F. C. Ogbalu, a teacher of Igbo language and culture and the founder of the Society for the Promotion of Igbo Language and Culture; C. G. I. Eneli, a history graduate of the University College, Ibadan; and E. C. Ezekwesili, the principal of the college and a history graduate of the University of Southampton, UK, took him under their wings. At Ibadan, J. D. Omer-Cooper, J. C. Anene, J. F. Ade Ajayi, and Kenneth O. Dike mentored him through his studies. Staff and students in the entire school eloquently testified to his brilliance, enterprise, and intelligence.

Upon completion of his doctorate degree, Afigbo joined the Department of History at Ibadan as a lecturer grade two and was a shining star. However, his career at Ibadan was briefly interrupted at the outset of the Nigerian civil war years as he left the University of Ibadan for the University of Nigeria, Nsukka. During the civil war, he joined forces with the Republic of Biafra, where he served in the Directorate for Propaganda of the Ministry of Information. With the cessation of hostilities in 1970, Afigbo returned to his job at the university, and by 1972, at the tender age of thirty-five, became a professor of African history.

No sooner had Afigbo completed his doctorate degree than he charted a new course, tangentially different from the Ibadan School and its obtuse fascination with action/reaction thesis, for himself. Afigbo, in no less rigorous fashion, began to emphasize the study of peoples and cultures, the study of intergroup relations, the dynamic characteristic of myths and traditions, the need to situate and integrate historical studies in nation building, and the need for scholars to adapt their methods accordingly. Given this eclectic scholarship, Afigbo can be understood at many levels and from different perspectives.

More than any other African historian, Afigbo used the particular to explain the universal and the universal to explain the particular. In his celebrated work on the rise and expansion of the precolonial great states, he used the representative study of the Benin kingdom to demonstrate that noncentralized states and the so-called ministates of precolonial Africa comprise the basic ingredient in the growth, expansion, and development of the so-called great, centralized states. Similarly, his detailed study of the textile-production processes in southern Nigeria provided nuanced explanations of the sociocultural dynamics of the region. His keynote address at the Ghana Historical Society and the Omohundro Institute for Early American Culture centenary celebration of the abolition of the Atlantic slave trade continues to generate debate.

Afigbo combined a robust academic life with an equally robust and astounding public life. On the academic front, two years after earning his doctorate, he was appointed head of the Department of History and Archaeology, University of Nigeria, Nsukka; two years later, he was appointed dean of the Faculty of Arts and director of the Leo Hansbury Institute of African Studies, University of Nigeria, Nsukka, among other positions.

In public service, he served as pioneer director of research at the National Institute for Policy and Strategic Studies, Kuru, Jos. At different times, he was appointed, first, as commissioner for education and, later, as commissioner for local government in the government of Imo State; chair, Michael Okpara College of Agriculture, Umuagwo, Imo State; and sole administrator, Alvan Ikoku College of Education, Owerri, Imo State, Nigeria.

For his numerous contributions to educational and national development, Afigbo was awarded many coveted academic honors: honorary member of the Historical Association of Great Britain, fellow of the Historical Society of Nigeria, the Nigerian National Order of Merit, the (foundation) Fellowship of the Nigerian Academy of Letters. More than any other Nigerian cum African historian, Afigbo used his researches and publications to promote the cause of his people. In fact, in Nigerian academic circles, Afigbo is regarded, first, as a historian of the Igbo nation, with studies bordering on the different groups and peoples in Delta Igbo, Enuani Igbo, Ika Igbo, Ikwerre, and Ukwuani; then as a historian of southeastern Nigeria; and finally, as a historian of Nigeria and Africa. For his efforts in promoting scholarship to his people, among his numerous traditional titles are Ogbute-Okewe-Ibe, Ogbuzuo, and Olaudah.

After retirement, Professor Adiele Eberechukwu Afigbo helped to establish the Department of History at the Niger-Delta University. He died in

Enugu, Nigeria, in the early hours of Monday, 9 March 2009, after a brief illness.

[*See also* Ade Ajayi, Jacob Festus; *and* Dike, Kenneth.]

BIBLIOGRAPHY

Works by Afigbo

The Warrant Chiefs: Indirect Rule in Southeastern Nigeria 1891–1929. London: Longman, 1972.

Ropes of Sand: Studies in Igbo History and Culture. Ibadan, Nigeria: University Press, 1981.

The Igbo and Their Neighbours: Inter-group Relations in Southeastern Nigeria to 1953. Ibadan, Nigeria: University Press, 1987.

Groundwork of Igbo History. Lagos, Nigeria: Vista Books, 1992.

Image of the Igbo. Lagos, Nigeria: Vista Books, 1992.

Igbo History and Society: The Essays of Adiele Afigbo, edited by Toyin Falola. Trenton, N.J.: Africa World Press, 2005.

Myth, History and Society: The Collected Works of Adiele Afigbo, edited by Toyin Falola. Trenton, N.J.: Africa World Press, 2006.

The Abolition of the Slave Trade in Southeastern Nigeria 1885–1950. Rochester, N.Y.: University of Rochester Press, 2006.

Nigeria History, Politics and Affairs: The Collected Essays of Adiele Afigbo, edited by Toyin Falola. Trenton, N.J.: Africa World Press, 2007.

Works about Afigbo

Falola, Toyin, and Adam Paddock, eds. *Emergent Themes and Methods in African Studies: Essays in Honor of Adiele E. Afigbo*. Trenton, N.J.: Africa World Press, 2009.

Falola, Toyin, and Saheed Aderinto, eds. *Nigeria, Nationalism, and Writing History*. Rochester, N.Y.: University of Rochester Press, 2011.

ADEYEMI BUKOLA OYENIYI

Afonso I (d. 1543), leader of the Kongo kingdom, was born in the mid-fourteenth century. His birth name was Mvemba a Nzinga and he was the child of King João I Nzinga Nkuwu of Kongo and Nzinga a Nlaza, one of the king's wives. When the Portuguese ship captain Diogo Cão first arrived in 1483, Afonso was a high-ranking officer in the kingdom. He consented to be baptized by Catholic missionaries. When a royal court faction opposed to Christianity arose after João I's baptism in 1491, Afonso developed his authority in his own province of Nsundi. He allowed two Portuguese priests, Goncalve Vas and Rodrigue Anes, to live in his court.

Not surprisingly, Portuguese missionaries and officials gave Afonso support, especially after his father renounced Christianity. In Nsundi, Afonso used his privileged access to European trade goods to gain access to valuable high-grade copper located north of the Congo River and outside Kongolese royal control. Copper basins and ritual items were often used in bridewealth payments and so held great value in Kongo. Afonso received aid from the Portuguese government in wars with the Téké-speaking Tio kingdom in this early period, most likely over control of copper.

When João I died in 1506, a group of royal family members met to choose a new king, which had been the normal way a new king would be selected. Afonso I put together an army with the aid of his mother and seized the throne. His mother also helped her son by delaying the announcement of João's death for some time, which allowed Afonso time to secure the capital. His half-brother Mpanzu a Kitima, the leader of the nobles opposed to Christianity, launched a war against Afonso. The two forces clashed. According to a letter written by Afonso to the King of Portugal in 1509 that unfortunately has not survived, Mpanzu a Kitima's troops outnumbered Afonso's forces, but Saint James appeared in the sky and offered his spiritual intercession to Afonso's soldiers. Mpanzu a Kitima was defeated and Afonso had him executed. With his main rival dead, Afonso then turned to consolidating his hold over the entire kingdom. The inauguration of the slave trade with the Portuguese allowed Afonso to buy merchandise that increased his own patronage and thus allowed him to develop broad alliances inside and outside his territory.

Growing Portuguese demand for slaves for the sugar plantations on the Atlantic islands of São Tomé and Principe led Portuguese traders to come to Kongo in 1508. Afonso agreed to trade people to Europeans, as long as they respected his royal monopoly over the slave trade. Many of the initial slaves were prisoners of war from neighboring states, such as Mbundu. While the plantation owners of São Tomé were happy to buy slaves, they despised the idea of a Kongolese royal monopoly over the trade. They soon circumvented Afonso's control by acquiring slaves from Kongolese nobles, particularly aristocrats who ruled over the coastal Kongolese province of Nsoyo. Afonso became angry that the Portuguese would not accept his monopoly. In a well-known letter written to the Portuguese monarch João III in 1526, Afonso pleaded for his ally to close slave-trading forts built by the Portuguese in Kongo and that he command his subjects to respect Afonso's control over the slave trade. Afonso even went so far as to threaten to expel all Portuguese merchants from the Kongo kingdom, even though he continued to request that more priests be sent from Europe. Unknowingly, Afonso prepared the way for future trouble with Portugal by sending silver objects as gifts to Lisbon. This wrongly convinced the Portuguese that rich silver mines existed in Kongo, and future Portuguese invasions of the kingdom would be inspired by this incorrect assumption. When the Portuguese did not follow Afonso's recommendations, he begrudgingly permitted the Portuguese to purchase slaves from other Kongolese by the 1530s. However, he set taxes on these acquisitions and commanded that only official boats be used to transport the captives. One reason for Afonso's change of policy came from new slave markets located along the Malebo Pool on the Congo River that were created in the late 1520s. With these new institutions under royal administration, Afonso became again a proponent of selling people to Europeans.

From the late 1520s until Afonso's death in 1543, the king's ability to obtain large amounts of European merchandise and his endorsement of Christianity greatly enhanced his territory and influence. A range of neighboring kingdoms from the Tio north of the Congo river to the Mbundu-speaking chiefdoms to the south gave gifts to Afonso in order to receive European trade goods. Officials burned talismans and mystical power objects associated with indigenous spiritual traditions as a sign of Afonso's loyalty to Christianity. The king built new churches so that Catholicism could spread, even though the monarch had a series of concubines. While missionaries disapproved, Afonso could still maintain a number of alliances with prominent noble families by forming intimate relationships with aristocratic women. Priests made less effort to censure the king for his behavior, perhaps in part because Afonso had married one woman in a Christian ceremony. Afonso had numerous children linked to different leading clans as a result. He assuaged clerical anger by establishing Catholic schools that attracted many men from noble families as early as 1516. One of his own sons, Henrique Kinu a Mvemba, studied in Europe and entered the priesthood. In 1518, Henrique was named bishop of the Kongo territory by the Vatican and returned to Mbanza Kongo by the early 1520s. Thus, Afonso began to cultivate ties to the papacy that no longer depended entirely on Portugal and sought to use the church to uphold his power.

Afonso faced challenges in the last years of his reign. Although his sons occupied prominent provinces in the kingdom, they commenced to struggle with each other over the royal succession. Some Portuguese traders and nobles conspired to kill Afonso on Easter Sunday 1539, but the plot failed. He died of unknown causes in 1543. His rule thus brought a very ambiguous legacy that other Kongolese rulers followed, especially in regard to the Atlantic slave trade.

[See also João I.]

BIBLIOGRAPHY

Balandier, Georges. *Daily Life in the Kingdom of the Kongo from the Sixteenth to the Eighteenth Century.* Translated by Helen Weaver. New York: Pantheon Books, 1968.

Hastings, Adrian. *The Church in Africa, 1450–1950.* Oxford: Clarendon Press, 1994.

Hilton, Anne. *The Kingdom of Kongo.* Oxford: Clarendon Press, 1985.

Sundkler, Bengt, and Christopher Steed. *A History of the Church in Africa.* Cambridge, UK, and New York: Cambridge University Press, 2000.

JEREMY RICH

Afrax, Maxamed Dahir (1952–), Somali novelist, short story writer, critic, journalist, and founder of cultural and literary journals and institutions, was born in Jarriiban, Mudug region, Somalia, in 1952. His name is also given as Mohamed Dahir Afrah and Maxamed Daahir Afrax. He graduated from high school in Mogadishu in 1973. When the Siad Barre government introduced the first official orthography for the Somali language in 1972, Afrax founded the first bilingual Somali-Arabic monthly magazine using the new script, *Codka Jubba* ("The Voice of Jubba," 1972–1975). In 1976, Afrax's story "Guur-ku-sheeg" ("Pseudo-marriage") was serialized in the Somali national newspaper *Xiddigta Oktoobar* ("The October Star"), laying the basis for a lasting literary tradition of serialized fiction.

In this same serialized form he also first published his popular novel *Maanafaay*, the story of the girl Maanafaay, who, in the Mogadishu of the 1970s, strives to be modern *and* modest and only barely escapes those who try to ruin her life and reputation. Published in book form in 1981, it was, in terms of its techniques and content, the first "modern" novel in the Somali language. In 1979–1981, Afrax also wrote a regular newspaper column on theater criticism, a literary genre so unfamiliar to Somali artists of that time that they were initially rather hostile to it.

In this period, Afrax served as deputy director of Somalia's National Agency for Theatres, took a course in journalism, and produced a weekly cultural program (Kulmis) for Radio Mogadishu. He also published a historical novel in Arabic, *Nida' al-Hurriya* ("The Cry for Freedom," 1976); authored a play, *Durbaan Been ah* ("A False Drum," 1979); and wrote a novel titled *Galti-Macruuf* ("Country Bumpkin," 1981). It was this publication, which criticized the corruption of government officials, that led to Afrax's arrest and his escape and exile from the increasingly repressive political climate in Somalia. After brief stays in Italy and Romania, he joined other dissident literary figures such as the poets Mohamed Ibrahim Hadrawi, Mohamed Hashi Gaarriye, and Farah Gamute, in Ethiopia, where they vainly attempted to unify the divided armed opposition fronts that had emerged in opposition of the Barre regime.

From 1984 to 1990, Afrax lived in Aden (Yemen), where he completed a degree, worked as a writer and researcher for the Ministry of Culture, and was an active member of the Yemeni Writers Union, the Arab Writers Organization, and other professional organizations. While in Aden, Afrax made regular research visits to Djibouti, already a center for practitioners and students of Somali oral literature and culture. This research led in 1987 to the publication of his pioneering book, in Somali, on Somali theater.

In 1990, Afrax moved to London, where, at the School of Oriental and African Studies, he completed his PhD dissertation, "Literature in Transition: Continuity and Innovation in Post-independence Somali Drama and Poetry." In London, he founded *Halabuur*, the first bilingual Somali-English literary-and-learned journal on Somali literature and culture (1992–1995), which has now resumed publication in Djibouti (2007), and founded the first professional association for Somali writers, the Somali-speaking Club of International PEN (1997). In this same period, Afrax published a number of scholarly articles in English (see bibliography), as well as several books in Arabic and Somali, of which his *Dal dad waayey iyo duni damiir beeshay* ("A Country Betrayed by Its Leadership") of 2003 is the most widely read among Somalis.

From the 1990s onward, Afrax has promoted and attempted to provide an institutional basis for the concept of a "culture of peace" for Somalia, of which he was one of the major architects. In pursuit of this project, while keeping one foot in London where his wife and three children have continued to reside, he moved to Djibouti, where he founded the Halabuur Centre for Culture and Communication in the Horn. To the same end, namely to develop the potential of Somali culture and art as vehicles for peace and development, he has served as a consultant for UNESCO, United Nations Development Programme (UNDP), and the Government of Djibouti. In 2000, when the Djibouti-led Somali Reconciliation Conference—during which Afrax served as an adviser to the Djibouti Government—led to the formation of the Somali Transitional National Government of President Abdulkasim Salad Hassan, Afrax became a member of parliament and then Minister of State for International Cooperation (October 2000–July 2003). Today he continues to play a crucial role in Djibouti's literary and cultural development as a practicing writer, cultural adviser to the government, director of the Halabuur Centre and editor of its journal, and founder-president of the PEN Center of Somali-speaking Writers.

Afrax's lifetime goal has been the rehabilitation of Somali culture and the (re-)establishment of lasting Somali cultural institutions. He has been committed to the preservation and development of the Somali language, has helped to connect Somali artists and scholars worldwide, and worked with them to engage Somali youth, wherever they might be, in the process of fostering the Somali language as a language of art and scholarship. In his writings and professional life, Afrax is a quintessential representative of the modernity of the post-independence era. Thus he has always experimented with new literary genres and institutions and warned against the dangers of a stultifying and uncritical focus on the "Somali tradition."

Throughout his life, Afrax, like many other Somali artists, has spoken out against social discrimination and injustice, defended freedom of expression, and opposed censorship of any kind, whether based in repressive politics, restrictive conceptions of Somali tradition, or—increasingly influential in Somalia— narrow-minded interpretations of Islam.

BIBLIOGRAPHY

Works by Maxamed Dahir Afrax

Fan-masraxeedka Soomaalida: Raad-caac taariikheed iyo faaqidaad riwaayada caan-baxay (Somali Drama: A Historical Analysis and Literary Criticism of the Most Famous Plays). Djibouti, Somalia: Centre of Cultural and Artistic Promotion, 1987.

"The Mirror of Culture: Somali Dissolution Seen Through Oral Expression." In *The Somali Challenge: from Catastrophe to Renewal?*, ed. by Ahmed I.

Samatar, pp. 233–256. Boulder, Colo.: Lynne Rienner Publishers, 1994.

"Rural Imagery in Contemporary Somali Urban Poetry: A Debilitating Carryover in Transitional Verbal Art." *SOAS Literary Review* 1 (Winter 1999): 1–13.

Nadharat fi ath-thaqafah al-Sumaliyya (A Window on Somali Culture). 'Sharjah, U.A.E.: Department of Culture and Information, 2002.

"The Abwaan as Beacon: The Centrality of the Message in Somali Literature." *Horn of Africa Journal* 22 (2004): 1–63.

"Classification and Nomenclature of Somali Literary Forms: A Pending Issue." *Horn of Africa Journal* 23 (2005): 58–84.

"*Tala-seeg*" (Too Late). Halabuur: *Journal of Somali Literature and Culture* 2, nos. 1–2 (2007): 95–101.

"Theatre as a Window on Society: Opposing Influences of Tradition and Modernity in Somali Plays." *Halabuur: Journal of Somali Literature and Culture* 2, nos. 1–2 (2007): 74–83.

Works about Maxamed Dahir Afrax

Ibraahin, Yuusuf Axmed "Hawd." "'Maana-Faay': Muraayad Bulshadeenu iska Dhex Aragto." *Halabuur: Journal of Somali Literature and Culture* 2, nos. 1–2 (2007): 83–87.

Kapteijns, Lidwien. "A Window to Somali Society: The Novels of Maxamed Daahir Afrax." *Halabuur: Journal of Somali Literature and Culture* 1, nos. 2–3 (Autumn/Winter 1994): 50–58.

LIDWIEN KAPTEIJNS

African Eve (c. 200,000 years before present), conjectural early human, also known as Mitochondrial Eve, was proposed by Rebecca L. Cann and her fellow researchers in 1987. Using mitochondrial DNA (inherited only along the maternal line), Cann and her associates examined 147 individuals and produced a genetic evolutionary tree showing branching from two sets of individuals: one set of African ancestry and a second set of mixed African and "other" ancestry. The most parsimonious explanation of the tree was that modern humans originated in Africa from a single source, which Cann and her coworkers named "Eve," at a date between 140,000 and 290,000 years ago. Subsequent research has placed this date more accurately at approximately 200,000 years ago by comparing ten human genetic models. African Eve is a mathematical model, and not an actual fossil of human remains. Nonetheless, most scientists now agree that she is the most recent woman who is ancestral to all humans today and that she lived in Africa.

Controversy was immediate, particularly concerning the manner in which Cann et al. interpreted their genetic tree, the rate of mutation of mitochondrial DNA used in the study, the resolution of the tree, and so forth. In the early to mid-1990s several alternative trees were published, with several different "roots" outside of Africa. As knowledge of genetics increased and techniques improved, different approaches were applied to the problem of human origins, migration patterns and timing, and the presence or absence of genetic bottlenecks (times during which populations decreased markedly in size). Mitochondrial DNA from Europe, Africa, and Asia were analyzed independently, and it was found that a small number of groups of single mitochondrial DNA origin (monophyletic clades, or haplogroups) could be identified, refined, and used in the interpretation of migration patterns around the world in what has been called a phylogeographic approach to demographic history.

In 2000 Ingman et al. completely sequenced the mitochondrial DNA from fifty-three women. They found a distinct and unique sequence in each of these women and were able to construct a genetic tree based on these data. The first divergence occurred within sub-Saharan African women, followed by a branching of multiple individuals from other Africans, thus supporting the genetic African origin of modern humans proposed by Cann and coworkers in 1987. An additional sixty-six women were sequenced independently by J. L. Elson and coworkers (2001) with similar results.

African Eve was not the only woman of her species at the time she lived. Many studies, of nuclear DNA, of fossils, and of archaeological sites, indicate an ancient population in the tens of thousands at the time Eve was alive. The difficulty in lay interpretation likely comes from the fact that, although studies indicate a single female common ancestor of all living women today, these studies do not take into account the lines that died out and the fact that males do not pass on mitochondrial DNA. She is not the most recent common ancestor shared by all living humans; rather, Eve is proposed as the most recent common matrilineal ancestor, an important distinction. In the mid-1990s geneticists began researching the most common patrilineal ancestor of modern humans, now called Y-chromosomal Adam, to join African Eve in the human evolutionary line. Adam is thought to have lived between 60,000 to 90,000 years ago in sub-Saharan Africa; this time difference between most common matrilineal and patrilineal ancestors is likely due to the great difference in male and female fecundity. He was not the only male alive at the time, of course; he was simply the only male to leave an unbroken line to the present.

BIBLIOGRAPHY

Cann, R. L., M. Stoneking, and A. C. Wilson. "Mitochondrial DNA and Human Evolution." *Nature* 325 (1987): 31–36.

Elson, J. L., R. M. Andrews, P. F. Chinnery, R. N. Lightowlers, D. M. Turnbull, and N. Howell. "Analysis of European mtDNAs for Recombination." *American Journal of Human Genetics* 68 (2001): 145–153.

Ingman, M., H. Kaessmann, S. Pääbo, and U. Gyllensten. "Mitochondrial Genome Variation and the Origin of Modern Humans." *Nature* 408 (2000): 708–713.

ELIZABETH MILLER

Afrika, Tatamkhulu *See* Tatamkhulu Afrika.

Afua Kobi (c. 1815–1900), Asante ruler in present-day Ghana, was an *asantehemaa* (queen mother) who advised the Asante royal council to avoid war with the British in the late nineteenth century; she was particularly active from about 1834 to 1884. She was born into Asante aristocracy as the daughter of Asantehene (King) Owusu Afriyie and Asantehemaa Afua Sapon and became the ninth *asantehemaa* in that dynasty. She married Kofi Nti, a member of the ruling *asantehene*'s council. Between about 1835 and 1850 they had five children, including two who became *asantehenes* and one who was later *asantehemaa*. When Kofi Nti died, most likely in the late 1860s, she married Boakye Tenten, also a council member; but they had no further children. Her descendants continued to hold key positions in the twentieth century, when her great-great-grandson, Barima Kwaku Adusi, was elected to the Asante throne, known as the Golden Stool.

Initially, Afua Kobi's sons were not considered serious candidates for the throne. However, as conflict with the British escalated, a war party began to form; and they enlisted her son, Kofi Kakari, to become *asantehene*. Kofi Kakari was induced to make an oath that he would not seek the throne, but in 1867, after a period of royal intrigue and maneuvering that included executions and exile for other candidates, he was elected to the Golden Stool. Although Kofi Kakari had been supported by those who advocated war with the British, his own position regarding how to deal with British colonialism remained ambiguous. His mother, who was

greatly influential in her position as *asantehemaa*, was known to prefer a peaceful approach. She was willing to take action if needed and in 1872 was quoted as saying, in response to threatening behavior by the British governor, "I am only a woman, but would fight the governor with my left hand" (Aidoo, 1981, p. 71). A letter in a newspaper of the time referred to her as being "at the head of the peace party" (quoted in Wilks, 1975, p. 508).

In 1873 she made a powerful speech before the military chiefs including her son, Asantehene Kofi Kakari, arguing that going to war with the British would destroy Asante. She claimed that "From olden times it has been seen that God fights for Ashantee if the war is a just one. This one is unjust" (quoted in Wilks, 1975, p. 507). The chiefs decided to fight, and when they lost to the British, Kofi Kakari was replaced by Afua Kobi's younger son, Mensa Bonsu. She continued as a senior counselor and intervened again in 1881, telling the council that they should not go to war. The war party's role declined in the 1880s, and neither of her sons was notably successful during their reigns. Afua Kobi faced competition from her daughter (and Mensa Bonsu's sister) Yaa Akyaa, who contrived to get her own children named to the Golden Stool. Mensa Bonsu was removed from power in 1883, and Afua Kobi was deposed in 1884; she then went into exile, apparently with her son, Mensa Bonsu. Sometime before 1900 they both returned to Kumasi, where they lived outside of the circles of power until their deaths.

BIBLIOGRAPHY

Aidoo, Agnes Akosua. "Asante Queen Mothers in Government and Politics in the Nineteenth Century." In *The Black Woman Cross-Culturally*, edited by Filomina Chioma Steady, pp. 65–77. Cambridge, Mass.: Schenkman, 1981.

Stoeltje, Beverly J. "Asante Queen Mothers: A Study in Female Authority." In *Queens, Queen Mothers, Priestesses, and Power: Case Studies in African Gender*, edited by Flora S. Kaplan, pp. 41–71. New York: New York Academy of Sciences, 1997. Though not specifically about Afua Kobi, this article provides a useful overview of the role of the Asante queen mothers.

Wilks, Ivor. *Asante in the Nineteenth Century: The Structure and Evolution of a Political Order*. Cambridge: Cambridge University Press, 1975. A thorough and detailed account of Asante politics, it includes dynastic charts and family trees as well as exhaustive information on historic events.

KATHLEEN SHELDON

Agaja (d. 1740), king of Dahomey, was born some-time in the later decades of the seventeenth century. According to oral traditions collected in the nineteenth and twentieth centuries, Agaja succeeded his brother Akaba to the throne in large part because of his support from influential royal women. Na Geze, a royal princess married to the ruler of the city-state of Ouidah located directly south of Dahomey, supported Agaja's claims to power. Likewise, his eldest sister and Akaba's twin Na Hangbe also intervened on the behalf of Akaba's son Agbo Sassa. According to European slave traders' accounts and oral narratives, Agaja battled Agbo Sassa for the throne around 1718. Apparently, Hangbe denounced Agaja as a usurper, to no avail; and her son was forced to flee to the north.

Once Agaja had seized the throne, he launched a series of reforms within the kingdom and led numerous campaigns against Dahomey's neighbors. One of his biggest targets was the wealthy city of Ouidah. This urban settlement served as the main port of entry for European slavers seeking to buy slaves from Dahomey and surrounding kingdoms. Between Ouidah and Dahomey was the small kingdom of Allada. Dahoman armies under Agaja invaded Allada in March 1724, ostensibly to back the pretender to the Allada throne against Sozo, the ruler of the small state. Allada fell to its much more powerful northern neighbor. Agaja had Sozo beheaded. Bullfinch Lambe, an English agent of the Royal African Company trading firm in Allada, became a slave of Agaja. Lambe and an African interpreter known as Captain Tom provided Agaja with the linguistic knowledge to negotiate with European traders and governments. The king was so impressed by literacy that he toyed with developing a script for his language of Fon, but apparently this project never was completed. Agaja boasted to Lambe in 1725 that he had fought in over 200 battles, and given Dahomey's aggressive foreign policy under his reign, this was probably not an idle boast. Agaja had created a professional army of female and male soldiers armed with flintlock muskets, and he developed a special artillery regiment armed with European cannons.

Ouidah, Agaja's next target, was ill-prepared for Agaja's armies. According to oral accounts from Dahomey, King Huffon of Ouidah sent an enormous amount of luxury imported goods to Agaja and asked his rival in Dahomey if he had the riches to offer a similar gift. Agaja then supposedly had two long lines of skulls set on a path and commanded that Huffon's ambassadors walk past them. Agaja declared his riches were the spoils of war. He sent an ambassador to England to offer a trade alliance before he conquered Ouidah in 1727. The formidable kingdom of Oyo to the east then invaded Dahomey repeatedly and forced Agaja to pay tribute of 40 women, 40 guns, and 400 loads of cowries. In the meantime, Ouidah regained some autonomy. Agaja expressed to Lambe his interest in ending the international slave trade in favor of establishing plantations in his own kingdom once he heard of the wealth of sugar plantations in the Americas. At his death in 1740, Agaja had helped set the foundation for Dahoman wealth and military might for the next century and a half.

[*See also* Hangbe.]

BIBLIOGRAPHY

Bay, Edna. *Wives of the Leopard: Gender, Politics, and Culture in the Kingdom of Dahomey*. Charlottesville: University of Virginia Press, 1998.

Harms, Robert. *The Diligent: A Voyage through the Worlds of the Slave Trade*. New York: Basic, 2002.

Monroe, J. Cameron. "Continuity, Revolution or Evolution on the Slave Coast of West Africa? Royal Architecture and Political Order in Precolonial Dahomey." *Journal of African History* 48 (2007): 349–373.

JEREMY RICH

Agatharchides of Cnidus (fl. c. 200–140 BCE), grammarian, historian, and the author of the most important surviving accounts of ancient northeast Africa and the Red Sea basin. Unfortunately, little is known of the details of his biography. The only sources for his life are a few autobiographical remarks in the fragments of his works and a notice in Codex 213 of the *Bibliotheca* of Photius, the ninth-century CE scholar and patriarch of Constantinople. These references indicate that Agatharchides was born probably about 200 BCE in the city of Cnidus on the west coast of modern Turkey and that his origins were comparatively humble. Probably in the early second century BCE, he immigrated to Egypt where he came to the attention of an official and adviser of Ptolemy VI (r. 180–145 BCE) named Cineas, who made Agatharchides his protégé. It was probably Cineas who also introduced him to another Ptolemaic official, the historian and diplomat Heracleides Lembus, whom he served as personal secretary and reader. Thanks to the patronage of Heracleides, Agatharchides became a member of the Peripatetic school and a well-known figure in the intellectual life of Alexandria, where he lived until he was exiled in 145 BCE by Ptolemy VIII

(r. 145–116 BCE), probably for supporting his rival for the Egyptian throne, Ptolemy VII (r. 145–144 BCE). He seems to have spent the remainder of his life in Athens, where he completed his last work, *On the Erythraean Sea* (the Red Sea and Indian Ocean).

According to Photius, Agatharchides wrote six works. These included an epitome of the fourth-century BCE poet Antimachus of Colophon's *Lyde* (a poetic anthology of love stories from Greek mythology), a book on friendship, and a collection of excerpts from writers on natural and human phenomena. Nothing beyond their titles is known about these works. Photius also mentions a seventh work, an abridgement of *On the Erythraean Sea* in one book, but it is not clear if this work was by Agatharchides or a later writer. However, Agatharchides was best known in antiquity as a historian, and, fortunately, the evidence for his historical activity is relatively full.

Agatharchides' principal historical works were two large histories: *On Affairs in Asia*, which surveyed in ten books the history of Asian empires until the end of the wars of Alexander the Great's successors in the early third century BCE, and *On Affairs in Europe*, which treated in forty-nine books the history of the third and probably the first half of the second centuries BCE. Together, therefore, these works surveyed world history down to Agatharchides' own time. His third and final historical work, *On the Erythraean Sea*, was a more specialized work, treating in five books the history, ethnography, and geography of the southern portion of the *oecumene*, the portion of the inhabited world known to the Greeks.

African themes occupied an important place in Agatharchides' historical works. Already the first of his historical works, *On Affairs in Asia*, contained in its second book a detailed account of the Nile valley that included a summary of Ptolemaic knowledge of the customs and institutions of the inhabitants of Meroë—the capital of the kingdom of Kush—and their neighbors together with a survey of the history of Greek ideas of the causes of the Nile flood. Although lost in its original form, extensive excerpts from this account are preserved in the first and third books of the first-century BCE universal historian Diodorus's *Library of History*. These excerpts, which contain the fullest surviving account of the Kushite monarchy, are still of fundamental importance for the study of the history and culture of Hellenistic Kush. Agatharchides' most important contribution to African historiography, however, was *On the Erythraean Sea*.

Unlike Agatharchides' other historical works, *On the Erythraean Sea* is comparatively well known, thanks to the survival of an abridgment of its first and fifth books that is preserved as Codex 250 of Photius's *Bibliotheca*. In addition, extensive excerpts from the fifth book are contained in the third book of Diodorus's *Library of History*. Finally, there is further evidence for its content in the fragments of the *Geographoumena* of the second-century BCE geographer Artemidorus of Ephesus, who also made extensive use of Agatharchides' work for his account of the Red Sea. Although these sources suggest that the first four books of *On the Erythraean Sea* treated the history of Greek activity in the Nile valley south of Egypt and the Red Sea, from these four books only excerpts of Agatharchides' discussions of the origin of the name of the Erythraean Sea and the beginnings of Ptolemaic activity in Nubia from the first book survive. The evidence for the fifth book of *On the Erythraean Sea*, which treated comprehensively the history and cultural geography of both the African and Arabian coasts of the Red Sea and their hinterlands based on the reports of third-century BCE Ptolemaic explorers preserved at Alexandria, is, however, much fuller, with most of the book's content still extant.

Agatharchides organized the ethnographies in the fifth book of *On the Erythraean Sea* according to the Peripatetic theory that a people's interaction with its environment determined the nature of its culture. Included were three detailed ethnographies: the Ichthyophagi (fish eaters), peoples who inhabited the African coast of the Red Sea and relied on fish for their sustenance; the Troglodytes, nomadic pastoralists who lived in the Red Sea hills and were probably related to the later Beja; and the kingdom of Saba in modern Yemen (Kush was omitted because Agatharchides had already treated it in *On Affairs in Asia*). Brief accounts of various hunter-gatherer populations—each identified by food source—who inhabited the area between the Nile valley and the Red Sea, the most important animals of the area, the transportation of captured elephants to Egypt, and gold mining in the eastern desert of Lower Nubia rounded out the work.

The fifth book of *On the Erythraean Sea* was not a formal geography, and it did have significant deficiencies. Sometimes, for example, Agatharchides clearly misunderstood his sources. So, for example, he interpreted a description of a band of chimpanzees as an account of tree-dwelling natives. More seriously, his tendency to identify peoples by their principal food source meant that he probably artificially created separate ethnic groups by treating individual populations exploiting different resources within their territories as different peoples. Despite these problems, *On the Erythraean Sea* provided a uniquely detailed and vivid account of the Red Sea basin and its hinterlands. Together with his account of the upper Nile valley in *On Affairs in Asia*, Agatharchides' works contained descriptions of ancient northeast Africa that were not equaled for the comprehensiveness and quality of their ethnographies until the appearance of the medieval Arabic geographies. As a result, his works became the main sources for all later Greek and Roman accounts of the geography and ethnology of the region. Traces of their influence can still be identified in works such as Strabo's *Geography* (first century CE), Pliny the Elder's *Natural History* (first century CE), Aelian's *On the Nature of Animals* (third century CE), and even the *Aethiopica* of the novelist Heliodorus (fourth century CE).

[*See also* Alexander the Great; *and* Heliodorus of Emesa.]

BIBLIOGRAPHY

Works by Agatharchides of Cnidus
On the Erythraean Sea. Edited and translated by Stanley M. Burstein. London: The Hakluyt Society, 1989.
Über das Rote Meer, Übersetzung und Kommentar. Edited and translated by Dieter Woelk. Bamberg, Germany, 1966.

Works about Agatharchides of Cnidus
Desanges, Jehan. *Catalogue des Tribus Africaines de l'Antiquité Classique à l'Ouest du Nil*. Dakar, Senegal: Université de Dakar, 1962.
Desanges, Jehan. *Recherches sur l'Activité des Méditerranéens aux Confins de l'Afrique, VIe siècle avant J.-C.–IVe siècle après J.-C.* Paris: École Française de Rome, 1978.

STANLEY M. BURSTEIN

Agboyibo, Yawovi Madji (1943–), human rights activist and politician, was born in the southern Togolese town of Kouvé on 31 December 1943. His father, Soklou Agboyibo, and his mother, Doafio, were both Catholics from the Mina ethnic community. After completing his primary and secondary studies in Togo, Agboyibo traveled abroad for his graduate education. He received degrees from institutions of higher learning in France, the Ivory Coast, and Senegal. He was a lawyer by training and chose to remain in Togo under the brutal dictatorship of Étienne Gnassingbé Eyadéma in the 1980s.

Eyadéma's regime nevertheless allowed Agboyibo to run for a seat in the Togolese parliament in 1985 as an independent, even though Togo was a one-party state at the time. Two years later, Agboyibo formed the Commission Nationale des Droits de l'Homme (CNDH), a human rights organization that condemned many of the human rights violations of the Eyadéma regime.

Agboyibo received international attention for these efforts, and he served in Switzerland on an international subcommission for human rights created by the United Nations in 1988 and 1989. Agboyibo also served on the Pontifical Committee for Peace and Justice in Vatican City from 1990 to 1995. On 12 May 1993, he was awarded the German Africa Prize for his humanitarian efforts. He later became the co-president of the Windhoek Dialogue project, a partnership between an array of Christian centrist and center-right European parties such as the Christian Democratic Union of Germany and the French Gaullist Union pour un Mouvement Populaire (UMP; Union for a Popular Movement) party.

Agboyibo became a leading advocate for democracy in Togo in the early 1990s and stepped down from the leadership of the CNDH in 1990. He then formed the Front of Associations for Revival (FAR), an advocacy group calling for democracy in Togo. The collapse of Communism in the Soviet Union and Eastern Europe had helped inspire many Africans to form grassroots movements to push for democratic reforms. Agboyibo convinced Eyadéma to grant a general amnesty for political exiles and to create an agreement that allowed for multiparty elections in the summer of 1991. After this accord, Agboyibo turned the FAR into a political party, the CAR (Comité d'Action pour la Renouvea [Action Committee for Renewal]). Two years later, Agboyibo ran a campaign for the August 1993 presidential elections, but he ultimately chose to boycott the elections out of concern for fraud. Eyadéma had little trouble winning the contest. In February 1994, Agboyibo won a seat in the Togolese parliament, and his CAR party formed a majority coalition with Edem Kodjo's Togolese Union for Democracy (UTD) party. However, the majority fell apart when Kodjo accepted Eyadéma's offer to become prime minister. Agboyibo thus became one of the most prominent members of the opposition to Eyadéma in the 1990s.

This position placed him at risk. By 1997, it was widely assumed that Agboyibo would again run for the presidency in the upcoming June 1998 elections. He was attacked by unknown individuals in August 1997 after a meeting with the US Ambassador to Togo in Lomé. In November of the same year, soldiers inflicted serious injury on him just before he was scheduled to speak to CAR supporters. The CAR nominated Agboyibo as its presidential candidate in the spring of 1998. Officially, he received 9 percent of the vote, placing him in third place behind Eyadéma and longtime opposition leader Gilchrist Olympio. Agboyibo joined Olympio and the rest of the opposition leaders in condemning the rampant fraud that had marred the election. He even led over a thousand supporters in the streets to show publicly his frustration about the results. Agboyibo shared the sentiments of many Togolese when he claimed Olympio had really won the election, but Eyadéma held on to the presidency anyway.

After 2000, Agboyibo continued his struggle for democracy in Togo from his strong position in parliament. In January 2001, Agboyibo demanded that Eyadéma hold new parliamentary elections as the president had promised in 1999. However, Eyadéma refused to honor that request. The Togolese government charged Agboyibo with libel in the summer of 2001. Agboyibo had accused prime minister Agbéyomé Kodjo of commanding a private militia. A court found Agboyibo guilty and sentenced him to six months in prison. Protests by the Togolese people, international human rights groups, and Western countries led to his release in March 2002. Agboyibo then ran for president on the CAR ticket in June 2003 and again came third.

To the surprise of many in Togo and elsewhere, this dedicated opponent of Eyadéma regime agreed to serve under the new president Faure Gnassingbé, who had become president after his father Eyadéma's death in early 2005. In September 2006, Agboyibo became prime minister. He stepped down after one year, disillusioned by the younger Gnassingbé, who had promised political reform but had not done much to limit the authority of the president or combat corruption. He resigned from the Togolese parliament as well. The year 2008 marked another milestone as Agboyibo surrendered leadership of his own party. The CAR chose Agboyibo in January 2010 as its presidential candidate that year. Shortly before the election, he told a reporter for *Jeune Afrique* magazine: "We say that it is necessary to break with the idea of holding elections merely as spectacles. Each people make its own choice. When it was a question of choosing between Jesus and Barabbas, the people of ancient Judea chose the latter. And, they contributed to the crucifixion of poor Christ. We have our own Barabbas." Characteristically, Agboyibo politely declined to name specific individuals he had in mind. He did assert that ruling president Gnassingbé had become so unpopular even in the northern regions where his party had dominated that there was no way he could win fairly. In March 2010, Agboyibo lost again amid accusations of electoral tampering by the government, and Gnassingbé won another election widely viewed as a sham.

Agboyibo was instrumental in leading the fight for democratic reform in Togo and offered a new alternative to the long record of dissent set by Gilchrist Olympio. Agboyibo documented his career as well as the troubled history of Togolese politics between 1990 and 2010 in two books: *Combat pour un Togo démocratique* (1999) and *Gouvernance politique et sociale en Afrique, 20 ans après le sommet de la Baule: le cas du Togo* (2010).

[*See also* Gnassingbé Eyadéma, Étienne; Gnassingbé Eyadéma, Faure Essozimna; *and* Olympio, Gilchrist.]

BIBLIOGRAPHY

Abalo, Jean-Claude. "Yawovi Madji Agboyibo: 'Faure ne peut pas gagner ces elections.'" *Jeune Afrique*, 3 March 2010. http://www.jeuneafrique.com/Article/ARTJAWEB20100302194054/.

Agboyibo, Yawovi. *Combat pour un Togo démocratique: une méthode politique.* Paris: Karthala, 1999.

Agboyibo, Yawovi. *Gouvernance politique et sociale en Afrique, 20 ans après le sommet de la Baule: le cas du Togo.* Lomé, Togo: Fondation FAR, 2010.

Seely, Jennifer. *The Legacies of Transition Governments in Africa: The Cases of Benin and Togo.* New York: Palgrave Macmillan, 2009.

JEREMY RICH

Agegnehu Engida (1905–1950; some sources give 1902/3–1947), Ethiopian artist, was born in the Gondar Administrative Region of Ethiopia in 1905. Another form of his name is Agegnehu Engeda. Although relatively little is known about his life and work, Agegnehu's role as a pioneer among twentieth-century Ethiopian painters is noteworthy. At a time when the only opportunity for higher learning in Ethiopia was in church schools and the only training available to aspiring painters was through apprenticeship to church artists, the young Agegnehu Engida was sent to Paris to study painting at the École des Beaux-Arts from 1926 to 1933. According to Ladislas Farago, who interviewed Agegnehu in his home in Addis Ababa soon after the artist's return from France, Agegnehu's artistic abilities had been recognized by Haile Selassie, who arranged for him to study abroad. In 1926 Ras Tafari Mekonnen, the future Emperor Haile Selassie, was regent to Empress Zawditu and heir apparent to the throne. Zawditu's father, Emperor Menilek II, had initiated the practice of sending promising students abroad to study, with the understanding that they would return to Ethiopia to serve the government in various capacities. This practice was continued and expanded by Haile Selassie, to the benefit of several painters who would become the leading twentieth-century artists of Ethiopia. In this way European academic and modernist styles of painting were introduced into a country where religious art had been the dominant tradition for almost two millennia.

Farago's account of his visit with Agegnehu Engida and his wife in Addis Ababa reveals on the one hand a sincere interest in local traditions and respect for the artist's work and on the other hand an attitude of superiority and condescension toward all aspects of Ethiopian society. Nonetheless, Farago's account is valuable in shedding some light on the artist's career. During his visit to Agegnehu's combined house and studio in Addis Ababa, Farago saw a number of the artist's paintings, which included predominately portraits but also landscapes and scenes of daily life in Ethiopia. Farago reports that the artist's only model was his wife, whom he describes as "a typical Amharic beauty." A photograph of the artist at home published in 1935 shows him in traditional Amharic dress seated in a wicker chair before a wall covered with his paintings, densely hung salon-style one above the other, their frames almost touching (Biasio, fig. 47, p. 66). Of the dozen or so paintings visible in the photograph, all appear to be portraits, mostly of female subjects. Farago observes that the artist was inspired by the style of the French Impressionists, but eschewed their pastel hues for a more brilliant palette derived from Ethiopian painting traditions. However, this observation is not borne out by the few known extant paintings of the artist, which are relatively muted in tone and are indebted to the European academic style of realism. Academic realism was deemed outmoded by avant-garde artists active in Paris in the 1920s and 1930s and Impressionism, a style widely practiced in the late nineteenth century, was also passé. The experimental modernist styles of painting popular in Paris when Agegnehu Engida was studying in the city had no apparent impact on his art.

Although Agegnehu Engida brought back to Ethiopia a conservative style of European painting,

nonetheless he played an important role in helping to introduce western styles and techniques of painting into Ethiopia. He and other artists of his generation who taught art in Addis Ababa—notably the sculptor Abebe Wolde Giorgis (1897–1967), who also studied in France—provided an alternative for young artists who chose not to pursue either traditional religious painting or the popular folk art styles of painting that had first emerged in the late nineteenth century during the reign of Menilek II. The next generation of painters to study abroad and return to Addis Ababa to teach, among them painters Gebre Kristos Desta (1932–1981) and Skunder Boghossian (1937–2003), would be the ones to introduce abstraction and modernist styles such as cubism, expressionism, and surrealism into Ethiopian art.

After returning from Paris to Addis Ababa, Agegnehu Engida had several solo exhibitions. He received commissions for mural paintings in the Selassie church (Holy Trinity Cathedral) and the Parliament building as well as government commissions to design military uniforms and currency notes. In 1941 the Ethiopian government's Ministry of Education and Fine Arts established a Department of Fine Arts, with the purpose of incorporating art education into the school curriculum. Abebe Wolde Giorgis was appointed director of the department with Agegnehu Engida as his assistant director. Also in 1941, according to Taye Tadesse, Agegnehu Engida set up an informal art school with fifteen students and in 1956 Abebe Wolde Giorgis established a similar school. Although neither school lasted more than a few years, together they established a precedent for the establishment in 1957 of an important and enduring institution, the Addis Ababa Fine Arts School. Known today as the School of Fine Arts and Design of Addis Ababa University, the school was founded through the efforts of Ale Felege Selam Heruy, another painter who returned to Addis Ababa after his studies at the School of the Art Institute of Chicago.

Few works by the Agegnehu Engida are known to survive today. The National Museum of Ethiopia in Addis Ababa owns two portraits by the artist. One, a self-portrait, shows the painter with well-trimmed mustache and goatee, wearing a dark blue beret and wire-rimmed glasses. The other, a portrait of a woman named Aster Mengesha, needs conservation and is not currently exhibited at the museum. Recently a portrait of a woman making a basket held in a private collection in the United States was identified as one of the paintings that appear in the background of the photograph of the artist in his studio, referenced above.

[*See also* Boghossian, Skunder; Gebre Kristos Desta; *and* Haile Selassie I.]

BIBLIOGRAPHY

Biasio, Elisabeth. *The Hidden Reality: Three Contemporary Ethiopian Artists: Zerihun Yetmgeta, Girmay Hiwet, Worku Goshu.* Zurich: Völkerkundemuseum der Universität Zürich, 1989.

Debela, Achamyeleh. "The Addis Ababa Fine Arts School: A Critically Important Institution in the History of Ethiopian Art." In *Continuity and Change: Three Generations of Ethiopian Artists,* edited by Rebecca Martin Nagy, pp. 10–11. Gainesville: Samuel P. Harn Museum of Art, University of Florida, 2007.

Farago, Ladislas. *Abyssinia on the Eve.* New York: G. P. Putnam's Sons, 1935.

Taye Tadesse. *Short Biographies of Some Ethiopian Artists,* rev. ed., Addis Ababa, Ethiopia: Kuraz Publishing Agency, 1991.

REBECCA MARTIN NAGY

Ager Gum (c.1941–1996), Sudanese military figure and song composer, was an Agar Dinka woman from the Nyang section born of an Yibel mother in Dinkaland in South Sudan. She is perhaps the most famous female military commander in Southern Sudanese history and also one of the most famous song composers. She became a role model for younger twentieth-century women as an example of new female leadership in a rapidly changing society.

In the early 1960s Ager Gum was living as most other Dinka women did. However, she experienced a series of personal misfortunes. She was married three times, but all her marriages failed, in part because most of her children proved unable to survive the harsh health conditions of South Sudan, where preventative vaccinations and medicines were rarely available. The father of her sole surviving child, a son named Chol, demanded the return of the wedding cattle that comprised her bridewealth, thus divorcing her in the Dinka manner. The son stayed with his grandfather. After this humiliation Ager Gum resolved never to marry again and to "do something great so that my husband will see that he has not made me miserable." She left her native community and moved to Rumbek, where she became a "town person" and participated in a more cosmopolitan urban culture marginal to traditional Dinka ways. She began to compose songs, which as she saw

them were weapons of resistance against bad marriages, usually with the theme that men want sex rather than real relationships. She was about twenty-seven years old.

In 1968 Ager Gum joined the Anya Nya guerilla movement, the Southern Sudanese war against the North. She went to the bush and fought alongside the men. She was always there. If there was a battle, she was lucky not to get killed. Sometimes the men were killed and she would collect the weapons from her dead comrades and carry them back to camp. At this time her physique was robust; her height was approximately six feet two inches and her body equaled that of most Dinka men in size and strength. She was often seen carrying boxes of ammunition on her head and a gun on her back. Considered to be powerful politically as well as militarily, Ager Gum commanded respect from all. She was the only woman to be given a command position in the upper ranks of the Anya Nya officer corps, becoming a first lieutenant and then a captain.

During the peaceful interval of the 1970s when Southern Sudan enjoyed self-government Ager Gum served as chief warden of the prisons in the city of Wau. She also trained other women for participation in warfare. When the second civil war erupted during the early 1980s she resumed her military vocation and became a significant leader in the new resistance movement, the Sudan People's Liberation Army (SPLA). Over the course of the second civil war Ager Gum gradually rose to the rank of major general. At the early stages of the struggle she organized and trained women as scouts, to be sent across enemy lines into the southern cities occupied by northern troops to buy ammunition and medicine and to search for intelligence information. She then became an officer commanding troops in Rumbek and controlled SPLA battalions of both men and women.

At this time Ager Gum began to find new uses for her other gift, that of composing songs. Historically, Dinka women composed marriage and social songs while men composed war songs. As a military commander, however, Ager Gum now began to translate her own experience into songs, many of which have become well known within the Southern Sudan. Some songs were composed and sung to motivate and develop military leadership skills, a genre hitherto monopolized by men. Through the performance of her new warrior songs Ager Gum aimed to motivate the troops psychologically, and subsequently these songs were often played on SPLA radio. Other songs of Ager Gum were intended as social commentary. For example, on one occasion she composed and sang in protest when a Southern woman married one of the jellaba (northern Sudanese merchants resident in the south). This particular song was later sung very widely in several southern districts. Ager Gum's songs thus became well known and were frequently sung, and her lyrics were very influential—should anyone get on the wrong side of her, he might find himself insulted in a song that would be heard from one end of Southern Sudan to the other by everyone. Ager Gum is, to date, the most notable female military commander in Southern Sudanese history and also one of the most respected song composers.

BIBLIOGRAPHY

Collins, Robert O. *A History of Modern Sudan.* Cambridge, UK, and New York: Cambridge University Press, 2008.

STEPHANIE BESWICK

Aggrey, James Emman Kwegyir (1875–1927), intellectual, pan-African thinker, educator, and Christian preacher, was born in Anomabo, Gold Coast (now Ghana) on 18 October 1875. His father was Kodwo Kwegyir (1816–1896) of the Fante people who was the Omankyiame or hereditary spokesman for the paramount chief of Anomabo, and his mother was Abna Andua, scion of a chiefly family. At the age of eight, Aggrey left his home to attend the Methodist school in Cape Coast. In 1890 he started teaching in a rural village school and the following year returned to Cape Coast to become an assistant teacher at the Wesleyan Centenary Memorial School where he soon advanced to a senior position. At this early stage in his life Aggrey became interested in Christian ministry. He began preaching at sixteen and later assisted in the translation of a Fante-language New Testament. During this time Aggrey also became involved with the Aborigines' Rights Protection Society, where, as secretary, he was instrumental in running a campaign against the 1897 Public Lands Bill, which was subsequently defeated.

In 1898 Aggrey's desire to further his education brought him to Salisbury, North Carolina, to study classics at Livingstone College, the chief educational institution of the African Methodist Episcopal Zion (AMEZ) Church. Aggrey graduated at the top of his class in 1902 and was retained as a faculty member, teaching a number of subjects at Livingstone and Hood Theological Seminary until 1920. He was later awarded a master of arts degree and a doctorate of divinity by these institutions. Aggrey had an insatiable

appetite for learning and enrolled in summer classes at Columbia University in New York in 1904 and 1914–1919. At Columbia Aggrey took a wide range of courses, but was particularly interested in sociology and worked closely with the influential sociologist Franklin Giddings. At this time Aggrey also joined the Negro Society for Historical Research.

While a professor at Livingstone, Aggrey met Rosebud Rudolf Douglass whom he married in November 1905. The couple later had four children. Aggrey was ordained as an elder in the AMEZ Church in 1903 and began filling pulpits in African American churches. From 1914 to 1920 he served as the pastor of two rural churches, where he preached on Sundays.

Aggrey's return to Africa came about due to his inclusion on two commissions sponsored by colonial governments and the Phelps-Stokes Fund to survey the educational system in different parts of the continent. In all, Aggrey visited at least eighteen countries in western, central, southern, and eastern Africa during July 1920 to June 1921 and January to June 1924. He was chosen for these tours by the prominent educationalist Jesse Jones due to his views on African American education. Jones and the members of the Phelps-Stokes Fund promoted the Hampton-Tuskegee model, which sought to make accommodations for the perceived needs of the African American community, which was in conflict with W. E. B. Du Bois' model of higher learning. Sylvia Jacobs (1996) has argued, however, that Aggrey's personal view of education had elements of both models as he was interested in producing "socially efficient" students who were trained in "head, hand, and heart." Aggrey was also chosen because he believed in the necessity of racial cooperation. He famously illustrated this point by saying that when the black or white keys of a piano were played by themselves they could make merely a partial tune, but only when the keys were played together could a true harmony be created. Aggrey's intellect, understanding, and charm allowed him to win over both white and black audiences throughout his life.

News of Aggrey's tour with European leaders aroused the interest of thousands of Africans who came to hear him speak and preach. Aggrey's fame preceded him when he reached Gold Coast where an elaborate homecoming was arranged, installing him as Kyiame or spokesperson for the paramount chief of Anomabo. Indeed, even more important than his contribution to African education, Aggrey's greatest historical significance may be the personal impact he had on future African leaders. Numerous politicians of the mid-twentieth century had personal interactions with Aggrey in the 1920s and claimed direct inspiration from him, such as Nnamdi Azikiwe (the first president of Nigeria), William Tubman (president of Liberia), Sylvanus Olympio (the first president of Togo), Hastings Banda (the first president of Malawi), and Kwame Nkrumah (the first president of Ghana).

Moreover, it could be argued that Aggrey did more than any other single individual of his generation to raise an awareness of the concept of Africa in the minds of sub-Saharan Africans. Aggrey viewed Africa as a whole and encouraged the embrace of an African identity. Aggrey's concept of the African nation was taken up by political and welfare groups like the African Association of East Africa that sought to build continental unity by organizing along African lines while downplaying tribal, territorial, and other differences. Like other pan-African thinkers, Aggrey also firmly believed that Africa as a civilization could achieve greatness. He often told African audiences a story of an eagle that was raised as a chicken, and thought it was a chicken, only to later realize it was actually an eagle. Aggrey would plead with his African listeners that they should stop thinking they were chickens and realize that they were true eagles indeed. This inspirational story of Aggrey's was recounted in many parts of Africa throughout the twentieth century.

Between Aggrey's two educational tours to Africa he became a full-time student at Columbia and received his master's degree in sociology in 1922 and passed his preliminary doctoral examinations in 1923. During this two-and-a-half year period Aggrey was also one of the most popular Christian speakers in North America, giving several hundred talks to various missionary societies, church groups, and student conventions all across the eastern United States and Canada.

After the second Phelps-Stokes Commission, Aggrey returned to Gold Coast in October 1924 to help in the formation of the Prince of Wales School and College at Achimota in Accra. This school was meant to engender an education that would not only be academically rigorous, but would have a communal emphasis and include Africa-centered content in its courses in keeping with Aggrey's desire to include the best of both African and Western cultures. After Achimota had its formal inauguration in 1927, Aggrey returned to New York to write his doctoral dissertation. Soon after his return, however, he contracted meningitis and died suddenly on 30 July 1927. The death of this African intellectual and figure of racial solidarity was mourned that summer by blacks and whites on both sides of the Atlantic.

[*See also* Azikiwe, Benjamin Nnamdi; Banda, Hastings Kamuzu; Du Bois, W. E. B.; Nkrumah, Kwame; Olympio, Sylvanus Epiphanio; *and* Tubman, William.]

BIBLIOGRAPHY

Jacobs, Sylvia M. "James Emman Kwegyir Aggrey: An African Intellectual in the United States." *Journal of Negro History* 81, no. 1 (Winter-Autumn 1996): 47–61.

King, Kenneth. "James E. K. Aggrey: Collaborator, Nationalist, Pan-African." *Canadian Journal of African Studies* 3, no. 3 (Autumn 1969): 511–530.

Ofosu-Appiah, L. H. *The Life of Dr. J. E. K. Aggrey.* Accra, Ghana: Waterville Publishing House, 1975.

Smith, Edwin W. *Aggrey of Africa: A Study in Black and White.* London: Student Christian Movement Press, 1929.

ETHAN R. SANDERS

Agonglo (c. 1743–1797), king of Dahomey (in modern Benin), was the son of Kpengla, his predecessor as king of Dahomey (r. 1774–1789). His official "Queen Mother" (*kpojito*), appointed as such after his accession to the throne, was a woman called Senume, but it is not clear whether she was also his biological mother. Contemporary European sources give his name as Wheenoohew, but this is not recognized in Dahoman tradition. He was also alternatively called Adarunza, but this seems to be a generic surname which (also in other variants, such as Adahoonzou) was applied by Europeans to all kings of the dynasty (Agonglo being counted as Adarunza VIII).

Agonglo's accession to the throne was contested, with two other princes presenting themselves as candidates, and his political position at the beginning of his reign appears to have been insecure, requiring him to conciliate his senior officials and the populace more generally. In particular, he was obliged to repudiate policies of his predecessor Kpengla that had proved unpopular, especially his attempt to assert closer royal control over the operation of the supply of slaves for the Atlantic trade. As recorded in the contemporary account of Archibald Dalzel (1793), Agonglo promised to "administer justice with a rigorous and impartial hand," to respect the role of his chiefs as intermediaries between him and the people, and to reduce the influence of the royal women. He also proclaimed "full liberty of trade," repealing the taxes and other restrictions on private merchants imposed by his predecessor.

Agonglo also appears to have enjoyed only limited military success and was remembered in Dahoman tradition in the following century as "a weak monarch." In particular an attempt at rebellion against the subjection of Dahomey to the Yoruba kingdom of Oyo, in the interior to the northeast (in modern Nigeria), which had claimed tribute from Dahomey since the 1720s, was defeated. Agonglo's only major military success was the conquest of the town of Gbowele in Mahi, to the north of Dahomey, in 1795, and even this was effected only after several unsuccessful attempts. His difficulties were also compounded by the decline of the slave trade, which was a major source of revenue for the Dahoman monarchy, due to the disruption of shipping by war in Europe, and also to the elimination of what had lately been the principal market for slaves in the Americas, the French colony of Saint-Domingue (modern Haiti), through the rebellion of slaves there from 1791 onward, followed by the abolition of slavery in French colonies in 1794.

These economic problems may have played some role in the premature termination of Agonglo's reign, by murder—the only recorded instance of the assassination of a king in Dahoman history, and leaving Agonglo as the shortest-reigning Dahoman king, apart from Behanzin (r. 1889–1894) who was deposed by the French colonial conquerors. Agonglo had sent an embassy to the queen of Portugal in 1795, requesting that Brazilian slave traders should conduct their trade exclusively at the Dahoman port of Ouidah. The Portuguese response was accompanied by two Roman Catholic priests, who were charged to attempt to convert the king to Christianity. These arrived in Dahomey in April 1797 and were received by Agonglo, who declared his willingness to be baptized, "without delay," although it seems likely that this was motivated more by a desire to secure Portuguese friendship and trade than by any genuine interest in conversion. Shortly afterward, however, Agonglo himself died, within the royal palace at Abomey, on 1 May 1797, reportedly poisoned by one of the senior women of the palace, Na Hwanjile, the successor to the office of "Queen Mother" of the earlier king Tegbesu (r. 1740–1774). Hwanjile was reportedly acting in collusion with a brother of the king called Dogan, who hoped to succeed to the throne, although Dogan's attempt to seize control of the palace was then repulsed and he himself killed. How far Agonglo's overthrow was in fact provoked by his flirtation with Christianity, as the Portuguese missionaries believed, is unclear. It may be that it simply happened to coincide with the attempted coup d'état of Dogan. Agonglo was followed on the throne by two of his sons, who ruled in succession, his designated heir Adandozan (r. 1797–1818) and Gezo (r.1818–1858).

[*See also* Gezo; *and* Tegbesu.]

BIBLIOGRAPHY

Akinjogbin, I. A. *Dahomey and Its Neighbours, 1708-1818*. Cambridge, UK: Cambridge University Press, 1967. Still the main study of eighteenth-century Dahomey, including the only detailed narrative account of Agonglo's reign on pp. 178–186.

Dalzel, Archibald. *The History of Dahomy, an Inland Kingdom of Africa, compiled from authentic memoirs*. First published in 1793; reprinted, with a new Introduction by J. D. Fage. London: Cass, 1967. Contemporary account of the first two years of Agonglo's reign, pp. 222–230.

Law, Robin. *The Oyo Empire c.1600-c.1836: A West African Imperialism in the Era of the Atlantic Slave Trade*. Oxford: The Clarendon Press, 1977. For Agonglo's abortive rebellion against Oyo, see pp. 268–269.

Verger, Pierre. *Trade Relations between the Bight of Benin and Bahia from the 17th to 19th Century*. Translated by Evelyn Crawford. Ibadan, Nigeria: Ibadan University Press, 1976. Quotes extensively from contemporary records of the abortive conversion and murder of Agonglo, pp. 199–201, 225–231.

ROBIN LAW

Agualusa, José Eduardo (1960–), Angolan journalist and writer, was born in Huambo, Angola, on 13 December 1960. He considered himself to be African, Brazilian, Portuguese, and Luso-Afro-Brazilian. This multiculturalism that he defends comes from his Portuguese and Brazilian heritage. Before becoming a journalist and a writer, he studied silviculture and agronomy. It wasn't until the 1990s that he started dedicating himself entirely to his writing. He lived in Recife and in Rio de Janeiro between 1998 and 2000, although, according to David Brookshaw, there still exists debate surrounding the date of Agualusa's departure from Angola. According to Brookshaw, some believe that it was in 1975 during the general exodus resulting from Angola's newly acquired independence and the new Portuguese politics regarding the former colonies. Others claim that it was after the attempted coup against Agostinho Neto in 1977, and others say that it was in 1998, a date that still, according to Brookshaw, seems more congruent with his writings.

Agualusa's vast oeuvre encompasses poetry, theater, short stories, novels, guides, and investigations. He wrote his first novel, *A Conjura*, in 1989, which won the Angolan Prize Revelação Sonangol. The novel describes a failed revolt in Luanda during the eve of the twentieth century. His second book, *D. Nicolau Água-Rosada e outras estórias verdadeiras e inverosímeis*, is a collection of short stories published in 1990 that deals with both history and fiction and the passage from one to the other. His third book, *O coração dos bosques*, is a collection of poetry published in 1991 but written between 1980 and 1990, in which Agualusa redefines Angola through the problematization of national myths. In 1992 he published *A feira dos assombrados* and in 1996 *Estação das Chuvas*. After winning a literary grant in 1997 given by Centro Nacional da Cultura, he wrote and published during that same year *Nação Crioula*, one of his most renowned novels. It is written as an exchange of letters authored by Fradique Mendes, a fictional character created originally by Eça de Queiroz, the nineteenth-century Portuguese realist writer. The letters offer three perspectives from three different countries involved in the slave trafficking during the last three decades of the nineteenth century: Angola, Brazil, and Portugal. In 1990 Agualusa published *Fronteiras Perdidas, contos para viajar*, a book of short stories that deal with the crossing and the loss of frontiers, a theme that traverses all of his work. He received a grant from Fundação Oriente that allowed him to visit Goa for three months. There he wrote his novel *Um estranho em Goa*, that was published in 2000. This novel is written from the perspective of an Angolan journalist who visits Goa and in his visit tries to decipher an identity for its people: Portuguese, Indian, and Goan. In 2000 he published two books, *Estranhões e Bizarrocos*, which is a book of short stories for children, and *A Substância do Amor e Outras Crónicas*. In 2002 he published another collection of short stories, *O Homem que Parecia um Domingo*, and in 2003, *Catálogo de Sombras*. In 2001 he received a literary grant from the German institution Deutscher Akademischer Austauschdienst. With this grant he lived a year in Berlin and wrote the novel *O Ano em que Zumbi Tomou o Rio*, which was published in 2003. This novel focused on national issues pertaining to both Angola and Brazil at the same time that it problematizes the concept of race. *O Vendedor de Passados*, a novel published in 2004, works with the concepts of origin, past, and identities as well as with the misconception of a frozen history as it portrays the necessity for the continuous reinvention of the nation and its inhabitants. This is accomplished through the character of Pedro Gouveia, an Angolan-Portuguese who returns to Angola to avenge the murder of his wife and the torture of his daughter. In 2005 a collection of short stories originally published in Angolan and Portuguese newspapers and journals, *Manual Prático de Levitação*, was published. *As Mulheres de Meu Pai*, published in 2007, focuses on women, music, and magic to talk about Africa and its future. In 2008 Agualusa published *Na rota das especiarias*, a travel diary in which he searches for both the Portuguese and the people from Flores, Bali, and Timor. In 2009 Agualusa was invited as a writer in residence by the Fundação Holandesa para a Literatura and stayed in Amsterdam for two months where he wrote *Barroco tropical*, published in that same year. In 2010 he published *Um Pai em Nascimento*.

In 2004 *Geração W*, a play written by Agualusa, was performed for the first time by Teatro Meridional at the Biblioteca Orlando Ribeiro in Lisbon. In 2006 he founded, along with Conceição Lopes and Fatima Otero, their own publishing company, Língua Geral, dedicated exclusively to writers in the Portuguese language. By 2010 they had published forty-three authors. In 2007, along with Mia Couto, he co-authored the play *Chovem Amores na Rua do Matador* which was performed for the first time in FINTA 07, the 13th Festival of International Theatre of ACERT (Cultural and Recreational Association of Tondela). *Chovem Amores na Rua do Matador* is the result of a catalytic challenge initiated by Trigo Limpo, the theater group of ACERT, in 2006 with a call to create a new work for the dramatic genre. In 2008 he wrote another theater piece, a monologue entitled *Aquela Mulher*, which was performed in São Paulo at the Teatro Scesc Anchieta and directed by Antônio Fagundes. The monologue is based on Hillary Clinton and her political aspirations. That same year, Agualusa started writing chronicles for the journal *LER* and for the Angolan Newspaper *A Capital*. He also had a TV program for RDP-Africa called *A hora das cigarras*. His vast production has been translated to more than twenty languages worldwide.

[*See also* Couto, Mia; *and* Neto, Agostinho.]

BIBLIOGRAPHY

José Eduardo Agualusa website. http://www.agualusa.info/.

Brookshaw, David. "Frontiers Crossed
and Frontiers Lost: Some Thoughts on the Fiction
of Mia Couto and José Eduardo Agualusa."
In *A primavera toda para ti: Homenagem a Helder
Macedo*, edited by Margarida Calafate Ribeiro,
Teresa Cristina Cerdeira, Juliet Perkins, and Phillip
Rothwell, pp. 250–254. Lisbon: Presença, 2004.

Leite, Ana Mafalda. "Angola." In *The Post-Colonial
Literature of Lusophone Africa*, edited by Patrick
Chabal, Moema Parente Augel, David Brookshaw,
Ana Mafalda Leite, and Caroline Shaw, pp. 103–164.
Evanston, Ill.: Northwestern University Press, 1996.

Marcon, Frank. "Escritores angolanos, Fronteiras
Perdidas e identidades contemporâneas." *Tomo:
Revista do núcleo de pós-graduação e pesquisa em
Ciências Sociais* (2007): 103–122.

JARA MICHELLE RÍOS-RODRÍGUEZ

Ahhotep (1560–1530 BCE), queen of Egypt, is one of the most prominent women leaders in ancient Egyptian history. She possessed numerous titles that provide us with invaluable insights into her role and stature in the New Kingdom. She was referred to as "Peace of the Moon." Her father was King Tao I and her mother Queen Tetisheri. She was the sister and wife of her brother, Seqenenre Tao II, one of the pharaohs of ancient Egypt who died on the battlefield in a campaign that was aimed at expelling the Hyksos from Egypt. Ahhotep was the mother of Kamose and Ahmose, the subsequent kings of Egypt after the death of Tao II, and also the mother of Ahmose-Nefertari, wife of king Ahmose.

Some historians and Egyptologists considered Ahhotep the first of several of the most notable powerful and remarkable women of influence in the New Kingdom. While some consider her to be the matrilineal founder of the Eighteenth Dynasty in ancient Egypt, others regard the actual foundation of the New Kingdom to be the work of her mother, Tetisheri. The latter school of thought argues that Ahhotep consolidated the kingdom by holding it together during a time of warfare.

While the men in Ahhotep's life were at war she effectively ruled Egypt from the Kingdom's capital at Thebes in the south. She played an important role in consolidating power and holding the kingdom together during wartime. When Tao II died and Kamose succeeded him and carried on with a successful campaign against the Hyksos, she helped run the administration. However, Kamose did not survive long as he too died in war and Ahmose succeeded the throne. At the time of ascending the throne Ahmose was about ten years old and was

considered too young to undertake the responsibilities of kingship all by himself. Consequently, his mother, Queen Ahhotep, stepped in to act as regent until he was about sixteen years old and was of age to take leadership responsibility. It was at this time when Ahhotep acted as regent that she earned recognition for her significant contributions to the consolidation of the dynasty. Evidence abounds in legend but most of all in the inscription that was unearthed on a doorway at the Nubian fortress of Buhen linking the name Ahhotep with Ahmose and suggesting that they, indeed, shared co-regency.

Some historians have surmised from the evidence that while Queen Mother, Ahhotep may have acted as regent during Ahmose's formative years, she was effectively coopted into the day-to-day administrative duties of the kingdom in the years that followed. During the period when she acted as a regent there was great instability in the kingdom that called upon her to step in and maintain Theban control of Upper Egypt. For stability to be restored she had to bring down the rebels and other forces thought to be the threat and source of the destabilization of the dynasty. Further archaeological evidence that was excavated at Tell el-Dab'a testified to the fact that when Ahmose came of age, he took over some of the more pressing responsibilities that needed to be attended to. They included the fighting during the long campaign to expel the Hyksos from Egypt. Thus it became necessary that someone with total allegiance to the throne be charged with the responsibility of maintaining order and royal control in Thebes. That person would be Ahhotep.

Paradoxically, however, while the women of the royal court and family do appear in many Egyptian historical records and inscriptions there is still a dearth of information on the precise roles of women in the administrative structures of the dynasty. Given that the scribes were drawn only from the men explains the prevalent male biases that taint the artifacts and historical accounts that have been unearthed so far. On another level, there have been concerted efforts to study and interpret the documents, the inscriptions, and the nature of tombs in combination with the use of the latest scientific techniques to enable historians to access and reconstruct a comprehensible picture of Ahhotep's role and her contribution during the Eighteenth Dynasty. The re-reading of a stela that was erected at the Temple of Karnak by Ahmose and unearthing other artifacts in her tomb in Thebes, for instance, has added value to the biography of Ahhotep. The stela at Karnak that was unearthed by the Egyptologist George Legrain contains the following long inscription translated thus:

> Give praise to the Lady of Land, the Mistress of the shores of Haunebu, (her) name is raised over every foreign country, (and) who governs the people. The wife of the King, the sister of the lord (= king)—life, prosperity, health! The princess, the king's mother, the noblewoman, who knows things and takes care of Egypt. She looked after its (= Egypt's) soldiers and protected them. She brought back its (= Egypt's) fugitives and gathered its dissidents together. She pacified Upper Egypt and expelled its rebels. The king's wife, Ahhotep, may she live (Jánosi, 1992: 99).

This quotation not only succinctly summarizes the honor bestowed upon Ahhotep by Ahmose but also how she was generally perceived during the Eighteenth Dynasty and beyond. Not only was Ahhotep held in high esteem in Egypt but also in the surrounding regions such as the isles of the Aegean and the Mediterranean region, particularly for her role in the liberation of Egypt from the Hyksos. Some scholars have argued that she may have used mercenaries from Greece during the war. Indeed, the epithets that she was accorded can only be compared with similar accolades that were specifically given to the pharaoh. It has been argued that no other known queen or royal lady in the entire Egyptian history ever possessed the title "Mistress of the shores of Haunebu."

Historians have analyzed the second part of the text above in juxtaposition with other evidence and concluded that it must have been some special reason why Ahmose recorded the deeds of his mother the way he did. They have argued that if Ahhotep were not an instigator and initiator of important events such as the military action that took place at the end of the Seventeenth Dynasty, she would not have received such honor. The assertion is further strengthened by the excavation of a gold pendant with three large golden flies also known as the "fly of Valour" in her coffin. Notably, during the New Kingdom the "Golden Fly" symbolized great bravery and courage. The honorific award was given only for excellence in military service, a demonstration that Ahhotep possessed military prowess. It further speaks of how she was perceived and valued for her administrative skills that led to the successful control of Upper Egypt thus keeping it stable while the pharaoh was away fighting.

The comparison of the titles that are used in the quotation cited above and the actual historical events that took place indicate she deserved them. That they were well-earned in the recognition of her remarkable historical contribution to the kingdom cannot be gainsaid. Ahhotep left a lasting legacy of her power as is evident in her daughter and wife of King Ahmose, Ahmose-Nefertari, who appropriately emulated her mother's administrative prowess. Ahmose Nefertari retained much of the power base established at Thebes by Ahhotep and continued to play a prominent role throughout the rein of her husband and her son, Amenhotep I.

[*See also* Ahmose I.]

BIBLIOGRAPHY

Jánosi, Peter. "The Queens Ahhotep I & II and Egypt's Foreign Relations. *The Journal of Ancient Chronology Forum* 2 (1992): 99–105.

Shahawy, Abeer el, and Farid Atiya. *The Egyptian Museum in Cairo: A Walk Through the Alleys of Ancient Egypt*. Cairo: Farid Atiya Press, 2005.

Sweeney, Emmet. *The Pyramid Age*. New York: Agora, 2007.

Yurco, Frank. J. "Black Athena: An Egyptological Review." In *Black Athena Revisited*, edited by Mary R. Lefkowitz and Guy MacLean Rogers. Chapel Hill: University of North Carolina Press, 1996.

HANNINGTON OCHWADA

Ahidjo, Ahmadou (1924–1989), politician and first president of the Republic of Cameroon, was born in August 1924 in Garoua, an inland river port on the Benue River in the northern Sahel region of Cameroon. The son of a Fulani chief, he had a humble upbringing. He started his secondary education in Garoua and later switched to Yaounde, the national capital. After his secondary education, he served as a career civil servant until 1946, when he started taking an interest in politics. As a civil service worker, Ahidjo worked as a radio operator for the post office until 1946, when he ventured into territorial politics.

With his ever-growing interest in politics, Ahidjo was elected as the representative of the Benue region of northern Cameroon to the colony's first Representative Assembly, which was gradually transformed into the broad-based Territorial Assembly. Reelected in 1952, his growing popularity and powerful ambitions in Cameroon politics became clear in 1953, when he was elected to the Assembly of the French Union. In the French

Union, he served as one of its secretaries and was able to win the confidence of the other members, who eventually chose him as vice president of the house for the 1956–1957 session.

France granted Cameroon domestic autonomy in 1957 and André Marie Mbida, leader of the Democrates Camerounais Party (DCP), became the territory's first prime minister. Ahidjo, in his early career, had helped found a number of political associations in the north of Cameroon. He joined the DCP in 1956, and as a devout Muslim, he brought to the party both northern support and a national outlook. With Mbida as prime minister, Ahidjo became the vice-prime minister and minister of the interior in Mbida's government. In 1958, following a break with Mbida, he organized a new political party, the Union Camerounaise, which became the governing party when Ahidjo succeeded Mbida as prime minister. Although both Ahidjo and Mbida were somewhat acceptable to the French, Mbida was more supportive of a gradual process toward independence. Ahidjo was more attuned to the broader African desire for rapid decolonization.

On 1 January 1960, the former French Cameroon Trust Territory became an independent republic, and in May of that same year, Ahidjo was elected the first president of the new state. He was now able to act on his political philosophy, which espoused governance by a single-party state, a commitment to Pan-African ideals, and a somewhat vaguely defined brand of African socialism. When, on 1 October 1961, the Cameroon Republic and the former British Trust Territory of the Southern Cameroons merged to become the Federal Republic of Cameroon, he became president of the federation. This increased his political influence and paved the way for the establishment of a one-party system, a dream that he achieved in 1966 with the creation of the Cameroon National Union. After successfully dissolving all of the other political parties in the former East and West Cameroon, he established himself firmly at the helm of power; and this was accompanied by elements of dictatorship. He was by nature retiring and not given to personal ostentation and flamboyant public display. These qualities contributed to a political style marked not only by dignity and an air of quiet command but also by a capacity for occasional firm and even ruthless action, as demonstrated in 1962 when, at a single stroke, he jailed all four leaders of the opposition parties. His firm control of the state saw him not only as head of state but as commander-in-chief of the army and head of the higher Judicial Council. The executive, judiciary, and legislative arms of government were therefore directly under his control.

Ahidjo was a firm proponent of intra-African cooperation. He mediated in several conflicts on the continent with the aim of maintaining peace and cordial relations among the states. For example, he played a major role in the Nigerian Biafran War, a role that helped ensure that Cameroon regained governance of the disputed Bakassi Peninsula as compensation following the Maroua Accord between the two countries. His government played a key role in various regional organizations as well as in the broad-based Organization of African Unity.

In November 1982, Ahidjo took the nation by surprise when he announced his resignation and handed over power to his prime minister since 1975 and long-time associate, Paul Biya. Even though he resigned as head of state, he stayed on as the chair of the Cameroon National Union party. That decision resulted in a power struggle in which Biya accused Ahidjo of plotting against the government. When Ahidjo's attempt to spearhead a coup d'état against Biya failed, he went into exile in France in August 1983. In early 1984 a Cameroon court sentenced Ahidjo to death in absentia; though the sentence was later commuted to an indefinite term of detention, Ahidjo never returned to Cameroon. He died of a heart attack on 30 November 1989 in Dakar, Senegal.

Ahidjo's principal legacy was the establishment of Cameroon's one-party state. He was also the architect of the centralized governing structure and powerful presidency that continued under President Biya into the twenty-first century. The influence of the president cuts across every sector of government, the executive, judiciary, and legislature. This dominant role of the president has made the independence of the different branches of government very difficult; in the Cameroon political system, the legislature and judiciary are directly or indirectly answerable to the executive. In terms of economic development, Ahidjo modernized Cameroon through his reforms in the agricultural sector, road construction, and other improvements in infrastructure.

[*See also* Biya, Paul.]

BIBLIOGRAPHY

Ahidjo, Ahmadou. *Contribution à la Contribution Nationale*. Paris: Presence Africaine, 1964.

Aseh, Nfamewih. *Political Philosophies and Nation Building in Cameroon: Grounds for the Second National Liberation Struggle.* Bamenda, Cameroon: Unique Printers, 2006.

Kofele-Kale, Ndiva, ed. *An African Experiment in Nation Building: Bilingual Cameroon Republic since Reunification.* Boulder, Colo.: Westview Press, 1980.

Le Vine, Victor. *The Cameroons: From Mandate to Independence.* Berkeley: University of California Press, 1964.

Takougang, Joseph, and Krieger Milton. *African State and Society in the 1990s: Cameroon's Political Crossroads.* Boulder, Colo.: Westview Press, 1988.

NDEH MARTIN SANGO

Ahmad, ʿAisha Musa (1905–1974), pioneer Sudanese woman singer and activist during the struggle for Sudanese independence and the first woman to perform on the radio in Sudan. Born in 1905 in Kassala City in the eastern region of Sudan, Ahmad was the eldest among her seven siblings, including three brothers and four sisters. Among them was a sister Jidawiyya who played a crucial role with Ahmad in their journey as female musicians. Ahmad's family was originally from Nigeria and migrated to Sudan in the late nineteenth century as pilgrims on their way to the holy places in Saudi Arabia. Her father, Musa Ahmad Yahiyya, was from the Fulani-Sokoto ethnic group, while her mother, Hujra, was from Hausa. Ahmad's nickname is Aisha al-Falatiyyia, a reference to her father's ethnic group, the Fulani, or Fallata, as they are known in Sudan.

The documented history indicates that Sudan served as a crossroads to the holy places in Saudi Arabia, for West African pilgrims. During their stay in Sudan on their way to the holy sites, they worked in different professions such as agriculture, blacksmithing, and trade in order to cover their traveling expenses. Some of those pilgrims were *fuqaha* (sing. *faqih*, "religious scholar") who taught the Qur'an to Sudanese children. Ahmad's father was one of the *fuqah*, who established qur'anic schools in different places in Sudan, such as Omdurman, Kassala, and Gadarif. Along with her peers in the area, Ahmad attended her father's qur'anic school (known as *Khalwa*) in Al-Abassiya, Omdurman. Memorizing part of the Qur'an and excelling in its recitation, Ahmad's skill in language and sound would make a tremendous impact on her career as a singer. Soon after she started singing at age fourteen, Ahmad became famous and was in demand for wedding festivities. Women singers at that time, however, were looked upon as having loose morals. Ahmad's father strongly opposed her indulgence in the profession and decided to marry her off to keep her away from singing. When Ahmad obtained a divorce soon after her marriage and followed her love of music and singing, her father disowned her.

Ahmad's voice was discovered by Dmitri al-Bazaar, who worked for the Mochian Beck Music Company in Cairo, Egypt. In 1938, she traveled with al-Bazaar to Egypt and recorded several songs for the company. Soon her songs were on discs in coffeehouses, and in 1942 she became the first Sudanese woman singer to perform for Omdurman Radio Broadcasting, accompanied by her sister Jidawiyya, who played the stringed oud with the orchestra. The appearance of Ahmad and her sister on Omdurman Radio met with animosity and hostility from male singers, whose performances dominated the radio and the profession at large. One famous singer, Haj Mohammed Ahmed Saror, went so far as to refuse to enter any place Ahmed had visited, and he never again performed for Omdurman Radio after her show began. Ahmad's performance, however, captivated the audience, and her continued success helped legitimize Sudanese women's position in public radio and their role as respected active performers. Ahmad was also the first to introduce duets in Sudan, and in the 1960s she performed with the Sudanese singer Ahmed Abdel Raziq.

As an activist, Ahmed played crucial roles in supporting women's rights and independence from British colonial rule during World War II and against the Axis powers. In 1945 she performed at the Nile Canal in Cairo, Egypt, to support women's rights for work. The British government had promised the Sudanese people that if they did well in the war in East Africa, Sudan would be among the African colonized countries that would achieve its dependence. Many Sudanese participated in the war in pursuit of their freedom, and Ahmad and her sister Jidawiyyia went to the battlefield in East Africa to boost the spirit of the Sudanese soldiers with their music, singing against Hitler and Mussolini. She refused to accept the foreign occupation of her country, not only by the Germans and Italians, but also by the British. She also performed a song welcoming the Sudanese soldiers who came back from the battlefield with victory and pride to pave the road for Sudan independence.

Ahmad was among many delegates who represented Sudan on several occasions outside the country. She visited Egypt on an annual basis to record her songs, on topics of nature, love, and her nation, recording over one hundred songs for Omdurman Radio Broadcasting and more than fifty songs for Wadi al-Neel. Ahmad was married four times, though her only son from the first marriage died while young. Ahmad was a resident of Omdurman, where she lived in different neighborhoods, which include al-Abassiya, al-Arda, and al-Thawra. Before her father's death in 1970, she asked him for forgiveness and he did forgive her. Ahmad died on 24 February 1974. She is buried in Hamad a-Neel Cemetery at Omdurman.

BIBLIOGRAPHY

This entry is based mainly on personnel communication with Adil Harbi, associate professor at the Institute of Music and Drama, Sudan (Harbi is a nephew of Aisha Musa Ahmed and the son of Jidawiyya) and the curriculum vitae of Aisha Musa Ahmed.

Badri, Haga Kashif. *Al-Harakah al-Nisa'iyah fi al-Sudan / Women's Movement in the Sudan.* Khartoum, Sudan: Khartoum University Press, 1984.

Malik, Saadia. "Exploring Aghani Al-Banat: A Postcolonial Ethnographic Approach to Sudanese Women's Songs, Culture and Performance." Ph.D. diss., Ohio State University, 2003.

Muhammad, Baqie Badawi. "The Role of Oral Poetry in Reshaping and Constructing Sudanese History." *Folklore Forum* 20 (1996): 60–76.

Naqar, Umar. *The Pilgrimage Tradition in West Africa: An Historical Study with Special Reference to the Nineteenth Century.* Khartoum, Sudan: Khartoum University Press, 1972.

BAQI'E BADAWI MUHAMMAD

Ahmad al-Bakka'i al-Kunti (c. 1803–1865), Malian political leader and notable Muslim scholar, was the political head of the Timbuktu-area lineage, the Kunta confederation, during the years 1847–1865. He inherited this role from his brother, Sidi al-Mukhtar al-Saghir bin Sidi Muhammad (d. 1847), who had assumed the position from his father in 1824, himself heritor of the influence of the family's patriarch, his father, Sidi al-Mukhtar al-Kunti (d. 1811). His education in the Azaouad region of Timbuktu encompassed the Islamic disciplines including Arabic language, jurisprudence, and theology. The database of West African writings, West African Manuscripts, provides us with a sense of his intellectual literary productivity: in a sample of 180 manuscript titles there are 47 poems or collections, 41 devotional writings, 33 letters of political

polemics, 15 works on Sufism, mainly attacking the Tijaniyya, and 10 juridical decisions. At some point, probably in the late 1820s or early 1830s, we know he traveled to Sokoto where he met Uthman Dan Fodio's successor, Muhammad Bello, although it was his hospitality offered to the British-sponsored traveler Heinrich Barth by which he is best known to the world away from Timbuktu.

The Kunta influence in the Timbuktu region by the mid-nineteenth century rested on their commercial activities and their efforts, since the early 1830s, to serve as spokesmen for the autonomy of Timbuktu over the threats initially from neighboring Tuareg. From 1824 the Kunta had also been involved in disputes about the claims of suzerainty over Timbuktu by the Masina *mujahid* Ahmad Lobbo, whose forces were initially welcomed to the city in that year as a way to neutralize the Tuareg. But Masina's efforts to exert administrative control over Timbuktu led to an uprising in 1833 and, in effect, a loose Kunta hegemony over the Niger Bend until mid-century. In 1850 the Kunta, now under Sidi Ahmad al-Bakka'i, turned to al-Hajj 'Umar's forces to insure their autonomy. Demands by the 'Umarian administration soon led to a war of words and, ultimately, armed conflict that set a coalition of Kunta, Tuareg, and Fulbe forces under al-Bakka'i's control against the 'Umarians. This conflict led to the deaths of both al-Hajj 'Umar (in 1864) and Ahmad al-Bakka'i in 1865.

By mid-century an ideological divide had emerged between the Kunta and their southern neighbors that grew from name-calling disputes over each other's scholarly credentials and, increasingly, focused on their differing ways, or "paths" (*tariqa* in Arabic) to seek the will of Allah. For the Kunta, since the time of Sidi al-Mukhtar al-Kunti, the litany followed in Sufi prayer was based on the teachings of the twelfth-century Baghdad mystic 'Abd al-Qadir al-Jilani, after whom the Qadiriyya *tariqa* was named. Until al-Hajj 'Umar arrived back from his pilgrimage in the late 1830s the Qadiriyya was the only *tariqa* known in most of Islamic West Africa. Al-Hajj 'Umar brought home a different *tariqa*, the Tijaniyya, that by the late 1840s served to set his preaching and his followers apart from mainstream Qadiriyya practice. Tijaniyya prohibitions against the use of tobacco, a mainstay of Kunta commercial interests in the Saharan trade, and efforts to restrict the sale of tobacco in Timbuktu only added smoke to the ideological fire that al-Hajj 'Umar had lit in the name of Islamic reform in Segou. Such was the growing hostility between the Sufi *tariqas* that al-Bakka'i took it upon himself to write to the scholars of Marrakech to warn them of the dangers posed by the Tijaniyya. This was the setting in which Sidi Ahmad al-Bakka'i became the leader of Kunta interests in the Timbuktu region.

Soon after he assumed that role at his brother's death in 1848, al-Bakka'i was faced with a crisis over the visit of the explorer Heinrich Barth, who arrived in Timbuktu in 1853. The event marked the nadir of al-Bakka'i's formerly cordial relations with Masina's ruler Ahmadu III. His response to his southern critics of his hospitality for a Christian traveler was to assert himself as an enlightened defender of Christians and Jews as People of the Book, against those who sought scriptural justification for detaining them. In correspondence with Ahmadu III of Masina he argued that since the only enemy of the Muslim peoples at the time was Russia (the Crimean War had just begun), Barth, a German under English sponsorship, could not be detained but rather deserved *aman* (safe passage). His interest in engagement with Europeans in Saharan affairs continued to 1860, in an attempt to gain British assistance against the French advance (and control over commerce) in the central Sahara.

Most of what we know about al-Bakka'i comes from his voluminous (and largely polemical) correspondence with the *mujahedin* to the south. In the earliest exchanges there is little evidence of the antipathy that was to follow, although it does reveal intellectual sparring, first with Ahmadu Lebbu over what al-Bakka'i took as his pretensions to claim caliphal status. His attitude toward political power was founded on his father's writings that asserted a sovereign will only become an agent of corruption on earth; to seek the authority of the imamate is therefore to challenge the established powers ordained by God. Al-Bakka'i used this argument to question the legitimacy, first, of the Masina jihad and then of al-Hajj 'Umar's movement. Religious suzerainty in the region, in his view, was owed to the 'Alawi sultan in Morocco and/or the Ottoman sultan (both of whose interests he undertook to represent) because these were the largest Islamic polities of the time. In addition to warning 'Umar about the corruption that power would bring, al-Bakka'i objected to the exalted claims he made for the founder of the Tijaniyya, Ahmad al-Tijani. By the late 1850s al-Bakka'i was actively campaigning against the rising 'Umarian presence in the Middle Niger region, including his encouragement to the descendants of his former Masina nemesis

("pagans" in the eyes of the 'Umarians) to stand firm against the 'Umarians. This is among his actions that most scandalized the 'Umarians. Al-Bakka'i's most enduring influence may well be his demonization of the Tijaniyya and the confrontation between Qadiriyya and Tijaniyya that effectively marks the beginning of a politicization of *tariqa* affiliation in the Western Sudan that was to gain even greater momentum in the years following his death.

Ahmad al-Bakka'i was one of the last principal precolonial Muslim spokesmen in the Western Sudan favoring an accommodationist stance vis-à-vis the threatening Christian European presence and, until the last years of his life, an exponent of noninvolvement in temporal matters. He was also the last of the great Kunta shaykhs, whose prestige and religious influence were interwoven with the Qadiriyya and the economic fortunes of the Timbuktu region. His significance lies in his wide range and voluminous correspondence documenting these issues.

[*See also* Bello, Muhammad; Sidi al-Mukhtar al-Kunti; *and* Uthman Dan Fodio.]

BIBLIOGRAPHY

Robinson, David. *The Holy War of Umar Tal: The Western Sudan in the Mid-nineteenth Century.* Oxford and New York: Oxford University Press, 1985. By far the best account of al-Hajj 'Umar's movement and al-Bakka'i's career from an 'Umarian perspective.

Saad, Elias N. *A Social History of Timbuktu: The Role of Muslim Scholars and Notables, 1400–1900.* Cambridge, UK, and New York: Cambridge University Press, 1983. Surveys al-Bakka'i's career from the perspective of Timbuktu history.

West African Manuscripts. http://www. westafricanmanuscripts.org/. The Arabic Manuscript Management System, a bilingual, open-access database of over 24,000 Arabic manuscripts from West Africa including descriptions of 180 works authored by Sidi Ahmad al-Bakka'i.

CHARLES C. STEWART

Ahmad Baba al-Massufi al-Tinbukti (b. 1556), religious teacher and expert in Islamic law in Timbuktu, was born 26 October 1556 in the village of Araouane, a few days north of Timbuktu by camel caravan. His full name was Abu al-Abbas Ahmad Baba ibn Ahmad ibn Ahmad ibn 'Umar ibn Muhammad Aqit al-Sinhaji, al-Tinbukti. His father was Ahmad (1522–1583), his grandfather al hajj Ahmad (1458–1535), and his great grandfather Umar, the son of Muhammad Aqit, the celebrated patriarch of the Masufa Tuareg clan of Aqit (one of the most powerful families of Timbuktu).

Ahmad Baba was raised in Timbuktu, where he studied the hadith and Islamic law with his father and other Aqit family members. His most influential teacher was the famous scholar and historical figure Mahmud Bagayogo, author of numerous qur'anic commentaries, whose acts of courage are recorded in al hajj Mahmud Kati's *Tarikh al fattash*. Prior to the Moroccan invasion of 1591, little is known of Ahmad Baba's life in Timbuktu, other than that he was heir apparent to the office of *qadi*, the highest political office of Timbuktu, a position that previously had been occupied by various members of the Aqit family. (Even the Askiya Muhammad could not usurp the religious and political authority of the *qadi* of Timbuktu.) At the age of forty-one, Baba was exiled to Marrakech by order of the Pasha Mahmud Zarqun, probably because of the political influence of the Aqit family. He remained in Marrakech for fourteen years before being allowed to return to his homeland. After his first two years in exile, Baba was released from confinement and lived in Marrakech under open arrest.

It was at this time that his fame spread, both as a religious teacher and as an expert in Islamic law. During this time, Baba became especially noted for his expert *fatwas* on difficult legal questions, earning him wide respect from students, scholars, and political leaders throughout northwest Africa. But he was loath to assume any political office or render judgments that might be enacted during his period of detainment in Morocco. When he was finally allowed to return to Timbuktu in 1608, he disappeared from written history, presumably spending the remaining twenty years of his life teaching and writing.

During his lifetime, Baba is known to have authored at least forty-one manuscripts, although few of these have surfaced. His most famous contribution to Islamic scholarship is his biographical dictionary of the best-known Sahelian scholars of Maliki law, a book that remains one of the most important sources for biographical information about medieval Islamic scholars of West Africa. He also wrote works on Arabic grammar, as well as influential legal decisions regarding which ethnic groups of West Africa may be construed as pagan and, hence, legally enslaved or subjected to jihad.

Today, the public library of Timbuktu is named in honor of Baba, who remains the most famous West African scholar of the medieval period. According to John Hunwick, Baba's fame rests in part on historical accident, the fact of his banishment from Timbuktu and long period of exile in Marrakech, as well as the erroneous attribution to him of the authorship of the *Tarikh al-Sudan*, by Heinrich Barth in 1857. Hunwick's point is not that Ahmad Baba is unworthy of such wide renown but that he is only one noteworthy scholar among many others who resided in Timbuktu during its greatest era.

BIBLIOGRAPHY

Hunwick, John. "Ahmad Baba and the Moroccan Invasion of the Sudan (1591)." *Journal of the Historical Society of Nigeria* 2, no. 3 (1962): 311–328.

Hunwick, John. "A New Source for the Biography of Ahmad Baba al-Tinbukti (1556–1627)." *Bulletin of the School of Oriental and African Studies* 27 (1964): 568–593.

CHRISTOPHER WISE

Ahmad Bey the Bosniak (d.1662), Egyptian governmental official, was a leader of the Qasimiyya bey household and political faction. He rose to power in the under the Mamluks shortly before the death of the chieftain of an opposing faction named Ridvan Bey. Alternate forms of his name are Ahamad Bey bi-Qanatir al-Siba' and Ahmad Bey Bushnaq. Ahmad Bey appears to have been one of a number of Bosnian soldiers from the Ottoman capital inserted into the Qasimi faction in an effort to counter the rising power of the Faqari faction in general, and Ridvan Bey in particular. Turkish chronicles of the period refer to Ahmad Bey, his brother Sha'ban Bey, and his nephew Ibrahim Bey Abu Shanab all as "Yeni Kapth," an epithet that most likely refers to the Yeni Kapi quarter on the Marmara coast of Istanbul.

Ahmad Bey had grown to be the only rival of Ridvan Bey, the powerful faction leader of the Faqariyya political network and family. The two households had been in continuous conflict for an extended period of time, and with the inclusion of the Bosnian military forces into the Qasimi faction, the group finally had power to begin to claim gains against the Faqariyya. However, during the lifetime of Ridvan Bey, gains against the other family could only go so far as long as Ridvan Bey held the position of amir al-hajj (leader of pilgrimage to Mecca). Despite a number of attempts by the Qasimi and other groups to remove Ridvan Bey from the position, and thus weaken his power, it would only be after his death that any progress could be made.

Upon Ridvan Bey's death in 1656, the viceroy Abu'l-Nur Muhammad Pasha gave the position of amir al-hajj to the man who had been his rival in life, Ahmad Bey, who was now head of the Qasimiyya household. The Faqariyya household was, predictably, outraged, and sought the resignation of the viceroy from his position by violence. Having forced him from his position, the Faqariyya appointed a bey as acting viceroy, had Ahmad Bey exiled, and their own candidate for the position of amir al-hajj, Hasan Bey al-Faqari, was installed.

This triumph of the Faqariyya did not last long. Ahmad Bey was shortly recalled to Cairo and restored to his position as amir al-hajj. The two families were, formally, reconciled; however, this incident left the resentment between them burning hotter than ever. This situation was exacerbated when Ahmad Bey returned from a mission to Istanbul with an order from the sultan naming him treasurer of Egypt, thus angering the Faqariyya.

Another appointment, this time to succeed to the governorship of Upper Egypt with the transfer of its previous governor to Habesh, came in 1659. However, the current governor refused the transfer and was forcibly expelled by the viceroy at the time.

The Faqariyya, however, still had the loyalty of the janissaries, due to the protection money collected from the Cairo merchants from which they profited. This resulted in the resentment of the other imperial troops, allowing the Qasimiyya to forge an alliance against a common enemy, when opportunity presented itself in the form of a small rural dispute in which a janissary officer was involved. In 1660 the rivalries between these two groups came to a head. This would culminate a series of bloody battles throughout the Egyptian countryside. The Qasimiyya allied with the Azaban infantry troop against the janissary officers. The Faqariyya beys fled Cairo and were subsequently hunted down and killed. Ahmad Bey put three of these beys, who surrendered under a safe-conduct, to death at al-Tarrana. This victory would lead to near total Qasimiyya ascendancy in political power for nearly a generation.

However, still suspicious of the growing power of the beys in general, the Ottoman viceroy sought to prevent a repeat of Ridvan Bey's autonomous power. This general feeling was reinforced by the brutal way in which Ahmad Bey had dealt with his rivals.

Seeing Ahmad Bey as too strong a personality to have in a position of power, as well as a threat, the Ottoman viceroy began making plans against him. The retinue of the viceroy Ibrahim Pasha V (Shaytan Ibrahim) assassinated Ahmad Bey in July 1662.

The death of Ahmad Bey left both the Faqariyya and the Qasimiyya without forceful leadership and brought about a relative peace between the two during the latter half of the seventeenth century, until the revival of factionalism again occurred in the early eighteenth century. This power vacuum in Egypt's military elite was filled, however, by individuals outside the beylicate. Officers from the military forces began to infiltrate the provincial elite, and the power structure in Egypt was subtly but permanently altered.

BIBLIOGRAPHY

Holt, P. M. "The Beylicate in Ottoman Egypt During the Seventeenth Century." *Bulletin of the School of Oriental and African Studies, University of London* 24, no. 2 (1961): 214–248.

Holt, P. M. "Egypt, the Funj and Darfur: Ottoman Egypt." In *The Cambridge History of Africa*, edited by J. D. Fage and Roland Oliver, pp.14–40. Cambridge, UK: Cambridge University Press, 1975.

Whidden, James. "Egypt: Ottoman, 1517–1798: Malmuk Beylicate (c.1600–1798)." In *Encyclopedia of African History*, edited by Kevin Shillington, pp. 449–450. New York: Fitzroy Dearborn, 2005.

NESS CREIGHTON

Ahmad Bukr (d. 1722), sultan of the Sudanese kingdom of Darfur (c. 1682–1722) was born in Jabal Marra to Sultan Musa and an unknown woman; his full name was Ahmad Bukr bin Musa bin Sulayman. He built up Darfur as a regional power, energetically worked to expand the role of Islam, and invited new ethnic groups to settle in the sultanate.

As the youngest of his father's eight sons, Ahmad Bukr came to power after his oldest brother proved unfit. There are few fixed dates in his history but he was very successful in his military campaigns, routing such local rivals as the Gimr in a seven-year campaign, and driving the invading forces of Wadai out of his territory. They had reached the Kabkabiyya region (north of Jabal Marra), and he countered by sending to Egypt for firearms and to Bagirmi, a sultanate west of Wadai, for allies. To consolidate his hold on the west and north of his territory, he married Kaltuma from the ruling Angu clan of the Zaghawa of Kobe, a key group to the north of Jabal Marra.

Sultan Ahmad Bukr began a long process of transforming Darfur into a multiethnic and Muslim state by bringing the local ethnic leaders under the control of centrally appointed regional governors and encouraging the spread of Islam. He was the first Darfur sultan known to issue written documents. He wrote letters and issued grants of *jah* (tax-exempt status particularly for Muslim holy men and their followers). This appears to have been part of a broader policy of encouraging the immigration of foreign groups with desirable skills into the sultanate, including Fallata fuqara' from Bornu and Bagirmi, Bulala, and Arabs, as well as various groups from the Nile valley. The sultan also built mosques and schools and compelled "the inhabitants to observe the three principal Muslim prescriptions: circumcision, the Ramadan fast, and performance of the five daily prayers" (Nachtigal, vol. 4, p. 800).

He wanted to conquer Kordofan, a large region that lay between Darfur and the Nile, then in the possession of the Musabba'at, a rival dynasty that also traced its origins to Darfur. To do so he had to incorporate cavalry units more suitable for fighting on the savanna into Darfur's armies whose standard weapons had been spear, shield, and throwing knife. In preparation he gathered a large army and appointed his son Muhammad Harut (also known as Muhammad Dawra) as his successor and left him to rule in his absence. The sultan died en route to Kordofan, but his mission of conquest was carried out by his successors over the next century. He was buried in Turra, following the royal practice.

Sultan Ahmad Bukr had multiple wives and over one hundred sons. Four of his sons (interrupted by one grandson) ruled Darfur from 1730 to 1801. Muhammad Dawra succeeded him (c. 1720–1730), followed by Dawra's son 'Umar Lel (1730–1739), and then three more of the *awlad* Bukr: Abu'l Qasim (1739–1752), Muhammad Tayrab (1752–1786), and Abd al-Rahman (1786–1801). These transitions were rarely smooth, and the period was marked by civil wars.

BIBLIOGRAPHY

O'Fahey, R. S., and Jay L. Spaulding. *Kingdoms of the Sudan.* London: Methuen and Co., 1974. This early work lays out the chronology of the sultans of Darfur and explains the place of Kordofan in the histories of Darfur and Sinnar.

Nachtigal, Gustav. *Sahara and Sudan* Vol. 4: *Wadai and Darfur.* Translated by Allan G. B. Fisher and Humphrey J. Fisher. 4 vols. London: C. Hurst and Co., 1971–1987. This excellent traveler's account provides many details of the history and culture of Darfur.

GEORGE MICHAEL LA RUE

Ahmad ibn al-Amin al-Shinqiti (c. 1863–1913), Islamic scholar and historian from present-day Mauritania. His name is also spelled Sidi Ahmed ould al-Amin al-Shinqiti. The *nisba* (name extension indicating place of origin) al-Shinqiti does not refer to the town Chinguetti (Shinqit), but was given to him during his stay in the Arab world. All *bidan* (Moors) going abroad to the Arab world have the *nisba* al-Shiniqiti added to their names, no matter from which region or town of the so-called Bilad Shinqit ("The lands of Chinguetti"; present-day Mauritania, Western Sahara, and the Azawad region in northern Mali) they come from. In the Arab world they are generally called *shanaqita* and their country is known as Bilad Shinqit, even if locally different names were circulating in precolonial times.

Ahmad was born around 1863/64 in the Gibla region of what is today southwestern Mauritania (Trarza) and belonged to a scholarly family. He was from one of the Idaw Ali lineages (Idaw Ali Gibla / Ahl Abd al-Rahman) who consider themselves noble descendants of the Prophet Muhammad (*sharif*). The Idaw Ali Gibla made their living through Islamic scholarship, cattle breeding, and seasonal agriculture migrating between Li'gul and Lake R'kiz. While the region of Lake R'kiz and the northern banks of the Senegal River (Chemama) were used for seasonal grain farming, Li'gul—with its numerous small water places—was the most important grazing ground for their cattle. Nevertheless, the Idaw Ali Gibla were living a transhumant way of life, they ran a number of well-established Islamic schools as well as the most important Sufi center of the Tijaniyya-Hafiziyya (the dominant branch of the Tijaniyya among the *bidan* population until the 1950s). Both were to be found in their camp (*frig*) and moved according to the migration seasons. Growing up in this notable Sufi scholarly milieu, Ahmad received a superior Islamic education that began in his own family and was completed in one of the two most prestigious institutions of higher education (*mahdhara*) in the region that specialized in Islamic law (*fiqh*) and Arabic grammar (*nahw*), the school of Yahdhih bin Abd al-Wadud (d. 1939/40). Ahmad concentrated his studies on grammar, philology (*lugha*), classical Arabic literature (*adab*), and poetry (*shi'r*).

After finishing his education in the Gibla, he decided to continue his studies abroad. Called *ghurba*, the tradition of traveling to various scholars for educational purposes was common practice in the region. It is said that a boy achieved manhood only after completing his *ghurba*, which is often combined with the pilgrimage to Mekka (hajj). Around 1897 Ahmad traveled northward from Trarza, passing through Tidjikja, Chinguetti, and Smara, where he sojourned for a while among the community of Shaykh Ma al-Aynayn, the famous Fadhili shaykh and leader of a jihad against the French occupation. After his stay in Smara he left Bilad Shinqit and spent some time among Tijanis in Marrakesh and Fez. Around 1899/1900, he continued to Mecca and Medina to perform his pilgrimage. In the following three years, he wandered around, going from scholar to scholar in Syria, Turkey, and even Russia, and in the year 1902 or 1903 he decided to settle in Cairo. He stayed there until he died on 21 August 1913.

Ahmad was not the only *bidan* scholar to take up permanent residence in Cairo. The colonization of North and West Africa had led to the migration of numbers of scholars to the Hedjaz (Saudi Arabia) and Cairo. Among them were scholars from Bilad Shinqit, especially admired and respected in the Middle East for their traditional training in Islamic sciences and Arabic classical poetry. Ahmad had to establish himself in a highly competitive milieu, where different *bidan*, Maghrebin, and West African scholars tried to make their living. His main scholarly opponent in Cairo was the *bidan* scholar Muhammad Mawlud ibn al-Talamid al-Tirkizi who was a specialist in Islamic jurisprudence (*fiqh*). Like Ahmad, he was trained in the Gibla region but in the school specialized in the Islamic jurisprudence of Ijdud ibn Iktawashni al-Alawi (d. 1872/73). Muhammad Mawlud managed to make a good living in Cairo by taking a position as assistant to Muhammad Abduh, after the latter was named *qadi al-qudat*.

Ahmad's reserved attitudes toward Muhammad Mawlud are well reflected in his most famous book, *al-Wasit fi tarajim 'udaba' Shinqit*. This book has the appearance of a poetry collection with an ethnohistorical appendix, but the choice of cited authors and the kind of poetry reflects the worldview of a pious Idaw Ali Tijani who grew up in Li'gul. It consists of a number of biographical notes tendentiously divided into two parts: descriptions of the friends of the Tijanis and their opponents. Muhammad Mawlud is represented as a Tijani opponent and Ahmad portrays him as a morally deficient character. As a Tijani scholar, Ahmad even engaged in the scholarly debates of the Middle East by defending Sufism in general and the Tijaniyya in particular. His second most famous writing, *dar' al-Nabhani 'an haram Sayyid Ahmad Tijani*, is a polemical defense against the attacks of Shaykh Yusuf al-Nabhani (d. 1932) on the Tijaniyya. Ahmad was a Tijani *muqaddam* and his house in Cairo was an important meeting place for pilgrims with a Tijani background.

During his stay in Cairo, Ahmad developed a close friendship with Muhammad Tawfiq al-Bakri (d. 1932) with whom he shared his engagement in Sufism and interest in classical Arabic poetry. Another one of his famous friends was the writer Mustafa Lutfi al-Manfaluti (d. 1924), a pious graduate of the Azhar School of Islamic theology who was a poet, essayist, and novelist, famous for his neoclassical writing style. These two friendships reflect the diffuse Pan-Islamic and Arab nationalist intellectual milieu Ahmad was engaging in. His own self-consciousness of being Arab was reflected in his book *al-Wasit*. By presenting a collection of classical Arab poetry—all composed by poets of his region of origin—he strives to demonstrate that the cultural heritage of the Bilad Shinqit was like that of the Maghreb of Arab-Berber origin and neglects all sub-Saharan influences by keeping silent about the intensive connectivity in fields of religion, literary production, and economy between the two regions. Instead he introduces numbers of biographical notes emphasizing the *bidans* connectivity to North Africa and states that the Bilad Shinqit are part of the Greater Maghreb (Maghrib al-Aqsa), a quite contestable point of view for a number of *bidan* scholars at home. His intention can best be understood by his description of a conflict in Medina (Saudi Arabia) in 1899–1900, when mainly Algerians tried to refuse *bidan* pilgrims access to the Maghrebin *waqf* being held in town by claiming that Bilad Shinqit was part of sub-Saharan Africa and not the Maghreb. This sheds light on the difficulties Saharans had when moving to the heartlands of the Arab world, as the majority of them, if of *bidan* or Tuareg origin, followed a strategy of underlining their Arab origin.

Being a unique compilation of information about precolonial Mauritania, *al-Wasit* was already in the 1920s recognized by the French colonial administration as an important source for *bidan* history, geography, and anthropology and is now considered the most important printed source for the historiography of nineteenth-century Mauritania. A list of Ahmad's additional writings can be found in Miské.

[*See also* 'Abduh, Muhammad; *and* Ma' al-'Aynayn.]

BIBLIOGRAPHY

Ahmad ibn al-Amin al-Shinqiti. *al-Radd al-muhkam 'ala munkir al-aqsam fi al-radd 'ala al-Shaykh Yusuf al-Nabhani al-mu'tarid 'ala Sayyidna al-Shaykh Sidi Ahmad al-Tijani.* Cairo: Matba'at al-Taqaddum., n.d.

Ahmad ibn al-Amin al-Shinqiti. *al-Wasit fi tarajim 'udaba' Shinqit. Kalam 'ala tilka al-bilad takhdidan wa-takhdidan wa-'adatihim wa-akhlaqihim wa-ma ta'laqu bi-dhalika.* Originally published in 1911. Reprinted, Nouakchott, Mauritania: Mu'assasa Munir, 1989.

Ahmad ibn al-Amin al-Shinqiti. *El-Wasît: littérature-histoire-géographie-mœurs et coutumes des habitants de la Mauritanie, par Ahmed Lamine Ech-Chenguiti.* Extracts translated from the Arabic by Mourad Teffahi. *Etudes Mauritaniennes* 5. Saint-Louis, Senegal: Centre IFAN, 1953.

Beyries, J. "Proverbes et dictons mauritaniens." *Revue des Etudes Islamique* 1 (1930): 1–51.

Miské, Ahmed Baba. "al-Wasît (1911), Tableau de la Mauritanie à la fin du XIXe siècle." *BIFAN,* ser. B, 30, no. 1 (January 1968), 117–164.

Miské, Ahmed Baba. *Al Wasît: Tableau de la Mauritanie au début du XXè siècle.* Paris: C. Klincksieck, 1970.

Norris, H. T. "Al-Shinqiti." *Encyclopaedia of Islam.* CD-Rom edition. Leiden, Netherlands: E. J. Brill, 2003.

BRITTA FREDE

Ahmad ibn Ibrahim al-Ghazi (c. 1506–c. 1543), North African political and military leader, was probably born in 1506 in the area between Harar and the Ogaden. Ahmad ibn Ibrahim married the daughter of Imam Mahfuz, the governor of Zeyla, who collaborated with Islamic scholars from Arabia against his master, the Sultan of Adal. Ahmad bin Ibrahim was similarly inspired by the renewed Islamic spirit and when he gained control of Harar in 1525, he refrained from adopting a political title and used only the religious designation of imam. His followers and his chronicler later called him Sahib al-fath (the lord of the conquest) or al-Ghazi (the holy warrior), for it was his conquest of Ethiopia, between 1529 and 1543, that made him so significant. In Ethiopian history, he is known as Ahmad Gragn, the left-handed.

The first half of the sixteenth century was marked by the weakening of the Solomonian dynasty's rule in Ethiopia on one hand and the revival of Islam, both spiritually and politically, in nearby Arabia, on the other. The Ethiopian emperor Lebna Dengel (r. 1508–1540) was no longer capable of effectively exercising Christian-Ethiopian dominance over the Islamic sultanates in the south of the Horn, while the local Muslims were now inspired by religious scholars from Hadramawt, Yemen, and Mecca. In 1517 the Ottomans occupied Egypt and began to clash with the Portuguese in the Red Sea and the Indian Ocean. It was against this background that Ahmad ibn Ibrahim managed, in 1525, to lead an Islamic revivalist movement in the Horn and created a coalition of various ethnic groups around his town of Harar, motivated by the spirit of anti-Ethiopian jihad.

Uniting Somalis, Oromos, Sidamas, Afars, Hararis, and others—all also motivated by the desire to control the fertile highlands—Ahmad ibn Ibrahim led his Islamic armies into Ethiopia, conquering Shewa in 1529, Amhara in 1531, and Tigray in 1535. Emperor Lebna Dengel died isolated in a mountain fortress in 1540, and, with the exception of the Lake Tana islands, the entire Christian kingdom fell to the Muslims. According to Ethiopian records, nine out of every ten Christians were forced to convert to Islam and all churches were looted and destroyed.

Although Ahmad ibn Ibrahim enjoyed the support of Islamic scholars and of their fellows and superiors in Mecca and benefited from military aid sent by the Ottomans, he failed to consolidate his occupation of the country. Old ethnic rivalries and quarrels over booty undermined his unifying revolution. In 1540 the Portuguese sent four hundred warriors to help the new emperor Gelawdewos, who at the time was wandering like a refugee in his own country. The combined Christian force was initially beaten and the Portuguese leader, Christopher da Gama, was beheaded by Ahmad ibn Ibrahim in August 1542. However, on 21 February 1543 in the battle of Zantara, he himself was killed. Following his death, the entire Islamic enterprise in Ethiopia collapsed and the remnants of Ahmad ibn Ibrahim's army returned to Harar. The new ruler of the Islamic capital hastened to build new walls around the town, and local Islam in the Horn of Africa would not regain momentum until the modern era.

On the Islamic side, the memory of Ahmad ibn Ibrahim was eternalized by his Yemenite chronicler, Shihab al-Din Ahmad ibn 'Abd al-Qadir, better known as Arab Faqih, in his work *Futuh al-Habasha*. His legacy as the guardian of Islamic pride and resistance to Ethiopian-Christian domination was recycled locally mainly by Somali speakers, who refer to him as Ahmad Guray. Though it was never fully established that he was a Somali, he was adopted by modern Somali nationalists and Islamic activists as their forefather, a predecessor of Muhammad Abdille Hasan, the early twentieth-century father of Somali nationalism. On the Christian Ethiopian side, the conquest of Ahmad ibn Ibrahim was undoubtedly the most traumatic event in their history and his memory is revived whenever Muslims in the Horn and in the Middle East unite to restore their momentum in Africa.

One of the most important figures in the medieval history of the Horn of Africa, Ahmad ibn Ibrahim shaped a major chapter in local Islamic-Christian relations and his legacy endures to this day.

[*See also* Gelawdewos; *and* Lebna Dengel.]

BIBLIOGRAPHY

Arabfaqih, Shihab al-Din Ahmad ibn 'Abd al-Qadir. *The Conquest of Abyssinia: 16th Century*. Translated by Paul Lester Stenhouse with annotations by Richard Pankhurst. Los Angeles: Tsehai Publishers, 2005.

Arabfaqih, Shihab al-Din Ahmad ibn 'Abd el-Qadir. *Futuh al-habasha—Histoire de la Conquête de l' Abyssinie (XVIe siècle)*. Translated and edited by René Basset. Paris: E. Leroux, 1897.

Erlich, Haggai. *Ethiopia and the Middle East*. Boulder, Colo.: L. Rienner, 1994.

Trimingham, John Spencer. *Islam in Ethiopia*. Oxford: Oxford University Press, 1952.

HAGGAI ERLICH

Ahmad Zaki Abu Shadi (1892–1955), Egyptian poet, critic, broadcaster, painter, and physician, was born in the al-Hanafy district in Cairo. His father, Muhammad Abu Shadi, was the head of the Egyptian Bar Association and his mother, Amina Naguib, was a poetess. He completed his primary and secondary education in Cairo and was involved in antioccupation activities during his adolescence. He joined the faculty of medicine (named Qasr al-Aini) and then traveled to London in 1912 to complete his studies in medicine at the University of London where he obtained a certificate of honor from Saint George Hospital in 1915. He married a British woman and lived with her in Egypt until her death in 1945. Following his return to Egypt in 1922, he served in many governmental posts in such places as the Ministry of Health and the Faculty of Medicine, Alexandria University. In 1946 he immigrated to the United States and stayed there until his death on 14 April 1955.

Abu Shadi was not only a cultural figure; he was also involved in several social and scientific activities. He was a specialized physician in bacteriology and founded the first health laboratory in Egypt. He also studied beekeeping and co-established the International Bee Club in 1919, *The Bee World* journal, and the Egyptian Bee Club in 1923. During his stay at the United States he broadcast programs for Voice of America and taught Arabic studies at New York's Asia Institute. He was also interested in painting and held his only exhibition in New York in 1946.

Despite all these achievements, Abu Shadi lived a troubled life in a troubled world. Two years before World War I, he had to leave his homeland for a stay in Britain after suffering an emotional crisis when his sweetheart married another person. Ten years later, his father's fatal illness obliged him to return to Egypt and rebuild his literary and professional career. During the 1920s and 1930s he devoted his time, efforts, and money to promote Egyptian cultural and scientific life but his contributions were not recognized and were severely attacked by many of his contemporaries.

During World War II Abu Shadi was nearly forbidden from publishing his works widely and was subject to many forms of oppression due to his critique of the monarchic regime. These obstacles led him to leave Egypt only one year after the war had come to an end. Although Abu Shadi supported the army movement in July 1952, when he was encouraged to return to Egypt, he refused. Three years later, he died in the United States, his freely chosen exile, where he was buried.

Abu Shadi's popularity now is due to his cultural activities, not his literary works or scientific contributions. His name has always been related to the establishment of the Apollo group which took its name from Apollo, the Greek god of poetry. This group represented one of the most important Arab poetry movements in the first half of the twentieth century. Abu Shadi announced its establishment in Cairo in September 1932. A journal with the same name (*Apollo*) appeared the same year speaking on its behalf.

Apollo embraced young poets who later became very important figures in modern Arab poetry. Some of these poets are Ibrahim Naji (1898–1953), 'Ali Mahmud Taha (1902?–1949), Abu al-Qasim al-Shabbi (1909–1934), and Iliya Abu Madi (1889–1957). This was accompanied by Abu Shadi's call for a new poetry that would maintain the organic unity of the poem, address intimate human experience, praise nature, and use simple language.

To defend his call, Abu Shadi engaged in intellectual battles, the most notable of which were his battles with two of the most prominent classical Arab poets Ahmad Shawqi (1868–1932) and Hafiz Ibrahim (1872–1932), on one hand, and the founder of the Al-Diwan school of poetry, 'Abbas al-'Aqqad (1898–1964) on the other. Abu Shadi believed that both represented a poetical authority that should be criticized in order to open new horizons for the younger poets in the Arab world.

In December 1934 *Apollo* ceased to be published but the poetic movement that it initiated remained a tributary of Arabic poetry until the 1940s. After *Apollo*'s cessation Abu Shadi published other journals such as *Literary* (*'Adabyyah*), but it was not prominent.

Abu Shadi left a huge amount of poems, most of which were published in the following collections: *Qatrah min yara'* (A Drop of Quill), 1908; *Zaynab*, 1924; *Misriyat: nukhab min shi'r al-wataniyah* (Egypt: The Best of Patriotic Poetry), 1924; *Anin wa-ranin* (Whining and Ringing), 1925; *al-Shafaq al-baki* (Crying Twilight), 1925; *Shi'r al-wijdan: mukhtarat ra'i'ah* (The Poetry of Feelings: Wonderful Selections), 1925; *Mukhtarat min wahy al-'am* (Selections of This Year of Revelation), 1928; *Ashi'ah wa-zilal* (Rays and Shadows), 1931; *Al Shoala* (The Light), 1932; *Atyaf al-rabi'* (Shades of Spring), 1933; *Aghani Abi Shadi* (Abu Shadi's Songs), 1933; *al-Yanbu'* (The Fountain), 1933; *Anda al-fajr* (The Dawn's Dewdrops), 1934; *Fawqa al-'abab* (Above the Waves), 1935; *Al Kaen Al Thani* (The Second Creature), 1935; *'Awdat al-ra'i* (The Return of the Cowboy), 1942; and *Min al-sama'* (From the Sky), 1949.

Abu Shadi wrote long poems that have been published separately such as *Nakbat Navrin* (The Catastrophe of Navarino), 1924; *Mafkharat Rashid* (Rashid's Pride), 1925; *Watan al-Far a'inah* (Pharaoh's Homeland), 1926; *Akhnatun Fir'awn Misr* (Ikhnaton: The Pharaoh of Egypt), 1927. This is in addition to four volumes that were not published during his lifetime: *Nayruz al-hurr, wa-qasa'id ukhra* (Isis, The Free Newroz), 1988;

Anasheed Al Hayah (Songs of Life) and *al-Insan al-jadid* (The New Human), 1983. Moreover, he produced three volumes in English, two of which were published (*The Songs of Nothingness* and *Songs of Happiness and Sorrow*), while Songs of Love was not. Despite the huge number of poems and books he left, the majority of his writings remain unread except by specialists.

Abu Shadi was among the first to write opera librettos in the Arab world. He composed four operas, namely, *Ihsan: Ma'sat Misriyah* (Ihsan: An Egyptian Tragedy), *al-Zaba', aw, Zinubiya malikat Tadmur* (Zenobia: Queen of Palmyra) (a four-act historical opera), *Ardashir* (a romantic musical), and *al-Alihah* (The Gods)(a three-act symbolic opera); all of his four operas were released in 1927. In 1926 he wrote two ballads: *Maha* and *Abdo Bek*. He also translated Shakespeare's *The Tempest* into prose in 1929, and *Ruba'iyat 'Umar al-Khayyam* in 1931. He also wrote books on literary criticism such as *Masrah al-adab* (The Theater of Literature), 192?; *Shu'ara' al-'Arab al-mu'asirun* (The Contemporary Arab Poets), 1958; and *Qadaya al-shi'r al-mu'asir* (Issues of Contemporary Poetry), 1959. In addition to this, he produced many writings on Islam such as *Dirasat Islamiyah* (Islamic Studies), 1950; *Thawrat al-Islam* (The Revolution of Islam), 1959; and on history such as *Min nafidhat al-Tarikh* (From the Window of History), 1952.

[*See also* 'Aqqad, 'Abbas Mahmud al-; Ibrahim, Hafiz; Shabbi, Abu al-Qasim al-; *and* Shawqi, Ahmed.]

BIBLIOGRAPHY

Dusuqi, 'Abdul-'Aziz. *A'lam al-shi'r al-'Arabi al-hadith*. (The Great Figures of Modern Arab Poetry). Bayrut: al-Maktab al-Tijari, 1970.

Isa, Ali. *Ahmad Zaki Abu Shadi: bayna al-'ilm wa-al-adab*. (Ahmed Zaki Abu Shadi between Science and Literature). Cairo: al-Majlis al-Qawmi lil-Shabab, 2009.

Jayyusi, Salma Khadra. *Trends and Movements in Modern Arabic Poetry*. Leiden, Netherlands: Brill, 1977.

Nash'at, Kamal. *Abu Shadi wa-harakat al-tajdid fi al-sh'ir al-'Arabi al-hadith*. (Abu Shadi and the Innovation Movement in the Arab Poetry). Cairo: al-Majlis, 2005.

EMAD ABDUL-LATIF

Ahmed, Su'ad Ibrahim (1935–), Sudanese educator and human rights activist for women's rights and an advocate for freedom and democracy, was born on 30 May 1935 in Omdurman, one of three cities that constitute the capital of Sudan (Khartoum, Khartoum North, and Omdurman). Her parents were originally from the Nubian region in northern Sudan. Ahmed was the only female among her three siblings. She grew up in an environment that helped shape her future life as a liberal and progressive individual. Her father, Ibrahim Ahmed, was an engineer who worked as a teacher in Gordon Memorial College, Sudan. He played an active role in Sudan's independence movement and served as the first Sudanese Deputy to the Vice Chancellor of the University of Khartoum, the first chairman of the University of Khartoum Senate, a member of the Executive Council (the first Sudanese Parliament), and founder and president of Mutamar a-l Khiregeen (Graduates Congress). With this family background, Ahmed's freedom in pursuing education comes as no surprise, at a time when girls' formal education was looked upon with suspicion and distrust from the masses, because of its potential to alter traditional values.

After finishing elementary and intermediate levels of education, Ahmed attended the Catholic Sisters' School in Khartoum. However, her mother heard of the newly established Omdurman Secondary School for Girls (the first government secondary school) and decided to enroll her on its opening in July 1949. During her study in

Omdurman Secondary School, Ahmed excelled in sports, literature, and theater. In 1955 Ahmed was admitted to the University of Khartoum. Being active in literature and theater, she established the Society of Drama and Music, where she was elected as secretary in its first executive committee. She participated in numerous performances, including work in the trilogy of Abdullah El-Tayeb, Arabic professor at the University of Khartoum. During her university years, Ahmed was also active in the political arena. In 1956 she joined the Democratic Front, a coalition of communist and democratic students, and in 1957 she was elected a member in the Students' Union at the University of Khartoum. Ahmed rose quickly to become Deputy-Chair of the Union with responsibility for redrafting the Student Union's constitution.

In 1960, after graduation from college, Ahmed returned to her original home, Wadi Halfa, in the Nubian region, to work with the Social and Economic Survey team. The team's mission was to conduct a survey on the social and economic aspects of the region, carried out to help prepare for the construction of the Aswan Dam in neighboring Egypt. When the local people realized that they would be relocated from their region in order for the dam to be constructed, a fierce resistance emerged. The streets flooded with demonstrators expressing their rage against their relocation, and Ahmed was among the masses who took action in

Su'ad Ibrahim Ahmed, 1998. (AP Images)

this resistance. She was arrested, fired from her job, and deported from her native region. Upon her arrival in Khartoum, Ahmed volunteered to work for *Women's Voice*, a journal published by the Sudanese Women's Union. Al-Ahfad high school also hired her as a teacher. In 1962 she was granted a scholarship from the American Association of University Women Educational Foundation to carry out her graduate studies in the United States.

In 1963 after finishing her M.Sc. in Statistics and Measurement in Educational Psychology at the University of Wisconsin at Madison, Ahmed returned to Sudan, where she was appointed Lecturer in the School of Extramural Studies at the University of Khartoum, the first Sudanese woman Lecturer to be appointed at the University of Khartoum. As an active academic staff member, she helped found the University of Khartoum Academic Staff Organization. Stressing her desire to promote politically liberal ideas, she also worked on the creation of an Organization for Socialist Academic Staff and efforts to establish the Democratic Front of the Academic Staff. After Sudan's October Uprising in 1964, women in general, and particularly those in academia, were anxious to fight for their rights. Ahmed was among a group of dedicated women on the academic staff who were able to compel the authority in the University of Khartoum to grant women the right to join the university's pension scheme. It was a successful, progressive, and courageous step toward the achievement of women workers' rights.

Ahmed's work and activities were rich and diverse in the public sphere as well as in academia. In 1966 she was assigned as representative of the University of Khartoum at the meeting in Nairobi to partake in the creation of the Adult Education Association of Africa. In 1968 Ahmed worked as a consultant with UNESCO for Adult Education, Technology of Education, and Higher Education. While working in the Institute of Extra Mural Studies, she was extremely active in developing the institute, extending its role to include outreach offerings for Sudanese society at large. She created special courses for workers' education, courses for scientific awareness such as The World around Us, and Extra Mural Studies branches in neighboring towns, where she moved courses and seminars to various regions. She also founded film societies in Khartoum, al-Obeyed, Shendi, and Madani, and established special film shows for women and children.

Ahmed was a member of the Sudanese Women Union, but she disassociated herself from the union and criticized the way it operated as not being liberal enough to bring about emancipation for Sudanese women under the current Islamist regime. While the president of this union, Fatima Ahmed Ibrahim, described by Ahmed as conservative, stated that "progressives should use Islam to defeat the fanatic Islamists," Ahmed stressed a non-religious approach, saying, "We should face them with secular ideas."

Ahmed's political struggle has been grounded in liberal thinking that promotes freedom and free will. As a working member of the Central Committee of the Communist Party of Sudan, in 1969, when the local military regime dismissed seventeen members of the academic staff in the University of Khartoum, Ahmed confronted dictator Ja'far al-Nimeiry vehemently at a public meeting, condemning the dismissals of her colleagues for reasons of political affiliations. Six months later, she condemned the fourth presidential decree in a public debate with the then Minister of the Interior (considered one of the most extreme hawks in government), giving a clearly critical speech to the applause of those assembled. Her persistent denouncement of the unjust, however, often came at a high price. She was detained in jail several times, where one incarceration lasted for thirty months. During her prison time she maintained her courage and audacity, where she confronted injustice and defended her fellow inmates. To demand her release and to achieve better living conditions for herself and other female inmates, she launched several hunger strikes, one of which lasted for seventeen days.

Ahmed's struggle for achieving justice not only addressed the academic and political arena, but expanded to include cultural and social issues. Her support for cultural activities and work trades was represented in many actions, including her advocacy for art and artists, her efforts to spread the cinema to a wider audience, and her personal engagement in advocating the Nubian language, civilization, and culture. Her recent stand against the construction of Merowe Dam was evidence of her struggle to preserve not only Nubian civilization and culture, but also Sudan at large. The Merowe Dam is considered the second-most destructive, after the Aswan Dam, in terms of its negative impact on Nubian life. As Ahmed states, "the building of dams has turned into a struggle for Nubian identity," for it requires the eradication of ancient civilization and displacement of people. Ahmed is persistent in her struggle for human rights, democracy, and culture.

[*See also* Nimeiry, Ja'far al-.]

BIBLIOGRAPHY

This entry is based partially on Ahmed's curriculum vitae, which was prepared by Dr. Fatima Babiker Mahmoud and Dr. Mohamed Suliman, and personal communication with Ustaza Suad Ibrahim Ahmed herself.

Boulding, Chris, "Death on the Nile: New Dams Set to Wipe Out Centuries of History." http://www.independent.co.uk/Tuesday, 29 April 2008/.

Hale, Sondra. *Gender Politics in Sudan: Islamism, Socialism, and the State.* Boulder, Colo.: Westview Press, 1996.

Hale, Sondra. "Sudan." In *The Oxford Encyclopedia of Women in World History*, edited by Bonnie G. Smith. Oxford and New York: Oxford University Press, 2008.

Sidahmed, Abubakr. The Nubian Net, http://www.thenubian.net/who.php/.

BAQI'E BADAWI MUHAMMAD

Ahmed Dini Ahmed (1930–2004), nationalist leader and first prime minister of independent Djibouti, was born in the Mabla mountain area north of

Ahmed Dini Ahmed. Ahmed Dini Ahmed casting his ballot in the first genuine multiparty parliamentary elections in Djibouti, 2003. (AP Images/Mahamed Ahmed)

Obock, Afar. Ahmed Dini Ahmed was fired by an intense sense of social justice and fairness and worked at one time or another with all of Djibouti's early preindependence leaders with the objective of facilitating an independent government in which all ethnic groups would work together for the betterment of all citizens. The failure of his close friendship with Hassan Gouled Aptidon immediately after independence was a personal blow to both of them, but was probably inevitable in two such committed but divergent individuals. Ahmed Dini had a political career roughly parallel to that of Hassan Gouled. He completed his primary school in Djibouti and then worked as a nurse's aide. He became interested in politics at a young age. In 1959, after Gouled had been elected to the French National Assembly, Dini was elected vice president of the Governing Council.

He worked closely with Hassan Gouled after 1970, and some observers believed that his political reputation may have even been greater than that of Gouled. At the constitutional conference held in Paris in April 1977, the details of how the new state would be constituted and what the political powers of the president and the prime minister would be were not yet clear. After the legislative elections and referendum of 8 May 1977, Ahmed Dini was elected president of the Chamber of Deputies. After independence the Chamber of Deputies became the National Assembly, and Dini was named prime minister on 12 July. However, he was profoundly disappointed when he learned that his new title was virtually meaningless: when the president's office subsequently released the first acts of the new constitution, Dini saw that President Hassan Gouled had reserved for himself the dual roles of head of state and head of government.

The reaction of the Afar community was also quite negative, and the new government of the Republic of Djibouti (GROD) was zealous in putting down dissent. After the bombing of the popular Palmier en Zinc restaurant in December 1977, the repression of the Afars increased, and Ahmed Dini resigned his post along with four other Afar ministers. In August 1981 Ahmed Dini created the Parti Populaire Djiboutien, an opposition party that was immediately outlawed. He was imprisoned from 7 September 1981 to 3 January 1982. After that experience, Dini effectively retired from politics for nearly ten years.

The Front for the Restoration of Unity and Democracy (Front pour la Restauration de l'Unité et de la Démocratie, FRUD) was established on

8 August 1991 and Ahmed Dini soon became its president. Within several months, FRUD guerillas occupied northern Djibouti and most territory between Lake Abbé and Lake Assal. Despite efforts by the GROD to invoke a treaty signed at independence in which France pledged to assist the GROD in the event of foreign aggression, France stated it would not become involved in a civil war. Increasing age and ill-health prevented Dini from being a field commander and his major roles were publicizing the repression of Afars in Djibouti and negotiating with France, international organizations, and humanitarian agencies.

A peace treaty between the GROD and Ahmed Dini's FRUD was signed on 12 May 2001. The agreement called for rehabilitation of areas ravaged by war, introduction of at least two FRUD-Dini veterans into the cabinet, and greater decentralization of powers. Open-heart surgery, diabetes, and general poor health led to Dini's death in September 2004. His death was widely mourned throughout all ethnic groups.

[*See also* Aptidon, Hassan Gouled.]

BIBLIOGRAPHY

Aden, Mohamed. *Ourrou-Djibouti: 1991–1994, du Maquis Afar à la Paix des Braves.* Paris: Harmattan, 395

Coubba, Ali. *Ahmed Dini et la Politique à Djibouti.* Paris: Harmattan, 1998.

Shehim, Kassim, and James Searing. "Djibouti and the Question of Afar Nationalism." *African Affairs* 79, no. 315 (April 1980): 209–226.

WALTER CLARKE

Ahmed Ould Ahmed ʿAida (d. 1861), emir of Mauritania, was the oldest son and successor to the emir Sid'Ahmed, who was himself the son of ʿUthman, founder in the middle of the eighteenth century of the emirate of the Mauritanian Adrar (*Adrar tmar*, "Adrar of the dates"), which Sid'Ahmed institutionalized by stabilizing the title within the Ahl ʿUthman and by attaching to it emirate wealth, in particular goods paid as tribute from the *znaga*. Ahmed Ould Aida brought to the emirate a new renown in the Saharan west.

His surname, Ould Aida, was given to him by the second wife of his father, of noble *brakna* origin, either in reference to his mother, who was of the Liʿwaysyat, a *hassan* group of warrior gentry, or in reference to his nurse, and out of derision. He assumed it in defiance, and thus the name is found

among his descendants, the Ahl Ahmed Ould Aida. His bravery and his audacity allowed him to form, even while his father was still alive, a *hella* (an encampment that was a symbol of emirate authority), by relying on his maternal line and those close to it, the Awlad Qaylan Salmuni and their local ruling family, the Ahl Mageyya. Upon the death of his father, at the end of the 1820s, he easily installed himself as his successor, and his half brothers had to go into exile in the neighboring emirates of the Trarza and the Tagant.

His reign was marked by incessant wars and skirmishes with the powerful peoples of the north, as well as with his Jaʿvriyya "cousins" who contested the strengthening of the emirate authority. To the north, the Awlad D'laym followed the ancient movement of the *hassan* groups (Maʿqil Arabs, a branch of the Hilali, who occupied the Saharan west and imposed the *hassaniyya* Arabic dialect) toward the southern pastures along two axes: in the west, the Awlad al-Lab, under the direction of a prestigious chief, Ahmed Ould Lavdhil, called Rmuga, victoriously confronted the emirs of the Trarza and of the Adrar, sometimes allied. In the east, the Awlad Selim and the Awlad al-Mulat, other factions of the Awlad D'laym, regularly pillaged the Adrar, exposing themselves to victorious counterattacks (ghazi Tiraklin).

The conflict with the Jaʿvriyya took place, either openly or hidden, during the entire reign of Ahmed Ould Aida. They opposed him first by supporting the claims of his brothers, then by organizing the dissidence after their exile, to the Trarza in particular, for short periods followed by reconciliation, in the case of the Ahl Karkub, or during the entire reign, in the case of the Ahl Maʿyuv. The role of the large collateral *hassan* families of the emirate line was in general diminished. A few, like Ahl Ahmed Ould Lavdhil, close cousins of this line, had to practice the *tawba* (religious "repentance"), which is to say renounce arms and pillaging, and became closer to the "Maraboutique" *zawaya* groups. In general, the Adrar experienced a certain economic boom, marked by the planting of palm groves and the development of commerce in the nomad cities (*qsur*).

Dissidents and exiles fueled the conflicts between with emirates. The most famous during this era was between Ahmed Ould Aida and the emir of the Trarza, Muhammed al-Habib, whose reign was contemporary (1827–1860) with the former. Marked by feats of arms and acts of honor, more than territorial or political claims, this conflict, which took place around the 1850s, is inscribed upon the memory of the west Saharan nomads: the theft of the white trousers (*serwal*) of the emir of the Trarza brought as a trophy, or the felling of the palm trees of Kanawal and Amdayr, a symbol of the protection of the population of this region by the emirs of the Adrar.

When Ahmed Ould Aida died, French presence, from the valley of Senegal, became stronger. In 1860, shortly before his death, the emir received the mission of Captain Henri Vincent with benevolence, but did not allow him access to the *qsur* of the Adrar and refused to sign a political agreement. The succession, disputed among several sons of different mothers (Brakna, Li'waysiyat, or Idayshelli), was difficult. The eldest, M'hamed, whose mother was Brakna and who was favored by his father, was immediately assassinated by his brothers Muhammed and 'Uthman, whose mother was Li'waysiyat, backed by the Ahl Mageyya. With their aid and the aid of the Awlad D'laym, they imposed their authority for a short time, but they too were assassinated. There followed a period of troubles in the Adrar during which brotherhood movements again established themselves and recruited followers (Shaykh Muhammed Fadhil Ould 'Abaydi, Shaykh Sidi Muhammed al-Kunti, Shaykh Ma al-'Aynin, as well as the shaykh of the *tijaniyya*). Finally in 1872 Ahmed, son of M'hamed who was assassinated by his brothers, established his emirate authority, thanks to the maneuvers of his mother, Khadidja Bi, and the support of her brother the emir of the Tagant, Bakkar Ould Swayd Ahmed.

BIBLIOGRAPHY

Ba, Ahmadou Mamadou. "L'Emirat de l'Adrar mauritanien de 1872 à 1908." *Bulletin trimestriel de la Société de géographie et d'archéologie d'Oran* 53, nos. 190: 83–119 ; 191: 263–298.

Bonte, Pierre. *L'émirat de l'Adrar mauritanien. Harim, compétition et protection dans une société tribale saharienne.* Paris: Karthala, 2008.

Vincent, Capitaine Henri. "Voyage dans l'Adrar et retour à Saint-Louis." *Le Tour du Monde*, 2ème année, 1861, pp. 49–64.

PIERRE BONTE
Translated from the French by Jenny Doster

Ahmose I (fl. sixteenth century BCE), Egyptian pharaoh (reigned 1550–1525 BCE), son of the Seventeenth-Dynasty king Sekenenre Taa II and his consort Ahhotep, expelled the Hyksos kings from Egypt and reunited his divided country. In honor of this achievement the historian Manetho recognized him as the first king of the Eighteenth Dynasty, and the first king of the New Kingdom.

The Second Intermediate Period (c. 1650–1550 BCE) saw Egypt split in two. The Canaanite Hyksos dynasty controlled the north from the delta city of Avaris, while the insignificant Egyptian kings of the Sixteenth Dynasty controlled the south from Thebes. Immediately to the south of Egypt, the Nubians were hostile to the Thebans, and allied with the Hyksos.

A change of Theban royal family saw the start of the Seventeenth Dynasty, and the first serious challenge to Hyksos domination. King Sekenenre Taa II (r. c. 1560) probably fell in battle; his hastily mummified body displays head wounds inflicted by a Hyksos battle-ax. Sekenenre Taa II had married his sister Ahhotep, and she had given him four children; two daughters (Ahmose-Nefertari and Ahmose-Nebta) and two sons, both named Ahmose. It was the younger Ahmose who would eventually succeed his father, but first the crown passed to Kamose, a man with no proven link to Sekenenre Taa II. When, three years later, Kamose died (possibly another victim of the battlefield), Ahmose I succeeded him. At the same time the Hyksos king Apepi was succeeded by Khamudi.

Following Egyptian tradition, Ahhotep acted as regent for her son. On a stela recovered from Karnak, Ahmose described his mother as "one who has taken care of Egypt . . . she has pacified Upper Egypt, and expelled her rebels." This suggests that Ahhotep fought in defense of Thebes, an assumption that is supported by Ahhotep's burial equipment, which included a ceremonial axe, a gold dagger and sheath, and three golden flies of valor, the "medal" used to reward Egyptian soldiers.

Eleven years after inheriting his throne, Ahmose determined to reunify Egypt. His campaign is detailed in the autobiography inscribed in the el-Kab tomb of the soldier Ahmose, son of Ibana. The Theban army slowly forced its way northward. Avaris was besieged and eventually fell, and the Hyksos retreated into Palestine. Three years later, after another lengthy siege, Ahmose captured the Palestinian city of Sharuhen (near Gaza) and established a buffer zone that would discourage an eastern invasion. With his eastern border secure Ahmose reconfirmed his control over Nubia and suppressed two further insurrections, a small rebellion led by the foreigner Aata, and a potentially far more serious rebellion led by the Egyptian Teti-an.

With unity restored, trade links reestablished, and regular "tribute" from the eastern and southern territories, Egypt grew rich. A professional civil service was developed to provide a support for the expanding empire, and a professional army was established to defend its borders. Building works started along the Nile Valley, and Thebes, Memphis, and Abydos all benefited from Ahmose's generosity. Unfortunately Ahmose's workmen built mainly in mud-brick and most of his buildings are now lost.

Ahmose rewarded the local governors who had supported him against the Hyksos, and he rewarded the god Amen, the patron deity of Thebes and the inspiration behind his victories. An unprecedented series of offerings made Amen the wealthiest of Egyptian gods, while his Karnak temple was extensively refurbished. As Memphis continued to serve as the northern administrative center, Thebes now became Egypt's southern and religious capital.

Ahmose married both his sisters, and Ahmose-Nefertari became his consort. She bore many titles including King's Daughter, King's Sister, King's Great Wife, and God's Wife of Amen. The Donation Stela, recovered from the Karnak temple, tells us that Ahmose purchased the Second Priesthood of Amen to provide Ahmose-Nefertari with an endowment that was to be held by the queen and her descendents forever. A third religious position, Divine Adoratrice, brought her even more independent wealth.

After a quarter of a century on the throne Ahmose died and was buried beneath a small pyramid in the Dra Abu el-Naga cemetery. His son Amenhotep I took the throne under the guidance of Ahmose-Nefertari.

[*See also* Manetho.]

BIBLIOGRAPHY

Bourriau, J. "The Second Intermediate Period." In *The Oxford History of Ancient Egypt*, edited by Ian Shaw, pp. 184–217. Oxford and New York: Oxford University Press, 2000.

Bryan, B. M. "The Eighteenth Dynasty Before the Amarna Period." In *The Oxford History of Ancient Egypt*, edited by Ian Shaw, pp. 218–271. Oxford and New York: Oxford University Press, 2000.

Tyldesley, Joyce A. *The Pharaohs*. London: Quercus, 2009.

JOYCE TYLDESLEY

Aho, Justin (d. after 1962), Beninese political leader and historian, was born sometime in the late nineteenth century into a powerful Wegbaja family. His family claimed descent from Glele, the powerful ruler of the Dahomey Kingdom in the late nineteenth century.

Despite his important role in colonial politics and anthropological research in Benin from the 1930s until the 1950s, little published work sheds light on his early background. Aho served in the French military as a young man and spoke and wrote fluently in French. He probably received his primary and secondary education in Benin. Aho's entrance into politics came during the turbulent 1920s and early 1930s. Benin, known under French rule as the colony of Dahomey, became home to a small but very vocal movement of Western-educated African urban elites who called for improved legal and political rights for coastal Beninese elites. From the turn of the twentieth century to 1945, the vast majority of Beninese people did not have the right to vote and were governed by the strict *indigènat* legal code. While some activists such as Louis Hunkanrin were jailed for demanding legal reforms, others chose to closely collaborate with the French colonial government. Aho fell into the latter category.

Protests in the southern Beninese city of Porto-Novo in 1923 over high taxes and the creation of a lively opposition press deeply disturbed colonial officials. Dieudonné Reste, the governor of Dahomey from 1929 to 1930, sought out supposedly legitimate traditional leaders to counterbalance the growing influence of anticolonial dissidents. He reformed the institution of state-appointed chieftaincies. Henceforth, state-appointed chiefs were given high salaries rather than drawing their income from a part of the total amount of the taxes they collected. Aho volunteered to become the chief of the old Dahoman capital of Abomey. Reste considered Aho to be the most able of all the chiefs he hired, and Aho used his position as a means of obtaining several different administrative posts. Governor Reste's successors in the 1930s and 1940s heaped praise on Aho. The Beninese chief claimed to be the true heir to the throne of Dahomey and set about making legal claims on land seized by the French government from the old kingdom during its conquest in the early 1890s. Aho used this land to grow palm products and made a sizable fortune. He also tried with some success to monopolize access to advanced education to members of his own family.

Over the course of the 1930s, some nationalists chose to ally themselves with Aho. For example, the noted historian and novelist Paul Hazoumé gave speeches with Aho on Bastille Day 1935 in praise of French rule. However, Western-educated Beninese people made numerous legal complaints about

Aho's abuses of power. He overcame a serious legal challenge in 1936 and even managed to receive a promotion. Rumors spread among some of his subjects that he had secretly ordered the human sacrifice of a young girl named Télé Akapovi who had disappeared. A low-ranking colonial official investigated these charges, but Aho was ultimately exonerated. Aho allowed the noted American anthropologist Melville Herskovits to conduct research on Fon culture in the 1930s and 1940s, and Aho's brother René became Herskovits's main informant. René Aho provided oral narratives that justified Justin's claim to be the true king of Dahomey, a view not shared by most members of the sizable royal family.

When the French Fourth Republic allowed Africans to form political parties and receive limited representation in the French parliament, Aho's days as a tyrannical powerbroker had to adjust to the new political climate. He served, like his brother René, as an informant for various French anthropologists and permitted researchers to photograph and record ceremonies held at his court and allowed the old royal palace at Abomey to become a museum. Aho chose to back Sourou Migan Apithy's Parti Républicain Dahomey (PRD) in the 1950s against the more popular candidate among Fon-speaking communities, Justin Ahomadégbé's Union Démocratique du Dahomé (UDD). Although independence made state-appointed chiefs like Aho relatively powerless, he continued to claim to historians such as I. A. Akinjogbin that he was still the true king. It is unclear when and how Aho died, although he was still alive in 1962, when he met Akinjogbin in Paris. Aho's careful self-representations of a modern king proved valuable in the late colonial period to promote his own interests, but his support for researchers helped develop scholarship on the kingdom of Dahomey.

[See also Glele; and Hazoumé, Paul.]

BIBLIOGRAPHY

Akinjogbin, I. A. *Dahomey and Its Neighbors, 1708–1818.* Cambridge, UK: Cambridge University Press, 1967.

Manning, Patrick. *Slavery, Colonialism and Economic Growth in Dahomey, 1640–1960.* New York: Cambridge University Press, 1982.

Staniland, Martin. "The Three-Party System in Dahomey: II, 1956–1957." *Journal of African History* 14, no. 3 (1973): 491–503.

JEREMY RICH

Ahomadégbé-Tometin, Justin (1917–2002), Beninese politician, was born on 16 January 1917 in Abomey, the former capital of the kingdom of Dahomey, which was then part of French West Africa. He claimed to be a member of the large Dahoman royal family through his mother. During his political career, he would highlight this connection to obtain support from members of his own Fon ethnic community. Ahomadégbé came from a relatively affluent family. He attended primary school in Abomey and then was admitted into the prestigious École William Ponty secondary school in Dakar, Senegal. École William Ponty was widely regarded as the best secondary school in French West Africa during the colonial period. After passing his baccalaureate examinations, he went to dentistry school at the School of Medicine in Dakar. With the advent of World War II in 1939, Ahomadégbé served in the French army and attained the rank of sergeant before France's defeat in 1940. After he was demobilized, Ahomadégbé returned home and started his own practice as a dentist in the southeastern coastal town of Porto Novo. He was one of a handful of African medical professionals in Benin prior to independence in 1960.

After World War II, the French government's colonial reforms established territorial assemblies in each African colony and gave each African colony limited representation in the French parliament in Paris. Ahomadégbé joined the first Beninese political party, the Union Progressiste Dahoméene, in 1945. However, he almost immediately quit to form his own party, the Bloc Populaire Africaine. In 1952, he was elected as a representative in the Beninese territorial assembly. Four years later, he was elected mayor of Abomey and formed a new party with his future rival Emile Zinsou, the Union Démocratique Dahoméene (UDD). Ahomadégbé joined the UDD to the large Rassemblement Démocratique Africaine coalition of political parties in French African colonies. Ahomadégbé presented himself as the radical alternative to his more moderate rivals Sourou-Migan Apithy and Hubert Maga. The struggles between these three politicians would dominate Beninese politics for the next sixteen years. Apithy made southeastern Benin his fiefdom, while the north constituted Maga's center of power. Ahomadégbé also gained backing for closely associating himself with the old Dahomey kingdom and by playing up his supposed mystical resources. His rivals dubbed him "the monster" or "the wizard," which only further developed his reputation for supernatural force.

In the 1957 and 1959 legislative elections, Ahomadégbé's party grew more popular at the expense of Apithy. Maga then briefly made an alliance with Ahomadégbé in 1959, but this deal quickly fell apart in the following year. In 1960, Benin gained its independence. Ahomadégbé tried to use strikes in 1960 and his own position as president of the Beninese parliament as the means by which he could overthrow Maga and become president of Benin. Maga joined with Apithy to block Ahomadégbé's ambitions. In 1961, Ahomadégbé's UDD party was banned by the Beninese government, and Maga even had Ahomadégbé jailed on the grounds that Ahomadégbé had conspired to assassinate the president. Although this show trial actually allowed Ahomadégbé legal counsel, he was found guilty. In November 1962, Maga released Ahomadégbé from prison.

Ahomadégbé's incarceration had hardly cooled his appetite for power. He plotted with members of the military and the Beninese government to overthrow Maga. Apithy decided to support Ahomadégbé once Maga had stripped Apithy of the position of vice president in early 1963. At the end of 1963, the Beninese military under officer Christophe Soglo drove Maga from power. In the new government, Apithy became president and Ahomadégbé was named vice president. This new alliance rapidly deteriorated in 1964 and 1965. Ahomadégbé sought out military backing to push Apithy from the presidency. Ahomadégbé had promoted the idea of a single-party state since 1960, and naturally his rivals wanted nothing to do with this idea. By the summer of 1965, Apithy and Ahomadégbé's struggle had so divided the government that it could not function. Some members of the parliament proclaimed Ahomadégbé president in November 1965 and forced Apithy to resign, even as many protestors took to the streets of the Beninese capital of Cotonou against this act. Christophe Soglo again led the Beninese military in a coup in December 1965 against Ahomadégbé. His later flight from prison through the marshes of the Togolese-Beninese border to exile greatly damaged his reputation for mystical power. Many of his former supporters questioned Ahomadégbé's royal lineage and argued that the spiritual forces associated with the old Dahomey kingdom never would have allowed a favored son to suffer such indignities.

Ahomadégbé made his way to Paris, where he once again returned to political intrigue. Bitter at the fact that his former protégé Emile Zinsou became the civilian face of the military junta that took power in 1967, Ahomadégbé tried to engineer his return to power through his connections in the Beninese military. The military held presidential elections in 1968 but refused to allow Ahomadégbé to run. When Ahomadégbé's associate Basile Adjou Moumouni won the election, the military refused to honor the results. Various military factions had become so divided by 1970 that they agreed to bring Ahomadégbé, Apithy, and Maga back to run against each other. The results were disastrous. All three candidates employed violence against each other and their supporters. Finally, the warring candidates agreed to a complicated system in which each leader would serve as president for two years. After Hubert Maga's term as president ended in May 1972, Ahomadégbé took office. An economic recession combined with rampant corruption and continued military plots spelled doom for Ahomadégbé's return to the presidency. Military officers led by Mathieu Kérékou overthrew and jailed Ahomadégbé. He stayed in prison for the next nine years. Once he was freed, Ahomadégbé went into exile in Paris until Kérékou agreed to democratic elections in 1990. Although Ahomadégbé was now too old by Beninese law to run for president again, he held a seat in parliament from 1991 to 1995. He continued to lead his UDD party until his death in Cotonou on 8 March 2002.

[See also Apithy, Sourou Migan; Kérékou, Chaad Mathieu; Maga, Coutoucou Hubert; and Soglo, Christophe.]

BIBLIOGRAPHY

Banégas, Richard. *La démocratie à pas de caméléon: Transition et imaginaires politiques au Bénin*. Paris: Karthala, 2003.

Claffey, Patrick. "Kérékou the Chameleon, Master of Myth." In *Staging Politics: Power and Performance in Asia and Africa*, edited by Julia Strauss and Donal Brian Cruise O'Brien, pp. 91–110. London: I.B. Tauris, 2007.

Decalo, Samuel. *Historical Dictionary of Benin*, 3d ed. Lanham, Md.: Scarecrow, 1995.

Ronen, Dov. *Dahomey: Between Tradition and Modernity*. Ithaca, N.Y.: Cornell University Press, 1975.

JEREMY RICH

Aidid, Mohammed Farah (1934–1996), Somali politicomilitary leader who played a central role in the collapse of the state and the large-scale violence against civilians that accompanied it, was born in the Mudug region of Somalia, into the Habr Gidir clan. His name is also spelled Maxamed Faarax Caydiid. Little is known about his early life, other than that he served with the Italian colonial police force and in the 1950s received some training in Italy and in the Soviet Union. He served under Somalian president Mohamed Siyad Barre, rising to the rank of general. He was involved in the Ogaden War of 1977–1978, in which Somalia tried and failed to take over what is now Ethiopia's Region Five and is largely populated by Somalis.

In the 1980s Aidid began to turn against Siyad Barre, and when the president suspected him of plotting against him, he imprisoned Aidid for six years. As was the case of many who challenged the president, Barre eventually released him and removed him from Somalia by promoting him to a lucrative position, in this case an ambassadorship to India, from which he resigned in June 1989.

In December 1989 Aidid arrived in Addis Ababa and, with Ethiopian support and in close collaboration with the Somali National Movement that was fighting the military regime in Somalia's northwest regions, began to lead the militias of his own branch of the newly established United Somali Congress (USC) against Barre's regime in Mogadishu. Aidid is widely regarded as being responsible for the transformation of the struggle of opposition movements against the military regime into a campaign of clan cleansing. Aidid's forces targeted several different classes, most notably the Darod clan, of which Barre was a member. In the eyes of human rights groups and scholars, as well as many Somalis, Aidid was guilty of crimes against humanity (just as the leader of the military regime he helped overthrow was guilty of war crimes and human rights violations). Together with Ali Mahdi, leader of another branch of the USC and selected as interim president at the national reconciliation meetings in Djibouti in 1991, Aidid has been held responsible for the extended militia warfare that broke out within the USC and claimed the lives of an estimated thirty thousand people in Mogadishu alone.

When the United States, as part of the United Nations' peacekeeping force, intervened in Somalia at the height of a devastating famine in December 1992, Special Envoy Robert B. Oakley briefly courted Aidid, apparently hoping that the general would be able to defeat the other warlords. However, when developments did not go his way, General Aidid turned against the United Nations and the United States, which in turn held him responsible for the deaths of twenty-four Pakistani soldiers in 1992. Anti-American sentiment was further fueled by a devastating air attack by US fighter helicopters on a house where Aidid's advisers were trying to persuade him to make peace with the United Nations and the United States. Matters came to a head with a humiliating American defeat on 3 October 1993, when Somali forces killed eighteen US Army Rangers who were trying to capture Aidid. The image of an American soldier being dragged through the streets of Mogadishu prompted American policy makers to disengage from Somalia. That decision would have repercussions beyond Somalia's borders, notably in 1994, when the Bill Clinton administration chose not to intervene in the Rwanda genocide.

After the Americans left Somalia in 1995, Aidid briefly claimed the contested interim presidency as different militias fought over the economic resources of what had once been the Somali state. In August 1996 Aidid died as the result of wounds suffered in a gun battle in the streets of Mogadishu. His son Hussein Mohamed Farah, who had been educated in the United States and had joined the US Marines, serving in Somalia in the 1990s, succeeded his father and continued his struggle for the domination of Somalia.

[*See also* Siyad Barre, Mohamed.]

BIBLIOGRAPHY

Hirsch, John L., and Robert B. Oakley. *Somalia and Operation Restore Hope: Reflections on Peacemaking and Peacekeeping.* Washington, D.C.: United States Institute of Peace Press, 1995.

Mukhtar, Mohamed Haji. *Historical Dictionary of Somalia.* New ed. Lanham, Md.: Scarecrow Press, 2003.

Ruhela, Satya Pal, ed. *Mohammed Farah Aidid and His Vision of Somalia.* New Delhi, India: Vikas Publishing House, 1994.

KATHLEEN SHELDON

Aidoo, Ama Ata (1942–), Ghanaian poet, playwright, and short-story writer, was born Christina Ama Aidoo in a village in central Ghana, in either 1940 or 1942 (sources differ). Her father, Yaw Fama, was a local ruler and an educator who opened the first local school and encouraged his daughter to attend. By the time she was a teenager, she was writing poems and short stories, and she has said that she knew from an early age that she wanted to be a writer. Her first story, "To Us a Child Is Born," was published in 1958, when it won a prize sponsored by *The Daily Graphic*, a leading Ghanaian newspaper. She attended Wesley Girls High School in Cape Coast and the University of Ghana at Legon. In 1962 she attended the African Writers' Workshop at Nigeria's University of Ibadan, the result of a contest to which she had submitted "No Sweetness Here," one of her first short stories. She later earned a fellowship that allowed her to study creative writing at Stanford University in California, returning to Ghana in 1969.

One of Aidoo's earliest publications was a play, *Dilemma of a Ghost*, that was staged at the University of Ghana at Legon by the Students' Theatre in 1964. The play presents the conflict that develops when a young Ghanaian man returns from studies in the United States with his African American wife. She became more widely known with the story collection *No Sweetness Here* (1970) and the novels *Our Sister Killjoy Or Reflections from a Black-Eyed Squint* (1977) and *Changes: A Love Story* (1991), which won the 1992 Commonwealth Writers Prize (Africa region). She has focused on issues of cultural change and women's position in a modernizing society. In *Changes* the main character, Esi, is a professional woman in Accra who finds love with a married man, whom she marries herself, entering into a polygamous relationship. Some of Esi's friends react with shock and believe modern women who consider themselves feminists should never accept a polygamous marriage, while others see the value of turning to particularly African forms of love and family. Aidoo, in foregrounding this contradictory modern woman's choices, suggests that African culture will prevail over feminism in some instances, though the outcome is deliberately ambiguous. *Changes* has been the focus of a great deal of analysis by literary and women's studies scholars as a result. Aidoo also published essays, including the widely anthologized "To Be a Woman," which "qualifies easily as a manifesto of African feminism" (Allan, 1993).

Aidoo taught at universities in Kenya and Tanzania in 1968 and 1969; it was during that time that she had a relationship with the Kenyan biochemist Ernest Parsali Likimani (d. 1980), and they had a daughter, Kinna. Aidoo went on to coordinate the African Literature Programme at Cape Coast from 1972 to 1982. She briefly served as Ghana's minister of education from 1982 to 1983 but found herself in conflict with Ghanaian political authorities and moved to Harare, Zimbabwe, in 1983, where she lived for several years. She has taught at several American universities, including Oberlin College, the University of Richmond, and Xavier University in New Orleans. She had a visiting position as a professor of Africana studies and literary arts at Brown University from 2003 to 2010.

BIBLIOGRAPHY

Ahmad, Hena. *Postnational Feminisms: Postcolonial Identities and Cosmopolitanism in the Works of Kamala Markandaya, Tsitsi Dangarembga, Ama Ata Aidoo, and Anita Desai*. American University Studies, series 27, Feminist studies, vol. 8. New York: Peter Lang, 2010. Literary analysis of Aidoo's *Changes*.

Allan, Tuzyline Jita. Afterword to *Changes: A Love Story*, by Ama Ata Aidoo. New York: Feminist Press at the City University of New York, 1993.

Azodo, Ada Uzoamaka, and Gay Alden Wilentz, eds. *Emerging Perspectives on Ama Ata Aidoo*. Trenton, N.J.: Africa World Press, 1998.

Odamtten, Vincent O. *The Art of Ama Ata Aidoo: Polylectics and Reading against Neocolonialism*. Gainesville: University Press of Florida, 1994.

Wehrs, Donald R. *African Feminist Fiction and Indigenous Values*. Gainesville: University Press of Florida, 2001. Wehrs devotes a chapter to Aidoo's novel *Changes*.

KATHLEEN SHELDON

Akale Weld (1831–1919), Ethiopian traditional scholar, was born to Memher Sertse Weld and Wolete Kiros in Wabet, a rural village in north Shewa. He began his schooling at his home under his father. He left Wabet for Wadla and later Lasta, where he studied chant (*zema*) and Geez poetry (*qene*). His most significant ecclesiastical scholarship studies took place in Gonder, where he was certified in the four departments of the traditional Amharic commentary of scripture and church literature, namely, Old Testament (at Beata Mariam Church), New Testament (at Atatami Mikael Church), the Books of Scholars (at Elfign Giorgis Church), and the Books of Monks (at Hamere Noah Selestu Me'et Church). Throughout his study period, he taught *qene* at Yohannes Welde Negodgwad Church in Gonder.

When Emperor Tewodros II held court in Debre Tabor, it was customary that priests, teachers, and other higher dignitaries of the church in Gonder travel there to pay tribute. As one of the celebrated scholars in the town, Memher Akale Weld came to be acquainted with the emperor. Akale Weld's deep knowledge of scripture and wisdom in analyzing cases helped him to maintain a good friendship with the emperor. Emperor Tewodros was quite impressed by the excellence of the scholar and made him a member of his court. His respect and admiration is recorded in his famous couplet in which he compared Akale Weld with his famous chief commander and reliable hero Fitawrari Gebrie: "yimarutal ende Akaliye yiwagutal ende Gebrie" (As scholarly as Akaliye, as courageous as Gebrie). When Emperor Tewodros moved his seat to Makdela, Akale Weld accompanied him but soon left because of the emperor's quarrel with the majority of church clergy. He went to the Monastery of Debre Dimah in Gojjam and revised the commentary of books according to the tradition of the *lay bet* (upper house) style of Amharic commentary tradition, which is still famous in the area.

When Menilek II visited Shewa, Akale Weld returned to his native province to congratulate the emperor. He was welcomed by Menilek and named head of the church of Kundi Giorgis and later Firkuta Kidane Meheret. It was at this time that he played the most significant role in securing harmony between the emperors Menilek II and Yohannes. Besides his role as an active negotiator, Akale Weld initiated the re-Christianization of the Wello region, which had turned to Islam during the jihad waged by Ahmad ibn Ibrahim al-Ghazi in the fifteenth century. Both emperors agreed with his project and appointed him teacher and theologian of Wello. He founded Debre Berhan Boru Selassie as a center of educational excellence, which attracted numerous students from all over Ethiopia.

With the support of the Christianized rulers of the region, namely, Abba Watew (Haile Mariam) and Ras Ali (Ras Mikael), Akale Weld intensified the evangelization of Welo by sending his students into different places. He survived several assassination attempts by local Muslims who opposed his missionary activities in converting the people to Christianity. Besides his mission in Welo he also promoted doctrinal harmony and peace within the church in support of its missionary activities.

He was one of the influential scholars during the council of Boru Meda in 1878, which was convened to end doctrinal differences within the church. The major differences, which arose from the understanding of the divinity of Jesus Christ, were *sega* or *śost Ledet* (grace), which was the doctrine influenced by Debre Libanos (Shewa); *qebat* (unction), the doctrine supported by scholars of Gojjam; and the *sega* (grace), which was promoted by the Gonderines. These three positions were opposed to the established *tewahedo* (union) doctrine, which Akale Weld favored.

The majority of the Ethiopian archbishops who were ordained for some years after the church became autonomous were his pupils. Akale Weld died a natural death on 19 November 1919 and was buried in Boru Selassie.

[*See also* Ahmad ibn Ibrahim al-Ghazi; Menilek II; *and* Tewodros II.]

BIBLIOGRAPHY

Ahmed, Hussein. *Islam in Nineteenth-Century Wallo: Ethiopian Revival, Reform, and Reaction*. Leiden: Brill, 2001.

Aklilu, Amsalu. Akalä Wäld. In *Encyclopedia Aethiopica*, edited by Siegbert Uhlig. Vol. 1, p. 165. Wiesbaden, Germany: Harrassowitz Verlag, 2003.

Alehegne, Mersha. *Zena pappasat ityopyawyan* [*History of the Ethiopian Patriarchs*]. Addis Ababa: Mahibere Kidusan, 2004.

Caulk, Richard A. "Religion and the State in Nineteenth Century Ethiopia." *Journal of Ethiopian Studies* 10, no. 1 (1972): 23–42.

MERSHA ALEHEGNE

Aké, Claude (1939–1996), Nigerian professor of political science, was born in Omoku, Rivers state, Nigeria, on 18 February 1939. His father, Geoffrey Aké, was a politician, and his mother, Christiana, was a trader. His wife was named Anita; they had two sons. Aké attended Kings College, Lagos, and the University of Ibadan in Nigeria, then studied at the University of London and Columbia University in New York City, in 1962 and 1963, respectively. He earned a PhD from Columbia in 1966. Thereafter he enjoyed an academic career at different universities across the world. Aké served as an assistant professor of political science at Columbia University between 1966 and 1969, as associate professor, Carleton University, Ottawa, Canada, from 1969 to 1972, and as a visiting lecturer at the University of Nairobi, from 1970 to 1972, and the University of Dar Es Salaam, from 1972 to 1974. He was dean of the faculty of social sciences, University of Port Harcourt, Nigeria, from 1975 to 1989, visiting fellow at Oxford University in 1982, and the founder and pioneering director of the Centre for Advanced Social Sciences (CASS) at Port Harcourt from 1991 to 1996. Shortly before his death in 1996 Aké was a visiting lecturer at Yale University.

Claude Aké was a prolific writer who contributed immensely to the field of political science, notably in the political economy of Africa, political theory, and development studies. His major and groundbreaking publications include *A Theory of Political Integration* (1967), *Revolutionary Pressures in Africa* (1978), *Social Sciences as Imperialism: A Theory of Political Development* (1979), *A Political Economy of Africa* (1981), *The Political Economy of Crisis and Underdevelopment in Africa: Selected Works of Claude Aké* (1989), *The New World Order: A View from the South* (1992), *Democratisation of Disempowerment in Africa* (1994), *The Marginalisation of Africa: Notes on a Productive Confusion* (1996), and *Democracy and Development in Africa* (1996). His edited works include *Contemporary Nigeria: A Political Economy* (1984) and *Political Economy of Nigeria* (1985), among others. Aké also contributed numerous scholarly researched articles in local and internationally reputable journals and monographs. These include "Ideology and Objective Conditions" (1979), "Indigenisation: Problems of Transformation in a Neo-colonial Economy" (1985), and "Rethinking African Democracy" (1991). Notable among his monographs for the Centre for Advance Social Sciences was "Is Africa Democratising?" (1996).

Aké devoted the greatest part of his academic and intellectual writings to highlighting the sustainable development in Africa, poor leadership, poverty, illiteracy and inequality, injustice, rule of law, and democratization. Aké believed that African political leaders and intellectuals played prominent roles in its economic misfortunes. He thus emphasized the need for African leaders to pursue self-reliant development. African countries could achieve prosperity, Aké argued, through "people-centered" development policies that mobilized the vast majority of the population.

In addition to his life as a globetrotting scholar, Aké was an active participant in economic development efforts in his homeland. While a lecturer at Port Harcourt, Aké trained many young Nigerians and other Africans in the field of political science. During his long tenure as dean of the faculty of social sciences, the university became a hub of intellectual activity, with faculty members hosting a series of conferences and seminars.

Aké believed that political participation by the majority in politics and governance is a catalyst to societal transformation. He viewed politics as too serious a business to be left in the hands of a privileged few. It was based on this conviction that in 1989 Aké participated in the formation of a political association called People's Solidarity Party (PSP). The PSP sought to register as an official political party, but it was denied by the military government of General Ibrahim Badamasi Babangida. Consequently, Aké abandoned partisan politics and returned back to his roots, focusing on intellectual matters and scholarship.

Aké was also a passionate advocate of human rights and environmental protection. Growing up and spending much of his career in the rapidly industrializing and environmentally fragile Niger Delta had a strong influence over his human rights and environmental activism. He worked closely with the prominent Nigerian environmentalist Ken Saro-Wiwa to campaign against environmental pollution and degradation caused by oil companies operating in the Niger Delta area. Encouraged by Saro-Wiwa, from 1990 to 1995 Aké served on a commission set up by the Royal Dutch/Shell Oil Company to study the environmental impact of oil exploration activities on the Niger Delta. He resigned from the commission following Saro-Wiwa's execution by a military tribunal of General Sani Abacha's government. His resignation from the commission provided him with freedom to criticize both the activities of Shell Oil Company and the military government for not giving adequate attention and compensation to the people of the Niger Delta who had been economically, politically, and socially affected by environmental pollution.

A firm believer in revolutionary change in African societies, Aké was influenced by traditional Marxian theorists, such as Karl Marx, Frederick Engels, Vladimir Lenin, and Mao Tse-tung, as well as Neo-Marxists, such as Andre Gunder Frank. In his studies of African countries, Aké argued that there was a wide class disparity among African people. For him, elites in Africa misappropriated their positions to continue to exploit and dominate the mass of their peoples. In his 1978 book *Revolutionary Pressures in Africa*, Aké foresaw and predicted a revolution by the oppressed in different parts of African societies. However, the Marxian revolution predicted by Aké did not occur in his lifetime, and it appeared even less likely in the years after his death, in the face of competing ideologies of fundamentalist religion and free market capitalism in most African countries, notably Nigeria. The hardworking Aké combined both intellectualism and consultancy services. He offered consultancy services to international organizations, such as the World Bank, United Nations Development Programme (UNDP), United Nations Economic Commission, African Development Bank (ADB), and International Development Research Centre, Canada, among others.

Aké's scholarship won him several national and international awards. He was a member of the Social Science Council of New York, UNESCO, and won a Council for the Development of Social Sciences in Africa (CODESRIA) award. The federal government of Nigeria awarded Aké the highest academic honor for excellence: the National Merit Award for scholarship in 1992. Aké also won a Martin Luther King Award and was a Rockefeller Scholar and a Woodrow Wilson Scholar from 1985 to 1986. His *Political Economy of Africa* (1987) earned him a Choice Book award in the United States. Aké's final projects were on violence and ethnicity in Africa. His last book project, *Democracy and Development in Africa*, was published posthumously by the Brooking Institution in Washington, DC, in 1997. Several scholarships and awards have been established in Aké's name. These include an annual memorial award program and annual lecture funded by the Ford Foundation and the Claude Aké Award for Excellence in Political Science.

Within the international and national academic communities, Aké was held in high esteem for his contributions to scholarship. In the words of the scholar Aaron T. Gana (2003), Aké was "certainly the most quoted African political scientist; he bestrode the international social science community like a dinosaur." For every student of political science in Nigeria and Africa in general, Aké's work was indispensable. He was also immensely popular with graduate and undergraduate students both in Africa and abroad.

Aké died in a plane crash on 7 November 1996 while returning from a conference on conflict resolution in Africa organized by the Centre for Advance Social Sciences (CASS). An obituary appeared in the *New York Times* on 19 November 1996. Following his death David Apter, chair of the Yale Council on African Studies, described Aké as a scholar of "crackling intelligence and an outspokenly severe view of African politics and nevertheless, underneath that, a quality of understanding which was remarkably subtle and complex. But he was able to communicate the complexity in a straightforward manner." Ake was, in Apter's view, "Africa's leading political scientist—and its most courageous" (cited in Mwalino).

[*See also* Abacha, Sani; Babangida, Ibrahim Badamosi; *and* Saro-Wiwa, Ken.]

BIBLIOGRAPHY

Gana, A. T. "Claude Ake: A Tribute." In *Democracy and Development in Africa*, by Claude Ake.

Abuja, Nigeria: Spectrum Books Limited, 2003.

Mittelman, J. H. "A Tribute to Claude Ake." *Issue: A Journal of Opinion* 25, no. 1 (1997): 3–4.

Mwalino, W. "An Interview with Claude Ake." *West Africa Review*, 2, no. 1 (2000).

SULAIMAN Y. BALARABE KURA

Akhenaten (fl. fourteenth century BCE), pharaoh of Egypt during the Eighteenth Dynasty (c. 1377–1359 BCE; Low date: 1352–1334 BCE), was the son of Amenhotep (Amenophis) III and Queen Tiye (Teya). He was named after his father and succeeded to the throne initially as Amenophis IV.

Akhenaten was one of six children born to the royal couple, four girls and two boys. His older brother, Thutmose, destined for the throne as heir apparent, and his older sister, Sat-Amun, claimed their father's affection from an early age, and, as was customary for a crown prince, Thutmose took up duties as high priest of Ptah in Memphis. Perhaps because of his unsightly appearance, Akhenaten was deprived of the attention his parents might have shown, and little care was taken in assigning an entourage of companions. His main tutor was an otherwise unknown Parennefer, who hailed from a small town, rather than the capital. When the court abandoned the capital at Memphis and took up residence at the southern city of Thebes, in about Amenhotep III's twenty-ninth year, the young prince took part in the move, and was given an apartment in his father's new palace at Malqata.

The sudden death of his older brother catapulted Akhenaten into the position of heir apparent. He may have taken part in one of his father's three jubilees, celebrated in years 30, 32, and 36, but for the most part he remained an unknown quantity to his contemporaries. When his father succumbed to a grievous sickness in his thirty-eighth year, the young prince, probably in his mid- to late teens, succeeded to the throne as Nefer-khepru-re-wa-en-re, Amenophis the divine, ruler of Thebes.

The first five years of the new reign were signalized by dramatic changes in art and the belief system. For the first year the king is shown with his mother, the dowager queen Tiye, offering to the gods and performing acts customary to the imperial kingship. As was the practice of the times, the king's facial likeness, in Akhenaten's case a gaunt, horselike profile, was used by sculptors in their depiction of the gods. Very early in the reign the king married the beautiful Nefertiti, of unknown origin but probably somehow related to the royal family, and two daughters, Meretaten and Meketaten, were born in rapid succession. In his second year the king convened his court and made a dramatic announcement to the effect that he had experienced a revelation: all the gods, whom he claimed to have known intimately, have now all stopped, and only the sun continues as an active force in the universe. A building program was immediately set in motion in order to create, at Thebes, four new temples to the sun god in his form of the Living Sun-disk. One was dedicated to Nefertiti, two to the royal couple, and the largest was given over to a celebration of the jubilee planned for year 3. As the gods had now been relegated to oblivion, they would no longer require temple service, and so their incomes and personnel were diverted to the new sun temples, and religious art was purged of the mythological symbolism now deemed otiose and irrelevant. The new sole god, the Sun-disk, was denied any anthropomorphic representation in art in favor of a simple circle, from which sticklike arms splay down on the head of the king, now termed "the beautiful child of the Disk."

The king cryptically refers to criticism leveled against him in his second and fourth years; and by the beginning of his fifth year he was determined to abandon Thebes, a city redolent of the person and worship of the great king of the gods, Amun. Before departing, however, he mounted a program of general defacement of the name and images of Amun and changed his name from "Amenophis" to "Akhenaten" (useful for the Sun-disk). The king's choice for a new site identified a broad plain in Middle Egypt, on the eastern side of the Nile opposite Hermopolis, and here at the behest of the Sun-disk himself a new city took shape, Akhetaten, "the horizon of the Sun-disk." Here Akhenaten was free to indulge himself in the contemplation of his father the Sun-disk and to fashion a court and government from the new men, the nonentities, who had followed him to the new capital. Large sun temples centered upon sun courts and open to the sky, rapidly took shape, and sprawling country-style villas arose in surrounding suburbs. A broad north-south avenue, running from the king's palace in the north, connected the new city with the world beyond Egypt's borders.

Akhenaten's revolution produced no "religion" to be preached with evangelical fervor to the world, but rather a private statement of the king's relationship to his father, the sun, and how the latter created and sustained the cosmos. The king promulgated a "teaching" to his inner circle, but this has not come down to us. To the end he remained adamantly opposed to polytheism and its symbolism and to mythology.

The end of Akhenaten's reign is shrouded in darkness. Nefertiti may have fallen from favor, and we hear of another wife, Kiya. Of his six daughters only the first and third survived him, the latter to marry Tutankhamen, who may have been a half brother and who succeeded his father-in-law. The heretic king died in his seventeenth or early eighteenth year and was probably for a short time interred in a tomb he had carved for himself in the eastern mountains. He had left the country in a shambles economically, with government corruption rife, and was ever afterward to be remembered as "that enemy of Akhetaten." Shortly, in all probability, his body was taken back to Thebes, where it may have been secreted in a hastily prepared tomb in the Valley of the Kings.

[*See also* Amenhotep III; Nefertiti; Tiye; *and* Tutankhamen.]

BIBLIOGRAPHY

Aldred, Cyril. *Akhenaten, King of Egypt.* London: Thames and Hudson, 1988.

Redford, Donald B. *Akhenaten, the Heretic King.* 2d ed. Princeton, N.J.: Princeton University Press, 2009.

Reeves, Nicholas. *Akhenaten, Egypt's False Prophet.* London: Thames and Hudson, 2001.

Silverman, David P., Josef W. Wegner, and Jennifer Houser Wegner. *Akhenaten and Tutankhamun: Revolution and Restoration.* Philadelphia: University of Pennsylvania Museum of Archaeology and Anthropology, 2006.

DONALD B. REDFORD

Akintunde-Ighodalo, Folayegbe Mosunmola

(1923–2005), pioneering Nigerian feminist, civil servant, and democratic activist, was born on 17 December 1923 in Okeigbo, a small town in present-day Ondo State, Nigeria. Her full name was Felicia Folayegbe Mosunmola Idowu Akintunde-Ighodalo. Her parents were Benjamin Olojomo Akintunde, a farmer, and Sarah (Ogunkemi) Akintunde, a direct descendant of the war leader and uncrowned Ooni-elect Derin Ologbenla of the Giesi Ruling House of Ile-Ife. Fola, as she was known, was their fourth, but first surviving, child. Although her parents were early converts to the Christian Missionary Society (CMS) mission in Ondo, she grew up in a family compound whose members also included followers of traditional Yoruba religious practices and Islam. Her father encouraged her to be self-reliant and assertive even if her actions sometimes disregarded gender expectations.

Young Fola Akintunde attended the local mission school whose headmaster recognized her potential and persuaded her father to allow her to complete primary school at a time when girls were usually withdrawn after two or three years; she then won a full scholarship to Queen's College, the elite government secondary school for girls in Lagos. In 1941 she passed the Cambridge School certificate examination and went on to the United Missionary College, Ibadan, where she obtained her teaching credentials in 1943. During the next five years she taught at several girls' secondary schools in Lagos, Sapele, and Ile-Ife. In 1948 she reluctantly accepted an overseas government scholarship for a one-year diploma course at the Institute of Education, University of London, instead of the full university course that she desired.

While in London Akintunde participated in student organizations, particularly the Nigerian Union of Students of Great Britain and Ireland (NUSGBI) and the West African Students' Union (WASU), whose activities focused on decolonization, colonial development, and Pan-Africanism. She was a member of the NUSGBI delegation that attended the coronation of Queen Elizabeth II and served as a vice president of WASU (1953–1955). Her horizons broadened and she decided to switch from education to economics as a career. When the Colonial Office insisted that she abide by the terms of the bond she had signed in connection with her original education scholarship, she broke her bond, took a part-time job with the London post office, and enrolled in the School of Commerce, Regent Street Polytechnic. Meanwhile, she participated in the intense discussions among her fellow colonial students about postwar development and political autonomy. Embracing nationalist values, she rejected her Christian name, Felicia, in favor of her Yoruba name, Folayegbe, or its shortened form, Fola.

In June 1954 Akintunde obtained her BSc (External) in economics. By this time her intellect and organizational abilities had come to the attention of Saburi Oladeni Biobaku and Simeon Adebo who were in England to recruit a team of young graduates to pioneer the Nigerianization of the Western Region senior government service. She was the only woman selected for the group of twelve cadet officers, signaling a change in ideas concerning women's government employment.

Before returning home in July 1955 Fola Akintunde married Jeremiah Ighodalo and gave birth to her first child. Her husband remained in London to finish his professional training in accounting. The following month Fola Ighodalo (later Akintunde-Ighodalo) formally entered government service in Ibadan, the capital of the Western Region, as assistant secretary in the Ministry of Development. Initially she experienced much discrimination from her British superiors, who did not welcome the intrusion of female officers in the political administration, but her determination and hard work eventually won them over. She served in a wide variety of ministries, including trade and industry; education; works and transport; agriculture and natural resources; and home affairs and information. In 1958 she supervised the Secretarial Training School that produced the first crop of Nigerian confidential secretaries who took over from their British counterparts in the regional ministries. She helped design the industrial and agricultural policy that shaped regional development plans before the first military takeover in 1966. In 1968 she was promoted to the post of permanent secretary, becoming the first Nigerian woman to serve in that capacity, a milestone in the history of the country's women.

Akintunde-Ighodalo gained a reputation for honesty, diligence, outspokenness, efficiency, and fierce rejection of corrupt practices. Although her stand on corruption ensured stiff opposition within the government service, it also meant that senior administrators, including governors, appointed her to direct enterprises that they did not want to fail because of malpractice. Unfortunately, her strict discipline was also a major factor in her failure to be promoted to the coveted post of head of service. In 1976 she voluntarily retired from government service.

As permanent secretary Akintunde-Ighodalo became a model for young women to aspire to higher education, participation in public life, and professional occupations. She was sought after as a spokesperson on women's issues as well as development. She articulated the modern Nigerian woman's viewpoint through newspaper articles, conference papers, and speeches. Although her position in the civil service prohibited her from taking part in overt political activities, she was active in women's and church organizations. She acted as government liaison in the founding the Council of Women's Societies in 1957, which became the National Council of Women's Societies.

She was also active as an executive member of the Ibadan-based Women's Improvement Society and the foundation in 1959 of the Nigerian Association of University Women (NAUW), of which she served as president from 1980 to 1984.

After retirement Akintunde-Ighodalo established Folmalko Farms, a large poultry business that she ran according to scientific methods in keeping with policies she had pursued when she was in government service. In addition she led an active public life, serving as a member of the board of directors of numerous industries, including Nigeria Airways. In 1978 she was named to the three-member Justice Mohammed Commission of Inquiry into Student Unrest, which investigated clashes between University of Lagos students and the government in 1978.

Freed from the constraints imposed on government servants, she participated more actively in NAUW activities, church affairs, and the expansion of the poultry industry. In 1982 she was a founding member and chair of the Centre for Applied Religion and Education of Christians for a New Society, a group that pursues community development, as well as the Poultry Association of Nigeria. For all these groups, she served at various times as executive member, spokesperson, and patron. She believed that it was her duty to accept as many invitations as possible because they provided fora that sustained her contemporaries and encouraged young people in promoting democracy and community development, especially in the difficult years of the Ibrahim Babangida and Sani Abacha regimes.

Besides her activities in "modern associations," she maintained a deep interest in traditional Yoruba culture. In 1972 she received two traditional appointments, the first as Otun Iyalode of Ifetedo, and the second as Wabodu of Okeigbo. The latter title invested her with the responsibilities of head princess of the Giesi ruling house of Ile-Ife. In recognition of her service to Nigeria, General Olusegun Obasanjo invested her as an officer of the Order of the Niger in 1977. She died on 14 February 2005.

[See also Abacha, Sani; Babangida, Ibrahim Badamosi; and Obasanjo Olusegun.]

BIBLIOGRAPHY

Denzer, LaRay. *Folayegbe M. Akintunde-Ighodalo: A Public Life*. Ibadan, Nigeria: Sam Bookman Publishers, 2002.

Denzer, LaRay. "Women's Employment in Government Service in Colonial Nigeria, 1863–1945."

Working Papers in African Studies, 136. Boston: African Studies Center, Boston University, 1989.

Mba, Nina Emma. *Nigerian Women Mobilized: Women's Political Activity in Southern Nigeria, 1900–1965*. Berkeley: Institute of International Studies, University of California, 1982.

McIntosh, Marjorie Keniston. *Yoruba Women, Work, and Social Change*. Bloomington: Indiana University Press, 2009.

LaRAY DENZER

Akitoye (d. 1853), *ologun* (king) of the city of Lagos (in present-day Nigeria), was born early in the nineteenth century in the city that he would later rule. His father, Ologun Kuture, reigned over the port from roughly 1780 to around 1803. Akitoye's elder brothers Adele and Osinlokun battled for power in the first two decades of the nineteenth century. Eventually Osinlokun won this struggle. Akitoye only entered the competition for the throne in the 1830s, after the death of Osinlokun and his son and successor Idewu. The latter had no children. When Idewu's ambitious brother Kosoko tried to seize the crown, his numerous opponents in Lagos sought to find other candidates to prevent Kosoko from taking power. The aging Adele was named *ologun*, but only lived two years. Then various family leaders and chiefs selected Adele's son Oluwole to block Kosoko from becoming the king, but he only lived for a short time before being killed in an accidental gunpowder explosion in the palace. Only then did Akitoye come to power in 1841. Such a convoluted state of affairs indicates the limited popular support for Akitoye and the weaknesses of royal power. Kosoko quickly returned to Lagos aboard a ship owned by the notorious West African slave trader José Domingo Martinez, a Brazilian. Although Akitoye tried to appease Kosoko with a palace and titles, Kosoko still considered himself to be the true ruler and made preparations to overthrow Akitoye. While Kosoko turned to the neighboring kingdom of Dahomey and the Yoruba city of Ijebu for aid, Akitoye drew aid from the Egba confederacy of Yoruba cities. At the battle of Ija Omiro in 1845, Kosoko seized Lagos but failed to capture Akitoye, who fled to the city of Abeokuta.

Akitoye's short reign as king was hardly auspicious, but he would ascend to the throne once again. Kosoko's determination to continue selling slaves and maintain unrestricted trade angered the British government, which had sought since the 1820s to stop the transatlantic slave trade. Kosoko refused to agree to end the export of slaves when the British consul John Beecroft requested this concession. Akitoye wisely used British Christian Missionary Society missionaries and English traders based in the town of Badagry to present himself as an opponent of slavery and a friend of Britain. When this lobbying effort did not immediately produce results, Akitoye turned to Domingo Martinez, the very same slave trader who had helped Kosoko earlier on. When this plan failed, Akitoye again implored the English government to take action in a letter drafted by an English trader. This petition prepared the way for colonization, as Akitoye wrote Beecroft, "My humble prayer to you, Sir . . . is that you would take Lagos under your protection, that you would plant the English flag there, and that you would reestablish me on my rightful throne at Lagos. . . . I promise to enter into a Treaty with England to abolish the Slave Trade at Lagos, and to establish and carry on lawful trade" (Mann 2007, p. 94).

Beecroft commanded British warships to drive Kosoko from power in Lagos once he received permission from British foreign secretary Lord Palmerston in 1851. Palmerston had previously preferred Kosoko, but the latter's refusal to budge on the issue of slave trading made him no longer desirable to British interests. Badagry, Akitoye's sanctuary since 1845, was experiencing a civil war and so the former king wished to return to Lagos for his own safety as well as for his old position of power. The first British attack actually failed to capture the city, and British officials and military officers were concerned that a defeat of British forces would be a dangerous sign of weakness. In late December 1851 a second and more effective attack on Kosoko led to victory for Akitoye. Beecroft installed Akitoye as king in February 1852. Akitoye promised Beecroft to ban slave trading and human sacrifices at funerals or to various Yoruba deities. He also permitted missionaries in the city and removed some restrictions on European traders that had existed prior to the British victory. For the first time, African Protestants could hold services openly. Akitoye also promised not to allow anyone who owed debts to foreign traders to engage in commerce with anyone but their creditors until they paid off what they owed and that he would seize the property of debtors who refused to pay off their creditors. In return, foreign traders would have to pay a 3 percent duty on imports and 2 percent on exports to Akitoye.

Akitoye soon complained to his British liberator that Beecroft's representative in Lagos, Louis Frazer, was arrogant and not concerned enough about defending Lagos from the threat of Kosoko. Frazer disliked Akitoye and considered him to be a pawn of English traders seeking to embarrass Frazer to his superior Beecroft. This tension came to a head in May 1853. A dispute emerged after Akitoye had received a company of Egba soldiers and twenty slaves from his erstwhile ally Domingo Martinez. These slaves were disembarked in Lagos by an Afro-Brazilian slave merchant and a Hungarian national named Amadie. Akitoye declared that Amadie should be arrested for dealing in slaves and sent to Badagry. Frazer did not feel that Akitoye had the right to detain a European even though the British had banned slave trading in Lagos. Frazer sent a letter in June 1853 to his superiors complaining that Akitoye needlessly tried to interfere in trade. The king's decision to restrict entrance into the city as a security measure also vexed Frazer. Akitoye's decision to arrest the chiefs Ajenia and Possu, who were associates of Amadie, further angered the British officer. Kosoko nearly regained control of Lagos in 1853. However, superior British firepower put down Kosoko's attack and Akitoye returned to Lagos as king. Akitoye died on the night of 2 September 1853, apparently from an unknown illness. Some reports received by the British government's representative suggest he might also have committed suicide or was the victim of poison. In any event, his son Dosunmu was proclaimed king by the town chiefs and the British vice-consul. Akitoye's career exposed the fractured nature of political power in Lagos and the transition from limited European political involvement in West Africa toward the expansion of imperial power in the second half of the nineteenth century.

BIBLIOGRAPHY

Mann, Kristin. *Slavery and the Birth of an African City: Lagos, 1760–1900.* Bloomington: Indiana University Press, 2007.

Short, Giles. "Blood and Treasure: The Reduction of Lagos, 1851." *ANU Historical Journal* 13 (1977): 11–19.

Smith, Robert Sydney. *The Lagos Consulate, 1851–1861.* Berkeley: University of California Press, 1979.

Smith, Robert Sydney. "To the Palaver Islands: War and Diplomacy in the Lagos Lagoon in 1852–1854." *Journal of the Historical Society of Nigeria* 5, no. 1 (1969): 3–25.

JEREMY RICH

Aklilu Habte Weld (1912–1974), prominent politician in the post–World War II Ethiopian government, was born in 1912 in Bulga, central Ethiopia, to a family of modest means. He rose to the pinnacle of power as prime minister. He came of age at a time when Ras Tafari Mekonnen (the future Emperor Haile Selassie I) was planning to modernize the administration of the country by replacing the hitherto dominant traditional aristocracy by Western-educated civil servants. Accordingly, Aklilu was sent abroad for education, first in Egypt at the French lycée in Alexandria (1925–1931) and then at the Sorbonne (1931–1936) in Paris where he obtained a law degree and diplomas in economics and political science.

The Italian invasion of 1935 interrupted the emperor's program of administrative reorganization and forestalled Aklilu's chances of commencing his career as a government official. For much of the occupation period, he remained in Paris, serving at the Ethiopian legation there successively as press attaché, secretary, and chargé d'affaires. He fled Paris when the city fell to the Germans in 1940.

In the postwar period Aklilu Habte Weld quickly rose through the ranks under the patronage of his older brother Mekonnen Habte Weld, who had become the emperor's most trusted official owing to a network of informers and spies he commanded. Aklilu was named vice minister of the pen (the royal secretariat) in 1942 and vice minister of foreign affairs in 1943 in the first postwar cabinet. In these positions Aklilu demonstrated his diplomatic skills in the negotiations that led to the Anglo-Ethiopian Agreement (1944), at the Paris Peace Conference, and, as chief of Ethiopia's delegation, at the San Francisco United Nations conference (1945), the UN debates over Eritrea, and the UN General Assembly vote that joined Eritrea to Ethiopia in a federation (1952). He was appointed foreign minister in 1949 and deputy prime minister in 1958.

In December 1960 several high ranking officials, including Abebe Aregay, who at the time occupied the portfolio of prime minister, were killed in a failed coup d'état. Seizing the moment to advance his goal of replacing the aristocracy of birth by technocrats of merit, the emperor elevated Aklilu to the position of prime minister in 1961, with the rarely conferred title of *tsehafe te'ezaz* (scribe of orders) and retaining the portfolio of the Minister of the Pen. Aklilu thus held at the same time the modern office of prime minister and the traditional office of keeper of the great seal, in effect becoming the second most powerful person after the emperor. In 1966 the office of prime minister was transformed into that of head of government and Aklilu was given, at least in theory, the authority to appoint ministers and run the government autonomously from the crown. It was a chance to effect social and political reforms that the younger generation of educated Ethiopians was demanding at the time.

Even though Aklilu drew up a program of constitutional, administrative, and land reform in 1961 and presented it to the emperor, his government failed to implement it. Many observers believe the failure to respond to popular demand paved the way for the revolution of 1974 that ended imperial rule. Aklilu owed his education and position to the emperor and was unwilling to challenge his benefactor. As a person of humble origins, Aklilu was an object of resentment to the traditional nobility who viewed his advancement as undeserved and worked assiduously to undermine him. Lacking the intriguing and scheming skills needed to navigate the labyrinthine world of Ethiopian politics, Aklilu was not able to confront them. A Francophile at a time when Ethiopia was inexorably moving toward closer association with Britain and increasingly with the United States, he was gradually overshadowed by the rising Anglophile elite. When crises came, he was made a convenient scapegoat by an emperor who was more interested in retaining power than loyalty to those who had served him.

In 1973 Ethiopia experienced severe economic conditions that fueled popular unrest, strikes by students, teachers, and cab drivers. An atmosphere of chaos reigned in the capital, forcing the government to respond by reducing gasoline prices, dropping price controls on basic essentials, and raising military pay. When these actions did not stop the rising tide of popular discontent, the cabinet of Prime Minister Aklilu Habte Weld took the unprecedented step of resigning. The political vacuum thus created brought to power a group of noncommissioned officers and enlisted men. In November 1974 the junta executed without trial sixty ex-officials of the imperial government, including former Prime Minister Aklilu Habte Weld.

[*See also* Haile Selassie I; *and* Mekonnen Habte Weld.]

BIBLIOGRAPHY

Bahru Zewde. *A History of Modern Ethiopia, 1855–1974.* 2d ed. Oxford: James Currey, 2001. A thoughtful general history modern Ethiopia (1855–1991), the book blends narratives of political and diplomatic history with accounts of social and economic developments. It also weaves together the differing experiences of the people of present-day northern and southern Ethiopia.

Aklilu Habte Weld. *Aklilu Remembers: Historical Recollections from a Prison Cell.* Translated by Getachew Tedla. Uppsala, Sweden, 1994. An autobiographical memoir written by Aklilu in detention, the book provides a detailed account of the author's early life and his involvement in significant negotiations with foreign powers and his contributions to shaping the construction of Ethiopia's government in the post–World War II period.

Spencer, John H. *Ethiopia at Bay: A Personal Account of the Haile Selassie Years.* Repr. Los Angeles: Tsehai Publishers, 2006. A personal account of an American lawyer who served the Ethiopian government during the post–World War II period, the book provides an analysis of domestic challenges, external relationships, dominant personalities, and the effort to modernize the Ethiopian state.

EZEKIEL GEBISSA

Akosua, Adoma (c. 1773–c. 1838), queen mother in Ghana, where she served as *asantehemaa* from around 1809 until about 1819, when she was removed from office after being involved in a failed rebellion against Osei Tutu Kwame. Her father was Apa Owusi, who held the position of *mampon apahene*, or chief of the locality of Mampon; her mother, Sewaa Awukuwa, was a member of the Asante royal family. It appears from some sources that Adoma Akosua was married to a son of Asantehene Osei Kwadwo.

When the ruling queen mother, Asantehemaa Konadu Yaadom, died in 1809, there were two women with a strong genealogical claim to succeed her. One was Konadu Yaadom's own daughter, Yaa Dufi, and the other was Adoma Akosua. Adoma Akosua was a matrilateral cousin of Asantehene Osei Tutu Kwame (their mothers were sisters); as such she was eligible to be named *asantehemaa*, and she was selected for reasons that are not entirely clear. Akosua appears in the records a few years later when she purchased her natal town of Apa, most likely using some of the wealth she was able to accumulate as *asantehemaa*. Apa was then moved from the jurisdiction of Mampon to that of Kumase.

In 1817 Asantehene Osei Tutu Kwame determined that he had to travel to the Asante province of Gyaman, where the local ruler, Kwadwo Adinkra,

was taking actions that ran counter to Asante interests. He left Adoma Akosua in charge of the civil government while he pursued a military campaign. She began a relationship with another chief who wanted the throne himself, and she gathered seventeen royal wives and their families to support that effort. Other sources say she was maneuvering to place one of her sons on the throne. She prepared a funeral ritual for Osei Tutu Kwame, apparently hoping that the ceremony would lead to his actual death. When he learned of her actions, he sent his loyal supporters back to quell the rebellion. After he returned to the capital, he called a council that decided on a punishment of death for all those involved; the wives who had supported Adoma Akosua were decapitated. It appears that her sons also died at that time. While one report stated that Adoma Akosua was strangled (so as to avoid spilling royal blood), she was not killed at that time, but she and her descendents were barred from holding royal office. She lived in Kumase outside the royal ward until she died sometime around 1838; a further fifteen people were executed at her funeral. Her great grandson Osei Kwaku Goroso mounted a campaign to reclaim his royal heritage in the 1880s, but he failed and was exiled to the Gold Coast.

[*See also* Kwame, Osei; *and* Yaadom, Konadu.]

BIBLIOGRAPHY

"Adoma Akosua." *Asantesem: The Asante Collective Biography Project Bulletin* 11 (1979): 14–17.

McCaskie, T. C. "Anti-Witchcraft Cults in Asante: An Essay in the Social History of an African People." *History in Africa* 8 (1981): 125–154. See pp. 126–129 for an account of the attempted rebellion.

KATHLEEN SHELDON

Aku, Martin Andréas (1913–1970), Togolese medical doctor and politician, was born on 2 September 1913 in Lomé, the capital of the West African German colony of Togo. His parents belonged to a Ewe-speaking community. His father, Andréas Aku, was the first Togolese head of the Protestant Church of Togo and had been ordained by German missionaries. His mother was Caroline Aku.

Naturally, Aku attended Protestant missionary schools in Lomé from 1920 to 1928. The German Protestant pastor Gottfried Stoevesandt was so impressed with Aku's intellectual ability that he invited him to attend secondary school in Germany. His relatively poor but influential parents agreed. For the handful of Togolese students able to continue their education in Europe between World War I and World War II, the medical field was the most attractive subject of their studies. Aku passed the German baccalaureate examinations and then with the support of the Bremen Protestant mission entered medical school. He received his degree in medicine and had residencies in French and English hospitals. In 1938 he wrote a short autobiography in German about his experiences as a doctor. Aku spent the early years of World War II in Europe, but he returned to Togo in 1942. He continued his medical practice first at Anécho and later at the town of Palimé.

At the end of the war the French government decided to allow limited representation for its African colonies in the French parliament and the creation of territorial assemblies. Aku became the candidate of the Comité de l'Unité Togolaise (CUT) party in the first elections for representing Togo in the French National Assembly. The CUT party was largely made up of Ewe speakers, many of whom dreamed of creating an independent Ewe state that would combine territory from Ghana with Togo. Aku prudently distanced himself from such plans, but he did campaign for eventual independence for Togo and for immediate political reforms and autonomy. His main opponent, the future president of Togo Nicolas Grunitzky, was more conciliatory to the French. Aku easily won the elections of 10 November 1946 with 73 percent of all votes cast.

Aku paradoxically was conservative on issues that concerned the French African empire as a whole, even as he fervently called for political reforms in his homeland. The French government's efforts to create separate African and European electoral colleges in 1947 infuriated Aku. He rejected France's adherence to the US Marshall plan, abstained on the vote over France's entrance into the North American Treaty Organization, and opposed the exclusion of communists from the cabinet. Yet he joined coalitions of moderate African parliamentary deputies rather than adhere to the more radical Rassemblement Démocratique Africaine voting bloc.

With Ewe intellectual and popular agitation for intervention by the United Nations to form an independent Ewe nation in the late 1940s, French officials harassed CUT members suspected of supporting these plans. The government promoted the more moderate Parti Togolais du Progrès of Nicolas Grunitzky over Aku's CUT. Aku also faced competition from more dynamic leaders like Sylvanus Olympio in his own party. Aku lost the 1951 French

parliamentary elections to Grunitzky. Instead of remaining in politics, he returned to his medical practice. He worked as a doctor in Togo in the 1950s and later moved to Ghana. Aku died on 17 June 1970 in Lomé. While he had little influence on later developments in Togolese politics, Aku was a pioneer of Togolese democracy.

[*See also* Grunitzky, Nicolas; *and* Olympio, Sylvanus Epiphanio.]

BIBLIOGRAPHY

Firla-Forkl, Monika. *Siru Pedro Olympio, Matthias Yawo Anthony und Martin Aku. Drei togolesische Mediziner in Deutschland 1914–38 und ihr weitererLebensweg.* Stuttgart, Germany: Linden-Museum Stuttgart, 2005.

Tété-Adjalogo, Tètèvi Godwin. *Histoire du Togo, la palpitante quête de l'Ablodé, 1940–1960.* Paris: NM7 Editions, 2007.

JEREMY RICH

Akudri Dada, Yoane (c. 1898–1997), Congolese evangelist and translator, was born in Gombe, a village inhabited by Kakwa-speaking clans in the northeastern corner of the modern-day Democratic Republic of Congo. This community suffered greatly from slave raids launched by Zande chieftains like Zémio and Mopoï living to their north in the late nineteenth century. However, the threat of northern raiders was hardly the only challenge for the young boy. His name Akudri signified "one who waited" since he was born after his mother was pregnant for more than nine months. He also bore his father's name Dada, which means "one who has no family." This would indeed be Akudri's own fate, since an epidemic of meningitis killed his parents and all his siblings when he was very young. The boy barely survived himself. A grave was dug to prepare for his funeral by other people in the village, but he managed to recover before it was used. He grew up to be a gifted singer and dancer. Unfortunately for him, his efforts to improve his appearance backfired when his earlobes became infected after they were pierced.

Akudri met evangelical Protestant missionaries of the Africa Inland Mission (AIM) at the town of Adi. AIM missionaries had originally established a mission at the town of Kukulung'a near Adi in 1922, after having already established a series of missions in the eastern Belgian Congo. Akudri's gift for languages caught the attention of the English missionaries Dorothy and Kenneth Richardson. They hired him as their cook and domestic servant and discovered him to be both open to Christianity and a formidable orator in his own right. He was baptized by Reverend George Van Dusen in the Mite River with three other Kakwa people; these were the first converts to Christianity among the Kakwa. Prophetically, Akudri chose Yoane (John) after John the Baptist. He attended Bible school at the AIM mission at Blukwa.

Akudri greatly assisted the American missionaries Jim Bell and Ralph Davis in the early years of the Adi mission. He served as the missionaries' interpreter in both Kakwa and the commonly spoken lingua franca of Lingala. Akudri even dared go on an evangelization mission with the Americans north into Zande villages, the old enemies of Kakwa people. His stepmother pleaded with Akudri not to visit these foes of the Kakwa, but Akudri stayed in this region for six months before returning home. Akudri also supported AIM missionary efforts to acquire land in Adi with the permission of the colonial government. His preaching in multiple languages soon drew crowds throughout northeast Congo, and he aided AIM missionaries in translating biblical texts into Kakwa. Eventually, he would go on tours that brought him to Uganda, Kenya, Sudan, Tanzania, the Central African Republic, Canada, and the United States. His sermons in English would often include homespun lines such as the prayer, "To preach, O Lord, give the stuff, and nudge me when I've said enough." His magnificent skill with public speaking made him a favorite figure in AIM's efforts to raise money in North America for their missions. He was the first pastor ordained by AIM in the Congo.

Before Akudri became a minor international evangelical celebrity, he ran into difficulties in the 1930s. A Catholic priest accused Akudri of leading a sect that promoted insurrections against the Belgian colonial government. He noted that so many people attended his services that they had stopped working. While AIM missionaries enjoyed telling the story at the expense of their Catholic rivals, one should remember that several revolts against the Belgians were linked to African Protestant churches in other parts of the colony. Later the colonial government had problems with Akudri because he and other Congolese Protestants refused to grow tobacco as a cash crop and Akudri convinced officials to promote cotton cultivation instead. Ironically, poor prices and the unsuitability of much of northeastern Congo for cotton cultivation made it a highly unpopular crop among Africans as well.

Although the coming of independence only furthered his reputation inside the Congo, Akudri endured the same troubles that struck many Congolese in the early 1960s. Simba rebels associated with Christophe Gbenye swept into Akudri's home region in 1964. These rebels often killed Congolese Christians and missionaries alike as allies of what they deemed as the continued domination of Congo by Western imperialist countries. Some Simba soldiers jailed him in Kumuru prison, but he escaped. Later a Simba unit broke into the AIM mission at Adi in search of weapons they believed were hidden there. The soldiers detained and tortured Akudri and then tried to demand money from AIM by keeping him hostage. Simba officers received three thousand Congolese francs for Akudri's liberation, but the rebels decided to kill him anyway. After they managed to fail to shoot him, Akudri evaded their patrols and fled into Uganda. Several years later, after making a North American tour in 1970 describing his miraculous escapes from the Simba, Akudri became a victim once more when the Ugandan strongman Idi Amin promoted Islam and threatened churches like AIM that were hostile to state control. Akudri was tortured for a week by Ugandan security forces. Later rebels fighting Idi Amin in 1979 captured him during another revival tour and threatened to kill him again. Yet Akudri dodged execution yet again. So many examples of redemption made him a hero to Protestants throughout northeastern Congo. He nonetheless remained a very humble figure despite the acclaim. For example, he turned down a gift of a new car from some Americans touched by one of his sermons, on the grounds that he had traveled to the United States to preach the Gospel rather than to receive gifts.

Akudri lived to see one more war. During the combined efforts by Rwandan forces and Congolese rebels to overthrow Mobutu Sese Seko in 1997, Akudri finally died from a long illness in the town of Aba. He was buried at the Adi mission. In northeastern Congo, cassettes of his recorded sermons are still popular among many Protestants. His life of nearly a century thus articulated the rise (and tribulations) of Christianity in rural Congo.

[*See also* Amin, Idi Dada; Gbenye, Christophe; *and* Mobutu Sese Seko.]

BIBLIOGRAPHY

Anderson, Richard. *We Felt Like Grasshoppers: The Story of Africa Inland Mission.* Nottingham, UK: Crossway Books, 1994.

Brashler, Peter. *Akudri*. Marysville, Calif.: Cascade Publishing, 1990.

Richardson, Kenneth, and Yoane Akudri Dada. *Kuu ana'bo naga Mako awudyu*. London: British and Foreign Bible Society, 1930.

Way, Yossa. "Yoane Akudri Dada." *Dictionary of African Christian Biography*. http://www.dacb.org/stories/demrepcongo/f-yoane_akudri.html/.

JEREMY RICH

Akuffo, Fred (1937–1979), military leader and politician, was born on 21 March 1937 in the eastern Ghanaian town of Akropong. He attended secondary school at the well-known Presbyterian Boys' Secondary School located in Odumase Krobo, Ghana. After finishing his secondary education in 1955, he joined the Ghanaian army. Eventually he entered the elite Royal Military Academy officers' training school in Sandhurst, England, in 1958. Some of his fellow African cadets went on to organize the 1966 coup that overthrew the Nigerian First Republic. After graduating from Sandhurst in 1960 and receiving further military training in England in 1961 and 1967, Akuffo became the head officer of Ghana's Airborne Training School at Tamale, in 1965 and 1966, and then became the commander of the Sixth Infantry Battalion in 1969. He supported the coup led by his fellow officer General Ignatius Acheampong in 1972. In the following year Akuffo attended training at the National Defence College in India. Not all of his duties were strictly military in nature. For example, Akuffo managed Ghana's decision to change traffic laws that made drivers switch from driving on the left to driving on the right. His success in this difficult program helped lead him to a high position within the military regime. Akuffo became the commander of the Ghanaian army in April 1974 and then the chief of the Ghanaian defense staff in April 1976. On 9 October 1975 Acheampong made Akuffo a member of the Supreme Military Council that ran the country. Eventually he was widely recognized to be Acheampong's second-in-command.

On 5 July 1978 Akuffo led a palace coup against Acheampong and drove him from power. The former leader publicly announced his resignation and returned to his hometown in the Ashanti region after he was stripped of his military rank. This was the first time in Ghanaian history that one military government overthrew another. Akuffo accused Acheampong of corruption and "running a one-man show." Jerry J. Rawlings, an Air Force officer who eventually toppled Akuffo's regime,

expressed his opposition to the coup publicly but was not censured or punished for it. Akuffo brought some civilians onto the Supreme Military Council and released some political prisoners who had been jailed after the overthrow of Kwame Nkrumah in 1966. He also decided to continue plans to allow civilians to again control the government in a transition that was scheduled to end with presidential and legislative elections in July 1979. He claimed to respect democratic principles and criticized the 1979 Rhodesian elections that allowed very limited participation by Africans as a sham. Akuffo tried to steer Ghana's struggling economy away from the more socialist orientation of Acheampong, but his regime's policies to introduce a new devalued currency did little to curb Ghana's extremely high inflation rate. Austerity cuts initiated by Akuffo led to many strikes by September 1978, and his use of troops to break up a strike at the state-run electric power company further angered many people. Even Akuffo's decision to allow political parties to operate legally in December 1978 did not boost his flagging popularity. One reason for Akuffo's troubles came from his unwillingness to allow for legal investigations of corruption charges against high-ranking military officers. Another came from his unwillingness to challenge the structural adjustment policies mandated by the International Monetary Fund (IMF) that had greatly cut funding for social services. It should be noted that Ghana's large debt to the IMF hardly provided Akuffo with leverage to challenge structural adjustment policies. On 4 June 1979 a group of Air Force officers threatened to bomb Accra unless Akuffo and his supporters surrendered. The officers freed Rawlings, who was on trial for an abortive coup, and made him their spokesman. Akuffo gave in and was immediately arrested alongside many military officers associated with previous military regimes. Rawlings held a short trial of Akuffo and his former boss Ignatius Acheampong on corruption charges following the coup. On 26 June 1979 a firing squad executed Akuffo, Acheampong, and four other senior officers in front of a large crowd at a military firing range on the Atlantic Ocean near Accra. On 28 December 2001 the corpse of Fred Akuffo was reinterred after having laid in a cemetery at Nsawam Prison in Accra. His widow Emily requested then-president John Kufuor to have an official burial as a sign of reconciliation. The funeral celebrated Akuffo's life along with his dead colleagues Ignatius Acheampong and Akwasi Afrifa. While his predecessor Acheampong and his successor Rawlings had a much greater impact on Ghanaian history than Akuffo's brief period of rule on Ghana, Akuffo did demonstrate a mild reformist impulse that was overcome by his reliance on the army to stay in power.

[*See also* Acheampong, Ignatius Kutu; Kufuor, John; Nkrumah, Kwame; *and* Rawlings, Jerry John.]

BIBLIOGRAPHY

Austin, Dennis. "The Ghana Armed Forces and Ghanaian Society." *Third World Quarterly* 7, no. 1 (January 1985).

Gocking, Roger. *The History of Ghana.* Westport, Conn.: Greenwood Press, 2005.

Kandeh, Jimmy David. *Coups from Below: Armed Subalterns and State Power in West Africa.* New York: Macmillan, 2004.

JEREMY RICH

Akuffo-Addo, Edward (1906–1979), lawyer, chief judge, and president of Ghana, was born at Dodowa in the Greater Accra region of the Gold Cost (now Ghana) on 26 June 1906. His father was William Martin Addo-Danquah of Akropong, Akuapem. His mother was Theodora Amuafi, also from Akropong, Akuapem. After receiving his elementary education at the Presbyterian primary and middle schools at Dodowa, he enrolled in Achimota College in 1929, from where he was awarded scholarship to study mathematics, philosophy, and politics at Saint Peter's College, Oxford University. Akuffo-Addo was one of the first students at Saint Peter's College, matriculating in 1930, a year after the college was established. He went on to graduate with honors in philosophy and politics in 1933. He was later made an honorary fellow of the college, and in 1971 he was made a doctor of civil law at Oxford University.

In 1940 Akuffo-Addo was called to the Middle Temple Bar in London. However, he returned to the Gold Coast in 1941 to start a private legal practice in Accra. In 1947 he and his peers, Alfred Paa Grant, Emmanuel Obetsebi Lamptey, J. B. Danquah, William Ofori Atta, and Ebenezer Ako Adjei, founded the United Gold Coast Convention (UGCC), a political movement that spearheaded the campaign for the independence of the Gold Coast. In 1948 the movement appointed Kwame Nkrumah as its general secretary. He, together with his other five peers, would eventually be arrested and detained by the colonial authorities for their alleged role in the 1948 disturbances in the Gold Coast colony. Their arrest and subsequent detention in the northern part of the country made them popular and won them the accolade the "Big Six."

Between 1949 and 1950 Edward Akuffo-Addo became a member of the Gold Coast Legislative Council. Meanwhile in April 1948 he was appointed a member of an all-African constitutional commission headed by the Gold Coast jurist Mr. Justice Henley Coussey of the Gold Coast High Court, to draft a constitution for the country.

From 1962 to 1964 Edward Akuffo-Addo joined the bench and became a judge at the Supreme Court of Ghana. Edward Akufo-Addo was dismissed from the bench together with fellow judges Sir Arku Korsah (chief justice) and W. B. van Lare by Ghana's president Kwame Nkrumah in December 1963 for their acquittal and discharge two months earlier of Tawaia Adamafio, Cofie Crabbe, and Ako Adjei. The three acquitted men had been accused of masterminding the bomb attack on Nkrumah. Akuffo-Addo, Korsah, and van Lare had formed a three-man panel of the "Special Court" established in August 1963 to try the suspects.

Akuffo-Addo was then appointed to serve as chief justice of Ghana's Supreme Court from 1966 to 1970 by the National Liberation Council (NLC), the military government that assumed power following the overthrow of Nkrumah. In 1968 the NLC appointed him the chairman of the constitutional commission established to draft the 1969 Second Republican Constitution for Ghana. Additionally, he was made the head of the political commission of the NLC. He was also a member of the presidential transitional commission appointed by the NLC as it prepared to hand over power to the incoming Progress Party government led by Dr. Kofi Abrefa Busia in 1969.

Between 1970 and 1972, Edward Akuffo-Addo served as the president of Ghana with Dr. Kofi Abrefa Busia (1969–1972) as prime minister. Power resided with Busia, however, and Akuffo-Addo's presidency was a ceremonial one. He was married to Adeline Yeboakua Akuffo-Addo, *abontendomhemaa* of Kyebi and daughter of Nana Sir Ofori Atta I (1912–1943), *okyenhene* of the Akyem Abuakwa state in the eastern region of Ghana.

He died in Accra on 17 July 1979, leaving behind his widow, Adeline, and four children, one of whom is Nana Addo Dankwa Akuffo-Addo, a prominent lawyer and politician, who narrowly lost the 2008 presidential race in Ghana.

[*See also* Busia, Kofi Abrefa; Danquah, Joseph Boakye; Nkrumah, Kwame; *and* Obetsebi-Lamptey, Emmanuel Odarquaye.]

BIBLIOGRAPHY

Afrifa, Akwasi Amankwaa. *The Ghana Coup.* London: Cass, 1966.

Boahen, Adu. *Ghana: Evolution and Change in the Nineteenth and Twentieth Centuries.* London: Longman, 1975.

Buah, Francis. A *History of Ghana.* Rev. ed. London: Macmillan, 1998.

Daniels, Ebo. *Essays in Ghanaian Law: Supreme Court Centenary Publication, 1876–1976.* Legon, Ghana: Faculty of Law, University of Ghana, 1976.

EBENEZER AYESU

Al-. *'For many names that include the particle al-, see under the main element of the name, for example,* Suyuti, Jalal al-Din al-.

Alakija, Tejumade (1925–), Nigerian educator, civil servant, and women's rights activist, was born in Ile-Ife, Nigeria, on 17 May 1925. Her family was extremely affluent, as she was the daughter of Sir Adesiji Aderemi (1889–1890), the traditional king of the city of Ile-Ife, one of the most important sacred sites in the spiritual traditions of the Yoruba people. One of her sisters, Awujoola Adesomi Olagbaju, went on to become a schoolteacher and headmaster in her own right.

Alakija received her early education in Nigeria. She attended the Aiyetoro Primary and the Aiyetoro Central Schools in Ile-Ife from 1933 to 1937. She also studied at the Kudeti Primary boarding school in Ibadan for a time. Eventually Alakija moved to England in 1946, where she enrolled in Westfield College at the University of London. She acquired her undergraduate degree in 1950 in history and then proceeded to continue her studies at Oxford University, where she received a postgraduate degree in education in 1951. While at Oxford, she belonged to the G. D. H. Cole group known for promoting international activities. Cole was a professor of social theory at Oxford and a prominent socialist thinker.

She returned to Nigeria following her graduation from Oxford and joined the Nigerian colonial civil service. The educational arm of the colonial government placed her at the new public primary Queen's School in the city of Ede. Alakija spent two years there from 1951 to 1953 and was only one of two Africans teaching there. In 1954 she founded a secondary school for girls with the support of the Anglican Mission in the Ijebu-Ode diocese. Alakija supervised this school for four years and then taught at the Abeokuta primary school in 1958. There, the teacher redesigned the teaching certificate program for educators for the entire colony. In 1959 Alakija returned to the civil service and was posted in London to represent the Western Nigeria province.

With independence in 1960, Alakija returned to Nigeria and served as an assistant secretary for the Ministry of Public Works. She also served as a training officer in the Western Nigeria region for the civil service until 1962. Her father was at that time the governor of the Western Region. In 1964 Alakija was named the assistant secretary of the Ministry of Trade and Industry in Western Nigeria. As a trained administrator, she was relatively protected from the dangers associated with the political instability of the 1960s and the onset of military rule in 1966. Alakija became the chief investment officer in the Ministry of Trade in 1969, and she oversaw numerous industrial and other development projects. From 1976 to 1978 Alakija acted as deputy secretary of the Ministry of Health. She then transferred to the Ministry of Education, where she streamlined the admission system for universities throughout Nigeria in 1978 and 1979. She finally retired from government service on 30 September 1983, an end to a career filled with such awards as the service award of the Federal Republic of Nigeria that she received in 1980.

Through her education and high position, she came to know many leading Nigerian intellectuals and political leaders. For example, she knew internationally renowned novelist Wole Soyinka and engaged in discussions of Yoruba proverbs and praise names with him. In the 1990s Alakija entered administration in higher education. She became the pro-chancellor and chairman of the council at the University of Abuja from 1993 to 1997. In the first decade of the twenty-first century, Alakija acted as an informal adviser to Nigerian political leaders and continued to serve as the *iyalode* (female chief) of her home town. In a 2005 interview, she expressed her frustration about the corruption so pervasive in Nigerian politics, the failures of organization in the public educational system, and the lack of industrial development in the country. However, Alakija remained optimistic that the Nigerian people would eventually overcome these challenges. Many political leaders and well-known intellectuals attended her eightieth birthday party in 2005, and she was an elder stateswoman to younger generations of Nigerian feminists late in her life.

[*See also* Soyinka, Wole.]

BIBLIOGRAPHY

Falola, Toyin, and Ann Genova. *Historical Dictionary of Nigeria.* Rev. ed. Lanham, Md.: Scarecrow Press, 2008.

Interview with Tejumade Alakija. http://www.nigeria villagesquare.com/articles/achebe-foundation/the-achebe-foundation-interviews-14-mrs-tejumade-alakija.html/.

JEREMY RICH

Alara (fl. ninth century BCE), earliest ruler of the Kushite kingdom (ancient Sudan) attested in written sources. His personal name (also Alala, Arara, Aruru, or similar) is usually considered as native, so-called "Meroitic," and thus impossible to etymologize in the present state of knowledge about this language. However, some similar appellatives in Egyptian (the official language of Kush for several centuries, due to the long-continued colonization) suggest its rendering as Irery/Ireru ("Roarer," "Snarler"), possibly a metaphor for "lion."

The historical data about Alara is extremely scanty. No personal belongings of his have been attested so far. The tomb Ku. 9 (completely plundered in ancient times) that was found in the Kushite royal cemetery near the modern village of el Kurru (south of the Fourth Cataract of the Nile) has recently been attributed to him but this identification is hypothetical.

In fact, Alara is known only from several mentions in Kushite royal chronicles in Egyptian dated to the eighth to fourth centuries BCE. The earliest reference to him is in the short inscription on the funerary stela of Queen Tabiry (found in tomb Ku. 53 at el Kurru) who is introduced as daughter of Alara by Kasaqa, evidently his spouse. Tabiry is also called "the great/elder spouse of King Piankhy" (r. c. 747–702) who is known as the Kushite conqueror of Egypt and the first representative of the "Ethiopian" (the Twenty-fifth) Dynasty of the pharaohs, which for about eighty years governed both kingdoms on the Nile. Thus, Alara, the father-in-law of Piankhy, must have lived sometime in the first half of the eighth century, as he had been the ruler of Kush before Egypt was conquered.

Noteworthily, the names of Alara and his spouse on the stela of Tabiry are highlighted by the so-called royal circles (cartouches) but unlike the names of Piankhy and Tabiry they lack any distinctive royal titulary, which probably means that the political status of Alara was not recognized as kingly (in Egyptian terms) by his immediate successors. It is only in later monuments that he is called "king," perhaps accorded this title retrospectively in order to strengthen the authority of the ruling dynasty.

The main historical evidence about Alara consists of two stelae of his grand-nephew King Taharqa (r. c. 690–664), which were found in the temple complex of Gematen, near the modern village of Kawa (south of the Third Cataract). Both monuments are dedicated to Taharqa's building activities in this sanctuary after his accession to the throne, which in its turn is presented as a result of his ancestor's intercession. The records, evidently deriving from a single source, allege that Alara had somehow entered into a reciprocal relationship with the Egyptian god Amun-Re, whose support helped him to overthrow some "plotter" (perhaps a competitor in the fight for supremacy) and to "appear as king." At a certain point of his reign Alara, maybe in gratitude for his triumph, "dedicated" (some scholars think, consecrated as priestesses, but this is doubtful) several of his sisters to Amun-Re of Gematen and asked the god to "look upon the womb" of his sisters and help their descendants to "attain prosperity (and) appearance as king as you acted for me." According to one of the versions, Alara particularly favored one of his sisters (who may have also been his wife), the future "mother's mother" of Taharqa. The latter, upon his accession, ordered the (re)building of the main temple at Gematen, duty bound "to act for him that acts" and reverently "pronounce the names of his foremothers," the sisters of his great ancestor.

Some scholars take Taharqa's references to Alara as topical evidence merely illustrating the highest respect toward one of the glorious predecessors shown by one of the most remarkable Kushite kings of the "heroic" period. In some others' view, these accounts have historical depth and metaphorically relate the "initial covenant" between one of the Kushite chieftains and the god Amun-Re (i.e., the Egyptian priesthood in Kush or maybe more specifically in Gematen) as a result of which the traditional chiefdom was transformed into an Egyptianized kingdom and very soon developed into a major political power in the Nile valley.

The other surviving pieces of evidence are less informative. An inscription of King Irikeamannote (r. c. 431–405), also found at Gematen, states that in the course of his inauguration this king addressed the main god of the sanctuary with this request: "Give me a long life upon earth (now that) you have given me the like of what you (once) made for king Alara."

The latest reference is assumed to be in the stela of King Nastasen (r. c. 335–315), the last readable Kushite historical monument in Egyptian, now in the Berlin Ägyptisches Museum. The record mentions that on his way to the place of coronation Nastasen visited the (unlocatable today) birthplace of King Piankhalara (supposedly identical with Alara) whose "might" he afterward received, together with the crown, from the god Amun at the enthronement ceremony. It might be inferred from the same statement that Alara originally came from some "provincial" place (evidently not far from Napata, the main political and religious center of Kush at that time) for its name seems to have never been mentioned again elsewhere in royal annals.

The fact that the majority of the surviving sources somehow associate Alara with the transfer of supreme power suggests that the references to him in the monuments of his successors were made in order to legitimate their respective ascents to the throne. However, such allusions to so distant a male ancestor are extremely few in the Kushite royal monuments where references to female relatives were feasible (due to the dogma of the theogamous origin of the kings) with rarest exceptions, and which normally did not go beyond the parents' generation. The special piety toward Alara is probably to be assigned to the fact that over time his descendants ceased to think of him as an earthly king and came to venerate him as a semimythological progenitor with whom a new era in the history of Kush began.

[See also Piankhy; and Taharqa.]

BIBLIOGRAPHY

Morkot, Robert G. *The Black Pharaohs: Egypt's Nubian Rulers.* London: Rubicon Press, 2000.

Török, L. "Alara: Evidence for Reign." In *Fontes Historiae Nubiorum: Textual Sources for the History of the Middle Nile Region between the Eighth Century BC and the Sixth Century AD,* edited by Tormod Eide, et al. 4 vols., vol. 1, pp. 41–42. Bergen, Norway: University of Bergen, 1994–2000.

Török, L. *The Birth of an African Kingdom of Kush and Her Myth of the State. Cahiers de recherches de l'Institute de papyrologie et d'égyptologie de Lille,* Supplement 4. Lille, France: University of Lille, 1995.

A. K. VINOGRADOV

Alassane, Moustapha (b. 1942), Nigerois filmmaker, was born in Ndougou (Niger). A mechanic by trade, he revealed himself to be an inventive young man at an early age. When no film theater existed in his village, indeed at a time when most of his fellow villagers had never seen a film, Alassane drew characters on cardboard, cut them out, and offered his fellow villagers their first cinematic experience by animating a rudimentary set of puppets.

In 1960 Alassane met Jean René Debrix and with his support obtained employment at the Institut d'Afrique Noire (Ifan) in Niamey. Later on, two major figures exerted profound influence on the art and filmmaking career of Moustapha Alassane: Jean Rouch, a French engineer turned Africanist and advocate of "direct anthropology," and Norman McLaren, a Scottish-Canadian who made his first film at age twenty and later became the animation guru at the studios of National Film Board of Canada in Montreal.

Rouch was fascinated by Alassane's inventiveness and soon hired him as a technical assistant. With Alassane, he shared a great interest in image making and technical know-how. Rouch's advocacy for filmmaking out in the open, away from the glare of studio lights, was motivated by a deep questioning of French cinema of the early twentieth century. Alassane never did have access to studios, nor to the equipment that went with first-world filmmaking. His films had to be shot in the open spaces for economic reasons and, as stated earlier, shown to local audiences in similar spaces. Rouch was an anthropologist–new wave filmmaker, whereas Alassane remained true to the spirit of the Federation Panafricaine des Cineastes (Fepaci) charter throughout his career. Rouch died in 2004 in Niger, in a car accident with Alassane at the wheel. Dingare Maiga, one of the earliest actors used both by Rouch and Alassane, was also a passenger in the car.

In the historiography of African cinema, Alassane is known as the father of film animation on the continent, a man who spread the art of filmmaking, trained and encouraged local actors, and fostered the development of new production technologies in cities, villages, and among university students of the University Abdou Moumini. He is as much an innovative creator as a relentless educator. His filmography boasts some thirty works, including several shorts, feature films, and animated films that tell local stories in genres as diverse as the prevailing social realism of the Fepaci group, the gangster, the western, and the documentary.

The year 1962 was a vintage one for Alassane. He directed *La bague du roi koda*, a film about love and the abuse of power; *Aoure*, a fictional film describing the rites of marriage in a village, much in the vein of Rouch's "cinema direct"; and *La Pileuse de mil* and *Le Piroguier*, two documentaries chronicling local activities that have sustained entire communities for centuries. In 1963, fresh from the Montreal studios of the National Film Board of Canada, Alassane produced the first African animated film, *La mort du Gandji* (1965). The film is a playful short advocating the power of imagination over brute force. The drawings are sketch-like, the movement of the characters swift, the mutations of sceneries fluid. Yet behind the humor of humiliated characters lay serious undertones of social responsibility, community welfare, and democratic government. In 1966 *La mort du Gandji* was awarded the Antilope d'Argent at the first festival of Negro arts held in Dakar (Senegal).

In 1964 another documentary appeared, *L'arachide de Sanchira* (1964), followed a year later by an aesthetic first, *Le retour de l'aventurier* (1966). The latter film is a parodic western critiquing and perhaps also acknowledging the pervasiveness of Euro-American cinematic genres among African youths. Serge Moati, a French filmmaker-television host, later produced a "making of" of it. At the close of 1966 Alassane produced another animated film, mocking the trappings and pretensions of political power in the postcolonial period: *Bon voyage Sim* (1966). Four other films followed between 1967 and 1971: *Malbaza* (1967), *Les contre bandiers* (1969), *Deela ou Albarka* (1970), and *Jamya* (1971).

In 1972 Alassane produced his first feature film, *Femme, villa, voiture argent* (1972), probably one of his better known works throughout Francophone Africa. Coming in the era of general disillusionment of African populations after ten years of independence, the film satirizes power politics among the new leaders and exposes the vanity of the "nouveaux riches." Four other films appeared between 1973 and 1975: *Abimbolla ou Shaki* (1972), *Siberi* (1973), *Soubane* (1974), and *Toula ou le genie des eaux* (1974). In 1978 Alassane collaborated with Jean Rouch on another animated film, narrated by Rouch, *Samba le grand*. The film is an adaptation of the legend of Samba Gana, also recorded by Frobenius.

A relentless creator, Moustapha Alassane signed off on another nine films by 2003: *Agwane mon village* (1982), *Kakamba ou le semeur de discorde* (1982), *Gourimou* (1982), *Soolo* (2000), *Adieu Sim* (2000), *Les Magiciens de l'Adar* (2001), *Agaissa* (2001), *Kokoa* (2001), and *Tagimba* (2003).

Moustapha Alassane's inventiveness knows no bounds: Once he fabricated a replacement piece for one of Rouch's broken cameras. Surrounded by a group of eager young men, he later built a camera from scratch, using his own cutting table, a millet shredding machine, and all his animated characters. With the advent of computer-based modes of production, he had a desktop computer brought to Tahoua, taught himself how to use it, and trained others to use it. The art of filmmaking, for him, had to be wrested from the demands of big budgets that suffocate so many young talents on the African continent. As of 2011 Alassane lives in Tahoua, where he operates a hotel.

[*See also* Rouch, Jean.]

BIBLIOGRAPHY

Boyd, Debra. *Animation in Creation*. 19-minute DVD, 2004.

Teicher, Gael. *Moustapha Alassane, Cineaste*. Paris: Editions l'Oeil, 2003.

TV5 Plus Documentaires. *Moustapha Alassane*.

SADA NIANG

Albasini, João dos Santos (1876–1922), nationalist, journalist and indigenous rights advocate, was born in Magul, Mozambique, on 2 November 1876. His father, Francisco Albasini, married the granddaughter of the head of Maxacuene clan in the Portuguese colony's capital; her name is not recorded. João dos Santos was also known by his Ronga nickname, Wadzinguele. His grandfather João Albasini, a Portuguese trader, later established himself and a second family in the republic of the Transvaal where he became the vice-consul of Portugal. João dos Santos Albasini received a limited education at the Catholic Mission of Saint José Lhenguene; secondary education was not available in Mozambique. However, he was a keen reader especially of political tracts and gained great facility in writing both Portuguese and Ronga. Sometime around 1897 Albasini married Bertha Carolina Heitor Mwatilo but the marriage was unhappy and they divorced in 1917. They had two children.

As Albasini reached adulthood, Portugal defeated the Gaza kingdom that dominated the central and southern parts of Mozambique ruled by a succession of Nguni warrior-kings during the nineteenth century. This ushered in a period of stability and investment in the colony. Lourenço Marques (present-day Maputo), the capital, was rapidly transformed from a small African town with a few white settlers into a busy, European-dominated port on the Indian Ocean, a center of commerce with rail links to neighboring countries. After a brief period of employment at the post office, Albasini became a forwarding agent at the port.

The fall of the Portuguese monarchy and the brief period of republicanism (1910–1926) allowed liberal, democratic, and anarchistic ideas to circulate widely in the overseas provinces. Black intellectuals such as Albasini participated in the relatively free and open debate of the time. He was a founding member of the influential nationalist group Grêmio Africano (African Club) whose membership consisted mainly of mission-educated African and mixed-race men. With his brother José and Estácio Dias, he founded the group's newspaper, *O Africano* (The African), in 1908, the first to be entirely written and produced by indigenous people. Its masthead read "devoted to the defense of the native population of Mozambique." In 1918 the newspaper was relaunched as a weekly, *O Brado Africano* (The African Roar). Both papers took up the cry against Portugal's linking of citizenship to race manifested in the body of "native" law and the Assimilation Law (1919). This laws distinguished *civilizados* (civilized people) from *não civilizados* (the uncivilized); the first classification, referring mainly to Portuguese and other Europeans, had full citizenship rights while the second designating indigenous populations, mainly in rural areas, were accorded mainly customary rights, the equivalent of second-class citizenship. A third category was admitted for those who were able to acquire some education and become literate in Portuguese. Mainly urban, these were recognized as *assimilados* or assimilated: Albasini and his Grêmio cohort belonged to this in-between stratum. They fought against this discrimination, verbally demonstrating the incivility, immorality, and corruption of the so-called civilized.

Journalism was never Albasini's source of income but rather his passion and his voice. His first editorial lamented that colonial monies were not being invested in roads, schools, standpipes, or factories to benefit the population. Albasini declared: "Enough!" and called for an end to the humiliation of the colony's subjects kept in ignorance and subordination.

While denouncing corruption and abuses of power, Albasini promoted the importance of literacy, education, and the use of the law and litigation in order to protect and defend indigenous interests in the face of territorial encroachment and labor exploitation. He also championed the interests and rights of rural and urban African women.

Despite his scathing editorials, the republican administration recognized Albasini for his prominent position in the colony. At the port, the governor-general appointed him to the post of director of Native Labor Services. This aroused controversy among workers who saw this as a betrayal of Albasini's public stance against forced labor. From September to December 1909 he was made part of a research expedition to study rural social conditions in the southern district Sul do Save. In 1914 he was the only African appointed to the six-person commission to study and codify Mozambican law.

Albasini died of tuberculosis in Lourenço Marques on 16 August 1922. Posthumously, a collection of five of his letters was published as *The Book of Pain* in 1925. It gave insight into the private as well as public life of this passionate, troubled, and controversial individual. His entire body of work is known for its outstanding literary merit.

Two Maputo buildings carry his name, the Escola João Albasini and the railway workers shelter known by his Ronga name, but he has yet to be fully recognized as one of the country's first nationalist heroes, probably because he never directly challenged colonialism as opposed to colonial policies.

BIBLIOGRAPHY

Honwana, Raúl. *The Life History of Raúl Honwana: an Inside View of Mozambique from Colonialism to Independence, 1905–1975.* Boulder, Colo., and London: L. Rienner Publishers, 1988. Edited and introduced by Allen Isaacman, this is a personal account of the history of the African elite's struggle for recognition. Isaacman's introduction and footnotes provide background and detail.

Penvenne, Jeanne. "João dos Santos Albasini (1876–1922): The Contradictions of Politics and Identity in Colonial Mozambique." *The Journal of African History* 37, no. 3 (1996): 419–464. The most comprehensive source of information on Albasini.

Penvenne, Jeanne. " 'We are all Portuguese!' Challenging the Political Economy of Assimilation: Lourenço Marques, 1870–1933." In *The Creation of Tribalism in Southern Africa.* London: Currey, and Los Angeles: University of California Press, 1989. This essay sets the background for the Grêmio

Africano and provides an analysis of its and successor groups' significance for the independence struggle of the 1960s and 1970s.

ROSEMARY ELIZABETH GALLI

Alemayo Kahsay (1925–1991), Eritrean comedian, theater artist, musician, and sports teacher, was born on 1 February 1925 during the Italian colonial period in Eritrea in Abba Shawl, the poor segregated Eritrean quarters of the capital Asmara. His father was Kahsay Woldegebr, and his mother, Ghebriela Fitwi.

At the age of ten he attended an Orthodox Church school and then received four years of Italian schooling, the maximum period of formal education for Eritreans under Italian rule. Thereafter Alemayo worked as a messenger for an Italian lawyer and, at the age of seventeen, found employment as a stagehand in Cinema Asmara, then Teatro Asmara, an imposing Italian theater and center for Italian social and cultural life. Here Alemayo was exposed to European variety shows, operas, and cinema that fascinated him greatly, particularly the genre of comedy, such as the works of Charlie Chaplin and the Neapolitan comedian Totò.

Italian colonization was characterized by strict race segregation, particularly under Fascist rule (1922–1941), and Eritreans were only allowed in the elegant Italian quarters of Asmara as workers and servants. When an Italian actor failed to perform a complicated stage fall during rehearsal, Alemayo asked to do it instead. Though performing to full satisfaction, he was initially not allowed to act with the all-white company, but later participated in Italian variety shows, especially their *barzellette* (jokes) programs. With the beginning of the British Military Administration period in Eritrea (1941–1952) Eritrean-European cultural collaboration began to be easier, but for Alemayo these performances, and the training he received from Italian entertainers, were only a stepping-stone on the way to modern Eritrean theater arts. In 1945 he acted in a religious play, *The Birth of Christ* by Memher (Teacher) Abraham Redda, which was performed in the main language of the Eritrean highlands, Tigrinya. Though the play failed to draw wider public interest, Alemayo was proud to perform with his compatriots in his own mother tongue. This reflected his growing political consciousness and activities.

From 1941 to 1952 he was an active member of the Unionist Party that campaigned for the unification of Eritrea with Ethiopia. In the 1940s he also served as the president of its Youth League, the Unionists' vice president, and as its president for a time, receiving the honorary Ethiopian title *grazmach* (commander of the left wing, a military title) in 1972 for his commitment. In 1947, as part of his activities for the Unionists, Alemayo became the main actor and director of Berhe Mesgun's anticolonial play, *Eritrea's Past Property*, which portrayed the cruelties Eritreans suffered under Italian colonialism. When the play was banned by the British authorities, the idea emerged to set up a theater association independent of any party affiliations. Thus Mahber Tewas'o Dekebbat (Ma.Te.De. or The Native Comedy and Dramatic Association, in their own translation) was founded at the end of 1947 in which Alemayo played an important role. He worked as an actor, director, manager, and musician and also designed the posters for the association.

Though never making a living from theater—from 1955 to 1961 he was employed as a sports teacher in Mendefera, today's capital of the Southern Region, and then moved back to Asmara as head of sports affairs for Eritrean schools in the Department of Education—he devoted all his spare time to the stage. Alemayo became particularly famous for his comic skills and was widely known as Wetru Higgus ("Always Smiling/Happy") or the Eritrean Totò. Many of his comic sketches and songs were still remembered in the twenty-first century; he was also remembered as an accomplished boxer and sports referee.

After the demise of Ma.Te.De in 1957, Alemayo became a leading figure in successive theater associations, Mahber Memhiyash Hagherwawi Limdi (Ma.M.Ha.L.; Association for the Improvement of National Customs, 1957–1960) and most importantly as the cofounder, president, and artistic director of Mahber Teatr Asmera (Ma.Te.A., 1961 to c. 1974), the Asmara Theater Association. With its unique variety shows and high quality of performances, Ma.Te.A. was the most significant Eritrean theater association of the twentieth century and influenced modern performing arts in Eritrea beyond the turn of the millennium. In his capacity as educator, Alemayo also always supported theater and music activities of the young. In the 1960s he led a theater group of the Teachers Association, mounted school plays at the end of the academic year, and together with his colleague, friend, and fellow musician Memher Asres Tessema, initiated Students' Music Day. He also organized theater activities in Orthodox Church and Asmara Residents associations.

Alemayo is considered to be the founding father of modern Eritrean performing arts. Married to Abeba Okbaledet, with whom he had two sons and a daughter, Alemayo died on 3 May 1991 in Milan, Italy.

BIBLIOGRAPHY

Asres Tessema. *Te'amot: kab tarikh medrekhawi sne-Tibeb 'Ertra, 1940–1980* [Tea Time Snack: Stories of the Performing Arts in Eritrea, 1940–1980]. Asmara, Eritrea: Bet Sehefat, 2006.

Matzke, Christine. "The Asmara Theatre Association, 1961–1974: *Mahber Te'atr Asmera.*" In *African Theatre: Companies*, edited by James Gibbs. Oxford: James Currey, 2008.

Matzke, Christine. "Looking for 'Eritrea's Past Property' (1947): Archives and Memories in Eritrean Theatre Historiography." In *African Theatre 9: Histories 1850-1950*, edited by Yvette Hutchison. Oxford: James Currey, 2010.

Plastow, Jane. "Theatre of Conflict in the Eritrean Independence Struggle." *New Theatre Quarterly* 13, no. 50 (1997).

CHRISTINE MATZKE with MEMHER ASRES TESSEMA, TEDROS HAGOS, and YAKEM TESFAI

Alemseged Tesfai (1944–), Eritrean lawyer, writer, and researcher, was born on 19 October in the southern Eritrean market town of Adi Quala. His father was Tesfai Gebremichael, a government employee, his mother, Hiwet Tesfabruk, a housewife. Alemseged was the sixth of seven siblings, four boys and three girls. From the age of six he attended various elementary and secondary schools in Eritrea and Ethiopia before matriculating in 1962 from Haile Selassie Secondary School in the Eritrean capital, Asmara. After a nine-month work experience as a junior clerk with Ethiopian Airlines in Asmara (to avoid forced conscription into the Ethiopian military academy), he joined the Faculty of Law at Haile Selassie I University in the Ethiopian capital, Addis Ababa, graduating in September 1969 with an LLB (bachelor of laws). Thereafter Alemseged was briefly employed as a legal expert in the Ethiopian Ministry of Finance, a post he left in May 1970 to pursue graduate studies in the United States. At the time Eritrea was engaged in a liberation war against Ethiopia (1961–1991), then under the reign of Emperor Haile Selassie. Already nurturing strong feelings of nationalism and deeply resenting Ethiopian occupation, Alemseged took an MLC (Master of Comparative Law) at the University of Illinois, Champaign-Urbana, between

1970 and 1972, after which he started his PhD at the Land Tenure Center, University of Wisconsin, Madison.

In 1974, on having passed his preliminary PhD exams, he abandoned his academic career and returned to Eritrea to join the Eritrean People's Liberation Front (EPLF) as a liberation fighter. After his military training, he first worked as an organizer in the Front's mass organization section (1974–1975) before being assigned to the educational department. Initially a teacher with the Revolution School of the EPLF, he then became director (1978–1979) of the Liberation School in Keren, today's capital of the Anseba Region, and thereafter head of curriculum of the EPLF Education Division (1978–1981).

In 1981 Alesemged changed to the Division of Culture, where he was made responsible for the development and advancement of "revolutionary culture," especially literature and drama. Though without previous experience in the arts, he studied whatever literature was available during the war and began to write texts on literature and theater, among them the critical evaluations *Literature, Its Development, and Its Role in Revolution* (1982) and *Drama* (1983). His ideas on socialist realism strongly influenced writing and other cultural practices during the liberation struggle. He also wrote essays and fictional texts, such as the popular novel *Son of Hadera* (1983), and an essay about the sacrifices of war, "Heart of *Tegadalai* [Fighter]" (1988). Between 1981 and 1984 Alemseged wrote three plays, among them *Le'ul* (1982; performed 1983), a drama about a female factory worker and clandestine member of the EPLF, and the acclaimed *The Other War* (1984), which portrays the rising tensions in an Eritrean family during the liberation struggle when the daughter returns with an Ethiopian husband. The play was the first full-length production to be documented on video by the EPLF Cine-Section and was also distributed among Eritrean exile communities abroad. In 1997 it was premiered in English at the West Yorkshire Playhouse in Leeds, England. From 1982 to 1986 Alemseged became the deputy head of the Cultural Division, and from 1986 to 1987 he was its director. He also served on the editorial board of the EPLF magazine *Harbenya* (1987–1988) and was deputy director of the Tigrinya program of the EPLF Radio (1988–1991) until Eritrea was liberated in 1991.

As head of the Cultural Centre of the Provisional Government of Eritrea (1992–1993) Alemseged was engaged in finding new directions for post-independence culture, but was then called on to lead the Land Commission of the Government of Eritrea (1993–1996) which sought to find equitable ways to relocate land. In 1997 Alemseged moved to the Research and Documentation Centre in Asmara, where he became head of the History Project. In the same year, he won the Raimok Prize for Tigrinya literature, the highest national award, for a collection of short stories, plays, and essays on childhood and war, later published in English as *Two in Weeks in the Trenches* (2002). While from 1997 his major project was historical research that resulted in a trilogy on Eritrean history covering Eritrea under the British Military Administration period (1941–1952) and the Federation with Ethiopia (1952–1962), he also published articles on reconstruction, development, and politics in Eritrea, and continued to write fiction, especially children's literature. Married in 1982 to Abrehet Haile, a former liberation fighter and judge in the High Court of Eritrea with whom he had a son, Temesgen (1993-2009), Alemseged lived in Asmara after independence and was one of the major intellectual voices in the country.

BIBLIOGRAPHY

Alemseged Tesfai. *Two Weeks in the Trenches: Reminiscences of Childhood and War in Eritrea.* Translated from the Tigrinya by the author. Lawrenceville, N.J.: Red Sea Press, 2002.

Matzke, Christine. " 'Life in the Camp of the Enemy': Alemseged Tesfai's Theatre of War." In *War in African Literature Today: A Review*, edited by Ernest N. Emenyonu. African Literature Today, vol. 26. Oxford: James Currey, 2008.

Negash, Ghirmai. *A History of Tigrinya Literature in Eritrea: The Oral and the Written, 1890–1991.* Leiden, Netherlands: University of Leiden, 1999.

Plastow, Jane. "Alemseged Tesfai: A Playwright in Service to Eritrean Liberation." *African Theatre in Development*, edited by Martin Banham, James Gibbs, and Femi Osofisan. Bloomington: Indiana University Press, 1999.

Plastow, Jane, and S. Tsehaye. "Making Theatre for a Change: Two Plays of the Eritrean Liberation Struggle. In *Theatre Matters: Performance and Culture on the World Stage*, edited by Richard Boon and Jane Plastow. Cambridge, UK, and New York: Cambridge University Press, 1998.

CHRISTINE MATZKE

Alexander, Jane (1959–), South African sculptor and multimedia artist, was born in Johannesburg, South Africa. Her father's family emigrated from Germany (her paternal grandfather was Jewish). She studied at the University of the Witwatersrand, Johannesburg, graduating with a bachelor of fine arts degree and the Martienssen Student Prize in 1982 and completing her masters degree in 1988. She taught English and art at schools in Namibia and Cape Town before joining the Michaelis School of Fine Art, University of Cape Town, as a part-time lecturer in 1996. She holds a professorship in sculpture and is resident in Cape Town. An intensely private person, Alexander rarely gives interviews or explains her work verbally.

In 1986 Alexander gained attention with a solo exhibition in Johannesburg. It included *Butcher Boys* (1985–1986), a disquieting depiction of three white, life-size, naturalistic figures seated on a bench. These self-absorbed beings, possessing animal and human visual characteristics, bear signs of physical damage and abnormality. Now in the permanent collection of the South African National Gallery, Cape Town, this sculpture established the direction of Alexander's career: a commitment to probing the consequences of action and power relations.

After South Africa's readmission to world politics and culture in 1994 Alexander participated in the Havana Biennale (1994) and the Venice Biennale (1995). In 1995 she was awarded the prestigious Standard Bank Young Artist Award for Fine Art and produced a highly acclaimed touring exhibition featuring sculptures and photomontages. She gained the FNB Vita Art Now Award (1996) and the DaimlerChrysler Award for Contemporary Sculpture (2002). *African Adventure*, produced after winning the DaimlerChrysler Award, toured to Stuttgart and Berlin as well as within South Africa.

Alexander has participated in many international shows, notably The Short Century: Independence and Liberation Movements in Africa 1945–1994 (Munich, Berlin, Chicago, and New York, 2001–2002), Africa Remix: Contemporary Art of a Continent (Düsseldorf, London, Paris, Tokyo, Johannesburg, 2004–2008), How to Live Together (27th Sao Paulo Biennale, 2006), Belief (Singapore Biennale, Singapore, 2006), Zoo (La Centrale Electrique, Brussels, 2006), Triennial Beaufort 2006, PMMK Museum of Modern Art in Ostend, and the North Sea Coast of Belgium (2006), Re-Thinking Dissent (Fourth Gothenburg Biennial, Gothenburg, Sweden, 2007), Apartheid—The South African Mirror (CCCB Centre de Cultura Contemporània Barcelona, 2007–2008), and Jane

Alexander on Being Human (Galilee Chapel, Durham Cathedral, England, 2009).

Having worked during the pre-1994 apartheid regime, when South Africa was subject to an international cultural boycott, Alexander became part of a postapartheid South African cultural art scene that participates in global art events. Her art bears the imprint of a deep awareness of human injustice and irrationality but it is as simplistic to position as it is explicitly South African sociopolitical comment. The reception accorded to her works in global venues confirms that Alexander expresses human concerns and, while many of her references might originate in South African (and African) history and daily life, she explores stories of existence that resonate in all societies.

Alexander's work is essentially narrative but it communicates on the cusp of cause and effect, within tableaux where action is suspended and probable outcomes are evoked, not prescribed. Viewers are compelled to look and ponder relationships between protagonists, objects, and spaces. The actors are enigmatic, seemingly real and yet invariably deviating from recognizably human or animal forms. As hybrids or mutants, they are humanoid in posture and may wear clothes, but possess the features of birds, monkeys, dogs, and antelopes. "Reality" becomes conceptually problematic.

The disquietude generated by Alexander's forms is attributable to stillness; viewers wait for something to happen, aware that the events portrayed are staged and meaning is deferred. In early works, such as *Butcher Boys*, the forms seem to illustrate a moment of frozen time, but from the late nineties narrative is more overtly postmodern, complex, open-ended, and unpredictable. Characters, such as the antelope-headed Harbinger, or Monkey Boy, recur in different stagings and settings, making Alexander's oeuvre a work in progress and a process of continuous character reexamination. Her central protagonists are inserted into events to witness or participate in action, evoking empathy or hostility from viewers who are responsible for constructing meaning. In sculpting her tragic dramas, Alexander uses the traditional devices of the theater—characters (who may also function as types), clothing defining identity, masks revealing and concealing identity, objects facilitating and locating action, and space as setting. Time, required to generate action, is suspended, and dialogue is replaced by silence.

Although Alexander's sculptural installations are frightening in their references to fantasy and reality, they are beautiful in their attention to form, detail, and spatial manipulation. As tableaux that are installed in different interior spaces, their narrative implications change because local histories are introduced. In the former British officers' mess in The Castle, Cape Town, redolent with colonial architectural features, *African Adventure* acquired references to South Africa's long history of racial division and discrimination, but these issues were not overtly present when the work was shown in the Hayward Gallery, London, at Africa Remix. Similarly *Bom Boys* functioned differently in Cape Town's Irma Stern Museum than in medieval Durham Cathedral.

Freud's term, the "uncanny," explains the strong emotional effect produced by Alexander's tableaux. Her imagery arouses dread because the familiar is rendered alien. Possessing an immaculate sense of how sculpture functions as visual and tactile form in space, Alexander casts and models smoothly articulated surfaces, introduces found objects such as artificial eyes, beaks, horns, animal hide, hair, and clothing, as well as found objects fused and altered to discard functionality and attain new identity. The uncanny, through its process of defamiliarization, creates the ambivalence that disturbs viewers within and beyond Africa. Trying to produce meaning they must seek analogies in their own experiences of disgust, horror, irresolution, brutality, pain, and other emotions that scar personal and social existence. Viewers become uncomfortably self-conscious and aware that Alexander does not render social comment; instead she offers opportunities for her audience to reach moral judgments about human behavior and what it means to be human or inhuman.

BIBLIOGRAPHY

Alexander, Jane. *Jane Alexander*. Exhibition catalog for the DaimlerChrysler Award 2002. Essays by Simon Njami and Akiko Miki. New York: Distributed by Art Publishers, 2002. Now out of print but offers essays by writers from outside South Africa.

Arnold, Marion. *Women and Art in South Africa*. New York: St. Martin's Press, 1996. See chapter 7, Sculpting the Body, which contains a lengthy discussion of Alexander's early work, accompanied by six color and two black-and-white illustrations.

Njami, Simon, ed. *Africa Remix: Contemporary Art of a Continent*. Exhibition catalog. London: Hayward Gallery, 2005. Contains a double-page spread illustrating *African Adventure*.

Powell, Ivor, "Inside and Outside of History." *Art South Africa* 5, no. 4 (Winter 2007): 32–38. A well-illustrated, insightful, well-argued critique extending his eloquent essay in Alexander's Standard Bank Young Artist's catalog (1995), which is difficult to obtain.

MARION ARNOLD

Alexander, Neville Edward (1936–), South African intellectual and political activist, was born in Cradock, Eastern Cape, South Africa, on 22 October 1936. His father was David James Alexander, a carpenter, and his mother, Dimbiti Bisho Alexander, a schoolteacher. His maternal grandmother was one of sixty-four Oromo children who were enslaved in Ethiopia in 1888 and subsequently brought to Lovedale in the Eastern Cape. His maternal grandfather was a Presbyterian Church pastor.

Alexander grew up in Cradock where he was also educated at the Holy Rosary Convent. After completing his schooling at the age of sixteen he enrolled at the University of Cape Town where he excelled in German and History, graduating with a BA in 1955, a BA (Hons) in 1956, and an MA in 1957. Both of the latter degrees were in German. In 1958 he was awarded an Alexander von Humboldt Foundation fellowship to study for a PhD at the University of Tübingen in Germany, which he completed in 1961. He also completed a BA (Hons) degree in history by correspondence in 1971 during his imprisonment on Robben Island.

Alexander is best known for his political work and scholarly achievements on the "national question," the struggle for a democratic, nonracial, and anticapitalist South Africa. His work on the role of language in the process of building national unity is particularly significant. This work and his writing were shaped both by his academic studies and his membership in the Non-European Unity Movement (NEUM) and by his period of study in Germany where he read the important debates on national identity in the works of Johann von Herder and Johann Fichte and had the opportunity of meeting with the emergent figures of the German left-wing movement. It was also while he was there that he was introduced to the ideas of guerrilla warfare and the new modes of struggles that were developing in Algeria, Cuba, and other parts of the colonial world.

When Alexander returned to South Africa in 1961 he took up a teaching post at Livingstone High School in Cape Town and resumed his work in socialist political organizations. For seeking to open up the debate on armed struggle he and a number of colleagues were expelled from the African Peoples Democratic Union of Southern Africa (APDUSA) in 1961. He was instrumental in the formation of a study group in 1962 known as the Yu Chi Chan Club (YCCC) which was superseded by the National Liberation Front (NLF). He was arrested in July 1963 along with a number of NLF members and convicted in 1964 of conspiracy to commit sabotage. He was jailed on Robben Island from 1964 to 1974. The period of Alexander's incarceration on Robben Island coincided with that of Nelson Mandela, Walter Sisulu, and a number of the country's most important political activists. While the conditions of their imprisonment were initially restrictive and brutal, Alexander and his fellow prisoners succeeded in inaugurating a profound debate on the island on the political struggle and its quest for reconstituting South Africa as a free and democratic country. The nature and quality of this debate made the prison one of the country's leading sites of intellectual production. A full account of this development has yet to be undertaken.

Upon Alexander's release he was banned and placed under house arrest in Lotus River, Cape Town, until 1979. When this came to an end he chose to work on two related fronts. The first was in the arena of political and civic struggle and the second was in exploring the role of education and language in the national question. With respect to his political work, he sought to build a united front of the organizations working among the politically disenfranchised and the working class. This brought him into an important conversation with the leaders of the Black Consciousness Movement, including Steve Biko. It was out of this that he came to play a formative role in the establishment of the Disorderly Bills' Action Committee in the Western Cape and its successor, the Cape Action League, which itself was instrumental in the establishment of the National Forum, a coalition of left-wing organizations established on the principles of a united front. After the "reconciliation" talks between the African National Congress and the National Party, he was in the forefront of the establishment of the Workers' Organisation for a Socialist Azania (WOSA), an organization to which he remains committed.

On the education front, Alexander worked as the Western Cape Director of the South African Committee for Higher Education (SACHED), which also led to the establishment of a leading alternative higher education initiative called Khanya College. He subsequently established the National Language Project and the Project for the Study of Alternative Education in South Africa (PRAESA) located at the University of Cape Town. SACHED provided Alexander with the opportunity for exploring the concept of alternative education. When the student uprising was at its height in the 1970s and the 1980s it was to initiatives such as SACHED that they turned for guidance in developing new approaches to education. Through the NLP and PRAESA Alexander led the national debate around language policy and planning in South Africa. It was as a consequence of this that he came to play a leading role in language policy development with various government departments, including serving for a period as the chairperson of the new government's Language Plan Task Group. His most recent work focused on the tension between multilingualism and the hegemony of English in the public sphere.

Alexander's intellectual output is marked by a series of influential books and articles. Among the most seminal are *One Azania, One Nation*, written under the pseudonym No Sizwe, which presents a view of the distribution of power and privilege in terms of class, caste, and color; *Sow the Wind*, written in 1986, which was influential in the analysis and politics around the uprising in the country; and *An Ordinary Country*, published in 2002, which sought to reflect on the politics of South Africa's transition to democracy.

Alexander was the recipient of the Linguapax Prize for 2008 in recognition of his contributions to language policy, linguistic diversity, and multilingual education.

[*See also* Biko, Steve; Mandela, Nelson Rolihlahla; *and* Sisulu, Walter Max Ulyate.]

BIBLIOGRAPHY

Alexander, Neville Edward. "Non-Collaboration in the Western Cape." In *The Angry Divide: Social and Economic History of the Western Cape*, edited by Wilmot James and Mary Simons. Cape Town, South Africa: David Philip, 1989. An important essay by Alexander on the political tradition of noncollaboration in South Africa.

Alexander, Neville Edward. *An Ordinary Country: Issues in the Transition from Apartheid to Democracy in South Africa*. Pietermaritzburg, South Africa: University of KwaZulu-Natal Press, 2002. A critical commentary on the transition to democracy.

Chisholm, Linda. "Making the Pedagogical More Political, and the Political More Pedagogical: Education Traditions and Legacies of the Non-European Unity Movement." In *Vintage Kenton: A Kenton Education Association Commemoration*, edited by W. Flanagan et al. Cape Town, South Africa: Maskew Miller Longman, 1994. This chapter is about the pedagogical tradition of the Non-European Unity Movement and includes a short description of Alexander as a teacher.

Drew, Allison. *South Africa's Radical Tradition: A Documentary History*. 2 vols. Cape Town, South Africa: University of Cape Town Press, 1996. This overview helps to locate the socialist movement in South Africa historically.

No Sizwe. *One Azania, One Nation: The National Question in South Africa*. London: Zed Press, 1979. Alexander's first major scholarly intervention on the "national question" after his unbanning. Written while he was under house arrest, it develops a completely new analytic framework for understanding the relationship between race and class in South Africa.

Soudien, Crain. "The Contribution of Radical Western Cape Intellectuals to an Indigenous Knowledge Project in South Africa." Forthcoming in *Transformation: Critical Perspectives on Southern Africa*. An article that focuses on the contribution of Ben Kies and Neville Alexander to the concept of nonracialism.

CRAIN SOUDIEN

Alexander the Great (356–323 BCE), king of Macedon (336–323 BCE). The thirteen-year reign of Alexander III of Macedon fundamentally changed the political and cultural structure of western Asia and North Africa. The Persian Empire, whose rule had extended from the Mediterranean to the borders of India, disappeared and was replaced by a system of competing Macedonian-ruled kingdoms. As a result, the region's center of gravity shifted westward from its ancient focus in Mesopotamia and southwestern Iran to the shores of the Mediterranean. Equally important, Greek became the language of government and Greek culture became the new elite culture throughout this vast region.

Writing the history of Alexander's brief but remarkable reign is difficult. Primary sources are few. Of the many accounts written by his contemporaries and the numerous documents issued by his government that once existed, only fragments quoted by later writers and a few inscriptions survive.

Therefore, historians depend for their reconstructions on five Greek and Latin biographies of Alexander written between the mid-first century BCE and the second century CE: the seventeenth book of the *Library of History* of Diodorus (first century BCE), the epitome of the *Philippic History* of Trogus Pompeius (first century BCE), the *History of Alexander* of Quintus Curtius Rufus (first century CE), the *Life of Alexander* of Plutarch (second century CE), and the *Anabasis of Alexander* of Arrian (second century CE). We also lack sources that reflect the perspective of the Persians and the other peoples Alexander encountered. Nevertheless, the basic facts of Alexander's career are not in doubt.

Alexander was born in 356 BCE, the eldest child of Philip II (r. 360–336 BCE) of Macedon and his Epirote wife, Olympias. His upbringing was appropriate to his status as heir to the throne of Macedon; he was educated by a number of Greek tutors including the philosopher Aristotle and trained for his role as king and commander of the Macedonian army by his father. When he succeeded Philip II as king of Macedon in 336 BCE, Alexander had been well prepared to assume the role of king and to continue the invasion of the Persian Empire that his father had launched prior to his death.

Before resuming his father's Persian campaign, Alexander devoted the first two years of his reign to consolidating his hold on power. Rapid campaigns in the northern Balkans and Greece headed off rebellions by Macedon's Greek and non-Greek subjects and secured his appointment as *hegemon* ("leader") of the Corinthian League and commander of the war against Persia. With Macedon and Greece secure, Alexander crossed into northwest Asia Minor in spring 334 BCE at the head of an army of about thirty-five thousand men.

Between his crossing into Asia in 334 BCE and his death at Babylon in June 323 BCE, Alexander campaigned throughout the territories of the Persian Empire from Egypt in the west to northern India in the east. The campaign can be divided into three phases. The first, which lasted from 334 BCE to 330 BCE, is known to historians as the "Greek Crusade" and was marked by the great set battles of Granicus, Issus, and Gaugamela. It climaxed with the destruction of the Persian capital of Persepolis and the assassination of the Persian king Darius III by his own officers. The second phase, which lasted from 330 BCE to 327 BCE, saw Alexander adopt various aspects of Persian royal ceremonial and practice, despite Macedonian and Greek opposition, in order to attract Iranian support to counter fierce guerrilla resistance in central Asia. The third and final phase of the campaign began with the two years Alexander spent in India. It ended with his disastrous return to the west through Baluchistan. He died at Babylon, while planning an invasion of Arabia.

Within this remarkable career of conquest, Alexander's conquest of Egypt occupies a place of special significance. Egypt had repeatedly rebelled against Persian rule, the last time less than five years before its satrap, cut off from possible reinforcements and unsure of Egyptian support, surrendered Egypt to Alexander without resistance in late 332 BCE. Alexander spent only about six months in Egypt before departing for his final confrontation with Darius III in spring 331 BCE, but his actions during this period were varied and critical for the future of Egypt. Some were military, such as a reconnaissance expedition he dispatched into Nubia—which, incidentally, resulted in providing Greek geographers with the first certain evidence that rain south of Egypt was the cause of the Nile flood. Others were personal, such as his visit to the oracle of the god Ammon in the oasis of Siwah in the Libyan dessert, where the priests recognized him as the son of Ammon. The most important for the future of Egypt, however, was the foundation of Alexandria, the first and greatest of Alexander's city foundations.

For the site of Alexandria, Alexander chose an Egyptian village named Rhacotis, located near the Canopic mouth of the Nile at the westernmost point of the Delta, a location made famous by a passage in the fourth book of Homer's *Odyssey* (book 4, lines 351–360). Although Alexandria was intended from the beginning to have a multiethnic population that included both Egyptians and Greeks, it was organized as a Greek polis with citizenship limited to its Greek inhabitants. The same preference for Greeks and Greek culture characterized other aspects of Alexander's actions in Egypt. So while he sacrificed to the Apis bull at Memphis, thus signaling his intention to honor traditional Egyptian cults, he spent few resources on temple construction, a principal duty of pharaohs, and celebrated his conquest of Egypt with elaborate Greek-style games. Similarly, while he left local Egyptian officials such as *nomarchs* in place and welcomed the collaboration of Egyptian priests and aristocrats, even assigning responsibility for civil affairs to two Egyptians, military and financial affairs remained in the hands of Macedonian officers and an Egyptian-born Greek,

Cleomenes of Naucratis, whom Alexander later appointed as satrap when the two Egyptians left their offices.

Historians have proposed widely divergent theories concerning Alexander's ultimate goals, ranging from a belief popular before World War II that he wished to realize the philosophical dream of the unity of mankind to the contemporary view that he was a typically brutal conqueror with no goals beyond glory and personal aggrandizement. Part of the reason for this wide range of views is the already mentioned limitations of the sources. Equally important, however, is the fact that Alexander died before he could develop a final plan for the governance of his empire. Instead, he improvised various solutions to administrative problems as they arose during the course of the campaign. Thus, while his growing autocracy, which was heightened by his belief in his semidivine status as the son of Ammon, is certain, as are his efforts to supplement the limited Macedonian and Greek manpower available to him by encouraging collaboration by native elites, neither policy had been institutionalized at the time of his death. Paradoxically, therefore, Alexander's principal contribution to history was essentially negative. He destroyed the Persian Empire and with it the state system that had dominated ancient southwest Asia for two centuries, but it would be his successors who devised a new state system to replace it. The same situation was true for Egypt. Alexander freed Egypt from Persian rule, but he devised no new system of governance for the country, essentially adopting with few changes the organization already in place during the last years of Persian rule. As a result, those Egyptians who may have hoped for a restoration of native rule were to be disappointed. Alexander's conquest instead laid the foundation for a millennium of domination, first by the Ptolemies and then by Romans, that would end only with the Arab conquest of Egypt in 642 CE.

[See also Cleomenes of Naucratis; and Ptolemy I Soter.]

BIBLIOGRAPHY

Bosworth, A. B. Conquest and Empire: The Reign of Alexander the Great. Cambridge, UK, and New York: Cambridge University Press, 1988.

Bowman, Alan K. Egypt after the Pharaohs, 332 BC–AD 642: From Alexander to the Arab Conquest. Berkeley and Los Angeles: University of California Press, 1986.

Burstein, Stanley M. Graeco-Africana: Studies in the History of Greek Relations with Egypt and Nubia. New Rochelle, N.Y.: A. D. Caratzas, 1995.

Cook, J. M. The Persian Empire. London: J. M. Dent & Sons, 1983.

Fraser, Peter M. Ptolemaic Alexandria. Oxford: Clarendon Press, 1972.

STANLEY M. BURSTEIN

Alfa Yaya. See Diallo, Alfa Yaya.

'Ali 'Abd al-Latif (1896?–1948), Sudanese political leader and ex-army officer, was born in 1896 (or 1892 or 1894) in Wadi Halfa, a border town between Egypt and Sudan. Both his father, 'Abd al-Latif Ahmad (who is said to have been from the Nuba Mountains) and his mother, Sabr (who was of Dinka origin, the largest ethnic group in the South Sudan), were people from the marginalized areas in Sudan, who, as a result of the slave raids in the nineteenth century, had been uprooted from their original homes. Both had stayed for a while in al-Khandaq, a town in north Sudan, but in the course of social upheaval caused by the Mahdist movement (1881–1898) found their way to Egypt. At the time of 'Ali's birth, his father was serving in the Egyptian army, which at that time included many Sudanese soldiers of ex-slave origin. On the occasion of the conquest of Sudan by the Anglo-Egyptian forces and the overthrow of the Mahdist state (1898), the family returned to Sudan.

After his father's retirement, 'Ali was brought up in Khartoum under the guardianship of his maternal uncle Rihan 'Abdallah, an ex-officer of Dinka origin. 'Ali graduated from the military school in 1913, was commissioned a second lieutenant in 1914, and served in different places in Sudan such as the Nuba Mountains, Darfur, and the south. He was promoted to lieutenant in 1918 and around 1919 was transferred to the Fourteenth Battalion in Wad Madani, a town in the Gezira area, south of Khartoum. In 1921 a political friction arose between 'Ali and his British superior. He was suspended from his duty and summoned to Khartoum.

Politically, Sudan at that time was passing through its most critical juncture. So far, although Sudan was under Anglo-Egyptian Condominium, it was in effect a British rule, for Egypt itself had been under British occupation since 1882. As a result of the Egyptian 1919 Revolution, however, the situation began to change. In Sudan, while the British authorities resorted, in order to counteract the growing Egyptian influence, to social forces such as tribal and religious leaders and attempted to forge a sort of conservative, pro-British "Sudanese nationalism," aspirations for a more democratic type of nationalism developed among the Sudanese youth who were serving in the modern sector of society, such as junior officials and officers, and secret organizations such as the League of the Sudanese Union emerged. Although it is not clear whether 'Ali belonged to this league or not, he is said to have established, while he was in Wad Madani, an organization called the Sudan United Tribes Society. It is noteworthy that, perhaps because of his own social background, 'Ali seems to have been keen on the point that, among the Sudanese people, there should be no discrimination based on race or clan.

In May 1922 'Ali was arrested in Khartoum for submitting to a newspaper an article titled the "Claims of the Sudanese Nation." The article called for the self-determination of the Sudanese people and presented a number of social demands such as more education, the appointment of Sudanese officials to the higher posts, and the revision of the Gezira scheme (a large-scale cotton plantation that was being constructed by the British). Although he was put on trial on 14 June, deprived of his military rank, and imprisoned for a year, this enhanced his influence among the Sudanese masses. After his release from prison in 1923, he established in May 1924, together with 'Ubayd Hajj al-Amin, who had represented the progressive wing of the League of the Sudanese Union, a new organization, the White Flag League. Its aim was to achieve the national liberation of Sudan in cooperation with the Egyptian Wafdist government led by Sa'd Zaghlul, a strategy that was expressed as the "unity of the Nile Valley." In June and July the League launched on a series of activities such as collecting signatories, attempting to dispatch a delegation to Egypt, sending telegrams to the international community, and organizing popular demonstrations (the "1924 Revolution"). On 3 July 'Ali sent a telegram to British Prime Minister Ramsay MacDonald, in which he criticized "imperialistic tactics and capitalistic schemes intended to annex Sudan forcibly into British Empire." He was arrested the following day, accused of instigation, and was sentenced to three years imprisonment. Even in prison, throughout the year 1924, he remained the symbol of national resistance.

After the revolution was finally suppressed, 'Ali was tried again in April 1925 and was sentenced to additional seven years' imprisonment. Although his term expired in 1934, the British authorities did not release him, on the ground that he had become mentally unstable while in prison. In May 1938 'Ali was sent to Egypt and put in a mental hospital in Cairo, where he was forced to remain until his death on 29 October 1948.

'Ali married al-'Azza Muhammad 'Abdallah in 1916, and had two daughters. In the course of the 1924 Revolution, al-'Azza played her own role, taking part in demonstrations (one of the first Sudanese women to do so) and trying to hide her husband's documents when their house was searched.

[*See also* Zaghlul, Sa'd.]

BIBLIOGRAPHY

Abdin, Hasan. *Early Sudanese Nationalism 1919–1925.* Khartoum, Sudan: Khartoum University Press, 1985.

Beshir, Mohamed Omer. *Revolution and Nationalism in the Sudan.* London: Rex Collings, 1974.

Kurita, Yoshiko. *'Ali 'Abd al-Latif wa Thawra 1924.* Cairo: The Sudanese Studies Center, 1997.

YOSHIKO KURITA

'Ali Bey the Great (1728–1773), Mamluk leader of Egypt (1760–1773), was born in the western Georgian region of Abkhazia to a Christian family. His father was, according to most sources, a Christian monk. 'Ali Bey al-Kabir was kidnapped in 1741, at the age of thirteen, by Turkish soldiers. From there he was recruited into the Egyptian Mamluk forces, in which he gradually gained rank and influence over the next several years.

While in name the Ottoman viceroy held power in Egypt, the majority of real power in the country was held by the Mamluks, who had since the late seventeenth century held most administrative and military positions of rank. As such, the leader of the dominant faction of the Mamluk became the unofficial *shaykh al-balad.*

In 1745 an insurrection of the Janissaries lead to the eventual assassination of Ibrahim Kahya Bey, who had been the head of the Qazdughliyya. Upon his death, 'Ali Bey, who had been a Mamluk follower of Ibrahim, became the *shaykh al-balad* in 1757, attaining a supremacy over the other beys that had previously been unknown due to internal fighting. 'Ali Bey created a personal retinue by promoting his followers to the beylicate and removing factional advisories by force, if necessary. 'Abd al-Rahman al-Jabarti reports of 'Ali Bey that he sought to modernize his army by recruiting forces of mercenaries with modern firearms, which he paid by raising high taxes against the Egyptian landowners, merchants, and even peasants.

While he was challenged by a number of opposition groups in Upper Egypt, power was retained by 'Ali Bey long enough to actually pay back the Egyptian deficit to the Ottoman imperial treasury. This was the only concession asked by the Ottoman authorities, who abstained from interfering with 'Ali Bey otherwise. Once these were paid, however, by 1768 the viceroy attempted to have 'Ali Bey overthrown. In reaction, 'Ali Bey removed the Ottoman viceroy from office and took for himself the office of interim viceroy, thus solidifying his power in Egypt. However, he still did not seek an open political or military break with Istanbul and continued to acknowledge the sultan as ruler of Egypt, if only in name. Occupied in a war with Russia, the Ottoman forces did nothing to oppose 'Ali Bey's independent behavior.

When dynastic conflict erupted in the Hashemite family of the Hejaz, who were the traditional rulers of Mecca, 'Abd al-Hamid sought the assistance of 'Ali Bey, as viceroy, to resolve the conflict as would be normal protocol. However, 'Ali Bey saw in this a chance to increase the legitimacy of his rule by acting in his role as viceroy on the behalf of the sultan. As such, he proceeded to the Hejaz with a large force, resolved the dynastic dispute and removed the Ottoman governor of Jeddah. He then placed an Egyptian Mamluk bey, loyal to 'Ali Bey, in the governorship, thus giving him at least nominal control over both regions.

Bolstered by this success, he then set out to bring Syria under his control as well. In 1771 his expansionist motions brought him against the Ottoman troops that were defending Damascus, which he defeated. This was, at least in part, due to the authority of the Ottoman governor at the time, Uthman Pasha, being substantially undermined by the growing autonomy of northern Palestine, with which 'Ali Bey formed an alliance. This thus established his boundaries to the limit of the previous frontiers of the Mamluk sultanate.

Unfortunately for 'Ali Bey, his independence from other alliances made him both a tempting and an easy target. The Ottomans made an alliance with one of 'Ali Bey's closest supporters, Muhammad Bey Abu al-Dhahab, and turned him against 'Ali Bey. At roughly the same time, members of the Qasimi faction, along with other Mamluk rivals in exile who had retreated to Upper Egypt, allied

themselves with the Hawwara, a tribal group from the region, and began to move against Cairo. These two groups of forces came to form a coalition against 'Ali Bey and they defeated him in battle in 1772. The following year he was killed in Cairo on 8 May 1773.

'Ali Bey's innovations, particularly his military force building and its accompanying increased taxes, served to spark further political, economic, and social upheaval. Particularly, his rule marked a point in which the beys began to practice excessive expropriation and oppression and levied taxes that were often so excessive they forced peasants to flee their land.

BIBLIOGRAPHY

Crecelius, Daniel, and Gotcha Djaparidze. "Relations of the Georgian Mamluks of Egypt with Their Homeland in the Last Decades of the Eighteenth Century." *Journal of the Economic and Social History of the Orient* 45, no. 3 (2002): 320–341.

Crecelius, Daniel. *The Roots of Modern Egypt : A Study of the Regimes of 'Ali Bey al-Kabir and Muhammad Bey Abu al-Dhahab, 1760–1775.* Studies in Middle Eastern History, vol. 6. Minneapolis, Minn.: Bibliotheca Islamica, 1981.

Sicker, Martin. *The Islamic World in Decline: from the Treaty of Karlowitz to the Disintegration of the Ottoman Empire.* Westport, Conn.: Praeger, 2001.

NESS CREIGHTON

'Ali Dinar bin Zakariya (1865/70–1916), the last sultan of Darfur in western Sudan, was born between 1865 and 1870 in the village of Shawaya northwest of al-Fashir, the capital of northern Darfur. His mother's name was Kaltouma and his father, Zakariya, was the son of Sultan Mohammad al-Fadul (1801–1839). 'Ali Dinar had six sisters: Nur Alhuda, Taga, Gusura, Tibaina, and Umsalama. Very little is known about the early days of 'Ali Dinar before he rose to prominence during the Mahdist rule in Darfur (1882–1898). When his cousin Sultan Abulkhairat was killed in 1889, some suspected Ali Dinar's role in this, but he denied the accusation in his published autobiography (*Diwan Al madih fi Madh Al Nabi Al Malih*; "Poetry in Praise of the Handsome Prophet," 1913). In 1890 'Ali Dinar was inaugurated a sultan in Jebel Marra (home place of the Fur ethnic group). The new sultan was summoned to Al-Fashir, which was under Mahdist rule, to pay allegiance to the new administration. In 1891 'Ali Dinar arrived in al-Fashir and from there he was transferred to

Omdurman (the capital of Sudan during Mahdist rule) where he was kept captive by the Mahdists and was only able to return to Darfur after the defeat of the Mahdist army by the Anglo-Egyptian forces in 1898. 'Ali Dinar arrived in back in al-Fashir in 1898 and, after defeating three pretenders to the Darfur throne, was reinaugurated as the sultan of Darfur. 'Ali Dinar petitioned the Anglo-Egyptian forces to recognize his authority over Darfur and in getting assurances abut the borders of Darfur.

'Ali Dinar offered to pay the Sudan government a nominal sum of five hundreds pounds yearly in support. 'Ali Dinar maintained cordial relationship with Slatin Pasha, who was appointed inspector general of Sudan and was the key person in dealing with 'Ali Dinar regarding his relationship with the government. During Turkish rule in Sudan (1821–1885) Slatin Pasha was employed as administrator in Darfur. Both Slatin and 'Ali Dinar were kept captives by the Khalifa Abdullahi in Omdurman. Slatin fled from captivity to Egypt in 1895 and returned with the Anglo-Egyptian forces. In many of the correspondences between 'Ali Dinar and Slatin Pasha, the latter made several references to their friendship during their years of captivity in Omdurman. 'Ali Dinar didn't refer to such friendship with Slatin and in his first letter to the governor-general of Sudan he objected to the appointment of Slatin due to his past activities in suppressing Darfurian revolts against the Turkish rule. It is probable that both 'Ali Dinar and Slatin Pasha knew each other, but now they both needed each other in order to keep their posts. Although on several occasions Slatin requested to meet with 'Ali Dinar, the sultan was always apologetic and full of excuses and thus evaded meeting with any government official during his reign.

Prior to the arrival of 'Ali Dinar in al-Fashir from Omdurman, Darfur was in turmoil and hard living conditions were aggravated by Turkish and Mahdist policies in fighting insurgencies and the forced emigration and militarization that lead to the depopulation of Darfur. In one of his letters to Slatin Pasha, 'Ali Dinar stated that one of his grave concerns as sultan was to generate prosperity and to provide peace and security in all Darfur. The firmness through which such policies were enforced, whether toward specific individuals or specific ethnic groups, had led to the wide circulation of many stories in Sudan that depicted 'Ali Dinar as cruel and brutal. But the source of many of these stories could be ascribed to the competitors

over the throne, to Northern Sudanese traders, and later to the British government, which circulated many of such stories after the souring of its relationship with 'Ali Dinar prior to World War I.

'Ali Dinar's years of captivity in Omdurman brought him into direct contact with people from different places in Sudan and the observing of the remnants of modernity represented by the symbols left from Turkish rule in the Sudan such as buildings, printing presses, and the mint. The influence of his residence in Omdurman is evident in several ways: the construction of the two-story palace in al-Fashir with its lavish garden, the first of its kind in Darfur; the building of a dome that encompassed the grave of his father Zakariya, a practice that is prevalent among the Sufis of northern and central Sudan but not common in Darfur; the acquaintance with northern Sudanese elites such as Ali El Mirghani, the politico-religious leader of the Khatmiya sect, and Abuldrahman Al Mahdi, the son of the Mahdi and the politico-religious leader of the Mahdist sect; and boasting about an Abassid (Arab) origin in many of his letters, a tradition that is prevalent among northern Sudanese.

Administratively, 'Ali Dinar introduced many changes in the sultanate such as in the appointment of rulers, the organization of the *fugara* (Muslim holy men), the appointment of a grand judge, and minting his own coins. In dealing with other traditional rulers within the sultanate, 'Ali Dinar demanded that they should pay annual homage by attending the celebrations of Islamic festivals in al-Fashir in the company of the *fugara*. In showing his religiosity to the outside world, 'Ali Dinar sent three caravans to Mecca (1906, 1909, 1913), carrying the lavishly decorated *mahmal* (gifts to the residents of Mecca and Medina), which is an old tradition associated with the Darfurian sultans.

From his correspondence with Slatin Pasha, 'Ali Dinar showed his lust for luxury goods such as fabrics, jewelry, horses, and swords, many of which were later presented to Darfurian dignitaries and to his contemporaries in Egypt and Libya. 'Ali Dinar's fondness for music is evident in many of the letters requesting the dispatch to Khartoum of young Darfurians to be trained in playing music on bagpipes and brass instruments, in addition to the playing of the traditional kettledrums, a symbol of power that were played on specific festive occasions.

With the advent of World War I, the relationship between 'Ali Dinar and the Anglo-Egyptian Sudan government deteriorated due to his frustration with the government for not supporting him with arms and diplomacy against French encroachments on the western borders of Darfur. France indicated to Britain that it would not desist from its campaign of annexation unless Britain exerted direct control over Darfur. Added to this was the resignation of Slatin Pasha from his post and his allying his country with Austria, which was at war against Britain. With the departure of Slatin Pasha, there was an abrupt shift in the Condominium's policy toward ʿAli Dinar favoring a confrontational approach that undermined the sultan's ego. It was during this time that ʿAli Dinar showed signs of religious fervor that led him to send several writings for publication, including one about his miracles, and poetry in praise of Prophet Mohammad, in addition to an autobiography in which he preached to Darfurians to be thankful to God for deliverance from the harsh life under Mahdist rule.

In April 1915 ʿAli Dinar declared a jihad against the Condominium rule and thus cut all channels of diplomacy for settling his disputes with the colonial rule. The British were swift in collecting intelligence about Darfur and in preparing an army that defeated the sultan's forces in May 1916. ʿAli Dinar escaped with his huge family and many of his confidents to Jebel Marra. Although the colonial army tried to persuade ʿAli Dinar to surrender, the sultan was full of excuses for not submitting, but to buy time to avoid humiliation. In 6 November 1916 ʿAli Dinar's camp was located and in a brief assault the sultan was killed by the colonial forces.

[See also ʿAbd al-Rahman al-Mahdi; and Muhammad Ahmad ibn ʿAbdallah.]

BIBLIOGRAPHY

Arkell, A. J. "The Coinage of ʿAli Dinar, Sultan of Darfur, 1898–1916." *Sudan Notes and Records* 23, no. 1 (1940): 151–160.

Kapteijns, Lidwien, and Jay Spaulding. *After the Millennium: Diplomatic Correspondence from Wadai and Dar Fur on the Eve of Colonial Conquest 1885–1916.* East Lansing: Michigan State University Press, 1988. Letters exchanged between the rulers of Darfur and Wadai regarding the French threat in their lands.

Spaulding, Jay, and Lidwien Kapteijns. *An Islamic Alliance: ʿAli Dinar and the Sanusiyya, 1906–1916.* Evanston, Ill.: Northwestern University Press, 1994. Analytical study of the relationship between ʿAli Dinar and the Sanussiya of Libya.

Theobald, Alan Buchan. *ʿAli Dinar: Last Sultan of Darfur, 1898–1916.* London: Longmans, 1965. The main major published work on ʿAli Dinar and his relations with the Condominium government.

ʿALI B. ALI-DINAR

Alier, Abel (1933–), Sudanese judge and politician, was born in Bor, then a district of Upper Nile Province. Alier emerged as a prominent member of the Bor Dinka tribe and the southern Sudanese community more generally. He attended the renowned Rumbek Secondary School, which educated many southern Sudanese leaders. He also attended the Wad Saidna school in northern Sudan. His success in early education lead Alier to attend law school at the University of Khartoum and upon high achievement there was able to undertake and receive a Masters degree from the Institute of Advanced Legal Studies, Yale University, in the United States. He was also a research fellow in Land Law in the School of Advanced Legal Studies, University of London, from 1961 to 1962. In recognition for his role in government and achievements in academia the universities of Khartoum and Juba gave Alier an honorary doctor of laws.

After completing his studies Alier joined the Sudanese judiciary as a magistrate. Not long thereafter he became the first southern Sudanese appointed as a judge in the history of the country. Changing paths in 1965 Alier decided to leave his post in the Sudan judiciary in the High Court in 1965 to engage in politics. Due to his stature among southern Sudanese he took part in the Round Table Conference that was trying to negotiate a solution to the then ongoing war between the government and the Anyanya rebellion. Alier became the leading member of the government delegation. Due to this experience he was made a member of the committee established to recommend a constitutional and administrative solution to the war in southern Sudan and associated wider grievances. Alier continued to pursue his political aspirations by standing for election to the National Assembly in Khartoum to represent his home area. Elected to the assembly in 1968 Alier was then appointed as the Minister of Southern Affairs. In 1971, as the Minister of Southern Affairs and based on his previous experience, Alier was involved in the first peace negotiations to resolve the civil war with the Anyanya rebellion. He was made the head of the delegation to the Addis Ababa Peace Talks facilitated by the emperor of Ethiopia Haile Selassie. The Addis Ababa talks resulted in a resolution to the seventeen-year-long civil war between southern Sudanese groups and the government.

He concurrently was a member of various boards, committees, and organizations; of particular importance was his membership to the Political Parties Conference on Southern Sudan, the Constitutional Commission from 1966 to 1968, the board of directors of the Industrial Planning Corporation, and the National Scholarship Board. During this period he also became a founding member of the Southern Front, a political party of leading southern Sudanese, and was soon made the secretary-general.

Not long after the 1972 peace agreement Alier was appointed by the Sudanese president Ja'far al-Nimeiry as the president of the High Executive Council (HEC), the top administrative body for the semiautonomous Southern Sudan region. He was also made the second vice president of Sudan from 1971 to1982, along with being the first president of the semiautonomous Southern Sudan from 1972 to 1978 and then again from 1980 to 1982. Alier was the sole candidate for presidency of the HEC presented by Nimeiry.

Alier's government gradually lost support as the social and economic benefits expected from the Addis Ababa peace settlement were slow to materialize. This along with increasing opposition from other leading southerners, particularly Joseph Lagu and other former Anyanya leaders, caused Alier to eventually resign as president of the HEC after a poor showing in the elections in 1978. In 1980 Alier was once again elected to the head of the southern government and was appointed to the HEC after Lagu and other southern Sudanese had become combative toward the government in Khartoum and began to openly oppose Nimeiry.

After the agreement that ended the second civil war in Sudan (1983–2005), the Comprehensive Peace Agreement (CPA), Alier was made the head of the Sudanese National Electoral Commission with the mandate of implementing the CPA-mandated national election and referendum on Southern Sudanese status in Sudan. Academically and professionally Abel Alier is undoubtedly one of the most prominent southern Sudanese. Despite many southern Sudanese perceiving Alier in a negative light due to the fact that his roles have consistently seen him working with successive governments in Khartoum rather than joining the southern rebellions fighting against the government, his role is Sudanese history has been significant.

[*See also* Haile Selassie I; *and* Nimeiry, Ja'far al-.]

BIBLIOGRAPHY

Alier, Abel. *Southern Sudan: Too Many Agreements Dishonoured.* Reading, UK: Ithaca Press, 1992.

Collins, Robert O., ed. *Civil Wars and Revolution in the Sudan: Essays on the Sudan, Southern Sudan and Darfur 1962–2004.* Hollywood, Calif.: Tsehai Publishers, 2005.

Johnson, Douglas. *The Root Causes of Sudan's Civil War.* London: James Currey, 2003.

Lagu, Joseph. *Sudan: Odyssey Through a State: From Ruin to Hope.* Khartoum, Sudan: MOB Center for Sudanese Studies, Omdurman Ahlia University, 2006.

Wai, Dunstan M., ed. *The Southern Sudan: The Problem of National Integration.* London: Frank Cass, 1973.

MATTHEW LERICHE

Ali Gajideni (d. 1487), West African ruler of present-day northern Nigeria and southern Chad, Ali consolidated the power of the Sefuwa dynasty in Bornu after a long period of dynastic rivalry. By building the fortified town of Birni Gazargamo, he laid the foundation of the second Sefuwa empire. After the retreat of the Sefuwa court from Kanem to its immediate neighbour Bornu in about 1380, royal power rotated between the Idrisid and the Dawudid branch of the dynasty for thirty five years, and then the great officials of the state manipulated succession between the two families for twenty years and subsequently civil war ravaged the country for fifteen years. During these seventy years the Sefuwa resided in temporary encampments in the eastern part of Bornu. Finally the Idrisid Ali Gajideni, the son of Dunama IV, finally vanquished Uthman ibn Kade, the last Dawudid king, expelled all remaining members of the hostile Dawudids and their supporters from the country, and was for some time the king maker and thus ended the dynastic crisis.

Mai (king) Ali's most significant accomplishment was to build for the Sefuwa a new permanent capital. He founded Birni Gazargamo in the middle of two branches of the River Yobe and surrounded it by high earth walls measuring altogether a length of 5 miles (8 km). In its neighborhood he erected at Gambaru a separate palace for the queen mother, Magira, where she could witness the conformity of her royal son's undertakings with respect to the basic tenants of sacred kingship surviving under the Islamic veneer. Since the banks of both rivers were by that time inhabited by Chadic-speaking

Sao, the Sefuwa had to be on good terms with the autochthon inhabitants of the country not yet converted to Islam. But the benefits of a stable capital in a central position of the country outnumbered by far the inconveniences of a pagan neighborhood.

With a secure and permanent capital Ali could embark on a policy of tightening the administrative structure of the state. Overpowerful titleholders like the Kaigama had their authority reduced and a system of fief-holding was inaugurated, by which the major fief-holders (cima) themselves remained in the capital and administered their fiefs by representatives. Thus the great officials came under the strict control of the court, the administration of the state was better centralized, and the military levies were more effectively organized. Some sources mention heavy fights against the Bulala of Kanem but these combats did not result in substantial territorial gains for the Sefuwa. Ali's epithet Gajideni is only attested by the German scholar and traveler Heinrich Barth, who states that according to oral traditions, he was called Ali Gaji. If it is correct that Gajideni and Gaji are derived from Arabic al-ghazi "the conqueror," as suggested by some authors, this evidence would emphasize Ali's character as a great warrior king.

Succeeded by his son Idris Katakarmabe, Mai Ali is still remembered today as the consolidator of Sefuwa rule in their western province and the founder of the Bornu empire. Birni Gazargamo remained the state capital until 1808, when the Sefuwa were expelled from it by Fulani jihadists.

[See also Idris Katakarmabe.]

BIBLIOGRAPHY

Barth, Heinrich. *Travels and Discoveries in North and Central Africa.* 3 vols. New York: n.p., *1857–1859.*

Barkindo, B.M. "Early States of the Central Sudan: Kanem, Borno and Some of Their Neighbours to c. 1500 A.D." In *History of West Africa*, edited by J. F. A. Ajayi and Michael Crowder. 3d ed. Vol. 1, pp. 225–254. Burnt Mill, UK: Longman, 1985.

DIERK LANGE

'Ali ibn Ibrahim (c. 1821–1908), preeminent transSaharan merchant and caravan leader (*khabir*) from the Sudanese kingdom of Darfur, was born in Kubayh, the son of Ibrahim ibn 'Ali, a Tirayfi merchant from Kordofan who immigrated to Darfur, and an unknown mother. He was commonly known as *khabir* 'Ali. In the nineteenth century Darfur was Egypt's leading supplier of trans-Saharan goods including ivory, ostrich feathers, and slaves. In 1838, when Darfur's sultan Muhammad Fadl died, young 'Ali ibn Ibrahim had already crossed the Sahara along the route from Kubayh (Darfur's commercial capital) to Asyut in Upper Egypt, perhaps as part of a caravan led by his mentor, paternal uncle, and future father-in-law, Muhammad Kannun, or one of the lesser Tirayfi caravan leaders. 'Ali ibn Ibrahim allegedly heard the news of the sultan's death from Muhammad 'Ali, the viceroy of Egypt.

'Ali married six times and had numerous children. His first marriage was probably to his paternal cousin 'Aisha bint Muhammad Kannun in the preferred pattern of cross-cousin marriages. This fulfilled familial expectations and cemented his ties to his wealthy and influential uncle, a leading merchant and estate-holder in Kubayh. Muhammad Kannun had designated 'Ali ibn Ibrahim as his commercial successor and before his death in Egypt in 1850 selected his nephew to lead the return caravan to Darfur.

Leading trans-Saharan caravans from Darfur was a major responsibility. They crossed the desert with hundreds of merchants, several thousand laden camels, and valuable goods, including slaves. The *khabir* received a sultanic letter of appointment before each northbound journey, specifying his commercial and legal responsibilities. He represented the sultan in business matters, controlled the members of the caravan, selected the route, daily schedule, and camps, and ensured the safety of its people and goods. He received a drum as a symbol of his office, using it to signal the caravaneers en route. His responsibilities included selling all the caravan's merchandise: his own, the sultan's, and the other traders' goods. Several observers noted that the Darfur merchants insisted on being paid directly in cash: ". . . they have now learned to estimate its worth, and to dispose of their goods for ready money. With this they purchase other articles, often driving hard bargains. . . ." This change came around 1850, as 'Ali rose to prominence.

His two marriages to *mayram*s (royal women of Darfur) reflected his new status. When he married Sultan Muhammad al-Husayn's sister, Fatima Umm Dirays, he received a sultanic land grant dated 8 September 1852 of the *hakura* (estate) called Ungorei, near Kubayh along the route to the royal capital Al-Fashir. Another estate, Ni'ama, initially granted to the *mayram*'s first husband had reverted to her at the time of their divorce. His second royal marriage was to the sultan's daughter, 'Arafa bint al-sultan Muhammad al-Husayn. They planned to go together to Egypt and perhaps on to Mecca. But when the *mayram* reached Toma, a nearby village used as a staging point for the trans-Saharan caravans, she became ill and died. Grieving, Ali returned to al-Fashir where the sultan insisted that he proceed to Egypt. Either on this or another journey he performed the hajj to Mecca.

From 1850 to 1873 'Ali ibn Ibrahim was central to the economy of Kubayh and Darfur. Following in the footsteps of his maternal uncle, he used his commercial success as agent for the sultan to acquire more permanent wealth in the form of *hakuras* and political status through his royal marriages. His estates were well-located on good agricultural land adjacent to the seasonal river near the commercial capital. His most famous estate, Nabaru, just north of Kubayh, was irrigated by the use of low dikes and *shadufs* (manual water-lifting devices), and there his "eighty slaves with their wives" grew wheat that the trans-Saharan merchants preferred to the local millet. He had a large household, and his house in Kubayh had a good well, many storage rooms for household items and trade goods, and ample space to provide hospitality for his many business guests. He was one of the largest slave owners in Kubayh, with slaves in his household and on his various estates.

Surviving documents show that he played an important role in the commercial life of Kubayh as a merchant and in legal matters connected to trade. In 1863 he was a prominent witness in a dispute over debt between a Darfur merchant and a Coptic merchant from Asyut. He also served as legal guardian for the children of a Shingiti merchant (from the region of Senegal) who died in Kubayh.

In 1874 as Darfur fell to the forces of al-Zubayr Rahma Mansur and was occupied by Egypt, 'Ali's trans-Saharan trade diminished. He was seen but barely described by the German traveler Gustav Nachtigal. He increased his land holdings in this period, acquiring Nabaru and perhaps purchasing other land near Kubayh. When the Mahdist revolt began in 1882, some of the Kubayh merchant community fled westward to Wadai. In 1886 the Mahdist general Muhammad Khalid Zugl rounded up the remaining Kubayh residents, including 'Ali, to join the Mahdi's successor, the *khalifa* Abdullahi. They were taken to Abu Rof, a section of Omdurman where 'Ali was well treated, and acquired a large house, slaves, and some farmland on Tuti Island on the Nile. While performing the hajj a second time, he met the historian Naum Shucair in Egypt. In Omdurman, he interacted with other Darfur exiles, including 'Ali Dinar, who rejected his avuncular advice.

After the British army defeated the Mahdist forces at the battle of Omdurman in 1898, 'Ali Dinar returned to Darfur to restore the sultanate. But 'Ali, now in his seventies, awaited further developments. The British consulted him about possible alternative rulers when 'Ali Dinar was rumored to be gravely ill. By December 1902 'Ali sought permission to return home and eventually received it. In 1908 he died and was buried near Umm Dafasu, a market in al-Fashir.

[*See also* 'Ali Dinar bin Zakariya'.]

BIBLIOGRAPHY

La Rue, George Michael. "Khabir Ali at Home in Kubayh: A Brief Biography of a Dar Fur Caravan Leader." *African Economic History* 13 (1984): 56–83. Provides further details and documentation on his life.

O'Fahey, R. S., and Muhammad Ibrahim Abu Salim. *Land in Dar Fur: Charters and Related Documents from the Dar Fur Sultanate.* Fontes Historiae Africanae, Series Arabica, vol. 3. Cambridge, UK: Cambridge University Press, 1983. Provides analysis and discussion of the *hakura* system.

GEORGE MICHAEL LA RUE

'Ali ibn Yusuf ibn Tashfin (1084–1143), emir of the Almoravid dynasty from 1106 to 1143, was born in the Moroccan city of Ceuta to a mother who was a Christian captive from Spain. 'Ali inherited rule of the Almoravid state upon the death of his father, Yusuf ibn Tashfin, in 1106. Almoravid rule at the time of 'Ali's accession to power was at its zenith and encompassed a considerable portion of territory of the Islamic west, including Andalusia, the western region of North Africa, and portions of the *bilad al-Sudan*. Indeed, it is a commonplace of the classical Arabic chronicles that 'Ali's name was invoked from some two thousand pulpits at the outset of every Friday sermon. However, his rule was beset with a host of serious problems almost from the outset, ranging from quarrels among the various tribal factions that formed the backbone of the Almoravid regime, to doctrinal disputes, the oppositional stance adopted by several Sufi-inspired brotherhoods, the quickening tide of Christian reconquest in Iberia, and, of gravest consequence, the challenge posed to the Almoravids by the Mahdi Ibn Tumart and the Almohad movement.

Much of 'Ali's energy as ruler of the Almoravid state was focused on affairs on the Andalusian side of the strait, particularly the waging of jihad against the Christian armies of Iberia. In this regard he proved himself a skillful commander, just as his father had done some two decades earlier. 'Ali oversaw a total of four incursions into Iberia, the same number his father had undertaken, the first of which occurred during the year of his accession to rule. The jihad that 'Ali waged in Andalusia resulted in several important victories for the Muslim armies, most notably at the battle of Ulcés in 1108 when the Almoravids under the command of 'Ali's elder brother Tamim struck a decisive blow against the armies of Castile. The Almoravids won another victory at Fraga in 1134, led this time by Yahya ibn 'Ali ibn Ghaniya (d. 1149), a highly competent battlefield commander who would later serve as Almoravid governor of Andalusia following 'Ali's removal of Tamim from that sensitive position in 1126.

Alongside this impressive string of victories in Iberia, however, 'Ali suffered a number of disastrous reversals, the most prominent of which occurred at Cutanda in 1120. Such was the degree of 'Ali's focus on military operations in Andalusia throughout his reign that he maintained little more than a lightly armed rear guard around the Almoravid capital at Marrakesh. It is noteworthy that this contingent was composed largely of Christian mercenaries recruited from Christian Iberia. The great attention 'Ali attached to managing the affairs of Islamic Spain, to the neglect of North Africa, would in many ways prove to be the undoing of the Almoravid state. Following the return of Ibn Tumart from his sojourn in the Islamic east, and his subsequent creation of the Almohad movement centered initially in the near-impregnable fortress at Tinmal in the mountainous region south of Marrakech, 'Ali found himself in the increasingly untenable position of waging war on two fronts. The Almoravid armies, even had they been present in sizeable numbers, would have been highly unsuited to confront the Almohads in the rugged terrain south of Marrakech, a weakness Ibn Tumart was quick to exploit. Indeed, the few remnants of Almoravid military architecture that exist today, most notably the observation posts at Zagora, Tashghimout, and Amergou, bear witness to the fact that the Almoravids could do little more than watch as the Almohad tide grew in strength on their doorstep.

'Ali's father, Yusuf, comes in for frequent praise for his extensive reliance on Muslim jurists and men of religion when determining significant points of policy. The influence such jurists exerted over the direction of the Almoravid state would only continue to grow during the period of 'Ali's rule. Among the figures 'Ali relied upon were many of the leading lights of the Maliki school of Islamic jurisprudence, and his reign may rightfully be counted among the high points in the articulation of Maliki legal thought, a development that would come to an abrupt halt during the subsequent period of Almohad rule. Notable among the jurists who played an active role in the Almoravid state during 'Ali's rule were Ibn Rushd al-Jadd (d. 1126) of Cordoba, Abu Bakr ibn al-'Arabi (d. 1149) of Seville, and al-Qadi 'Iyad al-Sabti (d. 1148) of Ceuta. The fatwa literature of the period, in which the aforementioned jurists figure prominently, reveals the range and importance of the issues these men were summoned to rule upon, including whether one may rightfully substitute jihad for hajj, an indication that Andalusians were effectively avoiding the Almoravid call for jihad under the pretext of making the pilgrimage to distant Mecca. Other issues treated in the fatwas of this period include the extent to which Ash'arism might licitly be reconciled with Malikism; the place, if any, to be accorded to mystical Islam; and the status of *dhimmi* populations that have decided to emigrate from Islamic territory. It is worth noting that the fatwas on these issues record that many of these questions emanated directly from the Almoravid emir himself, a suggestion of the intensity with which doctrinal disputes rose to the fore during his rule. Particularly nettlesome was the controversy provoked by Abu Hamid al-Ghazali's influential revivalist treatise, the *Ihya' 'ulum al-din*. As is well known, the work contains a sustained critique of what al-Ghazali considered the sterility of much of the legal thought of his era. Not unexpectedly, the jurists of the Almoravid state reacted strongly to al-Ghazali's pronouncement, and the work was ultimately burned in public outside the great mosque of Cordoba with 'Ali's approval. However, his decision to condemn al-Ghazali's work was highly problematic, since it was al-Ghazali himself who had some three decades earlier provided the Almoravids with a fatwa that authorized their incursion into Andalusia and subsequent overthrow of the Muslim ta'ifa states.

Alongside the remarkable development of Maliki legal thought during the reign of 'Ali ibn Yusuf, we should make final note of the flowering of Andalusian letters that occurred at the same time. In contrast to his father, who, despite his considerable political cunning and skilled statecraft, was widely held to be a cultural illiterate, 'Ali received an extensive education in Arabic literature, and actively sought to revive the generous patronage extended to court poets during the *ta'ifa* period. In this we may discern the two great influences in the formation of 'Ali's character, that of his father, Yusuf, and that of the refined poet-king of Seville, al-Mu'tamid ibn 'Abbad.

[*See also* Ibn Tumart, Muhammad; *and* Yusuf ibn Tashfin, Abu Ya'qub.]

BIBLIOGRAPHY

Bosch Vilá, Jacinto. *Los Almoravides: Historia de Murruecos.* Tetuan, Morocco: Editora Marroquí, 1956.

Huici-Miranda, Ambrosio. "'Ali b. Yusuf y sus Empresas en el Andalus." *Tamuda* 3 (1959): 77–122.

Lagardère, Vincent. *Les Almoravides jusqu'au règne de Yusuf b. Tashfin (1039–1106).* Paris: L'Harmattan, 1989.

RUSSELL HOPLEY

'Ali Khurshid (c.1786–1845), Turco-Egyptian soldier and administrator, served in the Sudan as governor during the 1820s–1830s and adopted policies that largely set the course for the entire colonial period. Following Muhammad 'Ali's conquest of Sinnar and Kordofan in 1820–1821, Egypt's African empire expanded gradually over a period of sixty years. The exploitive motives of that expansion, and failure ever to extract the quantities of gold, ivory, and slaves that comprised its principal object, were reflected in attempts to administer the territories. The appointment of 'Ali Khurshid was a watershed in this process. His long period of loyal service was marked by pragmatism, a liberal and enlightened outlook, and energetic interest in developing the country.

In 1826, following military service in Greece, 'Ali Khurshid was named governor of Sinnar, a much larger territory (of uncertain southern and eastern borders) than the future province of the same name. Much of the northern Sudan was in disarray or ruin after the Egyptian conquest and the brutal suppression of revolt that had followed it. Despite his continuing campaigns, notably along the Abyssinian borderlands, and raids against the Dinka and Shilluk that extended Egyptian authority southward, 'Ali Khurshid's main aim was therefore to settle the country and revive the local economy. This he pursued by conciliating the Arab tribes: he granted amnesties, confirmed the authority of tribal chiefs, settled abandoned lands, and took counsel of Sudanese notables, one of whom, Shaykh Abd al-Qadir wad al-Zayn, he astutely promoted as chief intermediary. He encouraged trade by policing the caravan routes, resisting excessive demands from Cairo, establishing shipyards, and setting the stage for exploration of the upper Nile. Experiments in economic development, in the hope of at least balancing the books, were undertaken, with mixed—largely poor—results. The transformation of Khartoum from riverside village to administrative and commercial capital owed much to his industry and good government. He was repeatedly promoted, and the territories under his control were expanded, until in 1835 he was named *hukumdar* (governor-general) of the combined Sudanese provinces.

The eastern Sudan was the focus of 'Ali Khurshid's costly and inconclusive military campaigns. It was to this region, along the national borders with Abyssinia, that dissident Sudanese tribesmen habitually fled. Khurshid launched several campaigns against local potentates, whose independence was a constant threat. Reinforced from Egypt, he was finally compelled to pull back after Britain, fearing Abyssinian collapse, pressed Cairo to withdraw. In the spring of 1838 he went to Egypt on leave, but was superseded in the Sudan and never returned.

Remaining in the viceroy's favor, 'Ali Khurshid occupied important positions until his death. His personal success in the Sudan had contributed to the development of Egyptian administrative policy; Cairo's later ambivalence over the merits and dangers of centralizing power in the hands of one official far from its control illustrates the unique position he achieved.

BIBLIOGRAPHY

Holt, P. M., and M. W. Daly. *A History of the Sudan: From the Coming of Islam to the Present Day.* 5th ed. New York: Longman, 2000.

Hill, Richard. *Egypt in the Sudan, 1820–1881.* London: Oxford University Press, 1959.

M. W. DALY

Aline Sitoue Diatta (c. 1921–1944), Senegalese prophetess, was born in the southwestern Senegalese township of Kabrousse, a member of the Diola ethnic group. Today the Diola number approximately six hundred thousand people, primarily in

Senegal, but there are significant communities in Gambia and Guinea-Bissau. Generally, the Diola are considered the best wet rice farmers in West Africa, though they have been increasingly troubled by droughts since the 1930s. Although many Diola are Muslim or Catholic in their primary religious affiliation, they include the largest number of adherents of an indigenous African religion in the Senegambia region. Before the colonial occupation by the French, British, and Portuguese, the Diola had a tradition of direct revelation from the supreme being, but it was limited to male prophetic leaders. Shortly after colonization, in the last years of the nineteenth century and the first decade of the twentieth, women prophets began to gain influence, especially among the southern Diola. Most of these prophets focused on new rituals to obtain rain, to cleanse their communities of witchcraft and other life diminishing activities, and to heal the sick.

In many ways Aline Sitoue was not a person likely to be identified with the epithet "Emitai sent her," the literal translation of the Diola word for "prophet." When her visions of Emitai, the Diola supreme being, began, she was still a young woman, barely in her twenties, unmarried but with a child, in a society that condemned both men and women who had children out of wedlock. A bout with polio had left her lame and limited her ability to work in the rice paddies, a central concern in Diola families. She was one of the first women from her township of Kabrousse to seek work as a maid in Dakar, thus removing herself from Diola-dominated communities. As far as is known, she did not attend the Catholic school at Oussouye, though she was a cousin of the one of the earliest Christians in her township.

In short, she was not the type of person to whom Diola elders looked for leadership, but she lived in a time of severe crisis. Droughts and insect infestations had devastated Diola agriculture with increasing frequency during the 1930s and early 1940s. The rice harvest of 1941–1942 had been one of the worst since written record-keeping of such matters began. Forced conscription into the French army had dramatically increased in 1939 and 1940, along with French missionary efforts to convert the Diola to Catholicism. Forced labor and an increasing alliance between missionary and French officials under a Vichy administration threatened Diola elders during the period before Aline Sitoue began her teachings. Requisitions of cattle and rice at a time of severe drought and government pressures to grow peanuts threatened Diola economic well-being and sense of independence.

Aline Sitoue's visions from Emitai began in 1941 or 1942, when she was shopping in the Sandaga market in the heart of Dakar. She heard a voice that she identified as coming from the Diola supreme being, who commanded her to walk down to the Atlantic Ocean beach and dig in the sand. When she did so, water filled the hole whereupon Emitai told her that this was her mission, to bring rain to the drought-stricken Diola. Initially afraid of her visions, she returned home to Kabrousse and began to teach. Central to her teachings was the introduction of a new spirit shrine known as *Kasila*, which focused on the sacrifice of a black bull to Emitai. For six days and six nights, the length of the Diola week, everyone in the community abstained from most forms of work, ate their meals together, slept in the public square, and sang and danced ancestral songs. In contrast to a prior emphasis on choosing priests from elders of wealthy or influential families, Aline Sitoue opened the priesthood of her new shrine to everyone, women, men, and children, all of whom could be chosen as priests of this new shrine. She insisted that only Diola forms of rice, African varieties (*oryza glaberimma*), could be used at these rituals. She also revived the Diola day of rest, *Huyaye*, regarded as a day of rest for the land, not for people.

Aline Sitoue's most important policy was her rejection of the French-supported cash crop of peanuts, which threatened the Diola family mode of agricultural production in which men and women jointly farmed the rice paddies. Peanut farming was primarily a male occupation and many northern Diola men had abandoned rice farming to their wives and daughters. Aline Sitoue feared that this would devastate a Diola way of life that was focused on rice farming. The use of upland forest land for peanut cultivation also threatened Diola hunting, palm product collection (palm wine, branches, and palm oil), the gathering of herbal medicines and thatch, all of which were important to the Diola economy.

It was Aline Sitoue's opposition to French agricultural schemes and their fear of armed revolt that led to the decision in January 1943 to her arrest and the arrest of a number of her followers. She was tried and convicted under the Native Law Code (the Indigénat) for the crime of obstructing French colonial administrative initiatives. Her only defense was that she was only following what Emitai had commanded her to do. She was sentence to exile, initially at Kayes, and eventually at a detainment camp in Timbuktu in neighboring French Sudan, where less than a year later, she died of scurvy in 1944. News of her death was a carefully guarded secret until the 1980s.

Within months of her arrest, other women prophets arose in the area around the provincial capital of Ziguinchor in the Casamance region and among the northern, predominantly Muslim Diola of Tendouck. Since that time, more than two dozen women and men have claimed to be people "sent by Emitai," in the tradition of Aline Sitoue Diatta. Since the late 1970s the late Father Diamacoune Senghor and the Mouvement des Forces Démocratiques Casamançais (MFDC) have claimed Aline Sitoue as a Joan of Arc figure who sacrificed her life to liberate the Casamance from colonial rule. Senegalese leaders, in an effort to undermine the secessionist MFDC, have claimed her as a Senegalese national heroine, who gave her life to liberate Senegal from French colonial rule.

Aline Sitoue was not the first known person to have visions of the supreme being. But her emphasis on direct revelation provided an effective response to the intensifying challenges of French colonial rule during World War II, which inspired more than two dozen other prophets to call for religious reform in the Diola tradition and resistance to economic development schemes that threatened Diola autonomy. Aline Sitoue's story also illustrates the important role that religious leadership has played in challenging the expansion of a global economy.

BIBLIOGRAPHY

Baum, Robert M. "Aline Sitoué: A Diola Woman Prophet in West Africa." In *Unspoken Worlds: Women's Religious Lives*, edited by Nancy Auer Falk and Rita M. Gross, 3d ed., pp. 179–195. Belmont, Calif.: Wadsworth/Thompson Learning, 2001.

Girard, Jean. *Genèse du Pouvoir Charismatique en Basse Casamance (Sénégal)*. Dakar, Senegal: IFAN, 1969.

Waldman, Marilyn, and Robert Baum. "Innovation as Renovation: The 'Prophet' as an Agent of Change." In *Innovation in Religious Traditions: Essays in the Interpretation of Religious Change*, edited by Michael A. Williams, Collett Cox, and Martin S. Jaffee, pp. 241–284. Berlin: Mouton de Gruyter, 1992.

ROBERT M. BAUM

Alkali, Zaynab Amina (1950–), Nigerian creative writer and educator, was born in the Tura-Wazila community of Borno State, Nigeria. She completed her graduate education at Bayero University, Kano, receiving a doctorate in African literature. Professionally, she has served as principal of Shekara Girls' Boarding School, Kano, an assistant lecturer at Bayero University, and senior lecturer in English and coordinator of English and general studies at Modibbo Adama College, University of Maiduguri. Following twenty-two years of university work, Alkali took a three-year break and worked for the National Primary Health Care Development Agency in Abuja. In 2009 she was named dean of the Faculty of Arts at Nasarawa State University, where she teaches creative writing and African literature in English. During her childhood, Alkali's father converted to Christianity, but she became a Muslim in the 1960s. She asserts that both Christianity and Islam have influenced her own spirituality. In 1971 she married Dr. Mohammed Nur Alkali, director-general of the Nigerian Institute of Political and Strategic Studies, in Jos, Nigeria. The couple has six children.

Alkali sets her stories in the village and urban areas of northern Nigeria, exploring the challenges faced by communities caught in the age of rapid social change. Her works contribute to Nigerian literature preoccupied with circumstances surrounding women's lives, highlighting the intersection of traditional gender norms, religion, and the forces of modernization. There exists a rich literary tradition in northern Nigeria, but written Hausa dominates much of the regional writing. Thus, Alkali's writing in English makes her one of the few northern Nigerian writers who have received international attention. Despite her use of English, Islam frames the social and cultural context of Alkali's literature, similar to the work of her northern Nigerian literary peers.

Alkali's first novel, *The Stillborn*, was published in 1984. Winner of the Association of Nigerian Authors (ANA) prize for prose fiction in 1985, the work is set in northern Nigeria and explores the challenges of a young woman who tries to negotiate the tension between her family's desires, which are governed by traditional expectations, and her own independence and personal aspirations. The classic division between the traditional village and the modern city frames the story, and the central characters come to realize that the promise of urban material wealth is illusory. The novel offers a conservative critique of the urban forces that lead individuals into unsavory endeavors and unethical choices. Having waited four years for her husband to establish himself in the city, the protagonist Li finally joins him, only to discover that her relationship with him has completely deteriorated. Li returns to the village, eventually secures a degree from the Advanced Teachers College, and becomes an educated single parent and family matriarch. Her progression shows the fluidity of her identity and the extent in which modern technology (education) has combined well with village values.

Having proven her ability to provide financially for her extended family and contribute to the education of other women, Li chooses to temper her independence by reconciling with her husband and establishing a relationship of equality. Some critics have claimed that this plot element undermines both the text's feminist import and its message of resistance to gender oppression. However, such a reading misses a crucial perspective of the novel, which seeks to balance multiple allegiances. Li's decision to reconcile shows how young women can maintain their loyalty to some traditional values, such as marriage, while they seek to integrate modern sensibilities of female independence and educational achievement.

The topic of female education reappears in most of Alkali's stories. In the novel *The Virtuous Woman*, Alkali describes the journey of two Muslim girls who have won scholarships to attend a prestigious boarding school. Nana Ai, the protagonist, is a shy, dutiful, and obedient orphan raised by her grandfather, a sage who has steadfastly supported her education. The story highlights how female modesty, a virtue revered by Islamic principles, is not incommensurate with either female education or the public visibility and travel that such an education requires.

In the short story "Cobwebs," Alkali explores the complexities of female education as Mama, a young wife and mother, attends the University of Azir. The educational environment has altered Mama's worldview, encouraging her independence and giving her new goals. While the narrative seems to affirm her new social outlook, it notes the inherent challenges of female education as Mama experiences alienation from her five-year-old twin sons. Upon her return to the village, she recognizes their emotional distance from her and asks herself, "What was their place in her world-view?" Here the text offers no easy solutions to her multiple responsibilities and aspirations.

"The Vagabond" continues the thread of female education, noting how its denial often coincides with the tradition of early marriage. Fearing that advanced schooling would rob her daughter of femininity and appeal, a mother prohibits her daughter's attending college and marries her off as a young adolescent. The daughter, Bibi, becomes pregnant, loses her child in labor, and develops vesicovaginal fistulae, a medical condition common to young girls whose bodies are not physically mature enough to withstand the demands of childbirth. Emotionally scarred from the trauma, Bibi becomes a street vagrant, rapidly deteriorating into poor health. Here Alkali's message about the necessity of female education and the ills of early marriage are didactically clear.

Issues of polygyny prove to be central to Alkali's works as well. Never does she openly condemn the religiously sanctioned practice, but her portraits of it leave the reader with the undeniable impression that husbands routinely abuse the patriarchal privilege. In "Cobwebs" Mama's emotional distance from her husband while attending the university is exacerbated by his adding yet another co-wife. "Saltless Ash" highlights two co-wives conspiring to thwart their husband's plan to marry a third. "The House of Dust" describes how a widow discovers that her recently deceased husband actually had another family, one that he started twenty-six years before and managed to keep secret from her.

In all of her work, Alkali offers consistent insight into the lives of Muslim women in northern Nigeria. She also provides a vision on how such women can begin to improve the quality of their lives through greater education, self-reliance, and religious devotion.

BIBLIOGRAPHY

Brooke, James. "A Nigerian Shame: The Agony of the Childbride." *New York Times*, July 17, 1987, p. A7.

Garba, Ismail Bala. "Of Real Freedom and Gender Equality." *Jenda: A Journal of Culture and African Women Studies* 8 (2006). http://www.jendajournal.com/.

Loflin, Christine. "Zaynab Alkali." *Postcolonial African Writers: A Bio-bibliographical Sourcebook*, edited by Pushpa Naidu Parekh and Siga Fatima Jagne. London and Chicago: Fitzroy Dearborn, 1998.

Whitsitt, Novian. "Islamic-Hausa Feminism and Kano Market Literature: Qur'anic Reinterpretation in the Novels of Balaraba Yakubu." *Research in African Literatures* 33, no. 2 (2002): 119–136.

NOVIAN WHITSITT

Allafi, Agnes (1959–) Chadian politician and sociologist, was born on 21 January 1959. Her father, a high-ranking army officer in the army of dictator

François Tombalbaye from the early 1960s until the coup that led to Tombalbaye's death in 1975, was an extremely influential man. He remains extremely unpopular among many northern Chadians for his alleged brutality in crushing rebel groups. Allafi had nine siblings, many of whom went on to receive advanced educations. Since her father was often transferred on military postings, Allafi studied at Fort-Lamy, Sarh, the Chadian capital of N'Djamena, and she passed her baccalaureate examination at Bongor in December 1980. The chaotic political situation in Chad from 1980 to 1982 prevented her from immediately commencing her undergraduate education. She married a Protestant customs officer on 11 April 1981, and she had two children with him. She worked as a teacher in 1981 and early 1982. When the warlord Hissène Habré captured N'Djamena in October 1982, he almost immediately had Allafi's father executed. Habré's dreaded secret police, the DDS, killed her husband soon afterward.

She fled with some family members to neighboring Cameroon, where she lived in the border towns of Yagoua and Garoua. A French military officer who had known Allafi's father tried to sponsor Allafi to attend the University of Yaounde in Cameroon, but Allafi preferred to leave the country. Many of her relatives had been killed by Habré's government, and rumors had spread that Habré wanted Allafi kidnapped and brought back to Chad. She eventually moved in 1985 to Cotonou, the capital of Benin, where she earned a masters degree in sociology at the National University of Benin. The subject of her thesis was the application of article 124 of the Beninese constitution that ensured equal rights for men and women. She stayed in West Africa until the fall of Habré's government and the victory of rebel leader Idriss Déby in 1990.

Once she had returned to N'Djamena, she joined the provisional Conseil Provisoire de la République (CPS) in 1991. She served on the Health and Social Services Commission of the CPS, thanks to her training in sociology. Allafi also became one of the first female leaders within Déby's Mouvement Patriotique du Salut (MPS; Patriotic Salvation Movement) party, and she remained loyal to Déby for over two decades. In 1992 she joined the Ministry of Agriculture. Allafi later directed or cocoordinated several different agricultural development projects in rural Chad. She attended the Beijing International Conference on Women in 1995 as the leader of the Chadian delegation. On 1 January 1998, President Idriss Déby appointed Allafi Minister of Social Services, and she held this post for nearly two years before she resigned on 13 December 1999. She organized a Chadian women's conference in the southern Chadian town of Moundou in 1999, created a mock parliament for young people, and a women's caucus in the Chadian parliament. She again became Minister of Social Services from June 2002 to June 2003, when she was replaced by Déby in a typical reshuffling of his cabinet. Allafi remained a staff member in different branches of the Chadian government in the early twenty-first century. Her career showed how some educated women could make a political career for themselves in the Déby era.

[*See also* Déby Itno, Idriss; Habré, Hissène; *and* Tombalbaye, François.]

BIBLIOGRAPHY

Ngartebaye, Eugène Leyotha. "La participation de la femme à la vie politique au Tchad, 1933–2003." MA thesis, Catholic University of Central Africa, 2004.

Tubiana, Marie José. *Parcours de femmes: Les nouvelles élites: entretiens, 1997–2003.* Saint-Maur, France: Sépia, 2004.

JEREMY RICH

Alliali, Camille (1926–), Ivorian lawyer, diplomat, politician, mayor, and cabinet minister, was born in Toumodi, a town about 25 miles from Yamoussoukro, Ivory Coast's capital. The son of an ordinary Baoulé peasant, he attended a public primary school in Toumodi run by Kablan Koizan, one of the very first Ivorian primary school teachers in the colony. He attended middle school in Bingerville and the École Normale William Ponty in Dakar. While in Senegal he met Richard Mollard, a visiting French professor, who encouraged him to study law. He recommended the University of Grenoble because the climate was more congenial and Grenoble's serene surroundings were conducive to serious academic studies. Alliali did not want to go down the path of becoming a colonial administrator, an agent of oppression, at a time when the anticolonial struggle led by the Parti Démocratique de Côte d'Ivoire–Rassemblement Démocratique Africain (PDCI-RDA) was in full swing. Instead, he chose to pursue a career as a public defender in order to represent his parents and fellow citizens in court, defending them against perceived colonial injustices.

At the time of his graduation in 1953 one could not simply pass an examination and be called to the bar. Defense attorneys were appointed by a decree of the governor-general of French West Africa (AOF) in Dakar. Although the legal profession had very few members, among them only two Ivorians, Lucien Yapobi and Aka Lambert, it took more than a year before the governor-general appointed Alliali. Even then, it took the intervention of Jean Delafosse, a member of the Advisory Council of AOF and Alliali's future brother-in-law, for the appointment to be made at all. Once appointed, Alliali became a forceful defender of the rights of the PDCI militants who were being severely persecuted by the colonial government.

Throughout his career, Alliali held many influential positions, starting with the vice presidency of the Ivory Coast's Territorial Assembly from 1957 to 1959. He also represented the Ivory Coast in the Senate of the French Community from 1959 to 1961. He served as Ivorian ambassador to France from 1961 to 1963 and as the first deputy minister of foreign affairs from 1963 to 1966. He was probably the longest serving justice minister, having held the position from 1966 to 1990. He was elected mayor of Toumodi in 1980. A Baoulé, he was also a member of the PDCI Executive Committee as well as the party's political bureau and in the early 1980s was considered a possible successor to Félix Houphouët-Boigny as party president. Dutifully loyal to the party, he attempted to broker an agreement between the two Konans—former President Henri-Konan Bédié and former Prime Minister Konan Banny—as the 2010 presidential election approached so as to prevent the former ruling party from going to the polls represented by two presidential candidates. He arranged a meeting at his residence on 18 August 2010 and succeeded in smoothing the ruffled feathers of Konan Banny, thus allowing Bédié to contest the presidential election on 31 October 2010 as the PDCI's sole candidate.

[See also Bédié, Henri-Konan; and Houphouët-Boigny, Félix.]

BIBLIOGRAPHY

Bakary, Tessy D. "Elite Transformation and Political Succession." In *The Political Economy of Ivory Coast*, edited by I. William Zartman and Christopher Delgado, pp. 21–55. New York: Praeger, 1984.

Dieng, Amady Aly. "Côte d'Ivoire: Disciple d'Houphouet-Boigny—Par Camille Alliali." All Africa, November 7, 2008. http://fr.allafrica.com/.

CYRIL DADDIEH

Alloron (d. 1884), Sudanese leader, was the first prominent Bari private merchant, slave trader, and opportunist insurgent warlord. He rose to power during the 1860s by exploiting poisonous dynastic rivalries between Nyigilo and Subek, the royal sons of Lagunu, the unchallenged Bari leader in 1840, and their respective noble offspring. The faction of Nyigilo had enjoyed the support of Catholic missionaries up to their departure in 1860, but thereafter allied with the northern slave traders who at that time were establishing fortified trading operations throughout southern Sudan. It was to become an era, for the first time in Bari history, during which commoner traders such as Alloron found it possible to acquire economic and political power. However, the upstart was often reminded of his humble origins by the epithet "man without rain," implying that he lacked the arcane fructifying powers of royalty.

The arrival of Turks, northern Sudanese, and Europeans in southern Sudan during the 1840s posed many challenges to the southern societies they encountered, among them the Bari community of the White Nile above the great swamps of the *sadd*. In recent generations the Bari had experienced political and social centralization under a series of gifted leaders who, among other prerogatives, had laid claim to a monopoly over the import-export trade of their incipient realm. Locally produced iron and ivory were exchanged by royal agents for alien luxuries such as beads, salt, and cloth that derived ultimately from the Red Sea coast of Eritrea and from Zanzibar. The new arrivals from the north now offered a much greater abundance and variety of imports; however, they introduced a much larger demand for slaves. They also challenged the right of the Bari leadership to dominate the community's trade.

Alloron began his career as a consummate middleman, serving simultaneously as the official Arabic interpreter for his noble Bari masters and the authorized agent for the Khartoum-sanctioned slavelord Abu Su'ud. He administered the key river port of Gondokoro, from which base he obtained firearms from the north, hired hundreds of Bari mercenaries, and supplied Abu Su'ud with an ever-increasing number of slaves. The steady undermining of royal control over the administered trade of the Bari monarchs by commoner chiefs such as Alloron helped to destroy the sovereignty of the Bari noble clan.

In 1869 the Egyptian khedive Ismai'il appointed Samuel Baker to occupy southern Sudan and end the slave trade. Upon his arrival Baker clashed immediately with Alloron, who masterminded an extended and determined Bari resistance to the invaders. However, after suffering significant defeats Alloron eventually switched sides and offered his allegiance to Khartoum. At Baker's departure from Equatoria Province in 1874 Alloron became a devoted follower of his successor as governor, Charles Gordon. By 1878, however, Alloron had fallen out with the next provincial governor Amin Pasha, and in the struggle to follow almost obliterated him. In the end, however, he failed; Amin had Alloron seized by stealth and beheaded. The year was 1884, and the Bari monarchy of mid-century was but a memory.

[*See also* Baker, Samuel White; *and* Ismai'il.]

BIBLIOGRAPHY

Baker, Samuel White. *Ismailia: A Narrative of the Expedition to Central Africa for the Suppression of the Slave Trade, Organized by Ismail, Khedive of Egypt*. London: Macmillan, 1874.

Beswick, Stephanie. "The Nineteenth Century Rise and Fall of the Bari: War, Local Trade, Slavery, and the Destruction of the Bari." In *Sudan's Wars and Peace Agreements*, edited by Jay Spaulding et al. New York: Cambridge University Press, 2010.

STEPHANIE BESWICK

'Alluba, Muhammad 'Ali (c.1875–1956), Egyptian lawyer, politician, and champion of Arab and Muslim causes, was probably born between 1875 and 1878 (he himself was not sure of the date) in al-Minya province, where his father was a school principal. The family later moved to Asyut where his father entered commerce and became a mill owner. After attending a *kuttab*, in 1890 he enrolled in the Khedivial Secondary School in Cairo. He graduated in 1895 and progressed to the Khedivial School of Law, from which he graduated in 1899 and entered law practice in Asyut. Known for much of his life simply as Muhammad 'Ali, "'Alluba" was a surname he had legally registered in 1931 to distinguish him from others.

'Alluba's political sympathies originally lay with the Nationalist Party founded by Mustafa Kamil. He entered national politics when he was elected to the new Legislative Assembly in 1914. At the end of World War I, 'Alluba was deeply involved in the postwar struggle for Egyptian independence from Great Britain. An original member of the Wafd Party and briefly its treasurer, 'Alluba was part of the Wafdist delegation that went to Paris in 1919 to demand independence for Egypt. Along with others, by 1921 'Alluba broke with the autocratic leadership of the Wafd's Sa'd Zaghlul and thereafter became a fierce opponent of Zaghlul and the Wafd. In 1922 he was a founding member and at one point secretary of the rival Liberal Constitutionalist Party, with which he was affiliated until 1934 when he resigned and became an independent in Egyptian politics. A veteran of Egypt's political wars, his 1942 book *The Principles of Egyptian Politics* (*Mabadi' fi al-Siyasa al-Misriyya*) is regarded as an insightful critique of the Egyptian political system as it had evolved by the 1940s.

First as a Liberal and later as an independent, 'Alluba served as a minister in several Egyptian governments of the parliamentary era. As Minister of Charitable Foundations in the anti-Wafdist coalition ministry of Ahmad Ziwar in 1924–1925, in September 1925 he with the other Liberals resigned from the ministry in protest against the dismissal of his fellow Liberal minister 'Abd al-'Aziz Fahmi. By the 1930s 'Alluba was loosely associated with the group of anti-Wafdist, palace-inclined politicians led by 'Ali Mahir. He served as Minister of Education in Mahir's first ministry from January to May 1936 and again as Minister of Parliamentary Affairs in Mahir's ministry in office from August 1939 to June 1940. After World War II he again briefly served as Minister of Charitable Foundations in the coalition ministry of Mahmud Fahmi al-Nuqrashi from December 1947 to March 1948.

His prominence in domestic politics notwithstanding, 'Alluba is primarily remembered as an early Egyptian champion of Arab and Muslim causes and as an advocate of a more assertive Arab and Muslim foreign policy for Egypt. 'Alluba himself credited his greater sensitivity to the Arab and Muslim world from travel abroad. He first became involved in external issues in 1929–1930, when as a lawyer he presented the legal case on behalf of the Supreme Muslim Council before the "Wailing Wall Commission" set up to inquire into the 1929 intercommunal violence in Palestine. In 1931 he was an Egyptian delegate to the Islamic Conference held in Jerusalem; he was selected to serve on the conference's executive committee and as one of its vice presidents. He traveled to India to advocate for Muslim solidarity in 1933 and in 1934 was one of the Islamic Conference's mediators who attempted to resolve the border dispute and war between Saudi Arabia and Yemen.

In the later 1930s 'Alluba was one of the leading Egyptian defenders of the Palestinian Arabs in their struggle against the British Mandate. In 1937 he attended and was one the vice presidents of the Bludan Conference lobbying in support of the Palestinian Arabs and in the following year was the leading figure organizing the World Parliamentary Congress of Arab and Muslim Countries in Defense of Palestine that met in Cairo in October 1938. Subsequently he led the congress's delegation that went to London to argue the Palestinian Arab cause. When in 1943–1944 a Wafdist government began to promote greater inter-Arab state collaboration, a process that led to the formation of the League of Arab States in 1945, ʿAlluba was one of the organizers of the Arab Unity Society, a pressure group calling for greater Arab solidarity and cooperation. His long advocacy of Arab and Muslim causes was recognized by the Egyptian government in 1948, when after his resignation from the Nuqrashi ministry ʿAlluba was selected as Egypt's first ambassador to newly independent Pakistan. A respected elder statesman, Muhammad ʿAli ʿAlluba died in Cairo on 25 March 1956.

BIBLIOGRAPHY

Deeb, Marius. *Party Politics in Egypt: The Wafd and Its Rivals, 1919–1939*. London: Ithaca Press for the Middle East Centre, 1979. Contains information on ʿAlluba's role in domestic politics in the interwar era.

Gershoni, Israel, and James Jankowski. *Redefining the Egyptian Nation, 1930–1945*. New York: Cambridge University Press, 1995. Discusses ʿAlluba's advocacy of Arab and Muslim causes in the 1930s and 1940s.

Goldschmidt, Arthur Jr. *Biographical Dictionary of Modern Egypt*. Boulder, Colo.: Lynne Rienner Publishers, 2000. A brief biography with an extensive bibliography.

JAMES JANKOWSKI

Almeida, Germano de (1945–), lawyer and author, was born on 31 July 1945 on Boa Vista Island in the Republic of Cape Verde. Germano de Almeida was one of ten children of Anacleto Dias Almeida and Eugenia da Cruz Almeida. His father was a carpenter and his mother was a stay-at-home mother who took care of the children. It was very difficult for his parents to support ten children. Cape Verde was a small and poor country under Portuguese rule. There were not many jobs available. When Germano was sixteen years old, his father passed away after being sick for many years. Germano started working as a carpenter to help his family. He was very

smart, really enjoyed school, and because of this, Germano was chosen to be his teacher's assistant. He wanted to continue with school and be successful even if he did not receive support from his parents because of their financial conditions. It was difficult to further his education in his native island of Boa Vista because the education system did not go beyond the fourth grade. He attended high school in the capital city of Praia, on Santiago Island, as well as in São Vicente Island.

When he was eighteen years old, Almeida joined the armed forces and served his duty in Angola. While in Angola, he continued his passion for school and spent much of his time reading and working to earn money. In 1972 Germano's hard work paid off when he earned a scholarship to study law at the Universidade Classica de Lisboa, in Lisbon, Portugal. After completing his studies, Almeida returned to Cape Verde. In 1975 this small island nation became a newly independent state. Almeida was appointed Cape Verde's attorney general in 1976, a position he held until 1979. After serving as the nation's attorney general, Almeida moved to São Vicente and made this island his residence. He also began exercising his career as a lawyer.

Although he enjoyed his profession as a lawyer, Almeida was also fond of politics and writing. He incorporated real life political and social experiences into his writings. In 1983 Almeida founded the magazine *Ponto & Virgula* and published his first piece, *Estórias* (Tales), under the pseudonym Romualdo Cruz. In 1989 he became partner in the publishing house Ilhéu Editora, through which he released most of his works.

In 1989 Almeida released his first romance novel, *O testamento do Sr. Napumoceno da Silva Araújo* (English trans. *The Last Will and Testament of Senhor da Silva Araújo*, 2004). It would become the author's most internationally acclaimed literary work. The literature during this period focused primarily on real accounts of poverty, famine, and emigration. In this novel, he incorporated the hypocritical realities of the islands into a romantic and entertaining fictional story of a wealthy businessman on the island of São Vicente who passed away and left his entire fortune to his illegitimate daughter. In 1990 Germano released *O Meu Poeta* (My Poet), about the public and political affairs of the city of Mindelo, São Vicente. In 1991 Germano became the co-owner and director of *Agaviva*, a local newspaper.

Almeida published *O dia das calças coladas* (The Day of the Rolled up Pants) in 1992 and *Os dois irmãos* (The Two Brothers) in 1995, both based on Almeida's real-life experiences as a lawyer in the rural settings of Santo Antão and Santiago Islands. In *Estórias de dentro de casa* (Tales from Inside the House), published in 1996, Germano Almeida writes about domestic life in the city of Mindelo. In *A Ilha fantástica*, (The Fantastic Island), released in 1994, and *A família Trago* (The Trago Family), published in 1998, Almeida recounted his family life and youth experiences in his native island of Boa Vista. In 1997 Germano Almeida's first romance novel, *O testamento*, was adapted and released as a film. It won various cinematography awards in Latin America. In addition to *A família Trago*, Almeida also published *A morte do meu poeta* (The Death of My Poet) and *Estórias contadas* (Told Tales) in 1998. Almeida himself published *A morte do meu poeta*, which is about a poet who becomes a corrupt politician and is eventually eaten by a shark. His publishing company believed this work to be too critical of the ruling party at that time. *Estórias contadas*, a collection of fifty-five short stories was published by the Portuguese newspaper *Publico*.

Following *Estórias contadas*, in 1999 Almeida published another romance novel, *Dona Pura e os camaradas de Abril* (Ms. Pura and April's Comrades). In this novel, about Portugal's Carnation Revolution, which led to the transition from an authoritarian regime to democracy, Almeida once again demonstrated his ability to blur the lines between real life and fiction. As in most of his works, Almeida wrote in Portuguese but very often infused Cape Verdean *Crioulo* phrases to capture the essence and day-to-day affairs of Cape Verdean life.

Germano Almeida continued his account of Cape Verdean society in *As memórias de um espírito* in 2001, *A viagem pela história das ilhas* in 2003, *O mar na lajinha* in 2004, and *Eva* in 2006. His work *A morte do ouvidor*, released in 2010, was well received by critics. In 2010 Cape Verde's president Pedro Pires also honored Almeida with the medal for literary excellence. His works have been translated into several languages and published in several places such as Brazil, France, Spain, Italy, Germany, Sweden, Holland, Norway, Denmark, Cuba, the United States, and Bulgaria. Germano Almeida is considered a major writer of the Portuguese-speaking world because his fictional work, intertwined with real-life experiences, sarcasm, and humor, marked a new period in the Cape Verdean literary tradition.

BIBLIOGRAPHY

Almeida, Germano. Oral interview by author, 26 July 2010.

Batalha, Luis, and Jorgen Carling, eds. *Transnational Archipelago: Perspectives on Cape Verdean Migration and Diaspora*. Amsterdam: Amsterdam University Press, 2008.

Lobban, Richard. *Cape Verde: Crioulo Colony to Independent Nation*. Boulder, Colo.: Westview Press, 1995.

Lobban, Richard, and Marlene L. Lopes. *Historical Dictionary of the Republic of Cape Verde*. 3d ed. Metuchen, N.J.: Scarecrow Press, 1995.

TERZA SILVA LIMA-NEVES

Almeida, Ndalu de. *See* Ondjaki.

Alula Engida (1847–1897), Ethiopian military leader, is considered by many in Ethiopia as the country's national hero and "Africa's greatest general" of the last quarter of the nineteenth century, an era during which he was a pivotal figure in Ethiopia's internal and external affairs. This was a period of formative significance, during which the Ethiopian empire managed to stem Western imperialism, defeat Islamic neighbors, and double its territory. Ethiopia's victories at that time ensured her unique independence, but also solidified her traditional institutions, which remained almost unchallenged until the final decades of the twentieth century. He is better known as Ras Alula. *Ras* was the highest rank in Ethiopia of the time, similar to duke in medieval Europe. Another form of his name is Alula Engeda.

Alula was born into a peasant family in Tigray, but was talented and ambitious enough to climb the ladder of local administrative and military service. In November 1875 and March 1876 he helped to defeat an Egyptian invasion (the battles of Gundet and Gura) and was promoted to *ras* and appointed to oversee the Mareb Mellash, the future Eritrea (as the area was renamed by the Italians in 1890). During the next twenty years, he led nearly all the major battles against the Egyptians, the Sudanese Mahdiyya (Kufit, September 1885; Metemma, March 1889), and the Italians (Dogali, January 1887; Adwa, March 1896). A great tactician, he would lure his enemies out of their fortifications into an ambush in the open, where the Ethiopians enjoyed numerical advantage and superior firepower.

Alula lacked formal education (that is, church-based education during his lifetime) but made some achievements as a modernizer. Reorganizing Eritrea as a frontier province, he turned the village of Asmara into a busy capital, introduced various land reforms, cultivated trade with the coast, and developed working relations with the local Muslim traders and communities. He also had his hand in the empire's diplomatic affairs and was the architect of the Hewett Treaty of June 1884, in which Ethiopia undertook to relieve the Egyptians besieged by the Mahdiyya state in the Sudan, in return for a British promise of a free port in Massawa.

An important dimension of Alula's historical role was his contribution to the hegemony of Tigray in internal Ethiopian political competition during the days of Emperor Yohannes IV (1872–1889). Alula helped his master Yohannes threaten Menilek of Shewa in 1878 and 1882, and Tekle Haymanot of Gojjam in 1881 militarily, and thus ensure their partial loyalty. When Yohannes was killed in Metemma (March 1889), Alula led Tigray's revolt against Menilek, before succumbing to Shewa's hegemony in 1894. In the battle of Adwa, he was an adviser to Menilek II (1889–1913), a position he continued to hold until his death in a local battle between Tigrayan factions in 1897.

Alula's career reflected the advantages of Ethiopia's traditional culture as well as its shortcomings. The old system enabled talented individuals of any background to gain prominence while sidelining incapable sons of the nobility. But, lacking more stable institutions, it was continually immersed in personal intrigues. One example was the way Alula lost Asmara and Eritrea to the Italians in 1888–1889. The Italians, entrenched in coastal Massawa, were militarily incapable of penetrating mountainous Eritrea, but Alula's regime in Asmara was undermined by his Ethiopian rivals. They finally persuaded Yohannes to order Alula to abandon Asmara and join his campaign against the Mahdiyya. In Alula's absence, his Tigrayan-Ethiopian rivals invited the Italians to his capital; they captured the entire province without having to fire a shot.

In spite of thus losing Eritrea, the Ethiopian empire of the late nineteenth century, as mentioned, experienced primarily victories, and its traditional political culture would persist until the costly, brutal revolution of 1974. After the 1991 restoration of Tigrayan leadership in Ethiopia, Alula's reputation was revived. The establishment of independent Eritrea that year also gave the image of Alula an additional dimension—that of an Ethiopian oppressor of Eritreans. However, in the collective memory of most Ethiopians, Ras Alula remains a symbol of patriotism, bravery, and African pride.

[See also Menilek II; Tekle Haymanot (1917–1988); and Yohannes IV.]

BIBLIOGRAPHY

Erlich, Haggai. *Ras Alula and the Scramble for Africa: A Political Biography: Ethiopia & Eritrea, 1875–1897.* Lawrenceville, N.J.: Red Sea Press, 1996.

Gabre-Sellassie, Zewde. *Yohannes IV of Ethiopia: A Political Biography.* Oxford: Clarendon Press, 1975.

Zewde, Bahru. *A History of Modern Ethiopia, 1855–1974.* London: J. Currey, 1991.

HAGGAI ERLICH

Álvaro I (d. 1587), king of Kongo, was born in the middle of the sixteenth century. His birth name was Nimi a Lukeni Lua Mvemba. Little is known of his early life, and the name of his father has not survived. His mother, Isabel Lukeni Lua Mbemba, remarried King Henrique I of Kongo after Álvaro's father had passed away. Henrique I died fighting Téké warriors from the northern Anziku kingdom only a year after ascending to the throne in 1567. The Kongolese people already had suffered greatly during a civil war for the succession of the kingdom following the death of Diogo I in November 1561. It is unclear how Álvaro gained the throne. Between 1584 and 1588, the Kongolese ambassador to the Vatican, Duarte Lopes, claimed that Álvaro had been acclaimed king by a majority of the major noble families, but some historians believe he wrested power through force. In the same year, a large group of violent raiders known as the Imbangala (or Jaga in contemporary European sources) entered the Kongo kingdom from the east. The Imbangala defeated an army headed by Álvaro, sacked Mbanza Kongo, and slaughtered civilians and Kongolese soldiers alike. Historians have long debated the background of the invaders, but they appear to have been peoples disrupted by warfare and slave raiding from the Kwango River valley to the northeast of Kongo. The Imbangala may have offered a means for displaced warriors from outside Kongo and its northern neighbor Tio to overcome the coastal kingdoms' monopoly over direct trade with Europeans.

Álvaro fled to the Island of Horses on the Congo River, where famine and other hardships beset the survivors. Desperate, Álvaro turned to the Portuguese garrison on the islands of São Tomé and Principe for support. Roughly six hundred soldiers led by Francisco de Gouveia Sottomaio sailed to Kongo and vanquished the Imbangala bands from 1571 to 1573. Imbangala warriors later would become key players in kingdoms further south of Kongo in the seventeenth century.

After Álvaro returned to Mbanza Kongo, the king carefully walked a fine line between making concessions to Portugal and maintaining Kongolese autonomy. Unfortunately for his successors, Álvaro offered Portugal control of any of the mines in his country. Although no major sources of silver existed in Kongolese territory, Portuguese dreams of silver would ultimately inspire costly invasions well after Álvaro's death. The Portuguese government also claimed that Álvaro had granted Portuguese traders the right to trade without paying taxes, which seems highly unlikely. The Portuguese crown hoped to make Álvaro become a vassal of Lisbon. Kongolese nobles and Portuguese residents of the kingdom, including the king's confessor, Francisco Barbuda, banded together to defend the kingdom's independence. Álvaro's cause was helped by the fact that many Portuguese and Luso-Africans had moved to Kongo to escape the overbearing Portuguese governors of São Tomé and the new colony of Angola just south of Kongolese territory. For converted Jews like Duarte Lopes, Kongo provided a refuge from the discrimination imposed in Portuguese territories, especially after the merging of Spanish and Portuguese empires. This large community supported a strong Kongolese monarchy in order to ensure that commerce continued undisturbed. They also profited from the creation of a new slave route from the Kwango River through the east-central Kongolese province to the coast. Since the governor of Mbata continually fought its eastern neighbors, the fighting generated captives that could be sold. The establishment of the Portuguese colony of Angola in 1575 was a potential threat, and the port town of Luanda created an alternate point for exporting slaves not under the control of Álvaro. Even so, demand for Kongolese raffia cloth created a new market for Kongolese products. Álvaro I thus could acquire revenue through a number of different ways. He also eliminated an old rival of Kongo by ending the threat of the old Ngola kingdom that had made war on Kongo as late as 1572. Álvaro also sought, with limited success, to break free of the tutelage of Portugal in regards to relations with European countries, but most of his ambassadors to the Vatican fell victim to pirates and storms. An example of Álvaro's complex policy toward Portugal was revealed in his relations with the neighboring southern kingdom of Ndongo. Álvaro apparently sent representatives to Ndongo to encourage that kingdom to attack the Portuguese settlement of Angola. However, Kongo ultimately sent troops to Angola to battle Ndongo. The king's forces failed to conquer his neighbor.

Like other Kongolese monarchs, Álvaro I tried to cultivate close ties with missionaries and secular clergy. In comparison to his predecessor Afonso I, Álvaro had little luck bringing in many missionaries. Kongolese Christians in the second half of the sixteenth century had to cope with a tiny number of priests, which limited the spread of official church teachings. Bishop Gasper Cão visited the kingdom at the behest of Álvaro. Pope Sixtus V did not heed the pleas of Álvaro's ambassador, Duarte Lopes, to send missionaries to Kongo completely unconnected to Portugal, but the visit did pay dividends in another way in terms of advancing the Christianization of the kingdom. Italian writer Filippo Pigafetta found Lopes' stories of Kongo compelling enough to set down in writing in 1591 in the book *Relatione del reame di Congo*. This text made more church leaders aware of the needs of Kongo, and helped Álvaro II's efforts to gain legitimacy through building churches and supporting church activities.

Álvaro I managed to successfully place his son Álvaro II in an excellent position to inherit his throne. This was a difficult challenge, especially as his son's mother was a slave. One reason for his ability to place his favorite candidate was his military reforms. After the Jaga defeat, Álvaro formed a regiment of musketeers. These troops generally were Portuguese or of Luso-African descent. He also promoted slaves to leading positions in the government. One advantage of his multiple marriages to slave wives was that he could form his own household without depending on aristocratic families. Few rulers in the century after Álvaro's death could match his political acumen and restrain the threats of the Portuguese and noble families.

[*See also* Álvaro II Nimi a Nkanga.]

BIBLIOGRAPHY

Balandier, Georges. *Daily Life in the Kingdom of the Kongo from the Sixteenth to the Eighteenth Century.* New York: Pantheon, 1968.

Hastings, Adrian. *The Church in Africa, 1450–1950.* Oxford: Clarendon Press, 1996.

Hilton, Anne. *The Kingdom of Kongo.* Oxford: Clarendon Press, 1985.

Vansina, Jan. *Kingdoms of the Savanna*. Madison: University of Wisconsin Press, 1966.

JEREMY RICH

Álvaro II Nimi a Nkanga (fl. late sixteenth century), king of Kongo, was born in the middle of the sixteenth century to King Álvaro I and a slave wife. At the death of his father in 1587, Álvaro had to struggle against a number of male and female members of the royal family in order to ascend to the throne. According to a Jesuit at the court, Álvaro II defeated one of his brothers in a single-combat duel in order to claim the crown. To strengthen his power, Álvaro created a large army of Tio slave soldiers that grew to over sixteen thousand men. They were purchased at the Malebo Pool of the Congo River, on the outskirts of Kongolese territory. With this force, Álvaro could dominate the aristocratic families and the provinces in a much more centralized fashion than his predecessors. For example, Álvaro appointed royal judges to oversee tribunals in each province. Upon the death or expulsion of nobles, Álvaro's government claimed the property and slaves of the dead or exiled noble for the king. He also taxed European residents of the kingdom to increase his own revenue. In addition, Álvaro launched a series of eastern campaigns to gain tributes and defend Kongolese territory. To uphold his position as a Christian king, Álvaro inaugurated a brotherhood of knights in 1607, the Order of Christ. Although the king of Spain objected to the creation of this brotherhood, Álvaro remained firm. This order would survive for over a century after the collapse of the Kongolese state in the late seventeenth century.

Álvaro passionately worked for the full recognition of Kongo as a state equal to any European nation. Pope Sixtus V had rejected Álvaro I's request that Kongo receive an independent bishop without any interference from the Portuguese. In 1594 Álvaro II sent his close relative Antonio Vieira to Rome to convince the Vatican to grant Kongo a separate diocese, rather than continue to allow the Portuguese crown to choose new bishops for Kongo. Álvaro II also asked to become a vassal of the Pope alone rather than of Portugal, and that his monarchy receive relics and indulgences as a full-fledged member of Christendom, rather than be considered as on the margins of Christianity. Furthermore, he wanted his own confessor and the royal Saint James chapel at the capital of Mbanza Kongo to be free of interference from foreign bishops, so that it could serve as a nucleus for an authentically Kongolese Catholic tradition. Álvaro's position is illustrated by a 1613 letter he sent to the Pope: "[Álvaro] has been informed that the Portuguese in this country seek to bring about a division between himself and the King of Spain, so that the latter would be prompted to conquer the kingdom of Congo. For his own part, he has always shown friendship to this king and he has favored his subjects."

These policies received some support from the papacy. In 1596 Mbanza Kongo was declared the See of São Salvador, which henceforth would have its own bishop. Dominican missionaries received a warm welcome and many gifts from Álvaro's regime at first, but the relationship soon soured. Dominicans found the knowledge and conduct of Kongolese priests appalling. Álvaro accused the newcomers of rejecting their duty to travel around the kingdom and cut them off from royal financial support.

However, many of Alvaro's other requests and complaints did not receive much support from the Vatican. It did not help that a number of Álvaro's envoys never reached Rome or died soon after their arrival as a result of the hardships of the journey. Even the bishops did not always serve Álvaro's interests. Since the Portuguese government retained the right to select candidates for this position, these priests acted as an autonomous force in the kingdom that often opposed Álvaro's growing power. Luso-African priests born in Kongo viewed the European Dominicans as a threat and urged Álvaro to limit their influence.

Álvaro regularly wrote letters to the Portuguese government as well as to the pope. In these writings, he repeatedly criticized the affronts of the Portuguese governor of the colony of Angola, such as the occupation of mines in Kongolese territory. Álvaro also demanded that all Portuguese subjects who lived in Kongo for more than six years be treated as Kongolese citizens. If this occurred, long-time European residents of Kongo would henceforth be judged by Kongolese law. If the king had his way, all Jewish converts to Christianity (or "New Christians" as they were called) would have been expelled from his realm. The Portuguese government's use of Imbangala slave regiments also irked Álvaro, as he considered these soldiers to be rebellious and cruel. In the 1590s, Álvaro declared himself to be the protector of the chiefs on the Luanda islands that were just off the Portuguese-controlled shore. When the Portuguese governor of Angola freed a man who had tried to assassinate Álvaro, and whom the Kongolese king had sent to the colonial capital of Luanda for sentencing, Álvaro became irate. When Álvaro's ambassador in Madrid harshly criticized the Portuguese in 1605, the Spanish king had the man removed from the priesthood and stripped him of his diplomatic honors. Last but not least, Álvaro resented the fact that Portuguese ships controlled all communications between Kongo and Europe.

Álvaro had a mixed record of quelling internal opposition in his kingdom. Noble families resented their declining independence as the authority of Álvaro made itself felt throughout each province. The Silva clan posed a serious challenge to Álvaro toward the end of his reign. They controlled the Nsoyo coastal province after Manuel Silva received this territory from Álvaro at some point before 1591. The king's plan to assuage his rivalry with the Silva family failed, since Manuel recognized the value of making alliances with Portuguese traders independent of the inland royal capital. When leaders of the Silva clan rebelled against Álvaro, he lacked the means to defeat the insurrection despite his large army of slaves. Ántonio Silva, the lord of the eastern Mbamba province, also developed his own network of nobles and supporters. Álvaro ensured his throne would go to his son by a slave wife, Bernardo. At Álvaro's death in 1614 Kongo had reached the zenith of its power, but Álvaro's official heir Bernardo was overthrown by other nobles a year later. The resulting civil war was a sign of the chronic violence that accompanied succession disputes in the late seventeenth century.

[See also Álvaro I.]

BIBLIOGRAPHY

Balandier, Georges. *Daily Life in the Kingdom of the Kongo from the Sixteenth to the Eighteenth Century.* New York: Pantheon, 1968.

Hastings, Adrian. *The Church in Africa, 1450–1950.* Oxford: Clarendon Press, 1996.

Hilton, Anne. *The Kingdom of Kongo.* Oxford: Clarendon Press, 1985.

Vansina, Jan. *Kingdoms of the Savanna.* Madison: University of Wisconsin Press, 1966.

JEREMY RICH

Alypius of Thagaste (fl. late fourth/early fifth century CE), Christian bishop. What we know about Alypius of Thagaste comes mainly from Augustine's *Confessions* and *Letters.* Born into a curial family in the Roman town of Thagaste (present-day Souk Ahras, Algeria), in the province of Numidia, Alypius (whose name seems to indicate Greek origins) was

younger than Augustine (born in 354 CE). Augustine was also Alypius's teacher, first in Thagaste around 374–376), then in Carthage around 380. But Alypius was soon captivated by the Roman games, the gladiators and the chariot races in particular, and stopped attending Augustine's lessons because of an undisclosed argument between his father and his teacher. Alypius quickly resumed attending despite his father's injunction, however, and one day as he entered the classroom Augustine used the example of someone attending the games to make a point, which convinced Alypius to change his ways. Among the group of students who studied with Augustine in this period, Alypius was the most promising, and he established a durable friendship and intellectual companionship with his teacher. Augustine's influence is probably responsible for his conversion, at this time, to Manichaeism, a religion of Persian origins, which flourished during Alypius's lifetime, and of which Augustine was an adherent before his conversion to Christianity.

Toward the end of 382 Alypius left Carthage for Rome to study law, preceding Augustine. There friends forced him to attend gladiatorial games, which he came to greatly enjoy, despite his attempts to resist them initially. In 384 he obtained the position of assessor to an important imperial official (*comes largitionum Italicianarum*) in charge of finances in the diocese of Italy and Africa, where he became well known for his incorruptibility as well as his opposition to a powerful senator. In the fall of the same year, Alypius followed Augustine to Milan, and along with Nebridius, the three dedicated themselves to the study of philosophy. At this time, Alypius was already living in continence, contrary to Augustine. Augustine was so eloquent about the joys of marriage that Alypius, curious about Augustine's lifestyle, considered getting married, but he eventually abandoned the idea. He also abandoned Manichaeism at that time and made plans with Augustine and a small group of friends to live in a communal arrangement.

Still in Milan at the beginning of August 386, Augustine and Alypius were visited by Ponticianus, a fellow African who held an important position at court. Ponticianus noticed the Epistles of Paul lying on a table and told them the story of Saint Anthony. He further mentioned the suburban monastery that Bishop Ambrose (later Saint Ambrose) supervised, the existence of which they had ignored until then, and proceeded to tell them about some of his colleagues who, while at the court in Trier, had happened on a copy of the *Life of Anthony*. They had suddenly abandoned their position "in the world" and had immediately decided to imitate Antony and adopt his way of life.

This visit, coupled with the influence of Ambrose in Milan, occasioned the conversion of both Augustine and Alypius (who witnessed the famous "garden scene," the key moment of Augustine's conversion as recounted in his *Confessions*) to Christianity and the ascetic lifestyle. They then finally acted upon their project of communal life by retiring to the Cassiacum monastery in the fall of 386. This is also when Augustine composed his first important writings, a series of dialogues (*Contra Academicos, De ordine, De beata uita*) in which Alypius appears as a participant in the discussions; however, Augustine's writing was often interrupted by his frequent trips back to Milan. Making the reverse trip from Cassiacum to Milan barefoot, they both (along with Augustine's son, Adeodatus) received baptism from Ambrose on Easter, 24/25 April 387.

Before going back to Africa (fall 388), the now inseparable friends visited Rome, where they were surprised to find out that, contrary to Milan, where Ambrose had strictly forbidden the practice, the Christians of Rome could not be brought to respect the interdiction of funeral meals. Funeral meals were unacceptable to Christians because they evoked the funerary clubs that had existed for centuries and as such had strong "pagan" associations. Augustine and Alypius would eventually work to enforce Ambrose's ban of this practice throughout the North African dioceses. In Africa Alypius lived in Thagaste among the disciples of Augustine in his newly founded monastery, where he was before October 393. Earlier in 393 the Christians of an undisclosed municipality might have asked Alypius to become their priest or bishop, since Aurelius of Carthage wrote to Augustine that Alypius was allowed to remain in the monastery. Most likely in the same year, he visited Jerome in Palestine, undoubtedly as part of a pilgrimage to the Holy Land. Upon his return to Africa, he was elected bishop of Thagaste some time before the end of 395. Like many other fathers of the church in this formative period, Alypius—and Augustine with him—became a "monk-bishop," both overseeing the administration of his bishopric and supervising the Augustinian monastery of Thagaste. As such, Alypius most likely contributed to the writing of the *Rule of Saint Augustine*, which became the guiding document of the Augustinian monastic tradition. As bishop, he also actively participated in

the ecclesiastical conflicts that plagued the North African Christian communities of the late fourth and early fifth centuries, in particular against the Donatists and the Pelagians.

Alypius regularly participated in the annual ecclesiastical councils of the African church in Carthage, and his legal expertise made him an ideal candidate as a representative to the Conference of Carthage against the Donatists (411). Indeed, his Catholic colleagues chose him as one of the seven representatives (along with Augustine and Possidius) authorized to speak for the 286 bishops present. He justified this confidence by making numerous legal points during the procedures, including the request to read documents relevant to the origins of the schism from the archives. He participated in the council of Milevus against Pelagius in 416. And in May 419, at the council of Carthage, his colleagues selected him, along with Augustine, as representative of Numidia for an extended meeting (which lasted all summer) to discuss a series of problems the African church faced. He noted at this occasion that the African church lacked a Greek copy of the Acts of Nicaea and asked that messengers be sent to obtain such copies from Constantinople, Antioch, and Alexandria.

This extra session of the council of 419 also elected Alypius as a delegate to the court in Ravenna, and he left for Italy at the end of August. The exact nature of this mission is not clear. It involved civil authorities since he travelled to Ravenna, and again his legal background, as well as his previous experience with the imperial administration, made him an ideal candidate. Augustine would later write that Alypius could not fulfill all of his goals during this trip, but we do know of three requests that he made. First, he asked for and obtained a remission (*indulgentia*) involving the entire population of Carthage, which might be connected to taxation. Second, following a small group of people who had taken asylum in the church, and perhaps related to a criminal affair, the African bishops requested a clearer law regarding the privileges of asylum for churches. For this request, Alypius met the patrician Constantius in person (the future emperor, Constantius III) and *Sirmondian Constitution* 13 might have been issued in response. Third, Alypius might have also demanded legal clarification regarding the selection of *defensores civitatis*. Julian of Eclanum later criticized the African bishops for sending Alypius with eighty horses to bribe the officials at court.

On his return to Africa, Alypius visited Boniface in Rome and brought with him numerous Pelagian works for Augustine to refute. He also visited his successor, Celestius, on a further trip to Italy (at a disputed date in the 420s), once again to request legal help from the court against the criminal practices of merchants who captured citizens to sell them into slavery. After the death of Valentinus, around 422, Alypius became metropolitan bishop of Numidia by virtue of his seniority. Augustine wrote his last known letter to Alypius in 428/9, but while Possidius joined his dying master during the siege of Hippo by the Vandals, Alypius's subsequent whereabouts are unknown. The Catholic Church canonized him in 1584 and celebrates his feast day, along with Possidius's, on May 16.

[*See also* Anthony the Great; Augustine of Hippo; *and* Possidius.]

BIBLIOGRAPHY

Berrouard, M. F. "Un tournant dans la vie de l'Église d'Afrique : les deux missions d'Alypius en Italie à la lumière des lettres 10*, 15*, 16*, 22* et 23*A de Saint Augustin." *REAug* 31 (1985): 46–70.

Brown, Peter. *Augustine of Hippo. A Biography.* Berkeley: University of California Press, 2000.

Lancel, Serge. *Saint Augustin.* Paris: Fayard, 1999.

O'Donnell, J. J. *Augustine: Confessions.* 3 vols. Oxford: Clarendon Press, 1992.

ERIC FOURNIER

Amadi, Elechi (1934–), Nigerian author, educator, army officer, and administrator, was born in Mbodo-Aluu, today in the Ikwerre Local Government Area of Rivers State, on 12 May 1934 to Daniel Wonuchuku Wogbara Amadi, a farmer and haberdasher, and Enwene Wogazior. One of Amadi's relatives, Gabriel Ohabiko, was a "famous Aluu story teller and historian from whose lips he must have garnered a vast store of oral tradition" (Alagoa in Feuser and Eko, 1994). His primary education was at Saint Peter's School, Isiokpo. He went on to Government College, Umuahia, where he developed a keen interest in literature and began writing short stories and poems. After graduating from Umuahia, he spent a year at Survey School Oyo and earned a Land Survey certificate, before going on to study for a degree in physics and mathematics at the University College, Ibadan in 1955. At university, Amadi replaced his Europeanized name, Emmanuel Elechi Daniel, with the form reflective of his Ikwerre heritage: Elechi Amadi.

He joined the Mbari club and published poems in campus publications like *The Horn* and *The Beacon*.

In 1957, Amadi married Dorah Nwonne Ohale, with whom he had eight daughters and a son. After his graduation in 1959, Amadi worked as a land surveyor for the former East Regional Government of Nigeria. A year later, he embarked on a teaching career. In 1963, he joined the Nigerian armed forces and began to teach at the Military School, Zaria. That same year, he began to rework one of his short stories into his landmark novel, *The Concubine*. The novel, published in 1966, tells the story of Ihuoma, who seems perfect, but is hapless in love. Her husband and admirers die in circumstances ascribed to the vengeance of a jealous sea-god, Ihuoma's husband in the spiritual realm. The novel relies heavily on Ikwerre oral tradition, incorporating myth, proverbs, songs and a mode of storytelling reminiscent of indigenous modes. These aesthetic features, and the similarity of Ikwerre language and culture to those of the Igbo as recreated in Chinua Achebe's work, led several critics to label him a literary son of Achebe, despite the differences in their themes and creative thrust.

In November 1965 Amadi retired from the army with the rank of captain and decided to resume his career in education in the southeast. At the threshold of the Nigerian Civil War of 1967–1970, he became an active participant in Ogbakor Ikwerre, a cultural union that sought to contest the political and economic domination of the majority tribes over the riverine minorities of Nigeria through the creation of a Rivers State. He was soon branded a "saboteur" by the Biafran authorities. For over a year he endured persecution and illegal detention. After regaining his freedom, Amadi returned to the Nigerian Armed Forces and served with the Third Marine Commandoes until the end of the war. His second novel, *The Great Ponds* (1969), was published during this time.

Amadi became permanent secretary of the Rivers State Government in 1973 and remained in this post for a decade. That same year, he published his war memoirs, *Sunset in Biafra*, and his first play, *Isiburu*. The year 1977 marked the publication of *The Slave*, the last in his trilogy of novels exploring the vulnerability of humanity at the hands of forces beyond its control in a precolonial past. That same year, he published two light comedic plays, *Peppersoup* and *The Road to Ibadan*, and the more serious *Dancer of Johannesburg*. These three plays marked a shift in Amadi's creative sensibility, drifting from precolonial Ikwerre villages toward contemporary Nigeria. They were also his first works to be published by a Nigerian press.

Amadi's literary output in the eighties and nineties was less voluminous as a result of his various commitments in the Rivers State administration and at the Rivers State College of Education, in such positions as commissioner of education (1982), commissioner for lands and housing (1989), lecturer in residence (1984–1985), dean of arts (1985–1986), and head of the literature department (1991–1993). This period marked the publication of three works, *Ethics in Nigerian Culture* (1982), *Estrangement* (1986), a novel set in the aftermath of the Nigerian Civil War, and a short story, "An In-Law Arrives" featured in the 1994 festschrift, *Elechi Amadi at 55*. In 1991 Amadi married his second wife, Priye Iyalla, a lecturer in French, with whom he had three sons. He was awarded the Rivers State Silver Jubilee Award in 1992 and the Ikwerre Ethnic Nationality Merit Award for Literature in 1995.

The twenty-first century opened with a renewed zest for literary activity. Amadi published the play *The Woman of Calabar* (2002), *Speaking and Singing* (2003), a collection of critical essays and poems, and finished two science fiction novels, *When God Came* and *Song of the Vanquished*. In 2007 he was a key consultant on the Nollywood adaptation of *The Concubine*, directed by Joe Dudun and Oby Kechere. He also coedited and contributed to *Songs for Wonodi: an Anthology of Poems in Memory of Okogbule Wonodi*. Amadi has also translated the entire Anglican Book of Common Prayer and hymnbook into Ikwerre and has played a role in the production of vernacular texts for use in Ikwerre schools.

Despite the range and superiority of his literary production, Amadi's work has received less critical attention than might be expected for a writer of his caliber. This may be a result of his controversial declarations on political commitment as prostitution of art, his distance from literary vogues such as the colonial clash and the post-independence disillusion, and the canonical preeminence of Achebe over the first generation of Nigerian novelists. This neglect stands in stark contrast to the popularity of his work in West African educational institutions, as well as among the general West African public. Elechi Amadi has made literary history as the most versatile writer of his generation, one of the most mellifluous novelists to grace the African literary arena, and the sole Nigerian writer to set three consecutive novels in a timeless, precolonial world where gods, spirits, and the unborn cohabit in uncertain proximity.

[*See also* Achebe, Chinua.]

BIBLIOGRAPHY

Amadi, Elechi. *Speaking and Singing (Papers and Poems)*. Port Harcourt, Nigeria: Port Harcourt University Press, 2003.

Eko, Ebele. *Elechi Amadi: The Man and His Work*. Lagos, Nigeria: Kraft Books, 1991.

Feuser, Willfried, and Ebele Eko, eds. *Elechi Amadi at 55: Poems, Short Stories, and Papers*. Ibadan, Nigeria: Heinemann, 1994.

Seiyifa, Koroye, ed. *Critical Perspectives on Elechi Amadi*. Port Harcourt, Nigeria: Pearl Publishers, 2008.

TERRI OCHIAGHA

Amador (d. 1595) was the leader of a major slave revolt in 1595, which almost succeeded in defeating the Portuguese colonial authorities in São Tomé. The hitherto uninhabited island of São Tomé was discovered by Portuguese navigators around 1471, but the successful colonization of the island began only in 1493, when Portuguese colonists established sugarcane plantations to be worked by African slaves brought from the neighboring continent. In the sixteenth century the local sugar industry prospered; however, the island was marked by continuous political instability provoked by frequent power struggles among the governor, the Catholic bishop, and the town council, which was dominated by the sugar planters. Amador was a Creole slave, that is, a slave born on the island.

From the beginning, slavery provoked resistance, and smaller slave uprisings occurred before and after Amador's revolt. In addition, gangs of runaway slaves, locally known as macambos, established maroon communities in the inaccessible dense forests in the mountainous interior of the island and frequently assaulted the plantations and attacked the town. The colonial authorities created a local militia to defend the colony and fight the maroons in the interior. The slave revolt began at a time when the decline of the island's sugar industry had begun due to the emerging sugar plantations in Brazil and when the local authorities were weakened as a result of a conflict between the Catholic bishop, Francisco de Villanova (1590–1600), and the governor Fernando de Menezes (1593–1596). In August 1594, this conflict culminated in the excommunication of the governor by the bishop, who afterward felt threatened by his enemies and fled for his life to Lisbon. Subsequently, the governor's own authority was challenged by the town council. Amador took advantage of the resulting political divisions within the settlement.

The revolt began on 9 July 1595 when slaves led by Amador and two other slave leaders, Lazaro and Domingo, entered the parish church in Trindade and killed some white men attending Mass. Thereafter a growing number of slaves assaulted plantations and burned the sugar mills and plantation houses. Two days later, during a battle in the town between the rebels and the inhabitants, three white men were killed. The next day, the slaves continued burning plantations and sugar mills in all over the island. On 14 July the militia and armed inhabitants, including the local clergy, confronted the rebels commanded by Amador in another battle. The slaves fled, but were regrouped by Amador (who had proclaimed himself king of São Tomé) into four units; in an attempt to encircle the town, each unit, under the command of one of Amador's captains, was sent to one of the principal parts of the town. Again the defenders succeeded in forcing the slaves to retreat.

After two weeks of siege, Amador, with an army of allegedly five thousand slaves, waged the final assault on the town. On 28 July the armed inhabitants and soldiers, with pieces of artillery at their disposal, marched into the battle, which continued for four hours. Finally the slaves withdrew in flight pursued by the settler army. Many slaves were left wounded, and two hundred were dead, among them Lazaro, one of Amador's commanders. Adão, another of his captains, was taken prisoner and hanged. On 29 July more than four thousand slaves who had escaped entered the town willingly, to benefit from the clemency the governor had promised to all rebels who surrendered. Four other slave leaders were arrested and hanged.

Amador was betrayed by his companions and arrested. According to the only existing contemporaneous document of the revolt, on 14 August 1595 Amador was hanged and quartered, and his heart was placed on a pillow. About sixty of the island's approximately eighty-five sugar mills had been destroyed during Amador's revolt, which proved to be one of greatest slave uprisings in Atlantic history. The revolt accelerated the emigration of the São Tomé planters to Brazil, which had already begun a decade earlier, since sugar production in Brazil offered better economic prospects. After independence in 1975, the government of São Tomé and Príncipe considered Amador a national hero of the country's anticolonial struggle. Since 1976, when the Portuguese escudo was replaced by the new national currency, the dobra, the country's bank notes have depicted Amador's portrait, which was entirely created by a local artist after independence. In 2004 the National Assembly in São Tomé declared 4 January as a national holiday in homage of Amador. The date was based on a rather unreliable secondary source of the early nineteenth century, according to which Amador was executed on 4 January 1596.

BIBLIOGRAPHY

Garfield, Robert. *A History of São Tomé Island, 1470–1655: The Key to Guinea*. San Francisco: Mellen Research University Press, 1992.

Seibert, Gerhard. "A verdadeira origem do célebre Rei Amador, líder da revolta dos escravos em 1595." *Piá* 26 (January 2005): 10–11.

Seibert, Gerhard. "Está errada a data do novo feriado nacional em homenagem ao Rei Amador?" *Piá* 36 (September 2006): 20–21.

GERHARD SEIBERT

Amadu, Seku (1776–1844 or 1845), Muslim cleric, major jihad leader and state-builder in early-nineteenth-century Mali, also known as Seku Amadu Lobbo, was born to a modest family of herders and clerics in Molangol, a Fulbe village not far from Mopti, in the inner delta of the Niger River. This area came to be known as Masina. He studied the Qur'an with his grandfather, but then continued his Islamic education at Jenné, the most important center of commerce and education in the inner delta.

Masina was an area where the Niger River divided into many channels and flooded every rainy season. Fulbe pastoralists practiced transhumant pastoralism, bringing their herds into the delta during the long dry season. The only authorities in Masina were the Ardos, heads of small pastoralist groups. As the tentacles of the long-distance slave trade extended themselves deeper into West Africa, many Ardos developed bands of cavalry that raided for slaves and allied themselves to the slave-raiding Bambara state of Segu. The transhumant patterns of the Fulbe also made them vulnerable to the attacks of Tuaregs from the Sahara. Seku Amadu was one of a group of rural marabouts who preached Islam, tried to organize the victimized areas, and criticized the established order. They were not noted for their learning, but they had an intense commitment to an austere form of Islam. Amadu's criticism of the Jenné *ulema* led to his being barred from the Grand Mosque.

The jihad supposedly began when a noble stole the blanket of one of Amadu's supporters. When the noble refused to give it back, Amadu had him killed and then fled to the village of Noukouma, where he gathered his supporters and allies. The reform forces also gained legitimacy when they received a flag from Uthman Dan Fodio, whose successful jihad was a model for the Masina rebels. At Noukouma, Amadu's forces were attacked in 1818 by an army made up of the forces of the Ardos supported by Bambara from Segou. Oral traditions suggest that Amadu's forces were heavily outnumbered by the better-armed forces of Segou and the Ardos. For example, they had few horses and fought largely on foot. When Amadu prevailed despite these limitations, many of those oppressed by the Ardos and threatened by slave-raiding rallied to his standard. Traditions claim that his army expanded from about one thousand to over forty thousand, and an increasing number of its members were cavalry. Amadu freed any slaves who joined his army. His forces speedily established control over Masina, and in 1819 conquered Jenné after a nine-month-long siege.

Victory brought new challenges. Other jihad leaders, such as Uthman Dan Fodio, took over and reformed existing state structures. Amadu had to create a state. He needed a standing army to protect the transhumant patterns of his Fulbe supporters and to prevent slave-raiders from operating in the inner delta. To do that, he needed a tax base and an administration capable of collecting taxes. Fulbe groups were required to have a fixed residence. Only a few members of any family would migrate with the herds. Each community had to support at least one teacher. Increased education provided the state with the administrative staff it needed. Every market was placed under the control of an official, who regulated weights and measures. The state also controlled land and taxed trade. Fixed residency made tax collection easier, but it also led to the transformation of the community. Increasingly, Fulbe men devoted themselves to Islamic learning and to politics and were supported by *rimaibe*, slaves who gradually were transformed into a serf-like status. The *rimaibe* could not be sold and lived mostly in their own villages. They had to provide their masters and the state with a percentage of their crops. The army contained a permanent force of cavalry, which could be supplemented by the call-up of able-bodied men. It extended the authority of the state further south and up to Timbuktu, and in the process, provided more slaves for the agricultural economy.

The Dina, as it was called, was a strict Muslim regime. Alcohol and tobacco were banned and women were secluded. Islam was strictly enforced. Amadu shared authority with a council of forty Muslim clerics, two of whom always sat with him when he heard cases or transacted business. He built a new capital, which was called Hamdullahi, which means "praises to God." According to traditions, Amadu lived an unostentatious life, dressing and eating simply. He preserved a pastoralist's love for his herds.

[*See also* Uthman Dan Fodio.]

BIBLIOGRAPHY

Ba, Amadou Hampaté, and Jacques Daget. *L'empire Peul du Macina* [The Fulbe Empire of Masina]. Dakar. Bamako: IFAN, 1955. A classic account based largely on oral traditions.

Brown, William A. "The Caliphate of Hamdullahi, c. 1818-1864." Unpublished PhD thesis, University of Wisconsin, 1969. The best available source in English for Amadu and for the Caliphate.

Sanankoua, Bintou. *Un empire Peul: La Diina du Maasina* [A Fulbe Empire: The Dina of Hamdullahi]. Paris: Karthala, 1990. A good summary of what is known about the Dina.

MARTIN A. KLEIN

Amadu Bamba (1853–1927), Islamic religious scholar, was born Muhammad Ben Muhammad Ben Habib Allah in Khuru Mbacke, near the village of Mbacke Bawol in west- central Senegal in the early 1850s (1853 is the most commonly cited date). Bamba originated from a family of Fulbe ancestry with a long tradition of Islamic learning. The Mbacke clan left their ancestral land of Futa Tooro in northern Senegal and settled in the kingdom of Jolof among the Wolof (the majority ethnic group in Senegal) sometime in the second half of the seventeenth century. This migration affected the family in two major ways: first, the Mbacke gradually abandoned the nomadic lifestyle of Fulbe herders for that of sedentary Wolof farmers; second, they showed greater inclination toward Islamic learning and increasing assimilation to Wolof culture.

Amadu Bamba was the fourth child of Momar Anta Sali Mbacke and the second son of his mother, Jaara Buso. He grew up in a period of intense violence and rapid social change marked by the end of the Atlantic slave trade, confrontations between Wolof kings and Muslim state-builders, and the dismantling of traditional political and economic structures by French colonial conquerors. As is customary with learned families in the Muslim world, Bamba received most of his early education from his father, uncles, and other family members. He followed the classical curriculum of a young Muslim in West Africa, first pursuing qur'anic education between ages five and seven, and then taking up the study of specialized disciplines at the feet of renowned masters. At age twelve Bamba completed qur'anic training and went on to study Islamic sciences (*'uluum al-din*) that consisted of qur'anic exegesis (*tafsir al-Qur'an*), the study of the Prophetic traditions (*hadiith*), Islamic jurisprudence (*fiqh*), Islamic mysticism (*tasawwuf*), and biography and hagiography of Prophet Muhammad (*siira*). The curriculum also included the sciences of the Arabic language such as grammar, lexicography, composition, and poetry.

By the time the French completed their conquest of the Wolof states in 1886, Amadu Bamba had emerged as a respected Muslim scholar and teacher in the kingdom of Kajoor. He had authored numerous poems and pamphlets dealing with theology, education and ethics, mysticism and worship, and the hagiography of the Prophet Muhammad. All of these themes loom large in his writings, which have been estimated at forty-nine pieces, or over thirty thousand verses.

From the late nineteenth to the early twentieth centuries, the prestige and reputation of Amadu Bamba grew considerably. His popularity was rooted in his scholarly accomplishment as a Muslim learned man and his critical assessment of the Wolof kings and the Muslim establishment of his time. Bamba was concerned with the political, economic, and moral challenges that faced the increasingly dysfunctional Wolof society. He believed in the central role of Islam and the Muslim leadership to alleviate the crisis but he rejected jihad (holy war) of the sword and collaboration with rulers, which for him would only lead to more suffering and disorder. He proposed education of the soul (*tabiyya*) as the best instrument to achieve positive social change. In 1883–1884 he founded the Muridiyya—the only Sufi order originated by a black man—as a tool to develop and disseminate *tabiyya* education. Gradually, the Murid order became a magnet for Wolof Muslims attracted by Bamba's science, his *baraka* (gift of grace), and his

distant attitude toward the French rulers of colonial Senegal. His displacement between the areas of Kajoor, Bawol, and Jolof, apparently to avoid large concentrations of people around him and to dissipate colonial suspicion, further added to his aura.

The growth of the Muridiyya increasingly became an object of concern to the local African chiefs representing the French colonial administration in the rural areas of Senegal. Because of the chiefs' complaints, the Murids began attracting the attention of French administrators. The first colonial report on Amadu Bamba and his disciples was filed in 1889. Despite Bamba's efforts to assuage French misgivings about his intentions, he was arrested on accusations of planning jihad, and subsequently he was sent into exile and then confined to house arrest until his death in 1927.

During Amadu Bamba's lifetime, the Muridiyya had evolved into a hierarchical and highly disciplined organization led by his brothers, sons, and early companions, who oversaw thousands of disciples. After Bamba's death the strong bond between master and disciples provided the foundation for a continuous expansion of the order under the leadership of a *caliph* (the oldest male heir of the founder). The memory of his life, actions, and teachings, preserved through annual commemorative events (*magals*) attracting hundreds of thousands of Murids to his tomb in the holy city of Tuba, remains a cornerstone of Murid unity and dynamism. The development of the Muridiyya was also helped by improved and closer relations with the colonial and post-colonial state of Senegal and the order's domination of peanut production, which until recently fueled the Senegalese economy.

Amadu Bamba was a Sufi, and his path to Sufism was paved by his family traditions and his scholarship. While his ancestors belonged to the Qadiriyya (a Sufi order founded by Abd al-Qadir al-Jaylani [d. 1166] in Baghdad), his thought on Islamic mysticism was also influenced by other Sufi thinkers, including Abu Hamid al-Ghazali (d. 1111), whom he referred to in his writings as "the master." In his attitude as well as in his teachings, Amadu Bamba was careful to combine the two dimensions of legitimate Sufism outlined by Ibn Khaldun in his commentary on al-Ghazali, namely Sufism as a "science of praxis" rooted in Islamic law and Sufism as a science geared toward the education of the heart. He viewed *tasawwuf* (mysticism) as a central element of Islam, but one secondary to *tawhid* (science of the oneness of God) and *shari'a* (Islamic law), which he considered to be the soul and body of the religion. This preoccupation is reaffirmed in his teachings and his scholarly works, where *tawhid* and worship always come before *Ihsaan* (purification). Bamba's idea of Sufism was shaped by a desire to blend mysticism, *shari'a*, and participation in social life.

Amadu Bamba's conception of Sufism provided the philosophical underpinning of his method of education. For Bamba, the primary duty of a human being was to seek an education. However, the ultimate goal of education was to make good Muslims, who modeled their actions on the teachings of Islam in order to serve their community well. In Bamba's view, knowledge included the esoteric or mystical sciences as well as the exoteric sciences (the classical disciplines). Amadu Bamba also considered that the acquisition of knowledge without its implementation in practice was a waste of time. In *Munawir as-Suduur* (The Enlightenment of the Heart), he wrote, "Knowledge, good actions, and good behavior are the root sources of spiritual perfection." Bamba saw science and action as the twin foundations of a virtuous life. These two elements shape the pedagogy he gradually developed.

The educational system that Amadu Bamba promoted was a lifelong and holistic approach designed to transform the character and behavior of the disciples by touching their body and soul. It comprised three main stages: the first was exoteric education or *ta'alim*, which aimed at transmitting knowledge through the study of the Qur'an and the Islamic sciences, and the second was esoteric education or *tarbiyya*, which targeted the soul through education of the body and spirit. The third stage, *tarqiyya* (ascension), which was reached by only a small number of especially gifted disciples, allowed the elevation of their souls beyond the futility of material life and put them in a position of leadership in the community. This education was disseminated in the qur'anic schools, *daara tarbiyya* (working schools), and villages that Murid sheikhs built across the Murid heartland in west-central Senegal. Later when Murid disciples settled in greater numbers in cities across Senegal and beyond, the *dahira*, an urban institution that attend to religious and other socioeconomic concerns, became the locus for the propagation of Murid education.

Amadu Bamba's relationships with the colonial administration evolved roughly through three major phases that can be characterized as suspicion (1889–1895), repression (1895–1912), and surveillance and accommodation (1912–1927). The expansion of the Muridiyya in Kajoor and Bawol coincided with the establishment and consolidation of French power in those areas. Soon the African chiefs who ruled the countryside on behalf of the colonial administration perceived Murid sheikhs as a threat to their own power and prestige. The growing power of sheikhs of modest origins was particularly upsetting to the chiefs, especially to those among them who could claim aristocratic descent. The chiefs' hostility to the Murids prompted increasing scrutiny of Amadu Bamba and his actions by the French colonial administration. From 1889 to 1895 the relationship between the Murids and the French continued to deteriorate. Amadu Bamba made a trip to Saint-Louis in 1892 in an effort to mend fences, but colonial suspicion stoked by alarming reports of preparation for jihad from chiefs and field administrators added to the tension and culminated in his arrest in 1895.

From 1895 to 1912 French suspicion led to repression. Bamba was exiled to Gabon for seven years (1895–1902) and then sent to Mauritania between 1903 and 1907. But colonial repression only enhanced the cleric's prestige among Senegalese Muslims. Bamba was perceived as a martyr, and his capacity to survive the harsh years of exile was interpreted as evidence of God's protection. From a respected Muslim learned man, he gradually came to be seen as a saint and miracle worker. The saga of his tribulations at the hands of the French gave birth to rich oral and written literature that has inspired devotional paintings, found everywhere in Senegal and in the Murid diaspora, which magnify his heroic feats and demean colonial actions. By 1912 the French started to develop a more pragmatic approach in their relations with Amadu Bamba. The failure of coercion, the increasingly important role of the Murids in the peanut economy of Senegal, and the administration's confidence that they had a better understanding of Senegalese society and the role of Islam dictated this change.

In 1912 Amadu Bamba was sent back to his ancestral land of Bawol, but he was kept under house arrest in the colonial town of Diourbel. The French were willing to work out some type of accommodation with the Murids, but surveillance remained important. Surveillance was made necessary by the need to protect the Muridiyya from the contamination of the so-called radical and politically dangerous Islam of North Africa and the Middle East and by the necessity to control and contain the increasingly influential, but not totally trusted leader of the Murids.

From 1912 the relations between the Murids and the French took a new course. After renouncing coercion, the French reconsidered the goals and motives of Amadu Bamba, which were not actually incompatible with colonial rule. Bamba had indeed proclaimed numerous times in his writings and correspondence with the colonial administration that the only jihad he was interested in was the greater jihad (*jihad ul-akbar*), or jihad of the soul. He famously wrote in *Munawir as-Suduur*, "The warrior in the path of God is not who takes his enemies' life, but the one who combats his *nafs* (carnal soul) to achieve spiritual perfection." The end of Bamba's exile, and his relocation to Diourbel, contributed to creating an atmosphere of détente, which was enhanced by the ability of the Murids to gradually carve out for themselves a Muslim space in the land of infidels they believed Senegal had become after French colonization.

Amadu Bamba is among the most recognizable names in the history of Senegal. He is considered a saint and a national hero even by Senegalese who are not followers of the Muridiyya. His reputation is based on the memory of his accomplishments as a highly learned holy man who has suffered for his religion and country, as well as on the role of the organization he founded in contemporary Senegal. Though not the largest Sufi order in Senegal (it is second to the *Tijaniyya* block), the Muridiyya is today the most influential political entity and the most dominant economic force in the country. From a small rural organization of Wolof farmers in the late nineteenth and early twentieth centuries, it has now become a bustling global movement of over five million followers in Senegal and abroad. Murid businesses and religious events form integral parts of the economic and cultural lives of cities in Western Europe and North America such as Paris, Brescia (Italy), and New York City. The order's image also benefits from high-profile disciples such as renowned pop stars Youssou N'Dour and Akon and the soccer star El Hadji Diouf.

BIBLIOGRAPHY

Babou, Cheikh Anta. *Fighting the Greater Jihad: Amadu Bamba and the Founding of the Muridyya of Senegal*. Athens: Ohio University Press, 2007.

Copans, Jean. *Les arabouts de l'arachide*. Paris: Harmattan, 1988.

Glover, John. *Sufism and Jihad in Modern Senegal: The Murid Order*. Rochester, N.Y.: University of Rochester Press, 2007.

O'Brien, Donal B. Cruise. *The Mourides of Senegal: The Political and Economic Organization of an Islamic Brotherhood*. Oxford: Clarendon Press, 1971.

Ross, Eric. *Sufi City: Urban Design and Archetypes in Touba*. Rochester, N.Y.: University of Rochester Press, 2006.

Sy, Cheikh Tidiane. *La confrérie Sénégalaise des mourides*. Paris: Présence Africaine, 1969.

CHEIKH BABOU

Amanishaketo (fl. late first century BCE), queen of Meroe, reigned during the second half of the first century BCE. She is shown dressed in ceremonial clothes on the pylon of her pyramid, Beg. n. 6, spearing bound prisoners: this action illustrates clearly the queen's status as fully equal to the king in Meroitic ideology. Another form of her name is Amanishakheto.

In a second portrait found on the same monument (the original block is actually kept in Berlin) it is possible to observe the presence of three scars under her left eye. Considering that the practice of scarring was also employed for medical purposes, it has been hypothesized that Amanishaketo could have been the one-eyed kandake who fought the Romans during the 20s BCE, especially since Amanishaketo's presence inside the Dodekascoenus in that period is confirmed by a long inscription left by the same Kushite queen in Qasr Ibrim.

As the successor of Amanirenas and the mother of the kandake Amanitore, Amanishaketo was very active, with traces of her presence having been discovered in the temples of Kawa, Gebel Barkal, and Naga, sites that were probably visited by the sovereign on the occasion of her coronation journey, when she visited the main religious centres of the kingdom. The royal building activity of the queen is, moreover, attested not only by temple M 267, erected against the wall of the royal citadel in Meroe, but, most of all, by the palace that she built in Wadi ben Naga, along an important commercial route. This two-level square structure (61 x 61 meters) was excavated in 1960. A cartouche of Kandake Amanishaketo was found there, as was a monumental columned entrance followed by a ground floor entirely occupied by narrow corridors and rectangular rooms that were used as magazines to store various products, including elephant tusks. Nothing remains, however, of the upper floor, perhaps the living area, with the exception of some architectural elements.

Also attributed to Amanishakheto is a famous, if untranslated, inscription on a structure from the ancient Kushite capital. It is known as "Meroe's obelisk" and was recovered in front of the pylon of the Amun temple by Sir John Garstang during the excavations he conducted in 1911. On the upper portion of the monument the queen was probably represented in front of the god Amun and other deities, the stone—today preserved in Khartoum National Museum—has also a long Meroitic royal text inscribed on its four faces. Although this text still remains indecipherable, if we compare its structure to other similar ones, it seems likely that it celebrated the kandake and her military victories.

The primary known facts concerning Amanishaketo are, however, linked to the discovery in her pyramid of an important funerary treasure composed of refined shields, armlets, seal rings, earrings, amulets, and Hellenistic cameos. It was in 1830 that an Italian physician, Giuseppe Ferlini, arrived in the Sudan with Mohamed Ali's Egyptian army. Having completed his military service in Khartoum, Ferlini was allowed in 1834 to carry out archaeological researches (unfortunately, with questionable methods) in the region of the so-called "Meroe Island," a region surrounded by water (the Blue Nile, the White Nile, and the Atbara River) on three sides. At first he did not obtain results either in Naga or in Musawwarat es Sufra but, before leaving for Europe, he decided to conclude his investigations in Meroe by excavating one of the main pyramids of the royal cemetery. He chose Amanishaketo's monument which, according to the drawings made by the French traveler Cailliaud in 1821, was at that time one of the best-preserved examples.

According to Ferlini's report, inside the pyramid, under its peak, he found a wide collection of jewelry belonging to the queen; this rich, absolutely unique discovery persuaded the physician, who was more a treasure hunter than an archaeologist, to demolish the whole structure down to its foundations. After his return to Bologna, Ferlini tried to sell the treasure but, owing to the general ignorance of Nubian antiquities, the collection was only considered a bad imitation of pharaonic objects. Only after their examination by Richard Lepsius the authenticity of the pieces was accepted: between 1840 and 1844 they were sold, being bought in part by Ludwig I, king of Bavaria, for his royal antiquarium and in part by the Berlin Egyptian Museum.

Unfortunately, the news of Ferlini's discovery of gold objects encouraged other adventurers, who badly damaged the greatest part of the pyramids located in the royal necropolis without discovering anything else. In Amanishakheto's tomb there were also found four auloi, or Hellenistic flutes; the presence of these peculiar musical instruments, combined with the samples of Hellenistic craftsmanship included in the treasure, confirms that the period during which the queen ruled corresponded to the Roman epoch.

[*See also* Amanitore.]

BIBLIOGRAPHY

Shinnie, P. *Meroe, a Civilization of the Sudan.* London, 1967.

Török, László. *The Kingdom of Kush: Handbook of the Napatan-Meroitic Civilization.* Leiden, Netherlands: Brill, 1997.

Welsby, Derek A. *The Kingdom of Kush.* London: British Museum Press, 1996.

Wildung, Dietrich, and Karl-Hienz Priese. *Das gold von Meroe.* Berlin: Staatliche Museen zu Berlin–Preussischer Kulturbesitz. Ägyptisches Museum und Papyrussammlung. Staatliche sammlung Ägyptischer Kunst München Mainz, Zabern Verlag: 1992.

EUGENIO FANTUSATI

Amanitore (fl. late first century BCE–early first century CE), queen of Meroe, was crowned under the name of Merkare and reigned over the Meroitic empire in coregency with her husband, Natakamani, between the end of the first century BCE and the first decade of the first century CE.

As with the other Kushite queens, her title was *kdke* (kandake, or candace, probably translating as "regal sister"), an attribution common in Egypt among the royal brides during the Eighteenth dynasty and adopted later in Nubia by the brides of the Twenty-Fifth dynasty's black pharaohs and subsequently by the wives of the Napatan and Meroitic sovereigns.

The complete lack of written sources relating to her kingdom forces us to make exclusive reference to the archaeological remains, and above all to the reliefs in which Amanitore was represented. The images at our disposal first of all show her in the prominent role of invincible warrior. On the northern pylon of temple N. 300 at Naga, a place that the Meroites called Tolkte, Queen Amanitore is depicted killing her enemies with a sword while they beg for their lives; she dominates them with her gigantic, obese figure. Linant de Bellefons, nineteenth-century French explorer in Nubia, described the depiction thusly: "This woman is not as those represented in Egypt, tall and slender, but shows an exaggerated fatness and enormous sides." The steatopygous aspect of Amanitore that so much amazed Linant was in reality a common feature of the Kushite queens, perhaps purposely attained through eating habits, and considered in Meroe a tangible mark of power.

Amanitore's position in the imagery toward groups of prisoners confirms both her personal involvement in military expeditions and the possibility that, during her reign, Meroe may have organized numerous raids against the nomadic tribes of the desert, with consequent notable expansion of the Meroitic imperial borders.

According to the interpretation of the iconographic documentation provided by the Lion temple in Naga, it seems quite evident that it was the custom of the Kushite sovereigns to offer a great number of war prisoners to the temples. Some were sacrificed in honor of the divinities, while others were employed in temple activities such as the provisioning of water, farming, and pottery and textile production.

The aggressiveness of the Meroitic queens finds further confirmation in the classical sources: Strabo, who traveled with the Roman prefect Aelius Gallus in lower Nubia in 24 BCE (and therefore during an epoch not very distant from the years of Amanitore's kingdom), described with wonder a candace deprived of an eye, probably lost during the course of a battle in which she personally led the Kushite armies.

The reliefs from Naga, through the perfect symmetry of the images of the two coregents, confirm the complete parity between Amanitore and her husband Natakamani in the control of the state. The parallelism of the ruling royal couple was not represented only on the pylons of the temple: on the left side of the door that frames the entrance stands the king, while on the right frame, Amanitore faces him. It seems, therefore, proper to speak about a "masculine" part and a "feminine" part of the building. Natakamani is linked to the southern side, Amanitore to the northern side, exactly as is the case with the divinities represented in the temple: those of masculine sex are carved on the southern external wall, those of feminine sex on the northern external wall.

This concept is confirmed by the observation of the very interesting images placed on the western side of the temple: Natakamani to the south and Amanitore to the north, each of them followed by the prince, flank an unusual representation of Apedemak. The god, frontally placed, presents also two further lateral heads and arms turned to the royal couple. Beyond the more or less demonstrable Indian influences on this three-headed and four-armed iconographic composition, the relief underlines above all the symmetry of the scene: only through recourse to a doubling of the divine image was it possible to depict Apedemak turning, at the same time and without preference, his faces and blessing arms to the two sovereigns.

A further unique aspect of Amanitore is that she always shared with the king the exercise of religious functions: this can be deduced from the observation of the Amun temple (N. 100)—built in Naga by the royal couple—in which the queen and Natakamani, dressed in panther skins, both appear as priests in the act making offerings.

Excavations begun in 1995 inside temple N. 300 led to the important discovery of a fragmented stela in which can be seen the fingers of a goddess, perhaps Amesemi, bride of Apedemak, which was probably originally associated with the image of a Kushite queen. This last possibility could be confirmed by the first word of the third line of the Meroitic cursive text inscribed on the stela if it is read as "Amni," exactly the initial part of Amanitore's name. If this interpretation is correct, it is likely that the piece was very similar to the small commemorative sandstone stela of another queen, Amanishaketo, probably Amanitore's mother, that was recently found completely intact in the hypostyle hall of the Amun temple in Naga. On the reverse the queen's image is shown embraced by a protective goddess, Amesemi, who wears her typical crown surmounted by a falcon and the moon, as evidence of the divine benevolence toward the female royal ruler.

Like all of Meroe's rulers, Amanitore was the titular owner of a pyramid (Beg. 1) in the north cemetery of the ancient capital of Nubia: the reliefs on the walls of the chapel represent a funeral procession of priests bearing various insignias and images of the candace. The substructure consisted of an irregular staircase of thirty steps and two undecorated rooms, in which the archaeologists did not find the queen's body, but rather only human and animal bones.

Finally, it has been suggested that Amanitore could be the candace mentioned in the Bible (Acts: 26-40) whose eunuch was converted to Christianity and baptized by the apostle Phillip.

[See also Natakamani.]

BIBLIOGRAPHY

Adams, William Yewdale. *Nubia: Corridor to Africa.* London: Allen Lane, 1977.

Török, László. *The Kingdom of Kush: Handbook of the Napatan-Meroitic Civilization*. Leiden, Netherlands: Brill, 1997.

Žabkar, Louis V. *Apedemak, Lion God of Meroe: A Study in Egyptian-Meroitic Syncretism*. Warminster, UK: Aris and Phillips, 1975.

Zach, Michael. *Gedanken zur kdke Amanitore in Begegnungen Antike kulturen im Nital*. Leipzig, 2001.

EUGENIO FANTUSATI

Aman Mikael Andom (1924–1974), Ethiopian military leader, was born in the village of Tsazegga, some fifteen miles north of Asmara, the capital of Eritrea, an Italian colony at that time (1890–1941). Prior to the establishment of Asmara by Ethiopian general Ras Alula Engida in 1885, Tsazegga had for centuries been the headquarters of a local Christian family that succeeded in maintaining its autonomy. Educated in Khartoum, Aman returned to Ethiopia in 1941 with the British forces who defeated Mussolini's African empire and restored Emperor Haile Selassie to the throne. He proceeded to distinguish himself in a brilliant military career, commanding Ethiopian UN contingents in Korea and Congo. In the Ogaden battles against the Somalis in the early 1960s, General Aman willfully ignored Haile Selassie's orders by penetrating Somali territory. He was consequently "exiled" to the Senate in 1965, as was the practice with overly independent political figures. Aman continued to cultivate relations with the army's generals and was among the few high-ranking officers admired by the rank and file.

When the junior army officers established their secret battalion committees in February 1974, Aman was contacted by some of them, and on 3 July, they chose him as chairman of their 120-member Provisional Military Administrative Committee, better known as the "Derg." On 22 July, the Derg forced the emperor to appoint Aman as Minister of Defense, and when they deposed the emperor on 12 September, Aman officially became head of state. He was chosen by the young officers due to his mature age, popularity, reputation, and prestige, but a major split soon developed between Aman and a wing in the Derg led by Major Mengistu Haile Mariam. Aman, paternalistic and overconfident, saw himself as the new leader of Ethiopia and sought to reduce the Derg to an advisory council. Aman envisioned the establishment of a new republic based on administrative decentralization and elements of economic openness. He supported exercising leniency toward members of the imperial elite,

and solving the burning Eritrean issue—local Eritrean nationalists had revolted in 1961—by reestablishing autonomy for the province within the framework of a pluralized, yet united, Ethiopia. (Eritrea had been restored to Ethiopia by the UN in 1952 and enjoyed autonomy until 1962.) The Mengistu-led wing in the Derg opposed these policies and was in fact ready to accept Aman only as a representative figure and spokesman. Aman himself had only a few followers among the young Derg members, and while he was attending to major state issues, Mengistu's men terrorized their colleagues in the Derg and arrested or killed potential rivals in the various army units.

The major issue, however, remained that of Eritrea. As an Eritrean, Aman was familiar with local politics and with leaders of the Christian wing within the Eritrean People's Liberation Front (EPLF), the movement that would eventually lead Eritrea to independence under Isaias Afewerki. (Aman was married to a sister of Isaias's spiritual mentor, Dr. Biasolo.) During late August and early September 1974, Minister of Defense Aman made public appearances all over Eritrea, promising autonomy and preaching unity. On 9 September 1974, back in the capital, he presented a detailed nineteen-point plan to solve the problem. But Aman's attempt to persuade Eritrean leaders to remain Ethiopians was not successful, nor was he able to convince his younger colleagues in the Derg that his political approach was justified. Meanwhile the army in Eritrea under Brigadier General Teferi Benti worked with Major Mengistu, insisted on crushing the local nationalists, and asked for reinforcements. On 6 October, Aman went to Eritrea again, where the EPLF held demonstrations and rallies against his plan. Yet, still confident that the young officers would follow him, he tried to restrain the expectations for prompt and drastic changes. In public appearances as head of state, Aman supported gradual land reform and opening the economy to foreign investment. He opposed comprehensive nationalizations and refused to authorize executions of arrested officials. To the end, he resisted sending reinforcements to Eritrea.

The struggle between Aman and Mengistu broke into the open in the second week of November 1974. Aman's only chance was to mobilize support outside the Derg, mainly from some units of the Harar-based Third Division, which he had commanded in the 1960s. But in spite of the advice of his associates, Aman refused to start an open war. Instead, on 15 November, he confined himself to his

Addis Ababa house and waited for the young members of the Derg to come and beg him to return. On 23 November, the Derg sent troops to arrest him and in the ensuing gunfight, Aman and two of his associates were killed. That same night, fifty-seven of the top figures in the imperial regime were executed without trial, and the Derg ordered reinforcements sent to Eritrea. The fall of Aman thus opened the road for Mengistu Haile Mariam and revolutionary centralization, communist dictatorship, and endless internal wars.

[See also Alula Engida; Haile Selassie I; Mengistu Haile Mariam; and Teferi Benti.]

BIBLIOGRAPHY

Clapham, Christopher. Transformation and Continuity in Revolutionary Ethiopia. Cambridge, UK: Cambridge University Press, 1988.

Erlich, Haggai. The Struggle over Eritrea, 1962–1978: War and Revolution in the Horn of Africa. Stanford, Calif.: Hoover Institution Press, 1983.

Haile-Selassie, Tefera. The Ethiopian Revolution 1974–1991: From a Monarchical Autocracy to a Military Oligarchy. London: Kegan Paul International, 1997.

Ottaway, David, and Marina Ottaway. Ethiopia: Empire in Revolution. New York: Africana, 1978.

HAGGAI ERLICH

ʿAmara Dunqas (d. c. 1534 CE/AH 940), first ruler of the Funj kingdom (in present-day Sudan), was nicknamed "Dunqas," a term implying that one who came into his presence should bow down with an inclined head. In later years it would be said that ʿAmara's father's name was ʿAdlan, and that he came from Lul, a place on the White Nile. However, the kinship principles that brought ʿAmara to power were matrilineal; like all the members of his dynasty, he was eligible to rule because of his descent, through the female line, from a remote Funj ancestress, whom tradition remembered by the name of Bint ʿAyn al-Shams.

ʿAmara was said to have founded the kingdom in 1504–1505 and to have reigned until 1533–1534. Contemporary information about ʿAmara may be found in the account of the mystic and adventurer David Reubeni, whose controversial subsequent role in European Jewish history (while in the Sudan, Reubeni claimed to be a descendant of the Prophet Muhammad) may raise questions concerning the veracity of his Sudanese data—which, nevertheless, seem inherently plausible. According to Reubeni,

ʿAmara was a powerful king backed by many soldiers, whose effective writ extended from the remote south to the borders of Egypt. An important subordinate governate, destined to survive to the present, was ʿAmara's middle Nile tributary territory of Jaʿal, home to the Jaʿaliyyin.

The town of Sinnar existed in ʿAmara's day, and served as his treasury, but it had not yet become a fixed seat of government. Rather, the perambulatory capital of the new Funj kingdom accompanied ʿAmara as he moved about month by month from one part of his realm to another. The king was a devout Muslim. He cherished religious books in Arabic and was eager to offer patronage to Islamic holy men. On the other hand, his people did not conform to the standards of dress typical of the Islamic heartlands, nor did they follow a strictly orthodox diet.

From the perspective of neighboring lands during ʿAmara's reign and the years immediately surrounding it, the northern Nile Valley Sudan was perceived as a realm of dark-skinned Muslims ruled by a Muslim Nubian king.

BIBLIOGRAPHY

Holt, Peter Malcolm. The Sudan of the Three Niles: The Funj Chronicle, 910–1228/1504–1871. Boston: Brill, 1999.

O'Fahey, Rex Sean, and J. L. Spaulding. Kingdoms of the Sudan. London: Methuen, 1974.

Spaulding, Jay. The Heroic Age in Sinnar. Asmara: Red Sea Press, 2007.

Hasan, Yusuf Fadl, ed. Kitab al-tabaqat fi khusus al-awliya' wa'l-salihin wa'l-'ulama' wa'l-shu'ara' fi'l-Sudan ta'lif Muhammad al-Nur b. Dayf Allah. Khartoum: Khartoum University Press, 1971.

Spaulding, Jay, and Muhammad Ibrahim Abu Salim. Public Documents from Sinnar. East Lansing, Mich.: Michigan State University Press, 1989.

JAY SPAULDING

Amasis (fl. sixth century BCE), pharaoh of Egypt (570–526 BCE), as Herodotus (II, 172) reports, was from Siuph in the district of Sais. The name of his father is not known, but the mother's name, Tashereniset, survives on a statue of Amasis erected after he was made king.

There is no information about Amasis until the year 570 BCE. As Herodotus recounts (II, 161–69), that year, when Apries, then the pharaoh, was returning from an unsuccessful expedition against Cyrene, a Greek colony on the Libyan coast, the Egyptian army accused the pharaoh of having sent them to die. Thus, they chose the general Amasis as the new pharaoh. When Apries sent an embassy to Amasis, asking him to submit to the legitimate king, the general replied in a vulgar manner. A battle ensued at Memphis in which Amasis defeated his opponent's army, seized power, and took Apries prisoner. Later, Amasis had Apries strangled to death, to satisfy the demands of the Egyptian people.

As for indigenous sources, a royal stela from Elephantine refers to the struggle. Because it is particularly difficult to read, some details of the war are not clearly understood. Still, its version is more faithful to the sequence of the events than Herodotus's account. It gives Amasis's victorious perspective, according to which Amasis had to face Apries twice: the first time in an open battle, and a second time, three years later, when Apries returned accompanied by a Babylonian army, provided to him by the Babylonian king Nebuchadnezzar II. Amasis fought against the Babylonian army and defeated it in a river battle. He was then able to surround Apries in his ship, and the former pharaoh was killed in the subsequent fight. According to Herodotus and the royal stela, Amasis honored Apries with a royal burial in the temple of Neith at Sais, as had been done for all his predecessors in the Twenty-Sixth Dynasty.

As for Amasis, he had a long reign. Apart from the initial struggle for power, not much information is known about his reign. Demotic literature and Herodotus provide the image of a popular pharaoh, wise and able to understand human virtues and vices. On the verso of the *Demotic Chronicle* is a tale of Amasis intoxicated by a powerful wine and wanting to be entertained by a story. A similar story in Herodotus, possibly reflecting the same popular sources, shows the pharaoh drunk; when he is blamed for his behavior, he promptly responds that a bow cannot be in tension all the time, but needs to be loosened sometimes.

A demotic papyrus also refers to a Nubian expedition during his reign. As no other details are given, the precise objective and the outcome of the expedition are not known. Amasis is known to have extensively built at Philae, while other monuments are known from Tell el-Maskhuta, Edfu, and Abydos, among other places.

While Amasis somehow seemed to have initially overcome an anti-foreign movement, it has to be said that Amasis's reign was very favorable toward the Greeks and Carians. New settlements were built at Naucratis, and the king made donations to various temples in Greece (Delphi, Cyrene, and Lindos), like Necho II before him. He is also said to have married Ladice, daughter of the king of Cyrene. He also had other wives: Tentkheta, mother of his successor Psammetichus III, and Nakht-Bastet-Kheru, who gave birth to the general Amasis. During the last part of his reign, he sent his daughter Nitocris to be adopted as successor to the God's Wife Anknesneferibre, daughter of king Psammetichus II. Nitocris did not succeed to Ankhnesneferibre, as the priestly office was suppressed after the Persian conquest by Cambyses.

Amasis died in 526 BCE, and according to Herodotus (II, 169), his tomb was placed in the precinct of the temple of Neith at Sais, in the temple court, but not near the shrine, where the tombs of his predecessors were. He was succeeded by his son Psammetichus III, who ruled for only six months before being defeated at Papremis by the Persian king Cambyses. According to Herodotus, Cambyses proclaimed himself as the legitimate successor of Apries and felt himself, therefore, authorized to desecrate and burn Amasis's mummy. Cambyses also initiated a desecration campaign against Amasis's names, as the cartouches on monuments bearing his royal names have been hacked out.

[*See also* Cambyses II; Herodotus; *and* Psammetichus II.]

BIBLIOGRAPHY

Arnold, Dieter. *Temples of the Last Pharaohs*. New York and Oxford: Oxford University Press, 1999. List of the temples built by Amasis.

Gozzoli, Roberto B. *The Writing of History in Ancient Egypt during the First Millennium BC (ca. 1070-180 BC): Trends and Perspectives*. London: Golden House Publications, 2006. Discussion of the royal stela as well as historical interpretation of Amasis's importance and role as king.

Lloyd, Alan B. *Herodotus Book II: A Commentary*. Leiden, Netherlands: Brill, 1988. Commentary of Herodotus's History. Book II, relative to Ancient Egyptian History.

Lloyd, Alan B. "The Late Period." In *Oxford History of Ancient Egypt*, edited by Ian Shaw, pp. 369–394. Oxford and New York: Oxford University Press, 2000. Historical introduction to the period.

ROBERTO GOZZOLI

Amda Seyon I (d. 1344), emperor of Ethiopia (1314–1344), whose regnal name was Gebre Meskel ("Servant of the Cross"), was one of the outstanding rulers of the early Solomonic period (1270–1527) in Ethiopia. While his grandfather, Yekunno Amlak (r. 1270–1284), is credited with establishing a new dynasty, Amda Seyon ("Pillar of Zion") can be said to have established the medieval Ethiopian state.

Amda Seyon is generally believed to have succeeded his father, Wedem Re'ad, as emperor in 1314. The first years of his reign were devoted to wars against Muslim populations in the southwest of Ethiopia. Around 1320 he turned his attention to the northern parts of Ethiopia, particularly to Tigray province in the north and the areas around the ancient capital of Aksum, where his dynasty's claim to be the legitimate successors to the Solomonic kings of Aksum had not been accepted. Amda Seyon's victories there secured the claim of Solomonic descent for his successors for centuries.

Undoubtedly the most famous of Amda Seyon's military campaigns were those directed in the 1330s against the Muslim states of Ifat, Hadiyya, and Adal. Although couched in the rhetoric of religious war, these campaigns also had a clear economic rationale: establishing his control over the lucrative trade routes with the important port of Zeyla. Amda Seyon's victories inaugurated a period of 150 years of Christian supremacy in the Horn of Africa.

Amda Seyon's conquests (some claim that these were to a large extent a reclaiming of regions previously ruled by the Christian kings) produced a heterogeneous empire that faced numerous administrative and political challenges. Like other rulers of the period, Amda Seyon had no permanent capital city, but rather "wandered" in a tent city with his troops, stamping out rebellions and making his presence real and visible to his subjects. Although in some cases he was able to appoint loyal subjects and even his relatives as his administrative representatives, in others he simply placed local rulers under tribute. One of the innovations of his period appears to have been the development of a large royal army, which served as a counterweight to and lessened his dependence on the troops which local rulers were expected to provide in times of crises. He also made skillful use of his ability to distribute land rights within the kingdom, rewarding the faithful with new donations and confiscating those of subjects who were inefficient or disloyal.

Throughout his reign, Amda Seyon had an uneasy relationship with many members of the Ethiopian Orthodox *Tewahdo* Church, particularly monks associated with Debre Asbo (Libanos) in Shewa province and with the Egyptian Metropolitan *Abune* Yaqob. Although the precise reasons for his disputes which these clerics remain unclear—he was accused of polygamy and incest—his actions probably reflect yet another aspect of his tendency to enforce his will violently on his subjects. "Rebel" monastic leaders such as Filippos of Debre Libanos, Aron, Anorewos, and perhaps Beselote Mikael were summoned to court, threatened, punished, and exiled to non-Christian parts of the kingdom. Inadvertently, this resulted in a spread of Christianity to more regions.

Although the period of Amda Seyon's reign is often described as a time of religious revival and the production of Geez literature, the evidence for this is, at best, ambiguous. Unlike some of his successors, such as Dawit (1379/80–1413) and Zera Yaqob, he does not appear to have been a patron of literature. While the *Kebre Negest* (the *Glory of Kings*), which formulates the claim of Ethiopian kings to be descendants of King Solomon and the Queen of Sheba, can be dated to his reign, it appears to have been revived and elevated in importance by one of his rivals. Nor is there any clear evidence linking him directly to the other important literary works of his era. Even the famous account of his wars against Ifat, while based on an eyewitness account, may not have been composed during his reign. Moreover, as was discussed above, the monastic movements which thrived during his reign appear to have been more responses against his attempts to centralize control than the product of royal support. Indeed, he appears to have had little interest in the promulgation of Christianity.

Amda Seyon died in 1344 and was succeeded by his son Seyfe Ar'ad.

[*See also* Makedda; Yekunno Amlak; *and* Zera Yaqob.]

BIBLIOGRAPHY

Huntingford, George Wynn Brereton, trans. *The Glorious Victories of Āmda-Seyon, King of Ethiopia.* Oxford: Oxford University Press, 1965. While Huntingford's translation of the text is undoubtedly the best known and most accessible to the English reader, for scholarly purposes it is preferable to refer to Kropp (see below).

Kaplan, Steven. "The Glorious Violence of Amda Seyon." In *Violence and Non-Violence in Africa: Multidisciplinary Perspectives*, edited by Pal Ahluwalia, Louise Bethleham, and Ruth Gino, pp. 12–26. London and New York: Routledge, 2007.

Kropp, Manfred, ed. and trans. *Der siegreiche Feldzug des Königs Āmda-Seyon gegen die Muslime in Adal im Jahre 1332 N. Chr.* Corpus Scriptorum Christianorum Orientalium 538, 539 Scriptores aethiopici 99, 100. Lovanii: E. Peeters, 1994. Kropp provides a reproduction of the original Geez and translation as well as a very informative introduction to the text.

Tamrat, Taddesse. *Church and State in Ethiopia, 1270–1527.* Oxford: Oxford University Press, 1972. This remains the seminal work on the period.

STEVEN KAPLAN

Amenemhat I (twentieth century BCE), Egyptian pharaoh (reigned c. 1991–1961 BCE), was the founder of the Twelfth Egyptian Dynasty, the heart of the Middle Kingdom Period of Egyptian history (c. 2040–1640 BCE). The first of a new line of kings, Amenemhat (an alternative form of the name is Amenemhet) was of nonroyal birth. He was probably the vizier (chief minister) Amenemhat who in c. 1997 BCE led an expedition of ten thousand men to the Wadi Hammamat, between the Nile and the Red Sea, to procure stone for the sarcophagus of Mentuhotep IV, the last king of the Eleventh Dynasty, as recorded in inscriptions at the quarry site.

The Eleventh Dynasty kings had begun the process of reuniting Egypt after the period of political fragmentation known as the First Intermediate Period (c. 2100–2040 BCE). Amenemhat I took this process a step further. Like his predecessors, Amenemhat was of southern origin. Mentuhotep means "Mentu is satisfied," and Amenemhat means "Amen is in front," both Mentu and Amen being gods of Thebes in southern Egypt. But whereas the Mentuhoteps are known almost exclusively by monuments in the south, Amenemhat I, while not neglecting the sites favored by his predecessors, devoted his attention to both the north and the south. Monuments of Amenemhat I have been found from Khatana-Qantir in the Delta to Armant and Tod south of Thebes.

To herald the coming of a new age, the king adopted "Wehemmesut" as part of his royal name, which means "Repeating of births," or "renaissance." Amenemhat transferred the royal residence from Thebes to a new site in the north, which he called Amenemhat Itjtawy ("Amenemhat Seizes the Two Lands [Upper and Lower Egypt]"), closer to the ancient capital of Memphis. Nearby at el-Lisht, he erected a pyramid complex in Old Kingdom style, surrounded by the tombs of his officials.

An inscription in the tomb of a provincial governor, Khnumhotep of Beni Hasan, records how the king toured the provinces, "appearing like (the creator god) Atum himself," reapportioning the land, settling border disputes, and appointing new officials. At the same time that he stabilized conditions within Egypt, Amenemhat also consolidated his borders. He fortified his western border with Libya, sent his army into northern Sudan, established a trading outpost on the Red Sea coast, and sent expeditions to Sinai.

His lasting fame was guaranteed by the enduring popularity of three classical Egyptian literary compositions in which he plays a part: *The Prophecies of Neferty, The Teaching of King Amenemhat I for His Son Senwosret,* and *The Story of Sinuhe.* Hundreds of complete and partial copies of these works have survived, especially from the Ramesside Period (c. 1295–1070 BCE), when they were used as school texts to train scribes in the classical language. They were being read long after the king's monuments had fallen into ruin or had been subsumed into the constructions of later rulers. *The Prophecies of Neferty* is set in the time of the Fourth Dynasty king Sneferu (c. 2575–2551 BCE). Summoned before the king and asked to speak about the future, the sage Neferty describes the advent of Amenemhat I, after the trials and tribulations of the First Intermediate Period, in glowing terms as a new era: "The people of his time will rejoice, for this son of a man will establish his name for ever and eternity" (Simpson, p. 220). *The Teaching of King Amenemhat I for His Son Senwosret,* the most popular of all in antiquity, focuses on an attempt on the old king's life and sums up his accomplishments in autobiographical style: "I subdued lions, I captured crocodiles, I enslaved the men of Nubia, . . . and I forced the Asiatic tribes to cower away like dogs" (Simpson, p. 170). The Nubian king Piye (Piankhy) quotes this very passage in the great victory stela that he erected in the temple of Gebel Barkal in northern Sudan to commemorate his successful Egyptian campaign of 722 BCE. *Sinuhe,* which recounts the adventures of an Egyptian abroad, opens with the news of Amenemhat I's death after thirty years of rule while his son was campaigning in Libya. It is a classic description of the king's death and also a theological statement of the king's divinity: "The God ascended to his horizon, the King of Upper and Lower Egypt. . . . He penetrated the sky, being joined to the sun disk, the God's body being mixed with that of him who made him" (Simpson, p. 55). Scholars still disagree about whether the king died of natural causes or as a result of an assassination plot.

[*See also* Piankhy; *and* Pyramid Kings.]

BIBLIOGRAPHY

Arnold, Dorothea. "Amenemhat I and the Early Twelfth Dynasty at Thebes." *Metropolitan Museum Journal* 26 (1991): 5–48.

Franke, Detlef. "The Middle Kingdom in Egypt." In *Civilizations of the Ancient Near East*, vol. 2, edited by Jack Sasson, pp. 735–748. New York: Charles Scribner's Sons, 1995.

Simpson, William Kelley, ed. *The Literature of Ancient Egypt: An Anthology of Stories, Instructions, Stelae, Autobiographies and Poetry.* 3d ed. New Haven and London: Yale University Press, 2003. Excellent modern translations of the inscription of Khnumhotep II at Beni Hasan, *The Prophecies of Neferty, The Teaching of King Amenemhat I for His Son Senwosret,* and *The Story of Sinuhe.*

LAWRENCE M. BERMAN

Amenemhat III (mid-nineteenth century BCE), Egyptian pharaoh (r. c. 1878–1842 BCE), was also known as Amenemmes III (the Greek version of the name). Amenemhat III was the sixth king of the Twelfth Dynasty of Egypt's Middle Kingdom Period (a period which included Dynasties 11–13, c. 2050–1650 BCE). With a reign of forty-six years, Amenemhat III was the longest ruling king of the Twelfth Dynasty, a line of pharaohs who governed Egypt from the city of Itj-Tawy (modern el-Lisht). He was the son of Senwosret III (Sesostris III), with whom his early reign may have overlapped during a period of coregency. His mother may have been Senwosret III's chief queen, Khnumetneferhedjet-Weret II. The name Amenemhat (the king's birth name) means "Amun is foremost" and was used both by royalty and by commoners. The name indicates both the importance of the god Amun during the Middle Kingdom and the origins of the Twelfth Dynasty in the southern city of Thebes, where Amun-Re (Amun combined with the solar deity Re) had emerged during the early Middle Kingdom as the principal state god, with his main temple at Karnak. Amenemhat III's throne name was Nimaatre, meaning "One belonging to Maat and Re," which denotes an emphasis on the principle of *Maat,* or divine order (also prominent in the names of other Twelfth Dynasty pharaohs), and the enduring religious importance of the ancient sun god Re.

The reign of Amenemhat III represents the high point of unity and economic prosperity during Egypt's Middle Kingdom. Whereas earlier kings of the dynasty, including his father Senwosret III, were actively engaged in military affairs in Lower Nubia and Syria–Palestine, Amenemhat III appears to have devoted most of his attention to internal development. He was a prolific monument builder, although the remains of his once-extensive building program are poorly preserved. Like other kings of the Twelfth Dynasty, a particular focus for Amenemhat III was the Fayum region—a rich agricultural area centered around Lake Moeris—located on the western side of the Nile just south of the Middle Kingdom capital of Itj-Tawy. The bases of two massive seated statues of Amenemhat III, known as the Colossi of Biahmu, are located in the Fayum region. These statues may explain why later Greek and Roman historians, including Herodotus and Strabo, specifically connected Amenemhat III with the early development of the Fayum. Amenemhat III was deified and venerated in the Fayum during the later Ptolemaic Period (c. 332–30 BCE), when he was known as king Lamarres. He is, however, only one of a line of Middle Kingdom pharaohs who devoted significant attention to the Fayum.

Amenemhat III completed two pyramids. His first, at Dahshur (south of Memphis), may date to the period of coregency with his father. Its interior suffered from structural problems and was not used for the king's burial. Subterranean galleries were, however, used for burials of royal women of the period. The second pyramid—in which Amenemhat III was probably buried—was at Hawara, on the northern side of the entrance to the Fayum. The Hawara pyramid formed the prototype for later pyramids of the Middle Kingdom, with its emphasis on elaborate blocking systems for protecting the royal burial crypt. Hawara was also the location of the massive temple complex, known in later times as the "Egyptian Labyrinth," which stood at the southern face of the pyramid. This building, described by Herodotus, Strabo, and other classical authors, is now destroyed, but has been partially excavated since the nineteenth century. Fragments of numerous statues of the king and gods indicate that this temple was decorated with an extensive program of divine statuary. The Egyptian Labyrinth may represent a form of temple known as the "Mansion of Millions of Years," in which the king's mortuary cult is linked with the veneration of deities. The active building program of Amenemhat III is also reflected in the extensive series of mining and quarrying expeditions carried out during his reign, notably to the copper and turquoise mines in the Sinai, where a significant expansion was made during his reign to the temple of Hathor at Serabit el-Khadim.

Amenemhat III is represented through a more extensive corpus of statues than other pharaohs of the Twelfth Dynasty. Many of these employ a realistic style characteristic of the late Middle Kingdom Period, which is notable for its accentuation of the mortality of the king. While not properly portraiture, these statues appear to have emphasized the king's humanity in his role as an intermediary between humankind and the gods. Amenemhat III's reign is the first time in Egyptian history when we have the representation of the king in statuary as a high priest, exemplified by a well-known statue from Medinet el-Fayum showing the king wearing the leopard-skin cloak of a *Setem*-priest (a priest who presided over important funerary rituals). Many other new statue forms occurred during his reign, suggesting innovations in the mode of portraying gods and the king's relationship with divinities.

Amenemhat III was the last long-reigning pharaoh of Egypt's Twelfth Dynasty. The final two rulers of the dynasty were his children: Amenemhat IV and the female pharaoh Sobekneferu. Another daughter, Neferuptah, was buried in a pyramid near her father's at Hawara. Amenemhat IV may have had a coregency with his father; both kings are commemorated together in a temple at Medinet Maadi in the Fayum. Sobekneferu's short reign ended the Twelfth Dynasty. She was succeeded by a period of ephemeral kings who made up the Thirteenth Dynasty.

Egyptologists debate the factors behind the dramatic decline in the length of reigns subsequent to Amenemhat III. Internal problems in the dynastic succession are probable, in light of the atypical accession of a female pharaoh at the close of the dynasty. The institutions of government and rulership from Itj-Tawy, however, continued on unbroken during this time. Amenemhat III appears to have served as a model for later Middle Kingdom rulers, such as king Hor, whose burial was inside Amenemhat III's Dahshur pyramid complex, and king Khendjer, whose pyramid followed the design of Amenemhat III's Hawara pyramid. The king's deification and later veneration as Lamarres reflect the lasting memory of his prosperous reign and the continuity of oral legends affirming that reign.

[*See also* Senwosret III.]

BIBLIOGRAPHY

Freed, Rita. "Another Look at the Sculptures of Amenemhat III." *Revue d'Égyptologie* 53 (2002): 103–124. A comprehensive review of the unique royal and divine statuary of Amenemhat III.

Grajetzki, Wolfram. *The Middle Kingdom of Ancient Egypt*. London: Duckworth Egyptology, 2006. An authoritative and up-to-date overview of the history and archaeology of the Egyptian Middle Kingdom.

Tallet, Pierre. *Sésostris III et la Fin de la XIIe Dynastie*. Paris: Pygmalion Editions, 2005. A detailed and well-illustrated source on the final reigns of the Twelfth Dynasty.

Uphill, Eric. *Pharaoh's Gateway to Eternity: The Hawara Labyrinth of King Amenemhat III*. London and New York: Kegan Paul International, 2000. A discussion of the classical sources and archaeological evidence on the Egyptian Labyrinth.

Wegner, Josef. "The Nature and Chronology of the Senwosret III-Amenemhat III Regnal Succession: New Evidence from Abydos." *Journal of Near Eastern Studies* 55 (1996): 249–279. An examination of the historical sources regarding the debated coregency of Amenemhat III with his father Senwosret III.

JOSEF WEGNER

Amenhotep III (fl. fourteenth century BCE), was the ninth king (reigned c.1391–1353 BCE) of the Eighteenth Dynasty (c.1550–1295 BCE) of pharaonic Egypt. Upon ascending to the kingship in c. 1391 BCE, he bore the titulary "Neb-maat-Re; Amenhotep, Ruler of Thebes"; he is known in Greek as *Amenophis* and in Akkadian as *Nibmuareya*. His father was king Thutmose IV and his mother, Mut-em-wiya, was one of his father's minor consorts. Amenhotep came to the throne as a child, no more than about ten years old, and he reigned at least thirty-eight years.

Amenhotep III's reign is characterized as being a political and artistic highpoint of the Egyptian empire of the Eighteenth Dynasty, a period of peace following Egypt's aggressive expansion during the earlier reigns of Thutmose III and Amenhotep II. With the exception of a military campaign in Regnal Year 5 against Nubian tribes in Kush, Amenhotep's relations with his neighbors were peaceful.

In Year 2 of his reign, Amenhotep married Tiye, a noblewoman from the region of Akhmim whose father, Yuya, was highly influential at court; she

Amenhotep III. (Luxor Museum of Ancient Art, Egypt/ Bildarchiv Steffens/The Bridgeman Art Library)

remained as his Great Royal Wife throughout the king's reign and participated prominently in it. In addition to four daughters, Tiye bore the king's heirs Thutmose—who predeceased his father—and the future king, Amenhotep IV (Akhenaten).

The king maintained his residence at Memphis until Year 20, after which he lived at Malqata, on the Theban west bank, perhaps to supervise the massive building campaign undertaken in that region during the latter part of his reign. In addition to adding significantly to the Great Temple of Amun-Re at Karnak (including the third and tenth pylons), he commissioned the construction of the majority of the present temple of Luxor to celebrate his divine conception and birth, as well as his massive mortuary temple at Kawm al-Haytan, of which the two Colossi of Memnon are now the most impressive visible survivals; the chief architect of these works was Amenhotep, son of Hapu, who was later deified. Outside of Thebes, the king was responsible for a number of temple constructions in Nubia, such as at Aniba, Sedeinga, Sesebi, and

Soleb, while in Lower Egypt he was active at Bubastis, Athribis, Heliopolis, Memphis, and Saqqarah, although little of these now remain.

This burst in construction activity was at least in part associated with Amenhotep's *sed*-festivals, celebrated as a reaffirmation of the king's divine nature and renewal of his power in Years 30, 34, and 37 of his reign. The rite itself was observed in a festival hall especially constructed at the Theban residence of Malqata, although scenes of the festival are known from Soleb and the king's mortuary temple.

A great deal of information regarding Amenhotep's international relations is known thanks to the preservation of the king's diplomatic correspondence, as well as that of his heir, Amenhotep IV/Akhenaten. Known as the *Amarna Letters* due to the location of their discovery, these cuneiform tablets illuminate Egypt's relations with Babylon, Assyria, the north Syrian kingdom of Mitanni, the Anatolian kingdom of Arzawa, and several other locations. Of particular interest are the notices of Amenhotep's diplomatic marriage to Gilukhepa, the daughter of the Mitannian king Šuttarna II in Year 10, and to her niece, Taduchepa, the daughter of king Tušratta, some twenty years later. Similarly, he married two Babylonian princesses, a sister and a daughter of king Kadašman-Enlil I, and likewise a daughter of king Tarkhundaradu of Arzawa. These marriages served to maintain Egypt's prestige in the Near East, as well as strengthen its political alliances and trade relations with foreign rulers.

One of the most contentious aspects of the reign of Amenhotep III is the open question of whether toward the end of his life he ruled jointly with his son Amenhotep IV/Akhenaten. Those advocating such a coregency, in particular Cyril Aldred and W. Raymond Johnson, tend to argue on the basis of art-historical evidence, while those arguing against it tend to be historians who base their opposition on the textual evidence.

As early as Regnal Year 11 of his reign, Amenhotep III made reference to himself on both public and private monuments with the epithet *tjehen aten* "(the) Dazzling Aten" (literally, "the Dazzling Solar-Disk"). Coupled with this was the king's deification as a living god in Year 30 during his *sed*-festival, when he was identified and assimilated with the solar deity Re-Horakhty. This would have had an immense amount of influence over his son Amenhotep IV/Akhenaten, who established the cult of the Aten as the state religion, essentially a cult dedicated to his divine father.

After no more than thirty-nine years on the throne, Amenhotep III died and was buried in tomb KV 22, located in a western branch of the Valley of the Kings at Thebes. At some point during the Twenty-First Dynasty his mummy was removed from the tomb, rewrapped, and reburied in a private tomb at Dayr al-Bahri, along with most of the other New Kingdom rulers. His son Amenhotep IV/Akhenaten succeeded him on the throne, and his wife Tiye outlived him by as many as twelve years.

[See also Akhenaten; and Tiye.]

BIBLIOGRAPHY

Cohen, Raymond, and Raymond Westbrook, eds. *Amarna Diplomacy: The Beginnings of International Relations.* Baltimore: The Johns Hopkins University Press, 2000. An important collection of papers examining a number of topics, including the diplomatic marriages of Amenhotep III.

Kozloff, Arielle P., and Betsy M. Bryan. *Egypt's Dazzling Sun: Amenhotep III and His World.* Cleveland, Ohio: Cleveland Museum of Art, 1992. A catalog from a museum exhibition accompanied by a number of essential articles regarding the history, art history, and religious atmosphere of the king's reign.

Moran, William L., ed. *The Amarna Letters.* Baltimore: The Johns Hopkins University Press, 1992. Modern translations of the diplomatic correspondence from the reigns of Amenhotep III and his heir Akhenaten.

O'Connor, David B., and Eric H. Cline, eds. *Amenhotep III: Perspectives on his Reign.* Ann Arbor: University of Michigan Press, 1998. A fundamental collection of scholarly papers examining all aspects of the king's reign and its aftermath.

TROY LEILAND SAGRILLO

Amenhotep IV. *See* Akhenaten.

Ameniras (fl. first century BCE), was a Meroitic queen of the ancient empire of Kush. Her name is a Meroitic rendition of the supreme royal deity Amen-Ra. It is because of her exploits in defending Kushite sovereignty against Roman advances that the Meroitic title for queen mother *kandake*, translated as "candace," became popular during the Roman era and is alluded to in the New Testament Book of Acts.

Ameniras's existence is documented in four epigraphic sources. The most well known of these inscriptions is the famous Hamadab stela, discovered by the archaeologist John Garstang in 1910 in the vicinity of the ancient capital of the Kushite Empire, Meroe City. The stela, written in the ancient Meroitic language, has been interpreted by scholars as an account of Kush's military encounter with Rome. The text provides a Kushite perspective on the Roman-Kushite war that was waged between 25 and 21 BCE and celebrates the Kushite victory over Roman forces. The Hamadab stela also mention Ameniras's prince and coregent Akindad, who was believed to have shared the throne with her after the death of her husband, the king Teriteqas. The stela depicts Ameniras and prince Akindad standing before the royal deities Amun and Mut; below these images is a fresco of prisoners, believed to be Roman soldiers lying on their bellies in submission to the Meroitic rulers. In this text, and on a bronze naos discovered at a temple at the ancient site of Kawa in central Sudan, Ameniras is referred to as *kore*, the Meroitic word for "ruler." The other two inscriptions where her name is attested are a graffito on the temple of Dakka in Lower Nubia, and the Teriteqas stela from Meroe City, where she is referred to only as *kdke*, that is, "the Queen Mother of Kush." It is believed by scholars that the Hamadab stela and the Kawa inscription refer to a period when she was sole ruler of the Meroitic state with her son Akindad and the Dakka inscription and Teriteqas stela refer to a period when she was a coregent and Queen Mother alongside her husband Teriteqas.

The Greek geographer Strabo, writing in the early first century CE, provided a historical source that sheds light on the Roman-Kushite war and describes the activities of the "one-eyed" candace, queen of Kush, who resisted, with minimal success, Roman attempts to subjugate and annex the empire of Kush. The "candace" of Strabo's account is now identified as Queen Ameniras. Strabo, a personal friend of the Roman prefect of Egypt, Aelius Gallus, provided a pro-Roman perspective on the Roman-Kushite war and painted a picture of Kush as a vassal of Rome that only escaped total domination because of the benevolence of Caesar Augustus.

Strabo relates that Aelius Gallus's successor as Roman prefect of Egypt, Gaius Petronius, launched a counterattack against the Kushites who had invaded the Thebaid in Upper Egypt and took over the cities of Elephantine, Syene, and Philae after the withdrawal of troops from the Egyptian frontier to Arabia. According to Strabo, the Kushites had waited until a significant number of Roman troops were engaged in battle in Arabia under Aelius Gallus and "enslaved the inhabitants and threw down the statues of Caesar." Strabo reports that when the Kushites were asked why they had started the war, they responded by saying they were mistreated by the nomarchs of Upper Egypt. Strabo recounts that, in retaliation, Petronius's forces marched against the "Aithiopians" and their "one-eyed manly" Candace until they defeated them at Pselchis and reached the city of Napata. Strabo recounts that while en route to Napata, Petronious established a garrison at the fortress island of Qasr Ibrim and left provision for four hundred soldiers over a period of two years.

The Kushite Queen responded to Roman military presence by attacking the garrison and thereby provoking another military confrontation with the troops of Petronius, only to end in a stalemate. A reconstruction of historical events suggests that king Teriteqas led the initial march against Roman Egypt and was killed in battle, leaving the reins of Meroitic sovereignty in the command of Ameniras and her prince Akindad. After the standoff between Ameniras and Petronius at Qasr Ibrim, her ambassadors traveled to the island of Samos to establish peace with Augustus; they "obtained all they desired and Augustus even remitted the tribute which he had imposed." Certain scholars question whether Petronius actually reached as far south as Napata and to what extent he was presenting a favorable image to appease Roman sensibilities. Since Kush ultimately avoided being made a vassal state by Rome, it is reasonable to postulate that Petronius's victories in Kush were not as decisive as described by Strabo—Rome was forced to make concessions to the Kushites. Augustus decided to abandon the idea of making Kush a vassal state and therefore relinquished the tribute he had initially imposed and withdrew from northern Nubia. He settled for maintaining Roman military presence on the border of Egypt and Nubia in collaboration with Kushite officials and as a result was able to continue surveillance of the area.

For Kush, Queen Ameniras avoided having her entire northern province annexed by Rome and the humiliating responsibility of having to provide tribute to a foreign power occupying her land. The Kushite state also maintained unrestricted access to the major temples of Upper Egypt and Lower Nubia at Philae and Kalabsha, where the veneration of Isis was paramount to bolstering Kushite national identity. This unique relationship between Kush and Rome was unlike any other diplomatic arrangement between Rome and a state with which it had gone to war. Ameniras's historical significance stems from the fact that she had protected the territorial integrity and independence of the Kushite state and inaugurated a period of economic prosperity that encouraged the flourishing of trade, commerce, and intercultural exchange between Kush and the Mediterranean world. This era often is called the "golden age" of the Meroitic period; it would last in the heart of the Sudanic Nile Valley until the middle of the fourth century CE.

[See also Augustus; Petronius, Publius; and Strabo.]

BIBLIOGRAPHY

Burstein, Stanley M. Graeco-Africana: Studies in the History of Greek Relations with Egypt and Nubia. New Rochelle, N.Y.: Aristide D. Caratzas, 1995.

Eide, Tormode, Tomas Hagg, Richard Holton Pierce, and László Török, eds. Fontes Historiae Nubiorum: Textual Sources for the Middle Nile Region Between the Eighth Century BC and the Sixth Century AD, Vols 2–3. Norway: University of Bergen, 1994–1998.

Török, László. The Kingdom of Kush: Handbook of the Naptan-Meroitic Civilization. Leiden, Netherlands: Brill, 1997.

Török, László. Meroe: Six Studies on the Cultural Identity of an Ancient African State. Budapest: Studia Aegyptiaca, 1995.

Welsby, Derek. The Kingdom of Kush: The Napatan and Meroitic Times. Princeton, N.J.: Markus Wiener Publishers, 1996.

SALIM FARAJI

Amiin, Cabdi Muxumed (1935–2008), Somali poet, dramatist, actor, and political activist, was born in Gabiley in northwestern Somalia in 1935. His father, Muxumed Amiin, was a soldier. His mother, Muumina Kaahin, Muxumed Amiin's first wife, died when Cabdi, her only child, was still an infant. Cabdi's grandmother Murriya took care of him until he was a teenager. He lived in the towns of Berbera and Arabsiyo where he attended a qur'anic school. As a teenager he had to support himself through different kinds of hard physical labor.

In 1953 he moved to Hargeisa, then the capital of the British Protectorate of Somaliland, where he started composing his first poems. Soon after, in the same year, he moved to Mogadishu, the Somali capital. There he was recognized as a talented poet and artist and was employed by Radio Mogadishu. At the same time he joined the movement for national independence. He worked for Radio Mogadishu until 1971 when Waaberi Artists, Somalia's leading theater troupe, was established and he became a founding member. He continued to be employed as a poet and dramatist at the government-owned National Theatre Agency until he went into exile in 1982.

From 1959 to1960 Cabdi was married to Amina Salad, by whom he had one daughter, Muxubbo. In 1967 Cabdi married Faduma Ciise Abtidoon, to whom he remained married for the rest of his life and by whom he had seven children, four daughters and three sons.

Cabdi Amiin was a multitalented artist of great stature, who always responded to the major issues of common concern nationally, regionally, and globally. His plays and poetic oeuvre, which spanned five decades, mirrored and chronicled the different stages of modern Somali history. Cabdi's lifetime coincided with an unusually troubled period in Somali history, a period characterized by a series of upheavals, social unrest, rapid changes, and dramatic historical events. Cabdi was greatly influenced by and highly responsive to all these challenges.

In the 1950s, when Cabdi's consciousness was being shaped, Somalia was under colonial rule and the movement for independence was at its height. Cabdi was one of the young patriots who joined what was known as Horseed (Pioneers), the youth wing of the Somali Youth League (SYL), the most popular political party, which led the national drive for independence. He made remarkable contributions to numerous artistic performances aimed at mobilizing public support for the efforts toward independence and to raise funds for SYL. He composed his first significant poem, entitled *Dhulyohow* (Oh Land!), in response to the news that Britain, the colonial ruler of most Somali territories at the time, had handed over to Ethiopia the Somali areas known as Hawd and Reserved Area, an event that evoked an overwhelming outcry from all Somalis and prompted many other Somali artists to express their feelings in poems, plays, and music, lamenting the loss of this Somali territory.

Somalia became an independent state in 1960 but the Somali regime that replaced the colonial administration did not live up to the expectations of the Somali people. Many poets and artists voiced the disappointment of the general public through poetry and drama critical of the government's flaws and bureaucratic inefficiency. Cabdi Amiin was at the forefront of these artists as illustrated in his famous song entitled "*Kuwa daanka buuxsadey*" (1964; "Those who filled their mouths [with illegally acquired public funds]"). The song launches a fierce attack on corrupt government officials. Another song, "*Geeddiga wadaay*" (1962; "Lead the Caravan") was one of the most famous Somali songs produced in the 1960s.

Cabdi Amiin and other artists' ongoing critique of the government of the late 1960s is believed to have had a strong effect on the people and to have prepared the ground for the military coup of 1969 led by General Mohamed Siyad Barre. The coup was the beginning of a new era and Cabdi was one of the many artists who, with their art, warmly welcomed and supported the revolutionary policies of the new military regime. They believed that it would bring about the change they had championed. However, by the late 1970s the dictatorial nature of the military regime and its leader became apparent and the initial popular support turned into growing opposition.

Here again Cabdi chose to voice the feelings of the majority. He started writing poems, songs, and plays of dissent in which he initially used thinly veiled metaphors, as Somali artists usually do. Later, however, he grew bolder in his political criticism. The climax came when he produced a play called *Muufo* (Bread), which is known to virtually every adult Somali. Interestingly, this openly critical play was staged on 1 May 1980 at the National Theatre in Mogadishu, in the presence of the head of state, General Barre, and his cabinet. In his post-performance statement, President Barre was furious about the content of the play. Soon after the playwright and other key actors were arrested, though they were later released.

In 1982 Cabdi gave up his job as well as his seat as a member of parliament and went into exile. He joined the armed opposition organizations based in Ethiopia and then moved to Yemen. In exile, he created numerous poems and some plays; however, his most famous plays and poems came out after his return to Somalia in 1988. Among this new work, the most famous play, with the most significant political effect, was *Land Cruiser*, in which he attacked the status quo. This play too was staged at the National Theatre with the country's political and economic elite in the audience. The playwright was arrested again, together with the leading actress, Saado Cali. Many Somalis believe that *Land Cruiser* contributed to the downfall of Barre and his regime in early 1991. Unfortunately, however, after Barre's fall Somalia was torn by civil war and anarchy, perpetuated by warlords competing for power. In protest Cabdi tirelessly created poetry and plays denouncing these evils and calling for peace.

Cabdi Muxumed Amiin was an artist of great stature, who took it upon himself to fight for a just world, putting the common good above his individual interest. He was a man of principle and dignity, who acted as "a voice of vision in his time," to borrow a phrase from Wole Soyinka. He is remembered for his bravery and the way his art, with its simple, direct language, always captured the pulse of the people. He is the author of two published collections of poetry and a novella. He was a founding member of the Somali-speaking Centre of International PEN and chair of its chapter in southern Somalia. He died in Nairobi, Kenya, on 2 November 2008.

[*See also* Siyad Barre, Mohamed; *and* Soyinka, Wole.]

BIBLIOGRAPHY

Works by Cabdi Muxumed Amiin
Geeddiga Wadaay. Mogadishu, Somalia: Ministry of Culture and Higher Education, 1973.
Maxaa ka yar oo aan sheegtaa? Helsinki: Soof Publications, 2000.
Diiwaanka Hilin Hayaan. Stockholm: Omhassan Publisher, 2006.

Works About Cabdi Muxumed Amiin
Ahmed, Ali Jimale. *Daybreak Is Near: Literature, Clans, and the Nation-State in Somalia*. Lawrenceville, N.J.: Red Sea Press, 1996.
Faduma Ciise Abtidoon (Cabdi Muxumed's widow), Personal interview by the author, 2009.
                          MAXAMED DAHIR AFRAX

Amin, Ali (1914–1976), Egyptian journalist and newspaper magnate in collaboration with his twin brother, Mustafa Amin, was born in Cairo on 21 February 1914. Their father was Amine Youssef Bey, a prominent lawyer and politician, and their mother was a niece of nationalist leader Sa'd Zaghlul. The boys grew up in Zaghlul's Cairo villa, a political nerve center, eventually known as *Bayt al Umma* (the "House of the Nation"). In 1919 Zaghlul headed the national delegation that sought British permission to attend the Paris Peace Conference. Their arrest and exile sparked the 1919 "revolution" that inaugurated the constitutional monarchy (1923–1953). In 1922, the Amin twins embarked upon their first journalistic ventures, a series of handwritten magazines.

Ali attended the Royal Awqaf School from 1926 to 1928, but was expelled for participating in demonstrations against one of numerous minority governments. He attended several preparatory schools (one associated with the American University in Cairo) and then in 1931 traveled to England to study engineering in Sheffield. Upon graduation, he returned home to work in the government bureaucracy until 1944, when he and Mustafa founded the independent weekly newspaper *Akhbar al-Yawm*. Like many Egyptians, the brothers despaired at King Farouk's personal scandals and pushed the limits of censorship to relate veiled accounts of his misbehavior. The paper was seized twenty-six times between 1944 and 1952 and the editors were arrested numerous times, although never for long.

In 1948 the Amins inaugurated a popular weekly magazine, *Akhir Lahza*; soon after they purchased a competitor, *Akhir Saa*, and in 1951 launched the youth magazine, *al-Jil*. In early 1952 they founded the daily *al-Akhbar*. Independent and gossipy, it became the most widely read paper in Egypt, outpacing the venerable, more staid *al-Ahram*. *Akhbar al-Yawm* remained the Saturday edition.

The Amins cautiously supported the July 1952 Free Officers coup led by Gamal Abd al-Nasser and the abolition of the multiparty system in January 1953. *Al-Akhbar* published lurid accounts of the corruption of the previous regime and served as a mouthpiece for Nasser's regime during the pivotal crisis of March 1954. During the 1956 Suez Crisis, Nasser delegated Ali Amin to make overtures to the British government; Amin later served as roving ambassador to London.

In the 1960s, *al-Ahram* emerged as Egypt's paper of record, although *al-Akhbar* remained influential. The Amin brothers remained editors after the state nationalized all newspapers in 1960, a move they opposed, and spent long hours conversing with Nasser. As proponents of a free press, the brothers eventually ran afoul of the regime and were labeled foreign agents—Ali for the British and Saudis, Mustafa for the Americans. When Mustafa was jailed for life in 1965, Ali stayed in England. He remained an exile, occasionally writing for *al-Ahram* until Anwar al-Sadat pardoned his brother in 1974. Ali returned home and assumed editorship of *al-Ahram*, but it was never truly his paper, and he soon rejoined Mustafa at *al-Akhbar*. The brothers waged a campaign against abuses of the Nasser regime that was cautiously approved by Sadat, until in March 1976, as part of a wider move to rein in outspoken critics of high level corruption, Sadat dismissed both from the their editorial posts. They remained as staff writers, but on 3 April 1976 Ali Amin died of cancer. He is buried in Cairo. The Egyptian Press Syndicate awards an annual prize for journalistic excellence in the brothers' names.

[*See also* Amin, Mustafa; Nasser, Gamal Abd al-; Sadat, Muhammad Anwar al-; *and* Zaghlul, Sa'd]

BIBLIOGRAPHY

Amin, Mustafa. "If It Makes the President Happy." *Index on Censorship* 14 (5) (1985): 8–21.

Ayalon, Ami. *The Press in the Arab Middle East: A History.* New York: Oxford University Press, 1995.

Darwish, Adel. "Obituary: Mustafa Amin." *The Independent,* 15 April 1997.

JOEL GORDON

Amin, Idi Dada (c.1925–2003), military officer and President of Uganda from 1971 to 1979, was probably born in Koboko district near the Sudanese border in northwestern Uganda. Few facts about his parents, his birth date, or his upbringing can be confirmed. His mother, who was Lugbara and

Idi Dada Amin. Amin at an Organization of African Unity conference in Kampala, Uganda, 1975. (AP Images/Sayyid Azim)

originally Christian, separated from her father— who was Kakwa, Muslim, and possibly a convert from Christianity—shortly after his birth and raised Amin in southern Uganda.

As a Muslim belonging to both the Kakwa and the Nubian ethnic communities, Amin received little formal education and had halting command of several languages, including Swahili and English. He practiced polygamy and married at least six women: Malyamu Kibedi and Kay Adroa (both Christians prior to marriage) in late 1966 and Nora (her full name cannot be confirmed), a Langi, in 1967. He divorced all three, according to a Radio Uganda announcement on 26 March 1974. He married Nalongo Madina on 24 September 1972 and Sarah Kyolaba, a go-go dancer from the Suicide Mechanized Unit Jazz Band, on 2 August 1975 during the Organization of African Unity summit meeting. He fathered over thirty children.

Amin joined the Fourth (Uganda) Battalion of the King's African Rifles (KAR) on 20 December 1946 as an assistant cook. He was sent to Kenya as a private in 1947, becoming a corporal in 1948 and serving there until 1949, when he was deployed to British Somalia. He served again in Kenya from 1952 to 1955 during the Mau Mau crisis. Commended for his initiative, he was promoted to sergeant in 1953. In 1958 he was promoted to warrant officer platoon commander. In 1959 he advanced to the rank of *effendi* (warrant officer), the highest rank an African could achieve in the KAR during the colonial period. Other soldiers labeled him "Dada" ("sister" in Swahili) as a joking reference to his accounting to superiors for the women he brought into the barracks. During the 1950s he became an outstanding rugby player and boxer, holding the light heavyweight boxing championship from 1951 until 1960. His excellence in tracking, marksmanship, leadership, and athleticism, as well as his obedience to his superiors, endeared him to his British officers.

On 15 July 1961, two weeks after Benedicto Kiwanuka became the Protectorate's first African Chief Minister, Amin became one of the first two Ugandans to be commissioned as lieutenants, even though he lacked the required standard of education. Among Ugandan soldiers, Amin was second in rank only to Shaban Oppolot, who later became the first Ugandan commander of the army. He saw further service in Kenya in 1962, where he was threatened with a court martial for the deaths of three Pokot villagers. Sir Walter Coutts, the colonial governor, requested the opinion of Milton

Obote, the new Prime Minister, who preferred a reprimand. Immediately after independence occurred in October 1962, Amin was promoted to captain; in 1963 he advanced to the rank of major.

Following the January 1964 mutiny by First Battalion troops, Amin, who was not involved in the mutiny, became the Battalion's commanding officer, and the next month, lieutenant colonel. That June, he was made commander of signals at Headquarters and in September, colonel and deputy commander of the Uganda Army in charge of recruitment and training.

In one of his first actions, Amin brought almost all of the approximately three hundred dismissed mutineers back into the army. In February 1966, Parliament established a commission of inquiry into charges of corruption against Amin and suspended him for the duration. Obote, Parliament's real target, made Amin chief of staff of the Army and Air Force. When Buganda, one of the kingdoms within Uganda, threatened secession in the ensuing crisis, Obote ordered Amin on 24 May to investigate claims of secret arms in the Kabaka's palace. Fighting broke out resulting in many deaths, possibly because troops under Amin's personal command disobeyed Obote's orders.

In January 1967 Amin was promoted to brigadier and then to major general in April 1968. Fearing that Obote might remove him, Amin recruited soldiers loyal to him. When an unsuccessful attempt to assassinate Obote occurred on 19 December 1969, Amin, fearing a coup d'état also aimed at him, hid while Brigadier Pierino Okoya took charge of the Army in Amin's absence, later criticizing Amin for his disappearance. Amin was suspected in Okoya's murder on 25 January 1970. In early October 1970, Obote made Amin Chief of Defense Staff, removing him from command over troops. Just before Obote left for the Commonwealth Conference in Singapore in January 1971, he publicly insisted that Amin prepare an explanation for the disappearance of funds. Privately, he ordered Amin's arrest.

To protect himself, Amin responded by leading a coup d'état on 25 January 1971. He succeeded due to his intelligence network within the army, a personally loyal faction within the army and military police, and prior recruitment of supporters, largely from the West Nile region, many of whom were Nubian soldiers. The hesitation of civilian politicians and army units that Obote had left in charge gave Amin an additional advantage. The governments of Great Britain and Israel welcomed Amin's coup, because Obote had nationalized British companies and established warmer ties with the Sudanese government. In his early speeches, Amin insisted that his government would serve as a caretaker until new elections could be held. Cheering crowds in Kampala, including many Baganda, welcomed his rule, but public response elsewhere was muted.

Amin's first challenge as ruler was to expand his narrow political base. On 2 February 1971 he proclaimed himself president and appointed a council of ministers consisting of talented technocrats. He removed Obote's state of emergency and released five ministers Obote had imprisoned, as well as about fifty others held in political detention. He arranged the return and proper burial of the Kabaka's body in April 1971. By decrees in March and May 1971, he also reduced the percentage of government ownership of firms nationalized by Obote from 60 percent to 49 percent. These popular moves bought him civilian support temporarily.

Amin also took measures that increased public insecurity almost immediately after he took power. He suspended parts of the constitution, ruling by decree throughout his period in office. With his first decree on 3 February 1971 he gained absolute undivided authority, reducing the authority of other Army officers as well as bureaucrats. In another on 17 March 1971, Army officers were given the right to arrest anyone without prior authority. The Defense Council quickly emerged as the supreme policy body, frequently reversing Cabinet decisions. Amin promoted loyal soldiers, sometimes advancing them by as many as seven ranks.

Starting on the night of the coup, he targeted Acholi and Langi officers and ordinary soldiers. Hundreds were massacred in the first months—perhaps fifteen thousand soldiers and civilians by the end of his first year in office. Intensive recruitment in the first year increased the army about twice as quickly as older soldiers were killed. Soldiers harassed civilians with impunity throughout Amin's regime and prominent civilian officials, including the chief justice, the Anglican archbishop, and the university vice-chancellor, were murdered. An abortive invasion to overthrow Amin that began on 17 September 1972 resulted in a fresh wave of killings. So did an unsuccessful coup attempt on 23 March 1974.

Amin's decision to expel Indians resident in Uganda, both citizens and noncitizens, in October 1972 and allocate many of their businesses to his military cronies thoroughly disrupted the economy, causing scarcities of most consumer goods and rapidly accelerating inflation.

Amin made a noticeable and erratic impact on foreign politics. He switched his loyalties from Israel to Arab states in 1972 after Colonel Muʿammar al-Qaddafi, President of Libya, began supplying assistance in February. Amin was elected Chair of the OAU for a year at its meeting in Kampala in June 1975. On 4 July 1976 Israeli commandoes rescued all but three of the hostages held by Palestinian Liberation Organization hijackers of an Air France plane at Entebbe airport. Two were killed in the operation; the third, Dora Bloch, was murdered by two army officers who took her from Mulago Hospital. On 28 July 1976 Great Britain ended diplomatic relations with Uganda—the first time it had broken ties with a Commonwealth country. Amin turned to the Soviet Union as his main weapons supplier and to East Germany to organize his intelligence apparatus. But both Great Britain and the United States, which had closed its embassy in Kampala in 1973, permitted their nationals to continue to do business with Amin until 1978.

Threatened by the growth in Uganda's military, Kenya seized Soviet weapons intended for Uganda. The strain between the neighbors deepened in January 1976, when Amin announced that he might act on a 1902 colonial map indicating that Uganda had once included all of western Kenya to within twenty miles of Nairobi. Following a public speech by Jomo Kenyatta in February 1976, and the deployment of Kenyan troops and armor on its border with Uganda, Amin withdrew the warning.

In June 1976, he contrived a proclamation making him "President for Life." Discontent in the armed forces led Amin to make sweeping changes among his top officers in April 1978. Probably to outflank a mutiny in the Simba Barracks in Mbarara, Amin ordered an invasion of Tanzania's Kagera Salient across the border the following October that resulted in looting, rape, and the deaths of many Tanzanian civilians. The Soviet Union and East Germany responded by breaking their ties with Uganda in favor of an alliance with Tanzania. Despite their disadvantage in military equipment, the numerically superior Tanzanian Army, accompanied by a small force of Ugandan exiles, easily drove out the invaders. It forced the Ugandan army to retreat, invaded Uganda, and took Kampala on 11 April 1979. Amin fled to Libya, where he received asylum until the end of 1979, when he was forced to leave after a gun battle between his security guards and Libyan police.

He moved to Jeddah, Saudi Arabia. In violation of the terms of his asylum he attempted to return incognito to Uganda in early 1989, but was recognized and stopped at Kinshasa airport in the Democratic Republic of the Congo. When Uganda refused extradition, he returned to Saudi Arabia, where he died on 16 August 2003. He was laid to rest in Ruwais Cemetery in Jeddah.

Amin drove Uganda into ruin. He and his henchmen may have committed more than 100,000 murders. He greatly accelerated decline in the rule of law and the rise of corruption. He transformed the economy chiefly by removing the Indian trading network and wrecked it through mismanagement. During his regime, most Westerners mistook him for a clown and overlooked his murders. Ugandans did not.

[See also Kenyatta, Jomo; Kiwanuka, Benedicto Mugumba; Obote, Apollo Milton; and Qaddafi, Muʿammar al-.]

BIBLIOGRAPHY

Grahame, Iain. *Amin and Uganda: A Personal Memoir.* London: HarperCollins Distribution Services, 1980.

Jørgensen, Jan Jelmert. *Uganda: A Modern History.* London: Law Book Co. of Australasia, 1981.

Kasozi, A.B.K. *The Social Origins of Violence in Uganda: 1964–1985.* Montreal: McGill-Queen's University Press, 1994.

Kyemba, Henry. *A State of Blood: The Inside Story of Idi Amin.* New York: Putnam Publishing Group, 1977.

Martin, David M. *General Amin.* London: Sphere, 1978.

Omara-Otunnu, Amii. *Politics and the Military in Uganda, 1890–1985.* New York: Palgrave Macmillan, 1987.

NELSON KASFIR

Amin, Mustafa (1914–1997), Egyptian journalist, novelist, scriptwriter, publisher, and politician, was born in Cairo on 21 February 1914. He said, "When I hold my pen I feel that I hug the most beautiful woman in the world; I have therefore lived a long love-story. I cannot imagine myself live a single day without my pen . . . When I pass away I ask to lay my pen next to me in my tomb since I may need it when I write a journalistic research story about the resurrection day" (Mustafa, p. 6). Mustafa Amin, or *al-Ustadh* ("the teacher"), as he was often referred to by his colleagues and followers, was one of Egypt's most eminent journalists of the twentieth century. Many in the Arab world have regarded him as the father of Arab journalism. His pen,

Mustafa Amin kept reminding his readers, was mightier than the dictator's sword—a reference to the trials he endured under Nasser's regime.

Mustafa and his twin brother, Ali, were born in the house of his mother's uncle, Sa'd Zaghlul, considered by many Egyptians to be the nation's father. He spent his formative years in Zaghlul's house, and there he absorbed his great-uncle's nationalist sentiments, as well as his support for freedom of speech and a free press. As a boy he witnessed the nationalist uprising of 1919—a remarkable event in which his mother, whom he admired, participated by way of distributing manifestos.

While in high school (1928), the twin brothers led a demonstration against Prime Minister Muhammad Mahmud (leader of the Liberal Constitutionalist Party and the Wafd rivals). The two were consequently expelled from the royal high school.

That same year, Mustafa and Ali started their journalistic career with the publication of their first student journals. However, their independent journalistic activity was ended by Mahmud's government. In 1930, Mustafa Amin joined the news desk of the newspaper *Ruz al-Yusuf*. He went on to edit a number of other periodicals as well: *Al-Sharq al-Adna* ("the Near East"), *Sawt al-Haqq* ("the Voice of Truth"), *Sada al-Sharq* ("the East's Echo"), *al-Sharq* ("the East"), and *Al-Shabhb* ("the Youth") among others. In 1934, he joined *Ahkhir Sh'ah* after he was fired from *Ruz al-Yusuf*. In that year he also completed his BA studies at the American University in Cairo. In the period 1935–1938 he studied law in Egypt and earned an MA in political science, economy, and journalism at Georgetown University in Washington, D.C. During his studies in the United States, he also worked as foreign correspondent for the Wafdist paper *al-Misri*. In 1938 he completed his MA studies with distinction, and upon his return to Egypt he was appointed editor-in-chief of *Ahkhir Sh'ah*. However, his troubled relations with the establishment continued. In August 1938 he was jailed for six months, after he published an article disgracing the Crown Prince Muhammad Ali.

In 1939, after his release from prison, he was appointed chairman of the news section of *Al-Ahram*. Two years later he was nominated editor-in-chief of *Al-Ithnayni wa al-Dunya*, the most widespread satirical periodical at the time. In 1943 he published his first book, *Amrikh al-Dhhikah* ("Laughing America"), which within two months went through three printings. Mustafa was also politically involved, and in 1944 he was elected

Member of Parliament. He nevertheless never dropped his journalistic activity, and in 1946 the twin brothers bought *Ahkhir Sh'ah* from Muhammad al-Tabi'i. In November 1944 they debuted the Saturday weekly paper *Akhbar-al-Yawm*, which resembled Western-style Sunday newspapers. *Akhbar al-Yawm* and the Amin brothers became identical. Under their leadership, the paper had the largest circulation of any in the Arab world.

Mustafa dedicated a great deal of articles to the rights of Egyptian women. Mustafa believed that his campaign bore fruit with the appointment of the first female minister in the early 1960s (he possibly was referring to Dr. Hikmat Abu Zaid, Minister of Social Affairs, 1962–1965). *Akhbar al-Yawm* also campaigned in favor of voting rights for women.

The independent and often dissident thoughts expressed by the Amin brothers in their newspaper were coolly received by the establishment, including Wafdist governments and the revolutionary regime, and often led to the imprisonment of the twin brothers. For example, in 1951 Mustafa was arrested twenty-six times, which nearly caused the newspaper to go into bankruptcy. However, he honored Mustafa al-Nahhas, the Wafdist leader and Prime Minister (1928, 1930, 1936–1937, 1942–1944, 1950–1952), for uniting the people in a struggle against the dictatorships of Isma'il Sidqi (1930–1933, 1946) and Muhammad Mahmud (1928–1929, 1937–1939).

Shortly before the July 1952 revolution, the Amin brothers launched their new daily newspaper *al-Akhbar*. Like their weekly *Akhbar al-Yawm*, it was also very popular and enjoyed impressive circulation all over the Arab world.

Mustafa Amin's first meeting with Gamal Abd al-Nasser took place in Umm Kulthum's house, when the latter hosted a party to celebrate the release of the "besieged heroes of al-Faluja" at the end of the 1948 War—one of those heroes being Nasser himself. When the two were introduced to each other, Nasser was quoted as saying: "How could I not recognize you? All my money was spent on your newspapers. While we were besieged in al-Faluja, we used to smuggle one of our soldiers [behind enemy lines] in order to buy *Akhbar-al-Yawm*." Overall, however, Amin's relationship with the Nasser regime was complex. What started as mutual respect and appreciation disintegrated into mistrust and persecution. Mustafa Amin opposed Nasser's policy of state censorship. For Amin, the values of democracy and freedom of speech were sacred and were repeatedly lionized and defended in his writings and throughout his journalist activity.

In May 1960, Nasser's decision to nationalize the press, including *Akhbar al-Yawm*, was received magnanimously by Amin, who stated, "we now write in *Akhbar al-Yawm* feeling as though we were its owners, whereas in the past we wrote for the paper feeling its workers." This set him apart from most other publishers and newspaper owners.

In 1961, Mustafa Amin was appointed chairman of the board of directors of *Dar al-Hilal* leaving for the first time his own newspaper *Akhbar al-Yawm*. His successful journalism career continued to make headway under the revolutionary regime, and in 1963 he returned to occupy his previous position as chairman of the board of directors of *Akhbar al-Yawm*; he was also named general inspector of the newspaper's editorial board. However, at the peak of his journalistic career, while in the regime's service, Mustafa's lost his credibility with Nasser's government.

On 21 July 1965, Mustafa Amin was arrested following accusations that he delivered highly sensitive information to the American intelligence authorities. He was judged and sentenced on 21 August to life imprisonment with hard labor. During his interrogation he was severely tortured, and the attorney general demanded that he confess to something he had never done.

On 17 April 1974, President Muhammad Anwar al-Sadat pardoned Mustafa Amin; Salah Nasr, the head of the general intelligence agency who tortured Amin and forced his false confession, was jailed for ten years. Sadat's move was met with gratitude and appreciation by Mustafa: "With my release from prison I remembered the person who opened the door of freedom; he similarly did it to other hundreds of prisoners before me. He [Sadat] provided thousands of fired [workers] a slice of bread. His reign is worth the title of 'a transitional period'—the transition of the Egyptian army from defeat to victory, the transition of the Arab people from separation to unity, and the transition of the exploited [people] from oppression to justice."

A few weeks after Amin's release, Sadat reappointed him editor-in-chief of *Akhbar al-Yawm*. However, following the death of his brother Ali in 1976 from cancer, he focused mainly on writing daily columns in *al-Akhbar*. Mustafa was grateful to Sadat for his release, yet in line with his professional integrity he did not hesitate to criticize Sadat when the latter arrested other political prisoners.

"Liberty is not just for me but for others too. What benefit will democracy have if it is granted only for me and not for others?" Mustafa asked.

Mustafa Amin's attitude toward President Muhammad Husni Sa'id Mubarak was quite positive, but he did not hesitate to express criticism with regard to domestic affairs. Following his accession in 1981, upon the assassination of Sadat, Amin told those who asked him to comment about the new President: "Egypt has returned to the Egyptians." Amin fully endorsed Mubarak's foreign policy, but as far as internal policy was concerned, he advocated enacting a new constitution, which would ensure free elections and a free press and erase the final vestiges of autocracy. Amin continued to criticize state control of the press. However, he acknowledged that, under Mubarak, not a single word in his column was ever omitted by the censor, unlike in the period of Mubarak's predecessors, when words, lines, paragraphs and sometime entire columns were banned for publication.

He continued to write independently for *Al-Akhbhr* and *Akhbhr al-Yawm*. He also published literary essays and books, some of which discussed his difficult experiences as a political prisoner. He also wrote two screenplays: *The Crowd Idol* and *Fatma*. His short story "A First Year of Love" was adapted into a movie; some of his other stories were adapted for television.

The Amin brothers were engaged in various charity activities and humanitarian projects. Before his death, Mustafa Amin ordered in his will that his wife Isis Tantawi (whom he married in 1974 after his release from prison) would head the Mustafa and Ali Amin Charity Association.

Mustafa Amin died in Cairo on 13 April 1997. He was survived by his wife and two daughters, Safiyyah and Ratibah.

[*See also* Amin, Ali; Mubarak, Muhammad Husni Sa'id; Nahhas, Mustafa al-; Nasser, Gamal Abd al-; Sadat, Muhammad Anwar al-; Sidqi, Isma'il; *and* Zaghlul, Sa'd.]

BIBLIOGRAPHY

Amin, Mustafa. *Masa'il Shakhsiyyah.* [Personal Issues]. Cairo: Akhbar al-Yawm Publishing House, 1996.

Fawzi, Mufid. *Ha'ulh'—Hhwarahum Mufid Fawzi* [These – Conversed with Them Mufid Fawzi]. Cairo: Akhbar al-Yawm Publishing House, 1992.

'Amrus, Majdi al-. "Mustafa Amin—al-Inshn." [Mustafa Amin—the Person]. *Al-Kawhkib*, October 27, 1998.

Habib, Tariq. "Shaykh al-Sahafiyyina: Mustafa Amin." [The Journalists' Sheikh: Mustafa Amin] *I Ha'ula'* . . . *Min al-Alf Ila al-Ya'* [These Ones . . . From A to Z], pp. 157–167. Cairo: Akhbar al-Yawm Publishing House, 1996.

Jundii, Majidah al-. "Majidah al-Jundi Tuhawiru Mustafa Amin – al-Hurriyyah Qadimah" ("Majidah al-Jundi Converses with Mustafa Amin – the Liberty is Coming"), *Sabakh al-Khayr*, April 24, 1997, p. 11-13.

"Mustafa Amin—al-Bidhyah wa-al-Nihhyah." [Mustafa Amin—the Beginning and the End]. *Al-Akhbhr*, April 14, 1997.

Mustafa, Muhammad. *Mustafa Amin—Fikrah La Tamutu.* [Mustafa Amin—A Thought Which Will Not Die]. Cairo: Akhbar al-Yawm Publishing House, 1997.

Mustafa, Muhammad. *Nujum al-Suhuf—Shuhud 'Alh al-'Asr.* [The Newspaper's Stars—The Witnesses of the Era]. Cairo: Akhbar al-Yawm Publishing House, 1990.

Mustafa, Nawal. "Mustafa Amin." In *Rihlah Ila A'maqihim!* [A Journey to Their Depths], pp. 13–38. Cairo: Akhbar al-Yawm Publishing House, 1988.

Mustafa, Nawal. *Qissat Hayht 'hshiq al-Sahhfah.* [The Life Story of the Press Lover]. Egypt: Akhbar al-Yawm Publishing House, 1997.

RAMI GINAT

Amin, Qasim Mohammed (1863–1908), Egyptian social activist and writer, was born in Alexandria on 1 December 1863 to an Ottoman-Kurdish father, who served as an administrator in Kurdistan before working in the Egyptian army, and an Upper Egyptian mother, the daughter of Ahmed Bek Khattab, who belonged to a prestigious family in Egypt. Amin attended Ra'as Al Tin primary school in Alexandria and high school in Cairo, after which he studied at the School of Law and Administration in Cairo and was there granted his BA degree in 1881. Four years later, he received another degree in Law from the University of Montpellier in France. He worked as a lawyer shortly after his graduation and then traveled on a scholarship to France, where he enrolled in the University of Montpellier. In 1885, he completed his four-year study in law with distinction; upon returning to Egypt, he worked in the judiciary. He married Zeinab Amin Tawfik and had two daughters, Zeinab and Jelsen.

Amin was one of the most notable social reformers in Egypt. His writings, lectures, intellectual battles, and social activities were mainly dedicated to defending the rights of women in education, work, and public affairs; his work in this area was extremely influential in Egyptian society over the twentieth century, so much so that his pen names included the "woman liberator" and "Luther of the East."

Amin bore the burden of refuting the popular and deeply entrenched Egyptian belief that established women as inferior to men. He attempted to counter the passive image of women in Egyptian society that was based on historical and religious information. He advocated getting rid of the symbolic isolation symbolized by the al-Niqab (an article of clothing with which a woman covers every inch of her body, including her hands and face) and replacing it with al-Hijab (an article of clothing that allows a woman to uncover her hands and face) and breaking with the customary isolation of women in their homes through opening education and careers to them.

To accomplish his goals, Amin wrote two books that received broad attention in Egyptian society in the twentieth century. The first, which was published in 1899, is *Tahrir al mar'ah* (The Liberation of Women). According to Amin, this book had two objectives: first, to reform the traditions of society regarding women and the ways they should be treated and raised; and second, to invite Muslim scholars to take into account the needs of the nation concerning women. The publication of the book produced widespread intellectual debates; books, essays, and chapters in books were written to refute the ideas expressed in it. Islamists and conservatives, on one hand, considered Amin's ideas a break from the traditions of society and a departure from the teachings of Islam; they saw them as nothing but a blind imitation of the West. On the other hand, many intellectuals looked upon Amin's project as indispensable for modernizing Egypt. Controversy was raised regarding the authorship of some of the book's chapters, particularly those that tackled the religious perspectives of the liberation of women. Indeed, some researchers (Imarah, 1989) attributed those chapters to Muḥammad 'Abduh (1849–1905).

Amin's second book, *Al-Mar'ah al-jadida* (The New Woman; 1900), included Amin's response to the criticism leveled against *The Liberation of Women.* The book is almost a cultural comparison between the status of Western women and Egyptian women (and Eastern women in general) in terms of education, work, participation in public affairs, personal status, and family life. The book, moreover, enthusiastically argues that imitating some of the habits, laws, and manners of the West that do not conflict with the overall principles of Islam (not only those related to women, but to other aspects of society and individual conduct as well), is the only means to elevate Egyptian society and pull it out of its cultural crisis.

Amin wrote many articles that were published in the newspaper *al-Moa'yed*, which criticized the defects of Egyptian society. In 1894, he published *Les Egyptiens* in French, as a response to *L'Egypte et les Egyptiens* by C.-F.-M. d'Harcourt (1893), in which he criticized the habits, morals, and social lives of Egyptians in the late nineteenth century. In *Les Egyptiens*, Amin analyzes social phenomena and relates them to their economic and political origins. This work was not translated into Arabic until the mid-1970s.

Amin did not engage in politics directly. However, he is said to have belonged to the gradual reform movement that rejected military resistance to the British occupation, but rather called for cultural resistance, by bringing up a new generation of Egyptians armed with knowledge and awareness. From this came his great interest in pedagogical and educational charity projects, such as the Islamic Charitable Society (al-Jam'iyah al-Khayriyah al-Islamiyah), which attempted to constrict British occupation in a number of compulsory schools throughout Egypt, close several high schools, and to exert great efforts to establish the Civil University (now Cairo University), which was opened after Amin's death. He also was one of the most prominent advocates for establishing a legislative parliamentary assembly that could reduce the polarization of authority between the British and the Khedive and allow Egyptians to participate in the formulation of the policies that governed their country.

Qasim Mohammed Amin died on 23 April 1908.

[*See also* 'Abduh, Muhammad.]

BIBLIOGRAPHY

Amin, Qasim. *The Liberation of Women and the New Woman: Two Documents in the History of Egyptian Feminism.* Translated by Samiha Sidhom Peterson. Cairo: American University in Cairo Press, 2000. English translation of *Tahrir al mar'ah* and *al-Mar'ah al-jadida*, first published in 1899 and 1900, respectively.

Freedman, Estelle, ed. *The Essential Feminist Reader.* New York: Modern Library, 2007.

Imarah, Mohammed. *Qasim Amin: al-a'mal al-kamilah.* Cairo: Dar al-Shorouk, 1989.

EMAD ABDUL-LATIF

Amin, Samir (1931–), Egyptian economic theorist, was born in Egypt to an Egyptian father and a French mother, both of whom were medical doctors. Amin had his early schooling at Port Said and then proceeded to France, where he obtained degrees in political science and statistics before finally earning a doctorate in economics from the University of Paris in 1957. He joined the French Communist Party (FCP) but later broke away and eventually became involved with Maoist organizations. After his studies in France, Amin returned to Egypt to work for the government, but eventually had to leave the country for his antigovernment stance. He then worked for the Ministry of Planning in Mali between 1960 and 1963. Amin was later offered a research position at the Institut Africain de Développement Économique et de Planification (IDEP). In addition, he held professorships in Poitiers, Dakar, and Paris. In 1970, he was appointed director of the IDEP; he remained in this position until 1980, when he left to establish the Forum du Tiers Monde (Third World Forum; FTM).

Amin's work at the Third World Forum has been particularly influential. The organization eventually grew to one thousand members, with three hundred each from the continents of Asia, Africa, and Latin America. He served as the co-coordinator of organization for many years, during which time the focus of the organization gradually changed from a tri-regional one to a more global one. Amin's contributions at the FTM have been quite remarkable. At the level of both action and high-level scholarship, he has succeeded in breaking out of the usual insularity that marks Africa as a geographical space, and also in focusing on the world as a central site of reflection. Amin's scholarship is not merely concerned with the widespread effects of African underdevelopment. He argues that the causes of African and third-world underdevelopment generally can be traced to entrenched structural and historical conditions which continue to have a global impact. The Third World Forum also provides an avenue for engaging critiques of global capitalism. The organization eventually formed partnerships with similar-minded forces in the North.

Accordingly, and in conjunction with such forces, the World Forum for Alternatives (WFA) was established in Cairo in 1997. The Third World Forum became a member of the new organization, which has other partners in Europe such as the Centre d'Etudes Anti-Imperialistes (Center for the Study of and Initiatives in International Solidarity; CEDETIM), based in France.

The WFA was instrumental in organizing an event as a countermeasure to the goals and principles of the World Economic Forum meeting in Davos, Switzerland in 1999. The WFA's rallying cry on that occasion was "at the Davos for the billionaires you will also find a Davos for the underprivileged." This initial event attracted considerable media and international attention, despite the fact that the newly formed organization was still in its infancy. The direct outcome of this success was the formation of the World Social Forum by Brazilian associates in Porto Alegre and other similar organizations in Hyderabad in Asia and a European counterpart in Florence. These various organizations have been able to articulate powerful strands of opposition to neoliberal ideology and global capitalism. It is therefore erroneous to think that the antiglobalization movement was initiated in Seattle, as is often posited. Rather, the movement was started by third-world scholars and activists, such as Amin, from the continents of Africa, Asia, and Latin America. Amin also argues that neoliberalism in its present formation is not sustainable and in fact can only thrive on a foundation of negativity. He argues that the US pursuit of a policy of permanent war is primarily a reflection of the inherent violence of neoliberal ideology.

Samir Amin has been able to develop a key concept as an alternative to global capitalism. He proposes the concept of "delinking" as a way out of the impasse caused by neoliberalism. Delinking is indeed quite an interesting concept. The growth of global capitalism has widened enormously the gulf between the Northern hemisphere and the Global South (Africa, Central and Latin America, and much of Asia). Amin argues the idea of the poor regions of the South attempting to develop along models fashioned in the West is not the answer to third-world developmental problems. He also argues that delinking is not meant to lead to third-world parochialism. Instead, it serves as an alternative to the numerous failed economic models of the Bretton-Woods institutional order by supporting a program in which the North adjusts itself to developmental processes in the South. Amin concludes that this is a viable alternative to the current global order, which continues to perpetuate the divide between the center and the peripheries.

Samir Amin's contributions to the intellectual traditions of Africa are as numerous as they are diverse. During the course of his eventful career, he has published over thirty books that mainly focus on the historical as well as structural conditions that have led to the underdevelopment of the African continent. However, the reach and impact of his intellectual production are indeed global. Amin was an early convert to Marxism and this has infused his scholarship with a socialist orientation. He also decries the effects and ravages of global capitalism on regions of both the North and the South. Amin's invaluable contributions to humanity accordingly are not limited to only the vast scope of his astounding scholarship. He has also been intimately involved in forging new postmodern traditions of global activism that are now reshaping the world in both implicit and explicit ways.

BIBLIOGRAPHY

Amin, Samir. *Capitalism in the Age of Globalization.* London and New York: Zed Books, 1997.

Amin, Samir. *Empire of Chaos.* New York: Monthly Review Press, 1993.

Amin, Samir. *Eurocentrism.* 2d ed. New York: Monthly Review Press, 2010.

Amin, Samir. *The Liberal Virus: Permanent War and the Americanization of the World.* New York: Monthly Review Press, 2004.

Amin, Samir. *Specters of Capitalism: A Critique of Current Intellectual Fashions.* New York: Monthly Review Press, 1998.

Amin, Samir. *The World We Wish to See: Revolutionary Objectives in the Twenty-First Century.* New York: Monthly Review Press, 2008.

SANYA OSHA

Amina (c. 1533–c. 1583), *sarauniya* (queen) of Zazzau (present-day Zaria, Nigeria), was the legendary warrior and state builder who established the kingdom of Zazzau as a major Hausa state in the sixteenth century. Also known as Aminatu, she may have been born about 1533, but this is uncertain. She was the eldest daughter of Bakwa Turunku, the twenty-second *sarki* (ruler) of Zazzau (now Zaria). There are conflicting accounts about the gender of this ruler. Historian Abubakr Sa'ad believes that she was a woman and argues that she very likely was the *sarauniya* of Kufena, the predecessor kingdom to Zazzau. Among the estates under her authority was Turunku. When an interregnum occurred, she was either appointed ruler or seized control of Kufena and in 1537 moved her capital to Zazzau, which she named after her second daughter, to secure land for expansion and better water supplies. Her reign was mostly peaceful, except for a failed military invasion from the south by the Jukun of Kwarafara kingdom.

According to *Amina Sarauniya Zazzau* (1954), even in childhood Amina would crawl to the sarki's court whenever it was in session and remain there throughout the daily proceedings. Thus she acquired the skills of governance, diplomacy, and warfare, while other girls learned domestic skills and prepared for their futures as wives and mothers. Amina's political career began after Bakwa Turunku relocated her court to Zazzau. As the first born of the ruler, she was appointed as the *magajiya*, an honorific designating the eldest daughter of the ruler. At this time she was a teenager, perhaps no more than sixteen years old, the age when most Hausa girls would have been married. According to tradition, Amina had many suitors, but she rejected them to concentrate on politics and war. Later tales elaborate on this, alleging that during her military conquests she took a lover in every town and had them beheaded the morning after they spent the night with her.

It is uncertain when Bakwa died. The chronicle *Daura Makas Sariki* (Arnett, 1910) states that she reigned for thirty years, but the king list published in the *Gazetteer of Zaria Province* (1920) gives a much shorter reign of only three years (1536–1539). She was succeeded by Ibrahim (a.k.a. Ibrahima), who reigned for twenty-seven years (1539–1566), followed by Karama (a.k.a. Karma), Bakwa's younger brother, who reigned for a decade (1566–1576). Unlike his immediate predecessors, Karama favored expansion and aggressively pursued war. Amina became one of his most enthusiastic and able lieutenants, always among the first to arrive at the palace with her horsemen when the war drums sounded. Before long she was acknowledged as Zazzau's leading warrior and one of its wealthiest officials, because of the spoils and slaves acquired through war and the estates she already possessed in her capacity as *magajiya*.

When Karama died in 1576, some traditions state that Amina was the logical choice to succeed him. Almost immediately she set out to expand Zazzau's boundaries even further and embarked on a series of military campaigns. Expansion toward the north was blocked by the rising powers of Kano and Katsina, while the difficult terrain of the central Nigerian plateau prevented expansion toward the east. Thus her army attacked the peoples to the southwest and southeast. In *Infaku'l Maisuri* (1820 CE; English translation, 1922), Sultan Mohammed Bello described her conquests as "the most extensive of all the countries of Hausa," reaching the "Sea in the South and the West," which probably meant the confluence of the Niger and Benue rivers. Her conquests included Nupe, Bauchi, and Yauri. According to Bello, even Katsina and Kano paid her tribute, but historians of these two emirates insist that there is no documentary evidence of this.

Defeated leaders sent her tribute and luxurious gifts. The *Chronicle of Abuja* (1952) states that the ruler of Nupe sent her forty eunuchs and ten thousand kola nuts, marking the first time that these commodities appeared in Hausaland. Her era is associated with the rise of strong states, the growth of the trans-Saharan caravan trade, and slavery in Hausaland. Traditional accounts relate that she built huge earthen walls around her war camps and the towns she conquered. These became known as *Ganuwar Amina* (Amina's walls), a name still borne by the ruins of such fortifications, although archaeologists have determined construction dates considerably before, and sometimes after, her time. According to accounts of her exploits, she dominated much of Hausaland for thirty-four years and died in battle at Attagara, a place thought to be near present-day Idah. Her body was not recovered.

Very little is known about her style of governance, but Harris relates a Yauri tradition that provides intriguing clues. It claims that when Amina and her "thousand horsemen" arrived in their land, she advised them to appoint a sarki rather than continue living with no overt ruler and also to develop a new identity as *Yaurawa*, based on the term, *yaura*, which referred to the strips of dried meat they offered her as tribute. Previously, the Hausa called the inhabitants *rasawa*, which translates as "the lost."

Two questions arise about the life of Amina. First, did she in fact rule Zazzau? The *Chronicle of Abuja* and the two king lists published by Arnett do not include her name among the rulers, even though local traditions refer to her as ruling the lands she conquered. Certainly, at this time capitals and courts moved in tandem with a ruler at war. It is possible that she had assigned a male relative to act on her behalf in her absence from Zazzau and his (or their) name(s) may have become incorporated in the official lists with the spread of Islamic and colonial ideas about leadership and gender. Moreover, while the title *sarauniya* does mean "queen," it is also a generic term for a female chief or organizational head, which could possibly be adapted to conditions of military conquest.

Second, when did Amina hold sway in Hausaland? Contemporary historians of northern Nigeria believe that her military exploits took place in the sixteenth century. They have rejected previous claims of a fifteenth-century date, based on a reference in the *Kano Chronicle* that asserts that her state-building occurred during the reign of Sarki Dauda of Kano (c. 1421–1438).

Amina's life story has inspired a growing culture industry, one imbued with a strong romantic overtone that ignores existing scholarship. This includes sculpture, paintings, a postage stamp, a play, a glossy coffee-table volume devoted to African queens, children's anthologies of black women leaders, as well as the proliferation of biographical accounts on the Internet. Although Amina's biography has not yet attracted the scholarly attention received by Queen Daura, the legendary female progenitor of the Hausa states, the work of Heidi Nast on pre-jihadist female roles in Kano, and that of Antoinette Tidjani Alou on the *sarauniya* (Fr. *sarraounia*) title in Niger, demonstrate important methodologies for expanding our understanding of the legacy of female leadership and its importance in West African history.

[*See also* Kimpa Vita, Dona Beatriz; *and* Nzinga a Mbandi.]

BIBLIOGRAPHY

Abubakr Sa'ad. "Queen Amina of Zaria." In *Nigerian Women: A Historical Perspective,* edited by Bolanle Awe, pp. 12–26. Ibadan: Bookcraft; Lagos: Sankore, 2001.

Adeleye, R.A. "Hausaland and Borno 1600–1800." In *History of West Africa,* edited by J.F.A. Ajayi and M. Crowder, 2d ed., vol. I, pp. 556–601. London: Longman, 1987.

Alou, Antoinette Tidjani. "Niger and Sarraounia: One Hundred Years of Forgetting Female Leadership." *Research in African Literatures* 40 (2009): 42–56.

Anonymous. *Amina Sarauniyar Zazzau.* Zaria, Nigeria: Gaskiya Corp., 1954.

Arnett, E.J. "A Hausa Chronicle." *Journal of the Royal African Society* 9 (1910): 161–167.

Arnett, E.J, trans. *The Rise of the Sokoto Fulani. Being a Paraphrase and in Some Parts a Translation of the Infaku'l Maisuri of Sultan Mohammed Bello.* Kano: Kano Emirate Printing Dept., 1922.

Harris, P.G. "Notes on Yauri (Sokoto Province), Nigeria." *Journal of the Royal Anthropological Institute of Great Britain and Ireland* 60 (1930): 283–334.

Hassan, Alhaji, and Mallam Shuaibu. *A Chronicle of Abuja.* Revised and enlarged edition. Translated by Frank Heath. Lagos: Caxton Press (West Africa) Ltd., 1962; originally published for the Abuja Native Administration by Ibadan University Press, 1952.

Nast, Heidi J. *Concubines and Power: Five Hundred Years in a Northern Nigerian Palace.* Minneapolis: University of Minnesota Press, 2005.

Nigeria, Northern Province. *Gazetteer of Zaria Province.* Comp. E. J. Arnett. London, Dunstable, and Waterford: Waterlow & Sons, 1920.

Palmer, H. R., trans. "The Kano Chronicle." *The Journal of the Royal Anthropological Institute of Great Britain and Ireland* 38 (1908): 58–98.

Smith, Abdullahi. "Some Notes on the History of Zazzau Under the Hausa Kings." In *Zaria and Its Region: A Nigerian Savanna City and Its Environs,* edited by M. J. Mortimore, pp. 82-101. Occasional Paper No. 4, Department of Geography, Ahmadu Bellow University, Zaria. Published for the 14th Annual Conference of the Nigerian Geographical Association, Zaria, January 1970.

Smith, M.G. *The Affairs of Daura.* Berkeley, Calif.: University of California Press, 1978.

LaRAY DENZER

Amina bint al-Hajj ʿAbd al-Latif (fl. 1802–1812 CE), Moroccan female scribe, jurisprudent, and scholar, was a well-known inhabitant of nineteenth-century Tetouan. Her full name was Amina bint al-Hajj ʿAbd al-Latif ibn Ahmad al-Hajjaj.

Morocco had a long tradition of manuscript production, rivaled only by Egypt. Manuscripts in Arabic were created and copied there from the eighth down to the nineteenth centuries, when the arrival of lithography and machine printing virtually put an end to the professional scribe. Although the profession of scribe was normally the province of men in most parts of the Islamic world, in the western parts—Spain and North Africa—women played an important role. In the tenth century there were said to be a thousand women scribes in Cordova who were engaged in copying out Qur'ans. The names of some of these scribes are known, but little other information about them is available.

However, in a few cases we do have more information about women scribes. Amina bint al-Hajj ʿAbd al-Latif is a case in point. She was an eminent inhabitant of Tetouan during the reign of Sultan Sulayman (1793–1822) who sometimes worked as a scribe. Two works copied by her are known: the last part of al-Mundhiri's *Targhib wa'l-tarhib,* a collection of sayings of the Prophet in favor of good works and against evil ones, dated 1802, and a copy of the Qur'an dated 1812. The latter she signed in the most devout and humble way: "This blessed volume ... was copied ... by the hand of His (God's) wretched, servile, sinful scribe, of the nation (*umma*) of God, and of His nation, the lowliest, and most in need of Him during her life and for what remains of it." She was in fact an important religious scholar, *faqiha* (jurisprudent), social worker, and giver of advice who specialized in dealing with the problems of the women of Tetouan, which must have been marital, financial, legal, and sexual, as well as spiritual. According to the *Tarikh Titwan* (The History of Tetouan) by Muhammad Da'ud (1908–1984), she was taught by her father, who was a well-known scholar and *faqih* and instructed her in the Qur'an, Arabic, jurisprudence, (*fiqh*) and *hadith*, the teachings and traditions of the Prophet Muhammad.

Unlike most male jurisprudents, Amina was unmarried and remained so her entire life. She was buried at her home in the *Hawmat al-Mataymar* (Metámar Quarter), where her tomb was much visited, no doubt by her former female charges.

Among the descendants of the refugees from al-Andalus who settled in Tetouan, Fez and Marrakesh were several women who made their living, or supplemented their income, by working as scribes. The Moroccan historian Ibn 'Abd al-Malik (1237–1303) mentions several in his *Dhayl wa'l-Takmila* (The Supplement and Completion) : Sa'ida Sa'da bint Muhammad ibn Fayyuruh al-Umawi and her unnamed younger sister, whose ancestors came from Tudela in Spain, worked as scribes in Marrakesh; Warqa' was another descendant of a family who came from Toledo. She lived and worked in Fez and died in 1145–1146. We know little about them, other than their names, which were written at the ends of the manuscripts they copied.

Women scribes continued to work in Morocco until the end of the nineteenth century. For example, Fatima bint al-Shaykh Ahmad al-Badawi of Fez copied the *Sahih al-Bukhari* (a famous collection of sayings of the Prophet Muhammad) in 1886–1887, signing herself *khadimat al-'ilm* ("the servant of knowledge"). We know that her father was the director of a *zawiya* (a kind of retreat) in Fez, though not much more.

BIBLIOGRAPHY

Dā'ūd, Muhammad. *Ta'rīkh Ti.twān*. Tetouan, Morocco, 1959–1998.

al-Manūnī, Muhammad. *Ta'rīkh al-wirāqa al-maghribiyya*. Rabat, Morocco, 1991.

DAVID JAMES

Amo, Anton William (c. 1700–c. 1759), the first African and black professor and philosopher of the European Enlightenment, was born in the coastal Ghanaian town of Axim. The background of his travel to Europe can only be speculated about. It is only certain that Amo was given over to Herzog Anton Ulrich von Wolfenbuettel-Braunschweig in 1707 as a slave of the Dutch West Indies Company. At that time he could have been eight years old, because he was baptized on 29 July 1708 in Braunschweig. In addition to German, Amo could speak Hebrew, Greek, Latin, French, Dutch, and English.

In 1727, Amo entered the University of Halle, where he studied philosophy and law. On 28 November 1729, he presented his first disputation, *De jure maurorum in Europa* (*On the Rights of Black Peoples in Europe*), which unfortunately remains lost. In this work, Amo acts as an advocate of the equality of all people and peoples independent of their race. As a philosopher, Amo doubtlessly felt personally confronted by the central paradoxes of the European Enlightenment, specifically the immoral nature of slavery and the question of the legality of racial discrimination: the human trafficking to which he himself fell victim was not only irreconcilable with the laws of nature and human rights but also with the Enlightenment's spirit of humanism and its rationality. If this scientific lecture (which received no public comment) had not been lost, it could have doubtlessly contributed special meaning not only for political philosophy and legal theory but also for international law. It could have provided the basis for much intercultural and international debate about human rights, protection of minorities, racism, tolerance, migration, xenophobia, social exclusion, and so on. Amo was eager to depict the situation of people from Africa who were brought into European society with unparalleled arbitrariness and abuse.

In 1729, Amo left Halle and moved to Wittenberg, receiving his master's degree in philosophy in 1730. He then studied physiology, mathematics, medicine, and pneumatology (known as psychology today) at the University of Wittenberg, receiving a degree in medicine and science in 1733. Through his study of experimental natural sciences Amo became a materialist as well as a staunch opponent of Idealism, which was made clear in his doctoral thesis in 1734, *De humane mentis apatheia* (*On the Absence of Sensation in the Human Mind*). Amo developed his own materialistic position, without falling victim to atheism or radical empiricism.

In 1736 Amo published his lectures held at the University of Halle under the title *Tractatus de arte sobrie et accurate philosophandi* (*Treatise on the Art of Philosophizing Soberly and Accurately*). This work deals intensively with questions of ethics, morals, metaphysics, hermeneutics, aesthetics, and politics. Here Amo argues that philosophy is always related to knowledge. In addition, he states that each philosophical finding must be directed toward perfection, because perfection has its own destiny regarding the purpose of knowledge. A finding is only perfect if it is also useful. The purpose of philosophy therefore, in accordance with its usefulness, consists of the preservation and perfecting of the human species. By perfecting, Amo means natural as well as moral perfection. Natural perfection aims at self-preservation and safeguarding a basic existence as well as the just and intelligent actions that are associated with it, that is, intellectual exercises for the sake of truth. Moral perfection, however, refers to wisdom in the sense of conformity of knowledge with the Divine Being and has eternal bliss as its goal. The basis of the object in Amo's terms is the certainty of recognition that lies in itself. Consequently, part of this philosophy is the recognition of objects, that is, the understanding and comprehension of an object according to its unchanging nature. This means that one can only accurately recognize an object if one does not perceive or understand it in a way that contradicts its very essence. An object is then something that exists somewhat in relation to its own perception. It owes its existence to divine and human intention. In other words, the object itself, the activity of the soul, and the perception of it are all made available by intention. For Amo, hermeneutics were no mere interpretation philosophy, but rather an art that attends to the methodical understanding and reasoning of the object to be investigated. In this regard, he assigned the interpreter the tasks of (1) preserving mindfulness, (2) practicing contemplation, and (3) keeping track of the object of investigation. To maintain his or her credibility, however, the interpreter also had to note his or her credentials (sources) and witness (author) truthfully and not tacitly deny these references. Thus, without the trinity of author, text, and interpreter, hermeneutics are neither credible nor authentic. The interpreter is only credible if he or she emphasizes the author's originality and also seeks only the objective truth without partisanship or false credentials. Nevertheless, Amo warns against doctrinaire interpretation that merely follows the rules of logic and grammar when many questions relevant to knowledge remain unresolved.

Amo moved to Jena in 1739 and taught at the university there. Probably in 1747, Amo sailed to his native land. When exactly he died remains a mystery. In 1782 he was named in the memoirs of David Henrij Galandat, a Swiss ship's doctor who was serving a Dutch shipping company and reported on Amo's harsh life after his return to Axim.

BIBLIOGRAPHY

Amo, Anton William. *Tractacus de Arte Sobrie et Accurate Philosophandi.* Halle, Germany: ex Officina Kitleriana, 1736.

Amo, Anton William. *De Humanae Mentis "Apatheia."* Wittenberg, Germany: ex Officina Schlomacheriana, 1734.

Brentjes, Burchard. *Anton Wilhelm Amo. Der Schwarze Philosoph in Halle* [*The Black Philosopher in Halle*]. Leipzig, Germany: Köhler & Amelang, 1976.

Mabe, Jacob Emmanuel. *Wilhelm Anton Amo interkulturell gelesen* [*Wilhelm Anton Amo Read Interculturally*]. Nordhausen, Germany: Verlag Traugott Bautz, 2007.

JACOB EMMANUEL MABE

Amrouche, Fadhma (1882–1967), Algerian writer, was the illegitimate daughter of an impoverished, illiterate Berber peasant woman. A Muslim by birth, she converted to Christianity, produced one of the first, if not the first, autobiographies written by an Algerian woman, became a naturalized French citizen, and raised two children who became well-known French literati: Marguerite Taos Amrouche (known as Taos Amrouche), a poet, singer, and novelist, and Jean Amrouche, a writer and poet. But the circumstances of her early life were unpromising at best.

Amrouche was born in a remote village in the rugged mountains of Kabylia in northeastern Algeria in 1882. When the villagers discovered that Fadhma's mother, Aïni, was pregnant out of wedlock, they attempted to kill her as an adulteress, as custom cruelly dictated. But plucky Aïni placed herself under the protection of the local French colonial magistrate and laid charges against fellow villagers, including male family members, thus saving Fadhma's life. After the child's birth, her mother, a Muslim, took her to a Catholic convent so that she would have a better life than her mother believed she could provide. The presence of missionaries in the region is important to Amrouche's story. Colonial proselytizing among the Muslim population increased with Charles Lavigerie's (1825–1892) appointment in 1867 as archbishop of Algiers. Lavigerie, founder of the White Fathers and the Sisters of Our Lady of African Missions, or White Sisters, initiated an intense conversion campaign in the Kabylia, since it was wrongly believed that the Berbers retained elements of their ancient Christian belief and thus were more amenable to conversion than other Muslims. When the mission school did not work out satisfactorily, Amrouche's mother entrusted her to the care of secular French educators in a boarding school for girls near Fort National. Fadhma spent ten years at the school under the care of Madame Malaval, who tirelessly promoted indigenous female education. Amrouche became one of the first Kabyle girls to learn to read and write, and she earned her "certificate of study." But colonial administrators later closed the school, claiming that educating Muslim girls was a waste of money since it only produced women rejected by both societies, at best. At worst, they claimed, education bred native prostitutes, as educated Muslim women, shunned by their communities, turned to this option in desperation.

Devastated by the fact that her education had come to an end, Fadhma found work at a French Catholic mission run by the White Sisters. There she met her husband, Belkacem, also a Berber and already a convert, whom she married in 1899; she then converted to Catholicism. At first, the couple attempted to live with Belkacem's clan in the great extended family household in the Kabylia, but the fact that they were Christians, while the rest of the family remained Muslim, posed problems. As their economic situation deteriorated for lack of work, they moved with their growing number of children to Tunis in the years before World War I. Fadhma eventually bore eight children, many of whom did not outlive her. During World War II, Fadhma and most of the family were in Tunis, while her daughter, Marie-Louise, was stranded in Spain. Heartbroken by the death of several of her other younger children and agonized by the separation from her only daughter, Fadhma found solace in composing a poem for her, "The Swallow" ("L'Hirondelle").

In 1946, her son Jean, by then a recognized writer in France, asked Amrouche to write her memoirs. Although she agreed, she would not consider publishing the work until after the death of her husband, Belkacem, in 1958. She was also known for her talent as a singer and for possessing an inexhaustible repository of Kabyle oral traditions—songs, poetry, legends, and lore then in grave danger of disappearing.

Indeed, it was Fadhma who instilled in her daughter, Marie-Louise, a love for Berber oral traditions. Marie-Louise translated tales and proverbs passed down from her mother, as well as Fadhma's own poems, publishing them in a French collection appropriately entitled Le Grain Magique (The Magic Grain) in 1960; she also penned a number of other works, beginning with her novel in 1947, and became a well-known singer.

After the passing of her husband, Amrouche moved from North Africa to France. She died in Brittany in 1967; her memoirs were published posthumously the next year in Paris. In 1946, upon completing her memoir, Fadhma wrote to her son Jean: "I bequeath you this story, which is the account of my life, for you to do what you like with, after my death. This story is true, not one episode has been invented, all that happened before my birth was told to me by my mother as soon as I was old enough to understand. I have written this story because I think it deserves to be known to all of you . . . I wrote this story in memory of my beloved mother and of Madame Malaval who gave me my spiritual life [i.e., the gift of reading, writing, and education]" (Amrouche, My Life Story, 193).

From a poor Berber village in Algeria, to Tunisia, and then France, Fadhma Amrouche's life odyssey constitutes a unique chapter in the history of women, education, and colonialism; it embodies both the harsh realities of native society and the contradictions of French Algeria, particularly as they were experienced by women of humble origins. Amrouche's story shows that there existed small openings in the repressive armature of patriarchy that some women exploited to gain personal agency. Most importantly, Fadhma's efforts to preserve Berber oral traditions fed into Berber national identity, which was initially directed at the French colonial regime. After independence in 1962, however, the Algerian state attempted to suppress minority cultural expressions among the Berbers, as well as the rights of women in general. In the late twentieth and early twenty-first centuries, Amrouche was revered by Kabyle nationalists as one of the mothers of the movement because of her key role in saving and transmitting oral traditions that constitute the core of Berber cultural identity.

[See also Amrouche, Marguerite Taos.]

BIBLIOGRAPHY

Amrouche, Fadhma. Histoire de ma vie. Paris: Maspero, 1968.

Amrouche, Fadhma. *My Life Story: The Autobiography of a Berber Woman*. Translated by Dorothy S. Blair. English translation of *Histoire de ma vie*, first published in 1968. New Brunswick, N.J.: Rutgers University Press, 1989.

Amrouche, Jean. *Chants Berbères de Kabylie*. Tunis, Tunisia: Monomotapa, 1939.

Direche-Slimani, Karima. *Chrétiens de Kabylie: Histoire d'une Communauté sans Histoire. Une Action Missionnaire de l'Algérie Coloniale*. Paris: Bouchène, 2004.

JULIA A. CLANCY-SMITH

Amrouche, Marguerite Taos (1913–1976), Algerian writer and singer who brought Kabyle folk music of the rural Berber community to international audiences and one of the earliest modern Algerian female novelists, was born Marie-Louise Amrouche in Tunisia to a family of Roman Catholic converts who had fled Algeria to escape persecution. Her mother, Fadhma Amrouche, also a writer and musician, was an early influence. Amrouche adopted the nom de plume Marguerite Taos to underscore the influence of her mother; Marguerite was her mother's Christian name, which the latter was not allowed to use by the Catholic Church, ostensibly because she had not been baptized properly.

Despite her exile, the family returned to Algeria on prolonged visits, from which Amrouche and her brother Jean Amrouche, a poet, got acquainted with the oral literature of their native Kabyle Berber people. Amrouche obtained her *brevet supérieur* in Tunis in 1934 and went to France the following year to join the École Normale at Sèvres, working briefly as an assistant at a boarding school in Radès. From 1936, she collected, transcribed, and interpreted Kabyle songs, in collaboration with her brother Jean and her mother. She presented her repertoire in Paris and in Munich in 1937–1938. While at the Congrès de Chant de Fès in 1939, she received a scholarship to study at the Casa Velasquez in Spain. She conducted a comparative study of Spanish and Berber folk songs, making her first public appearance at the First Congress of Moroccan Music in 1939.

Amrouche's debut novel, *Jacinthe noire* (Black Hyacinth), was published in 1947, eight years after she finished writing it. A coming-of-age story, the novel describes the conflict of cultures in the wake of African contact with the West through the story of a young Tunisian girl who is sent to France for studies and encounters prejudice and differences in culture and lifestyle. She finished its sequel in 1950, but it was not until 1960 that *Rue des tambourins* (Street of the Tambourines) saw the light of day. Capturing intense alienation and dislocation of the colonial subject, the novel is based on the author's recollections growing up in Tunis and features a fearsome matriarch trying to marshal her extended family through a period of cultural and religious turmoil. The two novels express a yearning for the past, but the narrators are aware that it is impossible to recover "home" again.

Although a gifted writer, Amrouche experienced difficulties publishing her work. According to Clarisse Zimra (2002), Algerian female writer Assia Djebar observed in a 1988 public lecture that Taos Amrouche's brother, Jean Amrouche, could have been behind his sister's troubles in gaining critical acceptance in the tightly knit Parisian world of letters. Although they collected Kabyle folklore together in the 1930s, the work appeared under Jean's name when it was published in 1939. Her bold depiction of women characters and narrators unafraid to explore female sexuality did not sit well with the Maghrebi literary establishment. Her other two novels—*L'amant imaginaire* (The Imaginary Lover, 1975) and *Solitude ma mère* (Loneliness, My Mother, 1995)—took twenty years each to get a publisher. *L'amant imaginaire* deals with male–female relationships in the context of postcolonial alienation and homelessness. The narrator focuses on the betrayal by a man, who takes her virginity and abandons her. In self-accusation, the heroine suggests that she suffers her predicament because she has abandoned tranquil rural life in traditional Algeria. Yet it is clear that despite her nostalgia, she is aware that she cannot recover the uncontaminated Kabylia.

Published posthumously, *Solitude ma mère* presents a heroine who tries to unlock the predicaments of her adult life by exploring her childhood. As in her other works, it is suggested that the unrecoverable past would be the only place the modern Algerian woman can be at peace with herself. Marguerite Taos Amrouche's best-known work is *Le Grain magique* (The Magic Grain), which was published in 1966. It is a collection of legends, folk songs, poems, and proverbs from the Kabylie. She recorded six phonograph albums of her mother's songs, which she performed across Europe and registered in her name at the French copyright agency Société des Auteurs, Compositeurs, et Editeurs de Musique (Society of Authors, Composers, and Editors of Music, SACEM).

After Algerian independence, Amrouche's performance of Kabyle songs was seen as an expression of precolonial Algeria that demarcated Africa from the West. When the Senegalese poet, politician, and high priest of the negritude movement, Léopold Sédar Senghor, saw Amrouche perform at the First World Festival of Negro Arts in 1966, he remarked that the song bore witness to the unity of the whole Africa. But back in Algeria, the music was seen as an epitome of rising Berber ethnic subnationalism. She was not allowed to represent Algeria at the Pan-African Cultural Conference of 1969.

Like her novels, the music brought in sharp relief the contradictions of postcolonial artists. In the songs, she aspired to recover the vanishing voice of the Kabyle, but she also took liberties with her mother's originals. According to Jane Goodman, although as a singer Amrouche claimed that her vocal style was instinctive and as unadulterated by modern technique as the voice of a Kabyle indigenous singer, her music is said by some scholars to be unrecognizable in rural Algeria. By contrast, Westerners would easily compare it with European traditional chants. She saw herself as a cultural ambassador linking her native Maghreb to Europe, especially France. She performed the music in metropolitan venues, such as the Théâtre de la Ville in Paris and prestigious cathedrals across Europe. Trained in Western classical music, she oriented the Berber music to both the requirements of the Western academy and nationalism in Africa.

Besides her autobiographical fiction and music career, Amrouche produced programs for French radio and television, including *Chants sauvés de l'oubli* (*Songs Saved from Oblivion*) and *Hommage au chant profond* (*Homage to a Profound Song*). She died on 2 April 1976 in Saint-Michel-l'Observatoire, France.

[*See also* Amrouche, Fadhma; Djebar, Assia; *and* Senghor, Léopold Sédar.]

BIBLIOGRAPHY

Brahimi, Denise. *Taos Amrouche, romancière.* Paris: Joelle Losfeld, 1995.

Goodman, Jane E. *Berber Culture on the World Stage: From Village to Video.* Bloomington: Indiana University Press, 2005.

Zimra, Clarisse. "Amrouche, Taos." In *Encyclopedia of African Literature.* Ed. Simon Gikandi. London: Routledge, 2002, pp. 22–23.

EVAN MWANGI

Amu, Ephraim Koku (1899–1995), Ghanaian musicologist, teacher, and preacher, was born on 13 September 1899 in Peki Avetile in the Volta region of Ghana. He was one of the six children of Stephen Amuyao (popularly known as Papa Stefano in his community) and Sarah Akoram Amma. He was named Koku (Kwaku in Akan) because he was born on a Wednesday. Amu was baptized Ephraim by the Reverend Father Rudolf Mallet of the Bremen Mission, now the Evangelical Presbyterian Church, in Peki.

His father was a farmer and woodcarver, who made musical instruments, among other artifacts. Native music, drumming, and dancing were thus an integral part of Amu's daily life in his formative years and would greatly influence his future career. He began his basic education in the Bremen Mission School in 1906 at the age of six. Initially reluctant to attend, he was placed under the care of an older schoolgirl so he could learn to read and write. With her help he progressed impressively and soon completed primary school. His love of music was encouraged at the Bremen Middle Boarding School, which he attended from 1912 to 1915. A music teacher there, Theodore Karl Ntem, impressed Amu so much with his mastery of the organ that Amu approached him for lessons on how to play. The teacher obliged and asked Amu to work on his farm every Saturday as payment.

After passing his Standard Seven School Leaving Examination, Amu was admitted to the Basel Mission Seminary at Abetifi in the Eastern Region of Ghana to train as a teacher and preacher from 1916 to 1917. His dedication to his calling was evident in his willingness to walk from his home to the college, a journey that took five days at that time, when there were no roads or railway facilities. At the college, Amu was instructed in the theory of music and sight singing. He graduated from the college as a Presbyterian trained teacher-catechist and moved to Peki Blengo Middle Boarding School, his former school, to teach. He taught there until 1925 when he was transferred to the Scottish Mission Seminary at Akropong, where he taught music, nature study, agriculture, and the Ewe language. In 1933, Amu was dismissed from the seminary at Akropong for defying the orders of his superiors not to express or teach African culture in his work as a teacher and preacher. This followed two consecutive occasions where Amu appeared before the congregation at church to preach in his *kente* (traditional Ghanaian cloth) attire. He was also accused of teaching students of the seminary using unorthodox methods such as singing local songs and using local musical instruments, which the European missionaries viewed as pagan.

Amu soon received another offer to teach, however. And, after some time at the prestigious

Achimota School, he earned a scholarship to study at the Royal College of Music (RCM) in London, where he pursued mainly counterpoint and harmony. He graduated in 1941 with a diploma (the Royal College of Music Associate). He returned and taught for a while at the Achimota Teacher Training College before being reassigned to the School for Music. When in 1951 the Achimota College became part of the newly established Kumasi College of Technology (KCT), Amu moved to Kumasi to supervise the Music Department, which had then received its first batch of eight students who were transferred from Achimota to Kumasi. In 1958, however, the specialist course was moved from KCT to Winneba, but Amu remained in Kumasi researching traditional songs and materials in Asante, Brong Ahafo, Kwahu, Akuapem, and other languages.

When the Institute of African Studies (IAS) of the University of Ghana established the School of Music, Dance, and Drama, Amu joined as a senior research fellow; he taught and researched there until his retirement in 1971. During his career he was renowned for his composition of many Ghanaian songs, notably "Yen Ara Asasi Ni," which is an alternative to the Ghana National Anthem, and "From Gambaga to Accra," the Achimota School anthem. He is also credited with the development of two local Ghanaian musical instruments: Antenteben (bamboo flute) and Odurugya (cane-flute). His first publication was *The 25 African Songs*, published in 1932. He also won several national awards, the highest being the Order of the Volta, one of the most important honors awarded by the government of Ghana. Amu also earned honorary doctorates in music from the University of Ghana in 1965 and the Kwame Nkrumah University of Science and Technology in 1977. He died in his sleep on 2 January 1995 and was survived by his wife, Beatrice Martina Amu, and five children.

A courageous and visionary musicologist, Amu's life work was to gain national and international recognition for Ghana's rich cultural heritage, as expressed in its music.

BIBLIOGRAPHY

Agyemang, Fred. *Amu the African: A Study in Vision and Courage.* Accra, Ghana: Asempa Publishers, Christian Council of Ghana, 1988.

Vieta, T. Kojo. *The Flagbearers of Ghana: Profiles of One Hundred Distinguished Ghanaians.* Accra, Ghana: Ena Publications, 1999.

MAXWELL AKANSINA AZIABAH

Anatsui, El. *See* El Anatsui.

Andani II, Ya-Na Yakubu (1945–2002), king of Dagombas and victim of murder at Yendi, the capital of the Dagomba traditional area, was born in August 1945 at Saganarigu, a suburb of Tamale in present-day northern Ghana. His father was Andani Yakubu, also the king of Dagbon, who reigned from 1968 to 1969, and his mother was Zenabu Mahama, who hailed from Savelugu. He was named after his grandfather, Na Yakubu I (1824–1849). He was the first son of his father, who had about thirty children, and the only child of his mother. He attended Yendi Primary and Middle schools and taught as a pupil teacher for several years.

He became the Ya-Na, the title given to the king of the Dagombas, in 1974. The previous incumbent, Ya-Na Mahamadu Abdulai IV (1969–1974), was said to have been improperly installed as king. The matter was contested in court amid great tension, and the Acheampong military government set up the Justice Ollenu Committee to investigate the matter. Based on the committee's recommendation, the incumbent was removed from office as Ya-Na, and on 1 June 1974, Yakubu Andani was installed as Ya-Na Yakubu II by the kingmakers, in accordance with Dagomba tradition.

Before he became Ya-Na, he had already married three wives; shortly after his inauguration, they were sent to Zohi, a suburb of Yendi, where they were conferred with titles. The first wife obtained the title *Gbanzalun*, the second wife became *Katini*, while the third one was given the title *Sologu*. By the time of his death in March 2002, Ya-Na Yakubu II had twenty-six wives, and each of them was similarly conferred with titles in accordance with Dagomba tradition. The removal of Mahamadu Abdulai IV from office deepened the enmity between the royal members and supporters of Abdulai's lineage, known as Abudu Gate or Abudus, and the royal members and supporters of Andani (also known as Andani Gate or Andanis). In 1986, Ya-Na Yakubu II made an attempt to create unity between the two feuding camps, but it was not successful, as the meeting he called was attended by only his own supporters. In 1987, the Provisional National Defense Council (PNDC) Government assisted in forming a reconciliation committee aimed at creating unity between the two groups. This committee was attended by both sides, but failed to end the tensions. In 1989, fifteen years into his rule, Ya-Na Yakubu II was taken to court by Mahamadu Abdulai. The court ruled that Ya-Na Yakubu II should be removed from office. Yakubu appealed to the Supreme Court, which reversed the ruling of the court of appeal and restored him as Ya-Na.

Yakubu II enjoyed some significant successes during his reign. Between Yendi and Zabzugu (both in the Northern Region), the River Sabali (a tributary of the White Volta) used to flood over its banks, making it difficult for people to transact business at the other side of the river, or transport their farm produce to the market across the river. In 1990, Ya-Nana Yakubu II asked the PNDC government to bridge the river. His request was granted and the river was bridged.

Ya-Na Yakubu II realized that there was a need to elevate the divisional chiefs under him to the status of paramount chiefs. Paramount chiefs controlled a large area or province, whereas divisional chiefs controlled a small area such as a district or a village. Thus, between 1991 and 1993, he spent considerable time trying to accomplish this. Before he undertook this effort, Ya-Na Yakubu II was the only paramount chief in the whole of the Dagomba traditional area. He was the first chief among the then four paramount chiefs in the Northern Region to have undertaken this exercise. Yakubu II's own status was elevated to that of king. Even today, as a result of the Ya-Na's efforts, there are fifty-five paramount chiefs in the Dagomba traditional area.

The creation of paramount chiefs motivated the Konkombas, who were under the domain of the Ya-Na, to request for their own system of paramount chiefs, to be created at Saboba. Initially, Ya-Na Yakubu II refused to grant them this request, and this was one of the causes of the 1994 Konkomba-Dagomba war. The war started at Nakpayili, in the Nanumba traditional area, and spread to the Dagomba and Gonja traditional areas. The war claimed two thousand lives; numerous houses and properties were destroyed. Later, the Ya-Na gave the Konkomba three paramount chiefs.

Ya-Na Yakubu II also attempted to improve the literacy rate in the Northern Region, where the majority of citizens could not read or write. Along with Dr. Abubakari Alhassan, he appealed to the Danish government for some support. In response to this, the Ghana Danish community, which eventually developed a non-governmental organization (NGO) called School for Life, was established in 1995. School for Life designed a free educational program targeted at out-of-school children between the ages of eight and fourteen. The NGO offered a nine-month literacy cycle in the mother tongue, helping children to attain basic literacy skills and then integrate into the formal education system.

Ya-Na Yakubu II was also instrumental in the establishment of the University for Development Studies in Northern Ghana. Plans to set up a university in Northern Ghana had been planned since the Acheampong's regime (1972–1978), but had never been implemented. Yakubu II was unrelenting in his efforts to put pressure on the national government to establish the university. He led several protest delegations to Accra until the university was finally established in 1992.

Throughout his rule, however, the antagonism between the Andani supporters and the Abudu supporters continued to grow. When the deposed chief died in 1988, his remains were buried at the Gbewaa Palace (where the kings of Dagbon are buried). Thereafter, the Abudu group demanded that Ya-Na Yakubu II vacate the palace and allow them to perform funeral rites for Mahamadu Abdulai, which he persistently refused. In view of this, members of the Abudu royal family refused to recognize the Ya-Na as the king and rallied behind their new leader, Bolin-lana. Matters came to a head in March 2002, when it was time to celebrate the *Bugum*, or Fire Festival. Traditionally, it is the prerogative of the chief to commence the rituals and the celebration of festivals. However, before the festival, there was already tension and rumors that the two feuding factions were stockpiling weapons. As a result of this, the District Security Council, in collaboration with the Northern Regional Security Council, banned the celebration of the festival at Yendi on 24 March 2002. However, Ya-Na Yakubu II claimed that he was not informed about the ban and went ahead to commence the celebrations as tradition required of him. Violence broke out between the Andani royal family members and their supporters and the Abudu royal family members and their supporters on 25 March 2002 and continued until 27 March 2002. During this period, all means of communication to Yendi were seized. When the dust finally settled, it was discovered that Ya-Na Yakubu II had been beheaded, and twenty-two other people had been killed.

Ya-Na Yakubu II's murder shocked the nation. It highlighted the continuing relevance of traditional animosities in Ghanaian politics and the potential for such animosities to ignite violence. The violence also came to shape party politics, with the Andanis supporting the opposition National Democratic Congress, while Abudus backed the New Patriotic Party (NPP), which was then in power.

Ya-Na Yakubu II was finally buried in a state funeral in April 2006, once a compromise had been reached between the Andanis and Abudus concerning his successor. He was survived by 103 children.

[*See also* Acheampong, Ignatius Kutu.]

BIBLIOGRAPHY

BBC News. "Ghana King's Burial Ends Long Feud." http://news.bbc.co.uk/2/hi/africa/4906764.stm. 13 April 2006.

Mahama, Ibrahim. *Murder of an African King: Ya-Na Yakubu II*. New York: Vantage Press, 2009.

Sibidow, S.M. *Background on the Yendi Skin Crisis.* Accra, Ghana: Yenzow, 1969.

Staniland, Martin. *The Lions of Dagbon: Political Change in Northern Ghana*. Cambridge, UK: Cambridge University Press, 1975.

Yakubu, Abudulai. *The Abudu-Andani Crisis of Dagbo: A Historical and Legal Perspective of the Yendi Skin Affairs*. Accra, Ghana: MPC Ltd., 2005.

ABDULAI ABUBAKARI

Andrade, Mário Pinto de (1928–1990), Angolan essayist, poet, and militant anticolonialist, was born in Golungo Alto, Kwanza-Norte province, Angola. The son of José Cristino Pinto de Andrade, one of the founders of the African National League (Liga Nacional Africana), and Ana Rodrigues Coelho, he came to be known as a "Citizen of Africa." At two years of age, he moved with his family to Luanda, where he completed his primary and secondary school studies. The proto-nationalist ideas of his father, the growing urbanization of Luanda, and the heterogeneous racial and social atmosphere of the Luanda Catholic seminary constituted the primary elements that marked the formation of his personality.

In 1948 he traveled to Lisbon, where he began a course in classics in the Department of Letters and frequented the Casa dos Estudantes do Império (House of Students of the Empire), an institution created in 1944 to support students from the colonies, which quickly was transformed into a dynamic place for the anticolonial movements of Portuguese Africa, bringing together intellectuals and militants known as the "Generation of Cabral."

Among the activities of that time, Mário Pinto de Andrade, together with Amílcar Cabral, Agostinho Neto, and Francisco José Tenreiro, founded the African Students Center, the objective of which was to promote knowledge of African cultures and societies, integrated under the ambit of the anticolonial struggles. That effort also included

studies of African linguistics and the publication, organized in 1953 with Tenreiro, of the *Caderno de poesia negra de expressão portuguesa* (Book of Black Poetry in Portuguese), the first anthology of poets from the Portuguese African colonies and an essential source in the history of those literatures.

Dating from that time also was his relationship with filmmaker Sarah Ducados, better known as Sarah Maldoror, who made documentaries and films about the war in Angola, including *Sambizanga* (1972), to which Mário contributed by writing the script.

In 1954, persecuted by Polícia Internacional e de Defesa do Estado (PIDE), the Portugese secret police, Andrade moved to Paris, where he collaborated with the prestigious review *Presence Africaine*, which was founded in 1947 by the Senegalese intellectual Alioune Diop, and where he published a variety of articles on literature, nationalism, and anticolonial struggles under the pseudonym Buanga Fele. During that period, he met the major intellectuals of the Francophone Négritude movement, including Léopold Senghor and Aimé Cesaire. Andrade increased his political and cultural activities and participated in the major events of the time, such as the Afro-Asiatic Conference at Bandung in 1955; the First Congress of Negro Writers and Artists in Paris in 1956, for which he served as secretary; and the First Conference of Afro-Asiatic Writers in 1958 in Tashkent, where he and Viriato da Cruz represented Angolan writers. At the same time, he continued his studies in sociology at the École Pratique des Hautes Études in Paris.

In those years, marked by the first African nations gaining their independence, his anticolonial thinking became more radical, leading to his support of the creation, with Amilcar Cabral and others, of the Movimento Anticolonialista (MAC, Anti-Colonialist Movement). MAC was later reorganized as the Frente Revolucionária Africana para a Independência das Colónias Portuguesas (FRAIN, African Revolutionary Front for the Independence of the Portuguese Colonies), whose goal was the creation of a unitary movement to develop armed struggle in all of the Portuguese colonies. Between 1960 and 1962 Andrade was president of the newly founded Movimento Popular de Libertação de Angola (MPLA, People's Movement for the Liberation of Angola), a position he held until the presidency was handed over to Agostinho Neto upon his release from prison. Andrade was also secretary general of the Conferência das

Organizações Nacionalistas das Colónias Portuguesas (CONCP, Conference of Nationalist Organizations of the Portuguese Colonies), an organization that resulted from the dissolution of FRAIN in 1961.

His militancy in the MPLA was marked from an early date by his dissenting views in relation to ideas and strategies adopted by Neto, until in 1974 he wrote what became known as the "document of the discontented," which gave voice to a dissident current in MPLA that brought together a group called "Active Revolt," which also included Andrade's brother, Joaquim Pinto de Andrade. The group opposed the presidential approach in MPLA under Agostinho Neto, calling for a greater democratization of the movement. Pressured by presidential repression, in 1975 Mário Pinto de Andrade left Luanda, settling in Guinea-Bissau, where he held the position of Minister of Information and Culture until 1980, when he left that country following the coup by Nino Vieira. In permanent exile, he lived in Maputo where he lectured at the Universidade Eduardo Mondlane. After some years of ill health, he died in London on August 26, 1990.

In addition to his many essays published in reviews and journals, and his important study, *Origens do Nacionalismo Angolano*, which was published posthumously in 1997 in Lisbon, he edited and wrote prefaces for various anthologies of African poetry, as well as poems in Portuguese and Kimbundu. Most of his writings have been digitized and are available on the Web site of the Fundação Mário Soares.

[*See also* Cabral, Amílcar Lopes; Césaire, Aimé; Cruz, Viriato Francisco Clemente da; Diop, Alioune; Ducados, Henda; Maldoror, Sarah; Neto, Agostinho; Senghor, Léopold Sédar; *and* Tenreiro, Francisco.]

BIBLIOGRAPHY

Andrade, Henda Pinto de, ed. *Mário Pinto de Andrade: Uma Olhar Íntimo*. Luanda, Angola: Edições Cha de Caxinde, 2009.

Andrade, Mário de, and Marc Ollivier. *The War in Angola. A Socio-Economic Study*. Dar es Salaam, Tanzania: Tanzania Publishing House, 1975. Available at http://www.fmsoares.pt/aeb_online/visualizador.php?nome_da_pasta=019050&bd=BIBLIOTECA_DIGITAL

Laban, Michel. *Angola: Encontro com Escritores*. Porto, Portugal: Fundação Eng. António de Almeida, 1991.

Mata, Inocência, and Laura Cavalcante Padilha, eds. *Mário Pinto de Andrade: Um Intelectual na Política*. Lisbon, Portugal: Edições Colibri, 2000. Texts by Mário Pinto de Andrade, testimony, and studies of his work and his thought.

JESSICA FALCONI
Translated from the Portuguese by Kathleen Sheldon

Andrianampoinimerina (1745–1810), king of the Merina state of central Madagascar and a pivotal figure in its eighteenth-century expansion, was born around 1745 in the northern Malagasy town of Ikaloy. His father, Andriamiaramanjaka, was a member of the Zafimamy royal family of the northern independent kingdom of Alahamadintany. His mother, Ranavalonandriambelomasina, was the daughter of Merina monarch Andriambelomasina, who ruled Merina from roughly 1730 to 1770. He also was the nephew of Andriambelomasina's successor, Andrianjafy, who was the king of Merina from 1770 to 1787.

He stayed with his father in Ikaloy until he was roughly twelve, when he moved to the Merina court. As a young man, Andrianampoinimerina became a wealthy merchant and probably engaged in slave trading. At the same time, he presented himself as a defender of ordinary commoners fearful of slave raiding, threats from neighbors like the Sakalava kingdom, and unjust officials. Supposedly, Andriambelomasina had stipulated that Andrianampoinimerina would succeed him after Andrianjafy. Since most narratives about Andrianampoinimerina are derived from nineteenth-century sources approved by Andrianampoinimerina's supporters and royal successors, it should be noted that many of the descriptions of Andrianampoinimerina's legitimacy and benevolence had a clear ideological goal: to prop up the ruling dynasty in the nineteenth century. Slaves and some aristocrats joined Andrianampoinimerina's move to depose Andrianjafy in 1787. After a war that dragged on for three years or so, Andrianjafy either died in his southern base at Ilafy or died in exile.

As king, Andrianampoinimerina offered his subjects a more centralized form of government. He claimed that previous Merina rulers had only brought about *fanjakana hova*, a Malagasy term that translated roughly as "rule by the *hova*" (illegitimate and unqualified rulers). This term presented the king's predecessors as weak and unable to stem internal and external conflicts. He claimed that a central authority was needed to mend social and political tensions and referred to himself as a sun that shone over all of the subjects in a discussion with a French trader in 1808. One of his more successful efforts was to promote a common Merina identity among his different subjects, both slaves and free people. To cut off his aristocratic and royal rivals from trade opportunities that could threaten his own supremacy, Andrianampoinimerina tried to monopolize and regulate foreign trade in slaves and other items. Such policies hardly made him popular among aristocrats, but commoners and others fearful of being sold had reason to back the king.

Andrianampoinimerina also intervened regularly in local affairs on behalf of commoners against officials and nobles, which increased his popularity as a "people's king" rather than a king merely concerned about the elite. He also presented himself as the chief intermediary between the spirit world of ancestors and that of the living. While such policies, combined with a stronger military, solidified Andrianampoinimerina's grip on power in Merina, he was hated by neighbors such as the Sakalava for his campaigns of military expansion. These wars brought slaves, wealth, and new lands that could be given out to loyal Merina supporters at the expense of other peoples.

He died in 1810, after having at least thirty children. His son Radama I followed his father's policies of expansion and state-managed economics.

[*See also* Radama I.]

BIBLIOGRAPHY

Larson, Pier M. *History and Memory in the Age of Enslavement: Becoming Merina in Highland Madagascar, 1770–1822.* Portsmouth, UK: Heinemann, 2000.

Randrianja, Solofo, and Stephen Ellis. *Madagascar: A Short History.* Chicago: University of Chicago Press, 2009.

JEREMY RICH

Anek Mathiang Yak (fl. nineteenth century) was born into the Pagok Pathiong Gok Dinka community in South Sudan during the 1860s. This was the turbulent height of the nineteenth-century Turco-Egyptian slaving era. She was taken as a slave from her village and brought to Tonj, a prominent regional slaving post. She was later taken north to the Mahdist capital of Omdurman and spent three years as a slave at nearby Buri. Like most female slaves, Anek underwent the brutal circumcision operation and was married informally to a man in Northern Sudan. She learned to speak Arabic.

With the arrival of the Anglo-Egyptian colonial era, Anek escaped slavery and returned to her homeland. There she married a man named Dahl Marol and resumed a normal Dinka life. As time passed she convinced her people of the value of the skills she had learned in the north, particularly aggressiveness and fluency in Arabic; she gradually gained a position of prominence among the Pathiong Gok and was eventually recognized as a female chief in the Dinka tradition. The colonial headquarters for the region that included the homeland of Anek's people was Rumbek; a British administrator and a military unit of the colonial government were based there. The regime relied heavily upon the services of local leaders of the region, and in time Anek became a prominent administrative chief; she even established a residence in Rumbek itself. At one point, as was customary at the time, a British officer awarded her a golden sword for maintaining peace among her people, the Gok Dinka.

Anek came to prominence later in life when she clashed with a prominent rival male leader named Wuol Athian, a traditional priest and military leader of the Agar, another Dinka community under the authority of Rumbek. She argued a case against him at a public gathering of chiefs and won; she was awarded a gray cow. It was highly unusual for a woman to challenge such a prominent man publicly and win—and shameful for a man to lose. Anek's opponents organized against her. At the next annual gathering of the chiefs of the Rumbek region before the British authorities, a Dinka translator was induced to charge Anek (probably falsely) with the grave offense of having slapped Wuol Athian's buttocks. It was also said that the offended chief was now mobilizing his warriors to attack Anek's Pathiong Gok community. The colonial officials, to keep the peace, removed Anek from her chieftainship and appointed a male successor. Anek abandoned her urban residence and retired to obscurity in the countryside. However, she bequeathed a lasting legacy; thereafter the Gok maintained a tradition of choosing female chiefs with greater frequency than do most Dinka groups.

BIBLIOGRAPHY

Beswick, Stephanie. *Sudan's Blood Memory: The Legacy of War, Ethnicity, and Slavery in South Sudan.* Rochester, NY: University of Rochester Press, 2004.

STEPHANIE BESWICK

Angelou, Maya (1928–), autobiographer, poet, educator, playwright, essayist, actor, and director, was born Marguerite Annie Johnson in St. Louis, Missouri, on 4 April 1928. Her pen name derives from having been called "Maya" ("My") by her brother Bailey and from having being married for nearly three years to Tosh Angelos, a Greek sailor whom she met while she was a salesgirl in a record store. After the marriage to Angelos ended in divorce, she performed as a calypso dancer at The Purple Onion, a San Francisco night club, where she took the stage name that she still uses.

Maya Angelou's mother, Vivian Baxter, was a blackjack dealer and a nurse; her father, Bailey Johnson Sr., was a doorman, a cook, and a dietician for the United States Navy. Their marriage ended in divorce. When Maya was three and Bailey was four, the children, with name tags on their wrists, were sent by train from Long Beach, California, to Stamps, Arkansas, home of their paternal grandmother, Annie Henderson.

Angelou traces her life's story in a series of six autobiographies, the best known of which is also the first: *I Know Why the Caged Bird Sings* (1969). Here she describes her early years in rural Arkansas, spent under the supervision of Annie Henderson, a religious woman and owner of the general store in the African-American community. During a visit to her mother's family in St. Louis, the eight-year-old Maya is raped by Mr. Freeman, a friend of Vivian Baxter's. The child's politically influential family is suspected of murdering the rapist. In guilt and remorse, Maya becomes mute, unable to speak for five years. It is during her silence that she turns to writing. *I Know Why the Caged Bird Sings* ends with Maya's teen pregnancy by a local boy and the joyous birth of a son, Guy. The mother/son relationship sets up the major dynamics for most of the remaining autobiographies.

Gather Together in My Name (1974) follows Angelou's struggles with drug addiction, prostitution, and single motherhood. During a brief return to Stamps, Arkansas, she again seeks the protection of her grandmother, who sends her away for having recklessly broken the boundaries between the white and black communities by challenging the authority of a white, female clerk at the Stamps General Merchandise Store. It is the last time they see each other.

In *Singin' and Swingin' and Gettin' Merry Like Christmas* (1976), Angelou, now in her early twenties, embarks on her troubled marriage and divorce to Tosh Angelos. At the same time she blossoms professionally. Leaving her son Guy under the care of Vivian Baxter, Maya becomes the lead dancer in a 1954–55 European tour of George Gershwin's folk-opera *Porgy and Bess*. In *Singin' and Swingin'* Maya learns of the death of Annie Henderson, to whom she pays tribute in a passionate elegy. At the end of the third volume she leaves the tour and is reunited with her son, promising that she will never desert him again.

The fourth and fifth volumes focus on Maya Angelou's residence in Africa. *The Heart of a Woman* (1981), which is set in Egypt, Senegal, and Ghana, recalls her affiliation with the American Civil Rights Movement and her employment as a reporter for the *Cairo Observer*. As the title implies, it is in *The Heart of a Woman* that Angelou makes a full commitment to herself as a black woman writer.

The fourth volume also traces her troubled relationship with Vusumzi Make, a South African freedom fighter recently released from prison whom Maya meets at a party in New York. Despite his belief that, as a woman, she is inferior to him, she goes with him from New York City, to London, and then to Cairo. As they continue to disagree, she leaves Make and tentatively accepts a job offer in Liberia. But after Guy is almost killed in a car accident, she takes him to Ghana to recuperate.

In Ghana Maya depends more and more on her love for her son and on her growing love for Africa. She also establishes a strong friendship with Nana Nketsia, the impressive African vice-chancellor of the University of Ghana. The fourth volume ends in Ghana, with Guy recovering from the car crash.

All God's Children Need Traveling Shoes (1986), begins where *The Heart of a Woman* had ended, with the car crash that almost took her son's life. Angelou, who forms a coalition with the American expatriates living in Ghana, seeks her African roots among the Bambara people. The autobiography concludes at the Accra airport, with Guy staying on to complete his studies at the university and his mother, aware that she cannot control her son's destiny, looking westward toward the United States.

The sixth volume of her autobiography, *A Song Flung Up from Heaven* (2002), begins with Angelou's return to America, where she is reunited with Dolly McPherson and other close friends. She is griefstricken when two of her associates, the African-American leaders Malcolm X and Martin Luther King, Jr., are assassinated. Consoled by the novelist James Baldwin, she eventually begins to view her life as a record of the black female experience in America. The autobiographical series comes full circle; the last sentence of A Song Flung Up from Heaven is also the first line of I Know Why the Caged Bird Sings.

Many of her other books blend the genres of memoir, essay, and autobiography. Perhaps the most unusual of these is a cookbook, hallelujah!: the welcome table: A Lifetime of Memories with Recipes (2004), in which favorite recipes are introduced by vignettes about Grandma Henderson, Maya's brother Bailey, and other friends, including her third husband, the architect Paul de Feu.

In addition to being an internationally acclaimed autobiographer, Angelou is a well-known poet and a writer of children's books. Her volume Just Give Me a Cool Drink of Water 'Fore I Die (1971) was nominated for a Pulitzer Prize. In 1986, Random House published the first edition of her collected poetry.

Angelou has also written a number of poems that eulogize American leaders and artists, the most famous being "On the Pulse of Morning," an ode composed for the 1993 inauguration of President Bill Clinton. She was the first black and the first woman to achieve such an honor. In 2008 the London Observer invited her to write a poem about Hillary Clinton, the candidate whom Angelou had supported in the United States presidential race of that year. In 2009 she wrote "We Had Him," a remembrance dedicated to American performer Michael Jackson and read by the African-American actress Queen Latifah at the public memorial service held in Los Angeles, California.

The recipient of almost fifty honorary degrees, Angelou is Reynolds Professor at Wake Forest University in Winston-Salem, North Carolina. For the past several years she has been a featured speaker at the annual national convention of the AARP (American Association of Retired Persons). Other honors include a Yale University Fellowship, a Rockefeller Foundation Fellowship, and the 1983 Woman of the Year Award in Communications from the Ladies' Home Journal. Angelou published another cookbook, Great Food, All Day Long: Cook Splendidly, Eat Smart, in 2010.

BIBLIOGRAPHY

Braxton, Joanne M. Maya Angelou's I Know Why the Caged Bird Sings: A Case Book. New York: Oxford University Press, 1999.

Lupton, Mary Jane. Maya Angelou: A Critical Companion. Westport, CT: Greenwood Press, 1998.

Lupton, Mary Jane. "Spinning in a Whirlwind: Sexuality in Maya Angelou's Sixth Autobiography." MAWA Review 18 (2003): 1–6.

McPherson, Dolly A. Order Out of Chaos: The Autobiographical Works of Maya Angelou. New York: Peter Lang, 1990.

Saunders, James Robert. "Breaking Out of the Cage: The Autobiographical Writings of Maya Angelou." In Twayne Companion to Contemporary Literature in English, edited by R.H.W. Dillard and Amanda Cockrell. New York: Twayne-Thomson Gale, 2002.

MARY JANE LUPTON

Angoulvant, Gabriel Louis (1872–1932), French colonial administrator in the Ivory Coast, chronicler, governor, and deputy in the National Assembly, was born on 8 February 1872 in Longjumeau, near Paris. Not much is known about his childhood and early education. He attended the École coloniale (Colonial School) in Paris, which produced bureaucrats for service in the French empire, and earned a degree in administration. He also studied Chinese at the École des langues orientales (School of Oriental Languages) in Paris. He then embarked on a career in the colonial civil service.

Angoulvant served in several positions in Asia and Africa before he became governor of the Ivory Coast (Côte d'Ivoire) and then governor-general at different times of both French West Africa (Afrique Occidentale Française, AOF) and French Equatorial Africa (Afrique Équatoriale Française, AEF). He had little African experience prior to being posted to the continent. Angoulvant served as resident chancellor in Tonkin, vice consul in China, and secretary general of Djibouti, as well as tours of duty in the Congo, Guadeloupe, Saint-Pierre-et-Miquelon, and the French Indies.

His appointment as governor of the Ivory Coast, where France faced stiff resistance to its rule, especially from the Baulé, came on 25 April 1908 and lasted eight years. He was a political appointee named to succeed Governor Marie François-Joseph Clozel. A headstrong new governor, Angoulvant was in a hurry to prove his mettle and achieve tangible results. He sought to rectify the situation he had inherited in which the Ivory Coast made the least contribution to the colonial budget despite its enormous potential. By 1909, he had persuaded Governor-General William Merlaud-Ponty that a full-scale military conquest was necessary to unleash the colony's full economic potential. In contrast to Clozel, who, despite being a military officer, had pursued a policy of cooperation with

Baulé chiefs and other local notables, Angoulvant preferred the use of military force to accelerate the pace of development of the colony. He dealt harshly with anyone he perceived to be uncooperative. He directed his subordinates to intervene in succession disputes and impose loyal, hence preferred, chiefs. He drastically reduced the portion of taxes that chiefs previously received from 25 percent to 5 percent. He also imposed a tax on firearms and instituted obligatory communal labor. Angoulvant's tenure is associated with some of the worst excesses of French colonial rule in West Africa. He was ruthless in suppressing the Baulé insurrection from 1908 to 1910, resorting to not just military operations but also detentions, war fines, relocation, and burning entire villages.

Angoulvant's military campaigns against the Baulé decimated the local population, which was reduced from 1.5 million to 160,000 in the span of ten years. Perhaps alarmed by these excesses, there was reported tension between military officers and the governor throughout his tenure. Angoulvant was clearly unfazed by criticism from merchants, humanitarians at home, and even the military command. In 1916, Angoulvant recounted his exploits in *La Pacification de la Côte d'Ivoire, 1908–1915: Méthodes et résultats* (*The Pacification of Côte d'Ivoire, 1908–1915: Methods and Results*). He attributed the successful implantation of cocoa, coffee, and cotton and the exploitation of the forest—developments that catapulted Côte d'Ivoire to the head of the class as the most successful colony in French West Africa—to his use of force. The successful implantation of cocoa in the Gold Coast next door belies Angoulvant's claims.

Nevertheless, Angoulvant's superiors in Paris thought highly enough of him to appoint him the governor-general of French Equatorial Africa (AEF) on 15 May 1917. A few months later, when the governor of AOF, Joost van Vollenhoven, resigned on 11 January 1918, Angoulvant stepped into the position, only to retire within two years and return to France in 1920. He continued active involvement in politics and was elected deputy in the legislative elections on 11 May 1924 to represent French India. In parliament, Angoulvant caucused with the radical left and continued to focus on colonial issues and to participate in various commissions and other projects related to French overseas territories. He contributed to the organizing of the colonial exposition in Paris in 1931. He lost his bid for reelection on 22 April 1928 and died in Paris on 15 October 1932 at the age of sixty.

[*See also* Clozel, Marie François-Joseph.]

BIBLIOGRAPHY

Domergue, Danielle. "Un gouverneur pas comme les autres: Gabriel Angoulvant." *Annales de l'Université d'Abidjan* 1, no. 11 (1983): 231–242.

Groff, David H. "Carrots, Sticks, and Cocoa Pods: African and Administrative Initiatives in the Spread of Cocoa Cultivation in Assikasso, Ivory Coast, 1908–1920." *International Journal of African Historical Studies* 20, no. 3 (1987): 401–416.

Weiskel, Timothy C. *French Colonial Rule and the Baule Peoples: Resistance and Collaboration, 1889–1911.* Oxford, England: Clarendon Press, 1980.

CYRIL DADDIEH

Angula, Nahas (1943–), Namibian politician, senior cabinet minister and prime minister, was born on 22 August 1943 in the village of Onyaanya in the Oshikoto region (northern Namibia). He married Tangeni Katrina Namalenga, a pharmacist, with whom he had several children, and since 1999 she has been the executive officer of the Namibia Institute of Pathology. Nahas Gideon Angula grew up in northern Namibia during the country's occupation by South Africa. He is counted among the first generation of exiled Namibians who fled to Zambia via Botswana in 1965. By then he was already a member of the Youth League of the dominant Namibian liberation movement, the South West Africa People's Organization (SWAPO) of Namibia. While in Zambia, he graduated from the University of Zambia with a teaching degree; he then founded a SWAPO-sponsored educational center for Namibian refugees near Lusaka. From 1976 he worked as a civil servant for the United Nations, at the same time graduating with a MA from the Teachers College at Columbia University.

He then took up high-ranking party positions within SWAPO, eventually becoming a senior party official, which he remains. In 1980 he was elected to the party's Central Committee, and he held the position of Secretary for Education and Culture from 1982 to 1989. Since 1985 he has been a member of SWAPO's Politburo, the highest-ranking body of the party. As such he was influential in shaping the party's educational system of schools for exiled Namibians in various African and eastern European countries, as well as in Cuba. He was instrumental in designing new educational policies for a future independent Namibia. His experiences made him destined to become, with the return of SWAPO's external leadership in 1989 and Namibia's independence in March 1990, a long-term minister in the Ministries of (Higher) Education, Culture and Employment Creation for fifteen years. In 2005 he was appointed prime minister in President Hifikepunye Pohamba's cabinet. In 2010, he was again named prime minister in President Pohamba's second cabinet.

As minister of various education ministries he had to dismantle and transform one of the country's most challenging legacies: the discriminatory and ethnically based apartheid educational system. He oversaw the introduction of national curricula and examination systems as well as the establishment of numerous new institutions of higher learning, including colleges, vocational training centers, and research centers. His appointment in 2005 as prime minister followed his backing of Pohamba in a fierce internal SWAPO contest for presidential candidate and after he had buried his own aspirations for that position. Angula, who in 2002 won the highest number of votes in SWAPO's Central Committee, is regarded as a popular and moderate politician.

In keeping with his moderate views, he refrained from overtly glorifying SWAPO's achievements as ruling party during Namibia's first twenty years of independence and instead asked "whether the progress which was made is sufficient." He continues to regard youth unemployment, poverty, and inequality as "a threat to our social cohesion." Some critics point out that he is more of an intellectual than a managerial administrator, and as such there have been calls on the president to replace him as prime minister. Angula has published essays and edited volumes on educational and pan-African topics.

BIBLIOGRAPHY

Angula, Nahas. "Civil Society, Research, and Policy Formulation in Namibia." In *Exploring the Complexities of Education,* edited by Conrad Wesley Snyder, Nahas Angula, John Meyer, Demus Makuwa, and Onesmus Hailombe, pp. 2–12. Windhoek, Namibia: Gamsberg Macmillan, 1999.

Angula, Nahas, and Bankie F. Bankie, eds. *The African Origin of Civilisation and the Destiny of Africa.* Windhoek, Namibia: Gamsberg Macmillan, 2000.

Hopwood, Graham. *Guide to Namibian Politics.* Windhoek, Namibia: Namibia Institute for Democracy, 2007. Useful, regularly updated reference work on political parties, personalities, civil society organizations and statistics.

Insight Namibia. Independent analytically orientated political magazine, published in Windhoek since 2005.

DAG HENRICHSEN

Annabi, Amina (1962–), Tunisian musician, was born in Carthage, a suburb of Tunis, in 1962. North African women have long, rich traditions of vocal and instrumental music. At weddings and other joyous occasions, including religious festivals, female musicians sing, perform, and dance. In addition, the celebrated Tunisian singer and actress Habiba Messika (1893?–1930) composed songs during the period 1920–1930 that are still performed today. One of the most popular singers and composers in contemporary North Africa and Europe is another Tunisian woman, Amina Annabi, whose music—and life—fuses traditional Arab, Middle Eastern, and West African musical genres with Western music, particularly blues, jazz, reggae, rap, and rock and roll. Annabi's is a complicated story, however, since it is not merely the tale of a talented musician making it in the world music movement from the 1980s on. Her life is intertwined with the postcolonial reality of millions of North Africans who reside permanently in European nations; many were born there and are from second- or third-generation migrant families. Although they hold legal citizenship in France, the United Kingdom, Italy, Spain, or Belgium, their family origin as Muslims, Arabs, Berbers, or Africans often brings rejection or marginalization at worst—at best, partial social and cultural integration.

Annabi is the product of a "mixed marriage"— her father is French and her mother Tunisian. Her mother came from a family that boasted gifted female musicians and composers, including her grandmother. The social composition of Carthage in those days was very culturally diverse, with a large Mediterranean expatriate community; each community had its own diverse musical traditions, which Annabi intertwines with Tunisian–Andalusian Arab classical forms, such as "Maluf," in songs. In addition, Tunisia has hosted international summer musical festivals for decades in Carthage and Tabarka, which brought in vocalists like James Brown, Tina Turner, and Joan Baez, as well as Algerian and Senegalese musicians and performers from around the world. Since one of Annabi's uncles had been involved in the Tabarka music festivals, she met with the famed Senegalese musician Wasis Diop. In 1975 Annabi and her mother, a talented musician and composer, moved together to Paris, where in later years she was able to collaborate with Diop. Thus, the young woman was raised in a milieu saturated with heterogeneous musical influences.

In Paris, Annabi had organized her own group by 1978 and went solo in 1982. As importantly, she worked at France's leading world music station, Radio Nova. Her first recorded album, *Yalil* (*Night*), included songs like "Belly Dance" and, reflecting her own background, fused an eclectic range of musical styles characterized as "ethno-techno." She composed several of the songs for this debut album, and her musical collaborator and friend, Wasis Diop, wrote some of the musical arrangements. *Yalil* was released in over 20 countries; as a result, in 1991 she won the "Le prix Piaf" which named her "best female singer of the year" in France. That same year, she joined an international musicians' peace project to protest the first American invasion of Iraq. In addition, Annabi represented France at the 1991 Eurovision Song Contest held in Rome, where she at first was co-awarded first prize along with a Swedish singer but then was relegated to second place, something that triggered a small storm of protests. Again in 1994, she was invited to participate in a multiartist album entitled *Paris*, which celebrated the French capital. Thus, one sees a progression in her career—from first-prize winner to actually representing France and French culture in international competitions—by combining the musical traditions of former French colonies with those of Europe or the West. One of her most popular songs is entitled "Yanari," which means "Life Is Difficult"—a piece about migrants, immigration, visas, and the traumas of transnational families.

She has participated in a number of philanthropic causes, most notably a fund-raising concert held in 2000 for a French charity named "The Chain of Hope," which brings poor children in need of hospital treatment from Third World countries for free medical assistance in France. In July 2001, she toured the United States with French musical groups, performing in New York, Washington, D.C., and other major cities. She is also an actress, having appeared in at least thirteen films, for example, Bernardo Bertolucci's 1990 *The Sheltering Sky*, inspired by the Paul Bowles novel of the same title; the 2002 film *Dreams of Trespass*, based upon the book by the well-known Moroccan feminist writer Fatima Mernissi; and most recently, the 2009 film *Cairo Time*.

In many of Annabi's songs, she embraces the Orientalist and colonial depictions of the sensuous, depraved Eastern woman and inverts them by making musical parodies of older cultural stereotypes, which had implicit or explicit racist undertones. Together with a growing number of North African artists, such as the Algerian *raï* singer Khaled, Annabi has managed to break out of the postcolonial cultural and political ghetto experienced by so many African migrants residing in Europe through art and performance. In response to the lascivious French military depictions or the degrading colonial picture postcards of Algerian women, Annabi demands in one of her most famous songs, with irony, "Tell me, in the name of which nation do you raise your voice in my house; he who speaks the loudest is always the one who is right?" (from "Le dernier qui a parlé," or "He Who Has the Last Word").

BIBLIOGRAPHY

Abbassi, Hamadi. *Tunis chante et danse*. Tunis: Alif, 2000.

Hamrouni, Ahmed. *Habiba Messika: Artiste accomplice*. Tunis: 'Alam al-Kitab, 2007.

JULIA A. CLANCY-SMITH

Annan, Kofi Atta (1938–), Ghanaian Nobel Laureate and United Nations (UN) Secretary-General, was born in Kumasi in what was then the British Gold Coast colony. Along with his twin sister Efua Atta, he was born to Rose Annan, a Fante, and Henry Reginald Annan, an Ashanti/Fante. Both parents were Christian and descendants of chiefs. Annan's father was a commissioner of the Ashanti region and an employee of the United Africa Company, who rose through the ranks to become its director. After his retirement, Henry Reginald Annan also became president of the Ghana International Bank.

Ghana's declaration of independence in 1957 found Kofi Annan in Cape Coast, finishing his secondary schooling at Mfantsipim, the Methodist boarding school. The following year, he began his studies in Economics at the Kumasi College of Science and Technology, completing his degree in the United States at Macalester College, in St. Paul, Minnesota (1961). From there, he moved to Geneva to pursue graduate studies in Economics at the Institut Universitaire des Hautes Études Internationales. In 1972, he studied for a Master's degree at the Massachusetts Institute of Technology's Sloan School of Management.

Annan started his UN career in 1962 as a World Health Organization administrative and budget officer in Geneva. He went on to serve with the Economic Commission for Africa in Addis Ababa, Ethiopia and the UN Emergency Force in Ismailia, Egypt, before returning to Geneva to work for the

Kofi Annan, 2006. (AP Images/Keystone/Salvatore Di Nolfi)

United Nations High Commissioner for Refugees. Briefly back in Egypt with the UN Emergency Force, he was to interrupt his UN career for a period between 1974–1976, when he was appointed Director of Tourism in Ghana. Upon his return to the UN, he served in various senior administrative positions in New York, including as Assistant Secretary-General for Human Resources Management and Security Coordinator for the UN System (1987–1990). In 1990, he demonstrated his diplomatic resourcefulness when he successfully negotiated the repatriation from Iraq of about nine hundred UN staff and Western nationals caught in the aftermath of the invasion of Kuwait.

Nevertheless, Annan returned to administrative duties for another two years (1990–1992), during which he served as Assistant Secretary-General and Controller for Programme Planning, Budget and Finance. In 1992, he moved to the newly established Department of Peacekeeping Operations, first as deputy head (Assistant Secretary-General for Peacekeeping Operations, 1992–1993) and then as under-secretary-general (1993–1996). Not one to shun personal responsibility, Annan later spoke of the international community's "sins of omission" and his regret that "there was more that I could and should have done to sound the alarm and rally support" to prevent the 1994 Rwanda genocide. On the failure of the UN to prevent the Serbian massacre of eight thousand Bosnians in Srebrenica a year later, he would eventually accept partial responsibility for the tragedy, acknowledging the failure of

an approach that established "safe areas" without credible means of defense.

By 1996, UN Secretary-General Boutros-Ghali's relationship with the American President Bill Clinton's administration was damaged beyond repair, and it began to look for another African to replace the Egyptian diplomat. While Special Representative of the Secretary-General to the former Yugoslavia (November 1995–March 1996), Annan had successfully overseen the handover of peacekeeping duties from the United Nations Protection Force (UNPROFOR) to the NATO-led Implementation Force (IFOR). His moderate demeanor and managerial credentials further helped him secure American endorsement, and in December 1996, he was elected secretary-general, the first from the ranks of UN staff. He was also the first sub-Saharan African to hold the position. Seven months into his appointment, Annan promised a "quiet revolution." His institutional reform plan drew on his intimate knowledge of the UN's strengths and weaknesses. Building on the courageous but unpopular decision taken by his predecessor, Boutros Boutros-Ghali, in 1996, Annan oversaw the elimination of one thousand Secretariat posts in his first year on the job. He further reduced administrative costs and implemented the first negative-growth budget (1998–1999 budget cycle). In an unprecedented move, Annan appointed Canadian diplomat Louise Fréchette as his deputy to help him manage the operations of the Secretariat and to enhance the inter-institutional coherence of different UN programmes. In 1998, Annan reorganized humanitarian response to complex emergencies and natural disasters by creating the Office for the Coordination of Humanitarian Affairs and strengthening its mandate to include policy development and humanitarian advocacy. Two years later, Annan appointed former Algerian Foreign Minister Lakhdar Brahimi to address the strategic, operational, and organizational shortcomings of peacekeeping operations, which during his tenure would deploy about eighty thousand military and civilian personnel at an annual cost of US$4.47 billion.

Annan was conscious of the importance of public relations, and his charismatic presence contributed to an unprecedented popularization of the role of UN secretary-general. This in turn helped him build a wider constituency of support, notably with civil society, but also with the business community. In 1998, a group of prominent American business and political leaders placed an open letter in the *New York Times* praising the UN for "reforming its bureaucracy, cutting costs and becoming more efficient." Although falling short of the desired effect of paying off the full US$1.5 billion, the US Congress was pressured into releasing funds that covered part of America's share of UN debt. A year later, Annan announced the Global Compact framework for companies committed to sustainability and responsible business practices by endorsing ten principles in the areas of human rights, labor, environment, and, later, anticorruption. Annan's outreach to the business world was also evident in 1997, when media magnate Ted Turner pledged US$1 billion to set up the UN Foundation; meanwhile, grants from software mogul Bill Gates's Foundation continue to provide funding for UN health and development goals and projects to date. Annan's vision of public, private, and civil society partnership further materialized with the establishment of the Global Fund, dedicated to financing the prevention and treatment of HIV/AIDS, tuberculosis, and malaria.

NATO military intervention in Kosovo in 1999 raised questions about the consequences of the use of force without international consensus or clear legal authority. Responding to this and remembering the lessons of the Rwanda genocide, Annan (now secretary-general) asked member-states to rise to future challenges. He argued that the "collective conscience of humanity" justified intervention on humanitarian grounds so as to stop states from committing atrocities against their own people.

A few months later, developing nations denounced humanitarian intervention as illegal and a violation of state sovereignty. Annan had already upset certain African leaders in 1997 when, displaying guile and political courage, he had stated that the notion that human rights are a Western "imposition" or "plot" was "demeaning of the yearning for human dignity that resides in every African heart."

In 2000, Annan outlined his vision of the UN in an era of globalization. He called on heads of state to commit their nations to reducing extreme poverty and child mortality and to agree to a blueprint of time-bound targets that became known as the Millennium Development Goals, which were soon incorporated into global economic and social development discourse. When world leaders returned to New York to review progress in 2005, Annan displayed true leadership by asking developed countries to increase their spending on development and debt relief and the developing world to commit to better governance, the rule of law, and combating corruption. He asked for a new consensus on the proliferation of conventional weapons and terrorism, planting the roots for the adoption of the UN's first counterterrorism strategy. Annan reasserted his belief in the "responsibility to protect" as a basis for collective action against genocide, ethnic cleansing, and crimes against humanity. World leaders approved the principle, albeit with qualifications. His proposal for a strong Human Rights Council to replace the ineffectual Commission on Human Rights was also diluted and his recommendation to expand the Security Council ignored.

Iraq was an irritant for Annan throughout his tenure as UN secretary-general and, ultimately, his handling of the issue eroded the Bush administration's confidence in his leadership of the UN. In 1998, Annan traveled to Iraq to negotiate the reentry of UN weapons inspectors. When he said that he could do business with Saddam Hussein if it meant preventing a war, his Washington critics accused him of naïveté. Already under attack from the neoconservatives, he alienated the White House by declaring the American-led 2003 invasion of Iraq as "illegal" because it lacked Security Council approval. The Oil-for-Food program that had until then been hailed as successful came under scrutiny in 2005, and accusations of corruption and nepotism were directed at the UN; Annan's own son was implicated. Annan commissioned an inquiry under former Chairman of the US Federal Reserve Paul A. Volcker to investigate the accusations. The investigation dismissed claims of corruption with one exception, but high-lighted oversight and management failures, damaging UN credibility. It also found that Annan's son had intentionally deceived his father about his financial relationship with the company at the center of the allegations. In an effort to placate neoconservative calls for Annan's resignation, US president George W. Bush appointed abrasive UN critic John R. Bolton as American ambassador to the UN in 2005. A year later Annan responded to increasing US unilateralism in his final speech by declaring that "No nation can make itself secure by seeking supremacy over others" and urging the United States to respect human rights in its "war on terror."

Annan used his good offices to settle long-standing disputes and stalemates. In 1998, he set up a mission to promote the transition to civilian rule in Nigeria. In 1999, he helped resolve the deadlock between Libya and the Security Council, and was involved in the process by which Timor-Leste (East Timor) gained independence from Indonesia. In 2000, he certified Israel's withdrawal from Lebanon, and in 2006, his efforts contributed to securing a cessation of hostilities between Israel and Hezbollah. Also in 2006, his mediation of the dispute between Cameroon and Nigeria over the Bakassi peninsula met with success, but his earlier efforts to unify the divided island of Cyprus failed.

During his tenure, Annan challenged the community of states to reach consensus "in defense of our common humanity" in the face of massive human rights and humanitarian law violations. His most significant achievement, however, was that he rose to the diverse challenges of the early twenty-first century and, by institutionalizing his vision of human development, he put "the individual at the center of everything the UN is about," as he hoped he would. In 2001, both Annan and the UN were jointly awarded the Nobel Peace Prize for "for their work for a better organized and more peaceful world." Annan was also credited for being "preeminent in bringing new life to the organization."

Following his retirement as UN secretary-general at the end of 2006, Annan has been president of the Global Humanitarian Forum, and chair of the Africa Progress Panel, the Alliance for a Green Revolution in Africa, and the Prize Committee of the Mo Ibrahim Foundation. He is a member of the Elders Group, Chancellor of the University of Ghana, a Global Fellow at Columbia University, and the Li Ka Shing Professor at the National University of Singapore. He is also the recipient of a number of honorary degrees and awards.

Annan continued to lobby for better policies to meet the needs of the poorest and most vulnerable, especially in Africa. In 2008, he led the African Union Panel of Eminent Personalities, which mediated a power-sharing agreement between the Kenyan government and opposition after the unprecedented violence, ethnic animosity, and mass displacement that erupted following a disputed election the previous year. Annan mobilized international support, but ultimately his intervention was rightly hailed as "an African solution to an African problem."

Annan's first marriage, to Nigerian Titilola Alakija, with whom he had a son and a daughter, ended in divorce. He subsequently married Nane Maria Lagergren, a Swedish artist and one-time UN lawyer from a prominent Swedish family. Lagergren's uncle was the diplomat and humanitarian Raoul Wallenberg. From this marriage, he has a stepdaughter.

[*See also* Boutros-Ghali, Boutros.]

BIBLIOGRAPHY

Annan, Kofi A. *We the Peoples: The Role of the United Nations in the 21st Century.* New York: United Nations Publications, 2000.

Annan, Kofi A. "Two Concepts of Sovereignty." *The Economist,* 18 September 1999.

Chesterman, Simon, ed., *Secretary or General? The UN Secretary-General in World Politics.* Cambridge, UK: Cambridge University Press, 2007.

Eckhard, Frederick. *Kofi Annan.* Geneva, Switzerland: Tricorne, 2009.

Griffiths, Martin. "The Prisoner of Peace: An Interview with Kofi A. Annan." Geneva, Switzerland: Kofi Annan Foundation and the Centre for Humanitarian Dialogue, 2008.

Kille, Kent J. *From Manager to Visionary: The Secretary-General of the United Nations.* New York: Palgrave Macmillan, 2006.

Traub, James. *The Best Intentions: Kofi Annan and the UN in the Era of American World Power.* New York: Farrar, Straus and Giroux, 2006.

KATYA LENEY-HALL

Ansah, Kwaw (b. 1941), Ghanaian filmmaker, writer, producer, and director, was born in Agona Swedru in the Central Region of Ghana. His father, J. R. Ansah, was a professional photographer, a painter, dramatist, and musician, and his mother was a trader. Kwaw Ansah, after his Anglican elementary education in Agona Swedru, moved to Accra, where he completed his ordinary-level certificate examinations. While studying for his ordinary-level certificate, he worked as a fashion designer for the United Africa Company. He later entered London Polytechnic (now the University of Westminster) in 1963 to study theater design. Having decided to pursue a career in film production, he then enrolled in the American Academy of Dramatic Arts in New York and graduated two years later, in 1965, with a diploma in dramatic arts. That same year he was admitted to the American Musical and Dramatic Academy. It was while there that he understudied film production in R.K.O. studios in Hollywood, California.

He returned to Ghana in 1965, beginning his career as a production assistant and set designer for the Ghana Film Industry Corporation. While undergoing his career training in the United States, he produced his first two plays: *The Adoption*, produced off-Broadway in 1964 at the Hermon Theater in the United States, and *Mother's Tears*, which made an impressive debut in Accra in 1967. In 1973, Kwaw Ansah founded his own advertising company, Target Advertising Services, and in 1980 he made a breakthrough when he produced his award-winning motion picture *Love Brewed in an African Pot*, which tells a love story of people from diverse backgrounds, revealing the clash between indigenous traditions and Western influences in pre-independent Ghana. *Love Brewed in an African Pot* made Kwaw Ansah famous and earned him a number of international awards, such as the Oumarou Ganda Prize at the 1981 FESPACO (Panafrican Film Festival of Ouagadougou), the Jury's Silver Peacock award for feature films at the Eighth International Film Festival in India, and in 1985, it won the UNESCO film prize award in France.

In 1988, Ansah went further to produce his second fiction film, entitled *Heritage Africa*. This film won the first prize, *Etalon de Yennenga*, at FESPACO 1989 and also won the Organization of African Unity Best Film and Outstanding Film Award at the 1989 London Film Festival. The film also premiered at the CELAFI (Celebrating African Identity) Conference in Toronto, Canada, in 1992.

Since producing *Heritage Africa*, he then turned his attention to producing documentaries, beginning with *Cross Roads of People, Cross Roads of Trade*, which was funded by the Smithsonian Institute in 1994. He also has to his credit the documentary entitled *Hopes on the Horizon*, a continent-wide project that started in 1996 for which he served as co-executive producer. In an interview with Francois Pfaff (1995), he revealed his motivation for film production, namely to "revitalize African culture" since Africa was suffering greatly from foreign cultural intrusions and interventions.

His daughter, Gyasiwa Ansah, is also a filmmaker. She has been production manager for two of his films, *Harvest at 17* and *Cross Roads of People, Cross Roads of Trade*, a documentary.

Kwaw Ansah has functioned in several management capacities. He has been chairman of the Federation of African Filmmakers and has also been on Ghana's Board of National Commission on Culture. He continues to function as chairman of TV Africa, a privately owned commercial television network that he founded.

BIBLIOGRAPHY

"Cascade Festival of African Films." http://www. africanfilmfestival.org/Pfaff, Françoise and Kwaw Ansah. *Research in African Literatures, Vol. 26, No. 3, African Cinema*. Bloomington: Indiana University Press, 1995.

TV Africa. "Ghana" http://www.tvafricaonline.com/abouttvafrica.aspx.

MAXWELL AKANSINA AZIABAH

Antera Duke Ephraim (c. 1735–c. 1809), Atlantic merchant, was born and lived in Duke Town, a part of the trading community of Old Calabar, near the Cross River in what is now southeastern Nigeria. The names of his parents are unknown. His name is also given as Ntiero Edem Efiom. He married Awa Ofiong, whom he called his "dear wife," as well as two other wives whose names are not known. His only known child was a son, Duke Antera.

Antera grew up in a family prominent in the marketing of merchandise brought by Europeans in exchange for African slaves and other goods. In addition to the local Efik language, the young Antera learned to speak English through contact with the British captains and crew who called at Old Calabar. The fact that he could also read and write English suggests he may have received some formal education in England, as did the sons of other West African traders of this time. Antera's father, grandfather, and many other prominent Efik could speak English, but literacy was less common.

Antera was unique among the many coastal West African merchants of his day for keeping a diary of his daily activities, and the entries covering the period from January 1785 to January 1788 have survived. The original volume of the diary, which a Scottish missionary brought to Edinburgh sometime in the later 1800s, was lost during World War II, but a substantially complete copy survives, which has twice been published with annotations and background essays. Because the English he penned is often irregular in its grammar and spelling, these editions included renderings in standard English.

The diary is a valuable record of the views and activities of an African participant in the Atlantic slave trade. Because Antera kept it only for himself, the diary is also a remarkably candid account of an African society engaged in that trade. Antera referred to only a small portion of the several thousand slaves who were sold from Old Calabar each year in the 1780s, but he was more detailed about the personal and business relations between African merchants and European captains. On the whole these relations were generally peaceful—even cordial. The diary mentions twenty English captains by name and describes visits to their ships to negotiate the terms of the trade, including the collection of *comey*, the customs or port fee Europeans had to pay before they could trade. The diary describes meals and drinks that the Efik and Europeans shared, including a "new year" party on 25 December 1785, where the participants did "Drink all Day befor [until] night." When conflict occurred it was in the interests of both sides to settle it quickly, as happened when the English captains and the "Callabar gentllmen" agreed to cut off an ear of an African as a punishment for mortally wounding Captain John Ford's mate in July 1787.

The dairy also illuminates the relations between Old Calabar merchants and their inland African partners. Antera and his African agents traveled to markets and towns at the borders of the Efik territory, where they exchanged Atlantic trade goods (cloth, metals) for slaves, ivory, yams, and palm oil. Other Africans traded these imports and exports through networks of markets that covered a wide area. A series of entries for November 1785, for example, tell how Antera led a canoe fleet loaded with trade goods up the Cross River to buy slaves and yams at the market towns. Several other entries refer to Antera's agents buying slaves from a market on an overland route leading to the upper Cross River.

The diary's many references to the Ekpe (Leopard) Society attest to this unique membership organization's political, social, and religious importance. In this region of very diffused political authority, Ekpe provided a mechanism for reaching decisions and enforcing them. The diary records the first known instances when someone "blew Ekpe" on another trader, prohibiting that African or European from trading until a debt was paid or a dispute resolved. Most important Efik traders at that time paid initiation fees to members of Ekpe's four grades or "laws," and the society had branches in outlying communities. Because of its power ambitious men vied for Ekpe's key offices and for a share of the initiation fees and fines that were shared among members. Antera belonged to the highest grade of Ekpe, whose members often hosted the dinner parties with the European sea captains to promote good relations.

Another valuable contribution of the diary is its unvarnished record of the details of life and belief in Old Calabar. Antera sometimes wrote of ordinary domestic events. In October 1785, for example, he noted, "I have be angary with my Dear [wife] Awa Ofion[g]," and that he got angrier when she rudely responded to his mother's intervention. On the last day of January 1788, Antera noted, he sent two of his half brothers to the palm wine market. Other entries concern more momentous events. Several times Antera recorded instances of African men or women accused of witchcraft being forced to "drink doctor." Those who vomited up the poisonous concoction were considered innocent, while the others died. An entry dated 20 September 1787 tells of the death of his brother's wife after being made to drink doctor. The death and funeral of Duke Ephraim, the most powerful man in Duke Town in July 1786, is the biggest event recorded in the diary. Antera wrote "9 men & women go with him," referring to the human sacrifices that were buried with Duke Ephraim. It is likely when Antera died two decades later, other men and women were sacrificed to accompany him to the world of the spirits.

By keeping a diary for his own purposes Antera unintentionally left a rare insider's account of West African life in the late 1700s. Written with no polemical agenda, his accounts of how Africans partnered with Europeans in the sale of slaves into the Atlantic, of rough justice and human sacrifice, as well as of tender relations can shock, surprise, or move modern readers.

BIBLIOGRAPHY

Behrendt, Stephen. D., A. J. H. Latham, and David Northrup. *The Diary of Antera Duke: An Eighteenth-Century African Slave Trader.* New York: Oxford University Press, 2010. The original text of the diary plus a modern, annotated rendering and scholarly chapters on the larger trading networks and Old Calabar society.

Forde, Daryll. ed. *Efik Traders of Old Calabar*. London: Oxford University Press, 1956. The first edition of the diary with a translation, annotations, and essays by pioneering scholars of southern Nigerian history and society.

Latham, A. J. H. *Old Calabar, 1600–1891: The Impact of the International Economy upon a Traditional Society*. Oxford, England: Clarendon Press, 1973. A scholarly account of Old Calabar's participation in the Atlantic trades.

Sparks, Randy J. *The Two Princes of Calabar: An Eighteenth-Century Atlantic Odyssey*. Cambridge, Mass.: Harvard University Press, 2004. The adventurous voyages around the Atlantic and back home to Old Calabar of two Efik youths in the 1770s, who like Antera were literate in English and came from a family of merchants.

DAVID NORTHRUP

Anthony the Great (d. 356 CE) is widely considered the first anchoritic monk to be influential throughout the Christian Mediterranean world. The *Life of Anthony*, written by Alexandrian bishop Athanasius (d. 373 CE), became a model both for late antique hagiography and for the anchoritic lifestyle that subsequently flourished in the eastern Roman Empire. Anthony's fame also had a significant impact on the spread of monasticism in the western Roman Empire, where the *Life* was read by such patristic writers as Jerome and Augustine.

The main source for Anthony's life is Athanasius's *Life of Anthony*, written in Greek between the years 356 and 362. The influence of this work on the genre of Christian hagiography cannot be overestimated. It was quickly translated into Latin by Evagrius of Antioch, as well as into Coptic, Arabic, Syriac, and other languages of the eastern empire. Jerome was directly inspired by it to write the first hagiographies in Latin in the late fourth and early fifth centuries.

The *Life* records that, as a young man in the Fayum region of Egypt, Anthony was convinced to lead an ascetic life after hearing a reading of Matthew 19:21, in which Jesus says, ""If you want to be perfect, go, sell your possessions and give to the poor, and you will have treasure in heaven. Then come, follow me." He sold his inheritance from his recently deceased parents and gave the proceeds to the poor, setting aside only enough money to ensure the care of his younger sister. An additional New Testament verse, Matthew 6:34 ("Therefore do not worry about tomorrow, for tomorrow will worry about itself. Each day has enough trouble of

its own"), then convinced him to let go completely of his earthly attachments. Accordingly, he entrusted his sister to local women (whom later historians would call "nuns" due to their ascetic lifestyle) and retreated to a sparse shelter at the edge of his family's property. This initial retreat from civic life is only the first stage of Anthony's withdrawal, as he soon sought an abandoned tomb at the outskirts of his town and thereafter a ruined fortress at the edge of the desert. Anthony's final retreat was to a remote mountain in the inner desert, to the southeast of the Nile Delta and a short distance from the Red Sea. Even though Anthony withdrew into the desert to continue his battles against demons and his solitary quest for perfection, other monks, acolytes, clergymen, and petitioning villagers continued to seek him out for guidance at every stage of his withdrawal. He died around the age of 105 in the year 356.

Anthony became the most famous anchorite of Late Antiquity largely due to the quick and widespread dissemination of the *Life of Anthony*. An anchorite was specifically a monk who sought to live a religious lifestyle through solitude, asceticism, and—most importantly—retreat to the desert. The desert was a very potent physical and symbolic space in fourth-century Egypt. In the region of the Nile Delta and valley, the contrast between the fertile, inhabited space was starkly contrasted with the sterile, unpopulated land of the desert. The desert was therefore the place to go to escape people, but it was also the place to confront temptations and other tortures brought on by demonic manifestations. Anthony's retreat from society automatically marked him as an outsider, and his heroic battles against the devil gave him a holy aura that attracted people looking for an outsider to guide them. Anthony was not so remote in his desert retreat, however, that he did not take part in the religious debates of his day. For instance, during the Galerian persecutions of Christians around the year 306, Anthony traveled to Alexandria to support the Christians who had been jailed, leading the judges to ban his presence at court. Ultimately, it was the image of Anthony as desert monk which inspired so many imitators that Athanasius wrote that the desert was made a city by all the monks. Instead of duplicating the civilization of the towns, however, the monastic civilization of the desert was a place of spiritual exercise only.

Anthony was not the first religious hermit. The *Life* itself points to a hermit living in Anthony's town as the person to whom the young Anthony went for guidance on the ascetic life during the earliest stages of his retreat. Even the local women to whom he sent his sister probably practiced an early form of monastic communal life. Anthony was unique in combining the concept of the village holy person with the idea of desert retreat from the Old and New Testaments, to create the new figure of the desert anchorite.

Anthony is thus the best-known example and proponent of a new lifestyle that grew out of fourth-century religious and political developments. The peace of the Church, achieved by the emperor Constantine in 312, brought an end to the era of Christian persecutions and martyrdoms within the Roman Empire. A desire to escape or protest against ongoing theological debates coupled with the desire to achieve a new kind of martyrdom—the martyrdom of the flesh that was the central element of the anchoritic life. These factors led to the proliferation of anchorites in the Egyptian and Syrian deserts of the fourth and fifth centuries, especially in Nitria, Scete, and Palestine. Anthony's example also influenced the establishment of cenobitic monastic institutions in the upper Nile valley, which provided a monastic alternative to anchoritism in their emphasis on community life.

Athanasius's friendship and meetings with Anthony give first-hand validity to much of the *Life*. Athanasius also infused the work with his own theological agenda, denouncing Arians and Meletian schismatics through the words of Anthony to his followers. Although Anthony was involved in the debate against Arianism (which broke from the mainstream Church in its conception of the nature of the Trinity), he was more concerned with achieving spiritual perfection through desert asceticism. He therefore refused ordination as well as an invitation to visit the emperor Constantius.

The *Life*, through the words of Athanasius, reconstitutes many of Anthony's sermons, which are preoccupied with the battle against demons and the ascetic spiritual life. The fifth-century collection, *Sayings of the Desert Fathers*, also records many of his sayings, largely considered to be authentic. Anthony himself wrote several letters in Coptic that survive in the original and in Greek and Arabic translation, and possibly more, despite his portrayal in the *Life* as an illiterate layman. His feast days are 17 January in the Roman Catholic and Eastern Orthodox Churches and 30 January in the Coptic Church.

[*See also* Athanasius of Alexandria; *and* Augustine of Hippo.]

BIBLIOGRAPHY

Bartelink, G.J.M, ed. *Athanase d'Alexandrie: Vie d'Antoine*. Paris: Editions du Cerf, 1994.

Chitty, Derwas J. *The Desert a City: An Introduction to the Study of Egyptian and Palestinian Monasticism Under the Christian Empire*. Oxford: Blackwell, 1966.

Goehring, James E. *Ascetics, Society, and the Desert: Studies in Early Egyptian Monasticism*. Harrisburg, PA: Trinity Press International, 1999.

Migne, Jacques-Paul. SS. *patrum Aegyptiorum opera omnia*. [Anthony's letters in Greek.] *Patrologia graeca 40*. Paris: Migne, 1858.

STACEY GRAHAM

Antiochus IV (d. 164 BCE), Seleucid king of Syria (175–164 BCE), is an important figure in African history because of his involvement with Ptolemaic Egypt during the Sixth Syrian War of 170–168 BCE; although this was only a small portion of his career, it was nonetheless a significant moment in Egyptian history.

Antiochus was the youngest son of Antiochus III (ruled 222–187 BCE). His date of birth is not known but was around the end of the third century BCE. Like many members of the royal families of the Hellenistic East he spent time in Rome (in the 180s BCE), officially as a hostage. This was a typical procedure of the era, but it allowed a growing closeness between the Roman elite and eastern royalty and laid the ground for eventual Roman control of all the eastern kingdoms. When Antiochus III died in 187 BCE, his successor was his son Seleukos IV, the elder brother of Antiochus IV, but Seleukos soon proved himself a weak ruler. He offended both Rome and Pergamon, the former becoming more involved in the affairs of the Greek East and the latter moving into its most powerful period. Seleukos unsuccessfully attacked Pergamon, and this and other difficulties in his reign resulted in his assassination in 175 BCE. Eumenes II (the Pergamene king) and the Athenians promptly declared Antiochus IV king, perhaps even before his brother's death. At some time Antiochus IV gained the surname "Epiphanes," or "Renowned."

Antiochus inherited an unstable situation. The weak rule of his brother had undone many of the efforts of their father to return the Seleucids to their former greatness. The rising power of both Rome and Pergamon, as well as constant difficulties in the

Jewish territories of the southern Levant, seemed to make the situation untenable. Thus Antiochus continued a policy started by his father: involvement in the affairs of Ptolemaic Egypt.

From 205 BCE, the Ptolemaic kingdom had been ruled by Ptolemy V, who was an infant when he came to the throne. A tool of his advisors, the boy king had seen Antiochus III conquer the Ptolemaic territories in interior Syria and the Levant as a means of solidifying Seleucid power. But the Romans would not allow the Seleucids to be enhanced at the expense of the Ptolemies and attempted to negotiate a peace between the two kingdoms in 200 BCE. In response, Antiochos III had concluded a marriage alliance between his daughter, Cleopatra I, and Ptolemy V; this agreement was concluded at Raphia on the Egyptian-Levantine border in the winter of 194/3 BCE when Cleopatra was ten and Ptolemy sixteen. Although this linkage of the two great dynasties of the Hellenistic East was to be an important factor in the future history of the region (the royal couple were the great-great-grandparents of the last Ptolemaic ruler, the famous Cleopatra VII), for the moment it created an impossible situation by substantially altering the regional balance of power. Ptolemy V was assassinated by his staff at the age of thirty in 180 BCE; Cleopatra I died in 176 BCE at age twenty-eight. Their son Ptolemy VI, as weak as his father, inherited the rule, a year before his uncle Antiochos IV became Seleucid king.

Antiochus IV, now the senior member of the combined Seleucid-Ptolemaic families, moved over the next few years to take control of Egypt. Probably at this time he took the title "Protector of Egypt." He moved down the coast into Egypt and attempted to reclaim the dowry of his late sister Cleopatra I, which consisted of portions of interior Syria. Ptolemy requested Roman aid and the Senate forced the parties into negotiation. These were futile, and Antiochus continued expanding his control of Egypt, attempting to solidify his position before there was any aggressive Roman response. In the process he also captured Cyprus and advanced as far as Memphis in Egypt, perhaps being crowned pharaoh. He then moved against Alexandria. But the Romans were ready for him, and in July of 168 BCE, Popilius Laenas took up a position at Eleusis, outside Alexandria, and met with Antiochus. The Romans did not waste effort: they gave the king an ultimatum of complete and immediate withdrawal from Egypt. By effectively holding Antiochus hostage and not giving him

time to consider the matter, Popilius Laenas was able to enforce his will and the king withdrew. This event became a seminal moment in the expansion of Roman power in the East: the Ptolemaic kingdom survived, but for the remaining 138 years of its existence, it was beholden to Rome. Both the Ptolemies and the Seleucids entered into significant decline.

The remaining four years of Antiochus's rule did not concern Egypt. He had to contend with the Maccabean revolt in Judaea in 166 BCE and later campaigns in Armenia and the Iranian plateau, upon which he died in 164 BCE. His involvement with the Jewish territories is remembered in the biblical books of Maccabees and Daniel. A strong proponent of Hellenization and Greek culture, he was a major benefactor of the traditional Greek cities, although attempts at Hellenization among the Jews were less successful. Like his Ptolemaic relatives, he sought to hold together a kingdom collapsing in the face of expanding Roman power; when he died, the Seleucid territories were substantially smaller than when he began to rule.

As with much of the Hellenistic period, the ancient sources for Antiochus are scattered, largely Polybios 26-30, Diodoros 29-31, Livy 41-42, Josephus, *Jewish War* 1.31-40, and the biblical sources mentioned above.

[*See also* Ptolemy V.]

BIBLIOGRAPHY

Bevan, Edwyn Robert. *The House of Seleucus*. Chicago: Ares Publishers 1995 [reprint of 1902 edition]. Despite its great age, a still valuable study of the Seleucid kingdom.

Hölbl, Günther. *A History of the Ptolemaic Empire*. Translated by Tina Saavedra. London, Routledge 2001. The most detailed study of Antiochus's involvement in Egyptian affairs.

Mørkholm, O. *Antiochos IV of Syria*, Copenhagen: Gyldendal 1966. Although nearly half a century old, the only biography of the king.

DUANE W. ROLLER

Anyentyuwe (c. 1858–), Gabonese intellectual and catechist (one who instructs potential Christians before their admission to the Church), was born in the Glass neighborhood of Libreville, the capital of Gabon, a territory acquired by France in 1885. Sonie Harrington, her father, was a prominent trader who belonged to the coastal Omyènè-speaking Mpongwe ethnic group, which had occupied the

Gabon Estuary region for centuries. Her mother, who also belonged to a Mpongwe clan, died when Anyentyuwe was very young. Since Harrington traveled to central Gabon on a regular basis to represent different European trading firms, he placed his young daughters Ayentyuwe and Azize with the American-run Protestant mission school of Baraka. This school had been founded in the 1840s to educate Mpongwe girls and boys.

Anyentyuwe represented to many American Presbyterian missionaries a rare hope. Most female graduates of mission schools entered into romantic and sexual relationships with visiting European and West African men. The vast majority of European residents of the colony were male outside of the missions. These men sought out Mpongwe women who had been educated in mission schools, since they already knew European languages and had learned how to maintain a bourgeois European household. Some women entered these relationships in part because they sometimes provided more flexibility and material comforts than relationships with Mpongwe men. Since no missions had been established by American and European Christians between the coast of Cameroon and Cabinda before the 1870s, Mpongwe women in Libreville were particularly prized, and some lived with European officials and traders in an area extending from the Ivory Coast to the Independent State of the Congo by the 1880s. Anyentyuwe rejected such premarital intimate relationships as inherently sinful. Therefore, Anyentyuwe was seen as an unusual example of faithful Christianity.

After Anyentyuwe finished her studies, she became a teacher in Baraka by 1880. Rumors among American and Gabonese Protestants spread that she had entered sexual relationships with different European men, but she denied them. Unfortunately, the elderly American missionary William Walker, who had cofounded the Baraka mission in 1842, held a dour view of most Mpongwe women as promiscuous and deceitful. He doubted her conformity to mission norms on chastity and marriage and accused her of encouraging adolescent girls to drop out of school and become the mistresses of English traders. According to Anyentyuwe, she was raped by an African Christian associated with the mission. When she reported the incident to Walker, he categorically denied its veracity and ordered her to leave the mission in late 1881. This event was the beginning of a series of disappointing moments for Anyentyuwe involving the American Protestant community.

With no home and no surviving close family to help, Anyentyuwe struggled to make a living in the small port of Libreville. She had never learned how to farm because she had lived her whole life with missionaries. She gave birth to her only child, her daughter Iga, in late 1881. Like so many other women on the Gabonese coast, she entered into a series of relationships with different European and West African men. One man from Sierra Leone offered to marry her, but then he died suddenly. A Scottish trader sought to enter a romantic partnership with her, only to quickly leave her. Protestant missionaries described her as yet another fallen woman who had not lived up to her Christian upbringing. To improve her situation, she agreed to work as a store manager on the southern Gabonese lagoon of Sette Cama in 1887. There, a Frenchman demanded sexual favors and then accused her of theft in revenge for her refusal to accept his offer. She was briefly detained and brought back to Libreville, where the governor of the colony exonerated her.

After these unhappy episodes, she then went to work for the famed scholar and missionary doctor Robert Hamill Nassau. He had lived in Gabon since 1874 and had need of a governess to watch over his young child Mary. Between 1889 and 1899, Nassau and Anyentyuwe developed a very close personal and professional relationship. Through her friend's patronage, she built her own house. As Nassau began to write on Gabonese culture and social practices, he turned to Anyentyuwe for information on indigenous spiritual practices, ethnobotanical knowledge, and on the early history of the Protestant mission. Her accounts became an extremely valuable source for Nassau's ethnographic and historical writings, such as *Fetichism in West Africa* (1904) and *Tales Out of School* (1911). While Nassau vehemently denied any sexual aspect to their friendship, a range of Gabonese and American Protestants decried what they saw as a covert intimate affair that undermined the supposedly proper division between Africans and people of European descent. Anyentyuwe's outspoken defense of her behavior further alienated missionaries. For example, she responded to a rebuke about dressing in expensive European clothes by asking why missionaries had taught women to wear and mend dresses.

In 1899, Nassau took an extended furlough to the United States after managing the Baraka mission for much of the 1890s. A majority of the Presbyterian missionaries in German Cameroon and French

Gabon joined together to demand that Nassau not return to Libreville. They contended that Anyentyuwe and Nassau were lovers, even though they lacked evidence to back their accusations. The Presbyterian Church of the USA Board of Foreign Missions backed the charges and transferred Nassau to the southern Cameroonian port town of Batanga. To make matters worse, Anyentyuwe's daughter Iga entered a consensual sexual relationship with a British trader in Cameroon in 1898 against her mother's wishes. When the British trader left Cameroon due to illness, Iga was nearly raped by a ship captain on her return voyage to Libreville. Only Anyentyuwe's intervention saved her daughter.

With Nassau gone, save for several short interludes back in Libreville, Anyentyuwe became persona non grata at Baraka once again. She contracted an unspecified illness, perhaps leprosy, that left her an invalid by 1900. At her death in 1904, she was buried in the Baraka cemetery—a rare moment of generosity from a mission that had so questioned her during her life. Her experiences demonstrate the struggles of independent women in late-nineteenth-century Gabon.

[See also Nassau, Robert Hamill.]

BIBLIOGRAPHY

Jean-Baptiste, Rachel. "Une Ville Libre? Marriage, Divorce, and Sexuality in Colonial Libreville, Gabon; 1849–1960." PhD thesis, Stanford University, 2005.

Nassau, Robert. *My Ogowe.* New York: Neale, 1914.

Nassau, Robert. *Tales Out of School.* Philadelphia: Allen, Lane, and Scott, 1911.

Rich, Jeremy. "'Une Babylone Noire': Interracial Unions in Colonial Libreville, c. 1860–1914." *French Colonial History* 4 (2003): 145–170.

JEREMY RICH

Aoko, Gaudencia (1943–), a Luo woman, helped to found and lead two African-initiated churches. The third of four children, Aoko was born in July 1943 in the town of Awasi, nineteen miles east of Kisumu in Nyanza Province, Kenya. Her educational background is uncertain. In interviews she called herself "uneducated" and claimed to know neither Kiswahili nor English, suggesting that she did not attend school beyond the primary level. Young Aoko was winsome by all accounts—"photogenic," "tall with a smooth blackness," and a "beautiful well-proportioned face" (Dirven, 1970, p. 126).

Against Aoko's wishes not to marry, in 1957 her conservative father arranged a marriage to Simeo Owiti, a Catholic friend from Njoro near Nakuru. Three years later, the couple relocated south of the Kenya border to Bugire in the North Mara district of Tanganyika. Here, Aoko attended *Tatwe*, a Catholic mission run by the Maryknoll fathers, where she learned the catechism and was baptized.

Early in 1963, her two children, aged one and four, died mysteriously on the same day. Soon after, she divorced her husband. At this time, Aoko began to have visions of Jesus and Mary, who instructed her to start a new religion called "Maria Legio." Giving her the Christian name "Gaudencia," they commissioned her to baptize, exorcise, and heal the sick. In April 1963, at the suggestion of her husband's brother, Johannes Muga, Aoko made the ten-mile trip to see Simeo Ondeto, a religious leader living in Suna, Kenya.

She found Ondeto and his mother, "Mama Maria," at the homestead of Johanes Baru in South Nyanza. Ondeto surprised Aoko by greeting her by name, despite never having met previously. Ondeto and his mother identified themselves as the figures in her visions. "We are the persons you were seeing up there [in heaven]. We have descended here in a black man's image to visit you Africans, descendants of Esau" (Hinga, 1990, p. 94). They laid hands on the girl, blessing her as Jesus and Mary had done in her visions. They instructed her to baptize a crowd of people gathered outside the homestead. Thereafter, Aoko spent a month in South Nyanza baptizing, healing, and preaching.

The meeting with Ondeto and his mother marked the beginning of Aoko's ministry in the group for which she is best known—the Legio Maria Church, founded on the model of the Catholic lay association Legion of Mary. She drew thousands into the movement through her charismatic preaching and conducted mass baptisms according to the instruction of Ondeto and "Mama Maria." Within a year, Legio claimed nearly 100,000 members. By the 1990s it claimed 2 million. Reliable statistics are unavailable, but Legio probably numbers over 1 million today.

The church's success was due in large part to Aoko's charismatic leadership. Ondeto was detained for a time at Homa Bay, the target of government persecution. His mother, who died in 1966, was too old to travel widely. This left the task of proselytizing to Aoko, who drew large crowds throughout western Kenya and in parts of Uganda and Tanzania. Aoko came to be seen as a great moral reformer, especially in her home area of Central Nyanza. She condemned Catholic missionaries for requiring fees to administer the sacraments and said mass and heard confessions personally. She ordained priests; baptized women and men not in communion with the Catholic Church because of polygamous marriages; preached against social ills such as smoking, drunkenness, and land disputes; conducted healings and exorcisms; and burned witchcraft paraphernalia.

Aoko's peregrinations for Legio took her from rural western Kenya to the corridors of power in Nairobi and back again. Contemporary observers called her Legio's "most colourful figure," a "crowd-puller" of a "Luo girl" whose "magnetic style" kept "the listener spellbound" (Dirven, 1970, p. 126; Barrett, 1968, p. 149). Aoko's importance is reflected in Legio's first constitution (1964), which called her "Rt. Rev. Mama," one of "two extraordinary spiritual leaders" of Legio, and its "Auxiliary Spiritual Leader of the Faith."

In the late 1960s she faced attempts by male rivals to marginalize her. Men close to Ondeto, including Aoko's ex-brother-in-law, developed a church hierarchy of cardinals, archbishops, and bishops that excluded women from major leadership positions. In response, Aoko held a press conference in Nairobi in June 1968. She issued a statement as "leader and founder of the Legio Maria Church" rejecting the new arrangement, insisted that leadership be open to any adult with charismatic gifts, criticized Ondeto for calling himself "Jesus Christ," and leveled charges of embezzlement against him. Legio headquarters in Suna reacted swiftly, barring women from the priesthood and reducing Aoko's title to "Sister General" (Dirven, 1970, pp. 207, 237).

In response, Aoko resolved to establish a more egalitarian church, wherein anyone with spiritual gifts could lead. Her first two attempts to register a church failed. The Kenyan government rejected applications for the Legio Maria Orthodox Catholic Church in 1968 and the Holy Church of Africa, East Africa, in 1969. But Aoko's third attempt, in 1971, succeeded. She headquartered the new Communion Church at her natal compound in Awasi. It was small compared to Legio (about 800 followers in the 1980s) but had centers at Mpitano, Rapogi (South Nyanza); Imbo, Asembo (Central Nyanza); and Njiru, Kasarani (Nairobi) (Hinga, 1990, p. 351).

Aoko's egalitarian ideals and Christian activism bestowed a mixed legacy on this new church. As in Legio, mass in the Communion Church was conducted in Latin, and the church used Roman Catholic clerical titles. Aoko used the same hymns, prayers, rosary, and the twenty-four-beaded catena as before. But in contrast to Legio and the Roman Catholic Church, the Communion Church allowed female priests to celebrate Sunday mass. Many were veterans from Legio who had been forced out. Ondeto and his "Mama Maria" were revered, but their pictures were not on the altar. For Aoko, the Communion Church meant equality. All church members wore the same robes embroidered with the communion chalice, and all church members—even children—wore the white biretta reserved for cardinals in Legio.

Little attention has been paid to post-Legio Aoko. Feminist historiography treats her as representative of female African religious founders and leaders whose accomplishments were usurped by men. This is understandable as Aoko's break with Legio Maria effectively caused her disappearance in the press and scholarly literature. Nevertheless, she remained an influential religious leader and continued to defy convention. Contrary to Luo custom, Aoko established her own *dala* (homestead) on the basis of successful business ventures. She even took three wives, calling upon the cultural idiom of a "female husband." Her immediate family members called her *jaduong*, a title reserved for eminent male householders, and deferred to her authority in spiritual and domestic matters. She thus appropriated a traditionally male role in a society that excluded women and unmarried men from positions of power.

Scholars differ as to the significance of Aoko's career. Some see it as evidence for the opportunities afforded to charismatic women by African-initiated churches to transcend patriarchal norms. Others see in her later marginalization evidence for the merely "ephemeral" quality of such opportunities. Either way, it is clear that Aoko was a trailblazer who challenged the sexist and ageist prejudices prevalent in her society and within the Roman Catholic Church.

BIBLIOGRAPHY

Anderson, Allan H. *African Reformation: African Initiated Christianity in the 20th Century* (Trenton, N.J., 2001). A reference work that provides an excellent overview of African-initiated churches in sub-Saharan Africa, the chapter "East African Churches" includes a pithy discussion of Legio Maria and its founders complete with bibliographic references (pp. 142–166).

Barrett, David B. *Schism and Renewal in Africa: An Analysis of Six Thousand Contemporary Religious Movements* (Nairobi, 1968). Groundbreaking study featuring an excellent index and rare photographs of Aoko, her husband Owiti, Ondeto, and others. See also Barrett's *Kenya Churches Handbook: The Development of Kenyan Christianity, 1498–1973* (Kisumu, 1973), which includes information on Aoko's legal disputes with the other members of the Legio Maria Church and her new Communion Church (pp. 137, 243, 246).

Dirven, Peter J. "The Maria Legio: The Dynamics of a Breakaway Church among the Luo in East Africa." D.Miss. dissertation, Pontificia Universitas Gregoriana, Rome, 1970. The first academic study of Legio Maria, it discusses the relationship between Aoko and Ondeto and draws on newspaper reports, correspondence from missionaries, interviews with Legio members, and court and other government records.

Hackett, Rosalind. "Women and New Religious Movements in Africa." In *Religion and Gender*, edited by Ursula King, pp. 257–290 (Oxford, 1995). An anthropological and sociological examination of women's power and authority in African independent churches, this chapter includes a discussion (pp. 265–266) of Aoko's role in Legio and the Communion Church.

Hinga, Teresia Mbari. "Women, Power and Liberation in an African Church: A Theological Case Study of the Legio Maria Church in Kenya." Ph.D. dissertation, University of Lancaster, 1990. A well-documented study that includes the transcript of an interview with Aoko, firsthand accounts about her, newspaper articles, and an extensive bibliography.

Kustenbauder, Matthew. "Believing in the Black Messiah: The Legio Maria Church in an African Christian Landscape." *Nova Religio: The Journal of Alternative and Emergent Religions* 13, no. 1 (2009): 11–40.

Welbourn, Frederick B., and Bethwell A. Ogot. *A Place to Feel at Home: A Study of Two Independent Churches in Western Kenya* (London, 1966). Contains a short, two-page assessment of Legio Maria, naming Ondeto as founder and Aoko as having succeeded to the leadership while he was in prison (see pp. 147–148). For more on the colonial and precolonial background to religious-political movements in western Kenya, see Audrey Wipper, *Rural Rebels: A Study of Two Protest Movements in Kenya* (New York, 1977).

MATTHEW KUSTENBAUDER

Apion, Flavius (fifth–sixth centuries CE), Egyptian landowner and Roman imperial official, is the best attested member of a family of large landholders prominent in Egypt from the fifth to the seventh centuries. The Apionic estates were one of the dominant forces in the Oxyrhynchite *nome* or subprovince of Egypt during the Byzantine period. Its surviving papyrological documentation details the activities of these estates, their financial managers, their farmers, and other related figures. This material makes the Apionic estates, so-called "the noble house," one of the best documented economic institutions during Roman rule in Egypt. By recent count, the published material from the Apionic archive includes nearly 275 texts covering more than 180 years, from 436 to 620/1. The Apionic estates are likely to have been the largest in the Oxyrhynchite nome.

Procopius, a sixth-century Byzantine historian, describes Apion's role during the Roman Empire's war with Persia during the reign of Anastasius in 503–504 as that of the army's finance manager. He describes Apion as an Egyptian, preeminent among the empire's patricians and well known for his energy, adding that Anastasius had declared Apion a partner in his royal power. This impressive claim may be a classicizing attempt by Procopius to describe Apion's unusual role in the Persian war. Apion in this period held the title *patricius* and was appointed by Anastasius to the position of *praefectus praetorio Orientis vacans* (praetorian prefect of the East). The general Areobindus held the chief military command in the campaign against Persia; Apion's role was to provide his campaign with logistical support. The chronicle of pseudo-Joshua the Stylite reports that to do so, Apion came to Edessa to manage Roman military supplies. The presence of the Roman military in Edessa so strained the normal requisitioning processes that Apion ordered distribution of wheat to all Edessan households, so that the populace could make military rations at their own expense.

According to Theophanes, a later ninth-century source, Apion was soon caught in the midst of bickering Roman generals during this campaign. When the Persian king Kovades prepared for a major offensive, Hypatios and Patricius refused to come to the assistance of Areobindus, the highest ranking Roman military commander. Only Apion's persuasion kept Areobindus in the field, leading to the ultimate success of the Roman army and the withdrawal of Kovades. Apion continued to show himself crucial to the logistical operations of the Roman army in the field. Joshua the Stylite reports that in May 504, Apion returned to Egypt, where he directed the preparation and shipment of more military rations from Alexandria. Modern scholars have supposed that Apion's connections to Egypt—and particularly to its considerable agricultural resources—made him well suited to this task.

The level of imperial favor placing Apion in these posts did not last. Theophanes reports that in 505/6, Anastasius recalled Apion and Hypatius to Constantinople, reportedly because of their conflict with Areobindus. The chronicler Marcellinus notes that in 510, Apion was exiled. The reason is unknown, but it has been suggested that he conspired against Anastasius. Other chroniclers note that Apion was forcibly ordained a priest at Nicaea, presumably at the start of or during his period in exile. Theophanes notes that when Anastasius had died and Justin took the throne, Apion and several others were recalled from exile. Apion himself received appointment to the position of praetorian prefect of the east, one of the highest ranking positions in the imperial bureaucracy. In that capacity he appears as a recipient of imperial legislation recorded in the Codex Justinianus from 518.

Apion's prominence in imperial affairs served his family well in later generations. His son Strategios was apparently a confidant of the emperor Justinian, who in 533 chose him as his personal vicar and instructed him to preside over a church council aimed at reconciling the orthodox and monophysite factions of the eastern church (a debate that centered on the nature of Christ's divine and human aspects). Strategios, who participated in the reconstruction of the Hagia Sophia, is praised by Procopius as wise and noble. Apion's later descendants include his grandson, also named Apion, who held the consulship in 539; two honorary consuls in the 580s; and a correspondent of Pope Gregory the Great in the 590s and 600s.

Apion exemplifies the social and economic trends of the late Roman world in several ways. First, he seems to have been involved in the era's most pressing Christian theological controversy, that between the orthodox and the monophysites. Severus of Antioch dedicated a work to him and Paulus at some point between 508 and 510, implying that Apion was probably a monophysite in this period prior to his exile. Yet the testimony of Innocent of Maronea would indicate that Apion was converted to orthodoxy by Justin and Justinian, after his rehabilitation to imperial favor.

Second, Apion is representative of the rise of a bureaucratic landholding aristocracy in Roman late antiquity. In this model, high-ranking imperial bureaucrats accumulated considerable wealth in gold, which they subsequently invested in ever-growing agricultural estates. These estates were highly monetized enterprises relying on peasant wage labor. In the extreme form of this model, the great size of estates such as that of the Apions, upon which the Roman state became reliant for revenue collection in the provinces, threatened the long-term health of the empire by creating too great a barrier between the state and its sources of revenue. Aspects of this model have received challenge from various directions, but the dramatic growth of the estates of Apion and others like it is undeniable and provides scholars of late antiquity a valuable window into patterns of social connectivity and wealth acquisition in this period.

BIBLIOGRAPHY

Gascou, Jean. "Les Grands Domains, la Cité et l'État en l'Égypte Byzantine." *Travaux et Memoires* 9 (1985). A seminal study of the role of large landholders in relation to the state in late Roman Egypt, with an emphasis on the family of the Apions.

Martindale, J.R., ed. *The Prosopography of the Later Roman Empire: Volume 2, AD 395–527*. Cambridge, UK: Cambridge University Press, 1980. Compiles the basic primary source references to the life and career of Apion.

Mazza, Roberta. *L'Archivio degli Apioni: Terra, Lavoro e Proprieta Senatoria Nell'Egitto Tardoantico*. Bari: Edipuglia, 2001. The standard survey of the evidence for the large estates of the Apion family.

Ruffini, Giovanni. *Social Networks in Byzantine Egypt*. Cambridge, UK: Cambridge University Press, 2008. Uses network analysis to trace the growth of the Apion family's power in the sixth century.

GIOVANNI R. RUFFINI

Apithy, Sourou Migan (1913–1989), Beninese politician, was born on 8 April 1913 in the southern Benin town of Porto Novo. He was from a relatively poor family from the Goun ethnic community. Apithy managed to acquire a high level of education despite his family's limited means, thanks to Catholic mission schools, beginning with the St. Joseph Primary School run by the White Fathers missionary society in Porto Novo. He was among the tiny number of Beninese who obtained an undergraduate education before World War II. He moved to France in 1933, where he passed the baccalaureate examinations after attending a secondary school in Bordeaux. Then, he studied accounting and politics at several institutions, including the École Libre des Sciences Politiques. He received his degree in accounting from the École National d'Organisation Économique et Sociale. He also married during this time and had two children. With the outbreak of war, Apithy served in a French artillery unit in 1939 and 1940. Afterward, he worked as an accountant for a French company in Dakar.

In 1945, the advent of limited political representation in territorial assemblies and the French parliament for French colonies like Benin, then known as Dahomey, offered new opportunities for Beninese men who had received an advanced Western education. Apithy became the protégé of Father Francis Aupiais, a French Catholic missionary, and both men were elected in the first elections for parliamentary representatives of the colony in Paris. He ran under the auspices of the French Section Française de l'Internationale Ouvrière, (SFIO) party. Although Apithy briefly joined the radical coalition of African parties known as the Rassemblement Démocratique Africaine (RDA) in 1946, he chose to join the more moderate Independants d'Outre-Mer alliance soon afterward. He also served in the Beninese territorial assembly from 1946 to 1960 and as a member of the High Council of French West Africa from 1947 to 1957. He tended to back most SFIO parliamentary members on Algeria and took a moderate line regarding the future independence of Benin in the late 1940s and early 1950s. In 1953, he was part of the French delegation to the United Nations.

In Benin during the 1950s, Apithy acted as a major power broker. He helped to start the Union Progréssiste Dahoméene (UPD), the first Beninese political party, but later formed his own party, Parti Républicain Dahoméen (PRD), in 1951. Apithy was a moderate opportunist who regularly changed his alliances. In 1956, he added to his portfolio the post of mayor of Porto Novo. Apithy then became president of the Beninese parliament in 1957. He had to share power with Hubert Maga and Justin Ahomadégbé-Tometin in parliament in the final years of French colonial rule in 1959 and 1960. While Apithy was the dominant figure in Porto Novo and southeastern Benin, Maga dominated the north and Ahomadégbé controlled the southwest. Apithy's legendary reputation for corruption and his equivocations regarding the proposed federation of Mali and Senegal alienated many of his previous supporters. Many in Apithy's own party turned against him. However, Maga assigned Apithy to be his government's Minister of Finances in 1960.

When Ahomadébé's UDD (Union Démocratique du Dahomé) party tried to seize power in the Beninese parliament in 1960, former rivals Maga and Apithy decided to join their parties together. They created the Parti Dahoméen de l'Unité (PUD) and banned the UDD. Although Apithy briefly became vice president, with Maga as president, Maga then chose to reduce Apithy's influence by transferring him to Benin's new diplomatic service in 1963. The extremely unstable political situation in Benin brought Apithy back at the end of 1963, when Maga was forced to step down from power. Beninese military officers supported Apithy and made him the new president on 25 January 1964, with his former opponent Ahomadégbé as vice-president. This new coalition of former foes proved as problematic as Apithy's previous partnership with Maga. By 1965, Apithy and Ahomadégbé were both turning different factions within the Beninese military against each other. The government became deadlocked in squabbling between the two men, which promoted military officer Christophe Soglo to mount a coup on 27 November 1965. Soglo claimed he wanted to prevent a civil war, which might have occurred if Apithy and Ahomadégbé had continued their bitter struggle.

Apithy fled to Paris immediately after the coup, which in the second half of the 1960s had become the home for many former African leaders overthrown in military coups. He stayed in France for five years. When a new military junta decided to hold elections in 1970, Apithy was permitted to return to run against his old colleagues and competitors Maga and Ahomadégbé. Apithy finished a distant third in the elections, but the results were meaningless, because the military chose to cancel the entire electoral process. Again, it appeared that a civil war would break out. Apithy did not help matters, particularly by suggesting that Nigeria should annex his home base of Porto Novo. Meanwhile, Maga threatened to encourage the secession of northern Benin as well. Maga, Ahomadégbé, and Apithy decided to share power in April 1970 through a byzantine plan in which each politician would serve as president for two years.

Apithy had to wait until 1974 for his turn at being the head of the government, but he never had the chance to assume power. Popular opinion rapidly turned against all three men, whose taste for luxurious cars and mansions alienated the majority of the people, who were living in poverty. The Beninese regime's decision to send a Togolese opposition figure back to strongman Étienne Gnassingbé Eyadéma further alienated people. Students protested against the government, while several different plots by different military units threatened to overthrow the shaky triumvirate. In 1972, Mathieu Kérékou and other military officers took over the country. Apithy was placed under house arrest and remained a prisoner until 1981. There, he lived in relative obscurity and poor health and spent much of his time writing. He managed to stay alive long enough to see the commencement of Kérékou's fall from power, but died on 12 November 1989 in Paris, only a few months before the rise of multiparty democracy in Benin.

[See also Ahomadégbé-Tometin, Justin; Gnassingbé Eyadéma, Étienne; Kérékou, Chaad Mathieu; Maga, Coutoucou Hubert; Soglo, Christophe.]

BIBLIOGRAPHY

Apithy, Sourou-Migan. *Face aux Impasses.* Cotonou, Benin: A.B.M., 1971.

Decalo, Samuel. *Historical Dictionary of Benin.* 3d ed. Lanham, Maryland: Scarecrow, 1995.

"Joseph, Sorou, Migan, Marcellin Apithy," Biographies des députés de la IVe République, accessed 26 March 2010, http://www.assemblee-nationale.fr/sycomore/fiche.asp?num_dept=166.

Ronen, Dov. *Dahomey: Between Tradition and Modernity.* Ithaca, NY: Cornell University, 1975.

JEREMY RICH

Appiah, Joseph Emmanuel (1918–1990), Ghanaian politician and diplomat, was born on 16 November 1918 and raised in Kumasi, the capital of Ghana's Ashanti region. His father was James Appiah, headmaster of the Wesleyan school in Kumasi and secretary of the Asanteman Council, a chiefly body that helped govern Ashanti. He was also secretary to his brother-in-law, the Ashanti king. His mother, who died when he was a child, was the niece of a prominent Cape Coast–based businessman, who, as head of Appiah's matrilineal family, played a central role in his upbringing. Appiah attended the elite Methodist secondary school at Cape Coast, Mfantsipim. He joined the management of the United Africa Company after graduation, was posted in Sierra Leone during World War II, and

traveled in 1944 to Britain, where he studied law and became a member of the Middle Temple. In the following decade, Appiah was an activist in the pro-independence West African Students' Union (WASU) and eventually became its president. He grew close to many leading British anti-imperialists and such African independence leaders as Hastings Kamuzu Banda (independent Malawi's first head of state), Jomo Kenyatta (independent Kenya's first head of state), and Kwame Nkrumah (independent Ghana's first head of state), as well as Pan-Africanist writers such as George Padmore and C.L.R. James. His also met his future wife, Peggy Cripps, who was a daughter of Sir Stafford Cripps, the postwar British Chancellor of the Exchequer. The two married in 1953, occasioning headlines around the world; it was considered the first "society" wedding to cross the color bar. They moved to Ghana a year later, a few months after the birth of their first child, Kwame Anthony Appiah. Three daughters—Ama, Adwoa, and Abena—followed over the next eight years.

Appiah, in his WASU period, was supportive of the United Gold Coast Convention, the political party that led the way to Ghana's independence. The party, established in 1946, was founded and headed by Joseph B. Danquah, a lawyer and philosopher who, like Appiah, was of Akan ethnicity; Kwame Nkrumah, of the small Nzima ethnic group, served as its general secretary. But, by 1957, the year when the Gold Coast colony (in combination with Ashanti and the Togoland trust territory) achieved independence as the Republic of Ghana, Danquah and Nkrumah (whose politics and policies were distinctly more radical than Danquah's) were leading separate parties. On his return to Ghana, Appiah split with his old friend Nkrumah and joined Danquah's party. He was elected to parliament, representing a district in the Ashanti region, and spoke vigorously in opposition to Nkrumah, condemning his increasingly authoritarian mode of governance. In 1958, Nkrumah's government passed the Preventative Detention Act, allowing incarceration without trial for political offenses; three years later, Appiah was arrested and, without any formal charges, was interned at Ussher Fort Prison, the same prison where, in 1948, Nkrumah himself had been held by the British. There, Appiah joined other luminaries of Ghanaian independence, such as Danquah (who was imprisoned again at the time of his death, in 1965). Appiah was released late the following year, but forbidden from engaging in politics outside of the governing party.

In 1966, after a period of economic stagnation, during which Nkrumah's unpopularity grew, a young Ashanti major, Akwasi Afrifa, organized a coup; Nkrumah, visiting Hanoi, Vietnam, at the time, retired to Guinea, becoming Sékou Touré's honorary co-president for life. Appiah returned to public service as a diplomat.

The next twenty years saw Ghanaian politics alternating between Nkrumahism, with an anti-Akan focus, and the Akan-based politics associated with Danquah, K.A. Busia, and Appiah. Late in 1969, Busia became prime minister of the Second Republic, elected under a constitution that Appiah, representing Ghana's Bar Association, helped draft. But Appiah declined to join Busia's Progress Party (Busia, he alleged, had mismanaged the opposition's finances). Instead, he ran with the Nationalist Party, which he founded. Its symbol was a broom, symbolizing the aim of sweeping away corruption, but his own constituency saw him as disloyal to the Ashanti cause and denied him a seat. His party took the capital, however, and, merging with another party, formed a united opposition Justice Party, with Appiah as its extra-parliamentary chairman. The Second Republic was beset by charges of corruption and abuse of power, as well as by economic reverses (including a large IMF-imposed devaluation), and early in 1972, while Busia was in London, the military returned to power, with another Ashanti officer, General I.K. Acheampong, serving as head of state.

For the next several years, Appiah engaged in diplomacy and conducted many investigations of multinational corporations operating in Ghana. In 1979, as Ghana was in a process of returning to civilian rule, Jerry Rawlings, a junior flight lieutenant of Scottish and Ewe ancestry, staged a coup; Acheampong and Afrifa were among those executed, and Appiah was briefly imprisoned and investigated. Rawlings, after stepping aside for a two-year period of civilian government, spent a dozen years as head of state. Appiah did not return to public life during this period and did not live to see the restoration of civilian rule that he had pressed for; he died of cancer on 8 July 1990 in Accra. His memoir, *Joe Appiah: The Autobiography of an African Patriot*, was published in 1990.

[*See also* Acheampong, Ignatius Kutu; Appiah, Kwame Anthony; Banda, Hastings Kamuzu; Busia, Kofi Abrefa; Danquah, Joseph Boakye; Kenyatta, Jomo; Nkrumah, Kwame; Rawlings, Jerry John; *and* Touré, Ahmed Sékou.]

BIBLIOGRAPHY

Appiah, Joseph. *Joe Appiah: The Autobiography of an African Patriot*. New York: Praeger, 1990.

Appiah, Joseph. *Antiochus Lives Again!: Political Essays of Joe Appiah*. Kumasi, Ghana: I. Agyeman-Duah, 1992.

HENRY LOUIS GATES, JR.

Appiah, Kwame Anthony (b. 1954), Ghanaian philosopher, educator, novelist, and poet, was born in London on 8 May 1954. His full name is Kwame Anthony Akroma-Ampim Kusi Appiah. Appiah's father was the prominent Ghanaian lawyer and politician, Joseph Emmanuel Appiah, who in Ghana served as a member of Parliament, an ambassador, and president of the Ghana Bar Association. His mother was the English novelist and children's writer, Peggy Cripps Appiah. Appiah was born in London while his father was a law student there, but the family returned to Ghana when he was a baby. Appiah's paternal and maternal forebears were politically distinguished in Ghana and England, respectively. His uncle, Otumfuo Nana Poku Ware II, succeeded his great-uncle, Otumfuo Sir Osei Agyeman Prempeh II, as king of Ashanti in 1970. His mother's father was Sir Stafford Cripps, Britain's chancellor of the Exchequer, who was involved in negotiating the terms of Indian independence. Appiah attended the University Primary School at the Kwame Nkrumah University of Science and Technology, Kumasi, Ghana, Ullenwood Manor in Gloucestershire, England, and Port Regis and Bryanston Schools in Dorset, England. He earned his bachelor's and doctoral degrees in philosophy at Clare College, Cambridge University, in 1975 and 1981, respectively.

Shortly after graduating from Cambridge, Appiah published his first book, a revision of his dissertation entitled *Assertion and Conditionals* (Cambridge University Press, 1985). A second book followed soon after, *For Truth in Semantics* (Blackwell, 1986), which drew on his Cambridge training in analytical philosophy and further established Appiah as a key philosopher in the field of language and logic. In 1989, he authored a textbook, *Necessary Questions: An Introduction to Philosophy* (Prentice Hall), that became seminal in the discipline. It was revised and published as *Thinking It Through* in 2003. *Avenging Angel*, a mystery set at Clare College and the first of Appiah's three novels, was published in 1991.

In 1992, a year after joining the faculty of the Department of Afro-American Studies at Harvard

University, Appiah published *In My Father's House* (Oxford University Press), an examination of the influence of African and African American intellectuals on the formation of contemporary African cultural life. This was considered his first foray into the field of African and African American cultural studies, a field to which he would return frequently in his subsequent work. His second novel, *Nobody Likes Letitia*, was published in 1994 (Constable), and his third, *Another Death in Venice*, in 1995 (Constable). In 1996, he coauthored *Color Conscious: The Political Morality of Race* (Princeton University Press) with political scientist and president of the University of Pennsylvania, Amy Gutmann.

A frequent collaborator of Henry Louis Gates, Jr., his classmate at Clare College and his colleague at Yale University, Cornell University (1986–1989), Duke University (1990–1991), and Harvard University (1991–2002), the two coedited the *Dictionary of Global Culture* in 1996 (Knopf), which was followed in 1999 by the landmark publication of *Encarta Africana*, a CD-ROM encyclopedia published by Microsoft, and available in book form as *Africana: The Encyclopedia of the African and African-American Experience* (Basic Civitas). *Africana* was the realization of a dream of W. E. B. Du Bois, according to Gates and Appiah, to produce an encyclopedia similar in scope to the *Encyclopedia Britannica*, but by and about people of African descent. Oxford University Press published a revised multi-volume edition of *Africana* in 2005.

In 2002, Appiah left Harvard to join the Princeton University faculty as Laurance S. Rockefeller University Professor of Philosophy and the University Center for Human Values. A year later, he served as coauthor on *Bu Me Bé: Proverbs of the Akan*, an annotated edition of 7,500 proverbs in Twi, the Asante language. He continued to publish books that straddled the disciplines of philosophy and cultural studies, with *The Ethics of Identity* (Princeton University Press, 2005); *Cosmopolitanism: Ethics in a World of Strangers* (Norton, 2006), which won the 2007 Arthur Ross Award of the Council on Foreign Relations; *Experiments in Ethics* (Harvard University Press, 2008); and *The Honor Code: How Moral Revolutions Happen* (Norton, 2010).

Appiah was the recipient of honorary degrees from the University of Richmond, Colgate University, Bard College, Fairleigh Dickinson University, Swarthmore College, Dickinson College, Columbia University, the New School, Colby College, and Berea College.

He was elected to the American Academy of Arts and Sciences, the American Philosophical Society, and the American Academy of Arts and Letters. He served on the boards of the PEN American Center, of which he became president in 2009, the National Humanities Center, and the American Academy in Berlin and was a trustee of Ashesi University College in Accra, Ghana. He was president of the Eastern Division of the American Philosophical Association and the chair of the Board of the American Council of Learned Societies. His numerous books awards included the Anisfield-Wolf Book Award and the Herskovits Award of the African Studies Association.

Appiah and his partner, Henry Finder, editorial director of the *New Yorker*, have homes in New York City and Pennington, New Jersey. Appiah is also a frequent contributor to the *New York Times Magazine*, the *New York Review of Books*, the *Washington Post*, and other publications.

[*See also* Appiah, Joseph Emmanuel.]

BIBLIOGRAPHY

Gates, Henry Louis, Jr., and Kwame Anthony Appiah. "Introduction." In *Africana: The Encyclopedia of the African American Experience*, edited by Henry Louis Gates Jr. and Kwame Anthony Appiah, pp. ix–xvi. New York: Basic Civitas Books, 1999. An introductory essay detailing the origins of the encyclopedia.

"Kwame Anthony Appiah." http://www.appiah.net. Appiah's own comprehensive Web site.

McPheron, William. "Kwame Anthony Appiah." Stanford Presidential Lectures in the Humanities and Arts. Stanford University Libraries, 2004. http://prelectur.stanford.edu/lecturers/appiah/. A useful overview of Appiah's books and his place in philosophy.

ABBY WOLF

Appian of Alexandria (second century CE), historian, composed an invaluable *Roman History* in Greek while living and working in Rome under the emperors Hadrian (ruled 117–138 CE) and Antoninus Pius (ruled 138–161 CE). What scant biographical details we possess derive from a few remarks about himself in his work, especially in the *History*'s Preface (Appian also evidently published an autobiography that has not survived). We catch a further, fleeting glimpse of his personality through extant letters exchanged with his friend Fronto, the Roman jurist and man of letters from Numidia (modern Algeria and Tunisia) in Africa, who helped to advance the historian's career by intervening on his behalf with Antoninus Pius. By Appian's own reckoning, he was a man of some stature in his native Alexandria, who in his late twenties or early thirties moved to Rome to pursue his career soon after Hadrian took power in 117. The precise nature of Appian's position in Rome is unclear, but he certainly practiced law at a fairly high level. Again, he proves the most useful informant about himself, reporting that he had "pleaded cases before emperors." It has been plausibly argued that this refers to a period of tenure as a lawyer working for the imperial *fisc*, or treasury. This would help explain his apparent interest in and familiarity with the finances of Rome (he alleges that the final book of his *History*, now unfortunately lost, included a discussion of imperial revenues).

Appian's *Roman History* was an ambitious undertaking, a full-scale history of Rome and the evolution of its empire in twenty-four "books" covering over eight hundred years. It encompassed the period from Rome's founding in 753 BCE and the monarchy down to the beginning of the reign of Augustus (and thus of the principate or Roman Empire) and the point at which Egypt became a Roman province in 30 BCE; the *History* concluded with an account of his native Egypt and events of the Empire's first century. A good deal of the work survives intact (an indication of how useful it was deemed to be), perhaps most significantly the five books detailing the Roman civil wars. Sadly, however, the entire latter part of the *History* (Books 18–24), including the four books of Egyptian history, is lost.

One of the most distinctive features of this work is the way in which it is arranged. The twenty-four books of the *History* fall into roughly three parts: one dealing with Rome's beginnings and the Republican wars of conquest through the first half of the first century BCE (Books 1–12); another with Rome's own civil conflicts from 133 to 30 BCE, from the time of the Gracchi down to the emergence of Augustus as Rome's first emperor (Books 13–17); and a third part (Books 18–24) covering Egyptian history and the first one hundred years of the Empire's history (roughly 30 BCE – 69 CE), with two concluding books about Dacia and Arabia, respectively, both of which had been brought under control in Appian's own time by the emperor Trajan (98–117 BCE). Both individual books and books grouped around a particular subject are conventionally referred to by a title (e.g., the *Aegyptiaka* or "Egyptian History") and, where there are multiple books, a separate numbering system (e.g., Books 13–17 are commonly referred to as *Civil Wars* 1–5). Appian deals with Rome's wars of conquest "ethnographically" or by region, beginning, after an initial book devoted to the Roman monarchy, with the conquest of the Italian peninsula (Book 3, the *Italika*) and moving through the successive stages in Rome's expansion beyond the shores of Italy (thus, for example, Book 7, the *Hannibalika*, chronicles the Second Punic War against Hannibal, the famous general from the North African city of Carthage; Book 9, Rome's wars with Macedonia; and Book 12, the struggle against Mithridates in Asia Minor). The account of Rome's civil conflicts between 133 and 30 BCE intervenes between the first twelve books and his four-book survey of Egyptian history, or *Aegyptiaka*, setting Egypt apart as a mark of both patriotic pride and practicality, since Egypt was a comparatively late acquisition for Rome, only becoming a province in 30 BCE, at the beginning of the reign of Augustus.

Appian was the beneficiary of an increasing tendency on the part of Rome to welcome Greeks (or, more properly, Greek-speaking Easterners) into the imperial administration, especially in Rome itself. Clearly a well-informed admirer of Rome and the Romans, he nonetheless writes from the perspective of a provincial, with an evident interest in his native Alexandria and Egypt. Although other Greek writers had composed histories of Rome, Appian is the first—and the first African—to write as an insider and participant in the imperial bureaucracy. In part, his aim appears to have been to educate his Greek readers in the history of Rome and of the empire—and perhaps to engender acceptance of, if not pride in, being part of that empire. The *Roman History*, while not a literary masterpiece and occasionally faulted for inaccuracies, is distinguished by a number of unique, welcome features; apart from the distinctive manner in which he organized the work, Appian is sensitive to social and economic issues to a degree not typical of his peers in either Greek or Latin (one reason why Karl Marx admired him). He is, moreover, no apologist for the sometimes brutal nature of Rome's rise to dominance in the Mediterranean. In terms of its importance to our understanding of the subject, Appian's history of Rome is among the most valuable we possess and Appian himself among the most notable authors to have emerged from Egypt during the Roman period.

[*See also* Augustus; *and* Hannibal.]

BIBLIOGRAPHY

Works by Appian

Appian. *Appian's Roman History*. 4 volumes. Translated by Horace White. London and Cambridge, MA, 1912 (multiple reprints). Greek text with facing English translation. The only complete English translation of Appian's *History* available.

Appian. *The Civil Wars*. Translated by John Carter. London,1996. Excellent, recent translation of the *Civil Wars* portion of Appian's *History*, with a superb introduction to both Appian and the historical period, notes, and bibliographical guidance.

Works about Appian

Bowie, Ewen L. "Appian." In *The Cambridge History of Classical Literature*, edited by P. E. Easterling and B. W. Knox. Vol. 1: Greek Literature, pp. 707–709, 888–889. Cambridge, UK: Cambridge University Press, 1985. Solid if brief account of Appian, his work, and his place in the literary and cultural milieu of the second century.

Gowing, Alain M. *The Triumviral Narratives of Appian and Cassius Dio*. Ann Arbor: University of Michigan Press, 1992. A detailed study of Appian's account of the period following the assassination of Caesar (44–35 BCE), with a good deal of general discussion about the historian and his work.

ALAIN M. GOWING

Aptidon, Hassan Gouled (1916–2006), Somali Issa Abgal Mamassan, president of the Republic of Djibouti (1977–1999), was born on 15 October 1919 in the village of Garissa in present-day Somaliland. His parents were nomads from the Loyada area, which is located at the frontier with the former British Somaliland. According to his official biography, he left the nomadic life as a young man, and "on his own," he was admitted to a Roman Catholic mission school in Djibouti, where he graduated from the primary school. As a young man, he earned his living doing odd jobs in the port and later taught in a primary school.

However, Hassan Gouled's true love was politics. In 1946, he joined the Club de la Jeunesse Somali et Dankali, a political group founded by Mahamoud Harbi. His philosophical differences with Harbi quickly became evident. He was elected representative in the Territorial Council (in which he served from 1952 to 1958), allegedly because he was not favorable to separation of the colony from the French Union. Disassociating himself entirely from the hotheaded Mahamoud Harbi, Hassan Gouled established his own party, the Défense des Intérêts Economiques et Sociaux du Territoire (DIEST). He ran for a seat in the Territorial Assembly in 1957, losing to someone who was backed by Harbi. In December 1958, Hassan Gouled was elected vice president of the Council of Government in Djibouti, a position he held for only four months. In April 1958,

Hassan Gouled Aptidon, 1986. (AP Images/Laurent Rebours)

he was elected as deputy for French Somaliland in the French National Assembly. While serving in Paris, Hassan Gouled attracted the attention of Charles de Gaulle, perhaps to his credit in the Assembly, but he was careless with his political alliances at home, and he failed to be reelected to the French National Assembly in the elections of 1962.

Hassan Gouled's unreserved support for a positive vote on the 1958 referendum on the maintenance of ties to the French union caused him to be called before his party to explain his position. He pledged that he would support a step-by-step evolution of the colony toward independence. He founded the Union Démocratique Issa (UDI) in 1959. Hassan Gouled was reelected to the Territorial Assembly in 1963, becoming Minister of Education in the Council of Government presided over by Ali Aref Bourhan, a position that he held until January 1967. At that time, the four Somali ministers in the Djibouti government announced their intention to vote "no" on the referendum vote, to be held on 19 March 1967. Hassan Gouled then symbolically shifted his party membership to the Parti Mouvement Populaire (PMP), a party that he had always opposed. Originally the party of Mahamoud Harbi, the PMP campaigned for independence in the referendum, but quickly disappeared afterward.

During the next ten years, Hassan Gouled carefully plotted his path to becoming the colony's preeminent independence leader. His first step was to found yet another political party, the Union Populaire Africaine (UPA). In 1971, he joined the UPA with the Ligue Pour l'Avenir et l'Ordre of Ahmed Dini Ahmed, a longtime Afar opponent of Ali Aref and an ardent champion of independence. Together, they established the Ligue Populaire Africaine (LPA), the first national multiethnic political party. Four years later, the LPA joined with the Action pour la Justice et le Progrès, a primarily moderate Somali grouping with strong ties to the business community, to form the Ligue Populaire Africaine pour l'Indépendence (LPAI). In order to broaden further the impressive coalition being put together, Hassan Gouled and Ahmed Dini traveled together to Mogadishu, where they met with leaders of the Front de Libération de la Côte des Somalis (FLCS), the armed radical group established by Harbi in 1958. Although it later fell apart after independence, when a key player was badly wounded in a shootout between FLCS factions, a secret agreement was signed guaranteeing certain key ministries to the FLCS after independence. Although it was not possible to implement the ministerial

appointment guarantees after the shootout, the FLCS flag was adopted as Djibouti's national banner.

Violent demonstrations in 1976 led to the resignation of Government Council president Ali Aref, thus removing the most prominent opponent of independence and potential obstacle to Hassan Gouled's domination of the pre-independence negotiations. As a temporary measure, Aref was replaced by Abdallah Mohamed Kamil, an Afar notary thoroughly committed to facilitating the path to independence. The formal process began with a roundtable conference in Paris on 28 February 1977, to set the timetable for independence and to establish the rules and procedures for the transfer of power. Although many representatives from the Djibouti side would have preferred a clearer idea of the shape of the independence government, Hassan Gouled declared that he would prefer to have those matters worked out in Djibouti rather than Paris. A referendum was held on 8 May 1977 to demonstrate the people's desire for independence. In the referendum, Hassan Gouled was elected to the new parliament, which proclaimed him President of the Republic at midnight on 26–27 June 1977.

Independence was celebrated with both joy and solemnity and a fireworks display at midnight on 26–27 June. A cabinet was formed, with Ahmed Dini named as Prime Minister. On 8 July, the office of the President released the first laws of the new state, in which the President is cited as both chief of state and chief of government. Ahmed Dini was profoundly disappointed to see that his role as prime minister was bereft of any real power. He resigned from the government a few months later. The disillusionment of the Afars would lead in 1991 to an active civil war with Ahmed Dini as leader.

Apart from his inability to put aside age-old Somali Issa–Afar rivalries, Hassan Gouled had a full plate of problems at independence: he had never been a pan-Somali supporter, and he had to hold Siyad Barre at arm's length while assuring the FLCS veterans that they were fully accepted in the new republic. Hassan Gouled had to assure Ethiopia that its access to the sea through Djibouti would not be threatened; he also had to maintain Djibouti's position as the sole state in the Horn with a fully convertible currency. While the Djibouti city population was (and still is) one of the most desperately poor urban areas in Africa, he had to maintain order, especially while his neighbors were occupied with fighting each other. Although it was hard for many other African states to accept, the continued presence of French military units in Djibouti was critical. He handled these complicated issues adeptly and successfully.

The one matter that Hassan Gouled appears not to have thought through was the possibility of a violent response by the Afar to their secondary role in the state apparatus. He sought to demonstrate his democratic spirit by including Afars in all of his cabinets and departments and in the national assembly. Since independence, every prime minister has been an Afar. Both Gouled and his successor have attempted to secure Afar loyalty through generous benefits for those who serve the state, including distribution of land and properties, exemption from taxes and fees, education, and foreign travel. For those judged ineffective or disloyal, they risk losing everything.

In domestic affairs, Gouled's most controversial decision was to outlaw *khat* in his first few months in office. The French had attempted unsuccessfully to halt the *khat* trade in 1956. This mild narcotic, produced in the Ethiopian highlands of Harrar, is consumed by a large majority of men and a few women in Djibouti. Its users claim that the fresh *khat* leaves curb thirst and hunger and facilitate conversation. *Khat* also severely affects productivity and consumes a significant portion of household incomes. The father of Djiboutian independence was unable to change a nation's habits, and after two years of general noncompliance, the law expired.

In the midst of the early months of the Afar-led civil war in 1991, Hassan Gouled started giving serious thought to the development of a multiparty constitution. He appointed a fourteen-member single party commission in January 1992, including some ministers and members of the national assembly. The commission deliberated in secret and produced a draft constitution for the president's review on 23 March. A month later, President Hassan released the draft and called for a referendum; the document was approved by 96 percent of the voters, and there was a high turnout of 76 percent. The Afar opposition was generally pleased and supportive of the new constitution. It provided a multiparty basis for the 1999 elections. Unfortunately, they complain now that the multiparty promises in the constitution have not since been implemented.

Djibouti's first president, afflicted by old age, failing eyesight, and general fatigue, retired in 1999 to his hilltop home at Arta, about 75 kilometers southwest of Djibouti town. Hassan Gouled was married monogamously for many years to Aicha Bogoreh. She balanced the austerity and intensity of her husband with a cheerful and magnetic personality. She was very active in charity work in the poor community of Djibouti town, and she worked hard for the rights of women. The first couple had no children. She died in 2001, and he followed in 2006.

[*See also* Ahmed Dini Ahmed; Bourhan, Ali Aref; Harbi, Mahamoud Farah; Kamil, Abdallah Mohamed; *and* Siyad Barre, Mohamed.]

BIBLIOGRAPHY
Agonafer, Fantu. *Djibouti's Three-Front Struggle for Independence, 1967–77* Ph.D. dissertation. School of International Studies, University of Denver, 1979.
Oberlé, Philippe and Pierre Hugot. *Histoire de Djibouti: Des origines à la République Paris*: Présence Africaine, 1985.
Osman, Sultan Ali. "Djibouti: The Only Stable State in the Horn of Africa?" and "Interview with President Hassan Gouled Aptidon," *Horn of Africa* 5 (1982): 48-59.
Thompson, Virginia, and Richard Adloff. *Djibouti and the Horn of Africa*. Stanford, Calif.: Stanford University Press, 1968.

WALTER CLARKE

Apuleius, Lucius (c. 125–180), Numidian author and orator, was born a citizen of Rome in c. 125 CE in the town of Madauros in the province of Africa, an area that had become Roman territory in 146 BCE. His home town was 140 miles (225 kilometers) southwest of ancient Carthage, the site of the modern city of Tunis. Perhaps as a child Apuleius learned first the native Berber dialect; certainly he heard Greek in his home and outside it, as well as the language of all government, Latin. This language became Apuleius's major one; he had, it seems, a solid but not equal facility in Greek. After schooling in Carthage, the major city of the province, Apuleius traveled to Athens, Greece, for further study, where he studied rhetoric and philosophy, to learn more especially about the thought of Plato. He then went to Rome for more education in rhetoric, all of it now in Latin. Such an education was possible because he came from a prosperous family: his father rose to the highest office in Madauros.

Still a young man, Apuleius returned to Carthage where, as a sophist, he gave public lectures to paying audiences on a wide range of topics. Like many sophists he traveled frequently in search of new audiences. Early in his career, while visiting Oea, the site of modern Tripoli on the coast of Libya, he was persuaded to marry Pudentilla, a wealthy widow perhaps ten years Apuleius's senior and the mother of his friend Pontianus. After their marriage, her late husband's relatives, who had intended to gain control of the money left Pudentilla by her husband, charged Apuleius in court with having used magic to influence her to marry him. The trial was held in the nearby town of Sabrata. Apuleius refuted the charges with basic information and logic, but in the flowery and elaborate style of writing found in most of his other writings and typical of this period of Graeco-Roman culture. We have no record of the court's verdict, but the writing of later commentators implies that Apuleius's eloquent defense was successful.

The elaborate style of Apuleius's writings reflects a movement called the Second Sophistic, which included the revival of the elaborate style of Greek speeches of the fifth and fourth centuries BCE, the classical age. Written in this highly artificial style is his *Florida* (Anthology), a collection of twenty-three notable passages from some of his speeches that well may have been delivered at Carthage in the 160s CE. The work, compiled by the author to show off his various talents, covers topics ranging from characteristics of the people of India to anecdotes from myth and history to the habits of parrots, and it reveals his imagination and virtuosity in the use of language.

Another surviving work of Apuleius, written in the style of the day, is the *de deo Socratis* (About the god of Socrates). It is a popular philosophical speech dealing with daemons, guardian spirits that function as intermediaries between man and gods, or divine voices within a person. Decorated with anecdotes and quotations from literature, the work takes up man's separation from the gods, the functions and kinds of daemons, and the characteristics of the personal daemon of Socrates. It urges individuals to be mindful of their own personal daemon in order to be guided to a better life.

Two other works should be noted that were quite likely written by Apuleius, though more in the style of a treatise than the artificial style of the works just considered. The *de dogmate Platonis* (About the teachings of Plato) is a summary in popular form of the system of Plato's thought with a mixture of ideas from Aristotle and the Stoics. Lacking literary color, it outlines Plato's thought about god, matter, the origin of the universe, the

human being, and ethics, including ways to teach virtue. The *de Mundo* (About the Universe) is a translation of a Greek work often wrongly attributed to Aristotle. The work deals first with the physical universe, then takes up the god of the universe as being unrivaled and the basis of continuous order. Like the work about Plato's ideas this work was intended to make Greek culture available to audiences who read Greek poorly or not at all.

Possibly the last and clearly the most famous of Apuleius's remaining works is *Metamorphoses* (Changes of Shape, often entitled *The Golden Ass*, "golden" meaning that it is a marvelous, splendid story). As far as is known, Apuleius was given the name "Lucius" by other writers, because it is the name of the main character of this work, the most famous of a half-dozen ancient novels left from antiquity. It follows the adventures of a young man as he travels about Thessaly, known as the land of witches. Apuleius spins tales of magic, folklore, crime, love, religion, the supernatural, and pure adventure. Early on the narrator, the curious Lucius, dabbles in magic and is transformed into a donkey, a form that persists through most of the novel. The style and tone of *The Golden Ass* change as Lucius encounters witches, amorous women, deceived husbands, corrupt priests, brave robbers, beautiful women, and other colorful characters. The gem of the entire work is the story of Cupid and Psyche (Love and Soul), narrated by an old hag who cooks for a gang of robbers. At the end of the novel Lucius regains human form and becomes a devotee of the Egyptian goddess Isis, whose worship had become widespread in the Roman Empire and who was reputed to have a particular hatred for donkeys due to their lust and curiosity. Whether this playful, romantic, irreverent, and fantastic collection of stories was assembled and presented merely to titillate and amuse with its variety of characters and situations or to convey a profound experience of personal redemption from the ills and temptations of the world, the work has gripped readers for some eighteen centuries. Possibly it was to Apuleius that a now destroyed ancient statue was erected in Madauros by people who recognized such talent in their native son: a fragment from the base of the statue has the phrase *philosopho platonico*, "to a Platonic philosopher."

BIBLIOGRAPHY

Harrison, Stephen J. *Apuleius: A Latin Sophist*. Oxford and New York: Oxford University Press, 2000.

Sandy, Gerald N. *The Greek World of Apuleius: Apuleius and the Second Sophistic*. Leiden, Netherlands, and New York: Brill, 1997.

Winkler, John J. *Auctor & Actor: A Narratological Reading of Apuleius' "Golden Ass."* Berkeley and Los Angeles: University of California Press, 1985.

R. CONRAD BARRETT

'Aqqad, 'Abbas Mahmud al- (1889–1964), Egyptian journalist, poet, and literary critic, was born in the Aswan region of Upper Egypt on 28 June 1889. His father, an archivist and money-changer, was Egyptian, and his mother was of Kurdish descent. 'Aqqad attended state primary school in Aswan, but since Aswan had no secondary school, his higher education was largely self-generated. With an inquisitive mind, and literate in Arabic, and to a lesser degree English (although his facility with that language improved over time), he read widely in his youth and afterward. An autodidact, his voluminous writings of later years demonstrate an interest in, and at least some knowledge of, a wide range of subjects.

In 1904, 'Aqqad left Aswan. He had a varied career in the decade prior to World War I; he worked in the Egyptian state bureaucracy, possibly attending the School of Arts and Crafts as well as a school for telegraphers, and by 1907 he was contributing to and editing various Cairo newspapers and periodicals. During World War I, 'Aqqad briefly worked for the censorship office, published his first collections of poetry, and also wrote for the Alexandrian newspaper *al-Ahali*. By 1919 he was a journalist at *al-Ahram*.

'Aqqad became a major figure in the world of Egyptian journalism, literature, and politics in the 1920s. An editor of the important Wafdist newspaper *al-Balagh* for much of the decade, he also contributed interpretive essays on numerous cultural topics to *al-Balagh*'s weekly literary magazine. The interpretive essay was the premier form of public discourse in early-twentieth-century Egypt, and 'Aqqad was one of its most prominent practitioners. Already a poet of note, he made his mark in the realm of Arabic literature in 1921 with the publication of the two-volume modernist literary manifesto *al-Diwan* (the Collection), coauthored with Abd al-Rahman Shukri and Ibrahim 'Abd al-Qadir al-Mazini. This work criticized the formalism found in the work of the neoclassical Arabic poets of the previous generation and instead called for Arabic poetry to reflect contemporary life and feeling. In politics, 'Aqqad was a staunch supporter of

the leading nationalist movement, the Wafd Party, led by Sa'd Zaghlul. He was made a member of the Egyptian Senate in 1925 and later elected to the Chamber of Deputies.

As was true of Egypt in general, the 1930s were a stormier decade for 'Aqqad. He was a vigorous defender of constitutional liberties and free speech during the period of more autocratic government under Prime Minister Isma'il Sidqi in the early 1930s and consequently served nine months imprisonment in 1930–1931 for his criticisms of the monarchy and the Sidqi regime. In the mid-1930s, 'Aqqad broke with the Wafd Party over the issue of internal corruption on the part of Zahglul's Wafdist successors; he subsequently became a vehement critic of the movement, claiming it had lost its nationalist purity. When other former Wafdists created the new Sa'dist Party in 1937, 'Aqqad affiliated with it and edited the party paper, *al-Asas*. He again served in Parliament, now as a Sa'dist deputy, during the period of Sa'dist-Liberal coalition governments from 1938 until 1942. When the Sa'dists returned to power in late 1944 he was made a Senator.

While he continued to engage in literary and social criticism, 'Aqqad's literary efforts in the 1930s and 1940s extended into the fields of history, fiction, and biography. His numerous publications during these decades reflected the breadth of his knowledge and interests. His substantial biography of his hero Sa'd Zaghlul, published in 1936, was for a long time the standard, if hagiographical, biography of the Wafdist leader. He published his one and only novel, *Sarah*, in 1938. In the 1940s, he joined the trend toward a more populist and Islamically oriented literature that had developed from the 1930s onwards, writing a series of biographies describing the *'abqariyyat* ("genius") of the Prophet Muhammad and other notable figures of early Islamic history such as 'Ali, 'Umar, and Abu Bakr. Yet throughout, 'Aqqad remained a defender of liberal values and democracy. His literary achievements were officially recognized in 1940, when he was made a member of the Arabic Language Academy. During the early days of World War II, in 1940, he published a polemic directed against Nazism and Hitler, titled *Hitlar fi al-Mizan* (Hitler in the Balance), and made a number of pro-Allies and anti-Axis broadcasts on Egyptian State Radio. In 1942, when an Axis invasion of Egypt seemed imminent, 'Aqqad briefly fled the country for the safety of the Sudan.

Although he remained a venerable public figure and his literary output continued undiminished, from the end of World War II onward 'Aqqad's influence in the worlds of Egyptian culture and politics gradually diminished. He was a supporter of the Egyptian Revolution of 1952 (July Revolution) and in turn was made chair of the poetry committee of the High Council for Arts, Literature, and the Social Sciences. In 1959, he was awarded the Egyptian State Prize for Literature. He died in Heliopolis on 12 March 1964.

A passionate polymath with strong, if not always well-grounded, opinions about numerous subjects, 'Aqqad's massive literary output reflected the range and vibrancy of the crosscutting currents that existed in Egyptian public discourse during the first half of the twentieth century. A vigorous modernist in the realm of literature who espoused an approach to poetry influenced by the English Romantics that emphasized giving free scope to the poet's feelings and imagination; a committed nationalist and democrat in the realm of politics who campaigned for Egyptian national independence and defended popular sovereignty and parliamentary democracy against its opponents; a social commentator who, early in his career, wrote approvingly of contemporary evolutionary thought, but who later became a champion of authentic Egyptian culture opposing periodic calls for the use of Egyptian colloquial Arabic in literature; a writer of a series of biographies extolling the "genius" of the early leaders of Islam: all these trends, coexisting in early-twentieth-century Egypt, can be found in the writings of 'Abbas Mahmud al-'Aqqad.

[See also Sidqi, Isma'il; and Zaghlul, Sa'd]

BIBLIOGRAPHY

Brugman, J. *An Introduction to the History of Modern Arabic Literature in Egypt.* Leiden, The Netherlands: E.J. Brill, 1984. A well-informed account both of the *Diwan* school of poets and of 'Aqqad's place in it.

Goldschmidt, Arthur Jr. *Biographical Dictionary of Modern Egypt.* Boulder, Colo.: L. Rienner, 2000. A brief biographical account with an extensive bibliography.

Safran, Nadav. *Egypt in Search of Political Community: An Analysis of the Intellectual and Political Evolution of Egypt, 1804–1952.* Cambridge, Mass.: Harvard University Press, 1961. An influential but controversial interpretation of 'Aqqad and his peers that argues for the idealism of his political commentary and the apologetic nature of his writings on Islamic history.

Semah, David. *Four Egyptian Literary Critics.* Leiden, The Netherlands: E.J. Brill, 1974. A thorough and insightful examination of 'Aqqad's theories about literature.

JAMES JANKOWSKI

Arafat, Yasser (1929–2004), Palestinian leader, was born in Cairo, Egypt, on 24 August 1929 to 'Abd al-Ra'uf, his father, and Zahawa Abu-Saud, his mother, who had emigrated from Palestine in 1927. Arafat himself was mysterious about his birthplace: sometimes he would say, "I was not born before I became Abu-'Ammar" and sometimes he insisted on being born in Old Jerusalem, next to the al-Haram al-Sharif, the Islamic sacred site (this version was adopted by official publications and Web sites of Fatah). Behind this obscurity probably lay the uneasiness of Arafat, as the leader of the Palestinian national movement, to acknowledge that he had not been born in Palestine and that his Palestinian parents had emigrated voluntarily out of personal, and not national, reasons from Palestine seeking a better living. His full name is Muhammad 'Abd al-Rahman 'Abd al-Ra'uf Arafat al-Qudwa al-Husayni. During the early 1950s, as a student in Cairo, he added the name Yasser (Yasir) after the faithful companion of the Prophet Muhammad 'Ammar Ibn Yasir—hence, his nom de

Yasser Arafat. (AP Images)

guerre, 'Abu-'Ammar. In July 1990 he married Suha Tawil, a Christian who converted to Islam following the marriage. They had one daughter, Zahawa, named after Arafat's mother.

When Arafat was four, his mother died in Cairo, and he was sent to spend periods of time with his late mother's family in Gaza and his father's family in Jerusalem. But most of his childhood passed in Cairo under the care of his elder and beloved sister In'am. Arafat used to say in interviews that in 1947 he joined the armed forces under the command of 'Abd al-Qadir al-Husayni (who was a remote relative of his), fighting against the Israeli forces in the vicinity of Jerusalem; but this statement is not corroborated by any other sources, including those who had been close to 'Abd al-Qadir and later documented their recollections.

Between 1950 and 1956, Arafat studied civil engineering at the Egyptian University (Fuad I). Heading a group of Palestinian students, he invigorated the activity of the General Union of Palestinian Students while serving as its chair. This activity is remarkable because retrospectively there originated the first formative nucleus of the ideology and organization of Fatah. They formed the core idea of Palestinian self-reliance, drawing lessons from the fatal consequences of relying on the Arab states' armies during the 1948 war (coined by the Palestinians as the *Nakba*, or the catastrophe).

The activity of the Union of Palestinian Students annoyed the Egyptian regime of Gamal Abd al-Nasser. Their budding ideology signified harsh criticism against any Egyptian (and in fact any Arab) interference and patronage in the Palestinian issue. Furthermore, these Palestinian students seized the opportunity to train themselves militarily in camps of the Muslim Brothers, the bitter rivals of the Nasserist regime.

In October 1959 Arafat and a few of his former Palestinian companions from the days of the students' union in Egypt joined some young Palestinians who had settled earlier in Kuwait and founded a clandestine group called Fatah. *Fatah* in Arabic refers to the great conquests crowned with victories during the golden age of Islam in the seventh century. But it is also a reverse acronym, meaning "The Palestinian National Liberation Movement." The main emphasis is on the Palestinian character and dimension of the liberation: the liberation is not only *for* the Palestinian but also *by* the Palestinians.

Indeed, the founders of Fatah, headed by Arafat, criticized harshly the dominant strategy devised and led by Nasser in the conflict with Israel. Nasser assumed that the ultimate aim of the liquidation of the state of Israel needed, as a necessary condition, a long period of political and military preparations in the Arab world under the dominance of Egypt. Then, the overall potential of the Arab world would be mobilized to achieve the anomalous aim of wiping out an established state before the international community would be able to interfere and prevent it. But the collapse of the union between Egypt and Syria proved to Arafat and Fatah what they had learned before in the wake of the 1948 war—that this Nasserite strategy was untenable. By establishing Fatah, they began to submit their own alternative strategy: in contrast to the suspension period needed according to Nasser's strategy, they insisted on launching sporadic guerilla operations ("military struggle" in Fatah's terms) against Israel. Israel would have to retaliate on the territories of the bordering Arab states, and the latter would have to defend their territorial sovereignty. Thus, they would be dragged by the Palestinian vanguard to an overall conflict notwithstanding their strong inhibitions. This strategy of "military struggle" was meant to emphasize the role of the Palestinians and to intertwine the strategy of the Palestinian self-reliance and self-help with the ideology of Palestinian self-determination and collective identity. Arafat was totally immersed in it, embodied it in his public as well as in his private life, and since then became known as the symbol and personification of Palestinian nationalism. He was so dedicated to this cause that his personal biography reads as a collective history of his people.

Guided by this rationale, Fatah headed by Arafat objected to the establishment of the Palestine Liberation Organization (PLO) in 1964 by Ahmad al-Shuqayri, who depended heavily on Nasser and in the eyes of Arafat was subservient to him. According to the idea of self-help, Arafat decided to surface from the underground by launching Fatah's first military operation in January 1965, to the dismay of both Nasser and Shuqayri. Hence, he refused to join the PLO headed by Shuqayri until the political decline of Nasser and his ally Shuqayri in the wake of the defeat of the Six-Day War between the Arabs and Israelis (1967). During 1968–1969 Arafat and Fatah took control of the PLO and disposed of the old guard of Shuqayri and his followers. They revised the Palestinian National Covenant in order to accommodate it to the main precept of Fatah, Palestinian national identity. Failing to establish a military foothold in the West Bank following the Six-Day War (Arafat himself infiltrated the West Bank during July–September 1967 but had to flee back on the verge of his being captured by Israel), Arafat and Fatah moved to Jordan in an attempt to build a kind of springboard ("secure base" in their terms) toward the West Bank and Israel. The fatal showdown with the Jordanian regime was inevitable, and the humiliated PLO, now led by Arafat and Fatah, was evicted in "Black" September 1970 and settled in Lebanon, exploiting the weakness of the Lebanese government.

A new turn in the interpretation of Palestinian self-determination evolved in the wake of the 1973 Arab–Israeli war. The Arab states devised in 1973–1974 the concept of the "phased strategy," which in fact laid the basis for a political process with Israel that gave precedence to the territories occupied in 1967. Arafat was compelled to accommodate the Palestinian attitude to the new circumstances and to adjust the concept of Palestinian self-determination in a way that would identify it with the establishment of a state even on part (22 percent on the West Bank and Gaza) of the Palestinian land. This new attitude, navigated by Arafat, caused frictions and splits within the PLO and even within Fatah itself. But Arafat was not deterred, and following the Lebanon War (1982) with Israel, when the PLO was evicted from Lebanon and settled in Tunis, he led the PLO to accept the concept of political negotiation as a means to secure the aim of a Palestinian state in the West Bank and Gaza.

This position culminated in November–December 1988, a year after the outbreak of the First Intifada (uprising) in the West Bank and Gaza. In November 1988 Arafat led the PLO as a whole to accept the canonical document Announcement of the Palestinian Independent State, which endorsed for the first time the concept of partition of Palestine into two states, in utter contradiction to the letter and spirit of the Palestinian Covenant. In December 1988 Arafat declared that he was ready to renounce terror and to accept Security Council Resolution 242 (November 1967), which was considered the generic term for a political process and settlement. The traditional position of the United States demanded the PLO's recognition of this resolution as a condition for "talking" with the PLO. Until then, the PLO had rejected (during the 1960s and 1970s) categorically Resolution 242 because it meant a final political settlement with Israel and because it totally ignored the Palestinians and their national rights while referring only to states (during the 1980s).

It seems that only a charismatic leader like Arafat could navigate the PLO to such a reversal in spite of the harsh protests and denouncements from within the PLO and outside it (mainly Hamas, founded at the end of 1987). More important for Arafat was the fact that his new attitude was fully welcomed by the Palestinians in the West Bank and Gaza (an area which, owing to the burgeoning Intifada, turned into the main Palestinian center of gravity).

This rationale led Arafat to the Oslo Agreement in September 1993, which included mutual recognition between Israel and the PLO. By it, Arafat and the PLO (based until then in the diaspora) integrated with the Palestinian population in the territories, gaining an initial foothold in Gaza and Jericho (Arafat and his entourage entered these areas in July 1994).

Soon, it became clear that Arafat had difficulty adjusting from being the revolutionary leader of a national movement to the head of an embryonic state and from centralist control to devolution of his powers in the framework of efficient governance. His critics among the local Palestinians indicated that he stumbled when he had to translate the lofty ideals and aspirations into feasible aims of day-to-day management.

The political effort to broaden the Oslo process into a comprehensive settlement with Israel under the brokerage of President Bill Clinton of the United States failed at Camp David (July 2000) and Taba (January 2001). Arafat's goals in these negotiations were clear-cut: the Palestinians had made substantial concessions by agreeing to relinquish 78 percent of their homeland according to the lines of 4 June 1967, leaving only 22 percent in the West Bank and Gaza Strip, which they were determined to keep. His position accepted the possibility of granting Israel minor territorial modifications for demographic or security reasons, provided such changes would not exceed 2 percent to 3 percent and that any alteration of borders was made in the context of mutual and equal swaps. In principle, Arafat attested to this position when he led the PLO in the midst of the Intifada to endorse willfully the "Arab Peace Initiative" adopted by the Arab Summit Conference in Beirut in March 2002 and every year afterward at all the Arab summits. This initiative calls to "establish normal relations with Israel" and "considers the Arab-Israeli conflict ended"—all these "in the context of comprehensive peace." As to the "Palestinian refugees" problem, an "agreed upon" solution must be achieved and a Palestinian state established along the 4 June 1967 lines.

The political void caused by the failures of the Camp David and Taba conferences was filled by the Second Intifada, which erupted in September 2000 not as a result of a premeditated decision from above (i.e., Arafat) but as a matter of a collective state of mind from below. Arafat lost control as the spiral of violence was aggravated, and Hamas fully exploited it to its advantage. Arafat, blamed by Israel as responsible for the violent escalation, was besieged by Israel in his compound in Ramallah for over two years. Secluded and frustrated, he fell ill and died on 11 November 2004 at the age of seventy-five. Many Palestinians and Arabs still believe that his death was unnatural and that he was poisoned by Israel, but this contention has never been proven.

[*See also* Nasser, Gamal Abd al-.]

BIBLIOGRAPHY

Abu Iyad (with Eric Rouleau). *My Home, My Land: A Narrative of the Palestinian Struggle*. Translated by Linda Butler Koseoglu. New York: Times Books, 1981. An intimate and penetrating view from within by a close companion of Arafat. Subjective but suggestive.

Abu Sharif, Bassam. *Arafat and the Dream of Palestine: An Insider's Account*. New York: Palgrave Macmillan, 2009.

Hart, Alan. *Arafat: Terrorist or Peacemaker?* London: Sidgwick and Jackson, 1984. Valuable source despite the fact that it "was written in co-operation with Yasser Arafat and the top leadership of the PLO" (as written on the cover). The testimony of In'am, the elder and beloved sister of Arafat, is unique.

Rubinstein, Danny. *The Mystery of Arafat*. South Royalton, Vt.: Steerforth Press, 1995. A concise and good summary.

MATTI STEINBERG

Arboussier, Gabriel d' (1908–1976), politician and anticolonial activist in French West Africa and French Central Africa, is important for his role in the emancipation of the territories of French West Africa and French Equatorial Africa from colonial rule between 1944 and 1960. He was born on 14 January 1908, in Djenné in the French Sudan (now Mali). His father, Henri d'Arboussier, was a French colonial administrator serving at the time as the territory's governor. His mother, Djavando, was a descendant of Al-Hajj Umar, a Muslim conqueror who had resisted the extension of French rule in West Africa. Gabriel spent his early years in Ouagadougou in Upper Volta (now Burkina Faso). There, at a public primary school, he began the mastery of the French language that contributed to his later reputation as one of the finest political orators of his time. Thereafter, he went to France to complete his studies for the secondary school diploma at Sorèze in the department of Tarn, where he distinguished himself for his brilliance. Subsequently, he earned the license in law at the University of Paris.

Upon his return to French West Africa, he served as an assistant or clerk in the colonial administration. Concurrently, he prepared for the competitive examination for admission to the National School of Overseas France in Paris, which educated the top level of colonial administrators. After coming in first on the examination, Arboussier enrolled there in 1938. Following graduation in 1941, he became an administrator in the Upper Volta. Then, in late 1944, he became the chief of staff in the office of Secretary-General André Soucadaux during the administration of Charles-André Bayardelle, the governor-general of French Equatorial Africa, in Brazzaville, the Middle Congo. Bayardelle encouraged and supported his successful candidacy as the deputy representing French citizens from Gabon and the Middle Congo in the elections of October 1945 for the First Constituent Assembly in Paris.

In that assembly Arboussier allied with the nine African deputies in Socialist Lamine Guèye's Bloc Africain and developed a close working relationship with the communists, who were one of the three main parties in the assembly. This alliance antagonized many of his European electors and led to his defeat in the elections of June 1946 for the Second Constituent Assembly, the voters in France and overseas having rejected the constitution proposed by the first assembly. While in Brazzaville Arboussier had become more widely known as the publisher of the monthly newspaper *Afrique Équatoriale Française Nouvelle*.

In early 1947, in alliance with Félix Houphouët-Boigny of the Côte d'Ivoire, Arboussier became the secretary-general of a new interterritorial African party called the Rassemblement Démocratique Africain (RDA), which was anticolonialist but not anti-French. Arboussier coordinated the work of the RDA deputies in the French National Assembly in Paris. He also had responsibility for helping the RDA leaders in French West and Equatorial Africa to organize the party at the local, provincial, and territorial levels using the model of the French Communist Party. Then, in late 1947, the RDA-dominated Territorial Assembly of the Côte d'Ivoire elected Arboussier as the territory's representative in the Assembly of the French Union. The assembly was a house of the French Parliament that advised the National Assembly and Senate on legislation concerning the overseas territories. This office enabled Arboussier to widen the audience for African advancement and emancipation among the representatives.

On 12 July 1952, Arboussier was ousted from his position as RDA secretary-general and expelled from the party because he insisted on retaining ties with the French Communist Party that were proving to be an increasing liability. As the French African territories moved toward self-government in 1957 and independence in 1960, the importance of relations with the communists diminished. In 1957 the RDA welcomed Arboussier back into the party. In September of that year he was appointed secretary of its coordination committee. Earlier, in June 1957, Arboussier had won election to the Grand Council of French West Africa, a legislative body created by the French Parliament under the terms of the Enabling Act reforms of June 1956. Arboussier served as a council member from June 1957 until November 1958, during which time he was first its vice president and then its president. During this period he became the right-hand man of Houphouët-Boigny. The Ivorian leader by this time was a cabinet minister in the government in Paris, where he was overseeing implementation of the reforms that were decolonizing Africa. In 1958, as vice president of the Grand Council of French West Africa, Arboussier rejoined the RDA leadership. After a referendum on 28 September 1958 abolished the federation of French West Africa and then transformed the eight territories into autonomous republics, Arboussier opted to become a citizen of Senegal. As independence drew near, he worked tirelessly with Léopold Sédar Senghor and Lamine Gueye of the Senegalese Socialist Party to organize the eight republics into a single federal state. But Houphouët-Boigny's rejection of such a course led instead to eight completely separate independent states.

Earlier, after the abolition of the federation of French West Africa, Arboussier had transferred his political activities to Senegal. There, in December 1958, he became the political director of the Mouvement Populaire Sénégalais. He was elected to a seat in the Legislative Assembly, which after independence in August 1960 became the National Assembly. Concurrently, he helped to create the short-lived Mali Federation between Mali and Senegal. He served as a member of the Federal Assembly of Mali from April 1959 to August 1960. Between 1960 and 1962 Arboussier was the minister of justice of Senegal. Thereafter, in Paris during 1963 and 1964, he served concurrently as Senegal's ambassador to France and deputy director of UNESCO. Between 1965 and 1967 he was the executive director of the United Nations' Institute for Research and Training. In 1974 he became ambassador of Senegal to the Federal Republic of Germany in Bonn. Arboussier died on 21 December 1976 in Geneva, Switzerland.

[*See also* Houphouët-Boigny, Félix; *and* Senghor, Léopold Sédar.]

BIBLIOGRAPHY

Arboussier, Gabriel d'. *L'Afrique vers l'Unité*. Paris: Éditions Saint-Paul, 1961.

Cornevin, Robert. "Gabriel D'Arboussier (1908–1976)." *Afrique Contemporaine* 1–2 (1977): 89.

Gardinier, David E., and Douglas A. Yates. *Historical Dictionary of Gabon*, 2nd ed. Lanham, Md.: Scarecrow Press, 1994.

Milcent, Ernest. *L'A.O.F. Entre en Scène*. Paris: Éditions Temoignages Chrétiens, 1959.

DAVID E. GARDINIER

Archinard, Louis (1850–1932), French general and architect of military conquest and the early colonial state in the French Sudan, was born in Le Havre, France on 11 February 1850. His father, also Louis Archinard, was born into a Protestant peasant family and moved to Le Havre, where he taught in a Protestant school. His mother, Sophie (née Cattelain), grew up in an artisanal family and also moved to Le Havre, where she too taught school. Le Havre benefited from the expanding Atlantic commerce, including the slave trade. In 1850, it was a major French port with deep connections with the colonial world, feeding the textile manufacturing sector in Normandy with imported raw materials, and exporting finished goods.

Archinard was admitted in 1868 into the École Polytechnique in Palaiseau, near Paris, which trained students to become civil or military engineers. The school stressed science in the service of the state. Although a relatively mediocre student, at age twenty Archinard entered the artillery corps of the Marine nationale, a relatively low-esteemed branch of the French military. Archinard's graduation and appointment as under-lieutenant coincided with the Franco-Prussian War (1870–1871). He served his first military assignment at the siege of Paris (19 September 1870–28 January 1871). France's defeat (28 January 1871), the fall of the Second Empire (1852–1870), and the founding of the Third Republic (1870) were formative events for Archinard.

Following the armistice, Archinard went for further artillery training, but he did not distinguish himself and his advancement in the military was slow. With the expansion of the Third Republic's colonial agenda, opportunities for Archinard's career improved. Promoted to captain, Archinard gained his first colonial experience in Saigon (1876–78), where he directed the armory.

Archinard returned to the École Polytechnique and served as inspector of courses. In 1880, Archinard headed to French West Africa, where his career blossomed together with the conquest of the Sudan, the vast interior of West Africa now known as the Republic of Mali. In 1876, Louis Alexander Brière de l'Isle, colonel in the infantry of the Marines, was appointed governor of Senegal. Brière saw France's control over its West African colony as tenuous and promoted aggressive territorial expansion. He appointed Gustave Borgnis-Desbordes, a colonel in the artillery of the Marines, as superior commander of the Upper River region, with a mandate for securing the hinterland of the colony through military conquest. Brière also sent Joseph Gallieni, captain of the artillery of the Marines, on a mission to the ruler of the Umarian Empire at Segou on the Niger River.

The Third Republic pursued an aggressive colonial agenda that reflected competing interests within the political leadership. Colonial successes brought France much-desired prestige and the promise of raw materials to feed the rapidly developing industrial base in the cities. Merchants benefitted from increased colonial commerce. Officers in the Marines saw their careers advance much more rapidly. The colonial lobby in the Third Republic was ascendant in the late 1870s and most of the 1880s, but it constantly confronted the challenge of securing sufficient budgetary credits to keep the military agenda moving.

When Archinard arrived in the Sudan in 1880, the French military presence consisted of a series of small, thinly stretched garrisons and an expeditionary column that pursued conquest during the dry season from roughly December through April. The French colonial army in West Africa consisted of a handful of French officers and enlisted men, and a mass of Africans soldiers. The core groups were the *tirailleurs sénégalais* (Senegalese Rifles), which had been founded by Governor Louis Faidherbe in 1857, a smaller group of Africans recruited into the cavalry (the *spahis*), and a large group of African auxiliaries, who joined the expeditionary column in the hope of sharing in the booty of lands conquered. The French colonial army benefitted from its technological superiority, especially repeating rifles and artillery. In 1880, Archinard's primary task was to erect military buildings and fortifications. During the 1880–1881 military campaign, Archinard saw action in which his command over the artillery proved decisive in breaching the walls of enemy fortifications.

Identifying friends and enemies in a world that the French did not understand, and in which they could not easily communicate with Africans, gave rise to the crucial roles played by African interpreters, employees, and soldiers. Interpreters were especially important, and several emerged as trusted companions. Mademba Sy (1852–1918), an employee of the Post and Telegraph Service, emerged as one of these core interpreters and became a favored adviser to Gallieni and Archinard.

During Archinard's first tour in the Upper River region (1880–1883), he became part of the inner circle of French officers closely associated with Colonel Borgnis-Desbordes. Archinard's career did not progress smoothly, however. While he was recovering from intestinal parasites in France, Archinard was passed over when Colonel Charles Boilève was appointed Borgnis-Desbordes's successor as superior commander of the Upper River region. Between 1883 and 1886, the military command of the Upper River was held by a series of relatively undistinguished one-year appointments until Gallieni was appointed from 1886–1888. The ever-widening reach of conquest raised the costs of supporting the military. Flashy military successes were important in fueling political support for military conquest.

Archinard remained in France and was posted to the office of artillery at Toulon. The Berlin West African Conference (15 November 1884–26 February 1885) provided momentum and the appearance of legitimacy to the Scramble for Africa. International recognition of the reality of the Scramble put extra pressure on the French military to move their agenda forward. Gallieni was quite successful, and he urged the appointment of Archinard as the next superior commander of the Upper River. In 1888, Archinard returned to the Upper River region to pursue the military's goals of conquering the two large African empires of the Sudan: the Umarians and the Samory. Archinard pursued strategies that led to the weakening of both by chipping away at the outlying provinces. By 1890, Archinard was ready for the conquest of the Umarian capital at Segou, which fell to the French in April, and captured several more Umarian garrisons.

In 1890, the governor of Senegal created a new, semiautonomous entity called the French Sudan, which gave the superior commander new administrative and fiscal powers. Archinard used his new authority to build a rudimentary colonial state that involved the French version of indirect rule. Most French military leaders harbored antipathy toward the Muslim leaders in the region, many of whom had aggressively resisted French conquest. The French military favored instead the animist Bambara, many of whom served the French as recruits in the Senegalese Rifles and as loyal auxiliaries. Using the powers of Republican France, Archinard sought to reestablish the Bambara kingdom of Segu, which had fallen to the Umarians in 1860. He appointed Marie Jarra, a descendant of the former Bambara rulers, as the new king of Segou. Within months, however, the French were faced with a massive rebellion in the Segou region. In 1891, Archinard tried again to rebuild African kingdoms in the region by appointing a distant Jarra to the throne in Segou and investing his loyal interpreter and adviser, Mademba Sy, as king in neighboring Sinsani (Sansanding).

Quite ill with parasites and most likely malaria, Archinard returned to France to recuperate. He was still too ill to return to the field in the fall of 1891 and was replaced by his longtime friend Colonel Gustave Humbert. Humbert was not as successful in carrying out headline-grabbing conquests, and political sentiment in Paris moved against further military expansion. Gallieni now sided with the colonial lobby, favoring peaceful expansion of commerce and French civilization. Archinard still had enough support to be recalled again to the Sudan, but with a clear warning from the colonial undersecretary of state not to exceed his orders and not to seek conquest beyond the approved areas. That was not, however, Archinard's agenda.

Archinard, now colonel, returned to the French Sudan in 1892 both as superior commander and as the inaugural governor of the new colony separated from Senegal. Archinard used his 1892–1893 campaign to finish the destruction of the Umarian empire at Nioro and Macina. Back in Segou, he ended the illusion of the restored Bambara kingdom by transforming the region into a colonial district, but he maintained Mademba Sy as king and crowned Aguibu as king of Macina. After conquering Macina, Archinard returned to France, where he made plans to destroy Samory Touré, a powerful military leader in West Africa.

In 1893, Albert Grodet, a civilian with no experience in Africa, was appointed governor. Archinard's role as the conqueror of the Sudan was ended by a profound shift in the colonial lobby, which had turned against aggressive military advances. After 1893, Archinard's military career assumed an honorable, but relatively anonymous and bureaucratic, character. Archinard served on the commission that drew up plans for the military conquest of Madagascar. The honor of leading that campaign went to Archinard's rival, Gallieni. In 1897, Archinard was promoted to general and posted to Cochinchina (the southern portion of French Indochina, today Vietnam) as commander of the brigade.

In 1901, at the age of fifty-one, Archinard married Marie-Mathilde Rue. At the age of fifty-four, Archinard became the youngest general in the central command in Paris. With the onset of the First World War, Archinard was mobilized as the inspector general of finances for colonial troops in the war zone. Having reached the mandatory age of military retirement in 1915, Archinard joined the reserves. In 1919, he was called out of retirement to help establish a new army in Poland. Archinard died on 8 May 1932, a year after the resurrection of his legacy as a central player in France's colonial expansion in French West Africa at the 1931 Colonial Exhibition in Paris.

Archinard is remembered as an aggressive leader of the French colonial conquest of the French Sudan and as the architect of the peculiar military version of indirect rule, which rewarded loyal supporters by inventing kingdoms for them. Archinard is also remembered as the central player in the practice of military imperialism, in which quest for prestige and advancement through glorious military adventures was pursued by disregarding civilian orders, if not outright insubordination.

[See also Faidherbe, Louis Léon César.]

BIBLIOGRAPHY

Cuttier, Martine. *Portrait du Colonialism Triumphant: Louis Archinard (1850–1932)*. Panazol, France: Éditions Lavauzelle, 2006.

Kanya-Forstner, Alexander Sydney. *The Conquest of the Western Sudan: A Study in French Military Imperialism*. London: Cambridge University Press, 1969.

Méniaud, Jacques. *Les Pionniers du Soudan Avant, Avec, et Après Archinard, 1879–1894*. Paris: Société des Publications Moderns, 1931.

RICHARD ROBERTS

Argwings-Kodhek, Chiedo More Gem (1923–1969), pioneering Kenyan lawyer and nationalist politician, was born in Gem, Siaya District, in present-day Nyanza Province of Kenya. The son of early mission converts, "Clem" was sent to a mission school at the age of seven and received his Cambridge School Certificate from St. Mary's College in Entebbe, Uganda, in 1936. The following year he enrolled at Makerere College in Kampala. After graduating with a teaching degree in 1940, Argwings-Kodhek spent the next seven years teaching in Nyanza and Rift Valley provinces. Future Kenyan president Daniel Arap Moi numbered among his pupils.

In 1947 Argwings-Kodhek won a government fellowship to study social sciences at the University of South Wales and Monmouthshire. Shortly after undertaking his studies, he applied to the authorities for permission to pursue a law degree instead but was denied; however, aided by friends, Argwings-Kodhek surreptitiously obtained a law degree in 1949 and became a member of the bar at Lincoln's Inn, London, in 1951.

While in Britain, Argwings-Kodhek married Mavis Tate, an Irish nurse, whom he brought to Kenya in 1952 despite the pervasive racism that confronted interracial couples in the settler colony. Soon after, Argwings-Kodhek sought employment in the attorney general's office but refused the ensuing offer of a salary inferior to that of his white colleagues. When Argwings-Kodhek started his own firm later that year, he became the first practicing African lawyer in Kenya.

His return coincided with the escalation of the Mau Mau conflict in central Kenya and the banning of the Kenya African Union (KAU). Following an antigovernment oathing campaign and assassinations of loyalists by Kikuyu militants, the government declared a state of emergency in October 1952 and arrested the largely Kikuyu leadership of the KAU, accusing them of masterminding the assassinations and coordinating the guerilla insurgency in the forests of Central Province and Nairobi. During the rest of the 1950s, Argwings-Kodhek and other politicians of a younger generation—mostly from the Luo ethnic group—resumed the KAU's efforts to build a mass nationalist movement.

As the government detained and prosecuted suspected Mau Mau militants during the first months of the emergency, Argwings-Kodhek began to take on their cases. Emergency regulations expanded the definition of a capital crime, and he found himself defending many ordinary people whose involvement in Mau Mau amounted to an attempt to survive in central Kenya's violent and polarized African milieu. Argwings-Kodhek provided criminal defense counsel for the majority of Mau Mau cases that were tried in colonial courts, most often for free and in spite of official obstruction, earning him the respect of the battle-hardened forest fighters as well as the enmity of the settler community, who dubbed him the "Mau Mau lawyer." For these endeavors he was disbarred in 1957.

By June 1955, the Mau Mau forest armies had been largely defeated, and the government lifted the ban on African political organizations—if only to encourage a moderate African politics organized on a district basis. Thus, Argwings-Kodhek's attempt in December 1955 to form the first African political party since the KAU, the Kenya African Nationalist Congress, was vetoed by the authorities. But in early 1956 he successfully registered the Nairobi District African Congress (NDAC), under which he would stand the following year for the colony's first African elections for the Legislative Council.

Using the NDAC as his platform, Argwings-Kodhek attacked the moderate African Legislative Council members who supported the government's glacial pace of political change and rallied Nairobi Africans around his "A–K Plan," a manifesto that demanded universal suffrage, civil rights, and increased social welfare for Africans. During 1956 and early 1957, Argwings-Kodhek was the leader of Nairobi African politics, and he seemed poised to lead a broad challenge to the authority of the old guard of African moderates in the Legislative Council. Yet, although the NDAC was the only organized political body in Nairobi in 1956, a leadership dispute crippled the organization just before the election—an event that observers suspected to be the work of Argwings-Kodhek's ambitious electoral opponent, the Luo trade unionist Tom Mboya. Ultimately, Mboya's better-organized Nairobi People's Convention Party (NPCP) bested Argwings-Kodhek, curbing his stint as leader of African politics in Nairobi.

Thereafter, Argwings-Kodhek began to shift his focus away from Nairobi politics. Having consolidated his political base in Central Nyanza with the help of his ally Oginga Odinga, a veteran nationalist and Luo power broker, he was elected to the Legislative Council in 1961. After the ban on colonywide African political parties was lifted in 1959, Argwings-Kodhek's NDAC folded into the Kenyan African National Union (KANU). During 1960 the KANU emerged as the main vehicle for African nationalist aspirations, distinguishing itself from the alliance of moderate Africans from smaller ethnic groups, Europeans, South Asians, and Arabs that composed the regionally minded Kenya African Democratic Union (KADU). Argwings-Kodhek was a KANU insider from the party's inception, and from his seat on its governing council he fought to keep the release of Kenyatta a precondition of KANU's participation in the Lancaster House constitutional negotiations. When the 1962 negotiations produced the MacLeod constitution and a brief period of coalition government, Argwings-Kodhek accepted a position as parliamentary secretary for the Ministry of Lands, Surveys and Town Planning. The position did not dampen his nationalist enthusiasm, however, for as late as 1963 he was charged under the penal code for threatening to "run down imperialists and their stooges with tractors if they were stumbling blocks on the road to freedom" (*Weekly Review*, 18 October 1976, p. 22). Yet, his nationalism did not translate to support for socialism, and in 1966 he surprised many observers when he declined to join Odinga in splitting from the KANU to form the Kenya People's Union, a socialist opposition party.

At independence in 1963, Argwings-Kodhek was elected to the National Assembly as a member of parliament for the Gem constituency. Over the next three years he held several high-ranking ministerial posts in the ministries for natural resources, health and housing, and internal security and defense before joining the cabinet as minister for natural resources in 1966. In the midst of these rotating appointments, Argwings-Kodhek and Tate divorced, and he married and had children with Joan Omondo in the mid-1960s. He was appointed minister of foreign affairs in January 1968 but served for just over a year. On 29 January 1969, Argwings-Kodhek died in a mysterious road accident in Nairobi's Hurlingham neighborhood. Argwings-Kodhek is most often remembered in Kenya for his courtroom contributions to the nationalist movement.

[*See also* Mboya, Tom; Moi, Daniel Torotich arap; *and* Odinga, Jaramogi Oginga.]

BIBLIOGRAPHY

Engholm, G. F. "African Elections in Kenya, March 1957." In *Five Elections in Africa: A Group of Electoral Studies*, edited by W. J. M. Mackenzie and Kenneth Robinson, pp. 391–459 (Oxford, 1960). A contemporary account of the electoral contest between Argwings-Kodhek and Mboya by a political scientist.

Goldsworthy, David. *Tom Mboya: The Man Kenya Wanted to Forget*. London: Heinemann, 1982. Provides a detailed account of the Argwings-Kodhek–Mboya rivalry in Nairobi, as well as examples of Argwings-Kodhek's activities in the internal politics of KANU during the 1960s.

Ogot, Bethwell. "C. M. G. Argwings-Kodhek." In *Historical Dictionary of Kenya*, pp. 21–22. London: Scarecrow Press, 1981.

Ogot, Bethwell. "Mau Mau & Nationhood: The Untold Story." In *Mau Mau & Nationhood: Arms, Authority & Narration*, edited by E. S. Atieno Odhiambo and John Lonsdale, pp. 8–32. Oxford: James Currey, 2003. Ogot includes a biographical sketch of Argwings-Kodhek as he appeals for a broader conception of who Kenya's "national heroes" are.

REYNOLDS L. RICHTER

Arinze, Francis (1932–), Nigerian Roman Catholic cardinal, was born on 1 November 1932 to Arinze Nwankwu (later baptized Joseph) and Bernadette Ekwoanya in the rural town of Eziowelle in southeastern Nigeria. Of humble beginnings, he was in his early years raised in the Igbo traditional religious system until he was nine, when he was baptized into the Catholic church by Father Michael Iwene Tansi, the first and only Nigerian, to date, to be canonized by the church. As a teacher and parish priest, Father Tansi could not but notice that the young Arinze was humble, hardworking, and intelligent since he came out in the first position in his class examinations. Arinze's aspiration to priesthood was largely a result of Father Tansi's influence and interest in him. His father was, however, initially opposed to that aspiration. As a cardinal, Arinze still remembers the terms of that opposition: "You will not become a priest because if you become a priest, you are not going to marry—number one—and you won't have children. And number two, you will be hearing all the bad things people do in your two ears and that's not good" (Arinze, p. 28). He eventually won his father's support but held on to his deep knowledge and appreciation of certain aspects of his Igbo traditional religion.

Arinze attended All Hallows Seminary, Onitsha, Nigeria, where he earned a degree in philosophy in 1950. He proceeded to Rome in 1955 to study theology at the Pontifical Urban University. While there, he was ordained a priest in 1958 by Gregoire-Pierre Agagianian who later became a cardinal. He remained in Rome after his ordination, earning a master's in theology in1959 and a doctorate in sacred theology, summa cum laude in 1960. His doctoral thesis "Ibo Sacrifice as an Introduction to the Catechesis of Holy Mass," which was later published as *Sacrifice in Ibo Religion* in 1970, was an indication of his deep connection to his homeland and the direction of his career in the church. After teaching liturgy, logic, and basic philosophy at Bigard Memorial Seminary in Enugu from 1961 to 1962 and serving as regional director for Catholic education for eastern Nigeria, Arinze went on to complete his formal education at the Institute of Education, London, earning a diploma in 1964.

On returning to Nigeria, he was ordained to the episcopate on 29 August 1965, thus becoming, at thirty-two, the youngest Catholic bishop in the world. As the titular bishop of Fissiana, he was named coadjutor to the archbishop of Onitsha, Charles Heerey, who died in 1967, again paving the way for Arinze to become the first native African to head a diocese. When the Nigeria-Biafra war broke out in the same year, Arinze suffered along with his Igbo people through the war, becoming a refugee himself and supervising the distribution of relief materials to other refugees, the sick, and the hungry in Biafra. When the war ended, his work as the archbishop of a fast-growing archdiocese of Onitsha, his presidency of the Nigerian Bishops Conference, his ability to work well with Muslims in the highly charged religious space of Nigeria all led Pope Paul II to appoint him the pro-president of the Vatican's secretariat for non-Christian believers, later renamed the Pontifical Council for Interreligious Dialogue. On 25 May 1985, he was named cardinal at the age of fifty-three.

Arinze's meteoric rise in the hierarchy of the Catholic Church can be ascribed to a number of factors. First, the church had become aware that its population, while declining in the Northern Hemisphere, was increasing in the south and that this was particularly so in Africa. By the beginning of the twenty-first century, two-thirds of the world's Catholics were living below the equator, which meant that numerically, Europeans no longer dominated the church. Second, although Arinze, like Pope John Paul II, was generally regarded as very conservative on matters of church doctrine, he was equally known to be well disposed to the idea that other religions have the obligation to hold on to their own ways of seeking salvation. Indeed he has been quoted as saying that Buddhists, Muslims, and Jews can get to heaven. His recognition that the Igbo religion has something useful to offer the Catholic Church is a case in point. His apartment in Rome is reported to be adorned with African carvings and masks. If it is true that Pope John Paul II's understanding of communism helped to keep that ideology in check, the thinking in the Vatican may have been influenced by the idea that the church at the present time needs in its top echelon, a man like Arinze, with a powerful ability to relate to other faiths, especially Islam. In Nigeria, approximately half the population is Muslim and half Christian. Last, Arinze's cosmopolitanism, his wide experience of the Catholic world, and his fluent use of English, Italian, French, German, and his native Igbo, not to mention his warm presence, were all factors in his meteoric rise within the church. As the Vatican analyst Gerard O'Connell noted in 2003, "The guy is very bright and astute and able to communicate in simple language. He has a great sense of joy" (Carroll, 2003). His service on the Pontifical Council for Interreligious Dialogue also made him popular and increased his visibility to the world public.

Arinze became even more visible and his status in the church continued to rise when as the president of the Special Assembly for Africa of the synod of bishops and member of the Committee of the Great Jubilee of the year 2000, he worked closely with individual bishops and priests from Africa and around the world. Greatly impressed with Arinze's leadership achievements, Pope John Paul II appointed him prefect of the Congregation of Divine Worship and the Discipline of the Sacraments, considered the fourth highest position in the Roman Catholic Church. He had, in 1999, received a gold medallion from the International Council of Christians and Jews for his outstanding achievements in interfaith relations. Indeed, Arinze's prominence within the church led many observers in the early 2000s to suggest that he might succeed the long-serving John Paul II. Had that happened he would have become the first African-born pope in fifteen hundred years, since Gelasius (492–496). Other African–born popes were Miltiades (311–314) and Victor (183–203).

At the time of Pope John Paul II's death, Cardinal Arinze was the only African cardinal who was considered papabile—eligible to be elected to the papacy. He was also one of the 27 members of the Roman Curia (the governing body of the church) and one of 115 cardinal electors who selected German Cardinal Joseph Ratzinger as John Paul II's successor as pope on 19 April 2005. Six days later, the new pope, Benedict XVI honored Cardinal Arinze by naming him Cardinal Bishop of Velletri-Segni, a position that Ratzinger vacated when he was elected pope, perhaps in recognition that Arinze had been one of his closest rivals for that position. Arinze's many publications include *Sacrifice in Ibo Religion* (1970), *The Church in Dialogue: Walking with Other Believers* (1990), and *Religions for Peace: A Call for Solidarity to the Religions of the World* (2002).

[*See also* Miltiades.]

BIBLIOGRAPHY

Arinze, Francis, and Gerard O'Connell. *God's Invisible Hand: The Life and Work of Francis Arinze*, an interview with Gerard O'Connell. Nairobi, Kenya: Paulines Publications Africa, 2003.

Carroll, Rory. "Cardinal Francis Arinze." *The Guardian* (London), October 3, 2003. Available at http://www.guardian.co.uk/world/2003/oct/03/catholicism.religion/.

Isizoh, Chidi Denis, editor. *Milestones in Interreligious Dialogue*. Rome and Lagos, Nigeria: Ceedee Publications, 2002.

Salvador, Miranda. "Arinze Francis." In *A New Catholic Encyclopedia: Jubilee Volume, The Wojtyla Years.* Detroit, Mich.: Gale Group in association with the Catholic University of America, 2001.

CHIMA ANYADIKE

Arkamani (Ergamenes II; fl. late third and early second century BCE), Kushite king of the Meroitic period, was a contemporary of Egyptian pharaoh Ptolemy IV and the fifth successor of Arkamaniqo (Ergamenes I), who was most noted for leading the Kushite expansion and reoccupation of Lower Nubia in the years 205–186 BCE. After Ptolemy II's ascent to power circa 274 BCE, Ptolemaic Egypt gained control over the long-disputed area of Lower Nubia and thereby provoked a retaliatory stance from Upper Egypt and the Meroitic Empire. Based on surviving inscriptions, it is clear that Arkamani styled himself as a restorer of Meroitic cultural traditions and political supremacy in Lower Nubia.

He achieved this primarily through two principal activities. First, he embarked upon an aggressive building campaign, in which he continued and completed construction of temples at Philae, Kalabsha, and Dakka, all located in Lower Nubia. Second, he provided military support to Upper Egyptian nationalists who launched an independence and secessionist movement from the central control of Ptolemaic Egypt.

The historical evidence pointing to Arkamani's rule can be found in the royal titulary (the naming system of Egyptian pharaohs) of five inscriptions located on temples at Philae, Dakka, and Kalabsha in Lower Nubia, and at his royal burial ground at Begarawiya near Meroe City, in the southern region of the Meroitic state. His throne names at each of these sites variously describe him as "The Kushite Whose Coming into Being is Divine," the "Living hand of Amun," and the "Beloved of Isis." It is believed by scholars that, before his succession to the throne, he served as the crown prince under his father, King Arnekhamani, and as a priest of the goddess Isis. This is based upon reliefs and inscriptions at the Kushite warrior god's temple Apedemak at Musawwarat in southern Kush, where he is identified as "Prince Arka."

Upon becoming king, Arkamani launched a campaign aimed at reestablishing Meroitic influence in Lower Nubia and reviving the primacy of traditional Kushite religion in the region as well. Although Ptolemy IV, as ruler of Egypt, had commissioned the construction of temples in the vicinity of Upper Egypt and Lower Nubia, from a Kushite perspective only the historic keepers of the Amun cult and classical pharaonic religion could legitimately raise temples to the gods—not foreign usurpers who only claimed to serve the ancestral gods because it was politically expedient. This sentiment was not only prevalent among the Kushites, but also among many Upper Egyptians, who had shared with Kush for centuries an unswerving dedication to the god Amun.

Arkamani, therefore, allied his foreign policy aims with the Upper Egyptians, who led a nationalist revolt against Ptolemaic rule, and in the years 205–186 BCE recaptured Lower Nubia. Hor-Un-Nefer (Herwennefer) and his son, Ankh-Un-Nefer (Ankhwennefer), led the independence movement. Hor-Un-Nefer was crowned king, with the royal titulary "Beloved of Amun." He served for six years. His son Ankh-Un-Nefer succeeded him on the throne and served as king until he was defeated by Ptolemy V. Both kings received Kushite military support, and under their rule the Theban priesthood was given refuge by the Meroitic kings Arkamani and Adikhalamani.

[See also Arkamaniqo; and Ptolemy II Philadelphus.]

BIBLIOGRAPHY

Burstein, Stanley Mayer. *Graeco-Africana: Studies in the History of Greek Relations with Egypt and Nubia.* New Rochelle: Aristide D. Caratzas, 1995.

Eide, Tormode, Tomas Hägg, Richard Holton Pierce, and László Török, eds. *Fontes Historiae Nubiorum: Textual Sources for the History of the Middle Nile Region Between the Eighth Century BC and the Sixth Century AD, Vol. 2.* Bergen, Norway: University of Bergen, 1994–1998.

Török, László. *Meroe: Six Studies on the Cultural Identity of an Ancient African State.* Budapest: Chaire d'Égyptologie , 1995.

Török, László. *The Kingdom of Kush: Handbook of the Naptan-Meroitic Civilization.* Leiden, The Netherlands: Brill. 1997.

Welsby, Derek A. *The Kingdom of Kush: The Napatan and Meroitic Times.* Princeton, N.J.: Marcus Wiener, 1996.

SALIM FARAJI

Arkamaniqo (Ergamenes; fl. second quarter of the third century BCE), whose name was translated as "Ergamenes" by contemporary Greeks, was a Kushite king who is considered the founder of the Meroitic period of ancient Nubian history. The transliteration of his name in ancient Egyptian is *ir ka imn*, which roughly translates as the "the active spirit of Amen." Arkamaniqo lived during the second quarter of the third century BCE; this assertion is primarily based upon his identification by the Hellenistic historiographer Agatharchides of Cnidus, who wrote that the "Ethiopian king Ergamenes" was a contemporary of Ptolemy II. There are also epigraphic sources that attest to his existence and reign in Kush at his pyramid burial at Begarawiya near Meroe City. His name is in cartouches inscribed in the mortuary cult chapel of this royal superstructure.

Arkamaniqo's pyramid was the first royal burial site in the region of Meroe City; this suggests that his rule represented a transitional period in Kushite history and the emergence of a new dynasty that could be called "Meroitic." Before his reign, Kushite kings and queens had been buried at El Kurru and El Nuri in the royal pyramids of Napata near Gebel Barkal, in the vicinity of the third and fourth cataracts of the Middle Nile. The primary source we have for the existence and events surrounding the life of Arkamaniqo is the writings of the Hellenistic historian Diodorus Siculus, who in the first century BCE recorded events relayed by Agatharchides.

Diodorus's account of Ergamenes is presented in the context of an ethnographic survey of Ethiopia (Kush) and its customs, traditions, and cultural practices. He states that the priests of Meroe, who were esteemed for their piety and austerity, would send oracular pronouncements in the name of the gods ordering the ruling monarch to be put to death. "Ergamenes king of the Ethiopians, who had received instruction in Greek philosophy," however, decided to oppose this tradition and marched on the sacred temples with an armed force and slaughtered all of the priests. Although Agatharchides's Ergamenes story was told through the historical lens of ethnic propaganda intended to present Greek philosophy as superior to Ethiopian traditions, it does suggest that Arkamaniqo's ascent to power was achieved through a military overthrow of the Amen priesthood of Napata. Other evidence to support this view is the fact the Arkamaniqo's throne name "The-heart-of-Ra-rejoices" was patterned after the throne name of the Twenty-Sixth Dynasty Egyptian king Amasis, who also came to power through a violent military takeover. This suggests that Arkamaniqo perceived himself as the herald of a new dynasty centered in the Meroitic heartland. The fact that he also relocated the royal burial grounds to the vicinity of Meroe also confirmed that Arkamaniqo represented a shift in power from southern Kush, and more important, the beginning of the Meroitic era of Kushite history.

[See also Arkamani; and Ptolemy II Philadelphus.]

BIBLIOGRAPHY

Burstein, Stanley Mayer. *Graeco-Africana: Studies in the History of Greek Relations with Egypt and Nubia.* New Rochelle: Aristide D. Caratzas, 1995.

Eide, Tormode, Tomas Hägg, Richard Holton Pierce, and László Török, eds. *Fontes Historiae Nubiorum: Textual Sources for the History of the Middle Nile Region Between the Eighth Century BC and the Sixth Century AD, Vol. 2.* Bergen, Norway: University of Bergen, 1994–1998.

Török, László. *Meroe: Six Studies on the Cultural Identity of an Ancient African State.* Budapest: Chaire d'Égyptologie, 1995.

Török, László. *The Kingdom of Kush: Handbook of the Naptan-Meroitic Civilization.* Leiden, The Netherlands: Brill. 1997.

Welsby, Derek A. *The Kingdom of Kush: The Napatan and Meroitic Times*. Princeton, N.J.: Marcus Wiener, 1996.

SALIM FARAJI

Armah, Ayi Kwei (b. 1939), Ghanaian novelist, translator, poet, and essayist, was born to an inter-ethnic Fante-speaking couple in the twin harbor city of Sekondi-Takoradi on the coast of western Ghana in 1939. His mother, Esi Bosoma Inse, was Akan, while his father was from the Ewe ethnic group. His name is also given as George Aryee Quaye Armah. His parents, both teachers, divorced after his father, under pressure from his family and clan, decided to take a second wife. Too small to join his father as required by traditions, the young Armah lived with his mother for about two years, accompanying her to the school where she taught and quietly sitting beside her in class. At age five, he was separated from his mother and sent to live with his father in Asankrangwa, a tiny rural town. When his father died in 1947 in a traffic accident, Armah's defiant mother took him and his siblings back to Sekondi, enrolling him in a school in Cape Coast to boost his chances of admission to a good high school.

In 1953–1958, he attended the most prestigious school in Ghana at the time, the Prince of Wales College (now Achimota School), near Accra (the Ghanaian capital), to get a secondary education. In 1959 he worked for eight months as a news writer for Radio Ghana, sometimes filling in as a news reader. In the same year, he won a Carnegie Corporation scholarship to join Groton School, an elite boys boarding school in Massachusetts, on the understanding that if he passed the requisite examinations he would be admitted to Harvard University as a second-year student. Although he got a merit scholarship at Harvard, Armah's educational expenses were to be paid for by a Mr. Richdale, a rich liberal with business interests in apartheid South Africa and father to one of Armah's classmates at Groton. Armah later turned down the offer on principle. Taking odd jobs to scrape through college, Armah graduated summa cum laude with a degree in sociology in 1963 from Harvard, where he wrote a BA thesis on William Blake and William Wordsworth. He also published short stories and sociopolitical commentaries.

Considering the future of Africa more important than a personal career, Armah left America in 1963 for Algeria, via Mexico, to work as a translator for a new magazine, *Révolution Africaine*. While there,

he developed severe liver and nervous problems that made him leave his new job. After five months of rehabilitation in Algiers and Boston, he went back to Ghana in 1964, where he was employed as a script writer at Ghana Television. During this period, he started writing novels.

Soon after joining Ghana Television, Armah became disillusioned with his job and the general bureaucratic malaise in the newly independent Ghana. He resigned as the scripts deputy departmental head, a development that led his mother to have him tied up and taken to a mental asylum in Accra. A friend of his, Ana Livia Cordero, arranged for his release from the asylum, and he briefly stayed in Legon, hosted by fellow writer Ama Ata Aidoo. Armah later taught literature at Navrongo School in 1967, hoping to nurture a new generation of leaders to take over from the current bureaucrats, who had dismally failed Africa. Unable to get a decent job in Ghana because of his revolutionary views, Armah left for Paris in 1967, taking up an editorial job at the French-language magazine *Jeune Afrique*.

In 1968, he joined Columbia University, graduating with an MFA in Writing and Translation in 1970. He taught for a semester at the University of Massachusetts before leaving for Kenya and then Tanzania, where he taught at the College of National Education in Chang'ombe until 1976. In Tanzania he learned Swahili and researched oral traditions, publishing his novels with the now-defunct East African Publishing House. After a short vacation in Ghana in 1976, he left for Lesotho, teaching creative and expository writing at the National University of Lesotho. He has been a visiting professor at the University of Wisconsin at Madison and Cornell University.

Like most prominent African writers, Armah's creative writing career started humbly with the publication of short stories and poems in journals such as *Okyeame* before having his work accepted by transnational outlets like *Harper's* and *The Atlantic Monthly*. His best known work is *The Beautyful Ones Are Not Yet Born* (1968), a modernistic allegorical novel that portrays in graphic scatological images of feces and mucous the moral and political rot eating at the vitals of new African nations. The protagonist is an anonymous railway office clerk, simply called "the man," who is pressured by his acquisitive family and fellow workers to accept the norms of society, bribery, and corruption in order to guarantee his family a comfortable life. In *Fragments* (1971), the protagonist, Baako, suffers similar social pressure when he returns from the United States, where he had gone for college education. *Why Are We So Blest?* (1972) is set largely in an American University and is focused on a disillusioned student, Modin Dofu, who has dropped out of Harvard.

Bleak in tone, Armah's first three novels depict the idealism and eventual destruction of young African intellectuals struggling to survive in postindependence Africa. His later work is much less pessimistic as he tries to offer prescriptive remedies for African woes. While most African writers have avoided the theme of slavery, Armah confronts it candidly in *Two Thousand Seasons* (1973). In this epic novel, told from the multiple perspectives of communal voices, Armah lambasts not only foreign invaders of Africa but also the feudalistic precolonial indigenous rulers who collaborated with Arabs and Europeans in enslaving Africans. For its part, *The Healers* (1979), written while Armah lived in Julius Nyerere's Tanzania, posits that it is only through unity that Africans can regain their salvation. *Osiris Rising* (1995) uses the Egyptian Isis-Osiris myth to depict the role of African intellectuals on the continent and the diaspora in redeeming Africa from the corruption of postindependence leadership. In his later fiction, African American women are presented as the ideal intellectual engines of African salvation and regeneration in Africa. *KMT: In the House of Life* (2002) is a quest for African glory in Egyptian heliographic through the work of the heroine Lindela (echoing Mandela's name).

Armah's *The Eloquence of the Scribes* (2006) is a memoir that chronicles the author's thirty years of research in African literary practice. In one of the chapters, he tears at metropolitan publishers for allegedly ripping off African writers. He recommends the development of community-based publishing firms for the development of African writing. He lives in the village of Popenguine in Senegal, from where he runs a Per Ankh, an African publishing cooperative.

[*See also* Aidoo, Ama Ata; Mandela, Nelson Rolihlahla; *and* Nyerere, Julius.]

BIBLIOGRAPHY

Lindfors, Bernth. *African Textualities: Texts, Pre-Texts and Contexts of African Literature.* Trenton, N.J.: Africa World Press, 1997.

Ogede, Ode. *Ayi Kwei Armah, Radical Iconoclast: Pitting Imaginary Worlds against the Actual.* Athens: Ohio University Press, 2000.

Wright, Derek. *Critical Perspectives on Ayi Kwei Armah.* Washington, D.C.: Three Continents Press, 1992.

EVAN MWANGI

Artaxerxes III (c. 405–338 BCE), Persian emperor (359–338 BCE), was the son of Artaxerxes II, who ruled the Persian empire from 404 to 359 BCE. He is also known as Artaxerxes III Ochus. His mother was Stateira. Artaxerxes III was one of three legitimate children of Artaxerxes II; the other two, Darius and Ariaspes, both were put to death near the end of their father's reign. Ochus, as he is known from most of the Greek sources, came to the throne after his father's death in 359 BCE; the exact date is not certain. He is rumored to have killed most of his living half brothers, their families, and most of his other relatives in order to prevent any disruptions, palace intrigues, or revolts.

During Ochus's reign he undertook to return the Persian empire to its former limits. To control the satraps (governors of the provinces), he ordered them to disband their mercenary armies. Most did, except for Artabazus, who eventually fled to the court of Phillip II of Macedon.

In 351 Ochus determined that Egypt, which had left the Persian fold sixty years earlier, should be reintegrated into the empire. However, his initial foray into Egypt ended in defeat. In the next few years there was a further revolt among the cities of Phoenicia and Cyprus, centered around Sidon. Ochus organized an army and laid siege to Sidon. The local ruler of Sidon, Tennes, betrayed his city, and the Persians entered the city and began a systematic destruction of the town, killing upward of forty thousand people, burning and sacking the city and selling the survivors into slavery. It is thought that this revolt had been aided by Nectanebo II, pharaoh of Egypt, and that Ochus meant to turn his attention toward the reconquest of Egypt, with Sidon as a stepping stone for that process.

Artaxerxes III Ochus gathered an army of 300,000 men, 30,000 cavalry, 300 triremes (warships), and 500 transport vessels. He set off for Egypt in 343 BCE and arrived in Memphis in the summer of 342 BCE. Nectanebo II was able to gather only 100,000 men (20,000 Greek mercenaries, 20,000 Libyans, and 60,000 Egyptians), but because the Persians delayed their attempt, Nectanebo II was able to fortify the Delta against landings on the beaches. In addition he brought up a number of boats that could be used for river fighting. The numerical superiority of Ochus's army was the deciding factor by which the Persians overwhelmed the Egyptian forces. Ochus arrived at the borders when the river was low and thus did not have to contend with the inundation flooding. The first battle was at the site of Pelusium, the gateway port on the eastern Delta. The defenders were able to hold out until rumors of a flanking maneuver caused the abandonment of the fort. The Greek mercenaries who were captured were paroled and allowed to return, with their property, to their homelands.

Ochus continued on toward the capitol at Memphis, where many of the Greek mercenaries abandoned Nectanebo II. The pharaoh gathered his treasure and fled south to Nubia, where he may have remained an independent ruler until 341 BCE, if we can trust an inscription at Edfu temple. Ochus reinstated a Persian administration in Egypt and appointed Pharandates as the satrap. In the classical sources, Ochus supposedly tore down the walls of the major cities and sacked all of the temples. He plundered them of both their valuables and their written records. These latter were then sold back to the temples for exorbitant ransoms. One source suggests that Ochus killed the Apis bull (around which a cult had formed that considered the bull an embodiment of a god) and had it cooked for a royal meal for himself and his generals. Another source says he killed the sacred ram at Mendes.

Ochus then became pharaoh of Egypt and the first king of the second Persian domination of Egypt, sometimes called the Thirty-First Dynasty. The reconquest of Egypt was a major military accomplishment as several earlier Persian rulers had attempted to regain Egypt and had failed miserably. With Egypt back in the empire, Ochus served notice to the Greek city-states that the Persian empire was reunified and a force to be reckoned with. In fact, both Thebes and Argos sent mercenary troops to aid Ochus in his Egyptian campaign, but Athens and Sparta did not. He continued sending envoys to the Greek city-states in order to impress them, as well as to gather additional information about their future plans.

Ochus returned to the Persian homeland and ruled for another four years. In 338 BCE, he was assassinated through a plot organized by his eunuch, Bagoas. He was succeeded on the throne by his son, Arses (Artaxerxes IV).

[*See also* Nectanebo II.]

BIBLIOGRAPHY
Briant, Pierre. *From Cyrus to Alexander. A History of the Persian Empire.* Winona Lake, Indiana, 2002.
English translation of *Histoire de l'Empire perse,* first published in 1996.
Dandamaev, M.A. *A Political History of the Achaemenid Empire.* Leiden, 1989. English translation of the original, first published in Moscow in 1985.
Mysliwiec, Karol. *The Twilight of Ancient Egypt. First Millennium B.C.E.* Ithaca: Cornell University Press, 2000. English translation of the 1998 German edition.
Vittmann, Günter. *Ägypten und die Fremden im ersten vorchristichen Jahrtausend.* Mainz am Rhein: Philipp von Zabern, 2003.

EUGENE CRUZ-URIBE

Asante, David (c. 1834–1892), pastor and missionary, was born around 1834 in Akuropon, the capital of Akuapem, north of Accra in present-day Ghana. The son of Owusu Akyem, a chief of the royal Asona clan, he possessed high social status but was excluded from succession to political posts because of the matrilineal structure of Akan societies. He shared this fate with all so-called Akan princes, who were among the first inhabitants of the Gold Coast to convert to Christianity and receive a European education, thereby creating a role for themselves as a new elitist avant-garde in precolonial Ghanaian societies.

From childhood, Asante's life was intertwined with the activities of the protestant Basel Mission, forerunner of the Presbyterian Church of Ghana, which established itself in Akuapem during the 1830s. He was one of the first pupils to enter the mission school in Akuropon in 1844 and was baptized David at Christmas 1847, again as one of the first converts from his hometown. He then joined the newly founded seminary, whose purpose was to train teachers and missionary assistants. Industrious and ambitious, Asante was sent to study at the Basel Mission Seminary in Switzerland in 1857. Alongside his European fellow students, he received instruction in German, Latin, Greek, and Hebrew in addition to various religious subjects. When he was ordained in June 1862, he possessed a European education of a level that was highly unusual for an African of his day.

After returning home, Asante's duties were those of any missionary responsible for spreading the Christian faith. However, he not only preached in the neighborhood of existing Christian communities but was also sent into the hinterland of the Gold Coast to prepare for the foundation of new mission stations. In the 1870s and 1880s Asante traveled widely, negotiating with chiefs of various peoples and states, a task appropriate to his extensive knowledge of indigenous societies. In his daily work as a pastor, Asante wielded a considerable amount of authority. His duties were not confined to religious functions, and he was also expected to supervise the everyday life of African Christians, ensuring that they adhered to the mission's regulations. Asante, who successively took charge of the Christian communities in Late (Akuapem), Kukurantumi, and Kyebi (Akyem Abuakwa), interpreted his role as pastor at least partly as that of a political leader of Christians vis-à-vis the indigenous authorities, thus combining his status as an educated Christian with that of an Akan of royal descent. In 1877, following a conflict with the ruler of Akyem Abuakwa, Asante was obliged to appear before a British colonial court. He was shown to have weakened the position of Okyenhene Amoako Atta by converting slaves of the ruler and enticing them to move to the Christian village close to the Akyem Abuakwa capital Kyebi.

Besides his missionary activities, Asante engaged in scholarly work in the field of linguistics, thus contributing to the establishment of his mother tongue, Twi, as a literary language. As a young man Asante was assistant to the German missionary and linguist Johann Gottlieb Christaller, helping him to collect Twi words and idioms. After returning from Switzerland, Asante kept up a close scholarly relationship with Christaller, advising the missionary in his linguistic work, which resulted in the publication of a Twi grammar and dictionary. Asante himself translated several books into Twi, including John Bunyan's *The Pilgrim's Progress* and a general history, which, together with Asante's letters to Christaller, constitute some of the earliest texts ever written in this language.

After the lawsuit of 1877, Asante was removed from Kyebi and never again given the opportunity to serve major mission stations. His career was further weakened by the fact that from the 1870s Africans employed by the Basel Mission were permitted only the role of pastors working under the supervision of European missionaries. By extending this ranking system to David Asante, he was deprived of the equal status with his European colleagues that he had enjoyed at a time when he was the only African clergyman working for the mission in the Gold Coast. From the point of view of personal ambition, Asante failed in his attempt to build up a successful career in the expanding sphere of European influence in his home country during the nineteenth century. In historical perspective though, he represents a class of Africans who took up the challenges of early colonialism with great self-confidence and can be regarded as the forerunners of a later postcolonial intellectual and political elite. David Asante died in his home town Akuropon on 13 October 1892.

BIBLIOGRAPHY

The Mission 21 Archives in Basel, Switzerland, house David Asante's manuscripts and publications.

Abun-Nasr, Sonia. *Afrikaner und Missionar. Die Lebensgeschichte von David Asante*. Basel: P. Schlettwein, 2003.

Ofosu-Appiah, L. H. "Asante, D." In *The Encyclopaedia Africana Dictionary of African Biography, Vol. 1: Ethiopia–Ghana*, pp. 202–203. New York: Reference Publications, 1977.

SONIA ABUN-NASR

Asantewa, Yaa (c. 1832–1921), *Ejisuhemaa* (female ruler) who led a formidable but ultimately unsuccessful armed resistance to British colonial rule of the Asante Kingdom (in present-day Ghana) from April 1900 until March 1901, was born at Besease, a small town south of Ejisu about 12 miles from Kumasi, capital of the Asante kindom. She and her brother Kwesi were the only children of Nana Atta Poo (mother) and Nana Kweku Ampoma (father). Through her mother in this matrilineal society, Yaa and her brother were members of the Asona royal clan of Ejisu. Based on the estimate that she was at least sixty years old at the time of the Asante-British War of 1900, she is believed to have been born about 1830, during the reign of Osei Yaw Akoto (1822–1833). She married Owusu Kwabena, a son of the Asantehene Osei Bonsu, and together they had one child, a daughter, Ama Seiwaa Boankra. Yaa was known as an accomplished agriculturalist who raised a variety of vegetables on her farm at Boankra, near Ejisu, and specialized in producing groundnuts and onions.

Yaa Asantewa's role as the leader of the resistance against the British annexation of Asanteman is best understood in the context of the Asante civil war of 1885–1888. Yaa's brother, Nana Kwesi Afrane Okpese, was one of the two principal war leaders who supported the Asantehemaa Yaa Akyiaa and her son Kwaku Duah III (enstooled as Prempeh) against the rival faction led by Atwereboana and his supporters from Mampon, Nsuta, and Kokofu. The faction headed by Kwesi Afrane Okpese prevailed in this dispute, leading to a greater profile for the town of Ejisu and its leader's new role as protector and defender of the occupant of the Golden Stool, symbol of the Asante nation. In about 1887, when the female stool of Ejisu became vacant, Nana Kwesi Afrane Okpese appointed his sister, Yaa Asantewa, as the *ohemaa* (female ruler, or queen mother).

Yaa Asantewa's daughter Ama Seiwaa produced eleven children, who were all members of the Asona royal clan through their mother. Of her eight daughters and three sons, Ama's son Kofi Tene was considered to be the reincarnation of his granduncle Kwesi Afrane, the protector of the Golden Stool. When her brother died, Yaa Asantewa used her prerogative as female ruler of Ejisu to appoint her grandson Kofi Tene (stool name Kwesi Afrane II) as the next Ejisuhene. As the new Ejisuhene, her grandson then assumed the role of guardian of the Golden Stool.

Thus, her own family's fortunes were directly threatened in 1896 when the British arrested the Asantehene, his mother, the Asantehemaa, and other chiefs, kings, and queen mothers, including her grandson, Kwesi Afrene II, and took them first to Elmina Castle at the Coast and then to Sierra Leone for imprisonment. Furthermore, with the arrest of her grandson, she became both king and queen of Ejisu as well as the guardian of the Golden Stool. It was in that position that she was assembled along with other chiefs and kings of Asante on 28 March 1900 when the British governor issued a series of announcements and demands to the assembled leaders. He told them that neither Asantehene Prempeh nor his rival in the previous civil war would be allowed to accede to the Asante throne; that the British resident would assume the Asantehene's power and prerogatives; that the Asante would be required to perform free labor for public works, road construction, and so on; that not only the war indemnity for the 1874 war and the costs of arresting Prempeh but the interest on the indemnity would have to be paid; and that the Golden Stool, symbol of Asante unity, would have to be surrendered to the British authorities.

At a meeting later that night at the home of the principal chief in Kumasi, Yaa Asantewa called on the assembled chiefs to resist the British by force of arms. She listed all the grievances the Ashanti bore against the British. According to an informant who was there at the meeting, she said:

> How can a proud and brave people like the Asante sit back and look while white men took away their king and chiefs and then humiliate them with demands for the Golden Stool? The Golden Stool only means money to the white man; they searched and dug everywhere for it. I shall not pay one *predwan* [£ 8 2s in Asante currency] to the Governor. If you the chiefs of Asante are going to behave like cowards and not fight, you should exchange your loincloths for my undergarments. (Boahen, 2003, p. 118)

Apparently shamed by her bold challenge, that night the chiefs swore an oath to fight to rid Asante of British rule. The war lasted from the first shots on 2 April 1900 to 3 March 1901 when Nana Yaa Asantewa was arrested, effectively ending all armed resistance.

Though the fighting had ended in November 1900, British troops continued to pursue Yaa Asantewa because they knew that as long as she remained at large, further resistance might coalesce around her. She maintained her freedom for a few months, however, when in a diversionary tactic, the main British forces hunting Yaa Asantewa followed the remnant of the Asante fighting forces northward while the elderly queen mother and a few trusted aides turned southeast and moved from place to place seeking refuge in obscure forest villages. For many years the story of Yaa Asantewa's capture recounted her arrest in the village of Sreso Timponu by British soldiers after being betrayed by two young bounty hunters. However, more recent scholarship suggests that Yaa Asantewa surrendered herself to the British to spare her daughter and grandchildren who were being held hostage in the fort at Kumasi. By the time she was locked into a cell in the fort on 3 March 1901, forty-five other leaders of the Asante resistance had already been arrested. She and fifteen other leaders of the rebellion as well as many of their dependents were exiled to the Seychelles on 22 May 1901, where she died twenty years later. Her remains and those of other Asante exiles were repatriated to Asante and given royal burials there when Prempeh I returned from exile in 1924.

In 1960 the Yaa Asantewaa Girls' Secondary School was established in her name in Kumasi, Ghana. In 2000 a museum dedicated to Yaa Asantewaa was opened at Kwaso, near Ejisu, Ghana, as part of the centenary celebrations of the Asante-British War of 1900.

BIBLIOGRAPHY

Akyeampong, Emmanuel, and Pashington Obeng. "Spirituality, Gender, and Power in Asante History." *International Journal of African Historical Studies* 28, no. 3 (1995): 481–508.

Boahen, A. Adu. *Yaa Asantewaa and the Asante-British War of 1900-1. Accra*, Ghana: Sub-Saharan Publishers, 2003.

Boahen, A. Adu. "Yaa Asantewaa in the Yaa Asantewa War of 1900: Military Leader or Symbolic Head?" *Ghana Studies* 3 (2000): 111–135.

Brempong, Arhin. "The Role of Nana Yaa Asantewaa in the 1900 Asante War of Resistance." *Ghana Studies* 3 (2000): 97–110.

Donkoh, Wilhelmina. "Yaa Asantewaa: A Role Model for Womanhood in the New Millennium." Paper presented at the African Studies Association Conference. Nashville Tennessee, November 16–19, 2000.

McCaskie, ThomasT. "Traditional Values and Women's Empowerment." Paper presented at the International Conference on the Centenary Celebration of Yaa Asantewaa, Kwame Nkrumah University of Science and Technology, Kumasi, August 2–3, 1999.

McCaskie, Thomas. "The Golden Stool at the End of the Nineteenth Century: Setting the Record Straight." *Ghana Studies* 3 (2000): 61–96.

LYNDA R. DAY

Asfaha Welde Mikael (1914–1997), chief executive of the autonomous Federa state of Eritrea (1952–1962) and Ethiopian government official, was born on 12 March 1914 in Segeneyti in Akkele Guzay, Eritrea. When he reached school age, he attended elementary school at Adi Keyih, Akkele Guzay, and secondary school at Keren Catholic School.

During the Italian occupation of Ethiopia (1936–1941), Asfaha accompanied General Nasi, who was posted as vice-representative in Ethiopia, and worked there until the defeat of Italy. Initially he worked as an interpreter, and later he held various high positions in Tigray until 1941. Upon the defeat of Italy and the reinstallment of Emperor Haile Selassie to the throne, Asfaha remained in Ethiopia, where he became an ardent supporter of the union of Eritrea with Ethiopia.

Asfaha was frequently dispatched to Eritrea by Ethiopia, particularly during 1941 and 1942, to persuade Eritreans to accept the union with Ethiopia. After many years in Ethiopia, Asfaha visited Eritrea in 1951 as a member of an Ethiopian mission to discuss the Eritrean situation with the British administration. In October 1952, just after the ratification of the Eritrean Constitution by the Emperor, Asfaha returned to Eritrea in the position of vice-representative of the emperor in Eritrea. This assignment was perceived by many Eritreans as an

intentional political act to undermine the Federation. The majority of the political parties in the 1940s struggled for independence, which was not realized. Although the federation was not of their choice, once it was endorsed the parties were eager to uphold it. The Federation for Eritreans represented their autonomy; it was a symbol of their separate identity, in which Eritrean languages, symbols, and forms of government were duly expressed. Therefore, the parties wanted to preserve the federation.

In his position as vice-representative in Eritrea, which he held from 1952 to 1955, Asfaha Welde Mikael worked closely with the representative of the emperor, Endargachew Messay, who made it clear in a 1953 speech that there would be no distinction between internal Eritrean affairs and Ethiopian affairs, that any Eritrean affair concerned Ethiopia too, and that he was determined to do everything within his power to promote union between the nations. Asfaha was in complete agreement with this sentiment, and both servants of the emperor worked relentlessly to frustrate the work of the first chief executive, Tedla Bairu. By supporting and protecting people who opposed federation, Asfaha Welde Mikael played a decisive role in undermining the chief executive's authority.

The Unionist chief executive, Tedla Bairu, was seen as being too pro-federation. Therefore he had to give way to someone more sympathetic to the Ethiopian cause, and Asfaha Welde Mikael succeeded him as chief executive, a post he held until the federal arrangement was abrogated in 1962. He was inaugurated on 18 August 1955. Asfaha retained also his position of vice-representative of the emperor, which had allowed him to take all the measures to dismantle the federation. Asfaha staffed his cabinet with hard-line unionists such as Dimetros Gebremariam, who became vice-president of the Assembly, and Araya Wassie, who as secretary of Interior, at once began to hunt down opponents of union. The Eritrean Assembly was soon purged of pro-Federation parliamentarians: many were forced into exile, while others were silenced or imprisoned. Within a very short time, Asfaha succeeded in dismantling the basic provisions of the Federation. Within three years, the Asfaha government had replaced the Eritrean Flag and Seal with Ethiopian ones (1958), substituted an Ethiopian penal code for the Eritrean (1959), and changed the title of chief executive to chief administrator (1959).

On 25 November 1962, Asfaha Welde Mikael read a statement written in Amharic for the Eritrean

Assembly, which proclaimed that the Federation has ceased to exist and that Eritrea has been united with its motherland, Ethiopia. Eritreans believed that the statement had been prepared by Ethiopia, and Asfaha ordered to read it to the Assembly, while Ethiopians maintained that the Eritrean Assembly voluntarily abrogated the Federation. Henceforth, Eritrea was converted into the fourteenth province of Ethiopia. The consequence of this action led to a thirty-year-long armed struggle.

After the abrogation of the Federation, Asfaha served in various ministries in the Ethiopian government, including minister of health and minister of justice. At the time of the military coup d'état that deposed the emperor, Asfaha was serving as a member of the royal advisory council. He was imprisoned by the military junta, along with many high officials of the imperial state, and upon his release he went into retirement.

Asfaha Welde Mikael died on 24 October 1997 and was buried on 25 October in Ethiopia. Asfaha Welde Mikael was until his death an unflinching supporter of union. Faithful to his beliefs, he voted against the independence of Eritrea in the referendum of 1993. While he remains loved and respected by Ethiopians, Eritreans remember the seven years of his governance as an era of pervasive suppression and terror, as well as a time when the pillars of the Federation were systematically dismantled. In Eritrean eyes, Asfaha was responsible for all the unbearable suffering, distraction, and death that followed the dismantling of the Federation.

[*See also* Tedla Bairu.]

BIBLIOGRAPHY

Bereketeab, Redie. *Eritrea: The Making of a Nation, 1890–1991.* Trenton, NJ and Asmara: The Red Sea Press, 2007.

Gebre-Medhin, Jordan. Peasants and Nationalism in Eritrea: A Critique of Ethiopian Studies. Trenton, NJ: The Red Sea Press, 1989.

Iyob, Ruth. Eritrean Struggle for Independence: Domination, Resistance, Nationalism. Cambridge, UK: Cambridge University Press, 1995.

Negash, Tekeste. *Eritrea and Ethiopia: The Federal Experience.* Uppsala, Sweden: The Nordic Africa Institute, 1997.

REDIE BEREKETEAB

Asham of al-Habasha, al-

Asham of al-Habasha, al- (d. 630), Christian king (*negus*) of Aksum, was contemporary to the Prophet Muhammad, who is said to have recited the ritual prayer (*salat*) for al-Asham upon his death. The original Ethiopic (Geez) form of his name is Elle Seham or, by approximative rendering of the latter's pronounciation, Ille Tsiham. The Arabic *Chronicle* of al-Tabari (d. 923) gives the text of two letters allegedly exchanged between the Prophet and al-Asham(a), called here *al-Najashi*, from Ethiopic *negasi*, an alternative form of *negus* that became specific for the ruler of Aksum linked to the so-called first hijra (emigration). In and after 615 two streams of early followers of the Prophet, including such prominent Islamic figures as the later caliph 'Uthman ibn 'Affan and Muhammad's daughter Ruqaya, fled to al-Habasha (Abyssinia). They went possibly to Aksum, the *Najashi*'s capital city, named also *Zar(a)f(a)r(a)ta* by al-'Umari (d. 1348) and al-Maqrizi (d. 1442), but never mentioned in this connection. There they took shelter from persecution by the Meccan leadership. The risk of their apostasy being thus averted, Muhammad would have uttered the famous hadith (traditional saying), "Leave the Ethiopians alone as long as they leave you alone," meaning that holy war (jihad) must not be waged on Ethiopians unless triggered by them.

In the course of time, the Ethiopian identity of the *Najashi* became somehow obscure in Islamic tradition, but the latter's Asham(a), Sahama, Samaha, etc., should be equated to Ethiopic Elle Seham and variants (Ze'elle Seham, Zeseham, etc.) of the local "king lists." In Tabari's *Chronicle*, the monarch's full name, corrupted, can be properly restored to Ashama ibn Al(l)a Hataz(a) or ibn al-Hataz(a), that is Ashama son of (Elle) Hetaza. His father, Hetaza, was also a king, known chiefly from his coinage, with gold pieces inscribed in Greek. Again, according to al-Tabari, al-Asham begot his successor Arha, that is, Armah, a ruler equally known from his coinage who is likely to have dispatched the last Ethiopian embassy to Constantinople, in 630/1, to congratulate the Byzantine emperor Heraclius on his recent victory over the Persians.

The *Sira* (Life) of Muhammad by Ibn Ishaq (d. 767 or 771), as revised and completed by Ibn Hisham (d. 828 or 833), yields more detailed information about the *Najashi*, whose father was killed immediately after he became king, while al-Asham himself was sold as a slave by his uncle, and only later recovered his throne. Whatever the value of such a tradition, the text has it that the Muslim émigrés, led by Ja'far ibn Abi Talib (a cousin of the Prophet), were treated hospitably by the *Najashi*, who refused to expel them as had been requested by Mecca. He questioned the newly converted Muslims about their creed, for which they had relinquished their own country and people without turning to Christianity or any other religion. On replying, Ja'far praised Muhammad and stated that Muslims worship God alone, with no associations at all (clearly a negative hint at polytheism and at the Trinity as well). In order to show the divine character of the Prophet's revelation, he also recited, as an ex-post anticipation, a few verses from chapter 19 of the Qur'an (the "sura of Mary"), with the same story of the birth of the Virgin Mary as the Gospel of Luke (1, 54ff.).

Thereupon, the Najashi and his bishops were moved to tears. Yet he later privately learned from 'Amr ibn al-'As (the future conqueror of Egypt) that, to the Muslims, "Jesus son of Mary" was a creature, not the son of God. In a further public occasion, Ja'far declared that Jesus was the servant of God, His apostle, His spirit, and His word. The Najashi had to acknowledge that, in this respect, the difference between Islam and Christianity did not exceed the length of the stick he was holding. Uneasy about this statement, the Ethiopians blamed him for betraying his religion, and rebelled, unsuccessfully, against him. Subsequently, he sent his son Armah to the Prophet, with sixty fellow Ethiopians (who would have all perished on their return when crossing the Red Sea), to let him know that, as for their embracing Islam, he held no power over his subjects, but was ready to come to the Prophet should the latter wish him to do so.

Speculating on these passages of the Sira, as well as on the letters transmitted by al-Tabari, which sport Islamic opening formulae, Muslim authors claim that al-Asham converted to Islam secretly, when, after reading a message directed to him by Muhammad, he testified to Muhammad being truly the Apostle of God and retained his throne only by keeping his conversion hidden. For this reason some Muslim jurists deemed that, far from being exempt from jihad, Ethiopia was, like Spain (al-Andalus), a land lost to Islam that must be rescued from its apostasy. No independent source, however, validates such circumstances, which rather echo the ancient lore on the six "kings of the world"— among them, indeed, the Najashi—to whom the Prophet sent an embassy in 628, summoning them to adopt the new religion. This is also the subject, before 711/2, of a much disputed mural painting in the Omayyad castle at Qusayr 'Amra (present-day Jordan), with the portrait of the Najashi.

In the Islamic sources great appreciation is expressed for the pious Najashi and his just rule. He appears as a classic bestower of gifts on eminent personalities of early Islam: in particular, he supposedly presented three spears to the Prophet himself, who gave two of them to the later caliphs 'Ali ibn Abi Talib and 'Umar ibn al-Khattab. The Persian rewriting of Tabari's Chronicle (achieved in 963) adds that the Najashi intended to build a church at Antioch and sent a ship laden with timber; the ship was wrecked at Jedda, and he donated the timber for the rebuilding of the Ka'aba at Mecca.

He died in October/November 630 and is buried at Negash, a village near Weqro (Enderta, Tigray), next to twelve first-hijra companions of the Prophet. The tomb of Ahmad Negash ("King Ahmad" or rather the "most praiseworthy king"), as he is styled there, is earliest introduced in 'Arabfaqih's coeval account of the 1533 victorious military campaign by the Islamic leader Ahmad ibn Ibrahim al-Ghazi or Grañ (the "Left-handed"). The site of an annual pilgrimage (ziyara) on the Shiite feast of 'Ashura' ("Tenth day" of the month of muharram), Negash is perhaps the most important holy place for the Muslims in the Horn of Africa. To them the tradition about Ahmad Negash confirms the comparative antiquity of their settlements as against the Christian state of Ethiopia, thus lending prestige to their homeland, the second region in the world to be reached by the message of Islam.

BIBLIOGRAPHY

Di Branco, Marco. "I sei prìncipi di Qusayr 'Amrah: fra tardoantico, ellenismo ed Islam." *Atti della Accademia Nazionale dei Lincei–Rendiconti Classe di scienze morali series 9, no. 18* (2007): 597–620. Reprinted in Marco Di Branco, *Storie arabe di Greci e di Romani. La Grecia e Roma nella storiografia arabo-islamica medievale*, pp. 231–254. Pisa, Italy: Edizioni Plus–Pisa University Press, 2009.

Donzel, Emery van. "al-Nadjashi." In *The Encyclopaedia of Islam*, edited by H. A. R. Gibb et al. Vol. 7, pp. 662–869. Leiden, Netherlands: Brill, 1992. With literature.

Donzel, Emery van. "Nagasi." In *Encyclopaedia Aethiopica*, edited by Siegbert Uhlig et al. 4 vols. Vol. 3, pp. 1109–1110. Wiesbaden, Germany: Harrassowitz, 2007. With special attention to the details of the Islamic legend.

Fiaccadori, Gianfranco. "'Ella Gabaz/('Ella) Hetaza." *La Parola del Passato* 61 (2006): 115–141. With discussion of sources and literature.

Fiaccadori, Gianfranco. "Ella Saham." In *Encyclopaedia Aethiopica*, edited by Siegbert Uhlig et al. 4 vols.

Vol. 2, pp. 262–263. Wiesbaden, Germany: Harrassowitz, 2005.

Gori, Alessandro. "Nagas." In *Encyclopaedia Aethiopica*, edited by Siegbert Uhlig et al. 4 vols. Vol. 3, pp. 1107–1109. Wiesbaden, Germany: Harrassowitz, 2007. On the burial place, with useful presentation of Muslim historiography on the subject as recently developed in both the Horn of Africa and the Yemen.

Raven, Wim. "Some Early Islamic Texts on the Negus of Abyssinia." *Journal of Semitic Studies* 33 (1988): 197–218.

GIANFRANCO FIACCADORI

Ashenafi Kebede (1938–1998), Ethiopian ethnomusicologist, composer, scholar, and teacher, was born in Addis Ababa. His paternal grandfather was *Liqe* Mekuwas Adinew Goshu, a renowned hero of the Battle of Adwa and a close confidant of Empress Taitu. His great grandfather, *Dejazmach* Goshu, served as a mentor and teacher to Emperor Tewodros. The most creative and artistic individual in his family was his mother, Fantaye Nekere, who composed verse and poetry. She taught Ashenafi about Ethiopian artistic forms, which he later drew upon for his work.

Ashenafi first showed an interest in music while attending Haile Selassie I Elementary School. After attending the Harar Teachers' Training School, he taught music at Haile Sellassie I University and the Addis Ababa YMCA before obtaining his BA in Music (1962) from the University of Rochester's Eastman School of Music in the United States. He returned to Addis Ababa to serve as the first official Director of the Yared School of Music (1963–1968). He received his MA (1969) and PhD (1971) in Ethnomusicology from Wesleyan University, also in the United States. His doctoral dissertation was titled *The Music of Ethiopia: Its Development and Cultural Setting* (1971). Due to the uncertain political climate in Ethiopia and the eventual overthrow of Emperor Haile Selassie's regime in 1974, Ashenafi decided to settle permanently in the United States with his family: his son Yared and his two daughters, Nina Ashenafi Richardson (a judge) and Senait Ashenafi (an actress).

Ashnenafi Kebede held several positions at American institutions, including assistant professor and director of the Ethnomusicology Program at Queens College, the City University of New York (1970–1976); professor of music and director of the Center for African American Culture at the Florida State University in Tallahassee (1977–1998);

executive officer of Ethius, Inc.; and chair of the International Arts Council for African and Afro-American Affairs. He received Fulbright awards, as well as grants from the Florida Fine Arts Council, the National Endowment for the Humanities, the Canadian National Music Council, the American Council of Learned Societies, and the United Nations Educational, Scientific, and Cultural Organization (UNESCO).

His publications include a novel, *Confession* (1964), and the scholarly works *YemiziKa Sewasiw* (1966, The Grammars of Music), and *Roots of Black Music. The Vocal, Instrumental, and Dance Heritage of Africa and Black America* (1982). He made an LP recording in 1969 entitled "The Music of Ethiopia: Azmari Music of the Amharas." He also published a number of scholarly essays, including "African Music in the Western Hemisphere" (1972), "The Bowl-Lyre of Northeast Africa. Krar: The Devil's Instrument" (1977), "The Sacred Chant of Ethiopian Monotheistic Churches: Music in Black Jewish and Christian Communities" (1980), "Modern Trends in Traditional Secular Music of Ethiopia" (1976*)*, and "The Azmari, Poet-musician of Ethiopia" (1975).

As a composer, he utilized musical concepts distilled from many cultures, illustrating the diversity of his creative output. His need to show the compassionate side of the human spirit served as his catharsis and antidote to trauma, for he was an eyewitness to many racial conflicts and social injustices that occurred during the latter half of the twentieth century—events in the wake of the Civil Rights Movement in the United States and the 1974–1991 revolution in his country of birth.

The public responded to Ashenafi as a composer in a somewhat contradictory manner. When he visited Budapest in 1967, its daily newspaper introduced him as the only African composer known to the European world. Hungarian critics nicknamed him the "Black Kodály" after their composer and educator, Zoltán Kodály (1882–1967). Emperor Haile Selassie designated Ashenafi as "National Composer" and awarded him the Haile Selassie I Foundation Grant for Outstanding Achievement in Cultural Affairs. Fifteen years later, Ashenafi spoke of his physical and mental isolation in the United States during the late 1970s and 1980s. He reconciled his dual sides, American and Ethiopian, by composing works transcending geographical and cultural boundaries, although he knew his audience might not comprehend his intentions when composing such works.

Inspired by concepts and musical idioms from Ethiopia, Japan, the Middle East, India, Europe (notably Hungary), and the United States, he incorporated their treatment of sound and text into his own compositions. He showed a preference for using the clarinet, flute, washint, mbilta, shakuhachi, koto, violin, xylophone, and voice. He claimed to have composed over one hundred works, but the majority have remained unpublished. English translations of his composition titles from the Amharic include: "Fire Fly," "Ethiopian String Symphony," "Peace Ethiopia," "Shoes of Ladder," "The Ulcer of Love," "Student Love," "The Life of Our Nation," "Koturasia for Koto, Violin and B-Flat Clarinet with Idiophonic Interjection in the Japanese Low Hira-joshi Tonality," "The Shepherd Flutist," "Pizzicati Orientale," "Fantasy for Aerophones: Ethiopian Washint and Japanese Shakuhachi" (also known as "Minuet for Flutes & Pipes [In the spirit of Ethiopian Washints and Embiltas]"); "Trio Concertina for Clarinet, Japanese Koto, Violin & Chamber Orchestra," "Nirvana Fantasy for Xylophone, Clarinet, Shakuhachi & Orchestra," "Eh ye ye–Soliloquy I" for voice, flute, and koto (1974), and "Mot (Death)– Soliloquy II" for voice, flute, and koto.

[See also: Haile Selassie I; Taytu Betul; and Tewodros II.]

BIBLIOGRAPHY

Tolossa, Fikre. "Ashenafi Kebede: A Composer with Soul." *Ethiopian Review* (1993 May): 20–22.

Kimberlin, Cynthia Tse. "The Scholarship and Art of Ashenafi Kebede (1938–1998)." *Ethnomusicology* 43 (1999): 322–334.

Zewde, Bahru, Richard Pankhurst, and Taddese Beyene, eds. "Ethiopian Music Traditions and Transitions: Event as Catalyst for Change." *Proceedings of the Eleventh International Conference of Ethiopian Studies*, vol. 2, pp. 643–652. Addis Ababa, Ethiopia, Addis Ababa University, 1994.

Fukui, Katsuyoshi, Eisei Kurimoto, and Masayoshi Shigeta, eds. "Four Contemporary Ethiopian Composers and Their Music: Asnakech Worku, Nuria Ahmed Shami Kalid a.k.a. Shamitu, Ezra Abate Iman, and Ashenafi Kebede." *Ethiopia in Broader Perspective: Papers of [the]13th International Conference of Ethiopian Studies*, vols. I–III, pp. 96–117. Kyoto, Japan: Shokado Book Sellers, 1997.

Olsen, Dale. "In Memoriam: Ashenafi Kebede (1938–1998)." *SEM (Society for Ethnomusicology) Newsletter* (1998):33–34.

CYNTHIA TSE KIMBERLIN

Ashurbanipal (fl. seventh century BCE), was a king of Assyria (668-628 BCE) and conqueror of Egpyt. Between 745 and 705 BCE, Assyria became a conquering imperial power. During the reign of Tiglath-Pileser III (744–727 BCE), Assyria seized control of Babylon to the south, invaded Urartu to the north, conquered parts of northern and southern Syria, and developed alliances that extended its influence to the borders of Egypt. Following Tiglath-Pileser's death, his successors—Sargon, Sennacherib, Esarhaddon, and Ashurbanipal—strived to consolidate and maintain this empire.

By the end of the eighth century BCE, Egyptian hostility to Assyria led to its support of revolts against Assyrian clients in Palestine, causing Esarhaddon, Ashurbanipal's father, to invade Egypt in 671 BCE and defeat the Twenty-Fifth Dynasty Egyptian pharaoh Taharqa (690–664 BCE), who came from Napata in Nubia (called Kush by the Egyptians and Meluhha by the Assyrians). After three battles, Assyrian forces captured Taharqa's capital city, Memphis, on 11 July 671 BCE. Taharqa fled to the south, leaving behind his son, his harem, and his treasury. Esarhaddon used the booty he gained from Egypt to finance the rebuilding of Babylon. The Assyrians appointed new rulers, governors, and officials, and imposed taxes on the Egyptians.

In 669 BCE, Esarhaddon died en route to Egypt, following rebellion once again under the leadership of Taharqa. The expedition was abandoned. Soon afterward, Ashurbanipal ascended the throne and moved to consolidate his authority. In 667 BCE, following Taharqa's attack on an Assyrian garrison at Memphis, Ashurbanipal ordered his forces to reconquer Egypt while he remained home at Nineveh and communicated his orders via the Assyrian messenger service. The Assyrian forces engaged Tarharqa's army at Kar-baniti (Saïs) on the eastern Delta border and then moved to take Memphis. Taharqa fled the city and took refuge at Thebes, hundreds of miles to the south. The Assyrian forces followed, augmented by allied Egyptian troops.

At this point in the narrative Assyrian sources break off, and conflicting accounts paint a picture of treachery and intrigue. It appears that en route, the Assyrian forces were faced with an internal plot to overthrow their army. Three allied northern Egyptian princes whom Esarhaddon had installed and supported now secretly attempted to communicate and plot with Tarhaqa to oppose the advance of the Assyrian army and its native allies, murder their commanders, and drive their forces from Egypt.

When the plot was uncovered and the messengers detained, the Assyrian army moved to crush the rebellion, rather than continue their march south to Thebes. Some of the rebellious leaders were captured and two of the three main instigators of the revolt, Necho and Sharruladari, were sent back to Nineveh. After this, there is nothing more in our sources regarding Sharruladari, who was probably either killed or detained under unfavorable circumstances. Saïs, Bintiti (Mendes), and Tanis—cities that supported the uprising—were severely punished and their inhabitants slaughtered. Only Necho was given clemency and gifts, including horses, chariots, and mules, and allowed to return home as a puppet vassal to rule at Kar-bel-matati (Saïs); his son, Nabu-shezibanni, later called Psammetichus I, was given the crown of the Delta city of Athribis. The third supporter of the revolt, Pakruru, appears in an Egyptian text, the Dream Stele of Tanoutamon (Assyrian: Tantamani), some years after the revolt as leader of the northern princes. It is not clear how he came to rule.

In 664 BCE Tantamani, who had succeeded Taharqa, resumed his uncle's efforts to drive out the foreigners and reunite Upper and Lower Egypt under a Napatian dynasty.

First he established himself in Thebes; he then invaded Lower Egypt, where he met a coalition of Delta kings in battle. Necho, his nemesis, was probably killed in the fighting, and soon afterward Pakruru, acting on behalf of the coalition, offered surrender. Tantamani later tried to extend his control over the entire Delta, but was rebuffed. When news of the Nubian advances reached Nineveh, Ashurbanipal ordered another invasion. Faced with overwhelming opposition forces, Tantamani fled Memphis, his army overtaken and routed. The Nubian escaped back to Thebes, but in 663 the Assyrian army captured and then sacked the city. The Assyrians, now in total control of the country, named Psammetichus I king of both Saïs and Memphis.

Assyrian interest in Egypt ended with the defeat of the Kushites at Thebes. There was no intention of moving further south and attacking Nubia, as the main motivation for their campaigns was to protect commercial interests in Phoenicia and Philistia from Egyptian interference. Much greater menaces lay to the East, and to this area Ashurbanipal now was forced to turn.

Hostility between political centers in Mesopotamia and Elam (modern-day southwestern Iran) had existed since the middle of the third millennium BCE. But during the period of neo-Assyrian ascendency, the two powers were allies. With the diversion of the Assyrian forces to Egypt (667), the Elamites, egged on by discontented Babylonian officials, invaded and laid siege to Babylon, but were quickly displaced when Ashurbanipal sent in troops. Later, Elamite kings, together with Arabian forces, allied with Ashurbanipal's brother, Shamash-shuma-ukin, the ruler of Babylon, in a major revolt against Assyria (652–648 BCE). Under siege for two years, Babylon finally fell in 648 BCE, and soon after Ashurbanipal devastated the Elamite capital at Susa.

Although seemingly at the height of its powers, soon after Ashurbanipal's death in c. 630 BCE the Assyrian empire collapsed; its capital cities were all in ashes by 612 BCE, destroyed by the combined forces of Babylonian and Median armies.

BIBLIOGRAPHY

Grayson, A. Kirk. "Assyria 668–635 B.C.: The Reign of Ashurbanipal." In *The Cambridge Ancient History*, 2d ed., vol. 3, part 2, edited by John Boardman et al., pp. 142–161. Cambridge, UK: Cambridge University Press, 1991.

Kitchen, Kenneth Anderson. *The Third Intermediate Period in Egypt (1100–650 BC)*. 2d. Warminster, UK: Aris and Phillips, Ltd., 1986.

Spalinger, Anthony. "Assurbanipal and Egypt: A Source Study." *Journal of the American Oriental Society* 94 (Jul.–Sept. 1974): 316–328.

IRA SPAR

Asmal, Kader (1934–), South African academic, human rights campaigner, and respected veteran of the African National Congress (ANC) in exile, was born in Stanger, a small rural town in what is now KwaZulu-Natal, South Africa. Asmal was a founder of the British and Irish antiapartheid movements. He was also an academic, who taught law for almost three decades at Trinity College Dublin, during his exile from South Africa.

In the broad array of constituencies and opinions that has historically constituted the ANC, Asmal has consistently stood for liberal constitutionalism and human rights. This position was most strongly associated with the ANC during the latter days of apartheid, when the international solidarity movement, based largely in Western countries, was at its height.

A key member of the ANC's Constitutional Committee during the post-apartheid negotiations period, Asmal directly influenced the content of the democratic constitution, which was hailed internationally as a truly progressive and liberal document. In President Nelson Mandela's government he was appointed Minister of Water Affairs, a relatively junior position in the cabinet, but one in which he nevertheless excelled. When Thabo Mbeki, the second post-apartheid president, decided to make education central to post-apartheid development, Asmal was appointed Minister of Education. Asmal resigned from parliament following the change of leadership in the ANC at its Polokwane conference in 2008, increasingly adopting the role of highlighting the disturbing practices taking hold in South African politics and in the ANC.

His work as Minister of Education received mixed reviews. He made important policy changes, but critics complained that he introduced too many changes simultaneously. His tenure began with a certain impatience to put the crisis-torn area of education on a firm footing of efficiency and excellence. A new history syllabus, more reflective of the democratic struggle and changes, was introduced. He criticized students and teachers for lack of seriousness, warning that teachers' classroom performance would be increasingly monitored and related to their pay, which brought Asmal into conflict with the large South African Democratic Teachers Union (SADTU). Nevertheless, Asmal introduced an outcomes-based approach to teaching and learning, called Curriculum 2005, arguing that it would encourage a more critically based learning environment.

These changes caused a huge uproar. Teachers complained that the new curriculum was too complicated and involved too much administration. Students' results did not improve, and most parents could not understand why these changes were really necessary, when basic skills were not consistently taught. After intensive public debate, President Jacob Zuma, who assumed power in 2009, reluctantly simplified the curriculum, reducing expectations for immediate and drastic changes. The crisis in education especially in poor areas persists.

In higher education, Asmal pursued changes to increase the number of black students entering universities, increase the number of black professors and staff members, and bring costs under control. He also encouraged students to attend further education and training institutions (technical/vocational colleges) rather than universities. His decision to incorporate some teacher training colleges into universities and close others was considered controversial. This move was later blamed for the critical shortage of teachers, as many left the

profession in frustration. The newly amalgamated institutions are still coping with the consequences of combining universities and colleges with dissimilar institutional histories.

Asmal's failings as minister of education did not deter him from continuing to act as a forceful liberal conscience in ANC politics. Since leaving parliament, he has criticized the erosion of the values upon which the democratic constitution was based, highlighting the "style of political engagement" in which ANC members have resorted to threats and even violence to silence factional rivals or those with whom they differ. Asmal has publicly criticized the repeated attacks on the judiciary, the decision by the police to bring back the military ranks used under apartheid, the minister of higher education's statements labeling academic freedom as at times "counter-revolutionary," and the government's decision to appoint of individuals with questionable track records to the post of national prosecutor, and to the judiciary. He became a victim of political smears when he criticized Fikile Mbalula, former ANC Youth League president and current deputy cabinet minister, for defending police militarization and for his campaign to secure the position of ANC secretary general. Mbalula referred to Asmal's views as the "rumblings (sic) of a raving lunatic," and those of "a bitter old man struggling to make peace with the realities of the day" (*Mail and Guardian Online*, October 28, 2009, from http://mg.co.za/article/2009-10-28-asmal-rues-tainted-political-atmosphere).

Asmal appreciates the liberal discourse of tolerance, reflection, and self-restraint. But ANC political culture has changed, shifting toward patronage politics and entrenching factionalism. In these current circumstances, Asmal's rational deliberation and measured self-restraint appear on the wane.

[*See also* Mandela, Nelson Rolihlahla; Mbeki, Thabo Mvuyelwa; *and* Zuma, Jacob Gedleyihlekisa.]

BIBLIOGRAPHY

Carter, Chiara. "Asmal Heads for New Pastures.") *Independent Online*, 2 March 2008. http://www.iol.co.za/news/politics/asmal-heads-for-new-pastures-1.391529

Davis, Gaye. "Asmal's Cry the Beloved Country." *Independent Online*, 13 April 2010, from http://www.iol.co.za/news/politics/asmal-s-cry-the-beloved-country-1.480382.

"Kader Asmal," South African History Online, accessed 4 June 2010, http://www.sahistory.org.za/pages/people/bios/asmal-k.htm.

"Mantashe: Asmal Welcome to Engage ANC," *Mail and Guardian Online*, accessed 4 June 2010, from http://www.mg.co.za/article/2009-10-23-mantashe-asmal-welcome-to-engage-anc.

THIVEN REDDY

Asma'u, Nana (1793–1864), the most prominent female Muslim scholar of the Sokoto caliphate in West Africa, was born a twin to a learned Fulani family in what is now northern Nigeria. Her full name was Nana Asma'u bint Shehu Uthman Dan Fodio. At the time of her birth her father, a Qadiriyya Sufi scholar and preacher, was undergoing deep spiritual experiences. It is said that these conditions led him to give his twin infants names other than the traditional gender-appropriate versions of Hassan and Hussein, after the twin grandsons of the Prophet Muhammad. Instead, Asma'u's name harkens back to Asma, the daughter of the first caliph, the Prophet's close friend, Abubakar. To many in the nineteenth century, Asma'u's name was a clear indication that the Shehu anticipated his daughter's adult role to be as important in promoting the cause of a just Islam in the region as was that of the historical Asma, who aided the Prophet Muhammad and Abubakar in their successful escape from persecution in Makkah and journey to Madinah.

Known by her honorific, Nana ("Lady"), Asma'u was educated by her mother and grandmother, as was the custom in the family, whose surname, Fodio, means "learned." Among the Fodios, both boys and girls were literate, and they wrote prose and poetry whose themes reflected the concerns of the time. The Shehu wrote over three hundred books on topics ranging from spiritual issues to warfare strategies. Asma'u's works number more than five dozen in various poetic styles, some with more than 130 couplets. Other poems of hers are in quatrains or quintains. Some involve the creation of verse endings known as *takhmis*, in which another author's poem is the basis for the addition of three more lines in which the second author retains the original rhyme and tone. This approach creates a new work that honors the first poem as it also expands upon it. One of Asma'u's works, written in the haste of impending battle as a reassuring response to her brother's poetic message, is an acrostic (in which the first letters of each line, read vertically, form a new line) based on the opening lines of Sura 94:5: "So verily with every difficulty there is relief." Asma'u's creative talents in composition were sophisticated and well honed.

In addition to her scholarship, Asma'u was active in the community. Like the Prophet Muhammad's energetic young wife Aisha, Asma'u was involved in the jihad battles orchestrated by her father the Shehu, her brother the Caliph Bello, and her husband, Commander Gidado; they valued her advice about strategies, and she was an eye-witness to battles. Asma'u also was instrumental in the organization of the community of over two hundred, who were often on the run, pursued by opposition forces in the region. Such itinerancy required not only feeding, clothing, birthing, and burying while on the move, but also caring for the wounded, finding a means of growing food and preserving foodstuffs for transportation, preparing and repairing saddles and weapons, and trying to maintain a sense of community cohesion and social equilibrium in the process.

Despite all these responsibilities, Asma'u is perhaps best remembered for her establishment of a cadre of women teachers of other women, a plan that brought together her scholarly abilities and community activism. These extension teachers were known as 'Yan Taru, led by directors known as Jajis. At a time when battles left many ethnic Hausa women widowed and homeless, resocialization was crucial to the preservation of the social order. The 'Yan Taru visited young women in their homes, bringing education to them when domestic responsibilities prevented their having sufficient freedom and time to attend classes elsewhere. Asma'u's poems formed the bases of their lessons.

Nana Asma'u not only functioned as a community leader during times of warfare and reformation in post-jihad northern Nigeria and as a community organizer and promoter of education among women, but she also was an accomplished and renowned scholar in her own right. She was known well beyond her region. Among her works was a letter from a Maghrebi scholar called Shinquiti, who praised Asma'u's erudition. Even in the twenty-first century, scholars in Morocco know the Fodio family name and appreciate Nana Asma'u's contributions to the body of works from the family. Her long poems described the history of the Sokoto jihad as it parallels the pattern of seventh-century jihad battles led by the Prophet Muhammad, provided her contemporaries with a relevant history of the early days of Islam, revered the attributes of Sufi women in history (including among them her contemporaries in the Sokoto community), and advised women new to Islam about appropriate behavior and attire. In elegies, Asma'u reflected on the most important beneficial characteristics of those who have died, whether famous in their time or little known. In all her works, the good person was revered for his or her goodness, regardless of gender or fame. Similarly, she advocated the necessity of the pursuit of knowledge for all, regardless of gender or position.

The effect of Nana Asma'u's activity in post-jihad northern Nigeria was an affirmation of women's roles as educators and scholars in a reformed Islamic community. It was the intention of the Shehu to promote Sunna among his family and followers; this involved the affirmation in their lives of the example of the Prophet Muhammad. Works by both the Shehu and Nana Asma'u demonstrated clearly that imitating the behavior and intentions of the Prophet Muhammad was prescribed for Muslims. That the Shehu's daughters were educated and active as scholars and teachers demonstrates his belief in women's intellectual and spiritual equity. The Shehu stated plainly that any man who declined to support the education of a woman in his household was not practicing Islam as he should.

In the twentieth century, Hausa women poets pointed to the example of Nana Asma'u in support of their scholarly activity, declaring that they needed no man's approval to pursue an education, because "Asma'u did not need permission to study." With the publication of Nana Asma'u's collected works at the end of the twentieth century, increasing numbers of women in higher education became interested in not only studying her poetry but also researching and perhaps publishing the works by Asma'u's sisters, still housed in the Fodio family archives. That Nana Asma'u's works were not published until two centuries after her birth, and that her sisters' works still have not been published, does not mean that women were not scholars. The Shehu's and Nana Asma'u's reverence for the pursuit of knowledge reflects the very first revelation conveyed to the Prophet Muhammad, "*Iqraa*, Recite! [. . .in the name of God]" (96:1). It can rightly be cited to support the importance of the active pursuit of knowledge among Muslim women in northern Nigeria, and in every community of devout Muslims.

BIBLIOGRAPHY

Boyd, Jean. *The Caliph's Sister*. London: Frank Cass, 1989.

Boyd, Jean, and Beverly Mack. *The Collected Works of Nana Asma'u, Daughter of Usman dan Fodio, 1793–1864*. East Lansing: Michigan State University Press, 1997.

Mack, Beverly. "Muslim Women's Knowledge Production in the Greater Maghreb: The Example of Nana Asma'u of Northern Nigeria." In *Women and Gender: The Middle East and the Islamic World*, edited by Margot Badran and Valentine Moghadam, pp. 2–30. Seneca Falls, N.Y.: Woodrow Wilson Press (co-publishing with Stanford University Press), 2010.

Mack, Beverly, and Jean Boyd. *One Woman's Jihad: Nana Asma'u, Scholar and Scribe*. Bloomington: Indiana University Press, 2000.

BEVERLY MACK

Aspelta (late seventh-early sixth century BCE), king of Kush, was the fourth Nubian ruler of the Napatan Period, a period of time spanning about four centuries (c. seventh–third BCE) during which Ancient Kush (a region covering more or less actual Sudan), which had previously ruled over pharaonic Egypt for more than a century during the Twenty-Fifth Egyptian Dynasty, became independent from its northern neighbor. Aspelta ruled probably at some point during the first half of the sixth century BCE, when Napata, a city located near the fourth cataract of the Nile, was the capital of the land.

Although his reign is fairly well documented in comparison with other contemporary Nubian kings, its exact length can only be postulated. Textual evidence shows that he reigned for at least three years, but historians have traditionally assigned him a reign covering more than two decades. He was at least still alive at around 593 BCE, when the Egyptian army led by the Twenty-Sixth Dynasty pharaoh Psammetichus II invaded Nubia. Written sources that deal with Aspelta are of various nature, but the most important ones in terms of historical content are the royal stelae that were found in or near the main Gebel Barkal temple in Napata (known as temple B 500) built for Amun, a major Egyptian god who was also worshipped by the Nubians, albeit under a local form. These documents include the Election Stela of year 1, the Banishment Stela of year 2, the Khaliut Stela, and the Adoption Stela of year 3, although the last mentioned document probably came originally from nearby Sanam. A fragmentary and unpublished royal stela, also dated to year 3, has recently come to light in Doukki Gel, just north of the Nubian town of Kerma, near the third cataract of the Nile.

Aspelta has left for posterity many colossal statues of himself. Most of them were unearthed from two cachettes in the Gebel Barkal temples; another one was found in a similar cachette in Doukki Gel in 2003. Aspelta's building activity was concentrated in those two areas. His palace in Gebel Barkal, which was burned down probably during or soon after the king's lifetime, is currently under excavation. Aspelta also erected temples in the royal residence of Meroe located between the fifth and sixth cataracts, where the capital of Kush was later transferred. Construction was probably carried even further south, in the vicinity of present-day Khartoum, where a sphinx and a statue were found. Aspelta was buried in the royal necropolis of Nuri, north of Sanam, where he built a twenty-eight-square-mile pyramid made of sandstone (tomb Nuri n°8), identified by foundation deposits dug at all four corners of the monument and containing objects with his name enclosed in a cartouche. In the innermost of the three underground chambers that were lined with funerary texts, the granite sarcophagus of the king was found, albeit without the mummy of its owner, which had been plundered; the text engraved on the sarcophagus displays a coherent and original blend of various Egyptian funerary compositions taken chiefly from the Book of the Day. Most of the beautiful gold inlaid objects found in the tomb of Aspelta are displayed in the Boston Museum of Fine Arts and the Sudan National Museum in Khartoum.

Aspelta's assumed father was King Senkamanisken. He was more likely than not the son of Queen Nasalsa, who is designated as queen mother on both the Adoption and Khaliut Stelae of Aspelta, on the one hand, and the Enthronement Stela of King Anlamani on the other, thus making the latter, who is the predecessor of Aspelta on the Kushite throne, his brother. A daughter of Nasalsa, Madiqen, the owner of tomb Nuri n°27, was also the king's sister. More speculative is the identity of Aspelta's wives who may have numbered up to four.

From a cultural point of view, Aspelta's rule exemplifies the great aptness of the Kushite royalty to adopt the prestigious Egyptian intellectual heritage and adapt it in order to suit specific Nubian needs. Having no written tradition of its own, the Kushites, who had lived for half a millennium under direct Egyptian control, used Egyptian hieroglyphics as their script and were greatly influenced by the Egyptian pantheon and architecture. This did not deter Aspelta from innovating in many

and subtle ways. More than in any other Kushite texts, his Election Stela emphasizes the greater role played by the king's brothers in the transmission of royal power, a fact that is corroborated by his kinship to the prior king; in Egypt, the heir apparent was traditionally the king's son. Unlike the Egyptian pharaohs, Aspelta underlines his matrilineal line of descent by listing his female ancestry all the way back to seven generations. The greater responsibility acquired by royal women, and especially king's sisters (a practice already common under the reign of Anlamani and even much earlier), is also illustrated by Aspelta's Adoption Stela, where a royal decree stipulates that the priesthood of Amun should be handed over from the king's sister Madiqen to his niece Henuttakhebit (sometimes mistakenly referred to as Kheb in the literature), and then passed on from generation to generation along the female line of descent. In the Election Stela, which is the richest and longest inscription of the reign, Aspelta exalts the local god Amun of Napata over the traditional figure of the Egyptian god Ra as the ultimate deity who chooses the future king to be. The text exhibits the far greater part played by the elite in picking out the new royal incumbent, a cultural feature that illustrates the somewhat collegial nature of Kushite kingship and caught the attention of later Classical authors, among whom the second-century BCE historian Agatharchides of Cnides (whose work has come down to us through Diodorus Siculus) stands out. In line, however, with a cultural trait typical of the Egyptian mentality, Aspelta shows great respect to a past (albeit here Nubian) ruler, by making sure that a proper cultic endowment be given to Khaliut, the deceased son of King Piye (Piankhy) of the Twenty-Fifth Dynasty. Aspelta's reappropriation of the Egyptian heritage is displayed through his use of Egyptian funerary texts, and in architecture, his pyramid is reminiscent of the shape of private tombs found at the Egyptian town of Deir el-Medineh, and later exported to Nubia.

Politically speaking, Aspelta's time as a ruler was not exempt from dispute and contestation. The Banishment Stela of Aspelta discloses the case of a family of priests being expelled from the temple of Amun of Napata at Gebel Barkal on order of the king, before being executed for having plotted to commit a crime the nature of which remains rather obscure. The hacking of Aspelta's (and sometimes Nasalsa's) name in both the Banishment and the Election Stelae, as well as the notable need for the king to legitimize his reign in the Khaliut Stela, all point to a controversial reign. Severed statues of the king that were found in Doukki Gel and Gebel Barkal, along with others dating from the reign of Taharqa to Anlamani, are more likely due to the destructive action of the invading Egyptian army of Psammetichus II than on account of some personal *damnatio memoriae*.

[*See also* Nasalsa; Piankhy; Psammetichus II; *and* Taharqa.]

BIBLIOGRAPHY

Bonnet, C. and D. Valbelle, *The Nubian Pharaohs: Black Kings on the Nile*. Cairo/New York: American University in Cairo Press, 2006. A well-illustrated book intended for general audience on the discovery and historical significance of the cachette at Doukki Gel, where a colossal statue of Aspelta was unearthed.

Dunham, D. *The Royal Cemeteries of Kush. Vol. II: Nuri*. Cambridge: Harvard University Press, 1955. Examines the tomb of Aspelta in Nuri and the catalog of finds.

Eide, L., T. Hägg, R. H. Pierce, and L. Török, *Fontes Historiae Nubiorum. Textual Sources for the History of the Middle Nile Region between the Eighth Century BC and the Sixth Century AD. Vol. I: From the Eighth to the Mid-Fifth Century BC*. Bergen: University of Bergen, 1994. Transliteration, translation and comments on all major written historical primary sources dating to the reign of Aspelta can be found in this invaluable edition

Török, L. *The Kingdom of Kush. Handbook of the Napatan-Meroitic Civilization*. Leiden/New York/Köln: Brill, 1997. No single book is devoted to Aspelta exclusively, but the most thorough study of the king and his time can be found in this more general work on the Kingdom of Kush.

JEAN REVEZ

Assis Júnior, António de (1877–1960), Angolan journalist, novelist, solicitor/lawyer, was born in Golungo Alto, Angola on 13 March 1877. His main work was as a solicitor advising the native population, mostly on issues regarding land expropriation by the settlers. As a journalist and writer, he took an active role in promoting social, economic, and political reforms during the second decade of the twentieth century, protesting against the practice of forced work and denouncing the abuses committed by colonial administrators as well as the preferential treatment given to the settler community. He worked as a judicial solicitor in Golungo Alto at the time that news broke regarding frightful atrocities being committed against white settlers, causing fear and uneasiness. He was arrested in 1917 under the accusation of leading a nativist movement whose purpose was to promote uprisings and spread rebellion in the colony. He narrowly escaped being deported.

A nationalist, Assis Júnior was cofounder of the Liga Angolana (Angolan League) affiliated with the Liga Nacional Africana (National African League). In 1922, High Commissioner Norton de Matos, an opponent of the Angolan League, ordered its dissolution, the arrest of Assis Júnior, and the deportation of several of its influential leaders. After these actions, organized nationalism in Angola went underground. The Liga Angolana (Angolan League) reappeared in 1929–1930 as the Liga Nacional Africana (National African League).

Assis Júnior is considered Angola's first important black or *mestiço* writer of prose fiction. His novel *O Segredo da Morta* (*The Dead Woman's Secret*), published in 1934, is a story of racial conflict and acculturation revolving around events that occurred in the 1890s. The novel has the subtitle *Romance de Costumes Angolanos* (*Novel of Angolan Customs*), which shows that the author meant to depict Angolan Creole society at the turn of the century. According to Russell G. Hamilton, "Assis Júnior offers a mixture of true events and detailed references to folklore, religious beliefs, and local customs in the area of Luanda, Sengue and Dondo." He used aspects of the African oral tradition and integrates Kimbundu proverbs and Kimbundu words and phrases into the story. Hamilton also points out that "the novel's digressions, narrative rambling, and plethora of seemingly insignificant details may somehow fit into the story-telling rhythm of an African oral tradition." Focusing on the link between orality as a cultural form and its insertion in written literature, the novel shows how elements introduced by modernity and social and economic development lead to cultural changes in the daily life of the population. *O Segredo da Morta* is unique to the times due to its cultural hybridism. Hamilton, cited by Corrado, emphasized the idea that Assis Júnior was sure of his Angolanness. He "was among the first *assimilado* intellectuals to foster a political and cultural conscience among *assimilados* and *mestiços* to formulate a conscience of Angolan nationality, and to elevate his cultural pretensions to the level of political conflict."

In addition to a large body of journalistic work and the compilation of a Kimbundu-Portuguese dictionary, Assis Júnior also published the *Relato dos acontecimentos de Ndalatando e Lucala* (*Account of the Events That Occurred in Ndalatando and Lucala*) in 1917. This book is an account of the effects of the rise of a colonial regime that was becoming more severe and violent. This text narrates the real causes that led to the wave of arrests of Angolan nationals that were supposedly involved in a nativist movement. From the pages of his *Relato dos Acontecimentos de Ndalatando e Lucala*, the idea emerges that the Euro-African society that had facilitated the implementation of the colonial regime had become such an obstacle to the control of Angola, that the authorities perceived them as a source of danger. Due to his civic positions and beliefs in favor of the natives, he was considered an outcast and sent to Lisbon, where he died in 1960.

[*See also* Ribas, Óscar Bento.]

BIBLIOGRAPHY

Chabal, Patrick, Moema Parente Augel, David Brookshaw, Ana Mafalda Leite, and Caroline Shaw. *The Postcolonial Literature of Lusophone Africa.* London: Hurst and Company, 1996.

Corrado, Jacopo. *The Creole Elite and the Rise of Angolan Proto-Nationalism, 1870–1920.* Amherst, NY: Cambria Press, 2008.

Hamilton, Russell G. *Voices from an Empire. A History of Afro-Portuguese Literature.* Minneapolis: University of Minnesota Press, 1975.

ORQUÍDEA RIBEIRO

Athanasius of Alexandria (c. 296–373 CE), bishop and patriarch of Alexandria, theologian, author, and doctor of the Church, is significant for his staunch opposition to Arianism, his prolific theological works, and his exile-ridden episcopate during a tumultuous time for Church and imperial politics. His most influential work is the seminal hagiography of Western monasticism, *Life of Anthony.*

Athanasius was born in Alexandria, Egypt, probably in the year 296, though possibly as late as 300. At an early age he came to the attention of Alexander, the patriarch of Alexandria, who ordained him as a priest and brought him into the patriarch's service. Alexandria in the fourth century cultivated a mixture of intellectual, philosophical, and religious schools of thought from its long-standing pagan, Jewish, and Christian communities. The city was economically vital as the main grain supplier for the imperial capital at Constantinople, and it ranked third among the four patriarchates in the early Church, after Rome and Constantinople and before Antioch. These factors contributed to a rich, diverse culture, out of which developed some of the major competing strands of late antique Christian theology. Athanasius was one of the main figures in the articulation of what became orthodox dogma for half the Christian world during the period between the Council of Nicaea in 325 and the Council of Chalcedon in 451.

Athanasius ascended to the episcopal throne in 328 amid growing political and theological conflicts in the Alexandrian Church. As bishop, Athanasius was both revered and reviled for his strong personality and outspokenness. Gregory of Nazianzus's *Homily 21* praises Athanasius as the perfect model of episcopal virtues. Recent scholarship, however, has shown that he was not above torturing and imprisoning his religious and political opponents. His insistence that he represented universal Christian orthodoxy was considered brash by those for whom doctrinal issues had not yet been decided satisfactorily. To Athanasius, "orthodoxy" exclusively meant the concept of Christ's divinity as defined by the Council of Nicaea 325; all other beliefs were automatically heretical.

The main disagreement centered on the nature of Christ: the Nicene Creed stated that Christ shared the same essence as God the Father, while the followers of Arius and many other Eastern clerics held that Christ and God were only of similar essence. Arius, a priest at Alexandria in the early fourth century, was initially condemned at the Council of Nicaea, though his theology remained influential in the Eastern Church after his death. Many of the Eastern emperors of the fourth and fifth centuries supported the Arian faction and were Arian Christians themselves, most significantly Constantius II. The Church in the West, however, including the pope at Rome and most Western bishops, continuously espoused the pro-Nicene position. Athanasius's opposition to Arianism therefore touched not only on theology but also on imperial politics. As a result, the bishop was exiled five times not only by Arian emperors (Constantius II, Valens), but pro-Nicene (Constantine I) and pagan (Julian) emperors as well.

His exiles lasted from one to eight years and were spurred by the Arian faction at Alexandria, resistance from emperors who were Arian or sympathetic to Arianism, and general imperial disfavor of the unrest Athanasius fomented in a city so vital to imperial interests. He used these periods of banishment as opportunities to strengthen relationships with ecclesiastical and political allies and to produce letters, orations, and other works in defense of his extremist position. For his first exile, he fled to Trier, where he found support from the Western emperor and pro-Nicene Western bishops. He returned West a few years later to spend an exile in Rome, during which he wrote the *Orations against the Arians*, the best example of the many works he wrote condemning heresy and defending his own position. Upon his return from the West, he composed the *On the Decrees of the Council of Nicaea*, which provides one of the best extant records of this council that became the doctrinal basis for the early Western (Catholic) Church.

Athanasius also spent many years among the new monastic foundations appearing throughout the Egyptian deserts in the fourth century. During his third exile from 356 to 362, for instance, he toured many of the monastic communities in Upper Egypt, in part to gain support for his cause from the emerging group of increasingly influential monks and abbots. His fourth exile brought him back to the desert, where he wrote for the monks the *History of the Arians* against Constantius. Athanasius was one of the first bishops to integrate the new forms of monasticism and new monastic leaders into the Church, either as advisors or as fellow clerics.

This new alliance between bishops in the city and monks in the desert can be seen in the *Life of Anthony*, written soon after Anthony's death in 356. This work almost single-handedly prompted the interest in desert ascetic monasticism in Egypt, the Middle East, and the West and served as the model for most Western hagiographies to follow. Athanasius had met the anchorite Anthony in person when Anthony came to Alexandria in 338 to show his support upon the bishop's return from exile. In the *Life*, Athanasius portrays Anthony as a staunch opponent of Arianism, lending the weight of the saint's authority to his own political and theological struggles.

Athanasius returned permanently to his see in 366, where he stayed until his death in 373. Upon his return, he wrote the *Festal Letter* No. 38, dated 367, which is significant for establishing a list of the books of the New Testament that would later become the definitive canon. As Athanasius approached the end of his life, the prominence of Alexandria in the theological debate was replaced with that of Cappadocia in Asia Minor, spearheaded by Basil of Caesarea, the new champion of Nicene Christianity in the East, and his friend, Gregory of Nazianzus, both of whom were heavily influenced by Athanasius. Athanasius's feast day is celebrated on May 15 (Coptic Church), May 2 (Catholic Church), and January 18 (Eastern Orthodox Church).

[*See also* Anthony the Great.]

BIBLIOGRAPHY

Barnes, Timothy D. *Athanasius and Constantius: Theology and Politics in the Constantinian Empire.* Cambridge, Mass.: Harvard University Press, 1993.

Brakke, David. *Athanasius and the Politics of Asceticism.* Oxford: Clarendon Press, 1995.

Drobner, Hubertus R. *The Fathers of the Church: A Comprehensive Introduction.* Translated by Siegfried S. Schatzmann. Peabody, Mass: Hendrickson Publishers, 2007.

Martin, Annik. *Athanase d'Alexandrie et l'église d'Égypte au IV*e *siècle (328–373).* Rome: École Française de Rome, 1996.

STACEY GRAHAM

Atieno Odhiambo, Elisha Stephen. '*See* Odhiambo, Elisha Stephen Atieno.

Atrash, Farid al- (1915–1974), leading male vocalist of his generation in Egypt, composer and box-office sensation with a career spanning five decades, was born in Suwayda, a village in the Druze stronghold of Southern Syria. He was the eldest child of Fahd al-Atrash, an Ottoman official related to the leading Druze princely clan and Alia al-Mundhir, a Druze from Beirut. At the end of World War I, Fahd al-Atrash was posted in the Turkish district of Demirci. Fearing arrest, he fled with his family to Beirut; on the sea passage from Izmir, Alia gave birth to a daughter, Amal, whose fame as the musical artist Asmahan would equal, if not surpass, her older brother's.

In 1923, against her husband's will, Alia took her children to Damascus and then to Cairo. She fled the violence that had followed the bombardment of the Druze stronghold in response to an attack on French forces led by the clan chief Sultan Pasha al-Atrash, Farid and Amal's great uncle. Traveling without papers, Alia invoked her family ties and reputedly received permission to enter Egypt with the personal approval of the Egyptian nationalist leader, Saad Zaghlul.

Despite their pedigree, the family rented a modest flat in a poor district. Alia supported her three children by taking in laundry and domestic work. She did manage to send Farid and Amal to the private College des Freres, registering them under an alias in order to secure scholarships. When their identity became known, a private benefactor paid their fees, allowing the family to move to better quarters.

In high school Farid and his sister displayed musical aptitude, traced to their mother, who sang and played the oud. Upon graduation, Farid enrolled in the Arab Music Institute. He studied oud with the master musician Riad al-Sunbati, who later composed some of Umm Kulthum's greatest numbers. Farid began performing in Cairo's theater district and worked his way up to the cabaret owned by Badi'a al-Masabni, the greatest belly dancer of the early twentieth century and a leading impresario of the era.

In his early career he gained notoriety primarily for his oud playing and his compositions, especially those written for Asmahan. The two often performed together. Farid remained in her shadow until she briefly abandoned her musical career in the mid-1930s to marry and start a family. Both had made a considerable impact on stage that was enhanced by recordings and radio play. In 1941 they costarred in the film musical Intisar al-Sahbab (Victory of Youth). This was their only screen appearance together. Asmahan, who died in an automobile accident under mysterious circumstances in 1944 at age twenty-five, made only one more movie. Farid made thirty-one films between 1941 and 1974, all musicals, screwball comedies, and tear-jerkers, many directed by Egypt's greatest cineastes, in which he romanced the Arab world's leading starlets.

His films to a great extent mirrored his personal life. In the 1940s and early 1950s they tended to be backstage melodramas filled with popular musical and comic character actors that culminated in the successful production of an operetta and successful wooing of a costar. Between 1947 and 1952, he costarred in six comic romances, all box office hits, with superstar belly dancer Samia Gamal. The two were romantically involved, but Farid never proposed marriage, fearing the impact upon his artistry. From the mid-1950s onward his films more often told tales of unrequited love, his role that of the loner. Failed romances, gambling debts, and increasing health woes began to dominate the popular press. Off screen he romanced deposed King Farouk's second ex-wife, Narriman, but her family rejected him. He later retracted a proposal to the singer-actress Shadia, citing poor health and fears that he would soon leave her a widow. In his final film he falls in love with the daughter of an old friend, but he steps back so she can marry a suitor closer to her age.

Farid remained a leading composer and live performer of popular music throughout the Arab world. His songs, those that are upbeat or those that are melancholic, a fusion of Western and classical Arab rhythms and scales, remain standards. His oud playing, his scales and modal progressions (maqamat), and improvisational style are still studied and appreciated as masterful. His mellow, expansive voice and vocal range and his ability to hold and modulate notes and induce a sense of ecstasy in listeners were matched by only a very few of his peers. Along with Umm Kulthum, Asmahan, Muhammad Abd al-Wahhab, and Abd al-Halim Hafiz, he dominated a golden musical era that has never been—and fans say never will be—replicated.

Farid al-Atrash kept a second home in Beirut; he died there on 26 December 1974 after completing his final film (the film was released posthumously). His photographs hanging in shops throughout the Levant recall his south Syrian origins and denote a special place of pride in the Arab east. But like so many other film, music, and stage stars who migrated to Egypt to find fame and fortune in the country's thriving film and recording industries, he mastered the Egyptian dialect, became intimately associated with Egypt, and was embraced as an Egyptian popular icon—a dapper bon vivant and tragic lover, with his puckish grin and plaintive voice. He is buried in Cairo, alongside his siblings.

[See also 'Abd al-Wahhab, Muhammad; Hafiz, Abd al-Halim; Kulthum, Umm; and Zaghlul, Sa'd.]

BIBLIOGRAPHY

Husain, Adil. Farid al-Atrash: Lahn al-khulud. Cairo: Amadu, 1992.

Zuhur, Sherifa. "Musical Stardom and Male Romance: Farid al-Atrash." In Colors of Enchantment: Theater, Dance, Music and the Visual Arts in the Middle East, edited by Sherifa Zuhur, pp. 270–296. Cairo: American University in Cairo Press, 2008.

JOEL GORDON

Aubame, Jean-Hilaire (1912–1989), Gabonese politican, was born on 10 November 1912 to a Fang family living near the colonial capital of Libreville. Orphaned by the age of eleven, Jean-Hilaire was educated at

Catholic school, in a similar fashion to his political rival Léon Mba. He did not have fond memories of his education, as demonstrated by his complaints about eating a monotonous diet of salted fish during the famines of the 1920s. Nevertheless, he remained a faithful Catholic throughout his life.

After working as a customs clerk in the 1930s, he took advantage of the limited political opportunities created for Gabonese people by World War II. He supported the Free French cause in 1940 when the colonial administration backed Vichy, and he became a close associate of Governor General of French Equatorial Africa Félix Éboué. After the war, the new French Fourth Republic allowed for a small number of deputies to represent colonies in the French parliament. In 1946, Aubame was elected deputy, after running a campaign in which he called for the expansion of schools and the creation of large villages to bring together the very scattered settlements where most rural Gabonese people lived. He would remain Gabon's representative in parliament until the Fourth Republic was overthrown by Charles De Gaulle and his supporters in 1958. In Paris, he stayed clear of the Ressamblement Démocratique Africaine (African Democratic Rally, RDA) party that had brought together most West African political leaders. However, Aubame favored the socialist and moderate policies of Léopold Senghor of Senegal as a rule.

After the 1947 *alar ayong* congress failed to politically unite Fang speakers from the Woleu-Ntem region with Fang people from Central Gabon and the Estuary region, Aubame became the most popular politician in Woleu-Ntem. This province, occupied exclusively by Fang clans, had begun to flourish economically thanks to cocoa farming in the 1940s after suffering greatly from war and famines. Aubame's resettlement plans were adopted by most people in the province between 1947 and 1949. Aubame helped to organize clans along European administrative lines, establish schools, and support clan leaders, often at the expense of state-appointed chiefs. He founded the Union Sociale et Démocratique Gabonaise (Gabon Democratic and Social Union, USDG) party in 1948, which remained with Léon Mba's Bloc Démocratique Gabonais (Gabon Democratic Bloc, BDG) a major party until the early 1960s.

While such moves only heightened his popularity in his home region, urban residents of Libreville and Port-Gentil as well as voters in other parts of Gabon became concerned Aubame would look after Woleu-Ntem's interests rather than their own. Aubame also became unpopular among colonial officials, even though his centrist position hardly made him a radical proponent of independence. Especially after 1956, settlers and administrators worked to back Léon M'Ba against Aubame's USDG. Aubame's long tenure in Paris placed him at a disadvantage against M'Ba's local organizing, and the French government's willingness to illegally interfere with elections posed an even greater challenge for the USDG. M'Ba also tried with some success to portray himself as less tied to French interests than Aubame, even though M'Ba became the preferred choice of the French administration by 1956.

After M'Ba's election as mayor of Libreville in 1957, there was a nearly even split between USDG and BDG members in the Gabonese territorial assembly. Even as the two parties struggled against each other, Aubame and M'Ba remained stalwart supporters of French-Gabonese ties. The two men agreed to support De Gaulle's 1958 referendum to maintain a vaguely defined Franco-African community rather than push for immediate independence. However, their struggles for political power deepened from 1958 to 1964.

Aubame and the USDG ran into a number of problems between 1958 and 1964. Although Aubame was appointed foreign minister by M'Ba in 1961 and remained at that post until 1963, he rejected the president's plans to merge the BDG and the USDG into one party. Settlers and the French government endorsed fraud and financial support to back M'Ba, since he was deemed the most loyal supporter of continued French influence in Gabon. M'Ba's authoritarian reforms of the Gabonese presidency greatly impeded the ability of Aubame and other USDG members in parliament to best the BDG's grip over power. Aubame also tried unsuccessfully to obtain support from the United States government as an alternative to continued French dominance after independence in 1960. By early 1964, the BDG had ensured by decree and by fixed elections its control over the Gabonese government. A small group of officers then chose to take power from M'Ba and install Aubame as the leader of Gabon.

The 17–18 February 1964 coup was undoubtedly the most important moment in Aubame's political career. It is very unlikely that he knew of the coup project until it took place, but he was willing to join the officers in the new government. M'Ba was detained and moved out of Libreville. However, the French government decided to protect French interests and not allow a successful revolution against a friendly regime, as had taken place in 1963 in Congo-Brazzaville. French troops invaded Gabon, took Aubame prisoner, and liberated M'Ba. Aubame was then sent into internal exile to do hard labor for ten years and was regularly beaten by guards. Omar Bongo commuted this sentence in 1972, but Aubame's political career was finished. He refused to become an opposition leader after his release from prison.

Rather than stay in Gabon, Aubame chose to rejoin family members living in Paris. He refused to enter the political arena again, to the chagrin of some opponents of Omar Bongo's single-party regime. He did visit Libreville in 1981 and was given a powerless position as advisor to Bongo, but he returned to France soon afterward. One small group of opposition extremists bombed Aubame's apartment in 1984, but he was not injured in the attack. He returned to Gabon shortly before his death on 16 August 1989. He remains one of the most important politicians in Gabonese history in the mid-twentieth century, and he is considered by many to be founding father of Gabonese opposition to authoritarian rule.

[*See also* Bongo Ondimba, Omar; Eboué, Félix; M'Ba, Léon; *and* Senghor, Léopold Sédar.]

BIBLIOGRAPHY

Ballard, John. "The Development of Political Parties in French Equatorial Africa." PhD diss., Fletcher School of Law and Diplomacy, 1963.

Bernault, Florence. *Démocraties ambigües en Afrique central: Congo-Brazzaville, Gabon, 1945–1965* [Ambigious Democracies in Central Africa : Congo-Brazzaville, Gabon, 1945-1968]. Paris: Karthala, 1996.

Biteghe, Moïse Nsole. *Echec au militaires au Gabon en 1964* [Defeat of the Military in Gabon in 1964]. Paris: Chaka, 1990.

Metegue Nnah, Nicolas. *L'histoire du Gabon des origines aux XXI siècle* [The History of Gabon From its Origins to the 21st Century]. Paris: Karthala, 2006.

JEREMY RICH

Augustine of Hippo (354–430), Christian bishop and theologian, was born Aurelius Augustinus on 13 November 354 CE in Tagaste (mod. Souk Ahras, Algeria) in Roman Africa, the son of Patricius and Monnica. The names of father and son are marked by emphatic affiliation with Rome (echoing the imperial title of Augustus and the high dignity of "patrician"), while the mother's name echoes the traditional Punic culture of Africa and one of its leading deities. Augustine died as bishop of Hippo Regius (mod. Annaba, Algeria) on 28 August 430. He never ceased to surprise his contemporaries, and he has astonished many more to this day.

As the older son in a family of some social pretensions but limited resources, Augustine should

Augustine of Hippo. *Meeting of Augustine and the Donatists* (dressed as eighteenth-century French clergy), painting by Carle van Loo (1705–1765) in the church of Nôtre-Dame-des-Victoires, Paris. (Giraudon/The Bridgeman Art Library)

have grown to manhood as a country squire of narrow horizons. But his parents were ambitious and found the money (from an influential friend) to send him away for education. He studied first at Madauros, an inland city known for literary culture and schools, and then in late adolescence at Carthage, the great city of the Roman province of Africa. The education of the time was traditional, literary, and could be utterly stultifying, but when talent and imagination were touched by it, the results could be dramatic. Augustine learned his Vergil and Cicero and learned to speak and write with a fluency and facility that only a few ancient writers or speakers ever matched.

University students from the provinces were required to leave Carthage for a year when their studies ended, and in that year Augustine took a common-law wife—name unknown—and sired a son, Adeodatus. He returned to Carthage and took up an academic career in the 370s. He flourished, wrote a few small books, and was socially better off than his father had ever been. But he was ambitious.

In 384, he moved from Carthage to pursue his career in Rome, where he was again successful but still ambitious. Pulling strings with influential friends, he won a nomination from the "prefect of the city" (effectively, mayor and first citizen of Rome) to appointment as professor of Latin rhetoric at Milan, which was then the site of the imperial court in the western half of the Roman Empire. (Emperors needed to be closer to the frontier in times of military uncertainty.)

When he reached Milan, he was joined by a retinue of family and friends, who recognized that this appointment would be the making of all of them. Augustine himself says that he expected at least a provincial governorship, and we have the example of another Latin professor, Ausonius, in that decade, who became "praetorian prefect"—effectively prime minister of the Roman government. With Augustine's talent, there were no limits. The common-law wife of a decade earlier was firmly sent packing to Africa by Augustine's mother, who arranged his engagement to a much more socially advantageous future bride. Augustine's surly response was to take a mistress in the meantime.

But in 386, Augustine resigned his professorship and fled to a country estate for a winter of reading and writing. When he returned to Milan in early 387, it was to present himself for baptism at the hands of the charismatic and powerful bishop Ambrose in the great Christian church of Milan—not, as some might have thought, to advance his

career in the now-Christian Roman government, but as the first step to abandoning that career. Upon baptism, he and his family made to leave Italy, delayed by a flurry of military unrest surrounding an attempted coup, but by 388 he was back in Africa, on his father's estate, reading and writing and going to seed. The natural future at this point was not fame and glory, but rustication and obscurity.

But his adolescent son died a year or two later and Augustine was restless. His religion sat heavy on him and he wanted to try the new "monastic" lifestyle of which he had heard but which he had never really seen. Visiting the coastal city of Hippo to speak to an old friend about becoming a monk, he was seized by the resourceful local Christians in church of a Sunday and compelled to accept ordination as priest and designated successor to the local bishop. Augustine broke down in tears, then fled: he was set on the quiet monastic life he had heard of.

He fled back to Tagaste, but his god pursued him and made it clear that he must accept ordination as a divine gift. Reluctantly he did so and turned his services and his pen to public ministry in the Christian Church. He belonged, as a good imperial functionary would, to the official church, a minority but protected community in Africa, in constant rivalry with what we call the Donatist Church, the traditionalist community at odds with the empire's officialdom and the empire's official church. First as priest until 395, then as bishop until 430, Augustine took up the tasks of his church with a will.

For twenty years he opposed the Donatists until, with the help of an imperial officer named Marcellinus, he engineered a great conference at Carthage in 411 to hear the issues between Donatists and Augustine's church, and the empire found for Augustine, suppressing then the Donatists and taking away their property. This victory was Augustine's greatest, if dubious, achievement as a bishop. He wrote and fought as well against Manicheans—members of an eccentric Christian sect Augustine himself had joined in his university days—"pagans" (a very Christian word that baffled the people it was applied to) and "Pelagians"— notionally the followers of a British monk named Pelagius whom Augustine thought was reading St. Paul on free will and predestination entirely wrongly; whether Pelagius himself was really a Pelagian in doctrine and whether he had real followers is a question of continuing scholarly debate.

In old age, Augustine continued to write until his last days, when he lay dying inside the walls of the city of Hippo as invading brigands called Vandals surrounded the city, destined to capture it after Augustine died and to take Carthage itself not long after, ruling in Africa for a hundred years.

But Augustine the bishop of Hippo is hardly the figure of most interest to modern readers and students. His luminous *Confessions* tell an intimate and personal version of the story given bloodlessly and from outside in the first paragraphs of this article. We all owe him a way of thinking and talking about the inner life, and Christians owe him a specific language and style and range of reference for that thinking and talking. Few readers are unmoved by the story of his inner struggle for understanding, faith, and forgiveness. As a child he hungers for religion, as an adolescent he finds fashionably shocking doctrines and zealous community among the Manichees, and as a grown man he remains preoccupied with theological and philosophical issues even as his career burgeons.

Accepting full formal membership in the Christian Church in 387 meant for Augustine—and this was a personal choice he made in a church that was much more tolerant—abandoning sex and the prospect of marriage in favor of a life of celibacy. He had non-Christian philosophical inspirations for this enthusiasm, but he responded as well to currents of thought in Christianity that were coming to the fore in his time. The way he wrote and spoke in the *Confessions* and over the next forty years about what was in part a purely personal inclination has had the effect of making an Augustinian skepticism about the flesh and its pleasures a lasting part of the Christian legacy.

But the *Confessions* also linked the resolution of religious doubt to intense religious experience in a way that would be paradigmatic for many as well. He describes and even enacts mystical contemplation in that work in a way that has proved powerfully influential.

His other great work, *City of God*, was a success in its own time for showing that Christianity could be defended against its critics using the vocabulary of those critics. If Cicero were Christian, *City of God* would be very much the book he could write. But in the following centuries the defense that Augustine offered proved also to be a compelling vision of human society transcending locality, nationality, and regime. A great strength of the Christianities that owe much to him is their ability to offer community without exclusivity and to give believers a sustaining belief and participation without requiring them at the same time to make affiliations of an ethnic, political, or other particularist nature. The vision of earthly peace and justice in book 19 of *City of God* has never been achieved, and Augustine himself explains both how it must remain an ideal but at the same time an ideal never fully to be achieved.

The most controversial of his writings are those in which he wrestles with the legacy of Saint Paul. The issue was personal. Did conversion mean a whole new life of purity and freedom from care (animated by what Calvin would call a doctrine of assurance) or did it free the believer only for a continuing struggle against temptation? In his first years as a Christian, Augustine tried to live as though the former were true, but from about the time he became bishop, he evolved a darker and more nuanced interpretation of life in the world in the in-between times separating Christ's first and second comings. Taking these ideas to their logical conclusion led him to arguments about freedom and predestination that many have found rebarbative and that communities owing him allegiance have often quietly backed away from. But even on his most contested pages, his writings have the power to capture real anxieties and vivid tensions of human experience that hold the reader's attention to this day.

Augustine left behind 5 million words of his writings that survive to us today. The mere fact of those works all being copied and copied repeatedly in many hundreds of medieval manuscripts is a sign of the influence he wielded. He should have lived and died a provincial bishop of limited renown, but his writings have made him a classic.

[*See also* Donatus; *and* Monnica.]

BIBLIOGRAPHY

Brown, Peter. *Augustine of Hippo.* London: Faber, 1967.

Fitzgerald, Allan D. et al., eds. *Augustine Through the Ages: An Encyclopedia.* Grand Rapids, Mich: William B. Eerdmans, 1999.

O'Donnell, James J. *Augustine: A New Biography.* New York: HarperCollins, 2005.

JAMES J. O'DONNELL

Augustus (63 BCE–14 CE), first emperor of the Roman Empire, was born as Gaius Octavius. He was the great-nephew of the childless Julius Caesar, who invited the boy to ride in his triumphal chariot in 46 BCE. Two years later, after Caesar's assassination and Octavius' posthumous adoption as his heir, the eighteen-year-old youth took the name

Gaius Julius Caesar Octavianus and began to recruit troops to avenge the murder of his "father." Thus, modern historians call him "Octavian."

In 43 BCE Octavian and Mark Antony, Caesar's former deputy, formed an alliance called the "Second Triumvirate" (for it also included Marcus Lepidus). The triumvirs ruled quite brutally, enforcing proscriptions of their personal and political enemies. Under Antony's military leadership the triumvirs soon defeated Caesar's assassins Brutus and Cassius at Philippi in northern Greece in 42 BCE.

The aftermath of civil war left Octavian with the difficult task of resettling troops in Italy and dealing with the inevitable resistance of locals who were losing their land. Meanwhile Antony had the easier diplomatic task of restoring relations with Rome's client states in the eastern Mediterranean. The most important, and richest, monarch was Cleopatra VII, pharaoh of Egypt and the last of the Greco-Macedonian Ptolemaic dynasty, lover of Julius Caesar at the time of his death, with whom Antony soon began a famous affair.

The rule of the triumvirs witnessed increasing hostility between Octavian in Italy and Antony in the East. Octavian's sister, Octavia, was even married to Antony to patch up their alliance, but Antony also married Cleopatra in Alexandria in an Egyptian ceremony. While Antony fought military campaigns in Asia with Cleopatra's financial support, Octavian wooed the loyalty of Romans and Italians with a devastating propaganda campaign against the Oriental excesses of Antony and Cleopatra, who "planned" to establish Alexandria as the new imperial capital. War became inevitable. In 31 BCE the forces of Octavian led by his trusted admiral Agrippa defeated Antony and Cleopatra at Actium. The next year Octavian invaded Egypt and, after Antony and Cleopatra committed suicide, he was installed as pharaoh of Egypt. He and his successors ruled Egypt as pharaohs for centuries to come.

The emperor took the treasury of the Ptolemies as his personal property and used it to pay his armies, while he diverted the agricultural surplus of the rich Nile valley to feed the Roman masses. These resources allowed Roman emperors to ensure the loyalty of the armies and the plebs for centuries. While the conquest of Egypt was a godsend for Rome, it was a calamity for Egypt, which would never again be as wealthy or as independent as it had been before the death of Cleopatra.

In 27 BCE Octavian "restored the Republic to the Senate and the Roman people" and he was given supreme military authority (*imperium*) and the new name of "Augustus." He had learned from the assassination of Julius Caesar to avoid the title of *King*—distasteful from its ancient Etruscan past—or *Dictator*, used by Caesar. He took such titles as *Imperator* (triumphant general) and *Princeps* (first man of the state) and the names of Augustus and Caesar. He learned to adapt traditional titles like *consul, proconsul, tribune,* and *pontifex maximus* (high priest) to disguise the fact that he held absolute monarchical power.

In 38 BCE Octavian took Livia Drusilla as his second wife and remained married to her for fifty-one years until his death. They had no children together, so his dynastic hopes rested on his daughter from his first marriage, Julia. Married to her father's old comrade Agrippa, Julia provided five grandchildren but the boys died in their youth and Augustus turned to Livia's son, Tiberius, as his successor. Two later emperors were descended from Augustus through his granddaughters: his great-grandson Caligula (r. 37–41 CE) and his great-great-grandson Nero (r. 54–68 CE).

Though a ruthlessly ambitious young man, Augustus was later a great sponsor of the arts. Poets like Horace and Vergil were personally devoted to him, and he rebuilt the city of Rome, turning it, he claimed, "from brick into marble." He had been in public life for fifty-eight years and ruled as "Augustus" for forty-one years at the time of his death. It was a career of extraordinary success, save only for a military disaster in 9 CE when three legions were destroyed in a German ambush. Nevertheless, Augustus rescued Rome after a century of civil and military unrest, and he established the framework of an Empire that survived for five centuries. The sixth Roman month (*Sextilius*) was renamed *Augustus* in his honor and remains a lasting tribute. At his death in 14 CE, he was proclaimed a god.

[*See also* Cleopatra VII; Julius Caesar; *and* Mark Antony.]

BIBLIOGRAPHY

Galinsky, Karl. *The Cambridge Companion to the Age of Augustus.* (Cambridge, UK: Cambridge University Press, 2005). This collection of articles by leading scholars examines the cultural as well as political aspects of Augustus' reign.

Mellor, Ronald. *Augustus and the Creation of the Roman Empire: A Brief History with Documents.*

(New York: Palgrave MacMillan, 2006).
A collection of ancient sources on Augustus.

Southern, Pat. *Augustus.* (London: Routledge, 1998).
A reliable biography.

Syme, Ronald. *The Roman Revolution.* (Oxford: Oxford University Press, 1939). This remains the most important overview of triumph of Augustus. Written during the height of European fascism, it is less sympathetic to Augustus than most other scholars.

RONALD MELLOR

Autshumao (c. 1600–1663), South African businessman, also known as Harry the Strandloper, was born a member of the Khoesan group known as the Goringhaikona, who lived mainly in the vicinity of Table Bay, where modern Cape Town is situated. The group was known to the Europeans as "strandlopers" (beachcombers) because they acquired the majority of their subsistence by harvesting the resources of the sea, including shellfish, sea fish, and marine mammals, including seals, for which on occasion they visited Robben Island in the bay. No doubt they also collected plants as appropriate. They had few, if any, cattle or sheep.

At the time of Autshumao's birth, European ships were beginning to use Table Bay with increasing frequency in order to take on fresh water and firewood and to leave messages for each other. This provided an evident opportunity for those Africans living in the neighborhood. Autshumao quickly came to take advantage of these circumstances and began to learn English. Around 1631 he accompanied the English captain John Hall on a return trip to Bantam in Java and was thus able to polish his linguistic skills. As a result, he was able to become an intermediary between the Europeans and the Khoesan of the South West Cape.

This role became increasingly institutionalized and profitable after 1652 when the Dutch East India Company established a permanent station in Table Bay, under the command of Jan van Riebeeck. On the one hand, Autshumao was able to install his niece, Krotoa (aka Eva), in the Dutch fort, which gave him important access to the protocolonial establishment. On the other hand, the company provided an important resource, both in terms of trade goods and directly, with which to build up his herds. Autshumao apparently organized the rustling of cattle, the murder of one of the Dutch stock herds, and various fraudulent dealings on a trading expedition; but nevertheless, the Dutch were forced to continue to use him as an interpreter. From time to time, he disappeared from the orbit of Dutch

control, spending time on the farther shores of False Bay. However, he was never rich enough, in cattle, to acquire a significant position within Khoekhoe society. As a result, he had no option but to exploit his position with the Dutch and continued to return to them. For a while this resulted in his incarceration on Robben Island, from where, in December 1659, he succeeded in escaping and joined other Khoekhoe in their resistance against the establishment of Dutch rule over the Table Bay hinterland. In the end, in 1660, peace was established and Autshumao was once again employed as an interpreter for the Dutch. He died, impoverished, in 1663.

After his death, and certainly after the publication of the diaries of Jan van Riebeeck, on which most knowledge about Autshumao is based, his role as a—rather picaresque—hero of resistance to colonialism has been developed. One of the ferries to Robben Island is named after him.

[*See also* Krotoa; *and* Van Riebeeck, Jan.]

BIBLIOGRAPHY

Elphick, R. *Kraal and Castle: Khoikhoi and the Founding of White South Africa.* New Haven, Conn.: Yale University Press, 1979.

Thom, H. B., ed. *Journal of Jan van Riebeeck,* 3 vols. Cape Town, South Africa: Balkema, 1952–1958.

ROBERT ROSS

Averroës. *See* Ibn Rushd.

Avila Laurel, Juan-Tomas (b. 1966), author and coordinator of activities at the Centro Cultural Español de Malabo (Spanish Cultural Center of Malabo, Equatorial Guinea), was born 6 November 1966 in Equatorial Guinea to Manuel Avila and Luisa Laurel, the eldest of five children. Reared primarily by his maternal grandmother due to his parents' separation, Avila Laurel spent his early childhood in Annabón (Equatorial Guinea), often having to share a bed with uncles and cousins due to the economic situation. His mother taught him how to read before he started school, and because of that he was considered very advanced for his age. He began his primary education in Annabón and in 1978, at the age of twelve, he moved to the capital, Malabo, with a great aunt to continue his education. Political instability of the country, especially the end of the bloody dictatorship of Francisco Nguema Macías in 1978, and the generally poor education system forced Avila Laurel to struggle to complete his education. He attended school in the afternoons after supporting his family as a street vendor during the day and studied at night by lamplight. After graduating from high school, he pursued a degree in nursing at the Escuela Nacional de Sanidad de Bata (The National School of Health of Bata) and worked as a laboratory technician in a hospital in Valencia, Spain, for several months. He returned to Malabo to continue his career as a laboratory technician. During the years that he worked in the health field, he also found time to pursue his interest in literature. After fourteen years as a laboratory technician, he took the job as an activities coordinator for the Centro Español de Malabo, where he is in charge of planning lectures, literary contests, and other activities for the center.

Avila Laurel's interest in literature and literary production began as an adolescent by participating in and winning several national and international literary contests. He won first place in the category of essay for the contest "12 años de independencia de Guinea Ecuatorial" organized by the Escuela Normal de Magisterio de Bata (Normal School of the Magistrate of Bata) in 1980. He also won first place in the category of theater (1986) with *Los hombres domésticos* (*Homeboys*) and first place in the category of poetry (1990) with *Voces del alma* (*Voices from the Soul*) in contests sponsored by the now defunct Centro Cultural Hispano-Guineano de Malabo (Hispano-Guinean Cultural Center of Malabo). On the international scene, he won third place in the category of narrative with *El desmayo de Judas* (*Judas Faints*) and honorable mention in the category of poetry with *Historia íntima de la humanidad* (*Intimate History of Humanity*) in the XXXV Certamen International Odón Betanzos Palacios (XXXV Odón Betanzos Palacios International Competition) in 1999.

His success in literary contests led the way for him to pursue a serious career in writing. Avila Laurel belongs to what is known as "*la nueva escritura guineana*." This generation of writers, for the most part, has lived solely under authoritative regimes in the country and does not express the type of nostalgia for a land and culture long lost, which is found in the works from authors of the previous generation. Writing only when he had time and living in a country where resources are scarce, Avila Laurel managed to publish a number of works in narrative, poetry, essay, and theater, including the following: *Poemas* (1994), *Los hombres domésticos* (1994), *Historia íntima de la humanidad* (1999), *La carga* (*The Burden*) (1999),

Áwala cu sangui (*Áwala with Blood*) (2000), *El derecho de pernada. Cómo se vive el feudalismo en el siglo XXI* (*The Lord's Right/Droit du seigneur. How Feudalism Lives in the 21st Century*) (2000), *El desmayo de Judas* (2001), *Nadie tiene buena fama en este país* (*Nobody Has a Good Reputation in This Country*) (2002), *El fracaso de las sombras* (*The Failure of the Shadows*) (2004), *Cómo convertir este país en un paraíso. Otras reflexiones sobre Guinea Ecuatorial* (*How to Convert This Country into a Paradise. Other Reflections on Equatorial Guinea*) (2005), *Guinea Ecuatorial. Vísceras* (*Equatorial Guinea. The Inside Story*) (2006), *Cuentos crudos* (*Crude Stories*) (2007), *Avión de ricos, ladrón de cerdos* (*Airplane of the Wealthy, Hog Thief*) (2008), and *Arde el monte de noche* (*The Mountain Burns at Night*) (2008). Although there is great variety in genre, there is one common theme in the writing of Avila Laurel: the reality of Equatorial Guinea. While some of his works such as *La carga* examine and criticize Spain's involvement in Equatorial Guinea's history and present-day situation, most of his works focus on the consequences of the dictatorships of Francisco Macías Nguema (1969–1979) and Teodoro Obiang Nguema (1979–present). His narrative works, usually with a direct tone and a touch of ironic humor, comment on the daily struggles of the Equatorial Guinean people. While all of his work is critical of how the Macías and Obiang regimes have affected the country as a whole, it is of special note that *Áwala cu sangui* is the only novel to date that focuses on the plight of the annobonés (Avila Laurel's ethnic group) people during the Macías regime.

In addition to writing, Avila Laurel also served as editor-in-chief of Equatorial Guinean literary journal *Revista de Cultura y Literatura El Patio* from 1999 to 2003 and was named the Joseph Astman Distinguished Faculty Lecturer at Hofstra University in 2003. He has also participated in conferences at several universities and centers for education in Equatorial Guinea and internationally: Centro Cultural Español de Malabo y Centro Cultural Español de Bata, Universidad Nacional de Guinea Ecuatorial, Universidad Nacional de Educación a Distancia (Equatorial Guinea), Universidad de Murcia (Spain), University of Missouri-Columbia (USA), Hofstra University (USA), Rutgers University (USA), Bates College (USA), Westminster College (USA), Drew University (USA), Kingsboro Community College (USA), Farleigh Dickinson University (USA), University of Seoul (South Korea), and University of Zurich (Switzerland). His participation in these conferences has greatly increased awareness about literature produced in the only Spanish-speaking sub-Saharan African country.

Considered perhaps the most influential Equatorial Guinean author that has chosen not to live in exile, Juan-Tomas Avila Laurel continues to seek avenues to publish and to educate the world about Equatorial Guinea.

[*See also* Nguema, Macías; *and* Obiang Nguema Mbasogo, Teodoro.]

BIBLIOGRAPHY

Avila Laurel, Juan-Tomas. Personal interview. 5 Mar. 2010. This interview was conducted through a series of e-mails.
Avila Laurel, Juan-Tomas. *Guinea Ecuatorial: Vísceras. Valencia*, Spain: Imprenta Romeu, S.L., 2006.
Ndongo-Bidyogo, Donato and M'bare N'gom Faye. *Literatura de Guinea Ecuatorial (Antología)*. (Madrid: SIAL Ediciones, 2000). This is the only anthology of Equatorial Guinean literature. It is an updated version of the first anthology complied by Donato Ndongo in 1984.
N'gom Faye, M'bare. *Diálogos con Guinea*. Madrid: Labrys 54 S.L., 1996.

NICOLE D. PRICE

Awaw (fl. late twentieth century–early nineteenth century BCE), earliest of the rulers of Kush (Ancient Sudan) so far attested in written sources. The form of the name is conjectural.

Awaw is briefly referred to as an enemy in the Egyptian "Execration Texts," compositions of magical spells meant to protect the unnamed "customer(s)" (most likely a royalty, perhaps a pharaoh) from any sort of harm made by, or expected from, any potential adversary anywhere in Egypt and/or beyond it. Exorcisms of this kind would be written in black ink on certain ritual objects (pottery vessels of various forms—bowls, platters, etc., or figurines of clay, alabaster, or limestone, representing bound prisoners), which, in the course of a mass ceremony, would be ritually broken up or otherwise damaged and buried afterward.

As several groups of finds show, the "Execration Texts" were composed of almost stereotypes for the given group of objects formulae. The variant of the text reconstructed from the sherds in the Berlin Ägyptisches Museum collection (fragments of approximately eighty inscribed vessels), presumably coming from the royal necropolis in Western

Thebes in Egypt, is considered the most complete. This recension includes four detailed lists of persons (rulers, their peoples, and certain social categories), thought to be potentially dangerous, among the Southerners (*nehsu*), North-Easterners (*aamu*), Libyans, and Egyptians (evidently, political adversaries). The fifth one records malevolent "things" and actions (words, dreams, etc.) to be neutralized by magical means.

The "standard" text opens with a nominal list of six southern rulers, each referred to with his entourage, the first one being "The ruler of the (land of) Kash, (called) Awaw, born by (his mother) Ku[ni?], begotten by (his father) [_ _ _]a, (and) all the fallen (men), that are with him."

The second section enumerates the dwellers of the southern lands, labeled "All "nehsu" (peoples) from <. . .>" which must have implied the (dark-skinned) peoples inhabiting the territory of the Ancient Sudan because the word "nehsu" never was applied to, for example, the western neighbors of Egypt, the Libyans. As in the previous case, the list begins with a reference to the "(land of) Kash," these two examples being the earliest attestation of the toponym better known afterward in the form "Kush." Most important, this place-name, which later became one of the main appellations of the cultural conglomeration gradually emerging in the Middle Nile valley, here refers to only one of the twenty-two enumerated "lands" of the Ancient Sudan. The fact that Awaw's name opens the list of the southern peoples' rulers, whereas his principality is put at the head of the long roll of (threatening) neighbors, must point to the high status of him and his realm among the powers, which the Egyptians considered menacing.

No specific complaints against neighbors were ever put forth, or hinted at, in the "Execration Texts." The ceremony, during which these spells (inscribed on the ritual objects to be broken up, and probably enchanted) were made use of, may have been a product of the Egyptians' public fears and actually did not imply a retribution for a real offence but rather its prevention, by means of magic, in the future.

This ritual must have been quite old but occasionally updated. Some early examples, inscribed statuettes datable to the Sixth Dynasty (ca. twenty-fourth–twenty-second centuries BCE), were found in the Giza necropolis, but they are not reported to bear any rulers' names. A version much closer to the Berlin recension was found on a series of statuettes from the Saqqara necropolis, dating to the

Twelfth Dynasty (ca. twentieth–eighteenth centuries) and thus somewhat later than the Berlin sherds. This time the spells also begin with a reference to the ruler of Kash, but his name and the name of his mother (Wetetrerses? and Teti, respectively) are quite different, whereas the father's name (Awaa) is rather similar to, and in one example is almost identical with, the name of Awaw from the Berlin inscriptions. It has, therefore, been deduced that the texts on the sherds and on the statuettes refer to father and son, his successor.

The real political status of Awaw is difficult to establish today. The title "heqa" (ruler), sometimes interpreted as "prince," applied in the "Execration Texts" to him, his (supposed) son, and all other non-Egyptian personages (the enemy Egyptians are presented with their functionary titles only and evidently did not belong to the category of "rulers"), is among the vaguest terms of Egyptian political lexicon. Depending on the context, as a metaphor, it could equally refer to a pharaoh, a god, or a "district governor," and so on. In any event, typologically this designation was below the title "king," which the Egyptians reserved for their own rulers, considering them superior to any foreign counterparts and often qualifying the latters as but "chieftains" (lit. "great (ones)").

The fact that the Sudanese lists take precedence over the lists of the "Asiatics," Libyans, and Egyptians seems to indicate that southern neighbors, and first of all the ruler(s) of Kash/Kush, were considered the main (potential) adversary— or rival—by the "customer(s)" at whose order the spells inscribed on the Berlin vessels and on the statuettes from Saqqara were compiled.

After Awaw and his (presumed) son, no rulers of Kash/Kush seem to have been attested for about two centuries. In the course of the intense Egyptian expansion under the pharaohs of the Twelfth Dynasty (twentieth–eighteenth century BCE, zenith of the Middle Kingdom), the early polities of the Ancient Sudan must have been suppressed. In fact, their development passed in latent state and naturally revived in the periods of political disintegration of the Egyptian empire (so-called Intermediate Periods) as the pharaonic administration's control of the southern lands was waning.

By the sixteenth century BCE (late second Intermediate Period in Egypt) an early state formation with the center in Kerma (south of the Third Cataract of the Nile) rose as a major political power in the Middle Nile valley, but after a period of remarkable growth and prosperity it was subdued by the first pharaohs of the Eighteenth Dynasty (late sixteenth–fifteenth centuries, the New Kingdom in Egypt), the native elite perhaps being partly incorporated in the system of indirect control.

Nevertheless,the real breakthrough in the evolution of indigenous statehood took place a millennium later, sometime in the late ninth–early eighth centuries BCE (Third Intermediate Period in Egypt), which resulted in the emergence of a new polity, with its capital first in Napata, between the Third and Fourth Cataracts, and later in Meroe, between the Fifth and Sixth Cataracts, which flourished until approximately the mid-fourth century CE. This cultural conglomeration, evidently the earliest, after Egypt, seat of civilization in Africa, retained several ancient self-appellations, the most common of which seems to have been "Kush." Some seventy royal names have been attested in the written monuments of this kingdom, which, at its height, controlled the territory from Aswan to Sennar and beyond. In a sense, all these kings were distant successors of Awaw, who ruled the core area of this territory at the time when it was only a "principality," though most important, of the Ancient Sudan.

[See also Alara; and Nedjeh.]

BIBLIOGRAPHY

Posener, Georges. "Ächtungstexte. (Execration Texts)" In *Lexikon der Ägyptologie, Vol. 1*, edited by Wolgang Helck, Eberhard Otto and Wolfhart Westendorf, pp. 67–69. Wiesbaden, Germany: Otto Harrassowitz, 1975.

Posener, Georges, ed. *Princes et pays d'Asie et de Nubie* (Princes and Countries of Asia and Nubia). Brussels, Belgium: Fondation Égyptologique Reine Élisabeth, 1940.

Säve-Söderbergh, Torgny. *Ägypten und Nubien. Ein Beitrag zur Geschichte altaügyptischer Aussenpolitik.* (Egypt and Nubia. An Essay on the History of Ancient Egyptian Foreign Policy) London: Lund Humphries, 1941.

Sethe, Kurt. *Die Ächtung feindlicher Fürsten. Völker und Dinge auf altägyptischen Tongefässscherben des Mittleren Reiches* (The Confounding of the Hostile Princes. Peoples and Things on the Ancient Egyptian Pottery Sherds of Middle Kingdom). Berlin: Verlag der Akademie der Wissenschcaften, 1926.

A. K. VINOGRADOV

Aways Mohamed, Sheikh (1847–1909), charismatic Islamic leader whose influence spread from

Somalia to the whole of East Africa and beyond. His full name was Aways Mohammed al-Qadiri.

He was born in Brava, a coastal town in Southern Somalia, the son of Mohammed Mahadh Bashir and Faduma Barow. The family had humble origins: some Italian sources claim that the father or one of his immediate forebears had been a freedman of the Tunni, the Somali clan settled in and around Brava. In the course of his life Sheikh Aways married several times. Five of his wives, Bay Aliow bint Bobo, Doyo bint Mahadh Abdallah, Amo bint Bana Tahir Bora, Fatima bint Mohammed Muhyiddin, and Hawa Shego, are mentioned in the Civil Register of the Court of Brava. Of his children, a daughter, Dede, was immortalized in verse by the judge and scholar Abd al-Aziz al-Amawi (who probably married her), and a son, Sha'ir, took over the leadership of the religious community of Beled Amin after his father's death, but he achieved only a limited renown.

As a young man, Sheikh Aways studied locally with Sheikh Mohammed Janna al-Bahluli, Sheikh Ahmed bin Haj Nur Jabhad, and Sheikh Mohammed Ta'yini al-Shashi, who encouraged him to pursue his religious education abroad. By 1870, Sheikh Aways was in Baghdad, where he became a disciple of Sayyid Mustafa ibn Sayyid Salman al-Kilani, a descendant of Sheikh Abdulqadir al-Jilani, the founder of the Qadiriyya brotherhood, and eventually obtained his full authorization to teach the brotherhood's spiritual knowledge and precepts. While in Arabia, he performed his first pilgrimage to Mecca and visited many saints' tombs in the Hadramawt and Hijaz.

Returning to Somalia in about 1881, he made his first base in Brava, where he attracted a large following. Later, Sheikh Aways mainly led a peripatetic life, moving from place to place with a large entourage of disciples. His missionary activity for the Qadiriyya took a revolutionary approach: he attracted the local populace with group-performed singing (dhikr) of didactic religious poems he composed in several Somali dialects. To better disseminate these compositions, he also devised a system of writing Somali in Arabic script. Concomitantly, he produced many religious poems in Arabic, which became part of the daily devotions of those affiliated to the Qadiriyya.

He also founded several religious-agricultural settlements (jama'a) of his Qadiri disciples throughout the Shebelle valley and in the Upper Juba region. Traveling abroad often, Sheikh Aways kept in contact with the most important religious scholars of his time, particularly those of Mecca and Medina. His hagiography records his visits to the Qadiriyya representative in Mecca, al-Sharif al-Sayyid Saleh Izziddin bin al-Sayyid Sa'id al-Kilani, and to Sheikh Abubakar ibn al-Sayyid Muhammad Shatta al-Dimiyatti. He also visited Zanzibar very frequently and was held in high esteem by Sultan Barghash and his successors, who often offered him their financial help.

Owing to his relentless missionary activity, his branch of the Qadiriyya (called Qadiriyya Uwaysiyya) spread to central and southern Somalia, Zanzibar, present-day Tanzania as far inland as Tabora and Ujiji, and south to the border with Mozambique, the eastern region of Congo, and the Comoro Islands. It is even reported that one of his disciples went to Indonesia on a proselytizing mission. According to his hagiography, he appointed no fewer than 520 deputies (khalifas), originating from a large variety of localities and ethnic backgrounds, a testimonial to the extensive network he had created with consummate organizational ability.

Despite his political sympathies for the Zanzibar sultans and his abhorrence of European colonialism, Sheikh Aways never came into direct confrontation with the foreign colonial powers in Somalia, unlike his major religious opponent, Mohammed Abdulle Hassan, who waged a twenty-year war against the British, Italians, and Ethiopians in Northern and Central Somalia. Originally affiliated to the Salihiyya brotherhood, Mohammed Abdulle Hassan later took up a more radical position against the views of traditional Islam, as preached by Sheikh Aways. From virulent exchanges of verse between the heads of the two movements, the dispute escalated into actual fighting. On 14 April 1909, a group of Mohammed Abdulle Hassan's followers killed Sheikh Aways and twenty-five of his disciples at the jama'a of Biyolay.

In an epoch and society where the status of a religious scholar was usually connected to lineage and family tradition, Sheikh Aways achieved his preeminent position thanks solely to his personal charisma. After his death, his popularity increased further, as did the fame of his miraculous deeds. Both in colonial and in postcolonial times thousands of pilgrims visited Biyolay every year to commemorate him on the anniversary of his death and to pray at his tomb.

BIBLIOGRAPHY

Cerulli, Enrico. *Somalia Scritti Vari Editi ed Inediti,* Volume 1. Rome, 1957.

Martin, Bradford G. *Muslim Brotherhoods in Nineteenth Century Africa*. Cambridge, UK: Cambridge University Press, 1976.

Vianello, Alessandra and Mohamed Kassim, eds. *Servants of the Sharia—The Civil Register of the Qadis' Court of Brava 1893–1900*. Leiden, Netherlands: Brill, 2006.

ALESSANDRA VIANELLO

Awe, Bolanle (b. 1933), Nigerian historian and educational administrator, was born to Samuel Akindeji Fajembola, an Ibadan man, and Mosebolatan Fajembola, an Ijesa woman, on 28 January 1933 in Ilesa, Osun State, Nigeria. Samuel Akindeji Fajembola was a manager with John Holt & Co., a merchant company, based in Liverpool, England; Mosebolatan Fajembola was one of the first female professional teachers to be trained in southwestern Nigeria. Awe had her early education at Holy Trinity School, Omofe, Ilesa; Saint James's School, Oke-Bola, Ibadan; C.M.S Girls' School, Lagos; and Saint Anne's School, Ibadan, between 1941 and 1951. Between 1952 and 1954, she attended the Perse School for Girls in Cambridge, England, and received an MA from the University of St. Andrews, Scotland, in 1958. Between 1958 and 1960, she did postgraduate work for a doctoral degree at Somerville College, the oldest of the University of Oxford's female colleges. She was awarded her PhD from Oxford in 1964; her unpublished doctoral thesis was "The Rise of Ibadan as a Yoruba Power in the Nineteenth Century."

Before completing her doctoral studies, Awe was appointed as an assistant lecturer in October 1960 at the University of Ibadan but left in 1967 for the School of African and Asian Studies, University of Lagos. She returned to the University of Ibadan, in 1969, as a senior research fellow in oral history at the Institute of African Studies. She rose to become the first female director of the Institute and served from 1983 to 1991. Awe, who became a research professor of history in 1977, was the founder and first president of the Centre for Documentation and Research on Women at the University of Ibadan.

In public life, Professor Awe served as commissioner for education, and, later, of trade, industries, and cooperatives in western states between 1975 and 1978. She was, in the 1980s, the founding chair of the Nigerian Commission for Women, which later provided the nucleus for the current Ministry of Women Affairs. In the 1990s, she served as the founding country director of the American-based John D. and Catherine T. MacArthur Foundation, where her initial focus was on reproductive health and the rights of women. She subsequently concentrated on the development of higher education in Nigerian universities, most notably at the University of Ibadan, the University of Port Harcourt, Ahmadu Bello University in Zaria, and Bayero University in Kano.

As a historian, Awe's emergence and growth could be attributed to well-tailored mentorship by history teachers and her own enterprise. At both Saint Anne's and the Perse School for Girls, she had history teachers who fired her imagination to pursue historical studies. She also learned much from her professors at Saint Andrews, who were often Oxford history graduates and encouraged her to take up postgraduate work at that university. Coincidentally, this was at a time when the Nigerian historians Kenneth O. Dike and Saburi Biobaku were publishing pioneering works that highlighted for Awe the importance of Africans themselves in the making of African history. Buoyed by these factors, she entered Oxford, determined to study African history, but it was a new field and those early students were barely tolerated. Hugh Trevor Roper, Regius professor of modern history at Oxford was, at the time, pontificating that sub-Saharan Africa had no history prior to European contact. However, Awe's own supervisor, Margery Perham, a historian who found much to fault in the British role in Africa, was very encouraging to her. Despite a paucity of written records on Africa, Awe was allowed to write her thesis on Ibadan using oral tradition, in the tradition of Jan Vansina. In a general sense, oral tradition, culture, and lore are cultural materials that are transmitted orally from one generation to another. In the tradition of Vansina, these cultural materials are believed to be held in common by a group of people over several generations, and they can be transmitted as history, literature, laws, and other knowledge, especially where writing system is lacking.

Working closely with E. J. Alagoa at the Institute of African Studies at the University of Ibadan, she examined oral sources for writing African history. Like no one else before her, she focused primarily on the contribution of women to Nigerian vis-à-vis African development, an effort that made her the foremost woman historian in and of Africa. Aided by United Nations concern for the role of women in development, especially the declaration of the years 1976–1985 as the UN's Decade of Women, Awe historicized the role of Nigerian women in precolonial, colonial, and, later, postcolonial periods. In all these she relied primarily on oral traditions. The general lack of information on women's contributions to development led her, in conjunction with others, to found the Women's Research and Documentation Center (WORDOC) at the University of Ibadan in the late 1980s.

Like Kenneth Dike, Saburi Biobaku, and J. F. Ade-Ajayi, Awe contributed immensely to the use of oral traditions in historical scholarship, especially in the construction and reconstruction of orally literate societies of Africa prior to the European intrusion. In addition, she emphasized the contribution of women to Africa's historical socioeconomic, cultural, and political developments, especially as prior writings tended to be silent on or dismissive of their contribution. She noted that oral traditions could reveal much about women's performance. After thirty-eight years as a scholar and as an administrator, Awe retired from the University of Ibadan in 1998. In retirement, she continued her passion for gender equity and continued to engage on gender issues in both African historical studies and in development issues. She was appointed by the federal government of Nigeria to serve as the pro-chancellor of the University of Nigeria, Nsukka in 2005.

Among other works, Awe authored *Yoruba Warfare in the Nineteenth Century* (Ibadan University Press, 1971); *The Iyalode in Ibadan Politics and Society, c. 1850–1997* (Sam Bookman Publishers, 1998); and the *Nigerian Women in Historical Perspective* (Bookcraft, 2001). Awe is married to Muyiwa Awe, an emeritus professor of physics, and the marriage is blessed with children and grandchildren.

For her services to Nigeria and Africa, Bolanle Awe received many national and international awards, including Fellow of the Historical Society of Nigeria (FHSN) and Fellow of the Nigerian Academy of Letters (FNAL). She is also an Advisory Board Member of the journal *Gender and History* and sits on the board of the Gender Institute at the University of Cape Town, South Africa. For her public service, the government of Nigeria conferred on her the national honor of Officer of the Federal Republic of Nigeria (OFR), one of Nigeria's highest national honors, in 1982.

[*See also* Ade Ajayi, Jacob Festus; Dike, Kenneth; *and* Vansina, Jan.]

BIBLIOGRAPHY

Awe, Bolanle. *Nigerian Women in Historical Perspective.* Ibadan, Nigeria: Bookcraft, 2001.

Falola, Toyin and Saheed Aderinto, *Nigeria, Nationalism, and Writing History.* Rochester, NY: University of Rochester Press, 2010.

Mba, Nina Emma. *Nigerian Women Mobilized: Women's Political Activity in Southern Nigeria, 1900–1965.* Berkeley: Institute of International Studies, University of California, 1982.

ADEYEMI BUKOLA OYENIYI

Awolowo, Obafemi (1909–1987), Nigerian trade unionist, nationalist, and political leader, was born in Ikenne, Western Nigeria on 6 March 1909. He survived a difficult childhood following the death of his father in 1920 and the breakup of his family and completed schooling by fending for himself. Awolowo worked as a house-help, fetched firewood for sale, apprenticed as a letter writer, and worked as a typist and clerk, teacher, news reporter, contractor, transporter, and produce buyer on the way to studying for a law degree at the University of London between 1944 and 1946. Through this harsh experience, he developed self-reliance and confidence, a fearless and defiant attitude to authority, as well as skills as a community and labor organizer, qualities that were to serve him in good stead as he thrust into the stormy politics of colonial Nigeria.

Obafemi Awolowo, 1959. (AP Images)

The 1930s mark the high point of colonial rule in Nigeria. British control of the economy through a United Africa Company (UAC)-led consortium of European firms squeezed out Nigerian entrepreneurs. Nigerians felt their economic domination and marginalization more deeply as European firms added local produce buying and extensive retail sales to their established control of banking. In a similar vein, a rising number of educated Nigerians were denied employment and promotion in the colonial public service and they were almost entirely excluded from the advisory parliament, the judiciary, or the executive council either in the colonial service or in the native councils. These conditions bred nationalist agitation among educated youth against the British colonial government and detestation of the older generation of educated elites led by Herbert Macaulay for their nonconfrontational accommodation of the colonial order. The Lagos Youth Movement (later Nigerian Youth Movement [NYM]) was formed in 1934 to address these many grievances. Awolowo joined as a founding member and became the leader of the Ibadan branch.

Awolowo organized the cocoa holdup of 1937–1938 to break the control of European firms over the purchase price of cocoa. In the same year, he led the Motor Transport Union in a strike against an increase in license fees, a government policy aimed at promoting railway transportation over commercial road transportation. In 1940 he organized a mass protest by farmers in the Western Provinces against the colonial government's prohibition of palm kernel oil export. When the colonial secretary of state for the colonies visited Nigeria in 1943, Awolowo delivered a memorandum on behalf of the Youth Movement demanding, among other things, better wages for Nigerian workers, expanded schooling opportunities in Nigeria, and scholarships for students to go abroad to study. These activities endeared Awolowo to ordinary people: farmers, vehicle drivers, and wage earners. More importantly, they launched Awolowo into the mainstream of Nigerian politics.

The Nigerian Youth Movement soon collapsed, a victim of internal rivalry among its national leaders, which increasingly widened ethnic divisions. The defection of its charismatic leader, Nnamdi Azikiwe, in 1941 along with many fellow Igbo members left the party dispirited and moribund. Awolowo had invested his energy and hopes in the NYM as the platform for national integration, where (in his words) ". . . all conscientious and right thinking Nigerian patriots and nationalists could unfold their ideas and display their talents for the common good." The ethnic divergence obliged a review of his political philosophy and strategy. His new thoughts were expressed in his influential book *Path to Nigerian Freedom* (1947), which he introduced with the statement, "Nigeria is not a nation. It is a mere geographical expression." In what was to become a lifelong political philosophy, Awolowo promoted federalism, based on the nationalities (not ethnic groups) that comprised Nigeria. For him, these nations were the natural building blocks of Nigerian unity.

In 1945 he led other Yoruba students in London to found the Egbe Omo Oduduwa (named after the Yoruba primogenitor), a cultural and political association to promote Yoruba unity within the impending Federation of Nigeria. His initial outreach to Yoruba leaders in Nigeria was rebuffed as many of them still supported the dominant nationalist organization, the National Council of Nigeria and the Cameroons (NCNC), led by Herbert Macaulay and Nnamdi Azikiwe. Further ethnic disagreements between the Yoruba and Igbo factions in the NCNC saw the Yoruba members defecting to form the Egbe (Association). This Egbe, led by recognized Yoruba elite, including Sir Adeyemo Alakija, I. O. Ransome Kuti, and Dr. Akinola Maja, secured the recognition of a wide spectrum of Yoruba traditional rulers and population. Awolowo's ideas, elaborated earlier in his draft constitution of the Egbe Omo Oduduwa, were adopted and he was appointed general secretary. The Egbe formed the hub of the Action Group (AG) political party that won the 1951 elections to the Western Nigeria House of Assembly and ran the internal self government of Western Nigeria (1952–1959) with Awolowo as the head of government business. When the Action Group won the independence elections in 1960 Awolowo became premier of the Western Region.

This pioneering experiment in Nigerian self-government established Awolowo as a deeply thoughtful and effective leader. The western regional government formulated and implemented policies including the reform of local government. It clearly defined the roles of traditional rulers, abolished the native court system, and regulated succession to chieftaincies. These reforms were no mean feats considering how central chiefs were to the colonial indirect rule system and the power and influence they had garnered. The party successfully implemented mass education projects including free and compulsory universal primary education, the expansion of educational facilities across all levels, free adult education programs, and the expansion of women's education.

Other credits to the government include infrastructural developments, the expansion of the road and telecommunications network, and establishing farm settlements and industrial and housing estates. Other feats like the building of Cocoa House, which at twenty-four floors was the first skyscraper and for a long time the tallest building in sub-Saharan Africa (completed 1965), Liberty stadium, Africa's first television service (1959), the University of Ife (1962)—renamed Obafemi Awolowo University at Ile-Ife after his death—established Awolowo as the arguably greatest Nigerian of the twentieth century. Needless to say, he was active with other nationalists at demanding for immediate end to colonial rule and national independence. In 1953 the AG and the NCNC allied over the granting of regional self-government. In 1956 the Action Group tabled a motion for internal self-government in the federation, a motion that failed because the conservative Northern People's Congress (NPC) opposed it.

However, Awolowo failed in his bid to become head of state in the 1959 federal elections, becoming instead the leader of the opposition in the federal parliament. Disagreements with his deputy and successor as premier of the Western Region, Ladoke Akintola, broke the Action Group from the Akintola faction forming the Nigerian National Democratic party (NNDP), which allied with the NPC to defeat the Action Group in the 1964 elections. Conflicts broke out in the region in protest against claims of election rigging. In 1964 Awolowo and several of his cohort were charged with treasonable felony and sentenced (some argue on trumped-up charges) for conspiring with Kwame Nkrumah of Ghana to topple the federal government in a coup or a communist revolution. The tensions deriving from these political crises and maneuverings led to Nigeria's first coup in January 1966, a counter coup (July 1966), and later the Nigerian Civil War, 1967–1971. Meanwhile, Awolowo was pardoned and released from jail by the Yakubu Gowon government to help resolve the national crisis. He joined the federal government as Minister of Finance and vice president of the Federal Executive Council. He is credited with effectively managing the war finances such that Nigeria conducted the war without recourse to external borrowing or a deficit budget.

Awolowo contested and lost the 1979 federal elections on the platform of the Unity Party of Nigeria, which he formed as successor to the Action Group. As in the First Republic, his party won the gubernatorial contests in the five western Nigeria states, which are predominantly Yoruba, and continued to pursue Awolowo's signature policies of free education at all levels, free public health, and social welfare. A final attempt at the Nigerian presidency failed in 1983. At his death in 1987 Awolowo was acknowledged as the most dominant figure in Nigeria's politics. A political opponent described him as the best president Nigeria never had. His ideas and the political organization he formed have continued to be central to political discourses in Nigeria.

Awolowo was certainly the most controversial political figure of twentieth-century Nigeria. His opponents label him a tribalist for his political affiliations in forming the Egbe and for the regional character of his Unity Party. It is difficult to determine in Nigeria's charged politics if those who so accuse him are any less parochial. He was also accused of encouraging the Igbos on to secession and then reneging on supporting them. Despite his denials and the historical reality, the image of being anti-Igbo sticks to Awolowo's image. The Balewa government, against which he led the opposition in the 1960s, labeled him a communist, for which reason he has been regarded with suspicion in Western circles. On the whole friends and foe alike agree that Awolowo was a skilled politician, organizer, and an effective administrator.

Among the Yoruba Awolowo has assumed an iconic status. He has been ranked next to Oduduwa, the mythical primogenitor among the leaders of the Yoruba of all times. His political family remains a force in Nigeria's politics; his political ideology and social and economic prescriptions remain the declared aspirations of successive Nigerian governments. His books, the last of which was written in 1985, remain the most coherent ideas for Nigeria's development. Most notable among his publications are *Awo: The Autobiography of Chief Obafemi Awolowo* (1960) and *My March Through Prison* (1985). In 1981 *The Selected Speeches of Chief Obafemi Awolowo* were published in three volumes by Fagbamigbe Publishers in Akura, Nigeria: volume one is *Voice of Reason*; volume two, *Voice of Courage*; and volume three, *Voice of Wisdom*.

[*See also* Azikiwe, Benjamin Nnamdi; Gowon, Yakubu Jack; Macaulay, Herbert; *and* Nkrumah, Kwame.]

BIBLIOGRAPHY

Jakande, L. K. *The Trial of Obafemi Awolowo.* London: Secker & Warburg; Lagos, Nigeria: John West Publications. 1966.

Oyelaran, Olasoge O. et al., editors. *Obafemi Awolowo: The End of an Era?: Selected papers from the National conference held at the Obafemi Awolowo University, Ile-Ife from 4th to 8th, October, 1987.* Ile-Ife, Nigeria: Obafemi Awolowo University Press, 1988.

OLUWATOYIN BABATUNDE ODUNTAN

Awutiek (d. c. 1921), chief of the Palyoupiny Malwal, created an early aristocratic Dinka state in the southern Sudan during the 1880s. Awutiek's uncle and predecessor Duang Marial had gained power by collaborating with slave traders such as Zubayr and with officials of the Egyptian colonial government. These lessons were not lost on the young chief Awutiek, who quickly realized the importance of firearms and purchased large quantities from Fertit middlemen, northern Sudanese traders, and Azande. He also acquired arms from Mahdists fallen in battle. Awutiek built a standing army. He set his warriors to regular military drills and maintained a strong, well-trained force. By 1892, having annihilating the last Mahdist force to venture into his territory, Awutiek extended his influence down the Chell and Loll Rivers as far as the Rek country in the eastern Bahr el-Ghazal. By the height of his power Awutiek controlled most of the diverse peoples living across a large section of the Southern Sudan between the Tonj and Pongo Rivers from northwest to southeast of Wau. Many smaller groups who came to live under the suzerainty of Awutiek adopted Dinka culture.

Awutiek formed a structure of administration by dividing his chiefdoms into a number of subordinate headships. He yielded a measure of autonomy to each chief, whose responsibility it was to collect and deliver tribute or taxes in the form of livestock, food, ivory, honey, wax, and labor. From his capital at Achamangu, Awutiek promoted and administered trade with neighboring Luo, Fertit, and Baggara merchants. He exchanged slaves, livestock, fish, ivory, rhinoceros horns, leopard skins, elephant and giraffe tails, ostrich feathers, chili, honey, and wax with northern traders in return for clothes, horses, donkeys, soap, and other items. Awutiek's trade allowed him to acquire enormous wealth and power and to maintain military and political control over his many subjects. As befitted his status, the chief acquired thirty wives, many of whom were Luo, while others comprised gifts from other southern clients. Those women acquired in raids (usually against the Baggara) were distributed among his military subordinates. As Awutiek's rule became

more centralized, he was able to restructure law in his territory; rather than merely fining those who committed offenses, he now executed some for key crimes. At the close of the nineteenth century, Awutiek was recognized as the most powerful leader in the region and many refugees from all quarters fled to his territory for protection. He represented the greatest military power in the erstwhile colonial provinces of Equatoria and Bahr el-Ghazal, northward to Jebel Telgauna, and east as far as the river port of Meshra el-Rek. However, he was soon to encounter new foreigners and hostile forces.

As the French began to penetrate the Southern Sudan from the Congo in 1897, they sought Awutiek's approval and friendship. Awutiek calculated he could increase his power much as his father and uncle had done, and he prepared to make alliances with these latest foreigners. As the only chief in the region willing to accept nominal French rule, the wily Dinka leader acquired sixty rifles and ammunition, ostensibly to consolidate his position against further Mahdist attacks. He further requested that the French establish a post in his territory at Achamangu. However, the French did not remain long, for in July 1898 they concluded an agreement with the British at Fashoda and evacuated the Southern Sudan.

The British newcomers, however, unlike the foreigners and traders of the past, proved unwilling to support Awutiek's aspirations to power. His representatives first met with British agents in 1900 and several diplomatic missions were exchanged. In 1902 Awutiek, now recognized as a "sultan" by the British, arrived in person at the administrator's offices in Wau accompanied by a retinue of forty-five followers and prepared to forge a new alliance. But the British were unwilling. Because the Malwal leader presented no military threat, the British preferred to ignore his requests for arms and recognition and to undermine his political and economic base. They had already begun to grant sanctuary to dissatisfied subjects of Awutiek who sought protection at Wau. They soon arrested a convoy of messengers delivering slaves from Sultan Zemio of the Azande to Awutiek. Shortly thereafter they cut off the chief's access to all trade goods by placing their administrative post, not in Awutiek's capital as the Sultan had requested, but further north in Aweil. This encouraged traffic to bypass the Sultan, and over the decades his influence faded and his realm collapsed. By February 1921 Awutiek, now referred to as a mere "chief" by the British, had died of old age.

BIBLIOGRAPHY

Beswick, Stephanie. "Violence, Ethnicity and Political Consolidation in South Sudan: A History of the Dinka and Their Relations With Their Neighbors." PhD diss., Michigan State University, 1998.

STEPHANIE BESWICK

Axmed, Cabdullaahi Yuusuf (b. 1934), fifth president of Somalia, was born on 15 December 1934 in the town of Gaalkacyo in the north-central Mudug region of Somalia; his name is also spelled 'Abdullaahi Yusuf Ahmed. He later joined the Somali army and was among the first cadet officials sent to Italy in 1954 where he stayed until 1957 for his military training. From 1963 to 1968 he attended the Staff & Command College in Moscow. As an army officer, Axmed participated in the Somali-Ethiopian wars of 1964 and 1977. He was decorated for bravery and received medals in both conflicts. He strongly disapproved of Siyaad Barre and his fellow officers, who overthrew the civilian government on 21 October 1969. Shortly after he came to power, Siyaad Barre arrested him and sent him to jail for six years. He was released from prison in 1975 and appointed manager of a state agency dealing with the importation of spare parts for government vehicles with the intention of keeping him on a short leash and curbing his influence in the army.

In early 1978 he led an aborted military coup to overthrow Barre's government along with other high-ranking military and police officers. He escaped first to Kenya and then to Ethiopia, where he founded Somalia's first armed opposition movement named the Somali Salvation Democratic Front (SSDF). In 1985, Axmed was arrested by the ruling military junta after he fell out of favor with Ethiopian president Colonel Mengistu Haile Miriam. His relationship with Ethiopia deteriorated after he refused to accept the Ethiopian annexation of the districts of Galdogob and Balanballe, which his forces captured from the Somali army in the early 1980s with the help of the Ethiopian army. He was kept in prison for five years until his release when the then-ruling Dergue was overthrown in 1991 by the Ethiopian People's Revolutionary Democratic Front of Ethiopia's current prime minister, Meles Zenawi.

In the 1990s, Axmed emerged as the preeminent leader of his native Puntland region and in 1998 declared the territory semi-autonomous. But unlike Somaliland, which declared its secession from Somalia, Puntland remained as an integral part of Somalia. On 23 July 1998, he became its president and served in this position until October 2004 when he resigned to become the president of Somalia. He won a landslide victory and got 189 votes from the Transitional Federal Parliament (TFG), while the closest contender got 79 votes; he was sworn in a few days later on 14 October 2004 in Nairobi, Kenya.

As president, he pledged to promote reconciliation and to set about rebuilding the country. However, his government was plagued by internal disagreements and conflicts with other power-holders in Somalia. He relocated the institutions of the TFG, along with his prime minister Cali Maxamed Geeddi and the speaker of the parliament Shariif Xassan Sheekh Aaden, from Nairobi first to the cities of Jowhar and Baydhaba and then, in late December 2006, to Mogadishu .

On 18 September 2006, a suicide car bomber crashed his vehicle into Axmed's convoy outside the National Parliament in Baydhaba. The attack killed five of Axmed's bodyguards, including his brother. Six attackers were also killed in the subsequent gun battle. The Islamic Courts Union, which had recently taken control of much of the country, was blamed for the attack. In December 2006, President Axmed defeated the Islamic Courts Union with the help of the Ethiopian army. The Ethiopian intervention was unpopular with many Somalis and was used by the opposition to mobilize Somalis in Somalia and in the diaspora (including the United States and Canada) for jihad (holy war) against the TFG under Axmed. As a result, the Islamist factions were greatly empowered and waged a violent guerilla campaign against Axmed and his Ethiopian allies, who responded with force—both sides of the war caused many casualties.

In December 2007, Axmed, who underwent a liver transplant in the 1990s, was admitted to a hospital in Nairobi for treatment of what his spokesman described as bronchitis, and on 4 January 2008 he collapsed in Baydhaba and was taken to London for treatment. Axmed's political problems were compounded by his failing health, and on 29 December 2008, he announced his resignation as president of Somalia before the Somali parliament in Baydhaba. In his speech, which was broadcast on national radio, Yuusuf expressed regret at failing to end the country's seventeen-year civil war as promised four years earlier.

Yuusuf was initially flown to his native Puntland and then arrived in Sana'a, the capital of Yemen, on 20 January 2009 along with his wife and seventeen family members and bodyguards. A Yemeni government official said that Yuusuf expressed a desire to live in Yemen, but no political asylum had been discussed as of 2010. The official added that he thought Yuusuf wanted to live in Yemen for a short period before perhaps seeking medical treatment in the United Kingdom.

[*See also* Mengistu Haile Mariam; *and* Siyad Barre, Mohamed.]

BIBLIOGRAPHY

Compagnon, Daniel. "Resources Politiques, Régulation Autoritaire et Domination Personnelle en Somalie: le Régime de Siyaad Barre (1969–1991)." PhD diss., Université de Pau et des Pays de l'Adour, 1995.

Daahir Cali Cumar (Deyr). *Qaran Dumay iyo Qoon Taalo-waayey [sic]*. Nairobi, Kenya: Mam and Bros, 1997.

Issa-Salwe, Abdisalam M. *The Collapse of the Somali State: The Impact of the Colonial Legacy*. London: Haan, 1996.

Wartorn Societies Project Somali Programme. *Rebuilding Somalia: Issues and Possibilities for Puntland*. London: Haan, 2001.

ABDIWELI ALI

Ay (fl. fourteenth century BCE), influential Egyptian courtier who served under the late Eighteenth Dynasty kings Amenhotep III, Akhenaten (Amenhotep IV), and Tutankhamen. Following Tutankhamen's untimely death, he claimed the throne, reigning for no more than four years (c. 1327–1323 BCE). After his death, his name was erased from Egypt's official history.

Ay's parentage is unconfirmed. However, there is strong circumstantial evidence to suggest that he was the brother of Queen Tiy, the commoner-born consort of Amenhotep III (reigned c. 1390–1352 BCE), and the father of Nefertiti, the commoner-born consort of Akhenaten (reigned c. 1352–1336 BCE). Queen Tiy's father, Yuya, routinely used the title "god's father," which, if it is to be read literally rather than as a priestly title, translates as "father-in-law of the king." Ay, too, routinely used this title and, while he makes no mention of any relationship with Nefertiti, his wife claims to have been the "nurse of the king's great wife Nefertiti, nurse of the goddess, ornament of the king."

Ay lived through the Amarna Period, the unorthodox time when Akhenaten worshipped—and expected his people to accept—the Aten: a genderless, faceless sun disk. The royal family was able to worship the Aten directly. Their subjects had to access the Aten via Akhenaten and Nefertiti, who now took the place of Egypt's traditional pantheon. This would not have posed a problem for the majority of the population who had little, if any, connection with state religion. But it was a problem for courtiers such as Ay who, needing to ingratiate themselves with the new regime, had to be seen to follow their king.

To honor the Aten, Akhenaten founded the new capital city of Akhetaten (ancient Akhetaten). His builders worked quickly, and by his regal Year 9 the city was functioning as Egypt's permanent capital, home of the Aten and of the bureaucracy that until now had been centered on Memphis. The elite courtiers were provided with spacious suburban villas and with elaborately decorated tombs cut into the Amarna cliffs. The geography of the cliffs meant that the tombs fell into two distinct groups, with the tombs of the priests and the officials of the royal residence included in the northern group and the tombs of the great state officials, Ay included, in the southern group. Forty-five elite tombs were started, but only twenty-four were inscribed and few were in any way completed. These forty-three must represent Akhenaten's innermost circle.

The most elaborate elite tomb belonged to Ay and Tiy. Here, Nefertiti features prominently on the decorated walls. In one remarkable scene Ay and Tiy stand together to receive golden necklaces from Akhenaten and Nefertiti. The receipt of gold was a public honor that had originally been reserved for victorious soldiers but that, at the start of the Eighteenth Dynasty, had been expanded to encompass high-ranking (male) officials. The fact that Ay and Tiy receive gold together is a clear indication that the couple was held in great esteem. Ay has five necklaces around his neck as he reaches out to catch another, and included in a pile at his feet is a pair of red leather gloves. The next scene shows Ay leaving the palace, wearing his gloves.

Another unusual scene shows what appears to be the royal harem: a group of women in two separate buildings whose doors are guarded, or perhaps protected, by men. The women are either making music or dancing, while the walls of their rooms are hung with lyres, lutes, and harps. Meanwhile, Akhenaten's vision of the Aten as the creator of all life was celebrated in *The Great Hymn to the Aten*, a lengthy poem preserved on the wall of Ay's tomb.

Akhenaten's last recorded date is Year 17; no official record of his death has survived, but it seems reasonable to assume that he died soon after. He was briefly succeeded by Smenkhkare and then by Tutankhaten.

Within a few years of acceding to the throne Tutankh-Aten (living images of the Aten) changed his name to Tutankh-Amen (Living image of Amen) and started a national restoration program designed to erase all memory of the Amarna "heresy." Given that he was less than ten years old at his accession, we must assume that he was guided in this policy by his courtiers, including Ay.

Tutankhamen died unexpectedly in his late teens or early twenties. Although several modern writers have suggested that Ay murdered Tutankhamen, there is absolutely no evidence to support this claim, and the most recent examination of Tutankhamen's mummy indicates that he probably died following an impact sustained in a chariot or boating accident.

Because his intended tomb was unfinished, Ay interred Tutankhamen in a modest private tomb in the Valley of the Kings (KV 62). Ay is featured on the wall of Tutankhamen's burial chamber, where he has donned the leopard-skin cloak of a priest to perform the "opening of the mouth" ceremony; a ritual that was traditionally the responsibility of the heir of the deceased and therefore confirmed Ay's right to rule.

Ay inherited Tutankhamen's throne, becoming "God's father Ay, Divine ruler of Thebes, beloved of Amen" while his wife, Tiy, became his consort. But Ay was already an old man who could never have been regarded as anything other than a temporary monarch. His highest regnal date is Year 4. He was buried in the Western Valley, an offshoot of the Valley of the Kings (tomb WV 23), in what was almost certainly Tutankhamen's original tomb. As his intended heir, his son or grandson Nakhtmin, had predeceased him, he was succeeded by Generalissimo Horemheb. Homemheb's queen, Mutnodjmet, may have been the identically named sister of Nefertiti; if so, Horemheb may have been Ay's son-in-law.

Ay and Tutankhamen made a valiant attempt to restore Egypt to its pre-Amarna position of strength, but they were too closely connected to the Amarna age to be separated from it. Akhenaten, Smenkhkare, Tutankhamen, and Ay were all omitted from the official lists of kings, which passed straight from Amenhotep III to Horemheb.

[See also Akhenaten; Amenhotep III; Nefertiti; and Tutankhamen.]

BIBLIOGRAPHY

Clayton, Peter. *Chronicle of the Pharaohs: The Reign-by-Reign Record of the Rulers of the Dynasties of Egypt*. London: Thames and Hudson, 1994.

Reeves, C. Nicholas. *Akhenaten, Egypt's False Prophet*. London: Thames and Hudson, 2001.

Tyldesley, Joyce A. *The Pharaohs*. London: Quercus, 2009.

Van Dijk, Jacobus. "The Amarna Period and the Later New Kingdom." In *The Oxford History of Ancient Egypt*, edited by Ian Shaw, pp. 272–313. Oxford, UK: Oxford University Press, 2001.

JOYCE TYLDESLEY

Ayankunle, Lamidi (1949–), master bata drummer and broker of Yoruba culture, was born on 6 August 1949 in the town of Erin-Osun in present-day Osun State, Nigeria. Ayankunle was born into a large extended family of traditional bata (double-headed, conically shaped drum ensemble) and dundun (double-headed, hourglass-shaped drum ensemble with tension straps) drummers. His father was Ige Ayansina and his mother was Awero Ayansina. Yoruba drumming lineages train their children in the art and profession of bata and dundun drumming. These families celebrate and worship orisa Ayanagalu (the spirit of the drum). Children born into an *Ayan* (drum family) lineage are given names beginning with the Ayan prefix, such as Ayankunle.

Passed down from generation to generation, bata is a five-hundred-year-old drumming, singing, and masquerade tradition from southwestern Nigeria. The fifteenth-century reign of Sango marks the earliest documented use of bata drum ensembles in royal contexts. One of the few compounds in Erin-Osun that continues to school its children in the art of traditional drumming, Ayankunle's family consists of about two hundred members, spanning five generations and five different towns in Osun and Kwara states. Bata is not just an instrument, however, but a powerful channel—one of the most powerful in the Yoruba arsenal—to help drummers broker between spirit and human realms. Thus, bata drummers have unique relationships with the spirits and the knowledge born of their roles as mediators between spirit and human domains. That ability has been perceived as a threat to Christianity and Islam; thus, bata has slowly become more common in secular and popular contexts due to dominance of Christianity, Islam, and modernity in Nigeria.

In the 1950s Ayankunle's father, Ayansina, collaborated with Ghanaian, Nigerian, and German professors of music in the documentation of bata rhythms and texts. In 1960 Ayankunle began to perform and travel locally and overseas with Yoruba popular theater groups based out of Osogbo.

Alongside his career as a master drummer in Erin-Osun, Ayankunle began teaching in the department of performing arts at the University of Ife and performing at national and international festivals for African arts and culture in the 1970s. In the 1980s, he began collaborating with German and US culture brokers and musicians.

The Ayankunle family exemplifies how the bata tradition has been reinvented from generation to generation. While the elders in the Ayankunle family want to ensure the continuity of the classical bata rhythms and texts, the younger generations have been playing bata in ritual and secular ceremonies as well as new contexts, inventing new fusions along the way. In order to understand and articulate this dynamism, especially young artists' attempts to merge bata with the popular musical genre of fuji, Debra Klein has documented the differences between two generations of artists. The "Yoruba Bata Generation," whose members were born in the 1940s and 1950s, came of age during a newly independent and imminently prosperous Nigeria. They have traveled the world as representatives of traditional culture since the 1960s, witnessed their tradition lose substance and meaning with the passing of each generation, and have come to see bata as an endangered culture form. Ayankunle's nine sons and other members of the "Bata Fuji Generation" came of age in the 1980s and 1990s during two military dictatorships in which Nigeria's political economy was in crisis. They have traveled minimally with their fathers, inherited the bata tradition and networks, invented bata and pop music fusions in order to keep their tradition relevant, and relate to bata as an evolving popular culture form. While the late 1990s was economically challenging for most Nigerians, the Yoruba Bata Generation sought refuge in overseas networks they had built around the celebration and perpetuation of Yoruba Bata: they successfully recast themselves as traditional performers in a global market. Meanwhile, the Bata Fuji Generation invented a new performance genre through which they revitalized their profession as purveyors of traditional culture during times of economic stress and cultural globalization.

In his late teens and early twenties during the late 1960s, Ayankunle was becoming a well-known and much respected master drummer. The postindependence years opened avenues for artistic creativity and experimentation in Nigeria, and Yoruba popular theater was thriving in Osogbo and Ibadan. Scouted by theater groups looking for local talent, Ayankunle was approached by several of the Yoruba popular theater directors and playwrights, including Kola Ogunmola and Abiodun Duro-Ladipo. While the unsolicited opportunity to perform with such well-respected theater troupes appealed to Ayankunle, his father exercised much ambivalence around his son's participation in such "popular" art. Despite his conversion to Islam, Ayankunle's father continued to practice, teach, and respect the orisa drum texts and ceremonies, cultural material he expected his son to carry on and transform. Accepting the invitation to perform with Ogunmola's theater, Ayankunle did not rehearse with the group every day but chose to spend the majority of his week in Erin-Osun playing for local celebrations so that he could stay connected with the culture of bata and practice his vast repertoire and improvisational skills.

Coming of age as a professional musician in the 1970s, Ayankunle began to perform and identify as a representative of traditional culture. When he was invited to participate in the international festival for Pan-African Arts and Culture, FESTAC '77, in Lagos, Ayankunle formed and became the leader of his first traveling ensemble called Yoruba Bata. During this time, the oil-rich Nigerian state took a keen interest in supporting and displaying local artists in festivals such as FESTAC and Nafest (Nigerian National Festival for Arts and Culture) that served to promote culture as a commodity. In the early 1980s Ayankunle began to collaborate with several artists and scholars within various local and global artistic communities in Nigeria, the United States, and Germany. Since the 1980s Nigerian, European and US students, artists, scholars, and tourists have lived and studied Yoruba bata, language, and culture with Ayankunle and his family. Rabiu Ayandokun, Ayankunle's younger brother, has also enjoyed a successful career as an international culture broker, versatile drummer, and purveyor of Yoruba bata. Since the 1980s Ayankunle and his groups, Yoruba Bata and Ayanagalu, have performed for festivals, schools, and museums around the globe in Algeria, Germany, Switzerland, Holland, Singapore, Russia, Austria, Italy, and throughout the United States.

Through his commitment to the practice and transmission of Yoruba Bata, Ayankunle has dedicated his life's work to the preservation and performance of what he terms *asa ibile*, traditional culture. Rooted in a Yoruba cosmology and worldview, Ayankunle's term for traditional culture evokes the past that can be easily recalled in the present.

Critiquing the modern Nigerian state for devaluing traditional culture and its practitioners, Ayankunle insists that his family and students of Yoruba culture practice traditional culture in its everyday, lived context so that it continues to thrive and change. By living, performing, and teaching bata Ayankunle consciously aims to prevent the disappearance of bata as a culture and art.

In the 2000s Ayankunle continued to travel the globe with his group Ayanagalu. Having started the Erin-Osun Bata Association in the early 2000s, Ayankunle has hosted and taught students of Yoruba culture, language, and performing arts in Erin-Osun.

[*See also* Duro-Ladipo, Abiodun.]

BIBLIOGRAPHY

Apter, Andrew H. *The Pan-African Nation: Oil and the Spectacle of Culture in Nigeria*. Chicago: The University of Chicago Press, 2005.

Barber, Karin. *The Generation of Plays: Yorùbá Popular Life in Theater*. Bloomington: Indiana University Press, 2000.

Beier, Ulli. *Thirty Years of Osogbo Art*. Bayreuth, Germany: Iwalewa, 1991.

Klein, Debra L. *Yorùbá Bàtá Goes Global: Artists, Culture Brokers, and Fans*. Chicago: University of Chicago Press, 2007.

Villepastour, Amanda. *Ancient Text Messages of the Yorùbá Bàtá Drum: Cracking the Code*. Farnham, UK: Ashgate Publishing Group, 2010.

DEBRA L. KLEIN

Aybak (d. 1257), first Mamluk Sultan of Egypt in the Bahri line of Mamluks, or slave rulers. His name is also given as Al Malik al Mu'izz Izz al Din. Although he ruled for a short seven years from 1250 to 1257, Aybak's rule built the system of military slave rulership that characterized government in Egypt for centuries. Originally known as Turkmani, he spoke Turkish as his native tongue. He had been bought from the region of Turkish-speaking tribes hundreds of miles form Cairo. Slave soldiers from these lands were favored over conscripted troops from Egypt because of their distance from local political and tribal obligations.

Creating a disciplined army that was expressly subject to the Sultan, however, resulted in a military that knew no loyalties except its own when the Sultan fell out of power. It was almost inevitable that these foreign regiments would eventually not only serve the ruler but come to rule themselves.

Aybak came to power as a loyal supporter of the penultimate Ayyubid Sultan and successor to Saladin, Al Sahih Ayyub. He was elevated commander of the Turkish slave soldiers and was trusted as a taste tester for the Sultan. He supported the claims of Shajar al Durr, the wife of Al Sahih Ayyub, who in a remarkable move proclaimed herself Sultana, or female sultan, after the murder of Turanshah, her son and designated successor. Lacking popular support for her rule, Shajar al Durr married Aybak and formally abdicated her official position after eighty days, although she continued to control and influence Aybak in significant ways. It was thus out of dynastic confusion that Aybak and these slaves of the Ayyubids began their rule. Aybak was given a new name to commemorate the formal beginning of his rule: Al-Malik al Mu'izz.

Like his successors, Aybak had a coterie of lieutenants who supported his rule even as they jockeyed with one another for power and influence as they awaited the eventual fall of their leader. These included Faris al Din Aktai, Baibars al Buduqdari, and Bilban al Rashidi. Despite his attempts to consolidate power, however, he did not receive the full support of the Egyptians or of the former Ayyubid ruling classes. Responding to the pressure, he installed a puppet Sultan in his place and built a large funerary monument to his former master in Cairo. He claimed that he was merely a "representative" of the caliph in Baghdad. Effective power, however, remained with Aybak and the Mamluks. Indeed, Ayyubid nobles attempted to wrest power back from the former slaves of their dynasty several times.

After several military engagements, however, Aybak was able to depose the puppet Sultan and prove the feasibility and effectiveness of Mamluk military rule. Aybak crushed internal rebellions in Upper Egypt, overwhelming restless and amateur rebels with the superior military prowess and training that was customary for Mamluks. Soon Aybak turned his attentions on the Mamluks themselves, especially as his hold on power was questioned and challenged by internal revolt. Aybak famously tricked the powerful Aktai to enter his citadel. He decapitated Aktai and threw his head out the window. He went after the Bahariyya Mamluks, the followers of Aktai, and plundered their property and wealth.

Aybak's death did not come from Mamluks or Ayyubid rebels as he had feared but from his own wife and original supporter, Shajar al Durr.

Aybak planned to marry the daughter of the Amir of Mosul, provoking Shajar's outrage. Although she had quietly remained somewhat behind the scenes as her husband consolidated power, she now accomplished in one swift order the dispatching of her husband and former confidant.

Although Aybak was generally disliked by the Egyptians who saw Aybak as a foreign usurper, his accomplishments were many and his legacy was well founded in a series of monuments and madrasas, or schools, founded in his name in Cairo. Aybak and Shajar al Durr had created an unlikely system of powerful slave soldier rulers. These rulers of Egypt and Syria and the Hijaz proved their worthiness neither through their bloodline nor through their closeness to the people they ruled. Rather their sheer abilities in the battlefield and their sheer persistence and ambition for power created a more stable system of rule despite often contentious and divisive successions. The Mamluks not only repelled the Mongols and defeated the Crusaders; they were the most powerful state in the medieval Middle East until the rise of the Ottomans.

[*See also* Saladin.]

BIBLIOGRAPHY

Ayalon, David. *The Mamluks: The Organization and Structure of a Moslem Military Society in the Middle Ages.* Jerusalem: Hebrew University, 1961.

Ayalon, David. *Islam and the Abode of War: Military Slaves and Islamic Adversaries.* Aldershot, UK: Variorum, 1994.

Irwin, Robert. *The Middle East in the Middle Ages: The Early Mamluk Sultanate 1250 – 1382.* London: Croom Helm Ltd., 1986.

Levanoni, Amalia. "The Consolidation of Aybak's Rule: An Example of Factionalism in the Mamluk State." *Der Islam* 71, no. 2 (1994): 241–254.

ALLEN J. FROMHERZ

'Ayyad ben Moussa (1083–1149), the most famous Maliki scholar to serve under Almoravid rule in Morocco, was born in the city of Ceuta on the North African Mediterranean coast. He achieved fame as a strict interpreter of Maliki law and as chief *qadi* (judge of religious law), both in Granada and in Ceuta. He was also a defender of Almoravid authority in the face of increasingly sharp criticism being leveled against the dynasty both in Spain and Morocco. Qadi 'Ayyad lived long enough to witness the fall of the Almoravids at the hands of the Almohad movement in 1147. He was taken captive

by the Almohads to their capital in Marrakech, where he died in 1149. It is thought that he was murdered by order of the Almohad caliph, 'Abd al-Mu'min.

'Ayyad's family originated in Yemen and migrated to the Islamic West at some point following the Islamic conquests, taking up residence in a variety of places, including al-Andalus, as well as in the Maliki strongholds of Fez and Qayrawan, prior to settling in Ceuta during the late tenth century. They achieved renown for their knowledge of the Qu'ran and of Islamic law, with a number of 'Ayyad's ancestors obtaining important religious appointments in the town. Thus, 'Ayyad had access to the best religious training in Ceuta, where he excelled as a student prior to departing his home town for further study in eastern Spain.

During his studies, 'Ayyad became acquainted with the current debate raging through Almoravid domains over the teachings of the Persian scholar Abu Hamid al-Ghazali. This scholar was well known as an advocate of the limited use of reason to interpret the Qu'ran, a proponent of the Sufi path, and a supporter of the position that any knowledgeable Muslim (not just the religious authorities) could represent the Islamic community. The teachings of al-Ghazali were deemed heretical by the Maliki jurists, and copies of his most famous works were burned in Almoravid cities at the beginning of the twelfth century. However, a number of religious scholars supported Ghazali's teachings as a means of protesting the excessive rigidity and literalism of the Maliki religious establishment under Almoravid rule. In concert with Andalusians chafing under Almoravid restrictions and Moroccan Berbers dissatisfied with Sanhaja dominance, such religious opposition would contribute to the rapid decline of Almoravid power following the death of Yusuf ibn Tashfin in 1106.

The decline of Almoravid fortunes was not yet evident to 'Ayyad, whose prestige continued to grow within Ceuta, until he obtained the position of chief *qadi* in 1121–1122. In this position, he began to produce a number of the most influential works of North African Maliki jurisprudence, some of which have survived (in part or in whole) to the present. A mark of his growing fame can be seen in his appointment as chief *qadi* in Granada in 1136. It was clear that 'Ayyad had won the support of the Almoravid administration, including the sultan, 'Ali ibn Yusuf. However, 'Ali's son, Tashfin ibn 'Ali, was governor in Granada, and he became disaffected with 'Ayyad after receiving numerous complaints regarding the severity of his judgments. Thus, 'Ayyad was relieved of his position only a few short months after receiving his appointment in Granada. Returning to his home in Ceuta, 'Ayyad was barred from political power for almost ten years, although he continued to produce a large number of commentaries and legal writings even while out of favor with the regime.

In fact, 'Ayyad may well have been a victim of the growing discontent with Almoravid rule that was then surfacing in al-Andalus. Maliki jurisprudence had established itself in southern Spain years before the Almoravids had made it the official interpretation of Islam in Morocco. For the most part, Andalusian Maliki jurists had become comfortable with the looser attitude toward Islamic standards practiced in Spain. However, the Almoravid dynasty had begun as a revivalist movement seeking to enforce a strict interpretation of Maliki law throughout Morocco and ultimately in al-Andalus. This harsh Malikism had proven essential for uniting the Sanhaja Berbers of the northern Sahara into an unbeatable fighting force that conquered a large empire. However, it did not go over as well in the refined cities of al-Andalus, where it was viewed as extreme and narrow, and the Sanhaja Berbers who supported its enforcement were seen as uncouth and ignorant. By allying himself so closely with the regime and its narrow Malikism, 'Ayyad also became a target for those who opposed it.

As governor of Granada, Tashfin ibn 'Ali was in the difficult position of having to enforce Almoravid rule while seeking to mollify Andalusian complaints. In Tashfin's pursuit of this task, 'Ayyad likely became more of a hindrance than a help, which explains his replacement as chief qadi. Against all odds, Tashfin strengthened Almoravid authority as governor of Granada over the course of nine difficult years, prior to returning to Morocco as heir apparent in 1138, and finally taking over as sultan in Marrakech in 1142. However, by that time, opposition from the Almohad movement had taken control of most Berber territories in the Atlas Mountains, and they had established a formidable army that won multiple battles against Almoravid troops. Meanwhile, without Tashfin's capable leadership, Almoravid authority in al-Andalus collapsed shortly after his departure. Tashfin's attempts to revive Almoravid fortunes came to a sudden end when he was killed in battle against the Almohads in 1145.

The death of his old enemy allowed 'Ayyad to experience a revival of his political fortunes and soon he was back in his old position as qadi of Ceuta. However, Tashfin's death also removed the final obstacle to the Almohad conquest of Almoravid domains. Within a couple of years, Ceuta had been overrun and Qadi 'Ayyad was exiled to the city of Tadla. Even there he was still considered to be dangerous, and the Almohad leadership eventually moved him to Marrakech, where he lived out the remainder of his life under house arrest, eventually dying under mysterious circumstances that suggest he may have been murdered.

[See also 'Abd al-Mu'min; and Yusuf ibn Tashfin, Abu Ya'qub.]

BIBLIOGRAPHY

Bewley, Aisha Abdarrahman. *Ash-Shifa of Qadi 'Iyad.* Granada, Spain: Madinah Press, 1991.

Castilla Brazales, Juan. *Indices de Tartib al-Madarik: Biografías de Andalusíes.* (Indexes of *Tartib al-Madarik*: Biographies of Andalusians) Granada, Spain: Consejo Superior de Investigaciones Científicas, Escuela de Estudios Árabes, 1990.

Talbi, Mohamed. *Biographies Aghlabides Extraites des Madarik du Cadi 'Iyad.* (Extracts of Aghlabid Biographies from the *Madarik* of Qadi 'Ayyad) Tunis, Tunisia: Université de Tunis, 1968.

Tunji, Muhammad. *Information sur la Definition des Regles de l'Islam par Abou El Fadl Ayad ben Moussaben Ayad El-Yahsoubi Es-Sebti; Mis a Jour et Presentation Mohamed ben Tawit Et-Tanji.* (Information on defining the rules of Islam by Abou El Fadl Ayyad son of Moussa son of Ayad El-Yahsoubi Es-Sebti; Updated and Presented by Mohamed ben Tawit Et-Tanji) Rabat, Morocco: 1981.

STEPHEN CORY

Azhari, Isma'il al- (1900–1969), Sudanese nationalist politician, scion of a prominent religious family, grandson of Isma'il al-Azhari (Mufti of the Sudan 1924–1932) and a descendant of Ahmad Isma'il al-Azhari (Isma'il al-Wali), a famous *alim*, was born at Omdurman. After secondary school at Gordon College in Khartoum, he studied at the American University in Beirut and, returning to the Sudan, became a mathematics teacher at the college. He soon became immersed in politics.

The scope for such involvement was enhanced by the Anglo-Egyptian Sudan's "condominium" status but circumscribed by the policies of its senior member, Britain. During World War I the British sought to minimize the Egyptian role; after anti-British uprisings in 1924 they sought to end it, by evacuating the Egyptian Army and curtailing the size and scope of a Sudanese educated class susceptible to Egyptian influence. But British efforts to channel political interest backfired. In 1938 members of the Sudan Schools Club in Omdurman founded the Graduates' General Congress to represent the educated elite's views. Al-Azhari was instrumental in the Congress's evolution from interest group to self-proclaimed spokesman for the Sudanese. In 1942 the Congress broke openly with the regime when it called for Sudanese self-government after the war and immediate sweeping reforms. This manifesto hastened the demise of the Congress, from which emerged the Sudan's first two political parties, the Ashiqqa, founded (1943) by al-Azhari, which formed the nucleus of the Unionists, and the Umma (1945), the political vehicle of the Mahdist sect and, by default, of other anti-Unionists.

Sudanese nationalism was inextricable from the overarching rivalry of the co-domini and of the two sectarian leaders, Ali al-Mirghani of the Khatmiyya and Abd al-Rahman, the son of the Mahdi. Al-Azhari's historic role was to plot a course between these poles and, by exploiting them, speed the achievement of Sudanese independence. By espousing the Unity of the Nile Valley—union with Egypt—with the clear but tacit support of Sayyid Ali, al-Azhari necessarily opposed all British plans for constitutional development. In doing so, he therefore opposed also the Mahdists and others who, despite their slogan of "the Sudan for the Sudanese," were prepared to cooperate with Britain to prevent an Egyptian takeover.

As leader of the Graduates' Congress, a founding member of the Ashiqqa, then leader of the National Unionist Party, al-Azhari was arguably the country's most skilled political operative. In an inherently weak position as a secularist with little personal following, he kept one step ahead of the British (who loathed him) and time and again made his rivals seem like stooges. Through boycotts, first of the Advisory Council for the Northern Sudan in 1944 (when he was arrested), the Administration Conference (1946), and the resulting Legislative Assembly (1948, when he was jailed), al-Azhari and his supporters succeeded in destroying their representative character and thus vitiating their effectiveness. Finally, when after the revolution of 1952 the new Egyptian government professed its support for Sudanese self-determination, al-Azhari and the unionists swept to power in the country's first parliamentary elections (1953). Their victory was owed to superior organization, deft propaganda, and the stigma of collaboration adhering to their principal opponents, but not to an overwhelming desire among northern Sudanese—let alone the non-Muslims of the South—for union with Egypt.

As prime minister, al-Azhari presided over the drastic "Sudanization" of the British colonial regime, arrangements for self-determination, and suppression of a bloody mutiny that erupted in 1955 in the Southern Sudan. Finally abandoning his Egyptian patrons, he managed to maintain his personal position and bring about the independence of the Sudan (1 January 1956) but, in doing so, lost the support of true unionists. The real powers in the land were "the two sayyids," and following their tactical rapprochement al-Azhari lost a parliamentary vote of confidence in July 1956 and had to resign.

Had he retired then, al-Azhari might have been remembered as the brilliant politician who defeated both co-domini to win independence for the Sudan. Instead he played the part of spoiler, first in opposition to his successor, Abdallah Khalil (1956–1958), who connived in the military coup of General Abboud (1958–1964), and later, during the second parliamentary period, as chairman of the council that functioned as head of state. In that role (in which he has been termed erroneously the "president of the Sudan"), al-Azhari maneuvered successfully to bring down opponents but never effectively to pursue a program of government. He died soon after the 1969 coup that swept away the regime he had done so much to discredit.

[See also 'Abd al-Rahman al-Mahdi; and Mirghani, Ali al-.]

BIBLIOGRAPHY

Abd al-Rahim, Muddathir. *Imperialism and Nationalism in the Sudan.* (Oxford, UK: Oxford University Press, 1969). Remains a useful Sudanese overview of the main developments.

Daly, M. W. *Imperial Sudan: The Anglo-Egyptian Condominium, 1934-1956.* (Cambridge, UK: Cambridge University Press, 1991). Surveys the period of al-Azhari's rise to power.

Warburg, Gabriel. *Islam, Sectarianism and Politics in Sudan since the Mahdiyya.* (London: Hurst and Co., 2003). This and other works by the same author detail the complicated politics of the nationalist movement.

M. W. DALY

Azikiwe, Benjamin Nnamdi (1904–1996), journalist and president of Nigeria, was born into the family of Obededan Chukwuemeka Azikiwe, a clerk with the Nigerian Regiment of the West African Frontier Force in the northern Nigerian Hausa town of Zungeru. Later known affectionately as Zik, as a child, Nnamdi learned Hausa before his parents sent him to Onitsha, their Igbo hometown, for his primary education in 1912. In 1918, he graduated from Christ Church School, Onitsha, and he briefly taught there as a pupil teacher (1918–1920).

His education also took him to the Efik town of Calabar, where he enrolled in the prestigious Hope Waddell Training Institute. Following his father's transfer to Lagos, Nnamdi moved with the family and enrolled at the Wesleyan Boys High School, Lagos (a predominant Yoruba town). By the time he graduated from high school, Nnamdi had acquired three major Nigerian languages—Hausa, Igbo, and Yoruba—and their speakers' cultures, a skill that later became an asset in his political career. After his high school education, Nnamdi joined the treasury department in Lagos as a clerk in 1921. There he began to experience discriminatory British colonial policies for the first time. Inspired by Rev. James Kwegyr Aggrey of the then Gold Coast (now Ghana), Azikiwe left Nigeria in 1925 for further

Benjamin Nnamdi Azikiwe, 2008. [AP Images/STR]

studies in the United States. By 1934, he had earned an associate's degree from Howard University in Washington, DC, bachelor's and master's degrees from Lincoln University in Pennsylvania, and another master's degree from the University of Pennsylvania. He enrolled for his doctoral studies at Columbia University, New York, but did not complete the program. In 1931, he taught political science and, later, African history and politics at Lincoln University. In the United States Azikiwe began to articulate his philosophical ideals and political goals. He also joined the Pan-African movement in support of African nationalism, racial equality, and justice.

Azikiwe returned to Nigeria in 1934, armed with a number of degrees and certificates and full of new ideas and optimism. Following his rejection for a teaching position at the King's College, Lagos, Azikiwe left for Accra in the Gold Coast where he accepted a job as the editor of *The African Morning Post* in January 1935. He held this position until 1937 when he was tried and convicted for the publication in his newspaper of an article deemed seditious by the British colonial government. Azikiwe won his case on appeal and returned to Nigeria. In Nigeria, he started the first press conglomerate, Zik's Press Ltd., publishing the first edition of the *West African Pilot* in November 1937. Through his chain of newspapers (*Daily Comet, Eastern Nigerian Guardian, Eastern Sentinel, Nigerian Spokesman, Southern Nigerian Defender*, and the *Nigerian Monitor*), writings, lectures, and speeches, Azikiwe launched a multipronged campaign against the excesses of the British colonial government in Nigeria. The *Pilot*, because of its wider circulation, became a tool to celebrate African achievements, to disseminate racial consciousness and nationalist ideas, and to fight against colonialism throughout the continent.

In his book, *Renascent Africa* (1937), Azikiwe articulated his ideas about the African revolution, which was to be accomplished in three transitional phases: the "Old Africa" as the Africa of yesterday; "Renascent Africa" as the twentieth-century Africa; and "New Africa" as the Africa of tomorrow. Renascent Africa would witness the transformation of its economic foundation and social order. He believed that Africa's greatness lay within the continent and that the New Africa had a major role to play in world affairs.

A charismatic and gifted orator, Zik became a major force in Nigeria's independence movement. In 1938, Azikiwe joined the Nigerian Youth

Movement (NYM), and later he served as its vice-president, but he left the organization in 1941 when he realized that most of its leaders were too moderate to lead Nigeria to independence. Sir Arthur Richards became the governor of Nigeria in 1943, and he was determined to crush the growing nationalist sentiments. In 1944, Zik and Herbert Macaulay, the foremost Nigerian nationalist and doyen of Lagos politics, founded the National Council of Nigeria and the Cameroons (NCNC), with Macaulay as president and Zik as general-secretary. Zik took over the leadership of the party after the death of Macaulay in 1946. Azikiwe began to identify himself with the labor movement in Nigeria and he supported the General Strike of 1945. In response, the colonial government banned the *Pilot* and the *Comet* for over a month for allegedly misrepresenting facts about the strike.

Zik's attacks on the government continued. He called for self-government within fifteen years, but the Richards Constitution, which allowed for an unofficial majority on the Legislative Council, sought to consolidate British control. Using his platforms as the leader of the NCNC and the proprietor of the Zik's Press, Azikiwe launched a campaign against the Constitution and the government. The tension between Zik and the government intensified to a point where he claimed that government was plotting to assassinate him. Such a claim made Zik a hero of many Nigerians, especially the youths, who formed the Zikist Movement to protect Zik and espouse his philosophical ideals.

In 1947, Zik won one of the Lagos seats of the Legislative Council, a position he held from 1948 to 1951. With the escalating tension in Nigeria and the neighboring Gold Coast, the British government announced that the Richards Constitution was going to be replaced. Zik was critical of this Constitution and many others after it for their divisive regionalism and the limited inclusion of Nigerians in government. He proposed a strong federal system with eight provinces rather than the three powerful autonomous regions, which he saw as a recipe for disaster and the balkanization of Nigeria.

Azikiwe was elected into the Western Nigerian House of Assembly in 1952 and also served as unofficial leader of government from 1952 to 1953. Zik was about to head the Western Regional Government when some Yoruba members of his party (NCNC) defected in support of a fellow Yoruba, Obafemi Awolowo, the founder of the Action Group (a leading political party in Nigeria).

The so-called carpet-crossing episode forced Zik to leave Lagos and return to the Eastern Region, where he served as premier from 1954 to 1959.

In January 1960, Azikiwe was sworn in as the president of the Nigerian Senate, and on 16 November 1960 he became the first indigenous governor-general and commander-in-chief of the Nigerian Armed Forces following the country's independence on October 1 of the same year. In 1963, Zik was selected to become the first president of the Federal Republic of Nigeria (1963–1966), although the actual power was in the regions and with the federal prime minister, Abubakar Tafawa Balewa.

Following the 1964 elections, marred by electoral malpractice, which could have led to the disintegration of the country, Azikiwe invited Balewa of the Northern People's Congress to form a government. Despite his efforts at reconciliation, there were violent outbursts in western Nigeria, leading to a military coup of January 1966 and a countercoup in July of the same year, which ended the First Republic. Further ethnic fighting directed against Eastern and Igbo residents living in northern Nigeria resulted in the outbreak of the Biafra-Nigeria War (1967–1970). Azikiwe's commitment to a strong united Nigeria was tested when he was caught between supporting his Igbo ethnic group or the federal government. He chose neither but acted as an arbitrator by brokering the Monrovia Accord with General Gowon, then head of federal Nigeria, which guaranteed general amnesty for all.

At the end of the war and following many years of military rule, Azikiwe remained an active political figure in Nigeria. He formed the Nigerian Peoples Party (NPP), and in 1979 he became its presidential candidate. He lost the election to Shehu Shagari of the National Party of Nigeria (NPN) but formed an uneasy alliance with the ruling party. Zik again ran for the presidency of Nigeria in the 1983 federal elections but was again unsuccessful. Following the military coup on 31 December 1983, he retired from active politics.

Azikiwe was also an author with an interest in advancing education and scholarship in Nigeria and Africa. He wrote more than twenty books and pamphlets as well as dozens of journal articles. Among the most important were *Liberia in World Politics* (1934; repr. 1970) and *Democracy with Military Vigilance* (1974). In 1970 he published *My Odyssey: An Autobiography*. Azikiwe founded the first indigenous degree-awarding institution in the country, the University of Nigeria, Nsukka (UNN) in 1960. He was a recipient of numerous academic awards, such as honorary doctoral degrees from Nigerian and foreign universities, including the Distinguished Professorship chair in International Affairs in 1994 by his alma mater, Lincoln University. In 1980, President Shagari conferred on him Nigeria's highest award, the Grand Commander of the Federal Republic (GCFR).

Nnamdi Azikiwe used his many skills to uplift the spirit of nationalism among Nigerians and other Africans, a contribution that earned him the title "The Zik of Africa." He became one of the most powerful voices for the liberation of Africa from all forms of external domination. He inspired a generation of revered African nationalist heroes, including Kwame Nkrumah of Ghana, Julius Nyerere of Tanzania, and Kenneth Kaunda of Zambia. A renowned Nigerian nationalist, a powerful orator and philosopher, a frontline politician, and a first-class journalist, Nnamdi Azikiwe remained a respected statesman and national icon until his death in 1996 at the age of ninety-one.

[See also Awolowo, Obafemi; Kaunda, Kenneth; Macaulay, Herbert; Nkrumah, Kwame; Nyerere, Julius; and Tafawa Balewa, Abubakar.]

BIBLIOGRAPHY

Azikiwe, N. Zik: A Selection from the Speeches of Nnamdi Azikiwe. Cambridge, England: Cambridge University Press, 1961.

Chuku, G. "Azikiwe, Nnamdi." In The Oxford Encyclopedia of African Thought, Vol. 1, edited by F. Abiola Irele and [Biodun] Jeyifo, pp. 116–119. Oxford, England: Oxford University Press, 2010.

Igwe, A. Nnamdi Azikiwe: The Philosopher of Our Time. Enugu, Nigeria: Fourth Dimension, 1992.

Ikenga, A. ed. Nnamdi Azikiwe: Tributes to an African Legend. Lagos, Nigeria: Minaj Publishers, 1996.

Olisa, M. S. O., and O. M. Ikejiani-Clark. eds. Azikiwe and the African Revolution. Lagos, Nigeria: Africana-Fep Publishers, 1989.

GLORIA CHUKU

'Aziz, al- (955–996), fifth Fatimid caliph of Egypt, was the first of the Fatimid caliphs to begin his rule in the newly founded Fatimid capital in Cairo. Born in Mahdiyya in North Africa, he traveled to Cairo in 974 with the Fatimid court when his father, the fourth Fatimid Caliph al-Mu'izz, moved the Fatimid capital from the Maghrib to Egypt. His full name was Al-'Aziz billah, Nizar Abu Mansur.

Al-'Aziz became the Fatimid caliph in 975 but, as the third son of al-Mu'izz, his succession was far from assumed. Al-Mu'izz's oldest son, Tamim, had been passed over for the succession because he was suspected of intriguing against his father with dissident members of the Fatimid court. Al-Mu'izz's second son, 'Abdullah, was the favored heir. But 'Abdullah died unexpectedly in 975 and al-Mu'izz formally recognized al-'Aziz as his successor. Al-'Aziz came to power in December 975 when he gave the *khutba* (Friday sermon) in his own name and publicly mourned his father's passing.

When al-'Aziz came to power, the Fatimid caliphate included Sicily, the Maghreb, Egypt, the Hijaz, and portions of Syria. The main goal of al-'Aziz's caliphate was extending and consolidating Fatimid power in Syria. During this period, Syria was difficult to control because it formed the frontier between three competing empires, the Fatimids of Cairo, the Abbasids of Baghdad, and the Byzantine Empire, and was held by various semi-independent military commanders. In addition, there was a small Isma'ili splinter group in Bahrain known as the *Qarmatiyya* who had split with the Fatimid Isma'ilis in 899 and who often supported enemies of the Fatimids.

Al-'Aziz first tried to conquer Damascus. The Turkish commander Alptakin who controlled Damascus was allied with the *Qarmatiyya* state. In 975, al-'Aziz sent the veteran commander Jawhar (d. 992), the general who had conquered Egypt for the Fatimids in 969, to Syria to retake Damascus. Jawhar suffered a humiliating defeat in a seventeen-month siege. Upon his return to Cairo, he blamed his defeat on the weakness of the Kutama Berber soldiers who had been longtime supporters of the Fatimids and formed the backbone of the early Fatimid military.

Thus, al-'Aziz undertook to lead the Fatimid army into Syria himself. In August 978, al-'Aziz's forces captured Alptakin and forced the *Qarmatiyya* to agree to peace. The *Qarmatiyya* had challenged both Fatimid power and legitimacy; the end of *Qarmatiyya* resistance in Syria was the significant result of this campaign. After this defeat, the *Qarmatiyya* were predominately reduced to a local power in Bahrain. However, Fatimid control over Damascus was still fairly nominal. One of Alptakin's former generals held power and recognized Fatimid rule without allowing direct Fatimid control.

Jawhar had blamed his Damascus defeat on the inadequacy of the Kutama Berber troops. Thus, after his victory, al-'Aziz took all of the Turkish soldiers he had captured under Alptakin's control and created a new Turkish force to balance the power of the Kutama Berber soldiers in Cairo.

In addition to his attacks on Damascus, al-ʿAziz also made several attempts to conquer Aleppo, which brought him into direct conflict with Syrian clients of the Byzantine Empire known as the Hamdanids. Al-ʿAziz besieged Aleppo in 983, but the Byzantines sent a force to support the Hamdanids, forcing the Fatimid army to flee. The Fatimids led another campaign against Aleppo in 991, but this attack also ended in defeat at the hands of the Hamdanids, assisted by the Byzantines. Despite these losses, al-ʿAziz continued to gather resources for another campaign into Syria, but the Byzantine support of the Hamdanids was too strong. In 995, during a campaign against Aleppo, the Byzantine Emperor Basil II (r. 976–1025) came to Aleppo to defend the city himself. While the Fatimids did not defeat the Hamdanid-Byzantine alliance at Aleppo, al-ʿAziz was able to acquire favorable treaty terms: the Byzantines lifted commercial restrictions against the Fatimids in Syria.

In addition to his Syrian campaigns, al-ʿAziz was also involved in diplomatic exchanges with the Buyids, Twelver Shiʿi amirs of Iraq who had conquered the Abbasid Caliphate in 945. This was significant due to the Shiʿi orientation of both leaders. Al-ʿAziz avoided direct conflict with the Buyids but attempted (unsuccessfully) to get the powerful Shiʿi Buyid amir ʿAdud al-Dawla (d. 983) to acknowledge Fatimid sovereignty. During an early phase of his reign, ʿAdud al-Dawla implied a willingness to accept al-ʿAziz's legitimacy as Imam, but as his power grew in Iraq, he took a more aggressive position against the Fatimids.

During al-ʿAziz's reign, Fatimid rule reached its greatest extent and Fatimid *daʿis* (missionaries) were active beyond the Fatimid frontiers. Al-ʿAziz was known as a wise ruler and highly competent administrator. His administration was staffed with Christians and Jews and al-ʿAziz had a very good relationship with the Coptic patriarch of Egypt. Despite Muslim opposition, al-ʿAziz allowed the Copts to rebuild the church of St. Mercurius near Fustat. However, al-ʿAziz's tolerance led to discontent, especially from the Sunni Muslims of Egypt. In 996, just after the death of al-ʿAziz, there was a Muslim rebellion that resulted in the plundering of several churches and the murder of several Christians.

Al-ʿAziz was known for his support of Shiʿi festivals in Cairo. He encouraged mourning ceremonies at ʿAshura, which commemorates the martyrdom of the Imam Husayn at Karbala (680). He also encouraged the celebration of the Shiʿi feast of al-Ghadir, which commemorates what Shiʿis consider to be the investiture of ʿAli b. Abi Talib (d. 661) by the Prophet Muhammad at Ghadir Khumm.

Al-ʿAziz died at the age of 42 while in route to Syria to fight the army of the Byzantine Emperor. He had ruled just over twenty-one years. He was succeeded by his son Abu ʿAli al-Mansur, who took the title al-Hakim bi-ʾAmr Allah (d. 1021). In Cairo, he established a large congregational mosque, which, after it was completed during his son's reign, became known as the Mosque of al-Hakim.

[*See also* Jawhar al-Siqilli.]

BIBLIOGRAPHY

Daftary, Farhad. *The Ismaʿilis: Their History and Doctrines*, 2d ed. (Leiden, Netherlands: Brill, 2007). This comprehensive overview of Ismaʿili history is the most recent account that includes the history of the full Fatimid Caliphate. It contains an extensive account the reign of al-ʿAziz.

Jiwa, Shainool. "Fatimid-Buyid Diplomacy during the Reign of al-ʿAziz Billah (365/975–386/996)." *Journal of Islamic Studies* 3 (1992): 57–71. This is the only study that addresses the relationship between the Fatimids and the Buyids during the reign of Al-ʿAziz.

CHRISTINE D. BAKER

Azzam, Abd al-Rahman (1893–1976), Egyptian diplomat, is best known as a pioneer of Egyptian Arab nationalism and the first secretary-general of the Arab League. His father, Hassan Bey, served as a member of Egypt's quasi-parliamentary bodies before 1914. His family owned considerable land in their hometown in Giza, as well as a townhouse in Helwan. Although scholars who emphasize the shallow basis of Egyptian Arab nationalism link Azzam's early Arabism to a strong consciousness of Peninsular origin, the Azzams regarded themselves as *fallahin dhawati* (an elite of rural origin). As was true of many sons of the ruling class in their modernizing journey, Azzam resisted his father's pressures to study at the religious university of al-Azhar. He attended state primary and secondary schools, St. Thomas's School of Medicine in London, and then, briefly, as a result of the interruption of World War I, the Qasr al-Aini School of Medicine in Cairo.

Abd al-Rahman Azzam. Azzam, far right, with King of Saudi Arabia Abdul Aziz Ibn Saud and King Faruq of Egypt, Port Tewfik, Egypt, 1946. Egyptian prime minister Mahmud Fahmi al-Nuqrashi stands at the left, facing the monarchs. (AP Images)

As a Nationalist Party activist in London and then Cairo, Azzam combined secular liberal territorial patriotism with liberal pan-Islamism. He was strongly supportive of the Ottomans, assuming that their nominal sovereignty over Egypt provided leverage against the British occupation. This emphasis on the complementary nature of local and broader identities would later inform his Egyptian Arabism. If Egypt had a leadership role within a larger ensemble, it would enhance Egypt's growth and independence.

Azzam acted upon his Ottomanism by traveling to the Balkans and Istanbul in 1913 (he wrote about anti-Muslim atrocities and promoted an autonomous Albania under the Egyptian Prince Fuad) and by fleeing across the desert in 1915 to join the Ottoman-Libyan struggle against the Italians and British.

Azzam arrived in Cyrenaica in December and joined Ottoman officers who were leading an army of the Sanussi religious order. His knowledge of Arabic and other skills made him indispensable to the Ottoman commander Nuri Pasha, the brother of Enver Pasha, one member of the triumvirate leadership of the Young Turks ruling in Istanbul. After Sayyid Idris, the head of the Sanussis, made peace with the British in 1917, Nuri and Azzam

moved to Tripolitania, where they sought to build up a centralized authority. When the Ottomans surrendered and left Libya in 1918, Azzam and a number of Tripolitanian chiefs founded the Tripolitanian Republic, the product of a coalition that Azzam helped to effect among various tribal factions. The Italians responded by promulgating the Fundamental Law of Tripolitania on 1 June 1919, granting the Libyans Italian nationality and civil and political equality. Although the Tripolitanians accepted this arrangement and dissolved the Republic, the Italians did not implement the law, and the efforts of Azzam and Tripolitanian leaders who formed the National Reform Party to pressure the colonizers did not succeed. The Italians were militarily victorious over all their chief opponents by 1924. Azzam and Sayyid Idris departed for Egypt in January 1923.

Azzam's Arab nationalism developed during this Libyan period and was given its first expression in *al-Liwa al-Tarabulsi,* the newspaper of the National Reform Party in which he played a major role as editor and writer. This Arabism, formulated in response to specific Libyan needs and in reaction to frictions with the Ottomans, was nevertheless transferred to Egypt as a kind of given to which Azzam referred naturally and readily. "I found myself fighting for an Arab cause," he commented in an interview shortly before his death. "In my early teens and twenties I fought for Egypt. Then during the wars for Egypt and Islam. Then, for Egypt and Arabism. There was no contradiction but a change of emphasis according to circumstances" (Coury, p. 173). Azzam became the most persistent advocate of Arabism among the Old Regime politicians, and within the context of a broad web of Egyptian and pan-Arab relationships.

Despite his long absence, Azzam quickly adapted to the new world of Egyptian politics established through the quasi independence granted by Britain in 1922. Elected to Parliament in 1924 as an independent, he nevertheless transferred to the Wafd Party and became one of its most accomplished parliamentarians. His position as a Wafdist was further consolidated by his pro-Wafdist journalism and his service as an emissary. He represented the Wafd at the Interparliamentary Conference in Rio de Janeiro (1927), at talks in Mecca relating to the restoration of strained Egyptian-Saudi relations (1928), as a delegate in London to present the Wafdist arguments against the dissolution of Parliament by the monarchy (1928–1929), and at the General Islamic Conference in Jerusalem (1931).

Azzam left the Wafd in 1932 on the occasion of the withdrawal of a group of leading dissidents. The rift reflected the disposition of Wafdists who were, variously, personally, and/or politically on amicable terms with the British, favorably disposed to the Palace and its allies, and willing to accept independence by stages. By 1936 Azzam was reconciled to abandoning Egypt's claims to the Sudan, he was accepting of a British-Egyptian treaty of friendship and military alliance, and he had forged close personal relationships with several British representatives. Whatever accounts for this split, Azzam spent the rest of his career as a political "independent" linked to the Palace and its politicians. He served as minister plenipotentiary to Iraq and Iran in the Ali Mahir ministry of 1936; as minister of Waqfs and Social Affairs in the Ali Mahir ministry of 1939–1940; as minister plenipotentiary in charge of Arab affairs in the Ahmad Mahir ministry of 1944–1945; and as secretary general of the Arab League from 1945 to 1952 (he was elected by the League's preparatory committee). Azzam's tenure as secretary general ended with the coming of the revolution of 1952 (he went into voluntary exile and did not return to Egypt until after Nasser's death). His inter-Arab ties, and particularly his ties to the

Saudis, nevertheless survived intact. He represented Saudi Arabia in its border dispute with Britain over Buraymi, and his daughter married a son of King Faysal ibn Abd al-Aziz in 1960.

Azzam's Arabism, eminently secular in spite of his earlier Islamism, was ultimately profoundly influenced by the interests and perspectives of an Egyptian ruling class confronting new social, economic, and political factors in the interwar period: the Arab world's potential as a market for Egyptian industry, labor, and investment; the solicitations of non-Egyptian Arabs seeking Egypt's support in anti-imperial struggles and willing to accept Egyptian leadership of a unitary movement; a corresponding Egyptian perception of the possibilities of creating a larger Arab ensemble to be led by Egypt and through which Egypt could gain many advantages; the pressure from below of new political forces, such as the Muslim Brothers, drawn from the lower middle classes and attaching new importance to the Arab world; concern about the Palestinian issue as such, based on sympathy for the Palestinians, and fear of Zionism as an imperial agent and threat to Egyptian power within the Arab East.

The rational calculus informing Azzam's Arabism was clearly reflected in the policies he promoted as secretary-general and as counselor to the Egyptian government: the use of the League to influence the Arab states to support the immediate withdrawal of British troops from Egypt; the Egyptian media's campaign against the Iraqi Hashemite government as a puppet of imperialism, echoed by Azzam as secretary general and favorably received by Iraqi pan-Arabists; the promotion of Egypt as the hub of a pro-Western regional bloc free from new treaties and bases; the decision to enter the war against Israel, in spite of a sense of serious weaknesses, on the assumption that failure to intervene would amount to Egypt's renunciation of Arab leadership, that the Egyptian ruling class would face the wrath of popular forces if it did not intervene, that Egypt needed to play a role in any final settlement to counter its trans-Jordanian and Iraqi rivals, and that the war was necessary as a "political demonstration" inasmuch as the conflict might be quickly resolved, and that even if this were not to happen, the Arabs might obtain better conditions as a result of military involvement.

Azzam represented a peripheral bourgeoisie mediating between dominant metropolitan powers and a mass base regarded as a source of support and a threat. If he and others challenged their

British masters in the late 1940s, it is attributable to the influence of an enraged public and to the belief that the weakness of Britain and the advent of the Cold War provided rich opportunities. In 1947 Prime Minister Nuqrashi asked the United States for massive military aid so that Egypt could take "its rightful place among the nations," and Egypt opted to leave the sterling bloc. Such readiness to integrate into a new subimperial system had its more purely domestic counterpart. In 1951 American intelligence noted that Azzam and other Egyptian politicians supported "a deliberate domestic political strategy" of controlled change to buttress the upper class of a "society [that] might well be characterized as reactionary capitalistic (in the opprobrious sense of the latter term)." Their program included increased subsidies for food and universal free education (Coury, pp. 428–429).

Even the British imperialists, for all their anger at his use of the League to their disadvantage, still remained aware of Azzam's continued (relative) usefulness. A Foreign Office memo of September 1947 asserted that the League served as a "convenient safety valve for Arab nationalist sentiment," and that Azzam, a known quantity, was easier to live with than "the more xenophobic elements which might replace him" (Coury, p. 406).

[*See also* Nasser, Gamal Abd al-.]

BIBLIOGRAPHY

Coury, Ralph M. *The Making of an Egyptian Arab Nationalist: The Early Years of Azzam Pasha, 1893–1936*. Reading, UK: Ithaca Press, 1998.

Doran, Michael. *Pan-Arabism before Nasser: Egyptian Power Politics and the Palestine Question*. New York: Oxford University Press, 1999.

Gomaa, Ahmed M. *The Foundation of the League of Arab States: Wartime Diplomacy and Inter-Arab Politics, 1941–1945*. London: Longman, 1977.

Louis, William Roger. *The British Empire in the Middle East 1945–1951: Arab Nationalism, the United States and Post-war Imperialism*. Oxford, UK: Oxford University Press, 1984.

Rogan, Eugene L. and Avi Shlaim, eds. *The War for Palestine: Rewriting the History of 1948*. Cambridge, UK: Cambridge University Press, 2001.

RALPH M. COURY

Bâ, Amadou Hampaté (1901–1991), Malian diplomat, ethnographer, devout Muslim, and defender of traditional African culture, was born in 1901 in Bandiagara, Mali, capital of the Toucouleur Empire of the Macina Fulani, which was founded by the Tidjaniya jihadist al-Hajj ʿUmar Tal. At the time of Bâ's birth, the French had been in control of Bandiagara for nearly a decade. His father, Hampâté, a Fulani militant from Fakala, died two years after Bâ was born. His mother, Kadidja Pâté, was the daughter of Pâté Poullou, a close personal companion of al-Hajj ʿUmar Tal. After her husband's death, Kadidja remarried Tidjani Amadou Ali Thiam, a Toucouleur Fulani and Louta chief, who became Bâ's adoptive father. At an early age, Bâ became intimate with Tierno Bokar Tall, the renowned "sage of Bandiagara," who was his lifelong teacher, spiritual guide, and personal mentor. In 1912, Bâ was enrolled in the French colonialist "School of the Hostages," remaining for a time in Bandiagara, before being transferred to nearby Djenné. In some accounts, Bâ is said to have been "taken hostage" by French colonizers, although this claim is disputed by Bâ's first cousin al-Hajj Sékou Tall, who claims that Bâ went voluntarily to the French school, after Tall's father gave him the option to refuse. Bâ graduated in 1915 and reunited with his parents in Kati, where he met a traditional storyteller named Koullel, who initiated him into oral storytelling traditions of the Fulani. It was during this period that Bâ earned the nickname of "Amkoullel" (or "Little Koullel"). In 1918, Bâ decided to enroll in the École Regionale, a French colonial school in Bamako. In 1921, he was selected for admission to the École Normale de Gorée in Dakar,

Senegal, but his mother refused to give him permission to attend. In response, the French colonial administration sent Bâ to Ouagadougou in the former Upper Volta, where he remained until 1932 as a French functionary. At the age of 31, Bâ secured a six-month leave of absence, during which Tierno Bokar Tall further initiated him into the esoteric teachings of Tidjaniya mysticism. Bâ's affiliation with Tierno Bokar deepened, a bond that would never be broken. In 1933, Bâ was transferred to Bamako, where he remained for four years, working as a translator for the colonial administration and as a personal secretary for the mayor of Bamako.

It was during Bâ's tenure in Bamako that controversy broke out over Tierno Bokar Tall's growing involvement with the Hamalliyya movement. The Hamalliyya were the followers of a man named Sheikh Hamallah, who sought to reform Tidjaniya Islam from within it. Although his reasons were spiritual and doctrinal rather than political, Tierno Bokar Tall aligned himself with the Hamalliyya movement at a time of great political tensions between the followers of Sheikh Hamallah and the Umarian Tidjaniya. Tierno Bokar's decision caused many difficulties for Bâ, who remained loyal to his teacher and who followed his teacher's decision to join the Hamalliyya movement. The French, who had targeted the Umarian Tidjaniya to serve as colonial administrators on their behalf, also perceived the Hamalliyya movement to run counter to their interests; hence, Bâ's involvement with the reformist sect caused trouble for him, not only with Umarian Tidjaniya notables but also with the French colonial administration that employed him.

Through the intervention of Théodore Monod, the French colonialist founder of the Institut Français d'Afrique Noire (IFAN; French Institute of Black Africa), Bâ was able to survive this difficult period of his political and professional life. In 1942, Bâ was appointed to IFAN, largely through the efforts of Monod. Under Monod's influence, Bâ also undertook the task of presenting Tierno Bokar Tall's views to the French reading public, which eventually resulted in the publication of *Vie et enseignement de Tierno Bokar: Le sage de Bandiagara* (1957, rewritten in 1980), later translated into English as *A Spirit of Tolerance: The Inspiring Life of Tierno Bokar*. During this period, Bâ also collected and transcribed oral tales and wrote a number of ethnographic studies of traditional African society. This work eventually led to the publication of *L'Empire Peul de Macina* (*The Fulani Empire of Macina*), which was published in two separate volumes in 1955 and 1962.

Bâ's involvement with the Hamalliyya movement also brought him into conflict with the growing, anti-Sufi, Wahhabi movement in the 1950s. Bâ evolved to become one of the most active voices against the threat of Wahhabi extremism in West Africa and the efforts of the Wahhabi to stifle traditional West African culture and expressions of Islam. Wahhabism is an Islamic fundamentalist movement originating in Saudi Arabia, of which al-Qaeda is an extreme branch. Bâ's perception of this growing influence in the region led him into close working relation with Marcel Cardaire, a French colonial administrator who also sought to eradicate Wahhabism in West Africa (albeit to serve French imperialist interests). Some criticized Bâ for collaborating with Cardaire in presenting Tierno Bokar Tall's views to French readers, but Bâ remained steadfast in his determination to disseminate the teachings of Tierno Bokar Tall. In 1951, Bâ traveled to France on a UNESCO (United Nations Educational, Scientific and Cultural Organization) scholarship, where he met important Africanists like Marcel Griaule, Germaine Dieterlen, and Louis Massignon. Following his tenure in France, he returned on a regular basis to give lectures at the Sorbonne on Fulani culture and civilization. At this time, he also collaborated with Germaine Dieterlen in authoring *Koumen*, an anthology of Fulani initiation stories. In 1958, Bâ founded the Institut des Sciences Humaines in Bamako, where he served as director. In 1960, Mali gained its independence from France; and from 1962 to 1966, Bâ served as the ambassador to Côte d'Ivoire for the newly established Republic of Mali. He was also elected to the executive council of UNESCO in 1961, where he served for ten years, working for the preservation of traditional African cultures. During this time, Bâ also contributed toward the establishment of a transnational system for the alphabetization of African languages. In 1970, Bâ retired from UNESCO's executive council in order to devote his time to ethnographic research and writing his memoirs. He took up residence in Marcory, Côte d'Ivoire, a suburb of Abidjan, but he continued to travel, staying for a time in his native village of Bandiagara, Mali. In 1974, Bâ won the Grand Prix Littéraire d'Afrique Noire for his novel, *L'étrange destin de Wangrin* (1973; English trans., *The Fortunes of Wangrin*). In his retirement, he composed his famous memoir, *Amkoullel: L'enfant peul*, which was published posthumously in 1991. Bâ also briefly collaborated with Yambo Ouologuem, the author of *Le devoir de violence* (1968), who was also born in Bandiagara. Bâ died on 15 May 1991 in Abidjan, Côte d'Ivoire. Since his death, his works have been translated into numerous languages throughout the world. He is widely venerated as a staunch defender of African culture, who sensed the urgency of preserving traditional knowledge that he feared might disappear. At a time when West African society experienced great political upheavals, Bâ proved adept at navigating his way through controversy, conflict, and intrigue. He did so without compromising his most cherished beliefs and moral principles.

[*See also* Ouologuem, Amadou Yambo; Tierno Bokar; *and* 'Umar Tal.]

BIBLIOGRAPHY

Austen, Ralph. "Amadou Hampate Ba: From a Colonial to a Postcolonial African Voice: Amkoullel, *L'enfant peul*." *Research in African Literatures* 31, no. 1 (2000): 18.

Bâ, Amadou Hampaté. *The Fortunes of Wangrin*. Translated by Aina Pavolini Taylor. Bloomington: Indiana University Press, 1999.

Bâ, Amadou Hampaté. *Kaïdara: A Fulani Cosmological Epic from Mali*. Translated by Daniel Whitman. Boulder, Colo.: Lynne Rienner, 1988.

Bâ, Amadou Hampaté. *A Spirit of Tolerance: The Inspiring Life of Tierno Bokar*. Bloomington, Ind.: World Wisdom, 2008.

Wise, Christopher. "Interview with Al-Hajj Sékou Tall." In *Yambo Ouologuem: Postcolonial Writer, Islamic Militant*. Edited by Christopher

Wise, pp. 231–241. Boulder, Colo.: Lynne Rienner, 1999.

CHRISTOPHER WISE

Bâ, Ma Diakhou (c. 1809–1867), leader of a Muslim jihad that briefly controlled the western part of Senegambia, was best known as Ma Ba, Maba Diakhou Bâ, or as Ma Ba Diakhou, with Diakhou being his mother's name. He is also called Amath Ba.

Ma Ba was born in a clerical family that had migrated from the strongly Islamic Futa Toro dominated by Halpulaaren, to a Wolof community in the Mandinka state of Badibu located on the north shore of the Gambia River. As a boy, he studied the Qur'an with his father and then at schools in the Wolof kingdoms of Kajoor and Jolof. He later in turn taught the Qur'an in Jolof, where his mother had been born. While there, he married Maty Ndiaye, the niece of the Burba Jolof, the head of the Jolof kingdom, and probably forged ties that proved useful in later conflicts. When his father died sometime in the 1840s, he was invited back to Badibu to assume his father's position. Though there were a number of Muslim clerical families long resident in the area, he seems to have quickly become an important teacher and one of the major leaders of the Muslim community during a period of tension.

Local traditions have it that al-Hajj 'Umar Tal visited the area in 1846 or 1847 and that he met Ma Ba in the village of Kabakoto, where the two prayed together for three days and three nights, after which 'Umar appointed Ma Ba his representative in the area. There is little evidence of later contact between the two, but when Ma Ba's jihad began, he founded Nioro (later renamed Nioro du Rip), which was named after 'Umar's capital. Furthermore, for more than a decade, Ma Ba continued to teach the Qur'an. This was, however, a period of tension between various Senegambian states and the important Muslim communities in their midst. The tensions were not new, but economic change was altering the balance of power. The end of the Atlantic slave trade weakened the rulers, while the beginning of the peanut trade gave resources to the industrious Muslim peasants who produced most of the peanuts. This income could be used to buy weapons. Many of the rulers felt threatened by increasingly assertive Muslim communities.

In early 1861, the British governor of the Gambia attacked the *mansa* (ruler) of Badibu to punish him for harassing Bathurst-based traders. During the operations, Ma Ba came aboard the governor's boat and agreed to accompany the expedition if his village were spared. After the *mansa* was defeated, Ma Ba helped arrange the peace terms. There are several stories about what happened next. One is that the *mansa's* son was sent to kill Ma Ba but got drunk and talked about his mission. The other is that the *mansa's* son seized the wife of a Muslim and demanded that Ma Ba send him a cow as a wedding gift. Ma Ba responded to the indignity with an insult, sending only a bowl of porridge and beans. The *mansa's* son was killed in an attack on Ma Ba's village, and Ma Ba immediately moved against the *mansa's* villages. Ma Ba's initial following consisted mostly of his students and those of other local marabouts, or Muslim leaders. They quickly swept through Badibu, burning villages that did not accept Muslim hegemony. Many members of the old warrior aristocracy and their slave soldiers were quickly driven across the Gambia River. Others took refuge at Bathurst or near the new French fort at Kaolack in Saalum.

Ma Ba's speedy success inspired other Muslims to join him and led to calls for his assistance. He quickly built up a force that cut across ethnic groups and included Muslims from all over western Senegambia. In May 1862, he moved into neighboring Niumi to aid a Muslim revolt. When the British sought to mediate, he said he would spare the lives only of those who converted. A month later, he withdrew from Niumi because of a conflict that erupted nearer to his base in northern Badibu. When a Muslim revolt in that area was defeated by the *bur* (ruler) of Saalum, the call once again went out to Ma Ba. In alliance with the defeated Muslims and with a dissident faction of the Saalum elite that converted to win Ma Ba's support, they defeated the army of the *bur* of Saalum and captured his capital of Kahone. That night, when the aristocrats got drunk celebrating their victory, Ma Ba withdrew.

This was typical of Ma Ba's behavior. Though he was over fifty years old when he turned to jihad, he was uncompromising in the pursuit of his goal. When a British emissary told him that his ravaging would lead to famine, he answered simply that "God is our Father, and he has brought this war. We are in his hands." Before battle, Ma Ba would sit on his prayer mat, surrounded by blind marabouts, who would chant praises of God and his Prophet Muhammad while Ma Ba wrote verses of the Qur'an, which were to serve as amulets and protect his soldiers from harm. He never actually fought, himself. Prisoners were given the choice of death or shaving their heads in a gesture of submission to Islam. If his success was based in the commitment of his followers to Islam, that was also his weakness.

He was more interested in leading a militant crusade to establish an orthodox Muslim community than he was in creating a stable state that would survive him. His demand that existing rulers convert to his more orthodox version of Islam was framed with typical Muslim humility. Thus, in 1864, he wrote the *burba* (ruler) of Jolof: "You are greater than I and than all of the kings of the East. . . . Come simply to me as a Muslim, and God will serve as a witness between us."

Some did come. Estimates of his strength in 1863 and 1864 ranged from eleven thousand to twenty thousand armed men. This made him an attractive ally. The most important was Lat Dior Diop, the young *damel* (ruler) of Kajoor, who was defeated by the French in December 1863 after opposing French construction of a telegraph line. When the French demanded that he expel Lat Dior, Ma Ba responded: "Lat Dior has converted, and he lives with me. . . . If he stays with me in order to make his salaam and read the Koran, we will be friends, because I love only the truth." Later that year, with Lat Dior playing a key role, Ma Ba's forces moved into Bawol, Jolof, and Kajoor in northern Senegambia. When the French protested, he responded:

I, Ma Ba, do not see what concerns you in the affairs of Jolof, Kajoor, Bawol, Siin, and the rest of Saalum. Tell me what concerns you. Are they Muslims or Christians? Do you love the infidels and detest the believers? As for me, I find in the laws of the Prophet that we should declare war on the infidels who are near.

Ma Ba regularly told the French that he would accept them as traders, but that they should not meddle in Senegal's religious conflicts: "Do not put yourself on the side of infidels, but only on the side of your property when damage is done you."

By mid-1865, Ma Ba controlled much of western Senegambia and was recruiting in the Futa Toro. In November 1865, a French military force landed at Kaolack and headed south, marching into an ambush supposedly planned by Lat Dior at Pathébadiane. The French survived this encounter because of their superior weapons, but they were forced to withdraw, suffering substantial losses and leaving most of their supplies behind. French prisoners were executed, and the following year many of Ma Ba's soldiers wore caps taken from the French army. In the subsequent two years, Ma Ba continued to exercise hegemony over most of western Senegambia while the French restricted themselves to fortifying strong positions and aiding African allies.

Most of Ma Ba's enemies were nominally Muslim, or at least made some obeisance to Muslim practice. They generally drank alcoholic beverages, and often they worshiped traditional deities but did not strictly abide by Islamic legal codes. The only state that totally resisted Islam was the Sereer kingdom of Siin. During the rainy season of 1867, Ma Ba invaded Siin. The French did not come to Siin's aid. Fortunately for Siin, however, a heavy rain dampened much of Ma Ba's gunpowder. Siin attacked before dawn and gradually prevailed in intense fighting. Early in the afternoon, Ma Ba laid out his prayer mat and began praying. When the battle was over, his dead body was found on the prayer mat. The *bur* of Siin had Ma Ba's head cut off and sent to the French. In later letters, the Bur Siin regularly reminded the French that Siin met the invasion alone and without French help.

Ma Ba was succeeded by his brother Mamour Ndari, who had difficulty in maintaining the unity of the state Ma Ba created. Many who fought with Ma Ba returned home or went elsewhere. Lat Dior returned to Kajoor, Albury Ndiaye to Jolof, and Fodé Kabba to the southern shore of the Gambia. Others often fought on their own, paying loose hegemony to Ma Ba's heirs in Nioro. Nevertheless, by the early 1880s, Senegambia was firmly Muslim. In that decade, the son of one of his followers, Amadu Bamba MbBacké, turned away from the path of war and began building a more peaceful Sufi movement, the Muridiyya. Ma Ba's family continued to play a major role in public and religious affairs. Ma Ba's heritage was a Senegambia strongly committed to Islam, though to an Islam more tolerant than he wanted.

[*See also* Amadu Bamba; Diop, Lat Dior; *and* 'Umar Tal.]

BIBLIOGRAPHY

Barry, Boubacar. *Senegambia and the Atlantic Slave Trade.* Cambridge, UK: Cambridge University Press, 1998. Excellent history of greater Senegambia.

Klein, Martin. *Islam and Imperialism in Senegal: Sine-Saloum, 1847–1914.* Stanford, CA: Stanford University Press, 1968. Contains a chapter on Ma Ba.

Klein, Martin. "Social and Economic Factors in the Muslim Revolution in Senegambia." *Journal of African History* 13 (1972): 419–442.

Quinn, Charlotte. *Mandingo Kingdoms of the Senegambia: Traditionalism, Islam, and European Expansion.* Evanston, Ill.: Northwestern University Press, 1972.

MARTIN A. KLEIN

Bâ, Mariama (1929–1981), Senegalese educator, novelist, and activist, was born into a well-to-do and ardently religious Lébou family, which had its own mosque in the family compound, bringing the neighborhood together for prayers several times a day. The Lébous, tall, regal, staunchly Muslim, and predominantly fishermen, are a subtribe of the Wolof ethnic group related to the Lébous of Saint-Louis (Ndar in Wolof) in the northern Sahel region of Senegal. They were the first inhabitants of the city of Dakar (Ndakarou in Wolof) in the Cape-Vert peninsula, composed of the villages of Ngor, Ouakam, and Yoff. Mariama's father was Niélé Bâ, born in 1892. Her mother died when Mariama was two years old. Hence, she never got to know her nor did she ever see a photograph of her. Niélé Bâ fought as a *tirailleur* (African infantry soldier) on the French side in World War I, becoming on his return to Senegal a deputy mayor of Dakar and finally a secretary in the Ministry of Health. This progressive and somewhat "assimilated" father wished for his daughter to have education the French way, and as far as she could go, in contradiction to the wishes of her grandmother, who wanted nothing more than an elementary education and traditional upbringing for her. Mariama Bâ would get both, which set her up for a lifetime dilemma over her attachment to two opposing worlds, that of tradition and that of modernity.

Thanks to Berthe Maubert, the headmistress of Bâ's elementary school, and in spite of her grandparents' determination to stop her further education while her father was away pursuing his career in Niamey, Niger, Bâ was able to take and pass the entrance examination to the L'École Normale des Jeunes Filles de Rufisque, coming in first of all the prospective entrants from the entire region of French West Africa. The founding headmistress of the Rufisque teacher training college was Germaine Le Goff, whom Bâ would later describe in her first novel, *Une si longue lettre*, as a woman who desired for the girls under her care a better destiny than the traditions they were beset with. Le Goff taught them rootedness in tradition and the past but also openness to new ideas and "universal culture" (Schwartz-Bart, 2003, p. 100). Le Goff encouraged Bâ's exceptional writing abilities; her classroom compositions became nothing less than veritable outpourings of emotion, vivid imagination, and understandable revolt against the ills of colonization in Senegal. In one such essay, inspired by two lines of verse by the French Romantic François-René de Chateaubriand (1768–1848)—"Combien j'ai douce souvenance/Du joli lieu de ma naissance" ("What sweet remembrance I have/Of the pretty place of my birth")—Mariama Bâ evoked childhood memories of her own birthplace: her grandfather's compound in Dakar. Bâ described the family setting, the path to the village slaughterhouse, the feasts, the dances, but also the dire want and the drudgery of life shaped by Islam, slavish imitation of French assimilationist culture, and the exigencies of tradition; she is especially unflattering about the lives of women, characterized by uncontrolled childbirth, rivalries, infighting, and domestic chores, a fate that her rebellious nature did not condone. A *cri du coeur* of a generation of Senegalese youth manacled by French values that devalued African civilization, Bâ's reflection on her childhood in Dakar says, "Then one day my father sent me to school and my life of freedom and simplicity was gone. My reason was whitened although my head remained black: but my blood, immune, remained pure, like the sun, pure, unaffected by exposure. My blood remained pagan in my civilized veins" (Ndiaye, 2007, p. 182). André Davesne, the school superintendent, was impressed and published the piece in the July 1947 edition of his journal, *Notes africaines*.

The French intellectual Emmanuel Mounier republished Bâ's essay in his Paris journal, *Esprit*. The famous French poet, novelist, and intellectual Maurice Genevoix (Prix Goncourt winner for his 1925 novel, *Raboliot*), cited large excerpts of it in his 1949 book, *Afrique blanche, Afrique noire*, as witness to a laudable and emerging aspect of Africa yet unknown to the world.

At the end of her teacher training program in Rufisque, Mariama Bâ taught in an elementary school in the native quarters of the Medina. Following ill health, she was transferred to the French West African regional inspectorate of education, where she remained until the end of her life. (Today a girls' school named in her honor stands on Gorée Island, close to the mainland of Dakar.) During the 1960s, as her children were growing up, she became active in women's rights struggles. From 1979 to 1981, she was a member of the Federation of Women's Associations and a member of the solidarity group Cercle Fémina. In 1980, she was the general secretary of the Dakar Soroptimist International Club and a member of Amicale Germaine Le Goff, which successfully applied to have the name of the Rufisque teachers training college changed to École Normale des Jeunes Filles Germaine Le Goff in honor of that educator.

Additionally, Bâ spoke up on women's rights by writing in the newspapers.

Mariama Bâ married Bassirou Ndiaye soon after graduating from the teacher's college, but the marriage failed; Bâ later wrote that her first husband wanted her to take the role of a traditional wife, even though they shared progressive ideals and theirs was a marriage born of romantic love. Her second marriage, to Ablaye Ndiaye, a scholarly and quiet medical doctor, did not last either, for essentially the same reasons. Her third marriage, to Obèye Diop, lasted for twenty-five years and produced nine children out of eight pregnancies, yet they too ultimately divorced. He wanted a traditional wife, her school diplomas, skills, and innate intelligence notwithstanding; and she wanted an enlightened and modern husband, instead of the traditional man she married.

It was around the time that her third marriage ended that Mariama began work on her seminal novel, *Une si longue lettre* (1979), which appeared in English as *So Long a Letter* (1980), was translated into numerous other world languages, and won a Japanese Noma Award for African publishing at the Frankfurt Book Fair in 1980. In this novel, Bâ denounces obstacles she saw in Senegalese women's paths: the brand of Islam that subjugates women; the complicity of men who refuse to give up their privileges and power; antiquated African traditions that foster outdated mores, such as polygyny, that do not promote women's happiness. She also attacks the assimilationist policies of the colonial masters, because they degrade indigenous African peoples and their countries (see the interview with Barbara Harrell-Bond in Azodo, ed., 2003, pp. 383–402). Nonetheless, imbued with a world-class vision, Mariama Bâ also praises all the peoples of goodwill and the traditions that foster human dignity and understanding across class, gender, sex, and racial boundaries.

In a speech titled "La fonction politique des littératures africaines écrites," given at a 1980 symposium, "La fonction politique de la litérature moderne de l'Afrique noire," Bâ explored the role of the writer as the mover and shaker of society, as the watchdog for abuses and ills of colonization and corruption, as the fighter for the preservation of the cultural patrimony and human rights, and the seer who proffers solutions for social problems. Women writers, she says, owe it to their kind to be catalysts for changing the situation of women. Africans in general should embrace publishing, in order to help reconstruct African history, through casting in stone landmarks that were ephemeral in the oral period. For this reason, continued Mariama Bâ, books are invaluable tools, weapons of reconstruction. It is through books and publishing that Africans can hope to be constantly nourished and develop as a people.

Cheikh Tidjane adapted *Une si longue lettre* into a film in Wolof titled *Bataaxalbi* (*The Letter*), which premiered on Dakar television on 2 November 1984. Bâ's second novel, *Un chant écarlate* (1981; English trans., *Scarlet Song*), was published posthumously; Mariama Bâ died earlier in the year of lung cancer. *Un chant écarlate* asserts the benefits of interracial marriages in fostering universal brotherhood and sisterhood. Mariama Bâ also eulogizes negritude and its unique meaning to black people everywhere as a laudable footstool on which to stand when Africa meets the world in its various forms.

Clearly, Mariama Bâ is not the first-person narrator, Ramatoulaye, of her first novel, as some critics say. What is evident, however, is that she has lent her energy to her protagonists, thanks to her activism and life experiences. Today, there are close to three hundred critical studies of Mariama Bâ's life and writings, especially about *Une si longue lettre*.

[*See also* Senghor, Léopold Sédar.]

BIBLIOGRAPHY

Azodo, Ada Uzoamaka, ed. *Emerging Perspectives on Mariama Bâ: Postcolonialism, Feminism, and Postmodernism.* Trenton, N.J.: Africa World Press, 2003.

Dia, Alioune Touré. "*Succès littéraire de Mariama Bâ pour son livre* Une si longue letter." *Amina* 84 (1979): 12–14.

Ndiaye, Mame Coumba. *Mariama Bâ; ou, Les allées d'un destin.* Dakar: Novelles Editions du Senegal, 2007.

Schwartz-Bart, Simone. *In Praise of Black Women.* Vol. 3: *Modern African Women*, translated by Rose-Myriam Réjouis, Stephanie K. Turner, and Val Vinokurov. Madison: University of Wisconsin Press, 2003.

Volet, Jean-Marie. "Not To Be Missed." Review of *Mariama Bâ; ou, Les Allées d'un Destin*, by Mame Coumba Ndiaye. At the University of Western Australia, School of Humanities, Web site on African literature: http://aflit.arts.uwa.edu.au/revieweng_ba09.html (August 2009).

ADA UZOAMAKA AZODO

Baamuta, Yusufu Ssemukasa (1894–1958), public servant, politician, and businessman in present-day Uganda, was born in the Kingdom of Buganda in 1894. His father, Thomas Ssemukasa, was a sub-county chief and general of Kabaka (King) Mwanga's army. His name, which was not a customary clan name, means "it is better to die on the battlefield than to die of a natural death." He was educated at an elite private school, King's College in Buddo, and at Sheffield College in England. Upon his return to Uganda he was a clerk in the protectorate government, but soon he became an outspoken politician and businessman who challenged the application of British administration in Uganda.

After several years of service to the protectorate government, Baamuta was appointed secretary of the Lukiiko (the Bugandan parliament). He was a vociferous defender of the rights afforded to the Buganda Kingdom under the terms of the Uganda Agreement (1900), which established the jurisdiction of British rule in Uganda. During the 1920s, he countered British officials who sought to extend protectorate government control over spheres such as taxation, appointment of chiefs, and economic policy. He was a friend and advisor to Kabaka Sir Daudi Chwa, and he married into one of the most powerful Bugandan families of the period by marrying the daughter of Sir Apollo Kaggwa.

Baamuta pursued a political ideology that accepted protectorate rule as a means of achieving greater development, but he opposed efforts by protectorate officials to dominate Buganda. He sought British training and guidance in order to achieve self-rule, and he vigorously rejected charges that Bugandans were incapable of such. In pursuit of these goals he came into conflict with the provincial commissioner John Postlethwaite in the late 1920s and was subsequently dismissed from his post in the Lukiiko on the insistence of the governor. Baamuta protested his dismissal and took his case to England, pressing for a commission to investigate whether actions of the protectorate government had violated the Uganda Agreement. He drew upon contacts such as Fenner Brockway, Sir Arthur Creech-Jones, and Norman Leys. He argued that British officials had overstepped their mandate in Uganda and that there was a disconnect between official British policy and the actions of protectorate officials in Uganda. He also hired a lobbyist and succeeded in having these issues raised in the House of Commons.

While he tried to expand his political base upon his return to Uganda, he also branched out as a newspaper columnist for the paper *Matalisi* and became a partner in the Buganda Cotton Company. The mandate of this company was to challenge the syndicate-based system of cotton ginning, which carved buying zones for ginneries. In addition, the Buganda Cotton Company became the first African-owned company to purchase and gin cotton in 1929; until this time cotton ginneries were exclusively owned by Europeans and Indians. Unfortunately, their cotton was spoiled during transport to England in 1930 and the company subsequently went bankrupt. Through his business venture, Baamuta applied his political ideology, seeking British guidance in order to gain self-sufficiency.

After his bankruptcy Baamuta retreated from political life and business, although he continued to educate farmers at the grassroots level on how to achieve greater self-sufficiency. He often held meetings at his home, where he taught farmers how the agricultural economy functioned both within Uganda and world markets, and his ideas were known throughout Buganda. He also offered guidance to young leaders like Ignatius Musaazi, whose Uganda African Farmer's Union protested against the cotton monopoly in the late 1940s. Musaazi also founded the Uganda National Congress political party in 1952. In 1945 Baamuta and fourteen others were deported, without trial, to northern Uganda after they were accused of leading strikes against the Bugandan government and plotting in the assassination of the prime minister, Martin Luther Nsibirwa. Baamuta denied his involvement and claimed that former political rivals were behind his deportation.

During the 1950s, the Ugandan protectorate government reformed the Ugandan legislative council in an effort to make it representative of all of Uganda and aid in the formation of a unitary state. While it was unpopular in Buganda, where calls for a federal government were favored, Baamuta was elected as a representative in 1954. In 1956 he introduced the first motion relating to independence, asking for self-rule by 1958 and independence within the British Commonwealth by 1960. He suffered an unknown illness two weeks after his motion was put forward, which left him bedridden until his death in July 1958.

[*See also* Chwa, Daudi; *and* Kaggwa, Apollo.]

BIBLIOGRAPHY

Postlethwaite, John. *I Look Back*. London: T. V. Boardman, 1947. Baamuta is not mentioned by name in this autobiography, but he is the son-in-law referred to on p. 108. Postlethwaite's portrayal of Baamuta as a corrupt and anti-British agitator should be taken with a grain of salt, because Postlethwaite was known to have a strong personality, and he clashed with several prominent Ugandans during his career as a protectorate official.

Scotton, James F. "The First African Press in East Africa: Protest and Nationalism in Uganda in the 1920s." *International Journal of African Historical Studies* 6, no. 2 (1973): 211–228. Baamuta has not been the subject of much scholarly attention. However, Scotton does mention his role as a newspaper commentator, and this coincided with the development of newspapers as a source of critique and opposition in Uganda.

KRISTOPHER COTE

Baard, Frances (c. 1908–1997), South African labor organizer and women's movement leader, was born in the diamond-mining town of Kimberley, the fourth of six children. Her father Herman Maswabi had come from Bechuanaland (now Botswana) to work on the mines and was a steward in the local Methodist church; her mother, Sara Voss, also Tswana, came from Kimberley. When her father's brother and sister-in-law died, Baard's family took in their children, and her parents sent her to stay with her father's sister in Ramotswa, a village not far from Gaborone, where she was confirmed in the local Lutheran church. After Baard, then around eight years old, suffered serious burns in a cooking fire, her mother brought her back to the family home in Beaconsfield, just outside of Kimberley. She attended a Methodist school, learning in both English and Tswana. Shortly after she returned, her mother passed away during the 1918 flu epidemic.

When Baard had completed Standard Six, she briefly attended Perseverance Training School. But her father died during her second year there, and her sister's husband found her a teaching position in the Orange Free State; she remained there for a year until she was let go because she lacked formal qualifications. At the time, she had two daughters, both of whose fathers had passed away when the children were very young.

Around 1939, Baard moved to Port Elizabeth, where she took a job as a domestic worker and met Lucas Baard, a Xhosa from Kimberley. They married in the Methodist Church in 1942 and moved to a house in New Brighton. Following her marriage and the birth of two more children, Baard found work in a food and canning factory—an industry that was booming during the war. Factory conditions at the time were harsh. Workers who peeled and canned the fruit had no plastic aprons or gloves and they often worked sixteen-hour shifts. When Ray Alexander organized a union at Baard's factory in 1948, Baard was elected organizing secretary for the African Food and Canning Workers Union. From then on, she worked in the trade union office, learning organizing skills, giving speeches, listening to workers' complaints, negotiating with management, and confronting the difficulties of keeping seasonal workers involved in the union—honing the political expertise that would equip her for a lifetime of political engagement. After the Group Areas Act came into effect in 1950, further hardening boundaries between different racial groups, Baard faced additional problems. Because the unions of workers defined as "African" and "Coloured" under South African law shared an office and refused to separate, she was constantly harassed by the police.

In addition to her trade union activities, Baard was drawn to attend a meeting of African National Congress (ANC) after her shock at seeing people forced to sleep outside on a cold, rainy night for lack of accommodation. She soon became involved in the ANC Women's League, at first going from house to house to talk with women about their problems, including lack of money, high rents, difficulty feeding their families, and men's problems with the pass laws. She also learned of the special hardships that widows faced, notably the threat of losing houses that could be registered only in men's names. Although Baard's husband took no interest in politics, he never tried to stop her from going to meetings. When he died suddenly in 1952 and she assumed sole responsibility for raising their two young children, her reputation as an activist protected her from being forced out of their house.

Baard's leadership role in both union and women's struggles resulted, in part, from the close ties between the Food and Canning Workers' Union, its African affiliate, and the broader political movements against apartheid during the 1950s. Thus, Baard organized protests against the Suppression of Communism Act in 1950 and two years later she took part in the Defiance Campaign against apartheid laws, a series of nonviolent actions in which small groups of people purposely violated segregation laws in order to draw attention to their inequities. During this campaign, she took responsibility for finding elderly people to care for children whose parents had been arrested. She also worked on the Bantu education boycott, helping parents to form the "cultural clubs" that provided an alternative to badly funded, segregated schools; became a member of the national executive committee of the South African Congress of Trade Unions (SACTU; a new union federation opposed to government-enforced segregated unions); and was a founding member of the Federation of South African Women (now known as FEDSAW).

Launched in 1954, this multiracial organization led women's struggles against the new requirement that African women join men in having to carry identity documents known as passes, which would regulate their freedom of movement and subject them to the constant threat of arrest. Baard attended the group's organizing meeting in Johannesburg in 1954 and worked on drafting provisions for the Women's Charter, a document that called not only for gender and racial equality but also for improved living and working conditions, better care for pregnant women and mothers, free education, housing with electricity and plumbing, and more affordable food. In 1955, Baard's union formally affiliated with the Women's Federation, thereby reinforcing her ability to combine labor organizing and other political work.

As part of the struggle against passes, Baard led campaigns of union women in Port Elizabeth, who went from door to door and organized in the factories to persuade women to refuse to accept passes. At this time officials were encouraging employers to demand passes from their workers even before it was legally required, and many women feared losing their jobs if they refused the new documents. When trucks came to issue the documents, Baard was among the leaders who stood next to the vehicles and explained to women the consequences of accepting passes. She was also in the forefront of the historic protest of 9 August 1956, when twenty thousand women assembled at the Union Buildings in Pretoria to rally against the apartheid government's plans to extend passes to women. Prior to the meeting, she went from branch to branch of the Women's Federation in Port Elizabeth, gaining women's support for the march, helping to raise funds for train fare, and collecting the signatures of women who were unable to attend for a petition endorsing her cause.

During 1955, as the South African government intensified its campaign against resistance movements, Baard was among 156 people arrested in the famous Treason Trial, along with Nelson Mandela and other antiapartheid campaigners. Among those released before the end of the trial (which occurred in 1961, when all defendants were acquitted), she continued her trade union and women's organizing until she was rearrested and banned in 1963. She spent a difficult year in solitary confinement, where she was denied reading materials and a light was kept on at all times, day and night. When finally taken to court, she adamantly denied the lengthy list of charges against her. At this point, she was returned to prison for another five years. Recalling this ordeal later, she said she was convinced that her interrogators were trying to kill her but she believed that her strong spirit enabled her to survive. Once she was released from solitary confinement, Baard was allowed to associate with the other political prisoners, who (like their counterparts on Robben Island) spent their time teaching reading and writing to those who were illiterate.

Rather than allow Baard to return to her home in Port Elizabeth at the end of her incarceration, authorities banished her to a tiny, filthy two-room shack in Mabopane, a township an hour outside Pretoria, far from her home and family. Her neighbors initially avoided her, fearing that she was a police informant. Persecuted for refusing to take a pass, flung into a hostile environment, and newly released from prison, Baard was penniless and jobless. Her house in Port Elizabeth had been appropriated, her furniture removed, and her children thrown into the street. One child was also arrested and jailed for being without a pass. In Mabopane, she worked for a time in a newly established textile factory. When the United Democratic Front, a new antigovernment coalition, was organized in the 1980s, Baard resumed her political activities against apartheid and against the corrupt "homeland" government of Bophuthatswana; she also continued her work on a variety of local community projects, including launching a day-care center called the Zenzeleni Community Center.

After apartheid ended, Baard's role in the struggle merited formal recognition. In June 2001, Kimberley's Diamantveld District Municipality was renamed the Frances Baard District Municipality, and on 9 August 2009 (South African Women's Day), a statue of her was unveiled by the Northern Cape Premier. The inscription on the granite plinth cites the famous remark from her autobiography: "My spirit is not banned—I still say I want freedom in my lifetime."

[*See also* Mandela, Nelson Rolihlahla.]

BIBLIOGRAPHY

Baard, Frances, as told to Barbie Schreiner. *My Spirit Is Not Banned.* Harare: Zimbabwe Publishing, 1986.

Berger, Iris. *Threads of Solidarity: Women in South African Industry, 1900–1980.* Bloomington: Indiana University Press, 1992.

Sideris, C., and D. Cachalia. Interview with Frances Baard, 15 July 1982. South African Institute of Race Relations Oral Archive No. 16.

Walker, Cherryl. *Women and Resistance in South Africa.* New York: Monthly Review Press, 1991.

IRIS BERGER

Baartman, Sara (1789–1815), an enslaved woman from South Africa, placed on public display in nineteenth-century Britain and France, where she became known as the "Hottentot Venus." "Hottentot" was a derogatory word used to describe groups now called "Khoisan" and likely derived from European disparagement of so-called click languages. She was born to a Khoisan family in an area north of the Gamtoos River valley in the eastern Cape Colony. Her name is written sometimes as "Saartjie" (Afrikaans); however, the Anglophone "Sara" is most commonly used. Her mother died when she was an infant, and her father was a cattle driver. A commando raid in 1810 by the Dutch Boers decimated her village, and Baartman, now orphaned, was sent to the Cape to be sold into slavery.

Pieter Cesars, a freed black, purchased her. She became a nursemaid for his brother, Hendrik Cesars, and his wife, Anna Catharina. The British physician Alexander Dunlop saw Baartman's unusually large buttocks and genitals (a condition known as "steatopygia") as a source of profit if exhibited in England. British culture was fixated at the time with spectacles of what were considered to be exotic physical features. When she arrived in London, she was exhibited at 225 Piccadilly. Her show consisted of singing and dancing in front of large crowds as the "Hottentot Venus." She became a well-known feature in British culture as ballads and cartoons were dedicated to her.

However, her scantily clad performances raised concerns of slavery and exploitation. Zachary Macaulay, a member of the African Institution, believed she was illegally transported and enslaved; the trading of slaves in the British Empire had become illegal in 1807. Supporters of Baartman took her case to the Court of the King's Bench in Westminster Hall in November 1810. Dunlop and Cesars claimed she was a servant and under contract. Baartman testified in Afrikaans and concurred with her two employers' position. The court ruled in her favor.

In September 1814, Baartman arrived in France, as Napoleon Bonaparte was losing his grip on his empire. In Paris, she became widely known and continued her work singing and dancing to large crowds. However, Baartman struggled, as she had difficulty with the language and had money and health issues. It has been speculated that the last years of her life were immersed in alcoholism and possibly prostitution to make ends meet.

Baartman died a year later in France, possibly of flu, bronchitis, or pneumonia. At her death, her body was taken to Georges Cuvier, a naturalist and zoologist. He dissected her body and conserved several of her organs, most notably her brain and genitals. This practice was not uncommon, as at that time racially based scientific thinking permeated the analyses of scholars of human and animal studies. Her dissection was used to justify the inferiority of Africans, most notably Khoisan. Her body parts were on display until the mid-1970s.

In 1994, when apartheid was dismantled in South Africa, President Nelson Mandela asked France for the return of Baartman's remains. Mandela saw Baartman as a heroic ancestor whose final resting place should be in her true homeland. After years of political and diplomatic wrangling, her body was returned and buried in the Gamtoo River valley in August 2002. Her story has become illustrative of the exploitation and distortion of African women's sexuality. Among the numerous popular and scholarly publications about her life, the writer Barbara Chase-Riboud has published a novel, *Hottentot Venus* (2003), while the film director Zola Maseko has made two documentaries concerning her public exhibition and the return of her remains to South Africa: *The Life and Times of Sara Baartman: The Hottentot Venus* (1998) and *The Return of Sara Baartman* (2003).

[*See also* Macaulay, Zachary; *and* Mandela, Nelson Rolihlahla.]

BIBLIOGRAPHY

Abrahams, Yvette. "Disempowered to Consent: Sara Baartman and Khoisan Slavery in the Nineteenth-Century Cape Colony and Britain." *South African Historical Journal* 35 (1996): 89–114.

Abrahams, Yvette. "Images of Sara Baartman: Sexuality, Race, and Gender in Early-Nineteenth-Century Britain." In *Nation, Empire, Colony: Historicizing Gender and Race*, edited by

Ruth Roach Pierson and Nupur Chaudhuri, pp. 220–236. Bloomington: Indiana University Press, 1998. Abrahams's two well-written articles examine how Baartman was perceived through a sexualized and racialized lens. Abrahams has organized many projects in South Africa related to Baartman.

Crais, Clifton, and Pamela Scully. *Sara Baartman and the Hottentot Venus: A Ghost Story and a Biography*. Princeton, N.J.: Princeton University Press, 2009. Seeks to unravel myths surrounding the historical understanding of her through extensive research. The authors seek to relate an accurate story about Sara Baartman and debunk assumptions that cannot be backed up with factual evidence. A good investigative and historical analysis. Also see Crais and Scully, "Race and Erasure: Sara Baartman and Hendrik Cesars in Cape Town and London." *Journal of British Studies* 47 (April 2008): 301–323.

Holmes, Rachel. *African Queen: The Real Story of the Hottentot Venus*. New York: Random House, 2007. A thorough and detailed examination of Baartman, using factual evidence and narrative. This book is similar in accuracy to Crais and Scully's book.

JODIE N. MADER

Baba, Sidiyya (c. 1862–1923), Mauritanian religious leader and founder of a school, was the grandson of his namesake known as "Sidiyya the Elder" (Sidiyya al-Kabir) and was raised by his uncles in the scholarly setting of his father and grandfather's camps in southwestern Mauritania. His father, Sidi Muhammad, died in 1869 during a cholera outbreak when Baba was seven years old, only one year after the death of Sidiyya al-Kabir. This was a moment when his lineage, the Ntisha'it, was one of the dominant ones within the larger Awlad Abyiri, a clerical lineage group that, during his grandfather's time, had risen to be among the most influential political forces in the region of Trarza (southwestern Mauritania). Sidiyya the Elder had spent a dozen years in the Kunta campus of the Azaouad, adjacent to Timbuktu, in the early nineteenth century and he brought back to the village that he founded at Boutilimit, in Trarza, many of the commercial and juridical skills that underpinned the Kunta influence in the region of Niger Bend. Baba grew up at a time when the French were making increasing inroads in the Senegal Valley, and it is clear from his later writings that he was not untouched by the moral and religious dilemma this posed. He read widely and thought deeply about the correct stance for a faithful Muslim to assume under European (Christian) colonial occupation.

His early qu'ranic studies were done under the supervision of a Moroccan scholar named Mulay Muhammad, who was a disciple of his grandfather; his legal education came at the hands of Muhammad b. Daddah, the chief jurist among the Ntisha'it. Oral tradition well into the twentieth century recalled his voracious appetite for reading and his fascination with the processes of modernization taking place at the end of the nineteenth and early twentieth century in North Africa and Egypt. Descendants say that the Egyptian modernizer Muhammad 'Ali was one of his inspirations. This may explain his willingness to engage with the French administration when others of his Muslim contemporaries in West Africa advocated militant opposition to Christian overrule. This may also explain his interest in history, both as a mechanism to preserve the past and as a way to understand change within southern Saharan society. French administrators (and Islamicists in the administration who met with him) remarked on his sharp and critical mind, his well-read opinions, and his openness in discussing Mauritanian society. The French Orientalist Louis Massignon published a summary of his family library at Boutilimit in 1918, remarking at the sophisticated collection of manuscripts the family had amassed there. The French came to rely upon his advice and assistance by the end of the century, but this collaboration was later to be roundly criticized in some quarters of Mauritania. Apologists claim that were it not for Baba's engagement with the French, all of Mauritania might have been swallowed up in an administrative unit dominated by Senegal.

For the French, in addition to his assistance, Baba was the titular head of the Qadiriyya *tariqa*, a Sufi or mystic brotherhood his grandfather had brought back from Timbuktu. The French were much alarmed by the possibility that a rival brotherhood, the Tijaniyya, which had resisted them in North Africa, might also oppose their interests in West Africa. There is little indication that Sidiyya Baba saw rivalry between the brotherhoods in the same way, but he (and his family) clearly benefitted from the fallout of French fears about Tijani influence. Similarly, when a local brotherhood, the Muridiyya, sprung up around the Senegalese Sufi shaykh, Amadu Bamba, it was to Sidiyya Baba that the French turned to serve as a mentor and supervisor of the Senegalese holy man during part of his exile from Senegal when he was brought to Mauritania.

Sidiyya Baba's controversial political role pales alongside his intellectual achievements, mainly demonstrated by his voluminous writings. The Arabic Manuscript Management System Web site attributes sixty titles to him that range across qu'ranic sciences, history, legal opinions (*fatawas*), devotional literature, Sufism, belief, and the Arabic language. Much of the history of Mauritanian society subsequently written was framed by his writing about the structure and phases of the Moorish past. Perhaps his most significant institutional legacy was the creation of a school, or *mahadra*, in Boutilimit that brought French support, Algerian instructors, and survived under the direction of his sons well after the independence of Mauritania. Indeed, this was the foundation for his family's education and the French-Arabic instruction that was implemented throughout the colony. Before his death in 1923 Baba and his wives produced a prodigious clan of eleven sons and twelve daughters, almost all of whom figured among the leading figures in the new state of the Islamic Republic of Mauritania in 1960.

[*See also* Amadu Bamba; Muhammad 'Ali; *and* Sidiyya al-Kabir al-Ntishai'i.]

BIBLIOGRAPHY

"Arabic Manuscript Management System." http://www.westafricanmanuscripts.org/. A bilingual, open-access database of over twenty-four thousand Arabic manuscripts from West Africa, including descriptions of sixty-six works authored by Shaykh Sidiyya Baba.

Marty, Paul. "Cheikh Sidia et sa 'voie' (Mauritanie)." *Revue du Monde Musulman* 21 (1915–1916): 29–134.

Stewart, Charles. "A Mauritanian Reformer: Shaikh Sidiyya Baba." *Tarikh* 7, no. 1 (1971): 65–70.

CHARLES C. STEWART

Baba 'Aruj (1474–1518), North African military leader, was born to a Muslim family on the Greek island of Mytilene. Baba 'Aruj, along with his younger brothers, Khayr al-Din and Ishaq, launched a successful corsair enterprise along the coast of North Africa in the early sixteenth century. Battling mostly against Spanish expansionism in the Maghreb, the brothers (generally known as the Barbarossas) conquered several strongholds along the coast, the most important of which was the city of Algiers. Their efforts directly led to the establishment of Ottoman authority in the North African provinces of Algiers and Tunis.

In the first decade of the sixteenth century, the situation appeared grim for Maghrebi Muslims. The Spanish had recently completed their conquest of the Iberian Peninsula, had expelled the Jews, and had also forced the remaining Muslims in Iberia to convert to Christianity. Their holdings in the New World were beginning to produce the wealth that would make Spain the preeminent empire of the century. Meanwhile the Spanish were expanding their influence along the North African coast, with the goal of eliminating Muslim rule in the Maghreb. Busily consolidating their new holdings in the eastern Mediterranean, the Ottomans appeared reticent to get involved in the west. It would take the efforts of a bold leader such as Baba 'Aruj to change their minds.

Historians know very little about the first three decades of Baba 'Aruj's life. He entered the light of history in 1504, when he and his brothers established a base in the Tunisian port of Goulette (Halq al-Wadi) in cooperation with the Hafsid sultan Muhammad b. Hasan. The Hafsids sponsored the Barbarossas with the intention of obtaining some of the booty taken through their corsair activities. By 1510, the Barbarossas had at least eight ships at their disposal, and their enterprise was so successful that the Hafsids allotted them a second base on the island of Jirba. In 1513, the Barbarossas and the Hafsids collaborated on a siege of the Spanish outpost in Bijaya (Bougie). Using twelve vessels, the Barbarossas established a naval blockade of the city, while the Hafsid army attacked by land. But the siege was turned back and 'Aruj lost his left arm in the battle. Nevertheless, he laid siege to the town a second time in the summer of 1514, supported by twelve ships and over a thousand Turkish troops, only to be frustrated again as a result of bad weather and the arrival of a Spanish relief force.

Operating from a base in Jiljilli, on the Gulf of Bijaya, 'Aruj began to expand his influence inland, with the intention of becoming a regional political ruler. These ambitions created conflicts with his Hafsid allies; so much so that the Hafsid governor of 'Annaba requested Spanish protection in 1516. Responding to an appeal from local Muslims, 'Aruj and his corsairs bombarded the Spanish outpost at the Peñon (a rocky island fortress) overlooking Algiers. But he was unable to defeat the Spanish, so 'Aruj moved his forces into the city, where he eventually quarreled with the Muslim ruler Salim al-Thumi. When al-Thumi looked to the Spanish to help him drive the corsairs from Algiers, 'Aruj had the Arab leader killed and exerted his authority by force. He consolidated his hold over the city by turning back a Spanish invasion led by Diego de Vera on 30 September 1516.

Thus, the Barbarossas had become the Muslim heroes of North Africa, seemingly the only hope for Maghrebi Muslims who feared imminent conquest by Spain. Their successes attracted the attention of the Ottoman Empire, which offered them official positions in their navy, along with military support. ʿAruj became the Ottoman governor of Algiers and was granted oversight of naval activities in the western Mediterranean. His prestige and future prospects had never seemed so high. Assigning authority over Kabylia in eastern Algeria to his brother Khayr al-Din, ʿAruj directed his attention toward the west and further showdowns with the Spanish. Toward the end of the year, he defeated the Spanish protégé Hamida al-ʿAwda, annexing the territories of Tanas and Milyana. His westward march seemed unstoppable.

In 1517, ʿAruj received an appeal for help from the inhabitants of Tlemcen, whose leader had allied himself with the Spanish. Entrusting Algiers to Khayr al-Din and the fortress of the Kalʿa of the Banu Rashid to Ishaq, ʿAruj and his troops took possession of Tlemcen. It all seemed too easy, and in fact ʿAruj had overextended himself by moving so far west. He seems to have sensed the danger he was in, so he sent an emissary to Fez with an appeal for aid from the Wattasid sultan. But no aid was forthcoming and ʿAruj would soon find himself unprepared for the Spanish counterattack that was heading his way.

In January 1518, the Spanish conquered the Kalʿa of the Banu Rashid, and ʿAruj lost access to his troops to the east. Not long afterward, a large Spanish force launched from Oran and, supplemented with tribal armies allied with Spain, laid siege to Tlemcen. ʿAruj and his troops were bottled up in the city for six months without reinforcements. Finally, in late summer 1518, ʿAruj escaped from Tlemcen with a few men. However, he was tracked down by Spanish soldiers and put to death. His ambitions had overcome his keen military sense, and ʿAruj had overextended himself with disastrous consequences.

Nevertheless, one should not underestimate the accomplishments of Baba ʿAruj. Through the efforts of ʿAruj and his brothers, the Ottoman Empire gained access to the Maghrebi provinces, which they would maintain into the nineteenth century. ʿArujʼs successor, Khayr al-Din, went on to have a successful career with the Ottomans, establishing Algiers as a regional power and being appointed admiral over the Ottoman navy in 1534. Though the empire had conquered Egypt in 1517, the Ottoman sultan seems to have been hesitant to commit troops to the distant lands of the Maghreb. However, the efforts of the Barbarossas not only forestalled Spanish conquest of North Africa, but they drew the Ottomans into the region, successfully keeping it in Muslim hands.

[*See also* Khayr al-Din.]

BIBLIOGRAPHY

Anonymous. *Fondation de la Régence dʼAlger: Histoire des frères Barberousse ʿAroûdj et Khair-ed-Dîn* [Foundation of the Regency of Algiers: History of the Barbarossa Brothers, ʿAruj and Khayr al-Din]. Translated by Jean-Michel Venture de Paradis. Algiers: Éditions Grand-Alger Livres, 2006.

Hess, Andrew C. *The Forgotten Frontier: A History of the Sixteenth-Century Ibero-African Frontier.* Chicago: University of Chicago Press, 1978.

Soucek, Svat. "The Rise of the Barbarossas in North Africa." *Archivum Ottomanicum* 3 (1971): 238–250.

Spencer, William. *Algiers in the Age of the Corsairs.* Norman: University of Oklahoma Press, 1976.

STEPHEN CORY

Babalola, Joseph Ayodele

Babalola, Joseph Ayodele (1904–1959), Nigerian religious leader, was born on 25 April 1904 in the town of Ilofa in southwestern Nigeria, to David Rotimi and Marta Talaba, both members of the large Yoruba ethnic community. His parents were Anglicans, and Babalolaʼs father was a church elder at the nearby town of Odo-Owa. Through his brotherʼs help, Babalola attended All Saints School in the larger city of Osobgo for a number of years, beginning in 1914. However, he never completed his secondary education. Instead, Babalola decided to learn a vocational trade, becoming a motor vehicle mechanic. After a short time, the local branch of the colonial public works department hired Babalola as a steamroller driver. He helped construct a road between the Nigerian towns Igbara-Oke and Isa and enjoyed a stable, if largely anonymous career.

That relative anonymity would vanish in 1928, when he became prominent in the Aladura revivals that had been sweeping through Yoruba communities since the Spanish influenza epidemic of 1918 and would continue through the 1930s. The Yoruba term *aladura* translates as "prayer" in English, and members of this movement emphasized both the power of prayer in providing the keys to material success and the importance of the Holy Spirit in healing and spiritually fortifying individuals. It never constituted a single church but instead was a movement that led

Yoruba-speaking Anglicans to leave the Church of England to form new denominations. Missionaries and many Western-educated Nigerian Christians argued that the Aladura prophets exaggerated their claims of spiritual gifts. Believers in the Aladura retorted that the Anglicans rejected divine healing, visions, and speaking in tongues, all of which could claim biblical foundation.

On 25 September 1928, Babalola started to struggle with headaches and insomnia for a week. He then had a dramatic experience while driving his steamroller. In his recollection of the incident, the engine stopped, and a loud disembodied voice called to Babalola three times commanding him to become a preacher. In keeping with Old Testament prophets who initially resisted such commands, Babalola only became convinced of the truth of this vision after the voice called to him multiple times. Much to the disappointment of his British supervisor, Babalola quit his job. Soon after leaving the public works department, Babalola had a second vision after the same mysterious voice told him to fast for a week. At the end, a man in a dazzling robe appeared before him and told him of his mission to drive away evil spiritual forces and to heal people of spiritual and physical illnesses. Babalola believed this man was Jesus Christ. The figure gave Babalola a bell to chase away malevolent forces and a bottle of blessed water that could heal people of any disease. The bell and the supernaturally infused water became important parts of Babalola's ministry. The former steamroller driver also claimed he regularly conversed with angels. One angel gave him a big yam to eat and told him that the yam was the tuber with which God fed the whole world. He further revealed that God had granted him the power to deliver those who were possessed of evil spirits. Babalola was told to go to Odo-Owa and start preaching. He was to arrive in the town on a market day, cover his body with palm fronds, and disfigure himself with charcoal paints. Babalola acted on these orders in October 1928 and called on people in the town to repent, but townspeople considered him to be suffering from a severe psychological problem rather than seeing him as a spiritual leader. A colonial official had him arrested, but then he was released. Soon after this, however, smallpox ravaged Odo-Owa, and some townspeople came to believe his message. Anglican missionaries disliked Babalola and doubted his gifts, but many Yoruba Anglicans preferred to follow Babalola.

In June 1930, Babalola left Odo-Owa for Lagos, the colonial capital of southern Nigeria.

Nigerian Pentecostals who had joined the United States–based Faith Tabernacle church welcomed Babalola as a minister who belonged to their tradition. Pastor Esinsinade baptized Babalola through full immersion, and Babalola soon became known for faith healing and preached all over southwest Nigeria. By this point, some Muslims and believers in Yoruba spiritual traditions had converted to Babalola's version of Christianity. At first, Babalola did not establish his own church. However, the Faith Tabernacle movement became divided over topics such as divine healing and accepting polygyny. This led to a meeting of the movement's council of leaders in July 1930. As these talks began, the meeting was interrupted by news that Babalola had resurrected a dead child. According to his followers, Babalola's prayer bell and healing water led to numerous other miracles. He also battled indigenous religious traditions in dramatic fashion. For example, in front of a local king's palace Babalola burned down a tree that was said to be a meeting ground of spirits. Methodist Wesleyan missionaries and some colonial officials joined Babalola's numerous critics, but he developed a large following throughout predominately Yoruba towns and cities. In 1932, an administrator had Babalola arrested and jailed for six months for leading antiwitchcraft campaigns in the Nigerian urban center of Benin City. After his release, he visited eastern Nigeria and eventually the Ghanaian city of Accra in the mid-1930s.

Nigerian members of the Faith Tabernacle like Babalola reached out to foreign Pentecostal missionaries, and Babalola joined the Apostolic Church based in Britain. However, Babalola left this denomination for the Christ Apostolic Church in 1943 after disputes over the use by missionaries of Western medicine caused controversy. Babalola argued that Western Pentecostals who relied on quinine and other medicines doubted faith healing. The CAC became one of the largest churches that originated in the Aladura revivals of the 1920s and 1930s. Babalola himself died in 1959, but the CAC expanded throughout Anglophone West Africa and eventually formed communities in Europe and North America. A university in Nigeria run by the CAC bore Babalola's name in the early twenty-first century. Despite Babalola's humble beginnings, he was a major figure in the rise of African-run independent churches in the twentieth century.

BIBLIOGRAPHY
Fatokun, Samson Adetunji. "The 'Great Move of God' in an African Community: A Retrospect of the

1930s Indigenous Pentecostal Revival in Nigeria
and Its Impact on Nigerian Pentecostalism."
Exchange 38, no. 1 (2009): 34–57.

Kalu, Ogbu. *African Pentecostalism: An Introduction.*
New York: Oxford University Press, 2008.

Peel, J. D. Y. *Aladura: A Religious Movement among the
Yoruba.* New York: Oxford University Press, 1968.

Shaw, Mark. *Global Awakening: How 20th-Century
Revivals Triggered a Christian Revolution.* Downers
Grove, Ill.: InterVarsity Press, 2010.

JEREMY RICH

Babangida, Ibrahim Badamosi (1941–), Nigerian
general, military ruler, and businessman was born
on 17 August 1941 in Minna, Nigeria, to Muhamadu,
a teacher, and his wife, Aishatu. After a childhood
in Minna, Babangida joined the Nigerian military
in 1962 and graduated from the Military Forces
Training College in Kaduna in 1963. He was then
sent to the Indian Military Academy in 1964 and to
the British Royal Armoured Center in 1966 before
returning to Nigeria in 1968, where he served as a
battalion captain and was wounded in 1969 at
Uzuakoli.

After the end of the Biafran civil war in 1970,
Babangida was promoted to major and taught at
the Nigerian Defence Academy. In 1972, he was
sent to the US Army Armor School at Fort Knox,
Kentucky, and upon his return was made a regimental commander in 1973. In 1975, General
Murtala Muhammed led a coup against the erstwhile head of the military government, Yakubu
Gowon, after the latter reneged on a promise to
return Nigeria to civilian rule. Muhammed
rewarded Babangida for his support by promoting
him to the army's armored corps commander. Both
Babangida and Olusegun Obasanjo were close
advisors to Muhammed when, on 13 February 1976,
Lieutenant Colonel Buka Suka Dimka engineered a
coup that killed Muhammed. Babangida and
Obasanjo were also targeted by the coup plotters,
yet they escaped and rallied loyal forces to defeat
the coup. Obasanjo was declared head of state and
Babangida remained head of the armored corps. In
1977, he completed his studies at the Command and
Staff College at Fort Leavenworth, Kansas, in the
United States.

In 1979, Obasanjo handed control of the Nigerian
state to civilian authorities under the elected president Shehu Shagari. Accused of corrupt policies
and deeply in debt after the collapse of oil prices
in 1981 and 1982, the Shagari regime became unpopular and was blamed for high unemployment.

Babangida helped orchestrate the overthrow of
Shagari's Second Republic and on 31 December
1983 led a coup that toppled the government and
installed Muhammadu Buhari as military head of
state. Babangida was subsequently promoted to
major general and made head of the Nigerian
Armed Forces.

The Buhari regime proved increasingly oppressive
and strained relations with the rest of the world.
Allegations of corruption, as well as investigations
into corruption in the military, coupled with increasing human rights abuses, including the imprisonment of dissidents and journalists without trial, led
Babangida to stage a bloodless coup against Buhari
in August 1985, after which Babangida placed himself
as head of the government.

Babangida's government at first sought to reverse
the excesses of Buhari's rule and vowed to restore
civilian rule by 1992. However, Babangida's rule
would be remembered as one of the most brutal
and repressive in Nigeria's history and would be
characterized by gross human rights abuses coupled with relatively open public debate over policy
issues. When responding to the financial crisis he
inherited, Babangida declared a referendum regarding acceptance of a structural adjustment program
(SAP) offered by the International Monetary Fund
(IMF). When Nigerians voted down the measure,
Babangida rejected the IMF's proposal and instituted his own SAP, which was almost identical to
the IMF's.

Babangida also released the journalists imprisoned by Buhari, but he embarked on a reign of
terror against the journalists who were opposed to
him. The most notable victim of this campaign was
Dele Giwa, killed by a letter bomb in 1986.

Babangida's attempt to transition to civilian rule
began with the establishment of political parties in
1989. However, once parties were allowed to form,
no fewer than thirteen parties formed, and
Babangida ruled that only approved parties, which
he himself created and named the Social Democratic
Party (SDP) and the National Republican
Convention (NRC), would be allowed to stand in
the parliamentary elections, which were held on
4 July 1992 with the SDP winning a majority in both
the Senate and the House of Representatives. The
run-up to the elections saw large-scale ethnic and
religious violence, prompting some journalists to
accuse Babangida of fomenting the violence as an
excuse to postpone the elections.

With presidential elections to be held in 1993,
the Independent National Electoral Commission

annulled the results of the first round of primaries, citing widespread fraud and vote irregularity as well as allegations of large-scale bribery. In April 1993, the SDP announced Moshood Abiola as its candidate for president, while the NRC selected Bashir Tofa. Presidential elections were finally held on 12 June 1993, resulting in Abiola's victory. Babangida quickly annulled the results without explanation and scheduled a new election but banned both Abiola and Tofa from running again. This act sparked widespread rioting, especially in the south of the country, which was brutally suppressed. On 26 August 1993, Babangida announced he would step down and handed power to Ernest Shonekan the next day. On 17 November, Sani Abacha, Shonekan's defense minister, took control of the government in another bloodless coup. Babangida, who was in Egypt during the coup, returned to Nigeria and settled in his home in Minna.

At the height of his powers, critics had given Babangida the nickname "Maradona" because his political tricks and feints resembled the devious skills of the Argentine soccer star Diego Maradona. But by the beginning of the twenty-first century, it appeared that his career had run its course. He did, however, seek a further presidential bid. In 2010, Babangida declared that he would seek the People's Democratic Party's nomination for the presidential elections in 2011. On 1 October of that year, a series of car bombs detonated in the capital, Abuja, during celebrations of Nigeria's Fiftieth Independence Day, killing at least eighteen people. Raymond Dokpesi, Babangida's campaign manager, was subsequently arrested for involvement in the bombing. This incident, coupled with widespread opposition from across the political spectrum, eventually persuaded Babangida to withdraw from the primaries, which were won by the incumbent, President Goodluck Jonathan.

[*See also* Abacha, Sani; Abiola, Moshood Kashimawo Olawale; Gowon, Yakubu Jack; Jonathan, Goodluck; *and* Obasanjo, Olusegun.]

BIBLIOGRAPHY

Diamond, Larry, Anthony Kirk-Greene, and Oyeleye Oyediran, eds. *Transition without End: Nigerian Politics and Civil Society under Babangida.* Boulder, Colo.: Lynne Rienner, 1997.

Falola, Toyin, and Matthew Heaton. *A History of Nigeria.* Cambridge, UK: Cambridge University Press, 2008.

Haynes, J. "Mobilising Yoruba Popular Culture: Babangida Must Go." *Africa: Journal of the International African Institute* 73, no. 1 (2003): 77–87.

Reno, William. *Warlord Politics and African States.* Boulder, Colo.: Lynne Rienner, 1998.

ROY DORON

Baba of Karo (c. 1890–1951), an intelligent Hausa woman of Karo village in the then Zaria Province of northern Nigeria, was born to a polygynous Hausa father of Kanuri descent, Tosho, who was a farmer and a qur'anic teacher. As a successful farmer, Tosho owned many slaves, who did most of the cultivation and marketing of his farm products. Paradoxically, his family prosperity depended on slavery and also evaporated because of slave raids and the final emancipation of slaves. Her mother, Fatsuma, was a secluded Muslim woman who prepared food and spun cotton for sale. Baba of Karo is also known as Baba Hasetu Dantsoho.

All that is known about Baba is based on interviews she granted to Mary Smith, the wife of Michael Smith, a Jamaican social anthropologist who did field research in northern Nigeria in the 1940s and 1950s. The interviews were carried out between November 1949 and January 1950 at Giwa town and Zaria city. They were recorded in Hausa almost verbatim as dictated by Baba and were later translated and published in English as an autobiography, *Baba of Karo: A Woman of the Muslim Hausa*, with an introduction by Michael Smith and elaborate endnotes, which help to contextualize certain segments of the story.

Baba revealed intimate information about her life and aspects of Hausa history in the nineteenth and twentieth centuries. She outlined her childhood and adult experiences, family genealogy, and complex kinship relationships. Typical of Hausa daughters of secluded Muslim wives, Baba started work at an early age, selling a variety of processed foods for her mother. She also traded in foodstuffs for herself before she got married. As required by custom and religious obligations, Baba's father arranged her first marriage to one of her kinsmen, Duma Sidi, around 1904, when she was fourteen years old. She later divorced him in spite of her family's objections because she wanted to leave her village and experience town life. She maintained a friendly relationship with him due to their kinship ties, even after she married her second husband, Malam Maigari, an Islamic teacher and farmer. As a secluded married woman, Baba engaged in spinning and weaving of coarse cotton and in food preparation. Her many adopted daughters sold the products for her. She also accompanied her husband on many of his religious trips. After a few years of marriage, Baba divorced Malam Maigari and later married two more husbands: Yari Malam Hasan, a prison warden and farmer, with whom Baba lived for fifteen years, and Ibrahim Dantsoho. Dantsoho was a farmer and a polygynist; he could not build a hut for Baba, so they lived separately. Baba lived in her younger brother's compound, and he occasionally supported her financially. She also reared a few goats inherited from her father, spun cotton, and sold firewood. While she had no children of her own, midwifery was part of her kinship obligations. Sometimes she helped in the delivery of her relatives' children, but mostly she attended to the mother and child after birth, for periods lasting up to three weeks.

In telling the story of her life experiences, Baba sheds light on many aspects of precolonial Hausa society and the changes brought by British rule. Hausa women's political role was limited—while some served as messengers of local chiefs (*jakadiya*), others became *magajiya* (heads of Bori-dancers or prostitutes). *Magajiya* in pre-Islamic Hausa was a female title usually held by a king's sister or daughter. But after 1900, when Hausa oral traditions acknowledged the existence of prostitution, *magajiya* became a title conferred on the female head of a group of prostitutes in a village or town or district. The autobiography also highlights the importance of pre-Islamic customs well into the twentieth century. In Baba's time, as in precolonial and postcolonial periods, the Bori cult and spirit possession played an important role in Hausa life and culture. At Hausa markets, ritual Bori dancing continued as ceremonies to appease the spirits, purify the marketplace, and retain its mystic character and commercial vitality.

Her story captures the ambivalence of the institution of marriage vis-à-vis the status of Hausa women. In a Hausa maiden's first marriage, where she was required by custom to accept whomever her family arranged for her to marry, or in betrothal marriage and marriage of alms, Hausa women's rights were undermined. But they enjoyed enormous freedom in their subsequent marriages and in divorce. Such freedom may have contributed to the instability of Hausa marriages and the high incidence of divorce. Among the different forms of marriage in Hausa society were parallel, patrilateral, and matrilateral cross-cousin marriages. First marriages for Hausa girls came between the ages of thirteen and fourteen years.

Often their parents arranged such marriages to paternal or maternal kinsmen. There was also a marriage of alms, where daughters were given away in marriage as gifts to respected Muslim men as an act of religious piety, which ensured local prestige. The Hausa also practiced infant-betrothal marriage. Baba also reveals the nature of marriage ceremonies. This included the payment of the *sadaki*, the only payment required in Muslim law to be made by the bridegroom to the bride's guardian to legally establish a marriage and which must be returned to the husband upon divorce.

The autobiography indicates the pervasive Islamic influence in twentieth-century Hausa society. Marriages and the political system were guided by Islamic law. Through qur'anic teaching and conversion, pagan slaves and their children were acculturated into Hausa and Islamic culture and subsequently absorbed into their masters' families. Those who were adopted, as was the case with Usuman, Baba's first adopted son, enjoyed the same rights as biological children except inheritance rights. The status of a free woman who married a slave man never changed; she remained free just as her children did. Similarly, a slave woman who became her master's concubine and had children with him regained her freedom and could leave the man and marry. Slaves in Hausa society enjoyed such other rights as having their own quarters (*rinji*), where whatever they grew on their own plots belonged to them. There was a high incidence of slave raids and kidnapping in Hausa society even after Lugard's Slavery Proclamation, which declared children born after 1 April 1901 in the Protectorate of Northern Nigeria free. It did not end slavery but prevented masters or owners from recovering runaway slaves through the courts.

Baba died on 3 June 1951 and is remembered as a courageous woman of independent will whose intellect and sharp memory led to the production of an autobiography.

BIBLIOGRAPHY

Coles, Catherine, and Beverly Mack, eds. *Hausa Women in the Twentieth Century.* Madison: University of Wisconsin Press, 1991.

Robson, Elsbeth. "Sub-Saharan Africa: Hausa Societies." In *Encyclopedia of Women and Islamic Culture,* edited by Suad Joseph et al. 6 vols. Vol. 2: *Family, Law and Politics,* pp. 135–137. Leiden, Netherlands: Brill, 2005.

Smith, Mary F. *Baba of Karo: A Woman of the Muslim Hausa.* With an introduction and notes by

M. G. Smith and a foreword by Hilda Kuper. New Haven, Conn.: Yale University Press, 1981.

Williams, Pat. "Impact of Islam on Women in Hausaland and Northern Nigeria." In *The Foundations of Nigeria: Essays in Honor of Toyin Falola,* edited by Adebayo Oyebade, pp. 591–621. Trenton, N.J.: Africa World Press, 2003.

GLORIA CHUKU

Babikr Badri (1861–1954), Sudanese educator and memoirist, was born in a village on the Atbara, the son of Muhammad al-Sadiq al-Tayyib of the Rubatab tribe and Madina bint al-Nur. With them he moved in boyhood to Rufa'a on the Blue Nile. There, after a traditional qu'ranic education, he became an early adherent of Muhammad Ahmad, the Mahdi. He fought in major engagements of the Mahdiyya, including the decisive battle of Omdurman (Karari), after which he returned to Rufa'a. His famous memoir, *Ta'rikh Hayati*, remains an important eyewitness account for events of that and subsequent periods.

It is for Babikr Badri's long career as an educator that he is famous. He became headmaster of the first primary school at Rufa'a in 1903. Despite a traditional Sudanese upbringing he had a more liberal attitude toward girls' education than officials of the new Anglo-Egyptian colonial regime. And with little formal training as a teacher, he overcame both official and local Sudanese opposition to open the country's first secular girls' school in 1907, long before Khartoum or Omdurman had one. Largely through personal effort and dogged determination he oversaw successive improvements and expansion in this school and in girls' education generally. After World War I, when, in reaction to Egyptian nationalism and its apprehended results in the Sudan, the British curtailed the secular education of boys and the role of the educated elite, girls' education continued to expand. Babikr Badri led also by example, enrolling his own female relatives in government schools.

Babikr Badri was instrumental in establishing "modernized *khalwas*"—simple "subprimary" schools where there had been none—and extending *khalwa* education to the nomadic population, a system later abused by the regime to replace rather than complement the modern sector. He became an inspector in the department of education, a position requiring much travel in the northern Sudan, eventually including even the Nuba Mountains and as far west as Dar Masalit. In this role he increasingly turned his attention to administrative problems, including

teacher training and the production of textbooks and other materials.

He was, for a time, able to succeed remarkably in this work without compromising the political views born of a keen observation of the conduct and results of the colonial encounter. Balancing loyalty to the Mahdist cult with a critical view of British educational and administrative policy, he adhered to the attitude encapsulated in the slogan "the Sudan for the Sudanese" espoused by the Mahdi's son, Sayyid Abd al-Rahman. He incurred the wrath especially of the government's intelligence department because, although like all Mahdists he opposed attempts by Egypt and its Sudanese allies to foster a union between the two countries, he favored a time limit for British tutelage. The implicit evolution of the Mahdist cult into what would be called "neo-Mahdism" was not obvious, and British officials feared fanaticism. Official attempts to suborn Babikr Badri as a spy failed. Yet as a moderate he could not escape scorn from younger—and especially pro-Egyptian—elements of the Sudan's emerging nationalist "intelligentsia." For this period, as indeed for the colonial era generally, his memoirs are a rich primary source.

During the Revolution of 1924 Babikr Badri maintained his position as a leading moderate nationalist. His attempt to mediate the revolt of the Khartoum Military School's cadets was aborted, with loss of face. His position as a leading Sudanese official of a regime now increasingly set against the advancement in government of Sudanese was anomalous, and it was apparently largely for private financial reasons as much as love of education that he remained employed.

In 1927 Shaykh Babikr was appointed inspector of *khalwa*s for the entire country. His indefatigability now added to a legend already established as an educator; one trek in 1927–1928, performed entirely on donkey-back, lasted 127 days. He finally and reluctantly retired from government service in February 1929.

It was partly in response to the reactionary policies of the regime that Babikr Badri then embarked on the causes that occupied the rest of his life: the privately financed local schools of the *ahliyya* movement, and especially the private Ahfad girls' school, which moved from Rufa'a to Omdurman in 1932. It expanded in 1933 to include an intermediate section and, after government opposition was finally overcome, added a secondary course in 1943. Babikr Badri died in 1954. The Ahfad University for Women, founded in Omdurman in 1966 by his son, Yousef, may be seen as the culmination of his work.

[*See also* Muhammad Ahmad ibn ʿAbdallah.]

BIBLIOGRAPHY

Badri, Babikr. *The Memoirs of Babikr Badri*. Vol. 1. Translated by Yousef Badri. London: Oxford University Press, 1969. Deals with the author's life until the end of the Mahdiyya in 1898.

Badri, Babikr. *The Memoirs of Babikr Badri*. Vol. 2. Translated by Yusuf Badri and Peter Hogg. London: Oxford University Press, 1980. Takes the author's story from 1898 to his retirement in 1929.

Badri, Babikr. *Taʾrikh hayati*. Vols. 1–3. Umm Durmān: Author, 1961.

M. W. DALY

Badawi, Suʿad al-Fatih Mohammed al- (1932–), Sudanese intellectual, educator, political leader, and women's advocate, was born on 1 January 1932 in the city of El Obeid, Province of Kordofan, and raised by an Islamic family. Her grandfather, al-Shaykh Mohammed al-Badawi, was a prominent Islamic scholar, and his house in Omdurman was a gathering place for well-known Islamic scholars from North Africa, such as al-Shaykh Mohammed Abdu of Egypt. Al-Badawi's father, al-Fatih Mohammed al-Badawi, was a district commissioner who replaced the position of the British officer after Sudan independence in 1956. Although girls' formal education was boycotted by the masses for being based on Western values, he was an open-minded and progressive individual with liberal ideas regarding girls' education. In this atmosphere al-Badawi and her two sisters were raised.

As a district commissioner, al-Badawi's father's moved and worked in different regions of Sudan. This situation compelled al-Badawi to receive her elementary, intermediate, and secondary education in different cities of Sudan, including El Obeid, Berber, Atbara, Khartoum, and Omdurman. She studied in missionary schools and in one school run by the government. In 1956, al-Badawi obtained her BA degree from Gordon Memorial College, Khartoum, Sudan, and was one of four pioneering women who graduated from the Faculty of Arts. Upon graduation, she worked as a secondary school teacher. Despite the fact that most Muslim women in her country were confined to their homes, al-Badawi traveled and obtained degrees, including a BA, with honors, in Arabic in 1958 and an MA degree in Arabic in 1961 from the School of Oriental and African Studies at the University of London.

Upon her return from England, al-Badawi was appointed head of the History Department in the Institute for Training Intermediate School Teachers, then she became inspector of education at the Ministry of Education, in Khartoum, Sudan. In 1969 she worked as a consultant for the United Nations Educational, Scientific and Cultural Organization (UNESCO) in Saudi Arabia, after which she was assigned as expert for girls' education in Saudi Arabia. Al-Badawi continued her work in Saudi Arabia, holding the position of dean of the Girls' College of Education in Riyadh, where she was one of the founders of the college. She was also a chief editor of the college magazine.

In 1974, al-Badawi earned her PhD in Arabic from the University of Khartoum. In 1980 she was appointed as associate professor of Arabic in Omdurman Islamic University, Sudan, and worked as a deputy vice chancellor of the University of the United Arab Emirates. In 1983 she again returned to Sudan to serve as dean of the Girls' College Omdurman Islamic University, the first Sudanese woman to hold the position. During her sabbatical leave in 1991–1992, as postdoctoral fellow at the University of Edinburgh in Scotland, she conducted research in the Department of Islamic and Middle Eastern Studies, where she also taught Arabic language.

In 1952, al-Badawi was one of the founders of the Sudanese Women's Union and a member of its executive committee, where she served as treasurer. She worked in several positions in the union to improve the quality of life of the Sudanese girls and women. In 1952 al-Badawi was the first to represent the Sudanese Women's Union at the Arab Women's Conference in Cairo, Egypt. She was also among the delegation in Moscow representing the Sudanese Women's Union in the Soviet Women's Conference in 1957. In the same year, al-Badawi was head of the Sudanese Women Journalist Delegation to the United Kingdom and France. Because of political conflicts, al-Badawi and other members left the Sudanese Women's Union, and in 1964 she founded and became president of the National Women's Front, which stressed Islamic values. She also founded *al-Manar* magazine, where she worked as chief editor. Al-Badawi's advocacy for women's rights is remarkable. She has stressed that women are obligated to become ardent intellectuals and full participants in society. Al-Badawi has maintained a balance between her generally progressive position on women's rights and that of the conservative Islamic context. Al-Badawi produced a weekly program for television and radio broadcasting in Sudan. She has been a column writer in numerous Sudanese daily newspapers, including *al-Ayam*, *al-Rai al-Am*, and *al-Sudan al-Jadeed*.

In 1992–1993, al-Badawi worked as secretary general of the International Islamic Women Center; in 1995–2000, she was secretary-general of the International Muslim Women Union, and she established the International Muslim Women Union in Pakistan. She participated in a wide range of international conferences, where she presented papers such as "Problem of Girls' Education in the Arab Countries" at a UNESCO conference in Algiers, "Women in Society" in Morocco, "The Problem of Working Women" for the International Labour Organization in Switzerland, "Muslim Celebration of the Fifteenth Century of the Hijra" in Hong Kong, "African Women Leaders" for a Cross-Roads Africa seminar in the United States, "Women and the Market of Labor" in Qatar, and "Muslim Women Forum" in Indonesia. Inside Sudan, al-Badawi served as a member of several boards of trustees: Omdurman Islamic University, University of Khartoum, al-Nilain University, and the Holy Qur'an and Islamic Sciences University.

As a political leader, al-Badawi held many positions in Sudan's parliament. In 1981 she was a member of the Fourth People's Council, from 1980 to 1989 she served as member and head of the Education and Scientific Research Committee of the Constituent Assembly, and from 1996 to 2005 she was a member of the National Assembly. In 2004 she was a member of the Pan Africa Parliament in South Africa. In 2000 al-Badawi worked as advisor for Women and Child Affairs for the president of Sudan.

Underscoring her academic and public achievements, al-Badawi has been honored by various institutions both inside and outside Sudan. In Sudan, she received approximately twenty acknowledgments and awards, from both governmental and nongovernmental organizations, including the government's Two Niles Award and the Golden Star for Science and Arts, and the Shield of Excellency from the Saudi-Arabian government, the Pioneering Medal of Excellence from the United Arab Emirates, the Golden Medal for Arab Women Pioneer from the king of Bahrain, and an honorary membership in the British Journalist's Club. Al-Badawi is married with three children and is still pursuing her role as a political leader, women's rights activist, spokesperson, and intellectual.

Badawi has served her country, Sudan, in a range of capacities and roles, and she continues to do so in several different fields, including social, educational, and political. Her work has expanded to include countries on the African continent and beyond it, including Saudi Arabia, United Arab Emirates, Scotland, and Bahrain.

BIBLIOGRAPHY

Badri, Haga Kashif. *Al-Harakah al-nisaiyah fi al-Sudan* [Women's Movement in the Sudan]. Khartoum: Khartoum University Press, 1984.

Hale, Sondra. *Gender Politics in Sudan: Islamism, Socialism, and the State*. Boulder, Colo.: Westview Press, 1996.

Hall, Marjorie, and Bakhita Amin Ismail. *Sisters under the Sun*. London: Longman, 1981.

BAQI'E BADAWI MUHAMMAD

Badi III (d. 1716), Funj king nicknamed "the Red," saw the Funj kingdom (in present-day Sudan) reach its apogee of power under his rule (AH 1103/1692 CE to AH 1128/1716 CE). Badi was a competent ruler, if perhaps not the equal of his second predecessor and namesake, who had been reputed the wisest man in the kingdom. The king resided at the capital city of Sinnar in a great palace complex of packed earth surrounded in part by a palisade of thorn boughs and surmounted by a lofty five-story tower. Before the gates of the palace lay the *fashir*, a great open square where state festivals were held and where a great weekly market took place. Slave attendants policed the market while leading Badi's royal lions; it was considered judicious to give them something. On Fridays, Badi and his entourage processed across the *fashir* to the royal mosque for noonday prayers, after which he often spent the afternoon at his suburban riverside estates, where he enjoyed his gardens of lemon trees and imported roses or sharpened his aim as a practiced musketeer.

The days of Badi III are unusually accessible to historians through the eyes of numerous foreign visitors. Regular royally sponsored caravans to neighboring lands brought back exotic goods, ideas, traders, and craftsmen to Sinnar, which burgeoned into a huge and cosmopolitan metropolis characterized by tolerance and optimism. Each newcomer appeared before the king, who granted him a legitimate place in the realm by pronouncing his name and vocation formally and directly from the throne. (Under these circumstances the king's word was law.) The newcomer was then assigned to an official patron at court who supervised his economic activities and, if necessary, represented his legal and political interests.

The new urban culture centered at the capital, however, was controversial in several respects.

Merchants accustomed to the market practices of the Mediterranean or Red Sea chafed at the system of royally fixed prices, pegged to the gold ounce, that prevailed in Sinnar. They began to import coins, conspicuously of silver, that permitted traders both foreign and native to challenge the royal command economy with the logic of the free market. Increasing contact with the Islamic heartlands exposed features of Funj culture that seemed odd or even wrong by mainstream standards. In addition to royal restraints on trade, Funj sumptuary laws, dietary customs, kinship practices, and royal claims to legal authority were increasingly seen as controversial. Provincial lords, particularly in the north, resented their exclusion from the economic processes that gathered wealth at the royal capital.

It was said that Badi III was the first Funj king against whom a section of his own people revolted (1705–1706). The figurehead of the rebellion was a prince named Awkal, who had succeeded in escaping to Darfur when his half-brother assumed the throne. (Such princes, by law, were to be executed by a court official titled *sid al-qum*, precisely to avoid sedition.) The leader of the uprising was a high court official and royal kinsman, the *amin* Irdab, supported by the governors of the large and important provinces of the north and the White Nile. After initial setbacks Badi regained the upper hand and repulsed the rebels' assault on his capital. However, the underlying causes of the revolt were not addressed, and they would soon return to challenge the dynasty.

[*See also* Badi IV.]

BIBLIOGRAPHY

Hasan, Yusuf Fadl, ed. *Kitab al-tabaqat fi khusus al-awliya'*. Khartoum: Khartoum University Press, 1971.

Holt, P. M. *The Sudan of the Three Niles: The Funj Chronicle 910–1228/1504–1871*. Leiden, Netherlands: Brill, 1999.

O'Fahey, R. S., and Jay L. Spaulding. *Kingdoms of the Sudan*. London: Methuen, 1974.

Spaulding, Jay. *The Heroic Age in Sinnar*. Trenton, N.J.: Red Sea Press, 2006.

Spaulding, Jay, and Muhammad Ibrahim Abu Salim. *Public Documents from Sinnar*. East Lansing: Michigan State University Press, 1989.

JAY SPAULDING

Badi IV (d. 1762), king of Sinnar in present-day Sudan (r. AH 1136/1724 CE to AH 1175/1762 CE), was nicknamed "Abu Shulukh," perhaps because of conspicuous facial cicatrization. He assumed the throne as a youth on the death of his father, Nol. The regent Doka, remembered as "the Good Wazir," ruled the kingdom until 1142/1729–1730, and from the latter year until 1156/1742–1743 the regency was held by Badi's maternal uncle, Isma'il. Badi emerged from his minority in 1744 during the Second Ethiopian War; it was said that the Sudanese victory could be attributed to his leadership in prayer.

Upon his personal assumption of power Badi took steps to change fundamentally the organization of the government of Sinnar. He was the first king to personify the rejection of matrilineal succession among the nobility of Sinnar. Badi's father, Nol, although he himself belonged to the old elite, made his son Badi the first and founding member of a new patrilineal dynasty. It may be that Badi's own mother did not belong to the Unsab, the royal clan whose womenfolk alone could bequeath Funj noble status; from a traditional perspective the young king would have been by birth a mere commoner. As Badi matured he refused to sequester his sons in the palace in traditional fashion, and gossip accumulated concerning the public misdeeds of these conspicuous princes. While details are lacking, Badi took violent steps to cripple the power of the old Funj elite and conspicuously lashed out at the erstwhile regent Isma'il, who as Badi's maternal uncle under the traditional Funj constitution would have ranked as the *sid al-qum,* the official assigned to execute a monarch when rejected by his court. Normally the *sid al-qum* was banned from the court deliberations that decided a king's fate, but Isma'il during his highly anomalous regency would have been both young Badi's judge and executioner.

Badi's most lasting contribution was to change the composition of the royal court through which a king of Sinnar governed his realm. When Badi assumed power, the court comprised about twenty members. Some were high-ranking members of the royal clan (the absent *sid al-qum* was represented by an agent), while others were noblemen who served as provincial governors; slave officials who staffed the treasury, the arsenal, and commanded the standing army; or Islamic holy men who handled government records in Arabic and staffed the royal mosque. Badi tripled the size of the court by admitting two new constituencies; about twenty popular leaders of vernacular Islam, and a similar number of junior noblemen entitled *arbab*—men who, unless they won the hand of a Funj princess, would produce commoner offspring.

Now their status, like that of the king himself, became hereditary in the male line.

The abandonment of matrilineal Funj kinship discipline generated escalating discord among the quarrelsome new patrilineages. Badi was deposed and exiled by a coalition of disaffected elements dubbed the Hamaj ("non-noblemen") in 1175/1762 and assassinated soon thereafter.

[*See also* Badi III.]

BIBLIOGRAPHY

Hasan, Yusuf Fadl, ed. *Kitab al-tabaqat fi khusus al-awliya'*. Khartoum: Khartoum University Press, 1971.

Holt, P. M. *The Sudan of the Three Niles: The Funj Chronicle 910–1228/1504–1871*. Leiden, Netherlands: Brill, 1999.

O'Fahey, R. S., and Jay L. Spaulding. *Kingdoms of the Sudan*. London: Methuen, 1974.

Spaulding, Jay. *The Heroic Age in Sinnar*. Trenton, N.J.: Red Sea Press, 2006.

Spaulding, Jay, and Muhammad Ibrahim Abu Salim. *Public Documents from Sinnar*. East Lansing: Michigan State University Press, 1989.

JAY SPAULDING

Badr al-Jamali, Abu al-Najm (r. 1074–1094), commander of the Fatimid armies in Egypt and Syria, was the first in a sixty-year era of Muslim viziers and military rulers of Armenian origin, a position he assumed following his restoration of order in the Fatimid lands after a period of political and social turmoil. Nothing is known about his birth or childhood, save the patronymic Ibn (son of) 'Abdallah, which is sometimes included in his full name and title. He was father to at least two sons: al-Awhad, whom he likely executed after a brief rebellion, and al-Afdal, who succeeded him as military vizier. The earliest references to Badr's life begin as an adolescent Mamluk (slave-soldier) in the service of a Fatimid governor of Aleppo around 1020. This official, 'Aziz al-Dawla, had apparently begun recruiting Mamluks into his military from among those Anatolian communities that retained a sense of their Armenian identity but had, in fact, converted to Islam in centuries previous. Following a brief crisis of dynastic leadership in the Fatimid state, it is likely that Badr participated in the assassination of his master, after which he disappeared from the Syrian scene for another forty years. He reemerged on the scene in a position of power and prestige during the 1060s, ascending as high as the position of governor of Damascus on at least two occasions during that decade, all the while using his experienced army to hold the Fatimid line in Syria against the Seljuq Turks, then at the peak of their authority in Iraq.

It was during that same decade that the weakened Fatimid state, based in Cairo, had fallen into a state of political and economic chaos brought upon by a spate of incompetent civilian administration and a breakout of violent rivalry between the various ethnic factions of the standing army (including Berber, Sudanese, and Turkish soldiery). In 1073, facing the imminent collapse of his government and dynasty after a decade of decline, the caliph al-Mustansir (r. 1036–1094) called upon Badr al-Jamali as the only official with the administrative clout and—more important—military backbone capable of saving the Fatimids. Badr answered the caliph's summons and quickly took charge of the situation, backed by his own private army of battle-tested Armenian soldiers, which included both Muslim converts and Christians, and which quickly took up residence within the once-exclusive dynastic city of Cairo. Armed with a caliphal mandate as well as this deeply loyal army, he quickly restored order in Egypt. This was no bloodless affair: he ended the ethnic chaos that had torn apart the Fatimid military by chasing down and summarily executing most of the commanders of the various army contingents, then forcibly bringing under his control the remaining militias that had spread across Egypt in what were essentially regional enclaves.

When the dust settled, the victorious Badr al-Jamali assumed the powerful role of vizier, second in title only to al-Mustansir himself, and appointed with tremendous pomp and circumstance by the caliph. However, this was not a clerical vizierate like those that had marked all previous Fatimid regimes; this was a military vizierate, in which Badr assumed all of the responsibilities of running the state—including those unique to the Fatimids' Ismaili Shi'i identity, such as heading the *da'wa* (proselytizing mission of the faith)—but backed by an army loyal to him rather than to the caliphate. The Fatimid caliphate, once marked by powerful figures such as al-Mu'izz, al-'Aziz, and the controversial al-Hakim, was essentially relegated to the spiritual office of imam, with little practical clout in running the state. This system was his most important historical legacy, as it persisted throughout the so-called Armenian period, which lasted for several decades and, indeed, to the end of the Fatimid state in the 1170s. Badr adopted many honorific and practical titles during his reign as vizier, and yet it is telling that he is best remembered in the historical record by his military title, *amir al-juyush* (commander of the armies); all properties and military contingents beholden to him were henceforth and historically identified as *juyushi*.

Despite the fact that Badr al-Jamali's subsequent career is poorly documented in the historical record, including his death in 1094 long after appointing his younger son al-Afdal to succeed him (the same year as his patron al-Mustansir), there are several aspects of his vizierate that left a noteworthy mark on the Fatimid lands in Egypt (Syria and Palestine were lost to the Seljuk Turks early in his vizierate). First, he complemented military success with economic recovery, chiefly by instituting a period of agricultural tax reform that appears to have relieved the countryside's financial woes and allowed the Egyptian economy to grow significantly until late in his career. Second, he took seriously the unofficial mandate of Islamic rulers to leave their mark on the monumental landscape of their lands, commissioning several structures in Cairo that stand to this day as landmarks of the medieval city: *bab al-futuh* (Gate of the Conquests), *bab al-nasr* (Gate of Victory), *bab zuwayla* (Gate of Zuwayla, a locally quartered Berber tribe), and the modest Juyushi Mosque, perched atop the Muqattam Hills. Finally, perhaps as a result of his own early background and the affinity he had long enjoyed with his Armenian soldiers, Badr maintained a unique relationship with his non-Muslim subjects, especially the local Christian communities. It was he who requested that the Coptic Orthodox patriarch move his main residence from Alexandria to Cairo, ostensibly out of the practical matter of keeping this important confession leadership close to his own center of power. This does not seem to have led to significant antagonism; in fact, contemporary Coptic sources writing in Arabic, such as Abu al-Makarim (long misidentified as Abu Salih the Armenian) and the authors of the semiofficial *History of the Patriarchs of the Egyptian Church*, wrote of Badr in terms that one could describe as positively warm. The latter, for example, relates one incident in which the vizier personally oversees the reconciliation of the Coptic leadership after a bitter fight, in his own garden, and seals the occasion by give them a stern, well-reasoned sermon on how they should treat one another.

[*See also* 'Aziz, al-; Hakim, al-; *and* Mustansir Biallah, Ma'ad al-.]

BIBLIOGRAPHY

al-Muqaffa', Sawirus Ibn. *History of the Patriarchs of the Church of Alexandria*. Translated and annotated by Yassa 'Abd al-Masih and O. H. E. Burmester. Cairo: Société d'Archéologie Copte, 1943. This section of the Coptic Orthodox patriarchate's semiofficial history, which is strongest in its coverage of the tenth through thirteenth centuries, includes a detailed account of Badr's intervention with the Coptic leadership—a unique perspective and historical memory of the powerful commander.

Dadoyan, Seta B. *The Fatimid Armenians: Cultural and Political Interaction on the Near East*. Leiden, Netherlands: Brill, 1997. The most thorough examination of not only the "Armenian period" of Fatimid rule in Egypt but also the religious and political context of the Armenians themselves before, during, and after their ascendance to power in that era. A unique series of Armenian- and Arabic-language documents relevant to the period are included in the appendix.

Lev, Yaacov. *State and Society in Fatimid Egypt*. Leiden, Netherlands: Brill, 1991. While Dadoyan focuses on the Badr's rule in the context of the Armenian movement, and Walker (below) does so in the context of the sweeping narrative of Fatimid history, this text places Badr, as well as his predecessors and successors, squarely within the context of Egyptian society and domestic policy. An essential text on how the Fatimids, including Badr al-Jamali, related to the populace who remained most directly under their control.

Walker, Paul E. *Exploring an Islamic Empire: Fatimid History and Its Sources*. London: I. B. Tauris, 2002. A crucial text on the narrative and historiography of the Fatimids, including an efficient and well-contextualized discussion of the origin, impact, and legacy of Badr's vizierate.

KURT WERTHMULLER

Baeta, Robert (1883–1944), religious leader, was born in 1883 in the Togolese capital of Lomé. His full name was Robert Domingos Gonçalves Baeta. His family belonged to the small but influential Afro-Brazilian community who were the descendants of former slaves who had returned to West Africa. His family chose to send Baeta to mission schools run by the Protestant North German Mission (Norddeutsche Missionsgesellschaft), along with two of his sisters, who later became active in Christian ministry as well. Even though German military officers only established a protectorate over southern Togo over the course of the second half of the 1880s, North German Mission pastors had already established schools in southern Togo in the mid-nineteenth century. Baeta proved to be an impressive student. The German pastor Johann Conrad Binder worked with Ewe-speaking Togolese pastors such as Christian Aliwodzi Sedode to create a new generation of Ewe-speaking pastors. Nineteen men graduated from Binder's training college between 1871 and 1900, and Baeta stayed in Germany from 1897 to 1900 to further his theological training. Baeta was raised in the home of his fellow pastor Andreas Aku and married Sedode's only daughter, Henriette.

Baeta became an active defender of the interests of Western-educated coastal Ewe people. Although he strongly endorsed the benefits of German rule for promoting economic and educational opportunities for Togolese people, he also expressed his demands for improved rights for colonial subjects. He endorsed the call for vocational training advocated by the African American educator Booker T. Washington, whose ideas were also supported by colonial officials and German missionaries. Shortly before World War I, Baeta wrote a petition to the German governor of Togo, the Duke of Mecklenburg. Baeta demanded the abolition of the use of chains to imprison Africans, corporal punishment, forced labor, and recently introduced poll and income taxes. Many other affluent Ewe leaders signed the petition as well. The Duke of Mecklenburg promised to look into these matters, but the onset of war in 1914 put an end to German rule. French and English troops quickly subdued German colonial forces in the first months of the conflict.

Despite the consequent disruption of the North German Mission's activities in Togo, Baeta was ordained as a minister in 1917. Baeta remained an advocate of limited legal rights for Togolese people, and he praised the British military administration for ending forced labor and for considering the removal of unpopular chiefs. Baeta's flexibility proved useful after 1919, when France was awarded control over most of the former German colony. Although many Togolese resented the return of forced labor under French rule, Baeta accommodated himself and his church community to the new rulers. For example, Baeta lauded Governor Auguste Bonnecarrère, head of Togo from 1922 to 1927, as a wise authority who was willing to listen to the advice of prominent Ewe men. Rather than ask for the return of the North German Mission pastors who had been expelled from the colony,

Baeta called for the creation of an independent Ewe church to be aided by the French Protestant Société Missionnaire Evangélique de Paris rather than remain affiliated with the Germans or be absorbed by another missionary church, such as the French Methodists. Togolese intellectuals who called for the return of German rule disliked Baeta as a result. However, Baeta maintained friendly ties with his former mentors. In 1924, Baeta visited Germany and wrote about his experiences, and he endorsed German presentations of Togo as a model colony. Yet he stayed in the good graces of the French, and the colonial administration appointed Baeta on the largely powerless Conseil des Notables in the capital of Lomé. Baeta continued to call for legal rights for Togolese people, even though he did not join the violent 1933 protests against abusive chiefs in Lomé.

Baeta was a major figure in the formation of the independent Ewe church that later became the Église Evangélique du Togo. He wrote hymns, helped to obtain scholarships for Togolese students to attend schools in France and Germany, and served as the secretary to the head pastor Andreas Aku. Baeta had little respect for indigenous spirituality, in keeping with his education. He wrote in one essay, "These words [a biblical text denouncing 'heathendom'] also apply to my poor native country, which unfortunately still is filled with the darkness of heathendom and is dominated by it to by far the largest extent." Yet his hymns drew from traditional Togolese rhythms such as Akpessse and Agbadza. His death in 1944 was a milestone in the history of Togolese Protestantism, as Baeta was the last living male church leader who had emerged before World War I. One of his sons, Christian Baeta, became a major Protestant pastor in his own right, albeit in the neighboring country of Ghana.

[*See also* Aku, Martin Andréas.]

BIBLIOGRAPHY

Altena, Thorsten. *"Ein Häuflien Christen mitten in der Heidenwelt des dunklen Erdteils": Zum Selbst-under Fremdverständis protestantischer Missionare im kolonialen Afrika, 1884–1918* ["A Little Christian in the Middle of the Heathen World of the Dark Continent": From Self to Other Understandings of Protestant Missionaries in Colonial Africa, 1884–1914]. Münster, Germany: Waxmann Verlag, 2003.

Debrunner, Hans. *A Church between Colonial Powers: A Study of the Church in Togo.* London: Lutterworth Press, 1965.

Oloukpone-Yinnon, Adjai Paulin, and Jonás Riesz, eds. *Plumes allemandes: Biographies et autobiographies africaines* [German Pens: African Biographies and Autobiographies]. Lomé, France: Presses de l'Université de Lomé, 2003.

JEREMY RICH

Bagaza, Jean-Baptiste (1946–), president of Burundi (1976–1987), was born in Rutovu (province of Bururi), to a Tutsi-Hima family of the Bashingo clan. After primary and secondary studies in the Catholic schools of the capital, Bujumbura, he undertook a military career that led him to the École Royale des Cadets in Belgium from 1966 to 1971. Returning to his country the same year, he was named adjunct chief of staff for the Burundian army in 1972. On 1 November 1976, he overthrew General Michel Micombero, a Tutsi officer also from the commune of Rutovu, who had abolished the monarchy and installed the First Republic ten years earlier.

As head of the Supreme Revolutionary Council, Bagaza relied on the army, dominated by officers originating from the south of the country. He restructured the only political party, Union pour le Progrès national (UPRONA; Union for National Progress), for which he organized two national congresses, in 1979 and 1984. The constitution of the Second Republic, adopted by referendum in 1981, resulted in his election to the presidency.

He established a volunteer political system, the results of which have remained substantial, notably regarding the fundamental infrastructures that have made Burundi a truly modern country: the principal access routes of the country were paved, and hospitals and schools were built and equipped. Since rural farmers make up more than 90 percent of the population of Burundi, a plan for providing electricity to the countryside (with hydroelectric plants in Rwegura and Mugere) and the conveyance of water was put in place; a restructuring of rural society was launched based on communal villages (historically populations are rather dispersed in Burundi) and on the production cooperative. The results were, however, mixed.

Bagaza dreamed of a strong, independent economy. He encouraged the development of small industries through the growth of public investment and the promotion of private initiative. This policy was strongly supported by the institutions of Bretton Woods and Western backers but also by China and some Arab countries, such as Libya. The agricultural sector saw increased growing of coffee in the north and the center of the country, cotton and palm oil trees on the river plains of Lake Tanganyika in the west, and tea in the higher altitudes. The promotion of cash crops was accompanied by the promotion of agronomic centers, such as the Institut des Sciences Agronomiques du Burundi (Isabu) and Institut de Recherche Agronomique et

Jean-Baptiste Bagaza, 1996. (AP Images/Sayyid Azim)

Zootechnique (Iraz), created within the framework of the Communauté Économique des Pays des Grands Lacs (CEPGL; Economic Community of the Great Lakes Countries). A policy of reforesting was launched to endow the country with sufficient lumber and to fight erosion. At that time, Burundi enjoyed an improved economic situation aided by the high price of coffee, which favored the popularity of the president.

In social matters, Bagaza's regime is known for two major decisions made in 1978: the suppression of the *bugererwa* (dependent property tax), a popular measure for "returning land to those who cultivate it," and replacing the head tax with obligatory savings. In foreign policy, the Second Republic followed broad lines of diplomacy that affirmed "good neighbor relations, positive nonalignment, noninterference with the internal affairs of other countries, international cooperation, and the support of liberation movements." However, this course repeatedly suffered from Bagaza's strong enmity for presidents Mobutu Sese Seko of Zaïre and Juvénal Habyarimana of Rwanda. He turned to the nation of Uganda under the presidency of Yoweri Museveni to break his isolation in the region.

Despite its early popularity, the Bagaza regime quickly showed its flaws. It followed developmental policies detrimental to the large fissures of Burundian society, which continued to be divided by the thorny Hutu-Tutsi ethnic question. The rise of coffee cultivation deemphasized food production. Coffee production quadrupled between 1976 and 1987, while the banana industry, which was at the heart of the rural economy in the densely populated regions of the north and central regions, receded.

Finally, a crisis of opposition between the Catholic Church and the Burundian state sounded the death knell of the reputedly progressive regime. Between 1983 and 1987, the conflict between these two institutions deeply divided Burundian society. President Bagaza did not hide his determination to reduce the influence of the church, reproaching it for its "privileges of the colonial period" and even "for indirectly standing surety for foreign attacks against the maintenance of discrimination between Batutsis and Bahatus." The first targets of his policies were European missionaries, of whom up to three hundred were expelled beginning in 1979. The native-born priests were arrested and seminaries were nationalized, measures unheard of in a Christian country. The crisis assumed a diplomatic dimension and raised the indignation of the international community, which was prepared to denounce the regime. The impasse in the country was complete, and "ethnic" and "regional" tensions worsened.

It was in this tense situation that Bagaza, visiting Québec for a Francophone summit, was overthrown in his absence by another Rutovu native, Major Pierre Buyoya, on 3 September 1987. If other reasons (among them the malcontent of soldiers and noncommissioned officers threatened with early retirement) explain Buyoya's coup d'état, the political-religious conflict appeared, above all in foreign eyes, as the most tangible sign of the deterioration of the regime.

Ousted from power, Bagaza went into exile and was received in Uganda by Museveni, whom he had aided in taking power in Kampala. He returned to Burundi following the elections of June 1993, which brought the Frodebu (Front pour la Démocratie au Burundi) candidate, Melchior Ndadaye, to the presidency. The failure of Buyoya (the Uprona candidate) in this election constituted a victory for Bagaza, who had long been refused permission to return to the country. But the assassination of Ndadaye the following October plunged the country into an unprecedented sociopolitical crisis. In this context of civil war and the state's decline, Bazaga attempted a political return with the creation of Parena (Parti pour le Redressement National). But this organization recruited its members primarily from the Tutsi minority, which deprived it of the opportunity of embodying a real political opposition. In July 1996, the return to power of Bagaza's perpetual rival, Buyoya, through a second coup d'état, put a serious brake on his political ambitions. His party still existed, but it remained limited by its militant social program. As of 2010, Bagaza held a seat for life in the Senate, a privilege that the constitution adopted after the 2005 conflict accorded to all former presidents of Burundi.

[*See also* Buyoya, Pierre; Habyarimana, Juvénal; Micombero, Michel; Mobutu Sese Seko; Museveni, Yoweri Kaguta; *and* Ndadaye, Melchior.]

BIBLIOGRAPHY

Chrétien, Jean-Pierre. *Burundi, l'histoire retrouvée: 25 ans de métier d'historien en Afrique.* Paris: Karthala, 1993.

Manirakiza, Marc. *Burundi, la déviance d'un pouvoir solitaire: Le régime Bagaza (1976–1987).* Brussels, Belgium: La Longue Vue, 1997.

République du Burundi, Comité central du parti Uprona. *Actes du premier Congrès national du parti Uprona*. Bujumbura, Burundi, 1980.

République du Burundi, Ministère de l'information. *IIe République: Respect des engagements*. Boulogne, France, 1984.

ALEXANDRE HATUNGIMANA
Translated from the French by Desmond Hosford

Bagosora, Théoneste (1941–), Rwandan military officer, was born into a northern middle-class Hutu family in Gisenyi, Giciye Commune. He was the oldest of six children and the son of a teacher. He attended the Petit Séminaire (minor seminary) St. Pie X in the diocese of Nyundo for his primary education. Upon graduating from the minor seminary, Bagosora began his military training at the officers' training school in Kigali in 1962. In 1981 Bagosora traveled to France to attend the Études Militaires Supérieures de l'École de Guerre Française, where he received further training at the elite school. He was the first Rwandan to attend the foreign academy. Upon his return to Rwanda, he began his tenure as commander of the Kanombe military camp located outside of Kigali. He married Isabelle Uzanyinzoga, a Hutu from southern Rwanda, which caused friction between Juvénal Habyarimana and other hard-line northern Hutus in the government at the time.

Bagosora was known to harbor deep resentments against the Tutsi in Rwanda. He had publicly stated that the Tutsi were attempting to reinstate the monarchy, which, under Belgian colonial rule, had promoted and supported the oppression of the Hutu majority. He also argued that the Tutsi-dominated Rwanda Patriotic Front (RPF) in Uganda was preparing an attack to take back control of the Rwandan government. This claim lent a sense of urgency to his call for the killing of all Tutsi in Rwanda, to disrupt the ambitions of the RPF. Bagosora was a large supporter of Radio Television Libre des Mille Collines (RTLM), the controversial radio station that broadcast news and instructions throughout the ensuing genocide in 1994. It was Bagosora who suggested the radio be used to coordinate the genocide and incite violence against the Tutsi before and during the genocide. He was strongly committed to the racist ideology that claimed the Tutsi were inferior to the Hutu, and it was this thinking that drove Bagosora and defined his military ambitions and career.

Bagosora's training and close relationship with the Habyarimana government allowed him to become one of the most prominent actors throughout the planning and implementation of the 1994 genocide. In 1990 he became president of the Association for the Development of the Giciye and Karago communes (ADECOGIKA), an organization he founded in 1984 whose purpose was to funnel financial resources to the Bushiru region. His affiliation with ADECOGIKA allowed him to develop a strong base of support in the region of Bushiru. In 1991, he was appointed as chair of a commission whose task was to develop a decisive plan to deal with the Tutsi threat coming out of Uganda. By 1992, when a moderate government took over, he was ousted from the Habyarimana administration because of his extremist rhetoric and views. However, owing to his affiliation with Agathe Habyarimana's Akazu ("little house"), he was able to remain an active leader of the Hutu extremist wing of the government as cabinet chief in the Ministry of Defense. This post allowed him to continue to monitor the moderate members of the National Republican Movement for Democracy and Development (MRND) and stay abreast of developments relating to the conflict between Tutsi and Hutu. Given his position as a high-ranking Hutu leader and his influential standing in the Habyarimana administration, he was instrumental in the creation of the Interahamwe, the government-supported militia who were primarily responsible for the majority of killings during the genocide. Bagosora has also been identified as the person responsible for developing and distributing the lists of Tutsi and moderate Hutu who would be targeted during the genocide.

By 1993 Bagosora had developed a reputation as an active and determined member of the extremist wing of the MRND and a leading proponent of anti-Tutsi sentiment. He even earned the nickname "Colonel Death" after the Arusha talks in 1993. He traveled to Arusha, Tanzania, during the course of the negotiations in order to stay abreast of what was being discussed and identifying the individual Hutu leaders who were complying with Tutsi demands. It was there that he remarked his intention of returning to Rwanda and preparing for the apocalypse.

On 6 April 1994 Bagosora became the highest-ranking official in Rwanda after the death of President Juvénal Habyarimana. He had attained the rank of colonel and was in firm control of the Ministry of Defense. He immediately took control of the elite military units and began issuing commands for the Interahamwe to set up roadblocks throughout Rwanda. He mobilized the Interahamwe and began using RTLM to disseminate information through the use of mass communication. Bagosora was in close contact with officials from the United Nations and various international groups from the beginning of the genocide. He reported that the situation was confined to a few regions and that he was in firm control of the armed forces. However, it soon became apparent that he was providing false assessments to United Nations commanders while actively organizing the planned massacres of Tutsi and moderate Hutu. As the Tutsi-led RPF advanced further into Rwanda, Bagosora fled the country with the aid of French forces. He was evacuated on 2 July 1994 from Butare and remained abroad until 1996.

Bagosora's rhetoric, actions during the genocide, and affiliation with the Akazu all led to his arrest on 9 March 1996 in Cameroon. The Belgian government had filed an international arrest warrant for Bagosora for the killing of ten Belgian peacekeepers but withdrew the extradition request in July 1996 upon the arrest in Cameroon. Bagosora was transferred to the International Criminal Tribunal for Rwanda in Arusha, Tanzania, on 23 January 1997, where he was charged with conspiracy to commit genocide, genocide, complicity in genocide, war crimes, inhumane acts, and outrages. Bagosora stood trial along with three other prominent leaders of the 1994 genocide. Throughout the trial he consistently denied all charges and argued that no genocide had occurred in Rwanda. In December 2008, he was found guilty and sentenced to life in prison for genocide and crimes against humanity.

[*See also* Habyarimana, Agathe; *and* Habyarimana, Juvénal.]

BIBLIOGRAPHY

Melvern, Linda. *Conspiracy to Murder: The Rwandan Genocide*. New York: Verso, 2006.

Off, Carol. *The Lion, the Fox, and the Eagle: A Story of Generals and Justice in Rwanda and Yugoslavia*. Mississauga, Ont.: Random House Canada, 2001.

Prunier, Gerard. *The Rwanda Crisis: History of a Genocide*. New York: Columbia University Press, 1997.

Scherrer, Christian P. *Genocide and Crisis in Central Africa: Conflict Roots, Mass Violence, and Regional War*. Westport, Conn.: Praeger, 2001.

Wallis, Andrew. *Silent Accomplice: The Untold Story of France's Role in the Rwandan Genocide*. London: I. B. Tauris, 2006.

STERLING RECKER

Baha' al-Din Zuhayr (1186–1258), Arab-born Egyptian poet and calligrapher of the Ayyubid period, was born 27/28 February 1186 in Mecca. He is also known as al-Baha' Zuhayr. He moved to Qus, in upper Egypt, at a young age. Zuhayr's later *diwans* (a Persian term meaning "collection of poems") indicate some recollection of his time in Mecca; he likely moved to Qus when he became old enough to attend school. Qus was then a center of Islamic learning and culture. Zuhayr studied the Qur'an and Islamic literature but was most enthused by poetry. Zuhayr made friends with another poet and quoted substantially from the "ancient" poets such as Imru al-Qays (c. 501–544), some of whom were pre-Islamic.

Despite a fascination with poetry, Zuhayr also cultivated his position among the political elite. He dedicated his first praise poem to the governor of Qus. Zuhayr did not stop with the locals, traveling to places such as Damascus in 1215 and then moving to Cairo in 1227, notably after the capital of the Ayyubids had shifted from Damascus to Cairo in 1218. It should be noted that Zuhayr fancied himself a "court poet," and thus he sought appropriate employment with figures from the ruling dynasty. The Ayyubid sultanate had been founded by Saladin, the legendary Arab leader who fought the crusaders, retaking Jerusalem in 1187. The empire reached its peak in 1188, encompassing land from Tunisia to Yemen and northeastward to Turkey. The Ayyubids continued their campaigns against the crusaders until they were themselves destroyed by a Mongol invasion in 1260. Not surprisingly, then, some of Zuhayr's poetic materials included celebrations of Islamic victories over the crusaders, including Sultan Kamil's victory over the crusaders at Damietta, Egypt, in 1221. Damietta, like its more famous twin, Alexandria, at the mouth of the western Nile, sits where the eastern Nile meets the Mediterranean Sea.

While these early attempts at currying favor were largely ignored, Zuhayr's move to Cairo proved successful. Attached to Sultan Kamil's son and potential heir, al-Salih Ayyub, Zuhayr accompanied al-Salih on his expedition to Syria in 1232 and again in 1238–1239. This later expedition would prove fateful, as Sultan Kamil died in 1238 and a struggle for succession ensued, mainly between al-Salih (who was attempting to subdue Syria) and his half-brother, al-Adil II, who, having been in Egypt when his father passed, managed to gain the sultanate in Egypt. Al-Salih's troops mutinied against him at Nablus, a city in the Levant, and al-Salih was held under "house arrest" by his cousin, al-Nasir Dawud, for about a year. During this time, Zuhayr remained faithful to al-Salih, continuing to serve as poet and minister.

The political tides that seemed to run against al-Salih soon turned in his favor. Al-Adil II was unprepared and incompetent to handle the position of "sultan," and al-Nasir decided to release al-Salih, who returned triumphally to Cairo in 1240. Al-Adil II was assassinated by his own troops, and al-Nasir returned to Syria, leaving al-Salih firmly in control in Egypt. It should be noted that the internecine strife between the Egyptian and Syrian parts of the Ayyubid Empire was in part a result of the location of the crusader states in between, and various Muslim rulers showed a willingness to ally with the Christian kingdoms to tilt the balance of power (even temporarily ceding Jerusalem from 1229 to 1244 while they fought among themselves); this was a recurring theme in both the reality of Zuhayr's life and his poetry. Zuhayr, of course, returned with al-Salih and was rewarded for his faithful service by being appointed vizier (minister).

During the next decade Zuhayr was at the peak of his political and personal influence, staying with al-Salih at al-Mansoura. Al-Salih had managed to consolidate power effectively and proceeded to recapture Jerusalem from the Christians in 1244. Four years later, Louis IX (St. Louis) of France launched the Seventh Crusade in response. During this time of increased fear of an invasion of the Egyptian delta by the crusaders, a poorly worded poem by Zuhayr led to his dismissal by al-Salih. Al-Salih died a year later, in 1249; but his death only brought more chaos. Al-Salih's slave-wife, Shahar al-Durr, managed to orchestrate a Mamluk slave revolt against al-Salih's ephemeral successor, son al-Muazzam Turanshah, in 1250. This effectively ended Ayyubid rule in Egypt, but the Ayyubids retained power in Syria. Consequently, Zuhayr went to Syria, where he attempted to curry favor with al-Nasir Yusuf, the Ayyubid emir of Syria, but to no avail. He returned to Cairo and receded into obscurity, dying of a plague epidemic on 2 November 1258, at the age of 72.

Baha' al-Din Zuhayr's collection of poems, or *diwan*, was edited in Cairo in 1314. Copies of the collection have been preserved in Paris and elsewhere. Zuhayr's work, originally in Arabic, was translated into English in 1876–1877 by Edward Henry Palmer (1840–1882). At the time, Zuhayr's work was well known in the Arabic world but virtually unknown in Europe. Palmer, an English

Orientalist, came across Zuhayr's poems in Arabic and was struck with the "beauty of the language and freshness and originality of thought" (p. xi).

Zuhayr's poetry emphasized both form and message. In form, his poetry was metrical and harmonious, with a regular pattern and flow. Zuhayr made use of rhetorical devices, puns, and local idioms; his search for double meanings ironically led to his eventual downfall (with the poem misinterpreted by al-Salih, though the exact offense is uncertain). His works showed some evidence of mystical influences.

In message, Zuhayr's poetry often emphasized either the blessings or curses that befell him and his contemporaries. His chief interests were formal works that offered praise to high-ranking Ayyubid officials, less formal works that delved into love and social relations, and works that touched on fate (not surprising given his own rise to power and subsequent fall). Zuhayr's works touched on problems such as alcoholism and the absence of lovers; several of his poem titles translate as "To an Absent Friend" (with perhaps the suggestion of a "girlfriend"). There is no mention of his ever marrying, and his death "in solitude" befits a man whose life was spent mostly in hypothetical terms. Zuhayr's poetry can best be summed up as "satirical," rather than humorous, and for the most part was not especially orthodox in respect to religious matters. In some ways his life mirrored the rise and fall of the Ayyubids, and his poetry is reflective of his life experience. Zuhayr is generally regarded as the most celebrated poet of the period.

[*See also* Malik al-Kamil, al-; *and* Saladin.]

BIBLIOGRAPHY

Houtsma, Martijn Theodor, ed. *Encyclopedia of Islam.* Vol. 1. London: Luzac, 1960.

Palmer, E. H., trans. *Poetical Works of Beha-ed-Din Zoheir of Egypt.* Cambridge, UK: Cambridge University Press, 1877.

Smoor, P. "Baha' al-Din Zuhayr." In *Encyclopedia of Arabic Literature*, edited by Julie Scott Meisami and Paul Starkey, p. 127. London: Routledge, 1998.

Stetkevych, Suzanne Pinckney. *The Mantle Odes: Arabic Praise Poems to the Prophet Muhammad.* Bloomington: Indiana University Press, 2010.

ROBERT D. YOUNG

Bahta Hagos (d. 1894), Eritrean leader of anticolonial revolt against Italy and warlords from northern Ethiopia, and popular hero, was born in the town of Segeneity. The exact date of his birth is unknown: he was born between 1839 and 1850 into a rich peasant family. Bahta Hagos's parents, Hagos Andu and Weizero Wonau, were agro-pastoralists who owned farmlands around Segeneity and in the eastern escarpments. As a young man, he became renowned for his physical strength as well as for his skills as a cattle herder. Like a majority of the people in Eritrea in colonial times, Bahta Hagos was converted from Orthodox Tewahdo Christianity to Roman Catholicism in the 1870s.

Bahta Hagos rose to prominence after he killed *fitewrari* Embaye, the son of Araya Selassie Demsu—the Ethiopian emperor Yohannes IV's uncle and the governor of the Agame area in Tigray. After Embaye arrived at Segeneity in October 1875, he ordered that the people in the area supply his army with food, and he extorted money from them. As the people of the locality resisted his demands, serious clashes broke out between them and Embaye's army, during which Bahta Hagos was wounded. Despite his wounds, he killed Embaye with a spear; over twenty of Embaye's soldiers and about eight local men were killed in the skirmish.

Fearing acts of reprisal by Araya Selassie Demsu, Bahta Hagos, his brothers (Kahsu, Gebremedhin, and Sengal), and a dozen other followers fled to Agemeda, where they lived for many years. Bahta Hagos and his armed bands ambushed Araya's and Alula Engeda's convoys and managed to increase the number of firearms at their disposal. During all the turbulent years of raids by Tigrean warlords, such as the invasions by Araya's son Debbeb, Bahta Hagos continued to develop his military skills. He may have killed his own brother, Kahsu Hagos, because Kahsu was believed to have shown acts of treachery to Bahta Hagos. Several attempts to find peaceful solutions to the ongoing disputes between Bahta Hagos and the Tigrean Debbeb failed. In 1879 when Ras Alula Engeda was appointed by Emperor Yohannes IV of Ethiopia as the governor of the highlands of Eritrea, the domains of Bahta Hagos continued to fall under the influence of Alula, forcing Bahta Hagos to move from the Agemeda and seek protection from Kentibay Hamid of Habab, who enjoyed protection from the Egyptian forces in the area and who provided material and moral support to Bahta Hagos.

In 1885, Bahta Hagos was convinced by the Italians in Massawa to join forces with them. He was soon promoted to the position of *capo di banda* (chief of the native army). In the late 1880s, he played a pivotal role in the process of Italian occupation of the Eritrean highlands. On the bases of his loyalty and record of service, he was promoted to the post of administrator and chief of the local army in the province of Akkele Guzay. He was given the title *degiat* and became among the most loyal local chiefs under the colonial government.

However, Bahta Hagos started to feel dissatisfied about Italian economic and social policies in the colony. Among the main reasons for his discontent were Italian policies of expropriation of large arable land in the colony, assassination or imprisonment of a great number of Eritrean local chiefs, and "womanization" (forcing women to serve in Italian military brothels). He came to consider the Italian occupation not as a source of protection but as a great danger for the people of Eritrea.

In December 1894 he called up his countrymen to revolt against Italian colonial occupation. He imprisoned the colonial administrator of Segeneity and cut all telegraph and other communication lines that connected the town with other Italian military bases. With about two thousand armed men, he attacked the Italian base at Halai. The revolt continued only for few days, during which Bahta Hagos was killed. Although his followers attempted another military offensive from the nearby village of Koatit, they were defeated. Most of the remaining followers, including Bahta Hagos's brothers, escaped and took refuge in Tigray, from where they continued to ambush Italian forces in Eritrea.

Bahta Hagos's rebellion was among the factors that compelled the Italians to reconsider some aspects of their local administration, including their land policies. In 1895, the Italian colonist settlement policies were "officially" abolished, and the colonial government pardoned those who fought with Bahta Hagos. By 1903, land expropriation was formally abolished and the colonial government "officially" ordained the leasing or return of the confiscated land to the owners. Generally, the colonial government adopted policies of reconciliation with the local people. However, in practice, it continued to expropriate arable lands in various forms, such as land expropriated in the form of *demaniale* (state-owned land).

The slogan by which Bahta Hagos inspired his rebellion is still remembered: "Sengal, my brother, do not be so silly, / Gebremedhin, my brother, do not be so silly, / If you are once bitten by a WHITE SNAKE, / You will find no cure." Bahta Hagos is remembered by Eritreans as one of the early nationalist heroes whose resistance to Italian colonialism played a significant role in shaping the relationship between the colonizers and the subjects.

[*See also* Yohannes IV.]

BIBLIOGRAPHY

Caulk, Richard. "Black Snake, White Snake." In *Banditry, Rebellion, and Social Protest in Africa*, edited by Donald Crummey, pp. 293–306. Portsmouth, N.H.: Heinemann, 1986.

Misghenna, Yemane. *Italian Colonialism: A Case Study of Eritrea, 1869–1934: Motive, Praxis and Result.* Lund, Sweden: Studenlitteratur, 1989.

Negash, Tekeste. *No Medicine for the Bite of a White Snake: Notes on Nationalism and Resistance in Eritrea.* Uppsala, Sweden: University of Uppsala, 1986.

O'Mahoney, Kevin. *"The Ebullient Phoenix": A History of the Vicariate of Abyssinia, 1839–1860.* Vol. 3. Addis Ababa, Ethiopia: United Printers, 1982.

MUSSIE TESFAGIORGIS

Baikie, William Balfour (1824–1864), Scottish explorer, naturalist, surgeon, and philologist who opened up the Niger region to European trade and influence, was born in Kirkwall, Scotland, the eldest son of a Royal Navy captain, John Baikie. He was educated for a time at Kirkwall Grammar School in Orkney, but mainly privately, in company with his cousins. He gained a medical degree from Edinburgh University, where he also developed his interest in natural history. In 1848, together with Robert Heddie, he wrote the first part of a published study of the natural history of Orkney, *Historia naturalis Orcadensis*. In the same year he joined the Royal Navy as an assistant surgeon, serving on no less than five different ships in the Mediterranean before being appointed in the same capacity to Haslar Hospital, Portsmouth, from 1851 to 1854. It was from here in 1854 that, through the patronage of the influential Sir Roderick Murchison—then president of the Royal Geographical Society—he was appointed as surgeon and naturalist to an exploring expedition up the Niger and its eastern tributary, the Benue, as far as it was possible to travel on these rivers. An important purpose was to assess the possibilities for trade in the Niger region, to investigate its mineral and other resources, and to prospect the potential for cotton growing at a time when British manufacturers were searching for alternative sources to those of the United States in particular.

In 1854 Baikie joined the iron-screw steamer *Pleiad* at Sierra Leone as surgeon and naturalist.

He was accompanied on board by the Reverend Samuel Ayaji Crowther, a Yoruba-born member of the Church Missionary Society, who published a dictionary and grammar of Yoruba and translated the Book of Common Prayer and the Bible in to that language. Crowther, later made a bishop, was largely responsible for the spread of Christianity in the region. At Fernando Po, Baikie was obliged to take over the expedition from its original leader, the consul John Beecroft, who had died there. With no experience as a commander, he was undoubtedly nervous about such a responsibility, but he felt he had a duty to carry out the intentions of the expedition. He succeeded in navigating some 700 miles of river, including 250 miles on the Benue beyond the journeys of previous explorers. He recorded much scientific and topographic data, and notably, by requiring his crew to take daily doses of quinine against malaria, completed the four-month journey without loss of life. The efficacy of this was to prove crucial in the development of the region. His published account of the expedition in 1856 was the basis for his application to lead a second expedition in the following year.

The 1857 expedition in the steamer *Dayspring*, accompanied by a supply ship, the *George*, was primarily to establish trading posts along the river, but Baikie, under the influence of Murchison, had specific instructions to investigate the geology and potential mineral deposits of the area. However, at the Bussa rapids, near Jebba, the *Dayspring* was wrecked, and its crew marooned for a year, while the naval surveyor Lieutenant John Glover trekked overland to Lagos and Sierra Leone to bring help. At present-day Lokoja, where the Niger and the Benue meet, Baikie established a trading settlement and consular office. Those of the crew who had elected to stay cleared the first one hundred acres themselves, while houses and enclosures were built. Within the first three years some two thousand local traders came to do business, and this first trading post on the Niger thrived with the establishment of a regular market and the opening up of roads into the interior, which Baikie supervised. Here European traders frequently employed African entrepreneurs as agents and trade partners. Baikie's modest but determined personality and his willingness to integrate with the local community, including learning local languages, ultimately provided a springboard for the development of the chartered Royal Nigerian Company. Under the influential entrepreneur Sir George Goldie, the latter became the de facto government of the region through its trade monopoly.

Baikie undertook a number of exploratory journeys overland, including one of more than 600 miles on horseback to Kano. These were dangerous areas for non-Muslim European travelers, but Baikie's personality won him many friends among the local people, not least among various chiefs in and around Lokoja. He found time to translate parts of the Bible into several languages spoken in present-day Nigeria, including Hausa. At Lokoja, Baikie was a respected doctor, schoolteacher, and magistrate, becoming a leader in the town's affairs. In his detailed reports to the Foreign Office, he particularly attacked the practices of both European traders and African middlemen on the coast attempting to enforce their commercial monopolies.

However, by the end of 1861, Baikie was often the only European in the township and living at a basic subsistence level, although he was still determined to maintain a British presence there. But the onerous running of the trading station, largely on his own, took its toll. At his own request, Baikie was relieved by the arrival of HMS *Investigator* from England in August 1864. The vessel then took him to Sierra Leone, where he spent some time with an Orcadian friend, sorting out his notes and specimens. He contracted an illness, however, and died on 12 December 1864, at the age of 39. Quite apart from his scholarly records and his numerous books, his personal and often solitary contribution to the laying of foundations for European trade in the region, together with his medical breakthrough in combating malaria, was to become a turning point in the history of development of Nigeria. He is commemorated in St. Magnus Cathedral in his home town of Kirkwall by an impressive memorial paid for by public subscription.

[*See also* Crowther, Samuel Ayaji.]

BIBLIOGRAPHY

Baikie, William Balfour. *Narrative of an Exploring Voyage up the Rivers Kwo'ra and Bi'nue (Commonly Known as the Niger and Tsadda) in 1854*. London: Murray, 1856. The first comprehensive account of the geography, natural history, people, and customs of the Niger by a trained scientific observer, especially important for its contemporary description of Igbo institutions.

Crowther, Samuel A. *Journal of an Expedition up the Niger and Tshadda Rivers*. London: Church Missionary House, 1855. Provides Crowther's Yoruba perspective on the Niger expedition.

Hastings, A. C. G. *The Voyage of the* Dayspring. London: John Lane, 1926. This focuses on Baikie's last expedition in 1857, with a particular emphasis on the part played by Lieutenant John Glover, the ship's surveyor whose overland journey brought rescue to the marooned crew and who became the first governor of Lagos.

Lloyd, Christopher. *The Search for the Niger*. London: Collins, 1973. A readable account of the history of exploration of the Niger from earliest times, including the several expeditions involving Baikie and their aftermath, providing a geographical context for the latter.

Stafford, Robert A. *Scientist of Empire: Sir Roderick Murchison, Scientific Exploration and Victorian Imperialism*. Cambridge, UK: Cambridge University Press, 1989. An especially well-researched work, which, although referring to Baikie as only one of many travelers whom Murchison promoted at this time, provides the essential imperial background to his travels and the role of the Royal Geographical Society.

JAMES MCCARTHY

Bakanja, Isidore (c. 1880–1909), Congolese catechist and canonized saint of the Roman Catholic Church, was born in the village of Bokendela, a small town on the Busira River east of the modern city of Mbandaka between 1880 and 1890. His father, Iyonzwa, and his mother, Inyuka, belonged to a Boangi community that was part of the large Mongo linguistic group. Little is known of his early family life, but this region of northwestern Congo was rife with violence during his early years. Different Mongo chiefs and traders used violent means to gain access to dependents and access to trade. Since the Busira and Ruki Rivers emptied into the Congo River, this area had long been deeply connected with the Atlantic slave trade. Ivory was also in major demand, and the guns and trade goods obtained by Mongo chiefs in exchange for elephant tusks allowed them to purchase more slaves. The situation did not improve once agents of Leopold II of Belgium's Independent State of the Congo (ISC) arrived in the late 1880s. Leopold II gave the Société Anonyme Belge pour le Commerce du Haut-Congo (SAB) a monopoly over trade in a vast area that included Bokendela in 1888. The SAB established a major trading center in the town of Busira located northeast of Bokendela, and in 1893 it created the first experimental rubber plantation in the entire colony there. By cultivating rubber, the SAB hoped to alleviate the effect of declining amounts of ivory coming from the Busira River region. While the SAB did find great profits from its Busira operations, the company's brutal treatment of workers ultimately caused the end of Bakanja's life.

Bakanja decided in his early twenties to travel from Bokendela to the regional trade center of Mbandaka, as did many other young men seeking better opportunities than the SAB provided in rural areas. Once in Mbandaka, he worked as a mason for the colonial administration. He became familiar with Catholicism through the work of Belgian Trappist missionaries in the town. After he spent time learning the catechism, which featured prominent sections on the importance of Mary, Bakanja was baptized at St. Eugene's parish in Bolokwa-Nsimba on 6 October 1906. He accepted his first Communion and underwent the sacrament of Confirmation later in the same year. Following the teachings of the 1903 catechism provided by the Trappists, Bakanja wore a scapular and prayed the rosary frequently.

Against the advice of friends, Bakanja decided to become the house servant of a Belgian SAB agent named Reynders. Bakanja desired to live closer to his original home, and so traveled with Reynders first to the SAB plantations at Busira and then to another plantation at Ikili. At Ikili, the SAB manager was a man named Van Cauter, a virulent anticlerical opponent of the Catholic Church. This man considered Bakanja to be nothing more than an "animal of stupid priests." Reynders recommended that Bakanja downplay his faith, but the young convert refused to listen to these recommendations. When Van Cauter commanded Bakanja to take off his scapular and to stop speaking of his faith to other people, the Congolese man refused. A severe whipping followed as punishment, either by Van Cauter himself or by some of his other workers. Later, Bakanja chose to pray during a break from work. Van Cauter became enraged and had an African foreman flog Bakanja for his insolence 250 times with a hippopotamus-hide whip studded with nails. After this excruciatingly painful sentence, Van Cauter then had Bakanja placed in chains. (SAB agents regularly employed violence against Congolese workers, regardless of their religious sentiments.) Once Bakanja was released, his wounds became infected and his health deteriorated. When ordered to travel with Reynders to Isoko, he hid in the nearby rainforest for several days after slipping away into a marsh located by a dock. An African found him and learned that Bakanja had been tortured for working as a catechist. An SAB inspector named Dorpinghaus discovered the weakened fugitive after three days and placed him on a boat where he received some treatment for his injuries. The lashings were so serious

that they had left some bones exposed. Gangrene had set in by the time Bakanja reached the village of Ngomb'Isongo. Bakanja was then taken to Busira, where a local catechist tried to care for him the best he could. Two Trappist missionaries, Gregoire Kaptein and Georges Dubrulle, met the disabled man on 24–25 July 1909. Bakanja told his visitors, "The white man [Van Cauter] did not like Christians . . . Certainly I shall pray for him. When I am in Heaven, I shall pray for him very much." The priests heard his confession and administered the sacrament of Extreme Unction. Six months after his initial beatings at the hands of the SAB agents, Bakanja passed away on 15 August 1909. Even at the moment of his death, he continued to pray for the conversion of Van Cauter.

Since both the Independent State of the Congo and the Belgian administration that superseded the ISC in 1908 relied extensively on the Catholic Church to run schools and provide legitimacy to the colonial regime, Catholic missionaries had the necessary influence to call for Van Cauter's trial. Although the SAB disputed the charges of mistreatment raised by the Trappist priests, in 1913 a Belgian colonial court sentenced Van Cauter to a two-year prison term. Bakanja's body was reburied in a mission cemetery at the new mission of Bokote in 1917. His piety and his martyrdom made him a popular figure with Congolese and missionaries alike, perhaps since his story allowed the Church to shift attention away from its close collaboration with the colonial order. After a long effort to beatify Bakanja, an investigation was held in Mbandaka. Father Honoré Vinck, a missionary scholar with decades of experience in Congo, conducted research that led to a diocesan beatification trial of 1987. The case then was sent to the Vatican. John Paul II announced Bakanja's canonization on 24 April 1994.

BIBLIOGRAPHY

Claessens, A. "Isidore Bakanja, martyr? Etude critique des conflits entre la Mission des Trappistes et la Société Anonyme Belge du haut-Congo (Étude entreprise à l'occasion de la béatification d'Isidore Bakanja" [Isidore Bakanja, Martyr? A Critical Study of Conflicts between the Trappist Mission and the Société Anonyme Belge du Haut-Congo (A Study Made on the Beatification of Isidore Bakanja]. 2 vols. Paris: Mémoire de Maîtrise, Institut Catholique de Paris, 1978–1979.

Nelson, Samuel. *Colonialism in the Congo Basin, 1880–1940.* Athens: Ohio University Center for International Studies, 1994.

Shorter, Aylward. "Isidore Bakanja." *Dictionary of African Christian Biography* (2003). http://www.dacb.org/stories/demrepcongo/bakanja_isidore.html.

Vangroenweghe, Daniel. *Bakanja Isidore, martyr du Zaïre: Recit biographique* [Bakanja Isidore, Martyr of Zaire: A Biography]. Brussels, Belgium: Didier Hatier, 1989.

JEREMY RICH

Bakari, Mtoro bin Mwinyi (c. 1869–1927), East African writer and educator, was born in Dunda (in present-day Tanzania) around the end of the 1860s; he subsequently moved to Bagamoyo, a major caravan station and port city that served as the first capital of Germany's East Africa colony. When he left East Africa for Germany in 1900, he would drop his father's title (Mwinyi) and use his name as surname, thus calling himself simply Mtoro Bakari. While he became acquainted with people of diverse social and cultural background, he grew up in a Muslim family and increasingly identified himself with Islam and Swahili culture. Bakari not only acquired a thorough knowledge of Swahili language and tradition, but he also began to learn Arabic in a Qur'an school, studied higher Islamic sciences, and possibly worked as a teacher for a few years. In the mid-1890s, he organized a small trade expedition, apparently obtaining goods from a local merchant and not gaining sufficient profit to pay off this debt. Though living under difficult material conditions during the following years, he married and lived with his wife and daughter in Bagamoyo.

The political and economic situation of the 1890s was influenced by the colonial regime imposed after the war on the East African coast, which commenced in 1888. The fight against the German usurpers increasingly exposed to violence and destruction local populations that chose not to take up arms but had to escape attacks of the anticolonial forces, certainly including relatives and friends of Mtoro Bakari in Dunda. This is an explanation for the fact that Mtoro Bakari did not tend to see the colonial regime in a negative light around 1900 when he left German East Africa. In 1898 he even agreed to work as a tax collector, apparently for some months only. He later pointed out that this had been a rather "troublesome business" and that "everybody had hated" him.

Mtoro Bakari was the main author of the *Desturi za Wasuaheli* (Swahili Customs, published in Swahili and German in 1903) and also of two articles in the *Safari za Wasuaheli* (Swahili Travel Accounts, published in Swahili and German in 1901).

The opportunity of being employed to teach Swahili at the School of Oriental Languages (SOL) in Berlin was a chance to overcome his dire situation at home and start a new career. In Germany, Mtoro Bakari encountered the ongoing institutionalization process of the teaching and study of African languages, which was influenced by the emergence of Germany as an imperial power since the foundation of the SOL in 1887. His superiors, Carl Velten (1862–1942) and Carl Meinhof (1867–1944), held the position of "teachers" of Swahili and African languages, respectively, and were endowed with the title "professor" in addition. In 1909, Meinhof received the first professorship of African languages worldwide at the Hamburg Colonial Institute (HCI), which became part of the newly founded University of Hamburg in 1919. Apart from closely cooperating with Velten and Meinhof, Mtoro Bakari served as consultant for various well-known scholars at the beginning of their academic careers, including the linguists Martin Heepe (1887–1961) and Otto Dempwolff (1871–1938), the phonetician Giulio Panconcelli-Calzia (1878–1966), the ethnographer Bernhard Struck (1888–1971), and the expert in Islamic history and culture Carl Heinrich Becker (1876–1933). Between the winter semesters of 1905–1906 and 1908–1909, he took a leading role in a colloquium for missionary students in which he discussed various aspects of Islam and Christianity with Protestant clerics and missionary students.

Despite the increasing interest in the study of African languages, and despite the exceptional recognition he earned as a knowledgeable informant and proficient teacher at the SOL (1900–1905) and the HCI (1909–1913), Mtoro Bakari was not able to pursue an academic career. The racist reactions following his marriage to a German woman, Bertha Hilske, in 1904 not only forced him to leave the SOL but indirectly stimulated administrative measures against legal unions of "mixed couples" in the German colonies. When the Bakaris sought to return to German East Africa in September 1905, the governor prevented them from entering the colony because he was convinced that their presence would undermine the colonial order threatened by the beginning of the Maji Maji War, the most extended and violent case of resistance in the German colonies. Another important consequence of the marriage was the downgrading of African teachers south of the Sahara from their status as civil servants to "teaching" or "language assistants," who were employed for two years and received a substantial part of their payment after returning to their colony. In 1913, Mtoro Bakari himself was dismissed by his superiors at the HCI after he came in conflict with Martin Heepe, a German doctoral student who attempted to confer to him the role of an assistant in his Swahili class.

After leaving the SOL in 1905, Mtoro Bakari earned his living by teaching Swahili to private or missionary students and giving talks on East Africa at high schools and other institutions. The talks, which he continued to give after 1913, when he lived with his wife in Berlin, can be seen as indirect resistance to the racial and religious discrimination that was on the increase since the emergence of Germany as a colonial power. There is no evidence, however, that Mtoro Bakari ever made any anticolonial statements in public before his death on 14 July 1927. Future studies of his writings may show how far his ideas contributed to the colonial concerns of Carl Velten, who cooperated closely with him from 1900 to 1904 and published his texts; and in what respects his activities contradicted or undermined the colonial efforts of his professional environment.

BIBLIOGRAPHY

Allen, J. W. T. *The Customs of the Swahili People: The* Desturi za Waswahili *of Mtoro bin Mwinyi Bakari and Other Swahili Persons.* Berkeley: University of California Press, 1981.

Velten, Carl. *Desturi za Wasuaheli na khabari za desturi za sheri'a za Wasuaheli.* Göttingen, Germany: Vandenhoeck and Ruprecht, 1903.

Velten, Carl. *Safari za Wasuaheli.* Göttingen, Germany: Vandenhoeck and Ruprecht, 1901.

Wimmelbücker, Ludger. *Mtoro bin Mwinyi Bakari (c. 1869–1927): Swahili Lecturer and Author in Germany.* Dar es Salaam, Tanzania: Mkuki na Nyota, 2009.

LUDGER WIMMELBÜCKER

Bakary, Djibo (1922–1998), prime minister of Niger, was born in Soudouré, west of the capital, Niamey. Although he was the son of a village chief, Bakary was a *talaka* (a commoner), since his father did not hail from a noble family. Bakary was related by blood to Hamani Diori, Niger's later president. Although he was a member of the Zarma ethnic community, many people in western Niger regarded Bakary as a Songhay, a closely related ethnic group. Later, he used this to mobilize political support along the Niger River valley.

At the age of 7, Bakary was taken by his uncle to the city of Tahoua (central Niger), where he was enrolled in a colonial primary school. A diligent student, he learned to speak Hausa before continuing his education in the capital. It was here that his political consciousness began: one day he met his father, who had been sentenced to forced labor and was breaking rocks for the repair of a local road. The sight of his father, press-ganged in contravention of deep-seated rules of respect for seniority, stirred a willingness in Bakary to agitate against colonial injustices.

In 1938 Bakary entered the colonial "William Ponty" school in Senegal, where he graduated as a teacher in 1941. Here he came into contact with the international Boy Scouts movement, which encouraged his interest in activism. Upon his return home, Bakary worked as a teacher in Niamey and in the town of Birni N'Konni before being transferred to the city of Agadez in 1945. There, he came under the influence of a Senegalese marabout (Muslim cleric) and began to agitate against aspects of colonial rule such as forced labor and corporal punishment. After his transfer by the French to the city of Zinder, Bakary established a local section of the Parti Progressiste Nigérien (PPN; Nigerien Progressive Party), formed in 1946 to protest against abuses of the French administration and Niger's chiefs.

A dynamic organizer with an interest in the politics of French West Africa, Bakary supported the PPN's affiliation to the Rassemblement Démocratique Africain (RDA; African Democratic Rally,). He became a leader on the interterritorial scene and in 1947 assumed the position of PPN secretary-general. One year later the French dismissed him from his teaching post, which allowed him to devote his life to politics. In 1951, however, Bakary fell out with the rest of the party leadership over its decision to break with the French communists, with whom the RDA associated at the metropolitan level. Bakary and fellow activists, part of a semiurban proletariat eager to climb the social ladder, felt inspired by the help of communist trade unions. Having left the PPN-RDA, Bakary engaged in union work. With the help of his family he began a commercial garden in Soudouré and established a union for suburban agricultural laborers. In time, he gained positions in international communist organizations, such as the World Federation of Trade Unions. He was elected, as representative of the French communist trade union, to the metropolitan Economic and Social Council. In 1953 Bakary and Abdoulaye Mamani, a fellow activist from Zinder, initiated Niger's first mass strike action. This resulted in wage increases for private-sector workers (lower paid than teachers and civil servants) and helped to consolidate Bakary's reputation as a political leader.

In 1954 Bakary reentered the political scene with the Union Démocratique Nigérienne (UDN), which expanded in both urban and rural areas, bringing the politics of decolonization for the first time to the countryside. Here the party became known under the rallying call "Sawaba," a name borrowed from a kindred political group in Nigeria and related to the Hausa word *sawki*, meaning "relief"—that is, deliverance from misery or constraint. This alluded to Sawaba's inarticulate notions of social betterment that made it into the kind of quasi-millenarian movement aiming for the vaguely defined good life that characterized much of nationalist politics in Africa at the time. Bakary articulated his party's ideas in an impassioned discourse of inclusive nationalism, marked by Marxist- and unionist-inspired objectives focusing on the *talakawa* (commoners) in general and semiurban *petit peuple* (lower classes) in particular, as well as broad societal transformation. In this context, his enemies were not just the officials of the French administration but also Niger's chiefs—though appointed by the colonial bureaucracy representatives of ascribed authority and dependent on the status quo—and the better-placed, Western-educated *évolués*, who flocked to the PPN-RDA.

Bakary's politics were marked by daring criticism of colonial rule and deliberate association with Niger's humbler classes, in preference to the Western luxury styles that characterized most *évolué* politicians, whose background he actually shared. Like the ideology of his party, his nationalism was not regionally defined. This reflected not only the social core of Sawaba, present in cities across the country but also Bakary's own upbringing as a Hausa-speaking Zarma in central Niger who could pose as a Songhay.

Following maneuvers toward an electoral majority, Bakary brought the party to supremacy by grudgingly entering a coalition with chiefly interests that was dominated by Sawaba and sidelined the PPN-RDA. In 1956 he became Niamey's first mayor and in March 1957 won the first general elections under universal suffrage. Bakary was appointed prime minister, forming Niger's first autonomous government under supervision of the colonial governor. Having led the *petit peuple* to preeminence and not immune to their revolutionary fervor, he gave free rein to Sawaba's hardliners. However, following the Algerian crisis and the restructuring of France's empire in 1958, Bakary fell out with Charles de Gaulle over the Fifth Republic's constitution. This catered for a *communauté* of colonial territories and the metropole and discouraged the option of independence. Pushed by the grassroots, Bakary campaigned for a "no" vote in the subsequent constitutional referendum. In view of Niger's strategic importance the French retaliated with a gubernatorial coup d'état, support for the PPN-RDA (ready to follow the metropole), and harassment of Sawaba campaigners. Massive fraud and intimidation helped to produce a "yes" victory, forcing Bakary to step down. His party was neutralized in subsequent parliamentary elections, held under similar circumstances. With the PPN-RDA in power, repression continued, also after the belated arrival of independence. Sawaba was outlawed during the last year of formal French rule.

In the autumn of 1959 Bakary, facing trumped-up charges over campaign spending in the referendum, was forced into exile. He took up residence in Mali and, with his family living in Gao, began to organize opposition to Niger's French-supported regime by recruiting Sawaba refugees for guerrilla training and arranging education of Nigerien students in Eastern Europe. For this, Bakary used his international network, traveling widely and maintaining contacts with foreign heads of state. In March 1962 he met Ben Bella; in June 1963 he visited Cuba, he spoke at international conferences, and he met Gamal Abd al-Nasser and Kwame Nkrumah. Threatened with assassination in Bamako, in the autumn of 1962 Bakary began to reside for longer periods in Ghana, where he married his second wife. His first wife and children remained in Gao.

Occasionally visiting towns in Dahomey and Nigeria to discuss guerrilla missions with his men, Bakary ordered an onslaught on Niger's regime by his forces (September–October 1964). This decision was given by the arrest of preparatory units, which threatened to uncover Sawaba's clandestine infrastructure built up over the previous years. The precipitate invasion ended in disaster, and a failed attempt on the life of President Diori in April 1965 by a Sawaba commando signaled the end of the movement. Sawaba cadres and guerrillas were incarcerated and subjected to torture and maltreatment. Bakary's family in Soudouré was also harassed, especially one of his brothers, Sanda Hima, who had been involved in street scuffles with the PPN-RDA in the 1950s and was maltreated by police. When Kwame Nkrumah was toppled in Ghana, Djibo Bakary fled to the Bulgarian legation in Accra, from where he made his escape abroad. Seen in Algiers in 1966, he stayed in Dar es Salaam in 1967, after which he settled in Guinea, together with his family, being constantly on guard for assassination attempts. Several of his children were sent to Cuba for their education. In 1969 Bakary travelled to Tripoli to contact the Chadian rebel movement (Front de Libération Nationale du Tchad, known as FROLINAT), probably to discuss the possibilities of joint action. This came to naught and soon after Bakary gave up the guerrilla struggle.

He returned from exile in 1974 when the military toppled the PPN-RDA and Sawabists were released. One year later the military's paranoid leader, Seyni Kountché, had Bakary and leading Sawabists rearrested. While his comrades were detained in the Sahara, Bakary was incarcerated in the garrison in N'Guigmi, Niger's far east, and later in a penal camp in Agadez. This was followed by house arrest in Niamey, first in a government villa in the Terminus district, then his own home. In 1984 his house arrest was officially lifted, ending nine years of confinement, but political surveillance only came to an end with the death of Seyni Kountché (November 1987). Bakary attempted a comeback with the reintroduction of multiparty politics, but he failed in subsequent elections (1993), partly because of an inability to play second fiddle. What was seen as his personal arrogance soured Bakary's ties with some middle cadres. Several were angry over his contribution to the failed invasions of 1964–1965 and the sharp contrast of their personal trajectories, in which they bore the brunt of the PPN-RDA's revenge. In the only book he wrote, Bakary gave an account of Sawaba's history but stopped short of the guerrilla infiltrations in the 1960s. Perhaps this would have been treated in the projected second and third volumes, which, however, never saw the light of day.

Thus, it never became clear whether Bakary, threatened by Niger's regime with assassination more than once, was implicated in the attempt on the president's life in 1965, although it is quite likely that Sawaba's leadership was somehow involved. However, after his release, Bakary reconciled himself with Diori. During the 1990s he began to develop intestinal problems, for which he received medical treatment in France and Cuba. Weakened as a result of incarceration and exile, Djibo Bakary died in Niamey on 16 April 1998 and was given an official funeral in his native Soudouré. His brother Sanda Hima was buried beside him.

The importance of Bakary's Marxist-inspired nationalist ideology lay especially in his movement's broad program for transformation of a society marked by traditionalism and colonial repression, which contrasted with the acceptance of neocolonial status by the subsequent client regime. His ambitions as leader of Niger's first autonomous government also extended beyond the country. By far Niger's most charismatic politician, Bakary was somewhat of an enigma, despite his *évolué* background purposely associating himself with Niger's lower strata. Following the latter's short-lived supremacy, Bakary's trajectory thus illustrated the violent nature of Gaullist-designed decolonization and the limited changes it brought, including the destruction of the *petit peuple* as a political force.

[*See also* Ben Bella, Ahmed; Hamani, Diori; Mamani, Abdoulaye; Nasser, Gamal Abd al-; *and* Nkrumah, Kwame.]

BIBLIOGRAPHY

Bakary, Djibo. *Silence! On décolonise: Itinéraire politique et syndical d'un militant africain*. Paris: L'Hammatan, 1992.

de Benoist, Joseph-Roger. "Du Parti Progessiste Nigérien au *Sawaba*: Djibo Bakary parle." *Politique africaine*, no. 38 (1990): 97–110.

Fuglestad, Finn. "Djibo Bakary, the French, and the Referendum of 1958 in Niger." *Journal of African History* 14, no. 2 (1973): 313–330.

Fuglestad, Finn. *A History of Niger, 1850–1960*. Cambridge, UK: Cambridge University Press, 1983.

Walraven, Klaas van. "Decolonisation by Referendum: The Anomaly of Niger and the Fall of Sawaba (1958–1959)." *Journal of African History* 50, no. 2 (2009): 269–292.

Walraven, Klaas van. "From Tamanrasset: The Struggle of Sawaba and the Algerian Connection (1957–1966)." *Journal of North African Studies* 10, nos. 3–4 (2005): 507–527.

Walraven, Klaas van. "Vehicle of Sedition: The Role of Transport Workers in Sawaba's Rebellion in Niger (1954–1966)." In *The Speed of Change: Motor Vehicles and People in Africa, 1890–2000*, edited by Jan-Bart Gewald, Sabine Luning, and Klaas van Walraven, pp. 75–103. Leiden, Netherlands: Brill, 2009.

KLAAS VAN WALRAVEN

Baker, Samuel White (1821–1893), British adventurer, explorer, and administrator, was born in

Samuel White Baker, 1865. Photograph by Maull & Fox, 1865. (Private Collection/The Bridgeman Art Library)

London to Samuel Baker, a businessman, and his wife. Educated in England and Germany, and a civil engineer by training, he played a notable role in the history of the Upper Nile in the 1860s. His varied and peripatetic life as a planter, big-game hunter, writer, and controversialist may be studied in his extensive writings and the enormous literature on European travel in Africa.

His work in Africa began in 1861–1865 with explorations in the eastern Sudan, up the White Nile, (where he met James Augustus Grant and John Hanning Speke), and beyond to the Great Lakes. Credit for discovery of the source of the Nile has gone to Grant and Speke; Baker, famously accompanied by his second wife, Florence, explored and named Lake Albert Nyanza. For these adventures, embellished in several books, Baker was much acclaimed, and in 1869, as an expert and raconteur he accompanied the Prince of Wales to Egypt. With characteristic insouciance the Khedive Isma'il, under pressure to control the Upper Nile in the face of European encroachment and pressure to fight the slave trade, thereupon appointed Baker governor of Equatoria.

Baker's record there (1869–1873) was mixed, not least because his terms of reference were extremely unrealistic. These involved extending Egyptian administrative control to the Great Lakes; conquest or conciliation of the tribes along the way; neutralizing the rampant slave trading of Arab and other foreign merchants, in which some of those tribes were victims and others collaborators; and establishing a permanent Egyptian presence, through a chain of fortified stations, in order to defend Cairo's claims and encourage (and tax) legitimate long-distance trade. Through direct patronage by the Khedive, Baker obtained lavish provision for the expedition, but he was unable ever to overcome either the bureaucratic and natural obstacles to communication between Cairo and the Upper Nile or the chaotic conditions he encountered south of Khartoum.

Pervading Baker's detailed narratives of the Upper Nile, and indeed other sources for the history of that tumultuous period, is a sense of frustration born ultimately of ignorance of the nature of the tasks at hand. Baker routinely reported annexation of territories over which he had no control, basing his claim on single encounters with local notables or the lack of opposition to his passage. The making of camps on the Nile with permanent garrisons was depicted as establishing control of their hinterlands. Even so, provisioning of those camps, and maintaining the loyalty (and health) of Egyptian Army officers and soldiers, required enormous efforts of transport and constant interventions with faraway Cairo in the face of double-dealing in Khartoum and inevitable delays.

Baker's relations with the peoples he encountered in the Upper Nile were complicated by inept diplomacy and exotic standards. He took sides in the disputes of the Bari, wholly misunderstood the effect of his sudden appearance in Unyoro, imagined budding relations with the Baganda, and, throughout, despite railing against the slave traders, failed to appreciate their tenacity or the degree to which they had influenced local conditions. A dreamy imperialism overarched his activities—and his private correspondence and official reports—and distorted or omitted the mundane: how realistic were the prospects of "trade" between Lake Victoria and Cairo? And although Baker was the first Englishman in some of these parts, he was not the first foreigner (or "Turk"): locals' expectation of his early departure rendered his presence a nuisance to be put up with rather than a revolutionary alteration of the local power structure.

Like many other of Cairo's European officials in the Sudan, moreover, Baker was the wrong man for the (impossible) mission assigned to him. Although uncorrupted by the venality and cynicism that pervaded administration of the Sudan during the late Turco-Egyptian period, he was unsympathetic with the plight of those under his command and, as a Christian European, easily seen as inimical to their interests. Hot-headed, irascible, uncompromising, ignorant of local economics (and even geography), wholly unequal to Cairene intrigue, and impressed by his own exploits (as a Gold Medallist of the Royal Geographical Society, *pasha* of Egypt, and—absurdly—a local major-general), Baker in the Upper Nile appeared as a comet in the night sky: a flash of light, much remarked upon from afar but in local African terms signifying very little.

Baker's books nevertheless remain important sources for the period. Most notable are *The Nile Tributaries of Abyssinia* (London, 1867); *Ismailia* (London, 1874); and *The Albert N'yanza* (London, 1866).

BIBLIOGRAPHY

Gray, Richard. *A History of the Southern Sudan,
    1839–1889.* London: Oxford University Press, 1961.
    Although outdated, this remains the only survey of
    the period for the region and places the works of
    Baker in context.

Hill, Richard. *Egypt in the Sudan, 1820–1881.* London:
    Oxford University Press, 1959. Remains the
    standard work for the period. Hill's other works on
    the Europeans in the Sudan are also relevant.

M. W. DALY

Bakhita, Josephine (c. 1869–1947), freed slave and Roman Catholic saint in Sudan, was born in the Darfur region near Agilerei Mountain, northeast of Nyala. Her father was a wealthy Daju (black African Muslim) who owned numerous cattle and a farm cultivated by servants. She had three brothers and four sisters, one of whom was kidnapped into slavery around 1874. Around 1876, Bakhita, which means "fortunate" in Arabic and is not her original name, was herself taken by slave traders; and after a failed attempt to escape, she was bought by a merchant in al-Ubayyid, where she served his two daughters. She was subsequently purchased around 1879 by an Ottoman army officer, who moved with his household to Khartoum in 1882. In this family, she was treated brutally with whipping and scarification, but several months afterward she was acquired by an Italian consular agent, Callisto

Legnani. When he was forced by political events (the Mahdist movement) to leave Khartoum at the end of 1884, Bakhita implored him to take her with him.

They traveled together with a friend, the Catholic merchant Augusto Michieli, to the seaport town of Suakin; in 1885, Michieli took her to his young wife, Turina, in Zianigo near Mirano Veneto, where Bakhita took care of their daughter Alice, called Mimmina. In 1886, Michieli purchased a hotel in Suakin and was followed there later by his wife, Mimmina, and Bakhita; after the children had been sent back, Bakhita accompanied Mimmina to the Institute of the Catechumens in Venice on 29 November 1888. When Michieli's wife returned in 1889, planning to take both girls with her for good, Bakhita refused and was backed by the Cardinal Patriarch of Venice, on whose behalf the king's magistrate ruled on 29 November 1889 that Bakhita was free because slavery was outlawed both in Sudan and in Italy. After her baptism on 9 January 1890 as Giuseppina Margherita Fortunata (Italian for "the fortunate"), she was accepted as a novice of the Daughters of Charity of Canossa at the Institute of St. Magdalene in Venice on 7 December 1893. On 8 December 1896, she became a nun in this order. She was transferred to Schio in 1902, where she served as a cook.

Bakhita was then asked to put her life down in writing, which she did by telling it to Sister Teresa Fabris in 1910. It was published in 1919, added to by fragments of childhood memories given to Sister Marinannina Turco in September 1929, and by a series of interviews with Ida Zanolini for *Vita Canossiana*, a monthly publication of the Canossian missions, published in 1931. During World War I, the convent was used as a military hospital; Bakhita worked in the kitchen, the sacristy, and as assistant nurse. From 1922, she suffered from pulmonitis, and as a result of her weakened condition she served as a doorkeeper at the convent for the rest of her life. Nevertheless, she began to travel in 1933, speaking about her life and collecting donations; she was then widely known as La Nostra Madre Moretta ("our black mother"). Between 1935 and 1938, she was engaged to prepare young nuns for work in Africa; on 11 December 1936, she accompanied a delegation of missionaries to an audience with Benito Mussolini and Pope Pius XI before their departure to Addis Ababa. Spending her last years in a wheelchair struck by heavy illness, she died on 8 February 1947, in Schio. In 1959, her diocese initiated the investigation required to elevate her status to *venerabilis* (honorable). Pope John Paul II proclaimed the Decree of the Heroic Practice of All Virtues on 1 December 1978 and beatified her on 17 May 1992 on St. Peter's Square, followed by the pope's visit in Sudan on 10 February 1993, where he mentioned her in a speech about the necessity of tolerance and peace in the civil war–ridden country. She was canonized on 1 October 2000 as "Our Universal Sister" and adopted as patron saint of Sudan.

Bakhita's life story invited its symbolization as struggle for liberation, especially in a Christian eschatological direction, as the way from childhood happiness to suffering to freedom in God and the Church. In this sense, Pope Benedict XVI mentioned her in the encyclical *Spe Salvi*, and her life has been reproduced in books (Dagnino, 1992; Zanini, 2004), movies (*Bakhita*, 2009; *Two Suitcases*, 2008), and a musical (Philippines, 2000). Her name has been given to churches (Torit, Lokichoggio, Kenya), schools (Brampton, Ontario, Canada; Narus, South Sudan), festivals, and associations (Blessed Josephine Bakhita Women's Association in Egypt). For some, including South Sudanese Catholic refugees, she became a role model as a liberated black African female Christian, whose memory transcends her tribal past and the often faceless history of slavery.

BIBLIOGRAPHY

Bakhita, Giuseppina. *Il cuore ci martellava nel petto: Il diario di una schiava divenuta santa*, edited by Roberto Italo Zanini. Turin, Italy: San Paolo, 2004. New edition of the 1919 text.

Dagnino, Maria Luisa. *Bakhita Tells Her Story*. Rome: Casa Generalizia, 1992. This is the English translation of Bakhita's diary and her 1929 interviews, with an introduction by the editors; this publication is focused on the church-related aspects of her life, and it is primarily a missionary pamphlet.

Troutt Powell, Eve M. "Sainted Slave: Bakhita in the Memories of Southern Sudanese." In *Race and Identity in the Nile Valley: Ancient and Modern Perspectives*, edited by Carolyn Fluehr-Lobban and Kharyssa Rhodes, pp. 159–169. Trenton, N.J.: Red Sea Press, 2004.

ENRICO ILLE

Bakrii Saphalo (1895–1980), Islamic scholar in the Oromo region of Ethiopia, was born in the village of Saphalo in Harerge. His real name was Abubakar Usman Oda. He was destined to make the village of his birth the most famous place in Harerge. In fact, "Bakrii," the root form of which is cognate with "Abubakar," came to be inseparably linked with the name of his village. Thus, he was generally known as Shaykh Bakrii Saphalo, and indeed, few of his admirers ever knew his real name.

He received twenty years of advanced Islamic education, becoming a shaykh (scholar-teacher). He opened his first center of teaching in Saphalo in 1927. Eventually, he opened five centers of teaching in several places, becoming the most famous teacher in eastern Ethiopia. In addition to religious education and philosophy, his teaching ranged over geography, history, mathematics, astronomy, Arabic, and composition in the Oromo language. During his long life, Shaykh Bakrii married a number of wives, by whom he had twenty-five children (eleven sons and fourteen daughters), of whom only three sons and six daughters were still alive in 2011. Shaykh Bakrii believed in the education of women, and all of his daughters received basic Islamic education. Ten of his sons were highly educated, becoming shaykhs. Not only did he educate distinguished scholars and a gifted poet such as Shaykh Mohammad Rashad, but he also produced several works that shaped our understanding of the Oromo situation during the long reign of Emperor Haile Selassie.

Shaykh Bakrii Saphalo was a prominent traditional scholar who was also a prolific writer. His eight manuscripts deal with secular as well as religious subjects and were written mainly in Arabic, although some were written in Oromo. Unfortunately, only two of them have been published, in Mogadishu; therefore, they remain inaccessible to scholars in Ethiopia and beyond. When his main residence at Kortu was attacked by Ethiopian soldiers in 1978, all of his works there were burned; Shaykh Bakrii barely escaped with his life. What is more, the military regime's authorities collected Shaykh Bakrii's manuscripts from the people in the village of Kortu and destroyed them and detained or forced into exile anyone suspected of possessing his manuscripts.

More than his published and numerous unpublished works, the immense popularity of Shaykh Bakrii Saphalo was derived from two other sources: the appeal of his poems among the Oromo people and his invention of a writing system for the Oromo language. His invention of a writing system represented a direct challenge to the Ethiopian government's policy of banning writing in the Oromo language. Once the government found out about his writing system, it immediately banned it and subjected its inventor to ten years of house arrest in the city of Dire Dawa. However, his writing system continues to be used clandestinely in parts of Harerge, Bale, and Arsi regions.

Although contemporary Muslim Oromo scholars either were indifferent to the suffering of their people or encouraged them to endure it as being the will of Allah, Shaykh Bakrii was deeply involved in raising Oromo political consciousness. He believed most intensely in creating political awareness among the Oromo. His goal was to make the Oromo agents of their own liberation. He was a scholar who had a strong passion for freedom and the dignity of his people. In short, he was a qur'anic teacher by day and a revolutionary nationalist by night, who was influenced by the anti-imperialist and anticolonialist socialist rhetoric that swept the continent of Africa in the late 1950s and 1960s. Under the pretext of liquidating "narrow nationalists" and "reactionary" religious leaders, the Ethiopian military regime wanted to execute Shaykh Bakrii, as it executed so many prominent Muslim scholars in Harerge in 1978. He escaped to Somalia and was admitted to the refugee camp. The rigor and deprivation of the camp proved too much for the old scholar, who died on 5 April 1980, aged eighty-five, and was buried in an unmarked grave at a refugee camp in northern Somalia.

Bakrii Saphalo was a perceptive man and a scholar of traditional Oromo wisdom. He was a gifted poet, a man of unusual talent and energy, and a prolific writer, who was subjected to persecution by two successive Ethiopian regimes. As an activist scholar, his works reflect a deep-seated passion to spread knowledge among the Oromo. For him, knowledge was a powerful weapon for those in search of social justice, while ignorance was darkness imposed upon the Oromo by the Ethiopian rulers. He struggled for more than six decades to free his people through education. He wrote, taught, and preached tirelessly to uplift the spirit of his people and secure respect for their language, culture, human dignity, and national identity. He lived through seven decades during which writing, preaching, teaching, and broadcasting in the Oromo language was banned in imperial Ethiopia. Through many years of selfless efforts, he brought his unique talents, energy, optimism, dedication, and motivation to develop written literature in the Oromo language.

[*See also* Haile Selassie I.]

BIBLIOGRAPHY

Hassen, Mohammed. "Shaykh Bakrii Saphalo (1985–1980): A Prolific Scholar and Great Oromo Nationalist." *Journal of Oromo Studies* 10, nos. 1–2 (July 2003): 135–178.

Hayward, Richard, and Mohammed Hassen. "The Oromo Orthography of Shaykh Bakrii Saphalo." *Bulletin of the School of Oriental and African Studies* 44, no. 3 (1981): 550–566.

Muudee, Mahdi Hamid. Walaloo Bariisaa: *Bariisaa Poems*, Atlanta: Sagalee Oromoo, 1996.

MOHAMMED HASSEN

Balbus, Cornelius (c. 80 BCE–5 BCE), Roman official in Africa and Mauretania, was a member of a distinguished family from Gades (modern Cádiz in Spain). His uncle, of the same name, had been the first consul not born a Roman citizen (40 BCE).

The younger Balbus was a loyal follower of Julius Caesar, and he first appears in the historical record on 24 February 49 BCE when he visited Cicero at Formiae while carrying a message from Caesar to Rome. Balbus seems regularly to have been a courier for Caesar during the Roman civil war. He was wounded in the engagements around Dyrrhachion early the following year; his daring diplomatic negotiations with the Pompeians at this time earned him much credit. He probably continued on Caesar's staff during the latter's time in the East, including the period he was in Egypt, returning to Italy by 45 BCE, when he visited Cicero at his villa in Tusculum. Balbus was elected *quaestor* for 43 BCE and became part of the staff of C. Asinius Pollio in Farther Spain. He crossed over to Africa in order to enter into a well-financed negotiation with Bogudes II, the king of Western Mauretania, presumably to keep the king loyal to the Caesarian party in the uncertain period after Caesar's assassination. Bogudes had consistently supported Caesar—despite the fact that Caesar had had an affair with his wife—but it is not known how successful Balbus's mission was.

His career during the years immediately following is little known. He may have been *propraetor* in Spain in 40 BCE. He held a pontificate at some uncertain date and rose to the rank of consul before 21 BCE. By that year he was holding a proconsular command in Africa. There were persistent difficulties with the indigenous populations of North Africa, who tended to make incursions both into the allied kingdom of Mauretania and the Roman province of Africa. The issue was largely the age-old conflict between the transhumant peoples who had long lived in the region, and who needed free movement across the countryside, and the increasing agricultural and urban population, much of it Italian in origin. In particular, the Garamantes, known to the Greco-Roman world since the fifth century BCE, were a major source of difficulty, at least from the Roman point of view.

Balbus set forth against them from his provincial headquarters, probably late in 21 BCE, seeking Garama, their famous capital. He followed the existing trade routes that led southeast from the Roman territory, passing through the ancient city of Cydamis, and eventually reached Garama (modern Germa) in the Fezzan region of modern Libya, over 435 miles (700 kilometers) inland. Garama was wealthy and prosperous, a situation reflected today in the rich archaeological remains of the region, especially the tombs that extend over 62 miles (100 kilometers) along the Wadi el-Aghial, and a series of hilltop forts that were being replaced by oasis villages during Roman times. In the record of his triumph of 19 BCE, Balbus listed over twenty towns and tribes that he allegedly conquered; needless to say most if not all of these "conquests" were ephemeral, if they existed at all. Nevertheless, if he did reach Garama it was one of the deepest Roman penetrations into the Sahara to date.

Balbus returned to Rome to celebrate his triumph, the first person not born a Roman citizen to do so. He also was the last private citizen to have a triumph, because future ones were reserved for members of the imperial family. As commemoration he built the Theater of Balbus in Rome, which was dedicated in 13 BCE amid great festivities, although ironically the site was flooded on the day of dedication. Balbus, who was present at these anticlimatic ceremonies, then seems to have retired to his native Gades but used his immense wealth to endow construction in that city, including an entire new subdivision. In his retirement he may also have devoted himself to writing his memoirs and other literary works.

A Roman who spent little time in Rome, Balbus is typical of the upwardly mobile provincial aristocracy of the first century BCE. Much of his career was in Africa, and the record of his journey into the heart of the Sahara provides a valuable toponymic record of areas little understood even today.

[*See also* Julius Caesar.]

BIBLIOGRAPHY

Groag, Edmund, ed. *Prosopographia Imperii Romani.* 2d ed. Berlin: de Gruyter, 1970. The complete listing of the documentary evidence for Balbus's career.

Mattingly, D. J. "Garama." In *The Barrington Atlas of the Greek and Roman World: Map-by-Map Directory*, edited by Richard J. A. Talbert, pp. 545–546. Princeton, N.J.: Princeton University Press, 2000. The most recent evidence for the remains on Balbus's route and at Garama.

Scullard, H. H. *From the Gracchi to Nero.* London: Methuen, 1959. Still the best history of the era.

DUANE W. ROLLER

Ballinger, Margaret (1894–1980), liberal historian and politician active in South Africa, was born Violet Margaret Livingstone Hodgson on 11 January 1894 in Glasgow, Scotland. Her father, John Hodgson, emigrated to the Orange Free State, South Africa, shortly after Margaret's birth, working as a merchant while Margaret's mother, Lillias, raised their three young children in Scotland. After fighting against the British with the Irish Brigade in the Anglo-Boer War, John Hodgson went to the Atlantic island of Saint Helena as a prisoner of war. When war ended in 1902, officials repatriated him, but he was ostracized in his community. Six months after his return, he illegally boarded a ship bound for Port Elizabeth, where he worked as a bookkeeper. In 1904, John Hodgson's family joined him in the Cape. He harbored liberal political beliefs, supporting legal equality and the extension of a nonracial franchise in southern Africa.

After attending the Holy Rosary Convent in Port Elizabeth, Margaret Hodgson proceeded to the Huguenot College in Wellington and then Rhodes University in Grahamstown; she graduated from the latter with a bachelor of arts in history, with first-class honors, in 1913. Her mentor at Rhodes was the liberal historian William Macmillan, who built upon her father's political influence. From Rhodes she won a scholarship to Somerville College, Oxford, where she completed coursework in modern history in 1917; she could not receive a master's degree until advanced degrees opened to women in 1924.

Margaret Hodgson returned to Rhodes in 1917 to lecture in history and economics. Upon Macmillan's recommendation, she taught his courses, as he had left to chair the Department of History at the School of Mines in Johannesburg (which in 1922 became the University of the Witwatersrand, known as Wits). Hodgson was ousted from Rhodes in 1919 and replaced with a male colleague, on explicit account of her gender and lack of an advanced degree.

In 1920, Macmillan secured her an appointment as a lecturer in history and economics at Wits.

Hodgson and Macmillan together shaped Wits into a center of liberal inquiry, where scholars argued that legal segregation belied the social realities of South Africa's thoroughgoing economic integration. Hodgson also fought personally, and unsuccessfully, to equalize salaries between men and women at Wits. In 1926, Hodgson joined Macmillan in the Joint Council of Europeans and Africans, where she led in advocating for African educational access, child welfare, and employment access.

Two years later, Hodgson met William Ballinger, a British labor activist who had come to Johannesburg to advise the Industrial and Commercial Workers' Union. They became political allies, friends, and lovers.

In 1932, Macmillan left South Africa for London, disgusted by the political limitations of the Wits campus and of South African politics. In 1934, Hodgson and Ballinger also traveled to London, where they secretly eloped. On that trip they founded the Society of the Friends of Africa, a group consisting of British Labor activists and South African liberals who sought to advance an economically rooted developmental agenda for black South Africans. Upon her return, Margaret Ballinger lost her job at Wits, based equally on her politics and on her status as a married woman.

When Prime Minister J. B. M. Hertzog's government abolished the nonracial Cape franchise and replaced it with a system of white "native" representation in 1936, Ballinger found a new career. While many activists in the African National Congress and the Unity Movement advocated noncollaboration with this new measure, Margaret Ballinger was elected the "native" representative for the Eastern Cape, a post she held until the system's abolition in 1960. In 1953, she became the founding president of the Liberal Party, a group that sought gradual, elite-led reform through legal and legislative means. The party disbanded in 1968, after multiracial political groups became illegal.

While Margaret Ballinger provided a rare official voice for her constituents, playing a mediating role between Africans and the apartheid state, such efforts could not forestall increasing state repression, as the Sharpeville Massacre of 1960 and the ensuing State of Emergency revealed. But throughout her career, Ballinger remained convinced that a more just society might be achieved by working through extant systems than by rejecting them. By her 7 February 1980 death in Cape Town, she was a politically isolated woman in an explosive country.

Ballinger's struggles to navigate official authority—in academia or in Parliament—illuminate the difficulties of reforming a multiply unequal society from within its structures of power.

[*See also* Hertzog, James Barry Munnik.]

BIBLIOGRAPHY

Ballinger, Margaret. *From Union to Apartheid: A Trek to Isolation.* New York: Praeger, 1969. Ballinger's account of her career, illuminating both the narrowing political possibilities that liberal South Africans confronted and her enduring ideological commitment to liberalism.

Moulton, F. A. *Voices in the Desert: Margaret and William Ballinger: A Biography.* Pretoria: Benedic Books, 1997. A comprehensive account of the Ballingers' careers that attempts to recuperate the contributions of their generation of liberal activists.

Vigne, Randolph. *Liberals against Apartheid: A History of the Liberal Party of South Africa, 1953–1968.* New York: St. Martin's Press, 1997. The most detailed account and evaluation of the Liberal Party specifically and South African liberalism more broadly, written by a former member of the Liberal Party.

MEGHAN ELISABETH HEALY

Bambouté, Makombo (1932–), poet, short-story writer, and novelist, was born Pierre Makombo Bamboté at Ouadda on the River Pipi in the Haute-Kotto region of the French colony of Ubangi-Shari on 1 April 1932. The most prolific and best-known man of letters from the Central African Republic (CAR), he studied in Central Africa and then in France, where he obtained graduate degrees in international affairs, sociology, and journalism. Soon after returning to the CAR, he was appointed director of information (15 January 1965–11 January 1966), then director of the National Museum Boganda at Bangui. He then joined the foreign service and was appointed chargé d'affaires at the United Nations Educational, Scientific, and Cultural Organization (UNESCO) on 7 March 1970 before moving to Canada, where he taught at Laval University in Quebec. He sought asylum in Canada in 1973, during the rule of President Jean Bedel Bokassa, and he still lives there today.

His first publication, *La poésie est dans l'histoire* (Poetry Inspired by History, 1960), consists of a single poem that criticizes slavery and colonialism, a poet's reaction to Africa's history of suffering. In this poem, he speaks of himself as an embittered Bandia, the Bandia being rulers of the Nzakara people in southeastern CAR. His second book, *Chant funèbre pour un héros d'Afrique* (Funeral Lament for an African Hero, 1962), was a long anticolonial poem written in honor of the recently assassinated leader of the Belgian Congo's independence movement, Patrice Lumumba, who Bamboté greatly admired. Bamboté then wrote a series of short stories in 1963 and 1964, published in 1980 as *Nouvelles de Bangui* (Stories of Bangui), for which he was awarded with the Études françaises award (Montréal University, Canada). These stories offer a vivid and nostalgic depiction of the land of his childhood. They include an account of the death of Chief Sayo, the son of Bangassou, the king of the Nzakara, who was one of the author's relatives. He then published *Les randonnées de Daba (de Ouadda à Bangui)* (1966), which was translated into English as *Daba's Travels from Ouadda to Bangui* in 1970. *Daba's Travels* draws on Bamboté's own childhood and youth as it tells the story of a child going from the rural region of Upper Kotto in the far eastern part of the country to the capital city of Bangui and overseas to study.

The hero, Daba, is born in the remote rural region of Ouadda, where his mother often told him about terrible dry seasons when elephants, buffalo, and antelopes stampeded through the countryside in a frenzied search for water. Panthers also stalked the bush around the village, often carrying off valuable sheep. Feeling safe near his parent's hut, Daba listened to such stories over and over again. And as he grew up, well loved and protected, he gained strength of spirit and developed a deep love for his native village. But Daba was not destined to live his life in remote Ouadda. While still a young boy, he left his beloved home on the first of a series of journeys that would lead him farther and farther away. Daba's years at boarding school in the large town of Bambari are described. During vacations, Daba and his schoolmates traveled through the savanna and along muddy streams, often encountering lions, crocodiles, and elephants along the way. Daba eventually goes to France because Daba's parents wanted him to receive a French-style education, a rare and special privilege not often obtainable by poor village children.

Les deux oiseaux de l'Oubangui (Two Birds from Ubangi, 1968), is a story of unhappy love, but it also describes how two Central African children discover the lifestyle, customs, and values of their community. *Princesse Mandapu* (1972) (named after Bamboté's mother, Mandapu) is Bamboté's most acclaimed work of fiction. Described by one critic as "a loosely connected baroque narrative"

and by another as the best example of "the theatre of the absurd" in African Francophone literature, it is a story of conflict between two powerful men in a small Central African town in which Bamboté expresses criticism of postcolonial society. The novel is ostensibly set in the 1930s, but it appears to be a criticism of postindependence society in Central Africa. It describes scenes from the daily life of civil servants in the CAR that could be associated with colonial or postcolonial society.

In *Coup d'état nègre* (Black Coup d'État, 1987), a former director of information in Bangui at the time of the Saint Sylvestré coup d'état describes the scenes he witnessed on the night of 31 December 1965–1 January 1966, which brought Jean Bedel Bokassa to power. No other Central African has risked describing this tragic night when President David Dacko was forced to flee the town as a result of this coup. The commander of the gendarmes, Jean-Henri Izamo, was ready to take power but was lured into an ambush by the chief of staff, Colonel Bokassa.

Que ferons-nous après la guerre; ou, Éloge de l'animisme (What Will We Do after the War; or, Elegy to Animism, 1998) is a work of poetry that focuses on an old man who yearns to end his days with a view of the lions of his motherland. *Déclaration de guerre aux morts* (Declaration of a War unto Death, 2009), another work of poetry, is a heartbreaking indictment of an African reality where it has become almost natural that some white black kings be in the place of the true African princes who had real friendships and royal cousinhoods before the abuses of authority of the colonialist mercantilism that supported slavery. People are reduced to the appearances of the governmental costumes worn by their skeletons.

Other works by Bamboté include *Le soir des destructeurs* (Night of the Destroyers, c. 1964), *La Salamandre* (The Salamander, 1964), *Le grand état central* (The Great Central State, 1965), *Le dur avenir* (The Difficult Future, 1965), *Technique pour rien: suivi de Civilisation des autres* (Technique for Nothing [and] The Civilization of Others, 1973), and *Journal d'un paysan de l'Afrique centrale* (Diary of a Central African Farmer, 1974).

[*See also* Bokassa, Jean Bedel; Dacko, David; *and* Lumumba, Patrice Emery.]

BIBLIOGRAPHY

Ngate, Jonathan. *Francophone African Fiction: Reading a Literary Tradition*. Trenton, N.J.: Africa World Press, 1988.

Pereyra, Verónica and Luis M. Mora. "Bamboté, Pierre Makombo." In *Literaturas africanas, de las sombras a la luz* [African Literature: From Shadows to Light], pp. 166–167. Madrid: Editorial Mundo Negro, 1998.

Tchokongbo, Christophe. *Lectures de Princesse Mandapu de Pierre Makombo Bamboté: Analyse stylistique de la fiction narrative* [(The Reading of *Pincess Mandapu* by Pierre Makombo Bamboté: Stylistic Analysis of Fictional Narrative]. Villeneuve d'Asq, France: Presses universitaires du Septentrion, 2000.

RICHARD A. BRADSHAW and
JUAN FANDOS-RIUS

Banana, Canaan Sodindo (1936–2003), nationalist politician, first titular president of independent Zimbabwe, statesman, peace broker, clergyman, author, soccer administrator, academic, poet, and journalist, was born on 5 March 1936 at Esiphezini, in Essexvale (now Esigodini) District near Bulawayo in Southern Rhodesia. The versatile Banana's father, Aaron, was a migrant laborer from Malawi while his mother, Jese, was a Zimbabwean Ndebele woman. Banana married Janet Mbuyazwe in 1961; the marriage produced three sons and a daughter. Banana attended Mzinyati primary school and Tegwani High School. He trained as a teacher at Tegwani Training Institute and then attended Epworth Theological Seminary, resulting in his ordination as a Methodist preacher in 1962. Subsequently he worked as a Methodist schools manager, principal, chairperson of the Bulawayo Council of Churches, and member of the Rhodesian Christian Council and World Council of Churches. In the 1970s, Banana attained a BA with honors in theology through distance learning from the University of South Africa and an MA in theological studies from Wesley Theological Seminary in Washington, D.C.

Banana's breakthrough on the national scene came in 1972 when he was appointed vice-president of the African National Council (ANC). The Bishop Abel Muzorewa–led ANC was formed to coordinate African opposition to the 1971 Anglo-Rhodesian proposal for the settlement of the Rhodesian crisis. The ANC also sought to fill the political void created by the imprisonment of nationalist leaders and the proscription of leading political parties—the Zimbabwe African People's Union (ZAPU) and the Zimbabwe African National Union (ZANU)—by the Ian Smith regime. During the Pearce Commission hearings to test opinion on the Anglo-Rhodesian proposal, Banana assumed greater visibility as an articulate spokesperson for the ANC. Africans emphatically opposed the proposal, because it was a deal to maintain white socioeconomic privileges exclusively brokered by white people and for white people. The proposal did not guarantee African majority rule and universal adult suffrage, since it mandated the establishment of three voters' rolls based on race, qualifications, income, and property ownership. Voting qualifications on the African Higher Roll were so high that they excluded teachers and many other African professionals.

Frontline participation in the ANC triggered Banana's surveillance, harassment, and detentions by the colonial security establishment. In 1972, Rhodesian police impounded his passport. This persecution compelled Banana to skip the border into Botswana en route to Kasai Industrial Center in Japan and the United States, where he became a chaplain at the American University in Washington, D.C., between 1973 and 1975. While in the United States, Banana increasingly transformed into a radical priest espousing liberation theology ideals. Liberation theology maintains that salvation for a people is a holistic and multifaceted process that entails liberation from multiple forms of bondage that are spiritual, social, political, and economic in nature. Banana called for the church to move beyond ministering to its laity by playing an increasing role in the socioeconomic development of postcolonial societies. He inaugurated his reputation as a liberation theologian in 1974 when he published a book titled *The Gospel According to the Ghetto* and a modified version of the Lord's Prayer that encouraged Africans to resist white supremacy. Some of the poem's famous lines are as follows: "Teach us to demand our share of gold/forgive us our docility /as we demand our share of justice."

Banana returned to Rhodesia in 1975 and was imprisoned for having left the country without proper travel documentation. Upon release from prison in 1976 he was restricted to his rural home area. In September of the same year the Smith regime allowed Banana to attend the Anglo-American-brokered Rhodesian peace talks at the Geneva Conference as part of Bishop Muzorewa's ANC delegation. While in Geneva, Banana defected to the Patriotic Front, the ZANU-ZAPU alliance, and endorsed the liberation struggle. This was for two main reasons. First, he was against Muzorewa's willingness to bargain for piecemeal independence with the Smith regime and, second, he opposed attempts to elevate the ANC beyond its caretaker status as an organization that was supposed to facilitate the legal operations of ZANU and ZAPU.

In January 1977 Banana was arrested and detained at Gatooma Prison. He was transferred to Wha Wha Prison in May 1979, where he stayed until his release in November 1979. His release coincided with the Lancaster House Talks that ended the liberation struggle and paved the way for the internationally monitored elections for majority rule in 1980. On 18 April 1980 Banana became the country's first postcolonial president, while Robert Mugabe became the executive prime minister. Mugabe availed the presidency to Banana after the main opposition leader, Joshua Nkomo of ZAPU, turned down the post because it had no real power. Banana was also selected in order to foster an impression of ethnic balancing at the apex of the national political power hierarchy; he was affiliated with the Ndebele, while Mugabe was Shona.

As titular president Banana was quite popular. This was aided by his calm deportment and well-contrived self-projection as an affable but urbane theologian. He represented the country at numerous international events that included the marriage of the Prince of Wales to Lady Diana Spencer in 1981. He became the chancellor of the University of Zimbabwe and was awarded numerous honorary degrees. The undemanding nature of the presidency left Banana ample room to engage in some of his passions, particularly soccer administration. He supported the Zimbabwe Saints and established his own soccer team, the State House Tornadoes. After departure from the presidency he became patron to the Zimbabwe Football Association.

Perhaps Banana's most important achievement as president was his central role in ending the state-instigated violence, the Gukurahundi, in Matabeleland and Midlands Provinces in the 1980s. Prime Minister Mugabe deployed the Fifth Brigade, a military outfit whose officers were accountable to him rather than to the normal army chain of command, to counter purported PF-ZAPU aligned dissidence. The brigade embarked upon indiscriminate attacks on civilians; nearly twenty thousand civilians died in these counterinsurgency operations. Banana initiated unity talks between ZANU and ZAPU soon after the 1985 general elections. After protracted negotiations a national unity accord was signed on 22 December 1987.

Banana relinquished the presidency on 31 December 1987. Mugabe became executive president. For the next ten years Banana enjoyed relative quiet while playing important roles. He became professor of classics, religious studies, and philosophy at the University of Zimbabwe. Internationally, he led the World Council of Churches' Eminent Church persons on sanctions against South Africa in 1989 and was cochair of the United Nations Panel of Eminent Persons conducting public hearings on the operations of transnational corporations in South Africa. In the 1990s, the Organization of African Unity (OAU) appointed him its special envoy on war-torn Liberia.

Banana's image as a revered statesman suffered a major blow in 1997 when he was arrested on charges of sodomy. This was after his former aide-de-camp, Jefta Dube, was charged for the murder of his colleague who had taunted him as "Banana's wife." In mitigation, Dube claimed trauma induced by sexual assaults by Banana. He gave prurient details of how the former president drank, danced, and laced drinks with drugs before raping him while he was unconscious. During Banana's trial in 1998 overwhelming evidence emerged from State House gardeners, cooks, and aides as well as students and some colleagues at the University of Zimbabwe about Banana's nonconsensual homosexual escapades. Shortly before sentencing, Banana fled the country to South Africa, where he met President Nelson Mandela. He had allegedly received a tipoff that Zimbabwean authorities were plotting against his life. It is presumed Mandela encouraged the fugitive Banana to return and face justice after successfully interceding with the Zimbabwean authorities for a lighter sentence. Banana was found guilty of eleven counts of sodomy and other "unnatural acts" on men. He received a ten-year prison sentence. Nine years were suspended, and he ultimately served six months at Connemara Open Prison. He was released in January 2001. Until his death Banana denied that he was homosexual and that rape allegations leveled against him were "pathological lies" and "character assassination."

Imprisonment cost Banana heavily. His marriage floundered when Janet Banana sought political asylum in Britain in 2001; the University of Zimbabwe dismissed him as professor; the Methodist Church defrocked him; and the OAU rescinded his appointment as special envoy to Liberia. Banana died of cancer in London, on 10 November 2003. He was sixty-seven. The virulently homophobic President Mugabe described him as "a rare gift to the nation." Banana was buried with full military honors befitting a former head of state at his rural home in Matabeleland South. This entombment, far from the celebrated confines of the National Heroes Acre in Harare, where men and women far lower in stature and contribution to the liberation and development of Zimbabwe lie interred, was as dishonorable as it was vindictive.

[*See also* Mandela, Nelson; Mugabe, Robert; Nkomo, Joshua Mqabuko Nyangolo; *and* Smith, Ian Douglas.]

BIBLIOGRAPHY

Banana, Canaan S., ed. *Turmoil and Tenacity, Zimbabwe, 1890–1990*. Harare, Zimbabwe: College Press, 1989.

"Canaan Banana of Zimbabwe dead." http://news.bbc.co.uk/2/hi/africa/3258969.stm.

Chiwewe, Willard A. "Unity Negotiations." In *Turmoil and Tenacity, Zimbabwe, 1890–1990*, edited by Canaan S. Banana, pp. 242–87. Harare, Zimbabwe: College Press, 1989.

Nzombe, Shepherd. "Negotiations with the British." In *Turmoil and Tenacity, Zimbabwe, 1890–1990*, edited by Canaan S. Banana, pp. 162–196. Harare, Zimbabwe: College Press, 1989.

Sellstrom, Tor, ed. *Liberation Movements in Southern Africa: Regional and Swedish Voices, Interviews from Angola, Mozambique, Namibia, South Africa, Zimbabwe, the Frontline, and Sweden*. Uppsala, Sweden: Nordiska Afrikainstitutet, 1999.

Taylor, Rebecca. "Janet Banana: They Say Power Corrupts—and It Does." *Guardian*, January 22, 2002.

Zvobgo, Chengetai J. M. *A History of Zimbabwe, 1890–2000, and Postscript, Zimbabwe, 2001–2008*. Cambridge, UK: Cambridge Scholars, 2009.

TERENCE M. MASHINGAIDZE

Banda, Hastings Kamuzu (c. 1896–1997), physician and president of Malawi from 1964 to 1994, was born in about 1896 at Mphonongo, approximately 18 miles (29 kilometers) east of the headquarters of the present-day Kasungu district. Given the name, Kamunkhwala, denoting the medicine that his mother took to enable conception, Banda attended two local junior elementary schools of the Livingstonia Mission of the Church of Scotland. In 1908, he went to the more established school at Chilanga Mission where, in that year, Dr. George Prentice baptized him as Akim Kamunkhwala Mtunthama Banda. He was to drop all three names and replace them with Hastings Walter (after a Scottish missionary, John Hastings), before finally settling on Hastings Kamuzu Banda, substituting *kamuzu* (root) for Kamunkhwala.

In 1914, Banda passed three standard exams, a mandatory step to continue to the full primary school level, the satisfactory completion of which was the highest qualification one could attain in the British colony, then known as Nyasaland. In 1915, although one of the best students in his class, he was expelled from school, thanks to a misunderstanding of a missionary, Thomas Cullen Young. The highly disappointed Banda immediately left for South Africa hoping to study at Lovedale Institution in the Eastern Cape, where some of the distinguished African teachers in the Livingstonia Mission system had qualified. Using some of the established routes that Nyasalanders had used to go to South Africa in search of work, Banda walked to Southern Rhodesia where he worked for some time as a medical orderly at a hospital in Hartley. With his uncle and former teacher in Kasungu, Hanock Msokera Phiri, who had joined him by this time, Banda proceeded to Natal, where the two found employment at a colliery. After a brief period they left for the Johannesburg area. There he worked first in a gold mine and then as a clerk in its administrative office, his basic Livingstonia Mission education proving to be an asset to him and to his employers.

Still determined to improve his education, Hastings Banda studied privately and attained standard eight, the equivalent of the American grade nine. At the same time, he and Hanock Phiri joined the American-based African Methodist Episcopal Church (AME), a development that was to change his life forever, for it was through his contacts in the church that the young Banda came to nurture ideas of furthering his education in the United States. At an AME conference held in Bloemfontein in 1923, the two met Bishop William Tecumseh Vernon, then resident in South Africa, and this encounter resulted in two important decisions. First, Phiri was to go back to Nyasaland to establish a branch of the church, and Banda was to start planning for a journey to the United States, where he was to advance his education under the auspices of AME. The arrangements were confirmed at another church conference in the following year, and in 1925 Hastings Banda sailed from South Africa to New York, where he was met by church members who arranged for him to proceed to Xenia, Ohio, where he enrolled at the Wilberforce Institute. He completed his high school education in three years, and in 1928 enrolled at Indiana University as a premed student. By this time, the AME had stopped sponsoring his studies; instead, he depended on the goodwill of some businessmen and doctors in Ohio and on talks he gave in Indiana and Ohio, mostly on African culture. Initially he struggled academically, especially in chemistry because of his weak background in the basic sciences, but, always a disciplined and hardworking individual, Banda overcame problems and began to thrive. In some of his humanities courses, he wrote papers on Chewa life and culture and, because of this, Dr. Stith Thompson, a professor of folklore, put him in touch with his linguist and anthropologist colleague at the University of Chicago, Edward Sapir, whose graduate student, Mark Hanna Watkins, was working on the Chewa. Sapir arranged for Banda to be transferred to Chicago, the idea being that he should assist Watkins in his research.

In December 1931 Banda graduated from Chicago with a bachelor of philosophy degree in history, and in the following year, he went to Meharry Medical College in Nashville, Tennessee, qualifying as a doctor in May 1937. In order to practice in Nyasaland, part of the British Empire, he went to Scotland to pursue further studies. At Edinburgh University he received his licentiate of the Royal College of Surgeons (LRCS) and licentiate of the Royal College of Physicians (LRCP) in 1941. That same year he became an elder in the Presbyterian Church of Scotland, and he would maintain close links with Scotland, and Edinburgh in particular, throughout his career. Upon obtaining a British license he abandoned plans to return to Nyasaland for the time being, because he would be subjected to segregationist practices. Instead he worked in Liverpool (1941–1943) and in Tyneside (1943–1945) before moving to London, where he established a thriving practice.

Throughout his stay abroad, Banda had corresponded with Hanock Phiri and had maintained interest in the welfare of Kasungu and in the evolving African politics in Nyasaland. He supported the new Nyasaland African Congress (NAC) financially and gave advice to its leaders. He also became involved in Pan African politics, becoming friends with Kwame Nkrumah, Jomo Kenyatta, and George Padmore, among many others.

Banda, like the majority of Africans in Northern and Southern Rhodesia and in Nyasaland, had always opposed the idea of political union of the three colonies, and when European settlers in the region convinced the British government to establish the Central African Federation, Banda left London for Kumasi, Ghana, where he practiced medicine for five years. At the request of the

Nyasaland African Congress, he returned to Nyasaland as a hero ready to lead the struggle for decolonization. His arrival raised the political temperature of Malawi as anticipation for the end of colonial rule increased. In March 1959, Governor Robert Armitage declared a state of emergency, arrested Banda and many in the senior leadership of the ANC, and sent them to prisons in Gweru, Southern Rhodesia. Hundreds of other activists were sent to prisons and detention camps within Nyasaland.

Upon his release in April 1960, Banda, now head of the Malawi Congress Party (MCP), which in 1959 had replaced the NAC, embarked on a series of negotiations with Great Britain that were to lead to significant political changes. The first adult suffrage-based elections of 1961 led to a majority African legislature and government, and in 1963, Banda became prime minister, and the Central African Federation was dissolved. On 4 July 1964, Nyasaland became independent of British authority and changed its name to Malawi. Two months later, Banda and many of his senior ministers disagreed on the direction of domestic and foreign policies, including his conciliatory attitude toward white-ruled southern Africa. Some ministers resigned, he sacked others, and the country plunged into a major political crisis. As Banda regained control, he adopted a more hard-line attitude toward the dissenting ministers and their supporters. All the ministers who had disagreed with him, including Henry Chipembere and W. M. Kanyama Chiume, eventually left for exile abroad, and many of their supporters left behind were imprisoned without trial. Abuse of human rights became part of Banda's one-party rule and, in 1971, the constitution was changed to make him life president. That year he visited South Africa, much to the disapproval of most African nations.

Until about 1980, Malawi's economy expanded, Banda emphasizing both small-scale and commercial agriculture. However, a number of factors, including expensive projects, the expense and waste involved in managing many parastatal organizations, often arenas of patronage, and the general state of the world economy in the 1980s had adverse effects on the socioeconomic progress of Malawi. At the beginning of the 1990s, internal pressure for political reform mounted, especially after the Catholic bishops issued a Lenten letter in March 1992 decrying the abuse of human rights and arguing for the need for immediate change. Banda had long been backed by Western powers, but they, too, particularly after the breakup of the Soviet Union, seemed to abandon him and pressed for political reform. In 1993, he and his party lost a referendum on the introduction of a multiparty system, and in the first free elections for over thirty years, Banda lost to Elison Bakili Muluzu's United Democratic Party. Old and very frail, he retired from politics not long after this and, in 1996, he apologized to the nation for any abuses that may have been committed in his name; he also called for national unity and support for the new government. On 25 November 1997, Dr. Hastings Kamuzu Banda died at the Garden City Clinic, Johannesburg, South Africa, and on 3 December, he had a national funeral at the Heroes Acre in Lilongwe, the location of his mausoleum.

[*See also* Chipembere, Henry Blasius Masauko; Kenyatta, Jomo; Nkrumah, Kwame; *and* Padmore, George.]

BIBLIOGRAPHY

Baker, Colin. *Revolt of the Ministers: The Malawi Cabinet Crisis, 1964–1965*. London: I. B. Tauris, 2001.

Kalinga, Owen, and C. Crosby. *Historical Dictionary of Malawi*. Lanham, Md.: Scarecrow Press, 2001.

Power, Joey. *Political Culture and Nationalism in Malawi: Building Kwacha*. Rochester, N.Y.: University of Rochester Press, 2010.

Ross, Andrew C. *Colonialism to Cabinet Crisis: A Political History of Malawi*. Zomba, Malawi: Kachere Series, 2009.

Rotberg, Robert I. *The Rise of Nationalism in Central Africa: The Making of Malawi and Zambia, 1873–1964*. Cambridge, Mass: Harvard University Press, 1965.

Short, Philip. *Banda*. London: Routledge and Kegan Paul, 1974.

OWEN J. M. KALINGA

Banda, Rupiah (1937–), president of Zambia, was born 19 February 1937 at Gwanda in Zimbabwe (then known as Southern Rhodesia), where his Zambian parents had moved for work. Banda spent his early years in Zimbabwe but was sent to Zambia (then known as Northern Rhodesia) for his education. He attended primary school at Katete in Eastern Province, the region from which his family originated. He completed his secondary school education at the elite Munali School in Lusaka. After studying at the University of Addis Ababa in Ethiopia, he transferred to Lund University in

Sweden and graduated with a bachelor's degree in economic history in 1964.

While at university in Lund he served as the representative for northern Europe for the United National Independence Party (UNIP). As one of few individuals with a college degree at the time Zambia neared independence from Britain in 1964, Banda attracted the positive attention of Kenneth Kaunda, who would become the first president. Banda and his close friend Vernon Mwaanga were among the small group of Zambians who completed a diplomacy course run by the London School of Economics at the National Institute of Public Administration in Lusaka.

After the 24 October 1964 independence festivities, Banda journeyed to New York with Zambia's delegation for the formal admission of their country to the United Nations. Kaunda then appointed Banda as Zambia's ambassador to Egypt, where he served from 1965 until 1967. During his tenure in Cairo, he married Hope Mwansa Makulu in 1966, and they had three sons. In 1967 Banda was appointed Zambian ambassador to the United States, and at age 30 he was one of the youngest diplomats in Washington.

After serving as ambassador to the United States until 1970, Banda returned to Zambia and held several positions over the next few years, including general manager of the National Agricultural Marketing Board. In 1974 he was back in the diplomatic corps, taking over as Zambia's ambassador to the United Nations. During his tenure there, he met with South African representatives to discuss the conflicts in Namibia and Zimbabwe (then known as Rhodesia).

In May 1975 Banda was appointed as Zambia's foreign minister by Kaunda, replacing his old friend Mwaanga. During a September trip to New York, Banda met US secretary of state Henry Kissinger and explained to him that the Zambian government was willing to work with the South African government in order to facilitate a peace settlement in Rhodesia. Banda informed Kissinger that President Kaunda wanted the secretary of state to visit Lusaka, and Kissinger accepted. The two diplomats met and talked in depth at a conference in Paris in December 1975, and Banda greeted Kissinger at the airport when he arrived in Lusaka in April 1976. Banda's central role in arranging Kissinger's very important visit to Zambia was one of his greatest accomplishments as a diplomat.

In addition to the negotiations regarding Rhodesia, another major challenge for Zambian foreign policy during the 1970s was the civil war in Angola. Banda strongly opposed the socialist factions in the conflict, instead supporting Jonas Savimbi. Although South Africa also backed Savimbi, Banda's preference for Savimbi did not reflect his approval of the apartheid regime in Pretoria. Rather, it is best understood as opposition to the heavy-handed Soviet intervention on behalf of the Popular Movement for the Liberation of Angola. Like his president at the time, Kenneth Kaunda, Banda wanted to see a government of national unity prevail in Luanda instead of a socialist government essentially being inserted by the Soviets. After Cuban and Soviet intervention helped deal Savimbi's forces a costly defeat, the Zambian leadership eventually decided to recognize the new socialist government in Luanda. This turn of events contributed significantly to Kaunda's removal of Banda from the foreign minister position in mid-1976.

After another brief period out of government service, Banda was elected as a member of the Zambian parliament representing Munali in 1978. He was defeated in 1983 but then reelected to the seat in 1988 and served until 1991, when he and many other members of UNIP (including Kaunda himself) were defeated by the new Movement for Multiparty Democracy (MMD). While trying in vain to rejuvenate UNIP throughout the 1990s, Banda focused primarily on private business, family, and his favorite pastime, Zambian soccer.

After his first wife, Hope, died from cancer in 2002, Banda moved to his farm in Chipata. Not long afterward he met a history teacher named Thandiwe. The two soon married, and the second Mrs. Banda gave birth to fraternal twins. During these years Banda finally decided to join the MMD. In October 2006 the third president of Zambia, Levy Mwanawasa, appointed Banda as his vice president. After Mwanawasa died in August 2008, Banda took over the presidency. The ruling MMD chose Banda as its presidential candidate that September. Elections began in late October, and on 2 November Banda was declared the winner and became the fourth president of Zambia.

During the first two years of his presidency, Banda strongly supported economic development in Zambia, maintaining strong ties to longtime foreign allies such as the United States and China. His lifelong passion for soccer was evident, and he cheered along with the entire nation as the national team had some success at the Africa Cup of Nations in January 2010. His enthusiastic support for the national team, known as the Chipolopolo Boys,

may have earned him the respect of many average citizens; but some of his policies were not as popular. Among the complaints lodged against President Banda were accusations of tribalism and in particular the notion that he engineered the acquittal of Zambia's second president, Frederick Chiluba, who was being tried for corruption.

Regardless of the criticisms, Banda's first two years as Zambia's leader generally added to his legacy as one of the important political and diplomatic figures in the southern African nation's history. Entering mid-2010, he continued to spearhead his country's efforts to overcome major challenges such as poverty and widespread HIV/AIDS, which had lowered life expectancy in Zambia to about thirty-eight years. In 2010 Banda announced plans to run for reelection.

[*See also* Chiluba, Frederick; Kaunda, Kenneth; Mwanawasa, Levy Patrick; *and* Savimbi, Jonas Malheiro.]

BIBLIOGRAPHY
Information on Banda can be found in the *Post* newspaper (Lusaka, Zambia) at www.postzambia.com and at www.statehouse.gov.zm.

DeRoche, Andrew J. "You Can't Fight Guns with Knives: National Security and Zambian Responses to UDI, 1965–1973." In *One Zambia, Many Histories: Towards a History of Post-Colonial Zambia*, edited by Jan-Bart Gewald, Marja Hinfelaar, and Giacomo Macola, pp. 77–97. Leiden, Netherlands: Brill, 2008.
Mwaanga, Vernon. *An Extraordinary Life: The Life of Vernon J. Mwaanga*. Lusaka, Zambia: Multimedia Publications, 1982.
Phiri, Bizeck J. *A Political History of Zambia: From the Colonial Period to the 3rd Republic*. Trenton, N.J.: Africa World Press, 2006.

ANDY DeROCHE

Bandeira, Alda (1949–), politician and foreign minister of São Tomé and Príncipe, was born Alda Bandeira Tavares Vaz da Conceição on 22 September 1949. She was the daughter of a male nurse and his wife on the Àgua-Izé estate, Santana District, São Tomé Island. She married Noberto Costa Alegre, with whom she has two daughters. Bandeira attended primary school and secondary school in São Tomé and Luanda, Angola, respectively. From 1972 to 1974 she studied German philology at Lisbon University.

During her country's decolonization process, following the Carnation Revolution of 25 April 1974 in Portugal, Bandeira became one of the prominent student members of the radical Associação Cívica pró-MLSTP, which struggled for her country's total independence from Portugal under the leadership of the Liberation Movement of São Tomé and Príncipe (MLSTP, founded in 1972), whose leaders were exiled at that time in Libreville, Gabon. However, in March 1975, owing to a political conflict between the radical faction of the Associação Cívica and the comparatively more moderate leaders of the MLSTP, she and others were forced to leave São Tomé for exile in Mozambique. There, she attended a course in modern languages at Eduardo Mondlane University in Maputo, from 1975 to 1977. Subsequently, she earned an MA in modern languages and literature at Lisbon University, and in 1987, she gained a postgraduate degree in international relations at the Lisbon-based Instituto Superior de Ciências Sociais e Políticas. In the period from 1975 to 1982, Alda Bandeira worked as an English teacher at secondary schools in Maputo and São Tomé.

From 1987 to 1990, the last years of the one-party regime in São Tomé and Príncipe, she was director of multinational cooperation in the Ministry of Foreign Affairs. In the same period, from 1988 to 1990, she was national coordinator of the programs run by the US African Development Foundation in São Tomé. In December 1989, in the very beginning of the democratization process in her country, she was one of the ten founding members of the Grupo de Reflexão (GR), the archipelago's first opposition group to go public. In November 1990 when the GR transformed itself into the Partido de Convergência Democrática–Grupo de Reflexão (PCD-GR), she became a member of the executive committee of this then-major opposition party. Prominent activists of the former Associação Cívica who had returned from abroad in the early 1980s but had always remained outside the party framework of the MLSTP occupied key positions in the PCD-GR.

In the first democratic elections of 20 January 1991, Bandeira's party won a landslide victory with 54.4 percent of the votes, and she was elected deputy of the PCD-GR in the fifty-five-member National Assembly. From 1990 to 1992 she was minister of foreign affairs in the government of Prime Minister Daniel Daio (PCD-GR), while her husband was minister of economy and finance in this executive. In 1992 when, following the dismissal of Daniel Daio, Noberto Costa Alegre (PCD-GR) was appointed prime minister, she left the government

and occupied her seat in the National Assembly in order not to complicate her husband's job. Reportedly, she had repeatedly disagreed with some of the positions defended by her husband while he was minister of finance and wanted to avoid possible conflicts while he was head of government. However, she was executive director of the government's Social Dimensions of Structural Adjustment program from 1993 to 1995. The two governments of the PCD-GR were marked by consecutive conflicts with President Miguel Trovoada (1991–2001), although he and the party had been close allies during the democratic transition. Finally, on 2 July 1994, Trovoada dismissed the Costa Alegre government in order to put an end to the supposed "poor political relationship between president and prime minister."

Following the early elections of October 1994, Bandeira, who had been the most prominent woman in local politics since the political transition, became the parliamentary leader of her party, which had been reduced from thirty-three to fourteen seats in the National Assembly. At that time she was one of only three women in parliament. In 1995, she was one of the founding members of the women's organization Forum das Mulheres Santomenses. At the second congress of the PCD-GR in December 1995, she was elected unopposed, with 265 votes, as the new party president. In the following year, she ran as one of the five candidates in the country's second presidential elections, including the incumbent Trovoada and former president Manuel Pinto da Costa (1975–1991). When she publicly announced her candidacy, she declared that the president had to be a politician who was really concerned with the development of the country instead of engaged in old hatreds and personal caprices. She introduced her slogan, "With honesty and organization we shall put the country on its feet," and made clear that she would run in the election to win, in either the first or the second round. During the campaign she was the only one of the five candidates with a detailed printed political program. She ended third and gained a respectable result with 5,970 votes (16.1%); however, she did not meet the high expectations of her followers and supporters. In 1998 and 2002 she was reelected deputy in the National Assembly.

In the period 2000–2002 Bandeira taught at the Instituto Superior Politécnico, a local teachers' training college. In June 2001 she resigned as leader of the PCD-GR after an inner-party conflict about the question of whom the PCD-GR should support in the presidential elections held that year. In April 2002 she became foreign minister in the short-lived government of Prime Minister Gabriel Costa, who was dismissed in September that year. In the same year, she resigned as director of the local children's nongovernmental organization Amigos das Crianças, a post she had held since 1990. Since January 2008, when the local government created a Maritime and Port Administration Institute to supervise navigation in the archipelago's Exclusive Economic Zone and regularize the situation of the then-439 ships worldwide using the country's flag, Alda Bandeira has been director of this new government institution.

[*See also* Pinto da Costa, Manuel; *and* Trovoada, Miguel.]

BIBLIOGRAPHY

Ramos, João. *Quem é quem em São Tomé e Príncipe.* 3d ed. São Tomé: Mediateca, 2007.

Seibert, *Gerhard. Comrades, Clients and Cousins. Colonialism, Socialism, and Democratization in São Tomé and Príncipe*, 2d ed. Leiden, Netherlands: Brill, 2006.

GERHARD SEIBERT

George Bandele Areogun. (Photograph by David H. Curl)

Bandele Areogun, George (c. 1910–1995), Yoruba wood sculptor, was born in 1910 in Osi-Ilorin, now in Kwara State, Nigeria. He was the son of Areogun of Osi-Ilorin (c. 1880–1954), a significant master woodcarver of the premodern tradition of the northeast area of Yorubaland. He acquired the name George when baptized Catholic as a child, although his father remained a practitioner of the local Yoruba religion. His name is referred to in recent sources as George Bamidele Arowoogun, the patronymic added as a surname. His close collaborator and patron for four decades, Father Kevin Carroll (1920–1993), always referred to him simply as "Bandele."

Growing up in a successful carver's household, Bandele became apprenticed in his teens to one of his father's former assistants, Oshamuko, also from Osi-Ilorin, one of a group of villages called collectively Opin, which was within the Ekiti region. Both his familial ancestry and his artistic lineage descended within the well-developed woodcarving tradition of the Opin-Ekiti region. Nominally Christian, Bandele represents a blended, cross-cultural religious pluralism that still included some practices of the traditional religion and initiation into the local Ogboni society, a closed political and religious fraternity. During the late British colonial period (1930–1960), patronage of the traditional arts of Yorubaland declined, especially among the royal courts and various local religious shrines. With little specifically known about his early adulthood, Bandele, as a wood worker, undoubtedly put in time as a sawyer of lumber, as he did in later years when carving commissions were scarce.

In late 1947, Bandele heard of a newly established Catholic mission project run by the Society of the African Missions (SMA) in nearby Oye-Ekiti that sought talented local artists for their arts workshop. He applied for work with the project's de facto arts director, the Reverend Kevin P. Carroll, who asked to see a demonstration of his carving ability. Having worked with two unimpressive carvers during the preceding year, Carroll eagerly accepted Bandele based on his carving of a Yoruba military figure, thus beginning a collaborative artistic relationship that would last until the 1990s.

His new employer, the Oye-Ekiti Workshop, represented a unique seven-year experiment (1947–1954) in religious art adaptation to indigenize Christian imagery within Yoruba culture. The brainchild of Father Patrick M. "Doc" Kelly (1905–1988), the provincial of the SMA's Irish province, this African arts workshop project represented the first institutional attempt by the Catholic Church to decolonize its Eurocentric Christian visual culture in Africa. Having anticipated the global demise of European imperialism and the resulting independence of many non-European peoples, the highest levels of the Vatican endorsed a radically new direction of cultural adaptation, later termed "inculturation" in church usage, in the 1930s.

The policy of inculturation proposed that the church encourage Christianity to "bloom" within the local culture (and notably its artistic expression), rather than imposing European culture along with the spreading of the Gospel. Responding to this fresh encouragement of cultural pluralism from the highest level of the church, the art of Oye-Ekiti and its artists represents a significant development in this stage of Africanizing Christianity in the twentieth century, or, to change perspective, of helping a person figure out how to be both a Christian and an African at the same time, without having to become European in the process.

Deeply rooted in Opin-Ekiti carving tradition, Bandele's artistic challenge here centered on adapting Christian content to his strong traditional carving style. Father Carroll collaborated in this innovative process by asking Bandele to carve a conventional Christian Nativity grouping of the Holy Family and the Magi or Three Kings. With Carroll's encouragement, Bandele carved the kings in the form of three varied Yoruba *oba* (or kings), two on foot and one mounted, as Bandele had often carved such figures for veranda posts and other local commissions. The product of this unique collaborative genre is termed "Yoruba-Christian" art, since it fuses traditional Yoruba art and Christian content.

Quickly, Bandele became Carroll's premier artist, and woodcarvings became emblematic of the whole project, although the workshop employed dozens of artists also working on textiles, beadwork, pottery, and leatherwork. In 1949, Carroll and Bandele accepted the Vatican's invitation to send examples of their art production to a worldwide "Exhibition of Art of the Missionlands" in Rome the following year. The Oye-Ekiti Workshop's submissions featured a mixed media Nativity and kings grouping, incorporating carved figures by Bandele, but with the kings now clothed in rich West African woven textiles and traditional Yoruba beaded crowns crafted by the workshop specialists. This work impressed Vatican officials such that additional examples were ordered and displayed in Italian and Vatican museums.

Reflecting his great technical skill, including carving equally well with either hand, Bandele, as an invaluable informant, provided African art historians with descriptive information of his four-stage woodcarving process, detailed in Carroll's seminal 1967 work *Yoruba Religious Carving* (pp. 93–97). In 1950, at Carroll's urging, Bandele accepted an inexperienced young carver into a three-year traditional apprenticeship in the workshop; the student, Lamidi Olonade Fakeye, came from a distinguished carving lineage in nearby Ila-Orangun. Fakeye's demanding training regimen conducted by Bandele reflected an important aspect of the workshop's approach—that is, that workshop artists continue to accept commissions from local sources of patronage (shrines and royal courts) as well Carroll's Yoruba-Christian arts. In this way the workshop artists maintained their links with their own local communities. In 1953, Father Carroll also managed to effect reconciliation between Bandele and his father, who had been estranged for a period. At the same time Carroll also succeeded in recruiting the elderly Areogun in trying his hand at carving a Yoruba-Christian Nativity set, thereby clearly aligning the workshop within the noted Opin-Ekiti carving tradition.

In 1954, the SMA closed the Oye-Ekiti workshop owing to a backlash within the order, as well as opposition of some bishops and local Yoruba Catholics who associated Yoruba-Christian art with "paganism." The SMA encouraged Carroll to continue developing the experimental art form outside the workshop context, and for more than three decades Bandele continued his working relationship with Father Carroll. In addition to Yoruba-Christian art, Bandele and his former apprentice Fakeye (who later went on to an international career as a carver) created the contemporary art form called "Yoruba neo-traditional" sculpture. Bandele was survived by at least three sons at the time of his death in 1995, with some becoming carvers.

[*See also* Fakeye, Lamidi Olonade.]

BIBLIOGRAPHY

Carroll, Kevin Patrick. *Yoruba Religious Carving: Pagan and Christian Sculpture in Nigeria and Dahomey.* London: Geoffrey Chapman, 1967. Seminal source on Yoruba art, the Oye-Ekiti project, and its Yoruba Christian genre by the missionary who managed the workshop.

Costantini, Celso. *L'arte cristiana nelle missioni*. Vatican City: Tipografia Poliglotta Vaticana, 1940. Significant source by the originator of the inculturation policy, who headed the Vatican's ministry of missions, 1937–1958.

Fakeye, Lamidi Olonade. *Lamidi Olonade Fakeye*. Holland, Mich.: Hope College, 1996. The perspective of a participating workshop artist and apprentice of Bandele, which focuses mostly on his own later illustrious career.

Picton, John. "Art, Identity, and Identification: A Commentary on Yoruba Art Historical Studies." In *The Yoruba Artist*, edited by Rowland Abiodun, Henry John Drewal, and John Pemberton. Vol. 3, pp. 1–34. Washington, D.C.: Smithsonian Institution Press, 1994. Valuable source on the Opin-Ekiti carving tradition by a noted academic African art specialist and colleague of Kevin Carroll.

NICHOLAS J. BRIDGER

Bangassou (c. 1850–1907), a Bandia paramount chief (or "sultan") of the Nzakara kingdom, a precolonial polity spanning the Mbali River in the southeastern region of what is now the Central African Republic. Named Kpangba at birth, he adopted the name Bangassou ("blazing sun"). According to Nzakara oral history, his father was Mbali/Bali (Mbari/Bari) "the gazelle," son of Gwendi (or Boendi) "the taciturn," son of Beringa "the drunkard," son of Dunga "the quarrelsome," son of Gobenge, son of Pobdi, son of Bwanda "the healer," son of Agungu, son of Pongiet, son of Bongumu. These ancestors of Bangassou were members of the Bandia clan who left their Ngbandi homeland on the Ubangi River and conquered the Nzakara people.

The Bandia rulers participated in the growing slave trade of the nineteenth century and incorporated women and children into their polity, thus prospering while nearby peoples in stateless societies were raided by slave traders. The Nzakara often raided the Banda, and Bangassou's father, Mbali, was killed during a fight with a Banda group in about 1878, after which Bangassou became ruler.

In 1876, a slave raider, Rabih, from the southern Sudan, established a camp near the Chinko River and sent raiders into Nzakara territory. Bangassou proved an effective military leader and successfully resisted military threats by Rabih's marauders, nearby Zande rulers, and Belgian and French expeditions into Nzakara territory. Bangassou also crushed internal opposition to his rule. Kpakulu, head of the Bandia vou-Gounga lineage, revolted against Bangassou in 1884, but he was defeated. When Kpakulu led another revolt (1892), Bangassou had begun to obtain rifles from agents of the Congo Free State. Bangassou defeated Kpakulu and dismantled his chiefdom. In 1885 Bangassou's warriors also fought the Gboudou in the upper Mbali River region and the vou-Gouma on the Kotto River. In January 1889 Bangassou attacked the Gbodo (Yakoma) and forced them to move south of the Mbomou River, and then he established his headquarters at the confluence of the Mbali and Mbomou Rivers.

On 31 May 1890, a Belgian officer of the Congo Free State, Alphonse Van Gèle, established the post of Yakoma on the Ubangi River. On 14 June, Bangassou traveled to Yakoma with his brother Lengo to meet Van Gèle, his first encounter with a European. To obtain military support, weapons, and trade goods, Bangassou signed a treaty that placed the Nzakara kingdom under the protection of the Congo Free State. On 26 July Bangassou visited Yakoma again and offered to escort Van Gèle to his village on the Mbali River. Bangassou facilitated the advance of the Congo Free State into his region, and he sold its agents enormous quantities of ivory.

In January 1892 Bangassou attacked the riverine Kpatili people, who capitulated and agreed to provide the Nzakara with pirogue canoes for a small fleet. After a confrontation between the French and Belgians on 14 March 1893 near Bangassou's capital, Bangassou declared his opposition to French advances, but then he approached the French representative Victor Liotard to ask for French protection. In October 1893, however, Bangassou supplied a Congo Free State expedition to the Shari River with soldiers led by his son Mbali, who led the Belgian lieutenant Raphaël Stroobant to Bakouma.

After the French and the Congo Free State signed a convention on 14 August 1894, Bangassou's kingdom came under French protection. With more weapons from the French, the Nzakara attacked the Banda Ngbougou and Banda Langba and reached Mobaye. In 1898 he attacked the Banda Togbo on the Gbanga River, then the Banda Linda. When the famous French Marchand mission traveled east along the Ubangi River to Fashoda in the Sudan, Bangassou provided the French with much-needed porters. In May 1900 Bangassou sent an expedition to punish the Dendi villages of Ndayo, Plassa, and Sangbo, and in 1901 he attacked the Vidri and then the more distant Ouyou.

In 1901 a former noncommissioned Belgian officer, Achille Otto, became assistant director of the Compagnie des Sultanats du Haut-Oubangui (Company of the Sultanates of Upper Ubangi), a French concessionary company, and signed a convention with Bangassou that gave the company a monopoly on all trade by barter or money and all transport throughout Nzakara territory. Bangassou also ceded full power to the company to pursue, in his name, all receivers of stolen (or privately traded) goods. This agreement was declared illegal by the French minister of the colonies since it conflicted with the commercial treaty signed on 18 December 1898 between Bangassou and Albert Bonnel de Mézières, the French head of a commercial mission to the Bandia and Zandé sent by the Chad and Ubangi Syndicate, which granted it a monopoly of commerce with Bangassou. Nevertheless, Otto soon came to exercise unparalleled power and influence throughout Nzakara country.

Bangassou also delegated great power to Yakpakpa, his official go-between and interpreter from the first arrival of the Europeans. In 1902, Bangassou designated his son Mbali as his official heir, but Mbali died in 1904. In 1903 Bangassou's warriors attacked the Mbangui beyond the Kotto River. The next year his warriors fought with those of Sultan Hetman of Rafai in an attempt to incorporate all hunting lands east of the Mbali River into his kingdom, but the Nzakara were defeated at Lato. In 1905, however, Bangassou gained French recognition for his rule over the hunting lands east of Mbali.

On 8 June 1907, after being injured during an elephant hunt, Bangassou died in the presence of the French captain Jules Jacquier, the de facto ruler of the region. The real cause of Bangassou's death is contested by the royal family, which insists that Bangassou suddenly became ill and died, which seems more acceptable than death as a result of a hunting accident. Bangassou's designated heir Mbali having died, his youngest son, Labassou, a half-blind leper, claimed his right to rule, and Captain Jacquier allowed him to serve as interim ruler, but other sons of Bangassou, including Kété ("Little Bangassou"), the eldest son of Mbali and grandson of Bangassou, also claimed their right to rule. A council of nobles selected Labassou as Bangassou's successor, and he was confirmed in his titles and powers in the protectorate treaty of 23 February 1909. After Labassou's death in 1917, the French no longer recognized the Nzakara kingdom.

[See also Rabih al-Zabayr Fadl Allah.]

BIBLIOGRAPHY

Coosemans, Marthe, and Léon Marie Lotar. "Bangasso." In *Biographie Coloniale Belge.* Vol. 1, edited by F. Dellicour, p. 67. Brussels, Belgium: Institut Royal Colonial Belge, Librairie G. Van Campenhout, 1948.

de Dampierre, Eric. *Un ancien royaume Bandia du Haut-Oubangui* [An Old Bandia Kingdom in Upper Ubangi]. Paris: Plon, 1967.

RICHARD A. BRADSHAW and
JUAN FANDOS-RIUS

Bangoura, Hadja Mafory (1910–1976), leading activist in the anticolonial movement in Guinea, was born in Bramaya-Ouassou. She went to Conakry in 1936, where she eventually joined the Foyer de la Basse Guinée, a mutual aid association for people from Lower Guinea. She worked as a tailor in Conakry before she was involved in a group that supported Sekou Touré during the nationalist struggles of the 1950s. She is remembered as the woman who approached Touré during the general strike of 1953, which was a key event in the Guinean nationalist struggle. He asked her to help mobilize women to support the strike. At a meeting of the strike committee where the women's wing was present for the first time, Bangoura spoke for the women, saying they would defend the men's activities, and if the men were afraid, the women were prepared to take their places at the front of the strike. Despite her lack of formal schooling and consequent illiteracy, she was a strategic thinker who was able to articulate her perspective and who was renowned as a dynamic public speaker.

With Touré's backing, Bangoura became a leader within the Rassemblement Démocratique Africain (RDA; African Democratic Assembly), the anticolonial party that was active across Francophone West Africa. After the 1953 strike, the women's committees held their first congress and elected a board of Guinean women; Bangoura became president of the women's committees. At a 1954 party meeting, Bangoura reportedly called on the women to abstain from sexual relations if their husbands did not join the RDA.

As the anticolonial struggle escalated, women also became involved in urban street patrols and sometimes urban violence. Bangoura, who was also head of the Red Cross, housed people who were injured in anticolonial hostilities. She was particularly targeted by the French colonial officials, who referred to her as "the terrible woman of the RDA" (Schmidt, 2005, p. 136). In July 1955 she was arrested on a charge of giving anti-French literature to inmates in the Conakry prison, and she was sentenced to one year in jail plus a fine of 70,000 francs. Women in Conakry reacted to her arrest by marching to police headquarters, where they blocked the streets and faced fire hoses. When Bangoura was released on bail on 17 August, she was greeted with jubilation by her followers, who carried her home accompanied by dancing, drumming, and music. Her sentence was eventually reduced, and she served only twenty-eight days.

After independence in 1958, Bangoura held government positions as an active member of the Parti Démocratique de Guinée (PDG; Democratic Party of Guinea), including her election as one of seventeen members of the RDA-PDG's newly constituted national political bureau, where she represented Guinean women. In 1968 she was elected first president of the Union Révolutionnaires des Femmes de Guinée, and she was appointed minister of social affairs in 1971. She was married to Badara Bangoura, a chauffeur, and was the mother of three children. Bangoura is recognized in Guinea with a high school named in her honor, the Collège Hadja Mafory Bangoura.

[*See also* Touré, Ahmed Sékou.]

BIBLIOGRAPHY

Keita, Sidiki Kobele. *Le PDG: Artisan de l'Indépendance Nationale en Guinée (1947–1958)*. Conakry, Guinea: INRDG, Bibliotheque Nationale, 1978.

Schmidt, Elizabeth. *Mobilizing the Masses: Gender, Ethnicity, and Class in the Nationalist Movement in Guinea, 1939–1958*. Portsmouth, N.H.: Heinemann, 2005.

Touré, Ahmed Sékou. "Hommage à Mafory Bangoura." *Révolution Démocratique Africaine*, no. 96 (1976).

Touré, Ahmed Sékou. "Promotion Hadja Mafory Bangoura: Séminaire de Formation Idéologique." *Révolution Démocratique Africaine* no. 107. Conkary, Guinea: INRDG, Bibliotheque Nationale, 1978. This report includes several chapters on women and politics in Guinea, and a final section titled "Mafory l'Immortelle," that relates her contributions.

KATHLEEN SHELDON

Bangui, Antoine (1933–), Chadian politician and writer, was born in southern Chad on 22 September 1933. His father had problems with a state-appointed chief in his home village in the year before his son Antoine's birth, so he fled to the neighboring colony of Ubangi-Shari (the Central African Republic). His mother followed and carried Antoine hundreds of miles on the long journey south with his elder sister. His father nicknamed the boy Bangui after the capital of the colony where the family had found sanctuary. When a teacher asked the boy in 1940 what his name was, Antoine answered, "Bangui." The teacher threatened to expel Bangui for insolence, but his father persuaded the teacher to accept the name. Bangui attended schools in the Central African Republic until 1947, even though his family finally returned to Chad in 1946. Luckily for Bangui, he won a contest held by the colonial administration to send a few children to France to continue their education. He completed his secondary studies at Lycée Die in France in 1954, and then attended classes at the University of Grenoble. He transferred to a teachers college in Caen in 1955, and he graduated with a teaching certification in 1957. From 1957 to 1960, Bangui taught math in the Central African Republic and then came back to his homeland.

Bangui's college education made him a rare commodity in Chad, which had one of the weakest and poorly funded educational systems in the entire French colonial empire. The PPT regime of François Tombalbaye, which ruled Chad from 1960 until military officers overthrew and killed Tombalbaye in 1975, desperately needed trained professionals. Bangui became minister of education in 1962, only two years after he was hired to be an adjunct in the education ministry's office, and then was named minister for public works and transportation in 1963. Bangui's skill at writing helps explain why Tombalbaye chose to make him an ambassador to West Germany from 1964 to 1966. On his return to the Chadian capital of N'Djamena, Bangui worked as a senior member of Tombalbaye's cabinet for five years before he was named minister of planning and cooperation in 1971.

Bangui's comfortable life ended in 1972. Tombalbaye had grown paranoid. The president's inability to defeat the Libyan-backed Front de Libération Nationale du Tchad (FROLINAT; National Liberation Front of Chad), a rebel movement that grew in popularity thanks to Tombalbaye's favoring of southern Chadians and his draconian efforts to reshape Chadian society along the lines of Congolese dictator Mobutu Sese Soko, had alienated most Chadians, as did the strongman's disinterest in aiding people suffering from severe droughts. Bangui was arrested on a trumped-up charge of plotting a coup and then learned how brutal his government actually had become. He was tortured for three years until the death of Tombalbaye and was locked away in a small cell covered in excrement.

Immediately after the end of the old regime, he left Chad for France, where his family had been living in the city of Nice. Family members and friends encouraged Bangui to write about his experiences. The end result was his autobiography, *Prisonnier de Tombalbaye* (Prisoner of Tombalbaye), which was published in 1980 as part of the Monde noir poche series by the Hatier publishing firm. The well-known African studies publisher Seuil had initially published the book, but the French government then banned it. The book is a testimony to the horrors of state terror and remains Bangui's most well-known work.

Few Francophone African writers can survive on royalties alone, and Bangui was no exception. The new government brought Bangui back into public service as the Chadian ambassador to Romania. Since his main tasks consisted of working with perhaps twenty-five Chadian foreign exchange students, Bangui found time to write. He continued his autobiographical works in *Les ombres de Koh* (The Shadows of Koh), a description of his upbringing that features detailed discussion of African spirituality. He remained in this position until he resigned in 1980, in the midst of civil war. He left his position by simply leaving the key to the embassy under the door, since the chaos back home had stopped all payments of salaries for the diplomatic corps. Bangui then worked at various posts in the United Nations Educational, Scientific and Cultural Organization (UNESCO), which kept him outside of his homeland until his retirement in 1993. Although his duties gave him little time to engage in literary matters, Bangui remained interested in both literature and human rights.

At the age of 60, Bangui came back to Chad again. Unhappy with the way President Idriss Déby had asserted his power, Bangui formed the opposition Mouvement pour la reconstruction nationale du Tchad (MORENAT; Movement for the National Reconstruction of Chad) party. He ran unsuccessfully for president against Déby in 1996, and he braved threats and government-engineered obstacles on the campaign trial, such as a decision by the courts to not recognize him as a legally sanctioned candidate due to some minor bureaucratic issues. On 25 April 1995, government troops assaulted Bangui while he visited Logone Orientale province. Though he failed in the election, he succeeded in rallying opposition to Déby through his indignant critique of the corruption and repression of the Déby era. His 1999 book, *Tchad: élections sous sontrôle (1996–1997)* (Chad: Elections under Control [1996–1997]) made him a target of Chadian state harassment, and he was accused yet again of organizing a revolt. He helped to coordinate a coalition of opposition parties in the same year, the Coordination des mouvements armés et politiques de l'opposition (CMAP; Coordination of Armed and Political Movements of the Opposition). Bangui remained an active critic of Déby for the next decade, but chose to do so in France rather than risk his safety again. He did return briefly to N'Djamena as part of a delegation of rebel leaders and opposition figures on 30 July 2007, but he did not choose to reconcile with his longtime foe. In the small world of Chadian writers, Bangui was an elder statesman in the early twenty-first century. His advancing age did not stop him from defending human rights. One could argue he had gone full circle from a trusted associate of a Chadian dictator in his younger days to become a distinguished promoter of democratic reform in his declining years.

[*See also* Déby Itno, Idriss; Mobutu Sese Seko; *and* Tombalbaye, François.]

BIBLIOGRAPHY

Bangui, Antoine. *Les ombres de Koh* Paris: Hatier, 1983.

Bangui, Antoine. *Prisonnier de Tombalbaye* Paris: Hatier, 1980.

Bangui, Antoine. *Tchad: Élections Sous Contrôle (1996–1997)*. Paris: L'Harmattan, 1999.

Bénadji, Hubert, and Debra Boyd-Buggs. "Antoine Bangui or the Prisoner of Tombalbaye." In *Camel Tracks: Critical Perspectives on Sahelian Literatures*, edited by Debra Boyd-Buggs and Joyce Hope Scott, pp. 123–140. Trenton, N.J.: Africa World Press, 2003.

JEREMY RICH

Bankole, Ayo (1935–1976), Nigerian musician and composer, was born on 17 May 1935 in Jos, Plateau State, in the northeast of Nigeria. He is of the Yoruba ethnic group and was born into a family of music teachers and composers. His father, Theophilus Abiodun Bankole, was a prominent organist and choirmaster at Saint Luke's Anglican Church, Jos. His mother was a music tutor at Queen's School, Ede (now in Ibadan, southwest Nigeria), one of the elite female secondary schools in Nigeria. She was also an active musician. Bankole's maternal grandfather, Akinje George, was the organist and choirmaster at the First Baptist Church, Lagos.

In 1941, when Bankole was six years old, his father noticed that he had music talent and sent him to live with his grandfather, who gave him initial lessons in piano and harmonium. As a boy soprano in the choir at Cathedral Church of Christ in Lagos, Bankole showed a talent that was nurtured by the prominent Nigerian composer and musicologist T. K. E. Phillips. Bankole's father then moved from Jos to Lagos, where he became the organist and choirmaster at Saint Peter's Anglican Church, Faji, very close to the cathedral church where Bankole was a choirboy. The cathedral choir was a model for other churches, and so Bankole's father encouraged him to stay and remain under the tutelage of Phillips, who was the only professionally trained organist and church musician in Nigeria at that time.

In 1945 Bankole enrolled for his secondary education at Baptist Academy, Lagos. There he excelled as a music student and became the pianist and organist of the school. He excelled in solo competition as well and led the school musical group to win prizes and accolades in several music competitions, including the ones organized by the Nigeria Arts Festival. After his secondary education, he worked as a clerical officer in the Nigerian Broadcasting Corporation (NBC). At NBC he came in contact with notable musicians such as Christopher Oyesiku, Tom Chalmers, Arthur Langford, Leslie Perron, and most especially, Olufela Sowande, the prominent composer who trained him on the organ and greatly influenced him. These influences provided Bankole with the necessary foundation on which a promising career was built. By 1954 Bankole was already a popular figure in the church music scene in Lagos and had become an assistant organist at the Cathedral Church under T. K. E. Phillips. By 1957 he had composed and performed his first major works, *Ya Orule* and *Nigerian Suite*, both piano solos.

In 1957 Bankole was admitted to the Guildhall School of Music and Drama in London on a federal government of Nigeria scholarship, where he produced some of his earliest interesting compositions. Shortly on arrival in London, he became the organist and choirmaster at Saint James-the-Less, taking over from another prominent Nigerian musician, Akin Euba, who was heading home. Akin Euba had occupied the position after the exit of Olaolu Omideyi, another great Nigerian musician, who had studied organ at the Royal School of Church Music. At the Guildhall School, Bankole was exposed to the works of various European composers, which greatly influenced his compositions. He studied piano, composition, organ, and harmony. He was popular among his contemporaries at the Guildhall and other colleges of music in London, and between 1958 and 1961 he represented the Guildhall School of Music at several youth concerts organized by four colleges—the Royal College of Music, the Royal Academy of Music, Trinity College of Music, and the Guildhall School of Music. Bankole was awarded another scholarship to study music, at Clare College, Cambridge University, in 1961, where he graduated with a bachelor of arts degree in music in 1964. He was awarded a master's degree by the same college in 1967. Meanwhile he obtained the highest British professional qualification for organists, the Fellowship of the Royal College of Organists (FRCO) in 1964, shortly after his bachelor's degree. He was the second Nigerian to obtain that qualification, after Fela Sowande. He proceeded further to the University of California, Los Angeles (UCLA), on a Rockefeller Foundation Fellowship to study ethnomusicology. There he wrote and researched works that explored the adoption of African traditional instruments into contemporary compositions. At UCLA he was trained by Roy Travis, one of America's foremost composers.

Back in Nigeria, from 1966 to 1969 Bankole became a senior music producer at the Nigerian Broadcasting Corporation in Lagos before he left for academia. At NBC he produced a series of music programs on radio and brought indigenous African music to life. He was also able to get some of his works performed and recorded. He was a lecturer in the University of Lagos, Akoka, from 1969 to 1976. At the university he continued his research, which he started at UCLA, into Nigerian indigenous music, which culminated in the publication of scholarly papers including "An Introduction to the Appreciation of the Problems of Synthesis in Modern Nigerian Music" (1970), "Sango Festival: An Ethnomusicological Study" (1970), and "The Dawn of Nigerian Musicology" (1973). He documented the reports of some of his fieldwork in monographs such as "A Dictionary of the Musical Instruments in Nigeria," "River People of Nigeria," and "Edo Musical Culture." He was an external examiner to the University of Nigeria, Nsukka, in 1971; a visiting lecturer at Ohio State University from 1971 to 1972; and he received a federal government commission to compose the anthem for the second All-African Games in 1973. In 1974 Bankole was Nigerian composer-elect to the fifth Congress of Soviet Composers held in Moscow. He was involved equally actively in choir works in several prominent churches in Lagos as an organist and music composer during this period.

Bankole was renowned for his skill in fusing the elements of traditional Yoruba music with European style in his compositions. His list of compositions includes four cantatas, three toccatas, four sonatas, one opera, a requiem, several part-songs, songs for solo voice, and several other important works for piano, organ, and voices. He was remarkable for the simplicity of his compositions and the ability to achieve fine tastes and satisfying effects through the use of simple musical materials. His formative years were marked by his exposure to various styles and mediums of music in the Western European tradition, especially at the Guildhall and at Cambridge, and by his exposure to ethnomusicology while at UCLA. Of those years Bankole described himself as "experimenting to develop my creative mind and enhance my grasp of the principles of composition" (Bankole, 1977). Bankole's late period is most representative of his synthesis of his bicultural heritage. He drew freely from European styles and techniques and assimilated features of contemporary African traditions, which benefited his latter compositions immensely. Some of the most popular compositions in Bankole's career include *Christmas Sonata* (1959), *The Passion* (1959), *English Winterbirds* (1961), *Baba se wa ni omo rere* (Father Make Us Good Children, 1958), *Three Yoruba Songs* (1959), *Toccata and Fugue* (1960), *Fun mi ni ibeji* (Give Me Twins, 1970), *Ore ofe Jesu Kristi* (The Grace of Our Lord Jesus Christ, 1967), and Cantata No.4 *Festac* (1974).

Bankole and his wife, Toro, were killed in tragic circumstances on 6 November 1976 in Lagos.

[*See also* Sowande, Olufela.]

BIBLIOGRAPHY

Bankole, Ayo. "An Introduction to the Appreciation of the Problems of Synthesis in Modern Nigerian Music." Seminar paper presented at the University of Lagos, Lagos, Nigeria, 1970.

Bankole, Ayo. "Notes." *Sonata No. 2 in C: For Piano*. Ife: University of Ife, 1977.

Euba, Akin. "An Introduction to Music in Nigeria." *Nigerian Music Review* 1 (1977): 1–38.

Merriam, Alan. *African Music in Perspective*. New York: Garland, 1982.

Omojola, Bode. *Nigerian Art Music: With an Introductory Study of Ghanaian Art Music*. Ibadan, Nigeria: French Institute for Research in Africa, 1995.

Isola, Olusola O. Electronic interview with Ayo Bankole Jr. June–July 2010, Lagos, Nigeria.

OLUSOLA O. ISOLA

Banna, Hasan al- (1906–1949), founder and martyred leader of the Egyptian Muslim Brothers, the archetypical modern Islamist mass movement, was born in Mahmudiyya, a Delta town not far from Alexandria, in October 1906. His father, a devotee of a mystical Sufi order and graduate of the prestigious al-Azhar seminar in Cairo, owned a watch repair shop and sold gramophones, but he gave religious lessons by day. He oversaw young Hasan's memorization of the Qur'an and taught him the watch business. Hasan attended Qur'an school in the provincial city of Damanhur, but in keeping with his father's modernist religious sensibilities, he went on to government preparatory school, then, at age 14, enrolled in a junior teachers school in the Delta city of Damanhur. In 1924 he entered Dar al-Ulum, the teacher training college in Cairo.

Banna went on to pursue a career in the state educational sector, but his life became dominated by a calling to a religious and political reformation of Egypt. During the 1919 "revolution," he and fellow schoolmates participated in demonstrations against British rule. At an early age he became deeply impressed with the need to redress what educated Islamic modernists perceived to be incorrect popular religious practices. Banna and his friends took up a call for moral reform and a growing outcry, trumpeted in the press, against Christian missionary activity. In middle school they formed a Society for Moral Behavior. They challenged school dress codes, reported irreligious behavior to the authorities, and became consumed with prayer, fasting, and religious study. For Banna this meant abandoning certain mystical practices to which he had become attracted as a young boy. In Cairo he joined the Young Men's Muslim Association (YMMA), a response to the YMCA.

While posted to his first teaching post in the Ismailia, in 1927—educational authorities, aware of his troublesome tendencies, wanted him far from the capital—Banna laid foundations for a new mass movement that would surpass all other religious societies. The cafés became his pulpit; they were the sites where he preached and held informal study sessions. In the spring of 1928 Banna and six others founded the Society of Muslim Brothers and rented space to maintain an office and instruction center. They soon founded branches in adjoining communities and made ventures into the Delta countryside. In 1932 Banna gained a transfer to a Cairo school. Within a year the Muslim Brothers held its first annual conference and began to establish bylaws and lay groundwork for a nationwide organization, including summer youth camps. Banna assumed the title of "general guide" and began to tour branches on a regular basis. A man of boundless energy and charisma, a captivating orator who lived modestly, he embodied for many the physical and spiritual attributes of the modern Muslim.

The movement rapidly assumed a leading place in Egyptian political and cultural life. The Brothers petitioned royal and government officials to promote religious practice and defend the faith from secular challenges. Young missionaries canvassed towns and neighborhoods and movement leaders founded a series of journals. The Arab Revolt in Palestine in the late 1930s prompted the Brothers to adopt a more political focus. Banna corresponded with Palestinian leaders and dispatched delegations that laid foundations for the movement's regional growth. By the early 1940s the Muslim Brothers constituted a mass movement large enough to challenge established political parties. Banna considered standing for office on two occasions. In 1942 leaders of the Wafd, Egypt's majority nationalist party, persuaded him to abstain; in 1949 several Brothers did run but were defeated in a rigged poll.

As formal political life in Egypt disintegrated in the mid- and late 1940s the Brotherhood became caught in the middle of an escalating cycle of violence and chaos. Banna retained popularity and leadership throughout a series of defections and tried to maintain a firm grip on the movement, a seemingly impossible task. His writings, sermons, speeches, and petitions to government figures speak to a long-term educational call to shape Muslim personal practice and foster an "Islamic order" more closely adherent to religious principles and law. Many within the movement, particularly those who led the secret organization and the youth rovers, grew impatient. Banna's defenders insist that he fostered the paramilitary arm of the movement, an outgrowth of the scouting rovers, in order to instill discipline and promote self-defense. The Brothers did send irregulars to fight in Palestine in 1948 and, after Banna's death, to engage British forces in the Suez Canal zone after Egypt abrogated the 1936 Anglo-Egyptian treaty in November 1951. The extent to which the general guide lost control of militants within his movement during his lifetime remains disputed.

Indisputable is the role the Brothers played in the erosion of political stability in the dying days of the parliamentary era. By most accounts the movement numbered half a million formal adherents by 1948–1949 and could marshal an equal number of sympathizers. The Brothers had formed secret cells in the police and military, downplaying their religious social agenda in order to galvanize nationalist sympathizers.

Anwar al-Sadat and several comrades approached Banna to express solidarity and propose collaborative efforts. Gamal Abd al-Nasser, Khalid Muhyi al-Din, Tharwat Ukasha, and other founders of the Free Officers movement, which seized power in July 1952 and soon after toppled the monarchy and old political order, met regularly under Brotherhood auspices until determining to chart their own course independent of all existing political movements. They broke ranks with the Brotherhood in part because they viewed the Brothers' militant wing as too reckless.

In December 1948 a student member assassinated Prime Minister Mahmud Fahmi al-Nuqrashi, a response to his efforts to outlaw the movement. Later that year, in November, police authorities discovered an abandoned jeep containing papers that proved the existence of a heavily armed secret organization linked to the military and responsible for specific acts of political violence. The "jeep case" instigated harsher crackdowns on the movement. On 12 February 1949 police agents gunned down Hasan al-Banna on the steps of the YMMA in downtown Cairo. The Brothers regrouped under the leadership of Hasan al-Hudaybi, but internal divisions only intensified, drawing the society into a headlong showdown with the Free Officers that forced them underground and effectively ended their public role for nearly two decades.

[See also Muhyi al-Din, Khalid; Nasser, Gamal Abd -al; Nuqrashi, Mahmud Fahmi al-; and Ukasha, Tharwat.]

BIBLIOGRAPHY

al-Banna, Hasan. *Memoirs of Hasan al-Banna.* Karachi, Pakistan: International Islamic Publishers, 1981. Details the Muslim Brothers's early years.

Krämer, Gudrum. *Hasan al-Banna.* Oxford, UK: Oneworld, 2010.

Lia, Brynjar. *The Society of Muslim Brothers in Egypt: The Rise of an Islamic Mass Movement, 1928–1942.*

Reading, UK: Ithaca Press, 1998. Fills in important gaps.

Mitchell, Richard P. *The Society of Muslim Brothers.* Oxford, UK: Oxford University Press, 1969. Remains the classic account of the movement.

JOEL GORDON

Bannerman, James (1790–1858), a prominent trader in nineteenth-century Ghana, was born in 1790. His mother was a Ga woman from Accra who had family ties with the Alata chief in the neighboring town of Osu and the Asere chief of Kinka. His father was Colonel Henry Bannerman, a Scottish officer and a trader in the Royal Africa Company stationed at the British fort of Cape Coast. Bannerman's father's connections in the British government and his mother's connections in southern Ghana helped prepare the way for his rise as a businessman. Bannerman's ambitions were facilitated by the changing nature of trade between European nations and West Africa. The British government's efforts to close the international slave trade posed some challenges for coastal communities on the Ghanaian coast, although the stabilization of the Asante kingdom's borders had already led to a decline of slave exports from the region by the early nineteenth century. By the 1850s, the use of steamships and growing demand for palm oil and cash crops in Europe had led to expanded trade opportunities. Bannerman successfully competed with British companies before and after the coming of the steamer to Ghana, and he became a very prosperous slave owner.

British missionaries and the small British colonial administration based at Cape Coast had mixed feelings about Bannerman. On the one hand, his fluent command of English and his willingness to support British interests made him a valuable ally. He met his wife through the British government's war with the Asante kingdom. In 1826, Bannerman married Yaa Hom, a princess belonging to the royal family of the powerful Asante kingdom. Yaa Hom was a daughter of the Asante king Osei Bonsu, who was captured at the battle of Katamanso in 1826 by British troops. However, Bannerman felt that efforts to abolish slavery in Cape Coast by colonial officials like Governor Charles Macarthy in 1826 interfered with his rights as a property owner. Bannerman agreed to partially free his slaves and henceforth treated them as indentured servants. Later, Bannerman felt that Macarthy had exaggerated his authority to abolish slavery and that he had been tricked. In 1841, Bannerman wrote the British parliament that any effort to force people to give up their slaves would lead to an exodus of Africans out of British-controlled territory.

Despite the reservations on both sides, Bannerman eventually entered the colonial administration. The Colonial Office named him a justice of the peace at Cape Coast in 1842. He was named lieutenant governor of the Gold Coast in 1850, and he was an unofficial member of the Gold Coast Legislative Council from 1850 to 1856. During Bannerman's tenure as lieutenant governor, he defended Afro-English missionary Thomas Birch Freeman when he was attacked by priests of the southern Ghanaian deity Naanam Mpow in 1850. Bannerman arrested and jailed the priests. Although he was passed over in his bid to become governor, he continued to be an active voice of the coastal trading elite. His son Charles set up the *Accra Herald* newspaper in 1857, most likely with some financial support from his father. He died in 1858, and his family remained extremely prominent in Accra for the next century.

[*See also* Freeman, Thomas Birch.]

BIBLIOGRAPHY

Parker, John. *Making the Town: Ga State and Society in Early Colonial Accra.* Portsmouth, N.H.: Heinemann, 2000.

Reynolds, Edward. "The Rise and Fall of an African Merchant Class on the Gold Coast 1830–1874." *Cahiers d'études africaines* 14 (1974): 253–264.

JEREMY RICH

Baquaqua, Mohammah Gardo (b. 1824), writer and escaped slave, was born probably in 1824 in the town of Djougou, located in what is now northern Benin. Djougou was an important trading town with close commercial connections to the kingdom of Dahomey to the south and the sultanate of Nupe to the east. Baquaqua's family, which spoke Dendi as their first language, was deeply involved in long-distance trade. His mother was originally from the Hausa-speaking town of Katsina far to the east of Djougou, while his father claimed Arab descent. He probably spoke Hausa as well as the Arabic he learned in qur'anic school. Baquaqua traveled on caravans to the east and west of Djougou at the behest of his father. However, he did not want to follow his father's wish that he become a Muslim scholar, so he stayed with one of his maternal uncles, a well-connected Hausa trader who regularly visited Salaga and other trading towns.

Baquaqua appears to have never mastered Arabic writing, based on a few examples that have survived. Baquaqua eventually found a position in the palace of the local ruler of Djougou as a royal servant, where he developed a strong attraction to alcohol. Like many towns in northern Benin and Ghana, rulers often subscribed to indigenous spiritual practices outside of Islam.

How Baquaqua ended up a slave is difficult to determine, because he provided several different explanations to missionaries and other supporters of his cause in Canada, Haiti, and the United States. In one version, Baquaqua became embroiled in a civil war in the kingdom of Gonja, relatively close to Djougou. He was captured by one army but then freed through the intervention of his brother, a soldier, who found him a job as a servant. After a drinking party, he was kidnapped. Baquaqua also claimed that he had been stolen from his family as a young child. In any event, he was passed south between several owners through the trading centers of Alejo, Krikii, and finally the coastal town of Ouidah. This port served as the point where the kingdom of Dahomey sold slaves to Brazilian and Spanish ships in the nineteenth century. To evade British naval patrols seeking to block trans-Atlantic exports of slaves, Baquaqua was moved from Ouidah to a nearby lagoon. A Brazilian ship then carried him to the city of Pernambuco in northeastern Brazil sometime in 1845. Baquaqua's account is the only known written slave narrative of Brazilian slavery. He was purchased by a baker, who treated him with callous disdain. Baquaqua ran away for a short time and considered suicide. Eventually, a ship captain from Rio de Janeiro purchased him from the baker. Baquaqua had a new job as a cabin steward aboard the *Lembrança*, a ship that regularly visited the southern Brazilian coast. Under the name of José da Costa, Baquaqua then journeyed aboard the *Lembrança* from Rio to New York City; the ship was loaded with coffee.

When the ship docked in New York on 27 June 1847, a group of local abolitionists demanded that the crew release Baquaqua and several other slaves and began legal proceedings. Since New York was a free state, the abolitionists contended that all slaves aboard the Brazilian vessel were now free. Baquaqua fled the ship with another man but was placed in a jail while the court case continued. Although the New York judge Charles Daly ruled on 17 July 1847 that Baquaqua should be returned to his owner, Baquaqua managed to escape from prison in the meantime.

Whether or not he received help in evading prison is unclear. He found shelter in Springfield, Massachusetts, from other abolitionists.

Eventually, American opponents of slavery provided Baquaqua with passage on a ship to Haiti. Disoriented and unable to speak French, Baquaqua found Haiti an unwelcome new home until he met several American Free Baptist missionaries. Baquaqua became a Protestant Baptist as a result of his association with the Judds, a missionary family. In 1849, the Judds helped Baquaqua return to New York to avoid being drafted into the Haitian army. Baquaqua lived in upstate New York from 1849 to 1853 and attended New York Central College in McGrawville (now McGraw). Churches and abolitionists funded his education. He eventually left the college. Baquaqua became increasingly frustrated with racism and the lack of economic opportunity in the United States. He moved to Canada by 1853 and then sought a way back to Africa. With the help of a Unitarian minister named Samuel Moore, he wrote his autobiography. For several years, he tried to go back to West Africa as a missionary for the Free Mission Society and later the American Missionary Association, but the funds never came together. In early 1855, Baquaqua took a ship to England, hoping he could convince English missionary patrons to allow him to return to his home. Several references indicate that he tried to find backing to go to the British colony of Sierra Leone in 1855 and 1856. He vanished from the historical record after 1857. Although much of his life remains obscure, his writings allow for a better understanding of the experience of African-born slaves in the Americas in the 1840s and 1850s.

BIBLIOGRAPHY

Law, Robin. "Individualising the Atlantic Slave Trade: The Biography of Mahommah Gardo Baquaqua of Djougou (1854)." *Transactions of the Royal Historical Society*, 6th ser., 12 (2002): 113–114.

Law, Robin, and Paul Lovejoy, eds. *The Biography of Mahommah Gardo Baquaqua: His Passage from Slavery to Freedom in Africa and America*. Princeton, N.J.: Markus Wiener, 2001.

JEREMY RICH

Baradiʻi, Muhammad al-. *See* ElBaradai, Mohamed.

Barakana, Gabriel (c. 1914–1999), religious and educational leader, was born to a family of chiefs in the town of Rusengo in eastern Burundi. The names and occupations of his parents are not known. He attended primary school in Rusengo from 1927 to 1933 and completed his secondary education at the Mugera seminary from 1933 to 1939. Barakana then decided to complete his theological training to become a Roman Catholic priest. He underwent training at the seminary in Nyakibanda from 1939 to 1947 and was ordained on 25 July 1947. Soon afterward, he went to the Vatican to study for a doctorate in canon law, which he received in 1950. Barakana thus became the first Burundian to ever receive a doctorate. Barakana decided to join the Jesuit Catholic religious order and officially became a member of this order on 20 May 1953 at Djuma in the Democratic Republic of the Congo (Zaire). He moved in 1955 to Eegenhoven, Belgium, where he completed a degree in philosophy and then attended the Catholic University of Louvain. He finished an undergraduate degree in the social sciences in 1958. Barakana then spent a year in France from 1959 to 1960.

On returning to Burundi in 1960, Barakana became a teacher and a spiritual director at the Collège du Saint Esprit secondary school. He held this position until July 1964, when he was named the rector of this institution of higher learning. From 1963 to 1965, Barakana served as the representative for Burundi at the Vatican II council in the Vatican, which brought about radical changes in the Catholic Church. Besides this work, Barakana helped establish the first university in Rwanda, beginning in 1961. On 10 January 1964, Barakana's dream was achieved, when the University of Burundi opened. The Burundian priest served as an administrator and taught classes in law there. In 1971, Barakana became the rector of this university. He supervised the development of new programs, such as an agronomy department.

One year later, the bloody genocide of 1972 took place in Burundi. Hundreds of thousands of people, largely Hutu, were killed by the military, which was dominated by Tutsi officers. Barakana was a close friend of President Michel Micombero, and some observers criticized that Barakana sought to whitewash the image of the ruling government during this catastrophe. However, he publicly condemned the slaughter of innocents, particularly of students, in a message to the nation on 9 May 1972. Barakana also sought unsuccessfully to convince his old friend to stop the killings.

Barakana spent time in England and France from 1978 to 1981 but returned to form a new Marian movement in his homeland. Jean-Baptiste

Bagaza, ruler of Burundi in the 1980s, jailed Barakana on 30 July 1985 for criticizing the strongman's persecution of the church, particularly the Hutu clergy and laypersons. The Jesuits were driven from their property. Barakana was liberated on 27 March 1987. The civil war of the 1990s in Burundi deeply saddened Barakana, and his health deteriorated over the course of the decade. Barakana died on 29 September 1999 at Kiriri and remained one of the most popular Burundian priests of the twentieth century.

[*See also* Micombero, Michel; *and* Bagaza, Jean-Baptiste.]

BIBLIOGRAPHY

Chrétien, Jean-Pierre, and Jean-François Dupaquier. *Burundi 1972: Au bord des gènocides*. Paris: Karthala, 2007.

Ndayishimiye, Guillaume. "Hommage au Père Barakana, de la Compagnie de Jésus." *Tubane* 15, no. 101 (July 2009): 46–47. http://www.abayezuwiti.com/tub_101_juillet_09_page%20entiere_reduit%20%282%29.pdf.

JEREMY RICH

Baranyanka, Pierre (d. 1962), politician, business leader, and historian, was born in the late nineteenth century in Burundi. He belonged to the Batare royal family that had controlled Burundi prior to the entrance of German military officers in the 1890s. He originally came from southern Burundi as his father was a chief in the Vyanda region not far from the town of Bururi. He received a primary education at a German school at Gitega. After the Belgian government took over Burundi following World War I, Baranyanka became one of the most fervent supporters of the new administration in the entire colony. He was a firm supporter of Catholic missions and the development of cash-crop production. Baranyanka converted to Catholicism after undertaking instruction for four years. He established an extremely large coffee business that consisted of thirty-five thousand coffee bushes by 1935. A young Belgian tourist in 1949 expressed the views of most European authorities and settlers regarding Baranyanka: "The most renowned coffee belongs to Pierre Baranyanka, a chief who really understands what should be done. His skin color is the only thing that makes him different from us" (Gahama, 1986, p. 185). Baranyanka was a hero for many Europeans, but many of his subjects considered him to be an authoritarian figure.

The Belgian government had granted Baranyanka the power to settle legal cases, to collect taxes, to recruit and supervise forced labor details, and to act as a representative for the colonial regime. The Belgian administration named him the chief of the Nkiko-Mugamba region, a territory that had rejected both the Burundian monarchy and the Belgians under the leadership of Kilima. Baranyanka forced this region to fully accept colonial rule and helped put down a revolt in 1934 led by a woman named Inamujandi.

Baranyanka provided both logistical support and knowledge to Catholic missionaries, and he served in the 1930s as an informant for Belgian missionaries such as Peter Schumacher, a member of the Roman Catholic White Father missionary society who sought to reconstruct the precolonial history of Burundi and Rwanda. In 1943, Baranyanka wrote his own history of Burundi, titled *Intsinzi Kartenda*, along the lines of the Rwandan royal history written by the Catholic priest Alexis Kagame. The notable French historian of the Great Lakes region Jean-Pierre Chretien has described Baranyanka as a major figure in the historiography of his country. In the 1950s, Baranyanka engaged with the Belgian administration's tepid efforts to create and promote some democratic institutions. The prominent official Pierre Ryckmans viewed Baranyanka as far preferable to the Burundian king Mwambutsa IV, who seemed unreliable to the colonial government. Ryckmans's successor, Robert Schmidt, head of the colonial government in Burundi from 1944 to 1954, was just as determined to back Baranyanka. The government endorsed Baranyanka's Parti Démocratique Chrétien (PDC; Christian Democratic Party) party over the nationalist party, Union pour le Progrès national (UPRONA; Union for National Progress), in the late 1950s. In 1961, UPRONA had a triumphant victory over Baranyanka and the PDC in elections for the recently created legislature. UPRONA's leader, Prince Louis Rwagasore, was assassinated by a Greek trader on 13 October 1961, and many believed Baranyanka had either ordered or supported the assassination. He died in Bujumbura, the capital of Burundi, in 1962. He had five children and seven daughters. Baranyanka's son, Jean-Louis, was executed in 1963 for supposedly ordering Rwagasore's death. Another son, Charles, became a diplomat and a historian in his own right.

[*See also* Inamujandi; Kagame, Alexis; Mwambutsa IV Bangiricenge; *and* Rwagasore, Louis.]

BIBLIOGRAPHY

Chrétien, Jean-Pierre. *Burundi, l'histoire retrouvée: 25 ans de métier d'historien en Afrique*. Paris: Karthala, 1993.

Gahama, Joseph. *Le Burundi sous administration Belge*. Paris: L'Harmattan, 1986.

JEREMY RICH

Barbarossa. *See* Baba ʿAruj; Khayr al-Din.

Barends, Barend (c. 1770–1839), Griqua leader and hunter in the region that is present-day South Africa, was born around 1770. During the second half of the eighteenth century, his family was one of several families of mixed Khoekhoe and Dutch descent who came to prominence in the dry lands of Namaqualand and along the Gariep River, on the northern frontier of the Cape Colony. Among them were two brothers, known variously as Claas and Piet Bastard or Claas and Piet Barends (sometimes spelled Berends). They first appear in the archival record in the 1760s accompanying Dutch and French expeditions to the Gariep and as overseers on the farms of the Van Reenen family, who were then the Cape's most important butchers. In time the family grew in wealth, prominence, and size, primarily on the basis of hunting, stock farming, and trading to the Cape, so that it was able to acquire the horses, firearms, and ammunition necessary for survival and prosperity. By the late 1790s, the family had become ensconced as one of the leading clans along the middle reaches of the Gariep River, generally in alliance with the Kok family, which had similar roots, in rivalry with the followers of Jager Afrikaner, who were engaged in raiding into what was to become Namibia and basically attempting to maintain their independence from the colonial authorities.

One of the Barends brothers—it is not known which—was married to a daughter of Adam Kok I. They had at least one child, Barend, who was thus a nephew of Cornelius Kok I and a cousin of Adam Kok II. By around 1800, Barend Barends was moving further up the Gariep, into the region that became known as Griqualand West, and was increasingly recognized as the leader of the clan. At this stage he had about two hundred followers. In 1800 the missionaries of the (Congregationalist) London Missionary Society, William Anderson and Cornelis Kramer, arrived north of the river and established a church around the spring at Klaarwater, later known as Griquatown. This formed the basis of a more formal political entity than had previously existed, which would eventually crystallize into the Griqua captaincy. Barends became one of the magistrates within the polity, said to be the most determined and energetic. He was also a deacon of the church and lay preacher.

At this stage in his life Barends was a particularly successful elephant hunter and on occasion traveled as far as Cape Town to exchange the ivory so acquired for consumer goods, guns, and ammunition. Eventually, though, the attempts of the missionaries to establish a sedentary community under their own tutelage came increasingly into conflict with Barends's own aspirations and way of life. Barends reestablished his main residence at the spring known as Daniels Kuil, to the northeast of Griquatown and on the southern borders of territory inhabited by Batswana. Later, he moved further north to Boetsap in the Harts River valley. In 1820, he effectively relinquished his leading position in Griquatown, to be replaced by Andries Waterboer. He nevertheless attempted in vain to persuade a missionary to stay with him, free from the control of Griquatown. This never led to an easy relationship, even though Waterboer was recognized by the Cape colonial government and thus had a degree of monopoly over the legal arms trade north of the Gariep. Barends certainly maintained considerable independence and control over a substantial following, negotiated with dissidents from the Griquatown captaincy, and commanded mounted horsemen in the Griquas' battles against Tswana forces, both at the battle of Dithakong in 1823 and a year later in a struggle between the Barolong and the Bataung.

Following the battles of the early 1820s, Barends seems to have appreciated the opportunity to move beyond the old reliance on hunting and stock keeping to develop a degree of hegemony over the southern Batswana. In part, he was aided in this by the Wesleyan missionaries who had settled at Platberg, near Boetsap, to work among the Barolong and who acknowledged Barends as the local hegemon. However, this strategy was threatened primarily by the arrival in the region of Mzilikazi at the head of the Ndebele state. This established itself first in the region of the Magaliesberg, to the west of what is now Tshwane. Barends, by now old and rather deaf, was convinced that horsemen armed with guns would always prevail in battle against *assegai*-wielding foot soldiers. He also came to believe that he was called upon by God to liberate the Batswana from Ndebele domination—and, no doubt, replace it with his own. In the winter of 1831,

with a party of perhaps three hundred Griquas and numerous Tswana auxiliaries, he launched an attack on the Ndebele state, moving through country which he knew well from numerous hunting expeditions. The commando managed to surprise the amaNdebele, most of whose army was away on another expedition, and succeeded in capturing large numbers of cattle and women. Two nights into their return, however, they were surprised by the counterattack of a small force of veteran Ndebele warriors and massacred as they slept. Barend himself managed to escape, but his political role was played out.

Subsequent attempts to collect forces for a second attack on Mzilikazi failed. The greater part of his followers from Boetsap moved away to the east and settled at Lishuane in the Caledon River valley, in the neighborhood of a Wesleyan mission. The group was led by Barends's nephew and successor, Peter Davids, and Barends himself only joined the group in 1837, two years before he died.

Barends always impressed those literate observers who met him as a shrewd and determined politician, though except for his religious justification of the attack on Mzilikazi there is no real description of his character, nor has any likeness of him survived. He was, however, one of the most significant actors in the South African interior during the first third of the nineteenth century.

[*See also* Kok III, Adam.]

BIBLIOGRAPHY

Legassick, Martin Chatfield. *The Politics of a South African Frontier: The Griqua, the Sotho-Tswana, and the Missionaries, 1780–1840*. Basel: Basler Afrika Bibliographien, 2010.

Penn, Nigel. *The Forgotten Frontier: Colonist and Khoisan on the Cape's Northern Frontier in the 18th Century*. Cape Town, South Africa: Double Storey; Athens, Ohio: Ohio University Press, 2006.

Ross, Robert. *Adam Kok's Griquas: A Study in the Development of Stratification in South Africa*. Cambridge, UK: Cambridge University Press, 1976.

Smith, Andrew. *The Diary of Dr. Andrew Smith*, edited by P. R. Kirby. 2 vols. Cape Town, South Africa: Van Riebeeck Society, 1939–1940.

ROBERT ROSS

Barnard, Christiaan Neethling (1922–2001), South African surgeon who carried out the world's first human-to-human heart transplant, was born into an impoverished Afrikaner family at Beaufort

Christiaan Neethling Barnard. Barnard explaining a heart transplant at a news conference in Rodenbosch, Cape Town, South Africa, 1967. (AP Images/Cape Argus)

West, South Africa, on 8 November 1922. His father, the Reverend Adam Hendrik Barnard, was a clergyman of the Dutch Reformed Church for Coloured, or mixed-race, people, and his mother was Maria Elisabeth de Swart. He was educated at Beaufort West High School before training as a doctor at the University of Cape Town's medical school, where he graduated MB, ChB, in 1945. Having done his internship at Groote Schuur Hospital in Cape Town, he worked for a short time as a rural general practitioner in Ceres, in the western Cape, before returning to Cape Town to become senior medical officer at City Hospital and then registrar at Groote Schuur Hospital. In 1953 he gained his MD for his dissertation "The Treatment of Tuberculosis Meningitis." Later, he underwent advanced surgical training at the University of Minnesota, Minneapolis, before returning in 1958 to a joint post at the University of Cape Town and Groote Schuur Hospital, where, as well as surgical work and teaching, he did advanced work in research laboratories in perfecting on dogs surgical techniques he later used for human organ transplantation. In parallel with this, he made numerous visits to the United States, becoming familiar with pathbreaking transplantation work, including that of Norman Shumway and Adrian Kantrowitz. In his own epoch-making operation, Barnard built on

this pioneering work, being assisted by a more permissive medicolegal framework in South Africa than that which existed in the United States.

Barnard was associate professor and head of Groote Schuur's Department of Cardiothoracic Surgery when, in a five-hour operation on 3 December 1967, he performed the world's first human-to-human heart transplant. He was supported by a large team that included his younger brother, Marius, also a surgeon. The patient was Louis Washkansky, a fifty-five-year-old white man, and the donor heart belonged to Denise Darvall, a twenty-four-year-old white woman; that the race was white in each case of this epoch-making operation was seen as important within apartheid South Africa. The operation was a technical success, with Washkansky surviving eighteen days. Overwhelming media interest followed, and Barnard joined the jet set, conspicuously enjoying life as an international superstar.

The lifestyle and extramarital affairs of a celebrity surgeon shaped Barnard's marital history. His first marriage, to Aletta Louw in 1948, produced two children (Deidre, born 1950, and Andre, born 1951) but ended in divorce in 1969. A second marriage, to Barbara Zoellner in 1970, again yielded two children (Frederick, born 1972, and Christiaan, born 1974); but it too ended in divorce, in 1982. Barnard's third marriage, to Karin Setzkorn in 1988, produced two more children (Armin, born 1990, and Lara, born 1997) before ending in divorce in 2000.

Barnard became professor of surgical science in 1972, continuing to be involved in only a modest amount of heart transplantation; but this did include the world's first double heart transplant in 1974, where a donor heart acted as booster to a diseased patient heart. Many international awards followed, including the Dag Hammarskjold International Prize, the Kennedy Foundation Award, and the Milan International Award for Science. In 1983 advancing rheumatoid arthritis forced Barnard to give up surgery and retire as head of the Department of Cardiothoracic Surgery. He continued to act as a consultant at various institutions and was also active in his two philanthropic foundations. Barnard died following an asthma attack on 2 September 2001, while on holiday at Paphos, Cyprus.

Barnard's achievement was based on consuming professional commitment, surgical courage, and meticulous postoperative care for patients. Ironically, despite Barnard's opposition to racial discrimination, the operation conferred on apartheid South Africa a rare moment of positive media coverage and arguably helped modify perceptions of Africa as a backward continent. The first heart transplant was a medical milestone that catapulted Barnard's institution—Groote Schuur Hospital—and his country—South Africa—into an age of modern medical specialism. Before 1994, the country's highly developed surgical and transplantation expertise was skewed toward the white population; but in recent years, it has been extended to all races and is now being widened beyond that to other populations in the African continent.

BIBLIOGRAPHY

Barnard, Christiaan Neethling, and Curtis Bill Pepper. *One Life*. Cape Town, South Africa: Howard Timmins, 1969. Autobiographical account.

Logan, Chris. *Celebrity Surgeon: Christiaan Barnard—A Life*. Cape Town, South Africa: Jonathan Ball, 2003. Highlights connections between personal and professional life.

McRae, Donald. *Every Second Counts: The Race to Transplant the First Human Heart*. New York: Simon & Schuster, 2006. Dramatizes the first heart transplant in relation to surgical work in the United States.

ANNE DIGBY

Baro Tumsa (1938–1978) pharmacist, lawyer, and Oromo nationalist and political activist in Ethiopia, was mainly responsible for the formation of the Oromo Liberation Front, which in turn transformed Oromo cultural nationalism to political nationalism. He was born in the region of Wallaga. He lost both his parents while very young, and it was his elder brother, the Reverend Gudina Tumsa, who brought him up and provided him with the best education.

While at Haile Selassie I University, Baro Tumsa immersed himself in student politics as well as risky underground Oromo political activities. From 1964 to 1966 he served as secretary and president of the union of the university students in Addis Ababa. It was under his leadership that university students were radicalized and energized. More than many of his contemporaries, Baro Tumsa realized that the Oromo and other conquered people of southern Ethiopia were landless subjects without rights who were exploited economically, subjugated politically, and dehumanized culturally. To bring the plight and suffering of southern peasantry to public attention, in February 1965 Baro organized the first ever university student demonstration under the banner of "Land to the Tiller," which became the binding revolutionary slogan for Ethiopian student movements both at home and abroad until the revolution of 1974. It was the political genius of Baro Tumsa that he framed the peasant problems as the burning issue of the 1960s and early 1970s.

After graduation in 1966, Baro Tumsa served in the Ministry of Health, where he modernized the policy dealing with the licensing, import, and distribution of pharmaceuticals. It was his interest in policy issues that sparked his interest in studying law at Haile Selassie I University. While working and undergoing legal training, Baro Tumsa was also an active member of the Macha and Tulama Association (1963–1967), the first countrywide Oromo civic organization. When the association was banned in 1967, and some of its leaders executed and others detained for a decade, Baro Tumsa secretly brought together educated Oromo in a group known as "Walbarroo" ("Know Each Other"). He also formed a legal organization known as the "Dhidheessa Association," which secretly continued with the activities of the banned association. He was instrumental in the transformation of the banned association into an underground movement that organized members into study circles and cultural committees. For political agitation, the leaders of the underground movement produced literature in the Amharic, English, and Oromo languages, which played a crucial role in raising

Oromo political consciousness among educated elements at Haile Selassie I University.

When the February 1974 revolution started, the underground movement in Addis Ababa under the leadership of Baro Tumsa took advantage of the situation and contributed to the overthrow of the imperial regime in four ways. First, Baro Tumsa and his comrades effectively used the limited freedom of the press that flourished in Ethiopia for a few months for the purpose of exposing the appalling poverty to which the Oromo were subjected under the imperial regime Second, Baro Tumsa's friends in the Ethiopian parliament regularly challenged the regime's policies. Third, its members conducted agitation among university and high school students. Fourth, and most important, the underground members of the military and police forces were instrumental in organizing the committee of the men in uniform (*derg* in Amharic) that overthrew Emperor Haile Selassie in September 1974. It was under Baro Tumsa's leadership that the many underground groups in the capital developed into a coherent organization known as the "Oromo Liberation Front" in 1974.

By 1976 Baro Tumsa realized the importance of unity between the Oromo and other Ethiopians. For that purpose, he formed the "Oppressed Peoples of Ethiopia Revolutionary Struggle," which brought together the educated elements of the conquered people of southern Ethiopia. He was able to achieve so much because he was a well-tempered man, a good listener, and a gifted orator. He had a magnetic personality and physical presence, was a remarkable organizer, and had a uniquely charismatic way that inspired people and mobilized resources. In 1977 Baro Tumsa escaped arrest and joined the armed struggle conducted by the Oromo Liberation Front in Hararge. He was killed in 1978. His tragic and untimely death deprived the Oromo people of a universally admired, respected, and loved leader. Since his death the Oromo struggle has not again produced a leader of Baro Tumsa's caliber.

[*See also* Elemo Qilxuu.]

BIBLIOGRAPHY

Balsvik, Randi. *Haile Selassie's Students: The Intellectual and Social Background to Revolution, 1952–1977.* East Lansing: African Studies Center, Michigan State University, in Cooperation with the Norwegian Council of Science and the Humanities, 1985.

Guddinaa, Kulanii, and Mohammed Hassen. "Baaroo Tumsaa." In *Goota Oromiyaa*, edited by Daraaraa Maatii and Mohammed Hassen, pp. 56–72. Atlanta, Ga.: Oromia Publishing, 2008.

Hassen, Mohammed. "A Short History of Oromo Colonial Experience: Part Two. Colonial Consolidation and Resistance 1935–2000." *Journal of Oromo Studies* 7, nos. 1–2 (July 2000): 132–148.

Zog, Olana. *Gezatena Gezot Macha and Tulama Association*. Addis Ababa: Self-published, 1993.

MOHAMMED HASSEN ALI

Barquq (d. 1399), Egyptian sultan, was the first of a new dynasty of Mamluks or "slave" sultans of Egypt. Purchased in Crimea, Barquq, whose full name was al-Malik al-Zahir Sayf al-Din Barquq, was a Circassian. The previous series of Mamluks, starting with Baybars, were Kipchak Turks. Bought as a slave soldier, Barquq quickly rose through the ranks of the Burji regiment of soldier slaves. Unlike the Bahri regiment that supplied previous sultans, the Burji regiment had their barracks near the dungeons (*burj*) of the citadel in Cairo. It appears that Barquq's father, a man of some stature named Anas, may have willingly given his son up for sale. In fact, after Barquq came to power he invited his father to come to Cairo and join his court. Indeed, Anas would have been pleased to learn that his son was first purchased by the powerful marshal of the army Yalbogha al-ʿUmari. Barquq was imprisoned after his master fell from power. He was also involved in the assassination of Malik Ashraf Shaʿban in 1377. Assassination, infighting and conspiracy were rife throughout Mamluk history. Power and military prowess were valued highly. The stability of the state rested on a marshal system of slave soldiers maintaining the underlying viability of the system. Barquq was himself appointed marshal of the armies by Sultan Malik Mansoor Ali. By this time Barquq, the slave, would have become a slave owner himself. When the sultan died of plague in 1382, Barquq placed the sultan's brother on the throne with himself as regent. Finally, he claimed full power after a council of city leaders and the caliph pronounced him ruler.

Barquq soon gathered around him a powerful and intelligent group of advisors and councilors. Barquq appointed the famed historian and philosopher Ibn Khaldun (d. 1406) as head Maliki judge. He sponsored the building of several institutions including the Sufi Khanqah and Madrasa of Sultan Barquq, now in the center of Cairo. Nevertheless, he could not prevent the constant threat of revolt and treason that characterized the Mamluk period. With any regional ruler or charismatic solider able to rise through the ranks and attempt a seizure of power, the sultan had to be constantly vigilant. In fact, the tide seemed to turn decisively against Barquq when most of his own officers defected to the camp of the governor of Aleppo, Yalbugha al-Nasiri, in 1389. Left with a decreasing number of unmotivated soldiers and officers defending the Cairo citadel, Barquq fled the city. Barquq was eventually found and sent to prison at Karak in the Levant. Most assumed the sultan would never return. Ibn Khaldun, along with several other functionaries, swiftly condemned Barquq and professed their new loyalty to al-Nasiri. Only the disastrous and chaotic transition to power saved Barquq. Al-Nasiri lacked the decisive leadership needed to stem the street fighting between Mamluk generals that played out in Cairo. Barquq escaped from prison and gathered a group of Bedouin Arabs from the Levant. He finally reentered Cairo in triumph in February 1390, much to the mortification of those who had abandoned him. In fact, Ibn Khaldun was forced into writing a long poetic panegyric expressing his apology, and the apology of his fellows, for abandoning a man most assumed had disappeared from the political scene. Although he controlled Cairo, it still took several years for Barquq to eliminate his enemies. There is some evidence that Timurlane, the Mongol conqueror, encouraged these revolts against the resolute Barquq, creating a chaotic situation that would provide the easy and ripe conditions for Mongol conquest.

In 1393 Barquq received a disturbing embassy from a "Mongol rebel" named Timurlane. Soon Timurlane's power spread throughout the Middle East. The sultan of Baghdad, Ahmad bin Uways, took refuge in Cairo. Barquq, despite historical evidence of the consequences of killing Mongol ambassadors, put Timurlane's ambassador to death. He virtually assured a ferocious reaction by Timur. Timurlane nonetheless did not conquer Egypt; he was eventually defeated by the Ottomans. He did manage, however, to slaughter the inhabitants of Damascus in 1401. Ibn Khaldun would have been among the slaughtered had he not deftly negotiated his escape during a meeting at Timurlane's tent. Barquq died in June 1399, possibly during an epileptic fit. He was widely famous. There was even a biography of the sultan written in Latin in 1416 titled *Ascensus Barcoch*.

[*See also* Baybars I; *and* Ibn Khaldun.]

BIBLIOGRAPHY

Fischel, Walter. *Ascensus Barcoch: A Latin Biography of Mamluk Sultan Barquq of Egypt (d. 1399)*. Leiden: E. J. Brill, 1959.

Fromherz, Allen J. *Ibn Khaldun, Life and Times*. Edinburgh: Edinburgh University Press, 2010.

Williams, Caroline. *Islamic Monuments in Cairo: The Practical Guide*. Cairo: American University in Cairo Press, 2002.

Winter, Michael, and Amalia Levanoni, eds. *The Mamluks in Egyptian and Syrian Politics and Society*. Leiden: E. J. Brill, 2004.

ALLEN J. FROMHERZ

Barry, Kesso (1948–), daughter of El Hadj Ibrahima Sory Barry of Dara (1884?–1978), the last *almamy*, or king, of the Fulani of Fouta Djalon, and his third wife, Diello, was born in Mamou, Republic of Guinea (Guinea-Conakry), in 1948. Kesso, meaning "virgin" in Fulani, enjoyed a happy childhood in the royal slave-sustained and polygamous household of her father until the age of six, when she moved to Sogotoro with his authoritarian sister. For four years her aunt tried to reform her impulsive, headstrong niece through hard work and discipline but to little avail. Upon her return to Mamou, Barry quickly made her reputation as a "revolutionary princess." She joined her brothers in typically male activities, such as hunting and tax collecting, frequenting the cinema, and joyriding in her father's car, once almost killing a child. On her own initiative, she attended Mamou's qur'anic school and its public primary school. At the latter, much to her traditionalist environment's displeasure, the princess socialized with the (former) French colonizers' children, wore shorts in physical education, and took drama classes from a progressive Guinean teacher, who used her lessons to broach all kinds of taboo subjects.

Slightly older than was customary and already snubbed by her peers, Barry was initiated at the age of twelve through the ritual of clitoridectomy. She suffered much as first the traditional practitioner botched the operation and then her wound became infected, and she was too repulsed by the humiliations borne by her polygamous mother to share the latter's delight in her newly acquired marriageable status. Less concerned with Guinean politics and the implications of Sékou Touré's (1922–1984) antifeudalist course for her family than with her own gender predicament, the young princess sought for ways to escape from Mamou's conservative, patriarchal society.

At thirteen, she persuaded her father to enroll her at secondary school, first in the Guinean capital of Conakry and a year later in Dakar, Senegal. As it was not her primary goal to be educated but to be free, Barry quickly tired of her life as a boarder at Conakry and, with some effort, obtained her father's permission to train in shorthand typing in the livelier metropolis of Dakar. Initially, Barry lodged with the rather strict relatives of her father's Senegalese fourth wife, but before long she moved in with French acquaintances of her father's, the more accommodating Mr. and Mrs. Saint-Grémois. Mr. Saint-Grémois, who did not hide his admiration for the independent princess, improved Barry's mobility by buying her a Vespa in exchange for her help in negotiating business in Guinea and, unbeknownst to her father, took her on a (disappointing) visit to France.

By the end of her year in Dakar, the prospect of an arranged marriage and a life full of constraints in Mamou prompted Barry to marry Baïllo, a thirty-year-old entrepreneur from Mamou who appealed to her primarily because he worked in Conakry. Keeping her legal wedding in Dakar a secret from her family—she lied about her age at the registrar's office—Barry eventually swayed her reluctant family to arrange her traditional marriage to the socially inferior Baïllo. Although he helped to conceal that his virgin bride did not bleed during their wedding night, in no time he shattered his fifteen-year-old princess's romantic notions of love with his domineering and jealous behavior. Soon after the births, in quick succession, of a daughter, Bintou, and a son, Ousmane, the couple divorced and Barry and her children moved in with her brother's family.

To maintain her independence, she took a position as a secretary in the bauxite mining town of Fria, where she fell in love with her employer, the French industrialist Gérard Decoster. Although he initially ignored her advances, in 1966 Barry tenaciously followed him to Paris, where she supported herself by working as a fashion model. Although her Muslim family was disappointed with her remarriage to a white Frenchman, a nonpracticing Catholic to boot, Barry was relieved to permanently settle in France with her two children. In 1988 she presented her autobiography, *Kesso, princesse peuhle* (Kesso, Fulani Princess). Written in French, it was addressed to her third child, her and Decoster's then ten-year-old daughter, Sandra, for whom she recounted her life history, from her royal youth in Mamou to her high-society life in Paris.

Despite her optimistic opening statement that "nothing is sad around me" (p. 12) and her constant emphasis on her self-determination, the adult Barry unexpectedly concluded her memoir by deploring the "ambiguity" (p. 232) of her life between two cultures and by expressing her regrets over having left her native Guinea.

[*See also* Touré, Ahmed Sékou.]

BIBLIOGRAPHY

d'Almeida, Irène Assiba. "Kesso Barry's *Kesso*, or Autobiography as a Subverted Tale." *Research in African Literatures* 28, no. 2 (Summer 1997): 66–82. Argues that the subversiveness of Barry's autobiographical tale is undercut by her "divided cultural self"—that is, her inability to come to terms with the contradictions between her traditional past as a Fulani princess in Mamou and her Westernized life in France.

Barry, Kesso. *Kesso, Princesse peuhle*. Paris: Seghers, 1988. Barry's autobiography.

ELISABETH BEKERS

Barsbay (d. 1438), whose full name was al-Malik al-Ashraf Abu an-Nasr Barsbay, was one of the more ruthless and tragic of the Mamluk sultans of Egypt. He ruled the Mamluk Empire from Cairo between 1422 and 1438, a time of increasing external pressure on the sultanate. His early life, like that of many a Mamluk or slave soldier, was brutal. Years of imprisonment hardened his character and his resolve for power.

Upon his succession to the sultanate, Barsbay immediately banned Jews and Christians from participating in government service, despite centuries of tradition that kept Jewish and Christian families firmly inside the Mamluk power network. There is some debate about the reasons for Barsbay's ban. It may have been paranoia over the increasing influence of European pirates and merchants on Mamluk shores. Indeed, the property of all European traders, many from Genoa and Venice, was confiscated by the sultan as an immediate way of increasing the store of the depleted treasury. The impact of this policy on trade, however, may have eventually reversed the temporary fiscal gain.

Barsbay adopted a highly defensive posture, erecting a number of forts and watchtowers on the coasts and financing a new navy. He even attempted to expand and conquer new lands. His first and most focused ambition was the Island of Cyprus. Janus, the King of Cyprus, was captured and led through the streets of Cairo in disgrace. Barsbay agreed to a yearly tribute payment to spare the life of Janus and restore his kingdom. Barsbay was much less successful in his campaigns against the Turkish peoples in Mesopotamia, and his defeated army returned to Cairo in a highly disorganized fashion in 1433.

A religious and diplomatic dispute of great import soon consumed the Mamluks. The powerful Timurid sultan (successor to Timurlane) Shah-Rukh claimed the right to attend to the Kaaba in Mecca and to vest the Kaaba with a veil. Barsbay was particularly concerned that the Timurids had ambitions not only to expand into Arabia for religious purposes but to gain control over valued Red Sea trade.

Witnessing the breakout of plague in the 1430s made Barsbay a chronic hypochondriac. He executed two of his doctors and redistributed to the poor much of the tax revenue he had so ruthlessly taken from merchants during his reign. None of these measures prevented him from coming down with the illness that led to his death in 1438. The end of his reign left the treasury drained and the Mamluks in a weakened position to deal with European and Ottoman expansion. Barbay also, however, left behind several important monuments, schools, and other architectural wonders.

BIBLIOGRAPHY

Darrag, Ahmad. *L'Egypte sous le Regne de Barsbay*. Damascus: Institut Français de Damas, 1961.

Petry, Carl, ed. *The Cambridge History of Egypt*, Vol. 1, *Islamic Egypt, 640–1517*. Cambridge: Cambridge University Press, 2008.

Sabra, Adam. *Poverty and Charity in Medieval Islam: Mamluk Egypt, 1250–1517*. Cambridge: Cambridge University Press, 2001.

ALLEN J. FROMHERZ

Bartili al-Walati, Muhammad al- (1727/28–1805), Mauritanian teacher and Muslim scholar, was born to a scholarly family and reared in Walata, an oasis town in present-day eastern Mauritania. His full name was Muhammad abu 'Abd Allah ibn abu Bakr as-Siddiq al-Bartili al-Walati. The main lineages that claim descent from the Bartili (or Barittayl) are the at-Talib Jibril, the 'Ali Diggan, and the at-Talib 'Ali Bannan, who formed a network of scholarly families. All of these groups have played an important role in the cultural and political life of the region of Takrur, serving as muftis (Muslim scholars qualified to formulate legal opinions on matters

of Islamic law), imams, and especially teachers. In al-Bartili's time, the name "Takrur" came to signify a Muslim cultural region stretching from the mouth of the Senegal River in the west to the Niger River bend in the east, including much of present-day Mauritania, Mali, and Senegal.

Walata was situated on a trade route and was a caravan station, a pilgrimage route, and a major center of Islamic culture. In this city, Muhammad al-Bartili learned the main Islamic sciences: theology (*tawhid*), Islamic law (*fiqh*), exegesis (*tafsir*), reports of the Prophet (hadith), grammar (*nahw*), philology (*lugha*), rhetoric (*bayan*), prosody ('*arud*), and so forth. He attended meetings with theologians, traditionalists, and other great teachers of the town, which were highly influential on his thought. According to a biography written by one of his disciples, al-Bartili was a teacher, a religious man, and a pious sufi.

In the fourteenth century, the geographer Ibn Battuta described Walata as part of the *Bilad al-Sudan* (land of the blacks) and as an important commercial center whose inhabitants were mostly Berbers from the Masufa tribal group. According to the French historian Maurice Delafosse, Walata was founded in 1224 near the wells of Birou (another toponym used to describe Walata), located on the edge of a basin (the Hodh) some 270 miles west of Timbuktu. However, Timothy Cleaveland argues convincingly in his book *Becoming Walata* that the founding of this city goes back to an earlier era. After the tenth-century Almoravid movement, Berber-speaking nomads seized a larger role in trans-Saharan trade and increasingly settled into towns like Walata. From the fifteenth century Arabic-speaking nomads also moved into the region and gradually settled in the commercial centers. Small waves of migrants also came to Walata from other towns in the region when they experienced political upheaval, such as from Timbuktu in 1468 and 1591. Hence, Walata attracted more Arab nomads and became dominated by Arab and Berber settlers.

al-Bartili gave Walata a crucial place in his major work *Fath ash-Shakur fi Ma'rifat A'yan 'Ulama' at-Takrur* (*The Key Given by God for Making Known the Noteworthy Scholars of Takrur*). This important text, written in Arabic in 1800, is a synopsis of the intellectual and religious history of Takrur. It represents a sequel to *Kifayat al-Muhtaj* of the Timbuktu scholar Ahmad Baba (1556–1627) and the *Tarikh as-Sudan* of 'Abd ar-Rahman as-Sa'di (1596–1655), also of Timbuktu. The former is a dictionary of

Maliki scholars of western Africa through the six-teenth century, and the latter is a chronicle of the history of the Songhay Empire and the Moroccan conquest and occupation, emphasizing the role of Timbuktu. The *Fath* shifted the focus of these two earlier works to the northern part of western Africa, which al-Bartili called "Takrur," and emphasized the role of Walata and its Berber, Arab, and Mandé scholars.

The *Fath* contains 208 biographies of leading intellectuals who lived between the sixteenth and early nineteenth centuries. More than a simple col-lection of biographies, this work speaks eloquently of the different aspects of Saharan and sub-Saharan cultures in Mauritania and northern Mali and shows that this culture, like that of other parts of the Muslim world, was rich in learned men who participated in the development and flowering of Arab-Muslim intellectual life. Al-Bartili recounted the intellectual formation of these Takruri scholars, especially the role of teachers in the transmission of Islamic knowledge. Because of his insistent empha-sis on detail, al-Bartili's *Fath* constitutes an amaz-ingly rich bibliographical and prosopographical source. In addition to listing the writings of the subjects of his biographies (often the most com-plete lists yet known), al-Bartili listed the works they studied, in effect outlining the basic program of teaching and studying in the western Sahel in the period. At the time of al-Bartili in Walata, the grad-uate programs in the "university-mosque" and the subjects taught were the basis of Islamic studies and were similar to those of the major cultural cen-ters in the cities of the Maghreb such as Fez and Tunis. Most of the scholars described in the *Fath* were at the same time jurists and mystics (sufi). In this society, to possess Islamic learning was to have respect and influence because only the scholar with an insight into the essential nature of knowledge and mystical truth could be expected to know what mattered and what was required for the public welfare and for settling disputes in the Muslim societies of Mauritania, Mali, and Senegal.

The main activities of al-Bartili were those of a teacher, mufti, and writer. His teaching focused on theology, Maliki law, and grammar. He composed several books: *Sharh 'Ala Asma' Allah Ta'ala al-Husna* (a commentary on the most beautiful names of Allah); *Sharh 'Ala as-Sullam* (a commentary on a treatise on logic); *Nasab ash-Shurafa' dhurriyyat Mawlay ash-Sharif* (the genealogy of the 'Alawi Sharif of Morocco); *Ta'lif fi 'ilm as-Siyar* (a book on the art of biography); *Ta'lif fi 'ilm at-Tarikh* (a work on the science of history); *Nazm fi Nadb as-Siwak* (a poem on dental cure); *Fath ar-Rabb al-Ra'uf fi Sharh Qasidat Ma'ani al-Huruf* (a commentary on a poem on grammar); and the aforementioned *Fath ash-Shakur fi ma'rifat a'yan 'ulama' at-Takrur*.

The source of al-Bartili's political power and wealth was knowledge. People approached him to consult on legal issues because he was respected, heard, and often feared. He was a rich man who possessed many cows and other income from the gifts that he received for his services. Although wealthy, his disciples described him as a very gen-erous man who despised the things of this world and whose only concern was learning and books. He was a scholar who devoted his entire life to studying, teaching, and religious practice.

Al-Bartili died in March 1805 during an epidemic that swept through Walata and killed many people.

[*See also* Ibn Battuta, Muhammad ibn Abdullah.]

BIBLIOGRAPHY

Al-Bartili, Muhammad ibn Abu Bakr. *Fath ash-shakur fi ma'rifat a'yan 'ulama' at-Takrur*. Edited by Muhammad Ibrahim al-Kattani and Muhammad Hajji. Beirut: Dar al-Gharb al-Islami, 1981.

Cleaveland. Timothy. *Becoming Walata: A History of Saharan Social Formation and Transformation*. Westport, Conn.: Heinemann, 2001.

El Hamel, Chouki. *La vie intellectuelle islamique dans le Sahel ouest africain. Une étude sociale de l'enseignement islamique en Mauritanie et au Nord du Mali (XVIe–XIXe siècles)*. Paris: L'Harmattan, 2002.

CHOUKI EL HAMEL

Barudi, Mahmud Sami al- (1839–1904), Egyptian poet, diplomat, military commander, and politi-cian, was born in Cairo on 6 October 1839. His family claimed descent from a medieval Mamluk royal line, but his surname (*nisba*) refers to the dis-trict of Ityay al-Barud in Lower Egypt, of which his ancestors had once been tax farmers (*multazims*). His father, an artillery officer under Muhammad Ali, died in Sudan when al-Barudi was only seven years old. After primary education, al-Barudi entered the Military Training School in Cairo, in 1851, and graduated from it in 1855 with the rank of *bash-jawish* (sergeant-major). During the reign of the viceroy Sa'id (r. 1854–1863), he served in Istanbul as a diplomat and during this time acquired a lifelong enthusiasm for literature.

In 1863 the new viceroy, Isma'il (r. 1863–1879), visited Istanbul and recruited al-Barudi as commander of his Viceregal Guard in Cairo, with the rank of *binbashi* (major). In the following year he served in the Egyptian military missions sent to France and Great Britain. He quickly rose through the ranks to *amir-alay* (colonel) and in 1865 served in the war in Crete, where Egyptian forces helped the Ottomans to suppress the rebellion. He was decorated by the Ottomans for his distinguished service there. Later, Isma'il, now khedive, appointed him as private secretary and sent him back to Istanbul as a military diplomat. He also saw active service in the Ottoman army in 1877, during the war with Russia, and attained the rank of *amir al-liwa'* (brigadier general). After returning to Egypt, he undertook the task of reorganizing the general staff under the khedive Tawfiq (r. 1879–1892) between 1879 and 1882. At the same time he served as minister of Awqaf (religious endowments), using surplus funds for public works, including the building of housing, mosques, and the Khedivial Library in Cairo, later to become the National Library.

In February 1881, under pressure from the growing nationalist movement, led by army officers around Ahmad 'Urabi (1840–1911), the government of Riyad Pasha, Tawfiq's prime minister, was obliged to dismiss the unpopular minister of war, Rifqi Pasha, and appointed al-Barudi in his place. This was partly because Rifqi was from the hitherto privileged Turco-Circassian élite, whereas al-Barudi was regarded as a true Egyptian of Arab culture (in spite of his Mamluk ancestry). From then onward he became increasingly identified with the nationalist cause in Egypt. In February 1882, after the fall of the government of Muhammad Sharif Pasha, he was appointed prime minister, at the instigation of the nationalist party, with 'Urabi as minister of war. His administration then promulgated a new constitution and electoral law, with increased powers for the Assembly, especially in relation to the state finances. However, in May 1882 a further confrontation with the khedive precipitated his enforced resignation, and an Anglo–French joint note, threatening intervention, prevented him from continuing in a leading role. After the British invasion in September and the defeat of the nationalists, he was arrested, tried, convicted of rebellion, and sent into exile in Sri Lanka for seventeen years.

Throughout his military and political career, al-Barudi never lost his enthusiasm for literature, in general, and for Arabic poetry, in particular. A poet himself from an early stage, he developed a neoclassical style derived from his very extensive knowledge of the best Arabic poetry of past eras (of which he compiled a massive anthology). But if his style was conservative, the content and subject matter of much of his verse were contemporary, reflecting a concern for current events, problems, ideas, and emotions, both public and personal.

Even while in office, al-Barudi expressed some of his ideas on resistance to tyranny and the need for representative government in the form of poetry. During his long exile, he devoted himself much more to verse composition; in his poems of this period, he concentrated, understandably, on themes of longing and nostalgia for his homeland, with much fine evocation of the beauties of the Egyptian landscape. He also wrote moving elegies on the deaths of his wife and of his compatriot 'Abd Allah Fikri (1834–1890). Such themes, and his handling of them, are considered by some literary historians to anticipate the romanticism that developed later in Arabic literature.

In 1900 al-Barudi was pardoned by a decree of the Egyptian government and allowed to return to Egypt. By then he was blind, in poor health, and unable to resume any role in politics or public life. He died four years later in Cairo.

The collected poems of al-Barudi were not published until after his death, in two large volumes in 1915. They then quickly gained much favor among critics and devotees of Arabic literature, in Egypt and elsewhere. This was due to both their style and their patriotic content, which served as a model and an inspiration to poets and writers of subsequent generations.

[*See also* Isma'il; *and* 'Urabi, Ahmad Muhammad.]

BIBLIOGRAPHY

Badawi, M. M. *A Critical Introduction To Modern Arabic Poetry*. Cambridge: Cambridge University Press, 1975.

Khouri, Mouna A. "Revolution and Renaissance in al-Barudi's Poetry." In *Islam and Its Cultural Divergence: Studies in Honor of Gustave E. von Grunebaum*, edited by Girdhari L. Tikku, pp. 76–95. Urbana: University of Illinois Press, 1971.

Khouri, Mounah Abdallah. *Poetry and the Making of Modern Egypt (1882–1922)*. Leiden: Brill, 1971.

Moreh, Shmuel. *Studies in Modern Arabic Prose and Poetry*. Leiden: Brill, 1988.

Solaiman, Md. "Al-Barudi and the Neo-Classical
School in Modern Arabic Poetry." *Dhaka University
Studies* 56, no. 2 (1999): 185–196.

GEOFFREY ROPER

Bashir, ʿUmar al- (1944–), president of Sudan, was
born near the town of Shendi, north of the capital,
Khartoum, into a modest family. After school, he
decided to join the army, which was then in power
and offered good opportunities for a man with his
background. During his army career, Bashir studied in military colleges in Sudan and Egypt, and in
1973 he fought with the Egyptian army in the
October War with Israel. He also became a para-
trooper and served in southern Sudan during the
civil wars there.

During the 1980s Sudan was moving toward
becoming an Islamic state. In 1983 the then president, Jaʿafar al-Nimeiry, introduced sharia, Islamic
law. In the army there were sympathizers with this
move, and Bashir became a follower of the leading
Muslim ideologist of the time, Dr. Hasan al-Turabi.
With the war in the south going badly, it seemed
early in 1989 that the government might abandon
sharia for the sake of peace with the mainly non-
Muslim south. Turabi and his followers decided to
act, and Brigadier al-Bashir was told to stage a
coup, which he carried out on 30 June.

As leader of the coup, Bashir became president;
but it was widely believed that Turabi really ran the
government from behind the scenes. Whatever
the case, Bashir and his colleagues implemented
the policy of rapid Islamization. A new sharia code
was brought in, and all opposition was hunted
down; many were imprisoned and tortured, sometimes to death, forcing others to flee abroad. At the
same time there was a drive to both Arabicize and
Islamize the society with extensive changes in areas
such as education. There was also an escalation of
the war in the south, though government forces
still proved incapable of defeating the rebels, while
successive rounds of peace talks also proved unsuccessful. In foreign policy Bashir's government first
sided with Iraq following its invasion of Kuwait in
1990 and then cooperated for some while with Iran.
At the same time it hosted many radical groups
from neighboring countries in Sudan as well as the
Popular Arab and Islamic Conference, which was
supposed to play a leading part in creating a new
enlarged *umma*, Islamic community. Osama bin
Laden and al-Qaeda were among the groups staying in the country from 1991 to 1996, at which point
they left, following an unsuccessful assassination

attack on President Mubarak of Egypt in Addis
Ababa.

In 1999 Bashir found himself confronted by his
former mentor Turabi, who believed that it was
time for the military to withdraw from power.
Bashir and the military and security leaders around
him disagreed, dissolving parliament and imprisoning Turabi. Following that break, Bashir was persuaded by the international community, led by the
United States, to begin a peace process with the
south's Sudan Peoples Liberation Army/Movement.
The process started in 2002 and concluded with the
signing of the Comprehensive Peace Agreement
(CPA) in 2005. According to the CPA, northern
Sudan would remain under sharia but the south
would have secular laws as well as the right to a referendum in 2011 to decide if it wished to secede
entirely.

By then, however, a new war had started in 2003
in the Darfur region of western Sudan; rebels
rejected what they described as the dominance of
their rulers from the Nile valley area of the country.
Instead of seeking peace, Bashir was determined to
crush the rebels using local militias known as the
Janjaweed, meaning "devils on horseback." Over
the next two years it was reported that up to 300,000
people had been killed in Darfur, with over 2 million
more in displacement camps in the region or across
the border to the west in Chad. It caused an international outcry: US President George W. Bush
called the attempt to crush the rebels "genocide,"
while lengthy peace talks in Abuja, Nigeria, broke
down. The International Criminal Court (ICC) in
The Hague decided to investigate, and in 2008 the
court's chief prosecutor, Luis Moreno-Ocampo,
issued an international arrest warrant against
Bashir for war crimes and crimes against humanity.
It was the first time a serving head of state had been
indicted in this way. Bashir was enraged at the
charges against him and denounced the court, but
he had to be careful which countries he visited
from then on since those that had signed up to the
ICC would be expected to arrest him once he was
on their territory.

Under the terms of the CPA, Sudan had agreed
to hold multiparty elections for the first time since
1986; these finally occurred in April 2010. Bashir
stood as presidential candidate for the ruling
National Congress Party and was duly elected with
68 percent of the popular vote, but most of the
opposition parties withdrew from the elections,
claiming that they were not being fairly conducted.
Bashir nevertheless claimed a new legitimacy,

which he hoped would indicate his people's opposition to the ICC warrant against him. It left something of a dilemma for the international community, with regard both to the acceptability of the elections and to the question of whether to continue to seek Bashir's arrest.

President Bashir has ruled Sudan for longer than any other leader since its independence in 1956. He has been in charge as it pursued an aggressive policy of Islamism, and though that has now softened, he remains determined to retain sharia in the north. He has presided over an era of economic growth as since 1999 Sudan has become sub-Saharan Africa's third largest oil exporter, mainly to China and other parts of Asia. He has also made peace with the south, but the price is the separation of that region in 2011. Meanwhile, conflict still occurs in Darfur, and Bashir continues to be indicted by the ICC.

[*See also* Mubarak, Muhammad Husni Sa'id; Nimeiry, Ja'far al-; *and* Turabi, Hasan al-.]

BIBLIOGRAPHY

Anderson, G. N. *Sudan in Crisis: The Failure of Democracy.* Gainesville: University of Florida Press, 1999.

Collins, R. O. *A History of Modern Sudan.* Cambridge: Cambridge University Press, 2008.

Lesch, A. M. *The Sudan: Contested National Identities.* Bloomington: Indiana University Press, 1998.

Petterson, D. *Inside Sudan: Political Islam, Conflict and Catastrophe.* Boulder, Colo.: Westview Press, 2003.

PETER WOODWARD

Basilios (ca. 1883–1970), prominent Ethiopian church scholar, monastic head, and first Ethiopian archbishop and patriarch, was renowned for his chastity, his religious devotion, and his unflinching loyalty to Emperor Haile Selassie I rather than for his reforms and/or teachings.

Like most Ethiopian dignitaries, his early life is obscure. The available sources give different years ranging from 1877 to 1892 as his birth date. Similarly, a document of the Orthodox Churches Conference in Addis Ababa asserts that he stayed in exile in Jerusalem during the Italian invasion while Ba'eda-Maryam, who wrote a doctoral dissertation on his biography, asserts that he was a fugitive in his own country. There are also discrepancies in the dates of his early ordinations and appointments.

Son of *Debtera* (church precentor) Wolde Tsadeq Selomon and *Emmet* (lady, usually a widow) Wolette-Maryam Bayyu, Gebre-Giyorgis (as Basilios was known before he became patriarch) was born in the subdistrict of Metta-Mikael, northern Shewa. His father died early and he was brought up by his mother, who became a nun. He began his formal education at Koso-Maryam, a full-fledged church in the next subdistrict and subsequently studied *zema* (church music), *qene* (Ge'ez poetry), and tergum (exegesis of the Holy Scriptures) at the monastery of Debre Libanos, about 62 miles (100 km) north of Addis Ababa.

Upon completion of his studies, he was admitted to a probationary service in the same monastery for three years, at the end of which he formally took the vow to live in celibacy in 1913. In the next year he was ordained priest at the hands of the Coptic Metropolitan Matewos (Matthew) and began rendering his service at the church of Washa-Mikael in the same region.

In 1919, he is said to have been created archimandrite, but the evidence for any institution having been placed under his governance is lacking. His first appointment as abbot seems to have occurred in 1924 when he held the office of the newly founded church of St. Mary at Mount Managasha, about 18 miles (30 km) to the west of Addis Ababa. In 1930, he included the administration of the church of St. Gabriel near the imperial palace. In May 1932 he was sent to Jerusalem with the title of *rais* (dean/president) to head the Ethiopian monastery and churches in the Holy Land. In 1934, he was recalled and appointed *Itchegie* (head) of Debre-Libanos (thus becoming the fifty-ninth abbot of the monastery). He retained the office to the end of his life.

At the time of the outbreak of the Italo-Ethiopian war (1935–1936), he accompanied the emperor to the war front in the north and returned with him to the capital. Whether he departed with the sovereign to live in exile in May 1936 or stayed somewhere in the country during the Fascist occupation of Ethiopia (1936–1941) is not certain. It seems that he went into exile after the departure of the sovereign. In any case, he joined the emperor in the Sudan where the British had flown him from England in 1940 to rally his people around him and fight the Italians on the side of the Allies. He thus traveled with his master through the province of Gojjam to Addis Ababa and was reinstituted in his former position.

One of the major components of Haile Selassie's religious policy was to make the Ethiopian Orthodox Church autocephalic. Since the official establishment of the church in the first half of the fourth century, the spiritual head had been the patriarch of Alexandria who consecrated a Coptic metropolitan for Ethiopia. Several Ethiopian sovereigns throughout the centuries requested the See of Alexandria to consecrate Ethiopian bishops, but the only concession the Copts were willing to make was occasionally to appoint a few Coptic bishops to assist the metropolitan. Their assumption was that the church fathers who met at Nicaea had excluded the eligibility of Ethiopians to lead the episcopate. In the late 1920s, Ras Teferi (later Emperor Haile-Selassie I) succeeded in convincing the Copts to appoint at least some Ethiopian bishops; hence, four were consecrated bishops in 1929, and one more followed in 1930. Most of them were killed by the Italians who also expelled the Coptic Metropolitan Cyril (1929–1951) from the country.

After the liberation, the question of the appointment of Ethiopian prelates became crucial. The return of Metropolitan Cyril was opposed by the Ethiopian government on the grounds that he had let down his congregation at the time of distress. An agreement was reached with the See of Alexandria in 1948 to let him resume his office until his death after which he would be succeeded by an Ethiopian Archbishop. At the same time, five Ethiopians were consecrated bishops; among them was Itchegie Gebre-Giyorgis, who now took the name Basilios. Upon the death of Cyril in 1951, Basilios became the first Ethiopian archbishop. The negotiation between the Ethiopian government and the See of Alexandria continued, and in June 1959 Basilios was consecrated patriarch of Ethiopia.

His accomplishments included the acquisition of landed properties for the church, the reconstruction of ruined churches, the establishment of new ones, the consecration of prelates for all dioceses, and the promotion of missionary activities within and outside Ethiopia. Some sources attribute the last one to his assistant and eventual successor, Abune Tewoflos. In the last few years of his life, Basilios seldom appeared in public and the archbishop of Harar ran the affairs of the church on his behalf. A British historian alleges that he had become senile, while an Ethiopian writer in the service of the church states that he became blind because of diabetes. In any case he was bodily frail for most of his life. He died of illness in October 1970 and was ceremonially buried in the monastery of Debre-Libanos.

[See also Haile Selassie I; and Tewoflos.]

BIBLIOGRAPHY

Clapham, Christopher. *Haile-Selassie's Government.* London: Longman, 1970.

Ethiopian Orthodox Church Administration. *The Church of Ethiopia. A Panorama of History and Spiritual Life.* Addis Ababa, Ethiopia: Ethiopian Orthodox Church, 1970.

Heyer, Friedrich. *Die Kirche Aethiopiens. Eine Bestandsaufnahme.* Berlin: De Gruyter, 1971.

Interim Secretariat of the Oriental Orthodox Conference. *The Oriental Orthodox Churches Addis Ababa Conference, January, 1965.* Addis Ababa, Ethiopia: Artistic Printers, 1965.

Wondmagegnehu, Aymro, and Joachim Motovo. eds. *The Ethiopian Orthodox Church.* Addis Ababa, Ethiopia: The Ethiopian Orthodox Mission, 1970.

BAIRU TAFLA

Bassey, Okon Asuquo (1932–1998), Nigerian world featherweight boxing champion, more popularly known as Hogan "Kid" Bassey, was born in the village of Ufok Ubet, Creek Town, Calabar, Nigeria, on 3 June 1932. He was one of five children born to his parents, who were cultivators of modest means. At the age of eleven, Bassey moved to Lagos to live with a maternal aunt and to continue his education. Sending a child, often the eldest, to live with a relative in a town or city with better educational opportunities and with the expectation that the child would later assume responsibility for parents, siblings, or other relatives was common practice. It was in Lagos that Bassey encountered the sport of boxing. As a youth, he enjoyed school, although he was not a great scholar; sports, however, were his passion and he participated in soccer, swimming, running, jumping, and other athletics—first at school, then at a local boys' club. Although there was a boxing section at the club, Bassey came to boxing later and reluctantly.

An uncle of Bassey's, W. D. Cowan, who also lived in Lagos during this time, was an amateur boxer and had been involved in the founding of the Nigerian Boxing Club. Although his uncle and other boys at the athletic club encouraged him to take up boxing, the young Bassey refused initially. Once he took it up, however, Bassey immediately began to distinguish himself as a talented boxer, earning the nickname "Killer." In 1949, at the age of 16, and while still in school, Bassey turned professional. That same year he took the Nigerian flyweight title.

Becoming a professional, however, did not mean that Bassey could make a living from fighting;

indeed, in order to earn a steady income now that he was no longer a student, Bassey took a job as a clerk. In 1950 Bassey won the West African fly-weight title, defeating the Ghanaian Ogli Tettey in May. After defending his title against Tettey, Bassey moved up to bantamweight. In 1951 Bassey fought in Lagos against Steve Jeffra for the Nigerian ban-tamweight title. Later that year, Bassey defended his bantamweight title against Joe Bennetts. In August 1951 Bassey fought Steve Jeffra for a second time, again successfully defending his Nigerian bantamweight title. The following month he took the West African bantamweight title in a bout against the Ghanaian Young Spider Neequaye.

Although his professional status did not make Bassey wealthy, his rise in boxing was meteoric. Just two years after his professional debut, in December 1951, Bassey sailed to Liverpool, England, to continue his boxing career, his passage to the United Kingdom organized and paid for by a group of boxing fans who saw promise in young Bassey. Bassey was not the first Nigerian to journey to Britain with dreams of winning a major boxing title; indeed, in Liverpool Bassey became friends with a number of other Nigerian boxers, most importantly Israel Boyle. Boyle and Bassey remained lifelong friends.

Bassey was victorious in his European debut, just one month after landing on British shores, beating Ray Hillyard in the fifth round. Bassey con-tested 19 matches in his first year in the United Kingdom, losing only three fights. The following year, 1953, Bassey fought fewer matches, winning six out of a total 10 fights. Among Bassey's 1953 vic-tories was the surprise defeat of the Spanish south-paw Luis Romero, who had a reputation for being a very powerful puncher. In 1954, Bassey sustained only one loss out of eight matches. The following year he won all six of his matches, culminating in the British Empire featherweight title against Irishman Billy Kelly in Belfast on November 19. In 1956, Bassey again won all of his fights, except one, and that particular fight was stopped by the referee because of a cut on Bassey's eye. It was about this time that Bassey parted company with man-ager Peter Banasko, who had been with Bassey from the very first day he arrived on the Liverpool quay. Banasko, a former boxer of "mixed race," had a stable of black and mixed-race boxers. Bassey's new manager, who was white, George Biddles, was a highly well-connected sports figure.

In 1957, Bassey scored the biggest victory of all, the world featherweight championship. En route to the world title, Bassey fought two major matches in the month of April: first, he defended his British Empire featherweight title, then he traveled to the United States to fight Miguel Berrios, who was the heavy favorite to win, in the final eliminator before the world title. Bassey's opponent in the world title match was Hamia Cherif, who was favored to win. The fight took place in Paris during the Algerian war of independence. Although the overwhelming majority of spectators supported the French-Algerian Hamia, there were several notable indi-viduals in the crowd cheering Bassey. Rival Nigerian politicians Nnamdi Azikiwe and Obafemi Awolowo as well as Bessie Braddock, a British Labour Party Member of Parliament, were all in attendance. So struck was Braddock by Bassey's ease in winning admirers wherever he went that she sought, unsuc-cessfully, to persuade Bassey to make his home per-manently in Liverpool and enter local politics. In postwar Liverpool, where the left-wing Braddock had her constituency, race relations were a source of concern and blacks were disproportionately represented among the poor and marginalized.

Bassey successfully defended his world title against Ricardo Moreno in Los Angeles in April 1958. Moreno was a prodigious puncher, with a fight record of 33 fights and 29 knockouts; nevertheless, Bassey knocked Moreno out in the third round of the scheduled 15-rounder with a left hook to the jaw. Bassey earned $70,000 for the Moreno fight, the largest purse ever for a featherweight. In September 1958, Bassey fought and defeated American Willie Pep, former world featherweight champion, in Boston. Other notable opponents that year included American Camelo Costa and Mexican Ernesto Parra, both matches fought in the United States.

In March 1959, Bassey returned to the United States to defend his title against American Davey Moore. Bassey, the slight favorite to win, lost his title to Moore in a close fight. Bassey again lost in the rematch with Moore in August of that year. At the time, Bassey was severely criticized by the media for retiring in the tenth round. Subsequently, many have judged Bassey's decision a wise move given that his right eye was completely closed and his right hand damaged. Following his second defeat by Moore, Bassey retired altogether from boxing, becoming coach of the national amateur boxing team. Bassey trained numerous Nigerian boxers, including Olympic medalists Nojim Maiyegun (bronze, middleweight, Tokyo, 1964) and Isaac Ikhouria (double bronze, middleweight, Munich, 1972).

At his death in Lagos, Bassey was survived by his wife and eight children. Bassey married twice; his first wife, Maria, was a Liverpudlian of mixed ancestry (her father was Sierra Leonian and her mother was British). Bassey's second wife, Mary, was a fellow Efik; and she and Bassey remained married until his death in 1998.

Bassey's victory in 1957 made him the first Nigerian ever to win a major sporting title. Bassey became and remained Nigeria's first truly nationalist icon. In a 2000 poll Nigerians voted Bassey "Nigerian sportsman of the century." His victories were chronicled not only by news media in Nigeria and the United Kingdom but also by *Ebony* magazine (United States) and the South African magazine *Drum*. Bassey was made a Member of the Order of the British Empire (1958), Lion of Africa (Senegal, 1973), and Member of the Order of the Niger (Nigeria, 1979).

[*See also* Awolowo, Obafemi; *and* Azikiwe, Benjamin Nnamdi.]

BIBLIOGRAPHY

Bassey, Hogan. *Bassey on Boxing*. Nashville, Tenn.: Thomas Nelson and Sons, 1963.

Ejikeme, Anene. "Hogan 'Kid' Bassey: Nigerian Icon." In *Emerging Themes and Methods in African Studies*, edited by Toyin Falola and Adam Paddock, pp. 443–456. Trenton, N.J.: Africa World Press, 2008.

Mee, Bob. "Hogan Bassey: Obituary." *The Independent* (United Kingdom), April 6, 1998.

Omotoso, Ademola. *Hogan Bassey: A Boxing Legend*. Nigeria: Greylands, 2004.

ANENE EJIKEME

Bate Besong, Jacobs (1954–2007), playwright and poet of Anglophone Cameroon, was born on 8 May 1954 in Mamfe, which was then located in the British-administered territory of Southern Cameroons. In 1954 the territory established an autonomous region separate from the larger British colony of Nigeria and in 1961 the Southern Cameroons voted in a plebiscite to join the majority French-speaking Federal Republic of Cameroon (FRC) as the Federated State of West Cameroon (FSWC). The Anglophone population of the Southern Cameroons led by John Ngu Foncha believed that federalism, in the form of the FSWC, would assure their autonomy.

Mamfe was only 37 miles (60 kilometers) from the Southern Cameroons border with Nigeria.

Besong moved to and from the two newly independent nations. He attended Hope Wadell Institute in Calabar and Saint Bede's Secondary School in Kom, both in Nigeria. It was in Kom that he obtained his GCE A Level in 1976.

Two major events during his teenage years would greatly influence Besong's writing. The first was President Amadou Ahidjo's imposition of a one-party system in the FRC in 1966 and the resignation of Augustine Ngom Njua, Foncha's successor as prime minister of the Federated State of West Cameroon in 1967. But what infuriated him most was the 1972 referendum. It simply erased the Federal Republic of Cameroon and instituted the United Republic of Cameroon. This was an act of betrayal to the Anglophone minority. Among other dissidents, Albert Mukong highlighted what he viewed as the political crimes and gruesome practices of the United Republic in his book *Prisoner without Crime* (1974). Besong heard about these events while reading for a BA in English at the University of Calabar in Nigeria. He began to realize that writing was the best way for him to fight these injustices. So he drilled for combat by creating *The Oracle*, a literary journal he managed with his compatriot Babila Mutia. Upon graduating from the University of Calabar, he moved on to the University of Ibadan for an MA. Mutia contends that by end of the 1970s, Besong was torn by the issue of identity. Although military conscription was also obligatory in Cameroon, Besong carried out his service in Nigeria. By so doing he opened the door for criticism by the government in Yaoundé.

Besong's fame as a writer began to grow in the 1980s. During that time he taught in government schools in the Northern Province and Buea, and at Cameroon Protestant College (CPC), Bali. His writings echoed the problems particular to Cameroon's Anglophones who felt that they were hostages in a hostile Francophone republic. His first collection, *Polyphemus Detainee and Other Skulls* (1980), posits his nation as a prison. That Anglophone Cameroon had been swallowed by the United Republic was to Besong and others a morbid act. This became a source of inspiration for many of his best works, which are rooted in history and myth.

If his work at CPC was tarred by frustration, then his work in the public institutions of the north proved even more infuriating to him. Posted to Mayo Louti, the remotest corner of his country, Besong would go for years without a salary. Corrupt civil servants added to his troubles by deliberately slowing his tenure process. Whether in Bali or in May Louti, Besong taught, observed, and wrote. He revisited the particular history of Anglophones and saluted a fighter for that cause, Augustine Ngom Njua, in *The Grain of Bobe Ngum Njua* (1985). Njua's resignation from the federal government in 1967 when Cameroon was on the threshold of dictatorship was, for Besong, a symbol of bravery.

The 1980s also witnessed Besong's emergence as a cutting edge playwright. He mercilessly ridiculed the two presidents of Cameroon, Ahidjo and Paul Biya, as mediocre dictators. In *The Cruelest Death of Talkative Zombie* (1986), he attempted to turn them into national laughingstocks and thugs, describing them as nothing short of walking corpses who adopted political killings as their method of governance. Besong, however, did not spare Cameroonians on either side of the river Moungo. In *Beasts of No Nation* (1990) he casts an angry look at the marginalized Anglophones, depicting them as shit carriers in their own country, and portraying Francophones as locusts that devastate all.

In *Requiem for the Last Kaiser* (1991), his first work of the 1990s, an angrier Besong entrapped in the Northern Province saw Hitler as a suitable metaphor for the president of Cameroon. Even his transfer to Molyco Grammar School in Buea yielded no change in his uncompromising hostility to the government. The cruelty inflicted on him and his fellow compatriots fueled his anger. Having to survive for years without a salary just because a corrupt clerk wants a bribe proved particularly disheartening. Besong moved from satire to insults because neologism and other caustic mannerisms yielded no change. Unsurprisingly, *The Banquet* (1994) announced a veritable hurricane of invective, which he believed was necessary to rid the nation of what he viewed as historical garbage.

At the University of Buea, where he was finally recruited, Besong became a star but also made many enemies. When during student protests Gilbert Forlem and Aloysius Embwam were gunned down in 2005 he bravely stood for them. In a eulogy to these martyrs, Besong virulently attacked scholars who cared only for their careers and ignored unnecessary sufferings and injustices. He would pay for this severely but, as an intrepid fighter for his cause, Besong pursued his combat by publishing his plays *Change Waka* and *His Man Sawa Boy* (2003). Finally came *Disgrace* in 2007. Besong penned the following frontispiece for that volume: "These people leave nothing but deceit and disgrace as an inheritance for future generations."

Although the statement appears ostensibly to be from the Book of Jeremiah in Judaism's Tanakh and the Christian Old Testament, it is in fact entirely of Besong's creation. The scholar Innocent Futcha argues that the frontispiece reflects Besong's desire to be remembered as "Jeremiah in Cameroon." Like Jeremiah, Besong was a doomed prophet. He was laughed at by the very people he crusaded for, cruelly persecuted by the persecutors of his people, and lived his combat to his last breath.

On 7 March 2007 Besong listened mesmerized to thousands of adoring Anglophones and Francophones discussing *Disgrace*. They enthusiastically portrayed him as the "Crusader against injustice," "The Obasajong," "Jeremiah in Cameroon." Sadly, tragedy befell them all when in the early hours of 8 March, Besong and three other compatriots were crushed to death in a car accident on the Yaoundé/Douala road.

Besong was survived by his wife, Christiana, and five children: Dante Besong, June Besong, Cedella Besong, Harold Mandela Besong, and Eldridge Charles Besong. In naming some his children after great historical figures (Dante, Nelson Mandela, American black nationalist Eldridge Cleaver, and Cedella Booker, mother of Bob Marley) Besong hoped they would proudly carry on his fight.

[*See also* Ahidjo, Ahmadou; Biya, Paul; Foncha, John Ngu; *and* Mandela, Nelson Rolihlahla.]

BIBLIOGRAPHY

Ashuntantang, Joyce, and Dibassi Tande, eds. *Their Champagne Party Will End!: Poems in Honor of Bate Besong*. Bamenda, Cameroon: Langaa, 2008.

Babila Mutia. Remembering Bate Besong 1954–2007. http://yaounde.usembassy.gov/lns_011910.html.

Futcha, Innocent. "Bate Besong: Jeremiah in Cameroon (A Review of BB's *Disgrace*)." http://www.batebesong.com/2007/03/bate_besong_jer.html.

GILBERT DOHO

Bathoen I (1845–1910), Kgosi of the Bangwaketse, was born at Tswaaneng, southern Gangwaketse, in Botswana. The eldest son of Kgosi Gaseitsiwe's senior wife, Bathoen I was heir to the Bangwaketse chieftaincy. His mother was of the Batlhware people. He learned to read and write at a London Missionary Society mission (LMS) school. As the son of Kgosi, he became leader of the Maisantwa regiment, initiated in 1864 (Ngongco 1977: 277). Bathoen became chief of the Bangwaketse in July 1889 after the death of his father, Gaseitsewe. The key events of Bathoen's life related to the growth of British colonial power in this period. In 1885 Botswana became a British protectorate. Khama of Bangwato, Bathoen of Bangwaketse, and Sebele of Bakwena were key players during the period (1890–1891) when Britain's control over Botswana developed from a vague protectorate over the southern part to a more clearly defined (though still, in practice, very limited) government over the whole territory. The three *dikgosi* also made an important visit to England in 1895.

During 1890–1891 pressure intensified from several quarters for clearer British control. The *dikgosi* were naturally opposed, but they had to accept the situation. Sir Henry Brougham Loch, the high commissioner, recommended annexation as a colony, but the Colonial Office saw this as too expensive and favored handing over the protectorate to Cecil Rhodes's British South Africa Company (BSAC)—in other words making Bechuanaland a third part of Rhodesia together with Mashonaland and Matebeleland.

In February 1889, Sidney Shippard, the British Bechuanaland administrator, called the Batswana chiefs including Bathoen to Kopong where he put to them wide-ranging proposals including mutual defence, settlement of disputes, railways, telegraphic lines, roads, and medical services, with hut tax to pay for the British administration (Sillery 1952: 63). The chiefs accepted some of the proposals, but Bathoen, supported by the other chiefs, rejected hut tax.

The Kopong conference showed the British government the strength of opposition to encroachment in the *dikgosi*'s internal affairs. Therefore, trouble was expected from Bathoen when the protectorate administration decided to push ahead with the erection of the telegraphic line. Shippard, who visited Bathoen in May 1890, reported that the chief was entirely in the hands of European syndicates, from whom he received an annual income of £200. The Kanye Exploration Company had obtained from him a concession giving them a monopoly of construction of railway and telegraphic lines in his territory, and he refused to sanction Shippard's project, unless the administration could come to terms with the company (Sillery 1952). Shippard negotiated separately with Ikaneng of the Balete, who actually occupied the territory, who raised no objections to the telegraph and also agreed to supply laborers to construct the line from his capital Ramotswa to Ngotwane (river) junction. The high commissioner instructed Shippard to inform the chiefs that the telegraph line would be erected whether they wanted it or not and that the claims of European concessionaries could not be accepted. Bathoen later wrote to the Administration that he was not opposed to the telegraph line but had been unwilling to break his previous promises. (Schapera 1942: 17).

In August 1890 there was a border dispute with the Bahurutshe under Gopane, who were encroaching from the east. An enquiry by the official Witt Surmon, ruled in favor of the Bangwaketse. In a later border with the Barolong, an enquiry by J. S. Moffat initially ruled for the Barolong, which led Bathoen to visit Cape Town in 1892 where he appealed successfully to the high commissioner.

In 895 Bathoen I, Khama III and Sebele I travelled to England to protest to Joseph Chamberlain, the colonial secretary, at proposals to transfer the protectorate to the BSAC, fearing alienation of land and legalized liquor (Schapera 1942: 17). Chamberlain was unsympathetic, but the combination of a successful speaking tour sponsored by their missionary allies and Rhodes's discrediting by the Jameson Raid led to a settlement whereby the chiefs' territory would remain under the Queen's protection. They agreed to pay hut tax and to surrender some land to for the railway and for European settlement; and a colonial officer was to be posted at their town. European liquor would be banned from the Reserves.

The Anglo-Boer War of 1899–1902 had only a limited impact on the Bangwaketse, as was the case with most tribes, with the major exception of the Bakgatla. Men were stationed along the southern and eastern boundaries were never called upon, though later in the war Bathoen provided men to work with British transport wagons.

The year 1902 saw the beginning of a church dispute that threatened to split the Bangwaketse tribe. An LMS preacher, Mothowagae, refused a transfer to Lehututu, and the LMS reacted by dismissing him from the church. Mothowagae formed his own "King Edward Bangwaketse Free Church." The LMS refused a request to ordain Mothowagae on the grounds that he lacked qualifications and was guilty of schism (BNA, BNB RC 10/11, 1903). The new church became a challenge to the chief, a pattern that was to be repeated in later Botswana history, and was eventually suppressed by the chief with the support of the administration.

Bathoen also faced a challenge from Gobuamang of the Bakgatla-ba ga-Mmanaana at Moshupa when he abolished the practice of *bogwera* and *bojale* (initiation schools) in 1901. Gobuamang organized bogwera for his own people in open defiance to Bathoen's orders. (Apart from the issue of abolition, holding an independent initiation had long been considered a rebellious act.) The administration warned Gobuamang to be more obedient to Bathoen in future and threatened him with arrest.

Although schools had been established among the Bangwaketse by the LMS in 1860, progress was relatively low and Bathoen imposed an annual levy of two shillings per taxpayer to subsidize education.

Bathoen died on 1 July 1910 at the age of sixty-five and was succeeded by his son Seepapitso III, a young man of promise and good education (BNB S.42/1 1910–1911).

[*See also* Bathoen II Seepapitso Gaseitsiwe; Khama III; *and* Sebele I.]

BIBLIOGRAPHY

Maylam, P. *Rhodes, the Tswana and the British: Colonialism, Collaboration and Conflict in the Bechuanaland Protectorate, 1885–1899.* Westport, Conn.: Greenwood Press, 1980.

Ngcongco L.D. "Aspects of the History of the Bangwaketse to 1910." Unpublished PhD dissertation, Dalhousie University, April 1977.

Parsons, N. *King Khama, Emperor Joe, and the Great White Queen.* Chicago: University of Chicago Press, 1998.

Schapera I. "A Short History of the Bangwaketse." *African Studies 1 no.1*, (1942): 5–6.

Sillery, Anthony. *The Bechuanaland Protectorate.* London: Oxford University Press, 1952.

Botswana National Archives [Gaborone]

BNA, RC. 10/11 Kanye Church Dispute, 1903.

BNA, S.42/1 Death of Chief Bathoen I and succession 1910–1911.

BNA, File SGS.394, Letter from Sidney Shippard, British Bechuanaland Administrator to Henry B. Loch, High Commissioner, Cape Town, 6 June 1890.

MAITSEO BOLAANE

Bathoen II Seepapitso Gaseitsiwe (1908–1990),

Botswana leader, was born in Kanye to Seepapitso II, paramount chief of the Bangwaketse, and Mogatsakgari, daughter of Ratshosa, Khama III's son-in-law. Bathoen's grandmother, Gagoangwe, was the daughter of Kgosi Sechele of the Bakwena. Bathoen was thus of royal descent on both sides. In 1916, when Bathoen was eight, his father was murdered by his own brother, Moeapitso, in a palace intrigue. Moeapitso was jailed, and Kgosimotse Gaseitsiwe was appointed acting chief of the Bangwaketse until Bathoen reached adulthood. Bathoen spent much of his childhood in Serowe among his mother's people, the Bangwato.

Bathoen studied at Kanye Hill School, now Rachele Primary School, beginning in 1918; subsequently, in South Africa at Tiger Kloof (1919–1922) and Lovedale (1923–1927). During this time, two strong women served as regents: the queen mother, Gagoangwe, and (after 1924) Gagoangwe's eldest daughter, Ntebogang. After completion of his junior certificate, the Bangwaketse asked Bathoen to return home and take over chieftainship from Ntebogang. Although some of Ntebogang's councilors allegedly opposed Bathoen, a heated *kgotla* meeting in December 1927 decided that Bathoen should be installed; and he was enthroned in April 1928 by his uncle Mokgadi-a-Bome. After his installation, Bathoen banished Kgampu Kamodi, one of the councillors who had opposed him, to Kike, presumably as a warning to others. Former Botswana president Ketumile Masire, a Mongwaketse, recalls in his memoirs that at one Kanye *kgotla* meeting, where traditionally men had relatively free speech, he was shouted down by Bathoen when he attempted to contribute his ideas for innovation in agriculture. Although Bathoen was a modernist in some ways, he was intolerant of any perceived threat to his power.

In January 1933, Bathoen married Ester Mmafani Ntsieng of Thaba-Nchu in South Africa; a member of the royal family related to Kgosi Moroka of Barolong-ba-Tshidi. Bathoen and Mmafani had five children, Seepapitso (male), followed by Bonolo (female), Bonno (female), Seatla (male), and Bontleng (female).

To assert his authority and prove his worth to Charles Rey, one of the most dynamic and controversial Bechuanaland Protectorate resident commissioners (1930–1937), Bathoen embarked on a program of centralizing power at Ntsweng, Bangwaketse's capital. He undermined the Tswana tradition of ruling with advisors, mostly his uncles, and some commoners knowledgeable in traditional law and custom. Support from the protectorate administration allowed Bathoen to wield extensive powers, beyond those of precolonial *dikgosi*. Against the will of Bangwaketse traditionalists, he reintroduced his grandfather Bathoen I's law abolishing the *bogwera* and *bojale* initiation schools. He also banned the brewing of sorghum beer and the illicit alcoholic drink *khadi*. The alcohol ban probably served both practical purposes, as he believed that the brewing delayed development projects, and religious belief, as the Congregationalist church, to which he, like his father and grandfather, belonged, attached much importance to teetotalism.

When the administration introduced the Native Administration and Tribal Proclamations of 1934, which would have made the succession of chiefs subject to government approval and replaced *kgotla* justice by tribunals, Bathoen and Tshekedi opposed the proclamations in court, arguing that the high commissioner lacked the authority to make such radical changes. The courts ruled against them in 1937, but the case played a part in undermining the proclamations, which were never fully introduced. Bathoen and Tshekedi also worked to resist plans to transfer of the protectorate to South Africa.

Despite his iron grip on affairs in Gangwaketse, Bathoen is credited for setting the pace for most developments seen in Kanye today. Bathoen felt that Gangwaketse should develop with the changing times, and he showed keen interest in development projects. Projects in Kanye were based on what he had seen in his travels, and he utilized regimental labor and involved foreign experts where necessary. Bathoen was interested in the education of his people, believing that young children should be sent to school instead of herding cattle, working in the fields or going to initiation schools. In 1934 regimental labor built primary schools at Digawana and Mmathethe. Another development that captured Bathoen's interest was the construction of roads: in 1933 he built the Montshioa road that runs through Kanye Hill, and in 1947, in preparation for the British royal visit by George V, he cut the long road from Kanye to Lobatse. Regimental labor built many other roads in Kanye and its outlets.

It was also during the reign of Bathoen that the Bangwaketse started collecting water from standpipes, when most of Botswana was very rural. In 1950, Bathoen dug 12 dams in his territory for watering animals and domestic use. In partnership with Rowland, he built a fine stone and cement reservoir at the entrance of Kanye Hill as a memorial to his father, Seepapitso II. Bathoen was also credited by the Bangwaketse for building King George V Hall in 1941. He also contributed significantly to the development of agriculture in Gangwaketse. He encouraged competition among farmers by starting the first agricultural shows in the protectorate in 1938. Bangwaketse were encouraged to bring forward their surplus grain produce to be stored in huge silos built by their chief and used in times of drought. These silos still dominate the landscape in Gangwaketse to this day.

At independence Bathoen became disillusioned with the new Botswana Democratic Party government, realizing too late that it was sidelining chiefs. He abdicated the chieftainship and, in a bizarre alliance of traditionalists with radicals led by Kenneth Koma, became a leader in the Botswana National Front. Local support enabled him to win a parliamentary seat in 1969, defeating the then vice president Masire.

On retirement from active politics, Bathoen went back to his farming at Dithutlwe and Mogapinyana lands. He died in 1990. In his memory, the Bangwaketse named the community museum he initiated Kgosi Bathoen II Museum. Recently, the Bangwaketse embarked on a project to erect a statue in his honor at the royal place.

[*See also* Bathoen I; Khama III; Khama, Seretse; Khama, Tshekedi; *and* Koma, Kenneth.]

BIBLIOGRAPHY

Masire, Q. K. J. *Very Brave or Very Foolish? Memoirs of an African Democrat.* Gaborone: Macmillan Botswana, 2006.

Molefi, R., Morton, F., and Ngcongco, L. "The Modernists: Seepapitso, Ntebogang and Isang." In *The Birth of Botswana: A History of the Bechuanaland Protectorate from 1910 to 1966.* Gaborone: Longman Botswana, 1987.

Simmon, G. "Survival of Chieftaincy in Botswana." *Journal of African Affairs* 72 (1973): 179–185.

Tlou, T., and Campbell, A. *History of Botswana.* Gaborone: Macmillan Botswana, 1984.

Interviews Conducted in Kanye

Kelosiwang, subchief of the Bangwaketse, 18 February 2010.

Mathiba, subchief of the Bangwaketse, 18 February 2010.

Mokuwe, Bangwaketse elder, 18 February 2010.

MAITSEO BOLAANE

Batibo, Herman (1947–), Tanzanian linguist and academic, was born in Mwanza, Tanzania, on 1 January 1947, as the eighth child of Michael Masalu, medical assistant, and Melania Humbo. The family lived in the suburbs of Mwanza, a provincial town in the northwest of what was then Tanganyika. Before his birth, two of his father's cousins had come to visit the family, but, because his uncle had mistreated him when he lived with them as an orphan, his father turned them away with the words "batiboyi abakanibyaala" ("It is not them who gave birth to me"). These words were used to call the newborn child; in the Sukuma culture, Batibo's ethnic group, children are named according to events or circumstances at the time of birth. The long name was soon shortened to "Batibo" and used as his surname. At Batibo's christening, the Bavarian priest administering the baptism found the child so charming that he gave him his own Christian name, Herman, instead of Paul, which his parents had chosen.

Batibo started his primary education in 1954 at Mwanza Catholic Cathedral Boys Primary School. He then joined St Mary's Seminary at Nyegezi, which was considered the best postprimary school in the region. Several languages were taught at Nyegezi, including English, Swahili, French, Latin, Greek, German, and Spanish. The study and analysis of these languages played a major role in Batibo's future academic development. He went to the secular Ihungo Secondary School at the western side of Lake Victoria for his advanced-level education, completing this in 1967. Intending to be a teacher, he then joined the University of Dar es Salaam, specializing in French, geography, and education.

At the University of Dar es Salaam, Batibo was introduced to general linguistics by Trevor Hill, an associate of Michael A. K. Halliday. Hallidayan functionalism had a lasting influence on Batibo's views of language as a product of society and an important component of culture and human heritage. After completing his BA (Ed) in 1971, Batibo remained at the university as a teaching fellow in the Department of Foreign Languages and Linguistics, where he was supposed to specialize in French applied linguistics and was offered a scholarship to study at the University of La Sorbonne Nouvelle (Paris III) in France. He studied in Paris from 1971 to 1977 but, under the influence of Pierre Alexandre of the National Institute of Oriental Languages and Civilisations, he switched to African (Bantu) linguistics. He obtained his MA in 1974 and his PhD in 1977, with a thesis on the phonology and morphology of Sukuma (subsequently published in 1985). Among the scholars who influenced him during his studies in Paris were André Martinet, Bertil Malmberg, Serge Sauvageot, and Luc Bouquiaux. Batibo's PhD thesis, and his early work more generally, are characterized by his engagement with descriptive and theoretical linguistics and the analysis of the phonology of Sukuma, his first language. Batibo's work during this period contributed to the study of tone by drawing on data from Sukuma and explaining them with reference to the theoretical ideas of the time. In subsequent work, Batibo continued to address questions of theoretical phonology, with reference to Sukuma and later Swahili, Tswana, and other Bantu languages. Two further academic interests developed during his formative years as a student: comparative linguistics, in particular of Bantu languages, and the study of French.

In July 1976, he became a lecturer in the Department of Foreign Languages and Linguistics at the University of Dar es Salaam. From 1979 to 1985, he served as head of department, during which time his work became influenced by the emphasis on the development of Swahili, then a national political aim in Tanzania. Many of his publications from the 1980s onward relate to the analysis of Swahili, particularly in phonology, and to sociolinguistic and applied linguistic questions, including language planning and standardization, language pedagogy, and translation. Batibo contributed to the university's Swahili research institute and the national Swahili council, serving on advisory boards and working groups for both. At the same time, he continued to develop his interests in theoretical and comparative-historical linguistics, as well as in foreign language teaching, where he served in several functions concerned with the study of French, for which, in 1984, he was awarded an Ordre des Palmes Académiques by the French government for his services to the promotion of teaching French in Tanzania.

In 1994, Batibo joined the University of Botswana as professor of African linguistics. While continuing work on descriptive and theoretical linguistics, sociolinguistics, and the study of Swahili, Batibo extended his research in Botswana to language endangerment and language documentation, two topics which received widespread international attention in the 1990s. Batibo's work from this period constitutes a strong African contribution to this development through a range of articles, mainly focusing on smaller Bantu and Khoesan languages of Botswana, two collections of papers (jointly edited with Birgit Smieja and Joseph Tsonope), and his 2005 book *Language Decline and Death in Africa*, which provides an Africa-wide survey of language endangerment and shows that, in contrast to many other parts of the world, smaller African languages are under pressure not so much from main European or world languages like English and Spanish but from national and regional African languages of wider communication.

In addition to his own research, Batibo contributed to African linguistics through engagement in international scholarly exchange and the development of linguistics in Africa. He held visiting professorships at the universities of Bayreuth, Leiden, York, and California at Los Angeles; at London's School of Oriental and African Studies; and at the French National Research Centre in Paris, among others. Also, he was chair of the Linguistics Association for SADC Universities from 1991 to 1995 and president of the standing committee of the World Congress of African Linguistics from 2000 to 2009.

BIBLIOGRAPHY

Batibo, Herman. *Language Decline and Death in Africa: Causes, Consequences and Challenges.* Clevedon, UK: Multilingual Matters, 2005.

Batibo, Herman, and Birgit Smieja, eds. *Botswana: The Future of the Minority Languages.* Frankfurt/Main, Germany: Lang, 2000.

Batibo, Herman, and Joseph Tsonope, eds. *The State of Khoesan Languages in Botswana.* Mogoditshane: University of Botswana, 2000.

Chebanne, Andy. "Language Decline and Death in Africa [book review]." *NAWA Journal of Language and Communication* 1 (2007): 171–174.

Salami, L. Oladipo. "Language Decline and Death in Africa [book review]." *Language Policy* 6 (2007): 307–310.

LUTZ MARTEN

Battiads. The Battiad dynasty ruled the Greek city of Cyrene (or Kyrene) for nearly 200 years, from its founding around 630 BCE until the advent of a democratic government around 440 BCE. The main source for the fortunes of the dynasty is the detailed history of the city by Herodotus (4.150-67, 200-205), the most complete extant description of the foundation of a remote Greek city.

Battos I (ruled c. 630–590 BCE) led as a young man the original expedition from Thera, probably instigated by a prolonged drought on the island. He received the title "king" as leader of the project. His actual name may have been Aristotoles (Pindar, *Pythian* 5.87), but he came to be called Battos either because he stuttered (*battos* in Greek) or, as Herodotus believed, when he adopted an indigenous North African title. After learning of the fertility of the north coast of Africa, he and his settlers went forth in two pentakonters but in uncertainty returned promptly to Thera. A second attempt was made on the island of Platea (perhaps Gasr el-Bomba off eastern Libya).

The Platea expedition also did not do well, and its members returned to Greece and asked advice from the Delphic oracle, which told them to seek a settlement on the mainland. They did so, but six years later this also failed, and finally the Greeks ended up at the site of Cyrene. These attempts to found a city starkly reveal the rigors of the spread of Greek populations.

When Battos I died, kingship passed to his son Arcesilaus I (or Arkesilaos I), who is little known, and then to the latter's son (grandson of Battos I), Battos II the Fortunate (ruled c. 576–560 BCE). He enlarged Cyrene, collecting together all the Greeks who had settled on the African coast. Local resistance at this incursion of a substantial Greek population began to coalesce around the indigenous chieftain Adikran, who sought Egyptian help but in futility, as the Greeks, superior in military abilities, defeated the combined forces. This marked the beginning of Cyrene as a major Greek city. It expanded its territory to include much of the surrounding region, founded additional towns in the hinterland, and soon became the largest of all Greek states, with an economy based on horse breeding and the exotic herb silphium.

The reign of the son of Battos II, Arcesilaus II (Arkesilaos II), was marked by sibling rivaly and an expansionist policy that resulted in military disaster. He was strangled by his brother, who was promptly killed by Arcesilaus's widow. Yet the unfortunate king is immortalized on the "Arcesilaus Cup," a Lakonian vessel, now in Paris.

His son Battos III the Lame (ruled c. 550–530 BCE) became king in these unstable times. Reaction to monarchy was spreading throughout the Greek world, and Battos saw the powers of the king severely reduced. In reaction he made an alliance with the Egyptian king Amasis, who married his daughter Ladike. The wife of Battos III was the dynamic princess Pheretime, probably a cousin, who became the most prominent woman the dynasty would produce. She would be an active player in the political fortunes of her family and the city, supporting her son Arcesilaus III (Arkesilaos III) in his uncertain quest for royal power and eventually placing his son Battos IV the Beautiful (ruled c. 510–480 BCE) on the throne. By this time the Persians, who had conquered Egypt around 525 BCE, were interested in Cyrene. Pheretime had sought Persian support in avenging the death of her son (Battos's father), and this meant that despite a failed attempt by the Persians to conquer Cyrene, the city would remain essentially a Persian protectorate. Battos IV was succeeded by his son Arcesilaus IV (Arkesilaos IV; ruled c. 480–440 BCE), a victor at Delphi, who failed to remove the Persians and was killed in a democratic revolution, which brought an end to the monarchy and the Battiads.

Herodotus's account of the dynasty and the history of Cyrene provides a microcosm of the fortunes of a powerful and wealthy Greek state in the Archaic and early Classical periods. It is possible to see the original and difficult foundation of the city and the establishment of the dynasty, followed by the development of internal strife and the weakening of royal power that eventually led to the removal of the dynasty, while the city itself prospered and flourished. Because of Herodotus, more is known about the rise and fall of the Battiads than about any royal dynasty in the pre-Hellenistic world.

[*See also* Herodotus; *and* Pheretime.]

BIBLIOGRAPHY

Burn, A. R. *The Lyric Age of Greece*. London: Arnold, 1960. Still the best general study of the era.

Chamoux, F. *Cyrène sous la monarchie des Battiades*. Paris: de Boccard, 1953. The only detailed study of the Battiad dynasty.

DUANE W. ROLLER

Batumubwira, Antoinette (1956–), Burundian politician and diplomat, was born on 23 May 1956. Her parents belonged to a prominent Tutsi family. From 1979 to 1981, after she had completed her undergraduate studies, Batumubwira worked as a journalist for the newspaper *La Voix de la Révolution du Burundi*. She eventually received a master's degree in communication. In 1981, she became a public relations administrator for the United Nations information center in Bujumbura, the Burundian capital. She held this position until 1995, even after the Burundian civil war commenced in the early 1990s. She married Jean-Marie Ngendahayo, a prominent politician in his own right, who served as Burundi's foreign minister from 1993 to 1995. She joined the Conseil national pour la défense de la démocratie-Forces de défense de la démocratie (CNDD-FDD; National Council for the Defense of Democracy–Forces for the Defense of Democracy), a rebel movement that was opposed to the rule of longtime leader Pierre Buyoya. Although Batumubwira herself was a Tutsi, she rejected Buyoya as an autocrat. She left her homeland and became the head of public relations for ICO Global Communications. From 1999 to 2000, she became the head of communications for

the United Nation's office in the Comoros Islands. Batumubwira briefly worked as a consultant in 2002 for the United Nations Regional African Conference. Although she returned to her homeland, the bloody fighting that devastated Burundi in 2003 led her to leave her country. For a short period of time, Butumbwira lived in South Africa.

The FDD under the leadership of Pierre Nkurunziza agreed to participate in elections and end its armed struggle in 2004. Before the FDD's victory, Batumbwira was living in Finland as a political refugee with her husband and two children. During her stay in the city of Vantaa, she learned to speak Finnish after taking a five-month course. She also received three months of training at the Uudenmaa Employment and Economic Development Center. Batumubwira even worked as an administrator for the government economic development office, which trained her in 2003 to 2004. During her tenure there, she completed several reports on the integration of immigrants into Finnish society. In an interview in 2007 held after she returned to Helsinki as the minister of foreign affairs for her country, she noted, "I've been away from Finland only for a short while. When I now came here, everything seemed exactly the same. I was immediately able to orientate myself in the city" ("Foreign Minister," 2007). The FDD contacted well-educated exiles like Batumubwira to join the new government even before they had returned home.

As Burundi's minister of foreign affairs from 2005 to 2009, Batumubwira sought out international aid for Burundi's fledgling democracy. Her previous experience in Scandinavia and with the United Nations was useful as she toured many European and African countries. She supported the growing economic presence of the People's Republic of China and participated in the November 2006 Chinese–African ministerial summit in Beijing. Batumubwira also helped shape her country's application to join the British Commonwealth. On 25 February 2009, Batumubwira resigned from her post to become the head of the External Relations and Communications Unit of the African Development Bank. Her career is a testimony to the ways educated Burundian women had taken leading political roles in the early twenty-first century.

[*See also* Buyoya, Pierre; *and* Nkurunziza, Pierre.]

BIBLIOGRAPHY

African Development Bank Group. "Antoinette Batumubwira Appointed Head of AfDB Group's

External Relations and Communication Unit," accessed April 4, 2010, www.afdb.org/en/news-events/article/antoinette-batumubwira-appointed-head-of-afdb-group-external-relations-and-communication-unit-4336/.

"Foreign Minister of Burundi Wants Everybody to Participate in the Politics," *Formin.Finland.fi*, February 19, 2007, accessed December 8, 2010, http://formin.finland.fi/Public/Print.aspx?contentid=86842&nodeid=17482&culture=en-US&contentlan=2.

Reyntjens, Filip. "Briefing: Burundi: A Peaceful Transition after a Decade of War?" *African Affairs* 105 (2006): 117–135.

JEREMY RICH

Bayano (fl. sixteenth century), fugitive slave and leader of an anticolonial rebellion in Panama, was born somewhere in Africa in the early decades of the sixteenth century. Nothing is known of his life prior to his enslavement and transport to the Americas. However, some have contended Bayano may have been a Mande-speaking Muslim from West Africa.

A Spanish ship carrying Bayano and 400 other slaves headed to the thinly populated colony of Panama in 1552. Smallpox and mistreatment had killed many Native Americans living in Panama, and so the Spanish government hoped to bring in these slaves as workers to replace indigenous people. However, the isthmus of Panama region also by this time had become a favored destination of many *cimarrones* (runaway slaves). Slave revolts had already taken place in Panama in 1525, 1530, and 1549. Slaves outnumbered free people in many Panamanian locales. Bayano thus was well positioned to find allies. Luckily for him and his fellow prisoners, the ship that carried them to Panama ran aground. Bayano and numerous other slaves escaped to shore.

By 1553, Bayano had emerged as a formidable opponent of Spanish authority and slavery. Sources written by Spanish authors described Bayano as a very handsome and strong man who spoke Spanish well. His Spanish opponents assumed that Bayano had been a king or a leader in his homeland, and they called him *el rey negro Bayano* (the Black king Bayano). His followers treated him with fear and respect, and they may have numbered more than 1,200 people. Bayano established a fortress for his rebel slave community (*palenque*) in a thickly forested mountainous region on the Atlantic side of Panama. This fort proved to be extremely difficult for his Spanish opponents to capture. Only two narrow roads led up to the hill where the fort stood, and the settlement had high palisades. Inside, Bayano's followers had constructed large silos to store food in case they were besieged. He also set up a second hidden fort to protect children, women, and elderly people. It was never discovered until Bayano was finally captured. Bayano and his supporters led numerous raids against Spanish caravans and settlements. One of his favorite targets was caravans carrying gold and silver on the Camino Real highway in Panama that connected Peru with Mexico. Governor of Panama Alvaro de Sosa sent out three different military expeditions. All of them were defeated by Bayano and his warriors. One Spanish force managed to reach Bayano's territory, but the runaway slave leader vanquished the Spanish and killed the leader, Gil Sánchez. Only four European soldiers managed to return alive to Spanish settlements.

Bayano was undone by deceit rather than by combat. The Spanish government ordered Pedro de Ursua to defeat Bayano. Ursua was a veteran of numerous campaigns against different Native American communities, and he drew from Spanish rebels who had risen up against the governor in Peru to take on Bayano. Ursua set ambushes at sites where caravans had been previously raided by Bayano's forces, which worked to weaken the African leader. A captured slave then informed Ursua of the location of Bayano's fort. In October 1556, Ursua led 40 men to the location and offered Bayano a peace agreement to split Panama into two territories: Bayano's independent kingdom and Spanish territory. Bayano's men and their leader agreed to meet and discuss the offer, and Ursua then seized Bayano after the Spanish and African leaders of the revolt feasted and fraternized with one another. Ursua tricked Bayano again by telling him he would give the African his freedom if he lured other runaway slaves to his fort. Bayano called on slaves to come to his fortress, and many runaways heeded his call only to be reenslaved by the Spanish. The rebellion ended, and Bayano appeared to have been sent into exile in Spain, where he was said to have lived comfortably under house arrest until he died of natural causes. Slave rebellions continued in Panama despite Bayano's failure in the late sixteenth century. A river bears Bayano's name in Panama in the twenty-first century.

BIBLIOGRAPHY

Pike, Ruth. "Black Rebels: The Cimarrons of Sixteenth-Century Panama." *The Americas* 64, no. 2 (2007): 243–266.

Richardson, Annette. "Bayano." In *Encyclopedia of Slave Resistance and Rebellion, Vol. 1*, edited by Junius Rodriguez, pp. 45–46. Westport, Conn.: Greenwood, 2007.

JEREMY RICH

Baybars I (c. 1233–1277), fourth of the Bahri dynasty of Mamluk sultans of Egypt, was born a slave. His full name was al-Malik al-Zahir Rukn al-Din al-Salihi al-Bundukdari. Although his date of birth is uncertain, most scholars agree he was born around 1233 far away from Egypt in the steppes of the Kipchak Turkish nomads. Before being purchased by the sultan, he took the name of his first immediate master, a relatively minor character named Aydakin Bundukdar. After demonstrating exceptional qualities as a youngster, Baybars was purchased by the Ayyubid sultan and successor to Saladin, Malik Salih. He started as only one of many fellow Kipchak slaves who served the Ayyubids. In fact, there were so many Kipchak soldiers in Egypt that it stimulated the creation of Kipchak-Arabic dictionaries such as the thirteenth-century *Codex Cumanicus*. Soon after being purchased by Malik Salih, he would have been subjected to the code of strict military discipline and training expected of the Mamluks, or "slaves." One of his first assignments was in Syria, where he fought against crusaders. Rising quickly through the ranks, he witnessed the intrigues of the last Ayyubid prince to maintain power over his sprawling and fractious realm. He eventually came to command the entire Egyptian army. His strategy was decisive in the victory at Mansura in 1250 and the capture of Louis IX, the king of France.

After Mansura the political situation became exceedingly murky, which was certainly to Baybars' advantage. Sensing both weakness and an opportunity to take power, Baybars instigated the assassination of Turan Shah in 1250 and Sultan Kutuz in 1260. The assassination of Sultan Kutuz was especially bloody and calculated. Kutuz had just won the decisive and historic battle of ʿAyn Jalut against the Mongols, preserving Egypt and Africa from the horde. Sultan Kutuz's personal valor is recorded as one of the main reasons for the success at ʿAyn Jalut. Baybars was one of the rear commanders at the battle. As Kutuz was returning to Cairo in victory, a group of officers, including Baybars, assassinated the sultan in his tent. Baybars took power in 1260.

While the way in which Baybars ascended to the sultanate may have been bloody, historians agree that once he gained power he proved a highly capable ruler. Not only was he victorious against the crusading Franks, he instigated important and lasting reforms within his realm. Without a family, Baybars could concentrate on the consolidation of his own power, not the infighting of potential familial successors. He reformed feudal practices and consolidated the army's control over rapidly expanding conquered land. He managed his vast empire by rebuilding fortresses, floating warships, establishing a royal post, and even creating a pigeon delivery service. Several important madrasas and monuments bearing his name survive. He also endowed the famous Sufi Baybarsiyya lodge.

His many victories are recorded with both wonder and distress by Frankish chroniclers. He fought against the famed Jean d'Acre in 1263 and expanded and consolidated control over petty Muslim principalities at Karak and Hims. In 1265 he took the vital port city and beachhead of Caesarea from the Franks. He also demolished Haifa and took Arsuf and Safed near Lake Tiberias. He took Jaffa south of modern Tel Aviv in 1268. In a nearly final blow to Latin Christendom in the Levant, he took Antioch in the north. Until Baybars, Antioch had never left the control of the Christians. Baybars' victory was a something of a death knell to the Latins. He even managed to capture the allegedly impenetrable Krak des Chevaliers in 1271 with the aid of innovative, heavy trebuchets and mangonels. The great chapel of the Hospitallers was converted into a mosque. Having captured the fortress, it used the Krak as a forward base against Christian Tripoli. All that was left of the crusader states were remnants of the Antioch principality and the town of Acre. The Muslims now held all of the high ground, and it was only a matter of time before the crusaders were expelled completely. He also eliminated the threat of the Ismaili Assassins, capturing their fortress near Damascus.

Learning perhaps from his own calculated use of power under his previous patrons, Baybars set up a complicated system for traveling from place to place, changing his destination and route randomly to avoid intrigue and capture. He expanded Mamluk power far north into Anatolia and Cappadocia, defeating the Suljuks and Mongols, and south into Nubia. His power in the region was without rival. After a life of almost perpetual campaigning, he died in 1277 in Damascus after seventeen years of rule—a long time for the Mamluks. While the Abbasid Caliphate had fallen to the Mongols only decades before in 1258, Baybars' energy and power established Cairo and the Mamluks as worthy successors to the lost golden age of Baghdad. In fact, Baybars welcomed a refuge of the Abbasid family in 1258, formally transferring the Caliphate to Cairo and gaining authority as "keeper of the two holy mosques" of Mecca and Medina. Cairo's unrivaled position as the de facto capital of the Arab world would be maintained well into the twentieth century.

[*See also* Saladin.]

BIBLIOGRAPHY

Hillenbrand, Carole. *The Crusades: Islamic Perspectives.* Edinburgh: Edinburgh University Press, 1999.

Irwin, Robert. *The Middle East in the Middle Ages: The Early Mamluk Sultanate, 1250–1382.* London: Croom Helm, 1986.

Thorau, Peter. *The Lion of Egypt: Sultan Baybars I and the Near East in the Thirteenth Century.* London: Longman, 1992.

Winter, Michael, and Amalia Levanoni, eds. *The Mamluks in Egyptian and Syrian Politics and Society.* Leiden: E. J. Brill, 2004.

ALLEN J. FROMHERZ

Bayram al-Kha'mis, Mohamed (1840–1889), Tunisian author, teacher, reformer, jurisconsult, was born in Tunis in March 1840. His mother was the daughter of Mahmoud Khouja, a minister of Ahmed Bey. His father, Mustapha Ben Mohamed Bayram Ath Thalith III, was a wealthy landowner and merchant from a family of scientists and administrators. When he died in Tunis in 1863, he left his son symbolic capital comprising precious documents, land, properties, funds, merchandise, and social contacts.

Bayram's education was centered both in the family's extensive library and in the rich Tunisian cultural milieu. From an early age he studied the Qur'an, hadith, and Arabic. He studied with eminent professors from the Zeytouna University, such as Bayram que Mustapha, Bayram Ahmed, Mohamed Mouaya, Ben Tahar Mohamed Achour, and others, receiving excellent training in many subjects, both Islamic and non-Islamic. His family was well placed in the social and intellectual circles of Tunis at that time because they had been privileged with a monopoly on the exercise of Al Ifta (jurisprudence) for nearly a century. Thus, Bayram was initiated into the political, social, and cultural life of Ottoman Tunisia and of the Muslim world in contact with Europe.

In Tunis in 1861 he replaced his uncle as director of the Al Onquiya School. In October 1863 he was promoted to professor, second class, at the Zeytouna University. In 1867 he became professor, first class. Committed to the Tanzimat reforms then sweeping the Ottoman Empire, he wished to contribute to the work of Tunisian reformers of his time such as Khéreddine Attounsi, Ahmed Ibn Abi Dhiaf, and General Al Hussein. He became critical of the Hussaynid dynasty in power, seeing it as the source of the 1864 insurrection led by Ali Ben Ghadhahim, and of other social and financial problems in Tunis. He argued for social justice and the separation of powers, and he opposed the absolutism of the beys.

Under the government of Khéreddine Pasha, on 6 April 1874 Bayram was named director of the Jamiyat Al Awqaf (Ministry of Religious Affairs) to rationalize its management. On 14 July 1874 Prime Minister Khéreddine named him publisher of the first official Tunisian newspaper, *Attounsi Arra'id*. Accepting this new responsibility, Bayram threw himself at the reform project. He organized the library at Zeytouna and published in *Attounsi Arra'id* articles on all aspects of Tunisian social life. But an illness weakened him. The treatments he received in Tunis being limited, he decided in December 1875 to seek care in Europe, first in Italy and then in France, where he stayed from 1875 to 1878. He was greatly moved by his direct contact with the West, and undertook, in several ways and for several reasons, a comparison between his country and Europe.

Conscious of the dangers menacing the Ottoman Empire and the regency of Tunis on the one hand and the undeniable overall progress of Europe on the other, Bayram was not optimistic about the future of the Muslim and Arab world, even with radical reforms. Having returned to Tunis after his medical treatment, he began another trip, to colonial Algeria, where he spent ten days in Annaba.

Comparing countries and civilizations became a central concern for Bayram, and it encouraged him to refine his thinking. Despite his ill health, he defended modern schooling when the Sadiki school was founded. Khéreddine's resignation from government did not discourage him. On 10 February 1879 Bayram was named director of the Sadiki hospital. He continued to severely criticize certain ministers such as Mustapha Khaznadar.

But for Bayram the situation in the province of Tunis, and that of the Ottoman world in general, had become catastrophic by several measures, to the extent that England and France were preparing at all levels to occupy Egypt and Tunisia, respectively. Unhappy in his personal and familial life in Tunis, Bayram requested permission to leave Tunis on 14 October 1879, under the pretext of making a pilgrimage to holy sites.

Still focused on his political and reformist ideas and his role as interpreter of cultures, he left his country. He spent two years in Istanbul, where he was well respected and sought out. For unknown reasons he left Istanbul to live in Cairo, where his family—he was married to a cousin, with whom he had three children—joined him. In Cairo he became a judge and founded a newspaper, *Al Iila'm* (Information), and a publishing house. He published *Safwat Al Iitibar Bi Mostawdaa Al AMSAR Wal Al Akhbar*, an important work of travel literature and political economics.

Bayram made several trips in Europe, the Mediterranean, and the Muslim world. He is remembered as the author of travel literature. He died in Halwan, Egypt, on 18 December 1889 and was buried in Cairo.

[*See also* Ibn Abi Dhiaf, Ahmed.]

BIBLIOGRAPHY

Works by Mohamed Bayram Al-Kha'mis
Al iila'm (Information). Cairo, 1882–1897.
Safwat Al Iitibar Bi Mostawda Al Akhbar Wal Amsar [Handbook of facts about countries]. Cairo, 1892.

Secondary Sources
Abdeljlil, Ben et Kamel Moncef, Omran. *Mohamed Bayram Al Kha'mis: bibliougraphiya tahlilya* [Mohamed Bayram Al Kha'mis: Analytical bibliography]. Tunis, 1989.
Essnoussi, Zinelabidine. *Mohamed Bayram Al Kha'mis: Nosous wa Dirasatun* [Mohamed Bayram Al Kha'mis: Texts and studies]. Tunis, 1952.
Gasmi, Fathi. *Ech-Cheikh Mohamed Bayram Al Kha'mis. Hayatuhu wa Fikruhu Al Islahi* [Sheik Mohamed Bayram Al Kha'mis: His life and reformist thought]. Tunis, 1994.
Tlili, Bechir. "Une contribution à l'étude de la pensée sociale et politique de Bayram V (1840–1889)." *Revue de l'Occident musulman et de la Méditerranée* 15, no. 15/16 (1973): 327–343.

AHMED JDEY
Translated from the French by Sylvia Cannizzaro

Be'alu Girma (1938–1984?), Ethiopian journalist and novelist, was born on 22 September 1938 in Illubabor, southwest Ethiopia, of an Ethiopian mother and an Indian father. He first went to school in his home town, but he moved to Addis Ababa at age ten and became a boarder at the Princess Zenebe Worq Elementary School. He received a scholarship to General Wingate Secondary School in 1951, where he discovered his gift for writing. He next studied journalism and political science at Addis Ababa University and edited the college newspaper *News and Views*. He earned a bachelor's degree in 1962.

Following his undergraduate degree, Be'alu worked for the English-language newspaper *Ethiopian Herald*. In his student days, his forceful advocacy of policies at odds with government views had occasionally forced him to go into hiding. There was no free press, and censorship could be strict, especially after an attempted coup d'état instigated by the Imperial Bodyguard, which many students supported, at the end of 1960. Due to his academic brilliance, he earned a scholarship to study journalism and political science in the United States at Michigan State University in East Lansing, Michigan. He returned to Ethiopia with a master's degree in late 1963. He then worked in the Ministry of Information and became editor-in-chief of the weekly Amharic paper *Yezareyitu Ityopia* ("Ethiopia Today"). Two years later, he became editor-in-chief of *Addis Reporter*, a weekly journal that he made very popular with his investigative and critical reporting, which was new in Ethiopia. As a result, he earned the hostility of powerful people; he was suspended for a period, and his salary was reduced. After three years, he became editor-in-chief of *Ethiopian Herald*, and from 1970 to 1974 he was editor-in-chief of the Amharic daily *Addis Zemen* ("New Era"). In 1974, there was a revolution and military takeover in Ethiopia, and Be'lau Girma got caught up in the new movement.

While he was editor of *Addis Zemen*, Be'alu became interested in creative writing. In 1970, he published his first novel, *Kadmas bashager* ("Beyond the Horizon"), which describes the aimless life of students who finally find meaning in a more personally committed relationship. His second novel, *Yehillina dewel* ("The Bell of Conscience"), appeared in 1974. This work demonstrates features that would become characteristic of his later creative writing: attention to social problems and suggested solutions, often in defiance of government policies. In this novel he described how villagers who took matters into their own hands built a school without help from the authorities.

In the year of the revolution, Be'alu left *Addis Zemen* and became deputy general manager of the

Ethiopian News Agency. He was promoted to general manager within a year, a post that he retained until 1977, when he became permanent secretary of the Ministry of Information. After the 1974 revolution, he became gradually more politically involved. He wrote many speeches for the head of state, Mengistu Haile Mariam, but he also realized that the socialist government was becoming more and more dictatorial, and he could not always toe the line. He rewrote his second novel and called it *Haddis*, again stressing that local initiative could succeed when the government failed to help. This went against the policy of the increasing centralization of all aspects of social and economic life in Ethiopia.

Eritrea had long fought for independence, and the war there escalated. At first, Be'alu supported the government, as shown in two novels published in 1980, *YeQeyy kokeb tirri* ("The Call of the Red Star") and *Derasiw* ("The Author"). But he changed his views when he saw the self-seeking and ruthlessness of the ideologists and military leaders, and increasingly he supported the aspirations of the common people. His last novel reflects his observations in Eritrea and among the leaders in Ethiopia, and it manifested even more clearly than before a feature of all of his fictional writing: he always built his stories on real persons and events. In this novel, *Oromay*, it is easy to recognize the protagonists, from the head of state and his ideological props to the self-seekers around the center of power. The word *Oromay* may hint at Italian *oramai* ("now") or, more likely, be short for *ora o mai* ("now or never"), indicating that this was a decisive moment for the success or failure of the socialist revolution, which prediction proved to be correct, although the government struggled on until it was overthrown in 1991. Due to the critical nature of the book, it was soon banned, which made it only more popular, and it solidified opposition to the government. This would cost Be'alu dearly. He was abducted on 14 February 1984 and was never heard of again; it is believed he was killed soon after on orders from the government.

[*See also* Mengistu Haile Mariam.]

BIBLIOGRAPHY

Azeze, Fekade. "Be'alu Germa." In *Encyclopaedia Aethiopica*, Vol. 1, pp. 425–426. Wiesbaden, Germany: Harrassowitz Verlag, 2003.

Molvaer, Reidulf K. *Black Lions: The Creative Lives of Modern Ethiopia's Literary Giants and Pioneers*. Lawrenceville, N.J.: Red Sea Press, 1997, pp. 341–352.

REIDULF K. MOLVAER

Bédié, Henri-Konan (1934–), former diplomat, cabinet minister, president of the National Assembly, second president of Ivory Coast, and first president to be deposed by the Ivorian armed forces, was born in Dadiékro, in central Ivory Coast. A member of the Baulé ethnic group that dominated the Ivorian political economy since the early 1940s, Bédié was a favored protégé of President Félix Houphouët-Boigny.

He studied law and economics in France at the University of Poitiers, after which he joined the Ivorian civil service in the waning years of French colonial rule in 1960 and was sent to study at the French Foreign Ministry. Two months later, he was named councillor at the French Embassy in Washington. Only twenty-seven years old at independence in August 1960, Bédié became Ivory Coast's chargé d'affaires, and shortly thereafter ambassador to the United States. He also established the Ivorian mission to the United Nations in New York. He served as ambassador until he returned home in January 1966. He was then transferred to the political bureau of the ruling Democratic Party of Ivory Coast (PDCI) and named minister delegate for financial affairs. He was named the substantive minister of economic and financial affairs in 1968, a position he held until 1977. Simultaneously, he served as a governor of the International Monetary Fund in 1973–1974 and administrator of the World Bank for 1974.

Bédié's political career was nearly derailed in 1969 by a scandal involving the award of a doctorate degree in economics to him by the University of Poitiers, allegedly in exchange for a considerable sum of (public) money. He weathered that storm successfully and kept his ministerial position. However, on his watch, the government launched politically expedient development programs in cotton, rice, and sugar in the north of the country. The programs were designed to address a growing imbalance in the economies of the north and south that was beginning to threaten peaceful ethnic coexistence as early as the 1970s. The programs were a financial disaster for the country and politically damaging to Bédié. The sugar complex in particular was plagued by such high cost overruns and financial mismanagement that it was eventually declared bankrupt and liquidated. Bédié and two of his colleagues in the ministries of planning and agriculture were publicly rebuked by Houphouët-Boigny for their mishandling of the economy and relieved of their posts in 1977. The president subsequently arranged for Bédié to be appointed special adviser for African affairs at the International Finance Corporation of the World Bank.

The shift to competitive elections in 1980 revived Bédié's political career as he was elected to the National Assembly that year and chosen as assembly president the following year. He remained president of the National Assembly for fourteen years until the death of President Houphouët-Boigny on 7 December 1993. Bédié appeared on national television within a few hours of Houphouët-Boigny's death to proclaim himself president as mandated by the constitution. He faced stiff opposition to his bid from Prime Minister Alassane Ouattara. However, Bédié was backed by the country's supreme court, which confirmed him two days later. He moved quickly to consolidate his newfound power by naming a new government, thereby assuring himself international, especially French, support.

As president, Bédié unveiled an ambitious, but ultimately failed, plan to revitalize the ailing economy and turn Ivory Coast into "the elephant [read giant] of Africa." Simultaneously, he pursued a controversial and highly divisive *Ivoirité* (ultranationalist) agenda, which sought to distinguish between indigenous Ivorians and foreigners and to restrict public sector employment, land, and the franchise to authentic Ivorians only. He resorted to judicial and extrajudicial measures to quell growing opposition to his rule. He won the presidential election in 1995, but that victory was tarnished because the major opposition parties boycotted it to protest the banning of their candidates.

In December 1999, Bédié was overthrown in a military coup led by General Robert Gueï. With French assistance, Bédié fled to France. He returned to Abidjan in October 2001 to participate in the Forum for National Reconciliation. Still harboring presidential ambitions, Bédié worked quietly to regain control of the PDCI since his return from exile. He managed to beat back a serious challenge to his leadership from Laurent Dona Fologo (who, as secretary-general, presided over the affairs of the party during Bédié's absence), retired Admiral Lamine Fadika, and a group of self-proclaimed "renovators." Both Fologo and Fadika, who are northerners, wanted to end Akan domination of the party and provide new leadership despite their own advanced ages and involvement in the erstwhile ruling party for more than 30 years. As a result of their challenge, the eleventh party congress was twice postponed in March 2002. Eventually, the congress convened in April, with Bédié chosen as the party's president and, hence, its candidate for the next presidential elections.

In the political impasse that accompanied the attempted coup against Gbagbo from September 2002 to March 2007, Bédié generally backed President Laurent Koudou Gbagbo in his efforts to reach a negotiated settlement. Perhaps acutely aware of the power of incumbency or how the system can be used to punish opponents, he has kept a rather low profile. He has been neither viewed as a threat to Gbagbo nor implicated in any attempts to destabilize the country, although he has sometimes participated in opposition protest demonstrations against Gbagbo. While Bédié awaited the oft-postponed election to try to become president once again, Ivory Coast continued to reap the whirlwind from the *Ivoirité* policies which he and his successors had doggedly pursued since the 1990s.

As expected, Bédié was the PDCI candidate for the presidential election that was finally held on 31 October 2010, coming in third with 25 percent of the votes. He was thus eliminated from the runoff election on 28 November between incumbent president Gbagbo and former Prime Minister Alassane Ouattara. Interestingly, Bédié had made a pact with Ouattara before the first round pledging his full support to Ouattara in the event of a runoff in which he was not a candidate. This Bédié-Ouattara electoral alliance was symbolized by a name change so that Ouattara contested the runoff under the banner of the Rassemblement des Houphouétistes pour la Démocratie et la Paix (RHDP; Rally of Houphouetists for Democracy and Peace). Bédié kept his promise by encouraging his supporters to vote massively for Ouattara in the runoff. They appear to have followed his exhortation, giving Ouattara a significant electoral victory. Announced by the independent electoral commission and certified by the special representative of the secretary-general of the United Nations on 2 December, the results were overturned by Gbagbo's hand-picked Constitutional Council the next day, thus producing two presidents and plunging Ivory Coast back into political turmoil and escalating violence. After a lengthy standoff between Gbagbo's and Ouattara's forces in early 2011, Gbagbo was finally ousted and Ouattara was installed as president in April 2011.

[*See also* Gbagbo, Laurent Koudou; Houphouët-Boigny, Félix; *and* Ouattara, Alassane Dramane.]

BIBLIOGRAPHY

Bakary, Tessy D. "Elite Transformation and Political Succession." In *The Political Economy of Ivory Coast*, edited by I. William Zartman and Christopher Delgado, pp. 21–55. New York: Praeger, 1984.

Baulin, Jacques. *La Succession d'Houphouet-Boigny.* Paris: Eurafor Press, 1989.

McNeil, Donald G., Jr. "Ousted Leader of Ivory Coast Flees to Togo." *New York Times*, December 27, 1999.

CYRIL DADDIEH

Behanzin, Aouagbe (c. 1844–1906), king of the West African monarchy of Dahomey (now the Republic of Benin), was born around 1844, one of the many sons of Glele, king of Dahomey. There is great debate in oral traditions collected in the twentieth century regarding his early life. Some claimed that Behanzin, known as Kondo before he ascended to the throne, lived with Hehegunon, a powerful member of the royal family. Others contended Behanzin was raised by the deposed Dahomean ruler Adandozan, perhaps to discredit him. It is generally believed that Behanzin did not have a close relationship with his father. European travel accounts before the 1870s do not mention Behanzin, and instead suggest that Glele's son Ahanhanzo was the undisputed heir. However, Ahanhanzo died under mysterious circumstances during the mid-1870s. Some of Ahanhanzo's descendents blamed Behanzin for Ahanhanzo's death, while other accounts contend that smallpox took his life. This controversy is typical for the protrayal of Behanzin, who has been presented by the Beninese people alternately as a failed ruler who could not resist French authority and as a brave and capable leader of African resistance to European rule.

How Behanzin became the heir is also a matter of debate. According to one tradition in the royal family, Behanzin and Glele's son Sasse Koka were the finalists. Wegbelu, a powerful advisor to Glele (and Behanzin's future successor) declared that Behanzin would be a ruler less likely to wage unnecessary wars. However, Glele's decision to choose Behanzin did not end royal intrigues. Sasse Koka's extremely powerful mother, Visesegan, one of Glele's queens, still considered her son to be the future ruler of the kingdom and encouraged her son to challenge Behanzin. Glele's advanced age made it more and more difficult to settle this dispute; he almost never appeared publicly from 1875 until his death in 1889. In the meantime, Behanzin and Visesegan each sought out allies in the extensive Dahomean royal family and military. Changes in the royal bureaucracy led to even more tensions, as a newer class of male slave diviners and advisors competed with free ministers and members of the royal family. Behanzin developed a reputation for his command of supernatural forces, which helped him pull in members of different factions within the government. Although Behanzin is sometimes presented as a "traditionalist" leader opposed to Visesegan's supposedly friendly view of European trading interests, historian Edna Bay has argued that this neat division does little justice to either rival.

The situation was further complicated by the rapid expansion of British, French, and German colonies in West Africa from the early 1880s onward. French officials reestablished in the early 1880s a protectorate over the port of Porto-Novo, which had been a vassal to the interior Dahomey kingdom. In Porto-Novo and the more important Atlantic port of Whydah, another tributary state, influential trading families began to struggle with each other over their loyalties. Dahomey's influence became more and more precarious. Some groups turned to England, others to France, and another faction backed German commercial interests. The establishment of the German colony of Togo in 1884 further exacerbated tensions. After the Berlin Conference of 1884 made proof of effective occupation vital for sustaining European claims to land, the French set about gradually making these claims in the port cities of Whydah and Cotonou. Interestingly, Behanzin appears to have tried in 1888 to get support from the English government for taking the throne by sending a diplomatic delegation to the British colony of Lagos, which presented Sesse Kako as a bloodthirsty leader. The British ultimately chose after a year not to intervene on behalf of Behanzin.

Behanzin ascended to the throne after Glele's death on 30 December 1889, even though many in the royal family did not support him. This event coincided with a push by French official Jean Bayol to force Dahomey to accept a French customs post in Cotonou. Behanzin refused to meet with Bayol on the grounds that he had to perform various rituals on behalf of his father. Bayol took this as an insult. At the same time, in early 1890, Behanzin consolidated his authority over the government and apparently Sasse Kako died in the process. French troops fought off a larger Dahomean force that tried to retake Cotonou in March 1890. Rather than continue the struggle, Behanzin withdrew his forces from the Atlantic coast to protect the kingdom's capital of Abomey and the Dahomean heartland. A two-year stalemate ensued. Some French reports from 1891 indicate that Visesegan wanted to broker a deal with the French and remove Behanzin, but it is impossible to determine the accuracy of this view based on the few sources available.

What seems more clear is that the French military's unwillingness to launch an immediate attack further bolstered Behanzin's authority in his kingdom. So did Behanzin's clever decision to send several thousand of his soldiers and other subjects from 1889 to 1892 as workers to German and Portuguese colonies. German trading firms brokered these deals and sold Behanzin modern weapons, even a few machine guns. By 1892, Behanzin's army was one of the best armed forces of any independent African nation.

Under the command of Alfred-Amédée Dodds, a mixed-race Senegalese officer, the French launched an offensive against Behanzin beginning in August 1892. Dodds moved slowly through the kingdom and faced heavy resistance for over a year, even though the French officially deposed Behanzin on 3 December 1892 after the king paid a tiny fraction of the 15 million franc fine imposed on the kingdom. Behanzin fled north rather than accept defeat. At times in 1893, Behanzin appeared to be willing to make an agreement with the French, which angered many Dahomeans who wished to continue the struggle. Behanzin only agreed to surrender in January 1894, several months after Abomey had fallen to Dodds. A few days before the surrender, a war minister proclaimed himself the true king, officially deposed Behanzin, and accepted French rule. The French exiled Behanzin to Martinique, where the former ruler suffered greatly from various illnesses. He then was transferred to Algeria. He died on 10 December 1906. Although many Dahomeans viewed him as a failure, by the mid-twentieth century anticolonial activists considered him a hero.

[*See also* Glele; *and* Visesegan.]

REFERENCES

Amegboh, Joseph. *Behanzin: roi d'Abomey*. Paris: Afrique biblio club, 1975.

Barbou, Alfred. *Histoire de la guerre au Dahomey, 1888–1893*. Paris: J. Pegat, 1893.

Bay, Edna G. *Wives of the Leopard: Gender, Politics, and Culture in the Kingdom of Dahomey*. Charlottesville: University of Virginia Press, 1998.

Law, Robin. *Ouidah: The Social History of a West African Slaving Port, 1727–1892*. Athens, Ohio: Ohio University Press, 2004.

JEREMY RICH

Beit, Alfred (1853–1906), diamond magnate, financier, imperialist, and philanthropist in southern Africa, was born in Hamburg, Germany, the eldest of six children. His father was an affluent merchant. Beit performed poorly in school, and in his teens he was sent to be an apprentice at the office of Jules Porges and Company in Amsterdam. In 1875, Beit went to Kimberley, South Africa, as a representative of the firm. While in Africa he went into property speculation and joined up with a young German named Julius Wernher. These two men formed the Wernher, Beit, and Company firm, which was known for its deep-level mining and use of cyanide processing for treating gold ore. His most famous friendship was with Cecil Rhodes, an English financier. They formed the De Beers Mining Company. Much of Rhodes's success depended on the financial advice he received from Beit.

Together, Rhodes and Beit worked to drive out other mining competitors, such as Barney Barnato. Beit introduced Rhodes to Nathaniel de Rothschild, a well-known wealthy financier, in order to buy shares and remove Barnato from the competition. Eventually Beit, Barnato, and Rhodes came to an agreement and formed a new company, De Beers Consolidated Mines Limited, in 1888. (Beit became a life governor of this firm.) By 1889, Rhodes had a monopoly on all Kimberley mines in South Africa—90% of the world's production.

In 1889, during a period of growing diamond monopolies by both German and British firms, Rhodes and Beit formed the British South Africa Company. This company was created to enable colonization and to create economic spheres of influence across much of southern and central Africa. This happened at a time when the "scramble for Africa" was at its height, as many European powers were quickly monopolizing all areas of the continent.

A major debacle for Beit was the failed Jameson Raid of 1895. Beit, Rhodes, Leander Starr Jameson, and others hatched a plot to support an uprising in the Boer Republic of the Transvaal. The goal was to make the Transvaal a British colony in order to create favorable economic conditions for the foreign mining companies. The raid failed and the conspirators, including Beit, were indicted. In 1896, a House of Commons inquiry into the raid condemned Beit and Rhodes's actions. Beit stepped down as director of the British South Africa Company and paid an indemnity to the Transvaal Republic.

Beit died in England at the age of 53, never marrying or having children. Beit was known as a philanthropist, giving aid to science research and education. Both during and after his life, Beit gave money to establish a university in Johannesburg and in his hometown of Hamburg. He also created a professorship of colonial history at Oxford in 1905. After his death, a Beit Trust was set up which bequeathed large sums of money for development in Africa, specifically in Northern and Southern Rhodesia. Today Zambia, Zimbabwe, and Malawi are beneficiaries of this charitable trust.

[*See also* Rhodes, Cecil John.]

BIBLIOGRAPHY

Fort, George Seymour. *Alfred Beit: A Study of the Man and his Work*. London: Nicholson & Watson, 1932. An older biography, but still an important read on Beit. Most copies of this right now are on microfilm, so this is difficult to obtain.

Galbraith, John S. *Crown and Charter: The Early Years of the British South Africa Company*. Berkeley: University of California Press, 1974. Beit and Rhodes formed the British South Africa Company, and this book chronicles how this company came to fruition.

Meredith, Martin. *Diamonds, Gold, and War: The British, the Boers, and the Making of South Africa*. New York: Public Affairs, 2007. This is one of the more recent books on diamond mining in South Africa. It focuses mostly on Cecil Rhodes, but Beit figures prominently with regard to how mining was cultivated in the region. Also, the book discusses the relationship between Beit and Rhodes.

Stead, W. T. "Alfred Beit, Diamond King, Empire Builder." *American Monthly, Review of Reviews* 34 (1906): 300–303. This is a primary account written soon after Beit's death by journalist W. T. Stead. It gives an overview of Beit's life—though it is a bit slanted, as Stead opposed the Boer War and flagrant mining capitalism. However, Stead tries to give a balanced account of Beit's life.

JODIE N. MADER

Bekri, Tahar (1951–), Tunisian poet, critic, and essayist, was born in Majel Bel Abbès, near Kassérine, Tunisia, where his father was employed with the railway system. His family originates from Gabes, in southeast Tunisia. Bekri's mother died when he was ten years old, which affected both his personal and literary journeys. He attended the Lycée of Sfax, where he was active in various literary and artistic circles. At the age of eighteen he published his first poems, in the school's literary journal. He then attended the University of Tunis, where he majored in French literature. During the turbulent years following May 1967, the university was a hotbed of political activism. Bekri was arrested for his political opinions in 1972 and was sentenced and jailed in 1975. Upon his release in 1976, he left for France and has since resided in Paris, where he was granted political asylum. Bekri completed a doctorate in French literature in 1981. He returned to Tunisia for the first time in 1987 after the fall of the the the regime of Habib Bourguiba.

Bekri is generally recognized as one of the most talented and prolific writers of his generation. He is the author of more than twenty books in numerous genres, including poetry, essay collections, and art criticism. His poetry has been translated into a dozen languages, including Hindi and Turkish, and has been the subject of a number of doctoral dissertations. Bekri writes with equal mastery in French and in Arabic.

Bekri's literary evolution and production span three decades. His early poetry—collected in *Le laboureur du soleil* (1983; The Sun's Ploughman), *Le chant du roi errant* (1985; The Song of the Errant King), and *Le coeur rompu aux océans* (1988; Oceanworthy Heart)—is clearly autobiographical and intimate in tone, marked by a profound sense of the loss of both his mother and his motherland. In the 1990s, Bekri's poetry becomes more universal in its themes and scope. The early angst of exile and the unsettling feelings of transience and nomadism evolved into a sort of transcendental urbanity and cosmopolitanism. The poems in *La sève des jours* (1991; The Sap of Days), and *Les chapelets d'attache* (1993; The Anchoring Rosary), and *Les songes impatients* (1997; Impatient Dreams) are those of a poet attuned to the problems of the world, and those of a postmodern writer condemned to live between languages, cultures, and countries. The first decade of the twenty-first century saw over a dozen publications by Bekri, including *Marcher sur l'oubli* (2000; On the Tracks of Oblivion), *L'Horizon incendié* (2002; Incendiary Horizon), *La brûlante rumeur de la mer* (2004; The Burning Rumor of the Sea), *Si la musique doit mourir* (2006; If Music Must Die), and *Les dits du fleuve* (2009; River Sayings). As the titles suggest, Bekri's preoccupations in this decade were philosophical, concerned with man's place in the continuum of life, but without theorizing or moralizing. The central metaphor is of the sea, an evocation of his Mediterranean childhood, but also a metaphor for the poet. His multicultural poetic scope is also visible in his Arabic-language volumes such as *Poems to Selma* (1989) and *Diaries of Ice and Fire* (1997).

Bekri has traveled extensively and has attended numerous conferences and colloquia, both as poet and critic. Since the mid-1980s he has taught Arabic language and culture at the University of Paris X at Nanterre.

[*See also* Bourguiba, Habib.]

BIBLIOGRAPHY

Khaddar, Hédia. *Anthologie de la poésie tunisienne de langue française.* Paris: L'Harmattan, 1984.

Toso-Rodinis, Giuliana. *Voix tunisiennes de l'errance. Essais sur les poèmes de Tahar BekrisSuivis de deux lectures sur A. Meddeb et Chems Nadir et d'un message à M. Aziza.* Palermo, Italy: Palumbo, 1995.

HÉDI ABDEL-JAOUAD

Belay Zelleqe (1909–1945), Ethiopian patriot from Gojjam who resisted the Italian Fascist occupation, was born in the Borena district of Wello province. His father, Basha Zelleqe Laqew, had been a member of Lij Iyasu Mikael's bodyguard. His mother, Weyzero Taytu, came from nearby Borena-Sayent. Upon Lij Iyasu's overthrow in 1916, Zelleqe, with two sons, Belay and Ejjegu, moved to Chaqeta, near Taytu's birthplace. The family ran into difficulty in 1924, when it came into armed conflict with the local governor. Zelleqe was killed, and subsequently hanged, wherupon Belay, Ejjegu, and several kinsmen fled into the lowlands bordering the Blue Nile, where they became *shiftoch*, or bandits, bent on revenge.

Belay's fortune was greatly affected by the Italian invasion. After fifteen years of fighting as a *shifta*, he determined to join the struggle against the external enemy. An opportunity came when he learned that an Italian military convoy was traveling from the Debre Marqos, the provincial capital of Gojjam, to Bechena. He attacked the convoy, killed its guards, and captured their weapons. Encouraged by this success, he carried out numerous raids on the Italians, mainly in Gojjam, but also on the Shewa and Wello borders.

He was so successful that, like Ethiopian rebel leaders of the past, he attracted many followers. They addressed him as Le'ul Belay, or Princely Belay, and Atse Bagulbatu, or Self-made Emperor. He soon emulated Emperor Haile Selassie by awarding his men military-cum-court titles, such as *Kegnyazmach*, *Grazmach*, and *Fitawrari*, i.e., commander of the right wing, left wing, and advance guard. When his brother Ejjegu asked him what title remained for himself, Belay reportedly replied, "I need no further title—as my mother has already named me Belay, i.e., 'One who is above others.'" His men also gave him the honorific "horse-name" (nickname or popular name) of Abba Koster, or Master of Gravity (or Seriousness).

At the time of Britain's entry into the struggle, Belay was the principal Ethiopian patriot in eastern Gojjam, with a well-armed and well-trained army estimated at 2,000 to 7,000 men. He collaborated with the British, to whom he described himself as the Avenger of the Blood of Ethiopia, but they found him vain and ignorant. Their main objection, however, was caused by his traditional overlord, Ras Haylu, the leading Ethiopian collaborator, who allowed a column of Italian troops under Colonel Saverio Maraventano to escape by crossing the Blue Nile from Gojjam into Shewa. This seriously delayed the Allied advance on the Ethiopian capital.

After Ethiopia's Liberation in 1941, the Emperor awarded Belay the title of *Dejazmach* and appointed him governor of Bechena. Wishing to reward his comrades-in-arms, Belay attempted to appoint them to various administrative posts but was overruled by his superiors, who wanted him to appoint other nominees, which Belay refused to do. He was accordingly accused of rebellion. The Emperor, irritated by this act of insubordination, summoned the quarreling officials to Addis Ababa, but Belay and his friends refused to go. The Emperor thereupon dispatched an armed force to apprehend them, but Belay resisted on the Somma mountain. Many casualties ensued, after which the Emperor sent a delegation to negotiate. Belay had hoped for a pardon, but his case was heard in a special court, which sentenced him to death. This sentence was confirmed by the Emperor, who nevertheless commuted it to life imprisonment. Belay was incarcerated in the former palace compound of the emperor Menilek II, but soon escaped. He was later re-arrested, and he and his brother Ejjegu were publicly hung on 12 January 1945. His execution was bitterly received by many Ethiopian patriots and subsequently led the Derg, or post-imperial military regime, to name Addis Ababa's Gojjam road after him.

[*See also* Haile Selassie I; *and* Iyasu Mikael.]

BIBLIOGRAPHY

Hilton, Andrew. *The Ethiopian Patriots: Forgotten Voices of the Italo-Abyssinian War, 1935–41.* Stroud, UK: Sutton Publishing, 2007.

Mockler, Anthony. *Haile Selassie's War.* Oxford: Oxford University Press, 1984.

Pankhurst, Richard. "The Ethiopian Patriots: The Lone Struggle 1936–40." *Ethiopia Observer* 13, no. 1 (1970): 40–56.

Shirreff, David. *Bare Feet and Bandoliers: Wingate, Sandford, the Patriots and the Part They Played in the Liberation of Ethiopia.* London: Radcliffe Press, 1995.

RICHARD PANKHURST

Belinda (c. 1713—c.1790), author of the first known slave narrative by an African woman in the United States, and successful petitioner for reparations for her enslavement, was born around 1713. Some historians have argued that she was brought to the US from Ghana, because her petition noted that she had lived on the "Ria da Valta River," which they viewed as a reference to the Volta River. However, she recalled praying in a sacred grove "to the great Orisa who made all things" as a child. Orisa deities are associated with spiritual traditions among Yoruba-speaking communities in southwestern Nigeria and parts of Benin.

Regardless of the exact location of her original home, in her narrative she recalled her childhood as a happy one. This peaceful world of groves gave way to the hardships of the Middle Passage. European raiders came into her village when she was about twelve years of age, "whose faces were like the moon, and whose bows and arrows were like the thunder and lightning of the clouds" (cited in Finkenbine, 97). Perhaps Belinda misremembered her capture, but no other historical accounts mention European slave raiders in West Africa using such weapons. It is possible that, as some historians have suggested about the slave narrative author Olaudah Equiano, Belinda was not born in Africa at all. Yet it is significant that Belinda was referred to in her petition to the Massachusetts legislature as "African," and not, as was more common at the time, as a "Negro."

At any rate, Belinda's account suggests that the slave raiders decided to leave her parents behind as too old, and took the child to the coast of Guinea. The girl was terrified to see three hundred or so Africans chained up. After she crossed the Atlantic, she was purchased by a wealthy resident of the North American British colony of Massachusetts, Isaac Royall. He was a successful professor at Harvard College whose family owned a sugar plantation on the Caribbean island of Antigua. In contrast, by the standards of colonial Massachusetts

law, Belinda could not even own property, as she was a mere slave. She toiled for Royall for decades until the coming of the American Revolution. Royall, a loyalist, fled to England rather than accept the rebel regime. Belinda made her way to Boston, where many slaves, free African Americans, and sympathetic whites were drawing together petitions to abolish slavery and to provide a means for slaves to purchase their freedom. Anthony Vassall, a former slave who had been owned by Isaac Royall's sister Penelope, petitioned the Massachusetts legislature for ownership of some of the land that his old loyalist master had abandoned. It is likely Belinda knew of this case.

In 1783, Belinda submitted a petition to the Massachusetts state legislature demanding to be paid reparations from Royall's estate for unpaid labor. There is little doubt that Belinda was illiterate, as she signed this document with an X. The letter itself is written in a very dramatic way, by someone who clearly was familiar with drafting similar petitions. Historian Roy Finkenbine contends that a likely candidate for the real identity of the author was the famous Boston-based, African American activist Prince Hall. He was a former slave who had become a leading figure in the Boston African American community, and had much experience with this kind of legal proceedings. The Massachusetts legislature granted Belinda's request for an annual pension of fifteen pounds and twelve shillings from Royall's estate for one year. She successfully applied again in 1787 for a three-year extension of the same pension, and did so again in 1790. Then she vanished from the historical record.

Meanwhile, a greatly altered version of her petition, which included a reference to rape, circulated among English abolitionists. While Belinda had no connection to the men who altered her story to bolster support for the fight against slavery, the transatlantic movement of her petition demonstrates the international character of the antislavery movement. Her case also set a precedent for the demand for reparations for the victims of the African slave trade that have appeared periodically in the three centuries since Belinda's successful appeal.

[*See also* Smith, Venture.]

BIBLIOGRAPHY

Finkenbine, Roy. "Belinda's Petition: Reparations for Slavery in Revolutionary Massachusetts." *William and Mary Quarterly* 64, no.1 (2007): 95–104.

Harris, Sharon. *Executing Race: Early American Women's Narratives of Race, Society, and the Law.* Columbus, Ohio: Ohio State University Press, 2005.

JEREMY RICH

Belisarius (c. 505–565 CE), Byzantine general, was born in what is now western Bulgaria. He was the military commander during Emperor Justinian's reign (527–565 CE), whom we know best thanks to Procopius of Caesarea, the most notable historian of the period, who joined his staff as legal secretary (*assessor*) in 527 and remained with him during his campaigns in North Africa and, up until 540, in Italy. Hence Belisarius is the central figure in Procopius' *History of Justinian's Wars*, published in 551, where he appears full of promise early in his career, but as time wore on, there is an insistent undertone of criticism. In the same year in which Procopius completed *Justinian's Wars* in seven books, he also wrote a coda containing information that he did not dare publish. This closet history is first mentioned in the *Suda*, a tenth-century lexicon, which refers to it as Procopius' *Anekdota* ("Unpublished Works"). A copy was found in the Vatican Library and published in 1623, and it revealed Belisarius as a weak, uxorious man, cuckolded by his wife Antonina, a crony of the empress Theodora. Perhaps as late as six years after Procopius published his *Justinian's Wars*, he added an eighth book, in which his critical tone is more overt. It covers the events of the wars up to 552, when the Byzantines at last won a decisive victory in Italy. The general who won it, however, was not Belisarius, but Narses, a eunuch chamberlain, a great favorite of the empress Theodora, who turned out to be a brilliant tactician.

Belisarius enrolled in Justinian's corps of guardsmen while Justinian's uncle, Justin I, was still emperor, and in 527 he was appointed Duke of Mesopotamia, headquartered at the fortress of Dara on the eastern frontier, where the Byzantine Empire confronted Persia. He led the Byzantines to victory at Dara in 530, but the next year he suffered a defeat and was recalled to Constantinople in disgrace. In January of 532, Justinian faced an insurgency in Constantinople—the "Nika revolt," so called after the watchword of the rebels, Nika! (Conquer!). Belisarius was on hand to help suppress the revolt, and, having proved his loyalty, he was chosen to lead an expeditionary force against the Vandal Kingdom in North Africa.

The Vandals, who were Christians but followers of the Arian heresy, had invaded Roman Africa a hundred years earlier and imposed their rule on the Roman provincials there. Landowners from Africa were displaced and Catholics persecuted, and both urged Justinian to intervene. He took only limited risk, however. Belisarius' force totaled no more than 15,000 infantry and cavalry, plus some barbarian auxiliaries. Yet Belisarius landed in Africa before the Vandals were alerted to the danger, defeated them in two cavalry battles, and returned to triumph in Constantinople, bringing Vandal captives and treasure, including loot that the Vandals had taken when they sacked Rome in 455.

Justinian was now ready to invade Italy, which had been overrun by the Ostrogoths in the years 488–492. Like the Vandals, the Ostrogoths were Arians, but they treated the Catholics benevolently, and the Emperor Anastasius recognized their leader, Theodoric, as regent (*rex*) of Italy. But Theodoric's successors were weak, and Italy seemed an easy conquest. Belisarius conquered Sicily in 535; the next year he invaded Italy, where he captured Naples, occupied Rome, and then endured a siege lasting more than a year when the Goths counterattacked. The war in Italy dragged on until 540, when Belisarius tricked the Ostrogoths into surrendering their capital, Ravenna, to him and returned to Constantinople, where Justinian gave him a cool welcome. Meanwhile, in Africa, the Byzantines faced a Berber insurgency and unrest in their own army. Only in 548 did the Byzantines get the upper hand, and for fourteen years thereafter Africa was at peace.

Belisarius returned to Italy in 544 to deal with an Ostrogoth insurgency led by a new king, Baduila, and campaigned there for four years with inadequate forces. Bubonic plague, which reached Constantinople in 542 and Italy a year later, had hollowed out the Byzantine army, and Justinian had more important priorities than Italy. In 549 Belisarius returned to private life in Constantinople, his reputation darkened.

He had a last victory in 559, when a horde of Kutrigur Huns invaded Thrace and threatened Constantinople. Belisarius organized the defense and routed the Kutrigurs, but Justinian relieved him of his command after the victory. Three years later he was implicated in a conspiracy and was put under house arrest for six months before Justinian returned him to favor. He died in March 565, eight months before Justinian.

BIBLIOGRAPHY

Evans, J. A. S. *The Age of Justinian. The Circumstances of Imperial Power.* London/New York: Routledge, 1996.

Evans, James Allan. *The Power Game in Byzantium: Antonina and the Empress Theodora.* London/New York: Continuum, 2011.

Graves, Robert. *Count Belisarius.* London: Cassell, 1938.

Hughes, Ian. *Belisarius: The Last Roman General.* Yardley, Pa.: Westholme, 2009.

JAMES ALLAN EVANS

Bell, Rudolf Duala Manga (1873 or 1875–1914), paramount chief and anticolonial protest leader in present-day Cameroon, was born in Douala, Cameroon, the eldest son of chief Manga Ndumbe Bell (ruled 1897–1908). Duala Manga is best remembered for a struggle against the racist policies of the German rulers of Cameroon, who executed him on 8 August 1914. Beyond this dramatic conclusion to Duala Manga's life lay a precolonial heritage of international commerce by the Duala people, an embattled but—until its last years—successful adaptation to German rule, and an afterlife as a nationalist and ethnic icon.

Duala Manga was descended from a line of merchant rulers who dominated trade between European Atlantic shippers and the Cameroon hinterland from the seventeenth through the nineteenth centuries. The Duala—inhabitants of what eventually became the city of Douala, at the estuary of the Wouri River—lived in a group of mutually independent settlements, of whom the most prominent were Duala Manga's Bell (or Bonanjo) and Akwa (or Bonambele).

In 1884 Duala Manga's grandfather Ndumbe Lobe, along with most of the other Duala rulers, signed a treaty of protection with the German government. The Duala hoped that such an arrangement would stabilize the internal struggles among their leaders, but the Germans clearly intended to assert their power over the entire territory of Cameroon, a project that included ending the Duala trade monopoly over the river system extending inland from the coast. Immediately prior to colonial annexation, the Bells had succeeded in building the largest and most prosperous of the Duala trading networks, and thus stood to lose the most from the new regime. Duala Manga's father and predecessor in office, Manga Ndumbe, nevertheless managed to increase his power and wealth.

Despite their designation in the local pidgin lingua franca as "kings," the precolonial Duala rulers had not developed any kind of political order that could be designated as a state in either Douala or their inland trading stations. However, the Germans appointed Manga Ndumbe *Oberhäuptling* ("Paramount Chief") over much of Douala, as well as the region extending northwest of the city along the Mungo River. Moreover, during the early 1900s, Manga Ndumbe (along with many other Duala, but especially Bell, merchants) established cocoa farms along their old trade routes, thus assuring private incomes not dependent on exporting goods produced by other Cameroonian communities. Finally, the Duala gained further advantages within the colonial system by their early acquisition of European education. Manga Ndumbe had gone to school in England before the German annexation, and Duala Manga himself studied in Germany from 1891 to 1896, earning a secondary school diploma.

When Duala Manga succeeded to the Bell chieftaincy in 1910, he inherited all of his father's prerogatives and property. However, that same year the Germans laid out a plan for segregating the city of Douala by moving all its African inhabitants away from the banks of the Wouri River, an area which was to be reserved for Europeans and separated by a one kilometer barrier from the "native quarters." This proposal threatened the Duala economically, since their land and houses would be purchased at submarket prices, and undermined their status as Europeanized "people of the water," superior to inland Cameroonian populations.

Bonanjo, Duala Manga's own urban territory, was the first target of the German project, but in his opposition to this scheme, the Bell ruler was supported by all of the Duala elites. His main tactics were petitions, first to local administrators and then in 1913, by the dispatch of a personal envoy, Ngoso Din, to the metropolitan Reichstag (parliament). Duala Manga also sought support of some kind from other Cameroonian chiefs. All these actions infuriated the German authorities in Cameroon, who first deprived Duala Manga of his chiefly office and then tried him and Ngoso Din for high treason. The exact grounds for such extreme charges are unknown, because no records have survived of the proceedings leading to the sentence of hanging. A less drastic punishment would very probably have been imposed had the climax of the expropriation crisis not coincided with the outbreak of World War I.

The legendary phase of Duala Manga's biography began three months after his death, when British and French troops seemed to avenge him by driving the Germans from Cameroon. In subsequent decades he became the subject of a popular Duala hymn and a major monument while his son,

Alexander Ndoumb'a Douala (1897–1966), used Duala Manga's reputation to build his own somewhat nebulous political career. In general histories of Cameroon Duala Manga figures as a precursor of anticolonial nationalism; but for the Duala people, the achievements and tragedy of his life epitomize the memory of their intense and ambiguous relationship to German rule.

BIBLIOGRAPHY

Austen, Ralph A. "Duala vs. Germans in Cameroon: Economic Dimensions of a Political Conflict." *Revue Française d'Histoire d'Outre-Mer* 64, no. 4 (1977): 477–497.

Austen, Ralph A., and Jonathan Derrick. *Middlemen of the Cameroons Rivers: The Duala and Their Hinterland, c. 1600–c. 1960.* Cambridge, UK: Cambridge University Press, 1999.

DeLancey, Mark Dike, Rebecca Neh Mbuh, and Mark W. DeLancey. *Historical Dictionary of the Republic of Cameroon.* 4th ed. Lanham, Md.: Scarecrow Press, 2010.

RALPH AUSTEN

Bello, Ahmadu (1909–1966), Sarduana of the Sokoto caliphate and prime minister of northern Nigeria, was born on 12 June 1909 in the city of Rabbah in northern Nigeria. Bello's father Ibrahim was the grandson of Uthman Dan Fodio (1754–1817), the religious leader who founded the Sokoto caliphate in the early nineteenth century. Ibrahim was also the chief of Rabbah.

Like many northern Nigerian Muslim leaders, Ibrahim sought to build close ties with the British colonial administration, and sent his children to Western schools. Bello first attended to a Western primary school in the provincial capital of Sokoto. He learned to speak English fluently at Sokoto Middle School, but he also continued to develop his Muslim faith. Bello then graduated from Sokoto and decided to become a teacher. With his father's blessing, Bello enrolled at Katsina Teachers College, where he spent five years. Once Bello successfully finished his studies at Katsina, he worked as an English and mathematics teacher at the Sokoto Middle School from 1931 to 1934. British colonial officers, impressed by Bello's intelligence and his willingness to adapt to European influences, appointed Bello the district head of Rabbah in 1934. According to the British colonial government's principles of indirect rule, Bello was allowed to manage the day-to-day affairs of the region under the supervision of British administrators.

In 1938, the death of Hassan, the reigning sultan of Sokoto, led to a succession dispute among his close relatives. Bello tried to become sultan, but a majority of prominent family members and the British administration chose Bello's first cousin Abubakar. Bello still received the royal title of Sarduana ("Minister of Defense") and received the job of administering the district of Gusau. Bello's familiarity with both Hausa and English law became apparent in 1943. A British official accused Bello of embezzling tax revenue collected from fees on cattle in 1943. Instead of accepting these charges, Bello took his critic to court and a British appellate court reversed the guilty verdict handed out by the administrator in the following year. Bello returned to work as the head official of the caliphate on police and educational matters. Sultan Abubakar learned to respect Bello's acumen for managing these services, although he initially had felt qualms about working with his former rival.

The end of World War II in 1945 and the independence of India in 1947 strongly affected Bello's views regarding the colonial administration, as did a year of study in England in 1948. The British government provided Bello with a scholarship to take courses in public policy. Even before this trip, Bello had begun to support political action on behalf of northern Nigerians. Some Muslim, northern Nigerian intellectuals formed the Youth Social Circle in 1945 with Bello's tacit approval, and eventually this group merged with the larger Northern Peoples' Congress (NPC) party, which was created by Bello in 1951. The NPC claimed to stand for the interests of northern Hausa and Fulani communities against the better-educated and well-organized southern Nigerian political parties, such as the National Council of Nigeria and the Cameroons (NCNC) and the Action Group. Abubakar sanctioned Bello's decision to lead the NPC on his behalf, since the sultan lacked the Western education necessary to effectively negotiate with southern Nigerian political groups. Bello also had been chosen to replace the former prime minister of Sokoto in the Northern Nigerian House of Assembly in 1949. This institution only could advise the British government, but Bello used this position to review the proposed Nigerian Constitution in 1949 and 1950. The powerful influence of Bello and the sultan of Sokoto ensured that the NPC dominated the north. Interestingly, Bello chose to focus his attention on the northern regional assembly, rather than act as the main NPC national leader. He became the first premier of northern Nigeria in 1954. Bello carefully promoted an integration of Muslim and British law, and maintained a coalition of younger intellectuals and activists, as well as entrenched aristocrats and Muslim scholars.

By the late 1950s, Bello was struggling to promote the interest of northern Nigerian elites, even as he tried to maneuver toward becoming the next sultan of Sokoto. To demonstrate his piety, Bello invited many Middle Eastern Muslim scholars from Saudi Arabia and elsewhere to visit his domains, and he encouraged promising young students of Islamic theology to go abroad for their education. Bello thus was instrumental in bringing puritanical Wahhabi Muslim teachings to Nigeria; Nigerian adherents of Wahhabism would become extremely influential later in the twentieth century. He also cultivated strong ties with the international Muslim community, enjoying a particularly good relationship with the Saudi royal family. It is in this spirit that Bello became one of the founders of the World Muslim League and its first vice president. Within Nigeria, Bello also established the Jama'atu Nasril Islam (Society for the Victory of Islam), dedicated to converting non-Muslims (and non-Christians) in the north. For many Igbo Christians, Bello's missionary zeal was akin to that of this reformist ancestor, Uthman Dan Fodio.

Despite his importance as a Muslim leader both abroad and at home, Bello was at the time as more of a nationalist figure by his contemporaries. Fearing the growth of the Action Group, which primarily drew the support of Yoruba-speaking voters in southwest Nigeria, Bello formed a political alliance in 1959 with the NCNC, the party that dominated southeastern Nigerian politics. The agreements that led to independence for Nigeria in 1960 gave the northern half of Nigeria more representatives in parliament than eastern and western Nigeria combined. Bello's deputy, Abubakar Tafawa Balewa, became prime minister of Nigeria at independence and remained in this office until the Nigerian First Republic was overthrown by a military coup on 16 January 1966. Bello founded a university in 1962 in Zaria, named after himself.

Regional and personal disputes, as well as the struggle between the adoption of a centralized political model or a federalist system, had practically paralyzed the First Republic by the mid-1960s. Government crackdowns against protests against census-taking in 1963 angered southern Nigerians. The elections of 1964, marred by rampant fraud, also made many southern military officers wary of northern dominance. A group of officers, largely drawn from the Ibo ethnic community in eastern Nigeria, decided to seize power and drive out most members of the political elite deemed too corrupt and too threatening to be allowed to live. Bello, along with many leading northern Nigerians, was executed in the coup along with his first wife, Hafsatu. He left behind five children. As a result of Bello's close relations with Saudi Arabia, the Saudi king ordered prayers to be said for him in Saudi mosques.

Bello's legacy remained controversial in the early twenty-first century. Some celebrated his efforts to unify different cultural and political influences in a new nation, while others decried his use of state patronage and long-standing social hierarchies.

[*See also* Uthman Dan Fodio.]

BIBLIOGRAPHY

Bello, Amadu. *My Life*. Cambridge, UK: Cambridge University Press, 1962.

Falola, Toyin, and Matthew M. Heaton. *A History of Nigeria*. New York: Cambridge University Press, 2008.

Paden, John N. *Ahmadu Bello, Sardauna of Sokoto: Values and Leadership in Nigeria*. London: Hodder and Stoughton, 1986.

Reynolds, Jonathan T. *The Time of Politics (Zamanin Siyasa): Islam and the Politics of Legitimacy in Northern Nigeria, 1950–1966*. Lanham, Md.: University Press of America, 1999.

JEREMY RICH

Bello, Muhammad (c.1780–1837), political, military, and religious leader and first Caliph of the Sokoto Caliphate, was born in the town of Morona, now located in Niger, in 1780 or 1781. His father was the revolutionary Islamic cleric and leader Uthman Dan Fodio (1754–1817), and his mother was Hawwa bint Adam ibn Muhammad Agh. Bello received an advanced education in Islamic theology and law thanks to his father, and supported his father's call for a strict adherence to orthodox Sunni interpretations of Islamic practices. Bello praised his father as a loving parent: "His face was relaxed and his manner gentle. He never tired of explaining and never became impatient if anyone failed to understand" (Boyd, 1989).

When Uthman Dan Fodio launched a series of holy wars against the nominally Islamic sultans of Hausa cities, such as Kano, in northern Nigeria and southern Niger, Bello became an active lieutenant of his father, commanded troops of Hausa and

Fulani background against the city-states, and had the walls built in 1809 for Dan Fodio's base at Sokoto. When the Muslim cleric Muhammad al-Kanemi (1776–1837) of Borno wrote Dan Fodio criticizing the Sokoto leader's efforts to seize Bornu, he sent letters to Bello as well. Once most of the Kano cities had been captured, Dan Fodio proclaimed a new caliphate based on orthodox Sunni legal and religious principles.

When Dan Fodio died in 1817, he left provisions that split the large Sokoto caliphate between Bello and Dan Fodio's brother Abdullahi. Bello received the capital of Sokoto, while Abdullahi was granted the Gwandu region. Bello acted as the leader of the loosely knit caliphate, in which individual city leaders (emirs) would come to Bello asking for the right to lead their own campaigns, with the blessing of the caliph.

Bello had a series of fortresses built on the outskirts of his domains and consolidated the conquests of his father. It was under his reign that a synthesis between Hausa urban and Fulani rural culture took place, as many Hausa aristocratic families accepted the new order of the caliphate.

Bello tended to be somewhat less aggressive than Dan Fodio in terms of foreign policy, even as he sanctioned regular slave-raiding campaigns against other communities in central Nigeria, northern Cameroon, and the western Central African Republic who did not believe in Islam. Bello welcomed Scottish traveler Hugh Clapperton into his domains in the mid-1820s. 'Umar ibn Sa'id Tal, the Senegalese apostle of the Tijaniyya Sufi religious brotherhood, lived at Bello's court from 1831 to 1838 and deeply impressed the aging sultan. 'Umar Tal married Bello's daughter, and the son from this union would succeed him as ruler of the Tokolor empire.

Bello had a large family, including at least 10 children: Aliyu Babba, Aliyu Karami, Abubakar, Mu'azu Ahmadu, Saidu, Ibrahim, Fodio, Muallayidi, Yusufu, and Khadijah. Bello developed close family ties with some of his friends as well. Gidado, Bello's best friend since their childhood, when the two boys had studied together, married Bello's sister, the famous writer Nanu Asma'u.

Bello's personal asceticism and his narrow interpretations of Sunni law would be an inspiration for 'Umar Tal once he launched his own revolutionary movement in the late 1840s and 1850s. Bello died in 1837 at his fortress of Wurno.

[See also Asma'u, Nana; Clapperton, Hugh; Kanemi, Muhammad al- ; 'Umar Tal; and Uthman Dan Fodio.]

BIBLIOGRAPHY

Boyd, Jean. The Caliph's Sister: Nana Asma'u 1793–1865: Teacher, Poet, and Islamic Leader. London: Cass, 1989.

Last, Murray. The Sokoto Caliphate. London: Longmans, 1967.

JEREMY RICH

Bellow, Bella (1945–1973), Togolese singer, was born Georgette Adjoavi Bellow in the town of Tsévié, near the Togolese capital of Lomé, on 1 January 1945. Her parents were both from immigrant families, as her father's family had come from Nigeria and her mother's family had come from Ghana. Bellow was one of seven children and the eldest daughter. Even when she was very young, her strong vocal skills drew attention. Bellow soon was called on to perform in various cultural and artistic events in her hometown. By 1950, she had moved to Lomé to attend primary school at the Catholic Notre Dame des Apôtres school. She finished her secondary education by passing her baccalaureate examinations in 1966 after having attending the Lycée Sokodé in central Togo and the Lycée Bonnecarrière in Lomé. Like so many young female singers of the 1960s, Bellow was deeply influenced by the legendary South African vocalist Miriam Makeba. As she performed in numerous recitals from 1963 onward, Bellow attracted an increasingly large following in Lomé. In 1965, she made her first recording, singing in French and Ewe. In the same year, she sang at the Beninese independence day celebrations. At the 1966 World Festival of Negro Arts in the Senegalese capital of Dakar, Bellow represented her country. After a brief stint in Abidjan, Ivory Coast, in 1967, where she received a certificate to become a secretary, Bellow chose to make music her full-time career.

The ambitious Togolese record producer Gérard Akueson met Bellow and decided to make her an international star. Bellow's former secondary teacher Paul Ahyi, a famous painter in his own right, set up a meeting between Bellow and Akueson. The producer put together songs that drew equally from Broadway, jazz standards, and West African popular music. Songs like "Zelie," "Bem-Bem," and "O Senye" featured Bellow's vocal skills and Akueson's sensibilities. Naturally, these songs were put out on Akueson's record label Akue. Bellow toured much of West and Central Africa, amazing audiences in Benin, Mali, Gabon, the Democratic Republic of the Congo, and Cameroon.

She regularly held concerts at the legendary Olympia Club in Paris, the city where she recorded much of her music. In the late 1960s, Bellow toured Greece, Yugoslavia, Germany, and the French Caribbean islands of Martinique and Guadeloupe. Her first album under the name Bella Bellow, *Rockya*, came out in 1969. Bellow played to an enormous crowd of many thousands of people at a concert in Rio de Janeiro in 1971.

By the early 1970s, Bellow also had formed a romantic relationship with Togolese judge Théophile Jamier-Lévy. When she took time off from her frenetic schedule to stay with her family, Akueson was upset to lose his star. By 1971, Bellow had chosen to break away from Akueson to better control her own career. She formed her own group, Gabada, named after a music style from her homeland. Her independent work mixed African American spirituals, Togolese songs, and bossa nova into a compelling and unique sound. She also recorded songs with the legendary Cameroonian jazz performer Manu Dibango. Many Congolese musicians also adored her work. She married Jamier-Lévy in January 1972. They had one child together the same year, Nadia Elsa.

Bellow's meteoric rise in popularity was cut tragically short. On 10 December 1973, Bellow was in her chauffeur-driven car traveling through the southern Togolese town of Atakpamé. Her car was involved in an accident, and the entire car was overturned. Bellow's head hit the pavement, and she had a fatal cerebral hemorrhage. She was buried in the Catholic cemetery of Lomé. Although Bellow's life had ended, her legacy lived on. Numerous West African singers such as Angélique Kidjo and Afia Mala considered Bellow to be a central influence on their own work. The Togolese 10,000 CFA bill (the highest denomination of Togolese currency) features her portrait, as does a postage stamp. On 10 December 2004, a major celebration of Bellow's life took place that included a women's soccer tournament and a concert.

[*See also* Kidjo, Angélique; *and* Makeba, Miriam Zenzi.]

BIBLIOGRAPHY

Web site dedicated to Bella Bellow, acessed 5 April 2010, http://lavraisfamille.skyrock.com/2.html.

Satchivi, Ekoué. "Bella Bellow: La pionière de la chanson togolaise moderne." *UFC Togo site*, accessed 5 April 2010, http://www.ufctogo.com/Bella-Bellow-La-pionniere-de-la-210.html.

Stewart, Gary. *Rumba on the River: A History of the Popular Music of the Two Congos.* New York: Verso, 2000.

JEREMY RICH

Bemba, Jean-Pierre (1962–), Congolese politician, was born on 4 November 1962 in the town of Bokada, located in the Nord-Ubangi Province of the Democratic Republic of the Congo. His mother died when Bemba was very young.

Bemba was the son of Jeannot Bemba Saolona, one of the wealthiest businessmen in Congo during the long reign of Congolese dictator Mobutu Sese Seko. Saolona profited from the ill-fated nationalization of many foreign-owned businesses, and eventually he ran his own television stations and airline companies. Saolona's SCIBE-Zaire firm, one of the largest companies in Congo during the Mobutu era in the 1970s and 1980s, employed over 10,000 people. Saolona sent his son to Belgium for his education at the age of six. Bemba attended primary school in Belgium. He then spent one year of secondary school at the Institut Boboto in the Congolese capital of Kinshasa during the 1973–1974 academic year. Bemba then returned to Belgium, where he received his secondary school diploma from the Institut Jean Bergman in the Belgian city of Liège. After his graduation from secondary school in 1980, Bemba enrolled in an economics progam at the Institut Catholique des Hautes Etudes Commerciales (ICHEC) in Brussels. Bemba graduated from ICHEC in 1986 with an undergraduate degree and a special certificate in economics in developing countries.

After finishing his time at ICHEC, Bemba returned to Congo to help his father run his array of enterprises. Bemba worked as an administrator for and then president of SCIBE-Zaire. This huge venture's diverse holdings included coffee plantations, a small fleet of planes and boats, and various import/export operations. From 1991 onward, Bemba also began to form his own companies. Among these firms were the Comcell cellular phone company, the Courier Express messenger business, and the SBZ Cargo air freight business. Eventually, Bemba branched into communications with the Canal Kin TV and the CCTV television companies. He also worked as a personal assistant to Mobutu in the early 1990s.

Bemba left his homeland for Belgium in 1997, just before Mobutu Sese Seko fled the country. Bemba chose not to stay in Kinshasa once Laurent-Désiré Kabila's AFDL rebel movement, backed by Rwanda, Uganda, and the United States, captured the capital. Bemba's family was closely tied to Mobutu, and one of his sisters had married Mobutu's son Nzanga. At his home in the town of Rhodes-Saint-Genèse near Brussels, Bemba began to plan his first foray into politics. Bemba already had close business contacts in Uganda, and he developed close ties to Congolese rebel movements aligned with the Ugandan government of Yoweri Kaguta Museveni. The Ugandan government had turned on Kabila's regime, and Ugandan military officers chose to support the Congolese rebels.

Bemba formed the Mouvement de Libération du Congo (MLC) in May 1998 under the aegis of the Ugandan military. Bemba allowed the Ugandan army access to valuable mineral resources in northeastern Congo in return for military and logistical support. Bemba also had his own considerable personal fortune to help fund his war with Kabila's government. He joined forces with an older rebel group, the Rassamblement Congolais pour la Démocratie (RCD), which had formed after the initial revolt began in the summer of 1998. The République démocratique du Congo (RDC; Democratic Republic of the Congo) was originally supported by Rwanda and Uganda, but growing tensions between the two countries and quarrels among RDC leaders led to the creation of two rival RDC wings: the pro-Ugandan RCD-ML and the pro-Rwandan RCD-Goma. Bemba's MCL became the dominant partner among the Congolese groups who partnered with Uganda. Bemba originally formed the RCD in the large eastern Congolese city of Kisangani but moved his headquarters several times, in part due to Kisangani's vulnerability, as it was on the fluctuating border between Ugandan and Rwandan spheres of influence.

Bemba soon entered into disputes with the RCD-ML leadership. Bemba's autocratic hold over the MLC had little room for the more divided RCD-ML group. The MLC profited from the departure of Chadian pro-Kabila troops in 1999 and occupied much of northern Congo all the way to the border of Congo-Brazzaville after a span of only a few months. Ugandan aid was crucial for the MLC. Unlike the RCD-ML, Bemba received more popular support for his claims of being a native son of Congo seeking to throw out the Rwandans and the allies from the Congo He also exploited nostalgia for the brutal Mobutu regime and went so far as to make Mobutu's home city of Gbadolite the headquarters of the MLC.

Bemba greatly profited from the war from 1999 to 2002, even as his soldiers committed rampant human rights abuses (as did all armed groups fighting in the Congolese war). He became a close associate of the notorious arms dealer Viktor Bout. The violence of the MLC spread across the northern border of the Central African Republic (CAR) in 2002, when CAR president Ange-Félix Patassé called on Bemba to help him stay in power. MLC troops committed rapes, robberies, and murder in the CAR capital of Bangui and in many rural locations. These abuses led to an indictment from the United Nations International Criminal Court (ICC), even as Bemba denied that the troops who engaged in wanton slaughter and theft were still under his command once they entered the CAR. By 2002, the MLC had been negotiating with the Kabila regime for several years.

The mysterious assassination of Laurent-Désiré Kabila in January 2001 and the new regime of Joseph Kabila created a new playing field for negotiations to end the revolts. Through a series of long and convoluted meetings mediated by South Africa and other countries, Bemba agreed to end the armed revolt of the MLC in return for a position of vice president of finance in the new coalition government in 2003. Bemba's decision to make a separate peace with Kabila before many other rebels allowed him to reposition himself as a politician rather than a military leader. Bemba ran for president against Kabila in the Congolese presidential elections of 2006 and proved to be a far more popular candidate than many had expected. He officially finished second in the first and second rounds to Joseph Kabila in an election rife with electoral fraud. Bemba became a major opposition figure, and the Kabila regime and Bemba's supports soon battled one another in Kinshasa in 2006 and 2007. Bemba fled Congo in April 2007 after being charged with rape and murder by the Kabila government, but he was arrested by Belgian police in May 2008 on the International Criminal Court (ICC) charges. In November 2010, he pleaded not guilty to five counts of war crimes and crimes against humanity at the ICC in The Hague.

[See also Kabila, Joseph; Kabila, Laurent-Désiré; Mobutu Sese Seko; Museveni, Yoweri Kaguta; and Patassé, Ange-Félix.]

BIBLIOGRAPHY

Prunier, Gérard. *Africa's World War: Congo, the Rwandan Genocide, and the Making of a Continental Catastrophe.* New York: Oxford University Press, 2008.

Reyntjens, Filip. *The Great African War: Congo and Regional Geopolitics, 1996–2006.* Cambridge: Cambridge University Press, 2009.

Turner, Thomas. *The Congo Wars: Conflict, Myth, and Reality.* London: Zed Books, 2007.

JEREMY RICH

Bemba, Sylvain Ntari (1934–1995), Congolese (Brazzaville) novelist, politician, musician, and journalist, was born in Simiti, the regional capital of Lekoumou, Congo, on 17 February 1934. Bemba had a wife named Yvonne, and together they had a son, Richard (date of birth unknown). Little else is known about his personal life.

Bemba lived in Brazzaville for most of his life, where he worked as a journalist for *La Semaine Africaine* (African Week), a weekly newspaper, for over thirty years. Bemba's contributions for *La Semaine Africaine* span the period from 1964 to 1995. He also began writing fiction in the form of short stories, many of which gained national exposure for their portrayals of "average" Congolese women and men. Bemba wrote in the French language, and his work has won numerous awards, including his acclaimed short story "Le chambre noir" (1963; The Black Room), which was named "Best New Literature" by the literary magazine *Evidence*. Bemba was also awarded the prestigious Grand Prix Littéraire d'Afrique Noir for his first novel, *Rêves portatifs* (1979; Portable Dreams).

The themes explored in Bemba's work include racial exclusion, double consciousness (as described by W. E. B. Du Bois in 1897), the loss of cultural memory, and classicism as experienced between Africa and the West. Bemba's writing reflects an era of burgeoning independence throughout Africa, and his themes connect with and were influenced by those of similar Marxist and socialist writing which was prevalent in Africa during the 1960s and 1970s. Writers such as Frantz Fanon, Chinua Achebe, Aimé Césaire, and many others influenced Bemba's writing. Bemba was a major player in Brazzaville's intellectual circles, and his writing ultimately led him into politics. He became a member of the Parti Congolese du Travail (PCT; Congolese Labor Party), and enrolled at the École Normale de Preparation aux Carriers Administratives in 1971. Bemba went on to become the minister of Information in 1973. In 1975, Bemba accepted the post of minister of Cultural Affairs, which was taken over in 1977 by Jean-Baptiste Tati-Loutard, the renowned poet. Bemba and Tati-Loutard became close friends, and Bemba's prose poem

77 Sanglots pour Negrecongo (1995; 77 Tears for Black Congo), written to Tati-Loutard and published posthumously in 1996, was a reflection on the decline of the political state of the Republic of the Congo.

Bemba produced four novels in total: the aforementioned *Rêves portatifs*; *Le soleil est parti à M'Pemba* (1983; The Sun Has Gone to M'Pemba); *Les dernier des cargonautes* (1984; The Last of the Cargonauts); and *Leopolis* (1985). Bemba's final novel is an allegory on the life of Patrice Lumumba, the first prime minister of the Congo, who was assassinated in 1961. Bemba's writing also includes many plays, some of which were produced for French radio. The Office de Radiodiffusion-Télévision Française, or ORTF, produced several of Bemba's plays, including *L'enfer c'est Orfeo* (1970; Hell Is Orfeo), which was also performed on stage by the Theatre National du Congo in 1972.

Bemba's plays continue to be produced on major stages from Paris to Brazzaville. The Congolese theater director, Serge Aliune Limbvani, has directed two of Bemba's plays for the French stage: *Noces posthumes de Santigone* (1994; Posthumous Nuptials of Santigone) and *Valse interrompue* (Waltz Interrupted), a play based on Bemba's short story "Le chèvre et la léopard" (1995; The Goat and the Leopard). In 1996 Limbvani took *Noces* on tour across Africa. In addition, Bemba participated in a prestigious Playwright-in-Residence program through the Festival International des Francophonies in Limoges, France. During this three-month residence, Bemba produced *Le bruit des autres* (1995; The Noise of Others), his last play.

Bemba was also a musician and studied traditional Soukous (rumba) music. Bemba performed in Paris with Matingou Tintina, another Congolese musician, in a group called Rumbamberos. Bemba also authored a book, *Cinquante ans de musique au Congo-Zaire, 1920–1970* (1984; Fifty Years of Music from Congo-Zaire), which is a detailed anthology of the Congo's important contributions to music, including a comprehensive study of Rumba music sung in the Lingala language. The book is often cited by ethnomusicologists studying Soukous. In addition, in 1975 Bemba contributed to a show presented on Radio Francaise, entitled *La rumba fantastique*.

One of Bemba's final efforts was a contribution to a conference in Brazzaville on "Magic and Writing in the Congo," with the surrealist writer and literary critic Annie Le Brun and Radovan Ivsic, the surrealist poet. Bemba delivered an invited paper, entitled "Games of Magic and Magic of Play in the Creation of Poetry and Fiction in the Congo" at the conference, on 31 May 1995. Soon after, his oeuvre was celebrated by a symposium at the Marien Ngouabi University in Brazzaville, where over twenty academics gathered to discuss his life and work.

During the rise of Laurent-Désiré Kabila in Congo during the mid-1990s, Bemba eventually withdrew his membership from the PCT. This move led to a loss of favor with Kabila's administration. Bemba began writing political commentary for *La Semaine Africaine*, under the pseudonym Yves Botto. Eventually, the onset of leukemia prompted his friend Jean-Baptiste Tati-Loutard to push for Bemba to be exiled to Paris in 1995, where he could seek medical treatment.

Bemba died of leukemia at Val de Grâce Hospital on 8 July 1995, at the age of sixty-one. Yvonne Bemba died in 1996, and Richard Bemba currently resides in Paris. Sylvain Bemba left a legacy of over ten plays, four novels, numerous short stories, and leading commentary on his country's musical history. His contributions provide a glimpse into the history of one African country in transformation, and the changing attitudes and long-lasting spirit with which the Congolese people supported and demanded that transformation. Bemba's literature continues to provide an enriching witness to over four decades of racism, revolution, and regeneration in the Congo.

[*See also* Achebe, Chinua; Césaire, Aimé; Fanon, Frantz; Kabila, Laurent-Désiré; Lumumba, Patrice Emery; *and* Tati-Loutard, Jean-Baptiste.]

BIBLIOGRAPHY

Banham, Martin, ed. *A History of Theatre in Africa.* Cambridge, UK: Cambridge University Press, 2004. Banham provides key information regarding African theater and discusses Bemba's work in particular.

Devesa, Jean-Michel. "Magie et écriture au Congo." *Cahiers d'Études Africaines* 35 (1995): 941–942. This article discusses Bemba's participation in the surrealist-focused conference on magic in the Congo.

Gugelberger, Georg M. *Marxism and African Literature.* London: Currey, 1985. Gugelberger glosses important themes, writers, and ideologies reflected in the 1960s, 1970s and 1980s in Africa.

Thomas, Dominic. *Nation-Building, Propaganda, and Literature in Francophone Africa.* Bloomington, Ind.: Indiana University Press, 2003. Thomas's book discusses the political involvement of intellectuals across Francophone Africa, touching specifically on Bemba's involvement in the Congo.

Wylie, Hal. "The Dancing Masks of Sylvain Bemba." *World Literature Today* 64 (1990): 20–24. Wylie discusses the theme of masks in Bemba's work.

SHANNON OXLEY

Ben Ali, Zine el-Abidine (1936–), president of the Republic of Tunisia (1987–2011), was born on 3 September 1936 in Hammam Sousse. As a militant student and youth organizer for the Neo-Dustur nationalist party, he was arrested by the French. Following Tunisian independence in 1956, the party rewarded his services by sending him to France for a military education. Upon returning to Tunisia, he embarked on a career in the national army, attaining the rank of general and director general of national security from 1977 until 1980. Following a posting as ambassador to Poland, he returned to the national security field in 1984. Ministerial level appointments followed, including National Security in 1985 and the Interior in 1986. His designation by President Habib Bourguiba as prime minister in October 1987 placed him first in line for the presidential succession. When a medical team declared Bourguiba incapable of fulfilling his duties, Ben Ali assumed the office on 7 November. The ailing and increasingly erratic Bourguiba's departure evoked a sense of relief among many Tunisians. Ben Ali stepped into his predecessor's twin roles of head of state and head of the Parti Socialiste Dusturien, now renamed the Rassemblement Constitutionnel Démocratique (RCD). The pledge to legitimize other parties raised hopes for the advent of a measure of political pluralism previously unknown in Tunisia.

Hedi Baccouche, who had helped ease Bourguiba out, became vice president of the RCD and prime minister. Press restrictions were relaxed; thousands of political detainees were amnestied; and exiled opponents of Bourguiba were encouraged to return. Because Ben Ali's national security background convinced him of the importance of not making martyrs of adherents of the Mouvement de la Tendance Islamique (MTI), he invited its representatives to join government officials, leaders of civil society, and the heads of the secular parties in deliberations to formulate a broad set of political principles in advance of new elections. This National Pact, which acknowledged the centrality of Tunisia's Arab and Islamic heritages, was unveiled on the first anniversary of the "Historic Change" that had brought Ben Ali to power. It established pluralism, respect for human rights, and guarantees of basic freedoms as methods of avoiding past political shortcomings. The pact presented the Islamists with their first opportunity to enter the political arena and, to conform to laws prohibiting religious terminology in political party titles, the organization became the Hizb al-Nahda (Renaissance Party). The authorities granted several of its demands, but withheld formal recognition, and thus prevented it from contesting the 1989 elections. To further reassure Tunisian secularists, Ben Ali vowed not to allow religious groups to erode the rights long guaranteed by the 1956 Personal Status Code.

Running unopposed, Ben Ali won 99 percent of the vote and his party swept every seat in parliament, much to the distress of al-Nahda, whose candidates secured 15 percent of the national vote as independents. Of the secular opposition parties that competed, only the Mouvement des Démocrates Sociales had an organization capable of mounting a meaningful campaign. Together, they garnered a mere 5 percent of the vote. The elections established the Islamists as a political factor second in importance only to the RCD. As the MTI leader Rashid Ghannushi left Tunisia in disgust, he fired a parting salvo, proclaiming that Islamists would no longer be content with seats in a multiparty parliament—whose creation they now doubted—but would seek to control such a body. Similar comments enabled Ben Ali to cast himself as the defender of a progressive, secular republic under threat from religious chauvinism and to meld his vision of constrained pluralism with a modified version of his predecessor's authoritarianism. This role brought him the support of Tunisians who wanted an Islamist government no more than they had wanted the earlier regime's autocracy. It also won the sympathy of the West.

Soon after the elections, Ben Ali revived a structural adjustment program adopted in 1986. Critics, including Baccouche, warned that an overhaul of such magnitude could purchase economic success only by aggravating social ills. He was fired and many opposition politicians were jailed for their protests, but the economic slide was arrested and a healthy growth rate achieved by the end of the decade.

Despite Tunisia's strong relationship with the West, Ben Ali refused to support the dispatch of a multinational force to the Arabian Peninsula following Iraq's invasion of Kuwait in 1990, insisting that intra-Arab problems required intra-Arab solutions. For a time, Tunisia paid dearly for its stance as tourism declined and the United States drastically slashed economic assistance and terminated military aid altogether until 1993. Crucial aid from the Gulf States was also severely curtailed. In the continuing absence of political opportunities, extremists within al-Nahda pushed the movement to turn against the government with a ferocity not seen since Bourguiba's last days. Judging the situation on the verge of spiraling out of control, Ben Ali ordered a crackdown.

The descent of Algeria into a vicious civil war pitting militant Islamists against the secular government beginning in 1992 deeply disturbed Tunisians. As they looked across their western border in horror, they endorsed, or at least did not oppose, harsh measures to rein in al-Nahda. In 1992, amid accusations of torture and other human rights abuses, hundreds of the organization's members were imprisoned, and some executed, for plotting a coup to pave the way for an Islamic state. Few outside the organization expressed reservations about the state's dealings with al-Nahda. In exchange for protection from the "green threat" of Islamic radicalism, many Tunisians turned a blind eye to excesses committed by the authorities. Leaders of other opposition parties contented themselves with the collapse of so formidable a rival as al-Nahda and, anxious to shield their own organizations from a similar fate, concealed whatever misgivings they may have had.

In any event, even after years of recruiting and organizing, no opposition party—nor any combination of them—could survive a confrontation with the government or hope to prevail in an electoral challenge to the RCD. As a result, they agreed to a new electoral law guaranteeing opposition parties crossing a low threshold of votes a proportional share of nineteen set-aside seats in parliament. In this way, Ben Ali cultivated the appearance of pluralism without providing the concept with substance, pitting the opposition parties against each other for a prize of dubious worth: their seats in the legislature assured them of a presence, but denied them the opportunity to have any impact. In the presidential election, not even the pretense of pluralism was advanced. The candidacy of the sole politician who came forward to challenge Ben Ali was rejected and he ran unopposed for a second term.

The RCD captured more than 90 percent of the total vote. The success of the campaign against the

Islamists, a growing economy, and discernible progress in alleviating some of the country's most severe social inequities enhanced the stature of the party and contributed to the magnitude of its electoral triumphs. Ben Ali surrounded himself with modern, well-educated technocrats who had carved out careers in the liberal professions, academia, and business, but real authority remained unquestionably with the president and a small coterie of trusted advisers.

Two critical questions now faced Ben Ali. Could the party sustain its popular support, particularly among a mushrooming middle class, without converting its contrived pluralist system into a more genuinely participatory arrangement, and was he willing to pursue such a transformational agenda? When, with al-Nahda silenced for the moment, the government turned on outspoken secular political opponents and human rights advocates, the answer was clear. During the latter half of the 1990s, the government continued to maintain the appearance of promoting pluralism even as it tightened its hold over the limited opposition that it allowed to function legally.

The 1999 elections produced predictable results. The usual group of opposition parties held a meaningless total of some thirty seats among them. In the 1999 presidential elections, Ben Ali did face opposition—albeit perfunctory—for the first time. The heads of political parties represented in the outgoing parliament were permitted to stand for the presidency, but the two who did mounted uninspired campaigns. Most opposition voters preferred to support Ben Ali's inevitable victory rather than to cast a vote for the leader of a rival party, giving the president 99.44 percent of the vote. Three years later Tunisians again went to the polls, this time for a constitutional amendment enabling Ben Ali to continue as president at the end of his third term in 2004. With 99.52 percent of those participating assenting, the election pattern prevailing since 1989 repeated itself, with inconsequential variations, in 2004 and 2009.

During much of Ben Ali's rule, Tunisia's strong economy contributed to neutralizing opposition to the RCD, but in December 2010 a wave of antigovernment demonstrations that had begun in the impoverished central region of the country spread to Tunis and other urban centers. Thousands protested the deteriorating economy, with its lack of jobs and opportunity, the harshly repressive nature of the Ben Ali regime, and the culture of government corruption believed to reach into the president's family and

closest associates. The authorities' attempts to end the demonstrations led to clashes between protestors and the police and gendarmerie in which scores of citizens were killed. Several days of turmoil culminated in the intervention of the army, which refused to fire on the crowds. Deprived of the ability to enforce his will, Ben Ali fled abroad, along with key members of his family. Prime Minister Mohammed Ghannouchi briefly assumed the presidency, but was soon succeeded by Fouad Mezbaa as interim chief executive. Ghannouchi's initial efforts to create a government failed when protestors objected to the inclusion of key figures from the discredited and already largely dismantled RCD and in early February 2011 he named a cabinet purged of such individuals. By then the Tunisian protests, labeled the "Jasmine Revolution" had helped to spark similar populist movements elsewhere in the Arab world, most notably in Egypt, whose longtime president Husni Mubarak, was toppled under similar circumstances in early February.

[See also Bourguiba, Habib; and Mubarak, Muhammad Husni Sa'id.]

BIBLIOGRAPHY

Camau, Michel, and Vincent Geisser. *Le syndrome autoritaire: politique en Tunisie de Bourguiba à Ben Ali*. Paris: Les Presses de la Fondation Nationale des Sciences Politiques, 2003.

Denoeux, Guilain. "La Tunisie de Ben Ali et ses paradoxes." *Maghreb-Machrek* 166 (1999): 32–52.

Dunn, Michael C. "The al-Nahda Movement in Tunisia: From Renaissance to Revolution." In *Islam and Secularism in North Africa*, edited by John Ruedy, pp. 149–165. New York: St. Martin's Press, 1994.

Geiser, Vincent. "Tunisie: des élections pour quoi faire? Enjeux et 'sens' du fait électoral de Bourguiba à Ben Ali." *Maghreb-Machrek* 168 (April–June 2000): 24–26.

Hermassi, Abdelbaki. "The Rise and Fall of the Islamist Movement in Tunisia." In *The Islamist Dilemma: The Political Role of Islamist Movements in the Contemporary Arab World*, edited by Laura Guazzone, pp. 105–127. London: Ithaca Press, 1995.

"Tunisia." In *North Africa: Development and Reform in a Changing Global Economy*, edited by Dirk Vandewalle, pp. 177–202. New York: St. Martin's Press, 1996.

Ware, Lewis B. "Ben Ali's Constitutional Coup in Tunisia" *Middle East Journal* 42 (1988): 587–601.

Wilmots, André. *De Bourguiba à Ben Ali: l'étonnant parcours économique de la Tunisie, 1960–2000*. Paris: Harmattan, 2003.

KENNETH PERKINS

Ben Barka, Mehdi (1920–1965), Moroccan anticolonialist leader, was born in Rabat. Although he was raised in a family of modest income, he managed to attend a French elementary school for children of notable families at the age of nine. In 1938, he graduated from Moulay Youssef High School in Rabat. He attended Algiers University in Algeria, where he graduated with a bachelor's degree in mathematics in 1942. He returned to Morocco and taught mathematics at Gouraud High School and then joined the teaching faculty at the Royal College. In *La mémoire d'un roi: Entretiens avec Eric Laurent*, the late King Hassan II, who was one of Ben Barka's students, described him as a man with "a vast knowledge, a charming personality, and a passionate nature" (p. 108).

The year 1935 marked the beginning of Ben Barka's involvement in the national movement for independence. He was the youngest member of the committee that drafted and signed a manifesto demanding full independence from France. This manifesto was submitted by the National Party to the French Resident General on 11 January 1944. With other party members, Ben Barka was arrested and jailed for signing that document, but after he was released from prison, he became an active member of the Istiqlal (Independence) Party and devoted himself entirely to the party's newsletter in both Arabic and French until early in 1951 when, upon the orders of General Alphonse Juin, who described him as "the most dangerous enemy of the French protectorate in Morocco," he was arrested, jailed, and deported from Rabat.

With Abderrahim Bouabid and Abderrahman Youssoufi, two influential figures in the national movement, Ben Barka played a major role in the creation in 1955 of UMT (Union Marocaine du Travail), a leading labor union in Morocco in the 1950s and 1960s. He was also a member of the Istiqlal Party delegation that met in a conference chaired by Edgar Faure, President of the French Council, at Aix-les-Bains in France to negotiate a solution to the political crisis between France and Morocco caused by the deposition of Moroccan sultan Mohammed V and his exile to Madagascar.

In 1956, the year the country gained its independence from France, Ben Barka was elected chairman of a national council (l'Assemblée Consultative), which was considered a first important step toward electoral life in the Kingdom of Morocco, but because of his avant-garde political views, he was stripped of all of his duties after the council was disbanded in 1959. In 1959, Mehdi Ben Barka, with Abderrahim Bouabid and Abdullah Ibrahim, spearheaded a left-wing movement inside the Istiqlal Party, known as the January 25th Movement, that led to the constitution of UNFP (Union Nationale des Forces Populaires), a party that based its political values on socialist principles.

Ben Barka's campaign for the liberation of North African countries and the unification of the Maghreb was made evident by his participation in the Tangier Conference, which brought together the Istiqlal Party, the National Liberation Front (FLN) of Algeria, and the Neo-Destour of Tunisia in 1958. When exiled from Morocco in 1960, he focused his attention on building ties between UNFP and other liberation movements in Arab and African countries as well as socialist parties in Europe. When exiled a second time, in 1963, he chaired a preparatory committee for a tri-continental conference representing countries from Africa, Asia, and Latin America that was planned to be held in Havana, Cuba, in 1966.

For his socialist and democratic views, Ben Barka faced persecution, including imprisonment, a death sentence, and exile. He was ready to return to his country when he was kidnapped, at age forty-five, by the French police in Paris in October 1965. Former Moroccan Interior Minister General Mohamed Oufkir, who was accused of plotting this kidnapping and assassination, was tried by a French court in absentia and received a life sentence. Known as "L'affaire Ben Barka," this political assassination caused a huge scandal for the Moroccan and French authorities. The circumstances surrounding the assassination of this man still remain unresolved.

The name of Mehdi Ben Barka aligns itself with the names of political and union leaders like Patrice Lumumba, Félix Moumié, Amílcar Lopes Cabral, Che Guevara, and Salvador Allende in the struggle for independence and democracy in developing countries in Africa, Asia, and Latin America. Today Mehdi Ben Barka is a major political icon in Morocco, and he is fondly remembered at international meetings in his home country and abroad. For example, in October 2005 an international congress was organized in Paris to commemorate the fortieth anniversary of the kidnapping and assassination of Ben Barka.

[*See also* Mohammed V.]

BIBLIOGRAPHY

Ben Barka, Bachir, coord. *Mehdi Ben Barka en héritage: de la Tricontinentale à l'altermondialisme*. Paris: Editions Syllepse, 2007.

Ben Barka, Mehdi. *Ecrits politiques 1957–1965 (Political Writings)*, translated by Bachir Ben Barka. Paris: Editions Syllepse, 1999.

Laurent, Eric, ed. *La mémoire d'un roi: Entretiens avec Eric Laurent*. Paris: Editions Plon, 1993.

LAHCEN EZZAHER

Ben Bella, Ahmed (1916–), Algerian anticolonial leader and politician, was born on 25 December 1916 in the town of Maghnia in western Algeria. His family was relatively affluent, and he was the youngest child of five boys and several girls.

Although Ben Bella's father was a practicing Muslim, Ben Bella himself never managed to master Arabic. He attended primary schools in Maghnia and graduated in 1930. Ben Bella was a phenomenal football (soccer) player at school, and he seriously considered becoming a professional athlete. However, he ended up joining the French army and served in numerous campaigns during World War II. His bravery and skill made him a legend in his own unit, and he eventually reached the rank of Sergeant Major. At the Battle of Monte Cassino in Italy, he carried his wounded company commander 1500 yards to safety and then took charge of the company. Charles De Gaulle, his future nemesis, awarded Ben Bella the Médaille Militaire. Despite his impressive resume, the French military refused to accede to Ben Bella's request to become a commissioned officer at the end of the war.

Future disappointments awaited Ben Bella once he returned to Algeria in 1945. The French military, with the aid of European settlers, launched in May 1945 a bloody crackdown on Algerian protesters in Sétif and other cities that opposed the deportation of nationalist party leader Messali Hadj. The new French Fourth Republic's decision to continue a political system that greatly favored European settlers over the vast majority of Berber and Arab people further alienated Ben Bella. A local French official engineered the confiscation of Ben Bella's father's land, and Ben Bella became a fugitive after he shot the Arab to whom the official had awarded Ben Bella's family's property. He joined Hadj's illegal Parti Populaire Algérien (PPA) and joined a

Ahmed Ben Bella. Ben Bella, right, with Cuban Premier Fidel Castro, Havana, Cuba, 1962. (AP Images)

small nucleus of radical young men who felt the independence of their country would require a violent revolution. The aging Hadj had no control over this tiny group, the Organisation Secrète (OS), which began to organize armed robberies to raise money in the late 1940s.

On 4 April 1949, Ben Bella led a robbery in a post office in Oran that netted the OS 3 million francs (worth roughly 20,000 USD), which was then used to buy weapons. In 1950, French police officers captured Ben Bella, and he received a long jail sentence. Ben Bella escaped jail in 1952 by cutting through his prison window bars with a knife that had been smuggled into the jail in a loaf of bread. He then escaped to Egypt, where he was granted sanctuary by Arab nationalist leader Gamal Nasser. In Cairo, he met other political exiles such as Hocine Aït Ahmed and Mohamed Boudiaf. They were among the first members of the Front de Libération Nationale (FLN), a group of young nationalists tired of the failures and divisions that impeded Hadj's party, now known as the MTLD (Mouvement pour le Triomphe des Libertés Démocratiques). A series of meetings in France, Switzerland, and Algeria that included Ben Bella in the spring and summer of 1954 prepared the commencement of the FLN's war against France on 1 November 1954.

When the war began, Ben Bella headed the FLN's leadership outside of Algeria in Egypt and Tunisia. He skillfully called for a diplomatic effort that tied military actions with an internationalization of the conflict. In particular, Ben Bella hoped to draw in the United Nations and Arab nations to force France to abandon the war. He had difficulty retaining his leadership position, especially as FLN commanders actually fighting in Algeria competed with the exiled FLN for control over the war and the organization. Ben Bella was not invited to the Soummam Congress in August 1956 that brought together FLN leaders in Algeria. Even worse for Ben Bella, French military units in October 1956 intercepted a plane in neutral waters carrying Ben Bella and other members of the original founders of the FLN. Ben Bella spent the rest of the war in a French jail cut off from the FLN.

When the Évian Accords brought an end to the war in the spring of 1962, Ben Bella's long period of isolation proved to be an advantage. In the summer of 1962, he teamed with FLN military commander Houari Boumedienne to defeat the GPRA (Gouvernement Provisionel de la République Algérienne) section of the FLN, which claimed to be the movement's governing body. His increasingly

authoritarian policies alienated many veterans of the nationalist struggle, such as Ferhat Abbas, who resigned from the government in 1963. The new 1963 constitution gave Ben Bella greatly increased powers as president, much to the dismay of parliamentary representatives. Ben Bella approved a misguided border conflict with Morocco in the fall of 1963.

The exodus of most European settlers from Algeria in 1962 and the confiscation of their property by the Algerian government furnished Ben Bella with a very effective means of rewarding supporters and punishing critics, although the confused implementation of this land reform program limited its effectiveness. Some of his former comrades in the FLN, especially those associated Berber communities, launched guerilla warfare to challenge Ben Bella, but his supporters in the military crushed these threats. Likewise, the Algerian military put down a failed coup attempt in 1964 led by Colonel Mohamed Chaabani. Ben Bella purged many former associates from his inner circle and became convinced that his old ally Boumedienne aspired to replace him as the head of Algeria. Boumedienne removed Ben Bella from power on 19 June 1965 and kept him under house arrest.

Ben Bella was only freed in 1979 after Boumedienne died. He moved to France and formed the Movement for Democracy in Algeria (MDA) opposition party in exile in 1984. In 1990, he was allowed to return to Algeria and ran for president in the 1992 elections, which were ultimately annulled by the military and the FLN. By this point he was viewed rather as an elder statement than a true leader. During the civil war in Algeria during the 1990s, Ben Bella rejected the political Islamic Front Islamique du Salut and Groupe Islamique Armée movements. Ben Bella continued to have a high profile in international affairs in the early twenty-first century, as demonstrated by his role as a defense counsel during the trial of former Iraqi dictator Saddam Hussein in 2005.

[*See also* Boumedienne, Houari; Hadj, Messali; *and* Nasser, Gamal Abd al-.]

BIBLIOGRAPHY

Merle, Robert. *Ahmed Ben Bella*. Translated by Camilla Sykes. New York: Walker and Co., 1967.

Naylor, Phillip C. *The Historical Dictionary of Algeria*. 3d ed. Lanham, Md.: Scarecrow Press, 2006.

Ruedy, John. *Modern Algeria: The Origins and Development of a Nation*. Bloomington: Indiana University Press, 1992.

Stora, Benjamin. *Algeria, 1830–2000: A Short History.* Translated by Jane Marie Todd. Ithaca, N.Y.: Cornell University Press, 2001.

JEREMY RICH

Bendjedid, Chadli (1929–), Algerian political leader, was born on 14 April 1929 in the town of Bouteldja located near the port city of Annaba. His father was a small landowner who was able to provide his son with a primary school education in Annaba. However, the family had relatives in Tunisia, and it appears Bendjedid grew up in a relatively cosmopolitan household.

Bendjedid joined the French military after World War II and served in Vietnam. He reached the rank of noncommissioned officer and was back in Algeria when the Front de Libération Nationale (FLN; National Liberation Front) anticolonial armed movement launched its armed struggle against French rule on 1 November 1954. By early 1955, Benjdedid joined the armed wing of the FLN, where he rose in the ranks. He was promoted to regional commander in 1956 and assistant commander in 1957. He suffered serious wounds in combat in 1957, but survived. Bendjedid became a protégé of FLN military leader Houari Boumedienne and served with him in the Ghardimaou region of Tunisia. He became a friend of FLN military officer Tahar Zibri during the war as well, although later he strongly opposed Zibri's failed effort to seize power after independence in December 1967. Boumedienne named Bendjedid to the general staff of the FLN's northern military zone.

Bendjedid kept a low profile politically during the war as numerous internal fissures emerged within the FLN, but he remained very loyal to Boumedienne's clique of military and political leaders based in western Algeria and Morocco. He proved his value to Boumedienne immediately after the Évian Accords in the spring of 1962, when Boumedienne and his ally Ahmed Ben Bella launched a military strike against dissident FLN members. FLN guerillas inside Algeria had rejected the idea that FLN army units outside the country led by Ben Bella should be the leaders of the new country. Although Bendjedid was briefly arrested by FLN guerillas, he was freed by troops who supported Ben Bella. Ben Bella and Boumedienne rewarded Bendjedid for his loyalty by granting him military command over Oran in June 1964 after he briefly supervised the withdrawal of French troops from the Constantine region. Bendjedid crushed a rebellion by FLN dissidents in the summer of 1964, backed Boumedienne's coup against Ben Bella in 1965, and then battled Zibri's troops in 1967. Bendjedid accompanied Boumedienne on a state visit to Morocco in the same year. Once Morocco occupied the former Spanish colony of Western Sahara in1975 and Algeria chose to back the Polisario rebel movement in this region, Bendjedid's duties in Oran included surveillance of the Moroccan-Algerian border.

All in all, nothing in his past career suggested that Bendjedid would become a major force in Algerian politics. In a 2008 interview, Bendjedid claimed that he had never aspired to become Boumedienne's successor in 1978. He was shocked to learn that Boumedienne, who was diagnosed with a rare terminal blood disorder in that year, decided to name Bendjedid as his heir as he neared death. Some observers contend that Boumedienne's decision to elevate Bendjedid over the course of 1978 also arose from Bendjedid's connections with Kasdi Merbeh, the head of Boumedienne's dreaded Sécurité Militaire (SM) secret police. When Boumedienne died in December 1978, military and civilian leaders of the FLN negotiated for several months before Bendjedid won their approval to be become president of Algeria on 7 February 1979. Bendjedid was considered to be trustworthy by rival factions in the Algerian leadership precisely because of his low profile under Boumedienne.

Bendjedid was president of Algeria until 1992. Under his authority, the Algerian government abandoned the command economy model favored by Boumedienne in favor of promoting Western investment. The Algerian government brokered the end of the US hostage crisis in Iran, and Bendjedid was the first Algerian leader to visit France since independence. Bendjedid tried to defuse the long Western Sahara crisis with limited success. He broke up some major nationalized industries. In 1979 and early 1980, Bendjedid tried to present himself as a more democratic figure by liberating formerly influential political prisoners like Ben Bella and Ferhat Abbas and by seemingly rejecting efforts to promote the Arabic language at the expense of Berber communities. When some Berber protesters demanded further reforms, though, Bendjedid showed no qualms in sending in the army to brutally put an end to the unrest. The FLN over the course of the 1980s became even more dominated by the military and less ideologically focused than it was under Boumedienne.

The oil profits that had allowed the Algerian state bureaucracy to provide jobs to young people and patronage to potential dissidents dried up with the drop of oil prices in the mid-1980s. Workers launched numerous strikes beginning in 1985. Students protested the lack of democratic reforms, and promoters of a Muslim political state following the teachings of the Muslim Brotherhood actively criticized the secular and corrupt Algerian government. On 4 October 1988, rumors of a general strike and the combined frustration of many Algerians with the status quo led to a major series of riots. Bendjedid called on the SM and the army to crush these riots, which they did in an extremely violent way. The wave of disapproval about this crackdown forced Bendjedid to promise a move toward democratic elections. He authorized a new constitution in 1989, ended the FLN single-party state, and legalized the religiously oriented Front Islamique du Salut (FIS) political party as well as other political parties.

However, the military still wished to ensure its control over the supposed transition to democracy. This proved to be a serious problem by 1991. The rising popularity of the FIS, renewed displays of discontent from Berber communities, and the flagging fortunes of the FLN demonstrated by the resounding defeat of the ruling party in the December 1991 legislative elections spelled major problems for Bendjedid. Army leaders annulled the 1991 elections, which led FIS members to challenge the government. The same military elite forced Bendjedid to resign in January 1992. He kept relatively quiet during the bloody Algerian civil war of the 1990s but began to claim he was a democratic pioneer after the war ended in 2002. Many Algerians blamed him for preparing the country for civil war.

[*See also* Abbas, Ferhat; Ben Bella, Ahmed; *and* Boumedienne, Houari.]

BIBLIOGRAPHY

Evans, Martin, and John Phillips. *Algeria: Anger of the Dispossessed*. New Haven, Conn.: Yale University Press, 2007.

Naylor, Phillip C. *The Historical Dictionary of Algeria*. 3d ed. Lanham, Md.: Scarecrow Press, 2006.

Stone, Martin. *The Agony of Algeria*. New York: Columbia University Press, 1997.

Stora, Benjamin. *Algeria, 1830–2000: A Short History*. Translated by Jane Marie Todd. Ithaca, N.Y.: Cornell University Press, 2001.

JEREMY RICH

Benjelloun, Omar (1934–1975), Moroccan anticolonial leader, was born in a remote, small village in the region of Oujda, a major city on the border with Algeria. He was raised in a low-income family. He attended elementary school and high school in Oujda, where he met Abdelaziz Bouteflika, later the president of Algeria.

When Benjelloun graduated from high school in 1955, he moved to Rabat, the capital city of Morocco, to study at the Scientific Institute. In Rabat he met leading members of the national movement for independence such as Mohamed Elyazghi, who is currently a key figure in the USFP (Union Socialiste des Forces Populaires). At the end of his first year in college, which coincided with the year the country gained its independence from the French Protectorate (1956), Benjelloun, who chose to follow a career in the postal service and communication, seized an opportunity to get into a two-year training program at the French national school of communication (École Nationale de Communication) in Paris. In Paris, he engaged in rich intellectual and militant student activities; he met students of different nationalities, which allowed him to create a strong network of relations that culminated in the formation of AEMNA (Association des Etudiants Musulmans Nord-Africains), an association of Muslim students from North Africa, of which he was president. This association helped provide financial and emotional support to students from the Maghreb. As president of the AEMNA, Benjelloun attended an executive committee meeting of the International Student Association in Prague. Benjelloun also studied law at the Law School (Faculte de droit) in Paris.

In 1960, after he had graduated with a college degree in postal services and communication, Benjelloun went back to Morocco and was appointed associate regional director at the postal service in Casablanca. This new position paved the way for him to experience new political challenges and circumstances that made him a strong union leader. He first joined the Moroccan labor union UMT (Union Marocaine du Travail) but soon broke away from it and was one of the principal founders of CDT labor union (Confederation Democratique du Travail), the political action of which was based on socialist principles. His labor union activities, which were behind a series of strikes in many public sectors in the country, forced authorities in Casablanca to move him away from a growing labor union class in this major industrial and commercial city to Rabat, where he was appointed a regional director of the postal service. However, Benjelloun remained in close contact with his fellow party members in Casablanca, for he presided over local party meetings in several parts of the city.

In 1963, Benjelloun and several of his fellow party members were arrested and accused of an armed attempt to overthrow the monarchy. Benjelloun, Fqih al-Basri, and Mehdi Ben Barka, who was not in the country, received the death sentence.

Benjelloun was also known among his companions and Palestinian friends as "Omar the Palestinian" for his unwavering support of the Palestinian cause, especially after the 1967 war. He was instrumental in the creation of the newspaper *Palestine*, the first of its kind in the Arab world in those years.

Omar Benjelloun also practiced law. He joined a team of defense attorneys to defend students, workers, farmers, war veterans, teachers, and engineers who were accused of an armed attempt to overthrow the monarchy during the famous Marrakesh trial in 1971.

On several occasions, Benjelloun was arrested, tortured, and put on trial and sentenced to maximum penalties, including two death sentences. He escaped several assassination attempts, including one in 1973 when he received in the mail a parcel that had explosives in it. He was then chief editor of *al-Muharrir* and *Liberation*, the two official daily newspapers of the USFP.

Omar Benjelloun was an influential figure in the Moroccan left-wing political movement in the 1960s and 1970s, for he was a leading member of a militant student union known as UNEM (Union Nationale des Etudiants Marocains) and of UNFP (Union Nationale des Forces Populaires), a key opposition party in the history of Morocco. He was also an outspoken labor union leader known among students, workers, and intellectuals for his populist views, for he called for the establishment of a democratic state based on socialist principles. He was assassinated in Casablanca on 18 December 1975. According to Marvine Howe, a historian of the Islamic movement in Morocco, members of the Combatants of the Maghreb (al-Moujahidoun al-Maghariba), an extremist organization known for its fierce opposition to Marxist-Leninist views, are believed to have carried out the assassination. This organization had links with former college professor and Islamic revolutionary Abdelkrim Moutii, who is now in exile in Libya.

[*See also* Ben Barka, Mehdi.]

BIBLIOGRAPHY

Abu Yahda, Mohamed. *Ash-Shahid Omar Benjelloun: Awwalu Dahaya al-Irhab ad-Dini bi'l-Maghrib. (The Martyr Oman Benjelloun: The First Victim of Religious Terrorism in Morocco.)* Casablanca: Manshurat al-Ahdath al-Magribiyya, 2005.

Ghallab, Abdelkrim. *Tarikh al-Haraka al-Wataniyya fi 'l-Maghrib. (History of the National Movement in Morocco.)* Vols 1 & 2. Casablanca: 1976.

Howe, Marvine. *Morocco: The Islamist Awakening and Other Challenges.* New York: Oxford University Press, 2005.

LAHCEN EZZAHER

Ben Jelloun, Tahar (1944–), Moroccan writer, was born on 1 December 1944 in Fez, Morocco. His father was a merchant, and his mother an illiterate housewife whose life is narrated in his *Sur ma mère* (2008; On My Mother). Both parents were devout Muslims whom Ben Jelloun credited for creating a nurturing environment. After attending the local

Tahar Ben Jelloun, 2004. (AP Images/John Cogill)

Qur'anic school until the age of six, Ben Jelloun received a bilingual French-Arabic education in a Franco-Moroccan elementary school. In 1955, his family moved to Tangier. Ben Jelloun's secondary schooling was mostly French; he attended the Lycée Regnault, the oldest French high school in Morocco. After receiving his high school degree in 1963, he studied philosophy at the Muhammad V University in Rabat.

Morocco's post-independence history was marked by the Lead Years (1960s–1980s), a period of severe political repression that spanned most of King Hassan II's reign. Suspected of having organized student demonstrations in 1965, Ben Jelloun was drafted into compulsory military service in what he described as an army-run disciplinary camp in 1966. This is where he wrote his first poem, "L'Aube des dalles" (The Dawn of the Paving Stones), published in 1968 in *Souffles* (*Breaths*), the influential avant-garde literary journal founded in 1966 by poet Abdellatif Laâbi, which played a pivotal role in Moroccan letters and culture before being banned in 1972. This led to the publication of Ben Jelloun's first collection of poetry, *Hommes sous linceul de silence* (1971; Men Under a Shroud of Silence), by a press directed by Laâbi.

Upon his release in 1968, Ben Jelloun finished his studies and obtained his first teaching position as the first philosophy teacher at Charif Idrissi High School in Tétouan. In 1970, he was transferred to Mohamed V High School in Casablanca. Following Morocco's policy of Arabization post-independence, Ben Jelloun was notified that the teaching of philosophy would be conducted in standard Arabic effective fall 1971. While Ben Jelloun, a native speaker of the Moroccan Arabic dialect, read and wrote standard Arabic, he did not master the latter sufficiently to make it a language of instruction (nor of creative writing). Therefore, Ben Jelloun went to France. Some events of the first part of his life are recounted in the semiautobiographical *L'écrivain public* (1983; The Public Scribe).

In 1972, Ben Jelloun published his first article in the renowned French daily newspaper *Le Monde*, in the book review section, and became a regular contributor for the newspaper. Throughout the years, he wrote book reviews and opinion pieces on contemporary issues linked to the Arab-Muslim world and its diaspora, such as the Palestinians' plight, the French headscarf affair, the Persian Gulf War, the Algerian civil war, and immigration and racism in France. His regular contributions to *Le Monde* extended to Spanish and Italian newspapers starting in the 2000s.

His first novel, *Harrouda* (1973), his most hermetic text, was noted by prominent writers, including Roland Barthes and Samuel Beckett, and most importantly initiated his friendship with Jean Genet, who asked to meet him in 1974. Ben Jelloun subsequently recounted his friendships throughout his life in *La soudure fraternelle* (1994; Fraternal Welding or Praise of Friendship), and devoted one book to his relationship with Genet in *Jean Genet, menteur sublime* (2010).

In 1975, he obtained his doctorate in social psychiatry at the University of Paris VII. His thesis on the "emotional and sexual problems" of North African workers in France was later published as *La plus haute des solitudes* (1977; The Highest of Solitudes), after the manuscript was rejected by many Parisian presses, as immigration was far from a popular topic at the time. This and another essay, *Hospitalité française* (1984; French Hospitality), as well as the novels *La réclusion solitaire* (1976; Solitaire), *Les yeux baissés* (1991; With Downcast Eyes), *Les raisins de la galère* (1996; The Grapes of Hardship), and *Au pays* (2009; A Palace in the Old Village), constitute Ben Jelloun's take on the situation of North African immigrants and their children in France, as well as the ensuing racism and Islamophobia they encounter. Following the 1998 publication of his bestseller, *Le racisme expliqué à ma fille* (Racism Explained to My Daughter), prompted by his daughter Mérième's questions, he has been regularly invited to speak in schools. However, another essay in the same series, *L'Islam expliqué aux enfants* (2002; Islam Explained to Children), and Ben Jelloun's support for the 2004 French law forbidding the Muslim headscarf in public schools, suggest Ben Jelloun's limitations in his role as spokesperson and mediator between France and its Muslim population.

While his novel *L'enfant de sable* (1985; The Sand Child) was shortlisted for the Prix Goncourt, the most prestigious French literary prize, its sequel, *La nuit sacrée* (The Sacred Night), was awarded the prize in 1987, making Ben Jelloun the first Maghrebian writer to be a recipient and establishing his international renown. The prize brought him recognition that extended to Maghrebian literature in general, at a time when France was witnessing the increased popularity of the right-wing Front National political party and its anti-immigrant stance.

Ben Jelloun went back to Morocco and lived in Tangier with his family from 2006 to 2009, then returned to Paris. He had four children with his wife Aicha. One of them, Amine, was born in 1991 with Down syndrome and inspired the poem "Amine, mon fils trisomique." In 2007, he joined a Human Rights Watch committee. In 2008, he was elected to the Académie Goncourt, the jury that awards the prize by that name.

A prolific and versatile writer, Ben Jelloun published collections of poetry, short stories, novels, essays, children's books, and plays and collaborated on photo books. While there is a notable shift in his fiction from the complex postmodern early novels to the more realist later texts, Ben Jelloun's work overall privileges marginalized characters and focuses on the violence of exploitation and repression (be it gendered, sexual, economic, racial, or political), and draws references from both the Western and Arabic cultural traditions.

Despite the renown and prizes, including the International IMPAC Dublin Literary Award for *Cette aveuglante absence de lumière* (2000; *This Blinding Absence of Light*), his acclaim is not universal, as his work has been criticized by some as being a self-Orientalizing caricature of Moroccan society. Nevertheless, with some of his works translated in forty-three languages, Ben Jelloun is the most prominent Francophone North African writer in France, and the most internationally known.

[*See also* Hassan II.]

BIBLIOGRAPHY

Aresu, Bernard. *Tahar Ben Jelloun*. New Orleans, La.: Dept. of French and Italian, Tulane University, 1998.
"Ben Jelloun, Tahar." http://www.taharbenjelloun.org.
Ben Jelloun, Tahar. *Moha le fou, Moha le sage*. Paris: Seuil, 1978.
Bourget, Carine. "9/11 and the Affair of the Muslim Headscarf in Essays by Tahar Ben Jelloun and Abdelwahab Meddeb." *French Cultural Studies* 19:1 (February 2008): 71–84.

CARINE BOURGET

Benneh, George (c. 1935–), Professor Emeritus of Geography and Resource Development, University of Ghana, received his elementary education at Berekum Catholic Primary School from 1941 to 1949 and continued to Achimota Secondary School for the period of 1950 to1956. In 1957, he was one of four students who won the Shell Ghana Independence Scholarship and was subsequently admitted into the University College of Ghana in October of the same year to study for a bachelor's degree in geography. Upon completion of his degree program, he taught geography briefly at the Achimota School, and in October 1961 he left for the London School of Economics to pursue his postgraduate education. Benneh obtained his Doctor of Philosophy (PhD) in 1964.

In 1964 he was appointed lecturer in the Department of Geography at the University of Ghana. He became a senior lecturer in 1973, an associate professor in 1976, and a full professor in 1989. He was appointed Vice Chancellor of the University of Ghana in 1992 and retired in 1996. Before then he was the head of the geography department and senior tutor of Commonwealth Hall, dean of the faculty of Social Studies, director of a population impact project funded by the United States Agency for International Development (USAID), and Pro-Vice Chancellor, all at the University of Ghana.

His focus as an academic has been on population, poverty alleviation, environment, and land tenure and management. He has published over thirteen books and booklets and seventy other publications in the fields of geography, environment, land tenure and land use, population, education, and public administration. His books include *New Geography of Ghana, Sustainable Food Security in West Africa,* and *Sustaining the Future: Economic, Social and Environmental Change in Sub-Saharan Africa,* among others.

Professor Benneh also taught at other institutes and universities across the globe, including the University of Copenhagen; University of Pittsburgh; University of Michigan; University of Birmingham, UK; and University of New England, Australia. He was appointed the first rector of the Catholic University of Ghana in 2001, but could not assume duties due to ill health. He was also a member of the New York Academy of Science, Fellow of the Ghana Academy of Arts and Science, and a member of the European Academy.

Benneh was a member of numerous boards and committees both internationally and locally. He also consulted for many organizations including the World Bank; the United Nations Food and Agriculture Organization; the Economic Commission for Africa; the United Nations Educational, Scientific and Cultural Organization; and the United Nations University. He was Chairman of the Board of Directors of the Bank of Ghana, an external member of the Council of the University of Swaziland, and Chairman of the Experts Advisory Board on Population, Environment and Agriculture, one of six expert groups formed to make recommendations to the preparatory committee for the conference on population and development in 1994.

He received the United Nations Global 500 award at the first Earth Summit in Rio De Janeiro, Brazil, and was adjudged man of the year in 1997 by the American Biographical Institute. Professor Benneh was awarded an honorary doctor of letters degree by the University of Ghana, Legon, in recognition of his contributions as a teacher, researcher, and administrator to the development of the university in particular and the country as a whole.

Benneh was not solely an academic during his active years. In order to realize his desire to connect academic research and the development of the individual and society at large, he took up political appointments as a way of influencing policy making in Ghana. He was commissioner for Lands, Natural Resources, Fuel and Power and later minister for Lands, Natural Resources, Fuel and Power (1979–1981) and minister for Finance and Economic Planning (1980–1981).

Benneh was a distinguished academic who had as his guiding principle the desire to transform the worldview of people through research designed to solve societal problems, build institutions, and mentor the leadership that brings change to society. In recognition of his principles, some of his former students and colleagues and alumni of the University of Ghana established the George Benneh Foundation (GBF) to foster these ideals.

BIBLIOGRAPHY

Agbodeka, Francis. *A History of University of Ghana: Half a Century of Higher Education (1948–1998).* Accra, Ghana: Woeli Publishing Services, 1998.

Biographical profile of Emeritus Professor George Benneh: Retrieved on 07/07/10 from http://gbfghana.org/biography.html.

Mingle, Edmund. "George Benneh Foundation Launched." *The Ghanaian Times,* December 11, 2006.

SAMSON AKANVOSE AZIABAH

Bensouda, Fatou (1960–), lawyer, politician, and Deputy Prosecutor of the International Criminal Court (ICC) in The Hague, was born Fatou Bom Nyang in Banjul, Gambia. Her father, Omar Gaye Nyang, was a government driver and Banjul's most renowned wrestling promoter; a sports arena in the city was named after him. She attended the Gambia High School, and then studied law at the University of Ife, Nigeria, from 1982 to 1986, and the Nigeria Law School in 1986 and 1987. She was called to the

bar in Nigeria and the Gambia in 1987. She obtained an MA in Maritime Law from the United Nations International Maritime Organization (IMO) Institute.

Bensouda is an experienced prosecutor, having served as a public prosecutor, state counsel, and senior state counsel before her appointment as Deputy Director of Public Prosecutions of the Gambia. She was also Solicitor General and Legal Secretary of the Gambia from 1996 to 1998. While at the Justice Department, she represented the Gambia in many international legal negotiations, such as the formation of the Economic Commission of West African States (ECOWAS) Tribunal. She led the Gambia's delegation at the Preparatory Commission for the ICC. She also sat on the board of the African Centre for Democracy and Human Rights Studies (ACDHRS) based in Banjul, the Gambia, and served on the Governing Council of the Gambia Committee on Harmful Traditional Practices (GAMCOTRAP), a leading women's rights organization in the Gambia.

From 1998 to 2000, she was Gambia's Secretary of State for Justice and Attorney General (now called Minister of Justice and Attorney General), the second woman to hold the post. In this capacity, she earned the admiration of human rights groups for promoting the speedy prosecution of offenses against children and women. Between 2000 and 2002, she worked as a banker and in private legal practice in the Gambia. From 2002 to 2004, she worked at the International Criminal Tribunal for Rwanda (ICTR) in Arusha, Tanzania, as senior trial attorney, and won recognition for her zealous prosecution of those charged with rape of and violence against children.

Bensouda rose to international prominence following her election in September 2004 as Deputy Prosecutor of the ICC in charge of prosecutions. She was chosen over two other candidates, from Fiji and New Zealand. Her previous advocacy for the rights of women and children, her experience in dealing with civil organizations during her time as a prosecutor, and her fluency in French worked in her favor. At the ICC she has been instrumental in the prosecution of major cases, such as those against Congolese warlords Jean-Pierre Bemba and Thomas Lubanga. Fatou also made several fact-finding missions to Guinea-Conakry following the 2009 massacre of opposition demonstrators protesting against military rule.

In 2009, she was presented with the prestigious International Jurists Award for her contributions to the field of criminal law. She has described her election as the ICC's Deputy Prosecutor as a "victory for the Gambia and African women as a whole." Fatou is married to Phillipe Bensouda, a Gambian businessman of Moroccan descent.

[*See also* Bemba, Jean-Pierre.]

BIBLIOGRAPHY

"The Gambia's Legal Export." *The Independent* (Banjul), November 19–21, 2004.

Hughes, Arnold, and David Perfect. *Historical Dictionary of The Gambia.* 4th ed. Lanham, Md.: Scarecrow Press, 2008.

HASSOUM CEESAY

Ber, Sonni Ali (d. 1492), king of the sultanate of Songhai, was born sometime in the early decades of the fifteenth century. He ascended to the throne of the kingdom of Songhai in 1464. In the previous century, Songhai had been a vassal of its larger neighbor to the west, Mali, but Ber's immediate predecessors had reestablished Songhai's independence, and ruled from the city of Gao on the Niger River. Another form of his name is Sunni Ali Ber.

Ber was a tremendous military strategist. He developed a large fleet on the Niger, amassed a large army of slave warriors, and was the head of one of the most skilled and fearsome cavalry units in West Africa in his lifetime. Soldiers on horseback patrolled the entire kingdom, and often surprised Ber's numerous political enemies. Ber launched numerous invasions of territories to the west and south. When Umar, the Tuareg governor of Timbuktu, insulted Ber in a bellicose letter apparently intended to intimidate the Songhai leader, Ber chose to respond in 1467 by threatening to send an army to the gates of the famous center of trade and scholarship. The Tuareg sultan Akilu, whose family had captured Timbuktu from the old Malian kingdom several decades earlier, dismissed Umar to appease Ber. Umar then promptly swore loyalty to Ber and offered to support him against Timbuktu. In January 1469, Ber's troops arrived in Timbuktu, sending the city into a panic. Akilu fled to the Sahara, while Umar provided Ber's troops with boats to cross the Niger River and enter the city. Ber executed many of Umar's political enemies.

The Songhai sultan then turned his attention to Djenne, a major West African trade center located, like Timbuktu, on the Niger River. Over the course of the 1470s, Ber defeated a series of Peul-speaking leaders and finally added Djenne to his conquests

in 1477. Then, he forced Akilu and his successive Tuareg leaders into submission over the course of the late 1470s and early 1480s. Ber was the master of the western reaches of the southern Sahara by 1484. He authorized expeditions against Dogon communities and others that had never submitted to Mali. Naserre, the leader of Mossi-speaking communities that had long raided westward, was defeated by Ber in 1483 near Djenne.

Ber was an extremely controversial figure among his contemporaries and later generations of historians. He honored water spirits and various other spiritual beings as part of the indigenous religious practices of the Songhai people, even as he claimed to be a true believer in Islam. Oral traditions among the Songhai people collected in the nineteenth and twentieth centuryies praised Ber for his bravery and his unparalleled supernatural powers. His mother was an initiate to power associations that honored spirits. He tried to show respect for Muslim scholars, and was said to have commonly told his court, "Without Islamic scholars the world would cease to be good." Nearly all the sources about Ber from his lifetime were written by Muslim scholars, who found his religious views appalling. However, some inscriptions from Songhai previously neglected by scholars indicate that some Muslim scholars flourished during his reign, and that Timbuktu-based scholars writing after Ber's death may have radically edited their portrayals of the Songhai leader in ways that neglected the complexity of his relationships with both Muslims and indigenous spiritual traditions. Writers in Timbuktu considered Ber to be a false Muslim and a tyrant, however, and accused him of interfering with Muslim marriage laws.

Sonni Ali Ber drowned in the river Niger River on 6 November 1492. His son Sunni Ber, who assumed leadership upon his death, was overthrown by Muhammad Ture soon afterwards.

[*See also* Muhammed Ture.]

BIBLIOGRAPHY

Farias, P. F. de Moraes. *Arabic Medieval Inscriptions from the Republic of Mali: Epigraphy, Chronicles, and Songhay-Tuareg History.* Oxford: Oxford University Press, 2003.

Hunwick, John O., ed. *Shari'a in Songhay: The Replies of al-Maghili to the Questions of Askia al-Hajj Muhammad.* Oxford: Oxford University Press, 1985.

Kaba, Lansine. "The Pen, the Sword, and the Crown: Islam and Revolution in Songhay Reconsidered,

1464–1493." *Journal of African History* 25, no. 3 (1984): 241–256.

JEREMY RICH

Berhanu Zerihun (1933/4–1987), prolific Ethiopian writer in Amharic and journalist, was born in Gondar the son of a Christian Orthodox priest, Zerihun Mersha. Raised in a strict Orthodox manner, but in a happy family, he entered a church school at age 7. As a child he was not interested in sacred texts and devoted much of his spare time to reading new Ethiopian "secular" books. At age 12 he decided to go to a state school despite the extreme disapproval of his father; Zerihun Mersha relented after Berhanu had run away to seek education. Berhanu finished the eight-year elementary course in only four years (1947/8–1951/52). His first poem about a corrupt judge was published at this time in the newspaper *Yezareitu Ityopya (Today's Ethiopia)*.

Having successfully completed elementary school, Berhanu enrolled in the Addis Ababa Technical School. Alongside his studies, he was an editor of a school magazine and regularly contributed to newspapers like *Addis Zemen, Yezareitu Ityopya*, and *YeErtra Demts*.

After graduating in 1955/6, Berhanu worked for a year as assistant shop master at the Technical School and subsequently at the Mapping and Geography Institute for two years. He never ceased writing for newspapers, mostly for *Yezareitu Ityopya*. At this time he started to earn his living by writing. From 1959/60 to 1960/1 he was a deputy editor of *Yezareitu Ityopya*. In 1961/2 he became editor-in-chief of *Voice of Ethiopia*, and in 1963/6 editor of *Addis Zemen*. In 1966/7 he published a review of a book about the Emperor Tewodros II by Abbie Gubenna. In his review, he held that it did not matter whether Tewodros had been of royal blood but whether he was a good king. This position contradicted the Constitution, which stated that the Emperor *should* be of the ancient Ethiopian royal line, a fact that Berhanu allegedly did not know or more likely just ignored. He was tried, fined, and subsequently dismissed from his position as editor.

During his career as a journalist, Berhanu was a prolific writer. Among his first books were *Hulet Yeemba Debdabewoch* ("Two Letters of Tears") (1959/60); *Del keMot Behuala* ("Victory after Death") (1962/3), which dealt with the Sharpeville massacre in South Africa; and *Yebedel Fetsamie* ("The Fulfillment of Crime") (1964/5), which dealt with prostitution in Ethiopia. In 1965/6 he published *YeTewodros Enba* ("Tewodros's Tears"), which was well received and garnered multiple positive reviews.

Berhanu was reinstated as the editor of *Addis Zemen* after the revolution of 1974. In 1977/8 he was arrested for political reasons, since *Addis Zemen* did not reflect the political line of the government. After nine months in detention Berhanu was released and appointed editor of the magazine *Yekkatit*. In 1979/80 he was appointed editor of the international magazine *World Marxist Review*. After the revolution of 1974, Berhanu started writing a three-volume opus, *Maebel* ("The Flood") (Vol. 1, 1974; Vol. 2, 1980/1; Vol. 3, 1981/2). It was a political work—in fact, one of the first revolutionary novels in Ethiopia. It dealt with the problems of Ethiopian population, the inequities of the old regime, and the prospects of socialist development. All three volumes of *Maebel* were subsequently read on the radio.

Berhanu also wrote plays, among them "Moresh" (Codename, Password), which was staged by the National Theatre, and "Tatennyaw tewanay" ("The Troublesome Actor") in 1982/3, which was performed at the Hager Feqer Theatre. His play "Abba Nefso" (1977 Ethiopian Calendar) was dedicated to the famous Ethiopian patriot *qennazmach* (military commander) Balcha Safo. His last novel, *YeTangut Mestir* ("Tangut's Secret"), was published in 1986/7.

Berhanu began to suffer health problems in the early 1980s and died on 24 April 1987; he was buried in Trinity Cathedral in Addis Ababa. Despite his Marxist ideology, he "wanted to die as an Orthodox Christian" and he never "looked upon Marxism as a form of religion but only a solution for social development" (Molvaer, 1997, pp. 336–337).

Berhanu rejuvenated Ethiopian literature by introducing his own literary style, consisting of brief, clear sentences, at a time when an elaborate literary style was in fashion. His literary manner is sometimes referred to as *berhanigna*, i.e., "the language of Berhanu."

[*See also* Tewodros II.]

BIBLIOGRAPHY

Balashova, Galina. "Berhanu Zaryehun." In *Encyclopaedia Aethiopica*. Vol. 1, pp. 538–539. Wiesbaden: Harrassowitz, 2003. Includes detailed and comprehensive information about Berhanu's publications.

Gerard, Albert S. *Four African Literatures: Xhosa, Sotho, Zulu, Amharic*. Berkeley: University of California Press, 1971.

Kane, Thomas L. *Ethiopian Literature in Amharic.*
Wiesbaden: Harrassowitz, 1975.

Molvaer, Reidulf K. *Black Lions: The Creative Lives of
Modern Ethiopia's Literary Giants and Pioneers.*
Lawrenceville, N.J.: The Red Sea Press Inc., 1997.

MAXIM ZABOLOTSKIKH

Beyala, Calixthe (c. 1961–), francophone novelist,
was born in Douala, Cameroon, the sixth of twelve
children. Separated from her parents at an early
age, Beyala was brought up by her grandmother in
the New Bell district of Douala. She was educated
at the Camp Mboppi primary school in Douala and
then at the Lycée des Rapides à Bangui and the
Lycée Polyvalent de Douala. At the age of seventeen, Beyala left Cameroon for Paris, where she
completed the baccalaureate. Beyala had two
children, a son and a daughter, with the French
husband whom she later divorced. After her divorce,
she lived in Spain and Corsica, before returning to
Paris in the 1980s. Before becoming a professional
writer, Beyala had a number of different jobs,
including working as a florist and a model.

A prolific writer, Beyala's first novel, *C'est le soleil
qui m'a brûlée* (The Sun Hath Looked Upon Me),
was published by a Parisian publisher, Stock, in
1987. In 1992, Beyala moved to the commercially
more successful, mainstream Paris publishing
house Albin Michel, who commissioned *Le petit
prince de Belleville* (1992; Loukoum: The "Little
Prince" of Belleville) and its sequel, *Maman a un
amant* (1993; Mom Has a Lover).

On signing with Albin Michel, Beyala quickly
became a bestselling author in France and one of a
very small number of francophone African authors
to make a living from writing fiction. Beyala has
won numerous literary prizes, particularly for her
early novels, including the Grand Prix Littéraire de
l'Afrique Noire (1993), the Prix François Mauriac de
l'Académie Française (1994), the Prix Tropique
(1994), the Grand Prix du Roman de l'Académie
Française (1996), and the Grand Prix de l'Unicef
(1997). Three of Beyala's novels have been published
in English translation: *The Sun Hath Looked Upon
Me*; *Your Name Shall be Tanga*; and *Loukoum: The
"Little Prince" of Belleville*. The scope of Beyala's fiction is vast, ranging from the erotic fiction of
Femme nue, femme noire (2003; Naked Woman,
Black Woman) to a novel based on Robert Mugabe's
land reforms (2005; *La Plantation* [The Plantation]).
The best-known works are those published in the
1990s and set in the multiethnic neighborhood of
Belleville in Paris.

Despite her unprecedented success, the reception
of Beyala and her writings has been extremely
mixed, not only in France but also in Africa, the US,
and the UK. Among other things, she has been
labeled a plagiarist, a loudmouth, a pornographer,
and a man-hater. In 1997, her fellow Cameroonian
author, Mongo Beti, published a damning article in
the journal *Palabres*, in which he condemns Beyala
as a self-serving, overly ambitious writer lacking in
talent. Mongo Beti's article was written in the wake
of the events of 1996, when the controversy surrounding Beyala reached a peak: in May 1996, Beyala
was accused and found guilty of plagiarism. Charged
in the High Court in Paris with having plagiarized
Howard Buten's *Burt* in her novel *Le petit prince de
Belleville*, Beyala and Albin Michel were ordered to
pay Buten's publisher substantial damages plus additional costs. That same year, in November, Pierre
Assouline, editor of the French literary magazine
Lire, publicly accused Beyala of having committed a
second offense of plagiarism, claiming that she had
had borrowed heavily from Ben Okri's *The Famished
Road* in her novel *Les Honneurs perdus* (1996; Lost
Honors), which had just been awarded the prestigious Grand Prix du Roman de l'Académie Française.
Although Okri and his publisher chose not to pursue
the allegations, Assouline's campaign received considerable attention in the French press, generating
what became known as "l'Affaire Beyala" (the Beyala
Affair). Beyala subsequently satirized this episode
in her novel, *La petite fille du réverbère* (1998; The
Little Streetlamp Girl), in which she makes a thinly
veiled attack on Pierre Assouline through the ana-
grammatically named character, "Riene Poussalire"
(Nothing Makeshimread).

By the end of the twentieth century, Beyala was a
familiar face in the media in France. Despite the
negative attention she had received for her plagiarism, Beyala was making regular appearances on
talk shows on French television and radio. She was
also beginning to attract the French public's attention as a political activist, most notably in her role as
president of Collectif Egalité, the French black rights
movement she founded in 1998. In 1999, the Collectif
experienced considerable success in drawing the
French public's attention to the lack of black faces or
"visible minorities" on French television. A 1999
meeting with Hervé Bourges, then president of the
national broadcasting regulatory body, the Conseil
Supérieur de l'Audiovisuel (CSA), eventually led, in
May 2000, to a revision of the French terrestrial TV
channel remits to reflect the multiculturalism of
France. On 19 February 2000, Beyala, along with

Guadeloupean actor and director Luc Saint-Eloi, showed up uninvited to the twenty-fifth annual César ceremony (the French equivalent of the Oscars) to read a statement from Collectif Egalité on the lack of black actors in French films.

In 2001, Beyala's political ambitions took a new turn when she decided to stand for Secretary General of the Organisation internationale de la Francophonie, a position eventually filled by former Senegalese President Abdou Diouf. Beyala's political interests are reflected in her writings of this period, most explicitly in her two book-length essays, *Lettre d'une Africaine à ses soeurs occidentales* (1995; Letter from an African Woman to her Western Sisters) and *Lettre d'une Afro-française à ses compatriotes* (2000; Letter from an Afro-French Woman to her Compatriots).

In 2007, Beyala gained further notoriety with the publication of *L'Homme qui m'offrait le ciel* (2007; The Man who Promised Me the Moon), a novel allegedly based on her failed relationship with the well-known, married, French television presenter Michel Drucker. In May 2009, Beyala sued Drucker, claiming that he had failed to pay her 200,000 euros, which she was due for ghostwriting an unpublished book of interviews with the French philosopher Régis Debray. Beyala's case was thrown out of court, however, and she was ordered to pay Drucker the symbolic sum of one euro in damages.

[*See also* Mongo Beti; Mugabe, Robert Gabriel; *and* Okri, Ben.]

BIBLIOGRAPHY

Beyala, Calixthe. *Loukoum: The "Little Prince" of Belleville*. Translated by Marjolijn de Jager. Oxford: Heinemann, 1995. English translation of *Le petit prince de Belleville*, first published in 1992.

Beyala, Calixthe. *The Sun Hath Looked upon Me*. Translated by Marjolijn de Jager. Oxford: Heinemann, 1996. English translation of *C'est le soleil qui m'a brûlée*, first published in 1987.

Beyala, Calixthe. *Your Name Shall Be Tanga*. Translated by Marjolijn de Jager. Oxford: Heinemann, 1996. English translation of *Tu t'appelleras Tanga*, first published in 1988.

Hitchcott, Nicki. *Calixthe Beyala: Performances of Migration*. Liverpool, UK: Liverpool University Press, 2006.

NICKI HITCHCOTT

Beyene Haile (1941–), avant-garde Eritrean novelist, playwright, and painter-cum-sculptor, was educated in Eritrea, Ethiopia, and at the American University of Beirut, Lebanon, from which he graduated in 1963 with a degree in public administration and political science. Beyene Haile lived in Addis Ababa until Eritrean independence. In 1992, he moved to Asmara, where he worked as a management consultant and trainer while still pursuing his artistic career.

Beyene Haile is the author of three Tigrinya-language novels and a play. His 1965 debut novel, *Abidu' do Teblewo?* (Madness) differs from conventional Tigrinya writing in at least three fundamental ways. First, it takes an intellectual and artist as its main character, and tells his story with compelling force and narrative skill. Wounded by life, the central character of the novel, a bohemian artist called Mezgebe, uses his art to heal his wounds and those of others in a manner that borders on insanity. Another experimental and innovative element of the novel is its narrative structure. In sharp contrast to the literary convention of its day, the book begins with the "end," and moves forward and backward chronologically through flashbacks, images, and repressed and activated memories, as we see the protagonist striving to make sense of his life, which, for him, is synonymous with his work. Considering that Tigrinya literature at that time was entrenched in the mode of verisimilar linear narrative, this was quite revolutionary. Another significant element of *Madness* was the introduction of new concepts into Tigrinya. The genre of the novel, for example, came to be viewed as more than just narrative, and words such as "art" and "aesthetics" have become associated with it. The book also taught its readers that telling a story was a pleasure, but writing a novel also required dedication, ability, and hard work.

Beyene Haile's second novel, *Deqwan Tebereh* (2003; *Tebereh's Shop*) is, in a sense, an artistic and intellectual re-articulation of *Madness*. Like *Madness*, it is narrated using stream-of-consciousness and features artistic characters. But it also opens up new technical possibilities and thematic frontiers. It opens with the monologues of two writers, one dead, one living. In addition to the "association of ideas" device, it also uses magical realism and collage-like imagery to carry and coalesce the stories of different characters, some of whom are supernatural beings who move about freely in time and space, relating Eritrean history in an epic manner.

At the technical and narrative levels, the book is woven together with embedded stories that overlap each other; it too is packed with long, unpunctuated, breathless sentences, as well as dialogue, plays within the text, endless philosophical and psychological probing, and many learned allusions, which seem to converse with both African and Western authors and manuscripts. For this reason, the novel has generally been regarded as a "difficult" read. Indeed, as the author asserts through one of his characters, the novel's intricate, and sometimes intentionally opaque, parts are meant to be understood "like a song the meaning of which you don't understand but still like" (*Tebereh's Shop*, p. 50). Thematically, *Tebereh's Shop* deals with Eritrean independence, and particularly with the role and responsibility of intellectuals in the post-independence era.

The novelist's luminous experimentalism with ideas, narrative ingenuity, and linguistic density is repeated in his third novel, *Titsbit Bahgu* (2006; *Setting the Bar*). Sharing recurring themes with *Tebereh's Shop*, the primary concerns of *Setting the Bar* include the discovery of truth through the art of writing, the post-border-war crisis in Eritrea, and the role of intellectuals in society. But the novelist's voice, ridiculing of the nation's intelligentsia, is also heard in this novel, eliciting once again disparate reactions of endorsement and controversy among readers, while at the same time enhancing the writer's image as the young nation's *enfant terrible*.

Considered the most experimental novelist in Eritrean literature to have used (post-)modernist techniques in the tradition of Joycean "stream-of-consciousness," Beyene Haile is primarily known in Eritrea as a writer of great skill and philosophical depth; he has acquired cult status as a literary and intellectual guru. Intellectuals—and members of the intelligentsia generally—are depicted in his works as a group endowed with the capacity to act as agents of historical and social change in Eritrean postcolonial society, although a particular section of that group, which he calls *qelem-qemes* (pseudo-intellectuals), is treated with striking contempt and vilification. Though of undisputed talent, Beyene Haile's seemingly obsessive attacks on the intellectual class—and especially on the *qelem-qemes*—while taking a procumbent stance toward government, has raised questions in some readers, while others have criticized him for literary elitism.

BIBLIOGRAPHY

Dhar, Tej. "A Conversation with Beyene Haile." *Journal of Eritrean Studies*. 4: 1 & 2: (2005): 167–176.

Negash, Ghirmai. "A Great Novel in a 'Small' Language: Representations of the African Intellectual in the Eritrean Novel Tebereh's Shop." *Research in African Literatures* 40:3 (2009): 1–15.

Negash, Ghirmai. *A History of Tigrinya Literature*. 2d ed. Trenton, N.J.: Africa World Press, 2010.

Tesfalul, Abraham, Haile Bizen, and Elias Amare. Readings on *Titsbit Bahgu (Setting the Bar)*. Asmara, Ambasoira Hotel. Book Launch, December 22, 2006.

GHIRMAI NEGASH

Bhêly-Quénum, Olympe (1928–), Beninese journalist and writer, was born Codjo Agblo Tchikoton Marc Eustache Olympe Bhêly-Quénum in the southern Beninese town of Ouidah on 20 September 1928. He came from a very influential aristocratic Fon family, and his father was married to a number of wives: Bhêly-Quénum was the eleventh of his father's thirty children. His mother was a skilled trader. Bhêly-Quénum's maternal grandmother was a well-respected priestess in the *vodoun* indigenous religious tradition. Bhêly-Quénum's uncle Maximilien Quénum was a well-educated intellectual and ethnographer, even though his nephew's defense of *vodoun* never persuaded his staunchly Catholic relative. His paternal grandfather was a powerful political figure in the late nineteenth century.

Sometime in the early 1930s, his family increasingly called him Olympe. After completing his primary studies in Benin, he traveled to Nigeria and then Ghana. Bhêly-Quénum attended the Achimota Grammar School in Accra, where he mastered English. The London-based Unilever company hired Bhêly-Quénum to work as an assistant manager in economic capital of Benin, Cotonou, on account of his language skills. Bhêly-Quénum, however, had far grander ambitions than a career as a clerk. He wished to move to France, receive an advanced education, and become a writer. His mother supplied him with some money to supplement his savings.

In August 1948, Bhêly-Quénum arrived on the docks of Marseilles, a new arrival to France. He briefly considered moving to Aix-en-Provence, but he moved to Normandy instead. The following year, he met the famous surrealist André Breton by chance in Paris, and the much older Breton recommended that Bhêly-Quénum write down his dreams. He passed the first part of his baccalaureate examinations and received some notoriety for his athleticism. Bhêly-Quénum was the runner-up for the French championship in the high jump event in 1952. The Académie de Caen awarded him a scholarship to conduct research on palm oil production in French West Africa. He moved to Brittany and completed his baccalaureate examinations. After being rejected by the École Normale Supérieure d'enseignement technique, Bhêly-Quénum enrolled at the University of Caen. He eventually received a license to teach French, Greek, and Latin. Eventually, Bhêly-Quénum obtained an undergraduate degree from Université de Paris IV–Sorbonne in sociology and anthropology. In 1958, he received a teaching position in the Parisian suburbs. Bhêly-Quénum became an active observer of the political and literary intrigues of African intellectuals in France in this period, and this milieu inspired several of his later short stories and novels.

With the advent of Beninese independence in 1960, Bhêly-Quénum commenced a new career. Hubert Maga, president of Benin from 1960 to 1963, invited Bhêly-Quénum to become a diplomat on behalf of his homeland. Bhêly-Quénum received training as a diplomatic from the Institut des Hautes Études d'Outre-Mer, where his instructors included Edgar Faure and other well-known French politicians. He worked at several French consulates in Italy. However, Bhêly-Quénum ultimately preferred writing to diplomacy. Gabriel d'Arboussier, the Senegalese ambassador to France in the early 1960s, convinced Bhêly-Quénum to become the editor-in-chief of the magazine *La vie Africaine* in 1962. Financial problems and political disputes led to the closing of this journal in 1964. Bhêly-Quénum and his French-born wife Maryvonne ran another magazine, *L'Afrique actuelle*, from 1964 to 1968.

Bhêly-Quénum wrote prolifically. In 1960, he published his first novel, *Un piège sans fin* (Snares Without End). This novel was unusual for its time in its lack of openly political themes as it describes the life of a poet and musician who eventually kills his wife out of jealousy. Bhêly-Quénum included symbols and concepts from *vodoun* spirituality in this tragedy. His second novel, *Le Chant du lac* (The Song of the Lake) was an immediate sensation in West African literature after it was published by the renowned Présence Africaine literary enterprise in 1965. Ironically, given Bhêly-Quénum's later views about *vodoun*, *Le Chant du lac* viewed West African spirituality as an obstacle to social and political development. His 1968 collection of short stories, *Liaison d'un été et autres récits*, included an early story based on the dream that so interested Breton and an interracial romance that had a much more optimistic perspective on race relations than one might expect in the late 1960s. Interracial romance again was the central theme in 1979's *L'initié*. This novel explores how a West African doctor manages to reconcile his Western training with his knowledge of African spirituality after he returns home from France.

After a long hiatus from publishing, Bhêly-Quénum again wrote a series of stories and novels in the 1990s. His relative silence in the 1980s derived from his work for UNESCO (the United Nations Educational, Scientific and Cultural Organization). Once he retired from this position, he returned to literary endeavors. 1994's *Les appels du vodún* was a novel closely based on the beliefs and personalities of his extended family set in the late nineteenth and early twentieth century. Bhêly-Quénum had lived in southern France for decades, where he and his wife raised five children, but he still supported Benin's fledgling democracy. Even after he passed the age of 80, he remained a vocal observer of African affairs. In March 2009, Bhêly-Quénum wrote an open letter to Beninese president Thomas Boni Yayi in which he severely criticized his leadership and expressed his disappointment with the lack of tangible change in the dire poverty of Benin. Bhêly-Quénum also defended the value of *vodoun* against Yayi and other Beninese Pentecostal Christians who viewed these beliefs as demonic. Sharp distinctions between religious traditions hardly suited the author, as he boasted of being a Catholic, a Freemason, and a supporter of *vodoun* at the same time. He also mocked French president's Nicholas Sarkozy's ill-advised Dakar speech in 2007 in which the French leader claimed Africa had no history. He countered Sarkozy's complaint that there were more African doctors in France than in their home countries by noting how so many intellectuals of African descent had served France and lived in Europe for many decades. His career of over half a century has made him a giant of Beninese literature.

[*See also* Arboussier, Gabriel d'; Maga, Coutoucou Hubert; *and* Yayi, Thomas Boni.]

BIBLIOGRAPHY

Bhêly-Quénum, Olympe. Personal Web site, accessed 2 April 2010, http://www.obhelyquenum.com.

Huannou, Adrien. *La littérature béninoise de langue française.* Paris: Karthala, 1984.

Little, Roger. "The 'Couple Domino' in the Writings of Olympe Bhêly-Quenum." *Research in African Literatures* 29, no. 1 (1998): 66–86.

Malela, Buata. *Les écrivains afro-antillais à Paris (1920–1960): Stratégies et postures indentitaires.* Paris: Karthala, 2008.

JEREMY RICH

Bhunu (1876?–1899), king of Swaziland also known as Mahlokohla, who took the royal name Ngwane V, was born around 1876 to King Mbandzeni and Queen Labotsibeni Mdluli of Swaziland. Born at a time when British- and Dutch-descended Boer invaders were seeking to occupy the Swazi people's land, he was given the name Bhunu (Boer) because of his temper, which the Swazi people associate with Boers. In 1881, his father, Mbandzeni, invited Reverend Joel Jackson to start a mission school at Luyengo (uSuthu Mission) for Bhunu, but the young heir did not go to school. When his father died in 1889, Bhunu was fourteen years old and chosen to be his father's successor. He was not chosen because of his own credentials, but because of the character and credentials of his mother, Labotsibeni. To avoid bloodshed over the throne, the British and Transvaal governors showed the Swazi people their new king on 3 June 1890. His name as king was Ngwane V. Bhunu's capital was in Zombodze, his mother's home, but for administrative purposes he set up his own village at Ezabeni.

Bhunu ruled at the most difficult time in the history of the Swazi people. He started to rule just after the country was affected by the rinderpest (cattle plague) outbreak that lasted from 1894 to 1898 and depleted the main asset and wealth of the Swazi people, cattle. About 90 percent of the cattle in Swaziland died. His ruling time also coincided with the beginning of the Second Anglo-Boer War. He had a reputation as a headstrong ruler. Bhunu liked drinking and was often violent as a result, which, coupled with his strong-willed nature, made him unpredictable. As was tradition with each king, he founded a regiment for men of his age group and called it Ingulube. It was during his reign that the first European town, Bremersdorp (today called Manzini) was established and the questionable concessions granted to Europeans by Mbandzeni came to be regarded as legal and valid.

The relationship between Bhunu and his mother Labotsibeni was not a good one, and it turned into a state crisis when Labotsibeni's chief *indvuna* (minister), Mbhabha Nsibandze, was murdered on the night of 2 April 1898. The king was suspected of the killing. The matter was reported to the Commissioner for Swaziland, appointed by the Republic of South Africa, Johannes Krogh, whom the Swazi people called Nkoseluhlaza. To avoid confrontation with the Boers, Bhunu went with a small band of his warriors to some British men in Zululand. The British agreed to deal with the matter and argued with the Boers that they had no right to try a native king. Bhunu returned to his country after the Boers agreed to conduct a token trial and the British were assured of his safety. He was summoned to appear before Krogh on May 14, but he did not go until a week later on May 21. When Bhunu appeared he was accompanied by 2,000 of his warriors in full regimental regalia, whistling and singing their war songs. The Swazi people did not appreciate seeing their king treated like a commoner and therefore were ready for war. Bhunu denied any role in the murder and thereafter went to live with his regiments in Mampondweni in the Mdzimba mountain range. News leaked from those close to him that Bhunu wanted to declare war on the Boers, who could not dislodge him from his hideouts. Swazi elders reminded Bhunu of the warning by his great grandfather Sobhuza I not to harm white men. They were successful in persuading him to come out. He underwent an enquiry and was finally ordered to pay a fine of £1,646 for permitting violence.

In April 1899 Bhunu was invited by President Stephanus Johannes Paul Kruger to visit Pretoria. He went with about 1,000 of his warriors and his interpreter, Mattys Grobler. While there, Bhunu contracted with concessionaire Mattias J. Globelaar to supply Swazi labor for the Johannesburg mines at £10 per head. This was interrupted by the Anglo-Boer War, as all Europeans had to leave the country. On a return journey from Eshowe, Bhunu saw and liked Lomawa Ndwandwe, the daughter of Ngolotjeni of Zikhotheni. She later became his wife and bore him a son, Mona, on 22 July 1899. Bhunu died at the age of 23 years on 10 December 1899 during the Incwala Ceremony, leaving behind six widows with one child each. He was buried near his father at Mdzimba Mountain. His four-month-old son Mona was declared his heir and would reign in his own right as Sobhuza II starting in 1921, following the regency of Labotsibeni.

[*See also* Kruger, Stephanus Johannes Paulus; Labotsibeni; Sobhuza I; *and* Sobhuza II.]

BIBLIOGRAPHY

Booth, Alan R. *Historical Dictionary of Swaziland.* 2d ed. Lanham, Md.: Scarecrow Press, 2000.

Grotpeter, John J. *Historical Dictionary of Swaziland.* Metuchen, N.J.: Scarecrow Press, 1975.

Jones, Huw M. *A Biographical Register of Swaziland to 1902*. Pietermaritzburg, KwaZulu-Natal: University of Natal Press, 1993.

Matsebula, J. S. M. *A History of Swaziland*. 3d ed. Cape Town: Longman, 1987.

BETTY SIBONGILE DLAMINI

Biayenda, Émile (1927–1977), Congolese Roman Catholic cardinal, religious leader, and martyr, was born in the Lari village of Mpangala in the Congolese district of Kindamba. His mother Biyela and his father Sémo named him Biayenda, "the lost treasures" in Kikongo, to honor the early deaths of Biyela's parents. The couple had three children before Biyela's death, one of whom would later be executed by firing squad. Ultimately, Sémo married another woman, and Biayenda remained close with his half-brothers, including the poet Maxime N'Debeka.

Biayenda began his primary studies at Pangala in 1935 and then continued his education at the Catholic Mission School of Kindamba from 1937 to 1942. Léon Lebanitou, a schoolmate of Biayenda, recalled how serious the future cardinal was as a boy and how he concentrated on praying rather than playing soccer. Another former classmate remembered how Biayenda washed peanuts with soap before cooking them for a group of missionaries, since he assumed no European would want to eat grilled peanuts like the rural Congolese people did. After completing two years at the school of the Catholic mission of Boudji from 1942 to 1944, he felt a vocation for the priesthood. He attended seminary at Mbamou and Brazzaville from 1944 to 1958. During his studies, Biayenda attracted attention because of his empathy for others. For example, he volunteered to carry a heavy wet sack of sand for another student who had been punished with this task for talking during class. Bishop Michel Bernard ordained Biayenda on 26 October 1958.

Biayenda held a succession of posts from 1958 to 1965. He first served at Saint Marie de Ouenzé in Brazzaville and then moved to Saint Jean-Marie Vianney at Mouléké. At the same time, he was the diocesan leader of the Legion of Mary. After the 1963 revolution that overthrew former priest Fulbert Youlou's regime, the new clique of military officers suspected the Catholic Church of undermining the new government. Biayenda also decried the nationalization of all mission schools. Apparently Biayenda's work drew negative attention from some authorities. He was arrested by soldiers on 7 February 1965 along with a Swiss Catholic missionary. Biayenda was then beaten, nearly drowned, and subjected to other forms of torture on the false charges that he had disseminated anti-government pamphlets. His imprisonment lasted 44 days. After the release of the two priests, they took refuge at a convent. Troops then threatened the nuns, as former president Youlou had just escaped jail. The Catholic hierarchy chose to send Biayenda to France soon afterward to avoid future trouble. He received a degree in theology and a doctorate of sociology in Lyon.

In May 1969, Biayenda returned to Brazzaville. He worked for several months at the Holy Spirit parish of Moungali in 1970 before being appointed auxiliary Bishop of Brazzaville on 17 May 1970. When his predecessor Théophile Mbemba died on 14 June 1971, Biayenda became Archbishop of Brazzaville. Biayenda's fierce criticism of the corruption and brutality of the ruling Marxist-Leninist government made him many enemies, but persecutions of the Catholic Church declined under strongman Marien Ngouabi, who had taken power in 1968. Pope Paul VI considered Biayenda to be a crucial figure for leading peaceful resistance against the despotic regime. On 2 February 1973, Biayenda became one of the youngest men ever to become a cardinal. He continued to speak out publicly about the vicious and arbitrary actions of the government as well as the use of ethnicity to divide the nation. In 1972, he preached against the lack of compassion of many Congolese: "A lack of conscience is what kills Congolese society. . . ." Biayenda differed from many older missionaries in extending welcome to Kimbanguist and evangelical Protestant churches. A true believer in the changes that came to the Catholic Church with the reforms of the Vatican II council, he promoted the use of Congolese musical instruments and the African languages of Kikongo and Kituba. He also promoted schools specifically designed to serve the poor. Biayenda intervened on behalf of a group of people condemned to death in 1972. The prisoners included Biayenda's half-brother, Maxime N'Debeka. Their aged father Sémo was terrified of losing another child to state violence. However, Biayenda defended the rights of all the detainees rather than concern himself only with N'Debeka's case. N'Debekea survived and continued an active career as a novelist.

On 18 March 1977, President Marien Ngouabi was assassinated. Some of Ngouabi's family and associates accused Biayenda of convincing the late president to abandon the talismans that kept him safe from harm. Several seminarians warned

Biayenda that he should flee the country or at least take some precautions for his safety. The Cardinal refused. He told the young men, "If they want to take me, then it would be best if they came here [to my residence]." Biayenda also said that there would be harsh retaliation awaiting many innocent Christians if he fled the country. Two soldiers drove up to the Cardinal's residence on the night of 21 March 1977 and asked Biayenda to accompany them to army headquarters. He was then executed. Government authorities blamed one of Ngouabi's uncles for ordering the Cardinal's assassination. On 26 March 1977, the Congolese government had the alleged killers put to death. However, few Congolese believed that the executed men had anything to do with the actual death of Biayenda. The persons responsible for Biayenda's death most likely were never apprehended or punished.

Émile Biayenda had a long legacy. His murder drew the attention of the international press. Many younger Congolese men were inspired by his courage and faith to consider religious vocations. During the civil wars that devastated Congo-Brazzaviille in the 1990s, some Congolese claimed to have seen Biayenda in visions, in similar fashion to the celebration by Kikongo-speaking communities of older figures like André Matsoua. His tomb has become a pilgrimage site for Catholics from throughout Congo-Brazzaville. The Fondation Cardinal Émile Biayenda based in Brazzaville has promoted his beatification since the 1990s.

[See also Ngouabi, Marien.]

BIBLIOGRAPHY

Bazenguissa-Ganga, Rémy. Les voies du politique au Congo: Essai de sociologie historique. Paris: Karthala, 1997.

Fondation Cardinal Émile Biayenda. Le Mémoire. URL: http://www.biayenda.lautre.net/index.php.

Mayima-Mbemba, Jean-Claude. Assassinats politiques au Congo-Brazzaville: Rapport de la Commission ad'hoc de la Conférence Nationale Souveraine (25 février–10 juin 1991). Corbeil-Essonnes, France: ICES, 2005.

Tsiakaka, Adolphe. Émile Biayenda, Grandeur d'un humble. Strasbourg, France: Editions du Signe, 1999.

JEREMY RICH

Bi Kidude. See Fatuma Binti Baraka.

Biko, Steve (1946–1977), South African antiapartheid activist and founder of the Black Consciousness

Steve Biko, 1977. (AP Images/Cape Argus)

Movement (BCM), was born Stephen Bantu Biko in King William's Town in South Africa's Cape Province on 18 December 1946. His father, a clerk employed by the state, died when Biko was four. His mother, a domestic servant who worked in white homes around King William's Town, almost single-handedly raised her four children thereafter. Biko began his education locally, first at Brownlee Primary and later at Charles Morgan Higher Primary, before moving on to live at another settlement known as Alice, where he attended Lovedale Institute. While he was at Lovedale Institute, his older brother was arrested, expelled from school, and sent to jail for almost a year on the suspicion that he was a member of the military wing of the Pan African Congress (PAC). The police, on similar grounds, also questioned the younger Biko. He was, however, not jailed. He was, however, expelled from school only three months after enrolling at

Lovedale Institute. Following his expulsion from Lovedale Institute, Biko moved to the Catholic boarding school of St. Francis College in Marianhill, outside Durban. In the late 1960s, he entered the University of Natal to study medicine, but was expelled because of his political activities; he was already a radical student leader and a political activist. Over time, he became a key figure in the antiapartheid struggle, rising to fill the leadership vacuum created in South Africa by the incarceration of Nelson Mandela and other leaders of black opposition parties such as the African National Congress (ANC).

Although Biko developed a strong resentment toward white rule at about the time he was expelled from Lovedale Institute, he committed himself to politics thereafter, including at the University of Natal, mainly because of his distress at the lack of political and social improvements in the black community under apartheid. He soon realized that it was virtually impossible for black students to attain leadership positions, or even to experience equal treatment, within the then-dominant student organization in South Africa, the multiracial National Union of South African Students (NUSAS). Because of this, Biko led the formation of a nationally representative black student organization known as the South African Students' Organization (SASO) in 1968. In 1969, Biko was elected president of SASO. After holding this position for about a year, he was appointed the publicity secretary of the body. He left the university in 1972 before completing his planned medical degree, to pursue a full-time career of political activism.

Outside SASO, Biko founded or helped to found several other bodies, including the Black Community Programs and the Zimele Trust Fund, established in 1972 and 1975, respectively. Biko was a committed activist and full-time organizer, who did the grinding—but essential—work of attending general meetings, delivering presentations, helping in leadership training, and fostering contact with influential white liberals such as Donald Woods, a campaigning newspaper editor who would later write a powerful biography of Biko. He also formulated policy documents, drafted position papers, and issued press releases. Above all, Biko was central to developing and spreading the philosophy and political theory of what became known as the Black Consciousness Movement. In this, he was influenced by leading African and African-diaspora intellectuals, including Aimé Césaire, Frantz Fanon, Anton Lembede, Robert Mangaliso Sobukwe, and Kwame Nkrumah. He was also influenced by the Black Power movement, which developed in the United States in the 1960s and early 1970s.

The philosophy of Black Consciousness developed from Biko's conviction that liberation from apartheid would come only from black people themselves, and not through the leadership of whites, whether liberal or not. The true struggle against racism and apartheid, he argued, had to start with black psychological self-reliance, because centuries of deliberate oppression of blacks by whites had had a profound and negative psychological impact on the former. Blacks had been encouraged to accept various myths, including that of their inherent inferiority and the superiority of the written word and Westernized standards of history over black and African oral traditions. The philosophy of black consciousness also rejected the alleged "primitiveness" of African culture, and the claim that African faith and belief were simplistic compared to Western alternatives. In Biko's opinion, centuries of deliberate oppression, in essence, had forced blacks to hate themselves. This self-hatred had important political implications, for example, in promoting political disunity and in persuading blacks to accept as inevitable their subservient position in society. Only by destroying this sense of hopelessness, Biko argued, could blacks eliminate both racial prejudice and the institutional racist structures of apartheid. In place of the myth of racial inferiority, Black Consciousness promoted a sense of racial awareness and pride in African culture, achievements, value systems, religion, and personal appearance. Because of blacks' lack of power in South African society, such an emphasis on racial consciousness was not, in Biko's view, racism in reverse.

Crucially, the philosophy of Black Consciousness challenged established black opposition leaders. Nelson Mandela, the African National Congress, and the South African Communist Party viewed multiracial struggle against apartheid as both possible and productive. For Biko, the extreme racial polarization of apartheid required the abandoning of multiracial coalitions in favor of racially exclusive struggle. He also criticized African Bantustan leaders who, in his view, collaborated with the apartheid regime by embracing the Pretoria government's ethnic homelands policy. Black Consciousness was not about skin pigmentation alone, but about active self-realization and empowerment. As such, the philosophy had resonance for other non-white groups, such as "Coloured" and Indian South Africans. Moreover, Black Consciousness was not an end in itself, but rather a stage in Biko's dialectical model of history, in which the struggle of thesis (apartheid) against anti-thesis (Black Consciousness) would result in the synthesis of "true humanity."

By the early 1970s, a growing number of black South Africans had become disillusioned with traditional black leadership, and were drawn both to the ideology of Black Consciousness and Biko's militancy. As Biko's prominence rose, he became a direct threat to the apartheid regime. In addition to leading SASO, he helped form the Black People's Convention (BPC), in order to popularize the ideas of the Black Consciousness Movement among workers and unemployed youth as well as students. Although Biko did not participate in the Soweto student uprising of 1976, that revolt undoubtedly reflected the increasing influence of Black Consciousness. The spark of the rebellion—black Soweto students' resistance to Afrikaans as the language of instruction in their schools—exemplified Biko's ideas of black self-assertion.

Despite his criticisms of traditional black leaders, Biko also began forging links between the BPC, SOSA, and the ANC. Fearing that Biko and other leaders of the Black Consciousness Movement might establish a powerful national black alliance of workers, students, and urban blacks who could destroy apartheid, the authorities continually harassed and spied on him. From 1973 to 1975 Biko was banned from political activity and restricted to King William's Town under the provisions of the Suppression of Communism Act. The authorities tapped his phone, raided his home and office, and charged him for minor traffic offenses. Biko, however, refused to back down. For instance, following his restriction to King William's Town in 1973, he established an Eastern Cape branch of the Black Communities Program which organized classes in literacy, dressmaking, and health education. At the time of his restriction, Biko also enrolled in a law program offered by the University of South Africa.

Following the Soweto uprising, the government harassment of Biko intensified throughout 1976 and 1977, and he was detained twice under the Terrorism Act. On 18 August 1977, while traveling to Cape Town, he was again arrested, under the guise that he was distributing inflammatory pamphlets specifically aimed at inciting blacks to riot. He was detained in custody, interrogated, stripped, and beaten by white police officers for refusing to cooperate. Thirty days later, Biko died from a brain hemorrhage.

The apartheid regime had finally silenced Biko, but his death proved something of a turning point in the struggle for black freedom. His martyrdom and direct resistance to apartheid encouraged Black Consciousness supporters to continue challenging government oppression through protest and other means. His death in custody spurred many protests, including at his funeral, attended by thousands of black South Africans, Western diplomats, and the world's media, which was used as an occasion to legally demonstrate against the government's racist policies. The government experienced further humiliation during Biko's inquest, when more global attention was drawn to racial injustice in South Africa. While the white courts acquitted the police of any wrongdoing, a growing number of observers within South Africa and outside it refused to accept that verdict. Biko became a powerful symbol of righteous opposition to apartheid. His life—and death—was commemorated in a popular biography by Donald Woods, later adapted into a motion picture, *Cry Freedom* (1987) and by musical tributes, from English rock star Peter Gabriel, Irish folksinger Christy Moore, and Jamaican reggae artist Tapper Zukie, among others. While Biko's death did not alone sound the death knell of apartheid, it certainly galvanized opposition to the Pretoria regime both at home and abroad. As Nelson Mandela would later state of Biko, "They had to kill him to prolong the life of apartheid."

Biko was survived by six children. His widow, Nontsikelelo, testified in 1997 at hearings before the Truth and Reconciliation Commission, which was set up following the establishment of democracy in South Africa. At those hearings, several white policemen admitted that they had tortured and murdered Biko. By then, however, it was no longer possible under South African law to prosecute the guilty officers.

[See also Césaire, Aimé; Fanon, Frantz; Lembede, Anton Muziwakhe; Mandela, Nelson Rolihlahla; Nkrumah, Kwame; and Sobukwe, Robert Mangaliso.]

BIBLIOGRAPHY
Bernstein, Hilda. *Steve Biko*. London: International Defence and Aid Fund, 1978.
Biko, Steve. *Steve Biko: Black Consciousness in South Africa*. Edited by Millard Arnold. New York: Random House, 1978.
Biko, Steve. *I Write What I Like: A Selection of his Writings*. Edited by Aelred Stubbs. London: Bowerdean, 1996.

Juckes, Tim J. *Opposition in South Africa: The Leadership of Z. K. Mathews, Nelson Mandela, and Stephen Biko.* Westport, Conn: Praeger, 1995.

Pityana, Barney N., Ramphele Mamphela, Mpumlwana Malusi, and Wilson Lindy, eds. *Bounds of Possibility: The Legacy of Steve Biko and Black Consciousness.* London and New Jersey: Zed Books, 1992.

Woods, Donald. *Biko: The True Story of the Young South African Martyr and his Struggle to Raise Black Consciousness.* New York: Henry Holt and Company, 1991.

MOHAMMED BASHIR SALAU

Bilal ibn Rabah (late sixth century–c. 641), originally an African slave, is universally known in the Muslim world as the first muezzin (*muʿaddin*) in the history of Islam and a close companion of the Prophet Muhammad. The biography of Bilal can be reconstructed thanks to many different Islamic traditional sources.

Bilal was born in Mecca in the late sixth century. He was most probably the property of the rich Meccan trader Umayya b. Khalaf, head of the Jumah clan, whose goats and sheeps he used to pasture. He had an Ethiopian (or more generally a black African) origin, which explains his nickname "al-Habashi" (the Abyssinian). From his mother, Hamama, he is also frequently called Ibn Hamama (the son of Hamama). Bilal came to know Islam at its first inception and was one of the earliest converts to the new faith. His religious conversion provoked the wrath of his master, who brutally tortured him to make him forswear the Muslim creed. Bilal reportedly bore the suffering inflicted on him, steadily screaming: "God is One, God is One!" Abu Bakr, the father-in-law of the Prophet, saw Bilal bravely enduring torture and was struck by his fortitude and the strength of his faith. He thus decided to buy him from his owner and immediately freed him.

Once manumitted, Bilal became one of the most devoted companions of Muhammad, whom he accompanied and served without rest. In 622, he followed the Prophet to Medina in the *hijra* (emigration to Yathrib/Medina in 622). When the Islamic call to the five daily mandatory prayers (*adhān*) was established (623), Bilal was chosen by Muhammad himself as the first official muezzin because of the fascinating power of his beautiful voice, which was not overshadowed by his defective pronunciation of the "shin" and the "sin" sounds of Arabic. In subsequent years, Bilal took part in all the battles and clashes between Muslims and Meccan polytheists. In particular, in the famous battle of Badr in 624, he managed to kill his former master. In 630, when Mecca was eventually reconquered by the Islamic forces, he had the honor of calling the Muslim faithful to prayer, launching the *adhan* from the roof the holy Kaʿba.

After the death of Muhammad in 632, the biography of Bilal is unclear due to discrepancies among the sources, especially those of Sunni and those of Shiite orientation. According to some Sunni views, Bilal continued to act as a muezzin during the caliphate of Abu Bakr but interrupted this activity when ʿUmar became caliph. Other sources state that after the Prophet's departure, Bilal summoned people to prayer only once: when ʿUmar came to Syria or, according to a more Shiite-biased view, when he visited the shrine of the Prophet in Medina and Muhammad's grandchildren, al-Hasan and al-Husayn, asked him to recite the *adhan* on the roof of the mosque of their grandfather. Most of the sources agree on the fact that, during the caliphate of ʿUmar, Bilal moved to Syria, where he apparently took part in the military operations of the Muslims against the Byzantines. However, some Shiite sources affirm that he was in fact forced to leave the Arabian Peninsula as he refused to work for Abu Bakr and ʿUmar, thus openly supporting the claim of ʿAli b. Abi Talib to caliphate.

The date and the place of the death of Bilal are also much disputed. Sunni sources locate the death of Bilal somewhere in Syria (Damascus, Aleppo, or Darayya) between 638 and 642. Shiites are inclined to believe that Bilal died in Damascus in 641. The shrine of Bilal is nowadays located in the Bab al-Saghir cemetery of Damascus, where it is visited by pious pilgrims (mostly Shiite Muslims).

Bilal is a relevant figure in Islamic culture. As the first muezzin, he is considered the patron of all muezzins, and a deep-felt veneration is bestowed to him by muezzins all over the Muslim world. As a black companion of the Prophet Muhammad, Bilal is particularly revered by African and African American Muslims, for whom he became a key symbolic figure. Bilal thus entered the historical narratives of the oral tradition of the Islamized Manding people of Mali as the forefather of Sunjata, the founder of the Mali Empire; he is considered the founder and protector of the guilds of itinerant black musicians in Morocco (Gnawa); his help is invoked by the members of the black brotherhood of *sidi* Bilal in Tunis and elsewhere in North Africa during the healing rituals of their possession cults; black Muslims of India trace back their roots to Bilal and consider him their ancestor.

Moreover, for contemporary black Muslims, Bilal's life proves the crucial contribution of Africans to the birth of Islam, the absence of racial prejudice in the original Islamic thought, and the equality of all the human races in front of God. In the United States, the meditation on the personage of Bilal was one of the central stimulating factors of the ideological evolution of the Afro-American Islamic congregation of the Nation of Islam (NOI): Warith al-Din Muhammad (d. 2008), head of the NOI, wanted the members of his movement to become "Bilalians," and the name of the official newspaper of the group was changed into the *Bilal News*. The symbolic place occupied by Bilal in the black Islamic context and the connection of Bilal with Shiite Islam is evident in the name of the Bilal Muslim Mission, a Shiite missionary organization founded in 1964 in Tanzania by the Indian Shiite scholar Sa'id Akhtar Rizvi (d. 2002) with the aim of spreading Shiite Islam among Sunni or non-Muslim blacks in East Africa, North America, and Scandinavia. The organization publishes a periodical in Kiswahili called *Sauti ya Bilal* (The Voice of Bilal).

Conversely, for other (mainly white) Muslims, Bilal came to be considered the archetypical image of the kind-hearted and God-fearing colored servant who devoted his life to his righteous master (the Prophet Muhammad).

BIBLIOGRAPHY

Conrad, David C. "Islam in the Oral Traditions of Mali: Bilali and Surakata." *Journal of African History* 26 (1985): 33–49.

Curtis, Edward E., IV. "African-American Islamization Reconsidered: Black History Narratives and Muslim Identity." *Journal of the American Academy of Religion* 73 (2005): 659–684.

Obeng, Pashington. "Religion and Empire: Belief and Identity among African Indians of Karnataka, South India." *Journal of the American Academy of Religion* 71 (2003): 99–120.

ALESSANDRO GORI

Biléoma, Mariètou Mbaye. *See* Ken Bugul.

Bingu wa Mutharika (1934–), president of the Republic of Malawi, was born Brightson Webster Ryson Thom in February 1934 in the Thyolo district of the Shire Highlands, Malawi. Later, he changed his name to Bingu wa Mutharika to reflect his Lomwe origins and his nationalist sentiments. Bingu, as he is popularly known, attended local schools and, after his secondary education, he went to the University of Delhi, India, on a scholarship, and received a bachelor's degree in commerce and a master's degree in commerce and economics. Upon his return to Malawi, he became a civil servant, but after a few years he left for Zambia, where he also worked for the government. In the early 1970s, he joined the World Bank in Washington, working mainly in its loans section and, in 1978, he moved to the United Nations Economic Commission for Africa, Addis Ababa, Ethiopia. In the 1980s, he was one of the first employees of the Preferential Trade Area of East and Central Africa (PTA), becoming its secretary general in 1989. Five years later, he managed the transition of the organization to the Common Market for Eastern and Southern Africa (COMESA), of which he was the founding secretary general. At some stage during this time, Bingu obtained a doctoral degree from the Western Pacific University in the United States.

In 1997, Bingu wa Mutharika returned to Malawi, formed the United Party, and became its presidential flag bearer in the May 1999 elections. He lost, receiving 1 percent of the total vote. As a consequence, he disbanded the party and returned to the UDF, of which he had been a founding member. President Bakili Muluzi appointed him as deputy governor of the Reserve Bank of Malawi and, in 2002, he accepted the appointment as minister of economic planning and development. After Muluzi failed to change the constitution to allow him to run for a third term in the May 2004 general elections, he nominated Bingu to be the UDF's presidential candidate, much to the surprise of many observers. He won and formed his cabinet, which included some of the ministers in the preceding government. In January 2005, he left the UDF to form the Democratic Progressive Party (DPP), and many members of parliament and most cabinet ministers joined him.

Soon after becoming president in 2004, Bingu wa Mutharika impressed Malawians and external donors by his determination to improve the economy and, especially, by his effort to root out mismanagement, and to instill a culture of financial responsibility in the public sector. Donor agencies, some of which had either stopped aid to Malawi or had reduced it during the Muluzi era, resumed full assistance.

Besides cleaning all the urban centers in Malawi, his government rehabilitated roads and other transport infrastructures, and introduced a fertilizer subsidy system that greatly resuscitated smallholder production. This gave confidence to rural producers, resulting in, among other factors, an increase in grain reserves and, therefore, a return to food security in a country whose population continued to expand. Overall, the economy grew by 8 percent annually during the period 2004–2009, and the projections were that it would grow at 6 percent in 2010. However, a major problem that became evident in 2009 was the policy of fixed exchange rates, which affected foreign reserves and, consequently, the ability to import essential goods, including petroleum products and spare parts.

A significant feature of Bingu wa Mutharika's presidency was the strained relations with his promoter and predecessor, Bakili Muluzi. The tension between them emerged because Bingu felt that Muluzi was trying to influence policy and the style of governing. On his part, Muluzi did not like the nature of the new government's anti-corruption campaign, and some senior officials of the UDF wanted Bingu expelled from the party. However, before this could take place, he resigned from the UDF, established the Democratic Progressive Party, taking with him many prominent members of the party, leaving Muluzi's organization in a much weakened position. In 2005, the government, through the Anti-Corruption Bureau, began to investigate ex-president Muluzi on the grounds that he had personally misappropriated donor funds. Legal problems associated with this were to prevent Muluzi from trying to contest the presidency for a third time.

In May 2009, Bingu was reelected as state president, and his party won an overwhelming majority in the National Assembly. This gave him confidence to introduce controversial legislature that the previous parliament would most likely not have passed. In 2010, he modified the national flag from the original depicting a rising sun to one with a full sun; the colors were also altered slightly. Most Malawians did not receive this change well, partly because there was inadequate debate on the matter and also because they did not find the justification for it to be convincing. Still, Bingu used his office to ensure that it became a reality. He also enshrined into law a quota system in education, arguing that it would guarantee equity in the country. However, sections of the country, especially the north, viewed it as discriminatory in nature.

Throughout his presidency Bingu wa Mutharika had uneasy relations with his vice-presidents. In 2004, he virtually dismissed his 2004 running mate, Vice President Cassim Chilumpha, accusing him of undermining the powers of the government. In May 2009, Joyce Banda, formerly minister of foreign affairs and international cooperation, became vice president, but within a short time, relations between her and the state president cooled rapidly and, by the end of 2010, she was expelled from the DPP and held her office only in name. At the same time, Bingu influenced the party to consider adopting his brother, Minister of Education Peter Mutharika, a distinguished academic, as its presidential candidate in the 2014 elections.

The president's increasing tendency to make decisions of national importance without adequate consultation, his treatment of the office of the vice-president, and his occasional threats to journalists and to those who oppose him worried many Malawians. This was also one of the subjects of concern that the Catholic bishops of Malawi expressed in their pastoral letter of November 2010.

In May 2007, Bingu was Mutharika's wife, Zimbabwean-born Ethel, died after a long battle with cancer and, in January 2010, he married Calista Chapola-Chimombo, a former cabinet minister. Eight months later, he appointed her to a non-cabinet post, presidential adviser on maternal, infant, and child health, a position that Vice-President Joyce Banda held previously. Among the highlights of his second term was his election as chairman of the African Union in the period 2010–2011.

[See also Muluzi, Bakili.]

BIBLIOGRAPHY

Chinsinga, Blessings, M. Bratton, E. Gyimah-Boadi, R. Mattes, and Inter-University Consortium for Political and Social Research. *Afrobarometer Round 3 Quality of Democracy and Governance in Malawi, 2005*. Ann Arbor, Mich.: Inter-University Consortium for Political and Social Research, 2008.

Kalinga, Owen J. M. *Historical Dictionary of Malawi*, 4th ed. Lanham, Md.: Scarecrow Press, 2011.

Tsoka, Maxon G. "*Spot the Difference: A Comparison of Presidents and Governments' Performance since 1999 in Malawi*." Afrobarometer Briefing Paper no. 74. Ann Arbor, Mich.: Inter-University Consortium for Political and Social Research, November 2009.

Tsoka, Maxon G. *"Country Turning Blue? Political Party Support and the End of Regionalism in Malawi."* Afrobarometer Briefing paper no. 75. Ann Arbor, Mich: Inter-University Consortium for Political and Social Research, November 2009.

OWEN J. M. KALINGA

Bin Jallun, 'Abd al-Majid (1919–1981), Moroccan Arabic writer, journalist, and diplomat (not to be confused with the francophone writer Abdelmajid Benjelloun, born in 1944), was born in Casablanca. At the age of five months, he was taken by his parents to Manchester, where his father worked as a merchant. He attended primary school there, and became the darling of a small community of immigrants. The loss of both his mother and his sister while he was still young had a profound effect on him, reinforced by his reading of Charles Dickens; the emotional consequences of this loss can be found in his writings.

He returned to Morocco with his father at the age of nine. They took up residence in Fez, where Bin Jallun received his secondary education, and then enrolled in the ancient Islamic university of the Qarawiyin. The pervasive atmosphere there was one of traditional Arabic learning and culture, and this made a considerable impression upon the young Bin Jallun. During this period he published his first articles in local periodicals.

To complete his university education, Bin Jallun went to Egypt shortly before the outbreak of World War II, and enrolled in the literature faculty at King Fu'ad University (later Cairo University). There he was taught by distinguished Egyptian professors and writers. After graduating, he studied at the Higher Institute of Editing, Translation, and Journalism in the same university, and earned a diploma from the Institute.

While in Egypt he married 'Inayat Abu 'Amir, who bore him two sons: Wa'il in 1950 and Safwan in 1951. During this period he became an active nationalist. He was a founder of the Arab Maghrib Bureau in Cairo, for which he subsequently served as secretary-general from 1949 until Moroccan independence in 1956. In this capacity he attended the Afro-Asian Conference at Bandung in April 1955.

After returning to Morocco with his family the following year, he continued his literary and journalistic career, becoming editor of the daily national newspaper *al-'Alam* (The Banner), organ of the Istiqlal (Independence) Party, published in Rabat. In 1958 he was appointed Moroccan ambassador to Pakistan, where he stayed until 1962. He later worked in the Ministry of Foreign Affairs until his retirement. He died on 3 July 1981.

The creative writings of Bin Jallun fall into four categories. First, his short stories—notably the two collections *Wadi al-Dima'* (1947; Valley of Blood) and *Law-la al-insan* (1972; If Not for Mankind)—deal mainly with the colonial relationship between Moroccans and French, and have been criticized as excessively bitter and melodramatic, but the power of the prose is generally acknowledged. A few of them have been translated into French and/or English. Second are his autobiographical works, notably the two-volume *Fi 'l-tufula* (1957–1968; In Childhood), in novel form, which won the first Morocco Prize for Literature and is regarded as a classic of modern Moroccan Arabic literature. In addition to poignant memories of his early years in England, it also includes much social criticism of contemporary Moroccan life and attitudes. A French translation was published in 1992, and the section on Manchester appeared in English translation in the periodical *Banipal* in 1999.

Bin Jallun has also produced noteworthy poems, especially in the collection *Bara'im* (1963; Blossoms). These poems have been described as modern in subject matter but traditional in form, eschewing the style of the contemporary avant-garde. Finally, he has written notable historical and political books, of which *Ma'rakat al-wadi* (1976; Battle of the Valley) won another Morocco Prize for Literature. Other works include *Hadhihi Marrakish* (1949; This is Morocco); *Sultan Marrakish* (1952; The Sultan of Morocco); *Maris istiqlalak* (1957; Assert Your Independence); *Jawlat fi Maghrib ams* (1974–1975; Excursions in Yesterday's Morocco, 4 vols.); and *Mudhakkirat al-masira al-khadra'* (1976; Memoirs of the Green March), on the Moroccan popular invasion of Spanish Sahara in 1975. Some of these books have become part of the school curriculum in Morocco.

BIBLIOGRAPHY

Donohue, John J., and Leslie Tramontini. *Crosshatching in Global Culture: A Dictionary of Modern Arab Writers. An Updated English Version of R. B. Campbell's "Contemporary Arab Writers."* Beirut: Ergon Verlag Würzburg im Kommission, 2004.

Haywood, John A. *Modern Arabic Literature: An Introduction, with Extracts in Translation.* London: Lund Humphries, 1971.

GEOFFREY ROPER

Bin Shaykh, Tawhida (1909–2010), Tunisian physician, was born to an old, well-known family of Tunis. Her widowed mother played a pivotal in her education starting from primary school. Both Tawhida and her sister were enrolled in the School for Muslim Girls, an academic institution prized for its first-class education, which had opened in 1909 in the family's neighborhood. During the 1920s in Tunis, while Bin Shaykh attended secondary school, the feminist movement took off and was marked by a watershed event in 1924: Manubiya Wartani, a young Tunisian woman attending a public conference devoted to the question of feminism and women's rights, removed her veil and stood up in the crowd to make a speech. At about the same time, Bin Shaykh had a chance encounter that would utterly change the course of her life; she made the acquaintance of a respected French physician, Dr. Etienne Burnet, and his Russian wife, Lydia, both working and residing in Tunis. After she graduated from secondary school in 1928, Bin Shaykh wanted to engage in social work. The Burnet couple realized that she showed promise in the medical field. At the time, there was only one place in North Africa to obtain a medical degree—Algiers—but Bin Shaykh's family did not want her to go there. This left the School of Medicine in Paris, where the Burnets hoped the young woman would be able to enroll. But her family was of elite status, was socially conservative, and she had never been outside of Tunis. Thus, the idea of going to Paris, even with the Burnets, was unthinkable. Nevertheless, Bin Shaykh proved so gifted in secondary school that her professors made a collective visit to her family, urging her mother to allow her to pursue medical studies in Paris. Her mother agreed.

Certain male members of the extended family adamantly opposed the idea. Indeed, the day of her scheduled departure in 1928, when she was packing her bags in preparation for embarking on a ship to Marseille with Madame Burnet, and as a driver waited at the door to take her to the port, a delegation of male relatives arrived at the family house, including a most formidable religious personality, a shaykh from the Zaytuna Mosque. The shaykh rightfully characterized Paris as a city of perdition in arguing against allowing the young woman to study there. However, Bin Shaykh's mother, Haluma, stood firm and directed the shaykh to take the Qur'an to find a verse forbidding women from being educated. During the ensuing, and quite heated, discussion, Bin Shaykh secretly sent word down to the port for the ship to wait. And it did.

There were very few women in the Faculty of Medicine in Paris at the time, and most were French nationals. Many people in Paris wanted to make Bin Shaykh's acquaintance since she was regarded as something of a novelty: an Arab Muslim woman alone in the city without family and enrolled at the School of Medicine. In 1936 Bin Shaykh became the first North African Muslim woman to earn a French diploma in medicine. Bin Shaykh spent eight years in Paris where she met, through the Burnets, scientists, writers, and leading medical experts. She was honored by being named as an intern in one of the Parisian hospitals. After she was awarded her medical diploma in France, she returned to Tunis, where in 1937 she went into private practice, specializing in women's reproductive health and often providing free medical services for poor women. However, colonialism blocked her medical career. She did not even attempt to find a position in one of the European hospitals because they were controlled by the French. While there were several women doctors working in the Tunis hospitals, a Tunisian female physician had little chance of acceptance.

Bin Shaykh was active during the Tunisian nationalist movement, which was always intertwined with feminism, but, significantly, in her own fashion and on her own terms. She served as the editor of the women's journal, *Leila*, from 1937 on, signing her own articles written in French with the nom de plume, Leila. The journal, an illustrated weekly published from 1936 to 1941, was devoted to the emancipation of North African Muslim women. In 1942 she married and had three children. During the nationalist struggles of the early 1950s, she served as vice-president of the Tunisian branch of the Croissant Rouge/Red Cross. When the French army bombed a village in the Cap Bon in 1952 with great loss of life, Bin Shaykh went to the scene of the massacres and wrote up a detailed on-site report, which she submitted in person to French authorities in protest.

After independence from France in 1956, she established the first clinic for family planning in 1963 and was played a leading role in the Tunisian Association for Family Planning. Doctor Bin Shaykh was instrumental in creating family planning at the Charles Nicolle hospital and in 1970 the first clinic solely devoted to women's reproductive medicine was opened in Tunis due to her efforts. However, in keeping with her commitment to women's needs first and foremost, she refused a government post in 1970 when the Tunisian Prime Minister offered this plum to her, saying that she preferred to take care of her patients and exercise her profession as a physician. In 2000 Bin Shaykh was awarded the prestigious Prix Didon by the Tunisian state in recognition of her contributions. Bin Shaykh died on 6 December 2010 at the age of 101.

Bin Shaykh's intellectual and social odyssey from the old city of Tunis to Paris should be located in a transnational context of the early twentieth century when female education assumed a dominant position in global political and social reform movements; it also became central to the very practice of empire, and struggles over the nature and future of empire.

[*See also* Adda, Gladys; Amrouche, Fadhma; *and* Bouzid, Dorra.]

BIBLIOGRAPHY

Clancy-Smith, Julia. "Envisioning Knowledge: Educating the Muslim Woman in Colonial North Africa, c. 1850–1918." In *Iran and Beyond: Essays in Middle Eastern History in Honor of Nikki R. Keddie,* edited by Beth Baron and Rudi Matthee, pp. 99–118. Los Angeles: Mazda Press, 2000.

Huston, Perdita. *Motherhood by Choice: Pioneers in Women's Health and Family Planning.* New York: The Feminist Press, 1992.

Kazdaghli, Habib. *Mémoire de Femmes: Tunisiennes dans la vie publique, 1920–1960.* Tunis, Tunisia: Édition Média Com, 1993.

JULIA A. CLANCY-SMITH

Bint al-Shati'. *See* 'Abd al-Rahman, 'A'ishah.

Biya, Chantal (1970–), second spouse of Cameroonian President Paul Biya, was born on 4 December 1970 in the eastern Cameroonian town of Dimako. Her father was a French expatriate, Georges Vigouroux, while her Cameroonian mother, Rosette Marie Mboutchouang, was a beauty pageant winner. Biya grew up in the Cameroonian capital of Yaoundé. After the death of Paul Biya's first spouse, Jeanne-Irène, in 1992, Chantal entered into a romantic relationship with the authoritarian leader despite the thirty-seven-year age difference between the couple. Before their meeting, she had worked as a waitress and had few financial resources. On 23 April 1994, Chantal and Paul married in an elaborate ceremony. They had two children, Paul Junior and Anasthasia Brenda.

Chantal proved herself to be an able supporter and adviser to her husband. She was a figure whose flamboyant public presence infuriated opponents of Biya's regime, even as she succeeded in gaining a large popular following in Cameroon. Biya presented herself as a champion of Cameroon's poor, who made up an overwhelming proportion of the country's population. The Fondation Chantal Biya, founded soon after her marriage in 1994, provided large amounts of funding to improve medical care and research, especially on the AIDS virus. The foundation paid for the construction of a maternity wing of the main public hospital in Yaoundé, which was then named after her. She formed other charitable organizations such as the Cercle des Amis du Cameroun (CERAC) and the African Synergy group to promote public health campaigns against AIDS. When the Organization for African Unity met in Yaoundé in 1996, she held a summit of presidential wives. In November 2008, UNESCO named her a Goodwill Ambassador for Education and Social Inclusion, and she made many trips abroad as a result. Some popular performers, such as the musician K-Tino, sang her praises. There can be little doubt that her various altruistic associations were designed to add a positive image to her husband's troubled leadership.

Her extremely lavish tastes in fashion and her connections to Western celebrities made her a target of criticism. Biya's famous and extraordinary hair styling made her a favorite of Western journalists and photographers, as did her penchant for wearing the latest in haute couture fashions from Europe. She met with famous Americans such as Mia Farrow and well-known political wives such as Carla Bruni of France and Michelle Obama of the United States. A common name for small purses in Cameroon was *Chantal*, since she often carried them. Critics of Biya's husband's notoriously corrupt regime pointed to such occasions as further evidence of both the hypocrisy of Biya's altruism and the willingness of Westerners to turn a blind eye to repressive regimes in Africa. It is important to note that Biya's political role was no laughing matter, regardless of her tastes in dress. In January 2005, she greeted a large number of spouses of various military and civilian leaders of Cameroon in a well-organized ceremony that visually displayed a very elaborate hierarchy of political authority.

She headed the Jeunesse Active pour Chantal Biya, a youth organization that backed the president in his electoral campaigns. She was said to have a great deal of behind-the-scenes influence on her husband. When former German football star Lothar Matthaus's effort to become the coach of the

Cameroonian national team failed in 2010, he blamed the decision on Chantal Biya, who was said to have intervened after Matthaus became embroiled in a sex scandal. More important, she served as an effective means of propaganda by acting as her husband's representative to foreign audiences as well as ordinary Cameroonians. Her career was an example of the ambiguous legacy of African presidential spouses, who acted as dispensers of aid while enjoying the benefits of wealth attained through political privilege.

[*See also* Biya, Paul.]

BIBLIOGRAPHY

Eboko, Fred. "Chantal Biya: 'Fille du Peuple' et Égérie Internationale." *Politique Africaine* 95 (2004): 91–106.

"Fondation Chantal Biya." http://www.fcb.cm.

Verhoeven, Béatrix. *Chantal Biya: La Passion de l'Humanitaire*. Paris: Karthala, 2008.

JEREMY RICH

Biya, Paul (1933–), president of Cameroon, was born Paul Barthélemy Biya'a bi Mvondo on 13 February 1933, in the village of Mvomeka'a (Meyomessala), in French Cameroon. Biya was from a peasant background; his parents, Etienne Mvondo Assam and Anastasie Eyenya Elle Mvondo, had little money. However, through hard work, determination, perseverance, and dedication to education, the younger Biya was able to forge his way to the top. His rise from a humble background indicates the importance of education in promoting upward mobility in post-World War II Cameroon.

Biya, a Christian, began his education at the age of seven at a Catholic mission school in Ndem, some thirty miles from his home village. At school, his hardworking and devoted nature won the admiration of his tutor (a French national) who recommended him for admission into the prestigious Akono Junior Seminary. There is no record of his life at the seminary, but he eventually left for the famous Lycée Leclerc in Yaounde, the capital of Cameroon. He then attended the Sorbonne in France, where he obtained a BA in political science and a postgraduate diploma in law in the late 1950s and early 1960s.

While still in France, Biya met Jeanne-Irene Atyam, whom he later married. She was a philanthropist who assisted the poor and the needy; she was also involved in other philanthropic activities

Paul Biya, 2009. (AP Images/Remy de La Mauviniere)

in the health sector. In April 1994 Biya remarried, to Chantal Biya. He is the father of three children, Frank Biya, Paul Biya, Jr., and Anastasia Brenda Biya Eyenga.

Biya's educational achievements in Yaounde and Paris earned him a place in the Cameroon civil service in the early 1960s. He dedicated his life to public service as a career civil servant, eventually transitioning to a career in politics. He rose swiftly through the ranks of Cameroon's state bureaucracy, serving as Chargé de Mission in 1962 and as Permanent Secretary at the Ministry of National Education in 1965. He was nominated to the post of Prime Minister by President Ahmadou Babatoura Ahidjo in 1975. Biya succeeded Ahidjo as the second president of the Republic of Cameroon on 6 November 1982. The vacuum caused by Ahidjo's retirement pushed Biya into party politics.

As the successor to Cameroon's only other president, Biya felt a need to build a solid political foundation and unique political philosophy in order to consolidate his authority. His political ideas were sharply expressed in a book he wrote titled *Communal Liberalism* (1987), a work that was translated into English, French, German, and Hebrew. The book emphasized the importance of nation-building and good governance. Biya's presidential oath of office in 1982 struck a similar tone. In it he undertook to "democratize political life, to bring about social and economic liberalization, to introduce rigor in management and moral attitudes, and to reinforce international cooperation."

Biya's ability to pursue such a program was limited to some extent by the continuing role of his predecessor in Cameroon politics. When he handed over power to Biya, Ahidjo remained as the chairman of the Cameroon National Union (CNU), the only legal political party in the country during his tenure. In Ahidjo's view, the party chair should determine government policies, while the role of Biya, as the head of state, was only to implement these decisions. Disagreements over the powers of the president and those of the chairman of the party developed into a rift between Ahidjo and Biya. In 1983, this resulted in an attempted coup d'état by Ahidjo to regain power. Biya used his executive powers to dissolve the CNU and created his own new party, the Cameroon People's Democratic Movement (CPDM). Ahidjo went into exile and in his absence Biya sentenced him to death, a sentence later reduced to life imprisonment.

The creation of the CPDM following the New Deal Congress held in the city of Bamenda in 1985 marked the beginning of Biya's dominance in Cameroon politics. As president of the Republic and as the chairman of the ruling party, he had the power to attempt to implement the ideas of moral rigor and good governance outlined in *Communal Liberalism*. Yet the results have been disappointing. In many international surveys carried out since 1985, Cameroon has been noted for corruption, embezzlement, misappropriation of public funds, and poor governance. Cameroon was rated the most corrupt country in the world by Transparency International for the 1999–2000 financial year.

Biya maintained the one-party system of rule he inherited from his predecessor until 1990. Before a multiparty system was introduced, he won presidential elections in 1984 and 1988 with more than 99 percent of the vote. By 1990, however, demonstrations and civil disobedience campaigns organized across the country had forced Biya to accept a multiparty political system. In an important speech, he called on the ruling CPDM to be ready for competition. The transition from a one-party system to a multiparty one was marked by

bloodshed, however. For example, at the May 1990 launch of the Social Democratic Front (SDF) in Bamenda in the northwest region, armed government soldiers killed six SDF supporters. In addition to the SDF, the Union Nationale pour la Démocratie et Progrès (UNDP; National Union for Democracy and Progress), and the Unions des Populations du Cameroun (UPC; Union of the Peoples of Cameroon), approximately two hundred and fifty other political parties were eventually formed, though most of these parties have regional bases with limited national influence.

The emergence of political parties led to a growing demand for a national conference to discuss issues plaguing the state of Cameroon. Central to these discussions was the issue of creating an independent election body. Biya and his government resisted such a conference, but did agree to a tripartite conference involving all the opposition parties. Cameroonian politics in the 1990s and 2000s were characterized by much instability because of accusations and counteraccusations between the government and opposition on alleged election malpractices. Biya's CPDM has remained by far the most powerful party. In the 2004 presidential elections Biya won 71 percent of the vote. His closest rival, Ni John Fru Ndi of the SDF, won 17 percent. In the 2007 National Assembly elections, Biya's CPDM won 153 of the 180 seats available.

Biya's rule in Cameroon has been most significant for reintroducing multiparty elections and for liberalizing the state's role in economic matters. His educational reforms have notably reduced the rate of illiteracy. In the early twenty-first century Biya's critics, such as Ni John Fru Ndi, highlighted Cameroon's continuing problems regarding free speech and corruption. February 2008 witnessed a series of antigovernment strikes in protest of high fuel prices and unemployment, as well as President Biya's decision to amend the constitution in order to seek another term in 2011. Hundreds of protestors were arrested, and at least forty people were killed in the demonstrations.

[*See also* Ahidjo, Ahmadou; *and* Biya, Chantal.]

BIBLIOGRAPHY

Aseh, Nfamewih. *Political Philosophies and Nation Building in Cameroon: Grounds for the Second National Liberation Struggle.* Bamenda, Cameroon: Unique Printers, 2006.

Kofele-Kale, Ndiva, ed. *An African Experiment in Nation Building: The Bilingual Cameroon Republic*

Since Reunification. Boulder, Colo.: Westview Press, 1980.

Le Vine, Victor T. *The Cameroons: From Mandate to Independence.* Berkeley and Los Angeles: University of California Press, 1964.

Takougang, Joseph, and Milton Krieger. *African State and Society in the 1990s: Cameroon's Political Crossroads.* Boulder, Colo.: Westview Press, 1998.

NDEH MARTIN SANGO

Bizimana, Augustin (1954–), Rwandan Hutu politician and military leader, was born in Byumba Prefecture, Gizungu Commune, Rwanda. He is considered by many to be one of the key actors in the planning and implementation of the Rwandan genocide in 1994, and is one of the International Criminal Tribunal for Rwanda's (ICTR) most wanted perpetrators of the genocide. He has been accused of genocide, conspiracy to commit genocide, complicity in genocide, direct and public incitement to commit genocide, crimes against humanity including murder, extermination, rape, persecution, and "serious violations of Common Article 3 and Additional Protocol II (killing, outrages upon personal dignity)" (The Hague).

Between 1990 and 1994 Bizimana was allegedly involved in the planning of the genocide, including the preparation of lists which contained the names of Tutsi and moderate Hutu. Bizimana initiated his plans for Rwanda when he was appointed Defense Minister in July 1993. As Defense Minister, Bizimana had control over the distribution of weapons to the civilian population as well as control over the national military force, the Rwandan Armed Forces (FAR). It was within this capacity that Bizimana had the ability to develop and monitor the plan that would result in the extensive and targeted execution of Tutsi and moderate Hutu in April 1994. His role as Defense Minister placed him in the position of head of military intelligence, also known as G2, as well as the commander of the army of the hardline Hutu government. This military arm of the Hutu extremist government carried out the orders to kill Tutsi and moderate Hutu. Bizimana also commanded the six-thousand-strong Gendarmerie, a paramilitary force whose structure was based on the French model. The combination of these factors allowed Bizimana to play a significant role in the planning and implementation of the genocide. In addition to holding a powerful position in the Rwandan government, Bizimana was also an adept politician, as evidence by his actions during the months surrounding the genocide.

In late 1993 and into the early months of 1994, Bizimana admitted that the recruitment and training of militias was taking place, but he insisted that the training was for young males who were to be hired as rangers at the national parks, not for any military operations. When President Juvénal Habyarimana's plane was shot down on 6 April 1994, Bizimana was in Cameroon, attending an Olympic committee meeting, allowing Colonel Théoneste Bagosora to take control of the country, as the highest ranking military official in Rwanda at the time.

In the days and months leading up to the genocide, Bizimana had been conveying complaints to the United Nations command that alluded to the fact that the Rwandan Patriotic Front (RPF) were carrying out extensive campaigns of violence against Hutu throughout Rwanda. Additionally, by 16 May 1994, Bizimana was reporting to UN officials and the international media that the massacres in Rwanda had ended, even though there were clear indications that this was not the case. Bizimana was, in effect, the primary source of information for many international actors who were attempting to discern what was occurring in Rwanda in 1994. His statements often contrasted sharply with what outside observers, such as foreign media correspondents and officials from the United Nations, were reporting to their respective agencies.

Bizimana has been identified as a high-ranking and influential member of Agathe Habyarimana's *Akazu* ("little house"), a tight circle of prominent Hutu who surrounded President Juvenal Habyarimana's wife and were considered part of her inner circle. The members of the *Akazu* have been identified in numerous reports and trial proceedings as the masterminds behind the design and implementation of the genocide. Bizimana, along with Bagosora, has been accused of carrying out the planning and killing of several high-ranking political officials during the genocide, as well as coordinating the targeted killings of the Tutsi ethnic group and moderate Hutu who were seen as threats to the power of the Habyarimana regime. As Defense Minister, Bizimana ensured that the military did not interfere with the implementation of the genocide. Bizimana has since been identified as the second in line for responsibility of the genocide, just behind Bagosora. Bizimana was responsible for communications to representatives of the United Nations as well as the control of military operations throughout the country. Therefore, Bizimana had the ability to manage and control events on the ground through a combination of deliberate mis-communication and his post as Defense Minister. From early on it was apparent that Bizimana was skilled at avoiding questions and answers that might have implicated him or his military forces in any wrongdoing.

Like others in the *Akazu*, there is strong evidence that Bizimana collaborated with the French before and during the genocide. Military sources have noted that a French security officer, Captain Paul Barril, had been hired by Bizimana to train 120 men at a camp in northwest Rwanda. The training operation was code-named "Operation Insecticide," referring to the elimination of the Tutsi *inyenzi*, or cockroaches. Bizimana transferred $1,200,000 from an account in Nairobi to one in Paris in June 1994, allegedly as payment for Barril's services.

When Bizimana fled Rwanda ahead of the advancing Tutsi-led Rwandan Patriotic Front (RPF) he, along with other leading members of the *Akazu*, was guaranteed full protection by the regime of Daniel Torotich arap Moi in Kenya. A warrant was issued for his arrest by the ICTR, though as of 2011 he has yet to be arrested and tried at the ICTR in Arusha, Tanzania. Additionally, the United States government has offered a $5 million reward and protection for anyone who has information that will lead to the arrest of Bizimana. His capture would be considered a significant step toward reconciliation and justice for the survivors of the 1994 genocide.

[*See also* Habyarimana, Agathe; Habyarimana, Juvénal; *and* Moi, Daniel Torotich arap.]

BIBLIOGRAPHY

"Bizimana, Augustin." http://www.haguejusticeportal. net/eCache/DEF/8/946.html.

des Forges, Alison Liebhafsky. *Leave None to Tell the Story: Genocide in Rwanda.* New York and London: Human Rights Watch, 1999.

Prunier, Gérard. *The Rwanda Crisis: History of a Genocide.* New York: Columbia University Press, 1995.

Scherrer, Christian P. *Genocide and Crisis in Central Africa: Conflict Roots, Mass Violence, and Regional War.* Westport, Conn., and London: Praeger, 2002.

STERLING RECKER

Bleek, Wilhelm, and Lucy Lloyd (1827–1875), (1834–1914),

linguists active in South Africa, were born in Europe but compiled one of the most valuable South African archives. Wilhelm Heinrich Immanuel Bleek was born on 8 March 1827 in Berlin, the eldest son of the theologian Friedrich Bleek and his wife Augusta. Bleek had his early education in Berlin and received his Ph.D. in linguistics in 1851 from the University of Bonn, writing a thesis relating the Khoekhoe (then known as "Hottentot") languages of the Cape to North African languages. Lucy Catherine Lloyd was born on 7 November 1834 in Norbury, England, the daughter of Anglican minister William Henry Cynric Lloyd and his wife Lucy Anne, who died when Lucy was eight. Her father remarried, and he brought his growing family to Natal in 1849, where he became Archdeacon of Durban. Lloyd received her education privately in England and Natal.

Bleek left for Africa as a linguist on an 1854 Niger expedition, on which he grew gravely ill. During his recovery in England, he met the Anglican Bishop of Natal John William Colenso and Cape Governor George Grey. Colenso hired Bleek to assist him in writing an isiZulu grammar in 1855, and in 1856 Bleek moved to Cape Town to serve as Grey's interpreter and librarian. In Cape Town, Bleek avidly interviewed San (then so-called "Bushmen") prisoners to extend his doctoral work, and upon these interviews Bleek built an extensive vocabulary of their |xam language. In 1862, Grey bequeathed his collection of historical, anthropological, and linguistic books to the South African Public Library and appointed Bleek its curator, a post in which he served for the rest of his life.

Bleek and Lloyd met through Lloyd's sister Jemima, whom Bleek married in 1862. Lucy Lloyd, who never married, moved into their home in Mowbray, Cape Town. Lucy Lloyd was fascinated by Bleek's work, particularly when she learned that twenty-eight |xam-speaking prisoners were incarcerated at the jail in nearby Breakwater. Bleek and Lloyd asked colonial authorities if they might house one of the prisoners at their home in order to speak with him and to collect |xam folktales. First a young man named |a!kunta and then an older man named ||kabbo joined their household, followed by ||kabbo's relatives and other |xam-speakers. From 1870 to 1884, at least seventeen impoverished |xam-speaking men, women, and children lived in their household. Bleek and Lloyd recorded their personal narratives, genealogies, oral traditions, and history, and they took photographs.

After Bleek's death on 17 August 1875, Lucy and Jemima Lloyd extended the project, as Bleek had decreed that they should in his will. The Lloyds' sisters Fanny and Julia joined the household to assist them.

Lucy Lloyd succeeded Bleek as curator of the Grey Collection, receiving half his salary on account of her gender and lack of formal training; she was replaced by an ill-prepared man in 1880, who abandoned the work in 1882. Lucy and Fanny Lloyd left for England in 1883, broke and in poor health. Jemima Bleek and most of her seven children moved to Germany the next year, where her three sisters joined her.

In 1911, Lucy Lloyd published *Specimens of Bushman Folklore,* a compendium of texts from her collection; she was assisted by Wilhelm and Jemima's daughter Dorothea Bleek. Lloyd received an honorary doctorate in 1913 for this accomplishment from the University of the Cape of Good Hope, becoming the first woman to receive such a degree from a South African university. The awards committee praised her "masterly exposition of the folklore of a vanishing race that has remained primitive." She died on 31 August 1914 and was buried beside Wilhelm Bleek in Wynburg, Cape Town. Shortly after Lloyd's death, |xam died out as its surviving speakers assimilated into Afrikaans-speaking "Coloured" communities.

Dorothea Bleek worked to keep the family's archive on scholars' agendas. But it was not until the 1970s that scholars of Khoisan rock art began to rediscover Lloyd and Bleek's work, and in 1986 the anthropologist Roger Hewitt alerted the University of Cape Town to the value of the trove of notebooks in their library. Since then, the 13,000-page archive has become accessible at the University of Cape Town, and it has informed a range of innovative works on the intertwined histories of Khoisan people, rock art, linguistics, anthropology, orality, memory, colonial authority, and knowledge production. In 1996, amidst the opening of the Truth and Reconciliation Commission, the artist and archivist Pippa Skotnes opened an exhibition drawing upon the Lloyd and Bleek archive at the South African National Gallery, provoking discussion of the meanings of indigeneity in a democratic South Africa.

The colonial production and post-colonial resonance of Lloyd's and Bleek's collection reveal the interconnections of race, gender, and class in creating and sustaining a South African archive.

BIBLIOGRAPHY

Bank, Andrew. *Bushmen in a Victorian World: The Remarkable Story of the Bleek-Lloyd Collection of Bushman Folklore.* Cape Town: Double Storey, 2006. The most incisive and detailed historical account of Lloyd's and Bleek's lives and of their archive's production.

Bennun, Neil. *The Broken String: The Last Words of an Extinct People.* New York: Continuum, 2004. An accessible account of the history of the San and the meanings of the archive.

Skotnes, Pippa. *Claim to the Country: The Archive of Lucy Lloyd and Wilhelm Bleek.* Johannesburg: Jacana; and Athens, Ohio: Ohio University Press, 2007. A magisterial publication of archival texts, photographs, and letters with scholarly commentary.

MEGHAN ELISABETH HEALY

B.Léza (1905–1958), Cape Verdean musician and composer, was born on São Vicente Island (Cape Verde) on 3 December 1905. He was the son of João Vicente da Cruz and Rosa Antónia Lopes da Cruz, a domestic servant. Born on Saint Francis Xavier's day, he was named Francisco Xavier da Cruz, after the saint, and many of his works as a composer are registered under this name. However, B.Léza is the name he used throughout his life, and the name that keeps him alive in the collective memory of the Cape Verdean nation. B.Léza grew up on the streets of Lombo, a poor district whose population was largely composed of sailors, fishermen, domestic servants, and workers of the coal companies established by the British in the City of Mindelo (São Vicente Island) during the times of steam navigation. B.Léza was the product of a port city, an environment characterized by cosmopolitism and a Bohemian lifestyle. He attended classes at the Liceu Infante D. Henrique (a secondary school in São Vicente), something unusual for a young man with his background. The Liceu was the most important educational institution of colonial Cape Verde, with outstanding students such as the Cape Verdean writer Baltasar Lopes da Silva, who later became B.Léza´s friend.

In 1924 B.Léza was appointed to a position at the Repartição Superior dos Correios e Telégrafos (the Cape Verdean post and telegraph service). Two years later he was transferred to the Fogo Island, where he founded a recreational club that organized balls, recitations, and lectures. In 1931 B.Léza was discharged from that position, and he returned to São Vicente. In his home city, he worked as a tutor and dedicated himself to the composition of *mornas,* a musical genre considered a symbol of Cape Verde. In 1933, B.Léza published a book on *morna* music, entitled *Uma Partícula da Lira Caboverdiana* (A Small Piece of the Cape Verdean Lyre), where he stated that "everything that is Cape Verdean is expressed by 'Morna.'" He also brought in an innovation in the way *morna* was played. In an interview done in 1985, Baltasar Lopes da Silva remembered that B.Léza introduced into the formal structure of *mornas* a transition chord, called by Cape Verdeans a "Brazilian halftone." This was both an example of B.Léza's virtuosity and a sign of the influence exerted on him by Brazilian music. Many people believe that even B.Léza's name was influenced by the Brazilian accent when pronouncing the Portuguese word *beleza* (beauty).

In 1940, B.Léza traveled to Portugal in order to participate in the Portuguese World Exhibition. He was called to represent Cape Verde as the leader of a musical ensemble. The event, closely related to the Portuguese political regime known as *Estado Novo*, aimed at a public presentation of Portugal and its colonies. There is not much detailed information available about B.Léza's participation in the exhibition. But the Brazilian journalist Gláucia Nogueira indicates that B.Léza reacted against the plans of the event's organizers, who wanted to make the musical ensemble seem exotic by locating the musicians in a reproduction of a rural Cape Verdean hut, in the "Colonial Garden." B.Léza took his time in Portugal to care for his already serious health problems. He suffered from Pott's disease, a kind of tuberculosis that affects the spine. In 1942 he went through surgery in a Lisbon hospital.

B.Léza returned to Cape Verde in 1945. In this same year, he married Maria Luísa Calado dos Santos, whom he had met during his stay in Portugal. They had two children, Osvaldo and Veladimiro Romano da Cruz. The family went through very hard times. B.Léza fell into financial difficulties, aggravated by his health problems and his regular consumption of alcohol. But B.Léza benefited in these difficult times from his friendship with members of the local elite. The deputy Adriano Duarte Silva (1898–1961) supported B.Léza through his last years, when he was wheelchair bound. The composer would give in turn gratitude and music, such as the *morna* composed in the honor of Dr. Adriano.

B.Léza's wife and children left for Lisbon in 1956, aggravating his already poor health. It was in a hospital bed that B.Léza composed one of his most beautiful *mornas*, called *Lua Nha Testemunha*. In 14 June 1958, he died in the City of Mindelo. B.Léza continues to live in the many recordings of his compositions. Outstanding Cape Verdean singers (Cesária Évora, Bana, Titina, and many others) dedicated themselves to the *mornas* composed by B.Léza, such as *Bejo d'Sodade*, *Nôte de Mindelo*, *Miss Perfumado*, *Mar Azul*, and *Trás d'Horizonte*.

[*See also* Evora, Cesaria; *and* Silva, Baltasar Lopes da.]

BIBLIOGRAPHY

Cruz, Francisco Xavier da. *Uma Partícula da Lira Caboverdeana: Mornas crioulas inspiradas por saudades, sofrimentos e amores.* [A Small Piece of the Cape Verdean Lyre: Creole Mornas Inspired by Nostalgia, Suffering, and Love]. Praia, Cape Verde: Tip, 1933. An out-of-print work written by B.Léza himself describing some of his opinions and experiences as a musician.

Laban, Michel. *Cabo Verde: Encontro com Escritores.* 2 vols. Porto, Portugal: Fundaçao Eng. Antonio de Almeida, 1992. This book is an ensemble of interviews done with outstanding Cape Verdean writers. Some of them have met B.Léza personally and contribute facts and opinions about the composer.

Nogueira, Gláucia. *O Tempo de B.Léza: Documentos e Memórias.* Praia, Cape Verde: Instituto da Biblioteca Nacional e do Livro, 2005. The only book dedicated exclusively to the life of B.Léza, it has not been into English.

JULIANA BRAZ DIAS

Blixen, Karen (1885–1962), the Danish writer also known as Isak Dinesen, who lived in British East Africa (present-day Kenya), was born Karen Dinesen at Rungstedlund, Denmark, on 17 April 1885. Her father, Wilhelm Dinesen, was a military officer, landowner, and Member of Parliament; the Dinesens were an ancient Danish family of landed gentry. Her mother, Ingeborg Westenholtz, was the eldest daughter of the wealthy businessman and finance minister Regnar Westenholtz. Following the suicide of Wilhelm Dinesen in 1895, Ingeborg Dinesen raised her three daughters and two sons in a maternal household, where Karen was known as "Tanne." As a young woman, Karen Blixen attended art school, mastered several European languages, frequented the aristocratic circles of upper-class young people in Denmark, and began to publish short stories in Danish periodicals in 1907 under the pseudonym "Osceola." None of these early stories attracted particular attention, and she felt discouraged as a writer and as an artist.

In 1912, at the age of twenty-seven, Karen Dinesen announced her engagement to Baron Bror

Karen Blixen, 1959. (AP Images)

Blixen-Finecke of Näsbyholm in southern Sweden, her second cousin. The next year Bror Blixen travelled to British East Africa (BEA), which was recommended in booster literature as a land of opportunity for wealthy European settlers and large landholders. Financed by a family company and a substantial capital deposit provided mainly by the Dinesen family, and despite his limited knowledge and experience of agriculture and accountancy, Bror Blixen acquired a Swedish-owned coffee farm, MBagathi, just outside the government town of Nairobi. On 14 January 1914, Karen Dinesen arrived in Mombasa and married Bror Blixen that same day, arriving at her new home near Nairobi with the title of "Baroness Blixen."

The African letters Blixen sent to her family in Denmark chronicle a series of tragedies: the ill-fated attempt to establish a viable coffee plantation in the colony; the failed marriage; and the debilitating illnesses, which continued after Blixen was infected with syphilis by Bror Blixen and required that she return for treatment by specialists in Denmark. In 1921 the couple separated, against Karen Blixen's wishes. The family company dismissed Bror Blixen as manager and appointed Karen Blixen to run the Karen Coffee Company. By this time she had established a close relationship with Denys Finch Hatton, an English army pilot,

trader, and professional game hunter she met in Nairobi in 1918, and loved until his death in 1931, when his private airplane crashed. The letters describe in detail the life of the semi-aristocratic class of European settlers attracted to the Highlands that were promoted in booster literature as "White Man's Country" in the early twentieth century. These letters are the first accounts of the people, animals, and landscapes that would reappear in the memoir *Out of Africa*, illustrating Blixen's profound spiritual and aesthetic experiences in BEA. They also reflect Blixen's thinking on intellectual issues of the time: race and racism, humanitarianism and human rights, sexual morality and the future of marriage, class consciousness and nationalism, and philosophy and literature.

One of the notable features of the letters is Blixen's perspective on the domestication and consolidation of British authority in the colony. Although she mixed freely with the local settler elite (for example, Lord Delamere and Berkeley Cole were close associates) and shared the ecstasy of the safari hunt, her letters frequently reflect critically on British attitudes as an outsider, and oppose the increasing restrictions placed on the rights of Africans in such forms as the hut tax. Blixen writes at length of her strong feelings of affinity for the African people, and her sense of responsibility for those who worked on the farm and were dependent upon its fortunes. In the letters the reader observes an enlightened version of "first-generation" settler polemics: the presence of African people and specific tribal cultures are acknowledged; individuals are recognized with affection and respect. Blixen was identified as "pro-native" in the 1920s as a result of her support for independent native cultivation of their own lands, and her opposition to settler campaigns to restrict Indian immigration. Yet at the same time she writes of African peoples as dependent and available for the "civilizing mission" of the settler project; they are seen as being in need of the benevolent leadership and semi-feudal order that consolidates the European elite; and Blixen speculates on the presence of the Masai as a "dying race."

The edited collection of *Letters from Africa, 1914–1931* (published posthumously in 1981) begins with a letter written on board ship to Blixen's mother, five days before she arrived in Mombasa, and concludes with a letter to her brother Thomas as she prepared to leave Africa in July 1931 to return to Rungstedlund, grief-stricken by Hatton's death and uncertain how to reestablish herself in Europe financially, intellectually and emotionally. The farm was sold to a developer in 1931 and subdivided into residential plots; the district was named Karen in Blixen's honor. Financially the project, like the marriage, was a devastating failure; over a million dollars of family capital had been lost. On her return to Rungstedlujnd Blixen turned to tales she had been sketching throughout the 1920s and, in 1933, she completed the manuscript for *Seven Gothic Tales*, written in English and published in the United States under the pseudonym "Isak Dinesen" in 1934. It was an immediate critical and commercial success. After this she proceeded to write her celebrated autobiography *Out of Africa*, written in English under pseudonym and published to immediate acclaim in 1937.

By reading the *Letters* and *Out of Africa* together the transformation of Blixen's African experiences into Dinesen's highly selective and sensuous autobiographical account is very clear. Characters, events, and the author herself are recognizable but transformed. The influence of "tales" shapes the characterization of animals and humans in memoir, and a profound sense of loss and belatedness is apparent from the famous first sentence: "I had a farm in Africa, at the foot of the Ngong Hills." This version of colonial experience has a dreamlike and romantic quality; here is "the refined essence of a continent" where "everything you saw made for greatness and freedom and unequalled nobility." The autobiography is divided into five sections, clusters of autobiographical narratives and sketches organized chronologically, beginning with the lyrical first description of the Ngong farm and concluding with the traumatic sketches of her departure from the farm and the return to Europe.

Since its first publication, Dinesen's memoir has stood as the most powerful and seductive capture of Kenya, and an influential capture of African space and peoples for Western readers. It presents Africa as a transcendent empowering space for women, and the autobiography is a superb rendition of Africa in the pastoral mode. Although the house is progressively stripped bare in the final stories, and the narrator departs in mourning, Dinesen's mythic and sensual narratives, and her sense of oneness with the natural world, present one of the most stunning and seductive visions of how a European woman might declare "This is where I belong."

The case has been well-made by critics that Blixen was involved as a settler and then as a writer in a colonialist project that she simultaneously participated in, benefitted from, despised, and sought

to subvert. Other autobiographical accounts can be read alongside *Out of Africa* to amplify the historical, social, and literary context of the memoir. These include her contemporary Beryl Markham's *West with the Night* (1942), which describes the expansion and commodification of tourism and hunting by Finch Hatton and Bror Blixen; Alyse Simpson's *The Land That Never Was* (1937), a little-known memoir published in the same year as *Out of Africa* which describes the gap between the Kenya of the English imagination and the realities of the white pioneering society; and Elspeth Huxley's *The Flame Trees of Thika* (1959), which both reworks and renovates the romance of pioneering amid the emergence of African nationalism in the 1950s. Later memoirs, such as Kuki Gallman's *I Dreamed of Africa* (1991), indicate the ongoing influence of Dinesen's narrative of authentic belonging in Africa, and its association with white hunter mythography. Notable too is the memoir of Blixen's gifted cook Kamante Gatura, *Longing for Darkness: Kamante's Tales from Out of Africa* (1975). Recent feminist and psychoanalytic criticism also opens new perspectives on Dinesen's autobiography, finding there a more complex and self-reflexive text, with its innovative modernist uses of language and subjectivity. In 1985, Sydney Pollack's film adaptation of the autobiography renewed Dinesen's vision of the elite settler colony in Kenya as the essence of Africa.

Karen Blixen never returned to Africa. She became mistress of Rungstedlund upon the death of her mother in 1939. Her third book, *Winter's Tales* (1942), returned to Danish rural life and mythology, and a historical crime story, *The Angelic Avengers* (Danish edition, 1944; British edition, 1946; American edition, 1947), was published under the pseudonym Pierre Andrézel. A new book of African memoirs, *Shadows on the Grass* (1960), was conceived as the epilogue to *Out of Africa*. It draws on material left out of the first memoir, and includes updates on the African people in the original, along with several other tales written early in the 1950s and presented elsewhere. This was her last book; Karen Blixen died at Rundstedlund on 7 September 1962.

[*See also* Delamere, Hugh Cholmondeley; *and* Markham, Beryl Clutterbuck.]

BIBLIOGRAPHY

Aiken, Susan Hardy. *Isak Dinesen and the Engendering of Narrative*. Chicago: University of Chicago, 1990.

Kennedy, Dane. *Islands of White: Settler Culture and Society in Kenya and Southern Rhodesia, 1890–1939.* Durham, N.C.: Duke University Press, 1987.

Shaw, Carolyn Martin. *Colonial Inscriptions: Race, Sex and Class in Kenya.* Minneapolis and London: University of Minnesota Press, 1995.

Thurman, Judith. *Isak Dinesen: The Life of Karen Blixen.* Harmondsworth, UK: Penguin, 1984.

GILLIAN WHITLOCK

Blondy, Alpha (1953–), Ivorian reggae music star, was born in Dimbokro on 1 January 1953 to a Muslim mother and a Christian father. The oldest of nine children, he was named Seydou Koné, after his grandfather, and brought up by his grandmother, Cheri Coco, in the Muslim faith. Early signs of rebelliousness prompted his exasperated grandmother to call him "blondy," an apparent mispronunciation of "bandit" (troublemaker). Reunited with his father in Odienné in 1962, young Blondy spent the next ten years attending Saint Elisabeth High School, where he became involved in student politics and also developed an interest in music. Expelled from school for an altercation with his math teacher, Blondy went to Monrovia, Liberia, to study English. He proceeded to the United States, settled in New York in 1973, and enrolled first in Hunter College and later in the Columbia University's American Language Program to pursue a career as an English teacher. At the time he was seeking to please his father who considered teaching English a more dignified profession. However, the pull of music, especially reggae, was much stronger. Heavily influenced by Bob Marley, Blondy became a Rastafarian and supported himself financially by singing Marley's songs in Harlem nightclubs. He also practically lived on the street, playing a drum and singing in Central Park. He was hospitalized at New York's Bellevue Hospital and treated for drug addiction and mental health for about a year.

Discharged from the hospital, Blondy returned to Ivory Coast. However, his personal struggles were far from over. He was imprisoned for threatening the Ivoirian ambassador in New York who had raised doubts about his Ivoirian citizenship. He thought Blondy's English was too polished for an Ivoirian. Blondy's parents also had him institutionalized at Bingerville asylum in Abidjan for two years, convinced that their son's dreadlocks and apparent destitution after years in America were unmistakable signs of insanity. Blondy continued to write songs even while he was under the influence of powerful antipsychotic sedatives. Released from the asylum, Blondy's fortunes began to change when he was reunited with a childhood friend Fulgence Kassi who had become famous as a television producer. Blondy's career as a reggae artist took off when he appeared on Ivoirian television's talent show, *First Chance*. He began using the stage name "Alpha Blondy," with the addition of the first letter of the Greek alphabet. He recorded his first solo album in 1982, entitled *Jah Glory*, and began touring all over Africa. The album proved enormously successful in Africa, selling more than a million copies. It would later become a resistance anthem because of one of the songs on the album, "Brigadier Sabari," recounts Ivoirian police brutality that Blondy had experienced personally.

With his newly formed band, Solar System, Blondy recorded his second album, *Cocody Rock*, in 1984 in Paris. Reflecting Blondy's versatility as a musician, the band featured an international cast of musicians drawn from Cameroon, Ivory Coast, England, France, Jamaica, and Togo. Blondy returned to Abidjan in 1985 to record *Apartheid Is Nazism*. In 1986 he made a pilgrimage to Jamaica and recorded his third album, *Jerusalem*, with the Wailers at Marley's Tuff Gong Studios. Committed to using his music to promote unity between Christianity, Islam, and Judaism, he sang in Hebrew during a concert in Morocco in 1986. By the time he released *Revolution* in 1987, Blondy had established himself not only as Africa's premier international reggae artist but also a politically engaged musician and heir-apparent to his idol Bob Marley. Blondy spent the years between 1987 and 1989 giving concerts and recording *SOS Guèrre Tribale* in Abidjan.

Blondy dropped out from the music scene for several years during the 1990s to spend more time with his seven children. He sought psychiatric help at the beginning of 1993 following a bout with depression after a world tour. This new episode is reflected in his more spiritual and religious album *Dieu* (God) that included tracks such as "Heal Me," an apparent reference to his illness and recovery, a veritable cry for help. He released *Yitzak Rabin* in 1998 to commemorate the slain Israeli leader's efforts to bring peace to the Middle East and *Elohim* in 2000. It featured the single "*Journaliste en Danger*," a reference to the assassination of the journalist Norbert Zongo. Blondy celebrated twenty years as a recording artist with *MERCI* (Thank You) in 2002. While the album earned him a Grammy Award nomination for Best Reggae Album, he was unable to attend the ceremony in New York because of the political turmoil in Ivory Coast at the time. He celebrated the signing of the March 2007 peace agreement between Laurent Gbagbo's government and the rebels with *Jah Victory* in July. Blondy gave a concert in New York's Central Park on 19 July 2009. On 13 June 2010 a concert he gave to celebrate the peace and unity of the country drew such a huge crowd that twenty people were crushed to death in a melee. Like his idol Marley, Blondy has used his talent as a musician to promote global peace, love, and religious tolerance. At home he preaches national unity and social justice. He empathizes with the downtrodden, the impoverished, the dispossessed, and the marginalized of society. He rails against "tribalism," human rights abuses, corruption, and dictatorship in Africa and elsewhere. He coined the term "democrature" (democratatorship) to describe Africa's sham democracies. To this day, Blondy remains a staunch supporter of African unity.

Blondy was named United Nations Ambassador of Peace for Ivory Coast in 2005. He has worked tirelessly to promote reconciliation and reunification of his country, divided into two since the failed coup of 19 September 2002. A humanitarian to boot, he has set up a nonprofit foundation, Alpha Blondy Jah Glory Foundation, to promote social justice and alleviate generational poverty by giving people the tools they need to help themselves. The foundation's work is reflected in the Women's Self-Sufficiency Micro Loan Program and Tafari-Genesis Retreat Camp for Children in Ivory Coast and Burkina Faso. Blondy gives an annual free concert at Bassam beach called "festa" and his message of peace and global understanding is delivered in an assortment of African and European languages including his native Dioula, English and French, and sometimes in Arabic, Baulé, Hebrew, Malinke, Twi, and Wolof.

[*See also* Gbagbo, Laurent Koudou.]

BIBLIOGRAPHY

Tenaille, Frank. *Music Is the Weapon of the Future: Fifty Years of African Popular Music.* Translated by Stephen Toussaint and Hope Sandrine. Chicago: Lawrence Hill Books, 2002.

CYRIL DADDIEH

Blouin, Andrée (1921–), pan-African political activist and author who worked with several African heads of state during the decolonization era, was born in the village of Bessou, near Fort de Possel (present-day Possel), in the French colony of Ubangi-Shari (present-day Central African Republic, CAR) on 16 December 1921. Her father, Pierre Gerbillat, was a French businessman from Lyon. Her mother, Joséphine Wouassimba, was the daughter of Gbanziri chief Zoumague of Kuango. Her father paid bridewealth to marry Zoumague's daughter, but he then married a Belgian woman, after which Andrée, like many young *métisse* or Euro-African "mixed blood" girls at that time, was sent away to be raised and educated by nuns of the Order of St. Joseph of Cluny in the Republic of the Congo (Brazzaville), where she was registered as number twenty-two. For the next fourteen years, Andrée's education and upbringing was supervised by extremely strict and often cruel Catholic sisters in this orphanage, which was surrounded by three-meter-high walls topped with broken pieces of glass.

The ambiguous status of *métisse* individuals in French colonies—often despised but also privileged—was emphasized in 1937, when the French government decided to extend French citizenship to more of their *métisse* colonial subjects. Thus, when Andrée was sixteen years old, she was permitted to become a French citizen. In 1938, Andrée escaped from the orphanage and returned to live briefly with her father in Bangui, the capital of Ubangi-Shari, while his Belgian wife was in Europe.

Andrée left her father's house again after his wife returned from Europe, and soon thereafter, during World War II, she began living with an Alsatian businessman in Bangui, Charles Greutz, who started a trucking company and purchased land for a coffee plantation in Bangassou, a town about 800 kilometers (500 miles) east of Bangui.

Andrée's autobiographical account of her life in Ubangi-Shari during this period provides rare insights into the daily life of European businessmen, their *métis* children, and their African employees during the French colonial era. She bore two children, Rita and René, but René died before Andrée married Greutz on 14 August 1946. She then went with him to Alsace, where she was warmly welcomed by Greutz's family and friends. This was a striking contrast with the racism she had experienced in Africa.

After the war, Greutz returned to Bangui; in 1948, Andrée left Rita with her grandparents in Alsace and returned to Bangui to join her husband, who had given a room in his large new villa to a visiting engineer from the French Bureau of Mines,

André Blouin. Greutz was involved with another woman at this time, and Andrée felt in love with Blouin. She eventually left Greutz for Blouin, who was then transferred to Siguiri in what was then French Guinea. On 19 November 1952, Andrée married Blouin in Paris, after which she was known as Andrée Blouin. She bore two children, Patrick and Sylvaine, and brought Rita from Alsace to Siguiri.

The seven years Andrée resided in French Guinea in the 1950s coincided with the rise to power of Sékou Touré, who became the first president of the Republic of Guinea. In 1957, Andrée became an active member of the struggle for independence in Guinea, working with the Rassemblement Démocratique Africaine (RDA; African Democratic Rally), and she supported Touré's decision to reject General Charles de Gaulle's offer of membership for Guinea in a federal community with France at its head. When the RDA won legislative elections, Andrée's husband was relieved of his post as director of the diamond mines of Kerouane and reassigned to Madagascar, because of his tolerance or encouragement of his wife's political activities. However, when Guinea became independent in 1958, the Blouins resolved to return to Guinea. On the way there, they passed through Brazzaville, where Andrée became involved in an effort to reconcile rival leaders Abbé Fulbert Youlou and Jacques Opangault. Then she visited Bangui, where she met with Barthélemy Boganda, "founding father" of the Central African Republic, who had read about Andrée's political activities. Andrée soon became a go-between for a number of African leaders, including Boganda, Youlou in the Congo, and Félix Houphouët-Boigny in Paris.

The Blouins eventually returned to Guinea, where Andrée met several revolutionary leaders from the Belgian Congo (now the Democratic Republic of Congo, or DR Congo), including Antoine Gizenga, who asked her to go to Leopoldville (later Kinshasa) to join the political struggle there. While her husband worked for the new government of Guinea, Andrée went to Leopoldville in 1960 to take charge of the Feminine Movement for African Solidarity. She was encouraged by many African leaders, including Ghana's Kwame Nkrumah, to mobilize women in support of African unity. By May 1960 she had enrolled 45,000 members in the Feminine Movement in three provinces alone, and word of her work soon spread throughout the colony. She became Chief of Protocol for the government of the Congo-Leopoldville and a speechwriter for Deputy-Premier Gizenga.

The Belgians expelled Andrée from the colony just a few days before independence was granted on 30 June 1960, however, for her political activism.

By 8 July, Andrée was back in independent Congo-Leopoldville, where her advice and political expertise was welcome. Prime Minister Patrice Lumumba decided to raise the pay of all government employees except the military. The main garrison in Leopoldville soon mutinied against its white officers and attacked numerous European targets. Bands of mutineers roamed the capital looting and terrorizing the white population. This led to a military intervention into Congo by Belgian forces in an ostensible effort to secure the safety of its citizens. The intervention was a violation of the national sovereignty. It was Andrée who suggested that Lumumba ask the United States to pressure the Belgians into removing their troops from Congo-Leopoldville. In response to requests by Lumumba, the United Nations (UN) Security Council called upon Belgium to remove its troops and for the UN to provide "military assistance to the Congolese forces" and "to allow them to meet fully their tasks." Andrée's suggestion helped to prompt the entry of the UN soldiers into the Congo. With the fall of Lumumba and the rise of Mobutu by means of a military coup, Andrée fell from grace, and she received an order of expulsion in November 1960.

After Algeria won its independence on 3 July 1962, Andrée's husband took a job with the Algerian Department of Mines. Andrée began writing articles analyzing events in Africa. Over the next decades, she was an outspoken critic of neocolonialism in Africa. In 1983 she published her memoir, *My Country, Africa: Autobiography of the Black Pasionaria.* Once called the Madame de Staël of Sékou Touré's revolutionary movement, she was also one of several notable *métisse* in CAR history, including Jane Vialle, Marie-Josèphe Zani-Fe Touam-Bona, and Jeanne-Marie Ruth-Rolland, who fought for women's rights.

[*See also* Boganda, Barthélemy; Gizenga, Antoine; Lumumba, Patrice Emery; Mobutu Sese Seko; Nkrumah, Kwame; Ruth-Rolland, Jeanne-Marie; Touré, Ahmed Sékou; Vialle, Jane; Youlou, Fulbert; *and* Zani-fé Touam-Bona, Marie-Josèphe.]

BIBLIOGRAPHY

Assiba d'Almeida, Irène. "Andrée Blouin: Growing Up as a Métisse in Colonial Africa." In *Francophone African Women Writers*, edited by Irène Assiba d'Almeida, pp. 55–70. Gainesville: University Press of Florida, 1994.

Blouin, Andrée, and Jean MacKellar. *My Country, Africa: Autobiography of the Black Pasionaria.* New York: Praeger, 1983.

Drew, Allison. "Andrée Blouin and Pan-African Nationalism in Guinea and the Congo." In *Pan-African Biography*, edited by Robert Hill, pp. 209–217. Los Angeles: African Studies Association, 1987.

"The Female Touch." *Time Magazine*, August 15, 1960.

RICHARD A. BRADSHAW and
JUAN FANDOS-RIUS

Blyden, Edward Wilmot (1832–1912), peripatetic Liberian intellectual and diplomat, pan-African theoretician, and sometime British colonial official in Sierra Leone and Nigeria, was born on 3 August 1832 on St. Thomas in the Danish Virgin Islands to free parents of Igbo or Ewe origin. Thanks to the influence of an American Presbyterian missionary, the Rev. John P. Knox, Blyden decided, while in his teens, to become a Presbyterian minister himself but was thwarted in his efforts to enroll at the Rutgers Theological College because he was black. Thus, again influenced by Knox and the contacts of the latter in the American Colonization Society, he immigrated to Liberia in 1850. Here he would complete secondary education at the Presbyterian Church–sponsored Alexander High School, where he would then become a teacher.

Blyden's perception that his parents—his mother a teacher and his father a tailor—were of "pure" Negro African origin, his encounters with slavery on St. Thomas, in Venezuela, where he lived for two years, and then in the United States, where in addition to slavery he encountered virulent racism, stimulated in him a lifelong commitment to Negro race pride and the development of a racial ideology similar to what later on would be called Négritude. He assimilated the stated ideals of the founders of Liberia that this new country was destined to regenerate Africa and to become a showcase of black achievement.

Even though Blyden's formal education ended with graduation from secondary school, he became a lifelong, intensively achievement-oriented, and interdisciplinary autodidact. He qualified for ordination as a Presbyterian minister in 1858. Blyden's preparation for the ministry requiring him to learn Hebrew, Greek, and Latin stimulated him to become a competent classicist.

Aiming to refute or reinterpret such Biblical passages as Genesis 9:25 regarding the curse of Ham that whites cited to justify slavery, Blyden cited Psalm 68:31: "Ethiopia shall soon stretch out her hands unto God." Reaching outside the Bible, he also cited Homer regarding the "blameless Ethiopians" and Herodotus's assertion that the ancient Egyptians were black. Regarding the African origins of ancient Egypt, Blyden anticipated the theses of Cheikh Anta Diop and Martin Bernal. Citing the black African ancestry of St. Augustine of Hippo, he underlined the African contribution to Christian theology.

Soon after Blyden's arrival in Liberia, he began to publish articles on scholarly subjects in the country's one newspaper, the *Liberia Herald*, becoming its editor in 1855. He then published his first book in Monrovia in 1856, *A Voice from Bleeding Africa*. Other writings by Blyden found publishers in Great Britain, the United States, and Sierra Leone and would be widely read in missionary and scholarly circles. Wealthy admirers offered to sponsor him for university studies in Great Britain, but he declined the offers, believing that he would be more useful to Africa if he remained in Liberia. He became principal of Alexander High School in 1858 and professor of classics at Liberia College in 1862. In short, within six years of Blyden's first arrival in Liberia, he had established himself and was recognized as Liberia's premier intellectual.

Although Blyden served the Liberian state and its educational institutions in a number of capacities until his final retirement in Freetown in 1906, his relationship with the Americo-Liberian interracial elite that dominated the country most of the time from independence in 1847 until the end of the nineteenth century was troubled. He accused its members of attempting to reproduce in Liberia the same color prejudices as in the United States, deplored their unwillingness, despite lip service to the contrary, to include the native inhabitants of Liberia in the government and civil society that they were creating, and blamed the continued lack of development of the country on their frivolity. He was particularly critical of the octoroon, Joseph Jenkins Roberts, who served as the first and seventh president of Liberia (1847–1856 and 1872–1876) as well as holding other posts, including that of president of Liberia College. There was also a personal element to his negative feelings about the interracial elite. In 1856, he entered into what proved to be an unhappy marriage with Sarah Yates, the mulatto daughter of the Liberian vice-president. Not as well educated as he, she was unable to share or even to empathize with any of his intellectual pursuits.

In the meantime, Blyden developed a strong interest in the native peoples of Liberia, particularly the Mandinka, who sensitized him to Islam and the Arabic language that he began to study. In 1866, he obtained funding from the American Colonization Society and various British missionary associations to visit Egypt, Lebanon, and Syria, cutting short his 1864 appointment as Liberian secretary of state. He hoped to perfect his knowledge of Arabic and of Islamic culture and to observe the Negro heritage of ancient Egypt. Returning to Monrovia, he added Arabic to the curriculum of Liberia College, despite the opposition of Joseph Jenkins Roberts, now the college president.

Throughout Blyden's active career in Liberia, he took particular interest in and responsibility for encouraging emigration from the United States, to which he paid numerous visits, and the British West Indies; however, he increasingly insisted that only "pure" Negroes should settle in Liberia. His 1862 visit to the United States as Liberian commissioner for emigration hardened his racial attitudes. On one hand, the virulent racism he encountered confirmed his conviction that the only way for African Americans to escape from this racism was to immigrate to Liberia. On the other hand, he was confronted with the reality that the mostly interracial African American leadership, convinced in this second year of the American Civil War that the end of slavery was approaching, had little desire to leave the United States. The accidental publication of a report that Blyden wrote for the American Colonization Society in which he argued that mulattoes were unsuitable temperamentally and biologically for settlement in Liberia contributed to his 1871–1873 exile in Sierra Leone.

This period of exile that corresponded with the administrations of two very Afrophile British governors, Sir Arthur Kennedy and John Pope-Hennessey, stimulated a growing Anglophilism on the part of Blyden. Obtaining an appointment as a government agent, he led two expeditions into the interior, one of them reaching Timbo, the capital of the Futa Jalon Almamate. Had the British authorities followed up on Blyden's leads, Futa Jalon might have gone to Great Britain, as part of Sierra Leone, rather than to France. Blyden also founded a newspaper, *The Negro*, in Freetown.

Apparently Blyden did not perceive any contradiction between his developing ideas of African cultural and political nationalism and his efforts to extend British influence, first in Sierra Leone and later in the Lagos colony, where he also served as a native affairs agent in 1896 and 1897. When it seemed to him that the colonial conquest of all of Africa was inevitable, he argued that at least the parts of Africa under British rule would undergo rapid economic development thanks to British investment and would be permitted to evolve politically and culturally along their own lines until in time the British would withdraw. In 1905, Blyden proposed that Liberia become a British protectorate as a way to avoid dismemberment.

Back in Monrovia in 1873, Blyden resumed teaching at Liberia College and also, from 1875 to 1877, served as principal of a refounded Alexander High School. Then, in 1877 and 1878, after serving a first stint as Liberian minister to Great Britain where he was lionized, he returned to Liberia to serve simultaneously as president of Liberia College (1880–1884) and minister of the interior of Liberia (1880–1882). His failure to win election in 1884 as president of Liberia led to his second period of exile in Sierra Leone. Here in 1887 and 1888, he published what is considered to be his greatest work, *Christianity, Islam, and the Negro Race*, a compendium of previous writings going back to the 1860s plus two articles on Islam in Africa written for inclusion in this book. He argued that African Islam was well adapted to the realities of African social life and that Christianity, in order to be successful in Africa, would have to emancipate itself from the Eurocentric arrogance of many missionaries. He pursued this line of thought in a second influential book, *African Life and Customs*, published in 1908, asserting that polygamy in Africa, being a guarantee of family and social stability, should not be a barrier to membership in Christian churches. In Lagos in 1891, Blyden argued passionately for the establishment of an independent native pastorate that would permit African converts to Christianity to retain their traditional cultures. Lecturing in Freetown two years later, he coined the phrase "African personality."

In 1892, Blyden served briefly, once again, as Liberian minister to Great Britain. He paid a last visit to the United States in 1895, taught for a year at Liberia College (1900–1901), and finally, while serving as director of Muslim education in Sierra Leone from 1901 to 1906, took up one more diplomatic assignment for Liberia as its minister to Great Britain and France between June and September 1905. Although lionized in both countries, he was unable to prevent the French annexation of Liberian territory. Following medical treatment in Liverpool, he retired to Freetown, where he died on 7 February 1912.

Although in his later years Blyden's anglophilia alienated many of the younger members of the African westernized elites, his writings inspired such leaders of the West African nationalist movements as Kwame Nkrumah and Benjamin Nnamdi Azikewe. Léopold Senghor viewed him as a major precursor of Négritude.

[*See also* Augustine of Hippo; Azikiwe, Benjamin Nnamdi; Diop, Cheikh Anta; Nkrumah, Kwame; *and* Senghor, Léopold Sédar.]

BIBLIOGRAPHY

Blyden, Edward W. *African Life and Customs*. London: C. M. Phillips, 1908.

Blyden, Edward W. *Christianity, Islam, and the Negro Race*. Edinburgh: Edinburgh University Press, 1967.

Holden, Edith. *Blyden of Liberia: An Account of the Life and Labors of Edward Wilmot Blyden, LL.D., as Recorded in Letters and in Print*. New York: Vantage Press, 1967.

July, Robert W. *The Origins of Modern African Thought: Its Development in West Africa during the Nineteenth and Twentieth Centuries*. New York: Frederick A. Praeger, 1967.

Livingston, Thomas W. *Education and Race: A Biography of Edward Wilmot Blyden*. San Francisco: Glendessary Press, 1975.

Lynch, Hollis R. *Edward Wilmot Blyden: Pan-Negro Patriot (1832–1912)*. New York: Oxford University Press, 1970.

LELAND CONLEY BARROWS

Boakye, Kwasi (c. 1827–1904), traveler and writer from what is now southern Ghana, was born c. 1827 in or near the Asante capital of Kumasi. In contemporary documents, his name often appears as Aquassie Boachi. His father Kwaku Dua (c. 1797–1867) was *Asantehene* (King of Asante) from 1834 to 1867. According to the "History of Ashanti," prepared in the mid-twentieth century under the chairmanship of Asantehene Prempeh II (1892–1970), Kwasi Boakye belonged to the village of Atomfuo, 8 miles (13 km) east of Kumasi. This suggests that on his mother's side he came from the lineage of royal blacksmiths, which may explain why, in 1837, in accordance with his father's wishes, he and a close relative of the same age, Kwame Poku, were chosen to accompany a Dutch embassy under Major-General Jan Verveer on its return to Elmina on the coast. They were subsequently brought to the Netherlands, where they received a bourgeois education at a boarding school in Delft,

living in the house of the schoolmaster. (The Dutch connection with the Asante kingdom had deep roots, beginning with their establishment of trading and slave posts on the Gold Coast in the seventeenth century).

The two students underwent what Yarak (1987) has called "a process of almost total cultural alienation from their motherland." They also made contacts with the Dutch royal family and members of the aristocracy. An oil painting showing the two "princes" and Verveer was sent from the Netherlands via Elmina to Kwaku Dua in Kumasi, but it has since been lost. Both boys were baptized into the Reformed Church in 1843, and in the same year Kwasi Boakye, who was considered "very bright indeed," began to study civil engineering at the Royal Academy in Delft, passing his final examinations with distinction in 1847. In this year Kwame Poku, who had been less successful at school, returned to the Gold Coast; he committed suicide there in 1850.

Having befriended the duke of Saxe-Weimar-Eisenach while in the Netherlands, Kwasi Boakye continued his studies at the Royal Saxon Mining Academy in Freiberg (southeastern Germany). Just at the time when uprisings were taking place in many German cities (including nearby Dresden), a German periodical published an article entitled "Erinnerungen aus Aschanti" (Memories from Asante), based on a lecture given at the Weimar court by Kwasi Boakye's mentor in Freiberg, Professor Bernhard von Cotta (1808–1879), who evidently drew all his information from Kwasi Boakye. It included the music of a thirteen-bar Asante "people's hymn" (*Volkshymn*), written down (and arranged) by the composer Franz Liszt (1811–1886) "in accordance with the memories of Prince Aquassie Boachi." (Liszt himself had settled in Weimar the same year.) A year later another periodical published six long articles on "the Ashantis," again without direct attribution but acknowledging his permission to use his "notes concerning his fatherland."

In 1849 Kwasi Boakye petitioned the new Dutch king not to be sent back to the Gold Coast. In any case, Dutch gold mining on the Gold Coast terminated at this time. He was appointed "aspirant-engineer" in the new department of mines of the Dutch East Indies; but for racial reasons the term "extraordinary" was added to his job specification, with the aim of ensuring that he should always remain under the supervision of a European. This supervisor, a man whom he had known since his studies in Delft, inflicted many racial slights upon him in Batavia (present-day Jakarta). Eventually, in 1856, Kwasi Boakye travelled to the Netherlands in order to complain. It appears that while on the one hand he was able to win considerable sympathy in royal and aristocratic circles, this was not enough to outweigh the obstacles he encountered in bourgeois society. He was awarded a government pension and—six years after returning to the East Indies—agricultural land on the island of Java, where he began planting coffee in 1862. His plantation was not a great success, but he won friends among the local population and senior Dutch officials. He died in Batavia (today's Jakarta) on 9 July 1904, leaving three recognized children by local women. (His children received Asante names, but not in accordance with Asante naming practice.)

Apart from scientific reports on his research concerning coal beds on Java, his main publication was an ethnographic article on the Chinese living on the island, which appeared in German and Dutch in 1855–1856. He also left behind a nineteen-page manuscript for a lecture on Asante given to a student debating society in Delft in 1846. European contemporaries referred in the 1870s to the career of Kwasi Boakye as evidence that "it is possible for something good to come out of Ashantee," and after his death several people who had known him published their recollections. A historical novel based on his life appeared in Dutch in 1997 and has since been translated into German and English.

BIBLIOGRAPHY

Boachi, A. "Mededeelingen over de chinezen op het Eiland Java." *Bijdragen tot de Taal-, Land- en Volkenkunde van Nederlandsch Indië* 4 (1856): 278–295.

Boachi, A. "Notizen über die Chinesen auf der Insel Java." *Zeitschrift der Deutschen Morgenländischen Gesellschaft* 9 (1855): 808–823.

Japin, Arthur. *The Two Hearts of Kwasi Boachi.* New York: Knopf, 2000.

Jones, Adam. "Franz Liszt und die Musik Afrikas." *AfS-Magazin* 3 (1997): 24–27.

Jones, Adam. "Zwei indigene Ethnographen der Goldküste im 19. Jahrhundert: Kwasi Boakye und Carl Reindorf." In *Afrikaner schreiben zurück. Texte und Bilder afrikanischer Ethnographien*, edited by H. Behrend and T. Geider, pp. 27–40. Cologne, Germany: Köppe, 1998.

Yarak, Larry. "Kwasi Boakye and Kwame Poku: Dutch-educated Asante 'Princes.'" In *The Golden Stool: Studies of the Asante Center and Periphery*, edited by E. Schildkrout, pp. 131–145. New York: American Museum of Natural History, 1987.

ADAM JONES

Bocchoris (ruled 717–711 BCE) was second king of the Egyptian 24th Dynasty. The name Bocchoris is a Hellenized garbling of the prenomen, Wahkare, of Bakenranef, a son, though perhaps not the eldest, of Tefnakhte (725–717 BCE). Bocchoris came to power in the city of Sais in the western Nile Delta, the ancestral home of the family. After his father's abortive attempt to reunite Egypt and his defeat at the hands of the Kushite Piankhy (b. c. 719 BCE), the claims of the family to be the legitimate rulers of the country proved equivocal to say the least; for most of his short reign Bocchoris lived under the perpetual threat of being unseated by a new Kushite invasion. His sphere of authority was much attenuated, and he seems to have been disinclined to expand it. The Thebaid was now subservient to Kush through the office of Divine Worshiper of Amun, now held by the Kushite princess Amunirdis, and the principalities of Middle Egypt and the western oases likewise acknowledged the authority of the kingdom of Kush. Even in his own bailiwick, the Delta, Bocchoris had to suffer the continued independence of a dozen or so cantons, ruled by Libyan chiefs and assorted mayors and princes. If he is the fir 'u (i.e., Pharaoh) king of Egypt whom the Ashdod rebels courted in their incipient revolt against Assyria—and there are others of his contemporaries who would have sported this title—there is no evidence that he could, or did, give any real assistance. In fact, when the discomfited Ashdodite rebel fled to Egypt for asylum, he bypassed Sais and made straight for Kush in the south! Scarabs and vases with Bocchoris's name have come to light in Italy and the islands, but whether these indicate trade is doubtful. In spite of his political and military weakness, however, Bocchoris enjoyed the approbation of Memphis and its priesthood. This city had suffered heavily in the invasion of Piankhy shortly before Tefnakhte died, and it would be quite understandable if the inhabitants refused to countenance him or any of his descendants as overlords. In the event, they gave Bocchoris their approbation, and when an Apis bull died in his sixth year, it was his name that is found in the great hypogeum of the sacred bulls, the Serapeum. Bocchoris was not to be spared, however. While this very bull was being interred, Sabaco, Piankhy's brother and successor, who had come to the throne a year before, was marching north in a repetition of the Kushite invasion. Treating Bocchoris as an illegitimate rebel, Sabaco removed him from the throne and had him burned alive, the penalty prescribed by Egyptian law for treason.

While the contemporary evidence for the reign is sparse, the memory of Bocchoris lived on in legends which are difficult to assess as to their historicity. His ultimate fate certainly enhanced his role as the tragic hero, the object of sympathy, but he himself was remembered as a wizened, avaricious, and contemptible cretin, albeit noted for his wisdom. (If this is not a working of the motif of the "anti-hero," well known in Egyptian literature, it may be a folkloric interpretation of now lost representations.) In legend, Bocchoris became a kind of Egyptian "Solomon," a great lawgiver whose sagacity and fairness attracted litigants from both near and far and whose judgments were remembered for their excellence centuries later. In fact, Diodorus made him the fourth in a line of seven legendary experts in jurisprudence scattered throughout the three millennia of Egyptian history. Specifically, he is credited with drawing up the laws governing kingship and more closely defining the laws regulating contracts. While we can only guess at the origin and extent of the former, the laws on contracts, as described by Diodorus, appear to have been genuine attempts at ameliorating earlier, draconian laws regarding enslavement for unpaid debt. (The tradition may contain a modicum of truth: business documents within a generation of Bocchoris's death seem to show such legislation in practice.)

Other more fanciful, if not outlandish, yarns fasten upon the reign of Bocchoris. Occupation of the land by Assyrians, Persians, and Greeks in the seventh through fourth centuries BC gave rise to a species of folklore that looked for deliverance from foreign oppression. The ram of Mendes had prophesied under Bocchoris that Egypt would be invaded sometime in the future by vile northerners and would suffer the destruction of its cities before final salvation came in the person of a savior from the south. Because of a false association of Moses with Piankhy, the reign of Bocchoris was singled out as the time of the Exodus. The Jews, smitten by leprosy, had fled into the Egyptian temples, whence on an oracle of the gods they were ejected to alleviate a famine that had overwhelmed the land. Bocchoris eventually expelled them from the country, whereupon they journeyed north into Palestine and founded the city of Jerusalem. Other legends of questionable reliability have Bocchoris setting

up a contest between the two sacred bulls, Apis (at Memphis) and Mnevis (at Heliopolis), and leading, with his father, a military campaign into the Sinai desert. Traditions preserved in Eusebius that it was during Bocchoris's floruit that Milesian commercial activity began and that the Greek colony of Cyrene was founded are without historical foundation.

The subversion of Bocchoris's administration and his execution did not terminate his family's hold on the bailiwick of Sais. He and his father founded a dynastic sequence that, through the intermediary of his (supposed) son, Nechepso ("Necho the Saite"), was to become the great 26th or Saite Dynasty.

[*See also* Tefnakhte.]

BIBLIOGRAPHY

Janssen, J. M. "Over Farao Boccoris." In *Mélanges A. W. Byvanck*, pp. 17–29. Leiden: Brill, 1954.

Meulenaere, Herman de. "Bokchoris." In *Lexikon der Agyptologie I*, p. 846. Wiesbaden: Harrassowitz Verlag, 1972.

Ray, J. D. "Bakenrenef." In *Oxford Encyclopedia of Ancient Egypt*, edited by Donald B. Redford, Vol. 1, p. 162. New York: Oxford University Press, 2001.

Redford, Donald B. *Pharaonic King-Lists, Annals and Day-Books*. Mississauga, Ontario: Benben Publications, 1986.

Ridgway, David. "The Rehabilitation of Bocchoris: Notes and Queries from Italy." *Journal of Egyptian Archaeology* 85 (1999): 143–152.

DONALD B. REDFORD

Bocchus I (d. 80 BCE), king of Mauretania (c. 120–80 BCE), was the first powerful king of Mauretania, the vast region of northwest Africa including everything west of the Muluccha River. The earliest known event of his career is his involvement with the Greek adventurer Eudoxus of Cyzicus, who, after an attempt to circumnavigate Africa, was shipwrecked on the Atlantic coast of Mauretania and ended up at Bocchus' capital, Volubilis, probably around 115 BC. Although Eudoxus requested financing for further expeditions, Bocchus was not interested in exposing his kingdom to Greek adventurism and planned to exile Eudoxus to an island (perhaps one of the Canaries), but he escaped to the Roman city of Tingis.

In 112 BCE, war broke out between Rome and Jugurtha, the claimant to the Numidian throne, the territory just east of Bocchus' dominions.

Bocchus attempted to remain neutral, but was drawn into the war when refugees began showing up at his court. He concluded a marriage alliance with Jugurtha and sent envoys to Rome, marking the beginning of a cautious double game. The Romans were diffident toward his overtures, and Bocchus sent military aid to Jugurtha and assisted in his attack on the Roman commander, Gaius Marius, but this resulted in Bocchus' defeat. Marius sent his quaestor Lucius Cornelius Sulla to the king to cultivate a relationship, and eventually Bocchus betrayed Jugurtha and trapped him, handing him over to Sulla in 105 BCE, ending the war. He was rewarded with the northern portions of the Numidian kingdom, from the Muluccha River east to the boundary of the Roman province of Africa. Moreover, Sulla, who felt that his handling of Jugurtha made his career, ensured official Roman recognition of Bocchus' enlarged kingdom and encouraged Bocchus to dedicate a great sculptural group on the Roman Capitol showing the surrender of Jugurtha. This monument, which included gilded Nikes and a scene of Bocchus handing Jugurtha over to Sulla, was dedicated in 91 BCE, which was an important moment in the relationship between Rome and the foreign kingdoms— Bocchus well understood that official recognition on the Roman Capitol represented the highest level of Roman support. Some portions of the relief actually survive in the Palazzo dei Conservatori in Rome and in Vienna, and it was represented on coinage of Sulla's son Faustus in 56 BCE.

With the expansion of his kingdom, Bocchus developed a secondary capital at the Carthaginian trading center of Iol (later to be the Caesarea of Juba II). This created a territorial duality to Mauretania which has lasted into modern times, with Morocco representing the original western core and Algeria Bocchus' acquisitions of 105 BCE.

Little further is known about Bocchus' career. Information from that time is dependent on Roman historians, and after the settlement of the Jugurthine War, Roman interests turned elsewhere. The king may still have been on the throne when the Roman adventurer Q. Sertorius hid in Mauretania during 81–80 BCE. Sertorius had been in command of Hispania Citerior when he learned that Sulla was sending an army to depose him. Sertorius fled to Mauretania with 3,000 men but was promptly expelled, probably at the behest of Bocchus, as an opponent of Sulla would find no security in Mauretania. A few months later Sertorius returned to North Africa and made himself ruler of Tingis, a Roman-controlled city at the edge of the Mauretanian kingdom. His ability to do this may mean that Bocchus had died and there was no one in power able to expel Sertorius. In any case, he abandoned Mauretania, probably early in 80 BCE, when he received a call from the Lusitanians to be their commander against Rome.

The events surrounding Sertorius are indirect evidence for the death of Bocchus, probably late in 81 or early in 80 BCE. By the latter year a son, Bogudes I, seems to have been on the throne, and it may be that the kingdom was split between Bocchus' sons, with one (probably Bogudes I) ruling from Volubilis and another (the obscure Sosus, or Mastanesosus) ruling from Iol. Details are almost impossible to determine.

Bocchus is a fine example of the developing concept of the indigenous king allied with Rome. Like his in-law Jugurtha, he was affected by expanding Roman power and was able to use it to his own advantage, somewhat more successfully than Jugurtha. His dedication on the Capitol is a significant part of his legacy, for it is tangible evidence of the increasing power of Rome and the desire of those in power on its fringes to become romanized.

[See also Jugurtha.]

BIBLIOGRAPHY

Coltelloni-Trannoy, Michèle. Le royaume de Maurétanie sous Juba II et Ptolémée. Paris: CNRS Éditions, 1997. Although the emphasis here is on a later period of Mauretanian history, there is much information on the world of Bocchus I.

Roller, Duane W. The World of Juba II and Kleopatra Selene: Royal Scholarship on Rome's African Frontier. London: Routledge, 2003. The most recent study of the Mauretanian kingdom, collecting all the evidence for Bocchus I.

Sallust (Gaius Sallustius Crispus). Catiline's Conspiracy, The Jugurthine War, Histories. Translated by William W. Batstone. New York: Oxford University Press, 2010. The Oxford World's Classics edition.

DUANE W. ROLLER

Bocchus II (d. c. 33 BCE), king of Mauretania (ruled c. 64–33 BCE), a direct descendant (perhaps grandson) of the famous Bocchus I, inherited the eastern portion of the kingdom of Mauretania from his father Sosus around 64 BCE. A cousin (perhaps brother), Bogudes II, ruled western Mauretania from Volubilis. The earliest evidence for the reign of Bocchus II is the arrival in Mauretania of a dispossessed Roman P. Sittius, an investor in African grain who ended up the scapegoat for irregularities in the commodities market, standing trial twice, on one occasion being defended by Cicero. He fled to the court of Bocchus (who had been one of his suppliers of grain) in 63 BCE and became a military commander for the king.

Aside from this glimpse, little is known about the the king's early career. At some time he mounted an expedition along the Atlantic coast, returning with giant reeds and asparagus; the former he presented to his wife, probably the Greek princess Eunoë, Maura, with whom Julius Caesar later had an affair. The fact that Bocchus had a Greek wife indicates his far-flung connections.

In 49 BCE, as the civil war between Caesar and Pompey the Great (Gnaeus Pompeius) intensified, Caesar gave Bocchus official recognition as a friendly king allied with the Romans. Because of the king's involvement in the civil war, Pompeian forces invaded Mauretania in 46 BCE but were soon expelled. Bocchus (with the Roman refugee Sittius commanding part of his forces) invaded the kingdom of Numidia, just to his east, as its king, Juba I, was active on the Pompeian side. In 46 BCE Bocchus occupied the Numidian capital of Cirta (modern Constantine in Algeria). But Bocchus may also have been playing a double game—like many of the allied kings, he was not certain who would prevail in the Roman civil war—and sent assistance to the sons of Pompeius in Spain; his relative Bogudes II, king of western Mauretania, was in Spain with Caesar, and there may have been some family rivalry involved.

Meanwhile Juba I of Numidia had been defeated by the Caesarean forces and had committed suicide. By late 46 BCE the civil war appeared to be at an end, and both Bocchus and Bogudes had their kingships confirmed by Caesar. Portions of the dismembered Numidian kingdom were given to Bocchus. Both kings embarked on an intensive program of romanization, especially notable in their striking of coins with Latin legends. Although the two kings of Mauretania eyed each other uneasily, they ruled a vast region—extending 1500 km from the Roman province of Africa to the Atlantic—that had been exposed to Roman influence for over a century. Yet Caesar's death in early 44 BCE caused the brief stability of the region to evaporate; a local chieftain in western Numidia, Arabion, encouraged by one of the sons of Pompeius, seized control of portions of eastern Mauretania and seemingly drove Bocchus into exile for a brief period until the Romans eliminated Arabion.

The rivalry between Bocchus and Bogudes festered for several years, and as the new phase of the Roman civil war developed in the early 30s BCE, with the triumvirs Octavian and Mark Antony in opposition, Bogudes, encouraged by Antonius, invaded Spain, a center of support for Octavian. Bogudes' own subjects rose in revolt against him, and he abandoned his kingdom for good, joining Antonius in the East, to be killed in early 31 BCE in the actions before the Battle of Actium. Octavian gave his kingdom to Bocchus, which meant that everything west of the Roman province of Africa was now under his control. Yet Bocchus did not enjoy his enhanced status long, for he died naturally in 33 BCE, without an heir and leaving an immense power vacuum.

At this time Octavian was heavily engaged in the war against Antonius and Cleopatra VII, and thus nothing was done immediately about Mauretania, but in 25 BCE, when he could turn his attention to the west, he created a new allied kingdom, placing on the throne the son of the deceased Juba I of Numidia, Juba II (who may have been remotely related to Bocchus), and his wife Cleopatra Selene, the daughter of Antonius and Cleopatra. The royal couple had been raised in Rome and were thoroughly romanized.

Bocchus II is an important player in the events of the mid-first century BCE, demonstrating the involvement of the royalty on the fringes of Roman power in the Roman civil war as well as the inevitable romanization of these kingdoms.

[*See also* Bocchus I; Cleopatra VII; Juba I; Julius Caesar; Mark Antony; *and* Pompey the Great.]

BIBLIOGRAPHY

Coltelloni-Trannoy, Michèle. *Le royaume de Maurétanie sous Juba II et Ptolémée.* Paris: CNRS Éditions, 1997. Although the emphasis here is on a later period of Mauretanian history, there is much information on the world of Bocchus II.

Roller, Duane W. *The World of Juba II and Kleopatra Selene: Royal Scholarship on Rome's African Frontier.* London: Routledge, 2003. The most recent study of the Mauretanian kingdom, collecting all the evidence for Bocchus II.

DUANE W. ROLLER

Boesak, Allan (1945–), South African religious figure and antiapartheid activist, was born to Sarah and Willem Boesak in Kakamas, Northern Cape. When Boesak was young, his father, a teacher, passed away. His family moved to Somerset West, where, at age 14, Boesak became active in the Dutch Reformed Church. He studied at the Bellville Theological Seminary, graduating as a priest in 1967. He went on to obtain a doctorate in Holland at the Kampen Theological Institute and then returned to South Africa to assume an active role in the struggle against apartheid.

As leader of the Afrikaner-dominated Dutch Reformed Church (DRC), he was the major force in getting the World Alliance of Reformed Churches to declare apartheid a heresy in 1982. At the time, that body had not questioned South Africa's membership or the supportive stand of the DRC and the Nederduitsch Hervormde Kerk (NHK) toward apartheid and the ruling Nationalist Party. Boesak became an influential figure in South African internal opposition to apartheid. At the Transvaal Anti-South African Indian Council meeting in Johannesburg in early 1983, he called for the formation of a United Democratic Front (UDF), bringing together hundreds of antiapartheid organizations under a single umbrella, to oppose Prime Minister P.W. Botha's reformist constitutionalist proposals, which did nothing to dismantle apartheid. When the UDF was launched in Cape Town Boesak made a moving address, capturing the mood of opposition to apartheid developing in the country; he was elected patron of the organization.

The antiapartheid opposition, with the UDF in the lead, was arguably the most important factor in exerting pressure on the government to enter into negotiations and bring about the end of apartheid. Following the Soweto revolt in 1976, the state had embarked on a reinvigorated campaign to crush the Black Consciousness Movement (BCM), the radical, black nationalist ideology associated with Steve Biko and the primary internal oppositional current to apartheid in the 1970s. Over the next few years, the police and military repressed additional protests in the townships. However, local community-based organizations formed to build on the protest momentum that had swept black areas of the country in the previous decade. This time the campaigns focused on local issues, such as high rent and poor or nonexistent local government services, amid the ongoing student struggles against apartheid in education. The Botha government reforms, a desperate effort to win over black elites and prevent radical transformation, created a more open environment for grassroots organizing. By the mid-1980s, hundreds of community organizations were actively organized against apartheid, producing a vibrant civil society. Boesak's call that these organizations constitute a broad under the banner of the UDF created an image of an increasingly isolated apartheid government confronting a broad coalition of civil organizations demanding democracy. The Alliance identified with the African National Congress's (ANC) Freedom Charter, which had been adopted in 1956, and advanced a vision of postapartheid, liberal democracy in South Africa.

Like many civil leaders active in the antiapartheid struggle, particularly those affiliated with the Church, some controversy surrounds Boesak's role in the immediate postapartheid democratic period. He became the leader of the ANC in the Western Cape, the province most uncharacteristic of the rest of the country. Here the ANC was weak in voter support; the majority of voters were classified as "Coloured," while those classified "African" under apartheid were in a minority. The Western Cape was one of only two provinces in the country where the ANC did not win an overwhelming majority. In the first democratic election in 1994 the party of apartheid, the Nationalist Party, won control of the provincial government, mainly due to the support of the region's working-class, Coloured population. In following elections the ANC did make inroads into the Coloured community, and since 1999 various coalitions, some which included the ANC, have controlled provincial government. However, faced with these electoral challenges, the provincial ANC has become imbued with leadership and factional infighting. Boesak was unable to keep himself above these internal party conflicts.

Boesak became embroiled in a political scandal when he was convicted of fraudulently diverting international donor funds during the UDF years to companies associated with his wife. This was an emotionally draining trial for him and his family. He was unhappy with the ANC for not supporting his claim of innocence. His defense was that he was protecting UDF and ANC activists who had received the unaccounted-for money; he did not steal it himself. He was sentenced to six years in prison for fraud and theft, but served only two years, as he was controversially pardoned in the last years of the Mbeki administration. The opposition parties criticized the ANC of undermining the rule of law by favoring its own members. This conviction obviously tainted Boesak's image.

Upon his release from prison, Boesak was offered many different roles in public life, but he decided to resume his church-based work. He was favored to once again become the leader of the faction-riddled Western Cape ANC. When it was reported that he wanted to stand for the premiership of the province, relations with the ANC soured again. He joined the breakaway party from the ANC, the Congress of the People (COPE). In the 2008 elections he stood as its regional leader, but the party won only four seats in the provincial legislature. Consequently, the COPE also became mixed up with factional politics and in 2010 Boesak, frustrated, resigned from the party. In 2009, he announced the publication of his biography; however, Trevor Manuel, a former leader of the UDF and then cabinet minister, threatened legal action against Boesak due to the book's portrayal of him, and Boesak was compelled to delay the book's publication.

Reverend Allan Boesak occupies an interesting place in South African politics that exemplifies the uncertainties that may plague the transition to democracy. Boesak is perhaps most recognized for his charismatic leadership during the antiapartheid struggle, and the fiery sermons and rousing political speeches he delivered against apartheid. It could be argued that he is also known for being one of many icons of the antiapartheid struggle who fell from grace in the democratic society he helped bring about.

[*See also* Botha, Pieter Willem; Manuel, Trevor, *and* Mbeki, Thabo Mvuyelwa.]

BIBLIOGRAPHY

Gastrow, Shelagh. *Who's Who in South African Politics.* Johannesburg: Ravan Press, 1985.

THIVEN REDDY

Boganda, Barthélemy (1910–1959), leader of Ubangi-Shari's independence movement and "Father of the Central African Republic," was born on 4 April 1910 at Bobangui, Lobaye. His father Swalakpé and mother Siribé both belonged to the Mbaka (Ngbaka) ethnic group. Swalakpé, a local leader with five wives, died before Boganda's birth during an attack by colonial troops on his village. Siribé, the third of Swalakpé's wives, was beaten to death by a soldier shortly after her husband's death. An orphan, Boganda was taken into custody by the head of the French post at M'Baïki, Lieutenant Mayer, who entrusted him to the care of Father Gabriel Herriau of the Catholic mission at Bétou. In 1920 the Bétou mission was closed and Boganda

was taken to the St. Paul mission in Bangui, where he attended primary school until 1924. While at St. Paul's he was baptized, adopted the name Barthélemy (24 December 1922), and was strongly influenced by Monsignor Jean Calloc'h, who studied local languages and worked alongside Africans to grow crops. In addition to his mother tongue, Ngbaka, Boganda learned to speak Batéké, Lingala, Banda, Sango, and French, and he later studied Latin and Greek in seminary.

In 1924 Boganda left Bangui to attend the Maydi Catholic school in Kisantu (then in the Belgian Congo), and in 1928 he continued his preparation for seminary in Brazzaville (French Middle Congo). Returning to the St. Paul mission in Bangui in 1930, he taught catechism classes while continuing his studies. In 1931 Monsignor Marcel Grandin, head of the Catholic church in Ubangi-Shari, sent Boganda to the seminary at St. Laurent de Mvolyé, Cameroon, where he studied philosophy and theology while passing through the stages to become a priest. After graduating, he returned to Bangui, where he was ordained on 28 March 1938 and became the first Ubangian Catholic priest. Boganda then served as a priest at St. Paul's, Zongo (Belgian Congo), Mbaïki, Bambari, the Grimari-Bakala-Kouango region, and, finally (June–October 1946), in Bangassou.

After World War II, Ubangi-Shari gained the right to send representatives to various French assemblies, and Boganda asked Monsignor Grandin's permission to compete as a candidate for the French National Assembly. Eager to back Catholic candidates against secular, leftist rivals, Grandin agreed, and on 10 November 1946 Boganda won 47 percent of the vote and defeated three opponents. He was reelected to the National Assembly in June 1951 with 60 percent of the vote and again in January 1956 with 88 percent of the vote.

Devoting himself to his new career as a politician in Paris, Boganda did not take part in the first elections for a local assembly, Representative Council, in Ubangi-Shari, but he sponsored a list of candidates under the rubric *Action Économique et Sociale Oubanguienne* (Ubangian Social and Economic Action), led by Georges Darlan. On 15 December 1946, this list, backed by Boganda, won 77 percent of the vote and all fifteen seats in the local assembly.

Early in 1947 Boganda founded the *Union Oubanguienne* (UO; Ubangian Union), a party that became operative on 1 September 1947. A ten-member ruling committee was appointed by

Boganda, but Georges Darlan was named party president. Regional committees met locally, and all party members attended a national congress at least once a year. Two types of cooperative associations for production and marketing were created to provide revenue for the party. Darlan founded COTONCOOP (Coopérative des Producteurs de Coton, 22 February 1948) and then SOCOOMA (Société Coopérative de Consommation), and Boganda started SOCOULOLE (Société Coopérative de l'Oubangui-Lobaye-Lessé) (22 May 1948). After the Representative Council (Territorial Assembly) of Ubangi-Shari refused any funding for Boganda's SOCOULOLE but granted funds for Darlan's and Jane Vialle's cooperatives, Boganda left the Ubangian Union (15 October 1948).

Monsignor Cucherousset, who succeeded Grandin in 1948, decided to suspend Boganda from the priesthood in November 1949. By this time Boganda had assembled a small group of followers at Bangui, and, on 28 September 1949, he founded the Mouvement pour l'Evolution Sociale de l'Afrique Noire (MESAN; Movement for the Social Evolution of Black Africa), a party not initially welcomed by the French colonists or the colonial administration in Bangui. Then, in Paris, Boganda married his French secretary, Michelle Jourdain, who started working for him in August 1948.

On 10 January 1951, a confrontation occurred in a village called Bokanga over a few transactions between some Portuguese traders and representatives of Boganda's cooperative, SOCOULOLE. The head of the district of Mbaïki arrested Boganda and his wife Michelle, who had their six-month-old daughter with her. On 29 March, the local court sentenced Boganda to two months of imprisonment and his wife to two weeks of imprisonment for encouraging public disorder. This arrest greatly increased Boganda's popularity just five months before the next elections. In 1952 Boganda and MESAN members ran as candidates for Ubangi-Shari's renamed Territorial Assembly and won seventeen out of twenty-six seats. Then Boganda was elected one of the three representatives from Ubangi to the Grand Council of French Equatorial Africa.

Boganda's popularity among Ubangians was so great that when a riot broke out in Berberati in April 1954, Governor Louis Marius Pascal Sanmarco asked Boganda to accompany him to Berbérati in order to help restore calm after an Ubangian couple was allegedly killed by a Frenchman. Boganda addressed the angry crowd in Berberati, promising that justice would be administered to white as well as to black. This speech calmed the crowd, and Boganda gained the appreciation of the colonial administration for having defused a very dangerous situation.

In November 1956 Boganda was elected the first Ubangian Mayor of Bangui. In the 1957 elections Boganda and the MESAN won all fifty seats in Ubangi's Territorial Assembly; then Boganda was elected Chairman of the Grand Council of French Equatorial Africa. In 1958 French President Charles de Gaulle proposed replacing the Union Française with a federation of France and its overseas territories, the Communauté Française, and gave each territory the choice of becoming a member of this Community or completely severing relations with France. In July 1958 Boganda denounced the 1956 Loi Cadre (Overseas Reform Act), which introduced semi-autonomous rule in 1957, and demanded his people's right to self-determination and independence, but he agreed to let Ubangi-Shari join de Gaulle's Communauté. This decision was approved in a referendum by 98 percent of the colony's population.

Boganda also argued that Ubangi-Shari needed to join with other former colonies in Central Africa to form an economically viable and politically potent federation. As president of the Grand Council of French Equatorial Africa, Boganda proposed the establishment of an "Equatorial Republic" or "Equatoria" to include the former colonies of Ubangi-Shari, Middle Congo, Gabon, Chad, and perhaps even the Belgian Congo and Portuguese Angola, with a united federal government and legislative assembly. At the suggestion of a French adviser at the time (and future historian of the Central African Republic [CAR]), Pierre Kalck, Boganda chose the name "Central African Republic" for the state he dreamed of creating. In the Middle Congo, this idea was supported by Jacques Opangault, President of the Council of Government, but he was successfully opposed by Fulbert Youlou. Gabon's leaders declared themselves opposed to any form of federation. In November 1958 the High Commissioner of French Equatorial Africa called a meeting of all the leaders of the territories of French Equatorial Africa, which Boganda refused to attend, to inform them that each territorial assembly had to make a separate decision regarding independence. Thus, on 1 December 1958, greatly disappointed, Boganda proclaimed the territory of Ubangi-Shari alone to be the Central African Republic, a state within the Communauté, and he was elected provisional head of government. Boganda devised a flag, a national anthem, and a motto—*Zo Kwe Zo* ("People [are] All People" or "Equality for Everyone")—for the sparsely populated, landlocked republic.

A democratic constitution was passed by the Legislative Assembly in February 1959, and new elections were scheduled for April 1959, but on 29 March a small plane Boganda was traveling in exploded in the air over Boukpayanga, killing everyone on board. Those suspected of planting the bomb that caused this "accident" included Boganda's enemies and those who wanted a more pliable president. With the support of the colonial administration and French residents, David Dacko was selected to serve as the new head of government by the Legislative Assembly, which soon proclaimed Boganda to be the "Father of the Nation."

Boganda was a dynamic, eloquent, and energetic leader of the Ubangian people in their struggle for independence, but he was raised in Catholic missions and seminaries and assimilated French culture to such a degree that he shared with some colonialists and missionaries an expressed disdain for many Ubangian customs and religious beliefs. He eventually received the support of the vast majority of Ubangians and thus enjoyed a more popular mandate than perhaps any other African leader of his era, but his success encouraged him to regard himself as a messiah for his people and discouraged his tolerance of any opposition. His success in establishing a one-party state left a legacy that subsequent rulers of the CAR have been all too eager to follow.

[*See also* Dacko, David; Darlan, Georges; *and* Youlou, Fulbert.]

BIBLIOGRAPHY

Ballard, J. A. "The Development of Political Parties in French Equatorial Africa." PhD diss., Fletcher School of Law and Diplomacy, Tufts University, 1963.

Espérou, R. "La chute du F-BGZB." *Le Trait d'Union* No. 211 (September-October 2003).

Kalck, P. *Barthélemy Boganda, 1910–1959: Élu de Dieu et des Centrafricains.* Paris: Editions Sépia, 1995.

Pénel, J. D. *Barthélemy Boganda: Écrits et Discours, 1946–1951: la lutte décisive.* Paris: Éditions L'Harmattan, 1995.

Yagao-Ngama, L. "Le Mouvement d'Évolution Sociale de l'Afrique Noire (M.E.S.A.N. Parti Unique) et le pouvoir en République Centrafricaine." *Thesis*, Université de Paris X, 1974.

RICHARD A. BRADSHAW and
JUAN FANDOS-RIUS

Boghossian, Skunder (1937–2003), artist and educator, was born in Addis Ababa to an Ethiopian mother and an Armenian father who was a colonel in the Imperial Body Guard of Haile Selassie. Boghossian received early art training at Tafari Makonnen Secondary School and in private lessons with Stanislas Chojnacki, a historian of Ethiopian art and water-colorist, then librarian at the University College of Addis Ababa (later Haile Selassie I University and now Addis Ababa University), and with Jacques Godbout, a Canadian writer, filmmaker, and painter who taught French at the University College.

In 1955 Boghossian won second prize at an art exhibition held as part of Haile Selassie's Jubilee Anniversary Celebration and was awarded an imperial scholarship to study in London. After attending classes at St. Martin's School, the Central School, and the Slade School of Fine Art in London, the young artist decided to transfer his studies to Paris, where he attended the École Nationale Supérieure des Beaux-Arts and the Académie de la Grande Chaumière. However, his formative exposure to the avant-garde artistic and intellectual milieu of the city came from frequenting artists' studios, cafes, and jazz clubs. In these venues he absorbed the theories and ideas of African philosophers and writers such as Cheikh Anta Diop, Aimé Césaire, and Léopold Sédar Senghor, who celebrated the intellectual and cultural achievements of black Africa. With European, Latin American, and African artists such as André Breton, Alberto Giacometti, Roberto Matta, Wifredo Lam, and Gerard Sokoto, he explored theories of Surrealism, Negritude, and Pan-Africanism and their implications for the visual arts. In Paris, Boghossian also was exposed to collections of historical African art from various regions of the continent, enriching his fund of African imagery and symbolism beyond the artistic traditions of his Ethiopian homeland.

Skunder Boghossian enjoyed experimenting with a variety of materials and techniques and had in common with his Surrealist colleagues an interest in the subconscious mind, dreams, hallucinations, and creative flights of fancy occasioned by intentionally orchestrated "accidents" on the canvas or other painting surface. Boghossian drew from a rich mine of artistic sources that included Ethiopian Orthodox Church mural and manuscript paintings, other local artistic traditions of Ethiopia, the beliefs and creative expression of other regions of the African continent, fiction and philosophical writings of international authors, jazz, and the exchange of ideas with his fellow artists in Europe, Africa, and the Americas. He always referenced Africa in his work and commented to Elizabeth W. Giorgis in a conversation she recalled in 1997 that his works were "a perpetual celebration of the diversity of blackness." He is known as a brilliant colorist and master manipulator of different kinds of paint and other media on various surfaces such as canvas, skin, and bark. The complex representational and abstract imagery and layered, often jewel-like surfaces of his paintings evoke a sense of primordial genesis, cosmic energy, and solemn, sacred spaces.

Boghossian returned to Addis Ababa in 1966 and joined the faculty at the Addis Ababa Fine Arts School, which was founded in 1957 by painter Ale Felege Selam Heruy under the patronage of Haile Selassie. There he taught painting, drawing, graphics, and abstract design. With painter/poet Gebre Kristos Desta and other colleagues, Boghossian introduced modern and abstract art to Ethiopian audiences. He and his fellow modernists exhibited at the Fine Arts School and at the Creative Arts Center at Haile Selassie I University, a vibrant venue for sharing ideas and creative expressions among artists, poets, playwrights, and musicians.

In 1967 Skunder was awarded the Haile Selassie I Prize Trust Award for the Fine Arts, an award given to only two other painters, Afewerk Tekle and Gebre Kristos Desta, during its short ten-year history. Although he taught in Ethiopia for only three years (1966–1969), Boghossian's influence on both his peers and younger generations of artists was strong and enduring. Several students at the Fine Arts School followed Boghossian to the United States to study with him at Howard University in Washington, D.C., where he was appointed artist-in-residence in 1972 and taught from 1974 to 2001. Prior to moving to Washington, he had spent some time in New York, taught briefly at the Atlanta University Center Consortium in Atlanta, Georgia, and lived for a while in Montgomery, Alabama. During his long career at Howard University, Boghossian was profoundly influential on African American artists through his unique artistic production, inspired teaching, and generous mentoring.

Early in his career, Boghossian's work entered the collections of the Musée d'Art Moderne de la Ville de Paris (1963) and the Museum of Modern Art in New York (1965), in both instances as the first black artist collected by those institutions. Eventually his paintings would enter the collections of other leading museums in the United States,

including the National Museum of African Art, the Howard University Gallery of Art, the Studio Museum in Harlem, the Indianapolis Museum of Art, the North Carolina Museum of Art, and the Samuel P. Harn Museum of Art. Boghossian received early exposure through solo shows at the Merton Simpson Gallery in New York and the Galerie Lambert in Paris in the early 1960s, at the Studio Museum of Harlem in 1972, and through inclusion in UNESCO's 1983 international touring show *Artists of the World against Apartheid* as well as numerous other shows in the United States, Europe, and Africa. More recently Boghossian's paintings have been introduced to a wider audience through exhibitions such as *Seven Stories about Modern Art in Africa* (1995); *Transatlantic Dialogue: Contemporary Art in and out of Africa* (1999); *The Short Century: Independence and Liberation Movements in Africa 1945–1994* (2001); *Ethiopian Passages: Contemporary Art from the Diaspora* (2003); and *Continuity and Change: Three Generations of Ethiopian Artists* (2007).

[*See also* Afewerk Tekle; Césaire, Aimé; Diop, Cheikh Anta; Gebre Kristos Desta; *and* Senghor, Léopold Sédar.]

BIBLIOGRAPHY

Giorgis, Elizabeth W. "The Artist Skunder Boghossian: Expressions of Specificity and Universalism." *Ethiopian Register* 4, no. 11 (November 1997): 22–26.

Deressa, Solomon. "Skunder in Context." *Ethiopian BIR Business and Industry Report* 3, no. 1, (January/February 1997): 14–28.

Harney, Elizabeth. *Ethiopian Passages: Contemporary Art from the Diaspora*, pp. 36–38, 68–71. Washington, DC: National Museum of African Art, Smithsonian Institution, 2003.

Nagy, Rebecca Martin. *Continuity and Change: Three Generations of Ethiopian Artists*, pp. 56–59. Gainesville, FL: Samuel P. Harn Museum of Art, University of Florida, 2007.

REBECCA MARTIN NAGY

Boilat, David (1814–1901), missionary, parish priest, and religious educator, was born in Senegal on 16 April 1814, the same day that Napoleon Bonaparte left France for exile on the Island of Elba. Two years later Britain ended its occupation of Senegal and returned the fortified island territories of Gorée and Saint-Louis to France. The island of Saint-Louis du Sénégal, founded by France in 1659 as a strategic site in the period of the trans-Atlantic slave trade, gained a reputation as a cosmopolitan Atlantic port city shaped by patterns of intermarriage between African women (Signares) and European administrators, merchants, and soldiers. The son of Marie Monté, a "free mulâtresse," and Pierre Boilat, member of the merchant marines, David Boilat came from the small but growing class of mixed race inhabitants who closely identified with the Catholic Church and sought the privileges of French education despite their relative isolation from French culture.

In 1816, when France regained possession of its territories on the Senegambia coast, it also embarked on a new colonial project seeking at first to create a plantation colony and then a French settlement that would facilitate the supply of raw materials to French industry. Creating a reliable French-educated, property-owning intermediary class served these objectives. Boilat was part of the first generation to participate in new French schools established by Roman Catholic orders in Saint Louis during the 1820s. The clergy specifically targeted signares and their children for evangelism because of their attachment to local religious practices, including the wearing of talismans called gris-gris and the veneration of "idols." French officers, moreover, required Catholic orders to avoid confrontation with Muslims on the north bank of the Senegal River for fear of inciting holy war.

The second period of Boilat's life involved travel and seminary training in France. The religious order Sisters of Saint Joseph du Cluny provided education and medical services in the colony in the 1820s. The director of the order, Sister Anne Marie Javouhey, convinced the governor of the colony and the French Naval Minister to create a seminary in France for "young blacks" from Senegal who could become the future workers, teachers, and evangelists of the colony. The first group of Senegalese students arrived at the seminary at Bailleul-sur-Thérain (in the department of Oise) in the spring of 1825. Two years later, at age thirteen, Boilat left Senegal for the seminary with a second group of students including Arsène Fridoil and Jean-Pierre Moussa. These three constituted the first group of indigenous clergy. They survived the harsh winters when others perished, earned high marks in their studies, and gained notoriety with religious and political figures during their stay in France. Boilat, Fridoil, and Moussa continued their studies at the Congregation of the Holy Ghost Fathers (Spiritains) in Paris, where they were ordained priests. Perhaps as a sign of the curiosity

the group provoked, on one occasion the Senegalese clergy celebrated mass at the royal palace at Fontainebleu for King Louis Philippe and Queen Marie Amélie.

In late 1842, the three young men returned to Senegal after completing their studies in Paris. Five years earlier the Governor of Senegal had issued a decree establishing primary education in Saint Louis and Gorée. When Louis Edouard Bouët-Willaumez arrived in Senegal in 1843 to assume the governor's office, he carried orders from the naval ministry to create a secondary school in the colony. Bouët-Willaumez viewed the three Senegalese clergy as useful agents of France's civilizing mission and thus charged them with developing a secondary school in Saint Louis. He named Boilat inspector for public instruction in the colony.

During this period, Boilat and his fellow clergy traveled between Saint Louis and Gorée, the second oldest French port in Senegal. They provided services as parish priests and teachers for the population that most identified with the Church, namely signares, the mulatto population, and African Catholics. They also sought to convert the population of African workers in the island towns newly freed under the 1848 decree abolishing slavery "on French soil." Boilat designed a school according to the curriculum of secondary schools in France, which provided religious instruction and instruction in Latin. Boilat sought to prepare young Senegalese for further education in law, medicine, and business or to serve in military and administrative service just like their counterparts in France.

The Senegalese clergy encountered some resistance from the free black and Muslim inhabitants of Saint Louis who sought western education but disapproved of Christian evangelism. They also experienced the hostility of French clergy in the colony. The governor supported Boilat's work, but the Fathers of the Holy Ghost favored favored a French order called the Brothers of Christian Instruction, who provided primary education for young boys that focused on technical skills designed to produce laborers for the colony. Competition between the Senegalese clergy and the metropolitan clergy, as well as surmounting debts, contributed to the demise of the school. In 1845, Boilat relinquished his duties at the school. In 1849 the governor closed the school and reallocated funds to scholarships for a few exceptional students to pursue secondary studies in France.

Citing health reasons, Boilat left his parish duties in Senegal in 1845. Before returning to France he embarked on a tour of Senegambia including a one-year stay with his sister in Sierra Leone. During this period, Boilat compiled his research for the ethnography and began writing a grammar manual of the Wolof language, his maternal tongue. Boilat said that he wrote these works to contribute to science, commerce, industry, and religion and to facilitate communication between Europeans and the local population in Senegal. On 10 November 1853 Boilat began a position as priest in the rural parish of Dampmart (Seine-et-Marne). He published the ethnography the same year and the Wolof grammar in 1858. In 1868, Boilat petitioned his superiors to replace the priest of a small parish in the town of Nantouillet. Little is known of Boilat's later years. He supervised the church and religious functions of the parish and may have taught at the local secondary school. Boilat died on 19 December 1901 at age 87, having served as an ordained Catholic priest for sixty-one years and a parish priest in the French countryside for thirty-three years.

Boilat remained an obscure figure in Senegalese and French history until recently. Although much of his life remains a mystery, his contribution to knowledge and his commitment to evangelism shaped the lives of local communities in nineteenth-century Senegal and France. He pioneered western education in Senegal by insisting that Senegalese children have the same educational opportunities as children in metropolitan France. He argued for the benefits of evangelism in France's African colonies and as a native of Senegal saw himself as best suited for this work.

Boilat knew and understood the land and the people as well as the social and cultural customs. As a person of mixed racial ancestry, Boilat also understood and aspired to the social and cultural expectations of bourgeois society in metropolitan France. He embodied the idealistic notion of assimilation that characterized French colonialism in nineteenth-century West Africa. But he also experienced the limitations of being a Senegalese in French colonial and metropolitan societies increasingly shaped by ideologies of race.

Boilat is remembered in history as one of the first group of "indigenous clergy" that trained in France and returned to Senegal to spread Christianity. Although Christian evangelism proved difficult in this region long influenced by Islam, Boilat's 1853 account, *Esquisses Sénégalaises*, proved a lasting contribution for the study of Senegalese and Mauritanian history. This ethnographic study, close to 500 pages in length, provides an unparalleled view of the environment, people, trade, religion, customs, and societies of Senegal in the mid-nineteenth century from the perspective of someone intimately familiar with African and French society. Boilat wrote the work for metropolitan geographers, scientists, and observers interested in Senegal. Unlike European travelers' accounts of the period, Boilat's work provided an insider's view of the societies and cultures of the region. It includes Boilat's own color sketches illustrating the peoples and places of Senegal and Mauritania.

Boilat's biography encompasses four distinct periods: His young life and early education in Senegal (1814–1825), his training for the clergy in France (1825–1842), his return to Senegal and his career as a teacher, priest, and evangelist (1842–1853), and his later years spent as an African priest in the French countryside (1853–1901). His career shows the promise but also the limitations that the first generation of African clergy faced within French colonial society. Boilat could not complete his work in Senegal and instead lived as a person of mixed racial ancestry in remote and rural regions of France. His research and writings, however, leave us with a lasting record of the Senegalese people, language, and customs of the mid-nineteenth century. Long before Senegalese poet and Negritude author Léopold Senghor, Boilat appeared as the first great African writer in French and the first recognized Senegalese painter. His life and work exemplifies the paradox of nineteenth-century notions of cultural assimilation that justified the expansion of French empire through its mission to "civilize" primitive Africa but also ignored the accomplishments of individuals like Boilat. David Boilat, an evangelist, parish priest, artist, and scholar, was a person of his time and ahead of his time.

BIBLIOGRAPHY

Barry, Boubacar. *Senegambia and the Atlantic Slave Trade*. Translated by Ayi Kwei Armah. Cambridge: Cambridge University Press, 1998.

Boilat, P.-D. *Esquisses Sénégalaises*. Paris: Éditions Karthala; 1984 reprint of 1853 edition with introduction by Abdoulaye-Bara Diop.

Bouquillon, Yvon, and Robert Cornevin. *David Boilat (1814–1901): Le Précurseur*. Dakar, Senegal: Les Nouvelles Editions Africaines, 1981.

Brooks, George E. *Eurafricans in Western Africa*. Athens, Ohio: Ohio University Press, 2003.

De Benoist, Joseph Roger. *Histoire de l'Église catholique au Sénégal*. Paris: ClairAfrique et Karthala, 2008.

Jones, Hilary. "From mariage à la mode du pays to Weddings at Town Hall: Marriage, French Colonialism and Mixed Race Society in Nineteenth Century Senegal." *International Journal of African Historical Studies* 38, no. 2 (2005): 27–48.

HILARY JONES

Bokassa, Jean-Bedel (1921–1996), military officer, president, and emperor of the Central African Republic/Empire, was born on 22 February 1921 at Bobangui, Lobaye region, then in the French Equatorial African territory of the Middle Congo (now part of the Central African Republic) He was the son of headman Mindogon Mgboundoulou, who was murdered at the regional colonial headquarters in the Lobaye, and Marie Yokowo, who died a week after her husband. Bokassa belonged to the same Mbaka (Ngbaka) ethnic group as Central African Republic (CAR) leaders Barthélemy Boganda and David Dacko. His grandfather M'Balanga took care of Bokassa until 1921, when he

Jean Bedel Bokassa. Bokassa at his coronation ceremonies, Bangui, 1977. (AP Images)

entered the Catholic missionary école Sainte-Jeanne-d'Arc at M'Baiki. Bokassa then attended Bangui's École de St. Louis (1928–1929), which was run by Father Charles Grüner, and an *école missionnaire* at Brazzaville (1929–1939). Enlisting in the French army on 19 May 1939, Bokassa became a corporal (1940), sergeant (1941), staff sergeant (1944), company sergeant-major (1950), regimental sergeant-major (1954), second lieutenant (1956), lieutenant (1958), and captain (1961). He was baptized a Catholic in 1950 before leaving for Indochina, where he served until 1953. In 1954 he was sent to Fréjus, France, then to Brazzaville in 1957. On 27 December 1959, Bokassa was transferred to Bangui by the French Military and Technical Assistance program and was assigned (1 January 1960) to form the military cabinet of David Dacko, the head of government of newly independent CAR. On 1 January 1963 Bokassa was transferred to the CAR national army with the rank of major. Then, on 1 December 1964 he was promoted to colonel and named chief of staff of the national army.

Relations between Col. Bokassa and President Dacko soon became strained, however, and on 1 January 1966 Bokassa and Captain Alexandre Banza staged a coup d'etat and forced Dacko to resign. Numerous military officers and politicians were arrested, and the 1959 Constitution and the National Assembly were abolished. Many real or perceived opponents were incacerated in Ngaragba Prison, where several died. Bokassa ruled as president of the CAR (4 January 1966 to 4 September 1976) and named himself president (12 January 1967) and then secretary general (23 August 1967) of the Mouvement d'Évolution Sociale d'Afrique Noire (MESAN; Movement for Social Evolution of Black Africa), the nation's only legal political party. Bokassa also promoted himself to the ranks of Brigadier General (December 1967), Major General (December 1970), Three Star General (December 1971), and Field Marshal (May 1974). Bokassa often shuffled his cabinets and retained important ministerial portfolios for himself.

In April 1969, Lt.-Col. Banza was accused of plotting against Bokassa and was executed. In 1973, Col. Auguste Mbongo was dismissed from the government, accused of plotting against Bokassa, and put in jail, where he died a few months later. On 3 Febrary 1976, Bokassa's son-in-law, Captain Fidèle Obrou, led an unsuccessful plot to assassinate him at Bangui-M'Poko airport, for which Obrou and several collaborators were sentenced to death. Bokassa's foreign policy was initially anti-communist. He had fought for the French in Vietnam against communists, and he justified his coup in part by the need to counter growing Chinese communist influence in the CAR, an argument that appealed to the French and Americans in the Cold War climate of the 1960s. Bokassa also cultivated a close relationship with American diamond dealers and granted uranium mining licenses to the French. A pragmatist more than an ideologue, he eventually sought economic assistance from the Soviet Union, Yugoslavia, the People's Republic of China, and Romania. In September 1976, after a visit to Libya to solicit economic aid, he created a Central African Revolutionary Council, announced his conversion to Islam, and adopted the new name, Salah Addin Ahmed Bokassa. On 4 December 1976 a MESAN congress approved a new constitution that named Bokassa I emperor of the Central African Empire. One year later, on 4 December 1977, Bokassa I crowned himself and one of his wives, Empress Catherine, in a costly, controversial ceremony. Unpaid civil servants and angry students became more confrontational in the wake of these developments.

In January and April 1979 Bokassa responded to student protests with military force and was accused of beating incacerated students to death himself. France organized an African committee of enquiry which found fault with Bokassa, and then, on 20 September 1979, while Bokassa was visting Libya, French troops (in Operation Barracuda) deposed Bokassa and returned former President Dacko to power.

When Bokassa flew to France and landed near Paris, the French government refused to grant him asylum and his airplane was sent to Ivory Coast, whose president, Felix Houphouët-Boigny, agreed to host him. Bokassa was supported and defended by some French friends, including Roger Delpey, a former French Indochina veteran and writer who claimed that Bokassa was innocent and being framed.

In December 1983, with the help of Delpey and his friends, Bokassa tried to fly back to the CAR, but Ivory Coast's army intervened to stop him. Bokassa and his family were then sent to France, where they lived in one of his palaces for a while. In October 1986 Bokassa managed to slip away and fly back to the CAR, but at Bangui-M'Poko airport he was arrested by French Col. Jean-Claude Mantion, the head of President André Kolingba's presidential guard. In 1985 Bokassa published *Ma verite* (My Truth), in which he emphasized his military career in the French army, denied he had engaged in cannibalism or

beaten incarcerated students, and blamed all his problems on French President Giscard d'Estaing, who managed to get a court order to destroy 10,000 copies of Bokassa's book.

Bokassa was tried and, on 12 June 1987, found guilty of complicity in at least twenty murders, of having students arrested and imprisoned, of torture, and of embezzling more than three thousand million CFA (about $10 million) from the state. He was, however, acquitted of several murders that had been attributed to him and was judged not guilty of misappropriating the crown jewels and of cannibalism. Although sentenced to death by firing squad, on 29 February 1988 President Kolingba commuted the sentence to life imprisonment with hard labor. On 1 September 1993, President Kolingba—who had just been defeated in democratic elections—ordered all prisoners to be set free, including Bokassa. On 3 November 1996, Bokassa died of a heart attack at a medical clinic in Bangui.

Bokassa murdered real and suspected rivals, incarcerated an estimated 400 individuals, personally beat students to death, and was certainly much feared by many Central Africans during his period in power, but his rule is now looked upon by many Central Africans with a degree of nostalgia. He patronized and promoted people from various ethnic groups to a greater degree than his successors, and economic conditions, ethnic tension, urban crime, and rural banditry have all worsened since Bokassa was in power. Outside of the CAR, however, Bokassa has retained a notorious reputation, and far more has been written about him than any other Central African. His efforts to muzzle the press, his cozy and controversial relationship with President d'Estaing, his much mocked coronation, his "collection" of wives, his extravagance and showmanship, and his mercurial moods and dramatic behavior all drew the attention of the western media, for whom he fit the stereotypical model of African dictator.

[*See also* Boganda, Barthélemy; Dacko, David; Goumba, Abel; Houphouët-Boigny, Félix; *and* Kolingba, André.]

BIBLIOGRAPHY

Faes, G., and S. Smith. *Bokassa: Un empereur français.* Paris: Calmann-Lévy, 2000.

Loubat, B. *L'Ogre de Bérengo.* Nice, France: Alain Lefeuvre, 1981.

O'Toole, T. "Jean-Bedel Bokassa: Neo-Napoleon or Traditional African Ruler?" In *The Cult of*

Power: Dictators in the Twentieth Century, edited by J. Held, pp. 95–106. New York: Columbia University Press, 1983.

Titley, B. Dark Age: The Political Odyssey of Emperor Bokassa. Montreal: McGill-Queen's University Press, 1997.

RICHARD A. BRADSHAW and
JUAN FANDOS-RIUS

Bokeleale, Jean Itofo Bokambanza (c. 1920–2002) Congolese Protestant minister, was born near the town of Becimbola, located not far from the town of Lotumbe in the northwest Equateur region of the Democratic Republic of the Congo. Despite his major role as the head of the Église du Christ de Zaïre (ECZ), the church created at the behest of Congolese dictator Mobutu Sese Seko in 1970 that he presided over for roughly three decades, no single academic study has seriously considered his career. Most written sources have come from his host of detractors, further complicating understanding his life and controversial role as a religious leader. Bokeleale met a Congolese minister named Jean Bomenge in 1937, while the young man was organizing a party. Bomenge convinced Bokeleale to enter the Disciples of Christ mission school at the town of Lotumbe, not far from the provincial capital of Mbandaka. The boy wanted to socially advance through acquiring literacy. According to a Congolese Disciples of Christ minister, he passed through four years of primary school material in half the time thanks to his intelligence. Bokeleale then began to study at the Congo Christian Institute at Bolenge in 1939 and finished his secondary school education there in 1942, receiving very high grades.

Bokeleale became such a central figure within the Disciples of Christ that some Congolese joked that he was half-white. In the late 1950s, Disciples of Christ missionaries hoped Bokeleale would become a major leader of an African-led church. In 1961, Bokeleale left the Congo for Europe to study theology. He returned in 1963, having yet again finished his studies in half the time normally required. Twelve young leaders of the Disciples of Christ anxious to assert African leadership over the continuing American missionary presence chose to elect Bokeleale as the head of the Disciples of Christ in Congo. These men were Joseph Ekofo, Rock Elanga, John Entombodji, Laurent Bondole, Samuel Lotafe, Esaïe Efole, Zakarie Nkoko, Illiterate Rock Losangya, Dawel Yoka, Etienne Afino, Rock Mokondoko, and André Ebale. American missionaries supported his

election, although some were nervous about his self-confidence. He traveled to the United States frequently to preach at conferences and to maintain ties between the Congolese Disciples of Christ and its American counterparts. Bokeleale organized a women's organization known in the Mongo language as Eamanelo ea Bamato Bauma (EBB) and built a girl's high school in 1967. At the same time, Bokeleale bought a fleet of cars for his own use and built large homes for Disciples of Christ leaders like himself.

The November 1965 coup that brought Mobutu Sese Seko to power had led government officials to build alliances with many Protestant church leaders. Bokeleale became a close ally and advisor of Mobutu and profited from their mutual partnership. In 1968, he was elected President of the Church of Christ in Congo, in large part because he had mastered French far better than most other Protestant pastors of his generation, who thus could only draw regional support. Christian and Missionary Alliance pastors objected in 1969 to Bokeleale's efforts to consolidate his authority over various Protestant churches.

One year later, Mobutu appointed Bokeleale the head of the Eglise du Christ au Zaïre (ECZ), a coalition of forty-one Protestant churches that would henceforth be the sole Protestant church recognized by the government. Bokeleale closed the Conseil Protestant du Congo, a voluntary body of representatives from various churches that had no binding authority. He also eliminated any distinction between mission churches and African-led churches. Some missionaries and other Congolese Protestants recoiled at this new organization as a threat to local autonomy or doctrine. Other Congolese resented the heavy-handed efforts state authorities used to close down Protestant churches that refused to participate, as well as the state funding that Bokeleale could use as patronage. Many Protestants affiliated with Bokeleale received well-paying posts within Mobutu's regime. Bokeleale worked with various churches that refused to enter the ECZ, such as the Église Baptiste du Kivu, to try to convince them to join the state-sanctioned church over the course of the 1970s.

At the local and regional level, ECZ members gave out scholarships, aid, and jobs. Bokeleale made numerous public appearances in the United States and in Congo. For example, he spoke to members of a Protestant interdenominational conference in Kansas City. He assured a Swiss journalist in 1975 that Mobutu was the political messiah of the Congolese people. Perhaps as a shot to American missionaries, he told the African American–oriented magazine *Jet* that he opposed US missionary links with the CIA. Despite Bokeleale's and Mobutu's close ethnic and political ties, they had some disagreements over the course of the 1970s and the 1980s. In 1983, the annual synod of the ECZ even considered the removal of Bokeleale, supposedly with the blessing of Mobutu. Meanwhile, many Congolese Protestants at home and abroad resented him. For example, Bokeleale chose to cancel a meeting with French Protestant leaders in Lyon once he learned that many Congolese immigrants in the city belonged to anti-Mobutu opposition parties.

When a wave of grassroots protests and the end of US patronage after the fall of the Berlin Wall led to a national constitutional convention, Bokeleale tried to promote a very conciliatory and moderate relationship with Mobutu's MPR regime in 1990. This unpopular stance, the dwindling resources of Mobutu's government, and the increase in independent Pentecostal churches that eschewed Bokeleale's call for ecumenical dialogue and the consolidation of Protestant churches put him at a serious disadvantage in the 1990s. More tragically, his son Charles was shot to death by unknown assailants in Kinshasa in 1999. Bokeleale died in 2002 in Kinshasa, a year after he stepped down from the leadership of his church. Despite his long partnership with Mobutu's government, scholarships and several schools have been named after him. In 2009 he received a posthumous degree from the Université Libre du Congo at Kinshasa for his hard work for this institution of higher learning. A number of Congolese commentators have praised him publicly for his organizational skills since his death.

[*See also* Mobutu Sese Seko.]

BIBLIOGRAPHY

Kabongo-Mbaya, Philippe B. *L'Eglise du Christ au Zaïre: Formation et Adaptation d'un Protestantisme en Situation de Dictature.* Paris: Karthala, 1992.

Longman, Timothy. "Empowering the Weak and Protecting the Powerful: The Contradictory Nature of Christian Churches in Rwanda, Burundi, and the Democratic Republic of Congo." *African Studies Review* 41, no.1 (1998): 49–72.

Loombe Ifindi, Bosunga. *Qui êtes-vous, Mgr. Bokeleale?* Kinshasa, Democratic Republic of the Congo: Sodaz, 1985.

Nelson, Jack. *Christian Missionizing and Social Transformation: A History of Conflict and Change in Eastern Zaire.* Boulder, Colo.: Westview Press, 1992.

JEREMY RICH

Bol, Kerubino Kuanyin (1948–1998), southern Sudanese rebel leader, was born in 1948 near Gorgrial in what was then the Bahr el Ghazal Province of Sudan. He was from the Dinka ethnic group. Just before Sudan was grantedn independence in 1955, Kerubino decided to cease his formal education to join with the growing armed resistance groups that were developing in a southern rebellion against the Khartoum government, eventually called Anyanya, under the command of Joseph Lagu. After the 1972 Addis Ababa Peace Agreement brought a conclusion to the Anyanya rebellion, Kerubino was integrated into the Sudanese Armed Forces (SAF). He became a major in the SAF and was made the commander of the SAF detachment in Bor, Southern Sudan. While in Bor, the home of John Garang—the eventual leader of the Sudanese People's Liberation Army/Movement (SPLA/M)—Kerubino became involved in a conspiracy of Southern SAF officers and soldiers in case of the perceived need to rebel once again. The former Anyanya and integrated forces were to be redeployed as a part of the force integration process. Kerubino and many others perceived such moves as part of a strategy to dilute the influence of Southern leaders in the army. Kerubino, along with the former Anyanya forces at the SAF garrison in Pibor, in the eastern area of Jonglei, were the first to mutiny; they fled with Garang to Ethiopia. This incident, known as the Bor Mutiny, is considered the moment of the return to war and the beginning of the SPLA/M under Garang.

With the creation of the SPLA/M, Kerubino became one of Garang's high-ranking leaders and a trusted commander. He was considered a very effective field commander, and his often ruthless reputation was known to strike fear in opposition forces. He was given a high position initially due to his important role in both the initial Bor Mutiny and in opposing other Southern Sudanese armed groups that had also fled in the months surrounding the Bor Mutiny to organize renewed rebellion. In this role Kerubino was important in securing Garang as the leader of the majority of southern forces based in Ethiopia and in securing the backing of the Ethiopian government for the SPLA/M under Garang. Moreover, as a part of the agreement for support from the Ethiopian President Mengistu

Haile Mariam, Kerubino was also an important commander used to engage in fighting against some of the rebel forces operating inside Ethiopia against the government of Mengistu.

After several years of effectively working with Garang and the SPLA/M, and in particular his role in a string of impressive victories in 1987 over SAF forces in Blue Nile, which contributed to the SPLA/M's movement farther north, Kerubino was detained and imprisoned by the SPLA/M for conspiring against the SPLA/M leadership. While the circumstances remain unclear, Kerubino was detained on suspicion of working with others to unseat John Garang as the head of the SPLA/M. After the major successes of the previous year Kerubino and Garang had increasingly clashed as Kerubino consistently asserted himself among the leadership of the SPLA/M. In the turmoil that ensued after the 1991 split of the SPLA/M, where Lam Akol and Riek Machar—both top SPLA/M commanders—lead an attempt to unseat Garang, the location where Kerubino was being detained was no longer under the full control of the SPLA/M of Garang. Thus, in 1992, during the fighting among SPLA/M forces Kerubino was able to escape.

After escaping, Kerubino joined with Riek Machar's group in 1993 and thus brought to Machar a strong Dinka force that Machar believed would be able to operate in the populous areas of Bahr el Gahzal and bring support from the Dinka groups, which had up until that point generally sided with Garang. To the dismay of Machar, Kerubino was not able to bring over the wide support of the Dinka communities in his home areas and outside of maintaining an effective militia, Kerubino did not provide the kind of popular leadership Machar and others in the breakaway SPLA/M factions had hoped. Some time after aligning with Machar, Kerubino began to engage with the Sudanese Security Services in Gogrial, a garrison town controlled by the Sudanese Armed Forces at the time. Along with other groups associated with the breakaway SPLA/M groups aligned to Machar and Akol, Kerubino began working under the pay of the SAF and the other security organizations.

As Kerubino moved more in line with government forces many of his forces deserted to return to their home villages. This reduced Kerubino's forces substantially and resulted in him relying further on the support of the government security organizations. His operations also transformed into what many have characterized as the ruthless marauding of Bahr el Ghazal. The kind of violence that resulted

exacerbated the food shortages and famine caused by major drought hitting the region in the late 1990s. As a result Kerubino's forces became recognized as having been a main catalyst to the great suffering caused by the famine of 1998 in the region. Well documented by Human Rights Watch and other groups, the actions in the region by Kerubino have been described as a "scorched earth campaign against his own people in Bahr El Ghazal" (HRW, 1998).

During the height of the famine in late 1997 and early 1998 support for Kerubino in Bahr El Gahzal continued to wane. In an effort to regain his stature in January 1998 Kerubino negotiated a return to the SPLA in conjunction with an assault on Wau, surprising the SAF. Although the SAF was able to counter Kerubino's forces, the near defeat of SAF by forces under Kerubino's command in the area of Wau, the major garrison in the major town of Bahr el Ghazal was a significant success for the SPLA/M. By helping the SPLA/M to gain greater control of Bahr el Ghazal, the return of Kerubino became important. After his impressive action in almost capturing Wau, Kerubino was attached to the command headquarters. As leader of the SPLA/M, Garang's intention was to keep Kerubino close, as SPLA/M continued to lack confidence in Kerubino, despite their recognition of his effective field operations. Kerubino wanted to be in the field and began once again to quarrel with SPLA/M leaders. It was not long until ego and clashes between Kerubino and other SPLA/M leaders once again resulted in a split between him and Garang. Thus, in late 1998, likely coaxed by offers of financial resources by the SAF and government security personnel that he previously had worked with, Kerubino once again defected from the SPLA/M. Kerubino defected to join with the emerging group of southern forces known as the South Sudan Defence Forces (SSDF), receiving support and protection from Paulino Mateip, at the time a major general in the SAF and a major leader of forces in the Nuer areas of the Greater Upper Nile.

Many of the remnant groups that had been involved in the SPLA/M split in 1991 and many that had never been willing to join with the SPLA/M of Garang, particularly those forces known as Anyanya 2, had assembled under a loose leadership to form a group that, in 1997, had entered into an agreement (the Khartoum Agreement) with the government in Khartoum, asserting themselves as the authorities in whole of Southern Sudan. While the SSDF did not control enough territory they were a significant force in many key areas such as the oilfields, where SAF Major General Mateip's forces had become an important provider of security for the government and oil companies. Once with the SSDF Kerubino began operating as a major general in the SAF.

In September 1998 Kerubino was killed in Maniken area of Unity State (at the time known as Greater Upper Nile) as the SSDF forces of Mateip were fighting with the formerly loyal SSDF forces of Peter Gadet, an SSDF commander initially a deputy of Paulino Mateip. The defection of Gadet and his forces from Mateip's faction resulted in major fighting between various SSDF groups, and it was during Gadet's capture of the positions of Mateip's forces at Maniken that Kerubino was caught up in the fighting and killed, likely for supporting Mateip, who had just supported and protected Kerubino.

[*See also* Garang, John; Lagu, Joseph; Machar, Riek; *and* Mengistu Haile Mariam.]

BIBLIOGRAPHY

Burr, J. Millard, and Robert O. Collins. *Requiem for the Sudan: War, Drought, and Disaster Relief on the Nile.* Boulder, Colo.: Westview Press, 1995.

Human Rights Watch. "Sudan, Oil and Human Rights." Washington, D.C.: Human Rights Watch, 2003.

Johnson, Douglas H. *The Root Causes of Sudan's Civil Wars.* London: James Currey, 2003.

Young, John. "The South Sudan Defence Forces in the Wake of the Juba Declaration." HSBA Issue Brief No. 2 (October 2006). http://www.smallarmssurveysudan.org/pdfs/HSBA-SIB-2-SSDF.pdf.

MATTHEW LERICHE

Bomani, Paul (1925–2005), Tanzanian politician, was born in January 1925 at a mission station in Ikizu, Musoma, in colonial Tanganyika. He belonged to a Christian agricultural family of relatively comfortable means by the standards of the African population of Tanganyika, then under British administration. He received his education in Tanganyika in the early 1940s, receiving a Grade II certificate as a teacher from the Ikizu Secondary and Teacher Training School in 1945. In 1953, as a result of his work with the agricultural cooperative movement, he was given a scholarship to attend a course in cooperative development at Loughborough College in Leicester, United Kingdom. He married his wife, Hilda, in 1958, and they had nine children. His brother Mark Bomani also had a prominent

political career and currently works in Dar es Salaam as a lawyer in private practice.

Bomani's early adult life, beginning in 1947, was defined by his leadership in the agricultural cooperative movement that was particularly active in the Lake Province around the shores of Lake Victoria. An articulate and effective leader with a good head for business, his involvement in the cooperatives led into his lifelong political career. The cooperative movement became a leading political force in Tanganyika in the 1950s as the momentum of the independence movement began to grow. In 1950 Bomani was elected president of the Lake Province Cotton Growers Association, which was one of the most effective cooperative societies. In 1952 he was elected president of one of the most powerful ethnic associations in the territory at the time, the Sukuma Union. In 1954 he was appointed to the colonial Legislative Council (LEGCO) by the British governor-general. In 1955, after his studies at Loughborough, he was appointed general manager of the Victoria Federation of Cooperative Unions in Mwanza, helping farmers to coordinate their processing and marketing efforts.

As progress toward independence increased, the British administration sought to accelerate efforts at political reform to give Africans an increased voice in government. Bomani was appointed a member of the Rammage Constitutional Reform Committee, charged with seeking a path toward universal franchise in the territory. He continued as a leader of the expanding cooperative movement across the territory. He was elected to a seat in the LEGCO in 1958. After his reelection to the LEGCO in 1960, and with independence imminent, he was appointed minister of natural resources and cooperative development by Prime Minister Julius K. Nyerere.

In 1962 the Commonwealth territory of Tanganyika reconstituted itself as a fully independent republic, and under pressure from political factions in the country favoring rapid "Africanization," the government sought to replace British expatriate civil servants who had stayed on in their positions, contracted by the new independent government. Perhaps the most prestigious expatriate civil servant serving the Tanganyika government was the minister of finance, Sir Ernest Vasey. With the 1962 constitution Vasey was dismissed from his position and replaced by Bomani, in whom Vasey placed great confidence.

As minister of finance, Bomani oversaw budgets and planning, producing several multi-year national development plans in response to the changing ideological and economic conditions of the early years of Tanzanian independence. He was widely acknowledged to be intelligent, honest, and capable. As minister of finance he tempered the more energetic political ambitions that defined his early career in the cooperative movement. Although widely admired, Bomani never had the political clout of some of his more populist colleagues, nor did he have the influence and security of Nyerere's closest associates. His long tenure in the Tanzanian government was instead a testament to his competence and the underlying meritocratic tendencies of Nyerere's early government.

Bomani continued as minister of finance throughout most of the 1960s, taking on a slightly different role as minister of commerce, industry, and mining in 1970. During this time he also served as an advisory governor of the World Bank. During the most radical years of Nyerere's administration, Bomani was sent abroad as ambassador to the United States and Mexico from 1972 to 1983, where he was also elected president of the International Cotton Institute in 1980, a position he held until 1986. In the United States he worked to promote Tanzania's position in the struggle to end apartheid in South Africa. During his tenure as ambassador he applied his experience to scholarship. He received a master of arts degree in international relations from Johns Hopkins University, and served as a councilor on the Advisory Board of American University in Washington DC.

As Nyerere began to plan for his own retirement in the early 1980s, Bomani was brought home to a revolving selection of cabinet positions managing the economic sector during a time of profound structural change under an International Monetary Fund (IMF) austerity policy throughout the 1980s. His integrity and decorum were much needed during a period known for a sudden explosion of corruption under the more lenient policies of Tanzania's second president, Ali Hassan Mwinyi, elected in 1985. With the return of market-oriented economic policies, Bomani eventually retired from government service and was hired as chairman of the bankrupt Tanzania Breweries. He arranged a sale of the company to South African Breweries who kept him in his position of chairman while the breweries turned into one of Tanzania's most successful companies. With his scholarly credentials and vast governmental experience, he was appointed chancellor of the University of Dar es Salaam in 1993, a position he held until his death.

Paul Bomani died at the end of March 2005 and was buried in Mwanza as an elder statesman of international stature and one of Tanzania's most respected businessmen. He was admired widely as a prudent moderate during a period of tumultuous political pressures.

[*See also* Mwinyi, Ali Hassan; *and* Nyerere, Julius.]

BIBLIOGRAPHY

John Iliffe. *A Modern History of Tanganyika.* Cambridge, UK: Cambridge University Press, 1979.

PAUL BJERK

Bona Malwal (1928–), Sudanese journalist, politician, and government official, is the son of a Dinka chief from Twic Mayardit County in the province of northern Bahr El Ghazal, in southern Sudan. Bona has pursued careers in journalism, academia, and most prominently, politics. After the 2010 national election, he was named advisor to President ʿUmar al-Bashir, of the National Congress Party (NCP).

An accomplished student and athlete, Bona went to the US on scholarship. While there, he earned an MA in journalism and communications before returning to Sudan, where he became a leading southern Sudanese nationalist. Building on his academic training, Bona became the editor-in-chief of *The Advocate,* an early publication defending the human rights of southerners and calling for devolution of power to the south. He was a cofounder of the Southern Front and served as its first secretary-general. He was then elected to the national assembly in 1968, only to be dismissed one year later after the coup of General Jaʿfar al-Nimeiry as Nimeiri.

With the signing of the Addis Ababa Agreement in 1972, which ended rebellion in the south and brought the Anyanya forces of Joseph Lagu, an army officer who defected and joined the rebellion in the South, into the government, Bona was named State Minister for Culture and Information. He was also appointed to the Political Bureau of the Sudan Socialist Union, the sole political party allowed under Nimeiri, as Bona Malwal was seen as a southern figure amenable to working with the new government in Khartoum. A highly influential minister, Bona's star faded with the national reconciliation of 1976, which opened up roles in the government to other parties—the Umma Party, the Democratic Unionist Party, and the National Islamic Front. This reconciliation reduced Nimeiri's need for southerners to reinforce his authority, and so many posts that had been held by southerners were given to Nimeiri's new political allies. With Nimeiri's permission, Bona left for the US in 1978, where he pursued his writing.

Two years later, Bona returned to Sudan; he was appointed Minister of Finance and Economic Planning for the South. He only served for one year before his difficulty in accepting Nimeiri's dismantling of the Addis Ababa Agreement, and the government's increasingly Islamist stance, led him to open opposition, and he was subsequently jailed. Nimeiri's abrogation of the Addis Ababa Agreement in 1983 led to a resumption of the southern war with Dr. John Garang's Sudan People's Liberation Army/Movement (SPLM/A). In 1985, a popular insurrection in Khartoum overthrew the Nimeiri regime, and the Transitional Military Council (TMC) came to power. The TMC organized national elections for 1986, which resulted in the victory of the Umma Party under the leadership of Sadig Al-Mahdi.

Under this new democratic administration, Bona was free to pursue his political activities and journalism. In 1986, Bona became editor-in-chief of the *Sudan Times*, an influential daily published in Khartoum which called for a political settlement to the southern war, condemned the growing Islamist influence in Sadig's coalition government, and supported democratic rule. The daily also supported the SPLM/A, although Bona was never a member of the organization. Bona was outside the country when Hasan al-Turabi's National Islamic Front carried out its coup in 1989; he remained outside the country for many years before he reconciled with the regime and felt comfortable returning.

During his exile in the UK, Bona published several books, gave lectures at St. Anthony's College, Oxford, and established the *Sudan Democratic Gazette*. The *Gazette* condemned the National Front government, but also became increasingly critical of Dr. John Garang and the SPLM/A. Also during his exile in Britain Bona formed the Southern Sudan Democratic Forum, a fledgling party of southern Sudanese expatriates. Bona also urged Deputy SPLM/A Leader at the time Salva Kiir, his regional compatriot, to oppose Garang in a series of letters, which subsequently became public. This action created a division with Kiir and other southern leaders.

Bona was a critic of the Comprehensive Peace Agreement (CPA), but welcomed the National Islamic Front's (NIF; now National Congress Party, NCP) commitment to southern self-determination, and was thus able to reconcile with the regime in Khartoum and return to Sudan, where he was appointed presidential advisor to President al-Bashir. His influence in the NCP government, however, made him an object of suspicion in SPLM/A circles. Bona served as a co-director of the campaign to elect al-Bashir in the April 2010 election, on the grounds that al-Bashir alone ensured that the commitment to self-determination would be realized in the promised referendum of January 2011. In the elections Bona ran as a candidate in his home region of northern Bahr El Ghazal, but on 12 April he withdrew in the face of what he claimed was SPLM/A interference. Bona advocated self-determination, but in view of what he considered the corruption, tribalism, and political inequities in the south under the SPLM/A Government of South Sudan, he advocated a transitional period before independence is realized. In October 2010, Bona helped engineer a reconciliation between twenty-three southern parties and factions and the SPLM, and also worked on a program of political reform in the post-referendum period. After his long isolation from mainstream southern politics and the SPLM/A, his championing of this process again brought Bona into the public spotlight.

Bona Malwal has been a devout Catholic his entire life. His wife is a senior diplomat in the government of South Sudan. His son, Akui, was appointed ambassador to Ethiopia, and his daughter, Sandra, is a leading official in the Sudan People's Liberation Movement–Democratic Change party of Lam Akol, which was created in 2009.

Bona Malwal is the author of *The Sudan: A Link between Arab and Non-Arab Africa* (1975), *People and Power in Sudan: The Struggle for National Salvation* (1981), *The Sudan: A Second Challenge to Nationhood* (1985), and *Crisis in the Sudan: Re-Thinking the Future* (1994).

Bona Malwal's historical significance is assured by his long struggle for the rights of the southern Sudanese, including self-determination. Despite this, his role in the 2011 referendum on southern self-determination, which resulted overwhelmingly in favor of secession, has been limited; he split time between Khartoum and Europe, engaged as an advisor to the NCP on the South and commenting on political development. He has been a politician who relishes controversy, as evident by his public quarrels with former Prime Minister Sadig Al-Mahdi, John Garang, and the SPLM leadership more generally and his tactical alliance with the NCP.

[*See also* Bashir, ʿUmar al-; Garang, John; Kiir
Mayardit, Salva; Lagu, Joseph; Nimeiry, Jaʿfar al-;
and Turabi, Hasan al-.]

BIBLIOGRAPHY

Collins, Robert O. *A History of Modern Sudan.*
   Cambridge, UK: Cambridge University Press,
   2008.
Johnson, Douglas H. *The Root Causes of Sudan's Civil
   Wars.* London: James Currey, 2001.

JOHN YOUNG and MATTHEW LERICHE

Bongo, Pascaline (1956–), Gabonese politician and
foreign minister, was born on 10 April 1956 to Omar
(then Albert-Bernard) Bongo Ondimba and Louise
Mouyabi Moukala in Franceville, capital of the
southeastern Gabonese province of Haut-Ogooué.
At the time of her birth, her father, Omar Bongo
Ondimba, later president of Gabon, was a lieutenant in the French air force. Little public information
is available about her childhood and adolescence,
but she attended the University of California–Los
Angeles in 1979 with her younger sister Albertine.
Her father had purchased a home for roughly 2.2
million dollars US in Beverly Hills, California.
Shortly before moving to the United States, she
reportedly had a short romantic relationship with
the Jamaican reggae singer Bob Marley.

Pascaline Bongo finished her studies in the
United States and returned to Gabon. Although
little detailed information exists about her activities in the 1980s, she rose to prominence in her
father's government after the civil upheaval that
severely challenged Omar Bongo's power in Gabon.
In 1991, Omar Bongo named her the minister of
foreign affairs. Her residence in the United States
and her command of English proved very useful in
this post. For example, she served as the key organizer of American pop singer Michael Jackson's
visit to Gabon in 1992. She remained minister of
foreign affairs until 1994 and held various government positions in the years that followed. Besides
holding this ministerial position, Pascaline Bongo
played a pivotal role in the 1993 presidential election between Omar Bongo and his main political
rival Paul Mba Abessolé. She was appointed by
her father to be on the Gabonese government
commission to organize and supervise the election.
It is believed by some scholars and many Gabonese
people that she helped ensure that her father's
Parti Démocratique Gabonais (PDG; Gabonese
Democratic Party) won the election through fraudulent means.

While her brother Ali Ben Bongo (1959–) was
widely viewed as Omar Bongo's heir apparent from
the early 1990s until 2008, Pascaline Bongo proved
to be a very capable politician and financial advisor
in her own right. However, much of her work
remained outside of the public eye. She was a longtime board member of the Banque Gabonaise et
Française Internationale (BGFI), one of the most
important financial institutions in Gabon in the
late twentieth and early twenty-first centuries. She
also was an executive board member of Total
Gabon, the Gabonese branch of the extremely
influential Elf/Total French-based multinational
corporation. In July 2008, she was appointed the
director of the Gabon Mining Logistics (GML)
company by Omar Bongo. The GML was the leading force behind the partnership between the
Gabonese government and Chinese firms seeking
to build a giant iron ore mining complex in Belinga,
a remote region in the northeastern Ogooué-Ivindo
Province. As of March 2011, the complex has yet to
go into operation, but Pascaline Bongo would be
the director of one of the biggest iron mining companies in the world if the Belinga complex reaches
its full potential. She also has played a key role in
managing lobbying efforts in the United States on
behalf of Gabon. Jacqueline Wilson, the ex-spouse
of former American ambassador Joe Wilson, who
gained notoriety in the Valerie Plame scandal in
the United States regarding a false rumor about the
sale of uranium by Niger to Iraq shortly before the
second Gulf War, received over 60,000 US dollars
in 2001 from Gabonese funds through Pascaline
Bongo for lobbying efforts. It is rumored but
unclear if Pascaline Bongo was involved in the successful effort to use the firm of lobbyist Jack
Abramoff, convicted of corruption charges in 2006,
as a means for Omar Bongo to meet US President
George W. Bush in 2004. She was the director of
Omar Bongo's staff for the first decade of the twenty-
first century.

Despite her relatively low profile, Pascaline
Bongo's political activities were a source of controversy for the first decade of the twenty-first century.
A United States–based human rights organization
protested in May 2003 the Gabonese government's
decision to ban the sale of *Misamu*, a Gabonese
newspaper, allegedly for printing an article investigating the mysterious death of one of Pascaline
Bongo's aides. On 10 December 2008, a Gabonese
journalist for the independent newspaper *Le Nganga*
reported he was beaten by law enforcement authorities in the presidential palace in Libreville after he

published a story accusing Pascaline Bongo of embezzlement. According to the 27 November 2008 article, Pascaline Bongo had obtained 600 million CFA (the currency of Gabon, worth roughly 1,245,000 US dollars in January 2009) from the Gabonese government for a road-building project with a Gabonese company. The article claimed the money was never used for the project.

Bongo's activities in France repeatedly drew attention from French courts and police investigations. She was implicated in the Elf/Total oil company corruption scandal in France and fined 2 million euros by a French court in 2007. A series of legal investigations into the use of African government funds to purchase property and merchandise in France from 2006 uncovered a great deal of information regarding Pascaline's financial transactions. For example, she owned several apartments in wealthy Parisian neighborhoods and purchased a Mercedes automobile for 75,858 euros in September 2006. This vehicle was paid for by a check from the Gabonese government, signed by Omar Bongo's lawyer in France, François Meyer.

Pascaline Bongo married Paul Tongui, a longtime PDG stalwart who has served in a variety of important ministries, such as the ministry of the treasury, in February 1995. She also had two children with Jean Ping, former minister of foreign affairs and in 2008 president of the African Union, before her marriage to Tongui. One of their sons, Christophe Bongo Tarallo-Bongo, resides in Paris.

Though her public presence has been limited in Gabonese politics, it is clear Pascaline Bongo was one of the most significant figures in the Gabonese government from the late 1980s until 2009. Like her father, she was adept at joining together roles in the private and public sector. After her father's death in 2009, she remained a key advisor to her brother Ali Ben Bongo, who won the August 2009 Gabonese presidential elections.

[*See also* Bongo Ondimba, Omar.]

BIBLIOGRAPHY

Gardinier, David E., and Douglas A. Yates. *Historical Dictionary of Gabon*. 3d ed. Metuchen, N.J.: Scarecrow Press, 2006.

Monnier, Xavier. "Les chèques cadeaux du Omar Bongo." 3 December 2008. Online. Bakchich, accessed 13 January 2009, http://www.bakchich.info/article6053.html.

Reporters Without Borders. "Journalist Brutally Beaten by President's Men Leaves Hospital."

12 December 2008. Online. UNHCR Refworld, accessed 13 January 2009, http://www.unhcr.org/refworld/docid/494773801a.html.

Tuquoi, Jean-Pierre. "La bande à Bongo." *Le Monde*, 26 November 2005.

JEREMY RICH

Bongo Ondimba, Omar (1935–2009), president of Gabon, was born on 30 December 1935 in the village of Lewai (now Bongoville) in the southeastern Haut-Ogooué region (in present-day Gabon) to the Tèkè family. His father was Basile Ondimba and his mother Jeanne Ebori. He was the youngest of twelve children. His father died before Bongo reached puberty. As the Haut-Ogooué province belonged to the French Congo colony rather than Gabon from 1926 until 1947, Bongo studied in schools in the Congolese capital of Brazzaville rather than Libreville. Once he finished his studies in 1953, he became a postal clerk. After several years, he joined the French air force. By 1959 Bongo reached the rank of first lieutenant after serving in Chad and the Central African Republic.

Omar Bongo Ondimba, 2004. (AP Images/Xinhua, Rao Aimin)

With the coming of independence in 1960, Bongo chose to become a civil servant rather than run for political officer. In 1961, he supported candidates from the majority Bloc Démocratique Gabonais (BDG; Gabonese Democratic Bloc) party headed by President Léon M'ba. He held a range of different government posts before the 17–18 February 1964 coup, including Minister of Information and Tourism. Bongo was held prisoner briefly by supporters of the coup against M'ba but was freed when French troops intervened and restored M'ba and the BDG party to power. M'ba named Bongo vice president on 12 November 1966. There is great controversy about the relationship between M'ba and Bongo. While some have contended that French officials such as Jacques Foccart aided Bongo in his rise to power against the wishes of M'ba, Bongo always contended that the two men shared a common program of multiethnic unity and close ties to France. When M'ba died on 27 November 1967, Bongo succeeded him as president.

Like so many other African leaders in the second half of the 1960s, Bongo chose to form a single-party regime. In 1968, Bongo renamed the BDG party the Parti Démocratique Gabonais (PDG; Gabonese Democratic Party) and instituted a single-party government system that survived until 1990. The rapidly expanding export of petroleum, uranium, and manganese fueled Bongo's plans for economic development. From 1968 to 1990, Bongo's government closely supported French interests in Central Africa, and several thousand French troops were stationed in the country. He formed close relationships to Giscard d'Estaing, François Mitterrand, and other French political leaders. At times, Bongo's foreign policy drew opposition from other African states, particularly his support for the Biafran state's failed struggle for independence from Nigeria from 1968 to 1973. Bongo demonstrated his wealth by holding the Organization of African Unity conference in 1977. His preparations included completely leveling much of the center of Libreville to make way for new buildings, including his presidential palace. He also inaugurated the Transgabonais railway between Franceville, the capital of his home province of Haut-Ogooué, and the coastal capital of Libreville. This massive undertaking cost over a billion US dollars, well beyond initial projections. After nearly a decade of work, the railway was completed in 1986.

Despite such massive achievements, Bongo faced a range of critics. European journalists denounced Bongo as a plutocrat whose corrupt government regularly paid off French politicians. His ties to the French-based multinational corporation Elf/Total also became controversial. As president, Bongo relied on a feared secret police to repress dissent, particularly from the MORENA opposition party. Internal exile, torture, and executions were regularly used to maintain the PDG's undisputed grip on power. Bongo also relied on a careful division of major government posts among members of different ethnic groups and regions to ensure his hold on power. Bongo became one of the wealthiest men in the world thanks to his control of the mineral and oil resources of his country. His political acumen and wealth also made him a feared leader.

In 1973, Bongo converted to Islam and changed his name from Albert-Bernard Bongo to Omar Bongo. He added his father's name, Ondimba, in 2004. His change of religion has been cynically viewed as a move to insert himself closer to other members of OPEC. Bongo has contended that Islam better reflected his personal values than Christianity. He has provided financial support for the minority Muslim community in Gabon, largely made of West African immigrants. Bongo is widely believed to have connections to powerful indigenous supernatural diviners but has never publicly acknowledged this to be the case. He also is said to have strong connections with the Masons in France.

Bongo first married Marie-Josephine Kama (now known as Patience Dabany) in 1959, when she was 15 years old. Kama, later known as Josephine Bongo, was the mother of two children. Ali Ben Bongo (1959–) is now the Minister of Defense of Gabon. Their other child, Albertine Amissa Bongo (1964–1991), died under mysterious circumstances. Josephine Bongo chose to divorce her husband in 1986, and he quickly married Edith Lucie Sassou-Nguesso, the daughter of the then-leader of neighboring Congo-Brazzaville, Denis Sassou-Nguesso. Bongo is said to have fathered many children with a number of different women, so the exact number of his offspring is a matter of debate. One of his most well-known daughters, Pascaline Bongo, became one of his top advisors.

Bongo's challenges between 1990 and 1994, however, were hardly a matter of conjecture. In 1990, opposition leader Joseph Rendjambe was found dead, supposedly of a drug overdose. Many Gabonese people took to the streets in protest, particularly in the city of Port-Gentil. French and Gabonese troops battled this movement, but Bongo ultimately agreed to hold multiparty elections.

Bongo narrowly won the 1993 elections against his rival Paul Mba Abessolé. However, Bongo and the PDG held onto power in the 1998, 2002, and 2007 presidential elections by a wide majority. These elections were believed by many Gabonese critics to have been marred by rampant fraud. Bongo continued to be a target of disparagement after holding on to power for over forty years. In 2008, a French court launched an investigation of Bongo's financial holdings in Europe, which greatly embarrassed the regime. He became gravely ill in the spring of 2009 and died in a Spanish hospital on 8 June 2009. Bongo's rule defined Gabonese politics and society for five decades, and his longevity was a testament to his political skills and intelligence. Unlike other African strongmen of his generation, he weathered the wave of democratic movements in the early 1990s. At the time of his death in June 2009, Omar Bongo Odinga was the longest reigning leader in the world, having served for forty-two years—two years longer than Libya's Mu'ammar al-Qaddafi. His son Ali Bongo Ondimba won election on 30 August 2009 and maintained the power of the ruling PDG party.

[*See also* Bongo, Pascaline; Dabany, Patience; M'Ba, Léon; *and* Qaddafi, Mu'ammar al-.]

BIBLIOGRAPHY

Bongo, Omar. *Blanc comme Nègre: Entretiens avec Airy Routier*. Paris: Grasset, 2001.

Obiang, Jean-François. *France-Gabon: Pratiques clientélaires et logiques d'état*. Paris: Karthala, 2007.

Verschave, François-Xavier. *La Françafrique, la plus long scandale de la République*. Paris: Stock, 1998.

Yates, Douglas. *The Rentier State in Africa: Oil Rent Dependency and Neocolonialism in the Republic of Gabon*. Trenton, N.J.: Africa World Press, 1996.

JEREMY RICH

Boraine, Alex (1931–), South African religious and political leader, was born on 10 January 1931 in Cape Town, South Africa to Mike Boraine and Isa Blanche. He grew up in the working-class neighborhood of Brooklyn in an English-speaking household and had two brothers, both of whom were killed in World War II. As was typical for white families of his generation, his early years brought him into very little contact with South Africans from other racial groups, and the political consciousness in his family centered mostly around the divisions between the English and Afrikaner communities in South Africa. After completing

tenth grade, Boraine left school and worked at a variety of odd jobs. His father died when he was eighteen.

In that same year, after a childhood that was relatively nonreligious, Boraine attended a Methodist youth camp and experienced a dramatic conversion. His rise through the church was equally dramatic. Within a year he was a lay preacher. By age 20, he was a Sunday school superintendent and candidate minister. For the next two years, he served in rural South Africa and began to confront the complexity of racial relations in the country. He also struggled to reconcile his mainstream theological practice and perspective with these emerging concerns.

In 1953, Boraine went to Rhodes University in Grahamstown, South Africa, to complete a BA in theology and Biblical studies. There he met Jennifer Clark, whom he married five years later. In 1960, he left for England to complete a master's degree at Mansfield College, Oxford. A couple of years later, he left for Drew University in the United States to begin work on a doctorate in theology (completed in 1969).

Though his time as a student at Rhodes and Oxford challenged his theology, it was his time in the United States during the height of the civil rights movement that really changed the way Boraine thought about race, social justice, and religion. It was with this new perspective that he returned to South Africa in 1968 and became general secretary of the youth department of the Methodist Church. During his seven years in this position, Boraine increasingly mixed politics and religion, even briefly working with a young Steve Biko, activities that brought him into conflict with both church elders and the security police.

Despite tensions between Boraine and the church's more conservative leadership, in 1970 he was elected President of the Methodist Church of Southern Africa. He continued his political activism and traveled widely, addressing, in particular, the issue of forced removals of communities as part of apartheid social engineering. Two years later, in an unexpected move, he was seconded to the Anglo American Corporation, a major South African mining firm, to oversee the company's reform of the working and living conditions of its workers.

His time with Anglo American brought him into contact with ordinary miners as well as with some of the country's most prominent business and political leaders. In particular, he became known among "white liberal" opinion leaders, who in 1974 persuaded Boraine to run for Parliament under the Progressive Party's banner. Liberalism among white South Africans during apartheid represented an ambiguous position on the political spectrum. Liberals like the famous Helen Suzman rejected the apartheid policies of the National Party government but did not want to reject the existing political process outright and instead adopted a strategy of critique and reform from within.

Boraine won the seat and served in Parliament for the next twelve years. During his tenure, he continued focusing on issues of race relations and social justice, including child labor and labor migration policies. He and his party pushed for what he called "negotiation politics" at a time when the struggle against apartheid was reaching a boiling point. Boraine's focus on engagement and dialogue increasingly fell on deaf ears, and in 1986 Boraine decided reform from within was no longer viable, and he resigned from his Parliamentary seat.

After several months of consulting with political leaders from a range of positions, Boraine and Frederik van Zyl Slabbert, another member of Parliament who had resigned just before Boraine and for the same reasons, set up the Institute for a Democratic Alternative in South Africa (IDASA). IDASA was designed to promote the kind of dialogue and negotiation across racial, political, and class lines that had not been possible in Parliament. One of IDASA's major early successes was the Dakar Conference, a meeting between prominent white South African intellectuals, ministers, and business and opinion leaders and the leadership-in-exile of the African National Congress (ANC). The conference was one of several sets of discussions that occurred in the late 1980s between the ANC and South African leaders.

IDASA continued to support these kinds of engagements into the early 1990s. Boraine left in 1993 to form a new organization called Justice in Transition, which was devoted to thinking about how the experiences and memories of victims could be incorporated into the emerging transition away from apartheid. Justice in Transition played a central part in laying the groundwork for what would become the Truth and Reconciliation Commission (TRC).

The TRC was tasked by the new post-apartheid government with documenting the testimony of victims of apartheid, granting individual amnesties to those who confessed to human rights violations and making recommendations for reparations.

In 1995, Boraine was elected and served as TRC deputy chairperson alongside its chairperson, Archbishop Desmond Tutu. He worked with the TRC for two years.

In 1999, Boraine left for New York to work on a book about the TRC and teach courses in the emerging field of "transitional justice" at New York University Law School. During this time, transitional justice was of increasing interest to governments, nongovernmental organizations, and donor foundations. In 2001, with the backing of the Ford Foundation and others, Boraine helped establish the International Center for Transitional Justice (ICTJ) and became its first president. In 2003, he took up the position of chairman of the ICTJ Board and returned to Cape Town to become the director of the Cape Town office of ICTJ. He continues to work, travel, teach, and consult widely in the fields of post-conflict reconciliation and transitional justice.

[*See also* Biko, Steve; Suzman, Helen Gavronsky; and Tutu, Desmond Mpilo.]

BIBLIOGRAPHY

Boraine, Alex. *A Country Unmasked: Inside South Africa's Truth and Reconciliation Commission.* Oxford, UK: Oxford University Press, 2000.

Boraine, Alex. *A Life in Transition.* Cape Town, South Africa: Zebra Press, 2008.

Boraine, Alex, Janet Levy, Ronel Scheffer, and Institute for a Democratic Alternative for South Africa. *Dealing with the Past: Truth and Reconciliation in South Africa.* Cape Town, South Africa: IDASA, 1994.

Tutu, Desmond. *Truth and Reconciliation Commission Final Report.* Pretoria, South Africa: Truth and Reconciliation Commission, 1998.

CHRISTOPHER J. COLVIN

Boro, Isaac Adaka (1938–1968), Nigerian student leader, teacher, policeman, and revolutionary, was born in the Niger Delta Region community of in Oloibiri, on 10 September 1938. He was the son of Jasper Pepple Boro, a schoolmaster at Kaiama in the Kolokuma-Opokuma district of Bayelsa State in present-day Nigeria. He took the name *Adaka*, meaning "lion," when he began his revolutionary campaign to create an independent Niger Delta Republic and secede from Nigeria in 1966. The movement was crushed by the Nigerian armed forces in only twelve days.

Born in Oloibiri, the community near which oil was first discovered and exploited in the Niger

Delta, Boro became more and more agitated by the neglect that his Ijaw people (also known as Izon or Ijo) suffered from the federal government of Nigeria after the country gained independence from Britain in 1960. The Izon were possibly the most vociferous group expressing fear of neglect and victimization by larger groups during the negotiations for Nigeria's independence from Britain. The Willink Commission, set up by the British, declared the fears of neglect justified, and they recommended a special Niger Delta Development Board, of which Jasper Pepple Boro became a member. The Board was, however, without executive powers, and the federal government did not carry out its recommendations for development.

It was in this atmosphere of agitation for justice among the peoples of the Niger Delta that Isaac Boro grew up to be, first, a school teacher and a policeman. At the age of twenty-three, he entered the University of Nigeria to study for a degree in chemistry. His leadership skills soon became apparent, when, against great odds, he won election as leader of the student union, as a minority candidate. From this position he began to gain the attention of the political leaders, some of whom tried to use him. In the end he became more and more radicalized in the pursuit of the interests of his own Izon people of the Niger Delta. In his own words, "I was able to find out that a state for the Ijaws was an impossibility. . . . I learnt a lot of things which conclusively led to the first revolution in search of a state ever recorded in Nigerian history" (cited in Tebekaemi, 1982, p. 56).

Boro tried to educate himself in radical political action through contacts with left-wing Nigerian politicians and trade union leaders. He later paid visits to the embassies of countries such as Mu'ammar al-Qaddafi's Libya, and Fidel Castro's Cuba, during an unsuccessful trip to Kwame Nkrumah's Ghana. In the end, he had to create his own revolutionary organization from his own internal resources of courage and resolve. First, he formed the Integral WXYZ, assisted by Samuel Owonaru, Napoleon Selete, and Nothingham Dick. Each letter stood for an operation, idea, or objective in the planned revolution: W for Niger Delta Labour Advisory Council, intended to place youth in jobs; X for Niger Delta Forum for Political Education to issue propaganda in the press to promote the imminent revolution; Y for Niger Delta Oil Council for combat with the international corporations prospecting for oil and gas; and Z for Reserved Operation Zero, meaning the final call to revolution.

Reserved Operation Zero happened in an unplanned manner in response to the first Nigerian military coup d'état of January 1966. Boro organized the Niger Delta Volunteer Service within days of the announcement of the coup, during which the prime minister, Sir Tafewa Balewa, Ahmadu Bello (sardauna of Sokoto and premier of Northern Nigeria), and other political leaders were killed. According to Boro, "I knew the day had dawned on the Niger Delta. If we did not move then, we would throw ourselves into perpetual slavery. The only protector of the Ijaws, Sir Balewa, was dead" (Tebekaemi, 1982, p. 94).

By 23 February 1966, Boro had completed recruiting and training his Niger Delta Volunteer Service. They were fully aware of the difficulty of their war of liberation. They were ill equipped, poorly armed, without funds, and not fully trained. Indeed, it was virtually a suicide mission, albeit one that would create awareness of the neglect of the Niger Delta by the Nigerian political system. Boro, Owonaru, and Nothingham Dick were tried, convicted, and sentenced to death; but they were later pardoned by General Yakubu Gowon. During their imprisonment in Lagos, Boro managed to write his memoirs/autobiography, giving a full account of his war to liberate the Niger Delta. His junior brother, David Boro, carried documents from their father from Kaiama to Lagos, and Superintendent Idada of the maximum security prison in Sanki, Lagos, assisted. He titled it *The Creek Revolution: The Memoirs of Isaac Boro*. It was first serialized in part in the *Spear: Nigeria's National Magazine* in 1970. It has now become a classic of the Niger Delta militancy as *The Twelve Day Revolution by Major Isaac Boro*, edited by Tony Tebekaemi and first published in 1982.

Boro's service in the Nigerian Army to defeat the attempt of the Igbo of Eastern Nigeria to establish a Republic of Biafra is yet to be documented. Kathryn Nwajiaku-Dahou (2007) suggests that Boro was "recruited" by the federal government and thereby betrayed his earlier objective of an independent Izon state. She suggests that this inconsistency has created problems for current Izon nationalists in appropriating his legacy. Far from being "recruited," Boro, assisted by Owonaru, Nothingham Dick, Boardman Nyananyo, George Amangala, and others, organized a unit of Izon volunteers in Lagos and persuaded the federal authorities to permit them to liberate the Niger Delta areas occupied by the Biafran army. Indeed, the charismatic leader of the federal forces in the Niger Delta region, General

Adekunle, is thought to have resented Boro's independent spirit, success, and fame.

Boro's legacy remains his single-minded struggle to call attention to the plight of the Izon people of the Niger Delta within the Nigerian nation. He has become the standard and exemplar of struggle, militancy, as well as sacrifice and commitment to the welfare of the common people of the region. His statute now stands inside Boro Park in Port Harcourt, Rivers State; the Bayelsa State government established The Isaac Adaka Boro Foundation in Yenagoa; and the Niger Delta University has awarded Boro the posthumous degree of doctor of philosophy *honoris causa*.

[*See also* Qaddafi, Mu'ammar al-; *and* Tafawa Balewa, Abubakar.]

BIBLIOGRAPHY

Boro, Isaac Adaka. *The Creek Revolution: The Memoirs of Isaac Boro*. Serialized as "The Boro Story: A Spear Exclusive," in *Spear: Nigeria's National Magazine*. Lagos, Nigeria: 1970. The manuscript was received by Tony Momoh from David Boro.

Boro, Isaac. *The Twelve Day Revolution*, edited by T. Tebekaemi. Benin City, Nigeria: Idodo Umeh, 1982.

Nwajiaku-Dahou, Kathryn. "Remembering and Forgetting Isaac Boro: Multiple Strands in Contemporary Ijo Nationalism." In *History Concourse 2007: The Future of the Niger Delta: The Search for a Relevant Narrative*, edited by A. A. Derefaka and A. M. Okorobia. Port Harcourt, Nigeria: Onyoma Research, 2008.

E. J. ALAGOA

Bosman, Herman Charles (1905–1951), journalist, novelist, short story writer, and essayist, is one of South Africa's most enduringly popular writers. He is chiefly remembered for his storyteller figure Oom Schalk Lourens, a backwoods sage who, pipe in hand and a trick or two up his sleeve, beguilingly narrates some of the funniest and yet most moving stories in the entire canon of South African literature.

Born in Kuils River near Cape Town, Bosman spent most of his life in the Transvaal. He was educated at Jeppe High School for Boys, the University of the Witwatersrand, and Normal College, where he qualified as a teacher. In January 1926 the fateful decision was taken by the Transvaal Education Department to dispatch him as a novice teacher to the tiny farm school of Heimweeberg in the Dwarsberg area of the Marico district. The next six months in the young man's life were to prove momentous. His stay in the

Marico exposed him to a community poor in material wealth but rich in the art of storytelling. Stories about the Anglo-Boer and Native wars, about life in the Boer Republics of Stellaland, Goshen, and Ohrigstad, about local legend and lore, were all eagerly absorbed by the young schoolteacher over coffee on the farm veranda or in the parlor. Later in life he was able to draw on this rich reservoir of material in over 150 stories spanning some twenty years, and this work established his reputation.

In July 1926 Bosman returned to Johannesburg for a holiday, and it was at this point that his life took a drastic downward turn. He had brought a hunting rifle back with him from the Marico, and during an argument with his stepbrother David Russell, a shot went off and Russell was killed. Bosman was arrested, convicted of murder, and sentenced to death. His sentence was commuted to imprisonment with hard labor for ten years—a term later reduced to five years (of which he eventually served four)—but he spent some weeks on death row, and this and other brutalizing experiences in prison made a lasting impression on him. *Cold Stone Jug* (1949) is a fictionalized chronicle of his term in Pretoria Central Prison. This remarkable work, the precursor of an entire genre in South African literature (the prison novel), ranges in tone from the jocular and sardonic to the anguished, desperate cry of a young man on the edge of insanity.

Upon his release on parole in 1930, Bosman embarked on a series of journalistic ventures, among them the launching of some short-lived periodicals. One of these was *The Touleier* ("The Wagon-train Leader"), which carried his first Oom Schalk Lourens story, "Makapan's Caves" (1930). In October 1932 Bosman married Ellaleen Manson, and the two departed for London in 1934. For the next six-and-a-half years Bosman contributed a steady stream of stories and sketches for South African magazines, including "In the Withaak's Shade," "The Music Maker," and, perhaps his most famous story, "The Mafeking Road," a Boer War story that deals with the tragedy of a father who kills his own son during the Boer retreat from Mafeking.

In 1940 the Bosmans returned to South Africa, and in 1943 Bosman was appointed editor of a biweekly newspaper published in Pietersburg, in the then Northern Transvaal. This milieu provided the fictional settings of "Kalvyn" in his first novel *Jacaranda in the Night* (1947) and "Willemsdorp" in the novel of the same name (first published 1977; new unexpurgated edition 1998). In 1944, after divorcing Ella, Bosman married Helena Stegmann and began the most productive period of his career, producing some thirty Marico stories, the three works that were to appear in his lifetime—*Jacaranda in the Night*, *Mafeking Road*, and *Cold Stone Jug*—and eighty "Voorkamer" stories. The last are a series of "conversation pieces" that feature a number of Marico farmers who gather in Jurie Steyn's voorkamer (parlor), which doubles as the local post office, and hold forth hilariously on a number of topical subjects. These satirical pieces appeared regularly in the South African news weekly *The Forum* from April 1950 until Bosman's sudden death from heart failure in October 1951.

Mafeking Road (1947) is undoubtedly the work for which Bosman is best known. It was an instant success upon its first release and has gone into numerous editions and impressions from 1947 to the present. All but one of the twenty-one stories in the collection feature Oom Schalk Lourens, through whom Bosman is able to reflect ironically on the prejudices and weaknesses of the Marico community, which he nonetheless evokes with great sympathy and understanding.

Mafeking Road is rich in memorable stories, many of which contain references to events that are staple items in Boer folk history. These mainly concern the two Anglo-Boer wars and the various wranglings between the Boer people and the British authorities. In them Bosman demonstrates an all-embracing vision of South African society. The opening passages of "The Rooinek," for example, describe the Second Anglo-Boer War and the devastation caused to Boer farms in the course of the hostilities. The concentration camps into which the British herded many Afrikaner women and children are also briefly referred to. However, the bulk of the story concerns the actions of a young Englishman—the "rooinek" ("redneck") of the story's title—who comes to settle in the Marico in the midst of a community who are bitterly antipathetic to the English. He strikes up a friendship with a Boer couple to whose baby daughter he grows extremely attached. When the couple decide to join the community trek to German West Africa after disease has laid waste to their cattle, he goes with them. The family dies in the Kalahari Desert, and the Englishman's body is later discovered with them, clutching a bundle of rags he evidently believed in his feverish state was the little girl. Other stories show, in Bosman's inimitable ironic style, black South Africans getting the better of their white "superiors" ("The Prophet," "Yellow Moepels") or expose the hypocrisies and fallibilities of the supposedly God-fearing community he is describing ("Makapan's Caves," "Marico Scandal," and "Veld Maiden").

In a 1954 BBC program the South African poet Roy Campbell described Bosman as "the best short story writer that ever came out of South Africa." The last sixty-odd years have shown just how accurate Campbell's assessment was: Bosman is as popular today as he was in 1950s and 1960s, and his stature, firmly established by his gentle ironic humor, humane vision, and consummate literary artistry, is unlikely to diminish in the years to come.

BIBLIOGRAPHY

Bosman, Herman Charles. *Cold Stone Jug*. Cape Town: Human and Rousseau, 1999.

Bosman, Herman Charles. *Mafeking Road and Other Stories*. Cape Town: Human and Rousseau, 1998.

Bosman, Herman Charles. *The Complete Oom Schalk Lourens Stories*. Cape Town: Human and Rousseau, 2006.

Gray, Stephen, ed. *Herman Charles Bosman*. Johannesburg: McGraw-Hill, 1986.

Gray, Stephen. *Life Sentence: A Biography of Herman Charles Bosman*. Cape Town: Human and Rousseau, 2005.

CRAIG MACKENZIE

Botha, Louis (1862–1919), farmer, general, and first prime minister of the Union of South Africa, was born on 27 September 1862 near Greytown in the British colony of Natal. His paternal grandfather, Philip Rudolph Boot (or Both), was of German settler descent and had participated in the 1830s Boer Great Trek into the interior. The son of migrant trekkers Louis Botha and Salomina van Rooyen, Louis was the ninth of thirteen children. In 1869, the Botha family left Natal and settled on a farm near Vrede in the Orange Free State, where Louis lived until the age of twenty-two. Earlier, he had been schooled at a local German mission where he received only a very basic education.

Botha's minimal formal learning proved to be no handicap to the development of his exceptional aptitude for fieldcraft and understanding of the working of the highveld terrain. In 1886, he settled on his own farm east of Vryheid in the Boer New Republic, established on lands in northwestern Zululand that he and other Boer volunteer fighters had been granted by King Dinuzulu two years earlier as a reward for having campaigned for him in his successful battle against a rival, Zibhebhu, for the Zulu paramountcy. Botha had played his part well as a Zulu collaborator and African king-maker. In 1886 he married Annie Emmet, a woman of Irish descent, the same year in which he was elected the district field-cornet or militia official for Vryheid, a post he retained when the short-lived New Republic was incorporated into the South African Republic or Transvaal in 1888. A farmer with a pronounced nose for politics, Botha got his electoral start in 1896 when he and Lukas Meyer became Vryheid representatives in the South African Republic's Volksraad or parliament.

At the same time Botha was, if anything, even more set on soldiering. Here, he had cut his teeth in the small Anglo-Transvaal War of 1880–1881 when the Boers rebelled against recently imposed British rule. Although not yet in command, he seized the initiative in sabotaging river crossings to thwart advance incursions by the enemy. Further blooding followed in 1884 in his collaborationist expedition to Zululand. Although Botha had been wary of forcing Britain's hand in its standoff with the Transvaal in the 1890s, when war came in October 1899 he saddled up and left his farm to fight in a major colonial conflict that would transform him into an influential military and political figure.

Joining the Vryheid force under General Lukas Meyer as an ordinary citizen-soldier or burgher commando at the outbreak of the South African War or Anglo-Boer War of 1899–1902, the sudden incapacity of his commander provided an opening for Botha to make his reputation. Thrust into leadership on the Natal eastern front, Botha put up an extraordinary display of tactical improvisation to frustrate British attackers and save the republican position at Ladysmith. Later, when going on a retaliatory offensive, he displayed his shrewd grasp of conducting warfare against a more powerful adversary, that of pressing hard but knowing when to stop in action and not to be wasteful of the lives of his men. Within a few weeks, Botha assumed Meyer's command permanently and was appointed general. Continuing illness within the Transvaal general staff aided his further rise to Commandant-General by early 1900.

With a reputation for keeping his nerve and for regularly intervening personally in hostile engagements, Botha was in the thick of many of the war's decisive engagements, including the Battle of Spioenkop. While unable to check the British advance and conquest of Boer territory, his tactically skilled forays made it hard going for his imperial enemy.

When the republicans switched from conventional deployment to guerrilla warfare in 1900, Botha reorganized his remaining forces and kept up a skirmishing campaign, not only contriving to remain at large but also landing punishing blows upon his British pursuers.

At the same time, Botha knew the odds—that it was better to lay down the sword and to try to reach a fair peace than to fight on to an inevitable defeat that might ruin Boer society completely. In 1901, he met Britain's Commander-in-Chief, Lord Kitchener, for talks. Although ready to parley, he backed away from peace proposals containing terms found to be indigestible. But a year later, at the May peace negotiations at Vereeniging, Botha championed what he considered to be an honorable settlement with Britain. By now a diplomatically minded peace negotiator, his firm views on Anglo-Boer reconciliation and on the beneficial restoring of imperial ties were aired in 1902 in "The Boers and the Empire," published in the British journal *The Contemporary Review*. At the same time, Botha's African neighbors had become a grievance. During his wartime absence his opportunistic tenants had occupied his property, a seizure that the general had to end at gunpoint when peace came.

With the war over, Botha turned to the reconstruction needs of the annexed Transvaal and Orange Free State, touring Europe with other generals to raise funds from sympathetic pro-Boer populations. In 1904, with Jan Smuts and other Boer leaders, he founded Het Volk, a reconciliatory Afrikaner party committed to unified white self-government of South Africa. Backed by English-speaking allies, he became prime minister of the Transvaal in March 1907. Thereafter, he played a prominent role in the National Convention, which produced the constitution on which the Union of South Africa was formed in 1910. Botha became its first prime minister, forming the South African Party with Smuts. Although white supremacy and segregation were central to him, he was skeptical of rigidly segregated African reserves as they might deprive white commercial agriculture of cheap labor and land. In other relations with Africans, he was not entirely without sentiment. After Union he released from a Natal prison his now broken old acquaintance, Dinuzulu, fingered as a Zulu rebel in the 1904 anticolonial rising, and gave him farm accommodation in the Transvaal.

Botha's political leadership was caught up in increasingly bitter rows with Afrikaner nationalists over his pro-empire Afrikaner-Anglo

South Africanism. The First World War provided further aggravation, and it was just as well that he declined a place in the British War Cabinet. While he believed that involvement in the conflict could bring national advantage, his anti-British Afrikaner opponents were either neutral or pro-German. Whatever the political cost to be counted, he returned to soldiering, squashing an anti-war Afrikaner rebellion in 1914–15, and then personally leading Union forces in a successful invasion of German South West Africa in 1915.

Botha's health began to falter toward the end of the war, a strained period in which he had to contend with mounting republican militancy and urban African labor unrest. But wider statesmanship still pulled him. Joining the Allied delegations to the 1919 Versailles peace conference, he opposed punitive terms for Germany. This went down well with his domestic Afrikaner opponents.

He returned to the Union to considerable acclaim as an enlightened wartime leader. By then worn out and sickly, he succumbed to influenza and heart failure at his farm, Rusthof, in August 1919 in the presence of his close and devoted family. Ironically, in the previous year he had supported the opening by his daughter, Helen de Waal, of the Louis Botha Children's Home for victims of the Spanish influenza pandemic.

[*See also* Dinuzulu ka Cetshwayo; Kitchener, Horatio; *and* Smuts, Jan Christiaan.]

BIBLIOGRAPHY

Barnard, C. J. "Studies in the Generalship of the Boer Commanders." *Military History Journal* 2, no. 5 (1973): 151–156.

Botha, B. Williams. *Smuts and South Africa*. London: Hodder and Stoughton, 1946.

Engelenburg, F. V. *General Louis Botha*. Pretoria, South Africa: J. L. Van Schaik, 1928.

Meintjes, J. *General Louis Botha: A Biography*. London: Cassel, 1970.

BILL NASSON

Botha, Pieter Willem (1916–2006), South African Prime Minister (1978–1984) and executive state President (1984–1989), was born 12 January 1916 on a farm near the town of Paul Roux in Orange Free State. An Afrikaner by birth, Botha is commonly referred to as either "P.W." or "Die Groot Krokodil" (The Great Crocodile). His parents, Pieter Willem and Hendrina, were influenced greatly by the South African War (Second Anglo-Boer War).

Upon completing his education in the early 1930s, Botha worked as a reporter and a National Party organizer in South Africa's Western Province. He flirted briefly with a pro-Nazi organization named Ossewabrandwag in the years before World War II but ended his connections to the group in 1941. Following a stint as a government information officer during the war, Botha was elected to Parliament as a National Party representative in 1948. He was appointed Deputy Interior Minister ten years later—a position that put him on the frontlines of Prime Minister Hendrik Verwoerd's push to implement "grand apartheid" in the late 1950s and early 1960s. In 1966, Botha became Prime Minister John Vorster's Defense Minister and worked to escalate the South African government's presence in Angola after the collapse of Portuguese control in 1974. His efforts made him influential within the National Party, and at the height of the 1978 "Information Scandal"—when revelations about the nature and scope of Pretoria's propaganda initiatives forced Vorster's resignation—Botha emerged as the Party's choice to be the country's ninth prime minister.

Botha's tenure as head of government was controversial. He was an unrelenting reformer and an uncompromising autocrat who came to be reviled with equal intensity by white conservatives, white liberals, and nonwhite activists. Botha softened aspects of apartheid and curtailed white privilege in unprecedented ways—rewriting South Africa's constitution to grant economic and social rights to the Republic's nonwhite people—but he also curtailed free speech, militarized South African civil society, and expanded the government's commitments in Angola and Namibia.

Botha changed the Republic in three obvious ways. First, he fragmented white hegemony in South Africa. The National Party's dominance of white politics after 1948 stemmed from a patronage model that funneled government resources directly to supporters. Confronted with an unfavorable economic climate in 1978, Botha concluded that reform was necessary. His subsequent efforts sparked a backlash among many whites, and right-wing political parties—the Herstigte Nasionale Party and the Conservative Party, among others—proliferated during the 1980s, effectively ending the coalition that had given the National Party such influence over national affairs.

Botha also tried to reform race relations in South Africa. Unlike his predecessors, he acknowledged that the theory of racial stratification—contingent on the belief that groups could be segregated completely—was impossible to square with the realities of economic interdependence in South Africa. This realization led Botha to implement constitutional reforms that established a Tricameral Parliament, which divided legislative duties between a House of Assembly (whites only), a House of Representatives (Coloreds only), and a House of Delegates (Indians only). Each body was given power to pass laws that affected their community, while the executive branch of the government, with Botha as president, retained exclusive control of national security.

To critics, this arrangement was a transparent ploy to co-opt Botha's domestic opponents and consolidate his personal power. Indeed, while Botha relaxed some symbolic aspects of apartheid, his tricameral system purposefully denied a chamber of representation to South Africa's black majority. Botha instead accelerated the so-called Bantustan plan, granting nominal independence to three "tribal" nations, while secretly authorizing military action against black activists at home and abroad. For him, sharing power with black South Africans—especially the African National Congress (ANC)—was inconceivable. He did attempt to negotiate with imprisoned ANC leader Nelson Mandela, however, toward the end of his presidency.

Botha's greatest impact came in the realm of foreign affairs. His policies, which he termed the "Total Strategy," expanded South Africa's military presence in Namibia, deepened the Republic's actions in Angola, loosened restrictions on counterinsurgency, and secretly created a nuclear weapons program. Envisioned as a way to enhance Pretoria's power, Botha's initiatives instead amplified antiapartheid criticism around the world, setting the stage for the US Congress's Comprehensive Anti-Apartheid Act and the Soviet-American entente that led to the 1988 Tripartite Agreement, which forced an end to South Africa's adventures in Angola and Namibia.

Die Groot Krokodil did not leave politics quietly. After a minor stroke in January 1989, Botha tried to pass power to Finance Minister Barend du Plessis, only to have his National Party colleagues circumvent his wishes by electing Education Minister Frederik Willem de Klerk as their president. Marginalized within his own government and resented (for multifarious reasons) by large swaths of the white electorate, he tried unsuccessfully to regain power in 1989 before resigning abruptly in August. Botha and his wife, Elize, retired to the town of Wilderness in the Western Cape. After Elize's death in 1997, Botha remarried. His only subsequent involvement in national politics came in 1999, when he refused to cooperate with the Truth and Reconciliation Commission. He died in 2006.

[See also De Klerk, Frederik Willem; Mandela, Nelson Rolihlahla; and Verwoerd, Hendrik Frensch.]

BIBLIOGRAPHY

Pottinger, Brian. *The Imperial Presidency: P.W. Botha: The First 10 Years.* Johannesburg: Southern Book Publishers, 1988.

Prinsloo, Daan. *Stem uit die Wilderness: 'n Biografie oor oud-pres, PW Botha.* Mossel Bay, South Africa: Vaandel Publishers, 1997.

Rhoodie, Eschel W. *PW Botha: The Last Betrayal.* Melville, South Africa: S.A. Politics, 1989.

de Villiers, Dirk, and Johanna de Villiers. *PW.* Cape Town, South Africa: Tafelberg, 1984.

RYAN IRWIN

Botsio, Kojo (1916–2001), Ghanaian nationalist politician and diplomat, was born on 21 February 1916 in Winneba, a coastal town in the central province of the Gold Coast (present-day Ghana). His father, James Edward Botsio, was the registrar of the colonial district commissioner's court. His mother, Diana Ama Amina, was a trader. Kojo Botsio was schooled at the local Catholic primary and middle schools before attending the prestigious Adisadel College in the historic city of Cape Coast in 1929. He went on to train as a teacher from 1935 to 1936 at Achimota College, which also trained other future prominent Ghanaian leaders including his longtime political associate, Kwame Nkrumah, Ghana's first postindependence leader. After his training at Achimota, Botsio taught at the Catholic secondary school of Saint Augustine in Cape Coast for five years.

In the tradition of some educated colonial Ghanaians of the time, Botsio studied for his bachelor's degree at Sierra Leone's Fourah Bay College, at the time the only university in West Africa. In 1944 he went on to study at Brasenose College, Oxford University, where his got a postgraduate degree in education and geography in 1946. He had a stint as a teacher with the London City Council Secondary School in Fulham.

Kojo Botsio's path turned to West African student politics and nationalism when he became the warden of the West Africa Students Union (WASU) hostel in Camden, London. The WASU, which had been formed in 1925, was the main cultural and political organization for West Africans in the United Kingdom. Many future leaders of West Africa started their political training in the WASU. It was as a warden of the WASU hostel that Kojo Botsio met Kwame Nkrumah for the first time in 1945. The two were to become political collaborators after that, starting with the administration of the affairs of the West African National Secretariat (WANS), which was formed by Nkrumah in December 1945. This association sparked Botsio's interest in politics and spurred him on to a greater involvement in the nationalist struggle for independence.

Kojo Botsio returned to the Gold Coast in 1947 to take up an appointment as the vice principal of Abuakwa State College in Kibi. He combined his academic duties with political activism by helping out in the activities of the United Gold Coast Convention (UGCC), then the main nationalist organization in the Gold Coast. He worked mainly with his friend Kwame Nkrumah, who had also returned from London to work as the secretary-general of the UGCC in 1947. Botsio was also active in the formation of various youth associations. He was made the secretary of the Committee of Youth Organization (CYO), the UGCC's youth wing. The pull of nationalist politics proved too strong for Botsio so he resigned his post as vice principal of the secondary school to devote his attention to politics.

Kojo Botsio was among the more youthful nationalists who encouraged Kwame Nkrumah to break away from the conservative UGCC, which led to the formation of the Convention People's Party (CPP) in June 1949. He became the general secretary of the CPP. His active involvement in the CPP's declaration of nonviolent civil disobedience against the colonial state in January 1950 earned him a jail term. He was released from prison in time for him to join the CPP's campaign in the 1951 election which was won by the party and also secured him a seat in parliament as a representative of the Gomoa constituency.

He, together with Kwame Nkrumah and Komla Agbeli Gbedemah, became the towering figures of the CPP. From the formation of the first CPP government in 1951 to the end of the party's rule in 1966, Kojo Botsio occupied various ministerial positions. He was appointed the minister of education by Nkrumah in 1951. As the education minister, he directed the implementation of various programs that made primary education compulsory and free, and also led to the expansion of the educational infrastructure of the Gold Coast and the establishment of new schools. In the postindependence period, he handled various ministerial portfolios including social welfare and labor, transport and communications, trade and development, and foreign affairs. He was Ghana's foreign affairs minister from 1963 to 1965.

Botsio lost some of his political stature and influence in the post-1966 period, but he did not completely leave the political scene. He was jailed briefly immediately after the coup in 1966 that toppled the CPP government and also had another spell of imprisonment in the mid- to late 1970s for allegedly plotting to overthrow the military National Redemption Council government. He was a key player in the formation of the People's National Party, which won the elections of 1979. In the 1980s and 1990s he tried unsuccessfully to bring together all the political groupings and individuals that claimed political descent or inspiration from Kwame Nkrumah and the CPP.

He was awarded the national honor of the Star of the Volta in 1999 for his dedicated services to the nation. Kojo Botsio died on 6 February 2001 and was survived by his wife Ruth Whittaker Botsio and two children, Kojo Botsio Jr. and Merene Botsio-Philips, both barristers.

[*See also* Gbedemah, Komla Agbeli; *and* Nkrumah, Kwame.]

BIBLIOGRAPHY

Austin, Dennis. *Politics in Ghana, 1946–1964*. London: 1964.

Thompson, W. Scott. *Ghana's Foreign Policy, 1957–1966: Diplomacy, Ideology and the New State*. Princeton, N.J.: Princeton University Press, 1969.

Vieta, Kojo. *The Flagbearers of Ghana: Profiles of One Hundred Distinguished Ghanaians*. Accra, Ghana: Ena Publications, 1999.

EMMANUEL ASIEDU-ACQUAH

Boubacha, Djamila (1938–), Algerian activist, was born in the Casbah of Algiers to a middle-class family. Djamila Boubacha (also spelled Boupacha) is one of the many young Algerian women who mobilized in the fight against French colonialism under the aegis of the Algerian War of Independence (1954–1962). She was a liaison agent for the Front de Libération Nationale (FLN; National Liberation Front) whose main task was to act as a go-between for FLN fighters in the *maquis* (guerrilla army) and the civilian population in the cities, towns, and villages. She was arrested on 10 February 1960, at the age of twenty-two, and illegally detained for allegedly planting a bomb that was defused before it could detonate in the student restaurant at the University of Algiers. Her trial was scheduled for 17 June 1959, although there were no witnesses who could identify her, nor any proof that she had deposited the bomb.

At the El-Biar prison, Djamila was tortured over the course of thirty-three days by French paratroopers who were known for their use of extreme violence in interrogation. Djamila was beaten, kicked, and trampled by the paratroopers who broke her ribs, electrocuted her on her breasts and legs, plunged her head into salty water, and sexually assaulted her with a broken bottle (a practice called "the bottle treatment"). This use of extreme violence was customary in French-run prisons during the War of Independence, and was used to both extract information from prisoners, and to terrorize and shame the Algerian population as a whole.

Djamila Boubacha was not the first victim or survivor of such an ordeal. What made her story exceptional was the way it emerged into the public sphere, and was covered and presented by the media. Behind such coverage were the French feminist Simone de Beauvoir and the Tunisian lawyer Gisèle Halimi, whose principle achievement was the efficient exposure of a propaganda machine that hid all traces of the hideous, inhumane torture practices inflicted on Algerians on a daily basis in French prisons and detention centers.

Gisèle Halimi was asked to defend Boubacha during her trial by her brother. Despite many hurdles, Halimi took on the case, and encouraged her client to make her ordeal public. In a state of abject traumatic shock after her torture, Boubacha declared openly, "I have been tortured. I insist on a medical examination." Despite the usual practice of dismissing the victim's claims at the French court, Halimi succeeded in bringing the case to the attention of the Attorney-General in Algiers. However, she discovered that the colonial authorities were working hard to stifle the case.

In the meantime, Simone de Beauvoir was working to create a committee for Boubacha's defense, which brought together many leading French artists and intellectuals, including Jean-Paul Sartre, Louis Aragon, Geneviève de Gaulle-Anthonioz, Elsa Triolet, Gabriel Marcel, Simone Weil, Germaine Tillion, and Pablo Picasso (who, although Spanish by birth, lived most of his life in France). All expressed their disgust at the French torture practices. They petitioned to have the case transferred to France, for fear that, if she remained in Algeria, Boubacha would be tortured, otherwise threatened, or murdered before the trial, in order to silence her. After many attempts, the committee managed to transfer Boubacha to a prison in Caen, France, where she underwent a fresh medical examination. This confirmed that she had been tortured, a claim that was denied by the first medical examination she underwent in Algiers.

Following this determination, a petition presented to the court of appeal in Caen was upheld. At this point, the case took on an international dimension. The trial took place from 26 to 28 June 1961 at the Caen tribunal, where Boubacha identified her torturers. Nevertheless, the French court found her guilty of planting the bomb, and she was sentenced to death. In response to the sentence, an international movement of solidarity was launched, supporting not only Boubacha and women like her, but all the Algerian people, their right to independence, and the legitimacy of the nationalist cause.

Simone de Beauvoir and Gisèle Halimi coedited a book on Boubacha, which explored her ordeal through interviews with her and the publication of letters. The book bears Picasso's portrait of Boubacha on the front cover. A translation of the book into English by Peter Green, *Djamila Boupacha: The Story of the Torture of a Young Algerian Girl Which Shocked Liberal French Opinion,* was published in London in 1962. Simone de Beauvoir claimed that the book was a means of telling the international community the truth about the Algerian cause, so that they could no longer mumble the old excuse "we didn't know." In countries as far-flung as Japan and the United States, supporters of the Algerian cause demonstrated in front of French embassies, urging France to end its occupation of Algeria.

The signing of the Évian Accords between France and the National Liberation Front in March 1962 brought an end to the Algerian War of Independence and resulted in the granting of amnesty to all war prisoners, including Djamila Boubacha. However, the Accords also provided amnesty to the war criminals of the colonial machine, who at the end of the war went unpunished. In postcolonial Algeria, Djamila Boubacha is remembered as a heroine of the War of Independence. However, nothing is known about her actions in the postindependence era. A movie on the life of Djamila

Boubacha, directed by Caroline Huppert and based on the book by de Beauvoir and Halimi, was in production in 2011.

[*See also* Halimi, Gisèle.]

BIBLIOGRAPHY

Angeloff, Tania, and Margaret Maruani. "Gisèle Halimi: la cause du feminism." *Travail, Genre et Sociétés* 14 (2005): 5–25.

de Beauvoir, Simone, and Gisèle, Halimi. *Djamila Boupacha: The Story of the Torture of a Young Algerian Girl Which Shocked Liberal French Opinion*. Translated by Peter Green. London: 1962. [English translation of de Beauvoir, Simone, and Gisèle, Halimi. *Djamila Boupacha*. Paris: Gallimard, 1962.]

Codaccioni, Vanessa. "(Dé)Politisation du genre et des questions sexuelles dans un procès politique en contexte colonial: le viol, le procès et l'affaire Djamila Boupacha (1960–1962)." *Nouvelles Questions Feministes* 29:1 (2010): 32–45.

Lazreg, Marnia. *The Eloquence of Silence: Algerian Women in Question*. New York and London: Routledge, 1994.

ZAHIA SMAIL SALHI

Boudjedra, Rachid (1941–), Algerian writer, was born in Aïn Beida (Eastern Algeria) on 5 September 1941 into a middle-class family. After attending Qur'anic school and French primary school, he was sent by his father to Tunis, since an education that included Arabic and Arab culture was not possible in French-colonized Algeria. While at the elite Lycée Saddiki in Tunis between 1952 and 1959, Boudjedra came into contact with the essentials of Arab, ancient Greek, Latin, and French culture. He traveled to Spain in 1959, where he became involved in the Algerian War of Independence as a representative of the Front de Libération Nationale (FLN; National Liberation Front). Following independence in 1962, he returned to Algeria, where he began studying philosophy and mathematics. From 1967 to 1969 he continued his studies at the Sorbonne in Paris, where he wrote a thesis on Louis Ferdinand Céline and graduated with a degree in philosophy. He married a French woman, with whom he has one daughter. After several years of teaching philosophy in Morocco, Boudjedra returned to Algeria in 1975.

Boudjedra's career as a writer began with his book *La Répudiation* (1970; The Repudiation), which received a prize whose name, in retrospect, seems prescient: the *Prix des enfants terribles*, initiated by Jean Cocteau, recognizes literary works which depart from generally accepted norms and confront society with its own taboos. Understood in this sense, transgression is a program inherent to Boudjedra's work, put into practice on diverse levels. His literary work draws on a plurality of cultures and languages; in fact, he switched to writing in Arabic in 1981, after having published six novels in French. With this step, Boudjedra followed the Arabization policy of the Algerian government, out of personal conviction and the need to once more immerse himself in his native language. When it became clear in the mid-1990s that fundamentalists sought to exploit Arabic as a political weapon, Boudjedra returned to writing in French. His 1992 book *FIS de la haine* (FIS [Front Islamique du Salut; used here as a play on the French word *fils*, son] of hatred) is a violent diatribe against political Islamism.

Boudjedra's work suggests that he experiences the diversity and heterogeneity of the worlds he has moved among not as uprooting and dislocating, but as opening and broadening his horizons, which on the literary level in particular are boundless. He is probably the most modern of the Algerian authors of his generation; he has pressed ahead most resolutely in the endeavor to renew the novel, explore new narrative strategies, and attain formal perfection. Boudjedra has named as his influences the classic novelists of modernism and their precursors like Gustave Flaubert, Marcel Proust, James Joyce, and William Faulkner, but also Günter Grass and above all Claude Simon. In Simon's work Boudjedra sees the realization of the "Mediterranean" novel he envisions: a novel anchored in the climate and social reality of the Mediterranean region, while simultaneously employing the formal devices of postmodernism within a Maghrebian literary context. Schooled in the *Nouveau roman*, Boudjedra has developed a style which critics have described as "verbally excessive," often making the text virtually impenetrable for the reader. Words cascade for page after page, with very little punctuation to provide orientation, demanding from the reader enormous effort and perseverance. This is a stylistic trait particularly evident in Boudjedra's early work.

On the formal level, Boudjedra is concerned with appropriating what has gained currency under the term "world literature" in the postcolonial context. On the level of narrative content, however, he locates his texts very precisely in his own Maghreb culture. Tapping into what Jean Ricardou has characterized as the "reservoir" (the sum of determinants forming an author's personal profile in which historical, social, ideological, and emotional elements converge), Boudjedra creates a narrative cosmos which allows the social figurations and problems behind the individual fate to shimmer through. Even if the authorial gaze is fixed pointedly on the sexual morals, and thus the situation of women, in Algerian society, other contentious and explosive issues, such as the privileges of the ruling class or social evils, are also addressed. Thus, other struggles are carried out in the medium of this thematic. In *Les Funérailles* (2003; The Funeral), the horrific events during the embryonic civil war of the 1990s are depicted in shocking explicitness. The conclusion of this novel presents a turning point; in line with President Bouteflika's highly controversial policy of national reconciliation, the novel eschews probing into issues of guilt and responsibility, smoothing over problems with a classical happy ending. In his more recent texts (*Hôtel Saint Georges*, 2007; *Les Figuiers de Barbarie*, 2010), Boudjedra has moved backward in Algerian history from colonization to independence.

Boudjedra's other novels include *Topographie idéale pour une agression caractérisée* (1975; Ideal Topography for a Characterized Aggression); *L'Escargot entêté* (1977; The Stubborn Snail); *Les 1001 Années de la nostalgie* (1979; 1001 Years of Nostalgia); and *Le Vainqueur de coupe* (1981; The Cup Winner). His Arabic novels include *al-Tafakkuk* (1982; The Falling Apart); *al-Mart/La Macération* (1984/1985; The Maceration); *Laylat imra'a Ariqa/ La pluie* (1985/1987; Rain: Diary of an Insomniac); *Ma'arak zuqaq (La Prise de Gibraltar* 1986/1987; The Taking of Gibraltar); and *Fawda al-Ashya/Le Désordre des choses* (1990/1991; The Disorder of Things). He returned to writing in French in the novels *Timimoun* (1994); *La Vie à l'endroit* (1997; The Life Face Up); and *Fascination* (2000). Boudjedra also wrote poems, collected in *Pour ne plus rêver* (1965; In Order Not to Dream) and *Greffe* (1985; Graft), and a short play, *Mines de rien* (1995; All Casually). Notable nonfiction texts include *Journal Palestinien* (1973; Palestinian Journal); *Lettres Algériennes* (1995; Algerian Letters); and *Peindre l'Orient* (1996; To Paint the Orient).

In the early 1970s, Boudjedra distinguished himself as a screenplay author; his film *Chroniques des années de braise* was awarded the Palme d'Or in 1975 at the Cannes Film Festival.

[*See also* Bouteflika, Abdelaziz.]

BIBLIOGRAPHY

Abu-Haidar, Farida. "The Bipolarity of Rachid Boudjedra." *Journal of Arabic Literature* 20 (1989): 40–56.

"Actualité de Rachid Boudjedra." *Présence Francophone* 68 (2007): 5–114 [special issue].

Gafaïti, Hafid. *Boudjedra ou la passion de la modernité.* Paris: Denoël, 1987.

Gafaïti, Hafid, ed. *Rachid Boudjedra. Une poétique de la subversion.* Paris: L'Harmattan, 2000.

DORIS RUHE

Boughedir, Férid (1944–), Tunisian film critic and director, was born in Tunis on 11 March 1944. His father, Taoufik Boughedir, was a journalist, novelist, playwright, and an influential figure in cultural life. Boughedir attended a French secondary school in Tunis and lived in the family home in Halfaouine, an area of old Tunis that was later to provide the name for the director's first film. He went on to study French literature in Rouen and Paris and wrote two doctoral theses on African and Arabic cinema.

Boughedir first made a name for himself as a film critic, writing for, among others, the journal *Jeune Afrique*, which was published in Paris and distributed in francophone Africa. In his writing for this, he was an inexhaustible supporter of the cause of African cinema. He was involved in organizing the oldest pan-African film festival, *Les Journées Cinématographiques de Carthage*, in Tunis, which he attended first as artistic director and later as festival director. In his time, Boughedir has been assistant director both to the French director Alain Robbe-Grillet and to Spanish director Fernando Arrabal.

One of the key milestones of Boughedir's career as a director is his first fictional short film from 1975, *Nouzha raïka* (in French, *Le pique-nique*), a screen adaption of a short story by Tunisian novelist Ali Douagi. This short film figures as one of the episodes in the film *Au pays de Tararani*. In this work, Boughedir demonstrates his love for a vivid visual narration of everyday life, which the novelist's colourful style feeds into. It was also this work which earmarked Boughedir as one of the future leading lights of fictional film in Tunisia. Three documentary films then followed: the feature film, *Caméra d'Afrique*, in 1973; the short film, *Cinéma de Carthage*, in 1985; and another feature film, *Caméra arabe*, in 1985. The theme of these three films was film production.

In 1990 Boughedir directed his first feature film, *Asfour Stah* (in French, *Halfaouine: L'enfant des terrasses*, and in English, "Halfaouine: Boy of the Terraces"), which achieved critical and popular success in Tunisia, won numerous international awards, and made a name for Boughedir outside of his country. Through this film he established himself as a major figure in the world of cinema in Tunisia, where his film responded to calls for a cinematic portrayal of daily life. The film emphasizes, above all, the exuberance and humor of the people of the old town of Tunis and the crafty subversions employed by the women in a male-dominated environment where men make the rules. It was the film's ambition to avoid a clichéd portrayal of the relationship between men and women (one founded upon relations of dominance and submission), where public space is monopolized by men and private space reserved for women. What the film actually portrays is the power dynamics of relationships between men, subtly crossed with the issue of dominance between the sexes. This is done in scenes that draw attention to that which is not said; in old Tunis people make their way through life, never forgetting the detours they need to make in order to achieve their ends. Overseas, Boughedir's debut became a seminal film, one that seemed to herald the advent of a Tunisian cinema that would be both realistic and enjoyable to watch, deep yet light-hearted, and which depicted strong female characters who contradicted the stereotypical silent and subjugated Arab woman.

Boughedir's second feature film, *Saïf Halk el Wad* (in French, *Un été à la Goulette*, and in English, "A Summer in la Goulette"), was produced in 1996 and focused on a different theme from his first. This next film was set in a particularly ethnically mixed suburb of Tunis during the 1960s. The film shows how three communities of differing religions all live together in a small town on the coast where they come to spend their summers away from Tunis. It was an opportunity to depict some eccentric characters in this microcosm in order to accurately render the era. Of this work, which enjoyed both critical and popular success, the director has said "My modest ambition with *Un été à la Goulette* was to create a film which would be both joyful and emotive, and which would educate the viewer, exploiting the boundless possibilities of cinema" (quoted in a release from the Tunisian distributor, COTUDIC).

Boughedir's dream is to continue the art and manner of Chaplin in expressing the joy and the suffering of life at one and the same time.

BIBLIOGRAPHY

Bouchrara, Traki Zannad. "Halfaouine ou le corps citadin." In IBLA, review of Institut des Belles Lettres Arabes de Tunis, December 1990.

Boughedir, Férid. *Le cinéma africain de A à Z*. Brussels: Editions OCIC, 1987.

Boughedir, Férid. *Le cinéma en Afrique et dans le monde*. Paris: Editions Jeune Afrique, 1984.

Elena, Alberto. *El cine del tercer mundo*. Madrid: Ediciones Turfan, 1993.

Stone, Judy. *Eye on the World: Conversations with International Filmmakers*. Los Angeles: Silman-James Press, 1997.

HOUDA BEN GHACHAM

Boukpeti, Benjamin Kûdjow Thomas (1981–), slalom kayaker and first Togolese winner of an Olympic medal, was born in Lagny-Sur-Marne, France, on 4 August 1981. The son of a Togolese father and a French mother, he grew up in the department of Seine et Marne near Paris. When he was only ten years old, his parents introduced him to the sport of slalom kayaking. They placed their son in a kayak club in their hometown of Lagny-Sur-Marne. He passed his baccalaureate examinations and chose to turn his love for kayaking into a career. Boukpeti excelled at this sport, to the point that he was selected to join a training center in the French city of Toulouse. He also commenced his undergraduate studies in biology, and he received an undergraduate degree in cellular biology and animal physiology from Université Paul Sabatier in Toulouse.

He first entered international competition at the 16th annual world kayaking championship in 2000, where he placed 16th overall. After he underwent two surgical operations to repair injuries to his shoulders, Boukpeti decided to take the unusual step in 2003 of representing Togo rather than France in international kayaking competitions. Since his father was Togolese, this was a possibility, even though he only had visited Togo once as an infant. The French Olympic Committee had refused to allow Boukpeti on the French team because of his age. Togo itself did not have an Olympic team in kayaking, but Boukpeti received funding from the International Olympic Committee's Olympic Solidarity fund to attend the 2004 Olympics in Athens, Greece. He was a semi-finalist at Athens in kayaking, but he did not win a medal. Boukpeti ultimately placed 18th in the field. After 2004, he continued to compete in international slalom kayaking events. He joined the South African-based international kayaking team Amadonsa after it was created in 2005. Boukpeti placed 54th in the World Kayaking Championship in Australia in 2005, 56th in the 2006 World Kayaking Championship in the Czech Republic, and 22nd in the 2007 World Kayaking Championship in Brazil. The Olympic Solidarity Fund again provided financial assistance so that Boukpeti could compete in the 2008 Summer Olympics in Beijing. With several former champions from France all vying for one spot, this route proved much easier for him than trying to make the French team.

Boukpeti entered the 2008 Summer Olympics ranked only 54th in the world. However, he would surprise spectators around the world in the individual slalom kayaking event. He led the entire group of competitors going into the final race in Shunyi, China. A strong showing from German Alexander Grimm, ranked 3rd in the entire world, led to a gold medal for Grimm. However, Boukpeti finished third. He broke his paddle in two at the end of race out of joy that he had been the first black man ever to win a medal in the sport. Boukpeti also became the first Togolese national ever to win an Olympic medal. He also won the slalom kayaking African championship in the same year. The Olympic success made him a hero in Togo, although very few people in the country had heard of him—or his event—prior to the Sydney games. Outside of sports, Boukpeti completed a business management program at IFAG Toulouse and joined the Monaco-based Peace and Sport nonprofit organization. He put his business degree to use by helping to manage Team Amadonsa. This organization developed a partnership with the Togolese Ministry of Sport to set up a kayak training program in the African nation.

Houari Boumedienne. (AP Images)

BIBLIOGRAPHY

Benjamin Boukpeti personal Web site, accessed 1 April 2010, http://benjamin.boukpeti.free.fr/Benjamin_ Boukpeti.html.

"Togo Claims First Olympic Medal." BBC News Web site. 12 August 2008, http://news.bbc.co.uk/2/ hi/7556266.stm.

JEREMY RICH

Boumedienne, Houari (1932–1978), Algerian politician and anticolonial military leader, was born Mohammed Ben Brahim Boukharouba in the Algerian town of Aïn Hesseinia, near Guelma, on 23 August 1932. Although Boumedienne was fluent in French through his primary school studies at a public school, he also chose to attend Islamic schools where the language of instruction was Arabic. Unlike some other future Algerian leaders who lacked a firm command of classical Arabic, Boumedienne thus could express himself in both French and Arabic as a result of his education.

The brutal crackdown of Algerian nationalists by European settlers and the French military on 8 May 1945 dramatically shaped Boumedienne's life. Rather than accept eventually being forced to join the French military as a conscript, he moved to Tunisia, where he attended classes at the Zitouna University, known for its advanced courses in Islamic law and theology. After some time, Boumedienne attended the University of al-Azhar in Cairo, the most respected institution of Muslim learning in the Middle East. Although Boumedienne ultimately tried to reconcile Islam with secular nationalist and socialist ideals rather than follow the Muslim Brotherhood's pointed critiques of nationalism, he proved to be a far more orthodox Sunni Muslim than many of his later colleagues in the Algerian rebel movement.

Boumedienne only returned to Algeria in 1955, after the Front de Libération National (FLN, National Liberation Front) movement had already begun to lead an armed struggle for independence against European settlers and the French government. He became one of the lieutenants of Abdelhafid Boussouf, the FLN commander of the *Wilaya* 5 units fighting in the region of Oran. When Boussouf took on other assignments, Boumedienne became the commander of the Wilaya 5 forces in 1957. Boumedienne eventually became the chief of staff of FLN's forces in Algeria, thanks in large part to his tactical skill and his organizational ability. For part of the conflict, Boumedienne lived in Morocco and trained FLN troops under the protection of Morocco's ruler Hassan II. This sanctuary allowed Boumedienne to consolidate his authority over his military units. When the Évian Accords in the spring of 1962 ended the war and set a transition to independence, Boumedienne chose to back Ahmed Ben Bella against Hocine Ait Ahmed and other FLN veterans who distrusted the general staff of the army led by Boumedienne. Boumedienne crushed his dissident FLN military rivals in the summer of 1962, which ensured that Ben Bella could take power. Boumedienne was vice president of Algeria and minister of defense in Ben Bella's government. However, Boumedienne's support for promoting Arabic as the national language (against the opposition of Berbers or Amazigh people) and his dislike for Ben Bella's occasional compromises with opposition demands led him to seize power in a coup on 19 June 1965. By this point, Boumedienne had ensured that many top military posts were held by his supporters. Another reason for the coup was that Boumedienne and other members of his clique felt that Ben Bella had pushed them out of important positions.

Boumedienne was not a popular figure at first, as university students took to the streets to protest the coup. He promised to end Ben Bella's style of personal rule and instituted a new ruling body made up of military officers, the Council of the Revolution. He abolished the Algerian parliament and Ben Bella's constitution of 1963. From the summer of 1965 until the failed coup attempt against him led by Colonel Tahar Zbiri in December 1967, Boumedienne consolidated his power and created a system of local and regional assemblies that answered to his own cadre of national leaders.

After the Zbiri coup event and another assassination attempt in 1968, Boumedienne became a much more dominant figure. He was a firm believer in staffing important positions with well-educated technocrats rather than war veterans, as he sought to promote economic development through nationalizing major foreign-owned petroleum fields and other industries, such as the dramatic nationalization of French oil concessions in 1971. The FLN grew to over 300,000 members, but it had become an arm of the central government rather than a party that could challenge the Algerian leader. Boumedienne implemented a policy of "state capitalism," in which the government controlled most major businesses operating in the country. He strongly promoted the use of Arabic in schools and contended that Algerian and Arab identities were identical, to the chagrin of Berber or Tamazight-speaking people. His creation of a national charter over the course of 1975 and 1976 alienated many former FLN leaders, who considered it a legal means to ensure Boumedienne's grip over power, even as it provided clauses for equal treatment of men and women and freedom of speech. These freedoms were not respected in practice, as demonstrated when the government placed former FLN leader Ferhat Abbas under house arrest from 1976 to 1979 for publicly criticizing the charter.

Boumedienne's foreign policy was an eclectic mixture of radical leftist positions and a pragmatic effort to retain close economic ties with France and other Western countries. Especially in the late 1960s and early 1970s, Boumedienne presented Algeria as a center of Afro-Asian revolutionary movements, and many leftist artists from different parts of Africa considered Algeria to be an international cultural center. Yet Boumedienne also encouraged Algerian immigration to France and tried to convince Gaullist governments to not place major restrictions on the movement of Algerians to France. Although Boumedienne invited French president Valéry Giscard d'Estaing to Algiers in April 1975, France chose to support Morocco as its main ally in North Africa. When Morocco occupied the former Spanish colony of Western Sahara in the same year, Boumedienne invested heavily in supporting the anti-Morocco POLISARIO rebel movement. This conflict proved to be an economic burden, as did the drop of oil prices in the late 1970s. Boumedienne did not live to see the negative consequences of many of his policies, as he died of a rare blood disease on 27 December 1978.

[*See also* Ben Bella, Ahmed; *and* Hassan II.]

REFERENCES

Abun-Nasr, Jamil. *A History of the Maghrib in the Islamic Period*. Cambridge, UK: Cambridge University Press, 1987.

Francos, Ania, and J. P. Sereni. *Un algérien nommé Boumediene*. Paris: Stock, 197 6.

Naylor, Phillip. *The Historical Dictionary of Algeria*. 3d ed. Lanham, Md.: Scarecrow Press, 2005.

Ruedy, John. *Modern Algeria: The Origins and Development of a Nation*. Bloomington: Indiana University Press, 1992.

Stora, Benjamin. *Algeria 1830–2000: A Short History.* Translated by Jane Marie Todd. Ithaca, N.Y.: Cornell University Press, 2001.

JEREMY RICH

Bourguiba, Habib (1903–2000), Tunisian politician and anticolonial activist, was born on 3 August 1903 in the Tunisian town of Monastir, located roughly 100 kilometers south of the capital of Tunis. His family was relatively poor, but several of his seven siblings raised enough money to send Bourguiba to French-run schools in Tunis.

Bourguiba attended the College Sadiki middle school and the Lycée Carnot secondary school. After Bourguiba passed his baccalaureate examinations in 1924, he moved to Paris to study law and political science. Bourguiba spent three years studying before he received his law degree. During that time, he met a Frenchwoman named Mathilde Lorain, and they married in 1927. On 9 April 1927, Mathilde gave birth to their first child and only son, Habib Bourguiba Jr. He then returned with his new family to Tunis. Since the decade before World War I, Western-educated Tunisians had protested discriminatory policies on behalf of European settlers and demanded equal rights and Tunisian autonomy. Bourguiba became involved in this nationalist movement, although French officials had cracked down effectively on the Dustur nationalist party

over the course of the late 1920s. Quarrels within the Dustur leadership and its lack of a mass base also hampered the party by the time Bourguiba came home in 1927.

The young lawyer soon threw himself into political organizing and wrote numerous articles in the influential newspapers *L'Etendard Tunisien* (The Tunisian Flag) and *Sawt al Tunisi* (Voice of Tunisia) in 1928. A giant Catholic Eucharistic Congress at Carthage in 1930, which featured European settler children dressed as medieval crusaders and hostile rhetoric against Islam, angered Bourguiba. His newspaper editorials in French and Arabic drew accolades from frustrated Muslim Tunisians and harassment from the French police. In 1931, Bourguiba was charged with incitement of racial hatred, but he continued to promote eventual Tunisian independence. However, he became disillusioned with the collaboration of the Bey of Tunis's administration as well as the ineffectiveness of the Dustur party. He formed his own newspaper, *L'Action Tunisienne*, in 1932.

Bourguiba then led a breakaway party from the Dustur movement, known as the Neo-Dustur party, which was formed on 2 March 1934. The Neo-Dustur party developed cells among ordinary urban workers and rural farmers and exploited the calamities of the Great Depression to build support for its call for independence. The French administration arrested Bourguiba in September 1934 and exiled

Habib Bourguiba, 1979. (AP Images/Michael Lipchitz)

him and numerous other leaders to internal exile in the sparsely populated southern Saharan region of Tunisia. There, he languished until the electoral victory of the Popular Front left-wing coalition of socialists and communists in metropolitan France in the spring of 1936. The new government released Bourguiba and other Neo-Dustur leaders from internment. Bourguiba's message had not changed, but he received some new support from sympathetic French leftists, especially as he presented the Neo-Dustur party's demands in a conciliatory way. He also tried to play off anxieties about the threat of war with Germany and Italy in suggesting that reforms by the French administration would ensure the future loyalty of Tunisia. However, the colonial bureaucracy and the vocal protests of European settlers effectively blocked any changes to the status of Tunisia as a protectorate of France. In November 1937 and April 1938, Bourguiba called for general strikes to show popular support for the party. French military units violently put down the April 1938 protests, and Bourguiba was placed in jail and sent to France for trial in the spring of 1940.

German victory in France and the Axis occupation of Tunisia placed Bourguiba in a quandary. Should he aid the Nazi and Fascist cause, as they desired? Unlike some other Neo-Dustur leaders, Bourguiba prudently distanced himself from the new rulers of Tunisia, even as the Nazi military allowed him to return to his homeland in 1943. This choice paid off after the Allies recaptured Tunisia. Bourguiba contended that the French government should allow for more autonomy for Tunisia and prepare a transition to eventual independence. Bourguiba left Tunisia secretly in 1945 and sought out support from the Arab League, the newly created United Nations, and trade unions and politicians in the United States. Bourguiba contended that a free Tunisia would be a strong ally against communism, which made him friends in the United States. Bourguiba did not return to Tunisia until September 1949, when French officials hoped he could steer the Neo-Dustur party in a more moderate direction. Many Neo-Dustur members and leaders found Bourguiba's long sojourns abroad irritating and counterproductive, and the more radical figure Salah Ben Youssouf became one of Bourguiba's biggest rivals within his own party. Bourguiba had no formal role in the fruitless negotiations between the French government and the Neo-Dustur leadership. He left Tunisia again to build up international support in Asia, Europe, and the United States in 1951.

Bourguiba and the Neo-Dustur group found the instability of the French Fourth Republic government and its vacillations between reform and maintaining the empire difficult to deal with. The French administration took a hard line against the Neo-Dustur leaders again in early 1952. Bourguiba was placed in internal exile again from January 1952 until the spring of 1954. Some nationalists formed armed resistance movements during this time, and French Prime Minister Pierre Mendes-France chose finally in 1954 to halt the bloodshed by reopening negotiations. Bourguiba and other Neo-Dustur leaders spent a year in Paris hammering out a deal for independence that allowed the French military a continued role in Tunisia. He returned to Tunisia a nationalist hero in March 1955, but European settlers violently opposed the accords, and Ben Youssouf and other radicals felt Bourguiba was too moderate and bourgeois to lead the country. In November 1955, Bourguiba consolidated his grip over the Neo-Dustur party at a party congress and forced Ben Youssouf to leave for Cairo, where the former chief competitor to Bourguiba was assassinated under mysterious circumstances in 1961. France granted independence to Tunisia in 1956, and Bourguiba became the head of the government. In a shocking development, Bourguiba relied on French troops stationed in the country to root out sympathizers of Ben Youssouf in the first year of independence.

Bourguiba remained the leader of Tunisia from 1957 until 1987. He walked a careful line between close ties with Western countries and maintaining support in the Eastern Bloc and among non-aligned Arab nations during the Cold War, especially in the 1950s and 1960s. When Algerian nationalists formed the armed Front de Libération Nationale (FLN) movement that fought against continued French rule in nearby Algeria, Bourguiba allowed FLN troops to set up bases in Tunisian territory. French forces attacked these bases in July 1961 and killed Tunisian civilians in the process. Bourguiba demanded an apology from France and created an international controversy, even as French troops were still on Tunisian soil, until they finally evacuated in October 1963. The United States strongly pressured France to desist from further attacks in order to back Bourguiba, whom State Department officials viewed as a strong ally against communism. After the end of the Algerian war in 1962, Tunisia maintained friendly ties with both its former colonial ruler and the new Algerian government. Bourguiba also tried and failed to broker a lasting peace in Palestine and Israel in 1965 through the intervention of the United Nations.

In Tunisia, Bourguiba launched numerous social reforms such as the end of veiling for women and equal access to education. More traditional and Salafist Muslim clerics disliked what was deemed to be violations of Islamic law, but many Tunisians accepted these reforms on behalf of women's rights. Like many African regimes in the 1960s, Bourguiba moved from a firmly capitalist to a socialist economic model, especially by promoting heavy industrial projects in the phosphorus mining industry. These programs did not allow Tunisia to escape its dependence on industrial manufacturing imports from Europe. Bourguiba's plans did not include promoting democracy. His government maintained firm control over Muslim clerics and the famous Zitouna (Zaituna) Muslim University and used repressive measures to maintain the continued dominance of the Neo-Dustur party.

From the early 1970s until Bourguiba's forced retirement in 1987, Bourguiba's popularity declined among younger Tunisians. Bourguiba did little to curb the country's economic inequities. The brutal show of force by the Tunisian military against striking workers on 26 January 1978 further angered many ordinary people and left some military and party leaders concerned that Bourguiba's advanced age made him unfit to be president. Bourguiba's choice of Muhammad Mzali to promote free market reforms in 1984 led to social unrest over the cutbacks in social services and increased fears in the Tunisian elite of a possible revolution. Bourguiba dismissed Mzali under pressure from government authorities in 1986 and then launched a crackdown against the militant religiously oriented Mouvement de la Tendence Islamique in the same year. Interior minister Zine el-Abidine Ben Ali forced Bourguiba to step down on 7 November 1987. Bourguiba spent the rest of his life under house arrest, and lived in his hometown of Monastir from the spring of 1988 until he died on 6 April 2000. Bourguiba orchestrated the coming of Tunisian independence and its post-colonial authoritarian government.

[See also Ben Ali, Zine el-Abidine.]

BIBLIOGRAPHY

Anderson, Lisa. "Democracy Frustrated: The Mzali Years in Tunisia." In *The Middle East and North Africa: Essays in Honor of J. C. Hurewitz*, edited by Reeva Simon, pp. 185–203. New York: Columbia University Press, 1990.

Bessis, Sophie, and Souhayr Belhassen. *Bourguiba: Un si long règne (1957–1989)*. Paris: Jeune Afrique, 1989.

Brown, L. Carl. "Bourguiba and Bourguibism Revisited: Reflections and Interpretation." *Middle East Journal* 55, no.1 (2001): 43–57.

Hopwood, Derek. *Habib Bourguiba of Tunisia: The Tragedy of Longevity*. New York: St. Martin's Press, 1992.

Perkins, Kenneth J. *A History of Modern Tunisia*. New York: Oxford University Press, 2004.

Perkins, Kenneth J. *Historical Dictionary of Tunisia*. 2d ed. Metuchen, N.J.: Scarecrow, 1997.

JEREMY RICH

Bourhan, Ali Aref (1934–), Djiboutian political figure, was born in Djibouti, but he grew up in Tadjoura. Aboubaker Ibrahim Chehem Pacha, who facilitated the earliest agreements with France in the 1860s, was his great-grandfather. His grandfather was Bourhan Baye, the first mayor of the village of Djibouti. Bourhan completed elementary school and joined the Territorial Ministry of Education. Like many early political figures in the French colony, he first gained a reputation as an orator and debater in the *Club de la Jeunesse Somalie et Dankalie*, Mahmoud Harbi's political movement. In 1957, Bourhan was elected deputy for Obock and Tadjoura.

Reacting to the increasing radicalization of Harbi, Bourhan joined the political group led by Ibrahim Mohammed Sultan in 1958 and was again elected to the territorial assembly. In June 1960, by now a fervent supporter of General Charles de Gaulle, he was appointed vice president of the Council of Government, replacing Ahmed Dini Ahmed. He was forced to step down from this post in 1966, in the wake of the riots that began during de Gaulle's stopover in Djibouti on 25–27 August. During the intense campaigning for the 1967 referendum imposed by the French government, Bourhan took a firm position in favor of maintaining close ties with France. He was reelected to his previous post in the Council of Government in April 1967.

By mid-1976, Djibouti was the sole remaining French colony on the African mainland. Although there were many old-timers in the French administration who felt no need to change its status (notably Jacques Foccart, intelligence chief and prime specialist in African affairs for a succession of French governments), it was decided in Paris that the French territory of Afars and Issas could be set free. For the French, Bourhan had been a loyal and dependable leader since 1960, but it was no longer possible to pretend that the Afars represented the majority. Bourhan was forced to resign in July 1976, and Abdallah Mohamed Kamil took his place.

After independence, Bourhan lived for a while in France but eventually returned to private business in the Republic of Djibouti. In the early 1990s, he dabbled in politics, without notable success, perhaps misjudging the amount of lingering bitterness about the many years that Bourhan served as "France's man" in Djibouti.

Bourhan was arrested with ten other members of the Afar ethnic group by the Djibouti government and imprisoned after what Amnesty International termed an "unfair trial" in July 1992. The Cassation Court in Djibouti rejected his appeal in June 1993. After the failure of his appeals, Bourhan went on a hunger strike to protest the miserable conditions under which he and his fellow prisoners were being held. The Government of Djibouti came under heavy pressure from the Government of France, Amnesty International, and several other human rights organizations to liberate Bourhan and his collaborators. On 15 December 1993, Bourhan and twelve other detainees received a presidential pardon and were released. Bourhan continues to live in Djibouti.

[*See also* Aboubaker Ibrahim Chehem; Ahmed Dini Ahmed; Harbi, Mahamoud Farah; *and* Kamil, Abdallah Mohamed.]

BIBLIOGRAPHY

Aden, Mohamed. *Sombloloko: Djibouti La Chute du Président Ali Aref (1975–1976)*. Paris: L'Harmattan, 1999.

Adou, Abdallah A. *The Afar: A Nation on Trial*. Stockholm: Förf, 1993.

Dubois, Colette. "Jacques Foccart et Ali Aref, Un mariage d'intérêt?" *Les Cahiers du Centre de Recherches Historiques* 30 (2002).

WALTER CLARKE

Bouteflika, Abdelaziz (1937–), Algerian diplomat and politician, was born in the Moroccan town of Oudja on 2 March 1937. He was the first child of his mother and the second of his father. He had three half-sisters, four brothers, and one full sister. His parents came from the Algerian town of Tlemcen, just across the border from Morocco. He left school in 1956, when the Front de Libération Nationale (FLN, National Liberation Front) anticolonial movement called on Algerian students to boycott French public schools.

Bouteflika joined the FLN and became the political officer of the Wilaya 5 FLN unit fighting in and around Oran. By 1960, he became the head politician officer of Wilaya 5. Before the Évian Accords of the spring of 1962 led to Algerian independence, Bouteflika served as an intermediary between the imprisoned FLN leader Ahmed Ben Bella and the military commander Houari Boumedienne. Bouteflika's skills at assessing the political situation was demonstrated when he chose to back the Ben Bella/Boumedienne alliance against dissident FLN groups in Algeria in the short battle for power in the summer of 1962. After Ben Bella ascended to power, he rewarded Bouteflika with the ministry of youth and tourism in 1962. Bouteflika was then named foreign minister of Algeria, and he remained in this position until 1979. Ben Bella became distrustful of Bouteflika, whom he deemed to be too friendly to Western governments. However, Bouteflika was rescued by Boumedienne, who felt that Bouteflika's removal was a serious error.

When Boumedienne overthrew Ben Bella in June 1965, he kept Bouteflika as foreign minister. Bouteflika proved to be an extremely capable diplomat—a necessity given the Algerian government's decision to try to act as a leading force in third world radical leftist politics and quietly develop close economic ties with the United States and France simultaneously. He proved to be an extremely able negotiator in the discussions that led to the nationalization of French oil concessions in the southern Algerian Sahara in 1970 and 1971. Bouteflika proved to be far more conciliatory to France than many of his more leftist colleagues, and he was uncomfortable with Boumedienne's belief in a command economy even as Bouteflika secured aid from the Soviet Union. His job grew more difficult after 1976, when the Algerian government backed the Frente Popular de Liberación de Saguía el Hamra y Río de Oro (POLISARIO; Popular Front for the Liberation of Saguia el-Hamra and Río de Oro) rebel movement's struggle in Western Sahara, a former Spanish colony annexed by Morocco. At Boumedienne's death from a rare blood disease in December 1978, Bouteflika was considered to be a possible replacement, but his reputation as a thoroughly bourgeois and pro-Western figure appears to have ruined his chances to take power. After Chadli Bendjedid was named as the new president by the FLN and military leadership in February 1979, Bouteflika served as a minister without portfolio.

He fell out of favor with the military leadership in the early 1980s. The FLN Central Committee dismissed Bouteflika in December 1981. Bouteflika chose to leave the country in 1982 and was charged with embezzling state funds worth more than 12 million US dollars in 1983. Bouteflika only returned to Algeria in 1987, which appears to have been a move by Bendjedid to rebuild the divided FLN leadership. Bouteflika became a member of the central committee of the FLN once again in 1989, but he remained a minor player in the troubled transition to democracy that took place in 1990 and 1991. Bendjedid allowed for multi-party elections, but the rising popularity of the religiously oriented Front Islamique de Salut (FIS; Islamic Salvation Front) party and its substantial wins in the late 1991 legislative elections. The army annulled the elections, and FIS and other armed groups such as the Groupe Islamique Armée (GIA; Armed Islamic Group) went to war to overthrow the FLN government. When Algerian president Mohamed Boudiaf was assassinated by one of his bodyguards in 1992, rumor had it that Bouteflika was considered to be his replacement, but he apparently would not take the position unless he had control over the army.

Bouteflika returned to the headlines in 1999. General Liamine Zéroual, Boudiaf's successor, failed to bring the Islamist rebels to the bargaining table, and his government could not decisively defeat the FIS and GIA in battle. It is estimated that between 200,000 and 300,000 Algerians died in this bloody conflict. Zéroual decided to resign in 1999, and the government organized new elections in which Bouteflika ran as an independent candidate with the blessing of many military leaders. He won with 74 percent of the vote, but many opposition parties and the Islamist movements did not participate in the election. Bouteflika claimed to be in charge of the military and replaced numerous commanders in 2000. He tried to rebuild the ties between France and Algeria frayed by the bloody war.

Bouteflika was a strong ally of US efforts to battle al-Qaeda armed movements and their sympathizers after the 11 September 2001 attacks on New York and Washington. Bouteflika promoted reforms that included amnesty for FIS guerillas through the Civil Harmony Law of July 1999, which slowly put an end to the war by 2002. Bouteflika was harsher toward Berbers demanding democratic reforms in 2001 and used military force to crush these protestors. At times between 2000 and 2010, Bouteflika stated his willingness to investigate state authorities involved in torture and assassinations during the civil war and the Berber disturbances. However, his government proved unwilling to arrest and prosecute government law enforcement and military agents for human rights violations. In 2005, Bouteflika promoted a charter for national reconciliation that reasserted amnesty for participants in the FIS and GIA, save those charged with massacres, rapes, and bombings. Critics viewed this move as a means of whitewashing political violence. Bouteflika won the 2004 elections relatively easily, but most Berber communities boycotted the elections, and his government was accused in both elections of electoral fraud. The FLN and other parties approved a change in Algerian law eliminating presidential term limits in 2009, and Bouteflika won the presidential election later that year with an enormous majority, even as many opposition groups again refused to participate in what they deemed to be an electoral farce. Bouteflika had helped bring an end to the civil war, but he had not succeeded in convincing many Algerians that they lived in a real democracy.

[*See also* Ben Bella, Ahmed; Bendjedid, Chadli; *and* Boumedienne, Houari.]

BIBLIOGRAPHY

Aghrout, Ahmed, and Mohamed Redha Bougherira. *Algeria in Transition:Reforms and Development Prospects.* New York: Routledge, 2004.

Evans, Martin, and John Phillips. *Algeria: Anger of the Dispossessed.* New Haven, Conn.: Yale University Press, 2007.

Naylor, Phillip. *The Historical Dictionary of Algeria.* 3d ed. Lanham, Md.: Scarecrow Press, 2005.

Ruedy, John. *Modern Algeria: The Origins and Development of a Nation.* Bloomington: Indiana University Press, 2005.

JEREMY RICH

Boutros-Ghali, Boutros (1922–), Egyptian diplomat, jurist and scholar who, during 1992–1996, served as the sixth Secretary-General (SG) of the United Nations (UN), the first African and Arab to hold the position, was born in Cairo on 14 November 1922 into a distinguished Coptic Christian family. His grandfather, Boutros-Ghali Pasha, was the Egyptian minister for finance and, from 1894, foreign affairs. He was prime minister from 1908 to 1910 when he was assassinated by a nationalist angered with his advocacy of the extension of the Suez Canal Company's concession. Boutros Boutros-Ghali pointed out in an interview that "the reality was that the population was happy to get rid of a Christian" and his grandfather's assassination set off a wave of Coptic-Muslim clashes.

Boutros Boutros-Ghali. Boutros-Ghali talking to reporters on his last day in office at the United Nations, 31 December 1996. (AP Images/Marty Lederhandler)

Although not overtly religious himself, his family's history, status, and influence on the Coptic Church were to form Boutros-Ghali, who would later perceive his role as SG as providing intellectual and moral leadership to the global community. At the same time, his firsthand experience of the importance of tolerance would later translate into a commitment to the protection of minorities. As a member of the two hundred elite Egyptian families whose property holdings had been nationalized by the 1952 Egyptian Revolution, Boutros-Ghali was also denied his political rights, although these were later reinstated.

Boutros-Ghali received a law degree (Cairo University, 1946), a PhD in international law (Paris University, 1949), and diplomas in public law, economics, and political science (Paris University, 1947, 1948, 1949). He was appointed professor of international law and international relations, Cairo University (1949–1977) and visiting professor, Faculty of Law, Paris University (1967–1968). Other academic appointments include: vice president, Egyptian Society of International Law (1965–1993) and president, Centre of Political and Strategic Studies, Al-Ahram (1975–1977); director (1963–1964), Centre of Research; member (1978–2003) and (from 2004) president of the Curatorium, The Hague Academy of International Law; member of the International Law Commission (1979–1991), the

International Commission of Jurists (1975–1977), and the Institute of International Law (1975–1985; president 1985–1987), the Council and the Executive Committee of the International Institute of Human Rights (1975–1992), the African Society of Political Studies (1980–1991); and associate member of the Académie des Sciences Morales et Politiques, Académie Française (from 1989).

Boutros-Ghali served as Egypt's deputy prime minister for foreign affairs (1991) and minister of state for foreign affairs (1977–1991) under the presidency of Anwar al-Sadat. Days into his latter appointment, in October 1977, Boutros-Ghali accompanied Sadat on his historic trip to Jerusalem. (His predecessor had resigned shortly before in protest at Sadat's decision to visit Israel.) Sadat's speech before the Knesset marked the beginning of the rapprochement of the two countries. While Sadat and Israeli Prime Minister Menachem Begin retained control of the discussions, Boutros-Ghali acted as one of the principal advisers and lobbyists. A year later, sitting opposite Moshe Dayan, he attended the Camp David Summit Conference that negotiated the peace accords between Egypt and Israel, signed in 1979. Nearly thirty years later, Boutros-Ghali was questioning Israel's resolve to bring lasting peace in the region: the persistent offensives against Gaza and the restrictions imposed on contact between Gaza and the West Bank excluded the possibility of reconciliation; he no longer expected to see "the wall of separation" and "shame" fall in his lifetime. Boutros-Ghali thought that peace would come to the Middle East with a sincere and nonviolent dialogue, inevitably conceded to by Israelis due to demography. Ever the realist, he thought that in the meantime the Arab world would continue to focus its grievances around the Palestinian problem, excusing fanaticism and abuse, and thus further delaying its path to democratization and modernization.

Other political appointments include: member of the Egyptian parliament (1987–1991), the secretariat of the National Democratic Party (1980–1991), and the Central Committee and Political Bureau of the Arab Socialist Union (1974–1977); and vice president of the Socialist International (1990–1991). Boutros-Ghali led Egypt's delegation to UN General Assembly sessions in 1979, 1980, 1982, and 1990 and to meetings of the Organization of African Unity, the Movement of Non-Aligned Countries, and the Summit Conference of the French and African Heads of State.

Since his retirement as UN SG, Boutros-Ghali has been president, Society for International Development (1997–2000); secretary-general, Organisation Internationale de la Francophonie (1998–2002), and vice president of the Haut Conseil de la Francophonie (2002–2006); president, International Panel on Democracy and Development, UNESCO (from 1997); president, Institute for Mediterranean Political Studies (from 2002); chairman, South Centre (2003–2006); and president of the Egyptian National Council for Human Rights (from 2004).

Founder and editor of the weekly *Al-Ahram Iktisadi* (1959–1975) and the quarterly publication *Alsiyassa Dawlya* (1965–1991), Boutros-Ghali is also the author of numerous publications in law, international affairs, diplomacy, and political science. He is the recipient of a number of honorary degrees and awards.

Boutros-Ghali's election as UN SG satisfied a widely held feeling, especially in the developing world, that it was the turn of an African to hold the top UN job. At a time that the predominance of French as the language of diplomacy was coming into question, French President François Mitterand was a strong backer, crediting Boutros-Ghali with Egypt's entrance into La Francophonie in 1983. The former Soviet leader Mikhail Gorbachev was supportive because of Boutros-Ghali's contribution in restoring Egyptian-Soviet ties following the

expulsion of Soviet military advisers from Egypt in 1972. The United States and United Kingdom opposed his candidacy, but did not veto it in recognition of Egypt's role during the 1991 Gulf War.

The collapse of the Soviet Union created for the first time in many years the potential for consensus in the UN Security Council (SC). Seeking to take advantage of this, the newly elected SG outlined his vision of strengthening the UN's capacity for preventive diplomacy, peacemaking, and peacekeeping in *An Agenda for Peace* (1992), a report commissioned by the SC at its first meeting heads-of-state level. He introduced post-conflict peace building as a way of supporting structures that strengthen peace and prevent relapse into conflict. The concept has since been developed by academics and is now understood to combine conflict prevention, conflict management, and post-conflict reconstruction: a holistic framework that includes traditional peacekeeping, human rights reforms, the return of refugees, and electoral assistance in order to establish sustainable peace in war-torn societies. However, the intergovernmental, institutional, operational, and political implications of Boutros-Ghali's vision were not followed through.

Ill-conceived decisions such as intervention in Somalia soon shattered the nascent post–cold war opportunities noted by the council. In 1992, SC Resolution 794 authorized the multinational, US-led Unified Task Force to use "all necessary means" to guarantee the delivery of humanitarian aid in southern Somalia where warlords regularly looted food supplies destined for famine victims. On 3 October 1993, American Army Rangers serving alongside the UN force came under fire from Somali gunmen, sustaining eighteen casualties. The battle of Mogadishu and subsequent gruesome media coverage led to a shift in American foreign policy. The Clinton administration became reluctant to use military intervention in conflicts, particularly in the developing world. Ignoring the role of American officials who endorsed and even drove the military operations, they sought to shift responsibility to the UN. US Ambassador to the UN Madeleine Albright later accused Boutros-Ghali as "the first to embrace and the last to relinquish the unsuccessful strategy of confrontation with Aidid" (Albright, 2003).

A strong believer in the moral importance of the nation-state to the identity of human beings, Boutros-Ghali thought that in an era of globalization, the UN should seek "to preserve the nation-state as the very foundation of international life and to bring states together in an enlightened multilateralism that can enhance their specific interests while advancing the common cause" (Boutros-Ghali, 1993). But in 1994, the Republicans took control of the US House of Representatives and the Senate. They rejected the assertive multiculturalism the UN stood for, and asserted unilateralism in support of US national interests. When Boutros-Ghali pleaded with the US-led SC to increase the small UN force in Rwanda, it was reduced instead to a token presence. Nearly 1 million Rwandans died before the SC responded to the genocide. Boutros-Ghali believed that if the standby force for rapid deployment that he had proposed two years earlier had been agreed upon, the Rwandan genocide might have not taken place.

Boutros-Ghali increasingly thought that the UN was becoming a substitute for great power intervention and a scapegoat for problems created by it. In 1993, his proposal for a NATO-led force of seventy thousand that would take over from the underequipped and undermandated United Nations Protection Force (UNPROFOR) to protect the safe areas in Bosnia had been rejected. Rightly fearing that UN troops' lives would be at risk, he clashed with Albright over UN consent to NATO air strikes that would shield Bosnian Muslims while they were arming. In the wake of the strikes, more than 340 UN personnel were taken hostage. In fact, throughout the war, UNPROFOR suffered more than 200 casualties, most of them French. During a UN debate on the matter, Boutros-Ghali described, in French, US criticism of the mission as "vulgar."

By July 1995, the Bosnian conflict was reaching its climax. Nearly eight thousand men and boys were massacred in Srebrenica, the largest mass murder in Europe since World War II. In the same month, Boutros-Ghali was back in Rwanda: "How could I justify my absence from Bosnia or from United Nations headquarters in New York at this critical time? Reporters pressed me for an answer. . . . "Because," I said, "if I cancel this trip . . . the Africans will say that while there is genocide in Africa . . . the secretary-general pays attention only to Srebrenica, a village in Europe" (Boutros-Ghali, 1999).

Statements such as this gave his detractors, most notably Albright, ammunition to accuse him of dismissing the Bosnian conflict as "a rich man's war." But they also show Boutros-Ghali's principled determination to denounce double standards and speak his mind when he felt under pressure to pay lip service to America. For years, the United States had failed to pay its UN assessment contribution in full and on time, setting an example for over half of the other member states. With the UN on the verge of bankruptcy and peacekeeping operations hampered by underfunding and restrictive SC mandates, Boutros-Ghali felt that the US attempt to lay all the blame on UN bureaucracy and mismanagement was unjustified. Early on he had asked US President George H. W. Bush for a senior American administrator to address reform of UN finance. US Attorney-General Richard Thornburgh, later replaced by Melissa Wells, had been appointed under-secretary-general for administration and management. Under Boutros-Ghali's watch, the first high commissioner for human rights was appointed in 1994. To enhance the UN's cohesion and effectiveness in the field, Boutros-Ghali had appointed UN resident coordinators. He had also reorganized the secretariat with the establishment of departments for political affairs, peacekeeping operations, and humanitarian affairs (which later developed into the Office for the Coordination of Humanitarian Affairs). This involved the abolition of eighteen high-level posts, saving US$4 million. But the move had prompted protests from a number of ambassadors who interpreted the reforms as an assault on their countries' influence.

When he went public with the figures on UN arrears, Boutros-Ghali caused fury in the US Congress. According to the Clinton administration, Congress would refuse to pay the UN dues as long as Boutros-Ghali remained SG. By the time of the 1996 presidential election campaign, Republican presidential candidate Bob Dole regularly derided Boutros-Ghali, mocking the pronunciation of his name so as to prompt his audiences to boo him. As Albright remembers, "I concluded that if UN-US relations were going to improve, the SG would have to go." Another African, the Ghanaian Kofi Annan, became the candidate of choice for the United States so as to make it impossible to "argue that our effort to displace [Boutros-Ghali] was an affront to the entire continent" (Albright, 2003). Boutros-Ghali thus became the first UN secretary-general not to be elected to a second term in office.

Elsewhere, the UN had managed its relationship with the United States more successfully. Between 1992–1994, with significant help from the United States, the United Nations Special Commission destroyed large quantities of Iraq's chemical weapons and production facilities. Boutros-Ghali had warned early on that economic sanctions might not be "a legitimate means of exerting pressure on political leaders." When the military regime in Haiti rejected an accord facilitating the return of ousted President Jean-Bertrand Aristide, sanctions were nevertheless imposed. There, as in Iraq, sanctions drove the most vulnerable to smuggling and black-marketeering to make ends meet. At the same time that human rights observers were being deployed for the first time, the UN was contributing to the erosion of the moral fiber of these societies. Under the threat of a US military intervention, constitutional government was restored in Haiti in 1994 and the UN took over the command of the military operation from the US troops. Aristide was restored to office, although allegations of electoral irregularities, extra-judicial killings, and torture continued to destabilize the country. In 1996, with backing from the US, the UN-moderated Guatemalan peace accords ended the thirty-six-year civil war.

In August 1992 the SC endorsed Boutros-Ghali's recommendation, authorizing the stationing of UN observers in South Africa to work closely with the National Peace Secretariat, to put an end to violence and promote multiparty negotiations. The UN continued to play an active role up to and after the election of South Africa's first democratic and nonracial government. Under Boutros-Ghali, the UN deployed successfully in Cambodia and Mozambique. The UN Transitional Authority in Cambodia (UNTAC) assumed control of key administrative structures and oversaw the transition that led to the 1993 national elections and the restoration of civil rule following years of civil war and foreign intervention. The UN Operation in Mozambique (ONUMOZ) monitored a ceasefire and demobilized 76,000 government and Mozambican National Resistance fighters before overseeing the first multiparty elections in 1994. The UN Observer Mission in El Salvador (ONUSAL, 1991–1995) helped bring peace and democracy to a society that had been bitterly divided during a decade-long civil war. There, as in South Africa, Boutros-Ghali set up truth and reconciliation commissions, fearing that "the pursuit of justice can create new conflicts" and believing that "forgiveness is often more important than justice."

Security issues dominated the public agenda in the post–cold war years and with the publication of *An Agenda for Development* in 1994, Boutros-Ghali sought to refocus attention on development. He identified "finding the right blend of government direction of the economy and encouragement of private initiative" as "perhaps the most pressing challenge of economic development" and hoped that governments—no longer the paramount economic agents—would intervene when appropriate and retain "the responsibility to provide a regulatory framework for the effective operation of a competitive market system." Recognizing development's social, cultural, political, and environmental dimensions, he saw UN's potential to contribute to wider global debates on the environment, population growth, HIV/AIDS, and the role of women. The need for environmentally sustainable development was at the heart of the 1992 UN Conference on Environment and Development. Reaching conclusions ahead of its time, the forum acknowledged that poverty and excessive consumption damage the environment, and that alternative sources of energy must replace the use of fossil fuels linked to climate change.

During Boutros-Ghali's tenure and as a result of recommendations of the Vienna Declaration and Program of Action, adopted at the 1993 World Conference on Human Rights, the posts of UN high commissioner for human rights and special rapporteur on violence against women were established. The following year the UN International Conference on Population and Development called for universal access to reproductive health services and education, as well as the full involvement of women in the formation of sustainable development policy. The conference addressed issues at the time associated with social and cultural stigma, such as adolescent sexuality and HIV/AIDS. Women's empowerment and equality were also at the heart of the 1995 Fourth World Conference on Women. The conference broadened the definition of violence against women to include actions justified in the name of culture or tradition. It identified women migrant workers as a vulnerable group and introduced the term "girl-child," recognizing the inferior treatment of girls leading to social exclusion. The 1995 World Summit for Social Development signalled a commitment to put the conquest of poverty, employment, and the fostering of stable, safe, and just societies at the center of policy objectives.

Boutros-Ghali remained engaged in international affairs well into his eighties. A firm believer that democracy and development reinforce each other and that together they can contribute to the consolidation of peace, he did not think it was for the UN to provide a model for democratization or even to promote democracy in a particular country. He believed that every government should choose "the form, pace and character of its democratization process" and be allowed to define its own priorities (whether to give precedence to moving from an authoritarian to a multiparty system, or prioritize transition to a free market economy). Subject to democratic regulations in economic and social matters, and employed in "such a way as to close the gap between poor and rich countries," globalization could be a genuine asset. But in the highly politicized and security-driven agenda that prevailed, few in the north were willing to listen to his call for the redistribution of wealth.

Christian, Arab, African, diplomat, jurist, and scholar, Boutros-Ghali possessed the intellectual robustness, moral gravity, and realism to represent successfully such diverse constituencies, albeit only for a relatively short period as UN SG. In a bid to restore balance to the public debate about his tenure, Boutros-Ghali published his memoirs in 1999.

His first marriage to Leila Kahil, an archaeologist, ended in divorce. He subsequently married Leia Nadler, an Egyptian Jew from Alexandria who converted to Roman Catholicism. They have no children.

[*See also* Aidid, Mohammed Farah; Annan, Kofi Atta; *and* Sadat, Muhammad Anwar al-.]

BIBLIOGRAPHY

Albright, Madeleine (with Bill Woodward). *Madam Secretary: A Memoir.* London: Macmillan 2003.

Boutros-Ghali, Boutros and Peres, Shimon. *60 ans de conflit Israelo-Arabe; Tèmoignages pour l'Histoire. Entretiens croisés avec André Versaille.* Bruxelles: Éditions Complexe, 2006.

Boutros-Ghali, Boutros. *En attendant la prochaine lune. Carnets: 1997–2002.* Paris: Fayard, 2004.

Boutros-Ghali, Boutros. *The Interaction between Democracy and Development,* Paris: UNESCO, 2003.

Boutros-Ghali, Boutros. *The Papers of United Nations Secretary-General Boutros Boutros-Ghali,* selected and edited by Charles Hill. Vols. 1–3. New Haven, Conn.: Yale University Press, 2003.

Boutros-Ghali, Boutros *Démocratiser la mondialisation; Entretiens avec Yves Berthelot,* Paris: Éditions de Rocher, 2002.

Boutros-Ghali, Boutros. *Emanciper la Francophonie,* Paris: L'Harmattan, 2002.

Boutros-Ghali, Boutros. *Unvanquished: A U.S.-U.N. Saga,* London, New York: I.B. Tauris Publishers, 1999.

Boutros-Ghali, Boutros. *Egypt's Road to Jerusalem: A Diplomat's Story of the Struggle for Peace in the Middle East,* New York: Random House, 1997.

Boutros-Ghali, Boutros. *An Agenda for Development; Report of the Secretary-General,* UN doc. A/48/935, May, 6, 1994.

Boutros-Ghali, Boutros. "Don't Make the U.N.'s Head Job Harder." *The New York Times,* August, 20 1993.

Boutros-Ghali, Boutros. *An Agenda for Peace: Preventive Diplomacy, Peacemaking and Peace-keeping.* New York, 1992.

Burgess, Stephen F. *The United Nations Under Boutros Boutros-Ghali, 1992–1997.* Lanham, Md.: Scarecrow Press, 2001.

Lang, Anthony F., Jr. "A Realist in the Utopian City." In *The UN Secretary-General and Moral Authority; Ethics & Religion in International Leadership,* edited by Kent J. Kille, pp. 265–297. Washington D.C.: Georgetown University Press, 2007.

KATYA LENEY-HALL

Bouzid, Dorra (1933–), Tunisian nationalist, writer, women's rights activist, and artist, was born in the provincial city of Sfax, where her father worked in the Arabic publishing business and was an amateur actor, which helps explain her lifelong involvement in the arts. Her mother, Cherifa, was educated and quite unconventional; after her husband's death, she taught primary school in Nabeul from 1943 on, riding a bike to school while still wearing a black veil, which scandalized the conservative local community. Since there were no educational institutions for Tunisian girls in the town, Dorra Bouzid studied in the local French secular school from the age of four on, with students from a range of religious and ethnic backgrounds. After her father's death—his family had been opposed to Cherifa teaching school—Bouzid's mother received a post in Tunis just prior to World War II and married again, to Mahmoud Messaâdi (1911–2004), an important figure in contemporary Arabic literature as well as in the history of education in independent Tunisia.

In the capital, Bouzid and her sister attended a well-known French lycée, where they were often the only Arab Muslim girls in class. This was a period of heightened anti-French colonial activity, and since both her mother and stepfather were ardent nationalists, their home in Tunis became a center for political meetings. But Bouzid was also attracted to music, dance, and singing and enrolled for a time in the École des Beaux Arts in Tunis, where she excelled. Nevertheless, her mother decided that, since women needed to be financially independent, and could not make a decent living in the arts, her daughter should study pharmacy. In 1951, Bouzid enrolled in the School of Pharmacy in Paris, which at the time had only a handful of Muslim women students. This was a time of fierce North African anticolonialism, throughout both France and the Maghreb. North African university students studying in the metropole were highly politicized; this was where Bouzid became involved in oppositional politics revolving around labor organization, combined with demands for independence from France. She helped to organize a student newspaper in Paris and joined the Association of r North African Students). Thus, the idea of the "Greater Maghreb," made up of independent national states but united in purpose, came to be first enunciated by students in Paris.

With her diploma in pharmacy in hand, Bouzid returned to her native land to practice pharmacy during the tumultuous shift from empire and colony to independence. In order to understand the next phase of her public life and her involvement in feminist and activist journalism, we need to back up to consider the evolution of the women's press in Tunisia.

In December 1939, the first francophone feminist magazine, Leïla, was founded, but it was forced to cease publication during the war in 1941. In 1955, L'Action, a Tunisian political newspaper, introduced a column concerning women, "Leïla vous parle" ("Leïla Speaks to You"), which folded after five issues because of the lack of Tunisian women trained in journalism. However, the editor had made the acquaintance of Dorra Bouzid when she was a student in Paris, and recruited her to relaunch the column. Eventually, Bouzid's feminist column expanded to become an entire page, entitled "Feminine Action." On 13 June 1955, Bouzid, the newspaper's only female employee, published an article under the pseudonym Leïla entitled "Call for Emancipation Law," demanding rights for women. The next year, the new president of the independent Tunisian Republic, Habib Bourguiba, promulgated the Code of Personal Status, the most far-reaching, progressive transformation in family and women's law in the Arab and Muslim world.

On the occasion of the Code's promulgation, Bouzid published another piece, "Tunisian Women are Adults," which reminded readers that two Muslim clerics had collaborated in drawing up the new legislation. In 1959, Safia Farhat founded the magazine Faïza, which Bouzid joined as head editor after the third issue. Although it ceased publication

in 1967, it remained well-known throughout the Maghreb, and more generally across Africa, as the first Arab-African feminist francophone magazine. During the Algerian War of Independence, the magazine was very politically active, as was Bouzid. She played a leading role as a journalist at L'Action, which later became Jeune Afrique (Young Africa), and was asked to act as an informal diplomatic intermediary between Tunisia and Morocco when relations between the two nations were strained in the early 1960s.

For the past five decades, Bouzid has published innumerable articles and has been involved in a wide range of publications, including the founding Femmes et Réalités, as well as in international conferences convened for various causes the world over. She has also been a radio commentator in Tunisia and France. In addition, her stepfather, Messaâdi, was appointed to several key ministerial posts: from 1958 until 1968, he served as Minister of National Education, followed by Minister of Cultural Affairs in the 1970s. Bouzid's close relationship with her stepfather gave her access to the heart of power and politics, where she was able to intervene in the defense of women's and artists' rights.

As an expression of Bouzid's dedicated promotion of the arts, she edited a volume, École de Tunis: Un âge d'or de la peinture tunisienne (1995; The School of Tunis: The Golden Age of Tunisian Painting), which offers analyses of painters and their attempts to evolve a distinctively Tunisian style. Long involved in numerous artistic festivals, Bouzid was publicly recognized as a "pioneer" of dance in her country during the 2008 international festival "Le Printemps de la Danse," held in Tunis. As the award noted: "Due to Bouzid's efforts, dancers and choreographers have come to prominence in Tunisian arts."

Currently, Bouzid is writing her memoirs. It is difficult to situate Dorra Bouzid's life within any single category, as she has been involved in a wide array of political, social, cultural, and artistic causes since her days as a student in Paris; she continues to be committed to these causes.

[See also Bourguiba, Habib.]

BIBLIOGRAPHY

Boujmil, Hafedh, ed. Leïla: Revue illustrée de la femme, 1936–1941. Tunis: Editions Nirvana, 2007.

Bouzid, Dorra. "De 'Leïla' et 'Faïza' à 'Femmes et Réalités." Femmes et Réalités (September 1998): 8–9.

Bouzid, Dorra, éd. *École de Tunis. Un âge d'or de la peinture tunisienne.* Tunis: Alif, 1995.

Mamelouk, Nadia. "*Leïla*: 1936–1941 Bien plus qu'une revue féminine." In *Leïla: Revue illustrée de la femme, 1936–1941*, edited by Hafedh Boujmil, pp. 11–40. Tunis: Editions Nirvana, 2007.

JULIA A. CLANCY-SMITH

Boye, Mame Madior (1940–), first female prime minister of Senegal, was born in the coastal city of Saint Louis, Senegal. She came from a family of lawyers, including her father, one brother who worked for the Supreme Court of Senegal, and another brother who received an advanced law degree, became a professor of international law, and eventually became the head of the University of Dakar. Boye herself attended primary school in her home city before graduating from the Lycée Faidherbe secondary school and enrolling in an undergraduate law degree program at the University of Dakar in 1963. She then studied law at the Centre National d'Études Judiciaries (CNEJ) in Paris. Once she finished her studies in France, she returned to Senegal and began to work as an assistant prosecutor for the government. Boye became an assistant judge in a court at Dakar, and later rose to be president of the Senegalese Court of Appeals. During this time, she was a trailblazer as a female lawyer in Senegal and supported an array of feminist causes. One of her greatest accomplishments was the reform of the Senegalese family legal code, to include more protections for younger women and for wives.

Boye left her government posts in 1990, and obtained a position working for the Compagnie Bancaire de l'Afrique Occidentale firm. She remained an employee of this company for the next decade. She also had been for many years the president of the Association des Femmes Juristes du Sénégal, an organization of female lawyers. Boye married, had two children, and divorced her husband.

Boye emerged from her relative political obscurity in 2001. Even though she did not belong to any political party, the leader of the Parti Démocratique Sénégalais (PDS; Senegalese Democratic Party), Abdoulaye Wade, selected Boye to be his prime minister after he won the 2001 Senegalese presidential election. Wade had campaigned on a platform that included promises to offer more political opportunities for women, and Boye's nomination reflected one fulfillment of that pledge. She took the position in March 2001, but she found she had little influence, despite her impressive title.

Mame Madior Boye, 2002. (AP Images/Senegal TV-APTN)

A demonstration of the kind of criticism she received came in late July 2001, when the Senegalese government arrested two journalists for publishing a photomontage of a nude model with Boye's face superimposed on the image. Some observers charged that Boye was little more than a figurehead for Wade, who preferred early in his tenure to have relatively obscure ministers in order to better dominate the government.

The president and Boye worked together to reduce the number of ministers in the government. Wade dismissed her in favor of Idrissa Seck, but then appointed her as attorney general of Senegal. It was in this position that Boye found herself embroiled in a scandal for the next decade. On 26 September 2002, the transport ship *Joola* sank on the Senegalese coast in the southern Casamance region. Roughly two thousand people died in the disaster, mainly Senegalese, and a few French citizens as well. Many Senegalese complained that the government had done far too little to ensure the safety and maintenance of the *Joola*. Boye was removed from office in part for her alleged errors in this affair. She claimed at first that dangerous weather conditions had led to the disaster, but journalists and angry relatives of the victims claimed she was covering up for poor government oversight.

Boye then became a member of an African Union conflict resolution team in 2004. She visited the Darfur region of Sudan, the Democratic Republic of Congo, and other conflict zones to try to help mediate these different crises. Unfortunately for Boye, a French court indicted her for negligence in the *Joola* disaster in 2008, at the prompting of twenty-two families who had lost relatives in the tragedy. They claimed that she had not acted on reports highlighting the poor condition of the ship from the Ministry of Transport in 2001. Boye responded by arguing that she had acted on these communications, and had also ordered the *Joola* to not operate for over a year. The Senegalese government responded by threatening to act in a reciprocal manner toward French citizens charged with crimes against Senegalese citizens in France. On 15 June 2009, a French court of appeals in Paris cleared Boye of all charges. She declared, "I have nothing to reproach myself for in this case. On the contrary, others have much to excuse themselves for in their conduct towards me. I never fled from my responsibilities. I could have found scapegoats by blaming others for the accident and protected myself as a result. However, I did not do so because I would have found that inhumane."

Boye continued to work as an international lawyer; in January 2010, she monitored municipal elections in Tunisia. Two months later, she criticized the international community's lack of activity in Darfur. Boye's pioneering work managed to continue despite the legacy of the *Joola*. Her legacy as an activist is similar to that of Mauritania feminist Aïssata Kane.

[*See also* Kane, Aïssata.]

BIBLIOGRAPHY

Diop, Moumar-Coumba. *Gouverner le Sénégal: Entre ajustement structurel et développement*. Paris: Karthala, 2004.

Gellar, Sheldon. *Democracy in Senegal: Tocquevillian Analytics in Senegal*. New York: Palgrave Macmillan, 2005.

"L'ancien premier ministre Mame Madior Boye sur le naufrage du bateau *Le Joola*: 'Je n'ai rien à me reprocher, on m'accuse à tort!'" Nettali.net, July 3, 2009: http://www.nettali.net/Je-n-ai-rien-a-me-reprocher-on-m.html.

JEREMY RICH

Bozizé, François (1946–), military officer and President of the Central African Republic (CAR), was born François Bozizé Yangouvonda in Mouila, Gabon, on 14 October 1946. His father, Yangouvonda, a Baya (Gbeya) from Ouham region, served in the French colonial army and the colonial gendarmerie (police forces) in Gabon and then Bossangoa, near his hometown. Bozizé attended primary school at Tchibanga (Gabon) and continued his studies at Bossangoa and the Lycée Technique in Bangui. Joining the Central African army some time around 1966, he entered the École Speciale de Formation des Officiers d'Active (ESFOA) at Bouar in 1967, graduating as a second lieutenant in September 1969. After attending the Centre National des Commandos at Mont-Louis, France (1970–1971), Bozizé was promoted to first lieutenant (1 September 1970), and after officer training at the École d'Application de l'Artillerie at Chalons (1973–1974) and the Centre Interarmées des Sports at Fontainebleau (1975), he rose up through the ranks to captain (30 August 1976), commander (9 December 1976), lieutenant-colonel (April 1978), colonel (1 August 1978), brigadier general (17 August 1978), major general (1979), and two-star general (31 December 2004).

Bozizé served as commander at the CAR Army's training unit, head of then-President Jean Bedel

Bokassa's private safety unit, aide-de-camp (1976), director of the National Office for Ex-Combatants (that is, Veterans; 1977), and technical adviser to the Minister of National Defense (1977). After Bokassa's downfall in 1979, President David Dacko appointed Bozizé Deputy Chief of Staff of the CAR Army (28 September), Deputy Minister in charge of National Defense (30 October), and Minister of National Defense from July to September 1980.

Bozizé left the government briefly to study at the École Supérieure de Guerre in Paris (November 1980–September 1981). When General André Kolingba seized power, Bozizé was appointed Mininster of Information and Culture (December 1981–3 March 1982) in the new President's Comité Militaire de Redressement National (CMRN; Military Committee of National Recovery), but on 3 March 1982, Bozizé joined a coup against Kolingba, publicly accused the president of treason on Radio Bangui, and announced Ange Patassé's seizure of power. Patassé's supporters demonstrated in the streets of Bangui, however, and the Presidential Guard commanded by French Colonel Jean-Claude Mantion intervened to stop the coup. The next day, General Kolingba announced that the plot had failed.

Bozizé fled to Germany, France, and finally Benin where, in June 1983, he founded the Parti Révolutionnaire Centrafricain (PRC; Central African Revolutionary Party) which attempted to unite Patassé's Mouvement de Libération du Peuple Centrafricain (MLPC; Central African People's Liberation Movement) and Abel Goumba's Front Patriotique Oubanguien (FPO; Ubangian Patriotic Front) without success. In September 1983 a special session of the MLPC congress removed Patassé from the presidency and chose Bozizé as president of the MLPC executive committee. On 24 July 1989, Bozizé was arrested in a hotel in Cotonou; a month later he was repatriated to Bangui, imprisoned, released on 1 December 1991, and exiled to France. In August 1993 he returned to Bangui to run for president but won only 1.59 percent of vote, thus ranking seventh out of eight candidates.

Turning to business, Bozizé ran a gas station and managed a bus that ran between Bangui and Bossangoa, but after military mutinies in 1996, President Patassé called Bozizé back to service as inspector general of the army of the CAR (October 1996), vice-president of the army's representative assembly, and head of the committee for collecting weapons from former rebels and others. In February 1997, Bozizé was appointed Army Chief of Staff, but after an attempted coup by Kolingba supporters in May 2001, Patassé became suspicious of Bozizé and ordered his arrest on 26 October 2001. Bozizé fled north with loyal troops to Chad, where he hired mercenaries and prepared to overthrow the president.

On 15 March 2003, Bozizé seized power in Bangui and formed a union government backed by a coalition of political parties led by Goumba. Bozizé then called for a national conference (Dialogue national) that was held in Bangui in October 2001, and attended by three hundred and fifty delegates representing the government, political organizations, trade unions, civil society, and ethnic groups. In December, Bozizé named Goumba Vice-President and appointed economist Célestin Leroy Gaombalet as Prime Minister. A new constitution was approved by referendum in December 2004, and in 2005 Bozizé ran for president with the support of twenty-three political parties and a few independent political candidates who shared the slogan "Kwa Na Kwa" (KNK; Work and Work).

On 13 March 2005 Bozizé won 42.97 percent of the vote and, as front-runner, qualified for the second round against MLPC candidate Martin Ziguélé. On 8 May 2005 Bozizé was elected with 64.6 percent of the vote against Ziguélé's 35.4 percent. In the National Assembly, the pro-Bozizé KNK coalition controlled some 78 out of 105 seats. On 11 June 2005 Bozizé was sworn in for a five-year term, but soon thereafter opposition armies launched rebellions in the north of the country, which led to brutal reprisals. However, in December 2008, Bozizé offered peace agreements to rebel armies and held a Dialogue Politique Inclusif (political national conference) to settle disputes among all rebel armies and the government.

Bozizé's wife Monique ran for a seat in the National Assembly from Bimbo's second electoral district and, in the second round of voting on 8 May 2005, was elected with 67.7 percent of the vote. In September 2006, President Bozizé appointed his younger sister Yvonne Mboïssona as Minister of Environment and Tourism, then on 22 August 2007 Mboïssona founded the Union du Mouvement Populaire de Centrafrique (UMPCA; Union of Central African Popular Movement) to support her brother. Jean Francis, the president's son, was appointed Deputy Defense Minister in January 2008.

Bozizé initially enjoyed fairly widespread support, but brutal repression of rebels and their alleged supporters led many rural villagers to flee across borders or into the bush, resulting in greater refugee populations, famine, and illness. Members of Bozizé's Presidential Guard have allegedly committed many atrocities. Banditry in the countryside also increased and began to threaten even aid workers for the first time. As a result, Bozizé's popularity plummeted, but in January 2011, Bozizé won 64.37 percent of the vote in the presidential election, followed by former President Patassé with 21.43 percent. Bozizé was thus elected in the first round for a second five-year term from 15 March 2011.

[See also Bokassa, Jean Bedel; Dacko, David; Goumba, Abel; Kolingba, André; and Patassé, Ange-Félix.]

BIBLIOGRAPHY

Mehler, Andreas. "The Shaky Foundations, Adverse Circumstances, and Limited Achievements of Democratic Transition in the Central African Republic." In *The Fate of Africa's Democratic Experiments: Elites and Institutions*, edited by Leonardo A. Villalón and Peter VonDoepp, pp. 126–152. Bloomington: Indiana University Press, 2005.

N'Douba, Prosper. *L'otage du général rebelle Centrafricain François Bozizé*. Paris: L'Harmattan, 2005.

Serre, Jacques. *Biographie de David Dacko, premier président de la République Centrafricaine, 1930–2003*. Paris: L'Harmattan, 2007.

RICHARD A. BRADSHAW and
JUAN FANDOS-RIUS

Brahim, Mariam (1956–), Chadian medical doctor, was born on 16 June 1956 in the eastern Chadian city of Abéché. Her parents were Brahim Djadarab and Fatimé Fadoul. She had four siblings: her brother Issa Michel and her sisters Khalié, Sadié, Ibni Oumar Mahamet-Saleh, and Rakié. The entire family attended primary school in Abéché, and Brahim excelled in her education. Her family supported her studies, and she completed her secondary education at the Lycée Franco-Arabe at Abéché. Her father pressured her to study English, but she found the language impractical in eastern Chad. Even so, she learned the language, which would later prove to be extremely useful when she lived in Canada. Her commitment to school impressed her Chadian and foreign teachers. Missionaries and her family also strongly encouraged her. Since there were no final classes to prepare for the baccalaureate examinations in Abéché in the early 1970s, she had to go to the Chadian capital of N'Djamena

to study. In this class, practically all the other students were French expatriates. Her French teachers sometimes mocked her, claiming, for example, that women could not master geometry. Despite such discrimination, Brahim passed her examination in 1976. She considered entering an architectural program at the University of N'Djamena, but her cousin Abderaman Hamdane offered her a new idea. He had just finished his university studies in Leningrad. Hamdane told Brahim that Russian universities were excellent, and so she applied for funding to follow his example. After the fall of pro-Western dictator François Tombalbaye in 1975, the Russian government sought to build up support by providing educational opportunities for Chadian students. Brahim received a grant to study medicine in Russia, and so she left behind architecture for a new career. As of 2004, there were still no female professional architects in Chad.

Once in the Soviet Union, Brahim and a dozen other Chadian medical students first studied the Russian language in Rostov-on-Don. She then enrolled in a medical school in Leningrad known for its nationally famous pediatric program. She encountered many difficulties, not the least of which being her struggles with Russian grammar. Financial troubles also posed a major problem, as the Chadian government's support arrived intermittently between 1977 and 1979, when the civil war left Brahim cut off from state funding. Her husband and her father sent her money to survive. She graduated from the Russian medical school in 1983. This year marked another milestone from Brahim. She married her husband in Moscow. With Hissene Habre's victory in 1982 and the establishment of a brutal new government, Brahim and her husband decided not to return to their homeland. Her husband found work in the Republic of Congo's capital of Brazzaville, which was at the time under a Marxist-Leninist regime closely tied to Moscow. It was easy for Brahim to visit her spouse in Brazzaville. A former colleague from medical school working at a Brazzaville suggested that she apply for a job at the same facility. When a Russian expatriate abruptly left her post as a doctor there, Brahim replaced her. She continued to work in Brazzaville from 1986 to 1989. Brahim's husband then went to Canada to continue his training as a petroleum engineer in 1989, but Brahim decided to return to N'Djamena to care for her family. With the overthrow of Habre by Idriss Déby, Brahim's family was reunited in 1990. The new government appointed Brahim's husband ambassador to Russia in 1991, and Brahim took advantage by continuing her education and writing a thesis under a female medical professor at the Russian Academy of Sciences in Moscow. She received her doctorate in 1996 and then returned to her homeland in 1997. She had five children: three born in Russia, one in the Republic of Congo, and one in Chad.

From 1997 onward, Brahim worked as a pediatrician and as a professor at the University of N'Djamena medical college. Like the more internationally known female Chadian doctor Grace Kodindo, Brahim considered public health programs to be an extremely important part of her work. Chad has among the highest rates of infant mortality in the entire world. Kodindo and Brahim worked together from 1997 until 2006. Brahim coordinated a program to promote popular education for children's health throughout the country in 1999. Her work provided little time for other activities, including politics. She joked in an interview with anthropologist Marie-José Tubiana that she learned she was a delegate to the constitutional convention in the early 1990s by hearing the announcement on the radio. Her story demonstrates the sometimes ignored role of Russian-educated professionals in Africa, as well as the slowly growing number of female medical professionals in Central Africa in the late twentieth and early twenty-first centuries.

[*See also* Habré, Hissène; Kodindo, Grace; *and* Tombalbaye, François.]

BIBLIOGRAPHY

Marie-José Tubiana. *Parcours de femmes: Les nouvelles élites, entretiens, 1997–2003.* Paris: Sépia, 2004.

JEREMY RICH

Braide, Garrick Sokari Daketime (c. 1882/1885–1918), Nigerian religious leader, was born sometime between 1882 and 1885, most likely in Obonoma, a small Kalabari town in the Niger Delta region. Obonoma, in present-day Nigeria, was the home of his mother Abarigania, although some people suggested he was actually born in the nearby town of Bakana. Obonoma was known in the late nineteenth and twentieth century as a center of indigenous spirituality and the home of a powerful deity known as Oyu or Ogu. Braide was raised in Bakana, the home of his father Daketima Braide, a member of the Marian Briade house. As an adolescent, he belonged to the entourage of the paramount chief of Bakana.

Braide also shared the indigenous polytheistic beliefs of his parents and may have been initiated into the service of the deity Ogu by his mother. It is unclear how or when Braide abandoned these older traditions and became a convert to Christianity. African Protestants and missionaries held services in Bakana from 1886 onward, and it may have been through these occasional visits that Braide became attracted to the newly introduced faith. By the 1890s Braide expressed his willingness to receive instruction in Protestant teachings at the Saint Andrew's Sunday School in Bakana run by Moses Kemmer. There, he drew attention from his pastor and from other Christians for his self-discipline and his strict adherence to Christian doctrine. He always kept Sunday as a day of rest and began each working day with prayer at Saint Andrew's. Sometimes, he slipped into the church to secretly pray. Kemmer praised Braide as a model convert: "There is hardly any heathen man or woman and in some cases baptized persons who came under [Braide's] address did not quake for the moment. He has been instrumental in bringing many to the house of God of late" (Ludwig, p. 299). He managed to accomplish this even though the religious instruction was not in his own language of Kalabari. Until the 1920s, Protestant missionaries used Ibo as the main language of religious instruction throughout the Niger Delta region. Thus, Braide had to learn Ibo. Historian G. O. M. Tasie contends that these linguistic difficulties slowed down Braide's progress in the faith, since he only was baptized on 23 January 1910. After a two-year probationary period, Braide was confirmed by Anglican assistant Bishop James Johnson in 1912. He eventually became a member of the Bakana mission school committee by 1914.

Braide's conversion came at a time when most African pastors in the Niger Delta came from other parts of Nigeria or from Sierra Leone. Relatively few African ministers came from the Delta, which was a source of complaint for some African Anglicans there. Braide became popular with some Delta Christians because of his local roots. However, he also developed a following by 1909 for his forthright opposition to indigenous religious beliefs. When some Bakana residents planned to hold a dancing ceremony involving diviners, one of the ritual specialists declared he would use his arcane knowledge to prevent rain from interrupting the ceremony. Braide was said to have declared the diviner had no power to stop nature, and a sudden rain storm then made it impossible for the ceremony to take place after Braide prayed. On occasion, Braide preached at Bakana and worked as an assistant for his pastor Reverend Kemmer.

Braide's religious activity took a dramatic turn by late 1915. He declared that he was an instrument of the Holy Spirit and now could heal the sick. Crowds flocked to Bakana to be cured of illnesses through Braide's prayers and touch. Braide also regularly preached in Ibo and Kalabari. He also composed more than 170 hymns in Kalabari. One hymn became a standard invocation to Christ at the beginning of his services. He and the congregants dumped water blessed by Braide on shrines to local deities as they chanted, "Jesus has come and Satan has run away." His visions and prophecies did not endear him to some African and European clergy in the Anglican Church Missionary Society, who began to consider Braide to be an undisciplined and ill-trained problem. Other European and African Anglican priests at first felt Braide was a brilliant example of African ministry, since he was a simple fisherman rather than a graduate of advanced schools who might be more concerned with social advancement than his faith. Braide's own pastor Kemmer still remained close to him. Kemmer went so far as to believe that Braide had cured his own wife of an illness, and he compared his friend to the Jewish prophet Elijah. Soon, many Nigerians dubbed Braide "Elijah II." Braide accepted the title. Colonial administrators became extremely frustrated that Braide decried the use of Western medicine as a sign of a lack of confidence in Christ. They also bemoaned how sick people had flooded into Bakana to be healed. Some state-appointed Nigerian chiefs also complained that Braide was a threat to public order and that he had disrupted indigenous beliefs as well as their own involvement in selling gin and other imported liquors. Braide's willingness to hear legal disputes left local courts empty. Several thousand people accepted baptism because of Braide's efforts in 1915 and 1916 alone.

Braide soon was the leader of a movement and had support from assistants such as Danilabo Ngiangia and Moses Hart. These men soon were known as "servants of the prophet" and moved into other Niger Delta towns like Bonny. Mark Ichie Uranta brought Braide's message to Opobo. Like Braide, they smashed sacred objects of local deities and ran their own religious courses. Anglican Bishop James Johnson pleaded with Braide to tone down his claims at a Christmas Eve meeting in 1915, but Braide rebuked the Anglican leader and formed his own church by February 1916. By May 1916, Braide claimed that World War I was God's punishment for colonial rule. Braide was jailed from late 1916 to early 1918 for such comments. However, his popularity had not dimmed, and his followers joined the Christ Army Church to promote his teachings. Ironically, Braide had little control over the church. He was eclipsed by Sierra Leonean immigrant S. A. Coker, a man who distanced himself from Braide's radical pronouncements. Braide died on 15 November 1918, but his message remained an important example of independent Nigerian Christianity.

[*See also* Johnson, James.]

BIBLIOGRAPHY

Ayandele, Emmanuel Ayankanmi. *Holy Johnson, Pioneer of African Nationalism, 1836–1917*. London: Routledge, 1970.

Kalu, Ogbu. *African Pentecostalism: An Introduction*. New York: Oxford University Press, 2008.

Ludwig, Frieder. "Elijah II: Radicalisation and Consolidation of the Garrick Braide Movement, 1915–1918." *Journal of Religion in Africa* 23, no. 4 (1993): 296–317.

Tasie, G. O. M. *Christian Missionary Enterprise in the Niger Delta, 1864–1918*. Leiden: Brill, 1978.

JEREMY RICH

Brand, Johannes Henricus (1823–1888), South African lawyer and politician, was born in Cape Town on 6 December 1823. His father, Christoffel J. Brand, a member of a leading Cape family, was a noted journalist and parliamentarian and the first speaker of the Cape Parliament in 1854. Brand Sr. had presented a doctoral thesis to Leiden University in 1820 on the rights of colonists, which the British might have considered treasonable if it had not been written in Latin. By the 1840s he, along with a number of his fellow Dutch-speaking settlers, decided to cooperate with British rule, believing, accurately as it would turn out, that they would be able to dominate democratic institutions in the colony when they were eventually granted.

Jan, as he was known, followed his father to Leiden University in the Netherlands, where he studied law, and thereafter he was admitted to the British Bar. In 1849, he returned to Cape Town, where he began a career as a barrister. In 1851 he married Johanna Sibella Zastron; the couple eventually had eleven children. In 1854 he was elected to the newly constituted Cape Parliament, where he sat for ten years. Then, in 1864, he acceded to a request to stand for president of the Orange Free State (OFS), despite having never visited the territory. He was elected overwhelmingly, both then and in four subsequent elections, and remained president until his death in 1888.

The Orange Free State had been established in the aftermath of the Great Trek away from the British-controlled East Cape by more than 12,000 European settlers. But by the time Brand arrived there, its ruling class consisted of the mainly Dutch-speaking famers, many of whom were prosperous wool farmers, and the predominantly English merchants, particularly in Bloemfontein, the capital. It had become independent in 1854, but had not yet become an established political community. Brand was able to unite the various factions behind him. Almost single-handedly, he transformed the OFS into a well-run, modern mini-state, though one whose financial holdings were meager.

In addition to his state-building activities, Brand's political career revolved around three main issues. First, there was the triangular conflict between the Free State, Lesotho, and the Cape Colony. After the Free State had reversed the losses of previous wars, it was able to impose the Treaty of Thaba Bosigo (1866) on the Basotho and thus maintain control of a large tract of fertile country in the Caledon River valley. These borders survived the British decision to annex Lesotho, which was taken primarily to ensure that it did not become subservient to the Republic. Brand's protests against this were in vain, but the loss of land was eventually to condemn Lesotho to its subsequent grinding poverty.

Second, subsequent to the discovery of diamonds near what was to become Kimberley, there developed a long judicial conflict around the Western border of the Free State, to make clear in which territory the diamond fields were situated. Brand initially sent administrators to the new settlements around the mines, but they were evicted by the British. The Free State was not able to do more than make dignified protests at what Brand saw as British skullduggery. However, this, together with the conflict over Lesotho, ensured that the Free State burghers were in no way prepared to countenance the British plans for the Confederation of South Africa.

Brand was able to lead the opposition to this while remaining on sufficiently good terms with the British for them to offer him a knighthood, which he accepted. His judicial, diplomatic, and political activities were just as effective as the armed struggle of the Free State's northern neighbors in the Transvaal.

Finally, in the last years of his life, Brand had to deal with the effects of the discovery, in 1886, of gold in the Witwatersrand, in the Transvaal. For the Free State, the main question revolved around the conditions under which railways were to be allowed to cross its territory, and the tariffs which were to be raised. Brand's skilled negotiations eventually ensured a very advantageous deal for the Free State. Brand was not an Afrikaner nationalist in the way that position would come to be conceived by his twentieth-century successors. He did recognize, however, that the white inhabitants of the Orange Free State in his era were increasingly self-assured in their desire to maintain their state's independence. British actions had only exacerbated this recalcitrance. Brand had no objection to working with this way of thought—including against the Transvaal when this became apposite after 1886. Thus he came to personify the continuation of the Cape political position espoused by his father, of collaboration with the British in such a way as to negate the policies of British imperialism. In this he was surprisingly, if not inevitably, successful.

Johannes Henricus Brand died on 14 July 1888.

BIBLIOGRAPHY

de Kiewiet, Cornelius Willem. *The Imperial Factor in South Africa: A Study in Politics and Economics.* Cambridge, UK: Cambridge University Press, 1937.

Giliomee, Hermann. *The Afrikaners: Biography of a People.* Cape Town, South Africa: Tafelberg, 2003.

Goodfellow, Clement Francis. *Great Britain and South African Confederation, 1870–1881.* Cape Town, South Africa: Oxford University Press, 1966.

van Jaarsveld, F. A. The *Awakening* of *Afrikaner Nationalism, 1868–1881.* Cape Town, South Africa: Human & Rousseau, 1961.

ROBERT ROSS